49.00

Tests

SECOND EDITION

Richard C. Sweetland, Ph.D.
Daniel J. Keyser, Ph.D.
General Editors

Tests

*A Comprehensive Reference
for Assessments in Psychology,
Education, and Business*

SECOND EDITION

Test Corporation of America
Kansas City

Library of Congress Cataloging-in-Publication Data

Tests : a comprehensive reference for assessments in psychology, education, and business.

Includes indexes.
1. Psychological tests. 2. Educational tests and measurements.
3. Occupational aptitude tests.
I. Sweetland, Richard C., 1931–   . II. Keyser, Daniel J., 1935–
[DNLM: 1. Educational Measurement. 2. Psychological Tests. BF 176 T345]
BF176.T43   1986   153.9′3   86-14416
ISBN 0-933701-03-9 (library)
      0-933701-05-5 (hardcover)
      0-933701-06-3 (softcover)

Printed in the United States of America

Table of Contents

Preface

As this second edition of *Tests* is published, it seems appropriate to say a few words about the project's development and background and to recognize the contributions of the people who made the task possible.

Tests: First Edition was published in response to the need for a resource containing consistent codified information describing and cataloging tests available for use by psychologists, educators, and human resource personnel. The professional community received *Tests* enthusiastically. Within one year of publication, the first edition was in its third printing, indicating to us that thousands of professionals and libraries had come to rely on its quick-scanning, easy-to-read format. Committed to providing our readers with the most current information possible on assessment instruments, we launched a "search and find" effort that resulted in the 1984 publication of *Tests: Supplement*, a revision of the first edition containing information on more than 500 new tests.

Our ongoing "search and find" efforts, which have upturned information on hundreds of new tests; rapid developments in areas such as neuropsychology, computerized testing, and forensic assessments; and our continued firm commitment to providing users with quick access to current test information convinced us of the necessity of developing this second edition. We thank our readers for the numerous suggestions they have offered, particularly for contacting us with the names of assessment instruments not referenced in the previous editions. We especially are grateful to the many test publishers and authors who generously and graciously contributed their staff time, information, and support for this book.

Particular recognition must be given to Jane Guthrie and Kelly Scanlon who coordinated this project. Their persistence and dedication to quality proved to be a major factor in the fruition of this project.

Throughout the research and production of *Tests*, Eugene Strauss and Leonard Strauss have given encouragement, suggestions, and invaluable advice in all aspects of the business of publishing. Our thanks go to them for their continued association with Test Corporation of America. In addition, we wish to acknowledge Sam Pirnazar for his contributions as a consultant to the first edition.

Richard C. Sweetland, Ph.D.
Daniel J. Keyser, Ph.D
Editors

Introduction

Tests, a reference guide containing information on thousands of assessment instruments, is designed especially for psychologists, educators, and human resource personnel who search for tests to satisfy assessment needs. In addition, students, librarians, and other nonspecialists who need to familiarize themselves with the broad range of available tests will find the contents and format helpful. *Tests* does not attempt to review or evaluate tests; its purpose is to present concise descriptions in a quick-scanning, easy-to-read format. This second edition, which presents the tests of 437 publishers, not only revises the information contained in the first edition and *Supplement* but also presents descriptions of over 600 new or revised tests—an increase of 25%. Each of the descriptions, unless noted otherwise, was verified by the publisher of the test.

Regarding matters of style, the editors have chosen to use the commonly acceptable masculine pronoun and, in most cases, the word "subject" for the individual being assessed. In so doing, the editors do not intend to show any sexual bias or disregard for those being evaluated. British spelling has been retained in proper titles.

How *Tests* Is Organized

The assessments described herein are organized according to a system of primary classification and cross-referencing intended to make information as accessible to the reader as possible. Each of the book's three main sections—Psychology, Education, and Business—is divided into subsections. For example, Psychology contains 11 subsections; Education, 50 subsections; and Business, 12 subsections. Each test has been given a primary classification in one of the Psychology, Education, or Business subsections and is described in detail in that subsection. Each test may also be cross-referenced in up to two other subsections. For example, the Wechsler Adult Intelligence Scale, described within Psychology: Intelligence and Related is cross-referenced under Education: Intelligence and Related. The tests within each subsection are listed alphabetically according to title.

In order to establish subsections that would be practical and functional for the reader, considerable consultation was sought from professionals who use tests on a daily basis. Based on feedback from these sources, the subsections in this second edition have been expanded from 62 to 73 and some have been renamed, both to facilitate the reader's search for assessments and to reflect contemporary terminology.

Format and Content of Descriptions

The format and content of each test entry are designed to provide the basic information necessary to decide whether a particular test is appropriate to consider for a given assessment need. Each test entry is structured as follows: test title and author, a scan line with coded visual keys indicating the population for which the test is intended and whether the test is examiner- or self-administered, a purpose statement, a brief description highlighting the test's major features, timing information, scoring method, relevant cost and availability information, and primary publisher. Each of these components will be explained in greater detail.

The TITLE of each test is presented exactly as it appears in the test publisher's materials. For example, one would find the description of the REEL Scale under The Bzoch-League Receptive-Expressive Emergent Language Scale. Readers who are familiar with a test's common or popular name rather than its published title may find the Author Index useful if difficulty is encountered in finding the test.

The test AUTHOR(S) appear(s) in italics below the test title.

The SCAN LINE, which is set off by bars between the author(s) and the purpose statement, identifies the population for which the test is intended (child/adolescent/ adult and age or grade range) and indicates whether a test is examiner- or self-administered:

✍ : symbolizes that a test is self-administered.

☞ ✍ : symbolizes that an examiner is required.

The PURPOSE statement offers a succinct overview of the test's intended applications and what it purports to measure, assess, diagnose, evaluate, or identify.

The DESCRIPTION presents the number of test items, type of test format (paper-pencil, true-false, projective, oral, observational, etc.), factors or variables measured, materials used, manner in which the test is administered, foreign language availability, and special features.

The terms TIMED and UNTIMED indicate whether a test is administered with time limitations. For timed tests, the exact amount of time allotted for the subject to complete the test is indicated; for untimed tests, the amount of time usually required to complete the test is provided.

The SCORING line specifies the method used to score the test: *hand key, examiner evaluated, machine scored,* or *computer scored.* Hand key indicates that the test is scored using an answer key or template provided by the test publisher. An examiner-evaluated test is scored using an examiner's opinion, skills, and knowledge. A computer- or machine-scored test uses answer sheets that are scored by machine or computer. When a combination of these terms appears in the scoring line, the first listed is the primary method employed.

The COST line contains price information that is as accurate as the editors could establish at the time of the book's publication. Because the pricing structure for some tests (covering the various forms, kits, options, etc.) is so extensive, only representative costs are included here. The editors encourage readers to contact the publisher for complete cost information.

The PUBLISHER line identifies the test's primary publisher. When a publisher has indicated that a test is distributed by a firm other than itself, the name of the distributor follows that of the publisher. (The Publisher/Distributor Index contains complete address and telephone information.)

The editors attempted to confirm the accuracy of every test entry through direct correspondence with the test publisher. Entries that were not verified due to lack of publisher response contain a disclaimer to that effect following the name of the test publisher.

Indexes

Tests: Second Edition contains seven indexes and an out-of-print listing. The indexes were compiled based on information provided by test publishers in response to specific questions regarding special populations, in-print status, and other aspects of test development.

The TEST TITLE INDEX lists, according to the published test title, each of the tests described in this book.

The OUT-OF-PRINT listing contains the titles and authors of tests that the publishers have indicated are out-of-print.

The HEARING-IMPAIRED INDEX identifies tests that are suitable for or that may be adapted for use with hearing-impaired populations, as well as tests that assess the sense of hearing.

The PHYSICALLY IMPAIRED INDEX lists tests that are suitable for or adaptable for use with physically impaired populations, as well as tests designed to assess motor and/or orthopedic handicaps.

The VISUALLY IMPAIRED INDEX contains tests that are suitable for or may be adapted for use with visually impaired populations, as well as tests designed to assesss vision.

The FOREIGN LANGUAGE AVAILABILITY INDEX contains tests that are available in language versions other than English.

The AUTHOR INDEX lists all test authors except for corporate and institutional staffs.

In addition to page numbers, the PUBLISHER/DISTRIBUTOR INDEX provides addresses and telephone numbers.

The purpose of *Tests* from the outset has been to provide a quick reference for tests available in the English language. When the first edition of this volume was published, a decision was made to omit reliability, validity, and normative data—aspects considered too complex to reduce to the quick-scanning desk reference format. The editors were aware, however, that a fuller treatment of each test was needed and were encouraged by librarians, educators, psychologists, and forensic specialists to create the *Tests Critiques* series, which serves as a complement to *Tests* and as a vital component within the array of test review resources currently available. The editors strongly urge readers interested in reliability and validity or other in-depth technical information about a particular test to consult the appropriate volume of *Test Critiques* or contact the test author(s) or publisher.

How to Use This Book

The system of classification and cross-referencing used in *Tests* and the inclusion of the indexes just described are designed to accommodate both readers who need information about a particular test and those conducting a general search for appropriate assessment instruments. The following suggestions for using *Tests* are intended to minimize the reader's efforts to locate information.

1. The editors encourage readers to scan the sections of the book relevant to particular assessment needs. This "scanning-by-section" approach may be most helpful to readers who know how the particular tests for which they are searching are likely to be classified or for readers whose search is focused on an assessment area rather than on a particular test.

2. By following up on cross-references, readers may discover additional tests relevant to their particular assessment situations.

3. Readers who are unable to locate tests using the Test Title Index should consult the Author Index and/or the Publisher/Distributor Index if these elements are known.

4. Readers interested in assessment instruments for testing impaired populations or in the broad range of tests available for assessing specific handicaps can consult the appropriate indexes.

5. Tests that cannot be located by perusing the indexes may be found in the Out-of-Print listing.

6. If you are unable to locate the information you need, please write to The Test Corporation of America, 330 West 47th Street, Suite 205, Kansas City, Missouri, 64112 or call (816)756-1490 describing your specific need. The TCA staff welcomes the opportunity to assist you.

The Test Corporation of America fully supports the ethical and professional standards established by national and state professional organizations. The inclusion of specific restrictions on test accessibility noted in some descriptions in *Tests* usually has been requested by the publisher or author; the fact that a test description does not list restrictions does not imply that such restrictions do not exist. When ordering tests, the reader should ask each publisher for the standards or requirements for purchasing.

Order forms, catalogs, and further information regarding tests may be obtained from each publisher. Anyone interested in ordering a specific test should contact the publisher using the Publisher/Distributor Index, which provides mailing addresses and telephone numbers.

Although the information in this book was obtained from primary sources, the editors are aware of possibilities for error. Each test entry has been researched, screened, written, edited, and read by professional test administrators; however, the editors ask that the reader understand that the job of checking and insuring the accuracy of a book such as this is a process that will continue throughout the publication of subsequent editions. The editors welcome on an ongoing basis the submission of information about new tests and encourage test publishers and authors to apprise the Test Corporation staff of changes due to revisions of tests or errors in the test descriptions.

Psychology

The tests presented and described in the Psychology section have been selected on the basis of their appropriate usage in a clinical or counseling setting. In general, tests found in this section are those that might be used by a mental health professional rather than by an educator or human resources specialist.

The classification of tests on the basis of typical usage or function is, of course, arbitrary, and the reader is encouraged to review the Education and Business sections for additional assessment instruments.

Psychology Section

Child and Child Development

ASSESSMENT IN INFANCY: ORDINAL SCALES OF PSYCHOLOGICAL DEVELOPMENT
Ina C. Uzgiris and J. McV. Hunt

Child   Ages 3 weeks-2 years   

Purpose: Assesses the psychological and cognitive development of infants in the first two years of life. Used with severely retarded and handicapped individuals and to compare different populations of children.

Description: Six paper-pencil observational scales assessing an infant's psychological and cognitive development: The Development of Visual Pursuit and the Performance of Objects, The Development of Means for Obtaining Desired Environmental Events, The Development of Imitation, The Development of Operational Causality, The Construction of Object Relations in Space, and The Development of Schemes for Relating to Objects. The book *Assessment in Infancy* describes the six scales and provides the methodology for testing severely mentally retarded individuals and handicapped infants, analyzing language development, and comparing different populations of children. The record forms are designed for use with the book. Supplementary instructional films (16 mm. or video cassette) are available for each of the six scales. Examiner required. Not suitable for group use.

Untimed: Varies

Scoring: Examiner evaluated

Cost: *Assessment in Infancy* (274 pp.) $24.95; 5 record forms $15.75

Publisher: University of Illinois Press

THE BARBER SCALES OF SELF-REGARD FOR PRESCHOOL CHILDREN
Lucie W. Barber

Child   Preschoolers

Purpose: Assesses young children's level of development. Used to help parents recognize and develop a child's self-regard.

Description: Multiple-item paper-pencil assessment profile of seven developmental factors, each measured on a 5-point scale. The factors are purposeful learning skills, completing tasks, coping with fears, cooperating with parental requests, dealing with frustrations, social adjustment, and developing imagination in play. The scales were designed for parents with aid of professional educators. Worksheets direct parents to the next level of their child's development. Materials include the seven scales, a guide for parents, and a profile guide with instructions. An examiner's manual also is available. Self-administered. Suitable for group use.

Untimed: Varies

Scoring: Examiner evaluated

Cost: Parents' packet $5.00; manual $6.50

Publisher: Union College, Character Research Project

Information and availability unconfirmed; no publisher response.

BATTELLE DEVELOPMENTAL INVENTORY
Refer to page 462.

BAYLEY SCALES OF INFANT DEVELOPMENT
Nancy Bayley

Child   Ages 2-30 months

Purpose: Assesses early mental and psychomotor development. Used in the diagnosis of normal versus retarded development.

Description: Two-scale test of infant mental and motor development. The Mental Scale assesses sensory-perceptual behavior, learning ability, and early communication attempts. The Motor Scale measures general body control, coordination of large muscles, and skills in fine-muscle control of hands. The materials include a kit containing stimulus items and the Infant Behavior Record for noting qualitative aspects of behavior. Examiner required. Not suitable for group use.

Untimed: 45 minutes

Scoring: Examiner evaluated

Cost: Complete set (all necessary equipment, manual, 25 each of 3 record forms, carrying case) $350.00

Publisher: The Psychological Corporation

BEHAVIOR RATING INSTRUMENT FOR AUTISTIC AND OTHER ATYPICAL CHILDREN (BRIACC)
Bertram Ruttenberg, Beth Kalish, Charles Wenar, and Enid Wolf

Child

Purpose: Evaluates the status of low functioning, atypical, and autistic children of all ages. Used to evaluate children who will not or cannot cooperate with formal testing procedures.

Description: Paper-pencil inventory of observations taken over a two-day period assessing a child's present level of functioning and measuring behavioral change in eight areas: relationship to an adult, communication, drive for mastery, vocalization and expressive speech, sound and speech reception, social responsiveness, body movement (passive and active), and psychobiological development. Each of the eight scales begins with the most severe autistic behavior and progresses to behavior roughly comparable to that of a normally developing 3½- to 4½-year-old. The complete BRIAAC includes a manual, report forms, individual scale score sheet, total score sheet, intrascale and interscale profile forms, descriptive

guides, and suggested individual plans. Examiner required. Not suitable for group use.

Untimed: Two days

Scoring: Examiner evaluated

Cost: Complete kit (manual, all required forms) $175.00

Publisher: Stoelting Company

BEHAVIOUR STUDY TECHNIQUE
Isla Stamp

Child   Grades PreK-1

Purpose: Measures behavioral development and adjustment of preschool children. Identifies children in need of further testing and assistance. Used by kindergarten teachers.

Description: Multiple-item observational instrument for systematic evaluation of behavior in preschool children. Although intended for use by kindergarten teachers, a psychologist's manual that is available with the test presents a coding system enabling psychologists to classify children as apparently mentally healthy, in need of some help in adjusting, or urgently in need of referral for diagnosis and therapy. Australian norms are provided for preschool and first-grade children. The manual and score keys are restricted to use by psychologists. Materials include a questionnaire, teacher's guide (revised 1979), psychologist's manual, and score keys. Examiner required. AUSTRALIAN PUBLISHER

Untimed: Varies

Scoring: Hand key; examiner evaluated

Cost: Contact publisher

Publisher: The Australian Council for Educational Research Limited

THE BINGHAM BUTTON TEST
William Bingham

Child   Ages 3-6

Purpose: Measures child's ability to discern color, shape, size, and spatial relationships as an indication of preschool readiness.

Description: One jar and 10 buttons of different colors and sizes are presented by the examiner to the child, who is asked to maneuver the buttons to reveal the ability to determine how colors, objects, and space relate to each other. The test also is used in the diagnosis of problems with visual perception or motor skills. Examiner required. Not suitable for group use.

Untimed: 25-30 minutes
Scoring: Hand key
Cost: Complete set $4.00
Publisher: Bingham Button Test

BIRTH TO THREE DEVELOPMENTAL SCALE
Tina E. Bangs and Susan Dodson

Child   Ages 0-3

Purpose: Assesses developmental delay in the behavioral categories of oral language, problem solving, social/personal, and motor activities. Used for educational planning and diagnosis.

Description: 85-item scale for early identification of developmental delay. The factors measured include basic skills/perceptual motor, social/emotional/interest, auditory skills, reception, and expression. Materials include a manual, five different scoring forms, and one summary form. Data derived from the scale provide criterion-referenced feedback. Examiner required. Not suitable for group use.

Untimed: Not available
Scoring: Examiner evaluated
Cost: Complete kit $38.00
Publisher: DLM Teaching Resources

BOEHM TEST OF BASIC CONCEPTS—PRESCHOOL VERSION
Refer to page 462.

THE BRIGANCE® DIAGNOSTIC INVENTORY OF EARLY DEVELOPMENT
Refer to page 463.

BURKS' BEHAVIOR RATING SCALES, PRESCHOOL AND KINDERGARTEN EDITION
Refer to page 102.

THE BZOCH-LEAGUE RECEPTIVE-EXPRESSIVE EMERGENT LANGUAGE SCALE (REEL)
Kenneth R. Bzoch and Richard League

Child   Ages 0-36 months

Purpose: Assesses emerging factors of expressive and receptive language in children. Identifies children needing further evaluation.

Description: 132-item paper-pencil inventory measuring the development of language in infants. The child's overt speech and response behaviors are rated by a parent or individual who has daily contact with the child and has the opportunity to observe the child's language behavior. Test items consist of statements of language behavior typical of children ages 0-36 months. The evaluator rates each item as being present or absent. Three expressive and three receptive factors are measured for each of 22 age levels. Three scores are derived: expressive language quotient, receptive language quotient, and overall language quotient. Results also yield receptive, expressive, and combined expressive and receptive language ages. Self-administered by evaluator. Not suitable for group use.

Untimed: Varies
Scoring: Examiner evaluated
Cost: Complete kit $24.00; manual $14.00; 25 test forms $12.00
Publisher: Pro-Ed

CALLIER-AZUSA SCALE: G-EDITION
Robert Stillman (Editor)

Handicapped children

Purpose: Assesses the development of deaf-blind and severely and profoundly handicapped children. Used to plan developmentally appropriate activities and to evaluate a child's developmental progress, particularly at the lower developmental levels.

Description: Multiple-item paper-pencil observational inventory measuring 18 developmental subscales in five developmental areas: motor development (postural control, locomotion, fine motor, and visual motor); perceptual abilities (visual, auditory, and tactile development); daily living skills (undressing and dressing, personal hygiene, development of feeding skills, and toileting); cognition, communication, and language (cognitive development, receptive communication, expressive communication, and development of speech); and social development (interactions with adults, peers, and the environment). Each subscale is made up of sequential steps describing developmental milestones. Some steps are divided into two or more items describing behaviors appearing at approximately the same time in development. The developmental steps described in the scale take into account the specific sensory, motor, language, and social deficits of deaf-blind and severely and profoundly impaired children (scale items differ from behaviors typically observed among normal children at the same developmental level). Administration of the scale is based on at least two weeks of observation of spontaneously occurring behaviors typically appearing in conjunction with classroom activities. The scale must be administered by someone thoroughly familiar with the child's behavior. No specific testing expertise is required other than good observational skills and a knowledge of the child's repertoire of behaviors. The most accurate results are obtained if several individuals with close contact with the child (teachers, aides, parents, specialists) evaluate the child on a consensus basis. Scale items are rated according to the presence or absence of the specific behaviors listed. Age equivalencies are included only to provide a rough means of comparing functioning levels in different areas of behavior. Interpretation of scale results is based on the sequence in which the behaviors occur, not on the age norms for normal children. A profile sheet is provided for summarizing scale results. Self-administered by examiner. Not suitable for group use.

Untimed: Varies

Scoring: Examiner evaluated

Cost: Contact publisher

Publisher: Callier Center for Communication Disorders

Information and availability unconfirmed; no publisher response.

CATTELL INFANT INTELLIGENCE SCALE
Psyche Cattell

Child   Ages 3-30 months

Purpose: Assesses the mental development of infants.

Description: Test of early development rating infant verbalizations and motor control, such as the manipulation of cubes, pencils, pegboards, and other stimulus items. The test has been modified with items from the Gesell, Minnesota Preschool, and Merrill-Palmer scales and is applicable to a younger age range than the Stanford-Binet Intelligence Scale. Materials include a kit containing stimulus items. Examiner required. Not suitable for group use.

Untimed: 20-30 minutes

Scoring: Examiner evaluated

Cost: Complete set (all necessary equipment, 25 record forms, carrying case) $295.00

Publisher: The Psychological Corporation

COMMUNICATIVE EVALUATION CHART
Ruth M. Anderson, Madeline Miles, and Patricia A. Matheny

Child

Purpose: Assesses children's development of overall abilities in language and visual-motor-perceptual skills. Identifies children needing referral for clinical evaluation.

Description: Task-assessment and oral-response test measuring the development of skills required for speech development. The tasks are designed to cover the coordination of the speech musculature, development of hearing acuity and auditory perception, acquisition of vowels and consonants, and growth of receptive and expressive language. The test also evaluates a child's well-being, growth and development, motor coordination, and beginning visual-motor-perceptual skills. The examiner elicits responses from the child and evaluates the responses as present, not present, or fluctuating. It is occasionally necessary to consult with the parent, guardian, or pediatrician for pertinent information. The test is subdivided into nine levels of 14-36 items for each of the following age groups: 3, 6, or 9 months; 1, 1½, 2, 3, 4, or 5 years. Examiner required. Not suitable for group use.

Untimed: 5-10 minutes

Scoring: Examiner evaluated

Cost: Test $1.00; 50 tests $37.50

Publisher: Educators Publishing Service, Inc.

COMPREHENSIVE ASSESSMENT PROGRAM: BEGINNING EDUCATION ASSESSMENT (BEA)
Refer to page 466.

COMPREHENSIVE DEVELOPMENTAL EVALUATION CHART (CDEC)
Shirley Cliff, Diane Carr, Jennifer Gray, Carol Nyman, and Sandra Redding

Child   Ages 0-3

Purpose: Measures a child's developmental abilities. Used for evaluation by either transdisciplinary or conventional team approaches.

Description: Multiple-item observational instrument used to collect comprehensive data and follow a child's development. The chart includes evaluations of gross-motor skills, fine-motor skills, muscle tone, reflexes, parental attitudes, height and weight, receptive language, head circumference, expressive language, cognitive/social development, feeding, vision, hearing, and others. Examiner required. Not suitable for group use.

Untimed: 30 minutes

Scoring: Examiner evaluated

Cost: CDE packet (2 charts, manual) $12.00

Publisher: El Paso Rehabilitation Center
Information and availability unconfirmed; no publisher response.

DENVER DEVELOPMENTAL SCREENING TEST (DDST)
William F. Frankenburg

Child   Ages 0-6

Purpose: Evaluates a child's personal, social, fine- and gross-motor, language, and adaptive abilities as a means of identifying possible problems and screening for further evaluation.

Description: 105-item "pick and choose" test in which the items are blocks, a bell, a ball, a bottle, raisins, rattle, yarn, and a pencil. Items are presented to the child in chronological step-wise order to permit a more dynamic profile (i.e., a growth curve) of a child's development. The examiner observes what the child does with the items and makes recommendations based on perceived abnormalities. Examiner required. Not suitable for group use. Available in Spanish.

Untimed: 10-20 minutes

Scoring: Examiner evaluated

Cost: Kit $15.00; manual $8.00; 100 test forms $7.50

Publisher: Ladoca Publishing Foundation
Information and availability unconfirmed; no publisher response.

DEVELOPMENTAL ACTIVITIES SCREENING INVENTORY (DASI)
Refer to page 469.

DEVELOPMENTAL ACTIVITIES SCREENING INVENTORY-II (DASI-II)
Refer to page 469.

DEVELOPMENTAL ASSESSMENT FOR THE SEVERELY HANDICAPPED (DASH)
Refer to page 603.

THE DEVELOPMENTAL PROFILE II

Refer to page 470.

DIAL-DEVELOPMENT INDICATORS FOR THE ASSESSMENT OF LEARNING

Refer to page 471.

EGAN BUS PUZZLE TEST

Dorothy Egan

**Child   Ages 20 months-
4 years**

Purpose: Assesses developmental deficit, delay, and handicap in children. Used by community health professionals.

Description: Multiple-item response screening test consisting of a display board with a printed street scene and nine lift-out pieces for assessing comprehension of verbal labels, expressive verbal labels, comprehension of illustrated situations related to experience, expresses language response, and the beginnings of intuitive verbal thinking. Examiner required. Not suitable for group use. BRITISH PUBLISHER

Untimed: 7-8 minutes

Scoring: Hand key

Cost: Specimen set (Bus Puzzle board, manual, 25 answer sheets) £29.00

Publisher: The Test Agency Ltd.

EXTENDED MERRILL-PALMER SCALE

*Rachel Stutsman Ball,
Philip R. Merrifield,
and Leland H. Stott*

Child   Ages 3-5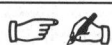

Purpose: Measures intelligence in children.

Description: 16-item task-assessment and oral-response test measuring the mental processes of evaluation and production with both semantic and figural units. The 16 tasks include tower building, ambiguous forms, food naming, dot joining, word meaning, pie completion, action agents, copying, round things, block sorting, following directions, 3-cube pyramid, 6-cube pyramid, action agents, stick manipulation, and design productions. Scores and percentile ranges are provided in six intervals from ages 3-5 for four specific abilities, each of which are tested by four of the tasks. The abilities are semantic production, figural production, semantic evaluation, and semantic production. The manual includes information on the development of the test items, instructions for administering and scoring, and case studies for 16 separate patterns of the four abilities at two age levels. Examiner required. Not suitable for group use.

Timed: 4-5 minutes

Scoring: Examiner evaluated

Cost: Complete kit (test materials, record forms, scoring forms, manual, carrying case) $345.00

Publisher: Stoelting Company

THE FIVE P'S: PARENT PROFESSIONAL PRESCHOOL PERFORMANCE PROFILE

Refer to page 473.

THE FLINT INFANT SECURITY SCALE: FOR INFANTS AGED 3-24 MONTHS

Betty M. Flint

Child   Ages 3-24 months

Purpose: Assesses an infant's mental health and the behavior of the mother (or other parent) as she interacts with the child.

Description: 74-item paper-pencil behavior scale assessing a child's sense of security and feeling of self-worth and parental behavior. When the "psychological parent" is other than the natural mother or father, the scale is of special value to physicians, social workers, and child care agencies responsible for adoption placements and foster care. Examiner required. Not suitable for group use. CANADIAN PUBLISHER

Untimed: Not available

Scoring: Examiner evaluated

Cost: Specimen set (manual, scoring booklet) $5.50

Publisher: Guidance Centre

HAWAII EARLY LEARNING PROFILE (HELP)

*S. Furuno, K. O'Reilly, C. Hosaka,
T. Inatsuka, P. Allman,
and B. Zeisloft*

Child   Ages 0-3

Purpose: Assesses self-help, language, motor, social, and cognitive skills of children. Used for early intervention, preschool placement, individual education prescriptions, and home plans.

Description: 650-item criterion-referenced inventory assessing the skills and behaviors of children. This visual assessment tool is used for planning, setting objectives, and recording progress. Two forms are available: chart and checklist. HELP Charts are a set of three charts displaying skills and behaviors. The HELP Checklist presents each developmental area in column format for easier interdisciplinary team assessment and recording. Cards and blocks are used as stimuli. Examiner required. Not suitable for group use.

Untimed: 8 hours

Scoring: Not available

Cost: Charts, checklists $2.95 each; activity guide $14.95

Publisher: VORT Corporation

HOME OBSERVATION FOR MEASUREMENT OF THE ENVIRONMENT (HOME)

*Bettye M. Caldwell,
Robert H. Bradley, and Staff*

Families of infants and preschoolers

Purpose: Measures the quality of the home environment for infants and preschoolers. Used for research and in clinical settings.

Description: 45- or 55-item inventory assessing the following aspects of a child's home environment: frequency and stability of adult contact, amount of developmental and vocal stimulation,

need gratification, emotional climate, avoidance of restriction on motor and exploratory behavior, available play materials, and home characteristics indicative of parental concern with achievement. The interviewer completes the inventory on the basis of a one-hour visit to the child's home while the child is awake. The parent is interviewed and parent-child interactions are observed during this period. Roughly two-thirds of the items are based on observed behaviors; one-third are based on parental report. All items are scored plus (+) or minus (–), depending on whether the behavior is observed during the visit or the parent reports that the conditions or events are characteristic of the home environment. The form for infants and toddlers (45 items) provides a total score and scores for six subscales: emotional and verbal responsibility of parent, acceptance of child's behavior, organization of physical and temporal environment, provision of appropriate play materials, parent involvement with child, and opportunities for variety in daily stimulation. The form for preschoolers (55 items) provides a total score and scores for eight subscales: learning stimulation, language stimulation, physical environment, warmth and affection, academic stimulation, modeling, variety in experience, and acceptance. Interviewer required. Not suitable for group use.

Untimed: 1 hour

Scoring: Examiner evaluated

Cost: Contact publisher

Publisher: Center for Child Development and Education

HOME SCREENING QUESTIONNAIRE (HSQ)
Refer to page 78.

HOUSTON TEST FOR LANGUAGE DEVELOPMENT

Margaret Crabtree

Child   Ages 0-6

Purpose: Assesses verbal and nonverbal communication abilities in children. Diagnoses problems resulting from emotional deprivation, neurological disabilities, retardation, auditory or visual-motor deficits or environmental linguistic influence. Used to plan specific intervention procedures and to monitor the child's progress.

Description: Multiple-item verbal and nonverbal checklist of communication abilities at two age levels. The Infant Scale consists of an observational checklist of linguistic and prelinguistic skills characteristic of normal infants up to 18 months of age. The 2-6 Year Test consists of 18 subtests that include both verbal and nonverbal tasks. The 18 subtests are Self-Identity, Vocabulary, Body Orientation, Gesture, Auditory Judgments, Oral Monitoring with Toys, Sentence Length, Temporal Content, Syntax, Prepositions, Serial Counting, Counting Objects, Imitates Linguistic Structure, Imitated Prosodic Patterns, Imitates Designs, Drawing, and Oral Monitoring While Drawing and Telling About Drawing. The manual provides normative data and information on reliability and validity. Individual child record forms serve as a work sheet, score sheet, and permanent record of the test performance. Examiner required. Not suitable for group use.

Untimed: 30 minutes

Scoring: Examiner evaluated

Cost: Complete kit (25 record forms, vocabulary cards, necessary manipulatives, manual) $82.75

Publisher: Stoelting Company

HUMAN FIGURES DRAWING TEST
Eloy Gonzales

Child   Ages 5-10

Purpose: Measures the cognitive maturation of children. Used by teachers, diagnosticians, psychologists, speech therapists, and other professionals.

Description: Paper-pencil test assessing the nonverbal conceptual ability of children through analysis of drawings of human figures. Because the test does not require speech, it is useful with children who have verbal problems or do not speak English. Examiner required. Suitable for group use.

Untimed: 10-15 minutes

Scoring: Hand key, examiner evaluated

Cost: Complete kit (examiner's manual, 100 scoring forms, storage box) $39.00

Publisher: Pro-Ed

HUMANICS NATIONAL CHILD ASSESSMENT FORMS: AGES 0-3 YEARS
Refer to page 476.

HUMANICS NATIONAL CHILD ASSESSMENT FORMS: AGES 3-6 YEARS
Refer to page 477.

INITIAL COMMUNICATION PROCESSES
Teris Schery and Ann G. Wilcoxen

Child

Purpose: Assesses early behavioral and communication (or pre-communication) processes for at-risk children and handicapped individuals of all ages who are functioning below the developmental level of three years. Used to plan and monitor intervention programs with children and delayed adults who may be autistic, severely or profoundly retarded, multiply handicapped, or learning disabled.

Description: 92-item observational inventory consisting of 10 subscales assessing the following areas of early behavioral and communication processes: auditory skills, visual skills, manual fine-motor skills, oral-vocal motor skills, manipulative object play skills, symbolic object play skills, problem-solving skills, affective development, communication skills-comprehension, and communication skills-expression. Interpretive profile distributions allow an individual to be compared with eight groups: autistic, severely/profoundly retarded, multiply handicapped, or trainable mentally retarded, each classified as having a mental age of above two years or below two years. The scales book describes each of the 92 items and provides space for recording the results for one student being observed several times or for six students being observed once. The objectives bank contains a detailed description of each of over 250 objectives with criteria for deciding upon attainment. The progress monitoring log serves as an index to the objectives bank and provides a sequential record of performance for one student on each of the more than 250 objectives. The manual includes a description of the scales, statistical data, and suggestions for interpreting the scores and planning for students. Examiner required. Not suitable for group use.

Untimed: Varies

Scoring: Examiner evaluated

Cost: Starter set (manual, objectives bank, scales book, progress monitoring log) $24.95

Publisher: CTB/McGraw-Hill

JOSEPH PRESCHOOL AND PRIMARY SELF-CONCEPT SCREENING TEST (JPPSST)
Refer to page 582.

KAUFMAN INFANT AND PRESCHOOL SCALE (KIPS)
Harvey Kaufman

Child

Purpose: Measures early high-level cognitive process and indicates possible need for intervention in normal children ages one month to four years and in retarded children and adults with mental ages of four years or less. Used by special education and early childhood teachers, psychologists, and physicians for a variety of screening purposes.

Description: Multiple-item task-assessment and observation measure of high-level cognitive thinking. The child is observed and asked to perform a number of tasks indicative of his level. All test items are "maturational prototypes" that can be taught to enhance maturation. The test covers general reasoning, storage, and verbal communication. The test yields the following scores: Overall Functioning Age (Mental Age) and Overall Functioning Quotient. Based on a child's performance on the scale, the manual suggests types of activities and general experience the child

needs for effective general adaptive behavior. Examiner required. Not suitable for group use.

Untimed: 30 minutes

Scoring: Examiner evaluated

Cost: Complete kit (manipulatives, stimulus cards, 10 evaluation booklets) $205.00

Publisher: Stoelting Company

KENT INFANT DEVELOPMENT SCALE (KID SCALE)
Jeanette M. Reuter and Lewis Katoff

Child Ages 0-1

Purpose: Assesses the developmental age of infants and young handicapped children chronologically or developmentally under one year of age. Used for developmental evaluation and prescriptive programming and as a basis for caregiver/professional conferences.

Description: 252-item paper-pencil inventory in which each item is a sentence stem that describes behaviors characteristic of an infant in its first year of life. Test items cover five behavioral domains: cognitive, motor, language, self-help, and social. The parent or caregiver marks the answer sheet to indicate which behaviors the child has acquired. A computer-scored printout lists items in order of developmental age by domain, compares the results for each domain and for the full scale with a normative sample of healthy infants, and furnishes developmental ages, a profile of strengths and weaknesses, and a timetable showing which developmental milestones will be achieved next. An interactive diskette is available. Examiner required. Suitable for group use. Available in Spanish.

Untimed: 30-40 minutes

Scoring: Hand key; may be computer scored

Cost: Contact publisher

Publisher: Kent Developmental Metrics

KINDERGARTEN BEHAVIOURAL INDEX
Refer to page 479.

KNOX'S CUBE TEST (KCT)
Refer to page 480.

KOONTZ CHILD DEVELOPMENTAL PROGRAM: TRAINING ACTIVITIES FOR THE FIRST 48 MONTHS
Refer to page 480.

LEXINGTON DEVELOPMENTAL SCALES (LDS)
Refer to page 480.

LINCOLN-OSERETSKY MOTOR DEVELOPMENT SCALE
Refer to page 561.

MARTIN DEVELOPMENTAL ABILITY TEST FOR THE BLIND
Refer to page 600.

MAXFIELD-BUCHHOLZ SOCIAL MATURITY SCALE FOR BLIND PRE-SCHOOL CHILDREN
Refer to page 601.

MCCARTHY SCALES OF CHILDREN'S ABILITIES
Dorothea McCarthy

Child   Ages 2.5-8.5

Purpose: Assesses intellectual and motor development of children.

Description: Measure of five aspects of children's thinking, motor, and mental abilities. The subtests are Verbal Ability, Short-Term Memory, Numerical Ability, Perceptual Performance, and Motor Coordination. The verbal, numerical, and perceptual performance scales are combined to yield the General Cognitive Index. Items involve puzzles, toy-like materials and game-like tasks. Six of the 18 task components that predict the child's ability to cope with school work in the early grades form the McCarthy Screening Test. Examiner required. Not suitable for group use.

Untimed: 45-60 minutes

Scoring: Examiner evaluated

Cost: Complete set (all necessary equipment, manual, 25 record forms, 25 drawing booklets, carrying case) $225.00

Publisher: The Psychological Corporation

MERRILL-PALMER SCALE
Refer to page 27.

MILLER ASSESSMENT FOR PRESCHOOLERS (MAP)
Lucy Jane Miller

Preschoolers

Purpose: Identifies children who exhibit moderate preacademic problems that may affect one or more areas of development. Used for screening by psychologists, physicians, occupational and physical therapists, speech pathologists, nurses, teachers, and trained support personnel. Used for comprehensive, clinical assessment by examiners with extensive clinical knowledge and experience.

Description: 27-item oral-response and task-performance test assessing preschooler's abilities in the following areas: neurological, sensory-motor, cognitive, and combined sensory-motor and cognitive. Provides standardized scores for the child's overall performance and for five performance indices: neurological foundations (abilities comprised of basic motor tasks and the awareness of sensations that are thought to provide the fundamental building blocks for more complex activities), sensory-motor coordination (more complex gross, fine, and oral-motor tasks that are not dependent on the interpretation of visual-spatial information), verbal cognitive abilities (memory, sequencing, comprehension, association, and expression in a verbal context), nonverbal cognitive abilities (memory, sequencing, visualization, and the performance of mental manipulations not requiring spoken language), and complex task abilities (the combination of sensory, motor, and cognitive abilities). In addition to the total score and five performance indices, normative information is provided to establish how a child's individual item performance compares to that of other children the same age.

In addition to the objective test items, a supplemental observations sheet is used to record subjective impressions about the quality of the child's performance, including movement, touch, vision, language, and draw-a-person (these observations are supplemental and should be administered only by examiners with clinical experience).

Test items are administered and scored with the aid of a scoring notebook. The record booklet includes a summary sheet, a family information and developmental history questionnaire, a supplemental observations sheet, and performance indices. The test also includes a card notebook; over 75 objects, including blocks, toys, and crayons, in a briefcase style portfolio and a carrying case; and an examiner's manual. Caution must be used in interpreting the results of the test when it is administered to populations not included in the normative sample, such as children for whom English is not the primary language or children with known physical, mental, or emotional dysfunction. The test may be used with the hearing, visually, and physically impaired, but no standardized score will be obtained. Examiner required. Not suitable for group use.

Untimed: 20-30 minutes

Scoring: Examiner evaluated

Cost: Kit (manual, scoring materials for 30 children) $249.00

Publisher: The Foundation for Knowledge in Development

MINNESOTA CHILD DEVELOPMENT INVENTORY (MCDI)
Harold Ireton and Edward Thwing

Child   Ages 1-6½

Purpose: Measures development of young child based on mother's observations. Used for clinical evaluation.

Description: 320-item paper-pencil yes-no format inventory completed by the mother to assess her child's current level of development. The inventory measures

the child's general development, gross motor, fine motor, expressive language, comprehension-conceptual, situation-comprehension, self-help, and personal-social skills. For use with mothers with a high-school education. A computerized version of the MCDI is now available for use with Apple computers. The computerized version contains a complete system for self-administration, scoring, and interpretation. Includes diskettes and a manual and produces a computerized MCDI Report. Self-administered. Suitable for group use.

Untimed: 20-30 minutes

Scoring: Hand key; may be computer scored

Cost: 10 reusable booklets $8.00; 25 answer sheets $6.00; 25 profile forms (specify male or female) $6.00; scoring templates $15.00; manual $12.00; computerized version $125.00

Publisher: Behavior Science Systems, Inc.

MINNESOTA INFANT DEVELOPMENT INVENTORY (MIDI)
Harold Ireton and Edward Thwing

Child   Birth-15 months

Purpose: Assesses infant development in the first 15 months. Used for pediatric review, infant screening, and educating parents about their child's development.

Description: 75-item paper-pencil inventory completed by the child's mother in order to measure the child's development in five areas: gross motor, fine motor, language, comprehension, and personal-social. The test does not yield scores. Instead, it provides a framework for making sound professional judgments and serves as a guide for interviewing the mother. For use with mothers who have a high-school education. Self-administered. Suitable for group use.

Untimed: 10 minutes

Scoring: Examiner evaluated

Cost: 10 reusable booklets $6.00

Publisher: Behavior Science Systems, Inc.

MULLEN SCALES OF EARLY LEARNING (MSEL)
Eileen M. Mullen

Child   Ages 15-69 months

Purpose: Assesses the learning abilities and learning patterns of children. Identifies learning disabilities, mental retardation, the manner in which a child learns, and the manner in which a child should be taught.

Description: Multiple-item oral-response task-performance test consisting of four separate scales of visual and language ability. The scales can be used together for comprehensive evaluation or separately to assess problems in visual discrimination and memory, fine-motor development, language comprehension and memory, and verbal ability. The Visual Receptive Organization Scale assesses visual discrimination, organization, sequencing, visual concepts, and short-term visual memory. The Visual Expressive Organization Scale assesses unilateral and bilateral fine-motor development and writing. The Language Receptive Organization Scale assesses listening, listening/looking, sequencing, verbal concepts, general knowledge, and short and long-term auditory memory. The Language Expressive Organization Scale assesses verbal ability, visual and oral vocabulary, abstract and practical reasoning, and short and long-term auditory memory. Examiner required. Not suitable for group use.

Untimed: Individual scales 12 minutes; complete test 45 minutes

Scoring: Not available

Cost: Complete kit (carrying case, 25 record forms, 25 Paths worksheets) $249.00

Publisher: T.O.T.A.L. Child, Inc.

THE NEONATAL BEHAVIORAL ASSESSMENT SCALE
T. Berry Brazelton

Ages 0-1 month

Purpose: Evaluates selected reflexes, motor responses, and interactive behavioral responses of newborn infants.

Predicts cognitive and emotional patterns in the infant. Used by medical professionals and paraprofessionals to teach parents about their newborn's state changes, temperament, and individual behavior patterns and to improve early health and developmental care.

Description: 47-item paper-pencil assessment procedure measuring neonatal reflex responses in a behavioral context. Twenty-seven behavioral items measure the infant's inherent neurological capacities, as well as responses to certain sets of stimuli. The behavioral section includes items that assess how soon the infant diminishes responses to stimuli of light, sound, and pinprick to the heel; auditory and visual items that determine how much and when the infant attends to, focuses on, and gives feedback in response to animate or inanimate stimuli; items assessing the degree and organization of the infant's motor coordination and control of motor activities throughout the examination; items assessing the infant's rate and amount of change during periods of alertness and state changes, color, activity, and peaks of excitement throughout the examination; items assessing how much, how soon, and how effectively the infant uses his own resources to quiet and console himself when upset or distressed (this category includes the graduated efforts of the caregiver to intervene and quiet the infant); and items assessing the infant's smiling and amount of cuddling behaviors. A second section of the scale includes 20 items assessing specific elicited reflexes and movements on a 3-point scale (hypoactive, normal, and hyperactive). All scale items are scored in a manner which takes into account the infant's state (ranging from deep sleep to intense crying) at the time of testing. Some of the 27 behavioral items are scored during a specific interaction with the infant (such as his head turning in response to a voice), but more are scored according to total continuous observations that are made throughout the entire assessment examination. For example, state changes, color changes, periods of alertness, and peaks of excitement are observed throughout the examination and scored at the conclusion. Repeated assessments (up to one month of age) are of considerably more value than just one assessment complete in the usual 20-30 minutes.

All persons using the scale must be trained in the proper administration of test items, order of examination procedures, optimal conditions of treating, and method of scoring. A list of trained examiners who can provide training may be obtained by writing directly to the principal investigator, Brazelton, at Children's Hospital Medical Center, 333 Longwood Avenue, Boston, MA 02115. It is essential that each examiner have a wide range of experience in assessing normal infants as a basis for scoring and interpreting the results of this scale. Examiner required. Not suitable for group use.

Untimed: 20-30 minutes per assessment

Scoring: Examiner evaluated

Cost: Contact publisher

Publisher: MacKeith Press; distributed in U.S.A. by Lippincott/Harper Publishers, Inc.

PEABODY DEVELOPMENTAL MOTOR SCALES AND ACTIVITY CARDS
Refer to page 483.

PIP DEVELOPMENTAL CHARTS
Dorothy M. Jeffree and Roy McConkey

Child   Ages 0-5

Purpose: Assesses the behavioral development of children. Identifies weaknesses in particular developmental areas. Provides a structured framework for recording a child's developmental progress. Used for screening and survey purposes.

Description: Paper-pencil inventory providing a behavioral checklist and profile of the most important stages of development in the first five years of a child's life. Development is measured in five main areas: physical, social, eye-hand coordination, play, and language skills. Each of these areas is subdivided into developmental sections, each beginning with a target behavior representing a "milestone" of development. Each section

then lists the behavioral skills that lead up to that milestone and the approximate ages at which the skills are "normally" acquired. The purpose of the charts is the evaluation and furthering of individual children's development, not normative comparisons. Use of the charts secures the active participation of the parents and is particularly useful when developmental delay or handicap is suspected. Self-administered by evaluator under supervision of a psychologist. Suitable for group use.

BRITISH PUBLISHER

Untimed: Not available

Scoring: Examiner evaluated

Cost: 10 charts £4.25 plus VAT

Publisher: Hodder & Stoughton

PRESCHOOL AND EARLY PRIMARY SKILLS SURVEY (PEPSS)
Refer to page 484.

PRESCREENING DEVELOPMENTAL QUESTIONNAIRE (PDQ)
Refer to page 486.

PRIMARY ACADEMIC SENTIMENT SCALE (PASS)
Refer to page 486.

PSYCHOLOGICAL STIMULUS RESPONSE
Eileen M. Mullen

Child   Ages 0-5

Purpose: Assesses the underlying intelligence and functional age of severely cerebral-palsied multihandicapped infants and young children and helps provide them with alternate ways of responding to questions and statements.

Description: Card-response test measuring language, visual processing, and general intelligence. Materials include a manual, vocabulary card booklet, response card booklet, and a protocol-score sheet book. The examiner shows the appropriate cards to the child. The child chooses one of three cards presented and, if mute, can respond with eye movements or by pointing. Examiner required. Not suitable for group use.

Untimed: 15 minutes

Scoring: Hand key

Cost: Complete set $35.00

Publisher: Meeting Street School, Rhode Island Easter Seal Society

---

A QUICK SCREENING SCALE OF MENTAL DEVELOPMENT
Katherine M. Banham

Child   Ages 6 months- 10 years

Purpose: Assesses a child's mental development. Identifies children in need of clinical evaluation. Used in clinics, hospitals, and special schools.

Description: Task-assessment and observational instrument arranged in five behavioral categories to measure a child's mental development. The test booklet consists of brief descriptions of behavior occurring in certain situations. The situations are to be checked and scored directly on the booklet. Instructions for administering are provided in the manual. Professional persons skilled in clinical interviewing procedures may administer the test, but persons trained in clinical psychology should interpret the results. The test provides a profile of scores in the five behavior categories for diagnostic purposes and educational guidance. Tentative norms for 50 children, along with the children's scores on the Cattell Infant Scale and the Stanford-Binet Scale, are provided. Examiner required. Not suitable for group use.

Untimed: 30 minutes

Scoring: Hand key

Cost: Specimen set $5.00; 25 tests $5.00

Publisher: Psychometric Affiliates

THE REVISED DEVELOPMENTAL SCREENING INVENTORY
Hilda Knobloch, Frances Stevens, and Anthony F. Malone

Child   Ages 4 weeks- 36 months

Purpose: Determines whether a child is functioning at age level. Screens for abnormalities requiring more detailed examination.

Description: Multiple-item yes-no assessment covering 20 age levels. Five areas are assessed: adaptive, gross motor, fine motor, language, and person-social. Preliminary questions answered by the child's parent or caregiver are followed by observation of the child's behavior. The evaluation begins at the child's chronologic age and proceeds to lower or higher age levels as needed. The maturity level is assigned by determining how well a child's behavior fits one age level constellation. Nine videotapes are available in addition to the questionnaire. Examiner required. Not suitable for group use.

Untimed: 10-30 minutes

Scoring: Examiner evaluated

Cost: 100 copies $40.00

Publisher: Gesell Developmental Test Materials, Inc.

REYNELL DEVELOPMENTAL LANGUAGE SCALES—SECOND REVISON
Joan Reynell

Child   Ages 1½-6

Purpose: Assesses expressive language and verbal comprehension. Used for evaluation of early development.

Description: Multiple-item two-performance tests of expressive and receptive language development: Verbal Comprehension Scale and Expressive Language Scale. Materials include the necessary toys and pictures. The test is suitable for use with hearing-impaired children. The test is a revision of the Experimental Edition of the scales. Examiner required. Not suitable for group use.

BRITISH PUBLISHER

Untimed: 1 hour

Scoring: Examiner evaluated

Cost: Complete kit (test materials, manual, 35 record forms) £166.75 (payment in sterling for all overseas orders)

Publisher: NFER-NELSON Publishing Company Ltd.

REYNELL-ZINKIN DEVELOPMENT SCALES FOR YOUNG VISUALLY HANDICAPPED CHILDREN

Refer to page 489.

RING AND PEG TESTS OF BEHAVIOR DEVELOPMENT FOR INFANTS AND PRESCHOOL CHILDREN

Katherine M. Banham

Child

Purpose: Measures the development of infants and preschool children and helps identify the social and motivational factors influential in a child's development. Used for clinical assessment of infant and child development.

Description: Task-assessment test measuring five categories of behavioral performance and ability: ambulative, manipulative, communicative, social-adaptive, and emotive. The test covers a wider range of items than standard intelligence tests in order to provide the clinical psychologist with diagnostic information. The scale yields a point score and a behavior age for the whole test, as well as for each of the five categories. A developmental quotient (D.Q.) may be derived from the full-scale behavior age. The test kit includes minimally culture-bound manipulation objects, manual, test booklet, and scoring sheet. Examiner required. Not suitable for group use.

Untimed: 45 minutes

Scoring: Hand key

Cost: Professional examination kit (25 tests, handbook) $20.00; 25 score sheets $5.00

Publisher: Psychometric Affiliates

ROCKFORD INFANT DEVELOPMENTAL SCALES (RIDES)

Refer to page 490.

S.E.E.D. DEVELOPMENTAL PROFILES

Child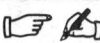

Purpose: Assesses the functioning level of children between the developmental ages of 4 weeks-6 years.

Description: Multiple-item paper-pencil criterion-referenced inventories for assessing gross-motor, fine-motor, adaptive reasoning, social and emotional, self-help, and speech and language skills. The test provides a functional appraisal of a handicapped child's abilities, monitors individual progress, and helps plan individual education programs. Items below the one-year level are presented in four-week intervals; between the one and two-year level, in three-month intervals; and between the two and six-year level, in six-month intervals. The test contains a graph for each development area and a master graph for a composite picture of the child's levels and progress. The profiles are compiled from various standardized assessment tools. Examiner required. Not suitable for group use.

Untimed: 1 hour

Scoring: Examiner evaluated

Cost: Complete kit (record forms, instructions, material list) $6.00

Publisher: Sewall Rehabilitation Center

THE SCHOOL READINESS CHECKLIST

Refer to page 491.

SCHOOL READINESS SCREENING TEST

Refer to page 491.

SCHOOL READINESS SURVEY

Refer to page 492.

SMITH-JOHNSON NONVERBAL PERFORMANCE SCALE

Alathena J. Smith and Ruth E. Johnson

Child   Ages 2-4

Purpose: Provides a nonverbal assessment of the developmental level of children. Used to evaluate hearing-impaired, language-delayed, culturally deprived, and handicapped children.

Description: 14-category examination using nonverbal tasks to measure the developmental level of a broad range of skills in young children. Each category consists of a series of subtasks presented in order of increasing difficulty. With the exception of two tasks, the examiner proceeds to the first task in the next category as soon as the child has failed two consecutive tasks. All but one of the tasks are untimed. The test measures strengths and weaknesses across a broad range of skills without constricting the evaluation by labeling the child with a single quantitative score. Norms are provided for both hearing-impaired children and normals. Examiner required. Not suitable for group use.

Untimed: 30-45 minutes

Scoring: Hand key; examiner evaluated

Cost: Complete kit (test materials, record sheets, manual) $105.00

Publisher: Western Psychological Services

STEPS UP DEVELOPMENTAL SCREENING PROGRAM (SUDS)
Shirley Cliff and Diane Carr

Child   Ages 0-3

Purpose: Screens children for a wide range of possible developmental problems. Can be used for evaluation by parents, social workers, and day-care center staff.

Description: Multiple-item observation test in which 32 question cards are used by trained volunteers to check various functions. Different test cards are provided for each two-week category for children under age 1 and for each three-month age category for children between ages 1-3. Each card contains questions screening areas of gross motor, fine motor, language, cognitive/social, vision, hearing, head circumference, congenitally dislocated hips, and convulsive disorders. The test frequently is administered during the waiting period in public health clinics, hospital clinics, and physicians' offices. Examiner required. Not suitable for group use.

Untimed: 5 minutes per screening

Scoring: Examiner evaluated

Cost: Kit (with manual) $60.00; 100 replacement cards $7.95; manual $10.00

Publisher: El Paso Rehabilitation Center

Information and availability unconfirmed; no publisher response.

STYCAR CHART OF DEVELOPMENTAL SEQUENCES (REVISED 1975 EDITION)
Mary D. Sheridan

Child   Ages 1 month-
5 years

Purpose: Assesses normal development of children. Used for clinical screening.

Description: Multiple-item chart indicating the steps in normal child development. The package includes testing procedures designed to supplement a general pediatric examination. The instrument is available as a wall chart or as a pocket-size pamphlet. It is not for public display in clinic waiting rooms. Available to medical doctors, speech therapists, and teachers of the deaf, blind, and physically handicapped. Examiner required. Not suitable for group use. BRITISH PUBLISHER

Untimed: Not available

Scoring: Examiner evaluated

Cost: Pamphlet and wall chart £2.45 (payment in sterling for all overseas orders)

Publisher: NFER-NELSON Publishing Company Ltd.

STYCAR VISION TESTS
Refer to page 662.

SYMBOLIC PLAY TEST— EXPERIMENTAL EDITION (SPT)
Refer to page 647.

VALETT DEVELOPMENTAL SURVEY OF BASIC LEARNING ABILITIES

Refer to page 496.

VINELAND SOCIAL MATURITY SCALE

Edgar A. Doll

All ages   Ages 0-30

Purpose: Measures successive stages of social competence and adaptive behavior. Used to measure individual differences which may be significant in cases of mental deficiencies and emotional disturbances in order to plan therapy or individual education.

Description: 117-item interview covering eight categories: Self-Help General, Self-Help Eating, Self-Help Dressing, Locomotion, Occupation, Communication, Self-Direction, and Socialization. The examiner interviews a parent, close relative, or other primary care-giver and enters each of their responses against each item listed in the record form. Raw scores are converted to an age equivalent score (social age), which may be used to compute a social quotient. Materials include a record form and manual. Examiner required. Not suitable for group use.

Untimed: 20-30 minutes

Scoring: Examiner evaluated

Cost: 25 record forms $8.00; manual $5.75

Publisher: American Guidance Service

VULPÉ ASSESSMENT BATTERY

Shirley German Vulpé

Handicapped children   Ages 0-6

Purpose: Evaluates the developmental status of atypically developing children.

Description: 1,127-item performance analysis/developmental assessment of functioning in eight developmental skill areas (basic senses and functions, gross-motor behaviors, fine-motor behaviors, language behaviors, cognitive processes and specific concepts, the organization of behavior, activities of daily living) and one environmental domain (environment). Information about an individual child is obtained through direct observation or from a knowledgeable informant. Examiner required. Not suitable for group use.

Untimed: Not available

Scoring: Examiner evaluated

Cost: Complete battery $20.00; 75 scoring pads $2.50

Publisher: National Institute on Mental Retardation

Intelligence and Related

ACER ADVANCED TEST B40

Refer to page 498.

ACER ADVANCED TEST N

Refer to page 498.

ACER HIGHER TESTS: WL-WQ, ML-MQ (SECOND EDITION) AND PL-PQ

Refer to page 499.

ACER INTERMEDIATE TEST F

Refer to page 499.

ACER INTERMEDIATE TEST G

Refer to page 499.

ACER JUNIOR A TEST

Refer to page 499.

ACER JUNIOR NON-VERBAL TEST

Refer to page 500.

ADVANCED PROGRESSIVE MATRICES (APM-1962)

J.C. Raven

Adolescent, adult

Purpose: Assesses the mental ability of people with above-average intellectual ability by means of nonverbal abstract reasoning tasks. Used for school and vocational counseling and placement and for research.

Description: 48-item paper-pencil non-verbal test in two sets. Set I contains 12 problems and is used as a practice test for Set II, which consists of 36 problems. In each problem, the subject is presented with a pattern or figure design with a missing part. The subject selects one of six possible parts as the correct one. Answer sheets are provided. Examiner required. Suitable for group use. BRITISH PUBLISHER

Timed: 40 minutes

Untimed: 60 minutes

Scoring: Hand key

Cost: 25 Set I tests £30.00; 25 Set II tests £70.00; 50 hand-scorable Set I and Set II record forms £4.50; plastic marking key £6.70 plus V.A.T.

Publisher: H.K. Lewis & Co. Ltd.; distributed in U.S.A. by The Psychological Corporation

AH4 GROUP TEST OF GENERAL INTELLIGENCE (REGULAR EDITION)
Refer to page 500.

AH5 GROUP TEST OF HIGH GRADE INTELLIGENCE
Refer to page 501.

ARTHUR POINT SCALE OF PERFORMANCE, FORM I
Grace Arthur

Ages 4-adult

Purpose: Measures intelligence of children and adults. Used as a nonverbal supplement to the highly verbalized Binet tests, especially with people with language, speech, emotional, or cultural problems.

Description: 10 nonverbal task-assessment subtests measuring intelligence: Mare-Foal Formboard, Seguin-Goddard Formboard, Pintner-Paterson 2-Figure Formboard, Casuist Formboard, Pintner-Manikin Test, Knox-Kempf Feature Pro-

file Test, Knox Cube Imitation Test, Healy Pictorial Completion Test 1, Kohs Block Design Test, and Porteus Mazes. The test is particularly useful as a supplement to the Binet scale in cases in which a child's environmental conditions vary widely from those of the average child. The comparison is of value whether it confirms the Binet ratings or reveals a disparity in verbal and nonverbal development. Examiner required. Not suitable for group use.

Untimed: Not available

Scoring: Examiner evaluated

Cost: Complete kit (tests, 50 record cards, manual) $415.00; 50 record cards $14.00

Publisher: Stoelting Company

BLOOM ANALOGIES TEST (BAT)
Philip Bloom

Adult

Purpose: Assesses high level verbal reasoning ability in adults.

Description: 50-item paper-pencil multiple-choice test providing rapid assessment of general intelligence level to a 5 sigma ceiling (top/3 million) without testing for factual knowledge or perseverance traits. Examinee chooses best response to a verbal analogy. Used to select members for high I.Q. societies, including Triple Nine Society, International Society for Philosophical Enquiry, Prometheus, and Mega. May require a general high-school education within the United States for representative scoring by examinees. Separate norms are provided for individuals who take the test while being timed and for those who take the test untimed. Self-administered. Suitable for group use.

Timed: 15 minutes

Untimed: Varies

Scoring: Hand key; scoring completed only by publisher

Cost: Test copies-free; scoring report from publisher $5.00

Publisher: Philip Bloom

THE BRITISH ABILITY SCALES, REVISED EDITION
Refer to page 503.

CATTELL INFANT INTELLIGENCE SCALE
Refer to page 6.

COGNITIVE DIAGNOSTIC BATTERY (CDB)
Refer to page 591.

COLOURED PROGRESSIVE MATRICES
J.C. Raven

Child, adult   **Ages 5-11 and adult**

Purpose: Assesses the mental ability of young children and older adults who are mentally subnormal or impaired. Used for school and clinical counseling and research.

Description: 36-item paper-pencil non-verbal test consisting of design and pattern problems printed in several colors, including the two easiest sets from SPM, and a dozen additional items of similar difficulty. In each problem, the subject is presented with a pattern or figure design with a missing part. The subject selects one of six possible parts as the correct one. Examiner required. Suitable for group use above age eight. Standard norms were developed in Great Britain; U.S. norms are available. BRITISH PUBLISHER

Untimed: 15-30 minutes

Scoring: Hand key

Cost: Specimen set (book of tests, 12 combined Coloured Matrices, Sections 1, 2, and 6 of manual, Crichton Vocabulary Scale Forms) £13.90 plus V.A.T.; 25 tests £86.00

Publisher: H.K. Lewis & Co. Ltd.; distributed in U.S.A. by The Psychological Corporation

COLUMBIA MENTAL MATURITY SCALE (CMMS)
Bessie B. Burgemeister,
Lucille Hollander Blum,
and Irving Lorge

Child   Ages 3½-10

Purpose: Assesses mental ability. Used with preschoolers, kindergartners, or children with physical or verbal impairments.

Description: 92-item test of general reasoning abilities. Items are arranged in a series of eight overlapping levels. The level administered is determined by the child's chronological age. Items are printed on 95 (6" x 19") cards. The child responds by selecting from each series of drawings the one that does not belong. Materials include item cards and a Guide for Administration and Interpretation, which includes directions in Spanish. The test may be administered by a classroom teacher. Examiner required. Not suitable for group use.

Untimed: 15-20 minutes

Scoring: Examiner evaluated

Cost: Examiner's kit (95 item cards, guide) $178.00; 35 individual record forms $20.00

Publisher: The Psychological Corporation

THE CULTURE FAIR SERIES: SCALES 1, 2, 3
Raymond B. Cattell and
A.K.S. Cattell

Ages 4 and older

Purpose: Measures individual intelligence for a wide range of ages without, as much as possible, the influence of verbal fluency, cultural climate, and educational level. Identifies learning and emotional problems. Used in employee selection and placement, special education decisions, and college, career, and vocational counseling.

Description: Nonverbal paper-pencil (except for part of Scale 1) tests arranged in three scales to cover the age range of four years to adult. Test items require only that the subject be able to perceive relationships in shapes and figures. Scale 1 (ages 4-8 and older retardates) differs from Scales 2 and 3 in that it is not wholly nonverbal or wholly group administered. It consists of eight subtests, four of which must be individually administered. A set of cards and some common objects are required for two of the subtests. Scales 2 and 3 contain four paper-pencil subtests of perceptual tasks: Completing Series, Classifying, Solving Incomplete Designs, and Evaluating Conditions. Scale 2 can be used with children as young as eight-years-old and with older children and adults. Scale 3 is more difficult than Scale 2 and obtains a greater refinement in the higher intelligence ranges. It is used with high-school and college students and adults of superior intelligence.

The choice of scales to be administered is based on the examiner's evaluation of the potential ability level to be tested. Scale 1 provides mental age and IQ scores; Scales 2 and 3 provide percentiles (by age), IQs, and special norms for untimed administration of Scale 2. Examiner required. Suitable for group use (except as noted for Scale 1). Available in Spanish.

Untimed: Scale 1 22 minutes; Scales 2 and 3 12½ minutes per form

Scoring: Hand key

Cost: Reusable classification test cards $8.60; 25 nonreusable test booklets $10.00; scoring key $1.50; handbook $2.25; 25 nonreusable test booklets $9.00; 50 answer sheets (all scales) $6.50; scoring keys (answer sheets) $1.05-$1.55; scoring keys (test booklets) $1.00; tape recording (Scale 2) $25.00; manual $5.80; and technical supplement $6.50

Publisher: Institute for Personality and Ability Testing, Inc.

EXTENDED MERRILL-PALMER SCALE

Refer to page 8.

FULL-RANGE PICTURE VOCABULARY TEST (FRPV)

R.B. Ammons and H.S. Ammons

Ages 2-adult

Purpose: Assesses individual intelligence. May be used for testing special populations, such as physically handicapped, uncooperative, aphasic, or very young subjects.

Description: 16-item test of verbal comprehension. Items are matched to drawings on 16 cards. The subject points to one of four drawings that best repre-

sents a particular word. The subject also may respond by indicating "yes" or "no" as the examiner points to each drawing. No reading or writing is required of the subject. Two parallel forms, A and B, which use the same set of stimulus plates, are available. Examiner required. Not suitable for group use.

Untimed: 5-10 minutes

Scoring: Hand key; examiner evaluated

Cost: Set of plates, with instructions, norms, and sample answer sheets $15.00; 25 answer sheets (specify Form A or B) $2.50

Publisher: Psychological Test Specialists

GOODENOUGH-HARRIS DRAWING TEST

Florence L. Goodenough and Dale B. Harris

Child, adolescent
Ages 3-15

Purpose: Assesses mental ability through nonverbal technique.

Description: Measures intelligence through three drawing tasks in three tests: Goodenough Draw-a-Man Test, Draw-a-Woman Test, and the experimental Self-Drawing Scale. The man and woman drawings may be scored for the presence of up to 73 characteristics. Materials include Quality Scale Cards, which are required for the short-scoring method. Separate norms are available for males and females. Examiner required. Suitable for group use.

Untimed: 10-15 minutes

Scoring: Hand key

Cost: Examiner's kit (test booklet, manual, Quality Scale Cards) $25.00; 35 tests $21.00; manual $11.00; Quality Scale Cards $16.00; text $36.00

Publisher: The Psychological Corporation

GRIFFITHS MENTAL DEVELOPMENT SCALES

Ruth Griffiths

Child   Ages 0-8

Purpose: Measures cognitive/intellectual development in infants and children.

Used to assess need for remedial treatment and to assess progress.

Description: Multiple-item test of intellectual development meauring social development, fine- and gross-motor skills, hearing, eye-hand coordination, and speech. The test is available on two levels. Scale 1 (27 items) is for children from birth to age two. Scale 2 (22 items) is for children from ages two to eight. Some items appear on both scales. Materials include toys, form boards, pictures, and models packed in a carrying case. There are different materials for each age group. Two books by the author, *The Abilities of Babies* and *The Abilities of Young Children*, are available separately. They describe the methods employed in the development and standardization of the scales. Examiner required. Not suitable for group use. Available in Swedish and Italian.
BRITISH PUBLISHER

Untimed: Varies

Scoring: Examiner evaluated

Cost: Kit (Scale 1, Scale 2, *Abilities of Babies* manual, *Abilities of Young Children* manual) $440.00; 25 booklets $32.50; 25 forms $20.00

Publisher: The Test Agency Ltd.; distributed in the U.S.A. by Test Center, Inc.

GROUP TESTS—1974

Child

Purpose: Assesses developmental intelligence. Used for psychological-educational evaluation.

Description: 6-subtest measure of general intelligence. Three subtests are verbal, three are nonverbal. The test provides three scores: verbal, nonverbal, and total. Materials include three series: Junior Series for Standards 4 to 6, Intermediate Series for Standards 6 to 8, and Senior Series for Standards 8 to 10. Examiner required. Suitable for group use.
SOUTH AFRICAN PUBLISHER

Timed: 2½ hours

Scoring: Hand key; examiner evaluated

Cost: (In Rands) Junior test 2,00; manual 1,20; norms 0,30; scoring stencil 1,60; 10 answer sheets 0,70; Intermediate test 0,70; manual for Intermediate and Senior 3,70; norms 0,30; scoring stencils Intermediate and Senior 1,10; Senior test 0,50; norms 0,30; orders from outside The RSA will be dealt with on merit

Publisher: Human Sciences Research Council

HAPTIC INTELLIGENCE SCALE
Harriet C. Shurrager and Phil S. Shurrager

Adult blind

Purpose: Measures the intelligence of blind and partially sighted adults. Used as a substitute for or supplement to the Wechsler Adult Intelligence Scale.

Description: Seven nonverbal (except for instructions) task assessments measuring the intelligence of blind and partially sighted adults. The subtests are Digit Symbol, Object Assembly, Block Design, Plan-of-Search, Object Completion, Pattern Board, and Bead Arithmetic. Wechsler's procedures were followed in establishing age categories and statistical treatment of the data. Examiner required. Not suitable for group use.

Timed: 1 hour, 30 minutes

Scoring: Examiner evaluated

Cost: Complete kit (25 record blanks, testing materials, manual) $475.00

Publisher: Stoelting Company

HEALY PICTORIAL COMPLETION TEST II
William Healy

All ages

Purpose: Measures mental ability and intelligence based on an individual's apperceptive ability. Used with all age groups and the mentally defective.

Description: 10-item task-assessment test of problems that are visual, nonlanguage, and ideational measures of important apperceptive abilities. The test consists of two boards containing a total of 11 5" x 3½" pictures representing the sequence of events occurring during the day in the life of a school boy. A square piece of each picture is missing. The child must complete each test picture by selecting the proper square from the accompanying 60 choices. There is only one correct choice for each picture, and the concepts embodied in the test items vary greatly according to difficulty. The 60 answer pieces are numbered on the back for scoring purposes. Examiner required. Not suitable for group use.

Timed: 20 minutes

Scoring: Examiner evaluated

Cost: Complete set (test, manual, carrying case) $87.00

Publisher: Stoelting Company

JENKINS INTERMEDIATE NON-VERBAL TEST: ACER ADAPTATION
Refer to page 507.

JENSEN ALTERNATION BOARD
Milton B. Jensen

Adolescent, adult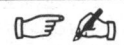

Purpose: Measures an individual's ability to understand and repeat patterns. Used to establish learning age levels and to demonstrate consistency in measuring impaired performance in certain mental pathologies.

Description: Nonverbal hand-eye-mental test using a switchboard device containing a row of five individually switched lights, a sequence selector switch, and a privacy panel to prevent the subject from seeing which series the examiner selects. A single-position warm-up exercise is administered as an example, followed by three test series, each with a different pattern. The patterns are repeated until learned and totals for each series and a combined score are computed. Examiner required. Not suitable for group use.

Untimed: 15-20 minutes

Scoring: Hand key

Cost: Apparatus $88.00

Publisher: Lafayette Instrument Company, Inc.

JUNIOR SOUTH AFRICAN INDIVIDUAL SCALES (JSAIS)—1979

Child   Ages 3-7

Purpose: Assesses cognitive functioning of children. Used for psychological-educational diagnosis.

Description: 21-scale measure of various aspects of a child's cognitive abilities. Twelve empirically selected scales yield the following IQ measures: General Intellectual Ability (GIQ), Verbal Ability (VIQ), and Perceptual-Performance Ability (PIQ), as well as estimates of memory and quantitative ability. Any scale or group of scales may be administered. Examiner required. Not suitable for group use.

SOUTH AFRICAN PUBLISHER

Untimed: Not available

Scoring: Hand key; examiner evaluated

Cost: (In Rands) manual-part 1, 11,00; part II 12,10; part III 8,00; 10 answer booklets 7,80; 10 profile sheets (specify 3-5 years or 6-7 years) 1,40; vocabulary set 8,40; picture puzzles 10,30; number and quantity concepts 8,90; picture series 4,10; visual memory 4,70 per set; picture riddles 8,50; orders from outside The RSA will be dealt with on merit

Publisher: Human Sciences Research Council

KAHN INTELLIGENCE TEST (KIT:EXP): A CULTURE-MINIMIZED EXPERIENCE
T.C. Kahn

All ages

Purpose: Assesses individual intelligence. May be used for special groups, such as the blind and deaf or individuals from different educational and cultural backgrounds.

Description: Performance measure of several aspects of intelligence, including concept formation, recall, and motor coordination. A special scale for assessment of blind subjects' intelligence is included. The test requires no reading, writing, or verbal knowledge. It uses the same materials as the Kahn Test of Symbol

Arrangement (KTSA): 16 plastic objects and a cloth strip containing 15 equal segments. The manual contains instructions for obtaining mental age, IQ, or developmental level. The test may be used only by psychologists, psychiatrists, counselors, and others with comparable training. Examiner required. Not suitable for group use.

Untimed: 15 minutes

Scoring: Hand key; examiner evaluated

Cost: Complete set $52.00; 50 record sheets $16.00; manual $5.00

Publisher: Psychological Test Specialists

KASANIN-HANFMANN CONCEPT FORMATION TEST (VYGOTSKY TEST) AND MODIFIED VYGOTSKY CONCEPT FORMATION TEST
Paul L. Wang

All ages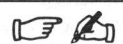

Purpose: Measures an individual's ability to think in abstract concepts. Used with uneducated adults, children, and special groups such as psychotic patients.

Description: Task-assessment test consisting of 22 blocks that the subject analyzes and sorts. The blocks are of different colors, shapes, and sizes but are alike in some way. The subject must determine the common factor and sort the blocks according to that factor. The Modified Vygotsky Concept Formation Test provides a new method of administering and scoring. The modification standardizes and simplifies the observation of the subject and adds a divergent thinking test. The modification is particularly useful in the study of mental retardation, schizophrenia, and cerebral organicity (e.g., frontal lobe pathology). Examiner required. Not suitable for group use.

Untimed: Not available

Scoring: Examiner evaluated

Cost: Test materials $52.00; Modified Vygotsky Concept Formation manual $7.50; 30 record forms $13.50

Publisher: Stoelting Company

KAUFMAN ASSESSMENT BATTERY FOR CHILDREN (K-ABC)
Alan S. Kaufman and Nadeen L. Kaufman

Child Ages 2½-12½

Purpose: Measures intelligence and achievement. Defines intelligence as ability of children to process information and solve problems. Used for psychological and clinical assessment of children, especially the learning disabled, mentally retarded, gifted, preschoolers, and minority groups and for neuropsychological research.

Description: 16 subtests of mental processing skills and achievement. There are three subtests of sequential processing, seven subtests of simultaneous processing, and six subtests of achievement (acquired knowledge, reading, and arithmetic). The examiner presents to the child a test plate containing a stimulus item and gives a verbal direction, and the child responds. Directions may be given in the child's native language or with gestures for the hearing impaired. The test yields four major scores: Sequential Processing, Simultaneous Processing, Mental Processing Composite, and Achievement. Each score has a mean of 100 and a standard deviation of 15. National percentile ranks, age and grade equivalents, and sociocultural percentile ranks are also available. Standardization is based on 1980 census data. Separate scales for mental processing and achievement were normed on the same sample. Materials include test plates bound into three easel kits, interpretive manual, 118 photo series cards, seven matrix chips, nine triangles, 25 individual test records, and a container. Examiners must have necessary qualifications to use the test. Not suitable for group use. A Spanish version is forthcoming in 1987.

Untimed: Varies

Scoring: Examiner evaluated; may be computer scored

Cost: Complete test kit $150.00

Publisher: American Guidance Service

LANGDON ADULT INTELLIGENCE TEST
Kevin Langdon

Adult

Purpose: Measures attention in reasoning of highly gifted adults. Used by individuals seeking information on their intelligence quotients or admission to societies such as Triple Nine, Mega, and Prometheus.

Description: 56-item paper-pencil multiple-choice test assessing common sense or judgment, spatial ability, inductive reasoning, verbal ability, intellectual sophistication, perseverance and, to a limited extent, creativity. A good command of English is required. Self-administered. Not suitable for group use.

Untimed: 10-20 hours

Scoring: Computer scored

Cost: Test booklet, answer sheet, computer-generated score report, statistical report $8.00

Publisher: Polymath Systems

LEITER ADULT INTELLIGENCE SCALE (LAIS)

Adult

Purpose: Measures general intelligence in adults. Used with individuals from the upper and lower levels of the socio-economic hierarchy and with the psychologically disabled.

Description: Six oral-response and task-performance tests assessing verbal and nonverbal intelligence. The verbal tests are Similarities-Differences, Digits Forward and Backward, and Free Recall-Controlled Recall. The nonverbal tests are Pathways (following a prescribed sequence), Stencil Designs (reproduction of designs), and Painted Cube Test (duplication of designs). Test results identify deficits in cognitive, psychophysical, or social areas and provide a measure of functional efficiency for psychologically disabled and superior individuals. Examiner required. Not suitable for group use.

Untimed: 40 minutes

Scoring: Examiner evaluated

Cost: Test kit (all test materials, manual, 100 record blanks) $132.00

Publisher: Stoelting Company

LEITER INTERNATIONAL PERFORMANCE SCALE (ARTHUR ADAPTATION)

Child   Ages 2-12

Purpose: Assesses general intelligence of nonverbal or non-English-speaking individuals.

Description: Multiple-item nonverbal intelligence test consisting of 54 subtests contained in two trays for measuring intelligence of individuals ages 2-7 (Tray 1) and 8-12 (Tray 2). The test requires no verbal instructions or responses. Individuals match blocks with corresponding characters in a wooden frame. Categories of matching are concretistics (matching of specific relationships), symbolic transformation (judging relationships between two events), quantitative discriminations, spatial imagery, genus matching, progression discriminations, and immediate recall. There are significant positive correlations between this test and the Stanford-Binet, Wechsler, Peabody Picture Vocabulary, and others. The test can be used with individuals who are deaf, cerebral palsied, non-English-speaking, culturally disadvantaged, mentally retarded, and mentally superior. Examiner required. Not suitable for group use.

Untimed: Varies

Scoring: Examiner evaluated

Cost: Complete set (test materials, manual, carrying case, 100 record forms) $385.00

Publisher: Stoelting Company

LEITER INTERNATIONAL PERFORMANCE SCALE (LIPS)
Russell G. Leiter

Child, adolescent
Ages 2-18

Purpose: Measures intelligence and mental age for all individuals ages 2-18, including the deaf, cerebral palsied, non-English-speaking, and culturally disadvantaged.

Description: Multiple-item nonverbal task assessment of intelligence in which the subject matches blocks with corresponding characteristic strips positioned in a sturdy wooden frame. The difficulty of the task increases at each level. The categories measured are concretistics (matching of specific relationships), symbolic transformation (judging relationships between two events), quantitative discriminations, spatial imagery, genus matching, progression discriminations, and immediate recall. Test materials include three trays of blocks and strips that make up the 54 subtests. Tray 1 covers ages 2-7, Tray 2 covers ages 8-12, and Tray 3 covers ages 13-17. Instructions for all age levels are delivered by easily learned pantomime. The LIPS yields Mental Age and I.Q. The Binet-type year scale has four tests at each year level from Year II through Year XVI and six tests at year XVII. The test kit includes all materials, wooden frame, carrying case, 100 record cards, manual. Examiner required. Not suitable for group use.

Untimed: 45 minutes

Scoring: Examiner evaluated

Cost: Complete kit $525.00; 100 record forms $16.00

Publisher: Stoelting Company

LOGICAL REASONING
Alfred F. Hertzka and J. P. Guilford

Adolescent, adult

Purpose: Measures critical thinking ability. Used for research and experiment.

Description: Multiple-item paper-pencil multiple-choice test measuring the "evaluation of semantic implications," which is defined as the ability to judge the logical soundness of meaningful conclusions. Norms are provided for high-school and college students for both part and total scores. The test is restricted to A.P.A. members. Examiner required. Suitable for group use.

Untimed: 20 minutes

Scoring: Hand key; may be computer scored

Cost: 25 tests $16.00; manual $1.00; 25 answer sheets $4.00; scoring key $2.50

Publisher: Sheridan Psychological Services, Inc.

THE MEGA TEST
Ronald K. Hoeflin

Ages 16 and older

Purpose: Assesses very high levels of intelligence in adults. Used as an admission test for those high-IQ societies for which ordinary intelligence tests lack sufficient ceilings.

Description: 48-item paper-pencil test of intelligence. The Mega test contains 24 verbal analogies, 12 spatial problems, and 12 numerical problems. The numerical problems include six descriptive problems and six number series. Subjects work on the test at their own pace at home or in a library. Participants may use any books they wish; pocket calculators are permitted. Computers are prohibited because not everyone has equal access to them. The test is administered to individuals by mail and scored only by the publisher. Self-administered. Not suitable for group use.

Untimed: 2-120 hours

Scoring: Hand key

Cost: Test booklet $1.00; score report $10.00

Publisher: Ronald K. Hoeflin

MERRILL-PALMER SCALE
Rachel Stutsman

Child   Ages 18 months-
4 years

Purpose: Measures intelligence in children. Used as a substitute for or a supplement to the Binet Scale.

Description: 19 task-assessment and oral-response tests measuring language skills, motor skills, dexterity, and matching. The 19 subtests are Stutsman Color Matching Test; Wallin Pegboards A & B; Stutsman Buttoning Test; Stutsman Stick and String; Scissors; Stutsman Language Test; Stutsman Picture Formboards 1, 2, and 3; Mare-Foal Formboard; Seguin-Goddard Formboard; Pintner-Manikin

Test; Decroly Matching Game; Stutsman Nested Cubes; Woodworth-Wells Association Test; Stutsman Copying Test; Stutsman Pyramid Test; Stutsman Little Pink Tower Test; and Kohs Blocks. The test deals directly with the problem of resistance in the testing situation and provides a comprehensive listing of the many factors influencing a child's willingness to cooperate. Refused and omitted items are considered when arriving at a total score, which may then be converted into mental age, sigma value, or percentile rank. The test is significant in its complete independence from The Stanford-Binet Scale. All subtests may be ordered separately. Examiner required. Not suitable for group use.

Untimed: Not available

Scoring: Examiner evaluated

Cost: Complete kit (tests, 50 record blanks, carrying case) $345.00

Publisher: Stoelting Company

MULTIDIMENSIONAL APTITUDE BATTERY—FORM L
Douglas N. Jackson

Adolescent, adult

Purpose: Assesses aptitudes and intelligence for adolescents and adults. Used for clinical and research purposes with normal and deviant populations, including prison inmates, neurotic, psychotic, and neurologically impaired psychiatric patients, persons in business and industry, and high-school and college students.

Description: Multiple-item paper-pencil multiple-choice test consisting of two batteries of five subtests each. The Verbal Battery includes the following subtests: Information, Comprehension, Arithmetic, Similarities, and Vocabulary. The Performance Battery subtests include Digit Symbol, Picture Completion, Spatial, Picture Arrangement, and Object Assembly. Verbal, Performance, and Full Scale IQs and standard scores for the 10 subtests have been calibrated to those of the WAIS-R and permit appraisal of intellectual functioning at nine different age levels, ranging from ages 16-74. Separate test booklets and answer sheets are provided for the two batteries. One battery of five subtests (seven minutes per test) can be administered in one sitting. An optional tape recording of instructions and timing may be used to administer all subtests. Scoring templates are available for hand scoring. Profiles and scoring sheets may be used for recording raw scores, converting scores to standard form, and recording IQs. The one-day scoring service provides a five-page computerized report for each individual tested, including a one-page summary for the counselor (tests may be submitted for scoring in any quantity). The manual contains instructions for administering the tests, interpretive and technical information, and norms tables and profiles. Online software is available. Examiner required. Suitable for group use.

Timed/Untimed: 70 minutes (7 minutes per subtest)

Scoring: Hand key; machine-scoring and computer analysis available

Cost: 70 test booklets (35 per battery) $87.50; 70 answer sheets (35 per battery) $28.00; manual $10.50; 35 record forms $6.00; scoring templates $12.50; computerized scoring (1-24 individuals) $3.25 each; cassette tape of instructions and timing $20.00

Publisher: Research Psychologists Press, Inc.

NATIONAL ADULT READING TEST
Hazel E. Nelson

Adult   Ages 20-70

Purpose: Measures the effects of dementia, alcohol, drugs, or illness on the intellectual functioning of adults.

Description: 50-item oral-response test measuring premorbid intelligence in the assessment of dementia. Test items comprise a list of 50 words whose pronunciation cannot be guessed by phonemic decoding but must be recognized in order to be read correctly. The individual reads the words aloud. The raw score predicts IQs that approximate closely to the premorbid IQ level. Examiner required. Not suitable for group use. BRITISH PUBLISHER

Untimed: Varies

Scoring: Examiner evaluated

Cost: Word cards £1.85; 25 answer sheets £3.65; manual £6.30

Publisher: NFER-NELSON Publishing Company Ltd.

NON-LANGUAGE LEARNING TEST
Mary K. Bauman

Visually handicapped individuals

Purpose: Measures nonverbal intelligence and learning abilities of blind and visually handicapped individuals.

Description: Multiple-item task performance test assessing shape discrimination, flexibility of thinking, and ability to profit from instruction and experience when using concrete materials. The test kit includes instructions and diagrams for constructing testing materials, instructions for administering the test, and rough norms. Examiner required. Not suitable for group use.

Timed: Varies

Scoring: Examiner evaluated

Cost: Test kit $5.00

Publisher: Associated Services for the Blind

NON-LANGUAGE MULTI-MENTAL TEST
E.L. Terman, W.A. McCall, and J. Lorge

Grades 2 and above

Purpose: Measures basic intelligence of illiterate or language-handicapped persons, including those who do not speak English or who are deaf. Used to determine linguistic handicaps.

Description: Multiple-item picture test of abstract thinking and relationships of pictorial symbols. The test may be adapted for either simple verbal or pantomime directions. Administration and timing are flexible. Two forms, A and B (verbal or pantomime), are available. Examiner required. Not suitable for group use.

CANADIAN PUBLISHER

Untimed: 30 minutes

Scoring: Hand key

Cost: Specimen test $1.00; 35 tests (Form A or Form B) $8.50

Publisher: Institute of Psychological Research, Inc.

Information and availability unconfirmed; no publisher response.

NON-LANGUAGE TEST OF VERBAL INTELLIGENCE
Refer to page 509.

NON-VERBAL ABILITY TESTS (NAT)
Refer to page 510.

OHIO CLASSIFICATION TEST
DeWitt E. Sell, Robert W. Scollay, and Leroy N. Vernon

Adult

Purpose: Assesses general mental ability. Used for evaluation of penal populations.

Description: Four-subtest performance measure of general intellectual ability. The subtests include Block-Counting, Digit-Symbol, Number Series, and Memory Span for Objects. The directions are given by the examiner. Some number reading is required. The test may be used in any situation where a culture-fair measure of intelligence is needed. Examiner required. Not suitable for group use.

Timed: 20 minutes

Scoring: Hand key

Cost: Specimen set $5.00; 25 tests $8.75; 25 answer sheets $7.00

Publisher: Psychometric Affiliates

PEABODY PICTURE VOCABULARY TEST-REVISED (PPVT-R)
Refer to page 511.

PICTORIAL TEST OF INTELLIGENCE
Refer to page 511.

PORTEUS MAZES
S.D. Porteus

All ages

Purpose: Assesses mental ability of verbally handicapped subjects. Used in anthropological studies and in research on the effects of drugs and psychosurgery.

Description: Nonlanguage test of mental ability in which the items are mazes. Materials include the Vineland Revision, Porteus Maze Extension, and Porteus Maze Supplement. The Vineland Revision, consisting of twelve mazes, is the basic test. The Porteus Maze Extension is a series of eight mazes designed for retesting and is not intended for use as an initial test. The Porteus Maze Supplement is designed for a third testing in clinical and research settings. Examiner required. Not suitable for group use.

Untimed: 25 minutes per scale

Scoring: Examiner evaluated

Cost: Basic sets (mazes and 100 score sheets), Vineland Revision $79.00; Porteus Maze Extension $58.00; Porteus Maze Supplement (no score sheets) $54.00; manual $36.00

Publisher: The Psychological Corporation

QUICK TEST (QT)
R.B. Ammons and C.H. Ammons

Ages 2-adult

Purpose: Assesses individual intelligence. May be used for evaluation of the severely physically handicapped, individuals with short attention spans, or uncooperative subjects.

Description: 50-item test of general intelligence. The subject looks at plates with four line drawings and indicates which picture best illustrates the meaning of a given word. The subject usually responds by pointing. The test requires no reading, writing, or speaking. Usual administration involves the presentation of 15 to 20 of the items. Items are administered until the subject scores six consecutive passes and six consecutive failures. Materials include plates with stimulus pictures and three alternate forms. Examiner required. Suitable for group use.

Untimed: 3-10 minutes

Scoring: Hand key; examiner evaluated

Cost: Complete kit (3 plates, 100 record sheets, instruction cardboard, item cardboard) $16.00; 100 record sheets $10.00; 3 plates $4.00; instruction cardboard $0.80; item cardboard $0.70; manual $5.00

Publisher: Psychological Test Specialists

ROSS TEST OF HIGHER COGNITIVE PROCESSES (ROSS TEST)
Refer to page 513.

SCHAIE-THURSTONE ADULT MENTAL ABILITIES TEST (STAMAT)
K. Warner Schaie

Adult   Ages 22-84

Purpose: Measures five separate factors of intelligence.

Description: Multiple-item paper-pencil test in two forms measuring verbal, spatial, reasoning, number, and word fluency abilities of adults. Form A (adult) is the original Thurstone Primary Mental Abilities Test, Form 11-17, with new adult norms. Form OA (older adult) is a large-type version of the original test plus two additional scales relevant for adults ages 55 and older. The test was used by Schaie for assessing the development of adult intelligence longitudinally and cross-sectionally. New normative data are based on 4,500 people from ages 22-84. Instructions have been written to enhance performance by older adults. Examiner required. Suitable for group use.

Timed: Form A 26 minutes; Form B 37 minutes

Scoring: Hand key

Cost: Specimen set $19.50; manual $12.50

Publisher: Consulting Psychologists Press, Inc.

SENIOR SOUTH AFRICAN INDIVIDUAL SCALE (SSAIS)—1964

Child, adolescent Ages 6-17

Purpose: Assesses general intelligence in children. Used for psychological-educational evaluation.

Description: 9-subtest measure of general intellectual ability consisting of five verbal subtests and four nonverbal subtests. Verbal, Nonverbal, and Total IQ scores may be obtained. Examiner required. Not suitable for group use. SOUTH AFRICAN PUBLISHER

Untimed: 50 minutes

Scoring: Hand key; examiner evaluated

Cost: (In Rands) complete kit (manual, tests 1-9, globite holder, 2 examples of the answer sheets, practice samples) 102,00; orders from outside The RSA will be dealt with on merit

Publisher: Human Sciences Research Council

SHIPLEY INSTITUTE OF LIVING SCALE
Walter C. Shipley

Adult   Ages 15 and older

Purpose: Measures the intellectual ability and impairment of adults and adolescents ages 15 and older. Used for clinical assessment and counseling in a wide variety of clinical, educational, personnel, and counseling settings.

Description: 80-item paper-pencil test measuring vocabulary and logical sequencing (abstract thinking) abilities. The test yields both an IQ estimate and a Conceptual Quotient (CQ), which expresses the extent to which the person's abstract thinking falls short of vocabulary. The CQ is particularly useful for assessing current impairment of intellectual functioning. Examiner required. Suitable for group use.

Timed: 20 minutes

Scoring: Hand key; may be computer scored

Cost: Kit (100 tests, manual, scoring key) $33.50

Publisher: Western Psychological Services

SLOSSON INTELLIGENCE TEST (SIT)
Richard L. Slosson

All ages

Purpose: Measures the mental age, IQ, and reading level of children and adults. Used by psychologists, guidance counselors, special educators, learning disability and remedial reading teachers to provide a quick assessment of a person's mental abilities.

Description: 195-item oral screening instrument consisting of questions arranged on a scale of chronological age from one-half month to 27 years. A basal age is established at the point before which the subject gives an incorrect answer after giving at least 10 correct answers in a row. Additional credit is given for correct answers above the basal age. The basal age and added months credit are used to determine mental age and IQ. Norms are not provided for infants below the chronological age of 2. The norms tables include alternate scoring systems, such as percentiles, normal curve equivalents, stanines, and T-scores. The results can be used to predict reading achievement, plan educational programs, predict success and acceptance in college, screen students for reading disabilities, and determine the IQs of blind individuals.
The SIT includes the Slosson Oral Reading Test (SORT), which yields a reading grade level ranging from primary to high school based on the ability to pronounce words at different levels of difficulty. The SORT also is used to identify reading handicaps. Item analysis is available to identify strengths and weaknesses in eight learning areas. Examiner required. Not suitable for group use.

Untimed: 10-20 minutes

Scoring: Examiner evaluated

Cost: Complete kit (manual, directions, 50 SIT score sheets, 50 SORT score sheets, expanded norms tables) $40.00

Publisher: Slosson Educational Publications, Inc.

THE SOUTH AFRICAN INDIVIDUAL SCALE FOR THE BLIND (SAISB)—1979
Refer to page 514.

SOUTH AFRICAN WECHSLER ADULT INDIVIDUAL INTELLIGENCE SCALE

Adult   Ages 18-59

Purpose: Assesses intelligence of Afrikaans and English-speaking South Africans.

Description: Multiple-item paper-pencil and performance test consisting of five verbal tests covering information, comprehension, arithmetic, digit span, and similarities and five performance tests covering picture completion, object assembly, block design, digit symbols, and picture arrangement. An IQ score can be obtained by adding the standard scores of the tests. Examiner required. Not suitable for group use.

SOUTH AFRICAN PUBLISHER

Timed: Not available

Scoring: Not available

Cost: Contact publisher

Publisher: National Institute for Personnel Research

THE STANDARD PROGRESSIVE MATRICES (SPM-1956)
J. C. Raven

Ages 8-65

Purpose: Measures an individual's mental ability through assessment of nonverbal abstract reasoning tasks. Used for school and vocational counseling and placement.

Description: 60-item paper-pencil nonverbal test in five sets of 12 problems each. In each problem, the subject is presented with a pattern or figure design with a missing part. The subject selects one of six possible parts as the correct one. The patterns are arrayed from simple to complex. The test often is used with the Mill Hill Vocabulary Scale. U.S. norms are available. Examiner required. Suitable for group use.

BRITISH PUBLISHER

Untimed: 45 minutes

Scoring: Hand key; may be machine scored

Cost: Specimen set (book of tests, 5 each of combined matrices and Mill Hill Vocabulary record forms, Sections 1, 3, and 5a of manual, sample machine-scorable record form) £15.20 plus V.A.T.; 25 tests £65.00; 50 record forms £4.50; plastic marking key £6.70 plus VAT)

Publisher: H.K. Lewis & Co., Ltd.; distributed in U.S.A. by The Psychological Corporation

---

THE STANFORD-BINET INTELLIGENCE SCALE, FOURTH EDITION
Robert L. Thorndike,
Elizabeth P. Hagen,
and Jerome M. Sattler

Ages 2-adult

Purpose: Measures an individual's mental abilities. Used to substantiate questionable scores from group tests, to provide more comprehensive assessment, and when the subject has physical, language, or personality disorders that prevent group testing.

Description: Verbal and nonverbal performance test assessing mental abilities in four areas: verbal reasoning (vocabulary, comprehension, verbal relations, absurdities), abstract/visual reasoning (pattern analysis, matrices, paper folding and cutting, copying), quantitative comprehension (quantitative, number series, equation building), and short-term memory (memory for sentences, memory for digits, memory for objects, and bead memory). Items are arranged according to item type and order of difficulty. The following scores can be obtained: raw and scaled scores for each of the 15 subtests, four content area scores, a composite of the four area scores, a composite of any combination of the four area scores, and a profile on all 15 subtests. Results identify children and adults who would benefit from specialized learning environments. Administered only by professionally trained, certified examiners. Examiner required. Not suitable for group use.

Untimed: 45-90 minutes

Scoring: Examiner evaluated

Cost: Examiner's kit (examiner's manual, four item books, manipulables, record booklet) $297.00; 35 record booklets $18.90; guide for administering and scoring $9.93; expanded guide for interpreting and reporting $15.00; technical manual $5.25; videotape $80.00

Publisher: The Riverside Publishing Company

STANFORD-BINET INTELLIGENCE SCALE: FORM L-M
*Robert L. Thorndike,
Lewis M. Terman,
and Maud A. Merrill*

Ages 2-adult

Purpose: Measures an individual's mental abilities. Used to substantiate questionable scores from group tests and when the subject has physical, language, or personality disorders which rule out group testing.

Description: 142-item verbal and nonverbal IQ test assessing language, memory, conceptual thinking, reasoning, numerical reasoning, visual motor, and social reasoning. In most cases, only 18-24 test items need to be administered to a subject. First, the basal age is established (year level at which all items are passed). Testing continues until the ceiling age is reached (year level at which all items are failed). Responses then are scored according to established procedures to yield mental age and IQ. The results identify children and adults who would benefit from specialized learning environments. Administered only by professionally trained, certified examiners. Examiner required. Not suitable for group use.

Untimed: 45-90 minutes

Scoring: Examiner evaluated

Cost: Examiner's kit (manual, large and small printed card material, miniaturized objects) $210.00; 35 record booklets $22.56; 35 record forms $13.56

Publisher: The Riverside Publishing Company

THE TEST OF NONVERBAL INTELLIGENCE (TONI)
*Linda Brown, Rita J. Sherbenu,
and Susan J. Dollar*

Ages 6-80

Purpose: Provides a language-free measure of intelligence and reasoning. Used with subjects suspected of having difficulty in reading, writing, listening, or speaking, including mentally retarded, stroke patients, bilingual and non-English speaking, speech or language handicapped, and learning disabled persons.

Description: 50-item response test assessing intellectual capacities in a format completely free of reading, writing, and verbalizing. The examiner pantomimes the instructions, and the subject responds by pointing to the selected answer. Test items use abstract symbols to present a variety of reasoning tasks, arranged in increasing order of complexity and difficulty. The test yields a TONI quotient and percentile ranks, accurately discriminating between retarded and normal subjects. Available in two equivalent forms. Examiner required. May be administered to small groups of up to five subjects.

Untimed: 20-30 minutes

Scoring: Hand key

Cost: Complete kit (manual, picture book, 50 Form A and 50 Form B answer sheets, storage box) $69.00

Publisher: Pro-Ed

WECHSLER MEMORY SCALE (WMS)
Refer to page 68.

WECHSLER SCALES: WECHSLER ADULT INTELLIGENCE SCALE (WAIS)
David Wechsler

Adolescent, adult
Ages 16-adult

Purpose: Measures intelligence in adolescents and adults.

Description: 11 subtests divided into two major divisions yielding a verbal IQ, a performance IQ, and a full scale IQ for individuals ages 16 and older. The verbal section of the test consists of the following subtests: Information, Comprehension, Arithmetic, Similarities, Digit Span, and Vocabulary. The performance or nonverbal section of the test consists of the following subtests: Digit Symbol, Picture Completion, Block Design, Picture Arrangement, and Object Assembly. Some units of the test require verbal responses from the subject, and others require the subject to manipulate test materials to demonstrate performance ability. Raw scores are converted into scale scores after the examiner records and scores the subject's performance. Examiner required. Not suitable for group use. Available in Spanish.

Untimed: 1 hour

Scoring: Examiner evaluated

Cost: Complete set (all necessary equipment, manual, 25 record forms) $155.00; attache case $50.00

Publisher: The Psychological Corporation

WECHSLER SCALES: WECHSLER ADULT INTELLIGENCE SCALE—REVISED (WAIS-R)
David Wechsler

Adolescent, adult

Purpose: Assesses intelligence in adolescents and adults.

Description: 11 subtests divided into two major divisions yielding a verbal IQ, a performance IQ, and a full-scale IQ for individuals ages 16 and older. The verbal section of the test consists of the following subtests: Information, Comprehension,

Arithmetic, Similarities, Digit Span, and Vocabulary. The performance or nonverbal section of the test consists of the following subtests: Digit Symbol, Picture Completion, Block Design, Picture Arrangement, and Object Assembly. Some units of the test require verbal responses from the subject, and others require the subject to manipulate test materials to demonstrate performance ability. Raw scores are converted into scale scores after the examiner records and scores the subject's performance. The WAIS-R is a revision of the 1955 edition of the WAIS. Examiner required. Not suitable for group use. Available in Spanish.

Untimed: 75 minutes

Scoring: Examiner evaluated

Cost: Complete set (all necessary equipment, manual, 25 record forms with attache case) $175.00; complete without attache case $155.00

Publisher: The Psychological Corporation

WECHSLER SCALES: WECHSLER INTELLIGENCE SCALE FOR CHILDREN—REVISED (WISC-R)
David Wechsler

Child, adolescent
Ages 6-16

Purpose: Assesses intellectual ability in children.

Description: 12 subtests divided into two major divisions yielding a verbal IQ, a performance IQ, and a full-scale IQ for children tested individually. The verbal section of the test consists of the following subtests: General Information, General Comprehension, Arithmetic, Similarities, Vocabulary, and Digit Span. The performance section consists of the following subtests: Picture Completion, Picture Arrangement, Block Design, Object Assembly, Coding, and Mazes. Some units of the test require verbal responses from the subject, and others require the subject to manipulate test materials to demonstrate performance ability. Raw scores are converted into scale scores after the examiner records and scores the subject's performance. The WISC-R is a revised form of the 1949 edition of the WISC. Examiner required. Not suitable for group use. Available in Spanish.

Untimed: 1 hour

Scoring: Examiner evaluated

Cost: Complete set (all necessary equipment, manual, 25 record forms, mazes, coding booklet, carrying case) $195.00; complete set without carrying case $175.00

Publisher: The Psychological Corporation

WECHSLER SCALES: WECHSLER INTELLIGENCE SCALE FOR CHILDREN: 1949 EDITION (WISC)
David Wechsler

Adolescent   Ages 5-15

Purpose: Measures intelligence for children ages 5-15.

Description: 12 subtests divided into two major divisions yielding a verbal IQ, a performance IQ, and a full-scale IQ for children tested individually. The verbal section of the test consists of the following subtests: General Information, General Comprehension, Arithmetic, Similarities, Vocabulary, and Digit Span. The performance section consists of the following subtests: Picture Completion, Picture Arrangement, Block Design, Object Assembly, Coding, and Mazes. Some units of the test require verbal responses from the subjects, and others require the subject to manipulate test materials to demonstrate performance ability. Raw scores are converted into scale scores after the subject's performance has been recorded and scored on the provided answer form by the examiner. The WISC-R is a more recently revised form of the 1949 WISC. Examiner required. Not suitable for group use. Available in Spanish.

Untimed: 1 hour

Scoring: Examiner evaluated

Cost: Complete set (all equipment, manual, 5 record forms and test blanks, carrying case) $225.00; complete without carrying case $175.00

Publisher: The Psychological Corporation

WECHSLER SCALES: WECHSLER PRESCHOOL AND PRIMARY SCALE OF INTELLIGENCE (WPPSI)
David Wechsler

Child   Ages 4½-6

Purpose: Assesses intelligence in children.

Description: 10 subtests divided into two major divisions yielding a verbal IQ, a performance IQ, and a full-scale IQ for children tested individually. The verbal section of the test consists of the following subtests: Information, Vocabulary, Arithmetic, Similarities, and Comprehension. A supplementary Sentences Test is available within the verbal section of test. The performance section consists of the following subtests: Animal House, Picture Completion, Mazes, Geometric Design, and Block Design. An Animal House Retest unit is available within the performance section. Selected subtests require verbal response, and other subtests require the subject to manipulate test materials to demonstrate performance ability. Raw scores are converted to scale scores after the examiner records and scores the subject responses. Examiner required. Not suitable for group use.

Untimed: 1 hour

Scoring: Examiner evaluated

Cost: Complete set (all necessary equipment, manual, 25 record forms, maze test, 50 geometric design sheets, carrying case) $175.00; complete set without carrying case $155.00

Publisher: The Psychological Corporation

WIDE RANGE INTELLIGENCE-PERSONALITY TEST (WRIPT)
Refer to page 216.

Neuropsychology and Related

ADULT GROWTH EXAMINATION (AGE)
Robert F. Morgan

Adult

Purpose: Measures an individual's body age. Identifies individuals needing further diagnostic screening. Used in employment and medical settings for initial screening purposes.

Description: Three blood pressure tests, a hearing test, and a vision test measuring body age (versus calendar age). Tests are administered in the following order: blood pressure, hearing, blood pressure, vision, and blood pressure. Administration requires a portable electronic blood pressure monitor allowing rapid accurate measurement without a stethoscope, a portable audiometric monitor with a variable volume dial up to 59 db for two frequencies—1000 cps and 6000 cps, and a portable visual near-point indicator (visual targets with pica type sentence—near point of clear focus tested). Raw scores for each of the subtests are converted to equivalent age scores. These scores are arranged in rank order with the median score being the tested body age of the individual being examined. The examination may be administered by trained paraprofessionals. The 1986 manual includes complete instructions for administration and scoring, conversion tables, and discussions of validity, reliability, and uses. Examiner required. Not suitable for group use.

Untimed: 10-15 minutes

Scoring: Examiner evaluated

Cost: $14.00; may be purchased as part of R.F. Morgan's *Growing Younger* book, NY: Stein & Day, 1983, $16.95

Publisher: Robert F. Morgan

ADULT NEUROPSYCHOLOGICAL QUESTIONNAIRE
Fernando Melendez

Adolescent, adult
Ages 16 and older

Purpose: Evaluates conditions that may suggest underlying brain dysfunctions or other organic conditions. Used as a symptom checklist for making appropriate referrals to other doctors and for further neuropsychological testing.

Description: 59-item paper-pencil questionnaire evaluating complaints, symptoms, and signs that may suggest brain dysfunction. The questionnaire also monitors the course of a person's recovery or decline over a period of time. The examiner asks questions and instructs the subject to elaborate when appropriate. Examiner required. Not suitable for group use. Available in Spanish.

Untimed: 10-15 minutes

Scoring: Examiner evaluated

Cost: Complete kit (forms, manual) $12.00

Publisher: Psychological Assessment Resources, Inc.

ANALYTIC LEARNING DISABILITY ASSESSMENT (ALDA)
Refer to page 576.

AUTISM SCREENING INSTRUMENT FOR EDUCATIONAL PLANNING
Refer to page 189.

BENDER VISUAL MOTOR GESTALT TEST
Lauretta Bender

All ages

Purpose: Assesses the visual-motor functions of individuals ages 3-adult. Also used to evaluate developmental problems in children, learning disabilities, retardation, psychosis, and organic brain disorders.

Description: Test consists of nine Gestalt cards. The examiner presents the cards to the subject one at a time and in order, and the subject reproduces on blank paper the configuration or design shown on each card. Responses are scored according to the development of the concepts of form, shape, and pattern and orientation in space. Analysis of performance may indicate the presence of psychosis and maturational lags. Scoring service is provided by Koppitz and Grune & Stratton. Examiner required. Slides may be used for group administration.

Untimed: 15-20 minutes

Scoring: Examiner evaluated; scoring service available

Cost: Test cards with manual of instruction $5.00; monograph and its clinical uses $12.00; slides with manual of instruction $15.00

Publisher: American Orthopsychiatric Association, Inc.

BENTON REVISED VISUAL RETENTION TEST
Arthur Benton

Ages 8-adult

Purpose: Measures visual memory. Used as a supplement to usual mental examinations and in experimental research.

Description: 10-item test of visual perception, visual memory, and visuoconstructive abilities. Items are designs that are shown to the subject one by one. The subject studies each design and reproduces it as exactly as possible by drawing it on plain paper. Materials include Design Cards and three alternate and equivalent forms, C, D, and E. Examiner required. Not suitable for group use.

Untimed: 5 minutes

Scoring: Examiner evaluated

Cost: Complete set (manual, 3 forms of design cards, 50 record forms) $30.00

Publisher: The Psychological Corporation

BEXLEY-MAUDSLEY AUTOMATED PSYCHOLOGICAL SCREENING (BMAPS)
William Acker and Clare Acker

Adult

Purpose: Assesses psychological defects resulting from organic brain damage. Used to evaluate chronic alcoholics and to screen new patients before referring them for further evaluation.

Description: Six computer-administered tests assessing psychological functioning: Visual Spatial Ability Test—Little Men, Symbol Digit Coding test, Visual Perceptual Analysis test, Verbal Recognition Memory test, Visual Spatial Recognition Memory test, and the Bexley-Maudsley Category Sorting Test (abstract problem solving). Three versions are available for use with the Commodore 4040 and 8050 disc drives and Apple II microcomputer systems. A specially designed patient keyboard, which clips over the Commodore Pet 4032 and 8032 computer, contains nine response keys and three masks for those tests that require fewer keys. Raw and standardized scores are available immediately upon completion of the test. The manual provides details of administration, scoring, and theoretical background. The test may be administered by psychologists, psychiatrists, and nurses. Examiner required. Not suitable for group use.
BRITISH PUBLISHER

Untimed: Varies

Scoring: Computer scored

Cost: Complete set (manual, disc, keyboard adaptor) £281.75

Publisher: NFER-NELSON Publishing Company Ltd.

THE BODER TEST OF READING-SPELLING PATTERNS
Refer to page 577.

THE BOOKLET CATEGORY TEST (BCT)
Nick A. DeFilippis and Elizabeth McCampbell

Adolescent, adult
Ages 15 and older

Purpose: Diagnoses brain dysfunction. Used for clinical assessment of brain damage.

Description: 208-item test of concept formation and abstract reasoning. Figures are presented one at a time to the subject, who responds with a number between one and four. This is the booklet version of the Halstead Category Test. The first four subtests may be used to predict total error scores if time limitations do not allow administration of the entire BCT. Examiner required. Not suitable for group use.

Untimed: 30-60 minutes

Scoring: Examiner evaluated

Cost: Complete set (2-volume manual, 25 scoring forms) $125.00

Publisher: Psychological Assessment Resources, Inc.

BOSTON DIAGNOSTIC APHASIA EXAMINATION
Harold Goodglass and Edith Kaplan

Adult

Purpose: Assesses the functioning of aphasic patients. Used for clinical evaluations.

Description: Multiple-item oral-response paper-pencil and task-performance test yielding 43 scores relating to recognized aphasic syndromes, including severity rating, fluency, auditory comprehension, naming, oral reading, repetition, paraphrasia, automatized speech, reading comprehension, writing, music, and parietal. The test also provides the following seven ratings: melodic line, phrase length, articulatory agility, grammatical form, paraphrasia in running speech, word finding, and auditory comprehension. The test manual, *The Assessment of Aphasia and Related Disorders*, includes information on the nature of aphasic deficits, common clusters of defects, statistical information, administration and scoring procedures, and illustrations of test profiles that correspond to major aphasic syndromes. Examiner required. Not suitable for group use.

Untimed: Varies

Scoring: Examiner evaluated

Cost: Complete set (manual, examination booklets, and Boston Naming Test) $27.50; 25 examination booklets $15.00

Publisher: Lea and Febiger

CALIFORNIA VERBAL LEARNING TEST, RESEARCH EDITION
Dean C. Delis, Joel H. Kramer, Edith Kaplan, and Beth A. Ober

Adolescent, adult
Ages 13 and older

Purpose: Assesses verbal learning and memory deficits and aids in designing and monitoring rehabilitation. Used with the elderly and the neurologically impaired.

Description: Multitrial verbal-learning task consisting of 16 categorized words used in immediate and delayed free-recall, cued-recall, and recognition trials. A second word list also is presented to obtain interference measures. Indices of learning strategies, error types, primacy/recency effects, and other process data are provided. Examiner required. Not suitable for group use.

Untimed: 35 minutes

Scoring: Examiner evaluated; may be computer scored

Cost: 25 record booklets $20.00; 25 scorings/reports $75.00; manual $15.00

Publisher: The Psychological Corporation

CALLIER-AZUSA SCALE: G-EDITION
Refer to page 5.

CANTER BACKGROUND INTERFERENCE PROCEDURE (BIP) FOR THE BENDER GESTALT TEST
Arthur Canter

Adolescent, adult
Ages 15 and older

Purpose: Assesses the probability of organic brain damage among individuals ages 15 and older. Used for diagnosis and to plan rehabilitation programs.

Description: 10-item paper-pencil test comparing the subject's results on the standard Bender Gestalt Test in which the subject is presented with stimulus cards and asked to copy the designs on a blank sheet of paper with the results of a Bender Gestalt Test in which the subject reproduces the designs on a special sheet with intersecting sinusoidal lines that provide a background "noise" or interference during the copying task. The difference between the standard and the BIP results provides the basis for defining the subject's level of impairment. Specific ranges of adequacy and inadequacy of performance are defined to permit a measure of impairment having a high probability of association with organic brain damage or disease. Scoring is a modification of the standard Pascal-Suttell system. Examiner required. Not suitable for group use.

Untimed: 20-30 minutes

Scoring: Examiner evaluated

Cost: Complete kit (25 tests, manual) $27.50

Publisher: Western Psychological Services

CARD SORTING BOX
Refer to page 974.

THE CHILD NEUROPSYCHOLOGICAL QUESTIONNAIRE
Fernando Melendez

Child, adolescent Ages 6-16

Purpose: Evaluates children suspected of having brain dysfunction. Used as part of a comprehensive evaluation that should include a neuropsychological and pediatric neurological examination.

Description: 41-item pencil-paper questionnaire reviewing possible complaints, symptoms, and signs that suggest underlying brain dysfunction. The test encourages the examiner to consider alternative problems and make appropriate referrals for further studies. The questionnaire can be used as a basis for

discussion with the child's parents. Examiner required. Not suitable for group use. Available in Spanish.

Untimed: 10-15 minutes

Scoring: Examiner evaluated

Cost: Complete kit (forms, manual) $12.00

Publisher: Psychological Assessment Resources, Inc.

COMMUNICATIVE ABILITIES IN DAILY LIVING (CADL)
Refer to page 623.

COMPLEX-ATTENTION REHABILITATION PROGRAM
Robert J. Sbordone and Steven Hall

Adolescent, adult

Purpose: Trains cognitively impaired and brain-injured adolescents and adults to improve their attentional skills.

Description: Computer-administered program that presents the patient with visual tracking tasks that increase in complexity according to the patient's performance. The patient uses a handheld joystick to keep a small circle within a constantly moving square. At the intermediate level, the task involves simultaneously tracking two squares of different sizes and speeds. At more advanced levels, the program trains the patient to utilize language and problem-solving strategies to perform the task. The program makes decisions such as whether to interpose a rest period, increase or decrease the complexity of the task, provide external cues, or terminate the session. It also contains a speech synthesizer option for vocal presentation to patients with reading problems. The program operates on an Apple (II + , IIe, IIc) computer system using only one disk drive. Examiner/self-administered. Not suitable for group use.

Untimed: Not available

Scoring: Computer scored

Cost: Complete program, including instructional manual $195.00; shipping fee $3.00

Publisher: Robert J. Sbordone

DEVELOPMENTAL TEST OF VISUAL-MOTOR INTEGRATION (VMI)
Keith E. Beery and Norman A. Buktenica

All ages

Purpose: Identifies children with visual perception, hand control, and eye-hand coordination problems. Used with children ages 12-15 and developmentally delayed adults.

Description: Multiple-item paper-pencil test measuring the integration of visual perception and motor behavior. Test items, arranged in order of increasing difficulty, consist of geometric figures that the children are asked to copy. The Short Test Form (15 figures) is used with children ages 2-8. The Long Test Form (24 figures) is used with children ages 2-15 and adults with developmental delays. The manual includes directions for administration, scoring criteria, developmental comments, age norms, suggestions for teaching, percentiles, and standard score equivalents. Examiner required. Suitable for group use.

Untimed: Varies

Scoring: Examiner evaluated

Cost: 15 Short Forms $13.41; 15 Long Forms $19.08; manual for both forms $11.16; monograph and stimulus cards $12.30; assessment work sheets $44.28

Publisher: Modern Curriculum Press, Inc.

DIAGNOSTIC ANALYSIS OF READING ERRORS (DARE)
Refer to page 544.

THE DIGIT-DIGIT TEST
Robert J. Sbordone, Steven Hall, and Mark Seecof

Child, adolescent, adult

Purpose: Assesses and trains complex attentional skills in normal, brain-injured, and cognitively impaired patients.

Description: Computer-administered test of complex attentional skills sensitive to the effects of traumatic brain injury and a variety of subtle neurological disorders in children. It is a numerical coding task in which the patient selects an appropriate stimulus (digit) within a horizontal array, identifies a second stimulus (digit) in a vertical array, and rapidly enters the latter digit on the keyboard. The program permits assessment and training of complex attentional skills which are typically impaired following brain injury. The program includes a training paradigm to teach the patient how to take the test. The patient's motor and cognitive processing speeds can be separated and compared. The program is designed for use with Apple (II +, IIe, IIc, III) and IBM PC computer systems. Examiner required. Not suitable for group use.

Untimed: Not available

Scoring: Computer scored

Cost: Complete program, including instructional manual $250.00; shipping fee $3.00

Publisher: Robert J. Sbordone

THE DYSINTEGRAL LEARNING CHECKLIST
Mary Meeker and Valerie Maxwell

Child, adolescent, adult

Purpose: Identifies students with potential learning problems. Used by pediatricians, neurologists, special education diagnosticians, and teachers.

Description: Multiple-item paper-pencil inventory of symptoms that are predictive of each of the four systems integrated into the cerebellum. The inventory, which identifies dysintegrated functions for learning, covers the following areas: vision, speech and auding, motoric, proprioceptor, and behavioral. Test results are coded to training materials for each system involved. Self-administered by examiner or parents. Suitable for group use.

Untimed: Varies

Scoring: Examiner evaluated

Cost: 10 checklists $3.50

Publisher: M & M Systems

DYSLEXIA SCHEDULE
Refer to page 580.

THE DYSLEXIA SCREENING SURVEY (DSS)
Robert E. Valett

Child   Grades 1-6

Purpose: Evaluates basic neuropsychological skills. Used for screening elementary pupils who may be dyslexic and to plan remedial strategies.

Description: 90-item paper-pencil test covering seven factors: functional reading level, reading potential, significant reading discrepancy, specific processing skill deficiencies, neuropsychological dysfunctions, associated factors, and development-remedial strategies. The test is administered individually in several steps, including a compilation of available information and subsequent testing of paper-pencil and body-movement tasks. The survey is recommended for use by special educators, remedial reading specialists, psychologists, and speech therapists. Use is not restricted. Remedial methods are presented in the test author's book, *Dyslexia*. Examiner required. Not suitable for group use.

Untimed: 30 minutes

Scoring: Examiner evaluated

Cost: 10 forms $7.95.

Publisher: David S. Lake Publishers

ELIZUR TEST OF PSYCHO-ORGANICITY: CHILDREN & ADULTS
Abraham Elizur

Ages 6-adult

Purpose: Differentiates between organic and non-organic brain disorders. Used by neurologists, psychologists, educators, counselors, and researchers.

Description: Multiple-item task assessment test using drawings, digits, and blocks to provide "uni-dimensional" measurements. Test tasks are easily performed by subjects so that results are not biased by intelligence factors. Sepa-

rate instructions are provided for administering to adults and to children. The test yields quantitative and qualitative results with cutoff points provided for classifying examinees as organic. Examiner required. Not suitable for group use.

Untimed: 10 minutes

Scoring: Hand key; examiner evaluated

Cost: Kit (25 protocol booklets, 1 set of test materials, manual) $49.50

Publisher: Western Psychological Services

ERROR DETECTION IN TEXTS (DETECT)
Rosamond Gianutsos,
Georgine Vroman,
and Pauline Matheson

Ages 10-adult

Purpose: Measures foveal imperception in patients with reading deficiencies and head injury and stroke victims.

Description: Paper-pencil test of ability to locate errors in a text. The patient reads 10 typewritten paragraphs and locates errors systematically placed in the left or right half of the page. Some errors are at the beginning of the word, others at the end. The test is available in two forms: A and B. The subject must be able to read simple English words. Examiner required. Not suitable for group use.

Untimed: 20-30 minutes

Scoring: Hand key

Cost: $10.00

Publisher: Life Science Associates

FACIAL RECOGNITION TEST
Arthur L. Benton

Adolescent, adult

Purpose: Assesses a subject's capacity to identify and discriminate photographs of unfamiliar human faces.

Description: Multiple-item multiple-choice test consisting of three parts: matching identical front-view photographs, matching front-view with three-quarter-view photographs, and matching front-view photographs taken under different lighting conditions. The test is available in a 27-item short form and a 54-item long form. The test is arranged so that the first 13 stimulus and response pictures presented comprise the short form. The test is administered orally by the examiner. Each correct response is assigned a score of 1; scores are corrected for age and education. Materials required include a spiral-bound booklet containing stimulus photographs and corresponding response choices, a record sheet, and a manual. Examiner required. Not suitable for group use.

Untimed: Varies

Scoring: Examiner evaluated

Cost: Contact publisher

Publisher: Oxford University Press

FINGER LOCALIZATION TEST
Arthur L. Benton

All ages

Purpose: Assesses subject's finger localization abilities.

Description: 60-item nonverbal test in three parts requiring the subject to indicate which of his fingers is touched by the examiner when (1) the subject's hand is visible, (2) the subject's hand is hidden from the subject's view, and (3) the subject's hand is hidden from the subject's view and the examiner touches a pair of the subject's fingers rather than a single finger. For each of the three phases of the test, the subject places his hand on the table, palm-side up with fingers extended and slightly separated. In the last two phases, the subject's hand is concealed by a curtain. For each of the three phases, the examiner firmly touches the subject's fingertip (two fingertips simultaneously in the third phase) for 2-4 seconds using the pointed end of a pencil. The patient responds by naming the touched fingers, pointing to them on an outline drawing of the stimulated hand, or calling out their numbers. Testing of spastic hemiplegic patients is restricted to the unaffected hand. Examiner required. Not suitable for group use.

Untimed: Varies

Scoring: Hand key

Cost: Contact publisher

Publisher: Oxford University Press

FREE RECALL (FREEREC)
*Rosamond Gianutsos and
Carol Klitzner*

Ages 10-adult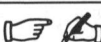

Purpose: Measures short- and long-term memory. Used to assess head injury or stroke as it affects verbal memory.

Description: Computer-administered test measuring short- and long-term retention. Subjects are required to memorize word lists and recall them after either a short delay or after an intervening task. Words are commonly used, monosyllabic nouns from the 1944 Thorndike-Lorge list. Examiner required. Not suitable for group use.

Untimed: 10-12 minutes

Scoring: Computer scored

Cost: $30.00

Publisher: Life Science Associates

FRENCHAY DYSARTHRIA ASSESSMENT
Refer to page 627.

===

FULD OBJECT-MEMORY EVALUATION
Paula Altman Fuld

Adult   Ages 70-90

Purpose: Measures memory and learning in adults regardless of vision, hearing, or language handicaps; cultural differences; or inattention problems.

Description: 10 common objects in a bag are presented to the patient to determine whether he can identify them by touch. The patient names the item and then pulls it out of the bag to see if he was right. After being distracted, the patient is asked to recall the items from the bag. The patient is given four additional chances to learn and recall the objects. The test provides separate scores for long-term storage, retrieval, consistency of retrieval, and failure to recall items even after being reminded. The test also provides a chance to observe naming ability, left-right orientation, stereognosis, and verbal fluency. Separate norms are provided for total recall, storage, consistency of retrieval, ability to benefit from reminding, and ability to say words in categories. Examiner required. Not suitable for group use.

Timed: 60 seconds for each first trial, 30 seconds for each second trial

Scoring: Examiner evaluated

Cost: Complete kit (testing materials, manual, record forms) $22.25; 30 record forms $6.25

Publisher: Stoelting Company

FULLERTON LANGUAGE TEST FOR ADOLESCENTS (EXPERIMENTAL EDITION)
Refer to page 628.

GARDNER STEADINESS TESTER
Richard A. Gardner and Andrew K. Gardner

Child, adolescent Ages 5-14.11

Purpose: Measures one aspect of activity level in children suspected of minimal brain dysfunction. Used in conjunction with a complete minimal brain dysfunction diagnostic battery.

Description: Nonverbal test measuring generalized hyperactivity, prolonged attention, motor impersistence, tremors, and choreiform movements. The examiner demonstrates the device to the child and shows him how to hold it correctly. The child is then tested for three 60-second periods with 15-second intervals of rest. The total contact time for the three trials is allowed to accumulate on the clock. At the end, the total time is recorded and the clock is reset. Materials consist of a special stylus and stylus plate, tone response, stop clock, timer, and control circuitry mounted on a fiberesin board. Examiner required. Not suitable for group use.

Timed: Total time 3½ minutes

Scoring: Hand key

Cost: Complete set $319.00

Publisher: Lafayette Instrument Company, Inc.

GOLDSTEIN-SCHEERER TESTS OF ABSTRACT AND CONCRETE THINKING
Kurt Goldstein and Martin Scheerer

Brain-injured patients

Purpose: Measures impairment of the brain's abstract and concrete reasoning functions. Used for assessment of patients with brain injuries.

Description: Battery of performance tests assessing abstract and concrete reasoning. The Goldstein-Scheerer Cube Test requires the subject to copy colored designs with blocks. The Gelb-Goldstein Color Sorting Test measures the ability to sort a variety of colors according to definite color concepts. The Goldstein-Scheerer Object Sorting Test requires the subject to sort a variety of simultaneously presented objects according to general concepts. The Weigl-Goldstein-Scheerer Color Form Sorting Test involves sorting different colored figures according to categories of color and form. The Goldstein-Scheerer Stick Test measures the subject's ability to copy figures composed of sticks and reproduce them from memory. Materials include all necessary equipment for the five tests. Examiner required. Not suitable for group use.

Untimed: 20-30 minutes

Scoring: Examiner evaluated

Cost: Complete set (all necessary equipment for all 5 tests, monograph, 50 each of 6 record forms) $325.00

Publisher: The Psychological Corporation

THE GRADED NAMING TEST
Pat McKenna and Elizabeth K. Warrington

Adult

Purpose: Identifies naming deficits. Indicates impaired language functioning in brain-damaged patients. Used with psychiatric, neurological, and geriatric patients.

Description: Multiple-item oral-response test assessing naming deficits in individuals, regardless of range of intellectual ability. Test items consist of picture stimuli that the patient is asked to name. Object pictures have been selected to prevent ambiguous answers. Items of sufficient difficulty are included to adequately assess patients with above average premorbid intelligence. Equivalent scores on the Wechsler Adult Intelligence Scale Vocabulary, the National Adult Reading Test, and the Schonell Graded Word Reading Test can be derived from a conversion table. Examiner required. Not suitable for group use. BRITISH PUBLISHER

Untimed: Varies

Scoring: Examiner evaluated

Cost: Manual £6.30; object picture book £13.90; 25 answer/record sheets £5.00 (payment in sterling for all overseas orders)

Publisher: NFER-NELSON Publishing Company Ltd.

GRASSI BASIC COGNITIVE EVALUATION
Joseph R. Grassi

Child   Ages 4-8

Purpose: Identifies cognitive deficits in children with brain dysfunction. Used by psychologists and educators for clinical assessment.

Description: Measures 27 traits in visual, auditory, and kinesthetic areas. The test is designed for children who are brain damaged, mentally retarded, cognitively disadvantaged, or learning disabled. Examiner required. Not suitable for group use.

Untimed: 30 minutes

Scoring: Examiner evaluated

Cost: Complete kit (25 record forms, manual) $35.00

Publisher: SWETS and Zeitlinger B.V.

GRASSI BLOCK SUBSTITUTION TEST
Joseph R. Grassi

Adolescent, adult

Purpose: Detects the early symptoms of organic brain pathology in adolescents and adults. Used for clinical screening procedures.

Description: Task-assessment test measuring abstract behavior as an indicator of organic brain pathology. Test materials consist of five specially designed semicubes and a manual. The manual is available from Charles C. Thomas Publisher. The examiner must be a clinical psychologist with training and experience in the concepts of abstract versus concrete behavior. Examiner required. Not suitable for group use.

Untimed: Not available

Scoring: Examiner evaluated

Cost: Test materials $30.00; manual $15.00

Publisher: SWETS and Zeitlinger B.V.

GROOVED PEGBOARD

Ages 5-adult

Purpose: Measures hand-eye coordination and fine-finger dexterity. Used as part of a clinical neuropsychological evaluation battery in brain damage, alcoholism, aging, and epilepsy.

Description: Multiple-operation, manual test using a 4" x 4" mahogany box with a shallow well in the lid and a hole plate containing 25 keyed slots oriented in random directions and a set of 25 keyed pegs. The subject inserts all 25 pegs into the slots with first one hand and then the other. Separate times are recorded for the dominant hand and the nondominant hand. The test is used with the Trites Neuropsychological and the Halstead-Reitan Test Batteries. It is also used to discriminate multiple sclerosis patients from those with other neurological diseases. Examiner required. Suitable for group use.

Untimed: 5 minutes

Scoring: Hand key

Cost: Complete kit $57.00; 30 replacement pegs $20.00

Publisher: Lafayette Instrument Company, Inc.

HALSTEAD CATEGORY TEST
Michael Hill

Purpose: Assesses individuals' perceptual ability to categorize graphic items.

Description: Multiple-item computer-administered test measuring an individual's ability to categorize along a number of different dimensions. The client observes a series of graphic items on the screen and chooses whether an object belongs to or differs from a set of objects. The series gradually increases in difficulty. Fifty sets of client scores may be saved on disk for later examination. Available for use with the Apple II Plus, IIe, and IIc computers and the IBM-PC and compatible computers. Examiner required. Not suitable for group use.

Untimed: Not available

Scoring: Computer scored

Cost: $199.00

Publisher: Precision People, Inc.

HALSTEAD-REITAN NEUROPSYCHOLOGICAL TEST BATTERY FOR ADULTS
Reitan Neuropsychology Laboratory and others

Adult

Purpose: Evaluates brain function and dysfunction in adults. Used for clinical evaluation.

Description: Battery of tests assessing adult neuropsychological functioning, including the Halstead Neuropsychological Test Battery, the Wechsler Adult Intelligence Scale, the Trail Making Test, the Reitan-Indiana Aphasia Screening Test, various tests of sensory-perceptual functions, and the Minnesota Multiphasic Personality Inventory. Materials include a category test projection box with electric control mechanism and projector; 208 adult category slides in carousels; tactual performance test (10-hole board, stand, 10 blocks); manual finger tapper; tape cassette for speech-sounds perception test; tactile form recognition test; and a manual for administration and scoring. The com-

ponents may be ordered separately. Examiner required. Not suitable for group use.

Timed/Untimed: Varies

Scoring: Examiner evaluated

Cost: Adult battery $1,106.00

Publisher: Reitan Neuropsychology Laboratory

Information and availability unconfirmed; no publisher response.

HALSTEAD-REITAN NEUROPSYCHOLOGICAL TEST BATTERY FOR CHILDREN
Reitan Neuropsychology Laboratory and others

Child, adolescent Ages 9-14

Purpose: Evaluates brain function and dysfunction in children. Used for clinical evaluations.

Description: Battery of tests assessing the neuropsychological functioning of children, including the Halstead Neuropsychological Test Battery, the Wechsler Intelligence Scale for Children, the Trail Making Test, the Reitan-Indiana Aphasia Screening Test, various tests of sensory-perceptual functions, and measures of academic achievement. The tests in this battery have been adapted from the Halstead-Reitan Neuropsychological Test Battery for Adults. Much of the equipment used for testing adults also can be used with the children's battery. Adaptations for use with this age group include new slides (stimulus material) for the category test, a new answer form for the speech-sounds perception test, a 6-hole board instead of a 10-hole board for the tactual performance test, and a shortened form of the Trail Making Test. Materials include all necessary equipment, test stimuli, slide carousels, recording forms, and manual for administration, scoring, and evaluation of all tests. The components may be purchased separately. Examiner required. Not suitable for group use.

Timed/Untimed: Varies

Scoring: Examiner evaluated

Cost: Older children's battery $1,056.00

Publisher: Reitan Neuropsychology Laboratory

Information and availability unconfirmed; no publisher response.

THE HEARING MEASUREMENT SCALE

Refer to page 610.

HOOPER VISUAL ORGANIZATION TEST (HVOT)

H. Elston Hooper

Adolescent, adult

Purpose: Assesses organic brain pathology of both hemispheres. Used for clinical diagnosis.

Description: 30-item pictorial test differentiating between functional and motivational disorders. The subject is presented with drawings of simple objects cut into several parts and rearranged and is asked to name the objects. Examiner required. Suitable for group use.

Untimed: 15 minutes

Scoring: Hand key

Cost: Complete (booklet, manual) $16.50; manual $7.50; booklet $10.00

Publisher: Western Psychological Services

HOUSTON TEST FOR LANGUAGE DEVELOPMENT

Refer to page 9.

ILLINOIS TEST OF PSYCHOLINGUISTIC ABILITIES (ITPA)

Refer to page 477.

INTERNATIONAL VERSION OF MENTAL STATUS QUESTIONNAIRE

T.L. Brink

Elderly adults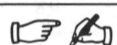

Purpose: Assesses confusion due to senile dementia in adults.

Description: 10-item oral-response test measuring short-term memory of elderly individuals, primarily in institutional and community environments. A Spanish translation is available. Examiner required. Not suitable for group use.

Untimed: 2-5 minutes

Scoring: Examiner evaluated

Cost: Free

Publisher: T.L. Brink

JORDAN LEFT-RIGHT REVERSAL TEST (JLRRT)

Refer to page 581.

JUDGMENT OF LINE ORIENTATION TEST

Arthur L. Benton

Adolescent, adult

Purpose: Measures subject's ability to judge line orientation (direction), one aspect of "spatial thinking."

Description: 30-item test available in two forms, H and V. Both forms present the same items, though in a somewhat different order (each form maintains an ascending order of difficulty). The subject is presented with pairs of partial lines, each of which represents (with respect to origin) a distal, middle, or proximal segment of a response-choice line. There are four types of test stimuli (line-segment pairs): HH (distal), LL (proximal), MM (middle), and mixed. The subject is scored on the number of completely correct responses. Materials required are a record sheet, manual, and spiral-bound booklet containing stimuli and multiple-choice response cards (includes five practice items). Examiner required. Not suitable for group use.

Untimed: Varies

Scoring: Examiner evaluated

Cost: Contact publisher

Publisher: Oxford University Press

JUMP: EYE MOVEMENT EXERCISE
Rosamond Gianutsos,
Georgine Vroman,
and Pauline Matheson

Ages 8-adult

Purpose: Assesses rapidity of eye movements. Used to assess head injury, stroke, or visual system damage.

Description: Computer-administered test of visual and oculomotor systems. Symbols flash at the left or right edge of the screen, and the subject judges whether they are the same or different. Rapid lateral saccadic movements are required, both left-to-right and right-to-left. The program finds and adjusts to the patient's ability level. Self-administered. Not suitable for group use.

Untimed: 8-12 minutes

Scoring: Computer scored

Cost: $30.00

Publisher: Life Science Associates

KAHN TEST OF SYMBOL ARRANGEMENT (KTSA)
Theodore C. Kahn

All ages

Purpose: Assesses personality dynamics and the extent of cerebral competence. Used for individual diagnosis and therapy, as well as vocational counseling.

Description: Multiple-task performance test of a subject's cultural/symbolic thinking. The subject is required to sort plastic objects of varying size, color, thickness, and translucence in several ways. The examiner evaluates the subject's symbol pattern and compares it to patterns of normal and clinical groups. For use only by clinical psychologists, psychiatrists, counseling psychologists, school psychologists, and others with professional competence in clinical assessment. Examiner required. Not suitable for group use.

Untimed: 15 minutes

Scoring: Hand key; examiner evaluated

Cost: Complete kit (plastic objects, felt strip, 10 individual record sheets, manual, clinical manual) $50.00; 50 record sheets $15.00; manual $4.00; clinical manual $6.00

Publisher: Psychological Test Specialists

KASANIN-HANFMANN CONCEPT FORMATION TEST (VYGOTSKY TEST) AND MODIFIED VYGOTSKY CONCEPT FORMATION TEST
Refer to page 25.

KENDRICK COGNITIVE TESTS FOR THE ELDERLY
D. Kendrick

Adult   Ages 55 and older

Purpose: Identifies early dementia and depressive psychosis of adults.

Description: Multiple-item paper-pencil oral-response test made up of two subtests detecting early dementia and depressive psychosis by assessing short-term memory and speed of responding. The two subtests, Object Learning and Digit Copying, are designed for longitudinal use in hospitals or clinics. The test is a major revision of the Kendrick Battery for detecting dementia in the elderly. Examiner required. Not suitable for group use.
BRITISH PUBLISHER

Untimed: 15 minutes

Scoring: Examiner evaluated

Cost: Complete set (manual, Object Learning Test, record form, Digit Copying Test) £28.25

Publisher: NFER-NELSON Publishing Company Ltd.

LATERALITY PREFERENCE SCHEDULE (LPS)
Raymond S. Dean

Ages 7-adult

Purpose: Assesses the lateral preference of individuals ages 7-adult in the performance of everyday activities that have neurological/neuropsychological implications. Used in diagnosing and planning the treatment of learning disorders, psychiatric syndromes, and a number of neurological disorders.

Description: 49-item paper-pencil inventory measuring the lateral systems used by individuals and estimating the degree of cerebral specialization. The six dimensions tested are general laterality, visually guided activities, visual, auditory, strength, and foot use. The individual indicates a preference for "right always" to "left always" on a 5-point Likert scale. A laterality score is calculated for each item and summed for each factor and for laterality in general. A third-grade reading level is required for self-administration. The test may be read to individuals with lower reading levels or dyslexia. Examiner/self-administered. Suitable for group use.

Untimed: 15 minutes

Scoring: Hand key

Cost: 100 forms $25.00; manual (includes scoring keys and interpretive devices) $15.00

Publisher: Raymond S. Dean, Ph.D.

LEARNING DISABILITY RATING PROCEDURE (LDRP)
Refer to page 583.

LIGHT-SWITCH ALTERNATION APPARATUS
Milton B. Jensen

Neuropsychiatric patients

Purpose: Measures "alternation-type" learning. Used with neuropsychiatric patients to determine degree of mental illness and potential for rehabilitation.

Description: Multiple-item task-performance instrument consisting of five two-position switches connected to five flashing lights that are used to provide learning tasks at five levels of difficulty: single position, single alternation, double alternation, and a 5-position series. Different and more complex learning tasks can be set up readily by altering the wiring circuit at the control panel (which is screened from the patient's view). Tentative norms are available for each of the five levels of difficulty. Scores of neuropsychiatric patients, when compared with

their scores on conventional tests of intelligence, provide an index of severity of mental illness and potential for rehabilitation. Examiner required. Not suitable for group use.

Timed: Varies

Scoring: Examiner evaluated

Cost: Contact publisher

Publisher: Lafayette Instrument Company, Inc.

LINE BISECTION (BISECT)
Rosamond Gianutsos, Georgine Vroman, and Pauline Matheson

Ages 8-adult

Purpose: Measures visual hemi-imperception. Used to assess head injury, stroke, or visual system damage.

Description: Computer-administered test measuring the presence of an intact visual system. The computer presents horizontal or vertical lines that have a visible gap somewhere near the center. The subject attempts to center the gap using the arrow keys. Examiner required. Not suitable for group use.

Untimed: 6-8 minutes

Scoring: Computer scored

Cost: $30.00

Publisher: Life Science Associates

LURIA'S NEUROPSYCHOLOGICAL INVESTIGATION
Anne-Lise Christensen

Adult

Purpose: Diagnoses type and severity of brain injury. Used as a basis for planning rehabilitational measures for brain-damaged adults.

Description: Oral-response and task-assessment test begins with a structure for preliminary conversation with the patient and continues with an assessment of the following neurological areas: motor functions, acoustico-motor organization, higher cutaneous and kinesthetic functions, higher visual functions, impressive speech, expressive speech, writing and reading, arithmetical skill, mnestic processes, and intellectual processes. Materials include a set of cards, manual, and text. Examiner required. Not suitable for group use.

Untimed: Not available

Scoring: Examiner evaluated

Cost: Contact publisher

Publisher: Munksgaard; distributed in U.S.A. by S.P. Medical and Scientific Books

LURIA-NEBRASKA NEUROPSYCHOLOGICAL BATTERY
*Charles J. Golden,
Arnold D. Purisch,
and Thomas A. Hammeke*

**Adolescent, adult
Ages 15 and older**

Purpose: Assesses a broad range of neuropsychological functions for individuals ages 15 and older. Used to diagnose specific cerebral dysfunction and to select and assess rehabilitation programs.

Description: Multiple-item verbal, observational test available in two forms : Form I (269 items) and Form II (279 items). The discrete, scored items produce a profile for the following scales: Motor, Rhythm, Tactile, Visual, Receptive Speech, Expressive Speech, Writing, Reading, Arithmetic, Memory, Intellectual, Pathognomonic, Left Hemisphere, Right Hemisphere, Impairment, and Profile Evaluation. Form II also assesses intermediate memory. The battery diagnoses the presence of cerebral dysfunction and determines lateralization and localization. Test materials include six stimulus cards, a tape cassette, comb, quarter, and stopwatch. A manual provides instructions for administering the test, evidence of reliability and validity, interpretive guides, and copies of the Administration and Scoring Booklet and the Patient Response Booklet. The Administration and Scoring Booklet includes the Profile Form and Computation of Critical Level Tables. It is used to record all scores during administration and provides verbal instructions to be read to the patient. The Patient Response Booklet is provided for

items requiring written answers. Microcomputer software is available for computer scoring of both forms. Examiner required. Not suitable for group use.

Untimed: 1½-2½ hours

Scoring: Hand key; may be computer scored

Cost: Complete kit Form I (manual, stimulus cards including Christensen cards, tape cassette, 10 scoring booklets, 10 response booklets, 2 answer sheets including publisher scoring and reports) $215.00; complete kit Form II (stimulus cards, tape cassette, manual, 10 patient response booklets, 10 scoring booklets, 2 answer sheets including publisher scoring and reports) $245.00

Publisher: Western Psychological Services

MEMORY SPAN (SPAN)
*Rosamond Gianutsos and
Carol Klitzner*

Ages 10-adult

Purpose: Measures concentration and short-term memory. May also be used as a retraining exercise with head injury or stroke patients.

Description: Computer-administered test providing assessment and remediation of memory deficits. A list of words appears on the screen one at a time. After the entire list has appeared, the patient tries to recall a certain number of words from the end of the list. On the first five trials, the patient is asked to recall the last two words; the number to be recalled increases by one for each set of five lists up to a maximum of seven. The patient must be able to read simple English words. Examiner required. Not suitable for group use.

Untimed: 8-12 minutes

Scoring: Computer scored

Cost: $30.00

Publisher: Life Science Associates

MEMORY-FOR-DESIGNS TEST (MFD)
*Frances K. Graham and
Barbara S. Kendall*

Ages 8.5-60

Purpose: Assesses perceptual-motor coordination. Used to differentiate between functional behavior disorders and those associated with brain injury.

Description: 15-item performance measure of perceptual-motor coordination. Items consist of designs on cardboard cards. The subject is shown a design for five seconds and then attempts to draw it from memory. This procedure is repeated for each of the 15 items. Diagnostic testing and evaluation should be closely supervised by a clinical or school psychologist, psychiatrist, neurologist, or pediatrician. Examiner required. Not suitable for group use.

Untimed: 10 minutes

Scoring: Hand key; examiner evaluated

Cost: Complete kit (revised general manual, 15 design cards, utility set of scoring examples and norms) $17.00; 15 design cards $15.00; scoring examples and norms $2.50; revised manual $5.00

Publisher: Psychological Test Specialists

MINNESOTA PERCEPTO-DIAGNOSTIC TEST (MPD), 1982 REVISION
Gerald B. Fuller

Ages 5 and older

Purpose: Assesses visual perception and visual motor abilities. Used to classify reading and learning disabilities, identify individuals with emotionally disturbed or schizophrenic perception, and differentiate between brain-damaged and non-brain-damaged individuals.

Description: 6-item paper-pencil test consisting of Gestalt designs on separate cards that the examiner presents individually to the subject. The subject draws each design on a separate sheet of paper. The drawings are scored for degrees of rotation, separation, and distortion, indicating whether perception is normal, emotionally disturbed, or brain damaged. The results also are used to classify reading and learning disabilities as visual auditory or mixed and to measure the maturational level of normal and retarded children. All scores are adjusted for both age and IQ. The test is available in separate scales for children (ages 5-12) and adults (ages 13 and older). Examiner required. Not suitable for group use.

Untimed: 6-8 minutes

Scoring: Hand key; examiner evaluated

Cost: Manual $12.50; cards $6.00; 50 record blanks $5.00

Publisher: Clinical Psychology Publishing Co., Inc.

MOTOR IMPERSISTENCE BATTERY
Arthur L. Benton

All ages

Purpose: Assesses motor impersistence.

Description: Battery of eight tests requiring the maintenance of a movement or posture: keeping eyes closed, protruding tongue (blindfolded), protruding tongue (eyes open), fixation of gaze in lateral visual fields, keeping mouth open, central fixation during confrontation testing of visual fields, head turning during sensory testing, and saying "ah." The procedure for each test is explained in the manual. Examiner required. Not suitable for group use.

Timed: Varies depending on test

Scoring: Examiner evaluated

Cost: Contact publisher

Publisher: Oxford University Press

NEUROLOGICAL DYSFUNCTIONS OF CHILDREN (NDOC)
James W. Kuhns

Child   Ages 3-10

Purpose: Assesses the neurological functioning of children. Identifies children needing further neurological evaluation. Used by school psychologists, education specialists, physicians, nurses, and occupational therapists and in school psychology training and pediatric residency programs.

Description: 18-item task-performance screening instrument measuring a range of neurological functions. For items 1-16, the child is asked to perform a variety of simple tasks, such as walking along a straight line, touching a finger to the nose, and following an object with the eyes. The tasks represent behavior capabilities minimally affected by environmental factors. Each task is evaluated with a "yes" or "no" response, depending on whether the child is functioning in a normal, healthy manner or is experiencing mild to moderate impairment in neurological functioning. In Item 17, the examiner measures the child's head circumference to determine any deviance from the chronological age normal range size as indicated on an included chart. Item 18 is a checklist of discriminating areas of information concerning the child's background. The screening and referral chart relates the child's scores to interpretive clusters and indicates whether referral to an appropriate professional (opthamologist, audiologist, physician, speech specialist, or neurologist) is needed for further evaluation. The manual includes complete information on administering and scoring the tests, interpreting the results, and technical data. Examiner required. Not suitable for group use.

Untimed: 50-60 minutes

Scoring: Examiner evaluated

Cost: Examiner's set (manual, 20 screening and referral charts) $35.00

Publisher: CTB/McGraw-Hill

NEUROPSYCHOLOGICAL SCREENING EXAM
John Preston

Adolescent, adult Ages 16 and older

Purpose: Assesses probable learning disabilities and neurological impairment. Used in clinical settings by mental health professionals with some neuropsychological background.

Description: Multiple-item paper-pencil test measuring the following neurological factors: level of consciousness, brain and behavioral abnormalities, handedness, verbal and language functioning, emotional problems, memory and cognitive functioning, and psychomotor development. The battery includes a screening exam (background information), examination record form, patient response record, stimulus cards, instructional audiotape for examiner, and three subtests from the Halstead-Reitan battery, which are purchased separately. Examiner required. Not suitable for group use.

Untimed: 50 minutes

Scoring: Examiner evaluated

Cost: Complete kit $38.00

Publisher: The Wilmington Press

Information and availability unconfirmed; no publisher response.

NEUROPSYCHOLOGICAL STATUS EXAMINATION (NSE)
Psychological Assessment Resources, Inc.

Adult

Purpose: Evaluates, organizes, and collates data pertaining to an individual's neuropsychological functioning. Used for a variety of neuropsychological assessments ranging from screening procedures to extensive work-ups and preparation for expert-witness testimony.

Description: 10-page multiple-item paper-pencil assessment evaluating neuropsychological information, such as patient data, observational findings, test administration parameters, neuroanatomical correlates, reports of test findings, clinical impressions, and recommendations for treatment. The instrument consists of 13 sections, including patient and referral data; neuropsychological symptom checklist (NCS); premorbid status; physical, emotional, and cognitive status; results of neuropsychological testing; diagnostic comments; and follow-up and treatment recommendations. The NCS is a two-page screening instrument used to assess the status of potential neurological/neuropsychological signs and symptoms. Each section was designed with consideration of base rate data for common findings in neuropsychological evaluations. The manual includes a discussion of the rationale of the logic underlying the structure of the instrument and provides suggestions for its most efficient use. Examiner required. Not suitable for group use.

Untimed: Varies

Scoring: Examiner evaluated

Cost: Examination kit (manual, 25 NSE and NCS forms) $13.50

Publisher: Psychological Assessment Resources, Inc.

NUMBER SERIES PROBLEMS (NSERIES)
Linda Laatsch

Ages 10-adult

Purpose: Measures simple problem-solving ability. Used to assess head injury, stroke, or visual system damage.

Description: Computer-administered test of problem-solving ability in which the subject solves addition (10, 12, 14, ?), subtraction (75, 70, 65, ?), and pattern (9, 8, 8, 9, ?) series. Two levels of difficulty are provided. The user receives feedback and can choose to receive a prompt. Scoring is separate for each type of series. Examiner required. Not suitable for group use.

Untimed: 5-12 minutes

Scoring: Computer scored

Cost: $35.00

Publisher: Life Science Associates

ORGANIC INTEGRITY TEST (OIT)
H.C. Tien

Grades K-adult

Purpose: Diagnoses organic brain dysfunctions, psychoses, and mental retardation. Used in neurology, psychometrics, and assessment of perceptual lag.

Description: 20-card verbal test based on Tien's theory of chromaphilia in brain damage. The examiner first shows the patient a card with one picture on it, then another card with two pictures on it, and asks the patient which of the pictures on the second card are like the pictures on the first card. Persons with perceptual problems are more likely to make choices based on color similarities; those with "perceptual lag" may be more likely to experience reading difficulties based on difficulty distinguishing form. The score is based on the percentage of correct answers. Low scores indicate dysfunction. Examiner required. Suitable for group use.

Untimed: 3-5 minutes

Scoring: Hand key

Cost: Complete set (includes 20 cards, manual) $37.50; postage and handling $2.50

Publisher: Psychodiagnostic Test Company

PAIN AND DISTRESS SCALE
Refer to page 206.

PAIRED WORD MEMORY TASK (PAIRMEM)
Rosamond Gianutsos

Ages 8-adult

Purpose: Measures associative verbal learning skills. Used with head injury and stroke victims.

Description: Computer-administered test of verbal associative memory. Pairs of unrelated words are presented for study. Later, the subject attempts to type the second word upon presentation of the first. Both the number of pairs and the study time can be adjusted to increase the difficulty of the task. Interference may be given between trials to prevent reliance on rote short-term memory skills. The subject must have some visual function, the ability to read simple English words, rudimentary keyboarding skills, and the ability to follow simple instructions. Self-administered. Not suitable for group use.

Untimed: 8-12 minutes

Scoring: Computer scored

Cost: $20.00 (minimum of 3 orders in Cat. #965 series)

Publisher: Life Science Associates

PANTOMIME RECOGNITION TEST
Arthur L. Benton

Adult

Purpose: Assesses a patient's ability to understand nonlinguistic pantomimed actions.

Description: 30-item test in which pantomimes, which are presented on a television monitor via a ¾-inch videotape cassette, depict a man pretending to use various common objects (spoon, pen, saw) followed by seven seconds of blank tape. Four types of response choices, which are presented as line drawings, are available for each item: correct choice (the object whose action is pantomimed), semantic foil (an object belonging to the same class of objects as the stimulus), neutral foil (an object whose use is pantomimed elsewhere on the test), and odd foil (an object whose use is not suitable for pantomime). The person points to one of the four line drawings after viewing the pantomime on the television monitor. Four practice items are provided in addition to the 30 test items. If a patient responds incorrectly to two or more practice items, the test should be terminated. Examiner required. Not suitable for group use.

Untimed: Varies

Scoring: Hand key

Cost: Contact publisher

Publisher: Oxford University Press

PEDIATRIC EARLY ELEMENTARY EXAMINATION (PEEX)
Melvin D. Levine

Child   Ages 7-9

Purpose: Assesses neurological development, behaviors, and health of children. Used by clinicians in health care and other settings.

Description: Multiple-item response test providing standardized observation procedures for characterizing children's functional health and its relationship to neurodevelopmental and physical status. The test enables clinicians to integrate medical, developmental, and neurological findings while making observations of behavioral adjustment and style. Examiner required. Not suitable for group use.

Untimed: 45-60 minutes

Scoring: Examiner evaluated

Cost: Complete set (manual, stimulus booklet, PEEX Kit, 12 record forms, 12 response booklets) $49.00

Publisher: Educators Publishing Service, Inc.

PEDIATRIC EXAMINATION OF EDUCATIONAL READINESS (PEER)
Refer to page 484.

PEDIATRIC EXAMINATION OF EDUCATIONAL READINESS AT MIDDLE CHILDHOOD (PEERAMID)
Melvin D. Levine

Child, adolescent Ages 9-15

Purpose: Assesses children's and adolescents' neurological development, behaviors, and health. Used by clinicians in health care and other settings.

Description: Multiple-item response test providing standardized observation procedures for characterizing children's and adolescents' functional health and its relationship to neurodevelopmental and physical status. The test assesses a wide range of functions, including neuromaturation, attention, many aspects of memory, motor efficiency, language, and other areas critical to the academic and social adjustment of older children. It is particularly sensitive to the often subtle developmental dysfunctions of junior high-school students. Examiner required. Not suitable for group use.

Untimed: 45-60 minutes

Scoring: Examiner evaluated

Cost: Complete set (manual, stimulus booklet, PEERAMID Kit, 12 record forms, 12 response booklets) $56.50

Publisher: Educators Publishing Service, Inc.

PERCEPTUAL MAZE TEST (PMT)
*Janice Smith, David Jones,
and Alick Elithorn*

Ages 7-adult

Purpose: Assesses perceptual and intellectual skills. Used for diagnosis and localization of cerebral damage, particularly right hemisphere damage.

Description: Multiple-item paper-pencil test of spatial abilities. Items are mazes consisting of a number of target dots superimposed upon the intersection of a lattice background. The subject's task is to find a path along the lattice that passes through the greatest number of target dots. Several forms are available: two parallel forms of the neuropsychiatric sets, NP1 and NP2, each with 12 test items; mirrored versions, NP1M and NP2M, also are available; the VC Series, VC1 and VC2, each consist of 18 items; mirror image sets VC1M and VC2M also are available. An automated version of the test for use on the Apple II, R.M.L. 3802, Nort Star Horizon, and other microcomputers is available. A special children's version of the PMT, with 16 items, is available for use with younger children. Examiner required. Suitable for group use.
BRITISH PUBLISHER

Untimed: 20-30 minutes

Scoring: Hand key

Cost: 100 neuropsychiatric sets $53.00; 100 VC Series $75.00; 100 children's version $75.00

Publisher: Medical Research Council

PHONEME DISCRIMINATION TEST
Arthur L. Benton

Adult

Purpose: Assesses a subject's phoneme discrimination abilities.

Description: Brief screening instrument consisting of 30 tape-recorded pairs of nonsense words spoken by an adult male. Of the 30 word pairs, 10 pairs are one-syllable words, and 20 pairs are two-syllable words. In 15 of the items, the word

pairs differ in only one phonemic feature. After each word pair is spoken, the subject vocally responds either "same" or "different," points to a card printed with either "same" or "different," nods, or gestures. One point is awarded for each correct response. Examiner required. Not suitable for group use.

Untimed: Varies

Scoring: Hand key

Cost: Contact publisher

Publisher: Oxford University Press

THE PICTURE STORY LANGUAGE TEST (PSLT)
Refer to page 253.

PORCH INDEX OF COMMUNICATIVE ABILITY (PICA)
Refer to page 639.

PORTABLE TACTUAL PERFORMANCE TEST (P-TPT)
Psychological Assessment Resources, Inc.

**Child, adolescent
Ages 5-14**

Purpose: Measures spatial perception in children.

Description: Multiple-task examination measuring spatial perception, discrimination of forms, manual or construction ability, motor coordination, and the ability to meet new situations. This portable version features a wooden carrying case, which can be set up for standardized administration. Examiner required. Not suitable for group use.

Untimed: Not available

Scoring: Examiner evaluated

Cost: Contact publisher

Publisher: Psychological Assessment Resources, Inc.

PRESCHOOL SCREENING INSTRUMENT
Refer to page 485.

PROBLEM SOLVING I REHABILITATION PROGRAM
Robert J. Sbordone and Steven Hall

Adolescent, adult

Purpose: Trains cognitively impaired patients to improve their problem-solving skills and ability to tolerate frustration.

Description: Computer-administered rehabilitation and training program in which the patient is visually presented with a series of tasks of increasing complexity requiring the use of a joystick. The first series of tasks involves moving a small square to a goal box. Initially, the patient is able to see both the goal box and the location of the square. At higher levels, visual cues are eliminated progressively, requiring the patient to develop effective problem-solving strategies to solve the task. At the intermediate levels, patients must improve their frustration tolerance and persistence to solve each task because the program creates invisible barriers and obstacles that obscure the goal box. The program has been designed to monitor the patient's progress and level of fatigue over many training sessions. The program also makes decisions, based on the patient's performance, to increase or decrease the complexity of the task, provide a variety of different cues, allow short rest periods, or terminate the session. It also remembers the patient's performance on previous training sessions, as well as the length of time since the last training session. A speech synthesizer option permits vocal presentation of cues and instructions to patients with reading difficulties. An analysis of the patient's problem-solving strategies at each of 10 levels of difficulty is provided. The program is designed for use with the Apple (II + , IIe, IIc) computer system. Examiner/self-administered. Not suitable for group use.

Untimed: Not available

Scoring: Computer scored

Cost: Complete program, including instructional manual $195.00; shipping fee $3.00

Publisher: Robert J. Sbordone

PROBLEM SOLVING II REHABILITATION
Robert J. Sbordone and Steven Hall

Adolescent, adult

Purpose: Trains high-functioning brain-injured patients to improve their sequential thinking, problem-solving, and cognitive flexibility skills. Designed for use with high-functioning brain-injured patients with residual frontal lobe dysfunction (problem-solving skills, poor sequential thinking, impaired self-critical attitude, and cognitive inflexibility).

Description: Computer-administered rehabilitation and training program which trains the patient to anticipate the consequences of his actions. It presents the patient with a series of problems (carrying passengers across a river in a boat) of increasing difficulty and complexity requiring the patient to consider as many as 10 different variables simultaneously. The program critically analyzes the problem-solving approaches utilized by the patient and determines their effectiveness. It also monitors the patient's level of cognitive fatigue. A speech synthesizer option allows vocal presentation to patients with reading difficulties. The program is designed for use with an Apple IIc or IIe with at least 64K of internal memory. Examiner/self-administered. Not suitable for group use.

Untimed: Not available

Scoring: Computer scored

Cost: Complete program, including instructional manual $195.00; shipping fee $3.00

Publisher: Robert J. Sbordone

PURDUE HAND PRECISION TEST
Refer to page 981.

QUICK NEUROLOGICAL SCREENING TEST (QNST)
Harold M. Sterling, Margaret Mutti, and Norma V. Spalding

Grades K-12

Purpose: Assesses neurological integration as it relates to the learning abilities of children and teenagers.

Description: Multiple-task nonverbal test of 15 functions, each involving a motor task similar to those observed in neurological pediatric examinations. The areas measured include maturity of motor development, skill in controlling large and small muscles, motor planning and sequencing, sense of rate and rhythm, spatial organization, visual and auditory perceptual skills, balance and cerebellar-vestibular function, and disorders of attention. Materials include geometric form reproduction sheets and flipcards printed with directions for administration and scoring. Scoring occurs simultaneously and neurodevelopmental difficulties result in an increasingly larger numerical score. Examiner required. Not suitable for group use.

Untimed: 20 minutes

Scoring: Examiner evaluated

Cost: Manual $12.00; 25 scoring forms $7.00; 25 geometric form reproduction sheets $3.50

Publisher: Academic Therapy Publications

THE RAIL-WALKING TEST
S. Roy Heath

Ages 6-adult

Purpose: Measures locomotor coordination. Screens for central nervous system disorder or injury.

Description: Task performance test assessing balance and motor coordination. The subject, shoes removed, is asked to walk "heel-to-toe" three times along each of three rails specifically constructed for the task. The first rail is four inches wide and nine feet long; the second rail is two inches wide and nine feet long; and the third rail is one inch wide and six feet long. Scores are based on the distance the subject walks without falling off. Special weight is given to each rail according to width. Directions are provided for local construction of the test rails. Examiner required. Not suitable for group use.

Untimed: 10 minutes

Scoring: Examiner evaluated

Cost: Instructions and norms $5.00

Publisher: S. Roy Heath, Ph.D.

RANDT MEMORY TEST
C. T. Randt and E.R. Brown

Adult   Ages 20-80

Purpose: Measures memory processes in neurologically impaired populations, including the elderly.

Description: Computer-administered test of memory changes in areas including process of association, primary memory deficits, recall vs. recognition memory, and transfer to and retrieval from secondary store memory. Test materials include picture recognition cards; documentation; a program for test administration control; response recording; and computation of scaled scores, standard scores, and summary of test scores. Norms are included for age decades from 20 to 80. Examiner/self-administered. Not suitable for group use.

Untimed: Varies

Scoring: Hand key; may be computer scored

Cost: Test, manual scoring $75.00; Apple computer scoring program $40.00

Publisher: Life Science Associates

REACTION TIME MEASURE OF VISUAL FIELD (REACT)
Rosamond Gianutsos and Carol Klitzner

Ages 8-adult

Purpose: Diagnoses and trains visual field deficits and blind spots. Used to assess head injury, stroke, or visual system damage.

Description: Computer-administered test detecting slowed response to visual stimuli. The patient presses any key on the keyboard to stop the "runaway numbers" on the screen. The numbers are presented in different locations in the visual field while the subject fixates on a point. Possible modifications include a hand-held or other specially arranged switch for responding. Examiner required. Not suitable for group use.

Timed: 8 minutes
Scoring: Computer scored
Cost: $30.00
Publisher: Life Science Associates

RECEPTIVE-EXPRESSIVE OBSERVATION (REO)
Refer to page 565.

RECOGNITION MEMORY TEST
Elizabeth Warrington

Adults   Ages 18-70

Purpose: Identifies minor visual and verbal memory deficits indicative of organic neurological disease. Used by clinicians with adults ages 18-70.

Description: Multiple-item response tests made up of two subtests based on pictures of words and faces and assessing verbal and visual recognition memory. The test enables clinicians to distinguish between right and left hemisphere damage and measures memory of verbally handicapped individuals. Examiner required. Not suitable for group use. BRITISH PUBLISHER

Untimed: 12-15 minutes
Scoring: Hand key
Cost: Complete set £33.30
Publisher: NFER-NELSON Publishing Company Ltd.

REITAN EVALUATION OF HEMISPHERIC ABILITIES AND BRAIN IMPROVEMENT TRAINING (REHABIT)
Ralph M. Reitan

All ages

Purpose: Diagnoses neuropsychological functions that may be impaired or deficient in both adults and children who may be suffering from brain damage or neurological dysfunction. Specific neurocortical training sequences are includes.

Description: Task-assessment and oral-response test measuring three fundamen-

tal areas of brain function: verbal and language functions (left hemisphere); visual-spatial, manipulatory, and sequential abilities (right hemisphere); and abstraction, reasoning, logical analysis, and ability to understand the essential nature of problem-situations (cerebral cortical functioning). Based on the results of the testing, five tracks of remedial training have been developed. Track A contains equipment and procedures that are specifically designed for developing expressive and receptive language and verbal skills. Track B also specializes in language and verbal materials, but includes elements of abstraction, reasoning, logical analysis, and organization. Track C includes various tasks that do not depend upon particular content as much as they do on reasoning, organization, and abstraction. Track D also emphasizes abstraction but uses material that requires the subject to deal with visual-spatial, sequential, and manipulatory skills. Track E specializes in tasks and materials that require the subject to exercise fundamental aspects of visual-spatial and manipulatory abilities. The training materials in each track are organized roughly from simple to complex; the subject is started at a level that is simple for him to perform satisfactorily. Examiner required. Not suitable for group use.

Untimed: Not available
Scoring: Examiner evaluated
Cost: Contact publisher
Publisher: Reitan Neuropsychology Laboratory
Information and availability unconfirmed; no publisher response.

REITAN-INDIANA NEUROPSYCHOLOGICAL TEST BATTERY FOR CHILDREN
Ralph M. Reitan and others

Child   Ages 5-8

Purpose: Assesses brain-behavior functioning in children. Used for clinical evaluation.

Description: Battery of tests assessing the neurological functioning of young children, including the Wechsler Intelligence Scale for Children, sensory perceptual tests, modifications of the Reitan-Indiana Aphasia Screening Test and the Halstead Neuropsychological Test Battery, and a number of additional tests (Color Form Test, Target Test, Matching Pictures Test, Progressive Figures Test, Marching Test, and Individual Performance Tests). This battery is related to the Halstead-Reitan neuropsychological test batteries for adults and older children, but a number of adaptations have been made for use with this age 5-8 group. The Category Test uses a different set of slides for stimuli and colored instead of numbered caps as the guide to lever choice on the answer panel. The Tactual Performance Test uses a 6-hole board in a horizontal instead of a vertical position. The Aphasia Screening Test deletes a number of items from the adult version, adds a number of simple procedures, and uses a different recording form. An electric finger tapping was devised because young children had trouble manipulating the manual apparatus. Materials include all necessary equipment, test stimuli, slide carousels, recording forms, and a manual for administration, scoring, and evaluation of all tests. The components may be purchased separately. Examiner required. Not suitable for group use.

Untimed: Varies

Scoring: Examiner evaluated

Cost: Young children's battery $1,115.00

Publisher: Reitan Neuropsychology Laboratory

Information and availability unconfirmed; no publisher response.

THE REVERSALS FREQUENCY TEST

Refer to page 586.

REVISED TOKEN TEST
Malcolm M. McNeil and Thomas E. Prescott

Brain-damaged adults Ages 20-80

Purpose: Assesses auditory disorders associated with brain damage and aphasia in adults. Used for designing rehabilitation programs and for research.

Description: Quantitative and descriptive test consisting of 10 subtests assessing auditory disorders associated with brain damage and aphasia. Percentile ranks are available for normal, right, and left hemisphere brain-damaged adults for each subtest and for overall performance. Examiner required. Not suitable for group use.

Timed: Not available

Scoring: Examiner evaluated

Cost: Complete kit (examiner's manual, administration manual, scoring forms, profile forms, 24 tokens, storage box) $58.00

Publisher: Pro-Ed

RIGHT-LEFT ORIENTATION TEST
Arthur L. Benton

All ages

Purpose: Measures subject's ability to discriminate between the right and left sides of the body.

Description: Test in which the subject is asked to point to lateral body parts on verbal command assessing three components of right-left orientation: orientation toward one's own body, orientation toward a confronting person, and combined orientation toward one's own body and a confronting person. Items range in difficulty from Level A (requiring identification of single lateral parts of one's own body) to Level E (requiring the combined operation of both the "own body" and "other person" systems of orientation). One point is credited for each correct response, including any corrections of an initially incorrect response. Two forms, A and B, are available; Form B is a mirror image of Form A (i.e., commands are reversed—right hand instead of left, etc.). Demands on the subject's motor skill are minimal and no naming ability is required. Modified versions (Form R and Form L) have been developed for use with hemiplegics. Materials required are a record form and manual. Examiner required. Not suitable for group use.

Untimed: 5 minutes

Scoring: Examiner evaluated

Cost: Contact publisher

Publisher: Oxford University Press

RILEY MOTOR PROBLEMS INVENTORY
Glyndon D. Riley

Child Ages 4-9

Purpose: Measures a child's oral, fine, and gross-motor skills. Used to determine whether further clinical evaluation is needed.

Description: Multiple-task verbal screening test providing a quantified system of observing neurological signs that may indicate a need for referral. The test measures the motor component as a factor in any related syndrome and differentiates between neurogenic and psychogenic disorders. Norms are provided for children ages 4-9. Cutoff scores are provided to indicate children who need further evaluation. Examiner required. Not suitable for group use.

Untimed: 5-10 minutes

Scoring: Hand key

Cost: Complete kit (100 record forms, manual) $19.50

Publisher: Western Psychological Services

RIVERMEAD PERCEPTUAL ASSESSMENT BATTERY
S. Whiting, N.B. Lincoln, G. Bhavnani, and J. Cockburn

Adolescent, adult Ages 16-69

Purpose: Assesses a wide range of perceptual abilities of adults. Used by occupational therapists for determining the degree of visual perceptual dysfunction and planning treatment.

Description: Multiple-item paper-pencil response test consisting of 16 subtests yielding information on different aspects of visual perceptual ability. The subtests are Picture Matching, Object Matching, Color Matching, Size Recognition, Series, Animal Halves, Missing Article, Figure-Ground Discrimination, Sequencing-Pictures, Body Image, Right/Left Copying Shapes, Right/Left Copying Words, Three-Dimensional Copying, Cube Copying, Cancellation, and Body-Image

Self-Identification. Items used during testing include illustrated sheets, picture cards, blocks, wooden figures, and a 3-D model. Assessment may be carried out in two sittings if preferred. Examiner required. Not suitable for group use. BRITISH PUBLISHER

Untimed: 45-60 minutes

Scoring: Examiner evaluated

Cost: Complete kit £258.75; manual £18.35; record forms £6.85

Publisher: NFER-NELSON Publishing Company Ltd.

SBORDONE-HALL MEMORY BATTERY
Robert J. Sbordone and Steven Hall

Adult

Purpose: Measures memory functions in normal, brain-injured, and cognitively impaired adults. Used for clinical assessment, cognitive rehabilitation, or research.

Description: Computer-administered test providing a fully automatic assessment of 18 discrete memory functions, including free recall of alpha-numeric stimuli over trials, delayed recall of alpha-numeric stimuli, memory loss due to proactive and retroactive interference, recognition memory of alpha-numeric stimuli, verbal memory errors, serial position learning, immediate word recognition memory, delayed word recognition memory, picture recognition memory, intentional word recognition memory, incidental word recognition memory, word origin memory, memory loss due to temporal delay or interference, immediate visual recognition memory for single and multiple geometric figures, types of visual memory errors, and storage versus retrieval memory deficits. The program either generates random stimuli or randomly selects test stimuli from a large pool and provides automatic cueing of the subject during testing.

A 12-page statistical and clinical analysis of the patient's performance, including a comparison of the patient's performance (in terms of Z scores) to age-matched organic, psychiatric, and normal controls is provided. In addition, the program utilizes powerful statistical techniques, such as signal detection and discriminant function analyses, to evaluate such factors as freedom from distraction, response bias, and test-taking efficiency. The battery is designed for use with Apple (II + , IIe, IIc, III) and IBM PC computer systems. Examiner/self-administered. Not suitable for group use.

Untimed: 45-50 minutes

Scoring: Computer scored

Cost: Complete program, including instructional manual $375.00; shipping fee $3.00

Publisher: Robert J. Sbordone

SEARCH FOR THE ODD SHAPE (SOSH)
Rosamond Gianutsos,
Georgine Vroman,
and Pauline Matheson

Ages 6-adult

Purpose: Assesses foveal imperception and differentiates scanning skill from shape examination and matching hemi-imperception. Used to assess head injury, stroke, or visual system damage.

Description: Computer-administered nonverbal shape comparison task. The subject scans an array of identical patterns for the "odd" one. Examiner required. Not suitable for group use.

Untimed: 8-10 minutes

Scoring: Computer scored

Cost: $30.00

Publisher: Life Science Associates

SEARCH-A-WORD (SAW)
Rosamond Gianutsos and
Carol Klitzner

Ages 6-adult

Purpose: Diagnoses hemi-imperception and visual attentional deficits. Used to assess head injury, stroke, or visual system damage.

Description: 30-task paper-pencil test of intact visual systems and central visual processing. The subject scans a 13"x13" character array and stops when a target three-character word is found. Materials

include the SAW test booklet, stopwatch, and a pencil. The subject must be able to read simple English words. Examiner required. Not suitable for group use.

Untimed: 8-20 seconds per task

Scoring: Hand key

Cost: $10.00

Publisher: Life Science Associates

SEARCHING FOR SHAPES (SEARCH)
Rosamond Gianutsos and
Carol Klitzner

Ages 8-adult

Purpose: Detects and treats differences in attention and responsiveness on the two sides of the visual field. Used to assess head injury, stroke, or visual system damage.

Description: Computer-administered test of visual systems and central visual processing. The subject looks at a shape in the center of the screen and searches for a match elsewhere on the screen as quickly as possible. Examiner then indicates whether or not the response is correct. The computer stores the search times for correct responses and the number of incorrect responses for later display. Examiner required. Not suitable for group use.

Untimed: 10 minutes

Scoring: Computer scored

Cost: $30.00

Publisher: Life Science Associates

SEGUIN-GODDARD FORMBOARDS (TACTUAL PERFORMANCE TEST)

Child, adolescent
Ages 5-14

Purpose: Measures spatial perception in children. Used in a variety of neuropsychological applications.

Description: Multiple-task examination of spatial perception, discrimination of forms, manual or construction ability, motor coordination, and the ability to meet new situations. The test materials consist of 10 sturdy blocks cut in the geometric forms of semicircle, triangle, cross, elongated hexagon, oblong, circle, square, flatted oval, star and lozenge, and a base with corresponding shapes cut into it. The child must place the blocks in the appropriate spaces on the formboard base. Two types of bases are available: one with raised geometric figures and one with flush geometric figures. Examiner required. Not suitable for group use.

Untimed: Not available

Scoring: Examiner evaluated

Cost: Raised formboard (used in Halstead-Reitan Battery) $99.25; flush formboard (used in Merrill-Palmer Scale) $68.50

Publisher: Stoelting Company

SELF-ADMINISTERED FREE RECALL (FRSELF)
Rosamond Gianutsos

Ages 10-adult

Purpose: Measures short- and long-term verbal memory in head injury and stroke victims.

Description: Computer-administered test of verbal memory in which the subject memorizes word lists and recalls them after either a short delay or an intervening task. This test is similar to FREEREC but is designed to be self-administered. The subject must be able to read simple English words. Self-administered. Not suitable for group use.

Untimed: 8-12 minutes

Scoring: Computer scored

Cost: $20.00 (minimum of 3 orders in Cat. #965 series)

Publisher: Life Science Associates

SEQUENCE RECALL (SEQREC)
Rosamond Gianutsos and Carol Klitzner

Ages 10-adult

Purpose: Assesses wide-range, nonverbal memory. Used to diagnose severe memory deficits.

Description: Computer-administered test of nonverbal memory. Shapes, short words, or pictures are presented one at a

time and are followed by a "menu" of items that may or may not have appeared. The subject is asked to indicate which ones appeared. Because it does not require reading aloud, this program can be used for diagnosis and treatment with patients unable to process verbal material, including non-English speakers, aphasics, and others. It can be set to a wide range of difficulty. Examiner required. Not suitable for group use.

Untimed: 10-15 minutes

Scoring: Computer scored

Cost: $30.00

Publisher: Life Science Associates

SERIAL DIGIT LEARNING TEST
Arthur L. Benton

Adolescent, adult

Purpose: Measures short-term memory in a clinical assessment of mental status.

Description: Test in which the examiner presents either eight (Form SD8) or nine (Form SD9) randomly selected single digits for a varying number of trials up to a maximum of 12 trials. Three alternate versions are provided for each form, the selection of which is based primarily on the subject's age and educational level. Generally, Form SD9 is given to patients under age 65 who have 12 or more years of education and Form SD8 to those age 65 or older and those under age 65 with less than 12 years of education. The manual provides exceptions to these criteria. Testing is discontinued after two consecutive correct repetitions. One point is scored for each "near-correct" response; correct repetitions are credited two points. Examiner required. Not suitable for group use.

Untimed: 5-10 minutes

Scoring: Examiner evaluated

Cost: Contact publisher

Publisher: Oxford University Press

SHAPE MATCHING (MATCH)
Rosamond Gianutsos,
Georgine Vroman,
and Pauline Matheson

Ages 6-adult

Purpose: Assesses foveal imperception associated with head injury, stroke, or visual system damage.

Description: Computer-administered nonverbal shape comparison task. Two detailed shapes are displayed one above the other. The subject has to decide whether they are the same or different in some small but distinct way. Examiner required. Not suitable for group use.

Untimed: 8-10 minutes

Scoring: Computer scored

Cost: $30.00

Publisher: Life Science Associates

SHERMAN MENTAL IMPAIRMENT TEST
Murray H. Sherman

Adult

Purpose: Measures mental impairment.

Description: Picture-card test providing a rapid measure for the objective determination of mental impairment. Examiner required. Not suitable for group use.
CANADIAN PUBLISHER

Untimed: 10 minutes

Scoring: Examiner evaluated

Cost: Set of cards $5.00; manual $2.00

Publisher: Institute of Psychological Research, Inc.

Information and availability unconfirmed; no publisher response.

SINGLE AND DOUBLE SIMULTANEOUS STIMULATION (SDSS)
Rosamond Gianutsos, Georgine Vroman, and Pauline Matheson

Ages 6-adult

Purpose: Assesses imperception due to unilateral visual field loss. Used to assess head injury, stroke, or visual system damage.

Description: Computer-administered test for intact visual systems and central visual processing. The subject indicates whether symbols appear on either the left,

right, both, or neither side of the screen. Examiner required. Not suitable for group use.

Untimed: 8-10 minutes

Scoring: Computer scored

Cost: $30.00

Publisher: Life Science Associates

SINGLE AND DOUBLE SIMULTANEOUS STIMULATION TEST (SDSST)
Carmen C. Centofanti and Aaron Smith

Child, adolescent, adult

Purpose: Assesses children and adults suspected of having central nervous system diseases or injuries. May be used for assessment with patients with confirmed lesions.

Description: Nonverbal touch-discrimination test measuring the accuracy with which a subject can identify single and double simultaneous tactile stimulation applied to the cheek and/or hand. The test assesses specific somatosensory functions and correctly identifies two of every three patients with diverse types of acute cerebral lesions and one of every two patients with chronic lesions, in addition to patients with other persisting functional deficits. The test can be especially useful when used in combination with the Symbol Digit Modalities Test. Examiner required. Not suitable for group use.

Untimed: 3-5 minutes

Scoring: Examiner evaluated

Cost: Complete kit (100 score sheets, manual) $19.50

Publisher: Western Psychological Services

SKLAR APHASIA SCALE: REVISED 1983
Refer to page 645.

SLOSSON DRAWING COORDINATION TEST (SDCT)
Richard L. Slosson

All ages

Purpose: Screens for serious forms of brain dysfunction or damage and aids in the diagnosis of visual-perceptual or visual-motor coordination problems. Also indicates the possibility of severe emotional disturbances.

Description: Multiple-item paper-pencil screening test identifying individuals suffering from serious forms of brain dysfunction or damage in which eye-hand coordination is involved. The subject is given 12 figures and asked to make three free-hand copies of each figure. The subject's copies are scored for degree of distortion indicative of brain damage or dysfunction, visual-motor coordination problems, emotional disturbances, or poor motivational attitude. Suggested cutoff scores are provided. The test is not intended as a definitive diagnostic instrument; therefore, it should be used in conjunction with the Slosson Intelligence Test (or other intelligence test) to cover problems in which eye-hand coordination is not a factor. Examiner required. Suitable for group use.

Untimed: 10-15 minutes

Scoring: Hand key

Cost: Complete kit (manual, scoring procedures, two score sheets, vinyl binder) $28.00

Publisher: Slosson Educational Publications, Inc.

SOUTHERN CALIFORNIA MOTOR ACCURACY TEST, REVISED 1980
A. Jean Ayres

Child   Ages 4-8

Purpose: Diagnoses perceptual-motor dysfunctions in atypical children. Used in clinical evaluations.

Description: Manual, reflex test measuring the degree of sensory-motor integration of the upper extremities of neurologically atypical children. Norms are provided for both left- and right-handed performance of children ages 4-8 at three performance speeds. A revised manual describes changes in both administration and scoring. The original test form may still be used, but only in conjunction with the new manual. Examiner required. Not suitable for group use.

Untimed: 10-15 minutes

Scoring: Hand key

Cost: Complete kit (25 tests, manual, line measure) $39.75

Publisher: Western Psychological Services

SOUTHERN CALIFORNIA SENSORY INTEGRATION TESTS (SCSIT)
Refer to page 566.

SPATIAL ORIENTATION MEMORY TEST
Refer to page 588.

SPEEDED READING OF WORD LISTS (SRWL)
Rosamond Gianutsos and Carol Klitzner

Ages 8-adult

Purpose: Diagnoses and trains visual scanning. Used to assess head injury, stroke, or visual system damage.

Description: Computer-administered test of four basic functions of visual information processing: anchoring at the margin, scanning horizontally, identification of words within the perceptual span, and monitoring the periphery. Words are presented by the computer in different positions on the screen. The user can vary word displacement from the center and display time. Once an individual's problems have been diagnosed, SRWL can be used for rehabilitation. Examiner required. Not suitable for group use.

Untimed: 10-15 minutes

Scoring: Computer scored

Cost: $30.00

Publisher: Life Science Associates

STANDARDIZED ROAD-MAP TEST OF DIRECTION SENSE
Refer to page 566.

STEADINESS TESTER—GROOVE TYPE
Refer to page 983.

STEADINESS TESTER—HOLE TYPE

Refer to page 984.

STIMULUS RECOGNITION TEST
T.L. Brink

Adult

Purpose: Assesses confusion due to senile dementia in adults.

Description: 10-item response test measuring short-term memory via recognition. The examiner presents oral and visual stimuli during the test. Examiner required. Not suitable for group use.

Untimed: 5-10 minutes

Scoring: Examiner evaluated

Cost: Set of stimulus cards and instructions $10.00

Publisher: T.L. Brink

SYMBOL DIGIT MODALITIES TEST
Aaron Smith

Ages 8-75

Purpose: Measures brain damage. Used to screen and predict learning disorders and to identify children with potential reading problems.

Description: Multiple-item test in which the subject is given 90 seconds to convert as many meaningless geometric designs as possible into their appropriate numbers according to the key provided. When group-administered, the test may be used as a screening device. The test may be administered orally to individuals who cannot take written tests. Since numbers are nearly universal, the test is virtually culture-free. Examiner required. Suitable for group use.

Timed: 90 seconds

Scoring: Hand key

Cost: Complete kit (100 tests, key, manual) $29.00

Publisher: Western Psychological Services

TACHISTOSCOPIC READING (FASTREAD)
Rosamond Gianutsos

Ages 10-adult

Purpose: Assesses areas of attention deficits, foveal imperception, and difficulty in planning and articulating words. Used with head injury and stroke victims.

Description: Computer-administered reading test in which the computer flashes a word and the subject types what he saw. The task speed adjusts to the subject's performance. The program may be used for retraining and has diagnostic capabilities. Self-administered. Not suitable for group use.

Untimed: 8-12 minutes

Scoring: Computer scored

Cost: $20.00 (minimum of 3 orders in Cat. #965 series)

Publisher: Life Science Associates

TACTILE FORM PERCEPTION TEST
Arthur L. Benton

All ages

Purpose: Assesses subject's ability to process nonverbal tactile information.

Description: Tactile form perception test using two parallel sets of 10 cards each to assess the subject's ability to process nonverbal tactile information. The cards, each of which presents a geometric figure made of fine-grade sandpaper, are placed face up in a covered box. The patient inserts either his right or his left hand into the box and examines the card for no more than 30 seconds. The patient then is allowed an additional 15 seconds to visually examine a multiple-choice card containing line drawings of the sandpaper figures. The patient uses the opposite hand to point to the line drawing which represents the sandpaper figure. When the patient has examined the first set of 10 cards, testing should continue with the second set of cards, using the opposite hand. If motor or sensory disability prohibits testing with the opposite hand, testing should be terminated. Each response is scored for correctness. Specific incorrect responses should be identified. Scores may be obtained for each hand separately and for both hands together. Examiner required. Not suitable for group use.

Timed: 45 seconds per card

Scoring: Hand key

Cost: Contact publisher

Publisher: Oxford University Press

TAPPING BOARD
Refer to page 984.

TEST OF PERCEPTUAL ORGANIZATION (TPO)
William T. Martin

Adult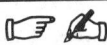

Purpose: Measures abstract reasoning abilities, psychomotor functioning, and the ability to follow specific, exacting instructions in an accurate manner. Identifies persons with emotional disturbance or perceptual-motor disabilities. Used for clinical research and screening purposes.

Description: 10-item paper-pencil test consisting of abstract reasoning and visual-motor tasks. Test items consist of written statements (instructions for plotting points on a map) presented in order of increasing difficulty. The subjects read the instructions and mark an "X" at each of the 10 coordinate points on a street map containing 54 one-inch square blocks confined within a 6 x 9 inch area. Objective scoring discriminates between persons with emotional disturbance and/or perceptual-motor disabilities and those with one or few of these problems. Subjective analysis of the test protocol identifies persons with emotional disturbances or intellect-abstraction problems. Clinical analysis must be done in terms of personality dynamics and visual-motor theory. A fourth-grade reading level is required. Examiner required. Suitable for group use.

Timed: 10 minutes

Scoring: Hand key; examiner evaluated

Cost: Examiner's set $25.00; 25 test forms $13.50; keys $2.50; 25 profile sheets $7.50; manual $6.00

Publisher: Psychologists and Educators, Inc.

TEST OF TEMPORAL ORIENTATION
Arthur L. Benton

Adult

Purpose: Assesses the accuracy of a patient's temporal orientation. Used as a component of a mental status examination.

Description: 5-item oral-response test in which the examiner asks temporal orientation questions (day of week, day of month, month, year, and time of day) and assigns points based on criteria provided in the manual. The test is used to disclose and interpret minor as well as gross temporal disorientation within a prescribed range of normal variation. The total number of error points constitutes the patient's obtained score, resulting in classifications ranging from normal to severely defective. Examiner required. Not suitable for group use.

Untimed: Varies

Scoring: Examiner evaluated

Cost: Contact publisher

Publisher: Oxford University Press

TESTS OF MENTAL FUNCTION IN THE ELDERLY

Adult

Purpose: Screens for impairment of mental functions in the elderly.

Description: 20-item paper-pencil and verbal test assessing 10 areas of mental function in the elderly: orientation, sentence learning, counting backwards, mental control, digit retention, 5-minute memory, digit copying, associated memory, simple arithmetic, and general knowledge. Items are contained on a series of paper sheets and are presented orally by the examiner. Responses are recorded by the exminer on the provided score pad. Comments regarding age norms and interpretation of test results are presented on the flip side of each test question sheet. Examiner required. Not suitable for group use.

Untimed: 15 minutes

Scoring: Examiner evaluated

Cost: Contact publisher

Publisher: Wyeth Laboratories, Inc.

THREE-DIMENSIONAL BLOCK CONSTRUCTION
Arthur L. Benton

All ages

Purpose: Assesses constructional apraxia.

Description: 3-item manual test in which three block models are presented one at a time to the patient, who is required to construct an exact replica of the model by using the appropriate blocks from a set of loose blocks on a tray. The set of loose blocks is placed to the patient's side, and the model to be copied is placed in front of the patient. The patient is instructed to arrange the loose blocks so that they look like the model. The maximum time allowed for the construction of each model is 5 minutes. If construction is not completed within that time, the model is removed and the next model is presented. Four types of errors are recorded: omissions, additions, substitutions, and displacements. The test is available in two forms, A and B. In Form A, Model 1 consists of a pyramid made from six 1-inch cubes; Model 2 is an 8-block four-level construction; and Model III is a 15-block four-level construction. In Form B, Model 1 is a pyramidal structure of six blocks; Model II is an 8-block four-level construction; and Model III is a 15-block four-level construction. One point is awarded for each block that is placed correctly. Examiner required. Not suitable for group use.

Timed: 5 minutes per model

Scoring: Examiner evaluated

Cost: Contact publisher

Publisher: Oxford University Press

TRIPLET RECALL (TRIPREC)
Rosamond Gianutsos and Carol Klitzner

Ages 10-adult

Purpose: Measures short- and long-term memory. Used to assess head injury or stroke as it affects verbal memory.

Description: Computer-administered test measuring short- and long-term retention. The task is easier than that in Free Recall and can be used for practice and remediation with patients for whom Free Recall is too difficult. Three words are presented one at a time and followed by 0, 3, or 9 words to be read, but not recalled, after a constant time interval. Examiner required. Not suitable for group use.

Untimed: 10-15 minutes

Scoring: Computer scored

Cost: $30.00

Publisher: Life Science Associates

TRITES NEUROPSYCHOLOGICAL TEST BATTERY
Ronald L. Trites

Ages 5-55

Purpose: Measures psychomotor steadiness and eye-hand coordination. Used to detect brain damage in children and adults, describe the extent of impairment, and document patient capabilities.

Description: 3-battery manual test of various aspects of steadiness and perceptual ability. Groove Type Steadiness Testers are used to measure eye-hand coordination and other psychomotor phenomena. The subject pushes a stylus through a gradually narrowing groove without touching the sides, in holes each of nine sizes. The units can be connected to a Tone Response device for immediate auditory feedback, and analyses can be made of the subject's total score to study the effects on steadiness of such variables as exercise, handedness, smoking, or alcohol consumption. The performance curve also can be analyzed for practice effects and fatigue. The third battery uses a Tapping Board, which has two 3½" square stainless steel plates on either end of an 18" fiberesin board. The subject is asked to tap the plates as rapidly as possible. A single impulse counter shows the effects of massed versus spaced trails, warm-up and fatigue effects, and end spurt. Social facilitation can be demonstrated by testing subjects alone or in groups. The manual presents age norms for subjects ages 5-15 with specific norms for males and females. Examiner required. Not suitable for group use. Available in French.

Untimed: Not available

Scoring: Examiner evaluated

Cost: Contact publisher

Publisher: Lafayette Instrument Company, Inc.

TWO ARM COORDINATION TEST
Refer to page 984.

VISCO CHILD DEVELOPMENT SCREENING TEST (THE CHILDS TEST)
Refer to page 497.

VISUAL ATTENTION TASKS (ATTEND)
Linda Laatsch

Ages 10-adult

Purpose: Diagnoses attention and vigilance deficits. Used to assess head injury, stroke, or visual system damage.

Description: Computer-administered test of attentional skills in which the examiner selects targets to which the subject responds and non-targets to which the subject inhibits response. The stimuli appear at selectable intervals, randomly or non-randomly. The task can be constructed to suit the level of the deficit. Examiner required. Not suitable for group use.

Untimed: 2-15 minutes

Scoring: Computer scored

Cost: $35.00

Publisher: Life Science Associates

VISUAL FORM DISCRIMINATION TEST
Arthur L. Benton

Adult

Purpose: Assesses a subject's capacity for discriminating complex visual forms.

Description: 16-item multiple-choice test in which each item consists of a stimulus design comprised of major and peripheral figures and four response choices: the correct foil (C), an incorrect foil involving displacement or rotation of the peripheral figure (PE), an incorrect foil involving rotation of a major figure (MR), and an incorrect foil involving distortion of the other major figure (MD). The subject's task is to discriminate among the response choices and identify the one design that matches the stimulus design. Items are scored 0, 1, or 2 points. Examiner required. Not suitable for group use.

Untimed: Varies

Scoring: Examiner evaluated

Cost: Contact publisher

Publisher: Oxford University Press

VISUAL MEMORY TASK (VISMEM)
Rosamond Gianutsos

Ages 8-adult

Purpose: Measures visual, nonverbal memory in head injury and stroke victims.

Description: Computer-administered test of visual memory. Irregular shapes are presented for study. The subject then "paints" the shape as recalled. Self-administered. Not suitable for group use.

Untimed: 8-12 minutes

Scoring: Computer scored

Cost: $20.00 (minimum of 3 orders in Cat. #965 series)

Publisher: Life Science Associates

VISUAL SCANNING (SCAN)
Linda Laatsch

Ages 10-adult

Purpose: Diagnoses visual scanning deficits. Used to assess head injury, stroke, or visual system damage.

Description: Computer-administered test of visual scanning deficits. Two formats are provided: TEXTSCAN and LINESCAN. In TEXTSCAN, letters move across the screen. The subject must respond when the target letter is briefly bracketed. In LINESCAN, a letter or number appears briefly at the right or left edge of the screen, and the same or a different letter or number appears at the opposite edge. The subject must indicate whether they are the same. The required scanning speed is adjustable over a wide range in both formats. May be used in retraining and for diagnosis. Examiner required. Not suitable for group use.

Untimed: 5-12 minutes

Scoring: Computer scored

Cost: $35.00

Publisher: Life Science Associates

WACHS ANALYSIS OF COGNITIVE STRUCTURES
Refer to page 497.

===

WECHSLER MEMORY SCALE (WMS)
David Wechsler and C.P. Stone

Adult

Purpose: Assesses memory functions. Used for adult subjects with special problems, such as aphasics, the elderly, and organically brain-injured individuals.

Description: Seven-subtest scale assessing memory functions and yielding a memory quotient. Two alternate forms, I and II, are available. A revised edition, available in one form, includes new subtests for measuring additional aspects of memory. Examiner required. Not suitable for group use.

Untimed: Not available

Scoring: Examiner evaluated

Cost: Specimen set (manual, design cards, both record forms) $8.00; 50 record forms $22.00 (specify Form I or

II); manual $7.00

Publisher: The Psychological Corporation

THE WESTERN APHASIA BATTERY (WAB)
Andrew Kertesz

All ages

Purpose: Evaluates an individual's ability to read, write, and calculate. Measures the language functions of content, fluency, auditory comprehension, repetition, and naming. Used to evaluate the severity of language impairment (aphasia) and the nonverbal skills of drawing, block design, and praxis.

Description: Three-part test covering oral language; reading, writing, calculation, and praxis; and nonverbal skills (apraxia, drawing, block design, calculation, Raven's matrices). The nonverbal part is optional. The oral part requires a stopwatch, four Kohs blocks, and a Raven's Colored Progressive Matrices test to measure spontaneous speech, comprehension, naming, repetition, and thus aphasia. The subtests require conversational speech in response to questions and a picture interview. The reading and writing tests measure functional communication, spontaneous speech and fluency, and comprehension. Examiner required. Not suitable for group use.

Timed: 1 hour

Scoring: Examiner evaluated

Cost: Complete set $56.50

Publisher: Grune & Stratton, Inc.

WISCONSIN CARD SORTING TEST (WCST)
David A. Grant and Esta A. Berg

Adolescent, adult
Ages 16 and older

Purpose: Assesses perseveration and abstract thinking. Used for neuropsychological assessment of individuals suspected of having brain lesions involving the frontal lobes. When used in conjunction with more comprehensive ability testing, the test can help discriminate frontal from nonfrontal lesions.

Description: Multiple-task nonverbal test in which the subject matches cards in two response decks to one of four stimulus cards for color, form, or number. Responses are recorded on a form for later scoring. The test provides measures of overall success and particular sources of difficulty. Examiner required. Not suitable for group use.

Untimed: Not available

Scoring: Examiner evaluated

Cost: Complete kit (card decks, response forms, manual) $75.00; manual $10.00

Publisher: Psychological Assessment Resources, Inc.

WORD MEMORY TASK (WORDMEM)
Rosamond Gianutsos

Ages 8-adult

Purpose: Assesses immediate memory in head injury and stroke victims.

Description: Computer-administered test of verbal memory. The computer displays a random list of words one by one. The subject then types the list in order. Both number of words in the list and duration of exposure are adjustable. The subject must have some visual function, the ability to read simple English words, rudimentary keyboarding skills, and the ability to follow simple instructions. Self-administered. Not suitable for group use.

Untimed: 8-12 minutes

Scoring: Computer scored

Cost: $20.00 (minimum of 3 orders in Cat. #965 series)

Publisher: Life Science Associates

Marriage and Family: Family

ADAPTIVE BEHAVIOR INVENTORY OF CHILDREN (ABIC)
Jane R. Mercer and June F. Lewis

Child   Ages 5-11

Purpose: Measures a child's social role performance in his family, peer group, and community.

Description: 242-item inventory in an interview format measuring six aspects of adaptive behavior, including family, community, peer relations, nonacademic school rules, earner/consumer, and self-maintenance. Items are divided into two sections. The first section is applicable to all children, and the second section consists of age-graded questions. The interviewer is usually a trained professional. The ABIC is one component of the System of Multicultural Pluralistic Assessment (SOMPA). Examiner required. Not suitable for group use. The manual includes the ABIC questions in both Spanish and English.

Untimed: Not available

Scoring: Hand key; examiner evaluated

Cost: Basic kit (manual, 6 keys, 25 record forms) $40.00

Publisher: The Psychological Corporation

ADOLESCENT-FAMILY INVENTORY OF LIFE EVENTS AND CHANGES (A-FILE)
Hamilton I. McCubbin, Joan M. Patterson, Edward Bauman, and Linda H. Harris

Adolescent   Ages 12-18

Purpose: Assesses the accumulation of life events and changes in a family from an adolescent member's perspective. Used in clinical and research settings to assess the stress adolescents may be experiencing as a result of family events and changes, to identify adolescents at risk for experiencing undesirable outcomes, as a pre- and postmeasure of family stress with intervention programs, and as a predictive tool for a wide range of criteria, including adolescent substance use, family member's health status, and family adaptation/maladaptation.

Description: 50-item self-report instrument consisting of six scales: Transitions, Sexuality, Responsibilities and Strains, Substance Use, and Legal Conflict. Adolescents answer "yes" or "no" to each item twice: if family life change occurred (1) during past 12 months and (2) before past 12 months. Three scores can be obtained: scale scores (identifying domains of family life most strained by life changes and events), total past life changes (provides an index of persistent stress in an adolescent's family), and a weighted stress score. Results can be compared to FILE assessment results (parents' perception of family stress). Examiner required. Suitable for group use.

Untimed: Varies

Scoring: Hand key

Cost: Test form $0.10; manual $15.00 ($10.00 for students)

Publisher: Family Stress, Coping and Health Project

THE AMERICAN HOME SCALE
W.A. Kerr and H.H. Remmers

Adolescent, adult
Grades 8 and above

Purpose: Evaluates the cultural, aesthetic, and economic factors of an individual's home environment. Used for counseling students and other individuals who may be experiencing problems due to their home environment.

Description: Multiple-item paper-pencil inventory assessing an individual's home environment. Construction of the test is based on profile and factor analyses. The test discriminates between sociological areas. The norms are based on over 16,000 eighth-grade students in over 42 American cities. Examiner required. Suitable for group use.

Timed: 40 minutes

Scoring: Examiner evaluated

Cost: Specimen set $4.00; 25 surveys $5.00

Publisher: Psychometric Affiliates

BORROMEAN FAMILY INDEX: FOR MARRIED PERSONS
Panos D. Bardis

Adolescent, adult

Purpose: Measures a married person's attitudes and feelings toward his immediate family. Used for clinical assessment, family and marriage counseling, family attitude research, and discussions in family education.

Description: 18-item paper-pencil test in which the subject rates nine statements about "forces that attract you to your family" on a scale from 0 (absent) to 4 (very strong) and nine statements about "forces that pull you away from your family" on a scale from 0 (does not pull you away at all) to 4 (very strong). Examiner/self-administered. Suitable for group use.

Untimed: 10 minutes

Scoring: Examiner evaluated

Cost: Free

Publisher: Panos D. Bardis

BORROMEAN FAMILY INDEX: FOR SINGLE PERSONS
Panos D. Bardis

Adolescent, adult

Purpose: Measures an individual's attitudes and feelings toward his family. Used for clinical assessment, family counseling, family attitude research, and discussion in family education.

Description: 18-item paper-pencil test in which the subject rates nine statements about "forces that attract you to your family" from 0 (absent) to 4 (very strong) and nine statements about "forces that pull you away from your family" from 0 (does not pull you away at all) to 4 (very strong). Examiner/self-administered. Suitable for group use.

Untimed: 10 minutes

Scoring: Examiner evaluated

Cost: Free

Publisher: Panos D. Bardis

THE BRICKLIN PERCEPTUAL SCALES: CHILD-PERCEPTION-OF-PARENTS-SERIES
Barry Bricklin

Ages 4-adult

Purpose: Measures a child's perceptions of each parent. Used with children from age six for family therapy and custody arrangements.

Description: 64-item response test assessing a child's verbal and nonverbal perception of parents in four areas: competence, supportiveness, follow-up consistency, and possession of admirable personality traits. An overall score based on nonverbal responses indicates which parent more frequently acts in the child's best interest. Each of the items is presented to the child on a separate card by means of a special card holder. Administration directions are printed on each card, as well as an "invisible grid" which scores the card automatically as the child responds. The test, which elicits nonverbal responses by means of a continuum stimulus, has been used with children as young as age 4 who understand the instructions. Examiner required. Not suitable for group use.

Untimed: 25-45 minutes

Scoring: Hand key

Cost: Complete kit (6 sets of cards—64 cards per set, 6 scoring sheets, BPS stylus, foam insert and test box, instruction manual) $49.00

Publisher: Village Publishing

CHILDREN'S VERSION/FAMILY ENVIRONMENT SCALE (CV/FES)
C.J. Pino, Nancy Simons, and Mary Jane Slawinowski

Child   Ages 5-12

Purpose: Evaluates the home environment of children. Used by guidance counselors, psychologists, clinicians, family therapists, and family educators.

Description: 30-item paper-pencil or oral-response test assessing 10 areas of family functioning along three dimensions: relationship dimensions (cohesion, expressiveness, and conflict), personal growth dimensions (independence, achievement orientation, intellectual-cultural orientation, active-recreational orientation, and moral-religious orientation), and system maintenance dimensions (organization and control). Questions are presented to the child in a pictorial nonprojective format. The manual describes clinical use, research, and test administration and scoring. Examiner required. Not suitable for group use.

Untimed: Varies

Scoring: Examiner evaluated

Cost: Test kit (manual, 10 reusable test booklets, 50 profiles, 50 examiner's worksheets, 50 answer sheets) $32.00

Publisher: Slosson Educational Publications, Inc.

DYADIC PARENT-CHILD INTERACTION CODING SYSTEM (DPICS)
Sheila M. Eyberg and Elizabeth A. Robinson

Child, adult

Purpose: Assesses the quality of interaction between parents and young children in the laboratory or clinical setting. Used to aid in evaluation of family functioning, monitor progress of treatment, and evaluate treatment outcome.

Description: Multiple-item paper-pencil coding system comprising a direct observation procedure for monitoring interactions between parents and young children. Data are collected by observing a parent-child dyad in three 5-minute semistructured situations that vary in the amount of parental control elicited: child-directed play, parent-directed play, and clean-up. Parents are observed for the following behaviors: descriptive statement, reflective statement, descriptive/reflective question, acknowledgment, physical positive, physical negative, labeled praise, unlabeled praise, critical statement, direct command, and indirect command. Each command is coded as to whether the child complies, noncomplies, or is given no opportunity to comply. Additional child behaviors observed include whine, cry, yell, smart talk, physical negative, destructive, and changes activity. Whether the parent responds to or ignores each deviant behavior also is recorded. In the manual, the behaviors listed above are operationally defined, examples are given, decision rules are delineated, normative data are provided, and research is summarized. Examiner required. Not suitable for group use.

Untimed: 15 minutes

Scoring: Examiner evaluated

Cost: Manual $14.50

Publisher: Psychological Documents, American Psychological Association

A FAMILISM SCALE
Panos D. Bardis

Adolescent, adult

Purpose: Assesses individual attitudes toward both nuclear and extended families. Used for clinical evaluation, marriage and family counseling, research on the family, and discussion in family life education.

Description: 16-item paper-pencil test in which the subject reads 10 statements about nuclear family relationships and 6 statements about extended family relationships and rates them according to his personal beliefs on a scale from 0 (strongly disagree) to 4 (strongly agree). The "familism" score equals the sum of the 16 numerical responses. The theoretical range of scores extends from 0 (least familistic) to 64 (most familistic). Separate scores may be obtained for "nuclear family integration" and "extended family integration." Examiner/self-administered. Suitable for group use.

Untimed: 10 minutes

Scoring: Examiner evaluated

Cost: Free

Publisher: Panos D. Bardis

A FAMILISM SCALE: EXTENDED FAMILY INTEGRATION
Panos D. Bardis

Adolescent, adult

Purpose: Measures attitudes toward the extended family (beyond the nuclear family, but within the kinship group). Used for clinical assessment, marriage and family counseling, family attitude research, and discussions in family education.

Description: 6-item paper-pencil test in which the subject reads a list of statements concerning extended family relationships and rates them according to his personal beliefs on a scale from 0 (strongly disagree) to 4 (strongly agree). The "familism" score is the sum of the six numerical responses. The theoretical range of scores extends from 0 (least

familistic) to 24 (most familistic). Examiner/self-administered. Suitable for group use.

Untimed: 5 minutes

Scoring: Examiner evaluated

Cost: Free

Publisher: Panos D. Bardis

A FAMILISM SCALE: NUCLEAR FAMILY INTEGRATION
Panos D. Bardis

Adolescent, adult

Purpose: Measures attitudes toward the solidarity of the nuclear family. Used for clinical assessment, marriage and family counseling, family attitude research, and discussion in family education.

Description: 10-item paper-pencil test in which the subject rates 10 statements about family relationships from 0 (strongly disagree) to 4 (strongly agree). The "familism" score equals the sum of the 10 numerical responses. The theoretical range of scores extends from 0 (least familistic) to 40 (most familistic). Self-administered. Suitable for group use.

Untimed: 5 minutes

Scoring: Hand key

Cost: Free

Publisher: Panos D. Bardis

THE FAMILY ADJUSTMENT TEST (ELIAS FAMILY OPINION SURVEY)
Gabriel Elias and edited by H.H. Remmers

Adolescent, adult

Purpose: Measures intrafamily homeyness-homelessness (acceptance-rejection) while appearing to be concerned only with attitudes toward general community life. Used for clinical evaluations and research.

Description: Paper-pencil or oral-response projective test measuring adult and adolescent feelings of family acceptance. The test yields 10 subscores: attitudes toward mother, father, relatives preference, oedipal, independence struggle, parent-child friction, interparental friction, family status feeling, child rejection, and parental quality. Subtest scores and clinical indicators of a number of adjustment trends, as well as an overall index of feelings of intrafamily homeyness-homelessness, are provided. Percentile norms are provided by sex for the following age groups: ages 12-13, 14-15, 16-18, and 19 and older. Interpretation is provided in terms of subtest profiles. Norms for specific parent-child relationships are provided also. No third party should be present if the test is administered orally. Examiner required. The paper-pencil format is suitable for group use.

Timed: 45 minutes

Scoring: Hand key; scoring service available

Cost: Specimen set (test, manual, key) $5.00; 25 tests $8.50

Publisher: Psychometric Affiliates

FAMILY ENVIRONMENT SCALE
Rudolf H. Moos and Bernice S. Moos

Adolescent, adult

Purpose: Assesses characteristics of family environments. Used for family therapy.

Description: 90-item paper-pencil test measuring 10 dimensions of family environments: cohesion, expressiveness, conflict, independence, achievement orientation, intellectual-cultural orientation, active-recreational orientation, moral-religious emphasis, organization, and control. These dimensions are further grouped into three categories: relationship, personal growth, and system maintenance. Materials include the Real Form (Form R), which measures perceptions of current family environments; the Ideal Form (Form I), which measures conceptions of ideal family environments; and the Expectancies Form (Form E), which measures expectations about family settings. Forms I and E are not published; however, reworded instructions and items may be requested from the publisher. Examiner required. Suitable for group use.

Untimed: Not available

Scoring: Examiner evaluated

Cost: Manual $6.50; key $1.50; 25 reusable tests $4.75; 50 answer sheets $3.50; 50 profiles $3.50

Publisher: Consulting Psychologists Press, Inc.

FAMILY INVENTORIES
David H. Olson,
Hamilton I. McCubbin,
Howard Barnes, Andrea Larsen,
Marla Muxen, and Marc Wilson

Families

Purpose: Measures various aspects of family functioning. Used for research and clinical work with couples and families.

Description: Series of nine paper-pencil measures of family functioning. Inventories available are FACES III: Family Adaptability and Cohesion Evaluation Scales; Family Satisfaction; Parent-Adolescent Communication; ENRICH: Enriching and Nurturing Relationship Issues; Communication and Happiness; FILE: Family Inventory of Life Events and Changes; A-FILE: Adolescent Family Inventory of Life Events and Changes; F-COPES: Family Coping Strategies; Family Strengths; and Quality of Life. The following information is provided for each inventory: conceptual development, construct validity, internal consistency (alpha) reliability, test-retest reliability, scoring procedures, cutting points, and national norms. A copy of each inventory is provided so they can be reproduced for research projects and clinical work. Permission to use and duplicate these inventories will be granted by the publisher upon receipt of an abstract form. Examiner/self-administered. Suitable for group use.

Untimed: Varies

Scoring: Hand key

Cost: Contact publisher

Publisher: Family Social Science

FAMILY INVENTORIES: ADOLESCENT FAMILY INVENTORY OF LIFE EVENTS AND CHANGES (A-FILE)
David H. Olson,
Hamilton I. McCubbin,
Howard Barnes, Andrea Larsen,
Marla Muxen, and Marc Wilson

Adolescent

Purpose: Measures level of stress in families of adolescents. Used for research and clinical work with families.

Description: 50-item paper-pencil self-report instrument that records life events and changes an adolescent perceives his or her family have experienced during the last 12 months. Changes are grouped in six dimensions: transitions, sexuality, losses, responsibilities and strains, substance use, and legal conflict. Examiner/self-administered. Suitable for group use.

Untimed: Varies

Scoring: Hand key

Cost: Contact publisher

Publisher: Family Social Science

FAMILY INVENTORIES: FAMILY ADAPTABILITY AND COHESION EVALUATION SCALES (FACES III)
David H. Olson,
Hamilton I. McCubbin,
Howard Barnes, Andrea Larsen,
Marla Muxen, and Marc Wilson

Families

Purpose: Assesses family functioning. Used for research and clinical work with couples and families.

Description: 20-item paper-pencil test of family adaptability and cohesion. Examinees respond by rating each item on a 5-point Likert scale. The authors recommend that FACES III be administered to all family members so that family member reports can be compared and couple and family scores can be used. FACES III is designed to obtain both perceived and ideal family functioning. A couple version is also available for couples without children. A seventh-grade reading level is required. Examiner/self-administered. Suitable for group use.

Untimed: Varies

Scoring: Hand key

Cost: Contact publisher

Publisher: Family Social Science

FAMILY INVENTORIES: FAMILY COPING STRATEGIES (F-COPE)
David H. Olson,
Hamilton I. McCubbin,
Howard Barnes, Andrea Larsen,
Marla Muxen, and Marc Wilson

Families

Purpose: Identifies effective problem-solving and behavioral strategies utilized by families in difficult or problematic situations. Used for research and clinical work with families.

Description: 29-item paper-pencil scale measuring coping skills via five subscales: acquiring social support, reframing, seeking spiritual support, mobilizing family to acquire and accept help, and passive appraisal. Examiner/self-administered. Suitable for group use.

Untimed: Varies

Scoring: Hand key

Cost: Contact publisher

Publisher: Family Social Science

FAMILY INVENTORIES: FAMILY INVENTORY OF LIFE EVENTS AND CHANGES (FILE)
David H. Olson,
Hamilton I. McCubbin,
Howard Barnes, Andrea Larsen,
Marla Muxen, and Marc Wilson

Families

Purpose: Assesses level of stress on family. Used for research and clinical work with couples and families.

Description: 72-item paper-pencil measure of family stress in nine areas: intra-family strains, marital strains, pregnancy and childbearing strains, finance and business strains, work-family transitions and strains, illness and family care strains, losses, transition in and out, and family legal violations. Family members indicate whether particular stressful events have occurred in their family. Examiner/self-administered. Suitable for group use.

Untimed: Varies

Scoring: Hand key

Cost: Contact publisher

Publisher: Family Social Science

FAMILY INVENTORIES: FAMILY SATISFACTION
David H. Olson,
Hamilton I. McCubbin,
Howard Barnes, Andrea Larsen,
Marla Muxen, and Marc Wilson

Families

Purpose: Assesses family functioning. Used for research and clinical work with couples and families.

Description: 14-item paper-pencil Likert-scale measure of satisfaction with one's family. Scores for satisfaction with family levels of adaptability and cohesion may be obtained in addition to the total score. Examiner/self-administered. Suitable for group use.

Untimed: Varies

Scoring: Hand key

Cost: Contact publisher

Publisher: Family Social Science

FAMILY INVENTORIES: FAMILY STRENGTHS
David H. Olson,
Hamilton I. McCubbin,
Howard Barnes, Andrea Larsen,
Marla Muxen, and Marc Wilson

Families

Purpose: Measures family members' perceptions of their family's strengths. Used for research and clinical work with families.

Description: 12-item paper-pencil measure of two aspects of perceived family strength: pride and accord. Family members use a 5-point Likert scale format to indicate degree of agreement with items relating to respect, trust, loyalty, pride, and sense of competency. Examiner/self-administered. Suitable for group use.

Untimed: Varies

Scoring: Hand key

Cost: Contact publisher

Publisher: Family Social Science

FAMILY INVENTORIES: PARENT-ADOLESCENT COMMUNICATION
David H. Olson,
Hamilton I. McCubbin,
Howard Barnes, Andrea Larsen,
Marla Muxen, and Marc Wilson

Adolescent, adult
Families

Purpose: Assesses family communication. Used for research and clinical work with couples and families.

Description: 20-item paper-pencil measure of two aspects of communication between parents and adolescents: open family communication and problems in family communication. Examiner/self-administered. Suitable for group use.

Untimed: Varies

Scoring: Hand key

Cost: Contact publisher

Publisher: Family Social Science

FAMILY INVENTORIES: QUALITY OF LIFE
David H. Olson,
Hamilton I. McCubbin,
Howard Barnes, Andrea Larsen,
Marla Muxen, and Marc Wilson

Adolescent, adult
Families

Purpose: Measures family members' perceptions of the quality of their lives. Used for research and clinical work with families.

Description: 40-item paper-pencil measure of satisfaction with quality of life in 12 areas: marriage and family life, friends, extended family, health, home, education, time, religion, employment, mass media, financial well being, and neighborhood and community. A 25-item form for adolescents is also available. Family members indicate their degree of satisfaction by rating items using a 5-point Likert scale. Examiner/self-administered. Suitable for group use.

Untimed: Varies

Scoring: Hand key

Cost: Contact publisher

Publisher: Family Social Science

FAMILY PRE-COUNSELING INVENTORY PROGRAM
Richard B. Stuart and Freida Stuart

Adolescent, adult

Purpose: Provides basic information about family members and establishes a basis for negotiating behavior changes. Used to counsel adolescents or families with adolescents and to evaluate counseling progress.

Description: Three separate paper-pencil test booklets to be filled out by family members: mother (103 items), father (84 items), and adolescent (86 items). The following factors are measured: specific positive behaviors of family members, specific positive changes desired, family members' assets for bringing about change, family's goals and ways family can help attain them, shared activities, decision-making style within family, communication within family, parental and adolescent attitudes toward responsibilities, and privileges given to the adolescent. The inventory emphasizes the positive aspects of relationships and contracting for behavioral change. Average reading skill is required. Self-administered. Suitable for group use.

Untimed: 45-60 minutes

Scoring: Examiner evaluated

Cost: 10 copies each of 3 booklets, guide $29.95

Publisher: Research Press

FAMILY RELATIONS TEST— ADULT VERSION
Eva Bene and James Anthony

Adolescent, adult
Ages 15 and older

Purpose: Assesses memories of early family relationships. Used in individual and family counseling sessions and as a research tool.

Description: Multiple-item test providing a systematic recollection of early family experiences. The subject chooses figures from a large group to represent the family. The subject then assigns item cards indicating like or dislike, love or hate, or jealousy to each of the different figures. Memories regarding parental competence also are explored. Item content facilitates recollection of childhood family feelings. Examiner required. Not suitable for group use.
BRITISH PUBLISHER

Untimed: 20-25 minutes

Scoring: Examiner evaluated

Cost: Complete kit (figures, item cards, 25 scoring sheets, 25 older children record sheets, 25 younger children record sheets, manual) £70.15 (payment in sterling for all overseas orders)

Publisher: NFER-NELSON Publishing Company Ltd.

FAMILY RELATIONS TEST— CHILDREN'S VERSION
Eva Bene and James Anthony

Child, adolescent
Ages 3-15

Purpose: Assesses a child's subjective perception of the interpersonal relationships in the family. Used for individual and family counseling and as a research tool.

Description: Multiple-item test of a child's perception of family relationships. The child is presented a set of family figures and a pack of cards with a single emotion, attitude, or sentiment printed on each card. The child selects a family figure to represent every member of the family. An additional figure is called "nobody." The child then assigns each family member the cards printed with an emotion, attitude, or sentiment. Scoring consists of counting the number of items in each attitude area for each figure. The results indicate the relative psychological importance of each family member; whether feelings are positive, ambivalent, or negative; and whether feelings are reciprocal. Materials include two item sets: one for children ages 3-7 and one for children ages 7-15. Examiner required. Not suitable for group use.
BRITISH PUBLISHER

Untimed: 20-25 minutes

Scoring: Examiner required

Cost: Complete set (family figures, item cards, 25 scoring sheets, 25 record sheets, 25 record/score sheets for younger children, manual) £70.15 (payment in sterling for all overseas orders)

Publisher: NFER-NELSON Publishing Company Ltd.

FAMILY RELATIONS TEST— MARRIED COUPLES VERSION
Eva Bene

Adolescent, adult

Purpose: Explores family interactions, particularly between spouses and among parents and children. Used for marital and family counseling and as a research tool.

Description: Multiple-item test measuring perception of family interactions. The subject chooses family figures representing the spouse and/or other family members. Item cards reflecting emotions, attitudes, or sentiments are assigned to each family figure. The test may be used with the children's and adult's versions to provide a more complete picture of present and past family relationships. Examiner required. Not suitable for group use.
BRITISH PUBLISHER

Untimed: 20-25 minutes

Scoring: Hand key; examiner evaluated

Cost: Complete kit (family figures, item cards, 25 record sheets, 25 scoring sheets, manual) £70.15 (payment in sterling for all overseas orders)

Publisher: NFER-NELSON Publishing Company Ltd.

FAMILY RELATIONSHIP INVENTORY (FRI)
Ruth B. Michaelson and Harry L. Bascom

Ages 5-adult

Purpose: Evaluates family relationships along positive and negative lines. Used as an aid in child-adult counseling, family therapy, youth groups, high-school instruction, and marriage and family enrichment programs.

Description: 50-item paper-pencil test measuring self-esteem, positive or negative perception of self and significant others, most and least esteemed family members, and closest and most distant relationships within the family. One numbered item is printed on each of 50 cards. Items 1-25 have positive valence, and items 26-50 have negative valence. The subject lists "self" and "family members" across the top of a tabulating form and assigns each item to self, significant other, or the wastebasket column and tallies the data on scoring forms with the help of a counselor. Materials include item cards, tabulating forms, scoring forms, a relationship wheel to graphically portray the responses, a Familygram to show family interrelationships, and a test manual. Examiner required. Suitable for group use.

Untimed: 30-45 minutes

Scoring: Examiner evaluated

Cost: Complete FRI kit (manual, 50 reusable item cards, 50 tabulating forms, 25 scoring forms, 50 individual relationship sheets, 25 Familygrams) $50.00

Publisher: Psychological Publications, Inc.

FAMILY VIOLENCE SCALE
Panos D. Bardis

Adolescent, adult

Purpose: Measures the degree of verbal and physical violence in an individual's family during childhood. Used for clinical assessment, marriage and family counseling, research on attitudes toward family and violence, and classroom discussion.

Description: 25-item paper-pencil test in which the subject rates 25 statements about family violence on a scale from 0 (never) to 4 (very often). The "family violence" score equals the sum of the 25 numerical responses. The theoretical range of scores extends from 0 (least violent) to 100 (most violent). Self-administered. Suitable for group use.

Untimed: 10 minutes

Scoring: Examiner evaluated

Cost: Free

Publisher: Panos D. Bardis

THE FLINT INFANT SECURITY SCALE: FOR INFANTS AGED 3-24 MONTHS

Refer to page 8.

THE HOME ENVIRONMENT QUESTIONNAIRE
Jacob O. Sines

**Child, adolescent
Ages 5-16**

Purpose: Assesses behaviorally relevant dimensions of children's psychosocial environments. Used to investigate sources of environmental stress.

Description: True-false paper-pencil test completed by the mother of the child being studied. The HEQ can be scored for 10 dimensions of the child's psycho-social environment that exert pressure on the child: p(ress) achievement, p aggres-sion-external, p agression-home, p aggression-total, p supervision, p change, p affiliation, p separation, p sociability, and p socioeconomic status. Two forms are available: HEQ-2R (123 items) for use with 2-parent families and HEQ-1R (91 items) for use with 1-parent families. Examiner/self-administered. Suitable for group use.

Untimed: 15-20 minutes

Scoring: Hand key

Cost: Specimen set (manual and norms, scoring keys, 25 each HEQ-2R and HEQ-1R) $30.00

Publisher: Psychological Assessment and Services, Inc.

HOME INDEX

Refer to page 672.

HOME OBSERVATION FOR MEASUREMENT OF THE ENVIRONMENT (HOME)

Refer to page 9.

HOME SCREENING QUESTIONNAIRE (HSQ)
*C. Cooms, E. Gay, A. Vandal,
C. Ker, and William F. Frankenberg*

Child   Ages 0-6

Purpose: Evaluates the quality of a child's home environment; used to indi-cate need for further evaluation.

Description: 64-item paper-pencil ques-tionnaire. Both forms have toy check lists. The parents fill out the questionnaire, which is then scored by an examiner. Sus-pect results must be followed by an evaluation of the home by a trained pro-fessional to see if intervention is needed. A 30-item blue form is available for chil-dren up to age 3, and a 34-item white form is available for ages 3-6. The ques-tionnaires are written at third- and fourth-grade reading levels. Self-administered. Not suitable for group use.

Untimed: 15-20 minutes

Scoring: Hand key

Cost: 25 questionnaires $4.50; manual $4.50

Publisher: Ladoca Publishing Foundation
Information and availability unconfirmed; no publisher response.

INTRA AND INTERPERSONAL RELATIONS

Refer to page 144.

THE JONES-MOHR LISTENING TEST

Refer to page 955.

LIFE INTERPERSONAL HISTORY ENQUIRY (LIPHE)
Will Schutz

Adult

Purpose: Evaluates an individual's retro-spective account of relationship to parents before age six. Used for counseling and therapy.

Description: Paper-pencil report of an individual's early relationship with parents in areas of inclusion, control, and affection at both the behavioral and the feeling levels. Separate scores are obtained for the father, the mother, and the respondent's perception of the relationship between the parents. Examiner/self-administered. Suitable for group use.

Untimed: Not available

Scoring: Hand key

Cost: Sample set (including keys) $4.00; 25 tests $9.50

Publisher: Consulting Psychologists Press, Inc.

MARYLAND PARENT ATTITUDE SURVEY (MPAS)
Donald Pumroy

Adult

Purpose: Assesses parents' attitudes toward the way they rear their children; particularly useful as a research instrument.

Description: 95-item paper-pencil test in which the subject chooses one of each pair of A or B forced-choice statements that best represent the parents' attitudes towards child rearing: indulgent, disciplinarian, protective, and rejecting. The survey indicates child-rearing "type" or approach. Materials consist of a cover letter, a copy of the research article, and scoring keys. Self-administered. Suitable for group use.

Untimed: 45 minutes

Scoring: Hand key

Cost: Complete set $2.00

Publisher: Donald K. Pumroy, Ph.D.

MATURITY STYLE MATCH: PARENT/SON OR DAUGHTER FORMS
Paul Hersey, Kenneth H. Blanchard, and Joseph W. Keilty

Adolescent, adult
Ages 12-adult

Purpose: Determines a parent's and child's perceptions of the relationship between parental style of influencing behavior and the child's maturity; used in family counseling.

Description: 6-category paper-pencil test measuring a parent's style in terms of telling, selling, participating, and delegating and the child's willingness and ability to handle certain activities and responsibilities. The subjects complete the inventory and compare their perceptions. The items are rated on a Likert-type scale ranging from "never" to "almost always." The test booklet includes scoring and interpretation material and a tape recording. Examiner/self-administered. Suitable for group use.

Untimed: Not available

Scoring: Hand key

Cost: 10-99 forms $1.95 each

Publisher: Center for Leadership Studies

MCMASTER FAMILY ASSESSMENT DEVICE (FAD)
Nathan B. Epstein, Lawrence M. Baldwin, and Duane S. Bishop

Adolescent, adult
Ages 12 and older

Purpose: Measures dimensions of family functioning. Used by therapists and researchers with individuals ages 12 and older for screening, identifying problems, and collecting clinically relevant information on the family system.

Description: 60-item self-report questionnaire assessing an individual's perceptions of family roles and functions. The questionnaire contains seven intercorrelated scales: Problem Solving (family's ability to resolve issues threatening its integrity and functioning), Communication (exchange of information among members), Roles (whether family has established behavior patterns for handling repetitive family functions), Affective Responsiveness (extent to which members experience appropriate affect over a range of stimuli), Affective Involvement (extent to which members are interested in and value others' activities and concerns), Behavior Control (way in which family expresses and maintains members' behavior standards), and General Functioning (overall health/pathology of family). Individuals rate items on a 4-point scale (strongly agree-strongly disagree) according to how well the item describes their family. The test has cut-off scores for identifying healthy and unhealthy families that have adequate sensitivity and specificity. A microcomputer scoring program allows interactive administration on a MacIntosh computer. The program, used with MicroSoft Basic, provides individual scores, a family mean score, and item analysis. Self-administered. Suitable for group use. Available in French, Spanish, Portuguese, Hungarian, and Afrikaans.

Untimed: 15-20 minutes

Scoring: Hand key or computer scored; examiner evaluated

Cost: Kit (test, reprints, scoring key, biannual updates) $20.00

Publisher: Brown/Butler Family Research Program

MEASURE OF CHILD STIMULUS SCREENING (CONVERSE OF AROUSABILITY)
Albert Mehrabian and Carol Falender

Child   Ages 3 months-
       7 years

Purpose: Measures major components of a child's arousability and stimulus screening. Used for research, counseling, and education program selection purposes.

Description: Multiple-item paper-pencil observational inventory measuring parents' descriptions of their children's arousability (responses of one parent are sufficient). Test results indicate the child's characteristic arousal response to complex, unexpected, or unfamiliar situations. Stimulus screening/arousability has been shown to be a major component of many important personality dimensions, such as anxiety, neuroticism, extroversion, or hostility. This test is based on the same conceptual framework used to develop the corresponding adult measure. Examiner required. Suitable for group use.

Untimed: 20 minutes

Scoring: Examiner evaluated

Cost: Test kit (scale, scoring directions, norms, descriptive material) $20.00

Publisher: Albert Mehrabian

MEASURES OF PLEASURE-, AROUSAL-, AND DOMINANCE-INDUCING QUALITIES IN PARENTAL ATTITUDES
Albert Mehrabian

Child   Ages 3 months-
      7 years

Purpose: Evaluates the emotional climate parents create for their children. Used for research and counseling purposes.

Description: Multiple-item paper-pencil self-report questionnaire consisting of three orthogonal measures of parental child-rearing attitudes. The test measures the levels of pleasure, arousal, and dominance experienced by the child. Three scores concerning parental attitudes are provided: pleasure-inducing, arousal-inducing, and dominance-inducing. Examiner required. Suitable for group use.

Untimed: 20 minutes

Scoring: Examiner evaluated

Cost: Test kit (scales, scoring directions, norms, descriptive material) $20.00

Publisher: Albert Mehrabian

MICHIGAN SCREENING PROFILE OF PARENTING (MSPP)
Ray E. Helfer, James K. Hoffmeister, and Carol J. Schneider

Adult

Purpose: Evaluates an individual's perceptions in areas that are critically important for positive parent-child interactions. Profiles segments of the individual's early childhood experiences and current relationships that seem to affect the individual's ability to interact with others. Used to identify those in need of further assessment.

Description: Multiple-item paper-pencil self-report questionnaire for parents and prospective parents. The questionnaire consists of four sections. Section A provides information about family characteristics, the respondent's health history, and relationships with employers, social agencies, and spouse. Section B provides information regarding respondent perceptions of childhood experiences and current interactions with family and friends. Section C (answered only by individuals having one or more children) provides information about the respondent's child (or children) and current parent-child interactions. Section D (answered only by individuals who do not have children) provides information with regard to the respondent's expectations for future interactions with prospective children. Section A requires various types of answers depending on the type of biographical information being requested. Sections B, C, and D use 7-point Likert scales to rate responses to individual test items. Computerized scoring generates four scores based on the responses in Section B: emotional needs met, relationship with parents, expectations of children, and coping. High scores indicate a potential for parent-child interaction problems and may be used to identify individuals in need of further assessment or counseling. Scores are not intended to diagnose specific problems, nor do they predict the future behavior of parents. The manual includes a discussion of the scale's background, development, and content; administration and scoring procedures; item measure characteristics; uses of the scale; and a list of available consulting services. Self-administered. Suitable for group use.

Untimed: Varies

Scoring: Computer scored

Cost: 25 questionnaires (including scoring service) $50.00

Publisher: Test Analysis and Development Corporation

MOTHER-CHILD RELATIONSHIP EVALUATION
Robert M. Roth

Adult

Purpose: Measures a mother's attitudes and how they relate to her children. Used for counseling and treatment programs.

Description: 48-item paper-pencil test measuring four areas of mother-child relationships: acceptance, overprotection, overindulgence, and rejection. The mother responds to each item on a 5-point scale ranging from "strongly agree" to "strongly disagree." Raw scores are converted to percentiles and T-scores for developing the profile. Examiner required. Suitable for group use.

Untimed: 30 minutes

Scoring: Hand key

Cost: Kit (25 forms, manual) $14.75

Publisher: Western Psychological Services

MOTIVATION AND POTENTIAL FOR ADOPTIVE PARENTHOOD SCALE (MPAPS)
B. W. Lindholm and J. Touliatos

Adult

Purpose: Measures individual motivation and potential for adoptive parenthood. Used by caseworkers evaluating persons seeking to adopt children.

Description: 72-item paper-pencil test based on the traits formalized by the Child Welfare League of America as standards for adoption services. The Motivation Scale is composed of items covering both positive reasons for wanting to adopt and lack of negative reasons for wanting to adopt. The Potential Scale covers attitude toward adoption and the natural parents of adopted children, acceptance and flexibility regarding the children that the applicants are willing to adopt, ability to use help relationships with one's family, relationships with one's spouse, relationships with one's friends, positive experiences with children, being able to enjoy and have a relationship with a child, being able to assume responsibility for others, and dealings with previous life situations. Self-administered. Suitable for group use.

Untimed: 20 minutes

Scoring: Hand key

Cost: Specimen set $8.00; 35 scales $14.00; manual $4.00

Publisher: Monitor

PARENT AS A TEACHER INVENTORY (PAAT)
Robert D. Strom

Adult

Purpose: Assesses parents' attitudes toward their parent-child relationship. Used with parents of children ages 3-9.

Description: Multiple-item pencil-paper inventory measuring parental attitudes in the following areas: feelings toward the parent-child interactive system, standards for assessing the importance of certain aspects of child behavior, and value preferences and frustrations concerning child behavior. Examiner required. Suitable for group use. Available in Spanish.

Untimed: 30-45 minutes

Scoring: Examiner evaluated

Cost: Starter set (manual, 20 inventory booklets, 20 identification questionnaires, 20 profiles) $27.50

Publisher: Scholastic Testing Service, Inc.

PARENT ATTACHMENT STRUCTURED INTERVIEW
Samuel Roll, Julianne Lockwood, and Elizabeth Jaffe Roll

Child   Ages 6-12

Purpose: Assesses a child's attachment to significant adults. Used in child custody cases.

Description: 50-item paper-pencil inventory measuring the strength of a child's attachment to significant adults and identifying the attachment figures. The test covers four aspects of attachment: responsiveness (who is engaged with the child in pleasant or neutral activities); confidence (who deals with the child in difficult situations); security (who provides a supportive, permanent, affective relationship); and hostility (who is involved in hurtful, frustrating situations). The examiner presents each question, which can be modified according to the child's age or comprehension level, and records the child's answers on an answer sheet. Distractor questions are included to overcome boredom or anxiety. The inventory is recommended for use by a psychologist trained in assessing children and as part of a complete assessment battery. Presentation of only half the questions at any one session is recommended. Examiner required. Not suitable for group use.

Untimed: 5-20 minutes

Scoring: Hand key

Cost: 25 intermediate forms, 25 scoring sheets, manual $32.95; postage and handling not included

Publisher: Samuel Roll, Ph.D.

PARENT: SELF/OTHER
Paul Hersey, Kenneth H. Blanchard, and John Donoghue, and Anna Donoghue

Adult

Purpose: Evaluates a parent's style, flexibility, and adaptability in terms of the child's maturity level.

Description: 12 situation, paper-pencil test measuring a parent's style (telling, selling, participating, delegating), flexibility, and adaptability in relation to the child's maturity level. The instrument is available in two forms (Parent Self and Parent Other) for each of three age ranges of child (early child, ages 0-8; intermediate child, ages 9-15; young adult, ages 16 and older). The forms are completed by a parent and a second person who observes the parent's behavior. The individuals score their responses, matrix the results according to instructions, and compare the results. Examiner/self-administered. Suitable for group use.

Untimed: Not available

Scoring: Hand key

Cost: 10-99 forms (specify form and child age level) $1.95 each

Publisher: Center for Leadership Studies

PARENTAL ACCEPTANCE-REJECTION QUESTIONNAIRE (PARQ)
Ronald P. Rohner

Ages 7-adult

Purpose: Assesses parental warmth in individuals ages 7-adult. Used for screening with clinical populations, in research studies with student and community populations, as a tool for parental education programs, in evaluating family problems, and in detecting potential child abuse.

Description: 60-item paper-pencil questionnaire measuring parental warmth in four scales: Warmth/Affection (20 items), Hostility/Aggression (15 items), Indifference/Neglect (15 items), and Undifferentiated Rejection (10 items). The test, designed to cut across social classes and available in 15 languages, can be combined with the formal interview (Parental-Acceptance Rejection Interview Schedule) and behavior observation. It is scored on a 4-point scale (almost always to almost never), with some reversed scoring to reduce response bias. Scores range from 60 (maximum acceptance, minimum rejection) to 240 (maximum rejection, minimum acceptance). Three versions are available: mother (includes father; reflects on what they do to child), adult (reflects back on childhood), and child (reflects on present actions in family). Examiner/self-administered. Suitable for group use.

Untimed: 10 minutes

Scoring: Hand key

Cost: Free

Publisher: Center for the Study of Parental Acceptance and Rejection

---

PARENTING STRESS INDEX (PSI)
Richard R. Abidin

Adult

Purpose: Identifies emotional pathology in children and parent-child systems under stress and at risk for dysfunctional parenting. Used with parents of children under age 10.

Description: 101-item paper-pencil screening and diagnostic instrument yielding a total index of stress and scores related to stressors associated with child characteristics (adaptability, acceptability, demandingness, mood, hyperactive/distractibility, reinforces parent), parent characteristics (depression, attachment, restriction of role, sense of competence, social isolation, relationship with spouse, parental health), and life stress events. The test is used clinically in medical centers, mental health centers, universities, and family programs for intervention, education, treatment planning, research,

child abuse risk assessment, and forensic evaluations for child custody. Self-administered. Suitable for group use.

Untimed: Varies

Scoring: Hand key

Cost: Specimen set (manual, 2 test booklets, 10 answer sheets, 10 profile sheets) $20.50

Publisher: Pediatric Psychology Press

PERCEPTIONS OF PARENTAL ROLE SCALES
Lucia A. Gilbert and Gary R. Hansen

Adult

Purpose: Measures perceived parental role responsibilities. Used with male and female adults for educational, counseling, and research.

Description: 78-item paper-pencil instrument assessing parental perceptions in three domains yielding 13 scales: teaching a child (cognitive development, social skills, handling of emotions, physical health, norms and social values, personal hygiene, and survival skills), meeting a child's basic needs (health care, child care, child's emotional needs, and food, clothing, and shelter), and serving as the interface between the child and the family and other social institutions (social institutions and family unit). The test takes into account current societal views about men's and women's roles. An eighth-grade reading level is required. Self-administered. Suitable for group use.

Untimed: 15 minutes

Scoring: Computer scored

Cost: Manual $15.00; 25 scales $8.00

Publisher: Marathon Consulting and Press

POTENTIAL FOR FOSTER PARENTHOOD SCALE (PFPS)
John Touliatos and Byron W. Lindholm

Adult

Purpose: Evaluates candidates for foster parenthood in terms of the quality of foster care they are capable of providing. Used by social workers to make foster care placement decisions and train foster family care workers and in research on foster care.

Description: 54-item paper-pencil rating scale measuring potential for foster parenthood along nine dimensions: health, employment and income, time, opportunities for cultural and intellectual development, opportunities for religious and spiritual development, marriage, ability and motivation for foster parenthood, flexibility, and working with the agency and the child's own parents. Each item presents a statement describing a positive quality of foster parents, such as "has physical ability to care for children" or "has had stable relationships with children." The social worker, rating the husband and wife separately, uses a 4-point scale ranging from "very different" (1) to "very similar" (4) to indicate the degree to which each statement accurately describes the candidates. Ratings can be made at any time during the placement process and are based upon the case worker's past experiences with applicants who have been successful and unsuccessful. Scores are obtained for the total scale and for each of the nine clusters. Cut-off scores are provided for identifying four types of candidates: excellent, good, fair, and poor. Use of the scale allows for comparison of different applicants, rating the same applicants at different points in time to assess possible changes, and the identification of a couple's strengths and weaknesses concerning potential for foster care. Self-administered by examiner. Not suitable for group use.

Untimed: Varies
Scoring: Examiner evaluated
Cost: Contact publisher
Publisher: John Touliatos, Ed. D.

PSYCHOSOCIAL ADJUSTMENT TO ILLNESS SCALE (PAIS)
Refer to page 169.

RELATIONSHIP PROFILE (EGOGRAM™)
N. Robert Heyer

Adult   Ages 18 and older

Purpose: Compares the personality traits of individuals in diadic relationships (couples, family members, work groups). Used in family and couples therapy for diagnosis and treatment; in business for training and counseling in work relationships.

Description: 50-item paper-pencil multiple-choice questionnaire for each member of a relationship diad. For each person, it measures the relative strength of six basic personality traits identified by Eric Berne, M.D., and widely used in transactional analysis. Graphic matching of profiles highlights areas of complementary ego state strength, as well as areas of dependency and unfilled needs in the relationship. A computer printout shows diagnostic guidelines and a measure of relationship stress. The test is normed for individuals ages 18 and older but may also be used for individuals ages 14-18. Self-administered. Suitable for group use. Available in Spanish.

Untimed: 10-16 minutes
Scoring: Computer scored
Cost: 10 sets $190.00; manual $24.00
Publisher: Psychological Measurement Systems

A RELIGION SCALE
Panos D. Bardis

Adolescent, adult

Purpose: Measures attitudes toward religion. Used for clinical assessment, family and marriage counseling, research on attitudes toward religion, and discussion in religion and social science classes.

Description: 25-item paper-pencil test in which the subject reads 25 statements about religious issues and rates them according to his beliefs on a scale from 0 (strongly disagree) to 4 (strongly agree). The score is the sum of the 25 numerical responses. The theoretical range of scores extends from 0 (least religious) to 100 (most religious). Examiner/self-administered. Suitable for group use.

Untimed: 10 minutes
Scoring: Examiner evaluated
Cost: Free
Publisher: Panos D. Bardis

THE SOCIAL BEHAVIOR ASSESSMENT SCHEDULE
Refer to page 179.

TAYLOR-JOHNSON TEMPERAMENT ANALYSIS
Refer to page 183.

TEST OF DIABETES KNOWLEDGE: GENERAL INFORMATION AND PROBLEM SOLVING (TDK)
Suzanne Bennett Johnson

All ages

Purpose: Examines an individual's knowledge of diabetes. Used with insulin-dependent diabetes patients and their families.

Description: 75-item multiple-choice paper-pencil test measuring an individual's factual knowledge of diabetes and ability to apply that knowledge. A seventh-grade reading level is required for the general information portion of the test, and a fourth-grade reading level is required for the problem-solving portion. Individuals with reading abilities below these levels may take the test by having an examiner read the items aloud. Examiner/self-administered. Suitable for group use.

Untimed: 20 minutes-1 hour

Scoring: Hand key

Cost: Test, scoring key, normative data $15.00

Publisher: Suzanne Bennett Johnson, Ph.D.

THERAPY ATTITUDE INVENTORY (TAI)
Sheila M. Eyberg

Adult

Purpose: Assesses the amount of satisfaction parents feel in response to parent training programs or individual parent-child interaction training. Used to evaluate therapy programs.

Description: 10-item paper-pencil inventory asking parents to rate their feel-

ings from one (indicating dissatisfaction or deterioration of condition) to five (indicating maximum satisfaction or improvement) regarding the following areas: acquisition of new disciplinary techniques, techniques for teaching their child new skills, relationship with their child, confidence in ability to discipline, intensity of current behavior problems, level of child's compliance, progress of child, general benefits of treatment program, satisfaction with type of program, and general feeling about the program. Space is provided for personal comments concerning the child and the treatment program. Self-administered by parent. Suitable for group use.

Untimed: 5-10 minutes

Scoring: Examiner evaluated

Cost: Free

Publisher: Distributed by Sheila M. Eyberg, Ph.D.

A VIOLENCE SCALE
Refer to page 186.

Marriage and Family: Premarital and Marital Relations

ABORTION SCALE
Panos D. Bardis

Adolescent, adult

Purpose: Measures attitudes toward many aspects of abortion. Used in clinical assessment, marriage and family counseling, research on attitudes toward abortion, and discussion in family education.

Description: 25-item paper-pencil test in which the subject reads statements about issues concerning abortion and rates them according to his personal beliefs on a scale from 0 (strongly disagree) to 4 (strongly agree). The score equals the sum of the 25 numerical responses. Theoretical range of scores extends from 0 (lowest approval of abortion) to 100 (highest approval). Examiner/self-administered. Suitable for group use.

Untimed: 10 minutes
Scoring: Examiner evaluated
Cost: Free
Publisher: Panos D. Bardis

BACKGROUND SCHEDULE
Marriage Council of Philadelphia

Adolescent, adult

Purpose: Aids counselors of couples by obtaining a wide range of relevant background material without using interview time to secure information.

Description: 39-item paper-pencil questionnaire used to obtain from couples in a relationship independent answers to questions about vital statistics, religion, activities shared with partner, occupation, siblings, parental data, interaction between self and parent before teens, during teens, and at the present time. The questionnaire is completed independently by the couple prior to their first interview. Not a psychological test. Self-administered. Not suitable for group use.

Untimed: 30 minutes
Scoring: Examiner evaluated
Cost: Schedule $0.20; 100 schedules $15.00
Publisher: Marriage Council of Philadelphia, Inc.

CALIFORNIA MARRIAGE READINESS EVALUATION
Morse P. Manson

Adult

Purpose: Measures a couple's readiness for marriage and indicates areas where potential difficulties are most likely to occur. Used for premarital counseling.

Description: 115-item paper-pencil inventory consisting of 110 true-false items and 5 projective completion items. The inventory measures strengths and weaknesses in eight areas of marriage readiness within three general categories: personality (character structure, emotional maturity, marriage readiness), preparation

for marriage (family experiences, dealing with money, planning ability), and interpersonal compatibility (marriage motivation and compatibility). In addition to providing scores for each of the eight areas measured, a total score indicating overall readiness for marriage is provided. Self-administered. Suitable for group use.

Untimed: 15-30 minutes
Scoring: Hand key
Cost: Kit (25 forms, manual) $15.00
Publisher: Western Psychological Services

CARING RELATIONSHIP INVENTORY (CRI)
Everett L. Shostrom

Adult

Purpose: Measures the essential elements of caring (or love) in the relationship between a man and a woman. Used for evaluation and discussion in marriage and family counseling.

Description: 83-item paper-pencil true-false test consisting of a series of statements that the subject applies first to the other member of the couple (spouse, fiance, etc.) and second to his or her "ideal" mate. Responses are scored on seven scales: affection, friendship, eros, empathy, self-love, being love, and deficiency love. Separate forms are available for adult males and females. Items were developed based on the responses of criterion groups of successfully married couples, troubled couples in counseling, and divorced individuals. Percentile norms for successfully married couples are presented separately for men and women. Means and standard deviations are presented for troubled couples and divorced individuals. The CRI is a component of the Actualizing Assessment Battery (AAB). Examiner required. Suitable for group use.

Untimed: 40 minutes
Scoring: Hand key
Cost: (manual, all forms) $5.25; 25 booklets (specify male or female) $12.50; 50 expendable profile sheets $8.00; 7 hand-scoring keys $14.00; manual $2.50
Publisher: Educational and Industrial Testing Service

COITOMETER
Panos D. Bardis

Adolescent, adult

Purpose: Measures knowledge of the anatomical and physiological aspects of coitus. Used for clinical assessment, marriage and family counseling, research on human sexuality, and discussion in family and human sexuality classes.

Description: 50-item paper-pencil true-false four-page instrument consisting of the questionnaire and a measure key. Examiner/self-administered. Suitable for group use.

Untimed: 12 minutes

Scoring: Hand key

Cost: Free

Publisher: Panos D. Bardis

COUPLE'S PRE-COUNSELING INVENTORY
Richard B. Stuart

Adult

Purpose: Provides couples with information regarding expected roles in the treatment process and collects data concerning the feelings and behaviors that may be relevant to marriage, relationship, and family counseling. Used prior to counseling and for periodic evaluation of progress in treatment.

Description: 133-item paper-pencil inventory covering the following areas of marital/family life: happiness with general areas of relationship, behaviors pleasing to each partner, level of communication, style of handling conflict, moods, effectiveness in everyday life, sexual satisfaction, level of agreement on child-rearing issues, willingness to change, goals for treatment, and commitment to relationship. The inventory emphasizes discovering the strengths of the relationship, as well as the problem areas. Average reading skill is required. Self-administered. Suitable for group use.

Untimed: 1 hour

Scoring: Examiner evaluated

Cost: Complete set (25 booklets, guide) $19.95; guide $1.95

Publisher: Research Press

A COURTSHIP ANALYSIS (CA) AND A DATING PROBLEMS CHECKLIST (DPCL)
Gelolo McHugh

Junior high school-adult

Purpose: Assesses adolescent couples' social problems. Used in family living and home economics classes, Sunday schools, youth groups, and premarital counseling to stimulate conversation.

Description: Courtship Analysis is a 150-item paper-pencil questionnaire allowing partners in courtship to report on the dynamics of their relationship by indicating the presence or absence of positive and negative character traits and behaviors of their partner. The Dating Problems Checklist is a 125-item paper-pencil questionnaire reporting on the dating atmosphere in which respondents socialize. The respondents indicate whether a particular attitude or situation exists and whether it is a problem for them. Examiner required. Suitable for group use.

Untimed: Not available

Scoring: Examiner evaluated

Cost: Specimen set (manual, 2 copies of each form) $2.00; 10 copies (specify test) $4.50; manual $1.00

Publisher: Family Life Publications, Inc.

Information and availability unconfirmed; no publisher response.

A DATING SCALE
Panos D. Bardis

Adolescent, adult

Purpose: Measures attitudes toward various aspects of dating. Used for clinical assessment, marriage and family counseling, research on attitudes toward dating, and discussion in family education.

Description: 25-item paper-pencil test in which the subject notes 25 statements about dating from 0 (strongly disagree) to 4 (strongly agree). The score equals the sum of the 25 numerical responses. Theoretical range of scores extends from 0 (least liberal) to 100 (most liberal). Examiner/self-administered. Suitable for group use.

Untimed: 10 minutes
Scoring: Examiner evaluated
Cost: Free
Publisher: Panos D. Bardis

DEROGATIS SEXUAL FUNCTIONING INVENTORY (DSFI)
Leonard R. Derogatis

Adult

Purpose: Measures and describes the quality of an individual's sexual functioning.

Description: 10 multiple-item paper-pencil subtests assessing the following factors related to an individual's sexual functioning: information, experience, drive, attitude, psychological symptoms, affects, gender role definition, fantasy, body image, and sexual satisfaction. Scaled scores from each subtest are combined to derive an overall sexual functioning score. Norms are available separately for men and women. Examiner required. Suitable for group use.

Untimed: 30-40 minutes
Scoring: Examiner evaluated
Cost: 10 reusable test booklets $30.00; 30 expendable test booklets $33.00; 50 answer sheets $10.00; 50 score/profile forms $11.00; manual $6.00
Publisher: Clinical Psychometric Research

ENGAGEMENT SCHEDULE
Marriage Council of Philadelphia

Engaged couples

Purpose: Aids counselors of couples engaged to be married by obtaining information about the couple's feelings and plans.

Description: 41-item paper-pencil questionnaire that secures independent responses from couples regarding their engagement, feelings about future in-laws, feelings about their own parents, confiding, affection, need for more information about sex, number of children planned, and sharing interests and activities. The questionnaire is not a measuring instrument for predicting future marriage possibilities or a psychological test. The schedule is to be completed independently in the waiting room prior to the clients' first interview. Self-administered. Not suitable for group use.

Untimed: 30 minutes
Scoring: Examiner evaluated
Cost: Schedule $0.20; 100 schedules $15.00
Publisher: Marriage Council of Philadelphia, Inc.

EROTOMETER: A TECHNIQUE FOR THE MEASUREMENT OF HETEROSEXUAL LOVE
Panos D. Bardis

Adolescent, adult

Purpose: Measures the intensity of an individual's love for a member of the opposite sex. Used for clinical assessment, marriage and family counseling, research on love, and discussions in family and sex education.

Description: 50-item paper-pencil test in which the subject reads statements concerning actual feelings, attitudes, desires, and wishes regarding one specific member of the opposite sex and rates them on the following scale: 0 (absent), 1 (weak), 2 (strong). The score equals the sum of the 50 numerical responses. The theoretical range of scores extends from 0 (no love) to 100 (strongest love). Self-administered. Suitable for group use.

Untimed: 12 minutes
Scoring: Examiner evaluated
Cost: Free
Publisher: Panos D. Bardis

FAMILY INVENTORIES: ENRICHING AND NURTURING RELATIONSHIP ISSUES, COMMUNICATION AND HAPPINESS (ENRICH)
David H. Olson,
Hamilton I. McCubbin,
Howard Barnes, Andrea Larsen,
Marla Muxen, and Marc Wilson

Families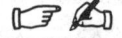

Purpose: Assesses marital functioning. Used for research and clinical work with couples and families.

Description: 125-item paper-pencil measure of 12 components of marital functioning: idealistic distortion, marital satisfaction, personality issues, communication, conflict resolution, financial management, leisure activities, sexual relationship, children and marriage, family and friends, equalitarian roles, and religious orientation. Degree of agreement with each item is indicated using a 5-point Likert scale. Examiner/self-administered. Suitable for group use.

Untimed: Varies

Scoring: Hand key

Cost: Contact publisher

Publisher: Family Social Science

GOLOMBOK RUST INVENTORY OF SEXUAL SATISFACTION (GRISS)
Susan Golombok and John Rust

Adult

Purpose: Assesses sexual functioning of adults.

Description: 28-item paper-pencil questionnaire used for developing a diagnostic profile. The test provides a main scale of dysfunction and 12 diagnostic subscales: impotence, premature ejaculation, anorgasmia, vaginismus, noncommunication, infrequency, male and female avoidance, male and female nonsensuality, and male and female dissatisfaction. Separate forms for males and females are provided. Self-administered. Suitable for group use.
BRITISH PUBLISHER

Timed: 10 minutes

Scoring: Examiner evaluated

Cost: Complete set (manual, 10 of each questionnaire) £20.65; manual £10.30

Publisher: NFER-NELSON Publishing Company Ltd.

GRAVIDOMETER
Panos D. Bardis

Adolescent, adult

Purpose: Measures knowledge of the anatomical and physiological aspects of pregnancy. Used in clinical assessments, marriage and family counseling, research on human sexuality and family classes.

Description: 50-item paper-pencil true-false test measuring knowledge of human pregnancy. Self-administered. Suitable for group use.

Untimed: 12 minutes

Scoring: Hand key

Cost: Free

Publisher: Panos D. Bardis

GROWING LOVE IN CHRISTIAN MARRIAGE
Richard A. Hunt and Joan A. Hunt

Adolescent, adult

Purpose: Enables a couple to explore and discuss perceptions and issues in their relationship. Used to elicit comparisons and similarities between partners as part of a counselor's sessions.

Description: Interactive computer presentation of four major components of a couple's relationship: clarifying goals and values, views of personality, conflict resolution, and expectations about wants and needs. The instrument requires an IBM compatible computer for administration, with the option for printing results, as well as seeing results, on the computer screen. The program is related to the authors' book for couples, *Preparing for Christian Marriage* (also titled, *Growing Love in Christian Marriage*.) Each partner enters own data directly into the computer. Examiner required. Suitable for group use.

Untimed: 20-30 minutes

Scoring: Computer scored

Cost: Computer program, couple's book $69.00

Publisher: Datascan

HARDING STRESS-FAIR COMPATIBILITY TEST
Chris Harding

Adult

Purpose: Measures an individual's intellectual, social, emotional, and philosophical orientation. Identifies and matches compatible pairs of individuals. Used for research and personal matching services.

Description: 46-item paper-pencil multiple-choice inventory assessing 10 factors related to the degree of compatibility between two individuals; intellective (tendency to think things through to a final conclusion), extroversion, sensitivity, idealism, goal setting, awareness (aware beyond immediate concerns), group detachment, advocacy (cooperative maturity), complexity (degree of inner defensiveness), and dominance-aggression. Tables printed on the back of the test identify 12 levels of compatibility: optimum compatibility, beginnings of identity fusion, complete mutual reciprocation, equivalent evaluations, "best friend" status, deep friendship possible, reciprocation with reservations in certain areas, awareness of others' viewpoint, indifferent relationship, mild antagonism, antagonism, and complete alienation. The scoring sheet contains data on norm distribution, formulae for matching, and explanation. Examiner required. Suitable for group use.

Untimed: Varies

Scoring: Computer scored

Cost: Outside the U.S. and Canada: inventory with computer scoring and matching service $10.00; inventory with scoring sheet available for research purposes free of charge; U.S. and Canadian residents may obtain information from Management Strategies Incorporated

Publisher: Harding Tests

THE LOVE ATTITUDES INVENTORY (LAI)
David Knox

Adolescent, adult

Purpose: Helps teachers and counselors teach the difference between romantic and realistic love. Used to promote discussion in adolescents and adults, family living and marriage classes, and marital and premarital counseling sessions.

Description: 30-statement paper-pencil questionnaire in which the individual agrees or disagrees with statements regarding love. Two additional long-answer questions require the individual to describe loving behavior. Examiner required. Suitable for group use.

Untimed: Not available

Scoring: Examiner evaluated

Cost: Specimen set (manual, 2 forms) $2.00; 10 LAI $4.50; manual $1.00

Publisher: Family Life Publications, Inc.

Information and availability unconfirmed; no publisher response.

MARITAL CHECK-UP KIT
Millard J. Bienvenu

Adult

Purpose: Identifies potential marital problems, facilitates communication, and encourages co-operative problem solving through positive intervention by a counselor.

Description: Six paper-pencil exercises that facilitate a positive approach to marital self-evaluation. Each form can be completed prior to or as part of marital counseling or enrichment sessions. The exercises include Positive Feedback Exercise (identifies positive personality traits), Marital Communication Exercise (identifies communication strengths and weaknesses), Marital Relationship Improvement Exercise (promotes understanding of individual feelings), Marital Relationship Assessment Exercise (promotes understanding of individual attitudes), Personality Pluses and Strengths (provides a self-evaluation of strengths brought to the marriage), and Feelings About Yourself (promotes discussion of feelings as they relate to spouse and marriage). Materials include forms for one couple and instructions. The exercises should be administered by a trained counselor. Examiner required. Not suitable for group use.

Untimed: Not available

Scoring: Examiner evaluated

Cost: Per couple $3.60

Publisher: Family Life Publications

Information and availability unconfirmed; no publisher response.

THE MARITAL COMMUNICATIONS INVENTORY
Millard J. Bienvenu

Adult

Purpose: Assesses communication in a troubled marriage and identifies communication problems. Stimulates group discussion in marriage enrichment programs and increases awareness of positive and negative communication patterns.

Description: 46-item paper-pencil questionnaire covering feelings, emotions, economics, communication patterns, and behaviors. The questionnaire also includes an optional socio-economic survey. Separate forms are available for males and females. Both husband and wife answer questions by indicating the frequency of communication in each area. Materials include questionnaire forms and a manual. Self-administered. Suitable for group use.

Untimed: Not available

Scoring: Hand key; examiner evaluated

Cost: Specimen set (manual, male and female forms, key) $2.00; manual $1.00; 10 forms (5 female, 5 male) $4.50

Publisher: Family Life Publications, Inc.

Information and availability unconfirmed; no publisher response.

MARITAL EVALUATION CHECKLIST
Leslie Navran

Adult

Purpose: Assesses common characteristics and problem areas in a marital relationship. Used as a survey instrument in clinical and counseling settings to initiate the consultation process and introduce the client to formal diagnostic testing.

Description: 140-item paper-pencil test organized in three sections: reasons for marrying, current problems, and motivation for counseling. Areas surveyed include interpersonal/emotional, material/economic, social, personal, money and work, sex, personal characteristics, and

marital relationship. The test is a component of the Clinical Checklist Series. Self-administered. Suitable for group use.

Untimed: 10-20 minutes

Scoring: Examiner evaluated

Cost: 50 checklists $12.95

Publisher: Psychological Assessment Resources, Inc.

MARITAL SATISFACTION INVENTORY (MSI)
Douglas K. Snyder

Adult

Purpose: Identifies the nature and extent of marital distress. Used in marital and family counseling.

Description: Multiple-item paper-pencil true-false test providing information concerning nine basic measured dimensions of marriage: affective communication, problem-solving communication, time together, disagreement about finances, sexual dissatisfaction, role orientation, family history of distress, dissatisfaction with children, and conflict over childrearing. In addition, a validity scale and a global distress scale measure each spouse's overall dissatisfaction with the marriage. The test is available in two forms: a 280-item version for couples with children and a 239-item version for childless couples. The results for both spouses are recorded on the same profile form, graphically identifying the areas of marital distress. Each spouse's scores can be individually evaluated as well as directly compared, thereby facilitating diagnostic and intervention procedures. Group mean profiles for each sex are provided for couples seeking general marital therapy, couples seeking divorce, couples with specific sexual dysfunctions, physically abused wives, and couples with specific distress around childrearing. The manual presents a number of case illustrations. Examiner required. Not suitable for group use.

Untimed: 30-40 minutes

Scoring: Hand key; may be computer scored

Cost: Complete kit (booklets, answer sheets, profile forms, key, manual) $60.00

Publisher: Western Psychological Services

THE MARRIAGE ADJUSTMENT FORM (MAF)
Ernest Burgess

Adult

Purpose: Measures a couple's level of adjustment to marriage. Used for marriage counseling.

Description: 93-item paper-pencil multiple-choice questionnaire covering vital areas of marital adjustment. Couples complete the form in the presence of the counselor. Materials include a questionnaire and instruction form. The questionnaire is available as part of a specimen set that includes the Marriage Prediction Schedule. Examiner required. Suitable for group use.

Untimed: Not available

Scoring: Hand key; examiner evaluated

Cost: Specimen set (MAF, MPS, instruction sheet) $2.00; 10 MAF (instruction sheet) $4.50

Publisher: Family Life Publications, Inc.

Information and availability unconfirmed; no publisher response.

MARRIAGE ADJUSTMENT INVENTORY
Morse P. Manson and Arthur Lerner

Adult

Purpose: Identifies causes of marital tension and distress. Used for marital and family counseling.

Description: 157-item paper-pencil multiple-choice test measuring 12 common marital problem areas: family relations, dominance, immaturity, neurotic traits, sociopathic traits, money management, children, interests, physical, abilities, sexual and incompatability. Clients indicate which of the problem statements apply to themselves, their spouse, or both. The test yields four evaluative scores indicating the severity of marital maladjustment. Self-administered. Suitable for group use.

Untimed: 10-15 minutes

Scoring: Hand key

Cost: Kit (25 forms, manual) $15.00

Publisher: Western Psychological Services

MARRIAGE ADJUSTMENT SCHEDULE 1A
Marriage Council of Philadelphia

Married couples

Purpose: Aids counselors of married couples by obtaining a wide range of relevant information.

Description: 34-item paper-pencil test that secures independent responses about the couple's shared activities, feelings about those activities, problem areas in the marriage, and the sharing of responsibilities. The test provides data on attitudes, feelings, and problem areas for the counselor to review as he continues to work with the couple. The schedule is completed independently by couples prior to the first interview. Not to be considered a psychological test. Self-administered. Not suitable for group use.

Untimed: 30 minutes

Scoring: Examiner evaluated

Cost: Schedule $0.20; 100 schedules $15.00

Publisher: Marriage Council of Philadelphia, Inc.

MARRIAGE ADJUSTMENT SCHEDULE 1B
Marriage Council of Philadelphia

Married couples

Purpose: Provides the counselor with information concerning a couple's feelings, attitudes, and behavior regarding sex.

Description: 36-item paper-pencil schedule. The counselor completes the inventory during the counseling hour by using an interview format to survey the couple's feelings, attitudes, and behavior. The schedule does not attempt to assess the couple's factual knowledge of human sexuality, nor does it provide a psychological basis for counseling. Examiner required. Not suitable for group use.

Untimed: Varies

Scoring: Examiner evaluated

Cost: Schedule $0.20; 100 schedules $15.00

Publisher: Marriage Council of Philadelphia, Inc.

A MARRIAGE ANALYSIS (BGMA)
*Daniel C. Blazier and
Edgar T. Goosmans*

Adult

Purpose: Evaluates the progress of marriage counseling. Used to increase marriage counseling effectiveness.

Description: 113-item paper-pencil multiple-choice questionnaire exploring a couple's marital relationship. The questionnaire investigates eight areas of marriage: role concepts, self-image, feelings toward spouse, emotional openness, knowledge of spouse, sexual adjustment and security, common traits, and meanings of marriage. The answers may be transferred to a profile sheet for visual assessment of marital adjustment. Materials include a questionnaire, manual, and profile sheet. Self-administered. Suitable for group use.

Untimed: Not available

Scoring: Hand key; examiner evaluated

Cost: Specimen set $1.00; 10 BGMA $4.50

Publisher: Family Life Publications, Inc.

Information and availability unconfirmed; no publisher response.

A MARRIAGE EVALUATION (ME)
Henry Blount

Adult

Purpose: Assesses a troubled couple's perceptions of marriage. Enables couples to evaluate the status of their marriage and identifies areas in need of immediate discussion.

Description: 60-item paper-pencil multiple-choice test assessing a couple's perception of their marriage. The topics

assessed include readiness for marriage, decision making, values, communication, personal growth, commitment, and expectation. Materials include a test, manual, and scoring instructions. Self-administered. Suitable for group use.

Untimed: 15 minutes

Scoring: Hand key; examiner evaluated

Cost: Specimen set 10 tests $4.50; manual $1.00

Publisher: Family Life Publications, Inc.

Information and availability unconfirmed; no publisher response.

THE MARRIAGE EXPECTATION INVENTORIES
P.J. McDonald

Adult

Purpose: Evaluates an individual's marriage expectations in premarital and marriage enrichment counseling.

Description: 58-item paper-pencil questionnaire investigating marital expectations in nine areas: love, communication, freedom, sex, money, selfishness, religion, relatives, and children. The respondents answer questions individually on separate forms and then share answers privately or in group discussion. The questionnaire is available in two forms: Form I for engaged couples and Form II for married couples. The two forms are identical except for wording. Materials include test forms and a manual. Self-administered. Suitable for use with groups of couples.

Untimed: Not available

Scoring: Examiner evaluated

Cost: Specimen set (manual, 2 copies of each form) $3.00; 10 tests (specify form) $4.50; manual $2.50

Publisher: Family Life Publications, Inc.

Information and availability unconfirmed; no publisher response.

A MARRIAGE PREDICTION SCHEDULE (AMPS)
Ernest Burgess

Adolescent, adult

Purpose: Measures a premarital couple's expectations of marriage. Used for compatibility evaluation in premarital counseling and in family living and marriage classes.

Description: 74-item paper-pencil multiple-choice questionnaire. The couple completes the form together, and answers and scores are discussed openly. Materials include a questionnaire and instruction sheet. The questionnaire is available as part of a specimen set that includes the Marriage Adjustment Form. Self-administered. Suitable for group use.

Untimed: Not available

Scoring: Hand key

Cost: Specimen set (AMPS, MAF, instruction sheet) $2.00; 10 AMPS (instruction sheet) $4.50

Publisher: Family Life Publications, Inc.

Information and availability unconfirmed; no publisher response.

THE MARRIAGE ROLE EXPECTATION
*Marie Dunn and
J. Nicholas DeBonis (revision)*

**Adolescent, adult
Grades 10 and above**

Purpose: Evaluates marital behavior expectations. Aids in evaluating potential marriage success. Used for premarital counseling and in high-school family living classes.

Description: 71-item paper-pencil multiple-choice test covering seven areas: authority, homemaking, child care, personal characteristics, social participation, education, and employment/support. Materials include the test, a profile, a manual, and a scoring key. The test is available in separate forms for males and females. Self-administered. Suitable for group use.

Untimed: 15-30 minutes

Scoring: Hand key

Cost: Specimen set (manual, 2 forms, 2 profiles, key) $2.00; 10 REI (5 male, 5 female) $4.50; manual $1.00

Publisher: Family Life Publications, Inc.

Information and availability unconfirmed; no publisher response.

MARRIAGE SCALE
J. Gustav White

Adult

Purpose: Compares the opinions, attitudes, and beliefs of premarital or marital partners. Used for premarital, marital, and family counseling.

Description: 21-item paper-pencil inventory measuring factors related to marital life and compatibility. Each partner is asked to rate on a 10-point scale statements pertaining to the following topics: mutual understanding, outlook on life, religion, love, intercommunication, objectional habits, pleasures, relatives, children, sex, occupation, interests, aesthetic tastes, finances, major plans, etc. After each subject completes his or her scale, each partner's profile is copied onto the profile of the other partner for a direct comparison of their responses. A four-page folder serves as a permanent file record. Not suitable for persons with below average reading ability. Self-administered. Suitable for group use.

Untimed: 10-15 minutes

Scoring: Hand key; examiner evaluated

Cost: Specimen set $4.50; 25 rating folders $13.50

Publisher: Psychologists and Educators, Inc.

MATE (MARITAL ATTITUDE EVALUATION)
Will Schutz

Adult

Purpose: Assesses the relationship between husband and wife or other closely related persons. Used for stimulating discussion and for analysis of relationships.

Description: Multiple-item paper-pencil inventories used for exploring the relationship between husband and wife or other closely related persons. Respondents indicate the kinds of inclusion, control, and affection they desire from their partner and their understanding of their partners' desires. The three dimensions tested are described in *The*

Interpersonal Underworld by Will Schutz. Examiner required. Suitable for group use.

Untimed: Not available

Scoring: Hand key

Cost: 25 test booklets $4.50; score keys $2.50

Publisher: Consulting Psychologists Press, Inc.

MENOMETER
Panos D. Bardis

Adolescent, adult
Grades 10 and above

Purpose: Measures knowledge of the anatomical and physiological aspects of menstruation. Used for clinical assessment, marriage and family counseling, research on human sexuality, and discussion in family and human sexuality classes.

Description: 50-item paper-pencil true-false test in which the subject marks the appropriate answers. Examiner/self-administered. Suitable for group use.

Untimed: 12 minutes

Scoring: Hand key

Cost: Free

Publisher: Panos D. Bardis

MIRROR-COUPLE RELATIONSHIP INVENTORY
Joan A. Hunt and Richard A. Hunt

Adolescent, adult

Purpose: Measures a couple's perceptions of self and each other. Used for counseling, premarital, and enrichment work with couples.

Description: 336-item paper-pencil test measuring content and process dimensions of marriage. The content areas are life-style, parents, career, money, sex, leisure, religion, friends, children, and future. The process areas are personality, self-awareness, security, freedom, problem solving, fight/flight, valuing self, valuing partner, stress, positive communication, negative communication, and satisfaction. One attitude scale measures bias of answers. A couple uses a guide-

book to discuss the computer-generated profile of scale scores and item answers. Self-administered. Suitable for group use.

Untimed: 30-45 minutes

Scoring: Computer scored; interactive computer-scoring disk available

Cost: Specimen set (includes scoring for one couple) $10.00; interactive computer scoring disk with booklets $69.00

Publisher: Datascan

PAIR ATTRACTION INVENTORY (PAI)
Everett L. Shostrom

Adult

Purpose: Measures aspects contributing to adults' selection of a mate or friend. Used for premarital, marital, and family counseling.

Description: 224-item paper-pencil test assessing the feelings and attitudes of one member of a male-female pair about the nature of the relationship. Percentile norms are provided based on adult samples. The inventory is a component of the Actualizing Assessment Battery (AAB). Examiner required. Suitable for group use.

Untimed: 30 minutes

Scoring: Hand key

Cost: Kit (3 male, 3 female booklets, 50 answer sheets, 50 profiles, manual) $14.25

Publisher: Educational and Industrial Testing Service

PARTNER RELATIONSHIP INVENTORY, RESEARCH EDITION (PRI)
Carol N. Hoskins and Philip R. Merrifield

Adult

Purpose: Evaluates the level of conflict within a relationship through each partner's perceived feelings about the other partner. Used for research and counseling, especially in conflict resolution in a test-retest situation.

Description: Paper-pencil test evaluating how successfully emotional and interaction needs are being met by an existing relationship. Three forms, each with separate male and female inventories are available. The Long Form contains 80 items describing the dynamics of the relationship. Individuals rate their agreement or disagreement with the items according to their own perceptions. Form I (40 items) has two alternate forms, and Form II (33 items) has four alternate forms. Examiner required. Suitable for use with groups of couples.

Untimed: 10-30 minutes

Scoring: Hand key; examiner evaluated

Cost: Guide $2.00; 25 Long Forms (specify male or female) $3.75; key $0.10

Publisher: Consulting Psychologists Press, Inc.

A PILL SCALE
Panos D. Bardis

Adolescent, adult
Grades 10 and above

Purpose: Measures attitudes towards oral contraceptives. Used for clinical assessment, marriage and family counseling, family attitude research, and discussions in family and sex education.

Description: 25-item paper-pencil test in which the subject reads statements concerning moral, sexual, psychological, and physical aspects of "the pill" and rates them on a scale from 0 (strongly disagree) to 4 (strongly agree). The score equals the sum of the 25 numerical responses. The theoretical range of scores extends from 0 (least liberal) to 100 (most liberal). Examiner/self-administered. Suitable for group use.

Untimed: 10 minutes

Scoring: Examiner evaluated

Cost: Free

Publisher: Panos D. Bardis

PRE-MARITAL COUNSELING INVENTORY
Richard B. Stuart and Freida Stuart

Adult

Purpose: Assesses a couple's relationship before marriage. Identifies basic discrepancies in attitudes and expectations, measures each partner's understanding of

the other and provides information that is used to help the couple negotiate a relationship contract before they marry to reduce the intensity of conflict after marriage.

Description: 16-page paper-pencil inventory administered separately to each member of a couple preparing for marriage. The factors covered include religious background, family background, relationships with others, past marital history, history of relationship with prospective marital partner, marital role expectations, division of duties within marriage, and confidence in ability to handle various aspects of marriage. An average reading skill is required. The manual describes use of the instrument in a three-session pre-marital counseling program. Self-administered. Suitable for group use.

Untimed: 1 hour

Scoring: Computer scored; examiner evaluated

Cost: 20 booklets, guide $19.95; guide $1.95.

Publisher: Compuscore

PREMARITAL COMMUNICATION INVENTORY
Millard J. Bienvenu

Adult

Purpose: Evaluates the level of communication within a premarital relationship. Used to prepare couples in the communication skills required for a successful marriage and to identify trouble spots in communication.

Description: 40-item paper-pencil questionnaire covering the following areas: differences, feelings, anger, sex, opinions, in-laws, beliefs, criticism, manners, problem solving, depression, economics, future expectations, child rearing, personal problems, and future adjustments. Materials include a questionnaire, manual, and scoring key. The inventory should be administered by a trained counselor or clergy. Examiner required. Not suitable for group use.

Untimed: Not available

Scoring: Hand key; examiner evaluated

Cost: PCI $0.35; guide $1.25
Publisher: Family Life Publications
Information and availability unconfirmed; no publisher response.

THE PREMARITAL COUNSELING KIT (PCK)
Millard J. Bienvenu

Adult

Purpose: Evaluates a premarital couple's relationship in preparation for marriage. Explores complexities of marriage with the couple through the guidance of a counselor or clergyman. Used for both premarital and marital counseling.

Description: Six separate forms comprising a series of counseling sessions. Form I compares the individuals' backgrounds and general indications of compatibility. Form II is a communication inventory designed to discover strengths and weaknesses in communication skills. Form III provides incomplete sentences for elaborating on areas of the relationship about which either person feels unsure. Form IV covers strengths and problem areas to be worked on in the relationship. Form V is an evaluation summary for the counselor. Form VI is the marriage preparation programming forum for specific recommendations of activities and discussion for the couple in preparation for marriage. The forms are recommended for use over a period of at least three counseling sessions. Self-administered. Suitable for group use.

Untimed: Not available
Scoring: Examiner evaluated
Cost: Introductory kit (manual and forms for one couple) $5.00; manual $2.50; PCK-5 (5 couples) $10.00
Publisher: Family Life Publications, Inc.
Information and availability unconfirmed; no publisher response.

RELATIONSHIP SATISFACTION SURVEY
Rose Lucas

**Adolescent, adult
Ages 16 and older**

Purpose: Assesses marital conflicts and issues. Used in couple, family, and marital counseling.

Description: 120-item paper-pencil survey assessing the following factors of a relationship: communication patterns, emotional factors, child rearing practices, habits, affection, career, finances, social-recreational activities, and values. The survey is most helpful when both partners cooperate in completing it. Self-administered. Suitable for group use.

Untimed: 25 minutes
Scoring: Examiner evaluated
Cost: 50 survey forms $15.00
Publisher: The Wilmington Press
Information and availability unconfirmed; no publisher response.

A RELIGIOUS ATTITUDES INVENTORY (CCEA)
W.E. Crane and J. Henry Coffer

Adolescent, adult

Purpose: Assesses religious belief for consideration in marital and premarital counseling. Determines religious compatibility and promotes discussion of religious attitudes. Used in marriage enrichment and religion classes.

Description: 107-item paper-pencil inventory covering such areas as responsibility, belief, and child rearing. Individuals respond to statements by indicating degree of agreement or disagreement. Scores are transferred to a profile sheet for comparison. Self-administered. Suitable for group use.

Untimed: Not available
Scoring: Examiner evaluated
Cost: Specimen set (manual, 2 profiles, 2 inventories) $2.00; 10 CCRA (includes profiles) $4.50; manual $1.00
Publisher: Family Life Publications, Inc.
Information and availability unconfirmed; no publisher response.

THE SEX ATTITUDES SURVEY (SAS)
Gelolo McHugh

Adult

Purpose: Examines sexual attitudes. Used in marital and premarital counseling, adult sex education, counselor-teacher training, and sexual and marital enrichment programs.

Description: 107-item paper-pencil survey which helps to promote understanding, growth, and sharing of sexual attitudes. The statements cover such areas as intercourse, sex roles, sex dreams, and homo- and heterosexuality. The subjects respond to each statement on an agree-disagree basis. Responses can be connected to form an individual profile for comparison of specific disagreements. Self-administered. Suitable for group use.

Untimed: Not available

Scoring: Examiner evaluated

Cost: Specimen set (manual, two forms) $2.00; 10 kits $4.50; manual $1.00

Publisher: Family Life Publications, Inc.

Information and availability unconfirmed; no publisher response.

SEX KNOWLEDGE AND ATTITUDE TEST (SKAT)
Harold I. Lief and David Reed

Ages 18 and older

Purpose: Assesses an individual's sexual knowledge and attitudes. Used as a research and educational tool.

Description: 106-item paper-pencil test assessing sexual knowledge (71 items) and attitudes (35 items). The sexual attitudes section contains four subsections: heterosexual relationships, sexual myths, abortion, and autoeroticism. Using medical students for the norm, attitudes are measured for conservatism vs. liberalism. The test should not be administered to individuals with less than a college education. Available in Spanish. Self-administered. Suitable for group use.

Untimed: 20-30 minutes

Scoring: Hand key; may be computer scored

Cost: Test booklet $1.00; answer sheet $0.25; manual $2.50; norms booklet $0.25; set of scoring keys $3.00; Sexual Performance Evaluation $2.00; SKAT related articles $3.00

Publisher: Marriage Council of Philadelphia, Inc.

THE SEX KNOWLEDGE INVENTORY—FORM X (SKI-X)
Gelolo McHugh

Adolescent, adult
Grades 10 and above

Purpose: Facilitates discussion of basic sex facts and the emotional aspects of sexuality. Used for marital and premarital counseling, college and high-school sex education, and counselor-educator training.

Description: 80-item paper-pencil multiple-choice test assessing knowledge of and attitudes toward sexual behavior. The test aids teachers and counselors in dispelling sexual myths and teaching facts. Self-administered. Suitable for group use.

Untimed: Not available

Scoring: Hand key; examiner evaluated

Cost: Specimen set (manual, test booklet, 2 answer sheets) $2.00; 1-9 test booklets $1.35 each; 10 answer sheets $3.00; key $5.00; manual $3.50

Publisher: Family Life Publications, Inc.

Information and availability unconfirmed; no publisher response.

THE SEX KNOWLEDGE INVENTORY—FORM Y (SKI-Y)
Gelolo McHugh

Adolescent, adult

Purpose: Measures knowledge and function of sexual anatomy and correct medical vocabulary. Used for marital and premarital counseling, pre- or posttesting for high-school and college sex education classes, and churches and clinics.

Description: 98-item paper-pencil inventory consisting of three parts. In Part I (20 items), the subject must match side view drawings of external and internal male and female sex organs with their correct names. Part II (30 items) consists of matching organ names or drawings with a description of their function. Part III (48 items) consists of matching vocabulary words covering all aspects of sexuality with their correct definition. Self-administered. Suitable for group use.

Untimed: Not available

Scoring: Hand key

Cost: Specimen set (manual, 2 tests, scoring key) $2.00; 10 tests $4.50; manual $1.00

Publisher: Family Life Publications, Inc.

Information and availability unconfirmed; no publisher response.

SEXOMETER
Panos D. Bardis

Adolescent, adult
Grades 10 and above

Purpose: Assesses knowledge of human reproductive anatomy and physiology. Used for clinical assessment, marriage and family counseling, research on sex knowledge, and discussion in family and sex education.

Description: 50-item paper-pencil test consisting of short answer and identification questions concerning human reproduction, anatomy, function, physiology, disease, birth control, and sexual behavior. Materials include the test form and answer key. Examiner/self-administered. Suitable for group use.

Untimed: 15 minutes

Scoring: Hand key

Cost: Free

Publisher: Panos D. Bardis

THE SEXUAL COMMUNICATIONS INVENTORY (SCI)
Millard J. Bienvenu

Adult

Purpose: Evaluates the level and type of communication about sexual matters within an established relationship. Used for marital counseling and enrichment programs.

Description: Paper-pencil test designed to help a couple overcome inhibitions in talking about their sexual relationship through an examination of their communication patterns. Part I consists of 30 statements concerning frequency and pattern of sexual communication and desire for change. Part II consists of incomplete sentences for a self-report of sexual feelings, ability to communicate, and desire for change. Part III surveys general background information to aid the counselor. Materials include the inventory, manual, and scoring key. The inventory should be used by trained psychologists only. Examiner required. Not suitable for group use.

Untimed: Not available

Scoring: Hand key; examiner evaluated

Cost: Marital form $0.35; guide $0.75

Publisher: Family Life Publications

Information and availability unconfirmed; no publisher response.

THE SEXUAL COMPATABILITY TEST
Arthur L. Foster

Adult

Purpose: Assesses a couple's sexual relationship. Used to plan sex therapy programs and to predict success of sexual treatment.

Description: 101-item paper-pencil test assessing the following factors: sexual satisfaction, sexual dysfunction, variety, communication, interests or desires, and a broad range of sexual activities. Couples must have an ongoing sexual relationship of at least one year. Materials include test form, answer sheet, and manual. Self-administered. Suitable for group use.

Untimed: 1 hour

Scoring: Hand key; examiner evaluated; may be computer scored

Cost: Complete test $45.00.

Publisher: The Phoenix Institute of California

THE SEXUAL CONCERNS CHECKLIST (SCC)
Lester A. Kirkendall

Adolescent, adult

Purpose: Determines an individual's most important sexual concerns in order for counselors or teachers to address clients' or students' specific needs. Used for sex education, sexual counseling, premarital and marital counseling, marriage enrichment programs, and research.

Description: Paper-pencil checklist containing human sexuality questions. Four forms containing statements of concerns appropriate to each of the following groups are available: male/female adolescents and male/female adults. The adolescent forms cover knowledge, attitudes, and specific problems related to adolescents. The adult forms cover the same areas, as well as sexual function problems. Self-administered. Suitable for group use.

Untimed: Not available

Scoring: Examiner evaluated

Cost: Specimen set (4 forms and manual $3.00; 10 forms (5 male, 5 female; specify adult or adolescent) $4.50

Publisher: Family Life Publications, Inc. *Information and availability unconfirmed; no publisher response.*

SEXUALITY EXPERIENCE SCALES
J. Frenken and P. Vennix

Adult Ages 18-55

Purpose: Assesses characteristics of heterosexual behavior. Used in counseling, therapy, and social and medical research.

Description: 83-item paper-pencil instruments measuring four dimensions of sexuality experience. SES-1 (21 items) measures restrictive sexual morality (rejection versus acceptance; SES-2 (15 items) measures psychosexual stimulation (seeking, allowing versus avoiding of symbolic sexual stimuli); SES-3 (29 items) measures sexual motivation (approach tendency versus avoidance tendancy in sexual interaction with partner); and SES-4 (18 items) measures attraction to own marriage (low versus high). SES-1 and SES-2 are administered to persons who have no sexual partners. The latter two are administered to persons who have durable heterosexual relationships. The tests, derived from item analysis and factor analysis, have 14 relatively independent subscales. Norms are available for married men and women ages 18-55 and for women complaining of sexual dysfunction and their male partners. Examiner/self-administered. Not suitable for group use.

DUTCH PUBLISHER

Untimed: Not available

Scoring: Computer scored

Cost: Manual $23.00; questionnaire for men (scoring form included) $0.75; questionnaire for women (scoring form included) $0.75

Publisher: SWETS and Zeitlinger B.V.

SOCIO-SEXUAL KNOWLEDGE AND ATTITUDES TEST (SSKAT)
Joel Wish, Katherine F. McCombs, and Barbara Edmonson

Developmentally disabled Ages 18-42

Purpose: Measures sexual knowledge and attitudes of the developmentally disabled of all ages. Used for educational and clinical counseling, planning, and placement.

Description: 227-page stimulus picture book presents realistic pictures illustrating "yes or no" and point-to response questions relevant to 14 socio-sexual topic areas: anatomy terminology, menstruation, dating, marriage, intimacy, intercourse, pregnancy and childbirth, birth control, masturbation and homosexuality, venereal disease, alcohol and drugs, community risks and hazards, and a terminology check. Subjects to be tested must have visual and verbal comprehension; expressive language requirements are minimal. This is a criterion test to determine what the subject knows, believes, and does not know about human sexuality. It does not establish standards. Normative data is based on developmentally disabled individuals ages 14-42, although the test also is valuable in determining sexual knowledge and attitudes of nonretarded persons of all ages. The manual presents data on reliability and item-total correlations for each subtest. Examiner required. Not suitable for group use.

Untimed: Open ended

Scoring: Examiner evaluated

Cost: Complete kit (record forms, stimulus picture book, manual) $100.00

Publisher: Stoelting Company

VASECTOMY SCALE: ATTITUDES
Panos D. Bardis

Adolescent, adult
Grades 10 and above

Purpose: Measures attitudes toward the social and psychological aspects of vasectomy. Used for clinical assessment, marriage and family counseling, research on human sexuality, and discussions in family and sex education.

Description: 25-item paper-pencil test in which the subject rates 25 statements concerning vasectomy on a scale from 0 (strongly disagree) to 4 (strongly agree). The score equals the sum of the 25 numerical responses. The theoretical range of scores extends from 0 (lowest approval of vasectomy) to 100 (highest approval). Examiner/self-administered. Suitable for group use.

Untimed: 10 minutes

Scoring: Examiner evaluated

Cost: Free

Publisher: Panos D. Bardis

Personality: Normal and Abnormal, Assessment and Treatment: Child

AUTISTIC BEHAVIOR COMPOSITE CHECKLIST AND PROFILE
Anita Marcott Riley

Autistic and emotionally
handicapped children

Purpose: Assesses behaviors associated with autism. Used with autistic, emotionally handicapped, and severely learning disabled students.

Description: 148-item inventories assessing a subject's interfering behaviors in eight categories: prerequisite learning behaviors; sensory perceptual skills; motor development; prelanguage skills; speech, language, and communication skills; developmental rates and sequences; learning behaviors; and relating skills. The checklist and profile help establish and support a diagnosis of autism, prioritize problem areas for intervention, and follow a student's behavior over time. Examiner required. Not suitable for group use.

Untimed: Not available

Scoring: Hand key

Cost: 20 test booklets $24.95

Publisher: Communication Skill Builders, Inc.

BAR-ILAN PICTURE TEST FOR CHILDREN
Rivkah Itskowitz and Helen Strauss

Child   Ages 4-10

Purpose: Assesses child's perceptions of home, school, peers, and family. Used for diagnosis, screening, and research.

Description: Multiple-item semi-projective interview instrument used for assessing emotional status, motivation and locus of control, interpersonal behavior and conflicts, attitudes towards significant others, feelings of mastery and competence, thought processes, and general level of activity. The test consists of nine basic drawings, six of which have separate versions for boys and for girls, depicting realistic situations from a day in the life of a child. The test was designed for use with children ages 4-10 but has been used successfully with children up to age 16. Examiner required. Not suitable for group use.

Untimed: 20 minutes

Scoring: Examiner evaluated

Cost: Folder with 15 test drawings $25.00; manual $9.00

Publisher: Dansk Psykologisk Forlag

THE BEHAVIOR OBSERVATION SCALE FOR AUTISM
Betty Jo Freeman

Child   Ages 2-5

Purpose: Assesses the presence of clusters of symptoms characteristic of the syndrome of autism.

Description: 24-item observational measure of behavior in four areas: solitary, relation to objects, relation to people, and language. Within each group, repetitive and nonrepetitive behaviors are coded separately. The scale is divided into three elements: recording, recognition, and measurement of behavior. Examiner required. Not suitable for group use.

Untimed: 30 minutes

Scoring: Examiner evaluated

Cost: Contact publisher

Publisher: Betty Jo Freeman, Ph.D.

BURKS' BEHAVIOR RATING SCALES, PRESCHOOL AND KINDERGARTEN EDITION
Harold F. Burks

Child   Grades PreK-K

Purpose: Identifies patterns of behavior problems in children ages 3-6. Used to aid differential diagnosis.

Description: 105-item paper-pencil inventory used by parents and teachers to rate a child on the basis of descriptive statements of observed behavior. The inventory contains 18 subscales: excessive self-blame, anxiety, withdrawal, dependency, suffering, sense of persecution, aggressiveness, and resistance and poor ego strength, physical strength, coordination, intellectuality, attention, impulse control, reality contact, sense of identity, anger control, and social conformity. This inventory is a downward extension of Burk's Behavior Rating Scale. Examiner administered. Not suitable for group use.

Untimed: 15-20 minutes

Scoring: Hand key

Cost: Complete kit (25 profile sheets and booklets, manual) $19.50

Publisher: Western Psychological Services

CALIFORNIA CHILD Q-SET
Jeanne H. Block and Jack Block

Child

Purpose: Describes individual behavior and personality in contemporary psychodynamic terms. Used for research in child development.

Description: 100-item formulation of personality descriptions. Items are descriptive personality statements sorted from most to least applicable to the subject. Materials include individual 2¼" x 3½" cards. Examiner required. Not suitable for group use.

Untimed: Not available

Scoring: Examiner evaluated

Cost: Q-Sort Deck $6.00

Publisher: Consulting Psychologists Press, Inc.

CHILD & ADOLESCENT ADJUSTMENT PROFILE (CAAP)
Robert E. Ellsworth

Child, adolescent

Purpose: Measures the adjustment of children and adolescents to life and the community. Used for evaluation of treatment programs.

Description: 20-item paper-pencil rating scale assessing a child's or adolescent's adjustment through five factored dimensions: peer relations, dependency, hostility, productivity, and withdrawal. The child may be rated every three months by a parent, teacher, or probation officer to evaluate the success of the child's mental-health program. The manual explains the rationale and validity of the scales and provides detailed norms for the general and clinical population with respect to adjustment to life and the community. Examiner required. Suitable for group use.

Untimed: 20-30 minutes

Scoring: Examiner evaluated

Cost: Manual $5.00; 25 scales and profile sheets $4.75

Publisher: Consulting Psychologists Press, Inc.

CHILD ANXIETY SCALE (CAS)
John S. Gillis

Child   Ages 6-8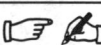

Purpose: Diagnoses adjustment problems in children. Helps to prevent emotional and behavioral disorders in later life by identifying children who would benefit from therapeutic intervention at an early age. Used for clinical evaluations and educational and personal counseling.

Description: Paper-pencil test measuring anxiety-based disturbances in young children. Test items are based on extensive research of the form anxiety takes in the self-report of 6-8-year-olds. An audiocassette tape is used to present the questionnaire items, and brightly colored, easy-to-read answer sheets are specially designed for use with children of this age group. The CAS manual contains reliability and validity information, scoring instructions, and percentiles and standard scores for both sexes separately and combined. Examiner required. Suitable for group use.

Untimed: 15 minutes

Scoring: Hand key

Cost: CAS professional examination kit $27.45; CAS manual $6.70; 50 hand-scoring answer sheets, scoring key $3.75; cassette tape $9.25

Publisher: Institute for Personality and Ability Testing, Inc.

CHILD ASSESSMENT SCHEDULE
Kay Hodges

Child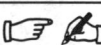

Purpose: Assesses the present episode of psychiatric illness. Can be used by clinicians to assess past episodes of illness as well.

Description: Diagnostic interview in three parts. In the first part, the interviewer asks the child approximately 75 questions about school, friends, activities and hobbies, family, fears, worries, self-image, mood, somatic concerns, expression of anger, and thought disorder symptomatology and then records the child's answers. In the second section interviewer obtains from the child information about the onset and duration of symptoms. In the third section, the examiner's observations about the child are recorded. This section consists of 53 items about insight, grooming, motor coordination, activity level, spontaneous physical behavior, estimate of cognitive ability, quality of verbal communication and emotional expression, and impressions about quality of interpersonal interactions. These items are scored by the examiner after the interview is completed. A parent form, which is similar in content to the CAS, is available for administration to parents. When both forms are used, they are administered to the parent and to the child individually. The clinician can make DSM-III diagnoses based on information from each form and can generate quantitative scores for various diagnostic clusters for use in making group comparisons. Examiner required. Not suitable for group use.

Untimed: 45-60 minutes

Scoring: Examiner evaluated

Cost: Manual, interview $7.50

Publisher: Kay Hodges, Ph.D.

CHILD BEHAVIOR CHECKLIST AND REVISED CHILD BEHAVIOR PROFILE
Thomas H. Achenbach and Craig Edelbrock

Child, adolescent   Ages 2-16

Purpose: Assesses the behavioral problems and competencies of children and adolescents.

Description: Five multiple-item paper-pencil multiple-choice and free-response inventories evaluating child behavioral problems from four perspectives. The Child Behavior Checklist assesses behavior from the parents' point of view; the Teacher Report Form assesses the child's classroom behavior; the Direct Observation Form employs an experienced observer to rate the child on the basis of a series of at least six 10-minute observation periods; and the Youth Self-Report (ages 11-18) gathers information directly from the child.

The four-page Child Behavior Checklist (available in two forms, one for ages 2-3 and one for ages 4-16) contains two pages of questions regarding the child's social history, interests, and school performance. Most items combine free-response questions about the child with multiple-choice rating scales for comparing the child with his peers. The last two pages of the checklist present 118 items (item 56 includes a-g) describing a variety of problem behaviors. Parents rate each item from 0 (not true) to 2 (very true) according to their child's behavior over the past six months (time period may be changed to suit user's aims). Responses are scored according to the Revised Child Behavior Profile, which yields scores for social competence scales and behavior problem scales as well as internalizing, externalizing, and total problem scores. Norms are provided in terms of T-scores.

The Teacher's Report Form, presented in a four-page format, gathers background information and assesses 118 items related to classroom behavior. The scoring profile includes standard scores, four general adaptive characteristics, eight behavior problem scales, internalizing and externalizing problems, and total problem scores.

The Direct Observation Form rates 96 problem behaviors from 0 (not observed) to 3 (severe intensity) for a 10-minute period and provides for scoring on-task behavior at 1-minute intervals. The observer writes a narrative description of the child's behavior during the observation period and then rates the behavioral items accordingly. Stable scores are obtained by averaging the ratings obtained on six different occasions. Individual item scores, total behavior problem scores, and on-task scores act as direct indices of behavior problems and change over time and provide a basis for group comparison.

The Youth Self-Report form, presented in a four-page format, gathers first-hand information related to the items on the Child Behavior Checklist. The scoring profile includes standard scores, three competence scales, behavior problem scales, internalizing and externalizing problems, and total problem scores. Separate manuals are available for the Child Behavior Checklist and Teacher's

Report Form. They discuss development and construction of the scales; the internalizing-externalizing dichotomy, factor loadings; standardization and norms; reliability and validity; effects of clinical status, socioeconomic status, and race; clinical cutoff scores, cluster analyses, profile patterns, and taxonomy; classification of children according to their profile patterns; distribution and correlates of profile types; clinical and research applications; and scoring procedures by hand and computer. Self-administered (except for the Direct Observation Form). All self-administered forms suitable for group use.

Untimed: Varies

Scoring: Examiner evaluated; computer scoring programs available

Cost: Sample packet (Child Behavior Checklist, Revised Child Behavior Profile scoring forms, Teacher Report Form and scoring profile, Direct Observation Form, and Youth Self-Report Form, scoring profile, instructions) $9.90

Publisher: Department of Psychiatry, University of Vermont

CHILD BEHAVIOR RATING SCALE
Russell N. Cassel

Child   Grades PreK-3

Purpose: Measures the behavior and personality adjustment of children. Used for research and to counsel both normal and emotionally handicapped children.

Description: 78-item paper-pencil inventory consisting of brief statements about behavior and personality that an evaluator (someone familiar with the child) applies to the child and answers on a 6-point scale ranging from "yes" to "no." The inventory yields a total personality adjustment score and a profile of the child's adjustment in five areas: self, home, social, school, and physical. Examiner required. Suitable for group use.

Untimed: 30-40 minutes

Scoring: Hand key

Cost: Complete kit (25 scales, manual) $14.75

Publisher: Western Psychological Services

CHILD OBSERVATION GUIDE
Refer to page 668.

THE CHILDREN'S ADAPTIVE BEHAVIOR REPORT (CABR)
Richard H. Kicklighter and Bert O. Richmond

Child   Ages 5-11

Purpose: Assesses adaptive behavior of children as reported by parents or guardians.

Description: Multiple-item interview tool used for soliciting perceptions of adults related to a child's adaptability in language development, independent functioning, family role performance, economic and vocational activity, and socialization. Since the five domains assessed match those in the Children's Adaptive Behavior Scale (CABS), the clinician can contrast adult perceptions with the child's performance on the CABS. Examiner required. Not suitable for group use.

Untimed: 20-30 minutes

Scoring: Examiner evaluated

Cost: Kit $19.95

Publisher: Humanics Limited

THE CHILDREN'S APPERCEPTION TEST (CAT-A)
Leopold Bellak and Sonya Sorel Bellak

Child   Ages 3-10

Purpose: Assesses children's personality. Used in clinical evaluation and diagnosis.

Description: 10-item oral-response projective personality test measuring the traits, attitudes, and psychodynamics involved in the personalities of children ages 3-10. Each test item consists of a picture of animals in a human social context through which the child becomes involved in conflicts, identities, roles, and family structures. Examinees are required to tell a story about each picture. The test also includes informational material on the history, nature and purpose of CAT, Ego Function Graph, test interpretation, use

of the Short Form, research possibilities, and bibliography. Examiner required. Not suitable for group use. Available in Spanish, Indian, French, German, Japanese, Flemish, Portuguese, and Italian.

Untimed: 20-30 minutes

Scoring: Examiner evaluated

Cost: Complete kit (pictures, manual) $16.00

Publisher: C.P.S., Inc.

THE CHILDREN'S APPERCEPTION TEST—HUMAN FIGURES (CAT-H)
Leopold Bellak and Sonya Sorel Bellak

Child   Ages 3-10

Purpose: Assesses children's personality. Used for clinical evaluation and diagnosis.

Description: 10-item oral-response projective personality test measures the traits, attitudes, and psychodynamics involved in the personalities of children. The test consists of 10 pictures of human figures in situations of concern to children: conflicts, identities, roles, and family structure. The test also includes a review of the literature concerning the use of animal vs. human figures in projective techniques, a discussion of the process of transposing animal figures to human forms, a copy of Haworth's Schedule of Adaptive Mechanisms in CAT Responses, and a bibliography. Examiner required. Not suitable for group use. Available in Spanish, Portuguese, Flemish, and Japanese.

Untimed: 20-30 minutes

Scoring: Examiner evaluated

Cost: Complete kit (10 pictures and manual) $16.00

Publisher: C.P.S., Inc.

THE CHILDREN'S APPERCEPTION TEST—SUPPLEMENT (CAT-S)
Leopold Bellak and Sonya Sorel Bellak

Child   Ages 3-10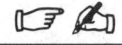

Purpose: Assesses children's personality. Used for clinical evaluation and diagnosis.

Description: 10-item oral-response projective personality test measures the traits, attitudes, and psychodynamics at work in the personalities of children ages 3-10. The test items consist of 10 pictures of animal figures in family situations which are common, but not as universal as those of the Children's Apperception Test. Among the situations depicted are prolonged illness, physical disability, mother's pregnancy, and separation of parents. The picture plates are constructed like pieces of a large jigsaw puzzle, with irregularly shaped outlines. Children who do not relate stories readily can manipulate these forms in play techniques. The test also includes informational material on test techniques and a bibliography. Examiner required. Not suitable for group use. Available in Spanish, French, Flemish, and Italian.

Untimed: 20-30 minutes

Scoring: Examiner evaluated

Cost: Complete kit (10 pictures, manual) $16.00

Publisher: C.P.S., Inc.

CHILDREN'S EMBEDDED FIGURES TEST (CEFT)
Stephen A. Karp and
Norma Konstadt

Child   Ages 5-12

Purpose: Assesses cognitive style in perceptual tasks. Used for measuring field dependence in studies of psychological differentiation.

Description: 25-item verbal/manual test of perceptual processes including field dependence/independence. The child's performance is related to analytic ability, social behavior, and body concept. Materials include cut-out models of two forms, 38 plates for the 25 items and 13 practice items, clear plastic envelopes to protect the plates, and a star rubber stamp. A washable ink stamp pad is required. The subject finds simple forms in complex figures and stamps the correct choice. Examiner required. Not suitable for group use.

Untimed: Open ended

Scoring: Examiner evaluated

Cost: Test kit (includes 50 record sheets and all test materials) $24.50

Publisher: Consulting Psychologists Press, Inc.

THE CHILDREN'S HYPNOTIC SUSCEPTIBILITY SCALE
Perry London

Child, adolescent
Ages 5-17

Purpose: Measures susceptibility to hypnosis in children and adolescents. Used for teaching, research, and experimentation.

Description: 22-item test containing instructions for inducing and testing the hypnotic state of children on two age levels. The instructions use permissive, nonauthoritarian language and gentle challenges. Items are of increasing difficulty, and testing may be ended after Item 12 if the child is not experiencing hypnosis. The test was adapted from the Stanford Hypnotic Susceptibility Scale Forms A, B, and C. Examiner required. Not suitable for group use.

Untimed: 50 minutes

Scoring: Hand key

Cost: Kit (25 scales and scoring and observation forms) $30.00

Publisher: Consulting Psychologists Press, Inc.

CHILDREN'S PERSONALITY QUESTIONNAIRE (CPQ)
Rutherford B. Porter and
Raymond B. Cattell

Child, adolescent
Ages 8-12

Purpose: Assesses personality development in children. Used for clinical evaluations and educational and personal counseling.

Description: 140-item paper-pencil test measuring 14 primary personality traits useful in predicting and evaluating the course of personal, social, and academic development. The traits measured include emotional stability, self-concept level, excitability, and self-assurance. Scores for extraversion, anxiety, and other broad trait patterns are obtained as combinations of the primary scales. Percentiles and standard scores are presented for both sexes together and separately. The test is available in four equivalent forms: A, B, C, and D. Each form is divided into two parts for scheduling convenience in school settings. A third-grade reading level is required. Examiner required. Suitable for group use. Available in Spanish and German.

Untimed: 30-60 minutes per form

Scoring: Hand key; scoring and interpretation services available

Cost: Contact publisher

Publisher: Institute for Personality and Ability Testing, Inc.

CHILDREN'S PROBLEMS CHECKLIST
John A. Schinka

Parents of children ages 5-12

Purpose: Assesses children's problems as reported by parent or guardian. Used as a survey instrument in clinical and counseling settings to initiate the consultation process and introduce the client to formal diagnostic testing.

Description: 190-item paper-pencil test completed by a parent or guardian and identifying problems in 11 areas: emotions, self-concept, peers/play, school, language/thinking, concentration/organization, activity level/motor control, behavior, values, habits, and health. The test is a component of the Clinical Checklist Series. It is available in a computer version for use with Apple II Plus, Apple IIe, and IBM PC computers. Self-administered. Suitable for group use.

Untimed: 10-20 minutes

Scoring: Examiner evaluated

Cost: 50 checklists $12.95; computer version (100 uses) $50.00

Publisher: Psychological Assessment Resources, Inc.

CHILDREN'S STATE-TRAIT ANXIETY INVENTORY
Charles D. Spielberger, C.D. Edwards, J. Montuori, and R. Lushene

Child, adolescent   Grades 4-8

Purpose: Assesses anxiety in children. Used for research screening and treatment evaluation.

Description: Two 20-item scales measuring two types of anxiety: state anxiety (current level of anxiety, or S-Anxiety) and trait anxiety (anxiety-proneness, or T-Anxiety). The S-Anxiety scales ask how the child feels at a particular moment in time, and the T-Anxiety scales ask how he generally feels. The inventory is based on the same concept as the State-Trait Anxiety Inventory and is used in conjunction with the adult form manual. Self-administered. Suitable for group use.

Untimed: 10-20 minutes

Scoring: Hand key; examiner evaluated

Cost: Manual $3.00; key $1.00; 25 expendable tests $4.00

Publisher: Consulting Psychologists Press, Inc.

THE DEVEREUX CHILD BEHAVIOR RATING SCALE (DCB)
Refer to page 593.

DIABETES OPINION SURVEY (DOS)
Suzanne Bennett Johnson

Child

Purpose: Measures attitudes toward diabetes in children. Used for clinical assessment and research in medical settings.

Description: 78-item paper-pencil Likert-scale test of five aspects of attitudes regarding diabetes: stigma, rule orientation, divine intervention, family interruption, and sick role. The lie scale from the Children's Manifest Anxiety Scale also is included in the DOS. The child expresses degree of agreement or disagreement with the attitude expressed in each item. A measure of parent attitudes may be obtained by using the Parent Diabetes Opinion Survey (PDOS). Examiner/self-administered. Suitable for group use.

Untimed: Varies

Scoring: Hand key

Cost: Sample $30.00

Publisher: Suzanne Bennett Johnson, Ph.D.

DIAGNOSTIC CHECKLIST FOR BEHAVIOR-DISTURBED CHILDREN: FORM E-2
Bernard Rimland

Child   Ages 3½-5

Purpose: Diagnoses infantile autism. Differentiates truly autistic children from autistic-type children.

Description: 80-item paper-pencil inventory assessing speech and behavior symptoms related to autism in young children. The checklist consists of questions (intended for the child's parents) covering social interaction and affect; speech, motor, and manipulative ability; intelligence and reaction to sensory stimuli; family characteristics; illness development; and physiological and other biological data. A total score is derived, as well as separate scores for speech and behavior. Cut-off scores and interpretive guidelines are provided to assist in diagnosing autism and other forms of childhood psychoses. Examiner evaluated. Not suitable for group use.

Untimed: Not available

Scoring: Scored by publisher

Cost: Contact publisher

Publisher: Institute for Child Behavior

EARLY SCHOOL PERSONALITY QUESTIONNAIRE (ESPQ)
Raymond B. Cattell,
Richard W. Coan, and IPAT Staff

Child   Ages 6-8

Purpose: Measures personality in children in the early school years. Used for clinical evaluation and educational and personal counseling.

Description: 160-item paper-pencil test measuring personality in children. Questions are read aloud by the teacher (an optional tape recording may be used instead), and the students mark their answers on the answer sheet. To use the answer sheet, children need only be able to discriminate the letter A from the letter B and to recognize pictures of a bird, cat, tree, flower, and other common objects. Percentiles and standard scores are provided for both sexes separately and together. The test is divided into two equal parts of 80 items each for scheduling convenience. Examiner required. Suitable for group use. Available in Spanish.

Untimed: Not available

Scoring: Hand key

Cost: ESPQ professional examination kit $12.15; manual $4.50; 25 answer booklets $6.50; 50 profile sheets $6.50; 2 scoring keys $6.75; tape recording $25.00

Publisher: Institute for Personality and Ability Testing, Inc.

FROST SELF-DESCRIPTION QUESTIONNAIRE
Barry P. Frost

Child, adolescent
Ages 8-14

Purpose: Diagnoses various aspects of a child's feelings of anxiety, aggression, and separation.

Description: 107-item paper-pencil true-false test covering 14 scales of anxiety: test, social, worry and tension, concentration, separation from family, spatial separation, body damage, free-floating, externalized aggression, internalized aggression, projective aggression, denial, affiliation, and submission. Materials consist of a booklet, answer sheet, and answer keys. Use is restricted to psychologists. Examiner required. Suitable for group use. Available in Spanish and Japanese.

Untimed: 15 minutes

Scoring: Hand key

Cost: Manual $2.50; 25 questionnaire booklets $15.00; 25 answer sheets $7.50; 4 keys $4.00

Publisher: Barry P. Frost, Ph.D.

FROST SELF-DESCRIPTION QUESTIONNAIRE: EXTENDED SCALE (FSDQ: EXTENDED)
Barry P. Frost

**Child, adolescent
Ages 9-14**

Purpose: Assesses personality variables, specifically anxiety, aggression, affiliation, and denial in children.

Description: 310-item paper-pencil test in three forms measuring externalized, internalized, and projective aggression; free-floating, body-damage, separation, test, concentration, and social anxiety; worry and tension; and denial and affiliation. The scales can be used separately or to follow-up on indications from the original Frost Self-Description Questionnaire. Form I (aggression) contains 85 items; Form II (four anxiety scales), 105 items; and Form III (three anxiety scales, denial, and affiliation) 120 items. Children are asked to read each question, decide if a description is true of how the child acts or feels, and mark an answer. The scales are appropriate for most children, except those with low intellectual skills. Examiner required. Suitable for group use.
CANADIAN PUBLISHER

Untimed: 20-30 minutes per form

Scoring: Examiner evaluated

Cost: Specimen set $20.00

Publisher: Barry P. Frost, Ph.D.

INTERMEDIATE PERSONALITY QUESTIONNAIRE FOR INDIAN PUPILS (IPQI)—1974
Refer to page 701.

JUNIOR EYSENCK PERSONALITY INVENTORY (JEPI)
Sybil B. G. Eysenck

**Child, adolescent
Ages 7-16**

Purpose: Measures the major personality dimensions of children. Used as a research instrument.

Description: 60-item paper-pencil yes-no inventory measuring extraversion-intro-version (24 items) and neuroticism-stability (24 items). A falsification scale (12 items) detects response distortion. Scores are provided for E-Extraversion, N-Neuroticism, and L-Lie. American norms are available for selected samples of majority and minority children. Examiner required. Suitable for group use. Available in Spanish.

Untimed: 10 minutes

Scoring: Hand key

Cost: Specimen set (manual, one copy of all forms) $5.00; 25 inventories $7.50; key $6.00; manual $2.50

Publisher: Educational and Industrial Testing Service

THE MEASUREMENT OF SELF-CONCEPT IN KINDERGARTEN CHILDREN (MSCKC)
Refer to page 481.

MICHIGAN PICTURE TEST, REVISED
Max L. Hutt

**Child, adolescent
Grades 3-12**

Purpose: Differentiates between emotionally maladjusted children and emotionally well-adjusted children. Diagnoses type and severity of conflicts and identifies children in need of rehabilitative/psychotherapeutic procedures.

Description: Oral-response projective test measuring school-age children for degree of emotional adjustment or maladjustment, areas of emotional conflict, and types of emotional conflict. Four "core" pictures presented to both sexes yield scores on several emotional areas. Eight additional pictures for boys and eight for girls yield information about areas and types of conflict. The students are presented with the picture cards one at a time and asked to create stories about them. Scoring employs simple objective methods along with characteristics of partially structured projective tests. Examiner required. Suitable for group use.

Untimed: Short form 15 minutes; long form 1 hour

Scoring: Hand key; examiner evaluated

Cost: Complete set $55.00; scoring forms $14.00; pictures $27.50; manual $21.00

Publisher: Grune & Stratton, Inc.

MISSOURI CHILDREN'S PICTURE SERIES (MCPS)
J.O. Sines, J.D. Pauker, and L.K. Sines

Child, adolescent
Ages 5-16

Purpose: Measures child personality characteristics. Used to screen school-age children for personality difficulties and to evaluate in terms of clinical diagnosis.

Description: 238-item test consisting of picture diagrams of everyday situations printed on 3 x 5 cards, which the examiner presents to the children, asking them to select those which look like fun and those which do not. The examiner separates the cards by color dividers to score the answers on the following scales: Conformity, Masculinity/Femininity, Maturity, Aggression, Introversion, Hyperactivity, Sleep Disturbance, and Systematic Complaint. The results yield information regarding the possibility of personality difficulties. The test is available only to psychologists, trained teachers, and counselors. Examiner required. Suitable for group use.

Untimed: 25 minutes

Scoring: Hand key

Cost: Specimen set $40.00

Publisher: Psychological Assessment and Services, Inc.

PEER NOMINATION INVENTORY OF DEPRESSION (PNID)
Monroe M. Lefkowitz and Edward P. Tesiny

Ages 8-11   Grades 3-5

Purpose: Assesses symptoms of depression in normal children. Used by researchers to collect epidemiological data regarding depressive symptoms in the general child population.

Description: 23-item inventory measuring depression, happiness, and

popularity. For each item, the child is rated on a 2-point scale (0 = not selected; 1 = selected) by his peers. Each rated child receives two scores: an item score and a total score (sum of item scores). Examiner required. Suitable for group use only.

Untimed: 30 minutes

Scoring: Examiner evaluated

Cost: One-time fee of $25.00 per administrator or institution

Publisher: Monroe M. Lefkowitz, Ph.D.

PERSONALITY INVENTORY FOR CHILDREN (PIC), REVISED FORMAT
Robert D. Wirt, David Lachar, James E. Klinedinst, Philip D. Seat, and William E. Broen, Jr.

Child, adolescent
Ages 3-16

Purpose: Evaluates the personality attributes of children and adolescents. Used by professionals for counseling and identification of learning and social disabilities.

Description: 600-item paper-pencil true-false inventory in four parts completed by the child's parents and providing comprehensive profiles based on the model of the Minnesota Multiphasic Personality Inventory (MMPI). Part I (131 items) yields scores for the Lie Scale and four factor scales: Undisciplined/Poor Self-Control, Social Incompetence, Internalization/Somatic Symptoms, and Cognitive Development. Parts I-II (280 items) yield scores for the Lie Scale, the four factor scales, Development Scale, and shortened versions of the following 14 scales: Achievement, Intellectual Screening, Somatic Concern, Depression, Family Relations, Delinquency, Withdrawal, Anxiety, Psychosis, Hyperactivity, Social Skills, Frequency, Defensiveness, and Adjustment. Parts I-III (420 items) yield scores for the Lie Scale, 4 factor scales, and full-scale versions of the 16 profiled scales. Parts I-IV (600 items) provide scores on all the scales in Parts I-III as well as 17 experimental scales, which are not profiled. Norms and profiles are available for two age groups:

ages 3-5 and ages 6-16. The revised format allows administration of three short forms of the inventory. Examiner required. Not suitable for group use.

Untimed: Not available

Scoring: Hand key; may be computer scored

Cost: Complete kit $125.00; 10 booklets $12.50; 100 profile forms $12.10 (specify ages 3-5 or 6-16); 100 answer sheets $12.10; scoring templates $29.50

Publisher: Western Psychological Services

PERSONALITY RATING SCALE
Sister Mary Amatora

Child, adolescent
Grades K-12

Purpose: Assesses personality strengths and weaknesses of children. Identifies children needing further psychological evaluation.

Description: 22-item paper-pencil test of personality functioning. The items are characteristics of good and poor habits of interaction acquired in childhood and strengthened in early adolescence that affect personality development and the process of maturation. The rating scale may be completed by the child, teacher, or peers. The test may be used with students in Grades K-3 with the special instructions provided in manual. Self-administered. Suitable for group use.

Untimed: 30-40 minutes

Scoring: Hand key; examiner and student evaluated

Cost: Specimen set $1.50; complete kit (35 scales, 35 pupil rating sheets, 3 class record sheets, key, manual) $6.90; additional manuals $0.50 each

Publisher: Employers' Tests & Services Associates

PIERS-HARRIS CHILDREN'S SELF-CONCEPT SCALE (PHCSC)
Ellen V. Piers and Dale B. Harris

Child, adolescent
Grades 4-12

Purpose: Measures a child's self-concept. Identifies problem areas in a child's self-confidence. Used for research.

Description: 80-item paper-pencil test assessing six aspects of a child's self-esteem: behavior, intellectual and school status, physical appearance and attributes, anxiety, popularity, and happiness and satisfaction. Items are written at a third-grade reading level and require a simple "yes-no" answer. Percentile and stanine scores are provided for the total score and for each of the six subscales. Scores can be used for research purposes or to identify extreme problem areas. The manual provides the information necessary for administering and interpreting the scale, as well as the information included in Research Monograph #1 concerning use of the scale with minority and special education groups. Examiner/self-administered. Suitable for group use.

Untimed: 15-20 minutes

Scoring: Hand key; may be computer scored

Cost: Kit (25 test booklets, 25 profile forms, scoring key, 2 computer answer sheets, manual) $43.00

Publisher: Western Psychological Services

PLAY AND TELL CARDS: A THERAPEUTIC GAME
Robert Gordon

Child   Ages 6-12

Purpose: Allows children to verbalize thoughts and fears in a nonthreatening environment. Aids in building a therapeutic relationship by stimulating dialogue and establishing rapport between child and therapist.

Description: 80-item interview guide consisting of cards presenting topics to be discussed during a game of checkers. After each move in the game, the child selects a card and discusses it with the therapist. The cards ask questions about home, family, emotions, relationships, school, values, safety, health, discipline, thought processes, conflicts, and fears. The checkers and board are not provided. Examiner required. Suitable for group use.

Untimed: Not available

Scoring: Examiner evaluated

Cost: Complete set (cards, instructions) $13.00

Publisher: The Wilmington Press

Information and availability unconfirmed; no publisher response.

THE PRESCHOOL BEHAVIOR QUESTIONNAIRE
*Lenore B. Behar and
Samuel Stringfield*

Child   Ages 3-6

Purpose: Screens preschool children for symptoms indicating behavior problems. Used by child psychologists to determine individual need and placement.

Description: 30-item paper-pencil observational scale consisting of behavioral statements, which a teacher or parent rates "doesn't apply," "applies sometimes," or "certainly applies" for the child in question. Measures hostile-aggressive, anxious, and distractible behaviors. Materials include score sheet, answer sheet, and manual. Self-administered by a parent or teacher. Not suitable for group use.

Untimed: 10 minutes

Scoring: Examiner evaluated

Cost: Complete kit (50 score sheets and answer sheets, manual) $10.00

Publisher: Lenore Behar

PRESCHOOL SELF-CONCEPT PICTURE TEST (PS-CPT)
Refer to page 703.

PSYCHOLOGICAL EVALUATION OF CHILDREN'S HUMAN FIGURE DRAWINGS (HFD)
Elizabeth M. Koppitz

Child   Ages 5-12

Purpose: Assesses a child's mental maturity, personality characteristics, and family relationships. Used to screen school beginners, as part of a psychological test battery, and to measure progress.

Description: Multiple-item paper-pencil test in which the child draws "one whole person" and answers three questions. The drawing is scored and analyzed for developmental items, emotional indicators, and content. The factors measured include mental maturity, self-concept, attitudes (concerns, anxiety, conflict), and interpersonal relationships. Examiner required. Suitable for group use. Available in German, Spanish, and Japanese.

Untimed: 5-12 minutes

Scoring: Examiner evaluated

Cost: Manual $29.50; 100 scoring sheets $19.50

Publisher: Grune & Stratton, Inc.

ROBERTS APPERCEPTION TEST FOR CHILDREN
*Glen E. Roberts and
Dorothea S. McArthur*

Child, adolescent   Ages 6-15

Purpose: Identifies emotionally disturbed children. Used for clinical diagnosis, particularly with children just entering counseling or therapy.

Description: 16-item oral-response test in which the child is shown cards containing line illustrations and is asked to make up stories about each. The illustrations depict adults and children in up-to-date clothing and emphasize the everyday, interpersonal events of contemporary life, including (in addition to the standard situations of the TAT and CAT) such situations as parental disagreement, parental affection, observation of nudity, and school and peer interpersonal events. Stimuli are chosen to elicit psychologically meaningful responses. The clinical areas measured and reported on the Interpersonal Chart are conflict, anxiety, aggression, depression, rejection, punishment, dependency, support, closure, resolution, unresolved indicator, maladaptive outcome, and deviation response. Other measures include the Ego Functioning Index, the Aggression Index, and the Levels of Projection Scale. The manual includes a number of case studies and examples. Examiner required. Not suitable for group use.

Untimed: 20-30 minutes

Scoring: Examiner evaluated

Cost: Complete kit (set of test pictures, 25 record booklets, manual) $60.00
Publisher: Western Psychological Services

ROGERS PERSONAL ADJUSTMENT INVENTORY— UK REVISION
Patricia M. Jeffrey, based on original test by Carl Rogers

Child Ages 9-13

Purpose: Assesses the personal adjustment of problem children. Used to initiate treatment programs and personality assessment.

Description: Multiple-item paper-pencil inventory assessing significant aspects of a child's personality, including attitude toward the environment; adjustment to peers, family, and self; and the manner in which the child approaches problems. Many test items have been completely rewritten, anglicized, and updated. Separate test forms have been developed for boys and girls. Examiner required. Suitable for group use.
BRITISH PUBLISHER
Untimed: Varies
Scoring: Examiner evaluated
Cost: Manual £10.90; 10 booklets (specify boy or girl) £9.60; 3 marking keys £5.35
Publisher: NFER-NELSON Publishing Company Ltd.

SCHOOL APPERCEPTION METHOD (SAM)
Irving L. Solomon and Bernard D. Starr

Child, adolescent Grades K-9

Purpose: Assesses the emotional and cognitive frame of mind of children and adolescents. Used for clinical evaluations.

Description: 12-item oral-response projective test consisting of 12 drawings and 12 alternates focused on school situations. The scenes are designed to elicit school-oriented fantasies, feelings, attitudes, and perceptions. The manual is included. Examiner required. Suitable for group use.

Untimed: Not available
Scoring: Examiner evaluated
Cost: Complete kit (24 pictures plus manual) $22.50
Publisher: Springer Publishing Company
Information and availability unconfirmed; no publisher response.

SCHOOL CHILD STRESS SCALE (SCSS)
Justin Pikunas

Child, adolescent Grades 1-8

Purpose: Measures the intensity of stress present in normal to severely retarded children. Used to identify children who need special adjustment counseling.

Description: Multiple-item oral-response questionnaire examining a child's levels of efficiency and adjustment in dealing with the stress often encountered by the severely retarded and mentally deficient. The examiner reads through the two-page instrument, questions the child, and records the answers. Examiner required. Not suitable for group use.
Untimed: 20 minutes
Scoring: Examiner evaluated
Cost: Testing form (includes guidelines for interpretation) $2.00; 25 forms $6.00
Publisher: Justin Pikunas, Ph.D.

SELF-CONCEPT ADJECTIVE CHECKLIST
Alan J. Politte

Child Grades K-8

Purpose: Measures personality and self-concept. Used for diagnosis, screening, and measuring changes due to therapy.

Description: 114-item paper-pencil test of self-concept in which the items are traits categorized as physical traits, social values, intellectual abilities, and miscellaneous. Children in Grades K-3 check "I Am" or "I Am Not" for each item. Children in Grades 4-8 have the additional choice of an "I Would Like To Be" column. The items may be rated by the student or an observer. Examiner required. Suitable for group use.

Untimed: 10 minutes
Scoring: Hand key; examiner evaluated
Cost: Specimen set $4.50; 25 rating checklists $13.50
Publisher: Psychologists and Educators, Inc.

STRESS RESPONSE SCALE
Refer to page 681.

Personality: Normal and Abnormal, Assessment and Treatment: Adolescent and Adult

ACTIVITY COMPLETION TECHNIQUE (ACT)
Joseph Sacks

Adult

Purpose: Assesses personality characteristics of adults. Used by clinicians for planning treatment, monitoring progress, and conducting research.

Description: 60-item paper-pencil or computer-administered sentence completion test covering four areas: family, interpersonal, affect, and self-concept. This revised form of the Sacks Sentence Completion Test yields 15 categories of information, including relationship with mother, relationship with father, heterosexual relationships, relationships with authority figures, hostility, anxiety, adequacy, future, and fantasy. The test provides an adjustment rating scale and is used to evaluate general personality characteristics and positive personality tendencies, such as self-actualization and activity-passivity. Available in Apple II Plus, IIe computer versions. Examiner/self-administered. Suitable for group use.
Untimed: 30-40 minutes

Scoring: Examiner evaluated
Cost: Kit (manual, 25 test forms, 25 rating sheets) $24.95; computer version $75.00
Publisher: Psychological Assessment Resources, Inc.

ACUTALIZING ASSESSMENT BATTERY (AAB)
Everett L. Shostrom

Adult

Purpose: Measures an individual's sense of actualization with himself and within his relationships with others. Used by therapists, marriage and family counselors, personnel administrators, and school psychologists for a wide variety of counseling situations.

Description: Four paper-pencil tests measuring 13 dimensions of a person's sense of actualization: being, weakness, synergistic integration, time orientation, core centeredness, love, trust in humanity, creative living, mission, strength, manipulation awareness, anger, and potentiation. The Personal Orientations Dimensions (POD) and the Personal Orientation Inventory (POI) primarily measure intrapersonal actualizing, and the Caring Relationship Inventory (CRI) and the Pair Attraction Inventory (PAI) primarily measure interpersonal actualizing. The AAB may be scored locally by using the POI, CRI, and PAI or may be sent to EdITS for scoring. Results are reported through the AAB Interpretation Brochure, a 6-page booklet containing descriptions and profiles for each of the four tests. Examiner required. Suitable for group use.
Untimed: Not available
Scoring: Hand key; may be computer scored
Cost: Contact publisher
Publisher: Educational and Industrial Testing Service

THE ADJECTIVE CHECK LIST (ACL)
*Harrison G. Gough and
Alfred Heilbrun, Jr.*

**Adolescent, adult
Grades 9 and above**

Purpose: Describes self and relations with others; used for personality assessment and research.

Description: 300-item paper-pencil test of up to 37 dimensions of personality, including four Method of Response scales, 15 Need scales, nine Topical scales, five Transactional scales, and four Origence-Intellectence scales. Items are adjectives that are checked if they apply to self, but they may be answered with reference to others. Scores need not be obtained on all 37 scales. Hand scoring requires users to prepare their own stencils. Self-administered. Suitable for group use.

Untimed: 15-20 minutes

Scoring: Hand key; computer scoring available

Cost: Manual $12.00; 25 check lists (hand scored) $5.25; 25 profiles $3.50

Publisher: Consulting Psychologists Press, Inc.

THE ADJUSTMENT INVENTORY: ADULT FORM
Hugh M. Bell

Adult

Purpose: Measures the personal and social adjustment of adults.

Description: Multiple-item paper-pencil self-report inventory assessing five areas of personal adjustment: home, health, social, emotional, and occupational. Items may be answered on the test booklet or on a separate answer sheet. Examiners must prepare their own scoring stencils for the answer sheets. Self-administered. Suitable for group use.

Untimed: 25 minutes

Scoring: Hand key

Cost: Manual and stencil for scoring test booklet $2.00; 25 test booklets $5.25; 50 answer sheets $5.25

Publisher: Consulting Psychologists Press, Inc.

THE ADJUSTMENT INVENTORY: STUDENT FORM
Refer to page 696.

ADOLESCENT ALIENATION INDEX (AAI)
F.K. Heussenstamm

Adolescent   Ages 12-19

Purpose: Identifies emergent or developing alienation in adolescents. Provides a measure of incipient estrangement that may give clues to personality disjunctures long before behavioral symptoms are evident.

Description: 41-item paper-pencil test in which students choose between two self-descriptive statements for each test item. The test covers facets of youthful alienation such as normlessness, meaninglessness, powerlessness, self-estrangement, and social isolation. Form A offers separate answer sheets for ease of test-taking and scoring. Form C offers consumable test forms designed for students with less sophisticated test-taking skills. Norms are based on suburban white, urban black, and rural Mexican-American high-school students and on black Job Corps enrollees. Self-administered. Suitable for group use.

Timed: 20 minutes

Scoring: Hand key

Cost: 35 forms (specify form) $10.00; 35 answer sheets (Form A) $4.00; scoring stencil (Form A) $3.00; scoring guide (Form C) $3.00; manual $4.00

Publisher: Monitor

ADOLESCENT DIAGNOSTIC SCREENING BATTERY
James J. Smith and Joseph M. Eisenberg

Adolescent   Ages 13-17

Purpose: Identifies diagnostic possibilities among those listed in DSM-III. Used with adolescents in clinical settings.

Description: Paper-pencil or computer-administered screening battery assessing symptoms important for diagnostic considerations. The system consists of a questionnaire for the adolescent and a questionnaire for the clinician. The adolescent's parent or guardian may provide independent information through the use

---

of the Child Diagnostic Screening Battery. The system is structured so that once data is entered in the computer, it is compared with all possible DSM-III diagnoses. A manual describing the use and application of the program and the use of printouts generated by the program is provided. Examiner required. Not suitable for group use.

Untimed: 15 minutes

Scoring: Hand key; may be computer scored

Cost: Total system $195.00; 10-day trial of system $15.00

Publisher: Reason House

ADOLESCENT EMOTIONAL FACTORS INVENTORY
Mary K. Bauman

Adolescent

Purpose: Measures emotional and personality factors of visually handicapped adolescents.

Description: 150-item paper-pencil or oral response questionnaire assessing the personal and emotional adjustment of visually handicapped adolescents. The inventory yields scores on the following nine scales: sensitivity, somatic symptoms, social competency, attitudes of distrust, family adjustment, boy-girl adjustment, school adjustment, morale, and attitudes concerning blindness. A validation score is also provided. The questionnaire is presented in large-print format. Instructions for tape recording the questions are included. Supplementary materials provided in the test kit include a discussion of the inventory and a discussion of personality assessment for blind adolescents. This test is an adolescent form of the Emotional Factors Inventory. Examiner required. The paper-pencil version is suitable for group use.

Untimed: Varies

Scoring: Examiner evaluated

Cost: Test kit (test booklet, scoring overlays, 10 IBM answer sheets, supplementary materials, and norms) $15.00

Publisher: Associated Services for the Blind

ADOLESCENT MULTIPHASIC PERSONALITY INVENTORY (AMPI)
Bruce Duthie

Adolescent   Ages 12-19

Purpose: Assesses personality characteristics in adolescents. Used for clinical evaluation in applied settings.

Description: 133-item paper-pencil true-false test of adolescent personality functioning. The AMPI has three validity scales (lie, fake, and defensiveness) and 10 clinical scales (hypochondriasis, depression, hysteria, psychopathic deviance, feminism, paranoia, psychasthenia, schizophrenia, mania, and social introversion). With the exception of the feminism scale, AMPI scales generally parallel their MMPI counterparts. A fourth-grade reading level is required. Examiner/self-administered. Suitable for group use.

Untimed: Varies

Scoring: Hand key; may be computer scored with IBM-PC compatible software

Cost: Start-up kit (manual, answer keys, 50 test booklets, 50 profile sheets, 2 computer interpretation coupons) $45.00

Publisher: Pacific Psychological

ADOLESCENT-COPING ORIENTATION FOR PROBLEM EXPERIENCES (A-COPE)
Joan M. Patterson,
Hamilton I. McCubbin,
and Richard H. Needle

Adolescent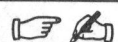

Purpose: Identifies behaviors adolescents find helpful in managing problems or difficult situations that happen to them or members of their families. Used in counseling, clinical, and research settings.

Description: 54-item self-report instrument covering behaviors for coping with problems. Items are grouped conceptually into seven behavioral patterns: developing and maintaining a sense of competence and self-esteem, investing in family relationships and fitting into the family lifestyle, investing in extra-familial relationships and seeking social support, developing positive perceptions about life situations, relieving tension through diversions, relieving tension through substance use and/or expression of anger, and avoiding confrontation and withdrawing. Examiner required. Suitable for group use.

Untimed: Varies

Scoring: Examiner evaluated

Cost: Manual $15.00 ($10.00 for students); assessment form $0.10

Publisher: Family Stress, Coping and Health Project

ADULT DIAGNOSTIC SCREENING BATTERY
James J. Smith and Joseph M. Eisenberg

Adult   Ages 18 and older

Purpose: Identifies diagnostic possibilities among those listed in DSM-III. Used with adults in clinical settings.

Description: Paper-pencil or computer-administered screening battery assessing symptoms important for diagnostic considerations. The system consists of two parts: a questionnaire for the patient and a questionnaire for the clinician. The structured interview is completed by the patient directly or by someone who has direct and sufficient knowledge of the individual referred for services. The system is structured so that once data is entered in the computer, it is compared with all possible diagnosis. A manual describing the use and application of the program and the use of the printouts generated by the program is provided. Examiner required. Not suitable for group use.

Untimed: 15 minutes

Scoring: Hand key; may be computer scored

Cost: Total system $195.00; 10-day trial of system $15.00

Publisher: Reason House

ADULT PERSONAL ADJUSTMENT AND ROLE SKILLS (PARS)
Robert E. Ellsworth

Adult

Purpose: Measures adults' adjustment to life and to the community. Used for evaluation of treatment programs.

Description: 31-item paper-pencil observational rating scale assessing eight dimensions of adult personal adjustment and role skills: close relations, alienation-depression, anxiety, confusion, alcohol/drug use, house activity, child relations, and employment. The scale is completed by a spouse, parent, or person close to the subject. The manual explains the rationale and validity of the scale and provides detailed norms for the general and clinical population with respect to adjustment to life and the community. Examiner required. Suitable for group use.

Untimed: 20-30 minutes

Scoring: Examiner evaluated

Cost: Manual $5.00; 25 scales and profile sheets $4.75

Publisher: Consulting Psychologists Press, Inc.

ADULT PERSONALITY INVENTORY
Samuel E. Krug

Adult

Purpose: Evaluates individual personality characteristics, interpersonal relations, and life-style. Used by professionals in industry, public service, health care, and education.

Description: Multiple-item paper-pencil inventory assessing personality characteristics in terms of the 16 Personality Factor psychometric profile. While maintaining continuity with the personality model underlying the 16 PF, the questionnaire itself has been redesigned using a systems development approach. Items have been shortened in order to increase the number of items on the inventory (for increased reliability) and the required reading level has been lowered to the fourth-grade level. The computer scoring service provides a nine-page verbal and graphic report examining significant individual characteristics, interpersonal relations, and life-style. Examiner required. Suitable for group use.

Untimed: Varies

Scoring: Computer scored

Cost: Contact publisher

Publisher: Institute for Personality and Ability Testing, Inc.

AFFECT SCALE
Ricardo Girona

Adolescent, adult
Ages 16 and older

Purpose: Assesses adult adjustment and self-concept. Used for educational and clinical screening and to evaluate psychotherapy progress.

Description: Multiple-item paper-pencil test using 18 pair-choices of adjectives or dimensions, each with a 7-scale intensity rating, to measure individual perception of self and others. Materials include scoreable booklets and scoring keys. Self-administered. Suitable for group use.

Untimed: 15 minutes

Scoring: Hand key; examiner evaluated

Cost: Scale $0.30

Publisher: Dr. Ricardo Girona

Information and availability unconfirmed; no publisher response.

AFFECTS BALANCE SCALE (ABS)
Leonard R. Derogatis

Adult

Purpose: Evaluates psychological adjustment and well-being in terms of mood and affect balance.

Description: 40-item paper-pencil self-report adjective mood scale assessing four positive affect dimensions (joy, contentment, vigor, and affection) and four negative affect dimensions (anxiety, depression, guilt, and hostility). Scoring and interpretation procedures are structured on the concept that healthy psychological adjustment is based on the presence of active positive emotions and

the relative absence of negative emotions. The overall score of the test is expressed as the affect balance index, reflecting the balance between positive and negative affects in terms of standardized scores. Examiner required. Suitable for group use.

Untimed: 3-5 minutes

Scoring: Examiner evaluated

Cost: 100 test forms $28.00; 100 profile sheets $20.00

Publisher: Clinical Psychometric Research

ALCADD TEST
Morse P. Manson

Adult

Purpose: Measures extent of alcohol addiction. Used for diagnosis, therapy, and research.

Description: Paper-pencil inventory measuring the extent of an individual's alcohol addiction by measuring areas of maladjustment. The test is not an instrument for detecting alcoholics. Examiner required. Suitable for group use.

Untimed: 5-10 minutes

Scoring: Hand key

Cost: Complete kit (20 tests, manual, key) $18.00

Publisher: Western Psychological Services

ANIMA INKBLOT SERIES
Wilfred A. Cassell

Adolescent, adult

Purpose: Assesses feminine consciousness in females and feminine characteristics in males. Used with adolescents and adults.

Description: 40-card test created by female artists for evaluating conscious-unconscious aspects of feminine psychology. The cards range from those with little structure regarding external visual reality to those with specific, interpersonal connotations. Wilfred Cassell's book, *Body Symbolism*, is included with the series. Examiner required. Not suitable for group use.

Untimed: 90 minutes

Scoring: Examiner evaluated; scoring service available

Cost: Cards, scoring sheets, *Body Symbolism* $95.00

Publisher: Aurora Publishing

ANIMA VIDEO SERIES
Wilfred A. Cassell

Adolescent, adult

Purpose: Assesses feminine consciousness in females and feminine mental characteristics in males.

Description: 40-item inkblot test presented in a video format entitled "Living Images" for evaluating conscious-unconscious aspects of feminine psychology. The test incorporates the Anima Inkblot Series, adding movement and a soundtrack developed by a female musician. A semihypnotic state of consciousness is created in which the viewer can respond without the potential contaminating effect of an examiner's presence. Scoring should be done by examiners experienced in projective techniques, hypnotherapy, and dream analysis. The tape includes two examples of how to respond and standard instructions. The tapes are available in a VHS and Beta video cassette format. A 16mm film version is available for teaching purposes. Examiner/self-administered. Not suitable for group use.

Untimed: 1 hour

Scoring: Examiner evaluated

Cost: Tape (state ½" or ¾" tape size) $95.00

Publisher: Aurora Publishing

ANXIETY SCALE FOR THE BLIND
Richard E. Hardy

Adolescent, adult
Ages 13 and older

Purpose: Measures manifest anxiety among blind and partially sighted people. Used for clinical evaluations by psychologists, psychiatrists, and trained counselors.

Description: 78-item true-false test measuring the level of anxiety present in blind and partially sighted children and recently modified adults. The subject is given a roll of tickets to be placed to the right or left of the table to indicate true or false as the items are read. Originally developed for use in residential schools with students of high-school age, the test may be used in other contexts as well. The test is still experimental in nature and must be used only by psychologists, psychiatrists, and other qualified counselors. Examiner required. Not suitable for group use.

Untimed: Not available

Scoring: Examiner evaluated

Cost: Scale $4.00

Publisher: American Foundation for the Blind

Information and availability unconfirmed; no publisher response.

ASSESSMENT OF SUICIDE POTENTIAL (RESEARCH EDITION)
Robert Yufit and Bonnie Benzies

Adolescent, adult
Ages 16-81

Purpose: Evaluates an individual's feelings about the past, present, and future. Used for the exploration and quantitative assessment of suicide potential.

Description: Multiple-item four-page paper-pencil or oral semi-projective measure of feelings about the present, future, and past. The TQ is composed of three types of items: multiple-choice, open-ended, and rating scales. The questionnaire provides an index of time perspective found to be related to suicide potential. Examiner required. Not suitable for group use.

Untimed: 15 minutes

Scoring: Examiner evaluated

Cost: Specimen set $4.25; manual $4.00; 25 expendable questionnaires $6.50

Publisher: Consulting Psychologists Press, Inc.

ASSOCIATION ADJUSTMENT INVENTORY (AAI)
Martin M. Bruce

Adult

Purpose: Evaluates the extent to which the subject is maladjusted, immature, and deviant in ideation; used as an aid to predicting potential deviant behavior.

Description: 100-item test in which the subject selects one of four words to use with a stimulus word, allowing the examiner to screen for ideational deviation, general psychosis, depression, hysteria, withdrawal, paranoia, rigidity, schizophrenia, impulsiveness, sociopathy, psychosomapathia, and anxiety. The answers are compared to "norms" to measure significant deviation. Available in Spanish and German. Examiner/self-administered. Suitable for group use.

Untimed: 10 minutes

Scoring: Hand key

Cost: Package of tests with IBM answer sheets $27.25; package of tests with hand key $27.25; manual $7.50; package of profile sheets $11.50

Publisher: Martin M. Bruce, Ph.D., Publishers

BECK DEPRESSION AND HOPELESSNESS SCALE
Aaron T. Beck, M.D.

Adult

Purpose: Assesses level of depression and the possibility of suicide. Used for clinical assessment and diagnosis.

Description: Multiple-item computer-administered instrument consisting of two scales: the Beck Depression Scale and the Beck Hopelessness Scale. The Beck Depression Scale measures the level of severity of dysphoric mood and assesses the current state of the individual's mood. The Beck Hopelessness Scale, when used in conjunction with the depression scale, indicates the level of depression and the possibility of suicide. The Beck Hopelessness Scale was developed on a large sample of patients who had attempted suicide. The program administers and scores the two scales and provides an interpretive printout of the test. The program may be used only on PsychSystems-supplied hardware, available in various configurations starting with single-users systems at approximately $25,000. A per-test fee (based on hardware configuration) also applies. Examiner required. Suitable for group use.

Untimed: Varies

Scoring: Computer scored

Cost: Contact publisher

Publisher: Center for Cognitive Therapy

BECK DEPRESSION INVENTORY
Aaron T. Beck

Adult

Purpose: Measures an individual's level of depression. Used for treatment planning and evaluation in mental health settings.

Description: 21-item inventory assessing the severity of an individual's complaints, symptoms, and concerns related to his current level of depression. The symptoms assessed are sadness, pessimism, sense of failure, dissatisfaction, feelings of guilt, expectation of punishment, self-dislike, self-accusations, suicidal ideas, crying, irritability, social withdrawal, indecisiveness, change in body image, work difficulty, insomnia, loss of appetite, weight loss, somatic preoccupation, fatigability, and loss of libido. A microcomputer printout indicates the severity of the depressed mood, lists major symptom complaints, and shows a table of responses. Questions are presented on an eighth-grade reading level. The test may be administered only on a psychometer. Self-administered. Not suitable for group use.

Untimed: 15-20 minutes

Scoring: Microcomputer scored

Cost: Contact publisher

Publisher: Center for Cognitive Therapy

BEHAVIOR STATUS INVENTORY (BSI)
William T. Martin

Adolescent, adult

Purpose: Measures behavioral traits of adults and adolescents in mental health settings. Used to evaluate emotionally disturbed, brain-damaged, and mentally retarded patients. Used to monitor patient progress in response to therapy.

Description: 91-item observational inventory assessing seven behavioral areas: personal appearance, manifest (obvious) behavior, attitude, verbal behavior, social behavior, work behavior, and cognitive behavior. An aide or staff member familiar with the individual can complete the questionnaire, rating each of the behavioral statements from 1 to 4 as it applies to the patient based upon observed behavior during the past week. Scores for each of the seven subscales and a Total Patient Asset Score are derived. Item analysis and subscale scores can be machine scored for one-time or ongoing patient and/or program analysis. Examiner required. Suitable for group use.

Untimed: No time limit

Scoring: Examiner evaluated

Cost: Specimen set $4.50; 25 forms $13.50; 25 profile sheets $6.00

Publisher: Psychologists and Educators, Inc.

BEM SEX-ROLE INVENTORY (BSRI)
Refer to page 218.

BERNREUTER PERSONALITY INVENTORY

Adolescent, adult

Purpose: Evaluates the normal adolescent and adult personality.

Description: Multiple-item paper-pencil inventory assessing the following six personality traits: neurotic tendency, self-sufficiency, introversion-extroversion, dominance-submission, self-confidence, and sociability. The nature of the traits measured are not readily detectable by the person taking the test. All required instructions are printed in the test booklet. Norms are provided for high-school and college students and adults of both sexes. Self-administered. Suitable for group use.

Untimed: Varies

Scoring: Hand key

Cost: Test kit (50 test booklets, hand-scoring stencils, manual) $33.00

Publisher: Stoelting Company

THE BIPOLAR PSYCHOLOGICAL INVENTORY (BPI)

Adult

Purpose: Measures psychological adjustment. Used for clinical evaluation and diagnosis, personnel screening, and police officer selection.

Description: Multiple-item paper-pencil or computer-administered self-report inventory assessing affect and behavior along 15 bipolar dimensions: honest/lie, open/defensive, psychic comfort/psychic pain, optimism/depression, self-esteem/self-degradation, self-sufficiency/dependence, achieving/unmotivated, gregariousness/social withdrawal, family harmony/family discord, sexual maturity/sexual immaturity, social conformity/social deviancy, self-control/impulsiveness, kindness/hostility, empathy/insensitivity, and valid/invalid. A narrative computer printout includes separate male/female formats, raw scores and percentile scores, a personal adjustment profile, a printout of answers to all questions, and a printout of significant (problem) items. The computer program is sold on disk (with backup disk and instructions) for use with Apple II computers with 48K, one disk drive, and printer (optical reader optional). Normative data are available for normal populations. Examiner required. Paper-pencil version suitable for group use.

Untimed: Varies

Scoring: Examiner evaluated; may be computer scored

Cost: Clinical sample kit (manual, test booklet, 5 answer sheets, set of scoring keys, profiles, scale items booklet, reliability-validity booklet) $20.00; computer program $250.00

Publisher: Diagnostic Specialists, Inc.

Information and availability unconfirmed; no publisher response.

THE BLACK INTELLIGENCE TEST OF CULTURAL HOMOGENEITY (BITCH)
Robert L. Williams

Adolescent, adult
Ages 16 and older

Purpose: Measures white Americans' sensitivity to the black experience and black Americans' identification with the black experience. Used in racial relations seminars or interracial workshops.

Description: 41-item paper-pencil multiple-choice test providing a culture-specific measure of racial attitudes. Two forms are available. Self-administered. Suitable for group use.

Untimed: 20 minutes

Scoring: Hand key

Cost: Complete set (20 tests, directions, key) $22.00; manual $3.75

Publisher: Robert L. Williams & Associates, Inc.

BLOOM SENTENCE COMPLETION ATTITUDE SURVEY
Wallace Bloom

Adolescent, adult

Purpose: Assesses adult and student attitudes toward self and important factors in everyday living. Used to identify change in an individual over time and to compare individuals and groups.

Description: 40-item paper-pencil free-response test consisting of sentence stems which the subject completes in his own words. The responses measure attitudes toward age mates or people, physical self, family, psychological self, self-directedness, education or work (depending on which version is used), accomplishment, and irritants. Two versions are available: one for adults and one for unmarried students. The scoring system facilitates use of the test as both an objective and a projective instrument. Examiner required. Suitable for group use.

Untimed: 25 minutes

Scoring: Examiner evaluated

Cost: Complete kit, specify version (30 test forms, 30 analysis record forms, manual) $25.50 each

Publisher: Stoelting Company

BRIEF SYMPTOM INVENTORY (BSI)
Leonard R. Derogatis

Adolescent, adult

Purpose: Evaluates psychological symptomatic distress. Used with medical and psychiatric patients and adult and adolescent nonpatients.

Description: 53-item paper-pencil self-report inventory assessing symptomatic distress in terms of nine symptom dimensions (somatization, obsessive-compulsive, interpersonal sensitivity, depression, anxiety, hostility, phobic anxiety, paranoid ideation, and psychoticism) and three global indices of distress (global severity index, positive symptom index, and positive symptom total). Score/profile forms and published norms are available by sex for four populations: nonpatient adult, nonpatient adolescent, outpatient psychiatric, and inpatient psychiatric. This inventory is a brief form of the SCL-90-R and may be used in conjunction with the matching observer's scales in the Psychopathology Rating Scales Series (the SCL-90-R Analogue and the Hopkins Psychiatric Rating Scale). Examiner required. Suitable for group use.

Untimed: 10-12 minutes

Scoring: Examiner evaluated

Cost: Manual $16.00; 100 test forms $28.00; 100 score/profile forms $22.00

Publisher: Clinical Psychometric Research

BULIMIA TEST (BULIT)
Marcia C. Smith and Mark H. Thelen

Adolescent, adult

Purpose: Assesses bulimia symptoms in adolescents and adults. Used as a screening device to identify individuals suffering from or at risk for bulimia, in clinical settings to aid in prevention and treatment, and in research.

Description: 36-item self-report forced-choice test consisting of five factors related to binges, feelings, vomiting, food, and weight and two factors related to laxative/diuretic abuse and regularity of menstrual cycles. Items are scored on a 5-point scale (5 = extreme bulimic direction; 1 = extreme normal direction). Examiner required. Suitable for group use.

Untimed: Varies

Scoring: Examiner evaluated

Cost: Contact publisher

Publisher: Mark H. Thelen, Ph.D.

CALIFORNIA BRIEF LIFE HISTORY INVENTORY (CBLHI)
Donald I. Templer and
David M. Veleber

Ages 12-adult

Purpose: Summarizes the life history of individuals ages 12 and older. Used for diagnosis and treatment planning.

Description: Multiple-item paper-pencil inventory in student and adult forms summarizing a client's background and present circumstances, medical/psychological history, family life, work or school, and substance abuse. Clients complete the inventory prior to the initial interview. Clinicians use the information for identifying problem areas and developing treatment plans. Self-administered. Suitable for group use.

Untimed: Varies

Scoring: Examiner evaluated

Cost: 25 student forms $7.00; 25 adult forms $7.00

Publisher: United Educational Services, Inc.

CALIFORNIA PSYCHOLOGICAL INVENTORY (CPI)
Harrison G. Gough

Adolescent, adult

Purpose: Assesses normal adult personality as an aid to educational, clinical, counseling, and vocational guidance.

Description: 480-item paper-pencil test of 18 socially desirable behavioral tendencies: dominance, capacity for status,

sociability, social presence, self-acceptance, sense of well-being, responsibility, socialization, self-control, tolerance, good impression, communality, achievement via conformance, achievement via independence, intellectual efficiency, psychological-mindedness, flexibility, and femininity. Assists counselors of non-psychiatrically disturbed clients by measuring personality characteristics important for social living and social interaction. Self-administered. Suitable for group use. Available in Spanish, Italian, and German.

Untimed: 45-60 minutes

Scoring: Hand key

Cost: Counselor's kit (includes 5 reusable tests, 25 answer sheets, 25 profiles, set of stencils, manual) $25.00

Publisher: Consulting Psychologists Press, Inc.

CALIFORNIA Q-SORT DECK
Jack Block; adapted by Daryl Bem

Adult

Purpose: Describes individual personality in contemporary psychodynamic terms. Used for research.

Description: 100-item test used to formulate personality descriptions. Items are descriptive personality statements on cards sorted from most to least applicable to the subject's experience. Materials include individual 2¼" x 3½" cards and a sorting guide. May be sorted by professionals or laymen. Examiner required. Not suitable for group use.

Untimed: Not available

Scoring: Examiner evaluated

Cost: Q-Sort Deck $4.75; guide and 50 recording pads $6.00

Publisher: Consulting Psychologists Press, Inc.

CARLSON PSYCHOLOGICAL SURVEY (CPS)
Kenneth A. Carlson

Adolescent, adult

Purpose: Assesses and classifies criminal offenders. Used to evaluate persons presenting behavioral or substance-abuse

---

problems and analyze the effects of intervention programs.

Description: 50-item paper-pencil questionnaire in a five-category response format with space for the respondent's comments. The scales measured are Chemical Abuse, Thought Disturbance, Antisocial Tendencies, Self-Depreciation, and Validity. The test is designed for offenders, those charged with crimes, and others who have come to the attention of the criminal justice or social welfare systems. The results are classified into 18 offender types. A fourth-grade reading level is required. Use is restricted to APA registered psychologists. Examiner required. Suitable for group use.

Untimed: 15 minutes

Scoring: Hand key

Cost: Complete set $15.00

Publisher: Research Psychologists Press, Inc.

CENTER FOR EPIDEMIOLOGIC STUDIES—DEPRESSION SCALE (CES-D)

Adult

Purpose: Measures symptoms associated with depression in adults. Used to identify high-risk groups for research and screening.

Description: 20-item paper-pencil test in which the subject is asked to rank his experiences and feelings for the past week on a 3-point scale ranging from "less than once a day" (0) to "most or all of the time" (3). Questions deal with symptoms of depressed mood, lack of energy, insomnia, and appetite loss. The scale may be read to a subject by an examiner or completed in privacy by the client. Scales are weighted for scoring and interpretation. Self-administered. Suitable for group use. Available in Spanish.

Untimed: 5 minutes

Scoring: Hand key

Cost: Contact publisher

Publisher: Epidemiology and Psychopathology Branch, NIMH

CHARACTER ASSESSMENT SCALE
Paul F. Schmidt

Adolescent, adult

Purpose: Assesses a person's moral strengths and weaknesses. Allows individuals to explore their moral character. Used in pastoral counseling and clinical psychology.

Description: 225-item paper-pencil test that measures a series of eight moral character strengths and weaknesses. The moral character strengths examined are humility, compassion, peacemaking, resourcefulness, enthusiasm, sexual integrity, and physical fitness and honesty. Weaknesses include pride, envy, resentment, greed, laziness, lust, gluttony, and denial. The subject reads each item and marks the answer true or false. Self-administered. Suitable for group use.

Untimed: 45 minutes

Scoring: Hand key: examiner evaluated; scoring service available

Cost: Test package $12.00; answer sheets $5.00; scoring service $5.00; manual $8.00

Publisher: Institute for Character Development

CHILD ABUSE POTENTIAL INVENTORY
Joel Milner

Adult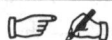

Purpose: Screens for physical child abuse potential in adults. Designed for use in social service, mental health, and research settings.

Description: 160-item paper-pencil forced-choice test of child abuse potential. In addition to the full CAP abuse scale, six descriptive factors are scored: distress, rigidity, unhappiness, problems with child and self, problems with family, and problems from others. Three validity scales are available and combine to make three response distortion indexes: faking good, faking bad, and random response.

A third-grade reading level is required. Examiner/self-administered. Suitable for group use.

Untimed: 12-20 minutes

Scoring: Hand key; may be computer scored

Cost: Contact publisher

Publisher: Psytec, Inc.

CLAYBURY SELECTION BATTERY
T.M. Caine, O.B. Wijesinghe, D. Winter, and D. Small

Adult

Purpose: Directs individuals toward psychological or psychiatric treatment that matches their personal styles. Examines the consistency between attitudes and work environment in the selection of therapists. Used also in vocational guidance settings.

Description: Three multiple-item paper-pencil questionnaires assessing personal interests, expectancies regarding treatment, and attitudes toward treatment. The Direction of Interest Questionnaire is a 14-item forced-choice inventory that distinguishes between two sets of interests: 1) ideas, imagination, theory, philosophy, unconventionality, and emotional problems and 2) facts, practical problems, biochemistry, common sense, engineering, domestic science, personal ambition, pain, and action. This questionnaire particularly is useful in vocational guidance. The Treatment Expectancies Questionnaire is a 15-item factor-analytically devised scale measuring an individual's expectancies regarding psychiatric or psychological treatment. The Attitudes to Treatment Questionnaire is a 19-item factor-analytically devised scale measuring staff attitudes toward psychological and psychiatric treatment and differentiates between psychological and organic approaches to patient care. The manual is based on *Personal Styles in Neurosis* by T.M. Caine, O.B. Wijesinghe, and D. Winter (Routledge and Kegan Paul, 1981) and provides a number of applications and a full account of the research basis of the questionnaires. Self-administered. Suitable for group use.
BRITISH PUBLISHER

Untimed: Varies

Scoring: Examiner evaluated

Cost: Manual £7.55; 50 Direction of Interest Questionnaires £5.65; 50 Attitudes Treatment Questionnaires £5.65; 50 Treatment Expectancies Questionnaires £5.65; 3 answer keys £5.65

Publisher: NFER-NELSON Publishing Company Ltd.

CLIFTON ASSESSMENT PROCEDURES FOR THE ELDERLY (CAPE)
A.H. Pattie and C.J. Gilleard

Elderly adults

Purpose: Assesses level of dependency in the elderly. Used by general practitioners, community nurses, health visitors, occupational therapists, social workers, and hospital personnel.

Description: Two multiple-item paper-pencil rating scales assessing cognitive and behavioral competence in the elderly. The Cognitive Assessment Scale is a short psychological test comprised of three sections: information/orientation, mental ability, and psychomotor. The psychomotor section utilizes the Gibson Spiral Maze. The Behavioral Rating Scale consists of 18 items measuring physical disability, apathy, communication difficulties, and social disturbance. The scoring procedure relates the level of cognitive and behavioral dependency to likely need for community or hospital care. Examiner required. Not suitable for group use.

Untimed: Varies

Scoring: Examiner evaluated

Cost: Contact publisher

Publisher: Hodder and Stoughton Educational; distributed in U.S.A. by The Psychological Corporation

---

CLINICAL ANALYSIS QUESTIONNAIRE
Raymond B. Cattell and IPAT Staff

Adolescent, adult
Ages 16 and older

Purpose: Evaluates personality and psychiatric/psychological difficulties. Used as a measure of primary behavioral dimensions in adults and adolescents. Used for clinical diagnosis, evaluation of therapeutic progress, and vocational and rehabilitation guidance.

Description: 272-item paper-pencil multiple-choice test measuring 16 personality factors (the 16PF factors) as well as hypochondriasis, agitated depression, suicidal depression, anxious depression, guilt, energy level, boredom, and five other dimensions in the pathology domain. Norms are provided for adults and college men and women. Special adolescent norms are provided for Part II. The manual contains profiles for a number of special groups, including alcoholics, narcotic addicts, various types of neurotic and psychotic disorders, criminals, and others. The test has been organized in two parts so that the entire test need not be given in a single sitting. A sixth-grade reading level is required. Self-administered. Suitable for group use.

Untimed: 2 hours

Scoring: Hand key; may be computer scored

Cost: 50 hand-scorable answer sheets $7.50; manual $11.90; scoring keys $8.50; computer profile and interpretation $10.00-$16.00; 25 reusable test booklets $19.50; for teleprocessing and computer software contact publisher

Publisher: Institute for Personality and Ability Testing, Inc.

CLINICAL CHECKLIST SERIES

Adolescent, adult

Purpose: Assesses personal, marital, and health problems. Used for initiating the consultation process and introducing the client to formal diagnostic testing.

Description: Multiple-item paper-pencil or computer-administered series of five checklists used, as appropriate, with adolescents and adults to identify relevant problems, establish rapport, and provide written documentation of presenting problems consistent with community standards of care. Checklists include Personal Problems Checklist—Adult, Personal Problems Checklist—Adolescent, Children's Problems Checklist, Marital Evaluation Checklist, and Health

Problems Checklist. Items are presented in terms understood by adolescents and adults from most educational and occupational levels. The checklists are available in computer versions for use with Apple II Plus, Apple IIe, and IBM PC computers. Self-administered. Suitable for group use.

Untimed: 10-20 minutes

Scoring: Examiner evaluated

Cost: 50 checklists $12.95; computer version (100 uses) $50.00

Publisher: Psychological Assessment Resources, Inc.

COMPREHENSIVE DRINKER PROFILE (CDP)
G. Alan Marlatt and William R. Miller

Adult

Purpose: Assesses alcoholism in men and women. Used for intake-screening in alcohol abuse treatment programs. Provides a basis for selecting, planning, and implementing individualized treatment programs.

Description: Multiple-item paper-pencil structured interview guide assessing an individual's history and current status regarding the use and abuse of alcohol. The profile measures items in the following areas: basic demographics, family and employment status, history of problem development, current drinking pattern and problem status, severity of dependence, social aspects of alcohol use, associated behaviors, relevant medical history, motivations for drinking and seeking treatment, and problem areas other than drinking. The Michigan Alcoholism Screening Test, which provides a survey of current drinking problems and summary score of problem severity, is part of the profile. The profile also yields scores on problem duration, family history of alcoholism, alcohol consumption, alcohol dependence, range of drinking situations, quantity and frequency of other drug use, emotional factors related to drinking, and life problems other than drinking. The profile is used by professionals and paraprofessionals, including physicians, psychologists, psychiatrists, social workers, nurses, and alcohol abuse counselors. Examiner required. Not suitable for group use.

Untimed: 1-2 hours

Scoring: Examiner evaluated

Cost: Interview kit (manual, 25 interview forms, 8 reusable card sets) $39.95

Publisher: Psychological Assessment Resources, Inc.

COMPREHENSIVE PERSONAL ASSESSMENT SYSTEM: ADJECTIVE SELF-DESCRIPTION (ASD)
Donald J. Veldman and George V.C. Parker

Adolescent, adult

Purpose: Evaluates an individual's assessment of his own personality traits.

Description: 56-item paper-pencil multiple-choice test of self-evaluated personality characteristics. The test measures seven factor-analytic derived traits. Self-administered. Suitable for group use.

Untimed: 15 minutes

Scoring: Hand key; may be computer scored

Cost: 100 forms $1.30; manual $2.25

Publisher: Research and Development Center for Teacher Education

COMPREHENSIVE PERSONAL ASSESSMENT SYSTEM: DIRECTED IMAGINATION (DI)
Donald J. Veldman and S.L. Menaker

Adolescent, adult
College student

Purpose: Assesses the concerns and attitudes of college-age students.

Description: 4-item paper-pencil projective test measuring a broad array of psychological characteristics. Each test item consists of a timed (4-minute) story-writing exercise, which provides a projective sample of the subject's thinking. Examiner required. Suitable for group use.

Timed: 16 minutes

Scoring: Examiner evaluated

Cost: 100 forms $3.90; manual $2.50

Publisher: Research and Development Center for Teacher Education

COMPREHENSIVE PERSONAL ASSESSMENT SYSTEM: ONE-WORD SENTENCE COMPLETION
Donald J. Veldman, S.L. Menaker, and R.F. Peck

Adolescent, adult
College student

Purpose: Provides information for clinical assessment of personality.

Description: 62-item paper-pencil projective personality test. Test items consist of sentences with single word blanks to be filled in by the subject. The test is primarily for the assessment of normal adults and adolescents. It is normed for college-age individuals. Self-administered. Suitable for group use.

Untimed: Not available

Scoring: Examiner evaluated; may be computer scored

Cost: 100 forms $3.90; manual $1.75

Publisher: Research and Development Center for Teacher Education

COMPREHENSIVE PERSONAL ASSESSMENT SYSTEM: SELF-REPORT INVENTORY (SRI)
Oliver H. Brown

Adolescent, adult

Purpose: Assesses adolescents' and adults' perception of their attitudes toward self and others.

Description: 48-item paper-pencil multiple-choice test evaluating a person's self-image of his phenomenological world. The test measures eight subareas. Self-administered. Suitable for group use.

Untimed: 20 minutes

Scoring: Hand key; may be computer scored

Cost: 100 forms $3.90

Publisher: Research and Development Center for Teacher Education

COMPUTERIZED STRESS INVENTORY (CSI)

Adult

Purpose: Assesses the level of stress in various areas of a person's life. Used in programs of stress management, illness prevention, and maintenance of wellness of normal, healthy adults.

Description: Computer-administered test of stress in over 25 areas of a person's life, including work, lifestyle, marriage, sexuality, friends and social life, self-esteem, and physical symptoms. A branching feature allows the program to adapt questions to the needs of the respondent. Each person's answers are analyzed individually to compile a 12-16-page CSI profile. An accompanying book that teaches 14 different stress management techniques is available. Examiner required. Not suitable for group use.

Untimed: 45-60 minutes

Scoring: Computer scored

Cost: Complete program (disks, instruction manual, two copies of *Stress? Find Your Balance*) $490.00

Publisher: Preventive Measures, Inc.

COMREY PERSONALITY SCALES (CPS)
Andrew L. Comrey

Adolescent, adult
Grades 10 and above

Purpose: Measures major personality characteristics of adults and high-school and college students. Used in educational, clinical, and business settings where personality structure and stability are important.

Description: 180-item paper-pencil test consisting of eight personality dimensions scales (20 items each), a validity scale (8 items), and a response bias scale (12 items). The eight personality scales are Trust vs. Defensiveness, Orderliness vs. Lack of Orderliness, Social Conformity vs. Rebelliousness, Activity vs. Lack of Energy, Emotional Stability vs. Neuroticism, Extraversion vs. Introversion, Masculinity vs. Femininity, and Empathy vs. Egocentrism. Subjects respond to items according to 7-point scales ranging from "never" or "definitely not," to "always" or "definitely." The profile presents a description of the personality structure of "normal" socially functioning individuals. Extreme scores on any of the scales may provide a clue to the source of current difficulties, predict future problems, aid in selection of therapy programs, and screen job applicants. Norms are presented as T-scores for male and female college students. Examiner required. Suitable for group use.

Untimed: 30-50 minutes

Scoring: Hand key; may be computer scored

Cost: (manual, all forms) $5.25; 25 reusable test booklets $14.25; 50 answer sheets $9.75; 50 computer answer sheets $10.50; 50 profile sheets $8.00; handbook $7.95; manual $3.00

Publisher: Educational and Industrial Testing Service

COPING OPERATIONS PREFERENCE ENQUIRY (COPE)
Will Schutz

Adult

Purpose: Measures individual preference for certain types of coping or defense mechanisms; used for counseling and therapy.

Description: 6-item paper-pencil test measuring the characteristic use of five defense mechanisms: denial, isolation, projection, regression-dependency, and turning-against-the-self. Each item describes a person and his behavior in a particular situation. The respondent rank orders five alternative ways he might feel; the alternatives represent the inventory's five coping mechanisms. Materials include separate forms for men and women. May be self-administered; however, an examiner is recommended. Suitable for group use.

Untimed: Not available

Scoring: Examiner evaluated

Cost: 25 tests (specify male or female) $9.50

Publisher: Consulting Psychologists Press, Inc.

CORNELL INDEX (REVISED)
Arthur Weider

Adult

Purpose: Evaluates an individual's psychiatric history. Identifies individuals with serious personal and psychosomatic disturbances. Used for clinical evaluations and research purposes.

Description: 101-item paper-pencil questionnaire measuring neuropsychiatric and psychosomatic symptoms. Administered in the form of a structured interview, analysis of responses provides a standardized evaluation of an individual's psychiatric history and differentiates statistically individuals with serious personal and psychiatric disturbances. Examiner required. Not suitable for group use.

Untimed: 5 minutes

Cost: 25 questionnaires $7.00; specimen set $5.00

Publisher: Arthur Weider, Ph.D.

CORNELL WORD FORM
Arthur Weider

Adult

Purpose: Assesses an individual's adaptive mechanisms. Used in a variety of clinical and research settings.

Description: Multiple-item paper-pencil test employing a modification of the word association technique. For each test item, the subject selects one word of a pair of printed responses that he associates with a given stimulus word. Analysis of the responses contributes to a descriptive sketch of the subject's adaptive mechanisms in a manner not easily apparent. Self-administered. Suitable for group use.

Untimed: 5 minutes

Scoring: Examiner evaluated

Cost: Specimen set $5.00; 25 copies $7.00; 100 copies $25.50

Publisher: Arthur Weider, Ph.D.

CORRECTIONAL INSTITUTIONS ENVIRONMENT SCALE (CIES)
Rudolf H. Moos

Adult

Purpose: Assesses the social environment of juvenile and adult correctional programs.

Description: 90-item paper-pencil true-false test of nine aspects of social environment: involvement, support, expressiveness, autonomy, practical orientation, personal problem orientation, order and organization, clarity, and staff control. Materials include four forms: the Real Form (Form R), which measures perceptions of the current correctional program; the 36-item Short Form (Form S); the Ideal Form (Form I), which measures conceptions of an ideal program; and the Expectations Form (Form E), which measures expectations of a new program. Forms I and E are not published, but items and instructions appear in the Appendix of the CIES manual. Items and subscales are similar to those used in the Ward Atmosphere Scale. One of a series of nine Social Climate Scales. Examiner administered. Suitable for group use.

Untimed: Not available

Scoring: Hand key; examiner evaluated

Cost: 50 reusable tests $4.75; 50 answer sheets $3.50; 50 profiles $3.50; key $0.75; manual $8.00

Publisher: Consulting Psychologists Press, Inc.

CROWN-CRISP EXPERIMENTAL INDEX (CCEI)
Sidney Crown and A.H. Crisp

Adolescent, adult

Purpose: Diagnoses psychoneurotic illness and personality disorder. Used for clinical screening and research, measuring change before and after defined intervention, and comparing defined groups. Used with a wide range of intelligence levels.

Description: 48-item paper-pencil questionnaire consisting of six subtests

designed to facilitate the rapid quantification of common symptoms and traits relevant to six conventional categories of psychoneurotic illness and personality disorder: free-floating anxiety, phobic anxiety, obsessionality, somatic anxiety, depression, and hysterical traits. The index provides a profile that can be related to the scores of defined groups. The manual includes reliability and validity data and statistics relating CCEI scores to age, sex, and social class. The questionnaire is restricted to senior staff members of any recognized medical or educational institution, medical doctors, and BPS and APA members. Examiner required. Not suitable for group use.
BRITISH PUBLISHER

Untimed: 5-10 minutes

Scoring: Examiner evaluated

Cost: Specimen set £3.00; 20 questionnaires £2.75 plus VAT; scoring template £.85 plus VAT; manual £3.50

Publisher: Hodder & Stoughton

CURRENT AND PAST PSYCHOPATHOLOGY SCALES (CAPPS)
Jean Endicott and The Department of Research Assessment and Training

All ages

Purpose: Assesses past and present psychiatric functioning. Used for diagnosis of psychopathology.

Description: 171 scales and checklist items measuring psychiatric signs and symptoms and covering a broad range of material similar to the Psychiatric Evaluation Form. Additional items cover history relevant to severity, prognosis, and diagnosis. The CAPPS is completed by the examiner after a clinical workup or through client interview. Examiner required. Not suitable for group use.

Untimed: 1-2 hours with interview

Scoring: Examiner evaluated; computer diagnosis available

Cost: Booklet with score sheets $1.00; score sheet $0.20; suggested procedure/training $0.20; instructions $0.40; Fortran program (scoring) $125.00; Family Evaluation Form (FEF) booklets $1.00; scoring system $1.50 plus postage and handling

Publisher: Department of Research Assessment and Training—N.Y. State Psychiatric Institute

CURTIS COMPLETION FORM
James W. Curtis

Adolescent, adult

Purpose: Evaluates the emotional adjustment of older adolescents and adults. Used in employment situations to screen individuals whose emotional adjustment makes them poor employment risks. Also used in educational and industrial counseling to identify individuals who would benefit from clinical treatment.

Description: Multiple-item paper-pencil free-response sentence-completion test measuring emotional adjustment. It is similar to a projective test, but is scored using relatively objective, standardized criteria. Examiner required. Suitable for group use. Available in Spanish and French.

Untimed: 30 minutes

Scoring: Examiner evaluated

Cost: Kit (50 forms, manual) $19.50

Publisher: Western Psychological Services

DEFENSE MECHANISMS INVENTORY
Goldine C. Gleser

Adolescent, adult
Ages 10 and older

Purpose: Assesses an individual's use of such defense mechanisms as projection and reversal.

Description: 10 vignettes (male and female forms) determining defense responses to a variety of situations are presented to the subject. Each vignette is followed by four questions: "What would you do?", "What would you like to do?", "What do you think?", and "How do you feel?" There are five possible responses to each vignette corresponding to the following five defense mechanisms: turning against an object, projection, principalization, turning against self, and reversal. Materials include adolescent, adult, and elderly male and female forms, answer sheets, and male and female profiles. Self-administered. Suitable for group use. Available in German, French, and Portuguese.

Untimed: 40 minutes

Scoring: Hand key

Cost: 10 test booklets (specify form and sex) $6.00; 5 answer sheets $6.00; 50 profiles $6.00; specimen set $6.00; scoring templates $10.00

Publisher: DMI Associates

DEPRESSION ADJECTIVE CHECK LIST (DACL)
Bernard Lubin

Adolescent, adult
Grades 10 and above

Purpose: Differentiates between depressed and nondepressed high-school and college students and adults. Used for counseling, group screening, and large-scale depression studies.

Description: Multiple-item paper-pencil checklist measuring transient depressive moods, feelings, or emotions. Seven parallel forms allow repeated measurement of these factors. The subject responds by checking the adjectives on the checklist that describe how he feels at the time of testing. Seven parallel forms, A, B, C, D (32 items each) and E, F, G (34 items each), allow repeated measurement. None of the adjectives appear on more than one of Forms A, B, C, or D or on more than one of Forms E, F, or G. Norms are presented for male and female normals and for depressed patients. Exmainer/self-administered. Suitable for group use.

Untimed: 5 minutes per form

Scoring: Hand key

Cost: Specimen set (manual, one copy of all forms) $5.50; 25 checklists (specify form) $6.50; key $2.50; manual $3.00

Publisher: Educational and Industrial Testing Service

DEROGATIS STRESS PROFILE (DSP)
Leonard R. Derogatis

Adult

Purpose: Measures the amount of stress an individual experiences in terms of interactional stress theory.

Description: 77-item paper-pencil test assessing 11 dimensions of stress grouped in the following three domains: environmental stress, personality mediators, and emotional response. In addition to 11 dimension scores and 3 domain scores, 2 global stress indices are also derived. An optical scan version is available for use with computer scoring and interpetation services. Examiner required. Suitable for group use.

Untimed: 12-15 minutes

Scoring: Examiner evaluated; may be computer scored

Cost: 100 self-scoring forms $40.00; 100 score/profile forms $18.00; 100 optical scan forms $45.00

Publisher: Clinical Psychometric Research

DESCRIBING PERSONALITY
Refer to page 699.

DIAGNOSTIC INVENTORY OF PERSONALITY AND SYMPTOMS (DIPS)
Ken R. Vincent

Adult

Purpose: Measures psychopathology in adults. Used for personality assessment in applied and research settings.

Description: 171-item paper-pencil true-false measure of symptoms characteristic of DSM-III diagnosis from both Axis I and Axis II. Scales corresponding to Axis I diagnoses are Alcohol Abuse, Drug Abuse, Schizophrenic Psychosis, Paranoid Psychosis, Affective Depressed, Affective Excited, Anxiety Disorders, Somatoform Disorders, Dissociative Disorders, Stress-Adjustment Disorders, and Psychological Factors Affecting Physical

Condition. Axis II disorders are collapsed into three major categories: Withdrawn Character, Immature Character, and Neurotic Character. Scores on two validity scales are also provided. Examiner/self-administered. Suitable for group use.

Untimed: Varies

Scoring: Hand key; may be computer scored with IBM-PC compatible software

Cost: Start-up kit (manual, answer keys, 50 test booklets, 50 profile sheets, 2 computer interpretation coupons) $45.00

Publisher: Pacific Psychological

DRUG USE INDEX (DUI)
*Frazier M. Douglass and
Khalil A. Khavari*

Ages 14-adult

Purpose: Measures polydrug use. Used by researchers, counselors, physicians, and therapists for diagnosis and planning treatment.

Description: Multple-item paper-pencil questionnaire assessing and predicting drug use. Individuals indicate their use of 19 different drugs and categories of drugs (including alcohol, tobacco, and over-the-counter drugs) on a scale of 0 (never) to 7 (several times a day). An overall drug use pattern is computed by summing across all drugs. The test is a predictive measure for use of 18 drugs or drug classes (except over-the-counter drugs). The questionnaire can be used for determining social and cultural variables that foster drug use and the kinds of drugs used. It also can be used for diagnosing and planning treatment for possible underlying psychiatric problems. Examiner required. Suitable for group use.

Untimed: Varies

Scoring: Examiner evaluated

Cost: One questionnaire provided free to each user; users may reproduce copies for their own use

Publisher: Khalil A. Khavari, Ph.D.

EATING DISORDER INVENTORY (EDI)
*David M. Garner,
Marion P. Olmsted, and Janet Polivy*

Adolescent, adult

Purpose: Assesses the psychological and behavioral traits common in eating disorders. Distinguishes individuals with serious psychopathology from normal dieters. Used in the treatment of individuals with eating disorders.

Description: 64-item paper-pencil self-report inventory consisting of eight sub-scales (Drive for Thinness, Bulimia, Body Dissatisfaction, Ineffectiveness, Perfectionism, Interpersonal Distrust, Interoceptive Awareness, and Maturity Fears) measuring specific cognitive and behavioral dimensions related to eating disorders. The inventory identifies individuals with serious eating disorders and differentiates between subgroups of eating disorders. Examiner required. Suitable for group use.

Untimed: 20 minutes

Scoring: Hand key

Cost: Kit (manual, scoring keys, 25 test booklets, 25 profile forms) $25.00

Publisher: Psychological Assessment Resources, Inc.

EDWARDS PERSONAL PREFERENCE SCHEDULE (EPPS)
A.L. Edwards

Adult   Ages 18 and older

Purpose: Assesses an individual's personality. Used for both personal counseling and personality research.

Description: Paper-pencil forced-choice test designed to show the relative importance of 15 needs and motives: achievement, deference, order, exhibition, autonomy, affiliation, intraception, succorance, dominance, abasement, nurturance, change, endurance, heterosexuality, and aggression. Self-administered. Suitable for group use.

Untimed: 45 minutes

Scoring: Hand key

Cost: Specimen set (schedule booklet, hand-scorable answer document and template; IBM 805 and NCS answer documents, manual) $12.00

Publisher: The Psychological Corporation

EGO STATE INVENTORY
David G. McCarley

Adolescent, adult

Purpose: Evaluates individual personality dynamics and interpersonal relations. Used in schools, industry, correctional institutions, and hospitals to acquire information about the internal dynamics of an individual from a transactional analytic view.

Description: 52-item paper-pencil multiple-choice test covering five ego states: punitive parent, nurturing parent, adult, rebellious child, and adaptive child. Each item consists of a cartoon drawing of two or more people in a recognizable social situation. One person in each of the cartoons is making a statement or asking a question, and the subject chooses from five possible responses the one he imagines the second person depicted in the situation would make. The test is hand scored with five stencils corresponding to the five ego states. Examiner required. Suitable for group use.

Timed: 20 minutes

Scoring: Hand key; examiner evaluated

Cost: Complete kit (workbook containing cartoons, manual with 5 scoring stencils, 100 answer sheets) $50.00

Publisher: Stoelting Company

EGO STATE PERSONALITY PROFILE (EGOGRAM™)
N. Robert Heyer

Adult   Ages 18 and older

Purpose: Assesses the personality traits of individuals ages 18 and older in terms of enduring characteristics called "ego states." Used in psychology for diagnosis, treatment planning, counseling, and therapy; in business for placement, career counseling, training, and team-building; and as a social research measure.

Description: 50-item paper-pencil multiple-choice questionnaire measuring the relative strength of six basic personality traits identified by Eric Berne, M.D., and widely used in transactional analysis: critical/judgmental, nurturing/caring, objective/logical, playful/impulsive, demonstrative/emotive, and conforming/compliant. The test yields a graphic profile. Differential ego state dominance indicates direction of subject's psychological aptitudes and typical behavior pattern in life and work situations; pronounced imbalance in a profile indicates the types of psychological problems and relationship difficulties to be found. The test is normed for individuals ages 18 and older, but it may be used also for individuals ages 14-18. Self-administered. Suitable for group use. Available in Spanish.

Untimed: 10-16 minutes

Scoring: Computer scored

Cost: 10 profiles (includes computer output and client guide) $70.00; manual $16.00

Publisher: Psychological Measurement Systems

EGO-IDEAL AND CONSCIENCE DEVELOPMENT TEST (EICDT)
R.N. Cassel

Adolescent   Ages 12-18

Purpose: Evaluates an individual's ego-ideal or conscience. Used as an index of parole or probation readiness for delinquents and to assess a person's knowledge of social expectations when confronted with problems.

Description: 80-item paper-pencil multiple-choice test measuring the extent to which the examinee agrees with the mainstream of U.S. society regarding solutions to social problems. The test consists of eight sections of 10 items each: home and family, inner development, community relations, rules and law, school and education, romance and psychosexual, economic sufficiency, and self-actualization. It yields a total score reflecting general agreement with society and eight section scores representing ego-ideal and conscience development. Two parallel forms are available. Interpretation forms, which describe the scale scores in detail and provide a normed profile for each examinee, are available. The manual describes the test rationale, gives directions for administering, scoring, and interpreting the test, and provides a complete description of the psychometric analyses of the instrument. Examiner/self-administered. Suitable for group use.

Untimed: 1 hour

Scoring: Hand key

Cost: 35 tests $30.00; 35 answer sheets $4.00; 35 interpretation forms $5.00; scoring stencil $3.00; manual $4.00 (specify form A or B for each item)

Publisher: Monitor

EIGHT STATE QUESTIONNAIRE: FORMS A & B (8SQ)
James P. Curran and Raymond B. Cattell

Adolescent, adult
Ages 17 and older

Purpose: Assesses the state of mind of adults and adolescents. Measures experimental manipulations of a person's moods and progress of related therapeutic intervention. Used for clinical evaluation and personal counseling.

Description: Multiple-item paper-pencil questionnaire measuring eight important mood states: anxiety, stress, depression, regression, fatigue, guilt, extraversion, and arousal. The questionnaire is available in two equivalent forms to allow for accurate retesting. Standard scores and percentiles are presented for men and women together, men alone, women alone, and male prisoners. A sixth-grade reading level is required. Self-administered. Suitable for group use.

Untimed: 30 minutes

Scoring: Hand key

Cost: Specimen set $6.35; manual $4.80; 25 reusable test booklets (for both Forms A & B) $12.50; 50 answer sheets $8.00; 50 profile sheets $6.50; and scoring key $5.25

Publisher: Institute for Personality and Ability Testing, Inc.

EMOTIONS PROFILE INDEX
Robert Plutchik and Henry Kellerman

Adolescent, adult

Purpose: Measures personality traits and conflicts in adults and adolescents. Used for counseling and guidance, therapy, and diagnostic evaluations.

Description: 62-item paper-pencil forced-choice test in which the subject chooses which of the two words presented in each item best describes himself. Four bipolar scales measure eight dimensions of emotions: Timid vs. Aggressive, Trustful vs. Distrustful, Controlled vs. Dyscontrolled, and Gregarious vs. Depressed. A unique circular profile displays percentile scores and compares the basic personality dimensions. Norms are provided on 1,000 adult men and women. Data also are given for certain special groups. Examiner required. Suitable for group use.

Untimed: 10-15 minutes

Scoring: Hand key

Cost: Complete kit (25 tests and profile sheets, manual) $17.50

Publisher: Western Psychological Services

THE EMPATHY TEST
Refer to page 914.

EYSENCK PERSONALITY INVENTORY (EPI)
H.J. Eysenck and Sybil B.G. Eysenck

Adolescent, adult
Grades 10 and above

Purpose: Measures extraversion and neuroticism, the two dimensions of personality which account for most personality variance. Used for counseling, clinical evaluation, and research.

Description: 57-item paper-pencil yes-no inventory measuring two independent dimensions of personality: extraversion-introversion and neuroticism-stability. A falsification scale detects response distortion. Scores are provided for three scales:

E-Extraversion, N-Neuroticism, and L-Lie. The inventory is available in two equivalent forms, A and B, for pre- and posttesting. The instrument also is available in Industrial Form A-I for industrial workers. College norms are presented in percentile form for Forms A and B both separately and combined. Adult norms are presented for Form A-I. Self-administered. Suitable for group use. Available in Spanish.

Untimed: 10-15 minutes

Scoring: Hand key; may be computer scored

Cost: Specimen set (manual, one copy of all forms) $5.50; 25 inventories (specify form) $6.50; keys $6.00; manual $2.50

Publisher: Educational and Industrial Testing Service

EYSENCK PERSONALITY QUESTIONNAIRE (EPQ)
*H. J. Eysenck and
Sybil B. G. Eysenck*

**Adolescent, adult
Ages 7-adult**

Purpose: Measures the personality dimensions of extraversion, emotionality, and toughmindedness (psychoticism in extreme cases) in individuals ages 7-adult. Used for clinical diagnosis, educational guidance, occupational counseling, personnel selection and placement, and market research.

Description: 90-item paper-pencil yes-no inventory measuring three important dimensions of personality: extraversion-introversion (21 items), neuroticism-stability (23 items), and psychoticism (25 items). The falsification scale consists of 21 items. The questionnaire deals with normal behaviors which become pathological only in extreme cases; hence, use of the term "toughmindedness" is suggested for nonpathological cases. Scores are provided for E-Extraversion, N-Neuroticism or emotionality, P-Psychoticism or toughmindedness, and L-Lie. College norms are presented in percentile form for Forms A and B both separately and combined. Adult norms are provided for an industrially employed sample. An 81-item

junior form is available for testing young children. Self-administered. Suitable for group use.

Untimed: 10-15 minutes

Scoring: Hand key

Cost: Specimen set (manual, one copy of each form) $5.50; 25 forms (specify form) $6.75; keys $8.00; manual $2.50

Publisher: Educational and Industrial Testing Service

FAMILY HISTORY—RESEARCH DIAGNOSTIC CRITERIA (FH-RDC)
*Jean Endicott and The Department of
Research Assessment and Training*

Adolescent, adult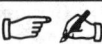

Purpose: Provides criteria for diagnosing mental disorders in family background. Used for psychiatric evaluation.

Description: 26-item checklist measuring the existence of mental disorders in family history. The clinician rates the items based on an interview of a family member about other family members. Examiner required. Not suitable for group use.

Untimed: 30-120 minutes, depending on the size of the family

Scoring: Examiner evaluated

Cost: Booklet with score sheet $1.50; parent work and data sheet $0.20; sibling work and data sheet $0.20; child work and data sheet $0.20; mate work and data sheet $0.20; summary data sheet 1 or 2 $0.20 each; sample set of all score sheets $1.10; case vignettes and keys $1.50 plus postage and handling

Publisher: Department of Research Assessment and Training—N.Y. State Psychiatric Institute

---

FEAR SURVEY SCHEDULE (FSS)
Joseph Wolpe and Peter J. Land

Adult

Purpose: Evaluates the manner in which an individual deals with fear-related situations. Particularly useful in behavior therapy.

Description: Multiple-item paper-pencil survey of a patient's reactions to a variety of possible sources of maladaptive emotional reactions. The reactions are unpleasant and often fearful, fear-tinged, or fear-related. The schedule reveals reactions to many stimulus classes in a short time. Examiner required. Suitable for group use.

Untimed: Not available

Scoring: Examiner evaluated

Cost: 25 response forms, manual $8.50

Publisher: Educational and Industrial Testing Service

FORER STRUCTURED SENTENCE COMPLETION TEST
Bertram R. Forer

Adolescent, adult
Ages 10-adult

Purpose: Evaluates personality dynamics and interrelationships of individuals ages 10 and older. Used for clinical evaluation.

Description: 100-item paper-pencil sentence-completion test available in separate forms for men, women, adolescent boys, and adolescent girls. The items are highly structured for wide coverage of attitude-value systems and to point out evasiveness, individual differences, and defense mechanisms. Objective interpretation is assisted by a checklist. Examiner required. Suitable for group use.

Untimed: 40-60 minutes

Scoring: Examiner evaluated

Cost: 25 tests $7.90; 25 checklists $7.90; manual $8.80 (specify adolescent or adult; male or female)

Publisher: Western Psychological Services

THE FORTY-EIGHT ITEM COUNSELING EVALUATION TEST: REVISED
Frank B. McMahon, Jr.

Adolescent, adult

Purpose: Assesses the personal and emotional problems of adolescents and adults. Used by high-school and college counselors.

Description: 48-item paper-pencil true-false personality questionnaire employing a "double-question" technique in which each item actually consists of two questions: (1) an introductory question probing a specific aspect of behavior or personality and (2) a contingency question which qualifies and amplifies the introductory question. Responses are evaluated in six problem areas: anxiety, compulsion, depression, socialization, goals, and inadequacy. The total score indicates severity of maladjustment, and subscores provide insights into each of the six problem areas. Examiner required. Suitable for group use.

Untimed: 10-20 minutes

Scoring: Hand key

Cost: Complete kit (25 tests, manual) $15.50

Publisher: Western Psychological Services

FUNDAMENTAL INTERPERSONAL RELATIONS ORIENTATION-FEELINGS (FIRO-F)
Will Schutz

Adult

Purpose: Evaluates an individual's characteristic feelings toward others. Used to assess both individual and interactional traits as an aid to counseling and therapy.

Description: 54-item paper-pencil test measuring six dimensions of an individual's feelings toward others: expressed significance, expressed competence, expressed lovability, wanted significance, wanted competence, and wanted lovability. Dimensions parallel the three dimensions of the FIRO-B. Examiner/self-administered. Suitable for group use.

Untimed: 15-20 minutes

Scoring: Hand key

Cost: Specimen set (includes tests and key) $5.25; 25 tests $4.50

Publisher: Consulting Psychologists Press, Inc.

GENERAL HEALTH QUESTIONNAIRE (GHQ)
D. Goldberg

Adolescent, adult

Purpose: Screens for psychiatric disorders among respondents in community settings, such as primary care, or among general medical outpatients.

Description: Multiple-item self-report paper-pencil measure of psychiatric problems. The test requires a minimum of subjective responses by the examinee. The items are aimed at detecting disorders that may be relevant to the subject's presence in a medical clinic. Three forms—GHQ-60, GHQ-30 (a short form) and GHQ-28—are available for research studies requiring more than one severity score. The test is available to psychiatrists, qualified medical doctors, and clinically experienced psychologists. Self-administered. Suitable for group use. BRITISH PUBLISHER

Untimed: Not available

Scoring: Examiner evaluated

Cost: Specimen set £7.55; 25 GHQ-28 £1.95; 25 GHQ-30 £4.15; 25 GHQ-60 £6.30 (payment in sterling for all overseas orders)

Publisher: NFER-NELSON Publishing Company Ltd.

GERIATRIC DEPRESSION SCALE
T.L. Brink

Elderly adults

Purpose: Diagnoses depression in the elderly.

Description: 30-item oral-response test assessing the level of depression in older adults. Questions seek "yes" or "no" responses. The test can be administered in oral or written format. The test can be used with other age groups, including adolescents, but loses validity as dementia increases. Spanish and French translations are available. Examiner required. Not suitable for group use.

Untimed: 5-15 minutes

Scoring: Examiner evaluated

Cost: Free

Publisher: T.L. Brink

GERIATRIC SENTENCE COMPLETION FORM (GSCF)
Peter LeBray

Elderly adults

Purpose: Assesses the personal and social adjustment of elderly adults. Used by clinicians working with the elderly in hospitals, long-term care facilities, outpatient settings, community care programs, and private offices.

Description: 30-item oral-response or paper-pencil projective test assessing elderly individuals' adjustment in four domains: physical, psychological, social, and temporal. The individual is asked to complete fragmentary sentence stems by using either written or verbal responses. The manual includes information on the development, structure, administration, and interpretation of the test and a number of clinical case illustrations. Examiner required. Suitable for group use.

Untimed: Varies

Scoring: Examiner evaluated

Cost: Manual, 50 forms $8.95

Publisher: Psychological Assessment Resources, Inc.

GIANNETTI ON-LINE PSYCHOSOCIAL HISTORY (GOLPH)
Ronald A. Giannetti

Adult

Purpose: Gathers information on an individual's background and current life circumstances. Used to obtain psychosocial history for general or psychiatric patients, evaluate job applicants' work history, criminal offenders' history of legal difficulties, or training applicants' educational history.

Description: Multiple-item multiple-choice and completion-item questionnaire presented on microcomputer diskette. Questions and their order of appearance are determined by answers to the preceding items. The examiner selects from the following areas to gather appropriate information: current living situation, family of origin, client development, educational history, marital history/present family, occupational history/current finances, legal history, symptom screening (physical), symptom screening (psychological), and military history. Questions are presented at an eighth-grade reading level. The length of the examination depends on the areas chosen for exploration and the extent of the individual's problems. A 3-12-page report presents the individual's responses in narrative fashion. Examiner required. Not suitable for group use.

Untimed: 30 minutes-2 hours

Scoring: Microcomputer scored

Cost: Microtest diskette (20 administrations) $130.00

Publisher: National Computer Systems/ PAS Division

GORDON PERSONAL PROFILE AND INVENTORY (GPP-I)
Leonard V. Gordon

Adolescent, adult

Purpose: Assesses aspects of an individual's personality that are significant in the functioning of the normal person.

Description: Paper-pencil measure of eight aspects of personality. The Personal Profile measures ascendancy, responsibility, emotional stability, and sociability. Four traits combine to yield the Self-Esteem score. The Personal Inventory measures cautiousness, original thinking, personal relations, and vigor. Respondents mark one item in each group of three as being most like them and one item as being least like them. Self-administered. Suitable for group use.

Untimed: 15 minutes per instrument

Scoring: Hand key; may be machine scored locally

Cost: Specimen set (booklet, manual for both profile and inventory) $54.00; 35 booklets, manual, keys $29.00; 35 answer documents $24.00; hand-scoring keys $10.00 (specify profile or inventory for each item ordered)

Publisher: The Psychological Corporation

GROUP ENVIRONMENT SCALE (GES)
Rudolf H. Moos

Adolescent, adult

Purpose: Assesses the social climate of therapeutic, social, or task-oriented groups.

Description: 90-item paper-pencil true-false test of 10 aspects of group social environments: cohesion, leader support, expressiveness, independence, task orientation, self-discovery, anger and aggression, order and organization, leader control, and innovation. These scales are grouped into three dimensions: relationship, personal growth, and system maintenance and system change. Materials include the Real Form (Form R), which measures perceptions of a current group; the Ideal Form (Form I), which measures conceptions of an ideal group; and the Expectations Form (Form E), which measures expectations of a new group. Forms I and E are not published, but reworded items and instructions may be requested from the publisher. One in a series of nine social climate scales. Examiner required. Suitable for group use.

Untimed: 20-30 minutes

Scoring: Examiner evaluated; hand key

Cost: Manual $6.50; key $1.50; 25 reusable tests $4.75; 50 answer sheets $3.50; 50 profiles $3.50

Publisher: Consulting Psychologists Press, Inc.

GROUP PSYCHOTHERAPY EVALUATION SCALE
Clifton E. Kew

Adult

Purpose: Evaluates behavior and ego strength as a measure of a person's suitability for group therapy techniques. Discriminates between patients who can function in a group setting and those who would be overwhelmed with anxiety in the group experience.

Description: Paper-pencil inventory measuring the cognitive, emotional, and behavioral aspects of a patient in terms of his group functioning ability. The therapist rates the patient from 0-4 in four areas: amount of communication and relatedness, and capacity for change and involvement. The therapist rates himself on amount of verbal activity and direction of therapist verbal activity. Suggested cut-off scores are provided for patients most and least suited for group therapy. Examiner required. Not suitable for group use.

Untimed: 5 minutes

Scoring: Examiner evaluated

Cost: Free

Publisher: Clifton E. Kew; distributed by Educational Testing Service

---

GROUP SHORR IMAGERY TEST (GSIT)
Joseph E. Shorr

Adult

Purpose: Evaluates a person's use of imagery and assesses self-image, areas of conflict, and strategies for coping with the world. Used for in-depth personality analysis.

Description: 15-item paper-pencil projective personality test in which the subjects (listening to a tape cassette) are asked to imagine a particular situation and then to expand (in writing) in a direct way upon the image evoked. These imaginary situations are used to reveal a wide range of personality variables, including the individual's personal world, relationships between self and others, self-image, sexual attitudes, and internal and external forces acting upon the individual. The responses are quantitatively scored according to degree of conflict within the subject's personality. The test is not limited by intelligence and is minimally culture bound. The manual includes instructions for scoring, a sample of the theoretical basis for in-depth personality analysis, and normative data. Examiner required. Suitable for group use.

Untimed: 1 hour

Scoring: Examiner evaluated

Cost: Complete set $44.50

Publisher: Institute for Psycho-Imagination Therapy

GUILFORD-ZIMMERMAN TEMPERAMENT SURVEY (GZTS)
J.P. Guilford and Wayne S. Zimmerman

Adolescent, adult
Grades 10 and above

Purpose: Measures personality traits. Used for personnel selection, vocational guidance, and clinical practice.

Description: 300-item paper-pencil measure of 10 factor-analytically derived traits that have proven to be most uniquely measurable: general activity, restraint, ascendance, sociability, emotional stability, objectivity, friendliness, thoughtfulness, personal relations, and masculinity/femininity. C-scale, centile, and T-scale norms are provided for high-school and college students and adults. The test is restricted to A.P.A. members. Examiner required. Suitable for group use.

Untimed: 45 minutes

Scoring: Hand key; may be computer scored

Cost: 25 tests $17.00; 25 answer sheets $5.50; 25 profile charts $4.00; manual $5.00; scoring set $6.00

Publisher: Sheridan Psychological Services, Inc.

THE HAND TEST, REVISED 1983
Edwin E. Wagner

Adolescent, adult
Ages 16-adult

Purpose: Measures an individual's attitudes and action tendencies that are likely to be expressed in overt behavior, particularly aggression. Used for diagnosis and screening.

Description: 10-item oral-response projective test using picture cards that present line drawings of hands in various positions. For each card, the subject explains what the hand is doing. The tenth card, which is blank, requires the subject to imagine a hand and describe what it is doing. Responses are scored on a variety of qualitative and quantitative indices to measure potential behavior toward persons and objects in the environment, pathological inefficiency, and social withdrawal. Reading skill is not required. Scoring takes a few minutes. The manual presents validity and reliability data on over 2,600 evaluations. Examiner required. Not suitable for group use.

Untimed: 10 minutes

Scoring: Examiner evaluated

Cost: Kit (25 scoring booklets, 1 set of picture cards, manual) $39.50

Publisher: Western Psychological Services

HARVARD GROUP SCALE OF HYPNOTIC SUSCEPTIBILITY
Ronald E. Shor and Emily C. Orne

College students, adult

Purpose: Screens large numbers of individuals for hypnotic susceptibility. Used for classroom demonstration and research.

Description: Multiple-item scale with instructions for inducing hypnosis. Subjects record their own responses. The test was adapted for group administration from the Stanford Hypnotic Susceptibility Scale Form A. Examiner required. Suitable for group use.

Untimed: 50 minutes

Scoring: Examiner evaluated

Cost: 25 response booklets $25.00; manual $6.00

Publisher: Consulting Psychologists Press, Inc.

HEALTH PROBLEMS CHECKLIST
John A. Schinka

Adult

Purpose: Assesses the health problems of adults. Used as a survey instrument in clinical and counseling settings to initiate the consultation process and introduce the client to formal diagnostic testing.

Description: 200-item paper-pencil test identifying health problems that may affect overall psychological well-being. The test, which can be used as a screening tool for medical referrals, covers 13

areas: general health, cardiovascular/pulmonary, endocrine/hematology, gastrointestinal, dermatological, visual, auditory/olfactory, mouth/throat/nose, orthopedic, neurological, genitourinary, habits, and history. The test is available in separate forms for men and women and in a computer version for use with Apple II Plus, Apple IIe, and IBM PC computers. The test is a component of the Clinical Checklist Series. Self-administered. Suitable for group use.

Untimed: 10-20 minutes

Scoring: Examiner evaluated

Cost: 50 checklists $12.95; computer version (100 uses) $50.00

Publisher: Psychological Assessment Resources, Inc.

HIGH SCHOOL PERSONALITY QUESTIONNAIRE (HSPQ)
Raymond B. Cattell and Mary D. Cattell

Adolescent   Ages 12-18

Purpose: Identifies adolescents with high potentials for dropping out of school, drug abuse, and low achievement. Used in correctional situations to facilitate parent-teacher, parent-officer, and parent-clinic cooperation.

Description: 142-item paper-pencil questionnaire measuring 14 primary personality dimensions, such as stability, tension, warmth, and enthusiasm. Scores for anxiety, extraversion, creativity, leadership, and other broad trait patterns are also obtained. The test is available in four equivalent forms, A, B, C, and D. Percentiles and standard scores are provided for boys, girls, and combined. A sixth-grade reading level is required. Examiner required. Suitable for group use. Available in Spanish.

Untimed: 45-60 minutes per form

Scoring: Hand key; scoring and interpretation services available

Cost: Professional examination kit $19.50; manual $9.25; 25 reusable test booklets $14.25; 25 machine-scorable answer sheets $5.50; 50 hand-scorable answer sheets $6.50; 50 hand-scorable answer-profile sheets $7.50; and 2 scoring keys $8.75

Publisher: Institute for Personality and Ability Testing, Inc.

HOFFER-OSMOND DIAGNOSTIC TEST (HOD)
Abram Hoffer, Humphrey Osmond, and Harold Kelm

Adolescent, adult
Ages 13-adult

Purpose: Diagnoses the degree and nature of psychiatric illness. Monitors treatment and establishes prognosis. Used by mental health practitioners to screen for mental illness.

Description: 145-item true-false test measuring the amount of paranoia, depression, and perceptual distortion in patients. Each item consists of a statement printed on a card. The subject reads each card and either answers on a separate answer sheet or places the card in a true or false box. If the patient is illiterate, the items may be read aloud. The test helps determine when a patient requires hospitalization or is ready to be discharged from the hospital. Materials include 145 test cards, a manual, score sheet, and test booklet. Self-administered under clinical supervision. Suitable for group use.

Untimed: 30 minutes

Scoring: Hand key

Cost: Complete test $36.50; HOD text $22.50

Publisher: Behavior Science Press

HOGAN PERSONALITY INVENTORY
Robert Hogan

College student, adult

Purpose: Assesses normal personality characteristics. Used for counseling, employment decisions, research, and self-development.

Description: 300-item paper-pencil true-false inventory assessing six primary traits: intellectance, adjustment, prudence, ambition, sociability, and likeability. The test contains one validity scale and six occupational scales (service orientation, clerical performance, sales performance, management performance, stress tolerance, and reliability). Test items are presented at an eighth-grade reading level. Hand-scoring materials allow the six primary traits and the validity scale to be scored and profiled. A two-page computerized profile report presents raw and percentile scores for six primary traits, one validity scale, and six occupational scales, and a list of 45 homogeneous item composites. Examiner required. Suitable for group use.

Untimed: 30-40 minutes

Scoring: Examiner evaluated; may be computer scored

Cost: Manual $8.50; 25 reusable test booklets $12.00

Publisher: National Computer Systems/ PAS Division

HOPKINS PSYCHIATRIC RATING SCALE (HPRS)
Leonard R. Derogatis

Adolescent, adult

Purpose: Evaluates the psychological symptomatic distress of medical and psychiatric patients in terms of the observer's judgment. Used in mental health settings for psychological screening and in treatment planning and evaluation.

Description: 17-item paper-pencil observational inventory assessing symptomatic distress in terms of nine primary symptom dimensions (somatization, obsessive-compulsive, interpersonal sensitivity, depression, anxiety, hostility, phobic anxiety, paranoid ideation, and psychoticism) and eight additional dimensions. Each dimension is defined by a brief descriptive paragraph coupled with verbal descriptive anchors at seven discrete scale points. This HPRS is a part of the Psychopathology Rating Scale Series, which includes the SCL-90-R, the SCL-90 Analogue, and the Brief Symptom Inventory (BSI). The nine primary symptoms assessed are common to all four scales. A brief version is available (B-HPRS) which rates only the nine primary symptoms. A microcomputer program (COMPAR-90) is available to calculate and assess differences in terms of standardized scores between HPRS or B-HPRS ratings of patients and self-ratings by the patients on the SCL-90-R or BSI. Examiner required. Not suitable for group use.

Untimed: 2-5 minutes

Scoring: Examiner evaluated

Cost: 100 HPRS forms $32.00; 100 B-HPRS forms $28.00

Publisher: Clinical Psychometric Research

HOW WELL DO YOU KNOW YOURSELF
Thomas N. Jenkins

Adolescent, adult
Grades 10 and above

Purpose: Assesses normal personality. Used for educational guidance.

Description: Multiple-item paper-pencil test measuring 17 personality traits: irritability, practicality, punctuality, novelty-loving, vocational assurance, cooperativeness, ambitiousness, hypercriticalness, dejection, general morale, persistence, nervousness, seriousness, submissiveness, impulsiveness, dynamism, and emotional control. Two additional measures of response style, consistency and test objectivity, are included. Examiner required. Suitable for group use.

Untimed: 20 minutes

Scoring: Hand key

Cost: Complete kit (3 test booklets of each edition and manual) $9.00; 25 tests (specify secondary, college, or personnel) $18.00; keys $6.00; manual $6.00

Publisher: Psychologists and Educators, Inc.

HUMAN RELATIONS INVENTORY
Raymond S. Bernberg

Adolescent, adult
Grades 10 and above

Purpose: Measures a person's tendency toward social or lawful conformity. Differentiates between conformist and nonconformist individuals.

Description: Multiple-item paper-pencil test measuring an individual's sense of social conformity. Social conformity is defined and tested in terms of moral values, positive goals, reality testing, ability to give affection, tension level, and

impulsivity. The test is constructed using the "direction of perception" technique, and the purpose of the test is effectively disguised from subjects to insure more valid results. The test discriminates between samples of law violators and ordinary conformists. Norms are provided for senior high-school boys, college students, regular churchgoers, Los Angeles police officers, male inmates of a California youth prison, adult male inmates of the Los Angeles County Jail, and adult female inmates of the Los Angeles County Jail. Examiner required. Suitable for group use.

Untimed: Not available

Scoring: Examiner evaluated

Cost: Specimen set $5.00; 25 inventories $5.00

Publisher: Psychometric Affiliates

HYPOCHONDRIASIS SCALE: INSTITUTIONAL GERIATRIC
T.L. Brink

Elderly adults

Purpose: Assesses hypochondriacal attitudes of institutionalized elderly.

Description: 6-item oral-response test measuring hypochondriacal attitudes, rather than behaviors, of the institutionalized elderly. The test can be administered in an oral or written format and used with noninstitutionalized elderly, young adults, and adolescents, although no precise validity studies have been performed with the latter two groups. A Spanish translation is available. Examiner required. Not suitable for group use.

Untimed: 1-3 minutes

Scoring: Examiner evaluated

Cost: Free

Publisher: T.L. Brink

IMPACT MESSAGE INVENTORY
Donald J. Kiesler, Jack C. Anchin,
Michael J. Perkins,
Bernie M. Chirico, Edgar M. Kyle,
and Edward J. Federman

Adolescent, adult

Purpose: Measures the affective, behavioral, and cognitive reactions of one individual to another. Assesses the personality and interpersonal style of an individual by measuring the attitudes and feelings the individual arouses in the respondent. Helpful in clarifying interpersonal transactions in any dyad, including teacher-student, friends, employer-employee, and therapist-client.

Description: 90-item paper-pencil inventory assessing one individual's reactions to the interpersonal or personality style of another person. Items describe ways in which people are emotionally engaged or affected when interacting with another person. Individuals respond on a 4-point scale ranging from "not at all" to "very much so" to indicate the extent to which each item describes the feeling aroused by the other person, behaviors they want to direct toward the other person, or descriptions of the other person which come to mind when in the other person's presence. Each test item describes a reaction characteristically elicited by a person high on one of the following 15 interpersonal dimensions: dominant, competitive, hostile, mistrusting, detached, inhibited, submissive, succorant, abrasive, deferent, agreeable, nurturant, affiliative, sociable, and exhibitionistic. Scores are derived for each of the 15 subscales as well as for 4 cluster-scores: dominant, submissive, friendly, and hostile. Kiesler has completed a revised manual, *Research Manual for the Impact Message Inventory.* The manual includes descriptions of the subscales and tables for converting raw scores to T-scores. Examiner required. Suitable for group use.

Untimed: 15 minutes

Scoring: Examiner evaluated

Cost: 25 question booklets (specify male or female) $9.00; 50 answer sheets $7.00

Publisher: Consulting Psychologists Press, Inc.

INCOMPLETE SENTENCES TASK
Barbara Lanyon and Richard Lanyon

**Adolescent, adult
Grades 7 and above**

Purpose: Identifies potential emotional problems in students from junior high-school through college to begin intervention before problems become too severe.

Description: 39-item paper-pencil test consisting of incomplete sentence stems that the subject completes in his own words. The test is both projective and psychometric and measures hostility, anxiety, and dependency. Scoring is based on examples for each item found in the manual. Two forms are available: a School Form (Grades 7-12) and a College Form (college-age adolescents). Norms are provided for three groups: Grades 7-9, Grades 10-12, and college-age adolescents. Self-administered. Suitable for group use.

Untimed: 15-20 minutes

Scoring: Examiner evaluated

Cost: Complete kit, specify form (30 test forms, manual) $17.00

Publisher: Stoelting Company

INTERPERSONAL CHECK LIST (ICL)
Rolfe LaForge and R. Suczek

Adult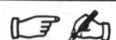

Purpose: Describes an individual's perception of another individual's personality. Used for clinical and social research.

Description: 134-item paper-pencil checklist for describing self or another person. Each item is categorized according to one of 16 interpersonal categories and one of four intensity levels. Summary variables are dominance, love, number of items endorsed, and average intensity of endorsed items. The subject is required to describe one or more persons, possibly self or a hypothetical person, by checking the items. The test may be duplicated. Examiner required. Suitable for group use.

Untimed: 15 minutes

Scoring: Computer scored

Cost: Test is free; technical report $12.00

Publisher: Rolfe LaForge

INTERPERSONAL RELATIONS QUESTIONNAIRE (IRQ)—1981

Adolescent   Ages 12-15

Purpose: Assesses personal adjustment in adolescence. Used for counseling and guidance.

Description: 260- or 100-item paper-pencil test measuring 12 components of adjustment: self-confidence, self-esteem, self-control, nervousness, health, family influences, personal freedom, general sociability, sociability with the opposite sex, sociability with the same sex, moral sense, and formal relations. Items are answered on a 4-point scale. A 100-item abridged questionnaire provides a more general indication of adjustment involving five components. Examiner required. Suitable for group use.
SOUTH AFRICAN PUBLISHER
Untimed: 2 hours; abridged questionnaire 1 hour
Scoring: Hand key; examiner evaluated
Cost: (In Rands) questionnaire 0,90; 10 answer sheets 0,80; scoring stencil (positive items) 4,20; scoring stencil (negative items) 4,30; test profiles 2,20; manual 7,70; orders from outside The RSA will be dealt with on merit
Publisher: Human Sciences Research Council

INTERPERSONAL STYLE INVENTORY—(ISI)
Maurice Lorr and Richard P. Youniss

Adolescent, adult

Purpose: Assesses an individual's manner of interacting with other people and style of impulse control. Used for self-understanding, counseling and therapy, personnel guidance, and research.

Description: 300-item paper-pencil true-false inventory assessing an individual's style of interpersonal interactions along 15 primary scales: Directive, Sociable, Help-Seeking, Nurturant, Conscientious, Trusting, Tolerant, Sensitive, Deliberate, Independent, Rule Free, Orderly, Persistent, Stable, and Approval Seeking. Each item is a statement describing ways

in which people relate and respond to each other. The individual reads each statement and decides whether it is mostly true or not true for himself. High-school and college norms are provided by sex. Self-administered. Suitable for group use.
Untimed: 30 minutes
Scoring: Computer scored
Cost: Test kit (5 reusable administration booklets; 5 computer scorable answer sheets; manual) $45.00
Publisher: Western Psychological Services

INTRA AND INTERPERSONAL RELATIONS

Child, adolescent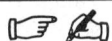

Purpose: Measures the relationship with self and parental figures. Used for counseling and assessment.

Description: Paper-pencil test of relationships with self and others. The scale also measures the relationship between the real and ideal selves and indicates self-acceptance. Examiner required. Suitable for group use.
SOUTH AFRICAN PUBLISHER
Untimed: 30 minutes
Scoring: Hand key; examiner evaluated
Cost: (In Rands) test booklet 2,20; manual 7,80; 10 answer sheets 0,30; scoring stencil 1,30; orders from outside The RSA will be dealt with on merit
Publisher: Human Sciences Research Council

INVENTORY OF ANGER COMMUNICATION (IAC)
Millard J. Bienvenu

Adolescent, adult
Ages 15 and older

Purpose: Helps individuals learn about their style of handling anger. Used as a counseling and teaching tool.

Description: 30-item paper-pencil multiple-choice questionnaire covers areas such as handling anger, confrontation, expression of feelings, and measurement of anger. Materials include a questionnaire, manual, and scoring key. Examiner/self-administered. Suitable for group use.

Untimed: 15 minutes

Scoring: Hand key; examiner evaluated

Cost: IAC $0.35; guide $1.50

Publisher: Counseling and Self-Improvement Programs/Millard Bienvenu, Ph.D.

Information and availability unconfirmed; no publisher response.

INVENTORY OF INDIVIDUALLY-PERCEIVED GROUP COHESIVENESS
Refer to page 918.

INVENTORY OF SELF-HYPNOSIS
Ronald E. Shor

Adult

Purpose: Assesses an individual's hypnotizability. Also used for inducing or demonstrating self-hypnosis.

Description: Multiple-item inventory in which subjects read instructions for inducing hypnosis, give themselves 12 suggestions, and rate their own performances. The inventory, adapted from the *Harvard Group Scale,* allows the subject to control the induction, which reduces anxiety. Self-administered. Not suitable for group use.

Untimed: 1½ hours

Scoring: Examiner evaluated

Cost: 25 instruction booklets $40.00; 50 response sheets $9.75

Publisher: Consulting Psychologists Press, Inc.

IPAT ANXIETY SCALE (OR SELF-ANALYSIS FORM)
Raymond B. Cattell, Ivan H. Scheier, and IPAT Staff

Adolescent, adult
Grades 10 and above

Purpose: Measures anxiety in senior high-school students and adults of most educational levels. Used for both clinical

diagnosis and psychological research on anxiety.

Description: 40-item paper-pencil questionnaire measuring the five principal 16 PF factors of anxiety: emotional instability (C-), suspiciousness (L +), guilt-proneness (O +), low integration (Q3-), and tension (Q4 +). Norms are provided for adult, college, and high-school populations, with both separate and combined sex tables. A sixth-grade reading level is required. Examiner required. Suitable for group use. Available in Spanish.

Untimed: 10 minutes

Scoring: Hand key

Cost: Anxiety Scale testing kit (handbook, nonreuseable test booklet, scoring key) $9.75; Anxiety Scale Handbook $7.25; scoring key $1.85; 25 nonreuseable test booklets $6.75

Publisher: Institute for Personality and Ability Testing, Inc.

IPAT DEPRESSION SCALE
Samuel E. Krug and James E. Laughlin

Adult

Purpose: Diagnoses depression in adults of most educational levels. Used for both clinical diagnosis and psychological research on depression.

Description: 40-item paper-pencil questionnaire diagnosing and measuring depression in adults. Norms are provided for adult, college, prison, and certain clinical populations. A fifth-grade reading level is required. Self-administered. Not suitable for group use. Available in Spanish.

Untimed: 10 minutes

Scoring: Hand key

Cost: Complete kit $8.25; manual $5.75; 25 nonreuseable test booklets $6.75; scoring key $1.85

Publisher: Institute for Personality and Ability Testing, Inc.

IPS SOCIAL HISTORY (SOCH)

Adult

Purpose: Gathers information necessary to assess an individual's social, medical, and psychological history.

Description: Multiple-item microcomputer program or paper-pencil test gathering personal information in the following areas: current status, childhood, education, military, criminal, substance abuse, personal relations with friends and family members, and self-descriptive adjectives. As a microcomputer program, a series of questions are presented on the answer screen, and the individual responds by pressing numbers on the keyboard. For paper-pencil administration, item responses are entered directly into the computer by clerical staff. A narrative report is produced describing major problem areas and psychological/medical history. This report then can be used as a guide during subsequent personal interviews or to identify topics needing further exploration. The test is available for use with OSI and APPLE computers. A national scoring service also is available. Examiner required. Paper-pencil version suitable for group use.

Untimed: Varies

Scoring: Microcomputer scored

Cost: Contact publisher for information concerning software requirements and administration costs

Publisher: Integrated Professional Systems, Inc.

IRRATIONAL BELIEFS TEST
Richard G. Jones

Adult

Purpose: Assesses an individual's irrational beliefs. Used for clinical assessment and diagnosis; personnel selection and evaluation; personal, marital, and family counseling; vocational guidance counseling; and educational evaluation and planning.

Description: Multiple-item paper-pencil test assessing an individual's irrational belief system along 10 dimensions derived from Ellis' Rational Emotive Therapy. Computer analysis provides scores and a narrative report based upon the 10 dimensions and a factor-analytic model. The report incorporates empirical rela-

tionships between the scales and other conditions such as stress, pathology, personality, motivation, organization roles, and decision styles. Examiner required. Suitable for group use.

Untimed: Varies

Scoring: Hand key; may be computer scored

Cost: Mail-in scoring service $12.00

Publisher: Test Systems International

JACKSON PERSONALITY INVENTORY (JPI)
Douglas N. Jackson

Adolescent, adult

Purpose: Assesses personality characteristics of normal people who have average and above-average intelligence. Used to evaluate behavior in a wide range of settings, including those involving work, education, organizations, interpersonal, and high-level performance.

Description: 320-item paper-pencil true-false test covering 15 substantive scales and one validity scale. The scales measured are Anxiety, Breadth of Interest, Complexity, Conformity, Energy Level, Innovation, Interpersonal Affect, Organization, Responsibility, Risk Taking, Self Esteem, Social Adroitness, Social Participation, Tolerance, Value Orthodoxy, and Infrequency. Materials include a manual, reusable test booklets, answer sheet, and template and profiles. Norms are based on random college sampling. High-school norms are available. This test differs from the Personality Research Form (PRF) in terms of the nature of the variables measured and is a further refinement of substantive psychometric and computer-based strategies for scale development. Examiner required. Suitable for group use.

Untimed: 1 hour

Scoring: Hand key

Cost: Complete set $25.00

Publisher: Research Psychologists Press, Inc.

JESNESS BEHAVIOR CHECK LIST
Carl F. Jesness

Adolescent

Purpose: Assesses the social behavior of adolescents. Used to evaluate behavioral change in school or institutional settings and for comparisons between self and observer ratings for use in counseling or research.

Description: 80-item paper-pencil rating scale measuring 14 bipolar behavioral tendencies: unobtrusiveness vs. obtrusiveness, friendliness vs. hostility, responsibility vs. irresponsibility, considerateness vs. inconsiderateness, independence vs. dependence, rapport vs. alienation, enthusiasm vs. depression, sociability vs. poor peer relations, conformity vs. nonconformity, calmness vs. anxiousness, effective communication vs. inarticulateness, insight vs. unawareness and indecisiveness, social control vs. attention-seeking, and anger control vs. hypersensitivity. Materials include an Observer Form for ratings by teachers and therapists and a Self-Appraisal Form for self-evaluation. Self-administered. Suitable for group use.

Untimed: 10-20 minutes

Scoring: Hand key; computer scoring service available

Cost: Specimen set (no key) $6.50; manual $6.00; key $10.00

Publisher: Consulting Psychologists Press, Inc.

KATZ ADJUSTMENT SCALES (KAS)
Martin M. Katz

Adult

Purpose: Describes and measures an individual's social behavior, symptoms, and performance. Evaluates personal and social adjustment. Used for both normal and mentally disordered persons.

Description: 225-item paper-pencil test consisting of five scales and a self-report form. The test measures the following factors: emotional stability, general psychopathology, belligerence, expan-

siveness, negativism, anxiety, helplessness, suspiciousness, withdrawal and retardation, nervousness, confusion, hyperactivity, bizarreness, level of performance, and satisfaction with level of socially expected activities. The test is administered to a relative or "significant other" in a position to observe the subject for at least seven weeks. It is used as an experimental study of various mental disorders as perceived by the United States and other cultures and the evaluation of treatments. The test may be administered by interview if the observer is illiterate. Materials include the scale, a list of references, and a brief manual. Self-administered. Not suitable for group use. Available in 12 European and Asian languages.

Untimed: 20-30 minutes

Scoring: Hand key; may be computer scored

Cost: Complete kit (scale, references list, manual) $15.00

Publisher: Martin M. Katz, Ph. D.

Information and availability unconfirmed; no publisher response.

KUNDU INTROVERSION-EXTRAVERSION INVENTORY (K.I.E.I.)
Ramanath Kundu

Adolescent, adult

Purpose: Assesses the introversion-extroversion dimension of adolescent and adult personalities. Used for clinical diagnosis, research, guidance, and placement.

Description: Multiple-item paper-pencil test measuring introversion and extroversion. A minimum English reading level is required. Self-administered. Suitable for group use.
PUBLISHED IN INDIA

Untimed: 15 minutes

Scoring: Hand key

Cost: (In Rupees) Specimen set 50-00Rs.; 25 reusable booklets 160-00Rs.; 10 manuals with scoring 100-00Rs.; 100 answer sheets 180-00Rs

Publisher: Ramanath Kundu

KUNDU NEUROTIC PERSONALITY INVENTORY (K.N.P.I.)
Ramanath Kundu

Adolescent, adult

Purpose: Assesses degrees of neuroticism. Used for clinical diagnosis, research, guidance, and employee selection.

Description: 66-item paper-pencil test measuring neuroticism. A minimum English reading level is required. The author plans to publish a new manual containing detailed information about the test. Self-administered. Suitable for group use.
PUBLISHED IN INDIA

Untimed: 15 minutes

Scoring: Hand key

Cost: (In Rupees) Specimen set 50-00Rs.; 25 reusable booklets 160-00Rs.; 10 manuals with scoring 75-00Rs.; 100 answer sheets 180-00Rs

Publisher: Ramanath Kundu

THE LEEDS SCALES FOR THE SELF-ASSESSMENT OF ANXIETY AND DEPRESSION
R. P. Snaith, C. W. K. Bridge, and Max Hamilton

Adult

Purpose: Measures severity of depression and anxiety. Used for individual counseling and therapy.

Description: 15-item paper-pencil test measuring patient's self-report of depression and anxiety. Four scale scores are obtained: Depression Specific Scale, Anxiety Specific Scale, Depression General Scale, and Anxiety General Scale. Specific scales provide a measure of the severity of diagnosed affective illness. Self-administered. Suitable for group use.
BRITISH PUBLISHER

Untimed: Varies

Scoring: Hand key

Cost: Specimen set (answer sheet, specific and general scale stencils manual) $8.80; keys $4.40; 50 answer sheets $8.40; manual $2.80

Publisher: Psychological Test Publications; distributed by The Test Agency Ltd.

LEITER RECIDIVISM SCALE

Adult

Purpose: Measures the potential for recidivism. Used by judges in criminal courts and at each stage of the correctional process to determine in a given case whether society would be best served by probation or incarceration.

Description: Multiple-item paper-pencil inventory assessing nine variables related to recidivism: instability, age-time ratio, social immaturity, social control (lack of control), vocational adjustment (lack of adjustment), personality dynamics, abnormal authority reaction, institutional adjustment, and offense level. An individual's recidivism score is the sum of his scores on the nine variables, each of which is a predictor of recidivism in its own right. Self-administered by a judge, probation officer, or correctional personnel. Not suitable for group use.

Untimed: Varies

Scoring: Examiner evaluated

Cost: Test kit (manual, 25 profile sheets, 25 record blanks) $24.00

Publisher: Stoelting Company

LEWIS COUNSELING INVENTORY
D. G. Lewis and P. D. Pumfrey

Adolescent

Purpose: Measures self-perceived problems of adolescents. Used for individual counseling and screening for pupils most in need of guidance.

Description: 46-item paper-pencil test measuring the need for professional help. Six Lie scale items are included, as well as a series of direct statements scored in six areas: relationship with teachers, relationship with family, irritability, social confidence, relationship with peers, and health. The pupil indicates whether he agrees or disagrees with each item. The inventory may be followed by Part 2, a short questionnaire allowing the pupil to expand on specifics about his perceived problems. Response patterns may indicate the type of help needed. Examiner required. Suitable for group use. BRITISH PUBLISHER

Untimed: Part I 10-15 minutes; Part II 15 minutes

Scoring: Hand key

Cost: Specimen set £10.30; 25 Part I forms £5.20; 25 supplementary questionnaires £3.00; 6 keys £11.25; manual £10.10 (payment in sterling for all overseas orders)

Publisher: NFER-NELSON Publishing Company Ltd.

LIFE EVENTS SCALE—ADOLESCENTS
R. Dean Coddington

Adolescent

Purpose: Assesses significant events occurring in an adolescent's life. Used for clinical evaluation and counseling of adolescents.

Description: 50-item paper-pencil questionnaire measuring the frequency of selected important events in an adolescent's family and social life. Scores are provided for three areas: family events over which the adolescent has no control (17 items), desirable extrafamilial events (18 items), and undesirable extrafamilial events (15 items). Total extrafamilial event scores and total scores are easily computed. Items are weighted for scoring purposes according to criteria provided by pediatricians, teachers, and mental health workers dealing with children and adolescents. Examiner required. Suitable for group use.

Untimed: 5 minutes

Scoring: Examiner evaluated

Cost: 100 test forms $20.00

Publisher: R. Dean Coddington, M.D.

LIFE POSITION IN TRANSACTIONAL ANALYSIS
Hunter H. Wood

Adult

Purpose: Measures a person's life position in the theoretical framework of transactional analysis. Used in situations where personality characteristics and predictions are relevant.

Description: 32-item paper-pencil true-false test consisting of a series of attitudinal statements with which the subject must either agree or disagree. Responses are evaluated to measure a person's life position on four scales: I'm OK, You're OK; I'm not OK, You're OK; I'm OK, You're not OK; and I'm not OK, You're not OK. Examiner required. Suitable for group use.

Untimed: 15-20 minutes

Scoring: Examiner evaluated

Cost: 30 forms $8.00

Publisher: Stoelting Company

MANSON EVALUATION
Refer to page 922.

MARTIN S-D INVENTORY
William T. Martin

Adolescent, adult

Purpose: Identifies persons with depressive and suicidal tendencies. Serves as a screening instrument for suicide prevention centers and mental health facilities. Also used for research on suicide and depression.

Description: 50-item paper-pencil inventory measuring behavioral and cognitive aspects related to depression and suicide. Subjects rate statements (both negative and positive) on a scale from 1 to 4 as they apply to their own beliefs and behavior. A total Adjusted Score is derived, with norms provided for normals, depressed persons, and psychiatric patients. Suggested cutoff scores are provided for persons considered depressed, moderately depressed, and significantly depressed. The inventory may be used in conjunction with the S-D Proneness Checklist. A pamphlet on suicide/depression also is available. Examiner required. Suitable for group use.

Untimed: 15 minutes

Scoring: Hand key; examiner evaluated

Cost: Specimen set $8.00; 25 tests $7.50; scoring templates $2.50; manual $6.00

Publisher: Psychologists and Educators, Inc.

MATHEMATICS ANXIETY RATING SCALE
Richard M. Suinn

Adolescent, adult

Purpose: Measures college students' anxieties regarding situations involving the use of mathematics. Used for screening and diagnostic purpose, research on mathematics anxiety, and as a means for developing anxiety hierarchies for desensitization therapy.

Description: 98-item paper-pencil test assessing the level of a student's mathematics anxiety. Test items refer to situations involving the use of mathematics. The student is asked to rate on a 5-point scale ranging from "not at all" to "very much" how anxious he is made by each situation. Norms are available for college students. Use is restricted to APA membership guidelines. Self-administered. Suitable for group use.

Untimed: 45 minutes

Scoring: Hand key

Cost: 100 scales $60.00

Publisher: Rocky Mountain Behavioral Science Institute, Inc.

MATHEMATICS ANXIETY RATING SCALE-A (MARS-A)
Richard M. Suinn

Child, adolescent   Grades 7-12

Purpose: Measures students' anxieties regarding situations involving the use of mathematics. Used for screening and diagnostic purposes and research on mathematics anxiety and as a means for developing anxiety hierarchies for desensitization therapy.

Description: 98-item paper-pencil test assessing the level of a student's mathematics anxiety. Test items refer to situations involving the use of mathematics. The student is asked to rate on a 5-point scale ranging from "not at all" to "very much" how anxious he is made by each situation. Norms are available for junior and senior high-school students by grade and by sex. Use is restricted to APA membership guidelines. Self-administered. Suitable for group use.

Untimed: 20-30 minutes

Scoring: Hand key

Cost: 100 scales $60.00

Publisher: Rocky Mountain Behavioral Science Institute, Inc.

MAUDSLEY PERSONALITY INVENTORY (MPI)
H.J. Eysenck

Adolescent, adult
Grades 10 and above

Purpose: Measures the personality dimensions of extraversion-introversion and neuroticism-stability in high-school and college students and adults. Used for industrial and educational prediction and screening, clinical evaluation, and research.

Description: 48-item paper-pencil checklist measuring two pervasive and independent dimensions of personality: extraversion-introversion (24 items) and neuroticism-stability (24 items). Test items are selected on the basis of item and factor analyses. Scores are provided for E-Extraversion and N-Neuroticism. College norms are presented in percentile and stanines. Norms for many clinical and occupational subgroups are included. Examiner required. Suitable for group use.

Untimed: 10-15 minutes

Scoring: Hand key

Cost: Specimen set (manual, all forms) $5.25; 25 inventories $6.50; keys $4.00; manual $2.50

Publisher: Educational and Industrial Testing Service

MEASURE OF ACHIEVING TENDENCY
Albert Mehrabian

Adult

Purpose: Assesses an individual's motivation to achieve. Used for research, counseling, and employee selection and placement purposes.

Description: Multiple-item verbal questionnaire assessing all major components of achievement. Test items are based on extensive factor-analytic investigation of most experimentally identified components of achievement. Examiner required. Suitable for group use.

Untimed: 15 minutes

Scoring: Examiner evaluated

Cost: Test kit (scales, scoring directions, norms, test manual) $28.00

Publisher: Albert Mehrabian

MEASURE OF AROUSAL SEEKING TENDENCY
Albert Mehrabian

Adult

Purpose: Assesses an individual's desire for change, stimulation, and arousal. Used for research and counseling purposes.

Description: Multiple-item verbal questionnaire measuring an individual's arousal-seeking tendencies. Test items are based on extensive factor-analytic and experimental studies of all aspects of change-seeking, sensation-seeking, variety-seeking and, generally, desire to master high-uncertainty situations. Examiner required. Suitable for group use.

Untimed: Varies

Scoring: Examiner evaluated

Cost: Test kit (scale, scoring directions, norms, descriptive material) $20.00

Publisher: Albert Mehrabian

MEASURE OF DOMINANCE-SUBMISSIVENESS
Albert Mehrabian and Melissa Hines

Adult

Purpose: Measures aspects of dominance and submissiveness in an individual's personality. Used for research, counseling, and job placement purposes.

Description: Multiple-item verbal questionnaire assessing personality characteristics related to dominance and submissiveness. Test items are based on extensive factor-analytic and experimental studies on aspects of dominance (controlling, taking charge) versus submissiveness characteristics. This measure has been shown to be a basic component of many important personality attributes such as extroversion, dependency, anxiety, or depression. Examiner required. Suitable for group use.

Untimed: 15 minutes

Scoring: Examiner evaluated

Cost: Test kit (scale, scoring directions, norms, descriptive material) $20.00

Publisher: Albert Mehrabian

MEASURE OF STIMULUS SCREENING (CONVERSE OF AROUSABILITY)
Albert Mehrabian

Adult

Purpose: Measures major components of arousability and stimulus screening. Used for research and counseling purposes.

Description: Multiple-item verbal questionnaire assessing the extent of an individual's arousal response to complex, unexpected, or unfamiliar situations. The test items are based on extensive factor-analytic and experimental investigations of all major components of arousability and stimulus screening. Stimulus screening/arousability has been shown to be a major component of many important emotional characteristics, such as anxiety, neuroticism, extroversion, or hostility. Examiner required. Suitable for group use.

Untimed: 15 minutes

Scoring: Examiner evaluated

Cost: Test kit (scales, scoring directions, norms, descriptive material) $20.00

Publisher: Albert Mehrabian

MEASURES OF AFFILIATIVE TENDENCY AND SENSITIVITY TO REJECTION
Albert Mehrabian

Adult

Purpose: Assesses an individual's interpersonal and social approach-avoidance characteristics. Used for research and counseling purposes.

Description: Multiple-item verbal questionnaire consisting of two subscales: affiliative tendency and sensitivity to rejection. The standardized sum of the scores on both subscales also provides a reliable and valid measure of dependency. Examiner required. Suitable for group use.

Untimed: 10 minutes per scale

Scoring: Examiner evaluated

Cost: Test kit (scales, scoring directions, norms, descriptive material) $20.00

Publisher: Albert Mehrabian

MILLON ADOLESCENT PERSONALITY INVENTORY (MAPI)
Theodore Millon, Catherine J. Green, and Robert B. Meagher, Jr.

Adolescent   Ages 13-19

Purpose: Evaluates adolescent personality. Used as an aid to clinical assessment and academic and vocational guidance. Identifies student behavioral and emotional problems.

Description: 150-item paper-pencil true-false test covering eight personality style scales, eight expressed concern scales (such as peer security), and four behavioral correlates scales (such as impulse control). The clinical version is available to those with experience in the use of self-administered clinical tests. Suitable for group use.

Untimed: 20-30 minutes

Scoring: Computer scored

Cost: Manual $12.50; clinical interpretive report $12.10-$17.00 depending on quantity and scoring method; guidance interpretive report $4.80-$9.35 depending on quantity and scoring method; 25 answer sheets $8.75

Publisher: National Computer Systems/ PAS Division

MILLON BEHAVIORAL HEALTH INVENTORY (MBHI)
Theodore Millon, Catherine J. Green, and Robert B. Meagher, Jr.

Adult   Ages 18 and older

Purpose: Assesses attitudes of physically ill adults toward daily stress factors and health care personnel. Used for clinical evaluation of possible psychosomatic complications.

Description: 150-item paper-pencil true-false inventory covering eight basic coping styles (e.g., cooperation), six psychogenic attitudes (e.g., chronic tension), three psychosomatic correlatives (e.g., allergic inclinations), and three prognostic indexes (e.g., pain treatment responsivity). The test is designed for use with medical patients by examiners experienced in the use of clinical instruments. Self-administered. Suitable for group use.

Untimed: 20 minutes

Scoring: Computer scored by NCS

Cost: Manual $12.50; interpretive report $11.45-$16.10 depending on quantity and scoring method; 25 answer sheets $8.75

Publisher: National Computer Systems/ PAS Division

MILLON CLINICAL MULTIAXIAL INVENTORY (MCMI)
Theodore Millon

Adult   Ages 18 and older

Purpose: Diagnoses emotionally disturbed adults. Used to screen individuals who may require more intensive clinical evaluation and treatment.

Description: 175-item paper-pencil true-false test evaluating adults who have psychological or psychiatric difficulties. The test covers three categories that include eight basic personality patterns (DSM--

III, Axis II) reflecting a patient's lifelong traits existing prior to the behavioral dysfunctions; three pathological personality disorders (DSM-III, Axis II) reflecting chronic or severe abnormalities, and nine clinical symptom syndromes (DSM-III, Axis I) describing episodes or states in which active pathological processes are clearly evidenced. This instrument is intended for use only with psychiatric-emotionally disturbed populations. The examiner must be experienced in the use of clinical tests. Interpretation is available exclusively from NCS, and test results are available immediately via Arion II tele-processing. Self-administered. Suitable for group use.

Untimed: 25 minutes

Scoring: Computer scored

Cost: Manual $12.75; interpretive report $16.25-$22.00; profile report $4.60-$6.30; 25 answer sheets $8.75

Publisher: National Computer Systems/PAS Division

THE MINER SENTENCE COMPLETION SCALE: FORM H
Refer to page 923.

THE MINER SENTENCE COMPLETION SCALE: FORM P
Refer to page 923.

THE MINNESOTA MULTIPHASIC PERSONALITY INVENTORY: NEW GROUP FORM (FORM R)
Starke R. Hathaway and Charnley McKinley

Adolescent, adult
Ages 16 and older

Purpose: Assesses individual personality. Used for clinical diagnosis and research on psychopathology.

Description: 566-item true-false test of 10 clinical variables or factors of personality: hypochondriasis, depression, hysteria, psychopathic-deviate, masculinity-femininity, paranoia, psychasthenia, schizophrenia, hypomania, and social introversion. Scores also are obtained on four validity scales: Question, Lie (L),

Validity (F), and Defensiveness (K). Items required for these 14 basic scores are grouped as items 1-399. Items used only in research are presented as items 400-566. Materials include a hardcover question booklet with step-down pages. Individual and Old Group Forms also are available. Personality scores are plotted on a profile sheet reflecting standard deviations from the mean. Self-administered. Suitable for group and individual use. Available in 45 languages.

Untimed: 45-90 minutes

Scoring: Hand key; examiner evaluated; may be computer scored

Cost: Test booklet $7.75; 25 answer sheets $5.00; 25 answer keys (includes manual) $12.50

Publisher: University of Minnesota Press; distributed exclusively by NCS Interpretive Scoring Systems

---

THE MINNESOTA MULTIPHASIC PERSONALITY INVENTORY: OLD GROUP FORM
Starke R. Hathaway and Charnley McKinley

Adolescent, adult
Ages 16 and older

Purpose: Assesses individual personality. Used for clinical diagnosis and research on psychopathology and mental health.

Description: 556-item true-false test of 10 clinical variables or factors of personality: hypochondriasis, depression, hysteria, psychopathic-deviate, masculinity-femininity, paranoia, psychasthenia, schizophrenia, hypomania, and social introversion. Scores are also obtained on four validity scales: Question, Lie (L), Validity (F), and Defensiveness (K). Subjects respond to items on a separate answer sheet. Individual and New Group Forms also are available. Personality scores are plotted on a profile sheet reflecting standard deviations from the mean. Self-administered. Suitable for group and individual use. Available in 45 languages.

Untimed: 45-90 minutes

Scoring: Hand key; examiner evaluated; may be computer scored

Cost: 10 test booklets $6.00; 25 machine-scored answer sheets $5.00; 25 hand-scored answer sheets $3.40; hand-scored answer keys $3.40; 25 case summary and profile forms $3.20; tape recorded version of MMPI $38.00

Publisher: University of Minnesota Press; distributed exclusively by NCS Interpretive Scoring Systems

THE MINNESOTA MULTIPHASIC PERSONALITY INVENTORY: THE INDIVIDUAL FORM (MMPI)
Starke R. Hathaway and Charnley McKinley

Adolescent, adult
Ages 16 and older

Purpose: Assesses individual personality. Used for clinical diagnosis and research on psychopathology.

Description: 550-item true-false test of 10 clinical variables or factors of personality: hypochondriasis, depression, hysteria, psychopathic-deviate, masculinity-femininity, paranoia, psychasthenia, schizophrenia, hypomania, and social introversion. Scores also are obtained on four validity scales: Question, Lie (L), Validity (F), and Defensiveness (K). Materials include 550 cards to which the individual responds. Personality scores are plotted on a profile sheet reflecting standard deviations from the Mean. Old and New Group Forms are also available. Examiner required. Available in 45 languages.

Untimed: 1 hour, 30 minutes

Scoring: Hand key; examiner evaluated; may be computer scored

Cost: 25 recording sheets $5.00; item cards $54.00; answer keys (includes manual) $18.00

Publisher: University of Minnesota Press; distributed exclusively by NCS Interpretive Scoring Systems

MINNESOTA-BRIGGS HISTORY RECORD WITH MARRIAGE SECTION
Peter F. Briggs

Adult

Purpose: Gathers the information necessary for compiling a comprehensive developmental record of the life of the individual under study. Used for counseling and research purposes.

Description: Multiple-item paper-pencil inventory consisting of seven scales of personal and developmental history. An optional marriage section is available. The standardized scoring system permits comparison of case histories and is compatible with multitrait, multimethod analysis. Self-administered. Suitable for group use.

Untimed: Varies

Scoring: Examiner evaluated

Cost: 10 history records $10.00; 50 history record answer sheets $3.50; 10 marriage sections $5.00; 50 marriage section answer sheets $3.50; user's guide (monograph #36) $4.00

Publisher: Clinical Psychology Publishing Co., Inc.

MISKIMINS SELF-GOAL-OTHER DISCREPANCY SCALE (MSGO-I & MSGO-II)
R. W. Miskimins

Adolescent, adult

Purpose: Measures a person's self-concept in terms of the way the person sees himself, the way he would like to be, and the way he believes others see him. Used for clinical diagnosis and research.

Description: Paper-pencil test assessing social, emotional, and general aspects of a person's self-concept. The test is available in two forms. MSGO—I contains 15 items and five blank items in which the subject or examiner can insert his own dimensions. MSGO—II contains 12 items and four blank items presented in a simplified format and worded for use with younger people, seriously debilitated individuals, or the educationally handicapped.
The two forms differ slightly in item content and administration but use the same rating procedure and yield nearly identical results. For each test item, the subject rates himself three times on a scale consisting of bipolar adjectives separated by a 9-point Likert scale.
When scores for all items have been combined, it is possible to determine

discrepancies between "Self" and "Goal" and between "Self" and "Others." A greater discrepancy indicates a lower self-concept. A profile of each subject's responses can be drawn, and interpretative data are available for the most common types of profiles. In addition, the MSGO-I yields 28 subscores (19 of which significantly distinguish between normal and psychiatric populations), and the MSGO-II yields seven subscores. Use is restricted to APA membership guidelines. Examiner required. Suitable for group use.

Untimed: Not available

Scoring: Hand key; may be computer scored

Cost: 100 scales and profiles (specify form) $50.00; manual $14.00

Publisher: Rocky Mountain Behavioral Science Institute, Inc.

MOONEY PROBLEM CHECKLIST
R.L. Mooney and L. V. Gordon

**Adolescent, adult
Grades 7 and above**

Purpose: Identifies individuals who want or need help with personal problems. Used for individual counseling.

Description: Multiple-item paper-pencil self-assessment of personal problems. The subjects read examples of problems, underline those of "some concern," circle those of "most concern," and write a summary in their own words. The areas covered vary from form to form but include health and physical development, home and family, boy and girl relations, morals and religion, courtship and marriage, economic security, school or occupation, and social and recreational. Materials include separate checklists for junior-high students, high-school students, college students, and adults. Self-administered. Suitable for group use.

Untimed: 30 minutes

Scoring: Hand key; may be machine scored

Cost: Examiner's kit (materials without separate answer documents, junior high, high school, college, adult) $4.00; examiner kit (separate answer documents, junior high, high school, college) $7.50; both kits include checklist and manual

Publisher: The Psychological Corporation

MULTIDIMENSIONAL PERSONALITY QUESTIONNAIRE (MPQ)
Auke Tellegen

Adolescent, adult

Purpose: Assesses the normal personality. Used in vocational counseling, personnel selection, and career development and as an adjunct to clinical personality tests in counseling, psychiatric, and medical settings.

Description: 300-item paper-pencil self-report inventory measuring factors of the normal personality. Questions are presented in dichotomous forced-choice format at an eighth-grade reading level. The questionnaire measures 20 scales, including 11 scales measuring primary personality dimensions (well-being, social potency, achievement, social closeness, stress reaction, alienation, aggression, control, traditionalism, absorption, and harm avoidance), 3 scales measuring higher-order personality traits (positive affectivity, negative affectivity, and constraint); and 6 scales measuring validity (index of invalid responding, associative slips, unlikely virtues, desirable response inconsistency, true response inconsistency, and variable response inconsistency). Norms are provided for college students and adults. Examiner required. Suitable for group use.

Untimed: 35-45 minutes

Scoring: Contact publisher

Cost: Contact publisher

Publisher: National Computer Systems/ PAS Division

MULTIMODAL LIFE HISTORY QUESTIONNAIRE
Arnold A. Lazarus

Adult

Purpose: Provides information on personal and social history of adults for clinical assessment, marriage and family counseling, and psychotherapy.

Description: 12-page paper-pencil questionnaire assessing client's behavior, feelings, physical sensations, images, thoughts, interpersonal relationships, and biological factors. The client completes the questionnaire during his own time rather than during the counseling session. The therapist assesses information to design a treatment program. Self-administered. Suitable for group use.

Untimed: 2 hours

Scoring: Examiner evaluated

Cost: 20 questionnaires $16.00

Publisher: Multimodal Publications, Inc.

MULTIPHASIC SEX INVENTORY
H.R. Nichols and Ilene Molinder

Adult

Purpose: Measures the sexual characteristics of male sexual offenders. Used to evaluate sexual deviance, assess progress in the treatment of sexual deviance, and assess the readiness of institutionalized sex offenders for release or for further intense treatment.

Description: 300-item paper-pencil true-false test of psychosexual characteristics from which 20 scales and a 50-item sexual history are derived. Six of the 20 scales are validity scales. The inventory also contains a treatment attitudes scale. The sex deviance scales include the Child Molest Scale, Rape Scale, and Exhibitionism Scale. There are five atypical sexual outlet scales: Fetish, Voyeurism, Obscene Call, Bondage and Discipline, and Sado-Masochism. The four sexual dysfunction scales include the Sexual Inadequacy Scale, Premature Ejaculation Scale, Impotence Scale, and Physical Disabilities Scale. There is also a Sexual Knowledge and Beliefs Scale. The 50-item Sexual

History Scale includes a sex deviance development section, marriage development section, gender identity section, gender orientation development section, and a sexual assault behavior section. An eighth-grade reading level is required; however, a taped version of the test is available for use by reading-impaired persons. Examiner/self-administered. Suitable for group use.

Untimed: 45 minutes

Scoring: Hand key

Cost: Complete kit (manual, 5 test booklets, 25 answer sheets, 25 profile forms, set of 14 scoring templates) $29.95; shipping and handling $3.00

Publisher: Nichols and Molinder

MULTIPLE AFFECT ADJECTIVE CHECK LIST (MAACL)
Marvin Zuckerman and Bernard Lubin

Adolescent, adult
Grades 10 and above

Purpose: Measures anxiety, depression, and hostility in high-school and college students and adults. Used for clinical evaluation and research application.

Description: 132-item paper-pencil inventory measuring affects of Anxiety (A), Depression (D), and Hostility (H). The inventory may be administered under two different test sets, In General and Today Now. The Today Now form measures current affect states and requires students to check the adjectives that describe how they feel at the time of testing. The In General form instructs subjects to check those adjectives which describe a more general state of their feelings. The Today Now form is sensitive to changes in affect resulting from examination anxiety among college students, perceptual isolation, therapy sessions, combat training, and intake of alcohol. College student and adult job applicant norms are presented in the form of T-score equivalents. Means and standard deviations are presented for a variety of clinical groups and experimental situations. The new MAACL-R contains trait and state forms that have been shown to differentiate patients with affective disorders from other types of patients and normals. The MAACL-R may be used in studies of stress and stress reduction, diagnosis and treatment of psychological disorders, and in basic reasearch on personality and emotions. Scales on the MAACL-R are Anxiety (A), Depression (D), Hostility (H), Positive Affect (PA), and Sensation Seeking (SS). The two summary scores are Dysphoria (A + D + H) and Positive Affect and Sensation Seeking (PA + SS). Examiner/self-administered. Suitable for group use.

Untimed: 5 minutes per form

Scoring: Hand key; may be computer scored

Cost: Contact publisher

Publisher: Educational and Industrial Testing Service

MYERS-BRIGGS TYPE INDICATOR (MBTI)
Isabel Briggs Myers and Katharine C. Briggs

Adolescent, adult
Grades 9 and above

Purpose: Measures personality dispositions and interests based on Jung's theory of types. Used in personal, vocational, and marital counseling, executive development programs, and personality research.

Description: 166- to 126-item paper-pencil or computer-administered test of four bipolar aspects of personality: Introversion-Extraversion, Sensing-Intuition, Thinking-Feeling, and Judging-Perceptive. The subjects are classified as one of two "types" on each scale. Results for the four scales may be expressed as continuous scores or reduced to a 4-letter code or "type." Individual report forms containing a profile sheet with a brief interpretation of the scores and a chart explanation of each of the 16 MBTI types are available. The test is heavily influenced by Jungian theories of personality types and the ways in which these types express their personality traits through perceptions, judgments, interests, values, and motivations. A theoretical background in dynamic psychology is helpful in maximizing the benefits of research

compiled for this test. Materials include Form F (166 items) and Form G (126 items), which eliminates 40 items not scored on the four standard scales. A software package containing a diskette, user's guide, and carrying case is available for use with the IBM PC and IBM-compatible personal computers. Self-administered. Suitable for group use.

Untimed: 20-30 minutes

Scoring: Hand key; scoring service available; may be computer scored

Cost: Counselor's kit (specify Form F or G: manual, key, *Introduction to Type*, 5 tests, 25 answer sheets) $27.50

Publisher: Consulting Psychologists Press, Inc.

MYERS-BRIGGS TYPE INDICATOR: ABBREVIATED VERSION (MBTI:AV)
Katharine C. Briggs and Isabel Briggs Myers

Adult

Purpose: Measures personality dispositions and interests based on Jung's theory of types. Used for personal, marital, and vocational counseling, especially in workshops, seminars, or other settings, where immediate feedback is needed or time restraints are important.

Description: 50-item paper-pencil self-report inventory assessing personality type along four bipolar scales: intraversion-extroversion, sensing-intuition, thinking-feeling, and judging-perceptive. Results for the four scales may be expressed as continuous scores or reduced to a 4-letter code or "type." An individual report form containing a profile sheet with a brief interpretation of the scores and a chart explanation of each of the 16 MBTI types is included. Test items consist of the first 50 questions of the MBTI Form G. Self-administered. Suitable for group use.

Untimed: Varies

Scoring: Self-scored

Cost: 25 test booklets $12.00; single copy $0.60

Publisher: Consulting Psychologists Press, Inc.

NEO PERSONALITY INVENTORY (NEO-PI)

*Paul T. Costa, Jr. and
Robert R. McCrae*

Adult

Purpose: Measures five major personality domains of adults. Used in clinical psychology, psychiatry, behavioral medicine, vocational counseling, and industrial psychology.

Description: 181-item paper-pencil test providing a general description of an adult's personality. Domains assessed are Neuroticism (N), Extraversion (E), Openness to Experience (O), Agreeableness (A), and Conscientiousness (C). Facet scales for the N, E, and O domains yield a more detailed analysis of personality structure. Domain N scales are Anxiety, Hostility, Depression, Self-Consciousness, Impulsiveness, and Vulnerability. Domain E scales are Warmth, Gregariousness, Assertiveness, Activity, Excitement, Seeking, and Positive Emotions. Domain O scales are Fantasy, Aesthetics, Feelings, Actions, Ideas, and Values. Two versions of the inventory are available. Form S, appropriate for men and women, is self-administered. Answers are provided on a 5-point scale. Form R is written for observer ratings by a peer, spouse, or professional. A computer version is available. Examiner/self-administered. Suitable for group use.

Untimed: 30 minutes

Scoring: Hand key; may be computer scored

Cost: Professional kit (manual, scoring keys, 10 reusable test booklets-Form S, 25 profile forms-Form S, 25 answer sheets) $42.00; computer version (25 uses) $75.00

Publisher: Psychological Assessment Resources, Inc.

NEUROTICISM SCALE QUESTIONNAIRE (NSQ)

*Raymond B. Cattell and
Ivan H. Scheier*

**Adolescent, adult
Grades 10 and above**

Purpose: Measures neuroticism in senior high-school students and adults of most educational levels. Used for clinical evaluation, personal counseling, and research on neuroticism.

Description: 40-item paper-pencil questionnaire measuring degree of "neurotic trend" in adults and adolescents. Standard scores are provided for men, women, and men and women together. A sixth-grade reading level is required. Self-administered. Suitable for group use.

Untimed: 10 minutes

Scoring: Hand key

Cost: Testing kit $8.50; handbook $5.75; 25 test booklets $7.75; scoring key $1.95

Publisher: Institute for Personality and Ability Testing, Inc.

NURSES' OBSERVATION SCALE FOR INPATIENT EVALUATION (NOSIE-30)

*Gilbert Honigfeld, Roderic D. Gillis,
and C. James Klett*

Adult

Purpose: Assesses the ward behavior of psychiatric inpatients. Used by nursing personnel to evaluate patient status and change.

Description: 30-item paper-pencil observational inventory assessing inpatient psychiatric behavior. Measures six factors: social competence (refuses to do the ordinary things expected of him; has trouble remembering), social interest (shows interest in the activities around him, tries to be friendly to others), personal neatness (keeps his clothes neat; is messy in his eating habits), irritability (gets angry or annoyed easily; is irritable and grouchy), manifests psychosis (hears things that are not there; talks, mutters, or mumbles to himself), and retardation (sits, unless directed into activity; is slow and sluggish). A global score, Total Patient Assets, is also calculated as a composite of the six factor scores. Scale items consist of statements about the patient's ward behavior and are rated on a 5-point scale from 0 (never) to 4 (always). Factor scores are based on two raters' combined scores in which each item receives unit weight. Profile forms convert raw scores to T-scores or centile ranks for normative comparison. Examiner required. Not suitable for group use.

Untimed: Varies

Scoring: Examiner evaluated

Cost: Contact publisher

Publisher: Behavior Arts Center

OBJECT RELATIONS TECHNIQUE
H. Phillipson

Adolescent, adult

Purpose: Assesses interpersonal relations. Used for individual therapy and counseling.

Description: 12-item projective test of interpersonal relations. Items are cards presenting important interpersonal situations in varying environmental and emotional contexts. The subject creates a story about each picture. Evaluation of the responses is based on object relations theory in psychoanalysis. Examiner required. Not suitable for group use. BRITISH PUBLISHER

Untimed: 1 hour

Scoring: Examiner evaluated

Cost: 12 plates £35.85; handbook £6.05 (payment in sterling for all overseas orders)

Publisher: NFER-NELSON Publishing Company Ltd.

OBJECTIVE ANALYTIC BATTERIES (O-A)
Raymond B. Cattell and James M. Schueiger

Adolescent, adult
Ages 14 and older

Purpose: Evaluates personality in adults and adolescents. Used for clinical evaluations, research on personality source traits, and personal counseling.

Description: 10 paper-pencil tests providing an objective measure of 10 personality source traits: ego strength, anxiety, independence, extraversion, regression, control, cortertia, depression, and others. The batteries are arranged in a kit, from which tests for half an hour, an hour, two hours, etc., may be scheduled, according to purpose and testing time. The handbook for the O-A Kit combines practical tests with broad developments in psychometry (defining validity, reliability, function fluctuation, state-trait differences) and in personality theory concerning the source-trait structures and their mode of interaction. The handbook is designed explicitly as supportive reading and realistic illustration for courses on personality theory. Norms are calculated directly for each of the 10 factors; the norm base covers ages 14-30 years; age trends are included for other situations. Examiner required. Suitable for group use.

Untimed: 30 minutes

Scoring: Not available

Cost: Professional testing kit $89.50; handbook $37.50; test kit $32.00; 10 expendable booklets (OA359) $8.50; (OA360) $4.75; (OA361) $4.50; 25 answer sheets (OA362) $8.00; audiotapes (OA363) $10.00; (OA347) set of 5 $45.00; score summary sheets for handscoring available from IPAT

Publisher: Institute for Personality and Ability Testing, Inc.

THE OFFER PARENT-ADOLESCENT QUESTIONNAIRE (OPAQ)
Daniel Offer, Eric Ostrov, and Kenneth I. Howard

Purpose: Measures parents' perceptions of their adolescent child's self-image.

Description: 50-item paper-pencil test of 12 areas of self-image: impulse control, emotional tone, body and self-image, social relationships, morals, sexual attitudes, family attitudes, mastery of the external world, vocational and educational goals, psychopathology, superior adjustment, and idealism. The test items require the parent to choose between six choices presented in a Likert-scale format and mark the appropriate space in the test booklet or on the answer sheet. The OPAQ usually is used in conjunction with the Offer Self-Image Questionnaire

(OSIQ) for Adolescents. Alternate forms are available for sons and daughters. Self-administered. Suitable for group use.

Untimed: 10-15 minutes

Scoring: Computer scored

Cost: Questionnaire $1.00; answer sheet $0.15; computer analysis $10.00 base fee and $1.00 per subject

Publisher: Institute for Psychosomatic and Psychiatric Research and Training, Michael Reese Hospital

---

THE OFFER SELF-IMAGE QUESTIONNAIRE FOR ADOLESCENTS
Daniel Offer

Adolescent   Ages 13-19

Purpose: Assesses teen-agers' self-image and personality adjustment. Used as an aid to clinical counseling.

Description: 130-item paper-pencil test evaluating five categories of personal imagery: psychological selves, social selves, sexual selves, familial selves, and coping selves measured on a scale of six responses ranging from "describes me very well" to "does not describe me at all." The test is standard scored. A low standard score indicates that the takers do not deal adequately with their environment. A high score indicates good ability to cope. Subjects read the front page of the booklet and provide the requested personal information, asking questions of the examiner if necessary. Software is available for computer administration and scoring. Examiner required. Suitable for group use.

Untimed: 40 minutes

Scoring: Examiner evaluated; may be computer scored

Cost: Manual $15.00; M/F questionnaire $1.00 each; answer sheet $0.15; scoring service per questionnaire $1.00, plus $10.00 base fee

Publisher: Institute for Psychosomatic and Psychiatric Research and Training, Michael Reese Hospital

THE OFFER TEACHER-STUDENT QUESTIONNAIRE (OTSQ)
Daniel Offer

Teachers

Purpose: Measures teacher perceptions of an adolescent student's self-image.

Description: 50-item paper-pencil test of the following areas of self-image as rated by a therapist: impulse control, emotional tone, body and self-image, social relationships, sexual attitudes, family attitudes, mastery of the external world, vocational and educational goals, psychopathology, superior adjustment, and idealism. The test items require the therapist to choose between six choices presented in a Likert-scale format and mark the appropriate space in the test booklet or on an answer sheet. The OTSQ usually is used in conjunction with the Offer Self-Image Questionnaire (OSIQ) for Adolescents. Self-administered. Suitable for group use.

Untimed: 10-15 minutes

Scoring: Computer scored

Cost: Questionnaire $1.00; answer sheet $0.15; computer analysis $10.00 base fee and $1.00 per subject

Publisher: Institute for Psychosomatic and Psychiatric Research and Training, Michael Reese Hospital

---

THE OFFER THERAPIST-ADOLESCENT QUESTIONNAIRE (OTAQ)
Daniel Offer, Eric Ostrov, and Kenneth I. Howard

Therapists

Purpose: Measures therapist perceptions of an adolescent client's self-image.

Description: 50-item paper-pencil test of the following areas of self-image as rated by a therapist: impulse control, emotional tone, body and self-image, social relationships, morals, sexual attitudes, family attitudes, mastery of the external world, vocational and educational goals, psychopathology, superior adjustment, and idealism. The test items require the therapist to choose between six choices presented in a Likert-scale format and mark the appropriate space in the test booklet or on the answer sheet. The OTAQ usually is used in conjunction with the Offer Self-Image Questionnaire (OSIQ) for Adolescents. Self-administered. Suitable for group use.

Untimed: 10-15 minutes

Scoring: Computer scored

Cost: Questionnaire $1.00; answer sheet $0.15; computer analysis $10.00 base fee and $1.00 per subject

Publisher: Institute for Psychosomatic and Psychiatric Research and Training, Michael Reese Hospital

OMNIBUS PERSONALITY INVENTORY (OPI)
P.A. Histe, T.R. McConnell, H.D. Webster, and G.D. Yonge

Adolescent, adult
Grades 11 and above

Purpose: Assesses selected personality factors, values, and interests of students relevant to an academic activity. Used to understand and differentiate among students in an educational context.

Description: 385-item paper-pencil inventory of 14 aspects of personality, including thinking introversion, theoretical orientation, aestheticism, complexity, autonomy, religious orientation, social extraversion, impulse expression, personal integration, anxiety level, altruism, practical outlook, masculinity-femininity, and response bias. An Intellectual Disposition Catagory is determined for each individual by combining his standings on six of the regular scales. Examiner required. Suitable for group use.

Untimed: 45-60 minutes

Scoring: Hand key; may be computer scored

Cost: 25 inventory booklets $23.00; 50 machine-scorable answer sheets $15.00; 50 hand-scorable answer sheets $17.00; manual $15.00; specimen set $15.00

Publisher: The Psychological Corporation

PAIN APPERCEPTION TEST
Refer to page 206.

PARENT DIABETES OPINION SURVEY (PDOS)
Suzanne Bennett Johnson

Adult

Purpose: Measures attitudes toward diabetes of parents with diabetic children. Used for clinical assessment and research in medical settings.

Description: 68-item paper-pencil Likert-scale test of eight aspects of attitudes regarding diabetes: attitudes toward medical staff, stigma, rule orientation/high supervision, divine intervention, family interruption, manipulativeness, reactions: observation/detection, and sweet consumption. The lie scale from the Personality Inventory for Children also is included in the PDOS. The parent expresses degree of agreement or disagreement with the attitude expressed in each item. A measure of child attitude may be obtained by using the Diabetes Opinion Survey (DOS). Examiner/self-administered. Suitable for group use.

Untimed: Varies

Scoring: Hand key

Cost: Sample $30.00

Publisher: Suzanne Bennett Johnson, Ph.D.

THE PERSONAL AUDIT
Refer to page 932.

PERSONAL DISTRESS INVENTORY AND SCALES
Alan Bedford and Graham Foulds

Adult

Purpose: Measures personal illness and personality deviance. Used for personality assessment, individual counseling, evaluation of treatment, and research.

Description: Four multiple-item paper-pencil tests of personality deviance. The Delusion-Symptoms-State Inventory

(DSSI) is an 84-item self-report instrument measuring a wide range of current symptomology. The test contains 12 sets of seven items each, corresponding to acute psychiatric symptoms. The Personal Disturbance Scale (DSSI/SaD) consists of the seven state anxiety and seven depression items from the full DSSI. Both total and separate scores for the two scales may be obtained. The DSSI/NS (Neurotic Symptoms) test is also derived from the DSSI and consists of the five sets of items measuring neurotic symptoms. The Personality Deviance Scales (PDS) cover Extrapunitiveness, Intropunitiveness, and Dominance. Each dimension consists of 12 items scored on a 4-point scale. Examiner required. Suitable for group use.

BRITISH PUBLISHER

Untimed: Not available

Scoring: Hand key; examiner evaluated

Cost: Specimen set (single copies of each manual and questionnaire, no keys) £14.50 (payment in sterling for all overseas orders)

Publisher: NFER-NELSON Publishing Company Ltd.

PERSONAL ORIENTATION DIMENSIONS (POD)
Everett L. Shostrom

Adult

Purpose: Measures attitudes and values in terms of concepts of the actualizing person, one who is more fully functioning and lives a more enriched life. Used to introduce humanistic value concepts, indicate a person's level of positive mental health, and measure the effects of various treatment and training techniques.

Description: 260-item paper-pencil two-choice test consisting of bipolar pairs of statements of comparative values and behavior judgments. The subject must choose from each pair the statement that is closest to his beliefs. Items are stated both negatively and positively; opposites are dictated not by word choice but by context. Test items are nonthreatening in order to facilitate communication of the results and provide a positive approach for measuring the following personality

dimensions: orientation (time orientation and core centeredness), polarities (strength/weakness and love/anger), integration (synergistic integration and potentiation), and awareness (being, trust in humanity, creative living, mission, and manipulation awareness). Test results indicate whether (and to what degree) an individual is actualizing or non-actualizing. The inventory is a component of the Actualizing Assessment Battery (AAB). Examiner required. Suitable for group use.

Untimed: 30-40 minutes

Scoring: Hand key; may be computer scored

Cost: Specimen set (manual, all forms) $5.50; 25 reusable test booklets $14.25; 50 NCS answer sheets $9.50; EdITS scoring without profile $0.80, with profile $1.00

Publisher: Educational and Industrial Testing Service

PERSONAL ORIENTATION INVENTORY (POI)
Everett L. Shostrom

Adolescent, adult
Grades 10 and above

Purpose: Measures values and behaviors important in the development of the actualizing person, one who is more fully functioning and lives a more enriched life. Used in counseling and group training sessions and as a pre- and posttherapy measure to indicate a person's level of positive mental health.

Description: 150-item paper-pencil two-choice test containing bipolar pairs of statements of comparative values and behavioral judgments. The subject must choose from each pair the statement that is closest to his beliefs. The inventory is scored for two major scales and 10 subscales: Time Ratio, Support Ratio, Self-Actualizing Value, Existentiality, Feeling Reactivity, Spontaneity, Self-Regard, Self-Acceptance, Nature of Man, Synergy, Acceptance of Aggression, and Capacity for Intimate Contact. College norms are presented in percentile scores. Adult mean scores and profiles are provided. Means, standard deviations, and plotted profiles are provided for clinically nominated self-actualized and non-self-actualized groups, as well as for many other clinical and industrial samples. The inventory is a component of the Actualizing Assessment Battery (AAB). Examiner required. Suitable for group use.

Untimed: 30 minutes

Scoring: Hand key; may be computer scored

Cost: Specimen set (manual, all forms) $5.75; 25 reusable test booklets $14.25; 50 profile sheets $8.00; set of 14 hand-scoring stencils $28.00; handbook $12.95; manual $3.25

Publisher: Educational and Industrial Testing Service

PERSONAL PREFERENCE SCALE
*Maurice H. Krout and
Johanna Krout*

Adult

Purpose: Assesses aspects of personality that are usually available only through projective tests. Used for clinical evaluations, vocational guidance, and industrial placement. Provides drawing analysis and specific material on basic issues.

Description: 100-item paper-pencil multiple-choice test consisting of 10 subtests of 10 items each. The test items are drawn from everyday activities relating to a variety of early experiences. The subject rates each item on a 3-point scale according to personal likes and dislikes. The responses indicate important attitudes and personality traits derived from those early experiences. The factors measured include adventuresomeness vs. security-seeking, communicativeness vs. taciturnity, optimism vs. pessimism, altruism vs. punitivism, emotional lability vs. emotional rigidity, aspiration level, assertiveness level, sentimentality, and impersonal affiliativeness.
A guide for interpretation is available, but more sophisticated approaches in terms of personality development and structure will yield more valuable insights from the scores. In industrial applications, specific subtests have proven most valuable in discriminating between workers who were well-motivated and successful with cer-

tain operations and those who were poorly suited for such work. Self-administered. Suitable for group use.

Untimed: 20 minutes

Scoring: Hand key

Cost: Test $0.35 (free guide with each set of fifty purchased)

Publisher: Johanna Krout Tabin, Ph.D.

PERSONAL PROBLEMS CHECKLIST—ADOLESCENT
John A. Schinka

Adolescent   Ages 13-17

Purpose: Assesses personal problems of adolescents. Used as a survey instrument in clinical and counseling settings to initiate the consultation process and introduce the client to formal diagnostic testing.

Description: 240-item paper-pencil test identifying common problems cited by adolescents in 13 areas: social, appearance, job, family, home, school, money, religion, emotions, dating, health, attitude, and crises. The test is available in a computer version for use with Apple II Plus, Apple IIe, and IBM PC computers. The test is a component of the Clinical Checklist Series. Self-administered. Suitable for group use.

Untimed: 10-20 minutes

Scoring: Examiner evaluated

Cost: 50 checklists $12.95; computer version (100 uses) $50.00

Publisher: Psychological Assessment Resources, Inc.

PERSONAL PROBLEMS CHECKLIST—ADULT
John A. Schinka

Adult

Purpose: Assesses the personal problems of adults. Used as a survey instrument in clinical and counseling settings to initiate the consultation process and introduce the client to formal diagnostic testing.

Description: 211-item paper-pencil test identifying problems in 13 areas: social, appearance, vocational, family and home, school, finances, religion, emotions, sex, legal, health and habits, attitude, and crises. The test is available in a computer version for use with Apple II Plus, Apple IIe, and IBM PC computers. The test is a component of the Clinical Checklist Series. Self-administered. Suitable for group use.

Untimed: 10-20 minutes

Scoring: Examiner evaluated

Cost: 50 checklists $12.95; computer version (100 uses) $50.00

Publisher: Psychological Assessment Resources, Inc.

PERSONAL QUESTIONNAIRE RAPID SCALING TECHNIQUE (PQRST)
David Mulhall

Adolescent, adult

Purpose: Measures changes in feelings, beliefs, and symptoms. Used for clinical and educational counseling.

Description: Multiple-item paper-pencil test of issues important to an individual. In cooperation with a consultant, the respondent defines a set of constructs to be measured. The constructs may include feelings or attitudes on behavior. The technique provides a framework through which the intensity of each construct can be measured. Two forms, PQ10 and PQ14, are available. Form PQ10 contains slightly fewer constructs. Availability is limited to experienced psychologists or persons with equivalent qualifications. Examiner required. Not suitable for group use.
BRITISH PUBLISHER

Untimed: Not available

Scoring: Hand key

Cost: Specimen set £17.20 (payment in sterling for all overseas orders)

Publisher: NFER-NELSON Publishing Company Ltd.

PET ATTITUDE SCALE
Donald I. Templer

Adult

Purpose: Measures an individual's attitudes toward pets.

Description: 18-item Likert-format scale indicating whether an individual has a favorable attitude toward pets. The test measures three factors: love and interaction, pets in the home, and joy of pet ownership. Self-administered. Suitable for group use.

Untimed: Varies

Scoring: Not available

Cost: Contact publisher

Publisher: Donald I. Templer, Ph.D.

PHSF RELATIONS QUESTIONNAIRE—1970
Refer to page 674.

THE PICTORIAL STUDY OF VALUES
Charles Shooster

Adult

Purpose: Examines personal values. Used for self-awareness programs, discussion groups, and research on values and mores. Suitable for illiterates and non-English-speaking persons.

Description: Multiple-item paper-pencil test measuring reactions to six basic value areas: social, political, economic, religious, aesthetic, and theoretical. Test items are composed of photographs. College norms are provided. Examiner required. Suitable for group use.

Untimed: 20 minutes

Scoring: Examiner evaluated

Cost: Specimen set $5.00; 25 tests $5.00

Publisher: Psychometric Affiliates

THE PICTURE IDENTIFICATION TEST
Jay L. Chambers

Adolescent, adult

Purpose: Assesses a person's effectiveness in dealing with combative, personal, and competitive motivational dimensions. Used for personality analysis and research in psychotherapy.

Description: Multiple-item two-part paper-pencil test in which the subject is presented a card with 12 photographs representing a variety of facial expressions (6 male, 6 female, ages 21-23). In Part I, the subject rates each facial expression on a scale ranging from "very positive" to "very negative." In Part II, the subject is given a list of 22 needs (based on Murray's Need System) and three time dimension items (past, present, future). The subject uses a scale ranging from "very definite expression of the motive" to "definitely does not express the motive." The ratings are computer analyzed by the author and yield two types of scores. A multi-dimensional scale analysis yields three dimension scales: Combative, Personal, Competitive. Specific attitudes scores are computed for each need. These attitude scores are correlated with target dimension need locations to provide an attitude score for each dimension. Self-administered. Suitable for group use.

Untimed: 45-60 minutes

Scoring: Computer scored

Cost: Manual $13.00; scoring and interpretation $3.00

Publisher: Jay L. Chambers, Ph.D.

PICTURE PERSONALITY TEST FOR INDIAN SOUTH AFRICANS (PPT-ISA)

Adult   Ages 16 and older

Purpose: Measures attitudes of Indian South Africans.

Description: Multiple-item paper-pencil projective test predicting job success in industry and business and indicating relations with significant others for clinical purposes. A picture album (one for males and one for females) is used for determining attitude towards demands, family relationships, father-son or mother-daughter relationship, mother-son or father-daughter relationship, attitude towards Indian authority, self-concept, sexual relationship, attitude towards white authority, social adjustment, and aggression. The test has 11 picture cards (constructs) that can be selected according to the purpose of the evaluation. Distinction can be made for Hindus, Mohammedans, and Christians. The test can be analyzed for positive (favorable), negative (hostile), and ambivalent

(unsure) reactions. An item analysis also can be performed. Individual testing is recommended for individuals who have only a primary school qualification. Examiner required. Suitable for group use.

SOUTH AFRICAN PUBLISHER

Untimed: 2 hours

Scoring: Hand key

Cost: Manual $6.70; test album (specify male or female) $41.30; 10 answer booklets $8.30

Publisher: Human Sciences Research Council

PIKUNAS ADULT STRESS INVENTORY (PASI, 1984)
Justin Pikunas

**Adolescent, adult
Ages 16 and older**

Purpose: Measures the intensity of stress present in adults and adolescents. Used to identify individuals needing counseling in order to deal more efficiently with stress.

Description: 3-page paper-pencil inventory examining the effects of stress on the subject's personal efficiency, adjustment, and physical health. A sixth-grade reading level is required. Test results are compared to a college student sample. Self-administered. Suitable for group use.

Untimed: 15 minutes

Scoring: Hand key

Cost: Testing form $1.00; 25 forms $8.00

Publisher: Justin Pikunas, Ph.D.

POLYFACTORIAL STUDY OF PERSONALITY
Martin M. Bruce

Adult

Purpose: Diagnoses personality as an aid in the clinical evaluation of an individual's relationship with others.

Description: 300-item pencil-paper true-false test measuring 11 aspects of psychopathology: hypochrondriasis, sexual identification, anxiety, social distance, sociopathy, depression, compulsivity, repression paranoia, schizophrenia, and hyperaffectivity. Self-administered. Suitable for group use.

Untimed: 45 minutes

Scoring: Hand key

Cost: Manual $6.90; IBM scoring stencil $12.50; package of profile sheets $10.50; package of IBM answer sheets $10.50

Publisher: Martin M. Bruce, Ph.D., Publishers

PORTEOUS PROBLEM CHECKLIST

Refer to page 675.

PROBLEM APPRAISAL SCALES (PAS)
Jean Endicott and The Department of Research Assessment and Training

Adolescent, adult

Purpose: Assesses psychiatric functioning. Used for diagnosis of psychopathology.

Description: Multiple-item measure of a broad range of psychiatric signs and symptoms consisting of 40 scales and one checklist item. The PAS covers the same areas as the Psychiatric Evaluation Form (PEF) and also includes items covering physical functioning and intellectual development. The PAS is completed by the examiner after a clinical workup. Examiner required. Not suitable for group use.

Untimed: After clinical workup, 3-5 minutes

Scoring: Examiner evaluated; computer scored for primary scales

Cost: Scale $0.50; interview guide $0.50; suggested procedures and instruction $0.40; summary scale scores/tables $0.50 plus postage and handling

Publisher: Department of Research Assessment and Training—N.Y. State Psychiatric Institute

PROFILE OF ADAPTATION TO LIFE—CLINICAL (PAL-C)
Robert E. Ellsworth

Adult

Purpose: Measures the personal and social adaptation of adults. Used as an intake screening instrument in clinical settings.

Description: 41-item paper-pencil self-report inventory providing scores on seven factorial scales: negative emotions, psychological well-being, income management, physical symptoms, alcohol/drugs, close relations, and child relations. The manual explains the rationale and validity of the scale and provides detailed norms for the general and clinical populations with respect to adjustment to life and the community. Self-administered. Suitable for group use.

Untimed: 20-30 minutes

Scoring: Self-scored or examiner evaluated

Cost: Manual $7.50; 25 scales and profile sheets $5.00; specimen set (manual, scale, and profile sheet) $7.75

Publisher: Consulting Psychologists Press, Inc.

PROFILE OF ADAPTATION TO LIFE—HOLISTIC (PAL-H)
Robert E. Ellsworth

Adult

Purpose: Measures an individual's adaptation to life in terms of the individual's lifestyle and spiritual awareness. Used by ministers and counselors working with people who are interested in health-related activities and spiritual awareness as part of their remedial program.

Description: Multiple-item paper-pencil self-report inventory assessing seven clinical scales (negative emotions, psychological well-being, income management, physical symptoms, alcohol/drugs, close relations, and child relations) and five scales relating to lifestyle and spiritual awareness (social activity, self-activity, nutrition and exercise, personal growth, and spiritual awareness). The seven clinical scales are the same as those contained in the Profile of Adaptation to Life—Clinical (PAL-C). The manual explains the rationale and validity of the scale and provides detailed norms for the general and clinical populations in terms of adjustment to life and the community. Self-administered. Suitable for group use.

Untimed: 20-30 minutes

Scoring: Examiner evaluated

Cost: Manual $7.50; 25 scales and profile sheets $5.00

Publisher: Consulting Psychologists Press, Inc.

PROFILE OF MOOD STATES (POMS)
Douglas M. McNair, Maurice Lorr, and Leo Droppleman

Adolescent, adult
Ages 18 and older

Purpose: Assesses dimensions of affect or mood in individuals ages 18 and older. Used to measure outpatients' response to various therapeutic approaches, including drug evaluation studies.

Description: 65-item paper-pencil test measuring six dimensions of affect or mood: tension-anxiety, depression-dejection, anger-hostility, vigor-activity, fatigue-inertia, and confusion-bewilderment. An alternative POMS-Bipolar Form measures the following mood dimensions in terms of six bipolar affective states identified in recent research: composed-anxious, elated-depressed, agreeable-hostile, energetic-tired, clear-headed-confused, and confident-unsure. The POMS-Bipolar Form is currently available for research use. Norms are provided for POMS for college and outpatient populations. Examiner required. Suitable for group use.

Untimed: 3-5 minutes

Scoring: Hand key, may be computer scored

Cost: Specimen set (manual, all forms) $5.25; 25 inventories (specify college or outpatient) $6.50; 25 profile sheets $4.75; keys $12.00; manual $3.00

Publisher: Educational and Industrial Testing Service

THE PROJECTIVE ASSESSMENT OF AGING METHOD (PAAM)
Bernard D. Starr,
Marcella Bakur Weiner,
and Marilyn Rabetz

Adult

Purpose: Assesses the adaptations, potential crisis situations, and areas of conflict unique to the phenomenology of aging. Used for clinical evaluation.

Description: 28-item oral-response projective test consisting of 31 drawings for use in clinical administration: 14 standard pictures with male/female alternatives and 14 alternates. The scenes are related to aging and elicit feelings, attitudes, and perceptions of the subjects that give clues to their emotional and cognitive frame of mind. Examiner required. Not suitable for group use.

Untimed: Not available

Scoring: Examiner evaluated

Cost: Complete kit (28 cards, manual) $35.00

Publisher: Springer Publishing Company

PROJECTIVE PERSONALITY TEST (ANALAGOUS TO THE TAT)

Adult

Purpose: Evaluates basic personality characteristics. Intended for use exclusively with Black African subjects.

Description: 16-18 picture cards provide the stimuli for a projective personality test analagous to the TAT. Each picture presents some degree of ambiguity to facilitate a variety of interpretations. Where humans are depicted, black characters are used except where the situation, according to the test publisher, "requires a Caucasian." There is one set of cards for each of the following groups: urban men, urban women, rural men, and rural women. Use is restricted to competent persons properly registered with the South African Medical and Dental Council. Examiner required. Not suitable for group use.

SOUTH AFRICAN PUBLISHER

Untimed: Open ended

Scoring: Examiner evaluated

Cost: Contact publisher

Publisher: National Institute for Personnel Research

PSYCHIATRIC DIAGNOSTIC INTERVIEW (PDI)
Ekkehard Othmer,
Elizabeth C. Penick,
and Barbara J. Powell

Adult

Purpose: Identifies frequently encountered psychiatric disorders. Used in all phases of diagnostic screening, intake, and followup.

Description: Multiple-item verbally administered oral-response test consisting of easily understood questions, most of which require only a "yes" or "no" answer. Clinicians and trained support personnel can quickly obtain diagnostic summaries evaluating the following 15 basic syndromes: organic brain syndrome, alcoholism, drug dependency, mania, depression, schizophrenia, antisocial personality, hysteria (Briquet Syndrome), anorexia nervosa, obsessive-compulsive neurosis, phobic neurosis, anxiety neurosis, mental retardation, homosexuality, and transsexualism. In addition, three derived syndromes are evaluated: polydrug abuse, schizoaffective disorder, and manic-depressive disorder. The questions for each of the basic syndromes are divided into four sections. If simple response criteria are not met, the interviewer omits the remainder of the questions for that syndrome and proceeds to the next syndrome. All positive syndromes are recorded on the Time Profile, which graphically displays which syndromes were positive, the patient's age when they were positive, and how long they were positive. Examiner required. Not suitable for group use.

Untimed: 15-60 minutes

Scoring: Examiner evaluated

Cost: Kit (reusable test booklet, 25 recording booklets, manual) $55.00

Publisher: Western Psychological Services

PSYCHIATRIC EVALUATION FORM (PEF)
Jean Endicott and The Department of
Research Assessment and Training

Adolescent, adult

Purpose: Assesses current psychiatric functioning. Used for the diagnosis of psychopathology.

Description: Multiple-item measure of a broad range of psychiatric symptoms consisting of 27 scales and two checklist items. The PEF measures the same areas as the Psychiatric Status Schedule and also includes characteristics of present illness and the major reason for admission. The PEF is completed by the examiner based on a clinical workup or client interview. Examiner required. Not suitable for group use.

Untimed: 25-50 minutes total interview

Scoring: Examiner evaluated; computer scored for summary scales

Cost: Booklet with score sheet $3.00; score sheet $0.30; manual of instructions $1.00; teaching tape and key $4.00; summary scale scores $0.55; editing/coding instructions $0.20; Fortran program $125.00 plus postage and handling

Publisher: Department of Research Assessment and Training—N.Y. State Psychiatric Institute

---

PSYCHIATRIC STATUS SCHEDULE (PSS)
Jean Endicott and The Department of
Research Assessment and Training

Adolescent, adult

Purpose: Assesses current psychiatric functioning. Used for the diagnosis of psychopathology.

Description: 321-item measure of psychopathology, organicity, and alcoholism or drug abuse. The subject's role as a wage earner, housekeeper, student, mate, and parent are also covered. Items are in true-false and checklist form. The interviewer answers the items based on a meeting with the subject. Materials include a 21-page stepdown booklet. The instrument covers many of the same areas as the Psychiatric Evaluation Form (PEF). Examiner required. Not suitable for group use.

Untimed: 30-50 minutes

Scoring: Hand key; examiner evaluated; may be computer scored

Cost: Booklet with score sheet $3.50; score sheet $0.30; suggested training procedures $0.20; manual $1.00; teaching tape and key $4.00; summary scale scores $1.50; editing/coding instructions $0.20; hand stencils $5.00; Fortran program $125.00 plus postage and handling

Publisher: Department of Research Assessment and Training—N.Y. State Psychiatric Institute

PSYCHOEPISTEMOLOGICAL PROFILE (PEP)
Refer to page 704.

PSYCHOLOGICAL SCREENING INVENTORY (PSI)
Richard I. Lanyon

Adolescent, adult
Grades 10 and above

Purpose: Identifies adults and adolescents who may need a more extensive mental health examination or professional attention. Used in clinics, hospitals, schools, courts, and reformatories.

Description: 130-item true-false test covering five scales: Alienation, Social Nonconformity, Discomfort, Expression, and Defensiveness. Materials include a manual, question and answer sheet, scoring template, and profile. Use is restricted to certified psychologists. Examiner required. Suitable for group use. Available in Spanish.

Untimed: 15 minutes

Scoring: Hand key

Cost: Complete kit $33.00

Publisher: Research Psychologists Press, Inc.

PSYCHOSOCIAL ADJUSTMENT TO ILLNESS SCALE (PAIS)
Leonard R. Derogatis

Adult

Purpose: Assesses the psychological and social adjustment of medical patients or their immediate families to a serious illness.

Description: 46-item paper-pencil self-report instrument or structured interview guide assessing the psychosocial adjustment of medical patients and their immediate families in terms of seven principal domains: health care orientation, vocational environment, domestic environment, sexual relationships, extended family relationships, social environment, and psychological distress. A total score summarizes overall adjustment to illness. The self-report form (PAIS-SR) and the interview guide (PAIS) measure equivalent items. Norms and profile/score sheets are available for lung cancer patients and renal dialysis patients for the self-report form. Examiner required. The self-report form is suitable for group use; the interview guide is individually administered.

Untimed: 20-30 minutes

Scoring: Examiner evaluated

Cost: Interview booklet $3.00; self-report form $0.70; score/profile sheets $0.20

Publisher: Clinical Psychometric Research

PSYCHOSOCIAL PAIN INVENTORY (PSPI)
Robert K. Heaton,
Ralph A. W. Lehman,
and Carl J. Getto

Adult

Purpose: Evaluates psychosocial factors related to chronic pain problems. Used in the treatment of chronic pain patients.

Description: 8-page multiple-item paper-pencil inventory assessing the following psychosocial factors considered important in maintaining and exacerbating chronic pain problems: several forms of secondary gain, the effects of pain behavior on interpersonal relationships, the existence of stressful life events that may contribute to subjective distress or promote avoidance learning, and components of past history that familiarize the patient with the chronic invalid role and with its personal and social consequences. Ratings take into account that patients differ in the degree to which they are likely to be influenced by potential sources of secondary gain. The inventory yields a total score. High scores predict poor response to medical treatment for pain. Examiner required. Not suitable for group use.

Untimed: Varies

Scoring: Examiner evaluated

Cost: Test kit (25 PSPI forms, manual) $18.00

Publisher: Psychological Assessment Resources, Inc.

PSYCHOTIC INPATIENT PROFILE
Maurice Lorr and Norris D. Vestre

Adult

Purpose: Measures the behavior patterns of adult psychiatric patients. Used with difficult patients and to evaluate treatment progress.

Description: 96-item paper-pencil inventory consisting of questions about the subject's behavior, which a nurse or psychiatric aide answers by indicating frequency of observation. Analysis of the responses provides objective and quantitative measures of 12 syndromes of observable psychotic behavior: excitement, hostile belligerence, paranoid projection, anxious depression, retardation, seclusiveness, care needed, psychotic disorganization, grandiosity, perceptual distortion, depressive mood, and disorientation. The 6-page test booklet is a revised and expanded version of the Psychotic Reaction Profile. Norms are provided for men and women, both drug free and drug treated. Examiner required. Suitable for group use.

Untimed: 20-30 minutes

Scoring: Hand key

Cost: Complete kit (25 forms, manual) $21.50

Publisher: Western Psychological Services

PURPOSE IN LIFE (PIL)
James C. Crumbaugh and Leonard T. Maholick

Adult

Purpose: Measures degree to which an individual has found meaning in life. Used with addicted, retired, handicapped, and philosophically confused individuals for purposes of clinical assessment, student counseling, vocational guidance, and rehabilitation.

Description: 34-item paper-pencil test assessing an individual's major motivations in life. Subjects must rate 20 statements according to their own beliefs, complete 13 sentence stems, and write an original paragraph describing their aims, ambitions, and goals in life. Based on Viktor Frankl's "will to meaning," the test embraces his logotherapeutic orientation in recognition of threat of the existential vacuum. Norms are provided for mental patients and normals. A fourth-grade reading level is required. Self-administered. Suitable for group use. Available in Spanish.

Untimed: 10-15 minutes

Scoring: Scoring service available

Cost: Specimen set (test, manual, bibliography) $4.00; 25 tests $5.00

Publisher: Psychometric Affiliates

QUIT SMOKING NOW PROGRAM
Robert Gordon

Adolescent, adult

Purpose: Evaluates a person's addiction to smoking cigarettes. Used by therapists to assist patients who wish to quit smoking.

Description: 40-item paper-pencil survey assessing the causes and nature of an individual's addiction to smoking and commitment to change during the attempt to quit. After the initial survey is completed, the therapist graphs on the Progress Chart the number of cigarettes smoked versus days of treatment. Monitoring cards are placed in front of patients' cigarette packages and are used for recording frequency and time of smoking. The test may be used in conjunction with hypnosis, behavioral techniques, and/or counseling. Self-administered. Suitable for group use.

Untimed: Not available

Scoring: Examiner evaluated

Cost: Kit (25 smoking surveys, 25 progress charts, 25 monitors, instructions) $18.00

Publisher: The Wilmington Press

Information and availability unconfirmed; no publisher response.

RESEARCH DIAGNOSTIC CRITERIA (RDC)
Jean Endicott and The Department of Research Assessment and Training

Adolescent, adult

Purpose: Provides criteria for the diagnosis of mental disorders and subtypes of disorders. Used for the diagnosis of affective and schizophrenic disorders.

Description: 25-item measure of present or previous illnesses. Items are a list of 25 diagnoses: present, past, and lifetime. The clinician checks the applicable diagnosis based on a clinical workup or Schedule for Affective Disorders and Schizophrenia (SADS) interview. Examiner required. Suitable for group use.

Untimed: After clinical workup, 10-15 minutes

Scoring: Examiner evaluated

Cost: Booklet $1.50; score sheet $0.25; checklist $0.50; suggested training procedures $0.25; case vignettes/training exercise #1 $7.50; case vignettes/training exercise #2 for testing $7.50; editing/coding instructions $0.25 plus postage and handling

Publisher: Department of Research Assessment and Training—N.Y. State Psychiatric Institute

ROGERS CRIMINAL RESPONSIBILITY ASSESSMENT SCALES (R-CRAS)
Richard Rogers

Adult

Purpose: Evaluates the criminal responsibility of individuals who may or may not, depending on their sanity or insanity at the time they committed a crime, be held legally accountable for their actions.

Description: Multiple-item paper-pencil inventory evaluating criminal responsibility. The instrument quantifies essential psychological and situational variables at the time of the crime that are to be used in a criterion-based decision model. This allows the clinician to quantify the impairment at the time of the crime, conceptualize the impairment with respect to the appropriate legal standards, and render an expert opinion with respect to those standards. Descriptive criteria are provided on scales measuring the individual's reliability, organicity, psychopathology, cognitive control, and behavioral control at the time of the alleged crime. Part I establishes the degree of impairment on psychological variables significant to the determination of insanity. Part II articulates the decision process towards rendering an accurate opinion on criminal responsibility with the ALI standard and includes experimental criteria and decision models for guilty-but-mentally-ill (GBMI) and M'Naghten standards. Results classify sane and insane individuals across age, sex and race, and all important legal variables. Examiner required. Not suitable for group use.

Untimed: Varies

Scoring: Examiner evaluated

Cost: Test kit (manual and 15 examination booklets) $22.00

Publisher: Psychological Assessment Resources, Inc.

ROTTER INCOMPLETE SENTENCES BLANK
Julian B. Rotter

Adolescent, adult

Purpose: Studies personality by using sentence completion.

Description: 40-item paper-pencil test of personality. Items are stems of sentences to be completed by the subject. Responses may be classified into three categories: unhealthy responses, neutral responses, and positive or healthy responses. The test is available in high-school, college, and adult forms. Self-administered. Suitable for group use.

Untimed: 20-40 minutes

Scoring: Hand key; examiner evaluated

Cost: 25 blanks (specify form) $8.00; manual $13.00

Publisher: The Psychological Corporation

S-D PRONENESS CHECKLIST
William T. Martin

Adolescent, adult

Purpose: Identifies persons with depressive and suicidal tendencies. Used by persons and agencies involved in suicide prevention. May be administered via telephone.

Description: 30-item paper-pencil inventory assessing a person's level of depression and suicide tendencies. Any trained counselor can complete the questionnaire, based on information gained through interviews and observation. The evaluator rates each of the statements on a 5-point scale ranging from "does not apply" to "most significant." Three scores are derived: Suicidal Score, Depression Score, and Total Suicide-Depression Proneness Score. Interpretative guidelines are provided with each form, including suicide correction factors. A pamphlet on suicide/depression also is available. Self-administered by examiner. Not suitable for group use.

Untimed: Open ended

Scoring: Examiner evaluated

Cost: Specimen set $4.50; 25 rating forms $7.50

Publisher: Psychologists and Educators, Inc.

SALAMON-CONTE LIFE SATISFACTION IN THE ELDERLY SCALE (LSES)
Michael J. Salamon and Vincent A. Conte

Elderly adults

Purpose: Assesses the quality of life of the elderly. Used with the elderly for screening, counseling, and treatment evaluation.

Description: 40-item paper-pencil multiple-choice sentence-completion inventory assessing elderly adults' reactions to their ecological, emotional, and social environments. The inventory evaluates the following areas, which are particularly important to the elderly: taking pleasure in daily activities, regarding life as meaningful, the relationship between desired and achieved goals, positive mood, positive self-concept, perceived health and financial security, and satisfaction with number and quality of social contacts. The inventory yields a total score and eight subscale scores. Examiner required. Suitable for group use.

Untimed: 20 minutes

Scoring: Examiner evaluated

Cost: Test kit (manual, 50 test booklets, 50 scoring sheets) $21.95

Publisher: Psychological Assessment Resources, Inc.

SCHEDULE FOR AFFECTIVE DISORDERS AND SCHIZOPHRENIA (SADS)
Jean Endicott and The Department of Research Assessment and Training

Adolescent, adult
Ages 12 and older

Purpose: Describes the psychopathology of the past week and the current episode of illness. Used as an aid in diagnosing and estimating prognosis and severity.

Description: Measure of recent psychopathology consisting of over 200 scales and many checklist items. The examiner rates the items based on a subject interview, case records, and a clinical workup. The instrument is similar in concept to the Schedule for Affective Disorders and Schizophrenia—Lifetime Version (SADS-L) and the Schedule for Affective Disorders and Schizophrenia—Change Version (SADS-C). The instrument must be used in conjunction with the Research Diagnostic Criteria (RDC). Examiner required. Not suitable for group use.

Untimed: 90-120 minutes

Scoring: Examiner evaluated; computer scored for summary scale

Cost: SADS booklet $2.00; SADS score sheet $0.30; SADS, SAD-L, RDC suggested procedures $0.50; SADS, SADS-L instructions $0.50; SADS, SADS-L, RDC Clars, $1.00; summary scale booklet $1.50; editing/coding instructions $0.40; Fortran program $125.00 plus postage and handling

Publisher: Department of Research Assessment and Training—N.Y. State Psychiatric Institute

SCHEDULE FOR AFFECTIVE DISORDERS AND SCHIZOPHRENIA—CHANGE VERSION (SADS-C)
Jean Endicott and The Department of Research Assessment and Training

Adolescent, adult

Purpose: Assesses change in psychopathological symptoms for the previous week. Used in diagnosis and treatment planning.

Description: Measure of symptom changes over the last week consisting of 29 scaled-items and several checklist items. Examiner rates the items based on a subject interview and clinical records. The instrument is one of a series of measures that includes the Schedule for Affective Disorders and Schizophrenia (SADS) and the Schedule for Affective Disorders and Schizophrenia—Lifetime Version (SADS-L). Examiner required. Not suitable for group use.

Untimed: 20-30 minutes

Scoring: Examiner evaluated; computer scored for summary scale

Cost: Booklet $1.00; score sheet $0.2υ; summary scale booklet $1.00; editing/coding instructions $0.20; Fortran program $125.00 plus postage and handling

Publisher: Department of Research Assessment and Training—N.Y. State Psychiatric Institute

SCHEDULE FOR AFFECTIVE DISORDERS AND SCHIZOPHRENIA—LIFETIME VERSION (SADS-L)
Jean Endicott and The Department of Research Assessment and Training

Adolescent, adult

Purpose: Assesses clinical history of psychopathology. Used for differential diagnosis of mental disorders.

Description: Measure of history relevant to diagnosis, prognosis, and severity of illness consisting of several scales and numerous checklist items. The examiner rates the items based on a subject interview, case records, and a clinical workup. Items are similar to those on the Schedule for Affective Disorders and Schizophrenia (SADS) and Schedule for Affective Disorders and Schizophrenia—Change Version (SADS-C). The instrument must be used in conjunction with the Research Diagnostic Criteria (RDC). Examiner required. Not suitable for group use.

Untimed: If not ill, 45 minutes; in an episode, 45-90 minutes

Scoring: Examiner evaluated; may be computer scored

Cost: SADS-L booklet $1.00; score sheet $0.25; editing/coding instructions $0.20; summary data program $125.00; editing program $125.00 plus postage and handling

Publisher: Department of Research Assessment and Training—N.Y. State Psychiatric Institute

SCHOOL MOTIVATION ANALYSIS TEST (SMAT)
Samuel E. Krug,
Raymond B. Cattell,
and Arthur B. Sweney

Adolescent   Ages 12-18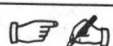

Purpose: Assesses the psychological motivations of adolescents. Used for clinical evaluation, educational and personal counseling, and psychological research on adolescent motivations.

Description: 190-item paper-pencil multiple-choice test measuring 10 important achievement, social, and comfort needs of 12- to 18-year-olds. Six of the needs are basic drives: protectiveness, caution, self-assertion, sexual identity, aggressiveness, and self-indulgence. Four are interests that develop and mature through learning experiences: interest in school, dependency, responsibility, and self-fulfillment. Test items consist of objective devices, which are less susceptible to deliberate faking or distortion than standard questionnaires or checklists. For each of the 10 interest areas, scores measure drive or need level, satisfaction level, degree of conflict, and total motivational strength. Norms are provided for males and females separately. A fourth-grade reading level is required. Examiner required. Suitable for group use.

Untimed: 46-60 minutes

Scoring: Hand key

Cost: Specimen set $11.25; handbook $9.50; 25 reuseable test booklets $25.00; 50 answer sheets $8.00; 3 scoring keys $9.75

Publisher: Institute for Personality and Ability Testing, Inc.

THE SCHUTZ MEASURES: ELEMENT B-BEHAVIOR
Will Schutz

Adult

Purpose: Measures a respondent's perception of his own behavior. Used for personal growth assessment, training, and development by counselors, psychologists, and team trainers.

Description: 54-item paper-pencil test consisting of behavioral descriptions that subjects are asked to rate as either "the way it is" or "the way I want it to be." The factors measured include expressed-received and perceived-wanted aspects of the behavioral dimensions: inclusion, control, and openness. This measure is an expansion of Fundamental Interpersonal Relations Orientation (FIRO) theory. Examiner/self-administered. Suitable for group use.

Untimed: 15 minutes

Scoring: Hand key

Cost: Complete set (materials for 10 participants) $30.00

Publisher: University Associates, Inc.

Information and availability unconfirmed; no publisher response.

THE SCHUTZ MEASURES: ELEMENT F-FEELINGS
Will Schutz

Adult

Purpose: Measures a respondent's perception of his feelings. Used for personality assessment, personal growth, and training and development.

Description: 54-item paper-pencil test consisting of behavioral descriptions that subjects rate according to how "I Feel" and how "I Want to Feel." The factors measured include expressed-received and perceived-wanted aspects of the feeling dimensions: significance, competence, and likeability. This measure is an expansion of Fundamental Interpersonal Relations Orientation (FIRO) theory. Self-administered. Suitable for group use.

Untimed: 15 minutes

Scoring: Hand key

Cost: Complete set (materials for 10 participants) $30.00

Publisher: University Associates, Inc.

Information and availability unconfirmed; no publisher response.

THE SCHUTZ MEASURES: ELEMENT R—RELATIONSHIPS
Will Schutz

Adult

Purpose: Measures two respondents' perceptions of their relationship. Used for team building, family therapy, conflict resolution, and training and development.

Description: 54-item paper-pencil test consisting of two forms: "Me to You" and "You to Me." The respondents rate descriptions of "the way it is" and "the way I want it to be" in terms of their relationship. The factors measured include expressed-received and perceived-wanted aspects of the behavioral dimensions inclusion, control, and openness and the feelings dimensions of significance, competence, and likeability. This measure is an expansion of Fundamental Interpersonal Relations Orientation (FIRO) theory. Self-administered. Suitable for group use.

Untimed: 20-25 minutes

Scoring: Hand key

Cost: Complete set (material for 10 participants) $30.00
Publisher: University Associates, Inc.
Information and availability unconfirmed; no publisher response.

THE SCHUTZ MEASURES: ELEMENT S-SELF—CONCEPT
Will Schutz

Adult

Purpose: Evaluates an adult's self-concept. Used in personal growth analysis, counseling, and training and development of counselors.

Description: 54-item paper-pencil test consisting of statements that examinees rate according to "I" and "I Want To." The factors measured include perceived-wanted aspects of the dimensions self-inclusion (presence), self-control (vs. spontaneity), self-openness (awareness), self-significance, self-competence, and self-like. This measure is an expansion of Fundamental Interpersonal Relations Orientation (FIRO) theory. Self-administered. Suitable for group use.
Untimed: 15 minutes
Scoring: Hand key
Cost: Complete set (material for 10 participants) $30.00
Publisher: University Associates, Inc.
Information and availability unconfirmed; no publisher response.

SCL-90-R
Leonard R. Derogatis

Adolescent, adult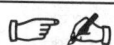

Purpose: Evaluates the psychological symptomatic distress of medical and psychiatric patients. Used for psychological screening and in treatment planning and evaluation in mental health settings.

Description: 90-item paper-pencil self-report symptom inventory assessing psychological symptomatic distress in terms of nine symptom dimensions (somatization, obsessive-compulsive, interpersonal sensitivity, depression, anxiety, hostility, phobic anxiety, paranoid ideation, and psychoticism) and three global indices of distress (global severity index, positive

symptom index, and positive symptom total). Score/profile forms and published norms are available by sex for four populations: nonpatient adult, nonpatient adolescent, outpatient psychiatric, and inpatient psychiatric. The SCL-90-R is the pivotal instrument in the Psychopathology Rating Scale Series, which includes the Brief Symptom Inventory, the SCL-90-R Analogue, and the Hopkins Psychiatric Rating Scale. The inventory is available in an optical scan version. A microcomputer scoring program is available for the IBM-PC and Apple computers. A psychometer diskette version is available from NCS/ Professional Assessment Services. Examiner required. Suitable for group use.
Untimed: 12-15 minutes
Scoring: Examiner evaluated; may be machine or computer scored
Cost: Manual $15.00; 100 test forms $28.00; 100 optical scan forms $40.00; 100 score/profile forms $18.00; microcomputer scoring program (SCOR90-1) $150.00
Publisher: Clinical Psychometric Research

SCL-90-R ANALOGUE
Leonard R. Derogatis

Adolescent, adult

Purpose: Evaluates the psychological symptomatic distress of medical and psychiatric patients in terms of observer's ratings. Used in mental health settings for psychological screening and in treatment planning and evaluation.

Description: 10-item paper-pencil observational inventory assessing symptomatic distress in nine primary symptom dimensions (somatization, obsessive-compulsive, interpersonal sensitivity, depression, anxiety, hostility, phobic anxiety, paranoid ideation, and psychoticism) and one global psychopathology scale. Each primary symptom is represented as a continuum along 100mm lines. The observer marks each continuum line proportionally. This inventory is a part of the Psychopathology Rating Scale Series and is intended to be used in conjunction with either the SCL-90-R or the Brief Symptom Inventory (BSI). The nine primary dimensions are the same as those measured on the other tests in the series. The test may be used by observers, such as physicians, nurses, or technicians, without extensive training in psychiatric disorders. Examiner required. Not suitable for group use.

Untimed: 1-2 minutes

Scoring: Examiner evaluated

Cost: 100 inventory forms $28.00

Publisher: Clinical Psychometric Research

THE SEEKING OF NOETIC GOALS TEST (SONG)
James C. Crumbaugh

Adolescent, adult

Purpose: Measures the strength of a person's motivation to find meaning in life. Used for pre- and posttesting of logotherapy programs with addicted, retired, handicapped, and philosophically confused individuals.

Description: 20-item paper-pencil test consisting of statements that the subject rates on a 7-point scale according to his or her own beliefs. The test is used in conjunction with the Purpose in Life Test to predict therapeutic success. The manual includes a discussion of the test's rationale, validity, reliability, administration, scoring, norms, and other technical data. A fourth-grade reading level is required. Self-administered. Suitable for group use.

Untimed: 10 minutes

Scoring: Scoring service available

Cost: Specimen set (test, manual) $4.00; 25 tests $5.00

Publisher: Psychometric Affiliates

SELF-INTERVIEW INVENTORY
H. Birnet Hovey

Adult

Purpose: Measures an individual's level of emotional adjustment and identifies individuals with neurotic tendencies. Used for self-awareness and counseling

programs with both psychiatric and normal patients.

Description: 185-item paper-pencil inventory containing a high loading level of unique content. A Composite Neurotic score is derived from subscores on current complaints, emotional insecurity, and guilt feelings. A Composite Maladjustment score is derived from subscores on pre-psychotic and psychotic behavior and childhood illness. Two validating scores are also provided: one on carefulness and one on truthfulness of response. Norms are provided for control groups. Examiner/self-administered. Suitable for group use.

Untimed: Not available

Scoring: Hand key

Cost: Specimen set $4.00; 25 inventories $5.00; 25 answer sheets $5.00; 25 profiles $5.00

Publisher: Psychometric Affiliates

SELF-PERCEPTION INVENTORY
William T. Martin

Adolescent, adult
Ages 12 and older

Purpose: Evaluates an individual's personality and general level of adjustment. Used for screening procedures, clinical research on personality, and evaluation of therapeutic progress.

Description: 200-item paper-pencil true-false test of personality. Test items consist of symptomatic and descriptive statements grouped according to the following syndromes: consistency, self-actualization, supervision, rigidity-dogmatism, authoritarianism, anxiety, depression, and paranoia. Subscale scores are provided for each syndrome. General Adjustment and General Maladjustment scores are derived from these subscales to provide an index of personality patterning. A fifth-grade reading level is required. Examiner required. Suitable for group use.

Untimed: 20-35 minutes

Scoring: Hand key

Cost: Examiner's manual (10 tests, 25 answer sheets, 25 profile sheets, keys, manual) $32.00; 25 tests $25.00; 25 answer and 25 profile sheets $6.00 each; keys $8.00; manual $6.00

Publisher: Psychologists and Educators, Inc.

SELF-RATING PSYCHIATRIC INVENTORY LIST (SPIL)
William W.K. Zung

Clinical patients

Purpose: Assesses psychiatric symptomatology. Used for diagnosis, evaluation of treatment outcome, and research.

Description: 88-item self-report paper-pencil measure of psychiatric symptoms for which subject checks one of the following: "none or a little of the time," "some of the time," "good part of the time," or "most or all of the time." Scores are obtained in seven areas: psychoticism, elation, depression, anxiety, neuroticism, emotional status, and drug abuse. Self-administered. Suitable for group use.

Untimed: Varies

Scoring: Hand key; examiner evaluated; may be computer scored

Cost: Contact publisher

Publisher: William W.K. Zung, M.D.

THE SENIOR APPERCEPTION TECHNIQUE (SAT)
*Leopold Bellak and
Sonya Sorel Bellak*

Adult

Purpose: Assesses personality in individuals age 60 and older. Used by psychiatrists, psychologists, physicians, nurses, and social workers for clinical evaluation and diagnosis.

Description: 16-item oral-response projective personality test measuring the traits, attitudes, and psychodynamics involved in the personalities of individuals age 60 and older. Each test item consists of a picture of human figures in situations of concern to the aged. The examinee is asked to tell a story about each picture. The test also includes informational material on technique, administration,

research possibilities, and a bibliography. Examiner required. Not suitable for group use. Available in Spanish and Japanese.

Untimed: 20-30 minutes

Scoring: Examiner evaluated

Cost: Complete kit (pictures, manual) $14.00

Publisher: C.P.S., Inc.

SENTENCE COMPLETION TEST
Floyd S. Irvin

**Adolescent, adult
Grades 10 and above**

Purpose: Assesses personality functioning. Used for clinical counseling and academic guidance.

Description: 90-item paper-pencil test measuring six aspects of personality: self-concept, parental attitude, peer attitude, need for achievement, learning attitude, and body image. Items are sentence stems, which the subject completes. They are scored on a 5-point scale ranging from outright positive to outright negative. Examiner required. Not suitable for group use.

Untimed: 15 minutes

Scoring: Hand key; examiner evaluated

Cost: Specimen set $6.00; 25 forms $7.50

Publisher: Psychologists and Educators, Inc.

SHORR IMAGERY TEST (SIT)
Joseph E. Shorr

Adolescent, adult

Purpose: Evaluates a person's use of imagery and assesses self-image, areas of conflict, and strategies for coping with the world. Used for in-depth personality analysis.

Description: 15-item orally administered/oral-response projective personality test in which the respondent is asked to imagine a particular situation and then to expand in a directed way upon the image evoked. These imaginary situations are used to reveal a wide range of personality variables: the individual's personal world, relationships between self

---

and others, self-image, sexual attitudes, and internal and external forces acting upon the person. Answers are recorded by the examiner and quantitatively scored according to the degree of conflict within the subject's personality. The test, which is not limited by intelligence, is suitable for use with the blind, illiterate, and physically handicapped. It is minimally culture bound. Examiner required. Not suitable for group use.

Untimed: 1 hour

Scoring: Examiner evaluated

Cost: Complete set $37.50

Publisher: Institute for Psycho-Imagination Therapy

SHORT IMAGINAL PROCESS INVENTORY (SIPI)
G. J. Huba, J.L. Singer, C.S. Aneshensel, and J.S. Antrobus

Adolescent, adult

Purpose: Evaluates the content and style of an individual's daydreams and general inner experience. Used for personal assessment, to study the relation of inner experience to other psychological functions, and to investigate group differences in imaginal processes.

Description: 45-item paper-pencil test consisting of five alternative responses covering three scales: Positive-Constructive Daydreaming, Guilt and Fear of Failure Daydreaming, and Poor Attentional Control. Responses are recorded in the question and answer booklet. Materials include profiles and scoring templates. Examiner required. Suitable for group use.

Untimed: 10 minutes

Scoring: Hand key

Cost: Complete kit $14.50

Publisher: Research Psychologists Press, Inc.

SINGER-LOOMIS INVENTORY OF PERSONALITY, EXPERIMENTAL EDITION
June Singer and Mary Loomis

Adult

Purpose: Assesses cognitive style or personality dispositions. Used in research.

Description: 120-item paper-pencil test measuring eight cognitive modes independently. The eight modes are Introverted Thinking (IT), Introverted Feeling (IF), Introverted Sensation (IS), Introverted Intuition (IN), Extraverted Thinking (ET), Extraverted Feeling (EF), Extraverted Sensation (ES), Extraverted Intuition (EN). Items are answered on a 5-point scale. A manual provides technical information, and an interpretive guide describes the eight Jungian modes that the test measures, as well as some combinations of different modes. Examiner required. Suitable for group use.

Untimed: 30-40 minutes

Scoring: Hand key

Cost: 25 booklets $12.00; 50 answer sheets/scoring forms $26.50; manual and interpretive guide $10.00

Publisher: Consulting Psychologists Press, Inc.

SITUATIONAL PREFERENCE INVENTORY
Carl N. Edwards

Adult

Purpose: Assesses an individual's preferred styles of social interaction. Used for counseling and research purposes.

Description: 28-item paper-pencil rating scale assessing preferred styles of social interaction. Each test item consists of a set of three statements, each representing a different style of interaction: cooperational, instrumental, or analytic. Individuals are asked to indicate which of the three statements they agree with most and which they agree with least, leaving the third statement unmarked (neutral). Independent scores are derived for each of the three interactional styles. Norms are available by sex for 14 populations. Self-administered. Suitable for group use.

Untimed: Varies

Scoring: Examiner evaluated

Cost: Contact publisher

Publisher: Carl N. Edwards

SIXTEEN PERSONALITY FACTOR QUESTIONNAIRE
Raymond B. Cattell and IPAT Staff

**Adolescent, adult
Ages 16 and older**

Purpose: Evaluates the normal, adult personality. Used for clinical evaluations, personnel selection and placement, vocational and educational guidance, marriage counseling, and psychological research on personality.

Description: Multiple-item paper-pencil test measuring 16 primary personality traits, including levels of assertiveness, emotional maturity, shrewdness, self-sufficiency, tension, anxiety, neuroticism, and rigidity. Test results have specific applications for business, psychotherapy, and education.

For business and industry, the 16PF predicts important job related criteria, such as length of time an employee is likely to remain with the company, sales effectiveness, work efficiency, tolerance for routine, and other specific measures. In diagnostic and therapeutic settings, measures are provided for anxiety, neuroticism, rigidity, and other behavior trends. Educators and school psychologists can use the 16PF to counsel college-bound and university students and to identify potential drop-outs, drug users, low achievers, etc. Occupational profile data (based on more than 11,000 cases) are summarized in the handbook for use in vocational and rehabilitation counseling. Four forms of the test are available. Forms A and B (187 items each) require a seventh-grade reading level. Forms B and C (105 items each) require a sixth-grade reading level. Form E (128 items) requires a third-grade reading level and presents shorter, more concrete items in a forced-choice format with large type.

Six types of computer-analyzed reports are available: the 16PF Narrative Scoring Report provides a complete report for each individual, including descriptions of all significant personality characteristics and relevant vocational and occupational comparisons; the Personal Career Development Profile provides information about individual strengths, behavioral attitudes, and gratifications to accomplish personal career development objectives; the Karson Clinical Report provides an in-depth analysis of underlying personality dynamics in clinical terms for use in psychiatric and psychological applications; and the Marriage Counseling Report examines individual and joint strengths and weaknesses in the personality organization of two individuals. A Human Resources Development Report and a Law Enforcement and Development Report are available.

The manual is a nontechnical guide for administration, scoring, and basic interpretation of Forms A, B, C, and D. The handbook, which must be ordered separately, is the primary source of technical information on the 16PF. A videotape recording of the Form A test booklet in American Sign Language is available. The Form E test booklet also is available on cassette tape. Examiner/self-administered. Suitable for group use. Available in Spanish and 40 other languages.

Untimed: 45-60 minutes

Scoring: Hand key; may be computer scored

Cost: 25 reusable test booklets (specify form) $16.50; 25 machine-scorable answer sheets (specify form) $5.50; 50 hand-scorable answer sheets (specify form) $6.50; 50 profile sheets $6.50; 50 hand-scorable answer-profile sheets (specify form) $7.50; contact publisher for information on computer reports

Publisher: Institute for Personality and Ability Testing, Inc.

THE SOCIAL BEHAVIOR ASSESSMENT SCHEDULE
Stephen Platt, Steven Hirsch, and Anne Weyman

Adult

Purpose: Assesses an individual's social functioning, changes in performance arising from psychiatric or physical illness, and the effects of the individual's behavior on other members of the household. Used by health visitors, medical doctors, occupational therapists, social workers, psychologists, and psychiatrists.

Description: Multiple-item semistructured interview guide assessing an

individual's behavioral disturbance and altered social performance. The test also evaluates the related difficulties suffered by the individual's household and close friends. Based on an interview with a relative or close friend (the informant), the schedule describes as fully as possible the patient activities and the extent to which his performance falls short of the main requirements of his role in the household or community. The effect of the individual's behavior on others (objective burden) is assessed in a section of the schedule that takes into account the changes that have occurred in the household and the lives of the informant and relatives. Distress caused to the informant (subjective distress) is rated on an item-by-item basis. Examiner required. Not suitable for group use.
BRITISH PUBLISHER

Untimed: Varies

Scoring: Examiner evaluated

Cost: Complete set (training manual, coding booklet, schedule, presentation wallet) £26.45

Publisher: NFER-NELSON Publishing Company Ltd.

SOMATIC INKBLOT SERIES (SIS)
Wilfred A. Cassell

Adolescent, adult

Purpose: Assesses an individual's body perception and general personality dynamics. Used to evaluate the psychopathological significance of somatic symptoms, conversion reactions, and sexual dysfunction.

Description: 20-item verbal examination consisting of 20 cards, each containing a carefully designed inkblot. The cards are presented individually to the subject, who describes his perceptions and associations to the examiner. The inkblots are oriented towards body perceptions. The subject's awareness of somatic similarities in the inkblots is used to provide clinical data of a projective nature regarding conscious-unconscious somatic attitudes, as well as general psychodynamics. The test is accompanied by Dr. Cassell's book, *Body Symbolism*, which describes scoring tech-

niques. An examiner qualified in projective techniques is required. Not suitable for group use.

Untimed: 45 minutes

Scoring: Examiner evaluated; scoring service available

Cost: Cards, scoring sheets $45.00

Publisher: Aurora Publishing

SOMATIC INKBLOT SERIES II
Wilfred A. Cassell

Adolescent, adult

Purpose: Assesses body perception and general personality characteristics of adolescents and adults. Used for determining conscious-unconscious health-related perceptions.

Description: 56-item verbal examination consisting of inkblot cards for assessing perceptions and associations related to anatomical structures. The anatomical structure is minimal for some cards to minimize the subject's tendency to develop a perceptual structure for seeing body parts. The cards are presented individually to the subject, who reports perceptions and associations to the examiner. Data provide information on psychopathology regarding how people experience conscious-unconscious health-related issues. The underlying principles of the test are outlined in Wilfred Cassell's book, *Body Symbolism*. An examiner qualified in projective techniques is required. Not suitable for group use.

Untimed: 90 minutes

Scoring: Examiner evaluated

Cost: Cards, scoring sheets $95.00

Publisher: Aurora Publishing

SOMATIC VIDEO SERIES II
Wilfred A. Cassell

Adolescent, adult

Purpose: Assesses body perception and related personality characteristics of adolescents and adults. Used for determining conscious-unconscious health-related perceptions.

Description: 56-item test presented in two videotapes ("Images I" and "Images

II") of 28 items each for evaluating body perceptions. The test incorporates the Somatic Inkblot Series II inkblots along with dreamlike video techniques making "lungs" breathe, "hearts" beat, and phallic symbols penetrate. The tapes include nature scenes and ambiant music producing a hypnotic-like state in which viewers' written responses are not contaminated by the presence of an examiner. The test can be administered in the standard or shortened version, which eliminates the nature scenes. Diagnostic and therapeutic use of the procedure are outlined in Wilfred Cassell's book, *Body Symbolism*. The tapes are available in VHS and beta video cassette. A 16mm film version is available for teaching purposes. An examiner qualified in projective techniques, hypnotherapy, and dream analogies is required. Not suitable for group use.

Untimed: Standard version 2 hours; abbreviated version 1 hour

Scoring: Examiner evaluated; scoring service available

Cost: Images I $95.00; Images II $95.00 (state ½" or ¾" film size)

Publisher: Aurora Publishing

SOUTH AFRICAN PERSONALITY QUESTIONNAIRE

**Adolescent, adult
Grades 10 and above**

Purpose: Measures general personality traits in the context of South African society. Used for employee screening and selection. Suitable for matriculants and higher.

Description: 150-item paper-pencil test consisting of bipolar forced-choice items measuring the following personality traits: social responsiveness, dominance, hostility, flexibility, and anxiety. Use is restricted to competent persons properly registered with the South African Medical and Dental Council. Examiner required. Suitable for group use.
SOUTH AFRICAN PUBLISHER

Untimed: Open ended

Scoring: Hand key; examiner evaluated

Cost: Contact publisher

Publisher: National Institute For Personnel Research

STATE-TRAIT ANXIETY INVENTORY, FORM Y AND FORM X
Charles D. Spielberger

**Adolescent, adult
Grades 7 and above**

Purpose: Evaluates individual anxiety levels as an aid to clinical screening for anxiety-prone students, as an indicator of current anxiety level of therapy and counseling clients, and as a research tool.

Description: Two 20-item paper-pencil tests of two aspects of anxiety: state (current level of anxiety, or S-Anxiety) and trait (anxiety-proneness, or T-Anxiety). The T-Anxiety scale asks the subject to indicate how he "generally" feels; the S-Anxiety scale asks how he feels "at a particular moment in time." The inventory is available in Form X and Form Y. Form Y, a revision of the original Form X, contains six different items on each of the two scales. The correlations between Form X and Form Y are 0.96 to 0.98. Self-administered. Suitable for group use. Form X is no longer available in English; a Spanish version is available.

Untimed: 15 minutes

Scoring: Hand key

Cost: Specimen set (includes tests, manual, key) $7.00; 25 tests $4.00; key $1.00; manual $6.75; 25 tests in Spanish $5.00; Spanish manual $12.50

Publisher: Consulting Psychologists Press, Inc.

STRESS ANALYSIS SYSTEM
P.B. Nelson, K.M. Schmidt, and Noel Nelson

Adult

Purpose: Used by adults to assess, understand, and deal with their own stress.

Description: Multiple-item paper-pencil test used by adults for developing a personal stress profile, pinpointing symptoms of stress, and managing stress. The test examines the amount of stress experienced from each of six sources: the Type A, controller personality; the anger-in personality; situational stress and life readjustments; corollary health habits; low accountability/victim syndrome; and interpersonal stress. Self-administered. Suitable for group use.

Untimed: 30 minutes

Scoring: Self-scored

Cost: SAS Kit (test, stress profile, and stress category information) $6.50

Publisher: Interdatum

STRESS EVALUATION INVENTORY (SEI)
Refer to page 941.

STRUCTURED AND SCALED INTERVIEW TO ASSESS MALADJUSTMENT (SSIAM)
Barry J. Gurland

Adult

Purpose: Identifies problems in social adjustment and rates them quantitatively. Used for clinical evaluations of mental patients.

Description: 32-page interview booklet including scales, profile chart, and instructions for administering and rating the interview. Eleven ratings are provided (five for deviant behavior, one for friction with others, three for distress, and two inferential) for five areas (work, social-leisure, family, marriage, and sex). An additional 11 overall ratings are provided. Examiner required. Not suitable for group use.

Untimed: Not available

Scoring: Examiner evaluated

Cost: 10 copies (scales, profile chart, instructions) $24.00

Publisher: Springer Publishing Company

Information and availability unconfirmed; no publisher response.

STUDY OF VALUES (REVISED 1964 BRITISH EDITION)
S. Richardson

**Adolescent, adult
Ages 16 and older**

Purpose: Measures an individual's basic personality values. Used for counseling and research.

Description: Paper-pencil test measuring six basic interests and motives: theoretical, economic, aesthetic, social, political, and religious. First published in 1931 and revised in 1951 and 1960, the current edition has a new scale form that was standardized in Great Britain. New items are added, but the form and intention of the original test are maintained. Examiner required. Suitable for group use.
CANADIAN PUBLISHER

Untimed: 20 minutes

Scoring: Examiner evaluated

Cost: Specimen set $13.70; 25 booklets $27.36; manual $11.01

Publisher: Institute of Psychological Research, Inc.

Information and availability unconfirmed; no publisher response.

SUBSTANCE ABUSE PROBLEM CHECKLIST (SAPC)
Jerome F.X. Carroll

Adult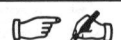

Purpose: Identifies client problems associated with substance abuse. Used for diagnosis, referral, and development of treatment plans for substance abusers and for research on treatment needs and outcomes.

Description: 337-item paper-pencil test of client problems in the following areas: motivations for treatment, general health, personal problems, social problems, job problems, problems relating to leisure time, religious problems, and legal problems. Each item lists a problem related to substance abuse; the examinee underlines those items that apply to him. The client indicates problems that are especially troublesome by circling the number next to the problem statement. Specific items/problems are later discussed individually by the client and counselor. A fourth-grade reading level is required. Examiner/self-administered. Suitable for group use.

Untimed: 40-45 minutes

Scoring: Examiner evaluated

Cost: 100 test booklets, clinical manual $45.00

Publisher: Eagleville Hospital

SUICIDE PROBABILITY SCALE (SPS)
John G. Cull and Wayne S. Gill

Ages 10-65

Purpose: Predicts the probability of suicidal behavior. Used by clinicians to assess the probability that an individual may harm himself.

Description: 36-item paper-pencil test in which the subject uses a 4-point scale ranging from "none or little of the time" to "most or all of the time" to indicate how often the behavior described in the statements would be descriptive of his behavior or feelings. The test itself does not mention suicide. Scoring yields an SPS Index, which translates into a probability of engaging in suicidal behavior. The manual presents cutoff scores indicating the level of probable suicide behavior, interpretive guidelines, and clinical strategies for each level. Examiner required. Suitable for group use.

Untimed: 5-10 minutes

Scoring: Hand key

Cost: Complete kit (25 tests, manual, 25 profile sheets) $31.50

Publisher: Western Psychological Services

SUINN TEST ANXIETY BEHAVIOR SCALE (STABS)
Refer to page 708.

SURVEY OF INTERPERSONAL VALUES
Leonard V. Gordon

**Adolescent, adult
Grades 10 and above**

Purpose: Measures individuals' values by assessing what they consider important in relationships with others. Used to measure values associated with adjustment and performance for selection, placement employment counseling, and research purposes.

Description: 30-item paper-pencil inventory assessing personal values. Each test item consists of a triad of value statements. For each triad, examinees must indicate most and least important values. The test assesses six values: support, conformity, recognition, independence, benevolence, and leadership. Self-administered. Suitable for group use.

Untimed: 15 minutes

Scoring: Hand key

Cost: 25 test booklets $31.00; scoring stencil $5.50; examiner's manual $10.00

Publisher: Science Research Associates, Inc.

SURVEY OF PERSONAL VALUES
Refer to page 943.

SYMONDS PICTURE-STORY TEST
Percival M. Symonds

Adolescent

Purpose: Evaluates the personality of adolescents. Used to obtain personal histories related to personality development.

Description: 20-item projective personality test consisting of 20 pictures for which the adolescent is asked to create stories. The test differs from Murray's TAT in that it is specifically for the study of adolescent fantasy. Quartiles are provided for 28 themes. Examiner required. Not suitable for group use.

Untimed: Varies

Scoring: Examiner evaluated

Cost: 20 picture cards, manual $9.95

Publisher: Teachers College Press

TASKS OF EMOTIONAL DEVELOPMENT TEST (TED)
Refer to page 681.

TAYLOR-JOHNSON TEMPERAMENT ANALYSIS
Robert M. Taylor and Lucille P. Morrison

**Adolescent, adult
Ages 11-adult**

Purpose: Provides a clinical assessment of personality. Used for premarital, marital, and family counseling, and educational and vocational guidance.

Description: 180-item paper-pencil test measuring common personality traits to assist in assessing individual adjustment and formulation of an overall counseling plan. The regular edition, for ages 15-adult, has a special feature allowing "criss-cross" testing in which questions are answered as applied to self and again as applied to significant other (e.g., husband's perception of both self and spouse and vice versa), thereby adding the dimension of interpersonal perception to counseling perspective. An eighth-grade reading level is required. The secondary edition, for ages 11-19 and adults who are poor readers, is presented in direct-question format with simplified vocabulary for lower-level readers. A fifth-grade reading level is required. Evaluation is presented as bipolar graphs of trait pairs: nervous/composed, depressive/light-hearted, active-social/quiet, expressive-responsive/inhibited, sympathetic/indifferent, subjective/objective, dominant/submissive, hostile/tolerant, and self-disciplined/impulsive. The following additional scales are available when the publisher's computer scoring service is utilized: emotional pressure (stress), adequacy of self-image (self-esteem), preference for privacy, outwardly poised, alienating, passive-aggressive, potential for marital adjustment, parenting effectiveness, leadership, and sales. Self-administered. Suitable for group use. Available in Spanish, French, German, and Portuguese.

Untimed: 20 minutes

Scoring: Hand key; may be computer scored

Cost: Basic package (manual, handscoring stencils, pens, ruler, 5 test booklets—regular or secondary, 50 handscorable answer sheets, 50 profiles) $70.00; practice scoring training packet $7.50; manual $50.00; 10 test booklets $6.50; 50 handscorable answer sheets $5.50; 50 computer scorable answer sheets $5.50

Publisher: Psychological Publications, Inc.

TEMPERAMENT INVENTORY TESTS
Robert J. Cruise and
W. Peter Blitchington

Adult

Purpose: Assesses an individual's basic temperament traits according to the four-temperament theory. Used by professionals and laymen in marital, vocational, social, moral, and spiritual counseling settings.

Description: 80-item paper-pencil test determining an individual's basic temperament traits. The test is available in a self-report form and a group form. The self-report form consists of a 42-page booklet, Understanding Your Temperament, containing the test and instructions for self-administration, self-scoring, and interpreting the scores from a Christian viewpoint. The group form, called the Temperament Inventory, is administered and scored with temperament templates by the examiner or group leader. Interpretive material is not included with the group form. Self-administered. Available in French, German, and Spanish.

Untimed: Varies

Scoring: Self-scored; examiner evaluated

Cost: *Understanding Your Temperament* $2.95; Temperament Inventory $0.60; set of temperament templates $2.95

Publisher: Andrews University Press

TENNESSEE SELF CONCEPT SCALE
William H. Fitts

Adolescent, adult
Ages 12-adult

Purpose: Measures an individual's self-concept in terms of identity, feelings, and behavior. Used for a wide range of clinical applications.

Description: 100-item paper-pencil test consisting of self-descriptive statements which subjects rate on a scale ranging from 1 (completely false) to 5 (completely true). The test is available in two forms: Counseling (Form C) and Clinical and Research (Form C & R). Form C is appropriate if the results are to be used directly with the subject. It provides a number of measures, including response defensiveness, a total score, and self-concept scales that reflect "What I Am," "How I Feel," and "What I Do." The scales include Identify, Self Satisfaction, Behavior, Physical Self, Moral-Ethical Self, Personal Self, Family Self, and Social Self. It does not require scoring keys. Form C & R yields the same scores as Form C as well as the following six empirical scales, which require special scoring keys: Defensive Position, General Maladjustment, Psychosis, Personality Disorder, Neurosis, and Personality Integration. Both forms use the same test booklet, but require different answer-profile sheets. The test may be administered to individuals regardless of whether they are psychologically disturbed or healthy. A sixth-grade reading level is required. Self-administered. Suitable for group use.

Untimed: 10-20 minutes

Scoring: Computer scored; hand key (only Form C & R)

Cost: Complete kit (10 reusable test booklets, 25 Form C answer-profile sheets, 2 computerized answer sheets, manual) $49.50

Publisher: Western Psychological Services

TEST ANXIETY PROFILE (TAP)
Refer to page 708.

THEMATIC APPERCEPTION TEST (TAT)
Henry Alexander Murray

Adolescent, adult
Ages 14-40

Purpose: Assesses personality through projective technique focusing on dominant drives, emotions, sentiments, complexes, attitudes, and conflicts.

Description: 20-item projective-type test in which a subject is shown pictures one at a time and asked to make up a story about each picture. The examiner records the subject's stories for later analysis. The projective test seeks to measure, among other things, the subject's temperament, level of emotional maturity, observational ability, intellectuality, imagination, psychological insight, creativity, sense of reality, and factors of family and psychic dynamics. Generally the subject is asked to make up stories based on 10 cards in each of two sessions. A trained examiner is required. Not suitable for groups.

Untimed: 1 hour per series

Scoring: Examiner evaluated

Cost: Specimen set $12.50; manual $1.50

Publisher: Harvard University Press

TIFFANY EXPERIENCED CONTROL SCALES
Donald Tiffany and Phyllis Tiffany

Adolescent, adult
Ages 11 and older

Purpose: Evaluates personality problems related to feelings of control.

Description: 32-item computer-administered measurement of an individual's perceived control of self and the environment. The test complements traditional personality assessment and is used in clinical psychology. The individual is briefed on using the computer keyboard, instructions are presented on-screen, and results are scored automatically. Available for Apple and IBM microcomputers. Examiner required. Not suitable for group use.

Untimed: 30 minutes

Scoring: Computer scored

Cost: Computer software package $225.00

Publisher: Applied Innovations, Inc.

TRAINING PROFICIENCY SCALE
James M. Gardner

Adult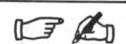

Purpose: Assesses an individual's ability to apply behavior modification techniques. Useful for in-service training and as a dependent variable in research.

Description: 30-item role-play test measuring an individual's ability to train another person using behavior modification techniques, including reinforcement,

---

shaping, and stimulus control. Examiner/self-administered. Not suitable for group use.

Untimed: 15 minutes
Scoring: Hand key
Cost: Scale $5.00
Publisher: Planet Press

TRANSACTIONAL ANALYSIS LIFE POSITION SURVEY (TALPS)
F.D. Kramer and B. Strade

Adult

Purpose: Measures an individual's life position as defined in transactional analysis "I'm OK" and "You're OK" dimensions. Used for personnel screening, personal assessment, and counseling aid and as a before-and-after measure for teachers presenting transactional analysis to large groups.

Description: 40-item paper-pencil test measuring attitudes toward self and others. Both "I'm OK" and "You're OK" scores are normed in percentiles for various age groups. The normed scores can be charted on a life position graph. The test is used as both a discussion-starter and as a tool for in-depth analysis. Self-administered. Suitable for group use.

Untimed: 10-15 minutes
Scoring: Hand key
Cost: Specimen set $8.00; 35 surveys $12.00; 2 scoring stencils $4.00; 35 report forms $6.00; manual $4.00
Publisher: Monitor

TRIADAL EQUATED PERSONALITY INVENTORY
United Consultants Research Staff

Adult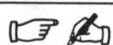

Purpose: Assesses personality. Used to predict job success and to measure personal adjustment.

Description: 633-item paper-pencil test of personality. Items are simple adjectives equated for response popularity. The test yields 21 self-image scores: dominance, self-confidence, decisiveness, independence, toughness, suspicion, introversion, activity, depression, foresight, indus-

triousness, warmth, enthusiasm, conformity, inventiveness, persistence, sex drive, recognition, drive, cooperativeness, humility-tolerance, and self-control. Examiner required. Suitable for group use.

Untimed: 50-120 minutes
Scoring: Examiner evaluated
Cost: Professional examination kit for 24 $50.00
Publisher: Psychometric Affiliates

A VIOLENCE SCALE
Panos D. Bardis

**Adolescent, adult
Grades 10 and above**

Purpose: Measures attitudes toward violence (words and actions aimed at property damage and personal injury). Used for clinical assessment, marriage and family counseling, research on violence, and discussions in social science classes.

Description: 25-item paper-pencil test in which the subjects rate 25 statements concerning various aspects of violence on a scale from 0 (strongly disagree) to 4 (strongly agree). The "violence" score equals the sum of the 25 numerical responses. The theoretical range of scores extends from 0 (lowest approval of violence) to 100 (highest approval). Examiner/self-administered. Suitable for group use.

Untimed: 10 minutes
Scoring: Examiner evaluated
Cost: Free
Publisher: Panos D. Bardis

WAHLER PHYSICAL SYMPTOMS INVENTORY
H.J. Wahler

Adult

Purpose: Discriminates between patients with medical ailments and those with psychogenic complaints. Used to screen new patients.

Description: 42-item paper-pencil test consisting of physical problems on which the subjects must rate themselves using a

6-point frequency scale ranging from "almost never" to "nearly every day." The test helps identify conversion hysteria, hypocondriasis, and psychophysiological reactions, as well as physically determined disorders. Self-administered. Suitable for group use.

Untimed: 15-20 minutes

Scoring: Hand key

Cost: Complete kit (100 inventory pads, manual) $22.50

Publisher: Western Psychological Services

WAHLER SELF-DESCRIPTION INVENTORY
H. J. Wahler

Adult

Purpose: Measures the extent to which individuals emphasize their favorable and unfavorable characteristics in self-evaluations. Used to identify individuals who may be overcompensating for real or imagined inadequacies or who have poor self-images.

Description: 66-item paper-pencil test consisting of descriptive statements which the subject rates on a 9-point scale from "not at all like me" to "beyond question very much like me." Scoring provides information about defensiveness, maladjustment, potential for change, and actual change during treatment. A sixth-grade reading level is required. Self-administered. Suitable for group use.

Untimed: 10-15 minutes

Scoring: Hand key

Cost: Complete kit (100 inventory sheets, manual, key) $23.40

Publisher: Western Psychological Services

WESTERN PERSONALITY INVENTORY
Morse P. Manson

Adult

Purpose: Diagnoses the presence and degree of alcoholism. Useful in alcohol rehabilitation programs.

Description: Paper-pencil test consisting of a six-page form that combines the "Manson Evaluation," which identifies the potential alcoholic personality, and the "Alcadd Test," which measures the extent of alcohol addiction, into one booklet. Examiner required. Suitable for group use.

Untimed: 15-20 minutes

Scoring: Hand key

Cost: Complete kit (25 tests, manual) $16.00

Publisher: Western Psychological Services

WHITAKER INDEX OF SCHIZOPHRENIC THINKING (WIST)
Leighton C. Whitaker

Adolescent, adult
Grades 8 and above

Purpose: Provides an index of schizophrenic thinking. Used for intake screening.

Description: 25-item paper-pencil multiple-choice test discriminating between schizophrenic and nonschizophrenic thinking. The test can be completed by anyone with an eighth-grade education. The test is available in two equivalent forms. A revised (1980) manual provides a discussion of relevant diagnostic issues and the development of the test, directions for administration and scoring, standardization and validity data, a discussion of diagnostic and clinical uses, case illustrations, references, and specimen copies of the test forms. Self-administered. Suitable for group use.

Untimed: 15 minutes

Scoring: Hand key

Cost: Kit (25 each form, key, manual) $29.50

Publisher: Western Psychological Services

WILLIAMS AWARENESS SENTENCE COMPLETION (WASC)
Robert L. Williams

Adolescent, adult

Purpose: Measures ethnic awareness and consciousness of black Americans.

Description: 40-item paper-pencil sentence completion test pertaining to black awareness as manifested in four factors: prowhite, antiblack, problack, and antiwhite sentiments. Self-administered. Suitable for group use.

Untimed: 20 minutes

Scoring: Examiner evaluated

Cost: Complete (tests, manual) $12.00

Publisher: Robert L. Williams & Associates, Inc.

Personality: Normal and Abnormal, Assessment and Treatment: Multilevels

ABERRANT BEHAVIOR CHECKLIST (ABC)
Michael G. Aman and Nirbhay N. Singh

Mentally retarded individuals

Purpose: Assesses the problem behaviors of mentally retarded individuals living in hospital and residential facilities. Used by psychologists, nurses, direct caregivers, and others to measure treatment effectiveness.

Description: 58-item paper-pencil symptom checklist assessing the problem behaviors of mentally retarded individuals and measuring treatment effectivness. The instrument contains five subscales: irritability; lethargy, social withdrawal; stereotypic behavior; hyperactivity, noncompliance; and inappropriate speech. Examiner required. Not suitable for group use.

Untimed: Varies

Scoring: Examiner evaluated

Cost: Complete kit (manual, 50 checklist/score sheets) $32.00

Publisher: Slosson Educational Publications, Inc.

ADOLESCENT SEPARATION ANXIETY TEST
Henry G. Hansburg

Ages 10-adult

Purpose: Evaluates the emotional and personality patterns with which individuals react to separation experiences. Used by clinical psychologists as a counseling tool when separation anxieties are suspected.

Description: 12-item verbal-response test consisting of illustrations of severe and mild separation experiences ranging from a picture of a child being transferred to a new class to a picture of a child and father standing at the mother's coffin. Each picture contains a set of 17 statements describing a range of possible feelings associated with the situation depicted. The subjects look at each picture and then tell the examiner which statements best describe their reactions. The test measures interaction of attachment, individuation, hostility, fear-anxiety-pain syndrome, defensiveness, and self-evaluation (self-esteem, self-love identity). The diagnostic categories most frequently used with the instrument consist of mild, strong, severe anxious attachment, hostile anxious attachment, hostile detachment, and excessive self-sufficiency or dependence. The test has been used experimentally with whole families. A 3-volume series on separation problems based on the use of the Separation Anxiety Test is available. Examiner required. Not suitable for group use.

Untimed: 20 minutes

Scoring: Examiner evaluated

Cost: Complete kit (Volumes I and II, boy test, girl test, evaluation pads) $22.50; Volume I ST of Adolescent Separation Problems $6.95; Volume II Separation Disorders $8.96; tests $3.00 (specify boy or girl); 30 evaluation sheets $6.00

Publisher: Robert E. Kreiger Publishing Company, Inc.

AUDITORY PROJECTIVE TEST
S. Braverman and H. Chevigny

Ages 4 and older ☞ ✍

Purpose: Assesses personality of blind people through a projective auditory technique. Parallels the Thematic Apperception Test (TAT).

Description: 3-part tape-recorded form of scenes from the Thematic Apperception Test. In the first part, the client listens to a scene spoken unemotionally in an artificial language between various role-playing characters, such as an older man and a young man, an older woman and a boy, and a man and a woman. As in other projective tests, the client is asked to develop a story based upon the stimulus presented. In the second section, English is used instead of the artificial language. In the third section, sound effects are presented, such as a stormy background with footsteps entering a house, a train with a whistle and screeching auto brakes, and running footsteps and gunshots. Interpretation consists of noting the themes, conflicts, style, and other aspects of the stories as they relate to the stimuli used. Examiner required. Not suitable for group use.

Untimed: Not available

Scoring: Contact publisher

Cost: Not available

Publisher: American Foundation for the Blind

Information and availability unconfirmed; no publisher response.

AUTISM SCREENING INSTRUMENT FOR EDUCATIONAL PLANNING
David A. Krug, Joel R. Arick, and Patricia J. Almond

Ages 18 months-adult ☞ ✍

Purpose: Assesses the behavioral, social, and educational development of autistic, mentally retarded, deaf/blind, and emotionally disturbed students. Used to establish IEPs, evaluate program effectiveness, and monitor student progress.

Description: Multiple-item paper-pencil observational inventory consisting of five subtests: Autism Behavior Checklist (ABC), Sample of Vocal Behavior, Interaction Assessment, Educational Assessment, and Prognosis of Learning Rate. The Autism Behavior Checklist contains 57 observable behaviors discriminating autism from other severely handicapped conditions, such as deaf/blind, severely emotionally disturbed, and mentally retarded. The Sample of Vocal Behavior assesses spontaneous verbal behavior in low-language developmentally delayed students. The examiner records 50 representative vocalizations in an unstructured setting. The sample is then analyzed for repetitive level, communicative value, vocal complexity, and syntactic complexity. The results yield a standardized language-age equivalency score. The Interaction Assessment provides a data-based assessment of social interaction between an adult and a child, recording observable behaviors such as self-stimulation, crying, laughing, gestures, toy manipulation, conversation, and tantrums. During a 12-minute period, the examiner observes the child for 10 seconds, then in the next 5 seconds codes the interval according to the student's behavior on a matrix coding sheet yielding a general social interaction profile. The Educational Assessment measures language performance and communicative ability. The student uses either sign language or verbal speech to answer the examiner's questions. The responses are interpreted quantitatively in the following areas: in-seat behavior, receptive language, expressive language, body concept, and speech imitation. The Prognosis of Learning Rate involves teaching each student a standardized task within a specific framework of responses. The student's learning acquisition rate is assessed in terms of responses to learn a black/white sequencing task. The observational methods involved in all five subtests allow all students to be "testable." Examiner required. Not suitable for group use. The Autism Behavior Checklist with instructions and profile is available in Spanish.

Untimed: Varies

Scoring: Examiner evaluated

Cost: ASIEP test kit (administration manual, 10 record form booklets, all materials needed for administration) $176.00; Spanish Edition of the Autism Behavior Checklist with 20 administration and scoring booklets $24.95

Publisher: ASIEP Education Company

BALTHAZAR SCALES OF ADAPTIVE BEHAVIOR II: SCALES OF SOCIAL ADAPTATION
Earl E. Balthazar

Mentally retarded children and adults

Purpose: Evaluates the coping behaviors of profoundly retarded adults and children. Used for program planning and progress evaluation.

Description: Multiple-item paper-pencil observational inventory assessing eight categories of social adaptation and coping behaviors: unadaptive self-directed behaviors, unadaptive interpersonal behaviors, adaptive self-directed behaviors, adaptive interpersonal behaviors, verbal communication, play activities, response to instructions, and checklist items. Ratings are based on direct observation of the individual in his own environment. Readministration of the scales is sensitive to changes in the individual's behavior. The manual provides instructions for use by technicians, teachers, and other paraprofessionals. Examiner required. Not suitable for group use.

Untimed: Varies

Scoring: Examiner evaluated

Cost: Complete kit (manual and materials for 25 subjects) $21.00

Publisher: Consulting Psychologists Press, Inc.

BARRON-WELSH ART SCALE
Frank Barron and George S. Welsh

Ages 6-adult

Purpose: Evaluates individual personality traits and measures creativity through figure identification. Used for counseling and research.

Description: 86-item paper-pencil test consisting of black-and-white figures to which the subject responds "like" or "dislike" for each. The test includes items from the Revised Art Scale. The items are also included in the 400-item Welsh Figure Preference Test. Examiner required. Suitable for group use.

Untimed: 15 minutes

Scoring: Hand key

Cost: 25 test booklets $17.25; 50 hand-scorable answer sheets $5.50; manual $15.00

Publisher: Consulting Psychologists Press, Inc.

BEHAVIORAL DEVIANCY PROFILE
Betty Ball and Rita Weinberg

Ages 3-21

Purpose: Diagnoses deviancy and disturbance in children and adolescents with moderate to severe social and emotional problems. Used to compare deviance of physical, psychological, and social factors in a child before and after intervention and to improve the observations of staff in mental health and educational programs.

Description: Multiple-item paper-pencil questionnaire in which the examiner records the child's observed behavior in four major developmental areas: physical and motor development, cognitive development, speech and language development, and social and emotional development. The profile looks at the total functioning of the child via a developmental and dynamic method. Severity of behavior, duration, and age appropriateness of the behavior are considered. Examiner required. Not suitable for group use.

Untimed: Observation time

Scoring: Examiner evaluated

Cost: Complete kit (manual, 15 record booklets) $15.25

Publisher: Stoelting Company

BEHAVIORAL INTERVENTION PLAN
James M. Gardner

Child, adolescent, adult

Purpose: Produces multimodal behavior intervention strategies for individuals of all ages. Used by professional mental health and education personnel for psychotherapy and behavior modification and management. May be used with handicapped and nonhandicapped individuals.

Description: 2000-item paper-pencil multiple-choice and fill-in-the-blank test assessing the severity of an individual's behavior problems, including aggression, destructiveness, and self-abuse. Test items focus on the person, the setting, and the behavior. Results are used for reducing the incidence and severity of the behavior problem. Examiner required. Suitable for group use.

Untimed: 30 minutes

Scoring: Computer scored

Cost: $150.00 per evaluation

Publisher: Planet Press

THE BLACKY PICTURES
Gerald S. Blum

Ages 5-adult

Purpose: Clinical assessment of personality dynamics. Used for psychodynamically oriented research.

Description: 68-item paper-pencil picture test of personality using a set of 12 pictures. The subject views the pictures, makes up a story and answers 6-7 multiple-choice or short-answer questions for each picture, and then sorts pictures according to preference. The instrument helps determine conflicts and defenses in the area of psychosexual development. The test also is suitable as a semistructured projective test of psychosexual stages of development. Materials include the pictures, inquiry booklets, record blanks, and a manual. The test may be administered individually or to groups using slides of pictures. The test is not yet available commercially. Examiner required. Suitable for group use. Available in Italian.

Untimed: 45 minutes

Scoring: Examiner evaluated

Cost: Complete set (12 pictures, inquiry booklets, manual, 25 record blanks) $32.00

Publisher: Psychodynamic Instruments

BODY ELIMINATION ATTITUDE SCALE
Donald I. Templer, Frank L. King, Robert K. Brooner, and Mark Corgiat

Adult

Purpose: Assesses attitudes related to body elimination.

Description: 26-item paper-pencil Likert-format scale measuring seven factors: fecal smell, personal hygiene, sight, dirty hair, animal feces, mucous-like discharge, and sound. Future research may indicate applications to Freudian and other personality theory and practical applications, including selection of persons for health care occupations and indications of psychosomatic disorders such as colitis and medical procedures such as ostomies. Self-administered. Suitable for group use.

Untimed: Varies

Scoring: Not available

Cost: Contact publisher

Publisher: Donald I. Templer, Ph.D.

BRISTOL SOCIAL ADJUSTMENT GUIDES, AMERICAN EDITION (BSAG)
Refer to page 667.

BRISTOL SOCIAL ADJUSTMENT GUIDES, BRITISH EDITION (BSAG)
Refer to page 668.

BURKS' BEHAVIOR RATING SCALES
Harold F. Burks

Child, adolescent Grades 1-9

Purpose: Identifies patterns of behavior problems in children. Used as an aid to differential diagnosis.

Description: 110-item paper-pencil inventory used by parents and teachers to rate a child on the basis of descriptive statements of observed behavior. Nineteen subscales measure excessive self-blame, anxiety, withdrawal, dependency, suffering, sense of persecution, aggressiveness, resistance and poor ego strength, physical strength, coordination, intellectuality, academics, attention, impulse control, reality contact, sense of identity, anger control, and social conformity. The Parents' Guide and the Teacher's Guide define each of the scales, present possible causes for the problem behavior, and offer suggestions on how to deal with the undesirable behavior from the point of view of the parent or teacher. The manual discusses causes and manifestations and possible intervention approaches for each of the subscales; use with special groups, such as the educable mentally retarded, educationally and orthopedically handicapped, and speech and hearing handicapped. Examiner administered. Not suitable for group use.

Untimed: 15-20 minutes

Scoring: Hand key

Cost: Complete kit (25 booklets and profile sheets, manual, 2 parents' guides, 2 teacher's guides) $23.50

Publisher: Western Psychological Services

BUTTONS: A PROJECTIVE TEST FOR PRE-ADOLESCENTS AND ADOLESCENTS
Refer to page 668.

THE C.P.H. (COLORADO PSYCHOPATHIC HOSPITAL) PATIENT ATTITUDE SCALE
Marvin W. Kahn and Nelson F. Jones

Adult

Purpose: Assesses a mental patient's attitudes toward hospital treatment. Used for examining ward programs and comparing occurrences in the hospital with the patient's social station in life and as a research tool.

Description: 45-item paper-pencil test assessing five attitude dimensions: authoritarian control and non-psychological orientation; negative hospital orientation; external control, cause and treatment; mental illness and treatment as the hospital supplies

regressive dependence; and let-down of control or therapeutic gain-arbitrary restriction. Items are scored on a 5-point Likert scale ranging from strongly agree to strongly disagree. Materials include scales and manual. Self-administered. Suitable for group use.

Untimed: 10-30 minutes

Scoring: Hand key

Cost: Specimen set $3.50

Publisher: Marvin W. Kahn, Ph.D.

CALIFORNIA ADAPTIVE BEHAVIOR SCALE
James M. Gardner

Child, adolescent
Ages 0-18 years

Purpose: Measures an individual's overall adaptive behavior. Used for assessment and placement.

Description: 353-item paper-pencil or computer-administered multiple-choice test assessing adaptive behavior and school and/or vocational readiness. An individual familiar with the person being rated uses a booklet or computer to assess self-help, socialization, language, gross-motor, perceptual motor, vocational, independent living, and academic skills. Can be purchased for Apple II, CP/M, or MS.DOS computers. Examiner/self-administered. Suitable for group use.

Untimed: 15 minutes

Scoring: Computer scored

Cost: Disk $350.00; mail-in service $10.00 per evaluation

Publisher: Planet Press

CARTOON PREDICTIONS (SICP)
Maureen O'Sullivan and J.P. Guilford

Adolescent, adult
Grades 10 and above

Purpose: Measures ability to understand a sequence of behaviors and predict the next step in the sequence. Used in research.

Description: Multiple-item paper-pencil multiple-choice test of an individual's cognition of behavioral implications—the ability to predict what is most likely to happen next in a sequence of behaviors. Each test item shows a single cartoon-like scene with characters in a readily grasped situation. The subject selects from among the alternative pictures the one that shows what is most likely to happen next in terms of the psychological states of the persons concerned. Norms are provided for tenth-grade and college students. The test is restricted to A.P.A. members. Examiner required. Suitable for group use.

Timed: 8 minutes

Scoring: Hand key

Cost: 25 tests $14.00; manual $3.50; 25 answer sheets $3.50; scoring key $2.00

Publisher: Sheridan Psychological Services, Inc.

CHILD DEVELOPMENT CENTER Q-SORT (CDCQ)
Frances Fuchs Schachter

PreK-adult

Purpose: Measures personality development at all ages and identifies personality types. Used by clinicians, counselors, and teachers to assess degree of normality and changes in the individual's personality picture.

Description: Multiple-item observational test consisting of 113 sort deck cards, each representing a personality characteristic. The examiner sorts the cards according to the prominence of each characteristic for the person being evaluated. A personality profile is developed based on the following seven factors: independence/dependence, affectivity, relations with people, relations with self, relations with inanimate objects, heterosexual relationships, ego, and superego. The personality profile of the person being evaluated is compared with that of an "ideal" individual of the same age and sex. The ideal profiles are based on a consensus of mental health experts for each developmental level. The test also yields an overall index of personality adjustment or psychological well-being to be used in evaluation and follow-up work. A complete test set includes a sort deck, distribution cards, manual, 30 record

forms, and ideal male and female profiles for the age level ordered. Examiner required. Suitable for group use.

Untimed: Open ended

Scoring: Examiner evaluated

Cost: Complete kit for each level $37.00 each

Publisher: Stoelting Company

THE CHILD DIAGNOSTIC SCREENING BATTERY
James J. Smith and Joseph M. Eisenberg

Child, adolescent Ages 2-17

Purpose: Identifies diagnostic possibilities among those listed in DSM-III. Used with children in clinical settings.

Description: Paper-pencil or computer-administered screening battery assessing symptoms important for diagnostic considerations. The system consists of two parts: a questionnaire for the child's parent or guardian and a questionnaire for the clinician. The clinician gathers information through a structured interview with the child's parent or guardian. The system is structured so that once data is entered in the computer, it is compared with all possible DSM-III diagnoses related to children. A manual describing the use and application of the program and the use of printouts generated by the program is provided. Examiner required. Not suitable for group use.

Untimed: 15 minutes

Scoring: Hand key; may be computer scored

Cost: Total system $195.00; 10-day trial of system $15.00

Publisher: Reason House

THE CHILDREN'S DEPRESSION INVENTORY (CDI)
Maria Kovacs

Child, adolescent Ages 8-13

Purpose: Assesses severity of depression in children and adolescents. Also used for

---

measuring progress during treatment and to classify for research purposes.

Description: 27-item paper-pencil inventory measuring an array of overt symptoms of child depression, such as sadness, anhedonia, suicidal ideation, and sleep and appetite disturbances. The examiner reads aloud three related statements, such as "I am sad once in a while," "I am sad many times," and "I am sad all the time." The child reads along silently and selects the statement that best reflects his feelings and ideas during the previous two weeks. The three choices for each item are assigned numerical values from 0-2, graded in order of increasing psychopathology. A total score (ranging from 0-54) is obtained by adding the numerical scores of the individual items. A first-grade reading level is required. Examiner required. Suitable for group use.

Untimed: Varies

Scoring: Hand key

Cost: Inventory and supplementary materials $2.50

Publisher: Maria Kovacs, Ph.D.

CHILDREN'S DEPRESSION SCALE
Moshe Lange and Miriam Tisher

Child, adolescent
Ages 9-16

Purpose: Measures depression in children. Identifies depressed children in need of further evaluation.

Description: 66-item (48 "depressive" and 18 "positive") scale measuring six aspects of childhood depression: effective response, social problems, self-esteem, preoccupation with own sickness or death, guilt, and pleasure. Items are presented on cards which the child sorts into five boxes ranging from "very right" to "very wrong" according to how he feels the item applies to himself. A paper-pencil questionnaire identical in content to the cards but appropriately reworded, is available for use with parents, teachers, or other adults familiar with the child. The complete set of materials includes 66 cards, five boxes, 25 record forms, and a manual. Examiner required. Not suitable for group use.

AUSTRALIAN PUBLISHER

Untimed: Varies

Scoring: Examiner evaluated

Cost: Contact publisher

Publisher: The Australian Council for Educational Research Limited

CHILDREN'S INTERACTION MATRIX (CIM)
William Fawcett Hill

Child   Grades 1-6

Purpose: Assesses grade-school children's suitability for assignment to counseling groups or other small groups. Used to determine group composition.

Description: 64-item paper-pencil test determining the child's overall acceptance of small groups, what the children talk about in the group, and their manner and degree of participation. The child reads statements describing a group situation and marks his reaction on the answer sheet scale. Examiner/self-administered. Suitable for group use.

Untimed: 20 minutes

Scoring: Hand key; may be computer scored

Cost: Monograph $4.00; manual $3.00; computer programs $2.00 each

Publisher: William Fawcett Hill

Information and availability unconfirmed; no publisher response.

COOPERSMITH SELF-ESTEEM INVENTORIES (CSEI)
Stanley Coopersmith

Ages 8-adult

Purpose: Measures attitudes toward the self in social, academic, and personal contexts. Used for individual diagnosis, classroom screening, pre-post evaluations, and clinical and research studies.

Description: 58- or 25-item paper-pencil test of self-attitudes in four areas: social-self-peers, home-parents, school-academic, and general-self. Materials include the 58-item School Form, 25-item School Short Form, and 25-item Adult Form. The School Form is suitable for use with individuals ages 8-15; the Adult Form is administered to individuals ages 15 and older. Self-administered. Suitable for group use.

Untimed: 15 minutes

Scoring: Hand key

Cost: 25 School Form test booklets $5.00; 25 Adult Form test booklets $3.50; keys-adult $1.25, school $2.00; manual $6.00

Publisher: Consulting Psychologists Press, Inc.

CULTURE-FREE SELF-ESTEEM INVENTORIES
James Battle

Grades 3-adult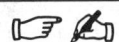

Purpose: Assesses the self-esteem of children and adults. Identifies individuals needing psychological assistance.

Description: Multiple-item paper-pencil test assessing five areas of self-esteem: general, school-related, peer-related, parent-related, and defensiveness. Raw scores for each subscale and a total score are obtained with acetate scoring template. Percentile ranks and standard scores are provided for children in Grades 3-9 and adults. Separate forms are available for children and adults; parallel forms are available for children for pre- and posttesting. The test may be administered orally or with a cassette tape to low-level readers. Suitable for group use.

Untimed: 10-15 minutes

Scoring: Hand key; may be computer scored

Cost: Test kit (25 each of forms A and B for children, 25 of form AD for adults, manual quick-scoring acetates, 25 computer-scorable answer sheets, oral administration on cassette tape) $51.00

Publisher: Special Child Publications

DEATH ANXIETY SCALE
Donald I. Templer

Adult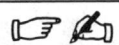

Purpose: Assesses anxiety related to death.

Description: 15-item paper-pencil scale measuring death anxiety as it permeates a wide range of life experiences. Examiner required. Suitable for group use.

Untimed: Varies

Scoring: Not available

Cost: Contact publisher

Publisher: Donald I. Templer, Ph.D.

EDUCATION APPERCEPTION TEST
Refer to page 671.

EMBEDDED FIGURES TEST (EFT)
Herman A. Witkin

Ages 10-adult

Purpose: Assesses cognitive style in perceptual tasks. Used in counseling.

Description: 12-item verbal-manual test of perceptual processes including field dependence-independence. The task requires the subject to locate and trace a previously seen simple figure within a larger complex figure. Performance is related to analytic ability, social behavior, body concept, and preferred defense mechanisms. Materials include cards with complex figures, cards with simple figures, and a stylus for tracing. A stopwatch with a second hand is needed also. Two alternate forms are available. Examiner required. Not suitable for group use.

Untimed: 10-45 minutes

Scoring: Examiner evaluated

Cost: Test kit (includes card set, stylus, 50 recording sheets) $14.00

Publisher: Consulting Psychologists Press, Inc.

EMOTIONAL FACTORS INVENTORY
Mary K. Bauman

Visually handicapped individuals

Purpose: Measures emotional and personality factors of visually handicapped individuals.

Description: 170-item paper-pencil or oral response questionnaire assessing the personal and emotional adjustment of visually impaired individuals. The questionnaire yields scores on the following seven scales: sensitivity, somatic symptoms, social competency, attitudes of distrust, feelings of inadequacy, depression, and attitudes concerning blindness. A validation score is also obtained. The questionnaire is presented in large-print format. Instructions for tape recording the questions are included. Supplementary materials provided in the test kit include a discussion of the inventory, instructions for administering and scoring the inventory, and a comparative study of personality factors in blind, other handicapped, and nonhandicapped individuals. Examiner required. The paper-pencil version is suitable for group use.

Untimed: Varies

Scoring: Examiner evaluated

Cost: Test kit (test booklet, scoring overlays, 10 IBM answer sheets, supplementary materials, and norms) $15.00

Publisher: Associated Services for the Blind

ENVIRONMENTAL DEPRIVATION SCALE
Gerald R. Pascal and William O. Jenkins

Ages 10-adult

Purpose: Clinical measurement of an individual's environmental deprivation. Predicts recidivism of offenders, mental hospital patients, and others who exhibit maladaption. Useful to pinpoint areas requiring intervention.

Description: 16-item paper-pencil test measuring environmental support/deprivation. Items include employment, income, debts, parental relationship, education, and fear. Behavior interviewing techniques are used in face-to-face contact with subjects. Scoring is a forced-choice technique: "0" for no deprivation and "1" for deprivation. Materials include manual and answer sheets. A juvenile version is available. Examiner required. Not suitable for group use.

Untimed: 40 minutes

Scoring: Hand key

Cost: Complete kit (25 test forms, manual) $35.00

Publisher: Behavior Science Press

EXPRESSION GROUPING (SIEG)
Maureen O'Sullivan and J.P. Guilford

Adolescent, adult Grades 10 and above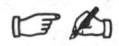

Purpose: Measures ability to understand facial expressions and body language. Used for counseling and research.

Description: Multiple-item paper-pencil multiple-choice test measuring the "cognition of behavioral classes," defined as the abiliity to look at a number of pictured expressions involving different parts of the body, deciding what psychological state or momentary disposition they indicate in common. Norms are provided for tenth-grade and college students. The test is restricted to A.P.A. members. Examiner required. Suitable for group use.

Timed: 10 minutes

Scoring: Hand key

Cost: 25 tests $14.00; manual $3.50; 25 answer sheets $3.50; scoring key $2.00

Publisher: Sheridan Psychological Services, Inc.

EYSENCK-WITHERS PERSONALITY INVENTORY
Sybil B.G. Eysenck

IQ range 50-80

Purpose: Evaluates personality structure and adjustment of subnormal patients (those with IQs between 50 and 80). Identifies individuals with tendencies toward mental illness or criminal or hostile behavior. Used for clinical diagnosis and screening.

Description: Multiple-item paper-pencil questionnaire measuring dimensions of a person's personality structure. The responses are scored on three scales: Neuroticism, Extraversion/Introversion, and Psychoticism. Norms are based on 400 subnormal patients with IQs of between 50 and 80. The inventory is restricted to senior staff members of any recognized medical or educational institution, medi-

cal doctors, and BPS and APA members. Examiner required. Not suitable for group use.
BRITISH PUBLISHER
Untimed: Not available
Scoring: Hand key; examiner evaluated
Cost: Specimen set £1.45; 20 question-naires £1.50 plus VAT; scoring key 70p. plus VAT; manual 60p.
Publisher: Hodder & Stoughton

FOUR PICTURE TEST
D. J. VanLennep and R. Houwink

Ages 10 and older

Purpose: Assesses personality. Used for diagnosis and individual counseling.

Description: 4-item projective test of personality in which the subject looks at four pictures for one minute. The pictures are removed, and the subject is asked to write a single story based on memory in which all four pictures are used. Materials include four picture cards and manual. Examiner required. Suitable for group use.
DUTCH PUBLISHER
Untimed: 30-45 minutes
Scoring: Examiner evaluated
Cost: Contact publisher
Publisher: SWETS Test Services

FRANCK DRAWING COMPLETION TEST
K. Franck

All ages

Purpose: Evaluates the relationship of sex role to mental illness in both children and adults. Used as a supplementary clinical tool for research purposes.

Description: 36-item paper-pencil projective personality test consisting of stimulus figures from which the examinee is required to make complete drawings. The drawings are analyzed according to a number of criteria to give a quantitative score, which may be placed on a masculinity-femininity continuum. The author's notes on some interpretations of the drawings are included in the manual to provide hypotheses for further

research. Materials include an eight-page expendable test booklet, scoring sheet, manual, scoring key, and specimen set. Examiner required. Not suitable for group use.
AUSTRALIAN PUBLISHER
Untimed: 15 minutes
Scoring: Hand key; examiner evaluated
Cost: Contact publisher
Publisher: The Australian Council for Educational Research Limited

FUNCTIONAL ANALYSIS OF BEHAVIOR
James M. Gardner

Child, adolescent, adult

Purpose: Provides a detailed and comprehensive description and analysis of individuals exhibiting severe behavior problems. Used with handicapped and nonhandicapped individuals for assessment and intervention.

Description: 90-item paper-pencil multiple-choice and fill-in-the-blank test. Computer analysis produces a functional analysis of behavior, including topography, course of the behavior, analysis of antecedents, severity of behavior, history of behavior, analysis of consequences, independent learning style, and suggested techniques. Completed by informant. Suitable for group use.
Untimed: 15 minutes
Scoring: Computer scored
Cost: $50.00 per evaluation
Publisher: Planet Press

FUNDAMENTAL INTERPERSONAL RELATIONS ORIENTATION—BEHAVIOR (FIRO-B)
Will Schutz

All ages

Purpose: Measures an individual's characteristic behavior toward others. Used in individual and group psychotherapy, in executive development programs, and as a measure of compatibility in relationships.

Description: 54-item paper-pencil test measuring six dimensions of an individual's behavior toward others: expressed inclusion, expressed control, expressed affection, wanted inclusion, wanted control, and wanted affection. Optional materials include the FIRO-BC, a form developed for use with children. Examiner/self-administered. Suitable for group use.

Untimed: 20 minutes

Scoring: Hand key

Cost: Specimen set (includes tests and key) $3.25; 25 tests (specify FIRO-B or FIRO-BC) $5.00

Publisher: Consulting Psychologists Press, Inc.

FUNDAMENTAL INTERPERSONAL RELATIONS ORIENTATION—BEHAVIOR CHARACTERISTICS (FIRO-BC)
Will Schutz and Marilyn Wood

Child, adolescent

Purpose: Measures characteristic behavior of children toward other people. Used with upper elementary and junior high school children for counseling and therapy.

Description: 54-item paper-pencil test containing six Guttman-type scales measuring the characteristic behavior of children in the areas of inclusion, control, and affection—the three dimensions of interpersonal behavior described by the author in his book, *The Interpersonal Underworld.* The test measures the relative strength of the needs within the individual. Because it does not compare a person with a population, norms are not provided. Examiner/self-administered. Suitable for group use.

Untimed: Not available

Scoring: Hand key

Cost: Manual $6.50; 25 test booklets $5.00; scoring key $4.00

Publisher: Consulting Psychologists Press, Inc.

GLOBAL ASSESSMENT SCALE (GAS)
Jean Endicott and The Department of Research Assessment and Training

Adolescent, adult

Purpose: Assesses general level of psychopathology. Used for diagnosis.

Description: Multiple-item measure of overall individual functioning. Information from family, case records, and clinical workup are used to rate the client's overall health or sickness on a 100-point scale. Examiner required. Not suitable for group use.

Untimed: After evaluation, 2 minutes

Scoring: Examiner evaluated

Cost: Scale $0.25; case vignettes and keys $1.50; instructions/examples $0.50 plus postage and handling

Publisher: Department of Research Assessment and Training—N.Y. State Psychiatric Institute

---

GRID TEST OF SCHIZOPHRENIC THOUGHT DISORDER
D. Bannister and Fay Fransella

All ages

Purpose: Identifies schizophrenic thought disorder. Used for diagnosis of schizophrenia.

Description: Multiple-item test of thought disorder based on ranking photographs of people on various dimensions. Eight photographs are presented to the subject, and the subject ranks the pictures from most to least likely to be kind. The subject then ranks the pictures for stupid, selfish, sincere, mean, and honest. Responses are scored on the basis of consistency and intensity. The relationship between the sorting categories, rather than the "correctness" of the sorts, is the most important evaluative factor. Materials include eight photographs. Examiner required. Not suitable for group use.

BRITISH PUBLISHER

Untimed: 20 minutes

Scoring: Examiner evaluated

Cost: Specimen set (pictures, manual, record sheet, analysis sheet) $9.60; set of pictures $4.80; 50 analysis sheets $8.40; manual $4.80

Publisher: Psychological Test Publishers; distributed by The Test Agency Ltd.

GROUP EMBEDDED FIGURES TEST (GEFT)
Philip K. Oltman, Evelyn Raskin, and Herman A. Witkin

Ages 10-adult

Purpose: Assesses cognitive style in perceptual tasks. Used in counseling.

Description: 25-item paper-pencil test of perceptual processes, including field dependence-independence. Performance is related to analytic ability, social behavior, body concept, and preferred defense mechanisms. Subjects find one of eight simple figures in the 18 complex designs. Examiner required. Suitable for group use.

Untimed: 20 minutes

Scoring: Hand key

Cost: Sample set (manual not included) $1.75; manual $6.00; 25 tests $16.50; scoring key $1.00

Publisher: Consulting Psychologists Press, Inc.

GROUP PERSONALITY PROJECTIVE TEST (GPPT)
R. N. Cassel and T.C. Kahn

Ages 11 and older

Purpose: Measures major personality characteristics. Used to screen potentially pathological personalities.

Description: 90-item paper-pencil test measuring seven aspects of personality, including tension, nurturance, withdrawal, neuroticism, affiliation, succorance, and total. Items are stick drawings accompanied by five descriptive or interpretative statements. The subject chooses the statement he believes is most accurate. Self-administered. Suitable for group use.

Untimed: 40 minutes

Scoring: Hand key; examiner evaluated

Cost: Examiner's set (manual, 7 scoring keys, 12 test booklets, 100 answer and profile sheets) $27.00; 25 test booklets $25.00; 100 answer and profile sheets $13.00; scoring keys $4.00; manual $4.00

Publisher: Psychological Test Specialists

HARTMAN VALUE PROFILE (HVP)
Robert S. Hartman

Ages 5-adult

Purpose: Assesses a person's capacity to value and indicates presence of emotional or existential problems. Used for mental health screening, personnel evaluation, research, educational program evaluation, assessment of special education class needs, and development of individual goals.

Description: Multiple-item paper-pencil or oral-response inventory measuring a person's capacity to value in terms of both intellectual and emotional capacities. Scores are provided on the following scales: World Concept-Self Concept Potentials, Cognitive-Affective Domain Relationships, Social-Emotional Handicaps, and Interpersonal Compatibility. Computer processing makes large scale screening possible, while in-depth analysis provides significant psychiatric and psychological insight. The profile is available in three forms (regular, card, and pictorial) making testing possible with subjects from ages five to adult. Examiner/self-administered. Suitable for group use. Available in Spanish.

Untimed: 20-30 minutes

Scoring: Hand key; examiner evaluated; may be computer scored

Cost: 35 profile forms $8.75; profile card form $12.00; profile pictorial form $15.00; 35 keys $5.00; manual $18.00; text $9.50

Publisher: Research Concepts

HILL INTERACTION MATRIX-A (HIM-A)
William Fawcett Hill

Adolescent, adult

Purpose: Assesses adolescents' and adults' suitability for assignment to counseling groups or other small groups. Used to determine group composition and diagnose problem members.

Description: 64-item paper-pencil test measuring an individual's overall acceptance of small groups, their discussion topic preferences, and participation tendencies. The subject reads statements describing a group situation and marks reactions on the 6-position answer sheet scale for each item. Hill Interaction Matrix-B is available with more sophisticated language. Examiner/self-administered. Suitable for group use. Available in German.

Untimed: 20 minutes

Scoring: Hand key; may be computer scored

Cost: Monograph $4.00; manual $3.00; computer programs $2.00 each

Publisher: William Fawcett Hill

Information and availability unconfirmed; no publisher response.

HILL INTERACTION MATRIX-B (HIM-B)
William Fawcett Hill

Adolescent, adult

Purpose: Assesses suitability of adolescents and adults for assignment to counseling groups or other small groups. Used to determine group composition.

Description: 64-item paper-pencil test measuring an individual's overall acceptance of small groups, the individual's discussion topic preferences, and style of participation. The subject reads statements describing a group situation and marks reactions on the 6-position answer sheet scale for each item. Hill Interaction Matrix-A is available with simpler language. Examiner/self-administered. Suitable for group use. Available in German.

Untimed: 20 minutes

Scoring: Hand key; may be computer scored

Cost: Monograph $4.00; manual $3.00; computer programs $2.00 each

Publisher: William Fawcett Hill

Information and availability unconfirmed; no publisher response.

HILL INTERACTION MATRIX-G (HIM-G)
William Fawcett Hill

Adolescent, adult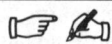

Purpose: Assesses verbal interaction in counseling/encounter groups. May be used to estimate current functioning of a group and to determine group development through repeated evaluation.

Description: 74-item paper-pencil test measuring the work mode, topic preference, risk-taking ration, and therapist/member interaction ratio of a group. The subject observes, listens or views a tape recording, or reads a transcript of a group session and marks the amount of interaction for each item on a 7-point scale. Examiner/self-administered. Suitable for group use.

Untimed: 20 minutes

Scoring: Hand key; may be computer scored

Cost: Monograph $4.00; manual $3.00; computer programs $2.00 each

Publisher: William Fawcett Hill

Information and availability unconfirmed; no publisher response.

HOLTZMAN INKBLOT TECHNIQUE (HIT)
W. H. Holtzman

Ages 5-adult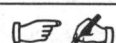

Purpose: Assesses individual personality. Used for diagnosis and therapy planning.

Description: 45-item projective measure of personality in which the examinee responds to 45 inkblots. Some inkblots are asymmetric, and some are in a color other than black. An objective scoring system has been developed. Materials include two alternate and equivalent forms, A and B, for a total of 90 stimulus cards. Examiner required. Not suitable for group use.

Untimed: Not available

Scoring: Examiner evaluated

Cost: Complete set (45 inkblots, 25 record forms with summary sheets, scoring guide) Form A or B $145.00; Forms A and B combined $275.00; monograph $45.00

Publisher: The Psychological Corporation

HOUSE-TREE-PERSON (H-T-P) PROJECTIVE TECHNIQUE
John N. Buck

Ages 3 and older

Purpose: Assesses personality disturbances in individuals ages 3 and older in psychotherapy, school, and research settings. May be used with the culturally disadvantaged, educationally deprived, mentally retarded, and aged.

Description: Multiple-item paper-pencil and oral-response test providing a projective study of personality. The test consists of two steps. The first, which is nonverbal, creative, and almost completely unstructured, requires the subject to make a freehand drawing of a house, a tree, and a person. The second step, which is verbal, apperceptive, and more formally structured, gives the subject an opportunity to describe, define, and interpret the drawings and their respective environments. Examiner required. Not suitable for group use.

Untimed: 15-20 minutes

Scoring: Hand key; examiner evaluated

Cost: Complete set (manual for administering and scoring; interpretive catalogs and manuals, 25 drawing forms, 25 interrogation folders, 25 scoring folders, 25 post-drawing interrogation folders, 25 two-copy drawing forms) $125.00

Publisher: Western Psychological Services

THE IES TEST
Lawrence A. Dombrose and Morton S. Slobin

Ages 10 and older

Purpose: Assesses the relative strengths of various personality forces. Used for individual diagnosis, clinical evaluation, and research.

Description: 57-item four-subtest projective measure of personality. Picture Title is a 12-item test in which the subject creates titles for pictures. Picture Story Completion requires the subject to select a cartoon to end each of 13 incomplete cartoon stories. Photo-Analysis consists of nine men's photographs with two objectively scored questions about each. Arrow-Dot is a set of 23 graphic problems requiring the subject to draw a line from an arrow to a dot goal without creating or crossing barriers. All responses are scored Impulse (I), Ego (E), or Superego (S). Use is limited to psychologists, psychiatrists, and other professionals in the areas of clinical and research psychology. Examiner required. Not suitable for group use.

Untimed: 30 minutes

Scoring: Examiner evaluated

Cost: Complete kit (Picture Title cards, Picture Story Completion cards, Photo-Analysis cards, 25 Arrow-Dot test forms, 25 record forms, separate instruction cards, general manual, heavy storage boxes) $43.50; 100 record forms $10.00; 25 Arrow-Dot forms $9.00; manual $6.00

Publisher: Psychological Test Specialists

IMAGERY AND DISEASE
Jeanne Achterberg and G. Frank Lawlis

Purpose: Evaluates the progress of disease. Helps patients mobilize their psychological resources to combat the progress of cancer, diabetes, and spinal pain. Bridges the gap between subjective holistic opinions and predictive science. Used for clinical evaluations, behavioral medicine, and rehabilitation counseling.

Description: Three paper-pencil and oral-response tests combining guided imagery/relaxation procedures, patient drawings of disease-related imagery, and a structured interview. After scoring the imagery and interview content, a total score is derived that reflects the overall quality of the patient's imagery and is highly predictive of long-term disease status. Examiner required. Not suitable for group use.

Untimed: Open ended
Scoring: Hand key
Cost: Handbook $17.95; testing materials
$20.00
Publisher: Institute for Personality and
Ability Testing, Inc.

INFORMATION TEST ON DRUGS AND DRUG ABUSE
Refer to page 316.

INTER-PERSON PERCEPTION TEST (IPPT)
F.K. Heussenstamm and R. Hoepfner

Ages 7-76

Purpose: Assesses individual and group status on interpersonal perception or social cognition. Used to evaluate changes accompanying sensitivity training, counseling, or psychotherapy. Also used to select personnel who must interact with people and for research purposes.

Description: 40-item paper-pencil multiple-choice test in which the subject is asked to select one of four alternative facial photographs expressing the same thoughts, feelings, and intentions as the given exemplar. The faces used for the 40 items are divided equally by sex and by ethnicity (10 each for Caucasions, Negroes, Mexican-Americans, and Oriental-Americans). Each item has been constructed with the aid of representatives of its respective age, sex, and ethnic group and has undergone intensive validation within samples of its representative group. The test is concerned primarily with abilities of social sensitivities and is relatively free of verbal intelligence aspects. Form AC uses faces of children and youths. Form AA uses faces of adults. Reusable forms are provided with separate answer sheets. Examiner required. Self-administered. Suitable for group use.

Timed: 20 minutes
Scoring: Hand key
Cost: Specimen set (specify form) $8.00; 35 tests (specify form) $40.00; 35 answer sheets (specify form) $4.00; scoring stencil (specify form) $3.00; manual $3.00
Publisher: Monitor

INTERPERSONAL BEHAVIOR SURVEY (IBS)
Paul A. Mauger, David R. Adkinson, Suzanne K. Zoss, Gregory Firestone, and J. David Hook

Adolescent, adult
Grades 9 and above

Purpose: Measures and distinguishes assertive and aggressive behaviors among adolescents and adults. Used for assertiveness training, marriage counseling, and in a variety of clinical settings.

Description: 272-item paper-pencil test in which the subject responds to statements written in the present tense to provide sensitivity to ongoing changes. The test yields eight aggressiveness scales (including one that measures general aggressiveness over a broad range of item content, including aggressive behaviors, feelings, and attitudes), nine assertiveness scales (including one that measures general assertiveness over a broad range of behaviors), three validity scales, and three relationship scales (Conflict Avoidance, Dependency, and Shyness). Two shorter forms are available: a 38-item form providing a general sampling of behaviors and a 133-item form providing information on all scales. The Profile Form provides a display of raw scores, T-scores, and percentiles. Norms are provided for adult males, adult females, high-school students, college students, and blacks. The manual presents validity and reliability data, interpretive guidelines, and a number of illustrated cases. A sixth-grade reading level is required. Self-administered. Suitable for group use.

Untimed: 10-45 minutes depending on form
Scoring: Hand key
Cost: Complete kit (5 booklets, 25 profile forms, 25 answer sheets, key, manual) $45.00
Publisher: Western Psychological Services

AN INVENTORY OF ATTITUDES TOWARD BLACK/WHITE RELATIONS IN UNITED STATES
James H. Morrison

Adolescent, adult

Purpose: Initiates discussions of black-white relations in training sessions. Used as a self-examination to sensitize a person to his attitudes towards race relations and for research.

Description: 28-item paper-pencil inventory measuring attitudes toward black-white relations in the United States on an integrationist-separationist continuum. Instructions are read to the subjects, who are allowed as much time as necessary to complete the test. The test requires a 10th-grade reading level. Self-administered. Suitable for group use.

Timed: 25 minutes

Scoring: Hand key

Cost: Specimen set (inventory, manual) $2.00; 20 tests (with manual) $4.00

Publisher: James H. Morrison

JENKINS ACTIVITY SURVEY (JAS)
C. David Jenkins,
Stephen J. Zyzanski,
and Ray H. Rosenman

Adult

Purpose: Identifies persons with the Type A behavior pattern associated with coronary heart disease. Used for research and clinical screening.

Description: 52-item paper-pencil test of several aspects of Type A behavior, including speed and impatience, job involvement, and hard driving and competitive. Items include questions about behavior found useful in medical diagnosis. Scores are associated with the individual's future risk of heart disease. Self-administered. Suitable for group use.

Untimed: Not available

Scoring: Scoring service available

Cost: 25 questionnaires $24.00; 10 questionnaires with prepared scoring certificates $135.00; manual $10.00

Publisher: The Psychological Corporation

THE JESNESS INVENTORY
Carl F. Jesness

Child, adolescent
Ages 8-18

Purpose: Evaluates personality disorders predictive of asocial tendencies. Used to classify disturbed children and adolescents for treatment.

Description: 155-item paper-pencil true-false test of 11 personality characteristics: social maladjustment, value orientation, immaturity, autism, alienation, manifest aggression, withdrawal, social anxiety, repression, denial, and asocial. The test distinguishes delinquents from nondelinquents. Administration requires either test booklets or a tape recorder and tape. Examiner/self-administered.

Untimed: 20-30 minutes

Scoring: Hand key; computer scoring service available

Cost: Specimen set (no key) $6.25; manual $6.00; key $10.00; cassette tapes $10.00

Publisher: Consulting Psychologists Press, Inc.

JUNG PERSONALITY QUESTIONNAIRE (JPQ)—1982
Refer to page 750.

LAW ENCOUNTER SEVERITY SCALE (LESS)
A.D. Witherspoon, E.K. de Valera,
and W.O. Jenkins

Ages 10-adult

Purpose: Assesses the severity of an individual's law encounter. Used for counseling purposes and follow-up studies with parolees and probationers.

Description: 38-item oral response test measuring the frequency, variety, severity, and consequences of any criminal offense. Items are classified in five groups, ranging from no encounter to felony offenses for which the offender is sentenced to prison for more than one year. Data are obtained through face-to-face interviews in which the examiner uses behavioral interviewing techniques. Can be used as a criterion for criminal acts. Examiner required. Not suitable for group use.

Untimed: 30 minutes

Scoring: Hand key

Cost: Complete kit (includes 25 test forms and manual) $25.00

Publisher: Behavior Science Press

LOUISVILLE BEHAVIOR CHECKLIST
Lovick C. Miller

Child, adolescent Ages 4-17

Purpose: Measures the entire range of social and emotional behaviors indicative of psychopathological disorders in children and adolescents. Used as an intake screening device.

Description: 164-item paper-pencil true-false inventory in which parents record their child's behavior by asking questions that provide relevant information on a number of interpretive scales. The inventory is available in three forms for three different age groups: Form E1 (ages 4-6), Form E2 (ages 7-12), and Form E3 (ages 13-17). The scales measured in Form E1 are Infantile Aggression, Hyperactivity, Antisocial Behavior, Aggression, Social Withdrawal, Sensitivity, Fear, Inhibition, Intellectual Deficit, Immaturity, Cognitive Disability, Normal Irritability, Prosocial Deficit, Rare Deviance, Neurotic Behavior, Psychotic Behavior, Somatic Behavior, Sexual Behavior, School Disturbance Predictor, and Severity Level. The scales measured in Form E2 are Infantile Aggression, Hyperactivity, Antisocial Behavior, Aggression, Social Withdrawal, Sensitivity, Fear, Inhibition, Academic Disability, Immaturity, Learning Disability, Normal Irritability, Prosocial Deficit, Rare Deviance, Neurotic Behavior, Psychotic Behavior, Somatic Behavior, Sexual Behavior, and Severity Level. The scales measured in Form E3 are Egocentric-Exploitive, Destructive-Assaultive, Social Delinquency, Adolescent Turmoil, Apathetic Isolation, Neuroticism, Dependent-Inhibited, Academic Disability, Neurological or Psychotic Abnormality, General Pathology, Longitudinal, Severity Level, and Total Pathology. General and clinical norms are provided for forms E1 and E2; Form E3 has only clinical norms. Norms are provided by sex and age for

Form E1 and by sex only for forms E2 and E3. The manual provides a number of case studies. Examiner required.

Untimed: 20-30 minutes

Scoring: Hand key; may be computer scored

Cost: Complete kit for all ages $170.00; kit, specify Form E1, E2, or E3 (reusable questionnaires, answer-profile sheets, key, manual) $57.50

Publisher: Western Psychological Services

MALADAPTED BEHAVIOR RECORD (MBR)
W.O. Jenkins, A.D. Witherspoon, E.K. de Valera, and John M. McKee

Ages 10-adult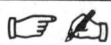

Purpose: Assesses behavioral maladaption and predicts the likelihood of habitual relapse of maladaptive individuals and groups. Used for counseling purposes with offender groups and drug and alcohol abuse cases and for predicting parole success.

Description: 16-item oral-response test measuring the following response categories: working conditions, amount of income, employer interactions, work attendance, alcohol use, gambling, money management, fighting, psychological adjustment, and others. Data are obtained through face-to-face interviews in which the examiner uses behavioral interviewing techniques. Each item is scored as "maladaption" or "no maladaption." A juvenile version is available. Examiner required. Not suitable for group use.

Untimed: 40 minutes

Scoring: Hand key

Cost: Complete kit (includes 25 test forms and manual) $35.00

Publisher: Behavior Science Press

MASLACH BURNOUT INVENTORY (MBI)
Christina Maslach and Susan E. Jackson

Adult

Purpose: Evaluates emotional exhaustion and cynicism among members of social service professions as an aid to research on cause, effect, and duration of "burnout" syndrome.

Description: 22-item paper-pencil test of three burnout aspects: exhaustion, personal accomplishment, and depersonalization. Each item is answered on the basis of how often the feeling described is experienced. A Demographic Data Sheet may be used to obtain general information. Examiner/self-administered. Suitable for group use.

Untimed: 20-30 minutes

Scoring: Examiner evaluated

Cost: Specimen set (manual, key, test, Demographic Data Sheet) $7.25; manual $16.00; 25 tests $5.00

Publisher: Consulting Psychologists Press, Inc.

MISSING CARTOONS (SIMC)
Richard de Mille,
Maureen O'Sullivan,
and J.P. Guilford

Adolescent, adult
Grades 10 and above

Purpose: Measures individual ability to understand social situations and make future predictions. Used for counseling and research.

Description: Paper-pencil multiple-choice test measuring three factors of social cognition listed in order of importance: cognition of behavioral systems (situations), cognition of behavioral units (momentary dispositions), and cognition of behavioral implications (predictions). Each test item shows a four-part cartoon strip with no verbal content with one picture missing. The subject selects the most appropriate alternative cartoon to complete the meaning of the strip. Norms are provided for tenth-grade and college students. The test is restricted to A.P.A. members. Examiner required. Suitable for group use.

Timed: 16 minutes

Scoring: Hand key

Cost: 25 tests $20.00; manual $3.50; 25 answer sheets $3.50; scoring key $2.00

Publisher: Sheridan Psychological Services, Inc.

MODES OF EXISTENCE TEST
S. Roy Heath

Adolescent, adult
Ages 12 and older

Purpose: Assesses personality in terms of temperament and emotional and intellectual maturity. Used for student and employee counseling when temperament and maturity are important factors.

Description: 11-item paper-pencil test measuring a person's self-concept of his personality. The test items consist of personality descriptions from which the subject is asked to select the three which most closely approximate the way he sees himself. The subject then ranks each of the three selected descriptions on a ladder chart according to how closely each represents his sense of self. The subject then selects and records which of the 11 personality descriptions are least like his sense of self. The examiner scores the responses according to three dimensions of temperament related to Heath's model of ego-functioning (group cooperative, group competitive, or group independent) and three levels of intellectual and emotional maturity (high, medium, and low). The test should not be administered to children under age 12. A sixth-grade reading level is required. Self-administered. Suitable for group use.

Untimed: 20 minutes

Scoring: Examiner evaluated

Cost: $2.00 per copy

Publisher: S. Roy Heath, Ph.D.

MUTUALLY RESPONSIBLE FACILITATION INVENTORY (MRFI)
Thomas D. Gnagey

Adolescent, adult
Ages 12-adult

Purpose: Helps an individual examine his role in helping maladjusted persons and provides assistance in planning personal goals and activities in such areas as teacher-pupil problems, family friction, and business relationships.

Description: Multiple-item paper-pencil test that systematically directs an individual's attention through an analysis of the areas most frequently disrupted in the maladjusting person. This process helps the individual focus his past interactions with the maladjusting person, plan for future growth, and instill positive self-direction in the maladjusting person. The individual uses the outline provided to analyze how he helps others grow in each of five categories (being needed, ability to "play by the rules," seeking positive relationships, involvement with others, and giving and accepting love) and to plan an approach to further personal growth. Self-administered. Suitable for group use.

Untimed: 30 minutes

Scoring: Examiner evaluated

Cost: Instructions, 20 inventories $8.00

Publisher: Slosson Educational Publications, Inc.

NON-VERBAL SCALE OF SUFFERING (N-V SOS)
Theodore C. Kent

Ages 5-80

Purpose: Assesses the level of subjective feelings of emotional distress in children and adults. Used as a pictorial screening instrument in a variety of settings to identify level of distress and provide clues of its origin.

Description: 24-item paper-pencil multiple-choice test of experienced suffering. Each item presents five nonverbal figures reflecting different degrees of distress, and subjects are asked to circle the drawing which best reflects their current feelings. Instructions may be given in any language; English and Spanish instructions are provided on the test blank. Examiner/self-administered. Suitable for group use.

Untimed: 10 minutes

Scoring: Hand key

Cost: 50 tests, manual $15.00; postage and handling $1.00

Publisher: Human Sciences Center

PAIN AND DISTRESS SCALE
William W.K. Zung

Adult

Purpose: Measures degree of pain and evaluates the characteristics of associated dysfunctions. Used in research and clinical settings to establish pain treatment programs and to monitor the effectiveness of such programs.

Description: 20-item paper-pencil self-report rating scale assessing the presence of somato-sensory pain and associated changes in mood and behavior. Scale items describe the 20 characteristics most commonly described by individuals when pain and associated distress are present. Individuals use a 4-point scale ranging from "none or little of the time" to "most of the time" to rate each item on the degree to which each statement describes their own feelings or behaviors. Items include both symptomatically positive and symptomatically negative statements. Standardized analysis provides an index of the pain and distress present. The manual includes directions for administering, scoring, and interpreting the scale; information concerning development, reliability, and validity; normative data; suggested applications; and a list of references for further research. Examiner required. Suitable for group use.

Untimed: Varies

Scoring: Examiner evaluated

Cost: Contact publisher

Publisher: William W.K. Zung, M.D.

PAIN APPERCEPTION TEST
Donald V. Petrovich

Adult

Purpose: Examines the emotional aspects of pain. Used in settings in which pain might be experienced or anticipated.

Description: 25-item oral-response projective test assessing pain's emotional aspects within a psychological context by measuring an individual's perception of intensity and duration of pain and by focusing on total reactions and not just thresholds. Items consist of picture cards dealing with three major groups of pain situations: felt pain sensations, anticipation versus felt-sensation of pain, and self-inflicted versus other-inflicted pain. Responses are recorded on the protocol sheet. Adult normative data are provided. Examiner required. Suitable for group use.

Untimed: 15-20 minutes

Scoring: Examiner evaluated

Cost: Complete kit (100 protocol sheets, set of plates, manual) $44.50

Publisher: Western Psychological Services

PERSONALITY DESCRIPTIONS
Union College Character Research Project

Child, adolescent Grades PreK-12

Purpose: Determines an individual's general personality characteristics, as well as those pertaining to religious orientation. Used for observing spiritual and character growth.

Description: Multiple-item paper-pencil projective self-description test of nine personality factors: outstanding characteristics, activities and interests, growing up, coaching and school, social relationships, emotional security and self-confidence, imagination and curiosity, community and vocational interests, philosophy of life (for junior and senior high), and home and family. The test is designed for eight age levels and separate male and female forms are available. Distinctive personality traits are obtained by modification process from age-level norms. Materials include age-level forms and instructions. Examiner required. Suitable for group use.

Untimed: 20-30 minutes

Scoring: Examiner evaluated

Cost: Each form $0.25 (specify age and sex); sample set of 16 $3.00

Publisher: Union College, Character Research Project

Information and availability unconfirmed; no publisher response.

PERSONALITY RESEARCH FORM (PRF)
Douglas N. Jackson

Adolescent, adult Grades 6 and above

Purpose: Assesses personality traits relevant to the functioning of an individual in a variety of situations. Used in self-improvement courses and guidance centers and for personnel selection.

Description: Multiple-item paper-pencil true-false test in five forms. Forms AA and BB contain 440 items covering 22 areas of normal functioning. Form E has 352 items in 22 scales. Forms A and B have 300 items in 15 scales. The 22 scales measured are Abasement, Achievement, Affiliation, Aggression, Autonomy, Change, Cognitive Structure, Defendance, Dominance, Endurance, Exhibition, Harm-Avoidance, Impulsivity, Nurturance, Order, Play, Sentience, Social Recognition, Succorance, Understanding, Infrequency, and Desirability. A 90-minute cassette tape with simplified wording is available for use with those who have limited verbal skills or sight or reading problems. Materials include a manual, reusable test booklet, answer sheets, profiles, scoring template, cassette tape, and tape manual. The test must be administered by a certified psychologist. Suitable for group use. Form E available in French.

Timed: Form E 1 hour; Forms A and B 45 minutes; Forms AA and BB 1 hour, 15 minutes; cassette tape 90 minutes

Scoring: Hand key; computer scoring available for some forms

Cost: Specimen set $25.00

Publisher: Research Psychologists Press, Inc.

PIKUNAS GRAPHOSCOPIC SCALE (PGS)
Justin Pikunas

All ages

Purpose: Assesses an individual's cognitive development, emotionality, and adjustment. Used by clinical and school psychologists to build rapport, test defi-

---

cits, and evaluate various forms of psychopathology.

Description: Nonverbal test using a single sheet containing 10 framed, partial drawings containing perceptual cues in various colors. The subject is asked to add to the drawings. The results provide an indication of self-expressive balance, intelligence, creativity, emotional disturbance, and some forms of psychopathology. Materials include the test, graphic scale, and manual. Two forms are available: PGSI (Grades K-8) and PGSII (Grades 9-adult). Examiner required. Suitable for group use.

Untimed: PGSI 20 minutes; PGSII 30 minutes

Scoring: Examiner evaluated

Cost: Specimen set (specify form) $6.75

Publisher: University Press of America

POLITTE SENTENCE COMPLETION TEST (PSCT)
Refer to page 703.

THE Q-TAGS TEST OF PERSONALITY
Arthur G. Storey and Louis I. Masson

Ages 6 and older

Purpose: Measures individual personality traits. Used for counseling, self-examination, and research.

Description: 54-card test measuring five factors of personality: assertive, effective, hostile, reverie, and social. By sorting cards, subjects are able to describe themselves both as they are and as they wish to be. The test was developed with norms for age, grade, occupation, and sex based on a wide range of subjects. Self-administered. Suitable for group use.
CANADIAN PUBLISHER

Untimed: 30 minutes

Scoring: Examiner evaluated

Cost: Specimen set (4 series of 54 tags, 4 paper boards, manual, list of directions, 25 answer sheets) $4.00; 25 answer sheets $10.00

Publisher: Institute of Psychological Research, Inc.
Information and availability unconfirmed; no publisher response.

THE REVISED BEHAVIOR PROBLEM CHECKLIST (RBPC)
Refer to page 677.

REVISED CHILDREN'S MANIFEST ANXIETY SCALE
Cecil R. Reynolds and Bert O. Richmond

Ages 6-19

Purpose: Measures level of anxiety in children and adolescents.

Description: 37-item paper-pencil true-false test of a range of anxiety-related dimensions. Scores are obtained for total anxiety, physiological anxiety, worry/oversensitivity, social concerns/concentration, and a lie scale. Separate norms are available in 1-year intervals for males and females ages 6-17; combined norms are available for ages 18-19. Examiner/self-administered. Suitable for group use.

Untimed: 10-15 minutes

Scoring: Hand key

Cost: Complete kit (manual, 100 test sheets, scoring key) $33.00

Publisher: Western Psychological Services

ROKEACH VALUE SURVEY
Milton Rokeach

Ages 11-adult

Purpose: Measures personal values and provides objective feedback about them in comparison with reference group. Used for value therapy, values clarification, and changing socially undesirable values.

Description: 36-item ranking test requiring minimum literacy. The respondent arranges values, which are printed on gummed labels, in rank order. The test assesses values divided into terminal ("comfortable life" and "world peace") and behavioral ("loving" and "ambition"). Self-administered. Suitable for group use. Available in Spanish, French, German, Czech, Japanese, Vietnamese, Russian, Hungarian, Swedish, Chinese, Lithuanian, and Hebrew.

Untimed: 15 minutes

Scoring: Examiner evaluated; may be computer scored

Cost: Test $0.50-$1.00 (depending on quantity)

Publisher: Halgren Tests

Information and availability unconfirmed; no publisher response.

ROKEACH VALUE SURVEY: FORM G
Milton Rokeach

All ages

Purpose: Measures human values concerning possible end-states of existence and modes of behavior. Used for value therapy, values clarification, and to identify socially undesirable value structures.

Description: 36-item label-ranking test consisting of two sets of 18 values (one set of terminal values and one set of behavioral values), printed on gummed labels, which the individual must arrange in order of personal importance. Terminal values include comfortable life, exciting life, sense of accomplishment, world at peace, world of beauty, equality, family security, freedom, health, inner harmony, mature love, national security, pleasure, salvation, self-respect, social recognition, true friendship, and wisdom. Behavior values include ambitious, broadminded, capable, clean, courageous, forgiving, helpful, honest, imaginative, independent, intellectual, logical, loving, loyal, obedient, polite, responsible, and self-controlled. Form G is a revision of Form D; the values "health" and "loyal" replace "happiness" and "cheerful." An extensive list of reference materials is provided. Normative data are available for many populations within American society. Self-administered. Suitable for group use.

Untimed: Adults 15-20 minutes; children 20-25 minutes

Scoring: Self-scored

Cost: Test kit (2 sets of 18 gummed labels with printed array for final rankings) $0.75-$1.00 each depending on quantity

Publisher: Halgren Tests

Information and availability unconfirmed; no publisher response.

RORSCHACH PSYCHODIAGNOSTIC TEST
Hermann Rorschach

Ages 3 and older

Purpose: Evaluates personality through projective technique. Used in clinical evaluation.

Description: 10-card oral-response projective personality test in which the subject is asked to interpret what he sees in 10 inkblots, based on the assumption that the individual's perceptions and associations are selected and organized in terms of his motivations, impulses, and other underlying aspects of personality. Extensive scoring systems have been developed. Although many variations are in use, this entry refers only to the Psychodiagnostic Plates first published in 1921. Materials include inquiry charts, tabulation sheets, and a set of 10 inkblots. A set of 10 Kodaslides of the inkblots may be imported on request. Trained examiner required. Not suitable for group use.

Untimed: Not available

Scoring: Examiner evaluated

Cost: Contact publisher

Publisher: Hans Huber; distributed in U.S.A. by Grune & Stratton, Inc.

ROSENZWEIG PICTURE-FRUSTRATION STUDY (P-F)
Saul Rosenzweig

Ages 4-adult

Purpose: Measures aggression in personality. Used in clinical counseling.

Description: Paper-pencil semi-projective technique assessing an individual's patterns of response to everyday frustration or stress. It consists of 24 cartoon pictures, each depicting two persons in a frustrating situation. One person is acting as the frustrator. The subject provides a reply for the anonymous frustrated person in the second picture. The instrument measures three types of aggression (obstacle-dominance, ego-defense, and need-persistence) and three directions of aggression (extraggression, imaggression, and intraggression). Nine factors, derived by combining the types and directions of aggression, constitute the score. The scoring guide is provided in the manual. Examiner required. Suitable for group use.

Timed: 15-20 minutes

Scoring: Hand key

Cost: Contact publisher

Publisher: Psychological Assessment Resources, Inc.

SCHEDULE OF RECENT EXPERIENCE (SRE)
Thomas H. Holmes

All ages

Purpose: Measures how often various stress-producing events have occurred in an individual's life during the recent past. Used for counseling and discussion purposes and as an aid to general health maintenance programs.

Description: 42-item paper-pencil inventory assessing the amount of psychological change (adaptive behavior) an individual has undergone in the recent past. Each test item is an event that causes change in a person's life that has been observed in a large number of patients preceding the onset of their medical illness or clinical symptoms. Test items include stress-related socially undesirable events and socially desirable events (birth of a baby or a promotion at work). The individual indicates for each item how often the event has occurred during a specific time period (ranging from less than 1 year up to 10 years). The inventory also may be used as a framework for a structured interview. The manual includes instructions for administering the test to individuals of all ages, sample test forms (both one-year and three-year versions), templates for scoring both versions, a report of the studies on which the test is based, and a list of suggested preventive measures for maintenance of health and prevention of illness based on test results. Examiner required. Suitable for group use.

Untimed: Varies

Scoring: Hand key

Cost: Manual $12.00; 50 one-year test scales with scoring template $10.00; 50 three-year test scales with scoring template $15.00

Publisher: University of Washington Press

SELF-ESTEEM QUESTIONNAIRE (SEQ-3)
James K. Hoffmeister

Grades 4-adult

Purpose: Evaluates how individuals feel about various aspects of themselves, including their capabilities, worth, and acceptance by others.

Description: 21-item paper-pencil self-report rating scale consisting of two subscales: Self-Esteem (12 items) and Self-Other Satisfaction (9 items). Items on the Self-Esteem subscale consist of statements, such as "Most of my friends accept me as much as they accept other people," that the individual rates on a 5-point scale from one ("not at all") to five ("yes, very much"). Items on the Self-Other Satisfaction subscale immediately follow items on the Self-Esteem subscale and take the form "Does the situation described in [the previous question] upset you?" These items are rated on a 5-point scale also. Scores are provided for both subscales according to the computerized convergence analysis process (a score is computed only if the individual has responded in a reasonably consistent fashion to the items used to measure that factor). The manual includes a description of the test's variables and content, directions for administering and scoring the questionnaire, information concerning development, validity, and reliability, and normative data. Examiner required. Suitable for group use.

Untimed: Varies

Scoring: Computer scored

Cost: 50 questionnaires (includes computer scoring service) $50.00
Publisher: Test Analysis and Development Corporation

SELF-OBSERVATION SCALES
*William G. Katzenmeyer and
A. Jackson Stenner*

Child, adolescent
Grades K-12

Purpose: Assesses the social maturity, self-acceptance, self-security, and affiliations of children and handicapped subjects. Used by schools and hospitals and in research.

Description: Multiple-item paper-pencil test measuring the areas of social maturity, social confidence, self-acceptance, self-security, school affiliation, teacher affiliation, and peer affiliation. Four forms are available: Primary (Grades K-3; 50 items), Intermediate (Grades 4-6; 60 items), Junior High (Grades 7-9; 72 items), and Senior High (Grades 10-12; 72 items). Subjects respond "yes" or "no" to each item. The Primary Form uses smiling/frowning faces to portray yes/no alternatives. Examiner required for Primary Form; other forms are self-administered. Suitable for group use.
Untimed: 25-30 minutes
Scoring: Machine scored
Cost: Complete kit (30 test booklets, scoring, manual) $42.00
Publisher: NTS Research Corporation

STANFORD HYPNOTIC SUSCEPTIBILITY SCALE
*Andre M. Weitzenhoffer and
Ernest R. Hilgard*

Adolescent, adult

Purpose: Measures hypnotic susceptibility. Used for teaching, research, and experimentation in hypnosis.

Description: Multiple-item test of subject's responsiveness to hypnotic suggestions. Includes verbatim instructions for inducing and testing hypnotic states. The subject's scores are based on a 12-point scale. The test is available in three forms: A, B, and C. Forms A and B

are equivalent; Form C contains more difficult items and a wider variety of hypnotic experiences. Restricted to APA guidelines. Examiner required. Not suitable for group use.
Untimed: 40 minutes
Scoring: Examiner evaluated
Cost: Manual and scales for Forms A, B, and C $12.00; complete kit, Forms A and B (manuals, scales, scoring sheets, interrogatory blanks for 50 subjects) $16.50; complete kit, Form C $12.00
Publisher: Consulting Psychologists Press, Inc.

STANFORD PROFILE SCALES OF HYPNOTIC SUSCEPTIBILITY
*Andre M. Weitzenhoffer and
Ernest R. Hilgard*

Adolescent, adult

Purpose: Assesses differential susceptibility to a variety of hypnotic state suggestions. Used for teaching, research, and experimentation in hypnosis.

Description: Multiple-item test of hypnotic susceptibility yielding 25 scores in six areas: agnosia and cognitive distortion, positive hallucinations, negative hallucinations, dreams and regressions, amnesia and post-hypnotic compulsions, and total susceptibility. The test is available in two roughly equivalent forms: I and II. Both must be administered to yield the profile. Profile scales may be used with subjects chosen by the Stanford Hypnotic Susceptibility Scale. Examiner required. Not suitable for group use.
Scoring: Examiner evaluated
Cost: 25 scoring booklets of each form $16.00; 100 profile sheets $9.75; manual (includes scoring booklet and profile sheet) $7.50
Publisher: Consulting Psychologists Press, Inc.

THE STERN ACTIVITIES INDEX (AI)
George Stern and Associates

All ages

Purpose: Measures personality in terms of the need-press paradigm of human behavior as conceptualized by Henry Murray. Used for counseling and research purposes.

Description: 300-item (long form) or 91-item (either of two short forms) paper-pencil inventory assessing personality along 30 basic need scales. The test items are descriptions of routine activities and feelings to which the individual indicates a personal "like" or "dislike." The long form provides scores on each of the 30 need scales (10 items per scale), 12 first-order scores (self-assertion, audacity-timidity, intellectual interests, motivation, applied interests, orderliness, submissiveness, closeness, sensuousness, friendliness, expressive-constraint, and egoism-diffidence), and four second-order scores (achievement orientation, dependency needs, emotional expression, and educability). The two short forms provide scores for the 12 first-order dimensions and four second-order dimensions. Short forms are used when administration time is a problem or when scores on the 30 basic need scales are not required. Short form SAI-1158SF is primarily for adults, but it can be used with individuals as young as age 12 who have a minimum seventh-grade reading level. Short form SAI-1173SF is used with younger children who have a minimum fourth-grade reading level. The long form requires a seventh-grade reading level. Self-administered. Suitable for group use.

Untimed: Long form 40 minutes; short forms 20 minutes

Scoring: Examiner evaluated; may be computer scored

Cost: Test booklet $0.50; answer sheet $0.10; profile form $0.10; technical manual $7.50; prices for computer and analysis scoring available on request

Publisher: Evaluation Research Associates

STROOP COLOR AND WORD TEST
Charles Golden

Grades 2 and above

Purpose: Evaluates personality, cognition, stress response, psychiatric disorders, and other psychological phenomena. Used to differentiate normal, non-brain-damaged psychiatric from brain-damaged subjects.

Description: Multiple-item response test of an individual's ability to separate word and color stimuli and react to them independently. The test consists of three pages: a Word Page containing color words printed in black ink; a Color Page with a series of X's printed in colored inks; and a Word-Color page on which the words on the first page are printed in the colors of the second page except that the word and color do not match. The subject is given all three pages and asked to read the Word Page. He then names the colors of the X's on the Color Page. Next he must name the color of the ink in which the words on the Word-Color Page are printed, ignoring the semantic meaning of the words. The test requires a second-grade reading level. Examiner required. Not suitable for group use.

Timed: 5 minutes

Scoring: Examiner evaluated

Cost: Complete kit (manual, 25 sets of 3 sheets) $45.00

Publisher: Stoelting Company

STRUCTURED-OBJECTIVE RORSCHACH TEST (SORT)

Ages 11-54

Purpose: Evaluates personality tendencies of white South Africans. Used in guidance, selection, and placement.

Description: Multiple-item paper-pencil test of mental functioning (8 components), interests (2 components), responsiveness (2 components), and temperament (13 components). The test was adapted from J.B. Stone's SORT and standardized for white South Africans of both sexes and both official languages (Afrikaans and English). There is a training course for interpreting the test. Examiner required. Suitable for group use.
SOUTH AFRICAN PUBLISHER

Untimed: 30 minutes

Scoring: Hand key

Cost: Test booklet $1.30; manual $5.30; 15 scoring stencils $22.10; 10 answer sheets $0.60; slides of the Rorschach inkblots $63.90; literature survey $7.10

Publisher: Human Sciences Research Council

SYMBOL ELABORATION TEST (S.E.T.)
Johanna Krout Tabin

All ages

Purpose: Assesses personality. Used for individual evaluation and cross-cultural research.

Description: 11-item projective measure of personality. Items are simple line figures. The subjects use each line figure as a beginning stimulus for their own drawings and answer seven brief questions aimed at eliciting feelings and associations. The factors measured include concepts of maleness and femaleness; views of interactions between same-sex, opposite sex, and mixed-groups; handling of aggression; diffuse and sexual anxiety; and self-concept. Examiner required. Suitable for group use.

Untimed: 30 minutes

Scoring: Examiner evaluated

Cost: Test booklet $0.75; guide $3.50

Publisher: Johanna Krout Tabin, Ph.D.

THE TEST OF SOCIAL INSIGHT: YOUTH EDITION AND ADULT EDITION
Martin M. Bruce

Ages 10-adult

Purpose: Measures the subject's understanding of and adaptation to acceptable patterns of culture in the United States.

Description: 60-item paper-pencil multiple-choice test measuring five ways of responding to interpersonal problems: withdrawal, passivity, cooperation, competition, and aggression. The potential conflict areas covered include home and family, authority figures, avocational contacts, and work interests. The Youth Edition is appropriate for individuals ages 10-18; the Adult Edition may be administered to individuals ages 18 and older. A fifth-grade reading level is required. Examiner required. Suitable for group use.

Untimed: 30-40 minutes

Scoring: Hand key

Cost: Manual $6.75; package of tests $29.50; package of profile sheets $10.50; IBM scoring stencils $8.75; IBM answer sheets $10.50

Publisher: Martin M. Bruce, Ph.D., Publishers

THEMATIC APPERCEPTION TEST (TAT-Z)—1976

Ages 10 and older

Purpose: Measures personality characteristics. Used for assessment and diagnosis of abnormal personality.

Description: 10-card projective measure of personality using the method of choosing cards which reveal, ter alia, the level of Westernization and adjustment to Western demands. The subject chooses pictures that relate to the following 10 areas: degree and direction of acculturation, family relationships, father-son relationship, mother-son relationship, attitude toward black authority, attitude toward white authority, self-concept, heterosexual relationships, social relationships, and handling of aggression. Examiner required. Not suitable for group use.

SOUTH AFRICAN PUBLISHER

Untimed: 2 hours

Scoring: Hand key; examiner evaluated

Cost: (In Rands) test album 18,80; answer book 0,30; manual 8,90; interpretation form 0,20; 10 shortened answer books 3,00; orders from outside The RSA will be dealt with on merit

Publisher: Human Sciences Research Council

THEMES CONCERNING BLACKS (TCB)
Robert L. Williams

Grades PreK-adult

Purpose: Assesses culturally specific attitudes of black people. Used as a personality or diagnostic test.

Description: 20-item oral-response projective test assessing black Americans' feelings and attitudes toward their ethnic experience in American society. Each test item consists of a picture card depicting some facet of the black experience. The subject is asked to elaborate on each card. When used as a diagnostic instrument, the test must be administered by a trained psychologist. May be administered to groups with slides and projector.

Untimed: 30 minutes

Scoring: Examiner evaluated

Cost: Complete (20 cards, manual) $30.00

Publisher: Robert L. Williams & Associates, Inc.

TWITCHELL-ALLEN THREE DIMENSIONAL PERSONALITY TEST (T-A 3-DPT)
Doris Twitchell-Allen

Ages 3-adult

Purpose: Evaluates the general personality structure of children and adults. Used for clinical diagnosis and research on personality.

Description: Four task-assessment and oral-response tests provide a projective evaluation of an individual's personality. Test materials consist of 28 small objects, all of an abstract nature (some are suggestive of human forms). The four subtests are Pre-Naming Story, in which the subject is asked to choose one or more of the objects and make up a story; Naming Test, in which the subject is asked to name all of the objects; Post-Naming Story, which allows the subject to tell a second story; and the Fein Testing of Limits, in which the examiner arranges a few of the objects in a vaguely suggestive pattern (according to test directions) and asks the subject to tell a story explaining the arrangement. The following types of responses are recorded by the examiner: gestures, general behavior, construction with the test forms, vocalizations (everything the subject says, not just the stories and names), sequence, and time. The test

may be administered to the blind with only minor procedural adaptations. Examiner required. Not suitable for group use.

Untimed: 1 hour

Scoring: Examiner evaluated

Cost: Complete set (instructions, recording forms) $115.00

Publisher: Doris Twitchell-Allen, Ph.D.

TWITCHELL-ALLEN THREE-DIMENSIONAL PERSONALITY TEST, 1985 REVISION
Doris Twitchell-Allen

Ages 3-adult

Purpose: Diagnoses critical areas of personality in children and adults. Helps teachers and human service personnel provide guidance in terms of an individual's current functional status and more permanent characteristics of personality.

Description: Four action and oral-response tests providing a projective evaluation of an individual's personality. Test materials consist of 28 small objects, all of an ambiguous or abstract nature (some are suggestive of human forms). The four subtests are Naming Test, in which the subject is asked to name 14 designated objects; Story Production, in which the subject chooses as many forms as he likes and makes up one story about them; Fein Testing Limits 1 (for intrafamilial relations), in which the examiner arranges three designated objects in a designated pattern (according to test directions) and asks the subject to tell a story about the examiner's chosen pieces; and Fein Testing Limits 2, in which the examiner begins a story using the three pieces from the previous test and asks the subject to complete it. The following types of responses are recorded by the examiner: gestures, general behavior, constructions with test forms, vocalizations (everything the subject says, not just the stories and names), sequence, and time. May be administered to the blind with only minor procedural adaptations. Examiner required. Not suitable for group use.

Untimed: 1 hour

Scoring: Examiner evaluated; may be computer scored

Cost: Complete set (carrying case, instructions, 5 sets of recording forms) $115.00

Publisher: Doris Twitchell-Allen, Ph.D.

VINELAND ADAPTIVE BEHAVIOR SCALES
Sara S. Sparrow, David A. Balla, and Dominic V. Cicchetti

Child, adolescent

Purpose: Measures the personal and social sufficiency of individuals from birth to adulthood. Used with mentally retarded and handicapped individuals.

Description: Multiple-item inventory in three forms assessing adaptive behavior in the following four domains: communication (receptive, expressive, and written), daily living skills (personal, domestic, and community), socialization (interpersonal relationships, play and leisure time, and coping skills), and motor skills (gross and fine). These four domains are combined to form the Adaptive Behavior Composite. An optional Maladaptive Behavior domain is included in the Interview Edition, Survey Form and Interview Edition, Expanded Form.

In the Interview Edition, Survey Form (297 items), a trained interviewer administers the inventory to a parent or caregiver in a semi-structured interview. The record booklet is used to record item scores and informal observations and contains a score summary page for recording and profiling derived scores. The Survey Form may be administered to individuals from birth to 18 years 11 months of age and to low-functioning adults.

The Interview Edition, Expanded Form (577 items) offers a more comprehensive assessment of adaptive behavior and provides a basis for preparing individual educational, habilitative, or treatment programs. The Expanded Form, like the Survey Form, assesses individuals from birth to 18 years 11 months of age, as well as low-functioning adults. Administration is similar to that of the Survey Form. Scores are recorded in the item booklet. The score summary and profile booklet includes a page for summarizing derived

scores and four program planning profiles, each of which identifies clusters of items describing activities that should be included in the individual programs. The Classroom Edition (244 items) assesses adaptive behavior of students ages 3-12 years 11 months. It is administered as a questionnaire which is completed independently by teachers. A qualified professional is required to determine and interpret derived scores. Each form has a manual with guidelines for administration, scoring, and interpreting results. Supplementary materials include an audiocassette presenting sample Survey and Expanded Form interviews; ASSIST microcomputer software programs for score conversion, profiling, and record management; the Technical and Interpretive Manual; and reports to parents explaining an individual's derived scores in relation to strengths and weaknesses. This instrument is the 1984 revision of The Vineland Social Maturity Scale. Examiner required. Not suitable for group use. The Survey Form, record booklet, and reports to parents for all three versions are available in Spanish.

Untimed: Varies

Scoring: Examiner evaluated

Cost: Survey Form Starter Set (10 record booklets, manual, 1 report to parents) $24.75; Expanded Form Starter Set (10 item booklets, 10 score summary and profile reports, manual, 1 program planning report, 1 report to parents) $40.25; Classroom Edition Starter Set (10 questionnaire booklets, manual, 1 report to parents) $18.50

Publisher: American Guidance Service

VISUAL-VERBAL TEST, 1981 EDITION
Marvin J. Feldman and James Drasgow

Schizophrenic patients

Purpose: Measures conceptual thinking and abstraction in schizophrenics. Used for diagnosis and assessment related to therapy.

Description: 42-item oral-response test measuring conceptual deviancy in schizophrenic patients. Each test item consists of a stimulus card depicting four items. Using three of the four items, the examinee formulates two different concepts for each card. The test items are based upon simple concepts such as color, form, size, structural similarities, naming, and position. Normative data are provided for normals, schizophrenics, and special groups. Examiner required. Not suitable for group use.

Untimed: 30-40 minutes

Scoring: Hand key

Cost: Complete kit (set of test cards, 25 protocol booklets, manual) $33.00

Publisher: Western Psychological Services

WELSH FIGURE PREFERENCE TEST (WFPT)
George S. Welsh

Ages 6-adult

Purpose: Evaluates individual personality traits through figure identification. Used for counseling and research.

Description: 400-item paper-pencil nonverbal test measuring an individual's personality traits by evaluating his preference for types of black-and-white figures. The subject responds by indicating "likes" or "dislikes" for each figure. Scales include Conformity, Male-Female, Neuropsychiatric, Consensus, Origence, Intellectence, Barron-Welsh Original Art Scale, Revised Art Scale, Repression, Anxiety, Children, Movement, Figure-Ground Reversal, Sex Symbol, and several measuring preferences for specific kinds of geometric figures. All scales need not be scored. The Barron-Welsh Art Scale (86 items) is available separately. Examiner required. Suitable for group use.

Untimed: 50 minutes

Scoring: Hand key

Cost: Experimental kit (includes 5 test booklets, 25 answer sheets, manual) $28.50; 10 reusable test booklets $22.75; 50 handscorable answer sheets $5.50

Publisher: Consulting Psychologists Press, Inc.

WIDE RANGE INTELLIGENCE-PERSONALITY TEST (WRIPT)
Joseph F. Jastak

Ages 9½-adult

Purpose: Measures general mental ability and personality structure. Used for clinical diagnosis and research relating personality to intelligence, academic achievement, and vocational aptitudes and performances.

Description: 10 paper-pencil subtests measuring verbal, numerical, pictorial, spatial, social competency, and other abilities. The test provides a "g" (global) or intelligence score and identifies the extent to which this general factor influences behavior. The test also provides cluster (lobal) scores for language, reality set, motivation, and psychomotor skills. In addition, the test offers several areas of special effectiveness: measuring mental abilities through a wide range of abilities; studying personality makeup; measuring changes in specific personality traits due to age, health, education, or other factors; demonstrating the role of group (lobal) factors in schooling, job selection, and social adjustment; studying variances contributing to the diagnosis of mental retardation, mental illness, learning disabilities, and antisocial and asocial behavior; showing how cultural neglect or environmental limits influence a person's overall functioning; and many research applications. Use is limited to educational and psychological professionals. Examiner required. Suitable for group use.

Timed: 50 minutes

Scoring: Hand key

Cost: Manual $20.50; 25 test forms $17.50; scoring stencil $12.50

Publisher: Jastak Assessment Systems

Research

ALTERNATE USES (AU)
Paul R. Christensen, J.P. Guilford,
Philip R. Merrifield,
and Robert C. Wilson

Adolescent, adult
Grades 7 and above

Purpose: Measures ability to produce spontaneously ideas in response to objects or other ideas. Used for research and experiment.

Description: Multiple-item paper-pencil test measuring spontaneous flexibility, defined as the ability to produce a variety of class ideas in connection with an object or other unit of thought. This ability is also known as the "divergent production of semantic classes." Forms B and C are equivalent. Norms are provided for sixth-grade, ninth-grade, and college students. The test is restricted to A.P.A. members. Examiner required. Suitable for group use.

Timed: 12 minutes
Scoring: Examiner evaluated
Cost: Manual $4.00; 25 tests (specify form) $8.00; scoring guide $1.00; scoring guide (specify B or C) $1.00
Publisher: Sheridan Psychological Services, Inc.

ASSOCIATIONAL FLUENCY (AF)
Paul R. Christensen and J.P. Guilford

Adolescent, adult
Grades 7 and above

Purpose: Measures the ability to produce spontaneously meaningful words. Used in research and experimental applications.

Description: Multiple-item paper-pencil test measuring the factor of "divergent production of semantic relations," which is defined as the ability to produce efficiently ideas bearing prescribed relations to other ideas or to produce alternate relations. Form A employs adjectives; Form B employs verbs (the forms are equivalent). In each case, the task is to list as many words as possible that bear a spec-

ified meaningful relation to the stimulus words. Instructions are included in the manual. Norms are provided for ninth-grade and college students. The test is restricted to A.P.A. members. Examiner required. Suitable for group use.

Timed: 4 minutes
Scoring: Examiner evaluated
Cost: 25 tests $7.00; scoring guide $0.75
Publisher: Sheridan Psychological Services, Inc.

BAY AREA FUNCTIONAL PERFORMANCE EVALUATION (RESEARCH EDITION) (BAFPE)
Judith S. Bloomer and
Susan K. Williams

Adult

Purpose: Assesses the abilities needed by psychiatric or neurological patients and mentally retarded adults to perform certain concrete intellectual functions satisfactorily in daily life. Used for counseling and in research on treatment and training programs in occupational therapy and special education.

Description: Two-category paper-pencil test in which the examiner observes the subject's general ability to act on the environment in goal-directed ways and to relate to other people. The examination consists of two major subtests: Task Oriented Assessment (TOA) and Social Interaction Scale (SIS).
The TOA consists of five tasks measuring general ability to be goal-directed. The five tasks (sorting seashells, filling out a bank deposit slip, drawing a house floor plan, copying a block design, and drawing a person in action) measure 10 functional components of behavior: paraphrase, productive decision-making, motivation, organization of time and materials, mastery and self-esteem, frustration tolerance, attention span, ability to abstract, verbal or behavioral evidence of thought or mood disorder, and ability to follow instructions leading to correct task completion. Examiner rates subject's performance on each task. Materials include a demographic data sheet.
The SIS is a behavioral rating scale assessing general ability to relate appropriately

to other people within the environment. Seven basic categories of social interaction are measured: response to authority figures, verbal communication, psychomotor behavior, independence/dependence, socially appropriate behavior, ability to work with peers, and participation in group or program activities. Each category is rated on a 5-point scale. The SIS is rated by a clinician who observes the client in a daily social situation. Examiner required. Not suitable for group use.

Timed: 40-60 minutes per client

Scoring: Examiner evaluated

Cost: Complete kit (includes reusable items, expendable forms for testing 25 subjects, manual) $96.50

Publisher: Consulting Psychologists Press, Inc.

BEM SEX-ROLE INVENTORY (BSRI)
Sandra L. Bem

Adult

Purpose: Measures masculinity and femininity. Used for research on psychological androgyny.

Description: 60-item paper-pencil measure of integration of masculinity and femininity. Items are three sets of 20 personality characteristics: masculine, feminine, and neutral. The subject indicates on a 7-point scale how well each characteristic describes him. Materials include a 30-item short form. Self-administered. Suitable for group use.

Untimed: 10 minutes

Scoring: Hand key

Cost: Manual $8.00; key $1.00; 25 expendable inventories $4.00

Publisher: Consulting Psychologists Press, Inc.

CALIFORNIA CHILD Q-SET
Refer to page 102.

CALIFORNIA Q-SORT DECK
Refer to page 123.

THE CLASSROOM ENVIRONMENT INDEX (CEI)
Refer to page 684.

COMMUNITY ORIENTED PROGRAMS ENVIRONMENT SCALE (COPES)
Rudolf H. Moos

Adult

Purpose: Assesses the social environments of community-based psychiatric treatment programs.

Description: 100-item paper-pencil true-false test of 10 aspects of social environment: involvement, support, spontaneity, autonomy, practical orientation, personal problem orientation, anger and aggression, order and organization, program clarity, and staff control. Materials include the Real Form (Form R), which measures perceptions of a current program; the 40-item Short Form (Form S); the Ideal Form (Form I), which measures conceptions of an ideal program; and the Expectations Form (Form E), which measures expectations of a new program. Forms I and E are not published, but items and instructions are printed in the Appendix of the COPES manual. Items are modified from the Ward Atmosphere Scale. One in a series of nine Social Climate Scales. Examiner required.

Untimed: 20 minutes

Scoring: Hand key

Cost: Manual $4.25; key $1.50; 25 reusable tests $4.00; 50 answer sheets $3.00; 50 profiles $3.00

Publisher: Consulting Psychologists Press, Inc.

COMPREHENSIVE PERSONAL ASSESSMENT SYSTEM: STUDENT EVALUATION OF TEACHERS I (SET I)
Donald J. Veldman and Robert F. Peck

Child, adolescent
Grades 3-12

Purpose: Used as a student evaluation of teacher behavior.

Description: Multiple-item paper-pencil test consisting of a set of 10 true-false questions. The test is for research purposes only and is not intended for use in administrative evaluation of teachers. Examiner/self-administered.

Untimed: 5-15 minutes

Scoring: Hand key; may be computer scored

Cost: 100 forms $10.00; manual $1.50

Publisher: Research and Development Center for Teacher Education

CONSEQUENCES (CQ)
Paul R. Christensen,
Philip R. Merrifield,
and J.P. Guilford

Adolescent, adult
Grades 7 and above

Purpose: Measures ability to produce spontaneously original ideas in response to associated ideas. Used for research and experiment.

Description: Multiple-item paper-pencil test measuring two factors: ideational fluency (divergent production of semantic units), and originality (divergent production of semantic transformations). Originality in this test is shown by giving remotely associated ideas that are likely to require revisions of other ideas. Ideational fluency is scored by count of obvious responses. Originality is scored by count of remote responses. The test is available in two equivalent forms, AI and AII. One manual covers both forms. The review set includes the manual and a portion of CQAI. Norms are provided for ninth-grade and engineering students. The test is restricted to A.P.A. members. Examiner required. Suitable for group use.

Timed: 10 minutes

Scoring: Examiner evaluated

Cost: 25 test booklets $12.00; manual $6.00; scoring guide $1.75

Publisher: Sheridan Psychological Services, Inc.

CORNELL CONDITIONAL REASONING TEST, FORM X
Refer to page 393.

CORNELL CRITICAL THINKING TEST, LEVEL X
Refer to page 393.

CORNELL CRITICAL THINKING TEST, LEVEL Z
Refer to page 394.

THE D48 TEST (RESEARCH EDITION)
Center for Psychological Applications, Paris

All ages

Purpose: Measures the g-factor in intelligence by assessing nonverbal reasoning skills. May be used with hearing-impaired or nonreading individuals.

Description: 48-item paper-pencil multiple-choice nonverbal analogies test involving pictures of dominoes. Items cover a wide range of difficulty and can be administered with a minimum need for language. Average scores range from 18 (fifth-grade students) to 31 (college students) correct answers. The manual provides norms and validity studies on French subjects. Examiner required. Suitable for group use.

Timed: 25 minutes

Scoring: Hand key

Cost: Experimental kit (5 test booklets, 25 answer sheets, manual, and scoring stencil) $12.00

Publisher: Consulting Psychologists Press, Inc.

DECORATIONS (DEC)
Sheldon Gardner, Arthur Gershon,
Philip R. Merrifield,
and J.P. Guilford

Adolescent, adult
Grades 10 and above

Purpose: Measures ability to add meaningful decorations to simple drawings. Used for research and experimentation.

Description: Paper-pencil test measuring the "divergent production of figural implications," which is the ability to add meaningful details to what is given. The subjects are presented with outlines of well-known articles of furnishings and asked to add decorative lines. Figural ideas, rather then artistic quality, is stressed. The test is scored by a simple count of acceptable responses. The test is restricted to A.P.A. members. Examiner required. Suitable for group use.

Timed: 12 minutes

Scoring: Examiner evaluated

Cost: 25 tests $13.00; manual $1.00; scoring guide $1.00

Publisher: Sheridan Psychological Services, Inc.

THE DEFINING ISSUES TEST OF MORAL JUDGMENT
James R. Rest

Adolescent, adult
Ages 13-adult

Purpose: Measures moral judgment concerning social issues. Used for research purposes only.

Description: 72-item paper-pencil test consisting of six short stories, each followed by 12 related statements. The stories present social problems or moral dilemmas, and the statements present a range of considerations to be taken into account as one tries to determine what a proper (morally "right") course of action would be in a given situation. Individuals indicate each consideration's importance by rating each statement on a 5-point scale ranging from "none" to "great." Individuals then rank in order of importance the four statements they consider the most important of the 12 statements provided for each story. The test provides scores for Stages (of moral development) 2, 3, 4, 4½, 5A, 5B, and 6; the most used index is a combination of Stages 5 and 6, a "principled" morality score ("P" score). An internal consistency check identifies individuals who are randomly checking responses or who do not understand the

directions. The test is inappropriate for use with individuals who are not fluent in English or do not have an eighth-grade reading level. The manual (available from Minnesota Moral Research Projects) contains information on administering and scoring the test, interpretation and sample analyses of test scores, reliability and validity, and norms for various groups. A detailed discussion of the rationale of test development, theoretical issues, and empirical findings is provided in *Development in Judging Moral Issues* (University of Minnesota Press). Examiner required. Suitable for group use.

Untimed: 40 minutes

Scoring: Examiner evaluated

Cost: Available free of charge to professional and student researchers affiliated with recognized institutions

Publisher: Minnesota Moral Research Projects

ENVIRONMENTAL RESPONSE INVENTORY (ERI)
George E. McKechnie

Adult

Purpose: Measures individuals' dispositions toward different physical/psychological environments. Used for research in retirement counseling, environmental planning, architecture, and urban design.

Description: 184-item paper-pencil inventory measuring people's attitudes toward the physical environment. Scores may be obtained for eight scales: Pastoralism, Urbanism, Environmental Adaptation, Stimulus Seeking, Environmental Trust, Antiquarianism, Need Privacy, and Mechanical Orientation. The subjects indicate their degree of agreement or disagreement on a 5-point scale. Currently intended for research use only. Self-administered. Suitable for group use.

Untimed: 30 minutes

Scoring: Hand key

Cost: Specimen set (no key) $7.50; manual $7.00; key $12.00

Publisher: Consulting Psychologists Press, Inc.

EXPRESSIONAL FLUENCY (EF)
Paul R. Christensen and J.P. Guilford

Adolescent, adult
Grades 7 and above

Purpose: Measures the ability to produce spontaneously statements of organized thought. Used in research and experimental applications.

Description: Multiple-item paper-pencil test measuring the factor of "divergent production of semantic systems," which is defined as the ability to produce efficiently appropriate verbal expressions of organized thought. Instructions are included in the manual. Norms are provided for ninth-grade students. The test is restricted to A.P.A. members. Examiner required. Suitable for group use.

Timed: 8 minutes

Scoring: Examiner evaluated

Cost: 25 tests $10.00

Publisher: Sheridan Psychological Services, Inc.

FAMILY RELATIONS TEST—ADULT VERSION
Refer to page 77.

FAMILY RELATIONS TEST—MARRIED COUPLES VERSION
Refer to page 76.

FAMOUS SAYINGS (FS)
Refer to page 916.

FLUENCY (FLU)
Paul R. Christensen and J.P. Guilford

Adolescent, adult
Grades 7 and above

Purpose: Measures divergent-thinking abilities in terms of words, expressions, and ideas. Used for research and experiment.

Description: Four paper-pencil multiple-choice tests measuring aptitudes for verbalized creative thinking. Each test covers a distinct area in the divergent-thinking process. The tests are Word Fluency (WF), Expressional Fluency (EF), Ideational Fluency (IF), and Associational Fluency (AF). Often referred to as the Christensen-Guilford Fluency Tests, the tests share a common manual and review set. All tests are administered in expendable booklets. The scoring guides are essential to decision as to acceptability of responses to test items. The test is restricted to A.P.A. members. Examiner required. Suitable for group use.

Timed: 24 minutes

Scoring: Examiner evaluated

Cost: 25 tests $8.00-$12.00; scoring guide $0.75; manual $6.00

Publisher: Sheridan Psychological Services, Inc.

GRIEF EXPERIENCE INVENTORY (RESEARCH EDITION)
Catherine M. Sanders,
Paul A. Mauger,
and Paschal N. Strong, Jr.

Adult

Purpose: Assesses attitudes and experiences related to grief. Used for research on grief and for training bereavement counselors.

Description: 135-item true-false paper-pencil inventory covering somatic and emotional content associated with the process of bereavement. The test yields three validity scales and nine symptom scales (Despair, Guilt, Somatization, Death Anxiety, Anger/Hostility, Social Isolation, Loss of Control, Depersonalization, and Rumination). Scale reliabilities are modest. Substantial normative data are provided. Examiner required. Suitable for group use.

Untimed: 20-30 minutes

Scoring: Hand key

Cost: Manual $9.50; 25 reusable tests $15.00; 50 answer sheets $8.50; 25 profiles $5.50; key $12.50

Publisher: Consulting Psychologists Press, Inc.

GUILFORD-ZIMMERMAN APTITUDE SURVEY (GZAS)
Refer to page 809.

THE HIGH SCHOOL CHARACTERISTICS INDEX (HSCI) AND THE ELEMENTARY AND SECONDARY SCHOOL INDEX (ESI)

Refer to page 687.

HUMAN INFORMATION PROCESSING SURVEY: HIP SURVEY

Refer to page 894.

IDEATIONAL FLUENCY (IF)
Paul R. Christensen and J.P. Guilford

Adolescent, adult
Grades 7 and above

Purpose: Measures ability to express meaningful ideas. Used in research and experimental applications.

Description: Multiple-item paper-pencil test measuring the factor of "divergent production of semantic units" by requiring the subject to produce efficiently many ideas fulfilling meaningful specifications. Instructions are included in the manual. Norms are provided for ninth-grade and college students. The test is restricted to A.P.A. members. Examiner required. Suitable for group use.

Timed: 12 minutes
Scoring: Examiner evaluated
Cost: 25 tests $10.00; scoring guide $0.60
Publisher: Sheridan Psychological Services, Inc.

INTERPERSONAL CHECK LIST (ICL)

Refer to page 143.

IRENOMETER
Panos D. Bardis

Adolescent, adult

Purpose: Measures attitudes and beliefs concerning peace (irenology is the study of peace). Used for discussion purposes.

Description: 10-item paper-pencil inventory in which an individual rates 10 statements about peace and its effects on individuals and society on a 5-point scale ranging from 0 (strongly disagree) to 4 (strongly agree). All statements express positive attitudes toward peace. The score equals the sum of the 10 numerical responses. Self-administered. Suitable for group use.

Untimed: Varies
Scoring: Self-scored
Cost: Free
Publisher: Panos D. Bardis

KATZ-ZALK OPINION QUESTIONNAIRE

Refer to page 687.

KIRTON ADAPTION-INNOVATION INVENTORY
M.J. Kirton

Adolescent, adult

Purpose: Evaluates an individual's adaptive and innnovative characteristics. Used for research in occupational psychology.

Description: Paper-pencil test measuring response to organizational change based on a scale ranging from an ability to "do things better" to the ability to "do things differently." Responses are related to concepts of creativity, problem solving, and decision-making. The test is a research tool and should not be used for evaluating individuals. Materials include a response sheet, manual, and key. Examiner required. Suitable for group use.
CANADIAN PUBLISHER

Untimed: 10-15 minutes
Scoring: Hand key
Cost: Specimen set $27.52; 25 response sheets $18.87; key $7.33; manual $18.20
Publisher: Institute of Psychological Research, Inc.

Information and availability unconfirmed; no publisher response.

KRANTZ HEALTH OPINION SURVEY (HOS)
David S. Krantz, Andrew Baum, and Margaret V. Wideman

College students, adults

Purpose: Measures preferences for different approaches to health care programs. Assesses the degree to which individuals wish to be involved (i.e., be informed and/or participate) in their own health care and medical treatment programs. Used for research purposes only.

Description: 16-item paper-pencil self-report inventory assessing preferences concerning personal involvement in medical care programs. The survey consists of two scales: Scale B (behavioral involvement) and Scale I (information). Scale B contains nine items and measures attitudes toward self-treatment and active behavioral involvement of patients in medical care. Scale I contains seven items and measures the desire to ask questions and be informed about medical decisions. The test items are rated on a binary agree-disagree format. An individual score for each scale and a total score measuring composite attitudes toward treatment approaches are provided. High scores represent favorable attitudes toward self-directed or informed treatment. Items refer to routine aspects of medical care and do not refer to severe or traumatic illness. Self-administered. Suitable for group use.

Untimed: Varies

Scoring: Examiner evaluated

Cost: Contact publisher concerning availability and prices

Publisher: David S. Krantz

LIGHT-SWITCH ALTERNATION APPARATUS
Refer to page 48.

MAKING OBJECTS (MO)
Sheldon Gardner, Arthur Gershon, Philip R. Merrifield, and J.P. Guilford

Adolescent, adult
Grades 10 and above

Purpose: Measures the ability to combine figural elements to produce specific objects. Used for research and experiment.

Description: Multiple-item paper-pencil test measuring the "divergent production

of figural systems." This test is parallel to those measuring expressional fluency in the verbal or semantic category. The factor might be called "figural expressional fluency" or, more precisely, "visual-figural expressional fluency." Given a collection of very simple figural elements, the subject is told to construct specified objects by combining those elements. The test is scored by a simple count of acceptable responses. Norms are provided for ninth-grade students and adults. The test is restricted to A.P.A. members. Examiner required. Suitable for group use.

Timed: 6 minutes

Scoring: Examiner evaluated

Cost: 25 tests $8.00; manual $1.75; scoring guide $1.00

Publisher: Sheridan Psychological Services, Inc.

MASTER ATTITUDE SCALES
Refer to page 689.

MATCH PROBLEMS (MP)
Raymond M. Berger and J.P. Guilford

Adolescent, adult
Grades 7 and above

Purpose: Measures an individual's originality in transforming figure conceptions. Used for research and experiment.

Description: Multiple-item paper-pencil test measuring the "divergent production of figural transformations," first known as "adaptive flexibility." The parallel ability in the verbal category is originality (divergent production of semantic transformations). The test is scored by simple count of acceptable responses. Norms are provided for ninth-grade students and young adult males. The test is restricted to A.P.A. members. Examiner required. Suitable for group use.

Timed: 14 minutes

Scoring: Examiner evaluated

Cost: 25 tests $12.00; manual $3.00; scoring key $1.25

Publisher: Sheridan Psychological Services, Inc.

MATCH PROBLEMS V (MPV)
Philip R. Merrifield and
J. P. Guilford

Adolescent, adult
Grades 7 and above

Purpose: Measures the ability to revise conceptions of figures, but at a lower level of difficulty than the Match Problems test. Used for research and experiment.

Description: Multiple-item paper-pencil test measuring the "divergent production of figural transformations," first known as "adaptive flexibility." The parallel ability in the verbal category is originality (divergent production of semantic transformations). This test is an alternate, shorter form of Match Problems and measures the same factor at a lower level of task complexity. The test is scored by a simple count of acceptable responses. Norms are provided for ninth-grade students. The test is restricted to A.P.A. members. Examiner required. Suitable for group use.

Timed: 10 minutes

Scoring: Examiner evaluated

Cost: 25 tests $8.00; scoring guide $1.25

Publisher: Sheridan Psychological Services, Inc.

MONEY ATTITUDE SCALE
Kent T. Yamauchi and
Donald I. Templer

Adult

Purpose: Assesses attitudes related to money. Used with adults in research.

Description: 29-item paper-pencil instrument assessing four money-attitude factors: power-prestige, retention-time, distrust, and anxiety. Self-administered. Suitable for group use.

Untimed: 15 minutes

Scoring: Hand key

Cost: $15.00

Publisher: Kent T. Yamauchi, Ph.D.

NEW USES (NU)
Ralph Hoepfner and J. P. Guilford

Adolescent, adult
Grades 10 and above

Purpose: Measures the ability to redefine and find new ways of looking at things. Used for research and experiment.

Description: Multiple-item paper-pencil test measuring the Structure-of-Intellect ability of "convergent production of semantic transformations," which involves the capacity to redefine. A low score on this test probably indicates "functional fixedness," which serves as an inhibitor in problem solving by preventing insights. Norms are provided for entering college students. The test is restricted to A.P.A. members. Examiner required. Suitable for group use.

Timed: 9 minutes

Scoring: Examiner evaluated

Cost: 25 tests $8.00; manual $0.75; scoring guide $1.25

Publisher: Sheridan Psychological Services, Inc.

PERTINENT QUESTIONS
Raymond M. Berger and
J. P. Guilford

Adolescent, adult
Grades 10 and above

Purpose: Measures conceptual foresight. Used for experiment and research.

Description: Multiple-item paper-pencil test measuring the cognition of semantic implications, the ability to see implications of a meaningful kind (e.g., anticipating, being aware of consequences, and making predictions). Norms are provided for college groups. The test is restricted to A.P.A. members. Examiner required. Suitable for group use.

Timed: 12 minutes

Scoring: Examiner evaluated

Cost: 25 tests $8.00; manual $1.25; scoring guide $2.50

Publisher: Sheridan Psychological Services, Inc.

PICTURE SITUATION TEST
Refer to page 935.

PLOT TITLES (PT)
*Raymond M. Berger and
J.P. Guilford*

**Adolescent, adult
Grades 10 and above**

Purpose: Measures ability to spontaneously produce original ideas. Used for research and experiment.

Description: Multiple-item paper-pencil test measuring two factors: ideational fluency (divergent production of semantic units) and originality (divergent production of semantic transformations). Originality in this test is seen in the production of ideas of high quality with respect to the criterion of "cleverness." Ideational fluency is scored by a count of nonclever responses; originality is scored by a count of clever responses. The test is available in two equivalent forms AI and B. Norms are provided for ninth-grade and architecture students. The test is restricted to A.P.A. members. Examiner required. Suitable for group use.

Timed: 6 minutes
Scoring: Examiner evaluated
Cost: 25 tests $8.00; manual $3.00; scoring guide $1.25
Publisher: Sheridan Psychological Services, Inc.

POSSIBLE JOBS (PJ)
Arthur Gershon and J.P. Guilford

**Adolescent, adult
Grades 7 and above**

Purpose: Measures the ability to elaborate upon given information. Used for research and experiment.

Description: Multiple-item paper-pencil test measuring "divergent production of semantic implications," which is defined as the ability to elaborate upon given information or to suggest alternative deductions or extensions. The test is scored by a simple count of acceptable responses. Norms are provided for ninth-

and tenth-grade students. The test is restricted to A.P.A. members. Examiner required. Suitable for group use.
Timed: 10 minutes
Scoring: Examiner evaluated
Cost: 25 test booklets $8.00; manual $1.75; scoring guide $1.00
Publisher: Sheridan Psychological Services, Inc.

PROVERBS TEST
Refer to page 512.

REACTION TIME TESTING
Refer to page 564.

REACTION TO EVERYDAY SITUATIONS TEST
Refer to page 937.

ROKEACH VALUE SURVEY
Refer to page 208.

THE SCALE OF BELIEFS IN EXTRAORDINARY PHENOMENA (SOBEP)
George Windholz and Louis Diamant

Adolescent, adult

Purpose: Measures belief in extraordinary phenomena and possible natural phenomena that evoke an aura of mystery and sensationalism. Used in research on personality traits.

Description: 35-item paper-pencil Likert-scale test measuring beliefs in extraordinary phenomena on the periphery of Western thought, such as astrology, ghosts, magic, and witchcraft and in possible natural phenomena such as ESP, UFOs, and some aspects of hypnosis, dreams, and death. Subject indicates level of agreement or disagreement with each item. Examiner/self-administered. Suitable for group use.
Untimed: 20 minutes
Scoring: Examiner evaluated
Cost: Free
Publisher: George Windholz, Ph.D.

SEEING PROBLEMS (SP)
*Philip R. Merrifield and
J. P. Guilford*

**Adolescent, adult
Grades 7 and above**

Purpose: Measures the ability to see and anticipate problems. Used for research on semantics.

Description: Multiple-item paper-pencil test measuring the cognition of semantic implications, the ability to see implications of a meaningful kind (e.g., anticipating, being aware of consequences, and making predictions). Norms are provided for high-school graduates. The test is restricted to A.P.A. members. Examiner required. Suitable for group use.

Timed: 4 minutes
Scoring: Examiner evaluated
Cost: 25 tests $8.00; manual $2.50; scoring guide $1.50
Publisher: Sheridan Psychological Services, Inc.

SITUATIONAL PREFERENCE INVENTORY
Refer to page 178.

SKETCHES (SKET)
*Arthur Gershon, Sheldon Gardner,
Philip R. Merrifield and
J. P. Guilford*

**Adolescent, adult
Grades 7 and above**

Purpose: Measures the ability to make abstract figures into recognizable objects. Used for research and experiment.

Description: 48-item paper-pencil test measuring figural fluency (divergent production of figural units), the ability to produce efficiently a variety of units of visual-figural information in response to specifications. Four basic, simple figures are given, each repeated 12 times. The taker is asked to transform each one into a recognizable object. The test is scored by a simple count of acceptable objects produced. Norms are provided for ninth-

grade students and young adult males. The test is restricted to A.P.A. members. Examiner required. Suitable for group use.

Timed: 8 minutes
Scoring: Examiner evaluated
Cost: 25 tests $14.00; manual $1.00; scoring guide $1.00
Publisher: Sheridan Psychological Services, Inc.

SLOAN ACHROMATOPSIA TEST
Munsell Color

Ages 6-adult

Purpose: Research test to screen the congenital achromat in populations that are completely colorblind and to measure how such persons see color.

Description: Visual-verbal test consisting of seven neutral gray scales each displaying 17 steps between black and white. The scales are mounted on red, orange, yellow, green, blue, and magenta color references. The subject is asked to select the gray on the scale which appears to match the color reference mounted behind it. Examiner required. Not suitable for group use.

Untimed: 3-4 minutes
Scoring: Examiner evaluated
Cost: Complete $88.00
Publisher: Munsell Color

SMOKING AND HEALTH
Refer to page 318.

SPORTS EMOTION TEST (SET)
E.R. Oetting and C.W. Cole

Athletes

Purpose: Evaluates emotional responses of athletes prior to and during competition. Used as a research instrument.

Description: 132-item paper-pencil rating scale measuring feelings of anxiety, concentration, intensity, and physical readiness. Subjects rate each response area on a 7-point scale according to how they feel at different times: 24 hours before, at breakfast, just before, and just after the start of the event and just after "something goes wrong." Examiner required. Suitable for group use.

Timed: 20 minutes

Scoring: Examiner evaluated

Cost: 100 scales and profiles $60.00; manual $12.00

Publisher: Rocky Mountain Behavioral Science Institute, Inc.

STUDY OF VALUES
Refer to page 707.

TEST OF BASIC ASSUMPTIONS
James H. Morrison and Martin Levit

Adolescent, adult

Purpose: Diagnoses philosophical preferences. Used to examine assumptions about reality or philosophy and for research and group discussion.

Description: 20-item paper-pencil measure of realism, idealism, and pragmaticism. Instructions are read to the subjects, who are allowed as much time as they need to complete the test. A minimum 12th-grade reading level is necessary. The test should not be used for prediction purposes. Self-administered. Suitable for group use.

Untimed: 40 minutes

Scoring: Hand key

Cost: Specimen set (manual, score sheet, test) $2.00; 25 tests (score sheets, manual) $4.30

Publisher: James H. Morrison

WORD FLUENCY (WF)
Paul R. Christensen and J. P. Guilford

Adolescent, adult
Grades 7 and above

Purpose: Measures the ability to produce spontaneously words useful in research and experimental applications.

Description: Multiple-item paper-pencil test measuring the "divergent production of symbolic units" by requiring the subject to produce rapidly words fulfilling specified symbolic (letter) properties. Instructions are included in the manual.

Norms are provided for ninth-grade students. The test is restricted to A.P.A. members. Examiner required. Suitable for group use.

Timed: 4 minutes

Scoring: Examiner evaluated

Cost: 25 tests $7.00

Publisher: Sheridan Psychological Services, Inc.

research

Education

Tests classified in the Education section generally are used in an educational or school setting to assess the cognitive and emotional growth and development of persons of all ages. Typically, professionals who use the tests listed in this section are school psychologists, school counselors, and classroom teachers.

As the classification of tests by function or usage is somewhat arbitrary, the reader is encouraged to check the Psychology and Business sections for additional tests that may be helpful in meeting assessment needs.

Academic Subjects: Business Education

CLERICAL SKILLS SERIES
Refer to page 7.

HIETT DIAMOND JUBILEE SERIES SHORTHAND TEST
V.C. Hiett

Adolescent   Grades 10-12

Purpose: Assesses the shorthand achievement of high-school and college students. Used as a mid-year or end-of-year exam.

Description: 125-item paper-pencil test of characters, dictation, and notes interpretation. Examiner required. Suitable for group use.

Timed: 40 minutes

Scoring: Hand key

Cost: Test $0.15 each; manual $0.20; key $0.20

Publisher: Bureau of Educational Measurements

HIETT SIMPLIFIED SHORTHAND TEST
V.C. Hiett

Adolescent   Grades 10-12

Purpose: Assesses the shorthand achievement of high-school and college students. Used as a first- and second-semester exam.

Description: 125-item paper-pencil test covering the reading and writing of the Gregg shorthand system. Examiner required. Suitable for group use.

Timed: 40 minutes

Scoring: Hand key

Cost: Test $0.15 each; manual $0.20; key $0.20

Publisher: Bureau of Educational Measurements

NATIONAL BUSINESS COMPETENCY TESTS AND ENTRANCE TEST
N.B.E.A. Competency Test Committee

Adolescent, adult
Grades 10 and above

Purpose: Measures knowledge and achievement related to a variety of business activities. Used for employee screening and educational evaluation.

Description: Multiple-item battery of five paper-pencil and task-performance tests measuring office skills. The tests, which attempt to simulate actual working conditions, include the Office Procedures Test, Secretarial Procedures Test, Typewriting Test, Accounting Procedures Test—Trial Edition, and Stenographic Test. Examiner/self-administered. Suitable for group use.

Scoring: Hand key

Cost: Review set (1 each of the five tests and their manuals/keys) $7.50

Publisher: National Business Education Association

NATIONAL BUSINESS COMPETENCY TESTS: ACCOUNTING PROCEDURES TEST (TRIAL EDITION)

Adolescent, adult

Purpose: Measures knowledge and skills related to accounting positions. Used for employee screening and educational evaluation.

Description: Multiple-item paper-pencil task-performance test in two parts assessing a variety of accounting knowledge and skills. Part 1 measures knowledge of basic accounting procedures and requires individuals to compute payroll earnings, prepare payroll reports, reconcile a bank statement, and complete a worksheet. In Part 2, individuals use source documents to make journal entries, post to a general ledger, prepare a trial balance, and make out a deposit slip. The test has optional questions on microcomputers in accounting. Examiner/self-administered. Suitable for group use.

Timed: Not available

Scoring: Hand key

Cost: Test booklet $0.75; manual/key $0.75

Publisher: National Business Education Association

NATIONAL BUSINESS COMPETENCY TESTS: OFFICE PROCEDURES
N.B.E.A. Competency Test Committee

**Adolescent, adult
Grades 10 and above**

Purpose: Assesses proficiency in entry-level office skills, excluding use of the typewriter. Used for student and program evaluations.

Description: Multiple-item paper-pencil test consisting of two parts. Part 1, Office Services, consists of 12 subtests. Each subtest requires the subject to perform a routine office task, such as checking, proofreading, telephoning, mail services, and completing a job application form. Part 2 consists of nine tasks involving computation and accounting services, including payroll, accounting forms, and computation. Responses are scored for accuracy, completeness, and neatness. Parts 1 and 2 may be administered on separate days. Examiner required. Suitable for group use.

Timed: Two 50-minute periods

Scoring: Hand key

Cost: Test $0.75; manual $0.75

Publisher: National Business Education Association

NATIONAL BUSINESS COMPETENCY TESTS: SECRETARIAL PROCEDURES TEST

Adolescent, adult

Purpose: Measures knowledge and skills related to secretarial positions. Used for employee screening and educational evaluation.

Description: Multiple-item paper-pencil and task-performance test in two parts assessing a variety of secretarial skills and abilities. Part 1 measures knowledge of basic secretarial procedures and editing skills, including punctuation, grammar, spelling, and word usage. In Part 2, individuals prioritize and complete five typing assignments and a calendar updating task. Examiner/self-administered. Suitable for group use.

Timed: Not available

Scoring: Hand key

Cost: Test booklet $0.75; manual $0.75

Publisher: National Business Education Association

NATIONAL BUSINESS COMPETENCY TESTS: TYPEWRITING
N.B.E.A. Competency Test Committee

**Adolescent, adult
Grades 10 and above**

Purpose: Assesses typing skills of advanced high-school and college typing students.

Description: Multiple-item test measuring typing speed and accuracy. The two parts of the test are designed to be administered on separate days. Part 1 consists of two 5-minute timed writing exercises requiring line-for-line copying. Part 2 requires a full class period and consists of five typing jobs to be completed as accurately as possible in the allotted time. The tasks include typing information on a form with horizontal lines, a business letter, a 3-column table with headings, a 2-page report manuscript with footnotes, and an invoice. Materials required are a typewriter, paper, carbon paper, and correction materials. Examiner required. Suitable for group use.

Timed: Two 50-minute periods
Scoring: Hand key
Cost: Test $0.75;manual $0.75
Publisher: National Business Education Association

NATIONAL BUSINESS ENTRANCE TESTS–STENOGRAPHIC TEST
N.B.E.A. Test Committee

Adolescent, adult
Grades 10 and above

Purpose: Assesses the ability to take dictation and transcribe it into business letters and interoffice communications. Used for selection and placement of stenographers.

Description: 13-item test requiring applicants to take shorthand notes and transcribe dictated material into usable letters under conditions similar to those found in the typical office. Twelve business letters and one interoffice communication are dictated at the rate of 80 words-per-minute. Applicants provide their own notebook and pencil for taking notes, and the entire dictation section (including pauses between items) comprises 30 minutes, 15 seconds. Applicants are given 90 minutes to transcribe the material into typed copy. At the beginning of the transcription period, applicants are given a transcription folder containing 12 sheets of letterhead paper, 8 manifold carbon sets, one sheet of white paper, and information regarding format and special requirements of the letters. Examiner required. Suitable for group use.

Timed: 2 hours
Scoring: Hand key
Cost: Test $0.75; manual $0.75
Publisher: National Business Education Association

THE OHIO VOCATIONAL ACHIEVEMENT TESTS IN BUSINESS AND OFFICE EDUCATION: ACCOUNTING/ COMPUTING CLERK
Refer to page 720.

THE OHIO VOCATIONAL ACHIEVEMENT TESTS IN BUSINESS AND OFFICE EDUCATION: CLERK-STENOGRAPHER
Refer to page 720.

THE OHIO VOCATIONAL ACHIEVEMENT TESTS IN BUSINESS AND OFFICE EDUCATION: DATA PROCESSING
Refer to page 721.

THE OHIO VOCATIONAL ACHIEVEMENT TESTS IN BUSINESS AND OFFICE EDUCATION: GENERAL OFFICE CLERK
Refer to page 721.

THE OHIO VOCATIONAL ACHIEVEMENT TESTS IN MARKETING EDUCATION: GENERAL MERCHANDISING
Refer to page 728.

REICHERTER-SANDERS TYPEWRITING I AND II
Richard F. Reicherter and Merritt W. Sanders

Adolescent   Grades 10-12

Purpose: Assesses the typing achievement of high-school students. Used as a first- or second-year exam.

Description: 150-item test measuring typewriting speed and accuracy. Items are presented in the form of work samples. Test requires a typewriter and an examiner. Percentile norms are available. Suitable for group use.

Timed: 36 minutes
Scoring: Hand key
Cost: Test $0.15; manual $0.20; key $0.20
Publisher: Bureau of Educational Measurements

RUSSELL-SANDERS BOOKKEEPING TEST

Raymond B. Russell and
Merritt W. Sanders

Adolescent   Grades 10-12

Purpose: Assesses the bookkeeping knowledge of high-school students. Used as a first- and second-semester exam.

Description: 90-item paper-pencil test of journalizing transactions, classification of accounts, adjusting and closing entries, and solving practical problems. Examiner required. Suitable for group use.

Timed: 40 minutes

Scoring: Hand key

Cost: Test $0.15; manual $0.20; key $0.20

Publisher: Bureau of Educational Measurements

SRA TYPING 5

Refer to page 874.

SRA TYPING SKILLS TEST

Refer to page 874.

STUDENTS TYPEWRITING TESTS

N.B.E.A. Test Committee

Adolescent, adult
Grades 10 and above

Purpose: Assesses typing skills of high-school and college students through the first four semesters of typing instruction.

Description: Multiple-item test measuring typing speed and accuracy. Test I, administered after the first semester of instruction, consists of two 5-minute timed writing exercises: one from printed copy and one from handwritten copy. Test II, administered after the second semester, consists of one 5-minute timed writing exercise and three exercises emphasizing accuracy rather than speed: typing a business letter with corrections, a tabulation, and a manuscript. Test III, administered after the third semester, and Test IV, administered after the fourth

semester, are similar to Test II and present appropriately more difficult typing tasks. Materials required are a typewriter, paper, carbon paper, and correction materials. Examiner required. Suitable for group use.

Timed: 35 minutes

Scoring: Examiner evaluated

Cost: 4 tests, manual $3.00; 1 test (specify semester level) $0.75

Publisher: National Business Education Association

WORD PROCESSOR ASSESSMENT BATTERY (WPAB)

Refer to page 887.

Academic Subjects: English and Related: Preschool, Elementary, and Junior High School

BASIC SKILLS TEST—WRITING-ELEMENTARY-FORMS A AND B

IOX Assessment Associates

Child   Grades 5-6

Purpose: Measures student's end-of-elementary school achievement in the basic writing skills. Also useful in determination of grade promotion and program evaluation.

Description: 35-item paper-pencil test measuring a student's ability to select complete sentences; spell, capitalize, and punctuate correctly; use verbs, adjectives, adverbs, and pronouns correctly; and express ideas in writing. An optional writing sample is provided. This test preceeds the IOX Basic Skills Test—Writing-Secondary Level. Examiner required. Suitable for group use.

Untimed: 30-45 minutes

Scoring: Hand key; may be computer scored

Cost: 25 BW-A2 $37.50; teacher's guide BW-G2 $3.95; 25 BW-B2 $27.50; test manual BTM-2 $3.95; 50 answer sheets BA-2 $6.95

Publisher: IOX Assessment Associates

CARROW ELICITED LANGUAGES INVENTORY (CELI)
Refer to page 620.

DENVER HANDWRITING ANALYSIS (DHA)
Refer to page 559.

DIAGNOSTIC SPELLING TEST
Denis Vincent and Jenny Claydon

Child

Purpose: Assesses spelling skills. Used for diagnosing individual student weaknesses.

Description: Multiple-item paper-pencil test of spelling skills. Items include editing and correcting a passage of text and recognizing common letter groups in nonsense words. The test also contains a questionnaire measuring attitudes toward spelling, a short dictation passage, and a short section measuring understanding of alphabetical order. Two parallel and equivalent forms, A and B, are available. Examiner required. Suitable for group use.
BRITISH PUBLISHER

Untimed: Not available

Scoring: Hand key; examiner evaluated

Cost: Specimen set (pupils' Forms A and B, manual) £5.20; 25 forms (specify A or B) £7.50 (payment in sterling for all overseas orders)

Publisher: NFER-NELSON Publishing Company Ltd.

DOS AMIGOS VERBAL LANGUAGE SCALES
Refer to page 261.

GATES-MCKILLOP-HOROWITZ READING DIAGNOSTIC TESTS
Refer to page 524.

GROUP LITERACY ASSESSMENT
Frank A. Spooncer

Child   Ages 10.6-12.6

Purpose: Measures overall ability of children at the stage of transfer from primary to secondary education to deal effectively with written material. Identifies students needing help, indicates standards within a school district, and suggests appropriate follow-up procedures for both class groups and individual students.

Description: Multiple-item paper-pencil test in two sections measuring written verbal abilities. In the first section, the student identifies and corrects mistakes in a simple story. In the second section, the story is continued as a modified cloze text. Children are required to use and combine pictorial, contextual, and grammatical cues offered by continuous prose. The test measures the students' ability to note significant details, carry information in short-term memory, and make inferential judgments and provides information about the student's spelling skills. Norms are presented as deviation quotients for ages 10.6-12.6 and reading age equivalents for ages 7-14. Scoring averages two minutes per paper. Examiner required. Suitable for group use.
BRITISH PUBLISHER

Untimed: 30 minutes

Scoring: Hand key

Cost: Specimen set £3.10; 20 test forms £1.90; manual £2.95

Publisher: Hodder & Stoughton

HOLLINGSWORTH-SANDERS JUNIOR HIGH SCHOOL LITERATURE TEST
Leon Hollingsworth and Merritt W. Sanders

Adolescent   Grades 7-8

Purpose: Assesses the literature achievement of junior high-school students. Used as a first- or second-semester exam.

Description: 115-item paper-pencil test of selection content, authorship, comprehension of quotations, and literary appreciation. Examiner required. Suitable for group use.

Timed: 40 minutes

Scoring: Hand key

Cost: Test $0.15; manual $0.20; key $0.20

Publisher: Bureau of Educational Measurements

HOYUM-SANDERS ELEMENTARY ENGLISH TEST
*Vera D. Hoyum and
Merritt W. Sanders*

Child   Grades 2-4

Purpose: Assesses the English achievement of elementary-school students. Used as a first- or second-semester exam.

Description: Multiple-item paper-pencil test covering sentence recognition, capitalization, punctuation, spelling, sentence usage, and alphabetization. Examiner required. Suitable for group use.

Timed: 40 minutes

Scoring: Hand key

Cost: Test $0.15; manual $0.20; key $0.20

Publisher: Bureau of Educational Measurements

HOYUM-SANDERS INTERMEDIATE ENGLISH TEST
*Vera D. Hoyum and
Merritt W. Sanders*

Child   Grades 5-6

Purpose: Assesses the English achievement of students. Used as a first- or second-semester exam.

Description: Multiple-item paper-pencil test for students in Grades 5-6. Factors measured include sentence recognition, capitalization, punctuation, contractions,

possessives, plurals, correct usage, and alphabetization. Examiner required. Suitable for group use.

Timed: 40 minutes

Scoring: Hand key

Cost: Test $0.15; manual $0.20; key $0.20

Publisher: Bureau of Educational Measurements

HOYUM-SANDERS JUNIOR HIGH SCHOOL ENGLISH TEST
*Vera D. Hoyum and
Merritt W. Sanders*

**Child, adolescent
Grades 7-9**

Purpose: Assesses the English achievement of junior high-school students. Used as a first- or second-semester exam.

Description: Multiple-item paper-pencil test covering sentence structure, capitalization, punctuation, grammar and usage, and alphabetization. Examiner required. Suitable for group use.

Timed: 40 minutes

Scoring: Hand key

Cost: Test $0.15; manual $0.20; key $0.20

Publisher: Bureau of Educational Measurements

THE HUNTER-GRUNDIN LITERACY PROFILES LEVELS 1, 2, 3, 4 AND 5
*Elizabeth Hunter-Grundin and
Hans U. Grundin*

**Child, adolescent
Ages 6½-13½**

Purpose: Assesses child's progress in reading and language development. Used for directing teaching towards a wider range of language and literacy skills.

Description: Battery of brief paper-pencil and oral tests measuring five components of literacy skills, including reading for meaning, attitude toward reading, spelling, free writing, and spoken language. The test is available on five levels: Level 1 (ages 6½-8), Level 2 (ages 8-9), Level 3 (ages 9-10), Level 4 (ages

10-11 +) and Level 5 (ages 11-12 +). The Reading for Meaning passage is different at each level. The score correlates with the Schonell Reading Test, Holborn Reading Scale, and the Neale Analysis of Reading Ability. Examiner required. Suitable for group use with the exception of the Spoken Language subtest, which must be administered individually. BRITISH PUBLISHER

Timed: Levels 1 and 2 40 minutes; Levels 3, 4, 5 35 minutes

Scoring: Hand key; examiner evaluated

Cost: Complete kit for each level (manual, keys, 35 tests for each area plus picture) $35.00. cumulative record included for Level 1

Publisher: The Test Agency Ltd.

KANSAS ELEMENTARY SPELLING TEST
Connie Moritz and Merritt W. Sanders

Child   Grade 3

Purpose: Assesses the spelling achievement of third-grade students. Used as a comparison measure.

Description: 85-item paper-pencil test of correct spelling recognition. Two sets of forms are available for each semester. Examiner required. Suitable for group use.

Timed: 15 minutes

Scoring: Hand key

Cost: Test $0.15; manual $0.20; key $0.20

Publisher: Bureau of Educational Measurements

KANSAS INTERMEDIATE SPELLING TEST
Alice Robinson and Merritt W. Sanders

Child   Grades 4-6

Purpose: Assesses the spelling achievement of upper elementary-school students. Used as a comparison measure.

Description: 85-item pencil-paper test of correct spelling recognition. Two sets of

forms are available for each semester. Examiner required. Suitable for group use.

Timed: 15 minutes

Scoring: Hand key

Cost: Test $0.15; manual $0.20; key $0.20

Publisher: Bureau of Educational Measurements

KANSAS JUNIOR HIGH SCHOOL SPELLING TEST
Mary T. Williams and Merritt W. Sanders

Adolescent   Grades 7-8

Purpose: Assesses the spelling achievement of junior high-school students. Used as a comparison measure.

Description: 85-item paper-pencil test of correct spelling recognition. Two sets of forms are available for each semester. Examiner required. Suitable for group use.

Timed: 15 minutes

Scoring: Hand key

Cost: Test $0.15; manual $0.20; key $0.20

Publisher: Bureau of Educational Measurements

LANGUAGE INVENTORY FOR TEACHERS (LIT)
Refer to page 632.

LISTENING COMPREHENSION TESTS IN ENGLISH FOR STANDARDS 5 AND 8

Child, adolescent

Purpose: Measures ability to understand spoken English. Used for educational evaluation.

Description: Multiple-item paper-pencil tests of listening comprehension for students in Standards 5 and 8. Pupils listen to recorded questions and mark answers on answer sheets. Materials include a cassette tape with questions for two alternate forms, A and B. Examiner required. Suitable for group use.

SOUTH AFRICAN PUBLISHER
Untimed: 50 minutes
Scoring: Hand key; examiner evaluated
Cost: (In Rands) Standard 5 manual 3,70; cassette 7,40; 10 answer sheets A 0,30; 10 answer sheets B 0,40; scoring stencils (specify A or B) 1,80; Standard 8 manual 4,00; cassette 7,40; 10 answer sheets A 0,30; 10 answer sheets B 0,40; scoring stencil A or B 1,80 each; orders outside The RSA will be dealt with on merit
Publisher: Human Sciences Research Council

METROPOLITAN LANGUAGE INSTRUCTIONAL TESTS
Refer to page 407.

NATIONAL ACHIEVEMENT TESTS: ENGLISH, READING, LITERATURE, AND VOCABULARY TESTS—VOCABULARY (GRADES 3-8)
Refer to page 415.

PARALLEL SPELLING TESTS
Dennis Young

Child   Ages 6.5-13

Purpose: Measures spelling skills at all levels of ability. Used for program planning and evaluation.

Description: Multiple-item paper-pencil test of spelling ability. Test items are selected from banks of sentences presented in the test booklet according to the level of ability of the students being tested. Twelve matched tests without overlap (a much larger number with partial overlap) can be formed. The abundance of material in the banks and the method of selecting a test render the results less vulnerable to practice effects and coaching. The test booklet also includes sections on examining and extending the results, an introduction to children's spelling errors and the assessment of spelling in children's writing, fundamental guidance on the teaching of spelling, and a method for systematically

charting the progress of children at all levels of ability over a period of six years (ages 6.5-13). Examiner required. Suitable for group use.
BRITISH PUBLISHER
Untimed: Varies
Scoring: Examiner evaluated
Cost: Test booklet £3.20
Publisher: Hodder & Stoughton

PHONOVISUAL DIAGNOSTIC TESTS
Edna B. Smith and Mazie Lloyd

Child   Grades 1-3

Purpose: Assesses students' knowledge of the sounds of letters. Used to determine strengths and weaknesses in the use of phonics.

Description: 24-item paper-pencil test measuring initial and final consonant sounds, short and long vowels, vowel spelling, 22 initial blends, and 14 final blends. The student writes 24 words as the examiner dictates them. Examiner required. Suitable for group use.
Untimed: 5-10 minutes
Scoring: Examiner evaluated
Cost: Complete set $4.50
Publisher: Phonovisual Products, Inc.

PROOFREADING TESTS OF SPELLING (PRETOS)
Cedric Croft, Alison Gilmore, Neil Reid, and Peter Jackson

Child   Ages 8-13

Purpose: Measures ability to discriminate between misspelled and correctly spelled words. Used for providing diagnostic information about individual spelling accomplishments.

Description: Multiple-item paper-pencil tests of spelling achievement. The items are reading passages containing misspelled words. The child is required to detect spelling mistakes, correct words identified as misspelled, and indicate lines of text without mistakes. Five non-overlapping tests for use with different grade levels are available. Each test consists of three or four paragraphs consisting of 12-14 lines of text; two lines contain no misspelled words. Examiner required. Suitable for group use.

NEW ZEALAND PUBLISHER

Timed: 30 minutes

Scoring: Hand key; examiner evaluated

Cost: Contact publisher

Publisher: New Zealand Council for Educational Research

RECEPTIVE ONE-WORD PICTURE VOCABULARY TEST (ROWPVT)
Morrison F. Gardner

Child   Ages 2-11.11

Purpose: Assesses receptive vocabulary of bilingual, speech-impaired, immature, withdrawn, and emotionally and physically impaired children.

Description: 100-item response test using 100 picture plates, each with four illustrations presented horizontally across the page. The child identifies the illustration that matches the word presented by the examiner. When used with the Expressive One-Word Picture Vocabulary Test, comparisons can be made between a student's receptive and expressive vocabulary skills. Examiner required. Not suitable for group use.

Untimed: 20 minutes

Scoring: Hand key

Cost: Test kit (manual, test plates, 25 English Record Forms) $45.00

Publisher: Academic Therapy Publications

THE SIMILES TEST
Refer to page 572.

SOUTH AFRICAN WRITTEN LANGUAGE TEST (SAWLT)—1981

Grades II-Standard 5

Purpose: Measures written language ability of English-speaking primary-school students. Used for educational guidance.

Description: Test of written language requiring the subject to write a passage in response to a stimulus photo. Materials include the stimulus photo, which should be provided to each subject in group administrations. Examiner required. Suitable for group use.

SOUTH AFRICAN PUBLISHER

Untimed: 30 minutes

Scoring: Hand key; examiner evaluated

Cost: (In Rands) manual 7,20; stimulus photo 1,20; writing pad 0,50; scoring pad 1,20; orders from outside The RSA will be dealt with on merit

Publisher: Human Sciences Research Council

SPELLMASTER DIAGNOSTIC SPELLING SYSTEM
Claire R. Cohen and Rhoda M. Abrams

Child   Grades 1-8

Purpose: Measures spelling abilities and diagnoses individual spelling difficulties. Used to plan instructional and remedial spelling programs and by classroom teachers, reading specialists, L.D. specialists, E.S.L. teachers, special education teachers, and adult education teachers.

Description: Multiple-item paper-pencil tests measuring eight levels of spelling abilities corresponding to grade levels 1-8. Diagnostic tests, irregular word tests, and homonym tests are provided for all levels. Diagnostic tests measure 160 phonic and structural elements in regular words. Each test contains a scoring key which identifies and analyzes errors. On the basis of the diagnostic tests, students are placed for individual or group instruction; other levels of diagnostic tests, irregular word tests, or homonym tests are administered according to individual need. Students can correct their own errors and find out why they made them. The testing and evaluating manual describes how to administer and score all tests. The teaching and learning manual provides specific teaching suggestions, learning activities, and approximately 5,000 supplementary words for individual study.

Correlation charts show how to use other published spelling materials. Examiner required. Suitable for group use.

Untimed: Varies

Scoring: Examiner evaluated; self-scored

Cost: Contact publisher

Publisher: Blue Star Enterprises

TEST OF WRITTEN ENGLISH (TWE)
*Velma R. Andersen and
Sheryl K. Thompson*

**Grades 1-6 and
older remedial students**

Purpose: Measures written language skills of elementary school children and older remedial students. Used to screen for mastery in areas of capitalization, punctuation, written expression, and paragraph writing.

Description: Multiple-item paper-pencil test in which the student corrects various errors of capitalization, punctuation, and usage and writes a brief paragraph. Items in each skill area are grouped according to difficulty from Grades 1-6. Remedial activities are provided for each of the areas tested. Items may be read by the students themselves or by the examiner so that poor readers can be accurately evaluated. A conversion table is provided for translating scores into approximate grade-level placement. Examiner required. Not suitable for group use.

Untimed: 30 minutes

Scoring: Hand key

Cost: Manual $12.00; 50 test forms $14.00

Publisher: Academic Therapy Publications

TEST OF WRITTEN SPELLING (TWS-2)
*Stephen C. Larsen and
Donald D. Hammill*

**Child, adolescent
Grades 1-12**

Purpose: Measures students' spelling abilities by using both words which are easily predictable by their sound and

words which are more irregular. Identifies the spelling strengths and weaknesses of students.

Description: 100-item paper-pencil test assessing student spelling performance with three groups of words: words readily predictable in sound-spelling pattern, words less predictable, and both types of words presented together. Standard scores and percentiles are provided for each of the three groups. Test items were developed after review of 2,000 spelling rules, with words drawn from 10 basal spelling programs. Examiner required. Suitable for group use.

Untimed: 20 minutes

Scoring: Examiner evaluated

Cost: Complete (manual, 50 answer sheets, class profile sheet, storage box) $32.00

Publisher: Pro-Ed

VISUAL MEMORY SCALE (VMS)
Refer to page 540.

VOCABULARY COMPREHENSION SCALE (VCS)
Tina E. Bangs

Child   Ages 2-6

Purpose: Evaluates a young child's comprehension of pronouns and words of position, quality, quantity, and size. Used for instructional programming and remediation work.

Description: 61-item test in which the subject responds to the examiner's spoken directions by manipulating the appropriate item, such as a card, dolls, cubes, cylinders, buttons in a box, a garage, a fence, a ladder, a tea set, which are included among the materials. The data collected can be used to plan activities for developing vocabulary needed to enter kindergarten or first grade. Suggestions for teaching unfamiliar words and concepts are included in the test manual. Examiner required. Not suitable for group use.

Untimed: Not available

Scoring: Examiner evaluated

Cost: Complete $52.00
Publisher: DLM Teaching Resources

WRITE: JUNIOR HIGH
CTB/McGraw-Hill

Adolescent   Grades 7-9   ☞ ✍

Purpose: Measures junior high-school students' writing and communication skills. Used to identify student needs and to implement correctional/remedial instruction.

Description: Multiple-item paper-pencil multiple-choice test and essay measuring a student's proficiency in written communication. The multiple-choice questions measure mechanics, punctuation, usage, vocabulary, spelling, organization, and format. The student also is required to write two essays in response to hypothetical situations. Examiner required. Suitable for group use.
Timed: 50 minutes per section
Scoring: Hand key; may be computer scored
Cost: Specimen set (objective test, writing topics, manual, computer-scorable and hand-scorable answer sheets, writing guide, class summary sheet, test reviewer's guide) $8.95
Publisher: CTB/McGraw-Hill

WRITING PROFICIENCY PROGRAM/INTERMEDIATE SYSTEM (WPP/IS)
Richard M. Bossone

Child, adolescent   ☞ ✍
Grades 6-9

Purpose: Assesses students' writing skills. Used by composition teachers.

Description: 70-item paper-pencil multiple-choice and essay test measuring writing skills objectives. The multiple-choice questions cover adjectives and adverbs, sentence fragments, pronouns, verb tense, subject/verb agreement, misplaced modifiers, conjunctions, sentence splices, capitalization, quotation and end marks, commas, topic/supporting sentences, sentence sequence, and use of transitions. The three writing exercises assess students' ability to use the descrip-

tive, narrative, and persuasive forms. The tests are an integral part of a program that includes instructional materials for the teacher. Examiner required. Suitable for group use.
Timed: 50 minutes
Scoring: Hand key; may be computer scored
Cost: Contact publisher
Publisher: CTB/McGraw-Hill

Academic Subjects: English and Related: High School and College

AMERICAN LITERATURE 50 Q TESTS

Adolescent   Grades 7-12   ☞ ✍

Purpose: Measures high-school students' content recall of a specific American novel. Used as a literature posttest.

Description: 50 paper-pencil multiple-choice questions for each of 167 titles compiled alphabetically and divided in two volumes. Tests are available for all titles, including *Across 5 Aprils, Christy, Ethan Frome, Intruder in the Dust, Rumble Fish, Swiftwater, Watership Down,* and *The Yearling.* Examiner required. Suitable for group use.
Untimed: 50 minutes
Scoring: Hand key
Cost: Two volumes of 75 tests each $30.00 per volume
Publisher: The Perfection Form Company

AMERICAN LITERATURE—ESSAY TESTS

Adolescent   Grades 10-12   ☞ ✍

Purpose: Measures students' content recall of a specific American novel and evaluates writing skills through paragraph organization and content. Used as a literature course posttest.

Description: Five paper-pencil essay questions covering each of 111 American literature titles, including *An American Tragedy, Black Like Me, For Whom the Bell Tolls, On the Beach,* and *Moby Dick.* Materials include test questions and guidelines. Examiner required. Suitable for group use.

Untimed: 50 minutes

Scoring: Examiner evaluated

Cost: Test, including guidelines $0.40

Publisher: The Perfection Form Company

BARRETT-RYAN ENGLISH TEST
E.R. Barrett, Theresa M. Ryan, E.R. Wood, and H.E. Schrammel

Adolescent   Grades 9-12

Purpose: Measures the English language achievement of high-school students. Used as a first- or second-semester exam for both survey and diagnostic purposes.

Description: 150-item paper-pencil multiple-choice test of punctuation, correct usage, capitalization, sentence structure, verb usage, grammar, and diction. Examiner required. Suitable for group use.

Timed: 50 minutes

Scoring: Hand key

Cost: Test $0.18; manual $0.20; key $0.20

Publisher: Bureau of Educational Measurements

BASIC SKILLS TEST—WRITING-SECONDARY-FORMS A AND B
IOX Assessment Associates

Adolescent   Grades 8-11

Purpose: Measures minimum competency of high-school students in the basic writing skills. Used for program evaluation.

Description: 20-item paper-pencil test measuring student's competency in using words correctly, checking mechanics, selecting correct sentences, and expressing ideas in writing. An optional writing sample is provided. This test succeeds the IOX Basic Skills Test—Writing-Elementary Level. Examiner required. Suitable for group use.

Untimed: 30-45 minutes

Scoring: Hand key; may be computer scored

Cost: 25 BW-A1 $37.50; 25 BW-B1 $37.50; teacher's guide BW-G1 $3.95; 50 answer sheets $6.95

Publisher: IOX Assessment Associates

BOOKLET OF GRAMMAR TESTS
Kenneth Stratton and George Christian

Adolescent   Grades 7-12

Purpose: Assesses skills in grammar. Used for indentifying student strengths and weaknesses as part of an educational evaluation.

Description: 10 paper-pencil tests of grammar skills. Both diagnostic and achievement tests are available in four areas: parts of speech, parts of the sentence, joining parts of the sentence, and punctuation and capitalization. Six other areas are covered by shorter tests designed to be used as measures of student knowledge: nouns, pronouns, verbs, adjectives and adverbs, prepositions, conjunctions and interjections, correct usage, and variety in sentence arrangement. Examiner required. Suitable for group use.

Untimed: Not available

Scoring: Hand key

Cost: Set of tests $3.95 each

Publisher: Stratton-Christian Press, Inc.

CLARKE READING SELF-ASSESSMENT SURVEY (SAS)
Refer to page 543.

COLLEGE ENGLISH PLACEMENT TEST
Oscar Haugh and James I. Brown

College freshmen

Purpose: Measures English composition skills of incoming college freshmen. Used to place college freshmen in English composition classes.

Description: Multiple-item paper-pencil test consisting of two parts. Part 1 is an objective test measuring English composition skills. Part 2, which is optional, consists of two essays. The test items reflect the results of a survey of college English professors concerning the relative importance of elements of composition in the assignment of freshmen to composition classes. The elements found to be vital in English composition and placement and their weight on the test are organization and paragraph structure (36%), syntax and grammar (17%), and conventions, usage, and capitalization (22%). The sections of the test are arranged to follow the actual steps in writing a composition. Examiner required. Suitable for group use.

Timed: Part 1 45 minutes; Part 2 50 minutes

Scoring: Examiner evaluated

Cost: Contact publisher

Publisher: The Riverside Publishing Company

COOPERATIVE ENGLISH TESTS
Educational Testing Service

Adolescent   Grades 9-14

Purpose: Measures high-school and college students' achievement in reading comprehension and written expression. Used to screen students who are advanced or lacking in basic English abilities and for placement in the appropriate level of instruction.

Description: 210-item paper-pencil test designed to assess a student's mastery of basic English skills. Four subtests are independently available: Reading Comprehension Part I, measuring vocabulary; Reading Comprehension Part II, measuring level and speed of comprehension in varied style and content; English Expression Part I, measuring effectiveness in conveying exact meaning; and English Expression Part II, measuring mechanics (usage, spelling, punctuation, capitalization). Two levels are available for

each subtest: Level 1 for Grades 12-14 and Level 2 for Grades 9-12. Examiner required. Suitable for group use.

Timed: 40 minutes per section

Scoring: Hand key; may be computer scored

Cost: 20 reusable test books $18.40 (specify level); 100 answer sheets $16.00

Publisher: CTB/McGraw-Hill

ENGLISH AND WORLD LITERATURE 50 Q TESTS
Wayne DeMouth

Adolescent   Grades 11-12

Purpose: Measures high-school students' knowledge of English and world writers. Used as posttests in regular courses.

Description: 50 paper-pencil multiple-choice questions covering each of 135 titles, including *Arms and the Man, Beowulf, Canterbury Tales, A Doll's House,* and *Jane Eyre.* Examiner required. Suitable for group use.

Untimed: 50 minutes

Scoring: Hand key

Cost: Test and key $0.40

Publisher: The Perfection Form Company

ENGLISH KNOWLEDGE AND COMPREHENSION
S. Chatterji and Manjula Makerjee

Adolescent   Ages 14-16

Purpose: Measures students' knowledge and comprehension of English.

Description: 67-item paper-pencil test arranged in two separately timed parts assessing knowledge and comprehension of the English language. Part I (20 minutes) consists of 29 items. Part II (1 hour) consists of 38 items. The test may be used with students whose native language is not English but who have been taught in English-language schools. Examiner required. Suitable for group use.
PUBLISHED IN INDIA

Timed: 1 hour, 20 minutes

Scoring: Hand key; examiner evaluated

Cost: (In Rupees) Complete kit (25 booklets, 100 answer sheets, key, manual) 90Rs
Publisher: Manasayan
Information and availability unconfirmed; no publisher response.

ENGLISH WORLD LITERATURE— ESSAY TESTS

Adolescent Grades 10-12 👉 ✍️

Purpose: Measures high-school students' content recall of a specific title in English world literature and evaluates writing skills through paragraph organization and content. Used as a unit posttest.

Description: Five paper-pencil essay questions covering each of 93 titles, including *Crime and Punishment, Dracula, Gulliver's Travels, The Hobbit,* and *The Stranger.* Materials include test questions and a guide book. Examiner required. Suitable for group use.
Untimed: 50 minutes
Scoring: Examiner evaluated
Cost: Test and evaluation guidelines $0.40
Publisher: The Perfection Form Company

HOSKINS-SANDERS LITERATURE TEST
Thomas Hoskins and Merritt W. Sanders

Adolescent Grades 9-12 👉 ✍️

Purpose: Assesses the literature achievement of high-school students. Used as a first- or second-semester exam.

Description: 150-item paper-pencil multiple-choice test covering the general literary content of 35 classical selections. Factors measured are content of selection, authorship, and recognition and understanding of selections by English and American authors. Examiner required. Suitable for group use.
Timed: 40 minutes
Scoring: Hand key
Cost: Test $0.15; manual $0.20; key $0.20
Publisher: Bureau of Educational Measurements

INTERPERSONAL COMMUNICATION INVENTORY (ICI)
Refer to page 917.

JOURNALISM TEST
Francis Miller and Kenneth Stratton

Adolescent Grades 10-12 👉 ✍️

Purpose: Assesses journalism skills. Used for diagnosing strengths and weaknesses and measuring student achievement.

Description: Multiple-item paper-pencil test of major journalism areas: judgment of news values, paragraphing, sentence variety, news sources, sports, judgment of feature values, speech-interview stories, editorials, make-up, headlines, terminology, copyreading, style, columns, and advertising. Item types include true-false and identifying errors. Examiner required. Suitable for group use.
Untimed: Not available
Scoring: Hand key
Cost: Test $0.39 each (minimum order of 10)
Publisher: Stratton-Christian Press, Inc.

MYTHOLOGY TESTS

Adolescent Grades 9-12 👉 ✍️

Purpose: Measures recall of information read in specific mythology texts. Used as a mythology unit posttest.

Description: 100-item and 50-item paper-pencil multiple-choice tests. There are separate tests for *The Greek Way* and *The Roman Way,* both by Edith Hamilton and *Gods, Heroes, and Men of Ancient Greece* by H.D. Rouse. Examiner required. Suitable for group use.
Untimed: 55 minutes
Scoring: Hand key
Cost: Books $2.50-$2.95 each; 50 Q tests $0.25; teacher guide $0.95; student guide $0.30
Publisher: The Perfection Form Company

NATIONAL ACHIEVEMENT TESTS: ENGLISH, READING, LITERATURE, AND VOCABULARY TESTS—COLLEGE ENGLISH FOR HIGH SCHOOL AND COLLEGE

Refer to page 414.

NATIONAL ACHIEVEMENT TESTS: ENGLISH, READING, LITERATURE, AND VOCABULARY TESTS—ENGLISH

Refer to page 414.

NATIONAL ACHIEVEMENT TESTS: ENGLISH, READING, LITERATURE, AND VOCABULARY TESTS—VOCABULARY (GRADES 7-COLLEGE)

Refer to page 415.

PURDUE HIGH SCHOOL ENGLISH TEST

R.D. Franklin, J.H. McKee, H.H. Remmers, and G.S. Wykoff

Adolescent   Grades 9-13   [☞ ✍]

Purpose: Measures the English language skills of high-school students and college freshmen.

Description: Multiple-item paper-pencil test measuring a student's knowledge and ability in five areas of English: grammar, punctuation, effective expression, vocabulary, and spelling. Fall and spring norms in terms of percentiles and standard scores are provided by grade and sex for high-school students. Norms for college freshmen and other interpretive data are included also. The test is available in two alternate forms, 1 and 2. Examiner required. Suitable for group use.

Timed: 36 minutes

Scoring: Hand key; may be computer scored

Cost: 35 test booklets $24.03; 100 self-marking answer sheets $50.10; 100 IBM 1230 answer sheets $27.30; IBM 1230 scoring mask $5.70; manual $4.86; 35 class record sheets $6.72

Publisher: The Riverside Publishing Company

READING, COMPREHENSION, GRAMMAR USAGE AND STRUCTURE, AND VOCABULARY TESTS

William A. McCartney

Adolescent   Grades 10-13   [☞ ✍]

Purpose: Assesses English knowledge or potential of students seeking to enter four-year colleges. Used to predict degree of success in freshman composition or other English classes and for admission and placement.

Description: 198-item paper-pencil battery of three tests designed to be used together but which may be taken separately to measure performance in the following areas: reading comprehension (48 multiple-choice items based on 16 short selections); grammar, usage, and structure (100 two-choice items based on logic of expression, idiom, and good taste); and vocabulary (50 five-choice items calling for recognition of synonyms). Examiner required. Suitable for group use.

Timed: Complete battery 2 hours

Scoring: Hand key; may be computer scored

Cost: Contact publisher

Publisher: William A. McCartney

Information and availability unconfirmed; no publisher response.

REPRODUCIBLE TESTS

Adolescent   Grades 9-12   [☞ ✍]

Purpose: Evaluates high-school students' content recall of specific books used in reading programs. Used as a posttest.

Description: 50-item paper-pencil two-page multiple-choice true-false and matching tests for each of 33 titles, including *The Bell Jar, Go Ask Alice, The Illustrated Man,* and *Old Yeller.* Materials consist of reproducible tests, answer sheets, and a scoring key. In some cases, the tests may be used as student self-tests. Examiner required. Suitable for group use.

Untimed: Not available

Scoring: Hand key

Cost: Each master $1.25

Publisher: The Perfection Form Company

SANDERS-FLETCHER SPELLING TEST
Gwen Fletcher and
Merritt W. Sanders

Adolescent   Grades 9-12

Purpose: Measures the spelling achievement of high-school students. Used as a first- or second-semester exam.

Description: 150-item paper-pencil test assessing student's ability to spell common words. Examiner required. Suitable for group use.

Timed: 30 minutes

Scoring: Hand key

Cost: Test $0.15; manual $0.20; key $0.20

Publisher: Bureau of Educational Measurements

SANDERS-FLETCHER VOCABULARY TEST
Gwen Fletcher and
Merritt W. Sanders

Adolescent
Grades 10 and above

Purpose: Measures the vocabulary proficiency of high-school and college students. Used as a measure of scholastic aptitude.

Description: 100-item paper-pencil test covering general vocabulary words. Examiner required. Suitable for group use.

Timed: 40 minutes

Scoring: Hand key

Cost: Test $0.15; manual $0.20; key $0.20

Publisher: Bureau of Educational Measurements

STRUCTURE TESTS, ENGLISH LANGUAGE (STEL)
Jeanette Best and Donna Ilyin

Adolescent, adult
Grades 10 and above

Purpose: Determines student knowledge of English-language structure. Used as an aid to assessing skill levels, diagnosing problems, and student placement.

Description: 50-item paper-pencil multiple-choice test available in beginning, intermediate, and advanced levels. There are two categories of difficulty for each level. The student selects which of three statements is written in correct English. The test can be used with an oral interview, such as the Ilyin Oral Interview Test. Examiner required. Suitable for group use.

Untimed: 30 minutes per test

Scoring: Hand key

Cost: Contact publisher

Publisher: Newbury House Publishers, Inc.

WALTON-SANDERS ENGLISH TEST
Charles E. Walton and
Merritt W. Sanders

Adolescent   Grades 9-13

Purpose: Assesses the ability of high-school and college students to use English grammar and structure correctly. Used as a first- or second-semester exam.

Description: 150-item paper-pencil test of spelling, pronunciation, punctuation, sentence structure, word forms, verbs, pronouns, and prepositions. Examiner required. Suitable for group use.

Timed: 50 minutes

Scoring: Hand key

Cost: Test $0.15; manual $0.20; key $0.20

Publisher: Bureau of Educational Measurements

WESTERN MICHIGAN UNIVERSITY ENGLISH QUALIFYING EXAM (EQE)
Bernadine P. Carlson

Adolescent, adult
Grades 15 and above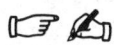

Purpose: Assesses level of English usage skills for graduate students and college juniors and seniors. Used for academic placement and as a criterion for graduation and an evaluation of skills for graduate work.

Description: 195-item paper-pencil multiple-choice test consisting of six parts: grammatical errors (30 items); punctuation for meaning (45 items); sentence structure (30 items); spelling (30 items); word usage, diction (30 items); and reading comprehension and rhetorical style (30 items). Test items consist of sentences taken from papers written by students in Grades 15 and above. The test may be used for pre- and posttesting in writing classes and with any type of skills handbook. A specimen booklet, which includes sample questions from each of the six parts, is available. Examiner required. Suitable for group use.

Timed: 1 hour, 40 minutes

Scoring: Hand key; may be computer scored

Cost: Contact publisher

Publisher: Bernadine P. Carlson

WESTERN MICHIGAN UNIVERSITY ENGLISH USAGE-ORIENTATION FORM (EUO)
Refer to page 852.

WORD UNDERSTANDING (WU)
R. Hoepfner, M. Hendricks, and R.H. Silverman

Adolescent   Grades 7-12

Purpose: Measures verbal comprehension and vocabulary. Used for personal and program evaluation.

Description: 32-item paper-pencil multiple-choice test consisting of two parts of 16 items each arranged in order of difficulty. Scores reflect the breadth and depth of vocabulary. Two forms are available: Form A is reusable, and answers are recorded on answer sheets. A lay-over stencil is available for scoring. Form C is consumable and used with subjects who may be expected to perform poor on answer-sheet tests. A response guide is available for scoring. The test has been normed on over 1,300 junior high-school students. Examiner required. Suitable for group use.

Timed: 4 minutes per part

Scoring: Hand key

Cost: Specimen set (specify form) $4.00; 35 tests (specify form) $8.00; 35 answer sheets (Form A) $4.00; scoring stencil (Form A) $3.00; scoring guide (Form C) $2.00; manual $2.00

Publisher: Monitor

WRITE: SENIOR HIGH
CTB/McGraw-Hill

Adolescent   Grades 10-12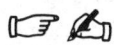

Purpose: Assesses the writing skills of high-school students. Used to identify student needs and to implement remedial instruction.

Description: Multiple-item paper-pencil multiple-choice and essay test measuring a student's proficiency in written communication. The multiple-choice questions measure mechanics, punctuation, usage, vocabulary, spelling organization, and format. The student also is required to write two essays in response to hypothetical situations. Examiner required. Suitable for group use.

Timed: 50 minutes per section

Scoring: Hand key; may be computer scored

Cost: Specimen set (objective test book, writing topic sheet, manual, machine-scorable and hand-scorable answer sheets, writing sample guide, class summary sheet, test reviewer's guide) $8.95

Publisher: CTB/McGraw-Hill

WRITING PROFICIENCY PROGRAM (WPP)
Richard M. Bossone

Adolescent   Grades 9-13   🖙 🖎

Purpose: Assesses students' expository writing skills. Used by composition teachers.

Description: Multiple-item paper-pencil multiple-choice and essay test assessing expository writing skills. The multiple-choice section measures sentence structure, word usage, punctuation and mechanics, capitalization, spelling, the paragraph, the essay, and business letters. The test is available in two forms: Test 1 for Grades 9-10 and Test 2 for Grades 11-13. The tests are an integral part of a program that includes instructional components for the teacher. Examiner required. Suitable for group use.

Timed: 50 minutes

Scoring: Hand key; may be computer scored

Cost: Contact publisher

Publisher: CTB/McGraw-Hill

Academic Subjects: English and Related: Multilevel

BENCH MARK MEASURES
Aylett Cox

Child, adolescent   🖙 🖎

Purpose: Assesses a student's general phonic knowledge, including reading, writing, and spelling, as a means of diagnosing particular deficiencies and to gauge progress during remediation.

Description: Three paper-pencil verbal tests arranged in sequence to cover four areas of remedial language: alphabet and dictionary skills, reading, handwriting, and spelling. The alphabet and reading sections must be administered individually, but the handwriting and spelling

schedules may be administered to groups. The kit contains step-by-step directions for administration, along with reading passages and spelling lists. The Guide to Bench Mark Measures contains a description of testing, scoring, and evaluation. The Graphs of Concepts and Multisensory Introductions shows the graphenes and concepts in the order taught in the Alphabetic Phonics curriculum. Summary sheets are used to record responses and mark errors. The examination was designed primarily for use with the Alphabetic Phonics curriculum, the three levels of which correspond to the Bench Mark's alphabet, reading, and writing schedules. The test can, however, be used with any student as a diagnostic tool and should be administered by a trained examiner in a quiet setting. The last two sections may be administered to small groups.

Untimed: 30 minutes-1 hour for each of the four levels

Scoring: Examiner evaluated

Cost: Complete kit $55.00; summary sheets $10.00; graph $1.25

Publisher: Educators Publishing Service, Inc.

BILINGUAL SYNTAX MEASURE (BSM)
Refer to page 260.

DIAGNOSTIC SCREENING TEST: LANGUAGE, SECOND EDITION (DSTL)
Thomas D. Gnagey and Patricia A. Gnagey

**Child, adolescent   🖙 🖎
Grades K-13**

Purpose: Determines a student's ability to write English and diagnoses common problems in the use of the language.

Description: 110-item multiple-choice paper-pencil test yielding six scores: total, sentence structure, grammar, punctuation, capitalization, and formal spelling rules. All subtests yield applied versus formal knowledge for a total of 12 scores in all. The examiner explains the procedure to individuals or groups and reads the test if the students have poor reading skills. Examiner required. Suitable for group use.

Untimed: 5-10 minutes

Scoring: Hand key

Cost: Manual, 50 test forms $27.00

Publisher: Slosson Educational Publications, Inc.

DIAGNOSTIC SCREENING TEST: SPELLING, THIRD EDITION (DSTS)
Thomas D. Gnagey

Child, adolescent
Grades 1-12

Purpose: Measures a student's ability to spell words and diagnoses common spelling problems.

Description: 78-item pencil-paper test measuring sight or phonics orientation for spelling instruction; relative efficiency of verbal and written testing procedures; analysis of sequential and gross auditory memory; and spelling potential. A pretest is available to determine the appropriate level of entry. The examiner, using the test form, pronounces 78 developmentally arranged words and the student spells them orally; the examiner then repronounces difficult words and the student writes them. When administered to groups, the test yields a grade equivalent score. The test is available in Forms A and B. Examiner required. Suitable for group use.

Untimed: 5-10 minutes

Scoring: Hand key

Cost: Manual, 25 Form A, 25 Form B $25.00

Publisher: Slosson Educational Publications, Inc.

DIAGNOSTIC SPELLING POTENTIAL TEST (DSPT)
John Arena

Ages 7-adult

Purpose: Assesses the spelling skills of students ages 7 through adult.

Description: Multiple-item paper-pencil test consisting of four subtests: Spelling,

Word Recognition, Visual Recognition, and Auditory-Visual Recognition. Tables are provided for converting raw scores to standard scores, percentile ranks, and grade ratings. Standard scores and percentiles may be plotted on a profile chart that compares spelling efficiency with requisite skills such as decoding, utilization of phonetic generalizations, visual recall, and matching auditory with visual representations. Two parallel forms are available for pre- and posttesting. The manual includes provisions for group administration of three of the subtests and presents a wide range of remedial activities. Examiner required. Suitable for group use.

Untimed: 25-40 minutes

Scoring: Examiner evaluated

Cost: Test kit (manual, Form A-1: 25 Spelling/Word Recognition Record Forms, Form A-2: 25 Visual/Auditory-Visual Recognition Record Forms, 25 Profile Sheets, in vinyl folder) $37.50

Publisher: Academic Therapy Publications

ENGLISH LANGUAGE SKILLS ASSESSMENT IN A READING CONTEXT (ELSA)
Donna Ilyin, Cecelia Doherty, Laurie Freid Lee, and Lynn Levy

Adolescent, adult

Purpose: Measures student understanding of the meaning and grammatical correctness of English language statements. Used to assess English as a Second Language.

Description: 25-item paper-pencil multiple-choice test in six versions: beginning conversation, beginning narration, intermediate conversation, intermediate narration, advanced narration, and advanced letter. The student selects one of four words which best completes the sentence in the conversation or story. The test has been used in federal accountability reports for funding. Self-administered. Suitable for group use.

Untimed: 30 minutes

Scoring: Hand key; machine scored

Cost: Contact publisher

Publisher: Newbury House Publishers, Inc.

ENGLISH PICTURE VOCABULARY TESTS (EPVTS)
M.A. Brimer and C.M. Dunn

Ages 2.9-adult

Purpose: Assesses listening vocabulary. Used by teachers and speech therapists for identifying reading difficulty and other verbal learning handicaps.

Description: Multiple-item response test measuring verbal comprehension in which the examinee matches a picture with a spoken word. The test is available on five levels: Test 1 (40 items) for ages 5-8.11; Test 2 (40 items) for ages 7-11.11 and available in versions for group and individual administration; Test 3 (48 items) for ages 11-18; and a full-range version (125 items arranged in order of increasing difficulty) for ages 3-18. No reading is required. Examiner required. Suitable for individual and group use depending on level.
BRITISH PUBLISHER

Untimed: Varies

Scoring: Hand key

Cost: Contact publisher

Publisher: Educational Evaluation Enterprises

ENGLISH PLACEMENT TEST
Mary Spaan, with Laura Strowe, A. Corrigan, B. Dobson, E. Kellman, and S. Tyma

Adult

Purpose: Assesses facility with the English language. Used to group low to intermediate proficiency adult nonnative speakers of English into homogenous ability levels as they enter an intensive English course.

Description: 100-item paper-pencil multiple-choice test of listening comprehension, grammar in conversational contexts, vocabulary recognition, and reading comprehension of sentences. A tape is available for use with the listen-ing comprehension items. Three forms (A, B, C) are available. Examiner required. Suitable for group use.

Timed: 1 hour, 5 minutes

Scoring: Hand key

Cost: Specimen set (examiner's manual, scoring stencil, test booklet, answer sheet) $5.00

Publisher: English Language Institute

ENGLISH PROGRESS TESTS SERIES

Child, adolescent
Ages 7-14

Purpose: Assesses the English skills of children. Used for measuring individual pupil progress.

Description: Series of 13 paper-pencil tests providing continuous assessment of reading skills. The English Progress Test A (ages 8-9) measures general progress in English. Test A2 (ages 7-9) covers rhymes, plurals, spelling, vocabulary, pronouns, tenses, and reading comprehension. Test B2 (ages 8-10) requires the child to provide rhymes and opposites, spell and punctuate, and write sentences. Test B3 (ages 8-9) assesses the ability to use words correctly. Test C2 (ages 9-11) requires written answers covering spelling, punctuation, vocabulary, and comprehension. Test C3 (ages 9-10) tests basic punctuation, vocabulary, and comprehension. Children also are required to join pairs of sentences into longer sentences and to construct acceptable sentences. Test D3 (ages 10-11) consists of 50 questions assessing the ability to use words correctly, elementary punctuation, and comprehension of both a poetry and a prose passage. Tests E (ages 12-13) and E2 (ages 11-12) each contain 12 different types of questions testing grammatical usage, written expression, vocabulary comprehension, and punctuation. Test F2 (ages 12-13) consists of "creative response" questions covering grammatical usage, written expression, vocabulary, comprehension, and punctuation. Test F3 (ages 12-13) assesses the ability to use words in a way that is contextually correct and to understand their meanings. Test G (ages 13-14) consists of 10 exercises assess-

ing English progress by various means, including comprehension passages, questions requiring correction for spelling and punctuation, and transforming direct speech to reported speech. Examiner required. Suitable for group use.
BRITISH PUBLISHER

Untimed: 40 minutes per test

Scoring: Hand key

Cost: Specimen set primary (Tests A2, A, B2, B3, C2, C3, D2, D3, pupils forms, sample manual) £4.15; specimen set secondary (Tests D2, D3, E2, E, F2, F3, G, pupil forms, sample manual) £4.15 (payment in sterling for all overseas orders)

Publisher: NFER-NELSON Publishing Company Ltd.

THE ENNIS-WEIR CRITICAL THINKING ESSAY TEST
Robert H. Ennis and Eric Weir

Adolescent, adult
Grades 7 and above

Purpose: Measures the ability to think critically. Used for teaching and in research.

Description: Paper-pencil essay test incorporating the following aspects of critical thinking: getting the point, seeing the reasons and assumptions, stating one's point, offering good reasons, seeing other possibilities, responding appropriately to/ avoiding equivocation, irrelevance, circularity, reversal of an if-then relationship, overgeneralization, credibility questions, and the use of emotive language to persuade. Examiner required. Suitable for group use.

Untimed: 40 minutes

Scoring: Examiner evaluated

Cost: Manual (includes scoring directions, 1 test, 1 scoring sheet) $9.95

Publisher: Midwest Publications

GRADED WORD SPELLING TEST
P.E. Vernon

Ages 6 and older

Purpose: Measures spelling ability. Used with students ages six and older, extend-

ing to the level of spelling reached by well-educated adults.

Description: 80-item paper-pencil test measuring students' ability to correctly spell words that are presented orally. Each word is placed in the context of a short sentence, and the test items are graded in order of difficulty. The particular items to be used on any one occasion are selected from the 80-word list according to the age and ability of the pupils to be tested; no pupil takes the whole test. The test is contained in a single reusable booklet and is designed to be administered orally. Full instructions for administration, scoring, and interpretation are provided. Norms are given as quotients (for chronological ages 5.6-17.6 +) and as spelling ages (5.7-15.10). Examiner required. Suitable for group use.
BRITISH PUBLISHER

Untimed: 30 minutes

Scoring: Hand key

Cost: Test booklet £2.10

Publisher: Hodder & Stoughton

THE INFORMAL WRITING INVENTORY
Refer to page 581.

INTERNATIONAL SOCIETY FOR PHILOSOPHICAL ENQUIRY VOCABULARY FORM A

Adult

Purpose: Measures knowledge of vocabulary at a high level of achievement (expected ceiling circa 170 A.Q.). Used as preparation for the supervised vocabulary test, Form B.

Description: 70-item paper-pencil multiple-choice test provides a high-level measure of linguistic aptitude. Subjects are asked to select from four choices the one word most closely "related" to the given test-item word. Norms are available for the top 6% to top 00.002% of the population. Answers and norms are printed on the back of the test form. Self-administered. Suitable for group use.

Untimed: Not available

Scoring: Self-scored

Cost: Test $3.00
Publisher: Harding Tests

INTERNATIONAL SOCIETY FOR PHILOSOPHICAL ENQUIRY VOCABULARY FORM B

Adult

Purpose: Measures knowledge of vocabulary at a high level of achievement. Provides best accuracy with the top 6% to top 00.13% of the population.

Description: 136-item paper-pencil multiple-choice test providing a high level measure of linguistic ability. Subjects are asked to select from three choices the one word most closely "related" to the given test-item word. Answers and norms are printed on the back of the test form. Examiner required. Suitable for group use.
Untimed: Not available
Scoring: Self-scored
Cost: Test $3.00
Publisher: Harding Tests

LANGUAGE PROFICIENCY TEST (LPT)

Refer to page 632.

LAURITA-TREMBLEY DIAGNOSTIC WORD PROCESSING TEST

*Raymond E. Laurita and
Phillip W. Trembley*

**Child, adolescent
Grades 1 and above**

Purpose: Identifies the level of categorical word processing that a student is able to utilize in spelling. Used for program planning, establishing IEPs, monitoring progress, and evaluating instructional programs in spelling.

Description: 64-item paper-pencil test using a dictation spelling format to assess the ability to discriminate among 15 vowel forms at five sequentially organized levels of difficulty. Criterion-referenced test items are based on an orthographic model that holds that spelling relies on a given set of word-processing generalizations.

The results are profiled on the Individual Progress Chart, which details the student's level of word processing ability, identifies categories of words that the student is ready to learn, and provides an estimate of the number of words in the student's spelling vocabulary. Suitable for group use.
Untimed: 20-30 minutes
Scoring: Examiner evaluated
Cost: Test kit (manual, 10 Individual Progress Charts, 20 record forms for pre- and posttesting) $25.00
Publisher: Leonardo Press

THE LISTENING FOR MEANING TEST

M.A. Brimer

Child   Ages 3-18

Purpose: Measures the level of intelligent verbal functions of which an individual is capable. Used by teachers, psychologists, or speech therapists.

Description: Multiple-item picture-response test using an individual's understanding of spoken English words as a means of measuring the individual's level of verbal functioning. The individual indicates which picture represents the meaning of a word spoken by the examiner. A focusing scale is used to determine at which point testing should begin within 10 hierarchically ordered scales of 12 items each. Examiner required. Not suitable for group use.
BRITISH PUBLISHER
Untimed: Varies
Scoring: Not available
Cost: Contact publisher
Publisher: Educational Evaluation Enterprises

MICHIGAN PRESCRIPTIVE PROGRAM IN ENGLISH (GRAMMAR)

William E. Lockhart

**Adolescent, adult
Grades 6 and over**

Purpose: Measures English grammar abilities and identifies skill deficits. Used to help students obtain a tenth-grade equivalency and pass the GED test in English grammar.

Description: Multiple-item paper-pencil test assessing the following high-school-level English grammar skills: capitalization, subjects, verbs, verb tense, moods, prepositions, case, possessive and indefinite pronouns, adjectives, adverbs, punctuation, synonyms, homonyms, plurals, and spelling. English study materials have allowed students to gain 0.8-3.0 years in English achievement for 24 clock hours of study. Examiner required. Suitable for group use.

Untimed: Varies

Scoring: Examiner evaluated

Cost: Test book $1.50; 7 response and prescription sheet booklets $2.00; answer key $1.00; English study materials $5.00

Publisher: Ann Arbor Publishers, Inc.

NATIONAL ACHIEVEMENT TESTS: ENGLISH, READING, LITERATURE, AND VOCABULARY TESTS—AMERICAN LITERACY TEST
Refer to page 414.

THE PICTURE STORY LANGUAGE TEST (PSLT)
Helmer R. Myklebust

Child, adolescent
Ages 7-17

Purpose: Determines a child's ability to express ideas through writing. Used to evaluate differences between learning disabled, mentally retarded, emotionally disturbed, reading disabled, and speech-handicapped individuals and to diagnose childhood dyslexia.

Description: Multiple-item paper-pencil test in which the examiner asks the subject to write the best story he can about a picture on an easel. Factors measured include number of words written, number of sentences, number of words per sentence, syntax accuracy, and success in expression of meaning. Administration suitable for groups of less than 10 children. Examiner required.

Untimed: 15-20 minutes

Scoring: Hand key; examiner evaluated

Cost: Test $20.50; 50 record forms $20.50; Development and Disorders of Written Language, Volume 1 and Volume 2 $38.00 per volume

Publisher: Grune & Stratton, Inc.

PRI READING SYSTEMS (PRI/RS)
Refer to page 553.

SPAR (SPELLING AND READING) TESTS
Dennis Young

Child, adolescent
Ages 7-15.11

Purpose: Measures children's ability to read and write. Identifies students needing remedial attention (designed to discriminate particularly among lower ability levels).

Description: Multiple-item paper-pencil test consisting of two sections (spelling and reading) that provide a complementary approach to testing literacy at a simple level. The spelling items are presented in the manual as "banks," allowing the user to select 10 matched tests without overlap and many more with partial overlap. The reading items follow the same format as Dennis Young's Group Reading Test and can be scored using the same templates. Two parallel forms, A and B, are available. Examiner required. Suitable for group use.
BRITISH PUBLISHER

Untimed: Not available

Scoring: Hand key

Cost: Contact publisher

Publisher: Hodder & Stoughton

SPELLING TESTS (ENGLISH)— 1964

Child, adolescent

Purpose: Measures ability to spell English words correctly. Used for educational evaluation and placement.

Description: Four paper-pencil tests of spelling ability. Series 2 is designed for Standards 1-3, Series 3 for Standards 3-5,

Series 4 for Standards 6-8, and Series 5 for Standards 9-10. Afrikaans-speaking students may need to be administered a series below their actual standard level. Two alternate forms, A and B, are available for each series. Examiner required. Suitable for group use.
SOUTH AFRICAN PUBLISHER

Timed: 45 minutes

Scoring: Hand key; examiner evaluated

Cost: (In Rands) 10 tests (specify form and series number) 0,30; manual 0,60; scoring key (specify form) 0,40; all orders outside The RSA will be dealt with on merit

Publisher: Human Sciences Research Council

THE STETSON READING-SPELLING VOCABULARY TEST (RSVT)
Refer to page 555.

===

TEST OF WRITTEN LANGUAGE (TOWL)
Donald D. Hammill and Stephen C. Larsen

Child, adolescent Grades 2-12

Purpose: Identifies students who have problems in written expression. Pinpoints specific areas of deficit.

Description: Paper-pencil free-response test in which students write a story about a given theme. The test yields information in six areas of writing competence: thematic maturity, spelling, vocabulary, word usage, style, and handwriting. The information is derived from an analysis of a sample of continuous writing, as well as from an analysis of subtest performance. Examiner required. Suitable for group use. Available in Spanish.

Untimed: Varies

Scoring: Examiner evaluated

Cost: Complete kit (examiner's manual, 50 student response sheets, 50 profile sheets) $50.00

Publisher: Pro-Ed

THE VOCABULARY GRADIENT TEST
Edgar M. VanVleck

Adolescent, adult

Purpose: Measures the size of an individual's vocabulary. Used with high school students and adults for placement or for personal information.

Description: 50-item paper-pencil multiple-choice test assessing the number of words known by an individual. Using an answer key provided, individuals can score their own tests and determine their percentile scores. Examiner/self-administered. Suitable for group use.

Untimed: 30 minutes

Scoring: Self-scored

Cost: Complete kit $6.00

Publisher: Polymath Systems

WOODCOCK LANGUAGE PROFICIENCY BATTERY (WLPB)
Refer to page 457.

===

WRITTEN LANGUAGE SYNTAX TEST
Sharon R. Berry

Hearing-impaired students   Grades K-12

Purpose: Measures hearing impaired students' command of the English language. Used for academic placement and evaluation of hearing impaired students.

Description: Multiple-item paper-pencil test assesing hearing impaired students' command of written syntax. The test includes three levels (1, 2, and 3) of assessment, as well as a preliminary exercise to determine which levels of the test are appropriate for a given student. The task that students perform entails viewing a picture, scanning a short list of randomly ordered English words, and using those words to form a sentence based on the picture. The manual includes information for administering and scoring the tests and interpreting the results. Picture stimuli are included on the test forms. Examiner required. Suitable for group use.

Untimed: Varies

Scoring: Examiner evaluated

Cost: Test kit (manual, one each of four levels of tests, one folder) $10.00; screening test (10 copies) $4.00; 10 tests (specify level) $6.00; 10 folders $4.00

Publisher: Gallaudet College Press

Academic Subjects: Fine Arts

FARNUM MUSIC TEST
Stephen Farnum

Adolescent   Ages 10-16

Purpose: Measures student musical achievement and ability as a way of helping teachers distinguish individuals with talent from those without.

Description: Multiple-item paper-pencil test covering music symbols, notation, tonal patterns, and cadence. The symbol section measures eye-focus speed and reaction speed to stimuli. The notation section measures the ability to differentiate between written notes and different notes played on the piano. With tonal patterns, the student identifies which of four tones has been changed. In the cadence section, the student indicates whether a tone should rise or fall to complete a musical phrase. Materials include a 16-page manual for testing, scoring, and selecting beginning band members; a 12-inch LP phonograph record; answer sheets; and correction keys. Examiner required. Suitable for group use.

Untimed: 40-45 minutes

Scoring: Hand key

Cost: Test kit $12.75; 100 answer sheets $12.00

Publisher: Bond Publishing Company

FARNUM STRING SCALE
Stephan Farnum

Child, adolescent
Grades 4-12

Purpose: Measures student performance and progress playing stringed instruments. Used to place individuals in orchestras.

Description: Performance test in which the student is presented with a series of musical exercises of increasing difficulty to sight-read. The performance level is recorded by noting the number of errors in the execution. Examiner required. Not suitable for group use.

Untimed: 10-15 minutes

Scoring: Examiner evaluated

Cost: Testing book $6.00; 100 score sheets $12.95

Publisher: Hal Leonard Publishing Corporation

Information and availability unconfirmed; no publisher response.

INDIANA-OREGON MUSIC DISCRIMINATION TEST
Newell H. Long

Child, adolescent
Grades 5 and above

Purpose: Assesses the development of a student's musical taste. Used in music appreciation classes.

Description: Multiple-item paper-pencil test in which the examiner plays a 12-inch LP record, and the students listen and record their responses on an answer sheet. Examiner required. Suitable for group use.

Untimed: 25-45 minutes

Scoring: Hand key

Cost: Complete (12-inch LP, manual, 3 answer sheets, 2 scoring keys) $12.50

Publisher: Midwest Music Tests

INSTRUMENT TIMBRE PREFERENCE TEST
Edwin E. Gordon

Ages 9 and older

Purpose: Assesses the timbre preference of students ages 9 and older. Used to help students select appropriate brass or woodwind instruments.

Description: Multiple-item paper-pencil test identifying the timbre preferences of students. Students listen to different melodic synthesized sounds on a cassette recording and indicate their preferences on an answer sheet. Results help students choose instruments that match their timbre preferences, which improves the performance of beginning band students and reduces dropout rates. Examiner required. Suitable for group use.

Untimed: 30 minutes

Scoring: Hand key; may be machine scored

Cost: Complete kit (cassette, 100 test sheets, scoring masks, manual) $35.00

Publisher: G.I.A. Publications

INTERMEDIATE MEASURES OF MUSIC AUDIATION
Edwin E. Gordon

Child   Grades 1-4

Purpose: Measures the music aptitude of children in Grades 1-4.

Description: Multiple-item paper-pencil test measuring and discriminating among the music aptitudes of children who obtained exceptionally high scores on the Primary Measures of Music Audiation. The test requires no language or music skills. Children listen to tonal and rhythm tape recordings, decide if pairs of patterns are the same or different, and circle an appropriate picture on the answer sheet. The manual contains information on converting raw scores to percentile ranks, interpreting results, and formal and informal music instruction suggestions. Examiner required. Suitable for group use.

Untimed: 24 minutes

Scoring: Hand key

Cost: Complete kit $57.00

Publisher: G.I.A. Publications

KWALWASSER MUSIC TALENT TEST
Jacob Kwalwasser

Grades 4-college

Purpose: Measures musical aptitude.

Description: 50-item aurally administered paper-pencil test assessing musical talent. Form A consists of 50 three-tone patterns, which are repeated with variation in pitch, tone, rhythm, or loudness. Alternate Form B (40 items) presents the same features in a more simplified form. A record player and an examiner are required. Suitable for group use.

Timed: 10 minutes

Scoring: Hand key; examiner evaluated

Cost: Contact publisher

Publisher: Belwin-Mills Publishing Corporation

MODERN PHOTOGRAPHY COMPREHENSION
Martin M. Bruce

Adolescent, adult

Purpose: Assesses knowledge of photography. Used for vocational guidance and as a measure of classroom progress.

Description: 40-item paper-pencil multiple-choice test measuring photographic understanding. Individuals are rated on a scale of superior, high average, average, and low average. Materials include a manual and grading keys. Self-administered. Suitable for group use.

Untimed: 20-25 minutes

Scoring: Hand key

Cost: 25 tests $25.75; manual $1.50; keys $1.10

Publisher: Martin M. Bruce, Ph.D., Publishers

MUSICAL APTITUDE PROFILE
Edwin Gordon

Child, adolescent
Grades 4-12

Purpose: Assesses the basic musical needs, abilities, and aptitudes of elementary and high-school students.

Description: 250-item paper-pencil test consisting of seven subtests arranged in three musical categories: tonal imagery (melody, harmony), rhythm imagery (tempo, meter) and musical sensitivity (phrasing, balance, style). Test items consist of short musical selections (played by professional artists) administered via audiotape. Scores are provided for each of the seven subtests. Examiner required. Suitable for group use.

Untimed: 110 minutes

Scoring: Examiner evaluated

Cost: Complete Musical Aptitude Profile (three full-track 7½ ips tapes on 7-inch open-recorder reels, manual, 100 MRC answer sheets, scoring masks, 100 record file folders, 100 musical talent profiles, two class record sheets) $170.52

Publisher: The Riverside Publishing Company

MUSICAL APTITUDE TESTS—MUSAT J AND MUSAT S

Child, adolescent

Purpose: Assesses musical aptitude. Used for educational evaluation.

Description: Two tests of musical ability. MUSAT J (Standards 1 to 5) measures ability to perceive seven aspects of music: interval, harmony, timbre, rhythm, duration, speed, and counting units. MUSAT S (Standards 6 to 10) measures 10 aptitudes: interval, harmony, timbre, rhythm, duration, speed, counting, loudness of tone, intonation, and selective listening. Materials include records containing music especially composed for this test. A record player is required for test administration. Groups should not contain more than 20 students. Examiner required. Suitable for group use.
SOUTH AFRICAN PUBLISHER

Untimed: Junior 1½ hours; Senior 2½ hours

Scoring: Hand key; examiner evaluated

Cost: (In Rands) Junior—complete kit (container and 2 records) 8,90; 10 answer sheets 10,90; 10 answer sheets 2 0,80; scoring stencils 1,80; manual 3,90; Senior—complete kit (container and 3 records) 11,20; 10 answer sheets I or II 0,70 each; scoring stencils 2,20; manual 3,90; orders from outside The RSA will be dealt with on merit

Publisher: Human Sciences Research Council

THE OHIO VOCATIONAL ACHIEVEMENT TESTS IN GRAPHICS COMMUNICATION: COMMERICAL ART
Refer to page 724.

PRIMARY MEASURES OF MUSIC AUDIATION (K-3)
Edwin E. Gordon

Child   Grades K-3

Purpose: Measures the music aptitude of students in Grades K-3.

Description: Multiple-item paper-pencil test diagnosing the musical potential of students with average to low musical aptitudes. The test requires no language or music skills. Children listen to tonal and rhythm tape recordings, decide if pairs of tonal or rhythm patterns sound the same or different, and circle an appropriate picture on the answer sheet. The manual contains information on converting raw scores to percentile ranks, interpreting results, and formal and informal music instruction. Examiner required. Suitable for group use.

Untimed: 24 minutes

Scoring: Hand key

Cost: Complete kit $57.00

Publisher: G.I.A. Publications

SEASHORE MEASURES OF MUSICAL TALENTS
C.E. Seashore

Grades 4-adult

Purpose: Assesses abilities fundamental to the development of musical proficiency.

Description: Six auditorily presented tests measuring aspects of auditory discrimination: Pitch, Loudness, Time, Timbre, Rhythm, and Tonal Memory. Scores are relatively unrelated to the amount of an individual's formal musical training. Materials include audio test stimulus on a record or reel-to-reel tape. Examiner required. Suitable for group use.

Untimed: 1 hour

Scoring: Hand key

Cost: Complete set (audio stimulus, 50 IBM 805 answer documents, key, manual), record version $65.00; tape version reel-to-reel $75.00

Publisher: The Psychological Corporation

SIMONS MEASUREMENTS OF MUSIC LISTENING SKILLS

Child   Grades 1-3

Purpose: Measures attainment of music listening objectives common to most primary-school music curricula.

Description: Multiple-item nonverbal criterion-referenced test of nine separate music listening objectives. All instructions and test items are tape recorded. Set includes a manual, five cassette recordings, 30 answer booklets, overhead transparencies of test pages, and a scoring mask. Examiner required. Suitable for group use.

Timed: Three 25-minute periods

Scoring: Hand key

Cost: $119.25

Publisher: Stoelting Company

WATKINS-FARNUM PERFORMANCE SCALE
Stephan Farnum and John Watkins

**Child, adolescent
Grades 4-12**

Purpose: Measures student performance and progress in playing musical instruments. Used to place individuals in musical groups.

Description: Multiple-item performance test in which the student is presented a

series of musical exercises of increasing difficulty to sight-read. The performance level is recorded by noting the number of errors in the execution. A second version, Form B, provides a different set of exercises. Examiner required. Not suitable for group use.

Untimed: 10-15 minutes

Scoring: Examiner evaluated

Cost: Testing book $9.00; 100 score sheets $7.00

Publisher: Hal Leonard Publishing Corporation

Information and availability unconfirmed; no publisher response.

Academic Subjects: Foreign Language and English as a Second Language

AATG FIRST LEVEL TEST

High-school and college students

Purpose: Measures knowledge of basic German. Used with secondary and college-level students.

Description: 70-item paper-pencil test assessing understanding of the German language by secondary-school students completing one year of study and by college or university students completing one semester of study. Examiner required. Suitable for group use.

Untimed: 1 hour

Scoring: Hand key

Cost: $1.75 per copy

Publisher: AATG (American Association of Teachers of German)

AATG NATIONAL GERMAN EXAMINATION FOR HIGH SCHOOL STUDENTS

Adolescent   Grades 9-12

Purpose: Measures German language achievement of high-school students in their second, third, and fourth year of study. Used to place transfer students, assess the progress of students and entire classes, and compare the results of various teaching methods.

Description: Multiple-item paper-pencil test assessing the German language competency of high-school students. Test sections include listening comprehension (via tape cassette), grammar, situational questions (testing reading as well as conversational skills), and comprehension of connected passages of approximately 200 words each. The questions in each section are of graded difficulty. The tests are administered once a year in January and may be administered in school or at an AATG chapter test center. In-school testing is accomplished under the direct supervision of the school's testing or guidance personnel. In the interest of security, all parts of the test must be returned (answer sheets are sent to American College Testing, and the test booklets and tapes are returned to the AATG Administrative Offices). Teachers who are unable or who prefer not to have their students tested in school may have their students tested at a chapter test center. ACT will send Regional Chairpersons (list available) a copy of all test orders submitted from their chapter area. Regional Chairpersons will establish chapter test centers and inform teachers who have requested this service when and where testing is to occur. Students are eligible to take the test designed for the level on which they are studying at the time of test administration. Students who take a test below their current level of work, or take more than one test, will be excluded from any awards program. ACT returns scores to test administrators and regional chairpersons in February. A total score, as well as scores for each section of the test, are provided. Practice tests are available. Examiner required. Suitable for group use.

Timed: 1 hour

Scoring: All tests scored by American College Testing (ACT) Program

Cost: $3.00 per student

Publisher: AATG (American Association of Teachers of German)

BASIC INVENTORY OF NATURAL LANGUAGE (BINL)
Refer to page 618.

THE BER-SIL SPANISH TESTS: ELEMENTARY TEST
Marjorie L. Beringer

Child   Ages 4-12

Purpose: Assesses the functioning level of children ages 4-12 in their own language.

Description: Multiple-item paper-pencil response test assessing receptive vocabulary and the ability to respond to directions. Writing samples, geometric figures, and figure drawing are included in the test. Directions are on cassette tape. Available in Spanish, Mandarin, Cantonese, Tagalog, Ilocano, Korean, and Persian translations. Examiner required. Not suitable for group use.

Untimed: 30 minutes

Scoring: Hand key

Cost: Complete kit $45.00

Publisher: The Ber-Sil Company

THE BER-SIL SPANISH TESTS: SECONDARY TEST
Marjorie L. Beringer

Adolescent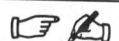

Purpose: Assesses Spanish-language abilities of junior and senior high-school students.

Description: Multiple-item paper-pencil test covering Spanish vocabulary, grammar, spelling, and punctuation, as well as basic mathematics processes and ability to draw a figure. The test is administered with cassette tape instructions. It is useful for curriculum planning and academic counseling. Available in Ilocano and Tagalog translations. Examiner required. Not suitable for group use.

Untimed: 20-30 minutes

Scoring: Hand key

Cost: Complete kit $45.00

Publisher: The Ber-Sil Company

BILINGUAL ORAL LANGUAGE TEST: BOLT-ENGLISH AND BOLT-SPANISH
Sam Cohen, Roberto Cruz, and Raul Bravo

Adolescent   Grades 7-12

Purpose: Measures English and Spanish oral language skills. Determines a student's level of bilingualism. Used for academic placement and planning and for reporting accurate results on enrollment and language dominance to federal and state agencies.

Description: Two multiple-item oral-response tests assessing oral language skills in English (BOLT-English) or Spanish (BOLT-Spanish). The tests assess oral language skills from simple sentence patterns to more complex syntactical forms of the language. Students are classified into one of four language categories: non-English/Spanish-speaking, very limited English/Spanish-speaking, limited English/Spanish-speaking, English/Spanish-speaking. The two tests are independent components of the same instrument and based on the same organization. Results of both tests are combined to determine a student's level of bilingualism. The summary page is used to record the level of bilingualism and to organize data for enrollment and language dominance reports. The test may be used on a pre/posttest basis to determine gain of proficiency in English and/or Spanish. Information concerning the results of field testing are presented in the technical reports. Examiner required. Not suitable for group use.

Untimed: 6 minutes

Scoring: Examiner evaluated

Cost: Classroom packets-English or Spanish (manual, picture booklet, 30 answer sheets, class record chart) $25.00; bilingual test summary page $0.50; technical reports $1.75

Publisher: Bilingual Media Productions, Inc.

BILINGUAL SYNTAX MEASURE (BSM)
Marina K. Burt, Heidi C. Dulay, and Eduardo Hernandez

Child, adolescent Grades K-12

Purpose: Measures children's mastery of basic oral syntactic structures in both English and Spanish. Used for diagnosis and placement in bilingual and other special language programs.

Description: Multiple-item measure testing strengths and weaknesses in basic language construction by using cartoon-type pictures and simple questions to elicit natural speech patterns. The test also places pupils in a proficiency level category (in both English and Spanish). Scores may be used for determining English readiness or program exit in bilingual and other special programs. The test is available on two levels: BSMI for Grades K-2 and BSMII for Grades 3-12. The manual provides proficiency ratings and equivalent Lau categories established by federal guidelines. Examiner required. Not suitable for group use. Available in English and Spanish.

Untimed: 10-15 minutes

Scoring: Hand key

Cost: Complete set (picture booklet, 35 English child/student response booklets, English manual, 35 Spanish child/student response booklets, Spanish manual, class records, technical handbook, expanding envelope) BSMI $123.00; BSMII $132.00

Publisher: The Psychological Corporation

BILINGUAL TWO LANGUAGE BATTERY OF TESTS
Adolph Caso

All ages

Purpose: Measures language proficiency in English and five native languages: Spanish, Italian, Portuguese, Vietnamese, and French. Assesses language dominance and determines point of bilinguality. Used with students and adults at any level of language proficiency for academic placement and evaluation and to determine LAU categories.

Description: Battery of criterion-referenced paper-pencil and oral response tests comparing proficiency in English with proficiency in any of five native languages. Tests for all languages consist of four parts (although the content in English is not necessarily the same as that in the native languages): phonetics (letter recognition and spelling), comprehension situations (opposites, similarities, comparisons, reading, and listening), writing sentences related to pictures, and an optional supplement measuring oral language proficiency (questions related to Limited English Proficiency Students). Students listen to directions presented on a pre-recorded tape (English on one side and the native language on the other) and write their answers in the student booklet of the appropriate language. The native language test is given first and the English test must be administered within two weeks. The battery may be administered at any time during the year, but optimal administration is in two sessions per school year (spring-fall) for three consecutive years. Results for both language tests are recorded on the student score profiles card, which includes the following charts: composite scores, proficiency levels, language dominance, point of bilinguality, and LAU category. A cassette player is required. Examiner required. Suitable for group use.

Timed: English test 21 minutes; native language test 21 minutes

Scoring: Examiner evaluated

Cost: Contact publisher

Publisher: Branden Press

CRANE ORAL DOMINANCE TEST (CODT)
Barbara J. Crane

Child, adolescent
Grades PreK-12

Purpose: Determines whether a student has a dominant language (Spanish/English) or is bilingual. Used to help instructors prescribe appropriate instructional materials and helps identify bilingual special education students.

Description: Multiple-item oral-response test identifying which language a student retains best, English or Spanish. The examiner reads from four (preschool) to eight (school age) words. Some of the words are in English and some are in Spanish. The student responds by repeating as many words as he can remember. Based on the results of 64 word-pair sets, the student is classified as monolingual non-English, dominant non-English, functionally bilingual, dominant English, or monolingual English. Examiner required. Not suitable for group use.

Untimed: 20 minutes

Scoring: Examiner evaluated

Cost: Complete for 30 pupils $32.07 (test booklets, score sheets, manual)

Publisher: Crane Publishing Co.

DOS AMIGOS VERBAL LANGUAGE SCALES
Donald E. Critchlow

Child, adolescent
Ages 5-13

Purpose: Measures a child's ability to understand English and Spanish words. Used to determine dominant language proficiency so that primary-language instruction, ESL programs, or remediation may be planned.

Description: 85-item verbal test in English and Spanish consisting of 85 word scales and their opposites. The examiner dictates each stimulus word, and the examinee responds with a word which has the opposite meaning. So that the test can be used in other English-speaking countries, words that have unique American-English spellings are excluded. The examiner must be fluent in English and Spanish. Not suitable for group use.

Untimed: 20 minutes

Scoring: Hand key

Cost: Manual $6.00; 25 recording forms $6.00

Publisher: United Educational Services, Inc.

EL CIRCO 1980
Educational Testing Service

Child   Grades PreK-1

Purpose: Identifies Spanish-speaking children's instructional needs in the areas of language and math. Used to evaluate early childhood bilingual curricula.

Description: Four paper-pencil tests assessing the language and mathematics skills of Spanish-speaking children. The Language Check is a pretest that determines whether the child's Spanish proficiency is sufficient to complete the exam. Para Quyge Sirven Las Palabras is a 38-item measure of the child's receptive language skills in Spanish. What Words Are For is a 30-item measure of receptive language skills in English. Cuyganto y Cuygantos is a 39-item measure of mathematical skills (counting, relationships, and numerical concepts). Examiner required. Suitable for group use.

Untimed: 15-30 minutes

Scoring: Hand key

Cost: Specimen set (copy of each measure, administration directions, and user's guide) $10.50

Publisher: CTB/McGraw-Hill

EMPORIA FIRST YEAR LATIN TEST
Bernadine Sitts, Lillian Wall,
Minnie M. Miller,
and Merritt W. Sanders

Adolescent   Grades 10-12

Purpose: Assesses high-school students' achievement in first-year Latin courses. Used as a first- or second-semester exam.

Description: 85-item paper-pencil test of Latin forms, syntax, derivatives, and simple paragraphs for comprehension. Examiner required. Suitable for group use.

Timed: 40 minutes

Scoring: Hand key

Cost: Test $0.15; manual $0.20; key $0.20

Publisher: Bureau of Educational Measurements

EMPORIA SECOND YEAR LATIN TEST
Bernadine Sitts, Lillian Wall,
Minnie M. Miller,
and Merritt W. Sanders

Adolescent   Grades 10-12

Purpose: Assesses the achievement of high-school students in second-year Latin courses. Used as a first- or second-semester exam.

Description: 90-item paper-pencil test of vocabulary, forms, syntax, derivatives, background material, and reading comprehension. Examiner required. Suitable for group use.

Timed: 40 minutes

Scoring: Hand key

Cost: Test $0.15; manual $0.20; key $0.20

Publisher: Bureau of Educational Measurements

ENGLISH FIRST AND SECOND LANGUAGE TESTS

All ages

Purpose: Measures understanding of English as a first or second language. Used for educational placement and guidance.

Description: 19 separate paper-pencil tests of English comprehension for each standard or level of pupil. Particular subtests vary but generally include Language Usage, Vocabulary, Reading Comprehension, and Spelling. Two alternate forms, A and B, are available for each standard. Examiner required. Suitable for group use.

SOUTH AFRICAN PUBLISHER

Untimed: Not available

Scoring: Hand key; examiner evaluated

Cost: Contact publisher; orders from outside The RSA will be dealt with on merit

Publisher: Human Sciences Research Council

EXAMINATION IN STRUCTURE
Charles Fries and Robert Lado

Adult

Purpose: Assesses problem areas in English grammar. Used with adult nonnative speakers of English.

Description: 150-item paper-pencil test of the basic structures of English grammar. Approximately 65% of the questions are multiple-choice; the remaining questions are completion items that test question words, negation, and sentence order. Three forms (A, B, C) are available while current supplies last. No manual or norms exist for the test. Examiner required. Suitable for group use.

Timed: 60 minutes

Scoring: Hand key

Cost: Specimen set (test booklet, answer sheet, scoring stencil) $5.00

Publisher: English Language Institute

FIRST YEAR FRENCH TEST
Minnie M. Miller and
Jean M. Leblon

Adolescent   Grades 10-12

Purpose: Assesses high-school students' achievement in first-year French courses. Used as an end-of-course exam.

Description: 100-item paper-pencil test of vocabulary, pronunciation, structure, and reading. Examiner required. Suitable for group use.

Timed: 50 minutes

Scoring: Hand key

Cost: Test $0.15; manual $0.20; key $0.20

Publisher: Bureau of Educational Measurements

FIRST YEAR SPANISH TEST
Oscar F. Hernandez and
Minnie M. Miller

Adolescent   Grades 10-12

Purpose: Assesses high-school students' achievement in first-year Spanish courses. Useful as an end-of-course exam.

Description: 100-item paper-pencil test of vocabulary, pronunciation, structure, and reading. Examiner required. Suitable for group use.

Timed: 50 minutes

Scoring: Hand key

Cost: Test $0.15; manual $0.20; key $0.20

Publisher: Bureau of Educational Measurements

FRENCH COMPREHENSION TESTS
H.C. Barik

Child   Grades 1-8

Purpose: Measures French listening comprehension. Used with students involved in French immersion programs or intensive French programs at early grade levels.

Description: 45-item paper-pencil multiple-choice test assessing listening comprehension in French. The answer choices are presented in picture form. The test consists of three sections: words and sentences, questions, and stories. Separate test manuals for the Primer (K) level and Level 1 are available. An optional reel-to-reel tape is available for test administration. Examiner required. Suitable for group use.
CANADIAN PUBLISHER

Untimed: 40 minutes

Scoring: Hand key

Cost: 35 Primer level tests $23.25; tape $16.00 (specify test); 35 Level 1 tests $25.85; manual (specify test) $6.00 (Canadian exchange)

Publisher: The Ontario Institute for Studies in Education

ILYIN ORAL INTERVIEW TEST
Donna Ilyin

Adolescent, adult
Grades 10 and above

Purpose: Measures the ability of secondary and adult students to communicate accurately in English. Used to assess abilities in English as a first or second language.

Description: 50-item verbal test in which the examiner shows paired pictures to the student, asks questions about them, and requires the student to respond, enabling the examiner to assess student comprehension and ability to use proper English grammar. Examiner required. Not suitable for group use.

Untimed: 30 minutes

Scoring: Examiner evaluated

Cost: Contact publisher

Publisher: Newbury House Publishers, Inc.

JAPANESE PROFICIENCY TEST (JPT)

Students, adult

Purpose: Evaluates American or other English-speaking students' level of proficiency in Japanese. Used for measuring achievement in language programs.

Description: 130-item multiple-choice paper-pencil test measuring two aspects of proficiency in Japanese: reading comprehension and Japanese character recognition. The stimulus material for the listening comprehension section is recorded in standard modern Japanese. Audio equipment is required for the listening comprehension stimulus material. Examiner required. Suitable for group use.

Timed: 2 hours

Scoring: Computer scored

Cost: $15.00 per examinee

Publisher: Educational Testing Service

LADO TEST OF AURAL COMPREHENSION
Robert Lado

Nonnative English speakers

Purpose: Measures nonnative English speakers' understanding of spoken English.

Description: 60-item paper-pencil multiple-choice test measuring nonnative English speakers' understanding of spoken English. The examinee chooses from picture responses for 20 items and from

written phrases or short sentences for the remaining 40 items. Three parallel forms (A, B, C), each accompanied by a tape recording, are available while current supplies last. Examiner required. Suitable for group use.

Timed: 40 minutes

Scoring: Hand key

Cost: Specimen set (examiner's booklet, test booklet, answer sheet, scoring stencil) $5.00; tape for administering test (specify A, B, C) $15.00

Publisher: English Language Institute

LANGUAGE ASSESSMENT BATTERY
Staff of the New York City Board of Education

Child, adolescent Grades K-12

Purpose: Assesses students' verbal abilities in English and/or Spanish. Identifies Spanish-speaking students who cannot participate effectively in English-speaking classrooms and provides a comparable measure of their communication skills in Spanish. Used for academic evaluation and placement of Spanish-speaking students.

Description: Multiple-item paper-pencil and oral response subtests measuring students' achievement of basic language skills: reading, writing, listening, comprehension, and speaking. The battery is available in an English edition and a Spanish edition. Test item difficulties are low in order to differentiate among students in the lower quartile. All items in both editions were carefully reviewed for vocabulary load, grammatical construction, appropriateness of Spanish usage, racial and gender bias, and correctness of item content. Both editions are presented in three levels: Level I for Grades K-2, Level II for Grades 3-6, and Level III for Grades 7-12. All Level I subtests are individually administered. The speaking subtests for Levels II and III are individually administered in order for the teacher to accommodate regional differences in vocabulary usage or dialect. The use of criterion-referenced interpretation and locally developed cut-off scores is recommended. Test development and related research are described in the technical manual. Examiner required. Levels II and III (except the speaking subtests) are suitable for group use.

Untimed: 41 minutes per edition

Scoring: Hand key

Cost: 35 Level I test booklets (specify English or Spanish Edition), examiner's directions, picture stimulus booklet $14.31; 35 Level II or Level III test booklets (specify edition), examiner's directions, picture stimulus card $25.26; 35 Digitek answer sheets (specify level and edition) $11.73; Digitek scoring masks (specify Spanish Levels II or III, English Levels II or III) $2.49; 250 NCS answer sheets $83.40; technical manual $7.20; examination kit $14.73

Publisher: The Riverside Publishing Company

LANGUAGE PROFICIENCY TEST (LPT)
Refer to page 632.

LANGUAGE PROFICIENCY TESTS (LPT)—1972

Adolescent

Purpose: Measures language proficiency. Used for educational placement and diagnosis.

Description: Multiple-item paper-pencil test of proficiency in English and Afrikaans. Separate materials are available for Standards 9 and 10. Examiner required. Suitable for group use.

Timed: 2½ hours

Scoring: Hand key; examiner evaluated

Cost: (In Rands) test (specify Standard 9 or 10) 0,40; manual 2,30; scoring stencil (specify Standard 9 or 10) 0,90; 10 answer sheets 0,60; orders from outside The RSA will be dealt with on merit

Publisher: Human Sciences Research Council

LISTENING COMPREHENSION GROUP TEST (LCGT)
Donna Ilyin

Adolescent, adult
Ages 14-85

Purpose: Measures the ability of nonnative speakers of English to comprehend and write English. Used as an aid to student placement, screening, and diagnosis.

Description: Two-part verbal-picture paper-pencil test used in English as a Second Language (ESL) and bilingual programs. The picture test (LCPT) measures listening comprehension by requiring the subject to look at a picture or series of pictures. The examiner makes a statement about each picture and then asks questions. The subject answers each question by selecting one of three pictures and either "yes" or "no," which are written on a separate piece of paper. The written test (LCWT) is intended for intermediate and advanced ESL students. Students look at a picture series, listen to a story, look at other related pictures, listen to the examiner's questions, and write one-sentence answers. Examiner required. Suitable for group use.

Untimed: Picture test 30 minutes; written test 45 minutes

Scoring: Hand key

Cost: Contact publisher

Publisher: Newbury House Publishers, Inc.

MICHIGAN TEST OF AURAL COMPREHENSION
John Upshur

Adult

Purpose: Measures an individual's understanding of spoken English. Used to predict the academic success of nonnative speakers of English.

Description: 90-item paper-pencil multiple-choice test of aural comprehension in which the student hears either a question or a statement and responds by marking the appropriate written answer choice. Three alternate forms (1, 2, 3), each accompanied by a tape recording, are

---

available. The test may be used in conjunction with the Michigan Test of English Language Proficiency. These materials are retired, nonsecure components of the Michigan Test Battery and should not be used for admission or placement purposes. Examiner required. Suitable for group use.

Timed: 25 minutes

Scoring: Hand key

Cost: Specimen set (examiner's manual, scoring stencil, test booklet, answer sheet) $5.00

Publisher: English Language Institute

MICHIGAN TEST OF ENGLISH LANGUAGE PROFICIENCY
John Upshur

Adult

Purpose: Assesses an individual's facility with the English language. Used to predict the academic success of advanced proficiency adult nonnative speakers of English.

Description: 100-item paper-pencil multiple-choice test of grammar, reading comprehension, and vocabulary. Available in eight alternate forms (D, E, F, G, H, J, K, L). These materials are retired, nonsecure components of the Michigan Test Battery and should not be used as an admission or placement test. Examiner required. Suitable for group use.

Timed: 1 hour, 15 minutes

Scoring: Hand key

Cost: Specimen set (includes manual, scoring stencil, test booklet, answer sheet) $5.00

Publisher: English Language Institute

MODERN LANGUAGE APTITUDE TEST (MLAT)
J.B. Carroll and S.M. Sapon

Adolescent, adult
Grades 9 and above

Purpose: Assesses the ease with which students will learn a foreign language.

Description: Five-part series of exercises in learning various aspects of language: number learning (aural), phonetic script

(audio-visual), spelling clues, words in sentences, and paired associates. The number learning and phonetic script exercises require the use of a reel-to-reel or cassette tape recorder. The spelling clues, words in sentences, and paired associates exercises may be used together as a Short Form. Materials include test tapes with instructions and auditory stimuli. Examiner required. Suitable for group use.

Untimed: Short form 30 minutes; complete test 1 hour

Scoring: Hand key; may be machine scored

Cost: Examination kit (test, IBM 805 answer document and key, practice exercise sheet, manual) $6.50; reel-to-reel tape $23.00; cassette tape $23.00; 25 test booklets $12.00; 50 IBM 805 answer documents $14.00

Publisher: The Psychological Corporation

MODERN LANGUAGE ASSOCIATION COOPERATIVE FOREIGN LANGUAGE TESTS
Educational Testing Service/MLA

Adolescent, adult
Grades 10 and above

Purpose: Measures a student's competency in French, German, Italian, Russian, or Spanish. Used for student evaluation and curriculum planning.

Description: Four subtests measuring a student's knowledge of common speech and writing structures and the receptive and productive aspects of vocabulary and idiom. The four subtests and the concepts they measure are the Listening Test (25 minutes), measuring understanding of taped statements, conversations, passages, and dramatic scenes; the Speaking Test (10 minutes), assessing fluency, pronunciation, and intonation; the Reading Test (35 minutes), measuring vocabulary and understanding of idiomatic expression; the Writing Test (35 minutes), requiring the student to fill in blanks, rewrite sentences, and rewrite paragraphs. The tests are available on two levels: L and M. Level L is used during the first and second years of language instruction in high school or the first and second semesters in college. Level M can be used during the third and fourth years of instruction in high school or the third and fourth semesters in college. Examiner required. Suitable for group use.

Timed: 1 hour, 45 minutes

Scoring: Hand key; examiner evaluated; may be computer scored

Cost: Specimen set, specify language (test books, handbook, norms, directions for administration and scoring, scoring key, and student bulletin) $8.95

Publisher: CTB/McGraw-Hill

ORAL LANGUAGE EVALUATION (OLE)
Nicholas J. Silvaroli, Jann T. Skinner, and J.O. "Rocky" Maynes

Child

Purpose: Assesses the English and Spanish language development of bilingual children. Used for academic planning and placement. Used by teachers with limited language evaluation experience and/or structural linguistic training.

Description: Multiple-item oral-response test assessing English and Spanish oral-language skills. Development is classified along a 6-point continuum of language development: labeling, basic sentences, language expansion, connecting-relating-modifying, storytelling-concrete, and storytelling-abstract. Part I (assessment) establishes a beginning oral language level in either English or Spanish. Part II (diagnosis) identifies pre-post test data and specific language responses that pinpoint specific oral language needs. Part II (prescription) provides the teacher with general and specific instructional activities and/or suggestions for helping students develop their oral language. Examiner required. Not suitable for group use.

Untimed: Varies

Scoring: Examiner evaluated

Cost: Manual $7.95

Publisher: EMC Publishing

PIMSLEUR LANGUAGE APTITUDE BATTERY
Paul Pimsleur

Child, adolescent
Grades 6-12

Purpose: Assesses aptitude for learning languages. Used for screening potential foreign language students and grouping for instruction.

Description: Battery of tests assessing aptitude for learning modern languages. The six parts include information on the student's grade-point average, interest in studying a foreign language, verbal ability, and auditory ability. Materials include a test tape providing auditory stimuli for Parts 5 and 6. Examiner required. Suitable for group use.

Untimed: 50-60 minutes

Scoring: Hand key; computer scoring service available

Cost: Specimen set (manual, test, class record, IBM 805 and 1230 answer documents) $8.00; basic scoring services $0.85 per student

Publisher: The Psychological Corporation

SECOND YEAR FRENCH TEST
Minnie M. Miller and Jean M. Leblon

Adolescent   Grades 10-12

Purpose: Assesses the achievement of high-school students in second-year French courses. Used as an end-of-course exam.

Description: 100-item paper-pencil test of vocabulary, pronunciation, structure, reading, and simple facts about France. Examiner required. Suitable for group use.

Timed: 50 minutes

Scoring: Hand key

Cost: Test $0.15; manual $0.20; key $0.20

Publisher: Bureau of Educational Measurements

---

foreign language and english as a second language

SECOND YEAR SPANISH TEST
Minnie M. Miller and
Oscar F. Hernandez

Adolescent, adult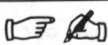

Purpose: Assesses knowledge of Spanish language and culture. Used to measure achievement in high-school and college students.

Description: Paper-pencil multiple-choice test of Spanish vocabulary, structure, and reading, as well as simple facts about Spain and Spanish America. Examiner required. Suitable for group use.

Timed: 40 minutes

Scoring: Hand key

Cost: Test $0.15; manual $0.20; key $0.20

Publisher: Bureau of Educational Measurements

SECONDARY LEVEL ENGLISH PROFICIENCY TEST (SLEP)
Educational Testing Service

Adolescent   Ages 12-17

Purpose: Assesses English language proficiency of nonnative speakers. Used as an admissions test by private secondary schools and as a placement test by both public and private secondary schools.

Description: 150-item paper-pencil test measuring two components of English proficiency: listening comprehension and reading comprehension (structure and vocabulary). The test does not measure productive language skills. A tape recorder is required to administer the listening comprehension sections. A cassette tape is included. Examiner required. Suitable for group use.

Timed: 1 hour, 20 minutes

Scoring: Hand key

Cost: Complete kit (reusable materials, 25 test booklets, 100 answer sheets, 1 cassette, 2 keys, manual) $100.00; specimen set (test booklet, answer sheet, tape, manual) $9.00

Publisher: Educational Testing Service

SPANISH AND LATIN AMERICAN LIFE AND CULTURE
Minnie M. Miller and Beulah Aiken

Adolescent
Grades 10 and above

Purpose: Assesses high-school and college students' achievement in Spanish and Latin American life and culture. Used as an end-of-course exam for Spanish classes.

Description: 100-item paper-pencil test covering Spanish and Latin American life and culture, including geography, history, art, literature, and customs. Examiner required. Suitable for group use.

Timed: 40 minutes

Scoring: Hand key

Cost: Test $0.15; manual $0.20; key $0.20

Publisher: Bureau of Educational Measurements

SPANISH/ENGLISH READING AND VOCABULARY SCREENING TEST (SERVS)

Child   Grades 1-4

Purpose: Determines whether a student's dominant language is English or Spanish. Used as a pretest to determine whether a student should be tested with a Spanish or English version of an achievement test.

Description: Multiple-item paper-pencil test indentifying which version, Spanish or English, of an achievement test is more appropriate for administering to a student. Three forms of the test are available. Form BC is designed for screening students in Grades 1-2. Form HS (Hand-Scorable) is designed primarily for third-grade students, who mark their answers in the test book. Form MS (Machine-Scorable) is designed for students in Grade 4 or above. Developed for use with CTBS—Espanol. Examiner required. Suitable for group use.

Untimed: Varies

Scoring: Hand key; may be computer scored

Cost: Multi-level examination kit (hand-scorable test books for Forms BC and HS, Form MC test book for use with answer sheet, CompuScan answer sheet, answer keys, technical report, examiner's manual) $14.25

Publisher: CTB/McGraw-Hill

TEST OF AURAL PERCEPTION FOR JAPANESE STUDENTS
Robert Lado

Japanese-speaking students

Purpose: Measures Japanese-speaking students' ability to detect the significant phonemic contrasts of English.

Description: Paper-pencil test diagnosing a student's ability to discriminate between various sounds in the English language. It is similar to the Test of Aural Perception for Latin-American Students, but it deals with the specific pronunciation problems common to Japanese speakers. The test is available while current supplies last. Examiner required. Suitable for group use.

Timed: 50 minutes

Scoring: Hand key

Cost: Examiner's booklet $4.00; 100 answer sheets $4.00

Publisher: English Language Institute

TEST OF AURAL PERCEPTION FOR LATIN-AMERICAN STUDENTS
Robert Lado

Latin American students

Purpose: Measures Latin American students' ability to detect the significant phonemic contrasts of English.

Description: Paper-pencil test diagnosing the ability of Latin American students to discriminate between various sounds in the English language. Useful for teachers of English who want to identify special class or individual pronunciation problems. The test is available while current supplies last. Examiner required. Suitable for group use.

Timed: 50 minutes

Scoring: Hand key

Cost: Examiner's booklet 4.00; 100 answer sheets $6.00; set of 3 scoring stencils $5.00

Publisher: English Language Institute

TEST OF ENGLISH AS A FOREIGN LANGUAGE (TOEFL)
Educational Testing Service

Adult

Purpose: Assesses proficiency in English for nonnative speakers. Used as a college admission and placement test.

Description: 150-item multiple-choice test measuring three aspects of English ability: listening, structure and written expression, and reading comprehension and vocabulary. Items involve comprehension of spoken and written language. Institutional TOEFL is available by special arrangement with ETS. Examiner required. Suitable for group use.

Timed: 2 hours

Scoring: Computer scored

Cost: Saturday $27.00 per student; Friday $35.00 per student; overseas $29.00 and $37.00

Publisher: Educational Testing Service

TEST OF ENGLISH FOR INTERNATIONAL COMMUNICATION (TOEIC)
Refer to page 847.

TEST OF SPOKEN ENGLISH (TSE)
Educational Testing Service

Adult

Purpose: Assesses nonnative speakers' proficiency in spoken English. Used to evaluate applicants for graduate level teaching assistantships and for certification in health-related professions.

Description: 24-item test assessing nonnative speakers' proficiency in spoken English. A test tape and a test book are used as stimulus material. The subject's answers are taped and evaluated by two raters at ETS. The test yields scores in three areas: grammar, fluency, and pronunciation. The institutional version, the Speaking Proficiency English Assessment Kit (SPEAK), is available for local testing. Two additional test forms, SPEAK II and SPEAK III, are available. Examiner required. Suitable for group use.

Untimed: Not available

Scoring: Computer scored; examiner evaluated

Cost: $45.00 application fee per test; SPEAK test form and rater training materials $300.00; SPEAK II and III $75.00 each

Publisher: Educational Testing Service

TESTS OF BASIC LITERACY IN THE SOTHO LANGUAGE—1982

Adolescent, adult

Purpose: Measures literacy skills of adults and Higher Primary Level students. Used for educational and vocational guidance.

Description: Multiple-item tests of literacy skills in three South African languages: South Sotho, North Sotho, and Tswana. Each test covers three areas: reading comprehension of items related to practical knowledge, reading comprehension of continuous prose and a cursive letter, and writing skill from dictation. Two forms are available for each test. Examiner required. Not suitable for group use. SOUTH AFRICAN PUBLISHER

Untimed: 1½ hours

Scoring: Examiner evaluated

Cost: Contact publisher; orders from outside The RSA will be dealt with on merit

Publisher: Human Sciences Research Council

Academic Subjects: Industrial Arts

EMPORIA CLOTHING TEST
Margaret C. Parkman, Patricia Duncan, and Merritt W. Sanders

Adolescent   Grades 10-12

Purpose: Assesses clothing course achievement and knowledge. Used as an end-of-course exam.

Description: 100-item paper-pencil multiple-choice test measuring knowledge of construction, choice of materials, finishes, design, care and repair of clothing, and care and management of household furnishings. Examiner required. Suitable for group use.

Timed: 40 minutes

Scoring: Hand key

Cost: Test $0.15; manual $0.20; key $0.20

Publisher: Bureau of Educational Measurements

EMPORIA FOODS TEST
Margaret C. Parkman, Patricia Duncan, and Merritt W. Sanders

Adolescent   Grades 10-12

Purpose: Assesses the foods course knowledge of high-school students. Used as an end-of-course exam.

Description: 105-item paper-pencil test of food preparation, nutrient values, meal planning, marketing, care, and preservation. Examiner required. Suitable for group use.

Timed: 40 minutes

Scoring: Hand key

Cost: Test $0.15; manual $0.20; key $0.20

Publisher: Bureau of Educational Measurements

EMPORIA INDUSTRIAL ARTS TEST
Elton Amburn, David E. Hill, and Merritt W. Sanders

Adolescent   Grades 10-12

Purpose: Assesses the industrial arts achievement of high-school students. Used as an end-of-course exam.

Description: 80-item paper-pencil test of woodworking, wood finishing, sheet metal working, and welding. Examiner required. Suitable for group use.

Timed: 40 minutes

Scoring: Hand key

Cost: Test $0.15; manual $0.20; key $0.20

Publisher: Bureau of Educational Measurements

INDUSTRIAL ARTS APTITUDE TEST (WOODWORKING)
Dale Hogan, Elton Amburn, and Kevin Hogan

Adolescent, adult
Grades 7 and above

Purpose: Assesses the woodworking aptitude of junior-high, high-school, and college students.

Description: 50-item paper-pencil test covering knowledge of terms, concepts, problem-solving techniques, and outcomes relating to woodworking classes. Examiner required. Suitable for group use.

Timed: 45 minutes

Scoring: Hand key

Cost: Test $0.15; manual $0.20; key $0.20

Publisher: Bureau of Educational Measurements

MACQUARRIE TEST FOR MECHANICAL ABILITY
Refer to page 977.

MASTERY TEST IN CONSUMER ECONOMICS
Les Dlabay

Adolescent Grades 8-12

Purpose: Measures knowledge of major consumer economics topics as set forth in various state education agencies and professional organization curriculum guides.

Description: Multiple-item paper-pencil test measuring achievement in consumer economics. The topics covered include the individual consumer in the market place; the consumer in the economy; personal money management; consumer credit; wise use of credit; food buying; housing; transportation; furniture,

appliances, and clothing; personal and health services; banking services; saving and investments; insurance; taxes and government; and the consumer in society. Each test item is keyed to one of these 15 topics. The results identify concepts that have been mastered and those on which students perform poorly. The manual includes a scoring key. The scoring service provides three alphabetical lists, class analysis data, and one set of pressure-sensitive labels. Examiner required. Suitable for group use.

Timed: 40 minutes

Scoring: Hand scored; may be computer scored

Cost: Starter set (manual, 20 test booklets, 20 answer sheets) $24.00; scoring service $1.00 per pupil

Publisher: Scholastic Testing Service, Inc.

NM CONSUMER RIGHTS AND RESPONSIBILITIES TEST (NMCRRT)
S. P. Klein

Adolescent Grades 9-12

Purpose: Measures understanding of consumer rights and responsibilities. Used for program evaluation and needs assessment.

Description: 20-item paper-pencil multiple-choice test measuring a student's understanding of consumer protection laws, economic conditions and terms, insurance, purchase payment plans, personal finance, and product information. The test booklets are reusable, and a lay-over stencil is used for scoring. Reliability and norms have been determined from samples of ninth- and twelfth-grade secondary students. Examiner required. Suitable for group use.

Timed: 20 minutes

Scoring: Hand key

Cost: Specimen set $5.00; 35 tests $10.00; 35 answer sheets $3.00; scoring stencil $2.00; manual $2.00

Publisher: Monitor

industrial arts

STUDENT OCCUPATIONAL COMPETENCY ACHIEVEMENT TESTING (SOCAT)

Adolescent

Purpose: Measures students' achievement in vocational education programs. Used for grade assignment, identification of curriculum strengths and weaknesses, and evaluation of job applicants.

Description: Multiple-item tests of skills and knowledge in 26 vocational fields: accounting/bookkeeping, agricultural mechanics, auto body, auto mechanics, carpentry, commercial foods, computer programming, construction electricity, construction masonry, drafting, electronics, general merchandising, general office, graphic arts, heating and air conditioning, home entertainment equipment repairs, horticulture, industrial electricity, industrial electronics, machine trades, plumbing, practical nursing, refrigeration, sewn products, small engine repair, and welding. Each test consists of a written section and a performance section. The multiple-choice written section covers factual knowledge, technical information, understanding of principles, and problem-solving abilities related to the occupation. The performance section is administered in a laboratory, school shop, or clinical setting and enables students to demonstrate knowledge and skills of competent craft persons. Mental aptitude tests are available for administration at the same time as the competency test. Examiner required. Suitable for group use.

Timed: Varies, depending on test

Scoring: Scoring service provided

Cost: Contact publisher

Publisher: National Occupational Competency Testing Institute

STUDENT OCCUPATIONAL COMPETENCY ACHIEVEMENT TESTING: ACCOUNTING/ BOOKKEEPING

Adolescent

Purpose: Measures students' achievement in vocational accounting/

bookkeeping programs. Used for grade assignment, identifying curriculum strengths and weaknesses, and evaluating job applicants.

Description: Two-part test measuring accounting and bookkeeping skills and knowledge. The multiple-choice written test covers processing purchases and payables, sales and receivables, cash receipts and cash payments, processing payroll and related records, inventory, operating mechanical and electronic accounting devices, and completing the accounting cycle. The student completes either the secondary or postsecondary level to end the written portion of the test. The secondary level covers daily journal, partnerships, departmental accounting, automated departmental accounting, general accounting adjustments, and cost accounting. The postsecondary level covers intermediate accounting practices, stocks, bonds, and securities. The performance test measures abilities in six areas for each level. The secondary level includes journalizing business transactions, posting from specialized journals, payroll procedures, banking and banking procedures, worksheet and statement preparation, and locating source data. The postsecondary level includes banking and banking procedures, worksheet and statement preparation, locating source data, aging accounts receivable, determining net income/loss, and advanced journal entries. Examiner required. Suitable for group use.

Timed: Written test 3 hours, performance test 3 hours

Scoring: Scoring service provided

Cost: Contact publisher

Publisher: National Occupational Competency Testing Institute

STUDENT OCCUPATIONAL COMPETENCY ACHIEVEMENT TESTING: AGRICULTURE MECHANICS

Adolescent

Purpose: Measures students' achievement in vocational agriculture mechanics programs. Used for grade assignment, identifying curriculum strengths and weaknesses, and evaluating job applicants.

Description: Two-part test of skills and knowledge in agriculture mechanics. The multiple-choice written test covers orientation and safety, agricultural mechanic skills, agricultural power and machinery, agricultural electrical power and processing, agricultural structures, and soil and water management. The performance test measures abilities in shielded metal arc welding, oxycetylene cutting, wheel bearings, electrical installation, agricultural structures, and farm level. Examiner required. Suitable for group use.

Untimed: Written test 3 hours; performance test 3 hours

Scoring: Scoring service provided

Cost: Contact publisher

Publisher: National Occupational Competency Testing Institute

---

STUDENT OCCUPATIONAL COMPETENCY ACHIEVEMENT TESTING: AUTO BODY

Adolescent

Purpose: Measures students' achievement in vocational auto body programs. Used for grade assignment, identifying curriculum strengths and weaknesses, and evaluating job applicants.

Description: Two-part test of skills and knowledge in auto body. The multiple-choice written test covers soldering and brazing, safety, welding, hand tools and power tools, math and science, body preparation and painting, basic knowledge, terminology, and customer relations. The performance test measures abilities in welding, sheet metal repair, panel construction, and painting. Examiner required. Suitable for group use.

Timed: Written test 3 hours; performance test 3 hours

Scoring: Scoring service provided

Cost: Contact publisher

Publisher: National Occupational Competency Testing Institute

---

STUDENT OCCUPATIONAL COMPETENCY ACHIEVEMENT TESTING: AUTO MECHANICS

Adolescent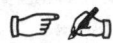

Purpose: Measures students' achievement in vocational auto mechanics programs. Used for assigning grades, identifying curriculum strengths and weaknesses, and evaluating job applicants.

Description: Two-part test of skills and knowledge in auto mechanics. The multiple-choice written test covers brakes, front end, engine repair, engine tune-up, automatic transmission, manual transmission/rear axle, electrical systems, and heating/air conditioning. The performance test measures abilities in brakes, inspection/lubrication, tune-up, and electrical systems. Examiner required. Suitable for group use.

Timed: Written test 3 hours; performance test 3 hours

Scoring: Scoring service provided

Cost: Contact publisher

Publisher: National Occupational Competency Testing Institute

---

STUDENT OCCUPATIONAL COMPETENCY ACHIEVEMENT TESTING: CARPENTRY

Adolescent

Purpose: Assesses knowledge and ability related to carpentry. Used for educational evaluation and employee screening.

Description: Multiple-item paper-pencil and task-performance test in two parts measuring competencies related to carpentry. The multiple-choice section (171 items) measures blueprint reading, preparation of specifications, building materials, hand and power tools, foundations, forms, rough framing, roof components, interior and exterior finish, and stair construction. The performance test measures layout of rafters, installation of door frames, engineer's transit, batter board elevation, stairway stringer, and sole plates. Examiner required. Suitable for group use.

Timed: Written test 3 hours; performance test 3 hours
Scoring: Scoring service provided
Cost: Contact publisher
Publisher: National Occupational Competency Testing Institute

STUDENT OCCUPATIONAL COMPETENCY ACHIEVEMENT TESTING: COMMERCIAL FOODS

Adolescent

Purpose: Assesses competencies related to commercial food service occupations. Used for educational evaluation and employee screening.

Description: Multiple-item paper-pencil and task-performance test in two parts measuring skills and knowledge related to food service and preparation. The multiple-choice written test (184 items) covers information on food preparation, food service occupations, sanitation, safety, equipment, service, purchasing, management skills, and specialty service. The performance test covers preparation of a cold salad, entree, quick bread, and table service. Examiner required. Suitable for group use.
Timed: Written test 3 hours; performance test 3 hours
Scoring: Scoring service provided
Cost: Contact publisher
Publisher: National Occupational Competency Testing Institute

STUDENT OCCUPATIONAL COMPETENCY ACHIEVEMENT TESTING: COMPUTER PROGRAMMING

Adolescent

Purpose: Measures competencies related to computer programming. Used for educational evaluation and employee screening.

Description: Multiple-item paper-pencil and task-performance test in two parts assessing knowledge and skills related to computer programming. The multiple-choice written test (150 items) measures general information, design, flowchart-

ing, operations, BASIC, COBOL, RPG, related mathematics, and problem solving. The performance test requires candidates to design a program, code it, test it, and output it. Examiner required. Suitable for group use.
Timed: Written test 3 hours; performance test 4 hours
Scoring: Scoring service provided
Cost: Contact publisher
Publisher: National Occupational Competency Testing Institute

STUDENT OCCUPATIONAL COMPETENCY ACHIEVEMENT TESTING: CONSTRUCTION ELECTRICITY

Adolescent

Purpose: Measures students' achievement in vocational construction electricity programs. Used for grade assignment, identifying curriculum strengths and weaknesses, and evaluating job applicants.

Description: Two-part test of skills and knowledge in construction electricity. The multiple-choice written test covers orientation; tools and equipment; blueprints; planning and layout; electronics; AC electricity; transformers; AC motors and starters; branch circuits; wiring methods; lighting, heating, and air conditioning; and low voltage. The performance test measures abilities in planning and layout, wiring methods, and service installation. Examiner required. Suitable for group use.
Timed: Written test 3 hours; performance test 3 hours
Scoring: Scoring service provided
Cost: Contact publisher
Publisher: National Occupational Competency Testing Institute

STUDENT OCCUPATIONAL COMPETENCY ACHIEVEMENT TESTING: CONSTRUCTION MASONRY

Adolescent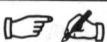

Purpose: Measures knowledge and skills related to construction masonry. Used for educational evaluation and employee screening.

Description: Multiple-item paper-pencil and task-performance test in two parts assessing competencies related to masonry. The multiple-choice written test (145 items) covers safety, tools and equipment, masonry materials, fastening devices, blueprint reading, interpretation of measurements, building site layout, construction methods, fireplace construction, maintenance of masonry structures, specialty construction areas of bricklaying, blocklaying, or stone masonry. The performance tests measure layout techniques, tools and equipment, building materials, construction techniques, and safety in choice of bricklaying, blocklaying, or stone masonry. Examiner required. Suitable for group use.

Timed: Written test 3 hours; performance test 3 hours, 15 minutes

Scoring: Scoring service provided

Cost: Contact publisher

Publisher: National Occupational Competency Testing Institute

STUDENT OCCUPATIONAL COMPETENCY ACHIEVEMENT TESTING: DRAFTING

Adolescent

Purpose: Measures students' achievement in vocational drafting programs. Used for grade assignment, identifying curriculum strengths and weaknesses, and evaluating job applicants.

Description: Two-part test of skills and knowledge in drafting. The multiple-choice written test covers interpretation of drawings, machine drawing, architectural drawing, mathematical calculations, electrical/electronic drawing, sheet metal drawing, mapping and cartography, and computer-assisted drawing. The performance test measures abilities in orthographic projection, auxiliary, threads, production/detail, and specialty areas. Examiner required. Suitable for group use.

Timed: Written test 3 hours; performance test 3 hours

Scoring: Scoring service provided

Cost: Contact publisher

Publisher: National Occupational Competency Testing Institute

STUDENT OCCUPATIONAL COMPETENCY ACHIEVEMENT TESTING: ELECTRONICS

Adolescent

Purpose: Measures students' achievement in vocational electronic programs. Used for grade assignment, identifying curriculum strengths and weaknesses, and evaluating job applicants.

Description: Multiple-item paper-pencil and task-performance test in two parts assessing knowledge and skills related to electronics. The 150-item multiple-choice test covers AC and DC circuits, solid-state circuits, digital circuits, and use of equipment. The performance test covers skills, including circuit construction, selection of components, tests and measurements, desoldering/soldering, economy of time, and safety. Examiner required. Suitable for group use.

Timed: Written test 3 hours; performance test 3 hours

Scoring: Scoring service provided

Cost: Contact publisher

Publisher: National Occupational Competency Testing Institute

STUDENT OCCUPATIONAL COMPETENCY ACHIEVEMENT TESTING: GENERAL MERCHANDISING

Adolescent

Purpose: Measures students' achievement in vocational general merchandising programs. Used for grade assignment, identifying curriculum strengths and weaknesses, and evaluating job applicants.

Description: Two-part test of skills and knowledge in general merchandising. The multiple-choice written test covers communication, human relations, merchandising, operations, management, and sales. The performance test measures abilities in the mechanics of completing a sale and handling money, human relations/communications, and product knowledge/selling. Examiner required. Suitable for group use.

Untimed: Written test 3 hours; performance test 40 minutes

Scoring: Scoring service provided

Cost: Contact publisher

Publisher: National Occupational Competency Testing Institute

STUDENT OCCUPATIONAL COMPETENCY ACHIEVEMENT TESTING: GENERAL OFFICE

Adolescent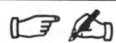

Purpose: Measures students' achievement in vocational general office programs. Used for grade assignment, identifying curriculum strengths and weaknesses, and evaluating job applicants.

Description: Two-part test of skills and knowledge in general office work. The multiple-choice written test covers typewriting and word processing, office procedures, communications, filing and records management, mail, computational skills, and interpersonal and employability skills. The performance test measures abilities in business correspondence, envelope preparation, tabulation, filing, machine calculation, and forms preparation. Examiner required. Suitable for group use.

Timed: Written test 3 hours; performance test 3 hours

Scoring: Scoring service provided

Cost: Contact publisher

Publisher: National Occupational Competency Testing Institute

STUDENT OCCUPATIONAL COMPETENCY ACHIEVEMENT TESTING: GRAPHIC ARTS

Adolescent

Purpose: Measures students' achievement in vocational printing programs. Used for grade assignment, identifying curriculum strengths and weaknesses, and evaluating job applicants.

Description: Two-part test of skills and knowledge in printing. The multiple-choice written test covers layout and design, composition, copy preparation, darkroom, stripping and platemaking, presswork, and finishing/paper. Three performance tests, which may be taken singly or in combination, are offered. The first test measures thumbnail sketches, rough and comprehensive layouts, typesetting, and paste-up. The second test measures line and half-tone negatives, stripping, proofing, and platemaking. The third test measures press preparation and clean up, printing, finishing operations, and packaging. Examiner required. Suitable for group use.

Timed: Written test 3 hours; performance tests 3 hours each

Scoring: Scoring service provided

Cost: Contact publisher

Publisher: National Occupational Competency Testing Institute

STUDENT OCCUPATIONAL COMPETENCY ACHIEVEMENT TESTING: HEATING AND AIR CONDITIONING

Adolescent

Purpose: Measures students' achievement in vocational heating and air conditioning programs. Used for grade assignment, identifying curriculum strengths and weaknesses, and evaluating job applicants.

Description: Two-part test of skills and knowledge in heating and air conditioning. The multiple-choice written test covers theory and fundamentals of air conditioning, oil heating, and gas heating; installation and service of air conditioning, oil heating, and gas heating equipment; electricity; solar heating; heat pumps; hydronic heating; psychometrics; and air movement. The performance test measures the ability to troubleshoot and repair a cooling and/or heating system and fabricate a heat exchanger. Examiner required. Suitable for group use.

Timed: Written test 3 hours; performance test 3 hours

Scoring: Scoring service provided

Cost: Contact publisher
Publisher: National Occupational Competency Testing Institute

STUDENT OCCUPATIONAL COMPETENCY ACHIEVEMENT TESTING: HOME ENTERTAINMENT EQUIPMENT REPAIR

Adolescent

Purpose: Measures students' achievement in vocational home entertainment equipment programs. Used for grade assignment, identifying curriculum strengths and weaknesses, and evaluating job applicants.

Description: Two-part test of skills and knowledge in home entertainment equipment. The multiple-choice written test covers basic skills, television receiver circuits, audio systems, radio receivers, tape players/recorders, television antennas, digital and logic circuits, safety, and customer services. The performance test measures the ability to perform color television setup procedures, diagnose and repair AM/FM receivers, and repair black and white televisions. Examiner required. Suitable for group use.
Timed: Written test 3 hours; performance test 2 hours, 45 minutes
Scoring: Scoring service provided
Cost: Contact publisher
Publisher: National Occupational Competency Testing Institute

STUDENT OCCUPATIONAL COMPETENCY ACHIEVEMENT TESTING: HORTICULTURE

Adolescent

Purpose: Measures achievement of students in vocational horticulture programs. Used for grade assignment, identifying curriculum strengths and weaknesses, and evaluating job applicants.

Description: Multiple-item paper-pencil and task-performance test of skills and knowledge related to horticulture. The multiple-choice written test (158 items) covers arboriculture, landscaping, nursery, turf, floriculture, floristry,

greenhouse management, vegetables, small fruit, and tree fruits. The performance test measures abilities in the same areas. Examiner required. Suitable for group use.
Timed: Written test 3 hours; performance test 3 hours
Scoring: Scoring service provided
Cost: Contact publisher
Publisher: National Occupational Competency Testing Institute

STUDENT OCCUPATIONAL COMPETENCY ACHIEVEMENT TESTING: INDUSTRIAL ELECTRICITY

Adolescent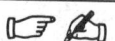

Purpose: Measures abilities related to industrial electricity. Used for educational evaluation and employee screening.

Description: Multiple-item paper-pencil and task-performance test in two parts assessing knowledge and skills related to industrial electricity. The multiple-choice written test (156 items) covers AC and DC current theory, test equipment, electrical drawings, general wiring, controls, generators, alternators, motors, and transformers. The performance test covers skills, including identification of tools and equipment, care and use of tools and equipment, diagrams, installation techniques, conduit, motor circuit, safety, and testing. Examiner required. Suitable for group use.
Timed: Written test 3 hours; performance test 3 hours
Scoring: Scoring service provided
Cost: Contact publisher
Publisher: National Occupational Competency Testing Institute

STUDENT OCCUPATIONAL COMPETENCY ACHIEVEMENT TESTING: INDUSTRIAL ELECTRONICS

Adolescent

Purpose: Measures students' achievement in vocational industrial electronics programs. Used for grade assignment, identifying curriculum strengths and weaknesses, and evaluating job applicants.

Description: Two-part test of skills and knowledge in industrial electronics. The multiple-choice written test covers basic theory, DC concepts, test equipment, AC concepts, vacuum tubes, solid state devices, power supplies and rectification, amplifier circuits and operation, digital electronics, and miscellaneous circuits and components. The performance test measures abilities in desolder PC board, component testing, oscilloscope, circuit timing, photosensitive transducer, logic circuit, and power supply. Examiner required. Suitable for group use.

Timed: Written test 3 hours; performance test 3 hours

Scoring: Scoring service provided

Cost: Contact publisher

Publisher: National Occupational Competency Testing Institute

---

STUDENT OCCUPATIONAL COMPETENCY ACHIEVEMENT TESTING: MACHINE TRADES

Adolescent

Purpose: Measures students' achievement in vocational machine trades programs. Used for grade assignment, identifying curriculum strengths and weaknesses, and evaluating job applicants.

Description: Two-part test of skills and knowledge in machine trades. The multiple-choice written test covers bench work, sawing, drilling, lathes, milling, grinding, and related theory. The performance test measures abilities in layout, measurement, drilling and hole forming, lathe operations, milling machine operations, bench work, and safety. Examiner required. Suitable for group use.

Timed: Written test 3 hours; performance test 5 hours

Scoring: Scoring service provided

Cost: Contact publisher

Publisher: National Occupational Competency Testing Institute

---

STUDENT OCCUPATIONAL COMPETENCY ACHIEVEMENT TESTING: PLUMBING

Adolescent

Purpose: Assesses competencies related to plumbing. Used for educational evaluation and employee screening.

Description: Multiple-item paper-pencil and task-performance test covering plumbing knowledge and skills. The multiple-choice written test (150 items) measures knowledge of assembly and layout, installation, planning, inspecting, evaluating, maintenance, and repair. The performance test measures drawing, layout, rough installation, and installation of a fixture. Examiner required. Suitable for group use.

Timed: Written test 3 hours; performance test 3 hours

Scoring: Scoring service provided

Cost: Contact publisher

Publisher: National Occupational Competency Testing Institute

---

STUDENT OCCUPATIONAL COMPETENCY ACHIEVEMENT TESTING: PRACTICAL NURSING

Adolescent

Purpose: Measures students' achievement in vocational practical nursing programs. Used for grade assignment, identifying curriculum strengths and weaknesses, and evaluating job applicants.

Description: Two-part test of skills and knowledge in practical nursing. The multiple-choice written test covers anatomy and physiology, medical/surgical nursing, basic nursing, maternal and child health, and personal/vocational relationships. The performance test measures abilities in making an occupied bed, taking vital signs, demonstrating sterile technique/indwelling catheter, administration of oral medication, administration of an intramuscular injection, administration of subcutaneous medication, tube feeding, perineal care, collection of clean catch/midstream urine specimen, and transferring patients from a bed to a wheelchair. Examiner required. Suitable for group use.

Timed: Written test 3 hours; performance test 3 hours

Scoring: Scoring service provided

Cost: Contact publisher

Publisher: National Occupational Competency Testing Institute

---

STUDENT OCCUPATIONAL COMPETENCY ACHIEVEMENT TESTING: REFRIGERATION

Adolescent

Purpose: Measures students' achievement in vocational refrigeration programs. Used for grade assignment, identifying curriculum strengths and weaknesses, and evaluating job applicants.

Description: Two-part test of skills and knowledge in refrigeration. The multiple-choice written test covers nomenclature; valves, gauges, controls; electricity; related math and science; installation and service; and safety. The performance test is divided into three parts measuring different aspects of troubleshooting and repairing refrigeration systems. Examiner required. Suitable for group use.

Timed: Written test 3 hours; performance test 3 hours

Scoring: Scoring service provided

Cost: Contact publisher

Publisher: National Occupational Competency Testing Institute

---

STUDENT OCCUPATIONAL COMPETENCY ACHIEVEMENT TESTING: SEWN PRODUCTS

Adolescent

Purpose: Measures students' achievement in vocational sewn product programs. Used for grade assignment, identifying curriculum strengths and weaknesses, and evaluating job applicants.

Description: Two-part test of skills and knowledge in sewn products occupations. The multiple-choice written test covers textiles, pressing, industrial sewing methods, operation of equipment, fitting garments, altering finished garments, and construction. The performance test measures abilities in machine usage, industrial sewing machine maintenance, industrial sewing methods, garment construction methods, taking body measurements, pattern alterations, and alteration of finished garments. Examiner required. Suitable for group use.

Timed: Written test 3 hours; performance test 3 hours

Scoring: Scoring service provided

Cost: Contact publisher

Publisher: National Occupational Competency Testing Institute

---

STUDENT OCCUPATIONAL COMPETENCY ACHIEVEMENT TESTING: SMALL ENGINE REPAIR

Adolescent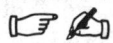

Purpose: Measures students' achievement in vocational small engine repair programs. Used for grade assignment, identifying curriculum strengths and weaknesses, and evaluating job applicants.

Description: Two-part test of skills and knowledge in small engine repair. The multiple-choice written test covers ignition, fuel, governors, starters, valves-ports-exhaust, engine block components-cooling, compression-lubrication, powered equipment mechanisms, shop procedures-safety, and theory-shop arithmetic. The performance test measures abilities in checking engine, checking and measuring parts, valve service, carburetor service, ignition service, invoicing parts, and use of time. Examiner required. Suitable for group use.

Timed: Written test 3 hours; performance test 3 hours

Scoring: Scoring service provided

Cost: Contact publisher

Publisher: National Occupational Competency Testing Institute

---

STUDENT OCCUPATIONAL COMPETENCY ACHIEVEMENT TESTING: WELDING

Adolescent

Purpose: Measures students' achievement in vocational welding programs. Used for grade assignment, identifying curriculum strengths and weaknesses, and evaluating job applicants.

Description: Two-part test of skills and knowledge in welding occupations. The multiple-choice written test covers welding terms and symbols, electricity, basic metallurgy, shielded-metal arc welding, oxyfuel welding, gas metal arc welding, gas tungsten arc welding, and safety. The performance test measures abilities in oxyacetylene welding and brazing, shielded metal arc welding, gas metal arc welding, and gas tungsten arc welding. Examiner required. Suitable for group use.

Timed: Written test 3 hours; performance test 3 hours

Scoring: Scoring service provided

Cost: Contact publisher

Publisher: National Occupational Competency Testing Institute

Academic Subjects: Mathematics: Basic Math Skills

ARITHMETIC TEST A/8

Adolescent, adult

Purpose: Measures general arithmetic ability.

Description: Multiple-item paper-pencil test assessing arithmetic skills. Norms are available on request. Examiner required. Suitable for group use.
SOUTH AFRICAN PUBLISHER

Timed: 30-40 minutes

Scoring: Hand key

Cost: (In Rands) 25 booklets 15,00; key 0,40

Publisher: National Institute for Personnel Research

ASSESSMENT IN MATHEMATICS
R. W. Strong and
Somerset Local Education Authority

Child, adolescent

Purpose: Assesses the mathematics competencies of primary and lower secondary students. Determines readiness to progress to new work.

Description: 86 multiple-item paper-pencil graded test sheets assessing student abilities in areas of work common to most instructional mathematics programs: number measure, probability and statistics, shape, and relations. The test sheets are printed as reproducible photocopy masters, providing a flexible assortment of graded tests for use in conjunction with existing instructional programs. The teacher's book provides the background to the tests, objectives and information for each test, and scoring procedures, including reduced reproductions of the pupils' sheets with correct answers indicated. Record cards are available for systematically recording each child's achievement and progress. Examiner required. Suitable for group use.

Untimed: Varies

Scoring: Examiner evaluated

Cost: Teacher's book, 86 pupils' sheets £16.95; 25 record cards £5.95

Publisher: Macmillan Education

ASSESSMENT OF SKILLS IN COMPUTATION (ASC)
CTB/McGraw-Hill

Child, adolescent
Grades 7-9

Purpose: Diagnoses a student's computation skill strengths and needs and identifies instructional prescriptions referenced to those needs. Used by junior high-school teachers.

Description: 72-item paper-pencil test in two sections measuring the computational skills students require to handle activities typically encountered at school and home and in community situations (i.e., reading a graph, buying records on sale, measuring shelves, or redecorating a room). The test is administered in two sections. Examiner required. Suitable for group use.

Timed: 50 minutes per session

Scoring: Hand key; may be computer scored

Cost: Specimen set (test book, manual, a machine-scorable and a hand-scorable answer sheet, class summary sheet, objectives matrix, text reviewer's guide) $8.95

Publisher: CTB/McGraw-Hill

BASIC MATHEMATICS TESTS SERIES

Child, adolescent
Ages 7-15

Purpose: Measures understanding of basic mathematical principles. Used for diagnosing individual children's abilities.

Description: Five paper-pencil tests measuring understanding of fundamental relationships and processes in mathematics. Test A (40 items), for ages 6-8, measures a range of math skills. Test B (40 items), for ages 8-9, assesses more complex relationships. Test C (50 items), for ages 9-10, covers area, graphical representation, symmetry, inequality, elementary knowledge of sets, and decimals and fractions. Test DE, for ages 10-12, covers symmetry, tabulation, fractions, elementary algebra, basic spatial ability, and graphical representation. Test FG (55 items), for ages 12-14, covers a wide range of mathematical thinking. Examiner required. Suitable for group use.
BRITISH PUBLISHER

Untimed: 1 hour

Scoring: Hand key

Cost: Specimen set primary (pupils Forms A, B, C, DE and manual) £3.30; specimen set secondary (pupils Forms DE, FG and manuals) £3.30 (payment in sterling for all overseas orders)

Publisher: NFER-NELSON Publishing Company Ltd.

BASIC NUMBER DIAGNOSTIC TEST
W.E.C. Gillham

Child   Ages 5-9

Purpose: Measures number skills of children ages 5-7 and of older children who are deficient in the use of numbers. Diagnoses children's strengths and weaknesses so that specific teaching objectives can be determined. Suitable for all children scoring below a 7½-year reading age on the Basic Number Screening Test.

Description: Multiple-item paper-pencil and oral-response test covering the basic number skills that a normally developing 7-year-old child should have mastered. The test items are arranged in approximate order of difficulty within 12 categories of skills progressing from reciting, copying, and writing numbers to dealing with simple addition and subtraction. The format allows close observation of the child's strategies and errors, thus providing a basis for remedial assistance. The test should be administered at regular intervals so that a child's progress can be charted and teaching requirements revised. Where appropriate, both test and retest items are provided. Approximate age-norms are provided. Examiner required. Not suitable for group use.
BRITISH PUBLISHER

Untimed: 15-20 minutes

Scoring: Examiner evaluated

Cost: Specimen set £1.60; 20 tests £4.60; manual £1.05

Publisher: Hodder & Stoughton

BASIC NUMBER SCREENING TEST
W.E.C. Gillham and K.A. Heese

Child   Ages 7-12

Purpose: Evaluates children's basic number skills. Used for survey and screening purposes. Identifies children needing further testing and possible remedial attention.

Description: Multiple-item paper-pencil test measuring proficiency with numbers and understanding of number concepts.

Two parallel forms, A and B, may be used simultaneously to minimize the risk of copying and for test-retest programs. Norms are presented as Number Ages (7:0 to 12:0). The manual contains instructions for administering and scoring the test. Examiner required. Suitable for group use. BRITISH PUBLISHER

Untimed: 30 minutes

Scoring: Hand key

Cost: Specimen set £2.00; 20 tests (specify form) £2.45; manual £1.05

Publisher: Hodder & Stoughton

BASIC SKILLS TEST—MATHEMATICS ELEMENTARY-FORMS A AND B
IOX Assessment Associates

Child   Grades 5-6

Purpose: Measures student's end-of-elementary school achievement in basic mathematics skills. Used for minimum competency testing, determination of grade promotion, or program evaluation.

Description: 30-item paper-pencil test measuring a student's performance in basic calculations with whole numbers, fractions, and decimals; word problems requiring single arithmetic operations and measurement units; and interpreting tables and graphs. This test preceeds the IOX Basic Skill Test—Mathematics Secondary Level. Examiner required. Suitable for group use.

Untimed: 30-45 minutes

Scoring: Hand key; may be computer scored

Cost: 25 BM-A2 $37.50; 25 BM-B2 $37.50; teacher's guide BM-G2 $3.95; test manual BTM-2 $3.95; 50 BA-2 answer sheets $6.95

Publisher: IOX Assessment Associates

BASIC VISUAL-MOTOR ASSOCIATION TEST
Refer to page 558.

BASICS OF OPERATIONS (GRADES 1-3)
B.J. Beeson and Sam Adams

Child   Grades 1-3

Purpose: Measures the ability of third- and fourth-grade students to add and subtract. Used to assess student progress and determine remedial needs.

Description: 335-item paper-pencil test measuring basic knowledge of addition and subtraction, as well as readiness for multiplication and division. The teacher reads the directions/questions in the beginning sections. Other sections may be completed independently. Examiner required. Suitable for group use.

Untimed: 30 minutes

Scoring: Examiner evaluated

Cost: Contact publisher

Publisher: Dr. Charles Sauls

Information and availability unconfirmed; no publisher response.

COMMON FRACTIONS
Sam Adams

Child, adolescent
Grades 6-8

Purpose: Measures the ability of students in Grades 5-8 to work with common fractions. Diagnoses individual needs in this area.

Description: 172-item paper-pencil test measuring 49 concepts and computational skills necessary for understanding and working with common fractions. The student may complete the entire test or that portion related to a particular operation. Examiner required. Suitable for group use.

Untimed: 45 minutes

Scoring: Examiner evaluated

Cost: Contact publisher

Publisher: Dr. Charles Sauls

Information and availability unconfirmed; no publisher response.

DECIMAL FRACTIONS
B. J. Beeson and
Lionel O. Pellegrin

Child, adolescent
Grades 6-8

Purpose: Measures the ability of students in Grades 5-8 to work with decimal fractions. Diagnoses individual needs in this area.

Description: 129-item paper-pencil test measuring 43 concepts and computational skills required to understand and work with decimal fractions. Examiner required. Suitable for group use.

Untimed: 45 minutes
Scoring: Examiner evaluated
Cost: Contact publisher
Publisher: Dr. Charles Sauls
Information and availability unconfirmed; no publisher response.

DIAGNOSTIC ABILITIES IN MATH (D.A.M. TEST)
Francis T. Sganga

Slow learners

Purpose: Measures knowledge of basic mathematics. Used for student placement and remediation.

Description: 220-item paper-pencil test in two sections. Part I is a timed test with 160 problems testing instant recall of fundamentals of addition, subtraction, multiplication, and division. Part II is a diagnostic test consisting of 60 problems covering whole numbers, fractions, and decimals. Examiner required. Suitable for group use.

Timed: Part I 30 minutes; Part II 3 hours
Scoring: Hand key
Cost: 10 test booklets, teacher instructions, answer key $22.95
Publisher: Mafex Associates, Inc.
Information and availability unconfirmed; no publisher response.

DIAGNOSTIC MATH TESTS

Child, adolescent

Purpose: Assesses skills in arithmetic.

Used for determining nature of specific pupil problems.

Description: Three paper-pencil tests of math ability: Diagnostic Arithmetic Tests (Standards 2 to 8); Diagnostic Tests in Basic Algebra (Standards 7 and 8); and Mathematics Tests, Diagnostic, Primary Level (Standards 1 to 5). Each test is divided into subtests. Aspects tested by the Diagnostic Tests in Basic Algebra are basic operations; simple algebraic expressions and linear equations; sets; exponents; number systems; ratio, rate, and proportion; substitution; and factors. Examiner required. Suitable for group use.

SOUTH AFRICAN PUBLISHER

Untimed: Not available
Scoring: Hand key; examiner evaluated
Cost: Contact publisher; orders outside The RSA will be dealt with on merit
Publisher: Human Sciences Research Council

DIAGNOSTIC MATHEMATICS INVENTORY (DMI)
John K. Gessell

Child, adolescent
Grades 1.5-7.5

Purpose: Assesses a student's mastery of mathematics. Used for providing diagnostic information for teachers and for prescribing group and individual learning activities.

Description: Multiple-item paper-pencil multiple-choice tests assessing a student's mastery of 325 objectives taught in traditional and contemporary mathematics courses. Each item tests one objective. The test is divided into seven overlapping levels spanning Grades 1.5-7.5. Recommended grade ranges are Level A, Grades 1.5-2.5; Level B, Grades 2.5-3.5; Level C, Grades 3.5-4.5; Level D, Grades 4.5-5.5; Level E, Grades 5.5-6.5; Level F, Grades 6.5-7.5; and Level G, Grades 7.5 and beyond for remedial students. Materials include practice exercises, a learning activities guide, and a guide to ancillary materials. Examiner required. Suitable for group use.

Untimed: Not available

Scoring: Hand key; may be computer scored

Cost: Multi-level examination kit $24.00; specimen set, specify level (test book, answer sheet, manual, practice exercises, teacher's guide, product overview, interim evaluation test)

Publisher: CTB/McGraw-Hill

DIAGNOSTIC SCREENING TEST: MATH, THIRD EDITION (DSTM)
Thomas D. Gnagey

Child, adolescent
Grades 1-10

Purpose: Determines a student's conceptual and computational mathematical skills.

Description: Multiple-item paper-pencil test in two sections: Basic Processes Section and Specialized Section. The Basic Processes Section consists of 36 items arranged developmentally within four major areas: addition skills, subtraction skills, multiplication, and division. Each area yields a separate Grade Equivalent Score and Consolidation Index Score and scores in nine supplemental categories: process, sequencing, simple computation, special manipulations, use of zero decimals, simple fractions, and manipulation in fractions. The Specialized Section consists of 37-45 items evaluating conceptual and computational skills in five areas: money, time, percent, U.S. Measurement, and Metric Measurement. The examiner explains the procedure and student completes the problems. The test is available in alternate forms, A and B. Examiner required. Suitable for group use.

Untimed: 5-20 minutes

Scoring: Hand key

Cost: Manual, 25 Form A, 25 Form B $25.00

Publisher: Slosson Educational Publications, Inc.

DIAGNOSTIC TEST OF ARITHMETIC STRATEGIES (DTAS)
Herbert P. Ginsburg and Steven C. Mathews

Child

Purpose: Evaluates the strategies grade-school children use to solve basic arithmetic problems. Used to plan instructional programs.

Description: Multiple-item paper-pencil test measuring the procedures children use to perform arithmetic calculations in addition, subtraction, multiplication, and division. Results provide a profile of each student's faulty calculational strategies and potential strengths. The examiner's manual includes an extensive section dealing with interpretation of test results, as well as suggested remedial approaches. Examiner required. Suitable for group use.

Untimed: Varies

Scoring: Examiner evaluated

Cost: Complete kit (examiner's manual; 25 addition, subtraction, multiplication, and division answer sheets; student worksheets) $55.00

Publisher: Pro-Ed

DIAGNOSTIC TESTS AND SELF-HELPS IN ARITHMETIC
Leo J. Brueckner

Child, adolescent
Grades 3-12

Purpose: Diagnoses and helps remediate specific weaknesses in fundamental arithmetic skills.

Description: Multiple-item paper-pencil set of four screening tests and 21 diagnostic tests of arithmetic skills. The four screening tests, which cover whole numbers, fractions, decimals, and arithmetic, identify specific tests for diagnosing difficulties. A self-help exercise accompanies each of the diagnostic tests (addition facts, subtraction facts, multiplication facts, uneven division facts, addition of whole numbers, subtraction of whole numbers, multiplication of whole numbers, division by two-place numbers, regrouping fractions, addition of like fractions, addition of unlike fractions, subtraction of unlike fractions, multiplication of fractions, division of fractions, addition of decimals, subtraction of decimals, multiplication of decimals, division of decimals, percent, and operations with measures). Examiner required. Suitable for group use.

Untimed: Varies

Scoring: Hand key

Cost: Specimen set $14.25

Publisher: CTB/McGraw-Hill

DMI MATHEMATICS SYSTEMS (DMI/MS)
CTB/McGraw-Hill

Child, adolescent
Grades K-8.9

Purpose: Identifies students' strengths in mathematics and diagnoses specific instructional needs.

Description: Multiple-item paper-pencil test measuring four strands of mathematics content: whole numbers, fractions, and decimals, measurement and geometry, and problem-solving and special topics. Each content area can be measured at two levels of specificity: category objectives assessment level and instructional objectives assessment level. The system is available on seven grade levels: Level A (Grades K.6-1.5), Level B (Grades 1.6-2.5), Level C (Grades 2.6-3.5), Level D (Grades 3.6-4.5), Level E (Grades 4.6-5.5), Level F (Grades 5.6-6.5), and Level G (Grades 6.6-8.9). The system is available in two formats. System, the graded approach, assesses skills by level, and materials are packaged according to the seven grade levels. System 2, the multigraded approach, assesses skills across levels, and materials are packaged according to the four strands of mathematics content. Examiner required. Suitable for group use.

Untimed: Not available

Scoring: Hand key; may be computer scored

Cost: Contact publisher

Publisher: CTB/McGraw-Hill

EARLY MATHEMATICAL LANGUAGE
Margaret K.R. Williams and Heather J. Somerwill

Child

Purpose: Assesses children's capacity to understand and use mathematical language. Used for preventive testing in the first years of schooling and for diagnostic testing with older children who are known to have difficulties in mathematics.

Description: Six multiple-item paper-pencil pupil test booklets assessing student knowledge and use of mathematical language in the following areas: position in space, weight and shape, number, volume and capacity, length, and time. The books are completely nonverbal, containing picture story sequences about the adventures of a family of bears. The test items are designed to stimulate and assess the use of relevant mathematical language. The teacher's book provides guidelines on using the pupil books and making the assessments, as well as suggestions for follow-up remedial work. Key pages from the pupils' books (printed as spirit duplicator masters) are available as worksheets for use as part of the assessments or for follow-up work as suggested in the teacher's book. Examiner required. Suitable for group use.

Untimed: Varies

Scoring: Examiner evaluated

Cost: Teacher's book, 6 pupil books £6.95; 16 worksheets £6.95; 25 record sheets £2.95

Publisher: Macmillan Education

EARLY MATHEMATICS DIAGNOSTIC KIT
David Lumb

Child   Ages 4-8

Purpose: Identifies problems related to learning mathematics. Used by teachers and educational psychologists for developing prescriptive programs.

Description: Multiple-item oral-response test assessing a child's understanding of

---

mathematics-related concepts, including perception of color, shape, size, and space; counting; conservation of number; matching; classification; addition, subtraction, multiplication, and division; fractions; time; representation; and language. The test provides information on weaknesses in early mathematical experience and understanding that could impede progress in learning mathematics. Although designed for younger children, the test can be used with older children with specific learning difficulties in mathematics. Materials include a Book of Test Items, which contains 110 plates covering the major areas of the early mathematics curriculum, a set of 40 assorted colored cubes, and a set of 3 small boxes. Examiner required. Not suitable for group use. BRITISH PUBLISHER

Untimed: 30 minutes

Scoring: Hand key

Cost: Complete kit (Book of Test Items, manual, 25 record booklets, colored cubes, 3 small boxes) £51.75

Publisher: NFER-NELSON Publishing Company Ltd.

EMPORIA ELEMENTARY ARITHMETIC TEST
Patricia M. Pease and Merritt W. Sanders

Child   Grade 1

Purpose: Assesses the arithmetic achievement of first-grade students. Used as a first- or second-semester exam.

Description: 130-item paper-pencil test of fundamental operations and reasoning problems. Examiner required. Suitable for group use.

Timed: 40 minutes

Scoring: Hand key

Cost: Test $0.15; manual $0.20; key $0.20

Publisher: Bureau of Educational Measurements

EMPORIA INTERMEDIATE ARITHMETIC TEST
Ruth Otterstrom and Merritt W. Sanders

Child   Grades 4-6

Purpose: Assesses the arithmetic achievement of elementary-school students. Used as a first- or second-semester exam.

Description: 130-item paper-pencil test of computation, comprehension, and problem solving. Examiner required. Suitable for group use.

Timed: 50 minutes

Scoring: Hand key

Cost: Test $0.15; manual $0.20; key $0.20

Publisher: Bureau of Educational Measurements

EMPORIA JUNIOR HIGH SCHOOL ARITHMETIC TEST
Ieleen Engleson and Merritt W. Sanders

Adolescent   Grades 7-9

Purpose: Assesses the arithmetic achievement of junior high-school students. Used as a first- or second-semester exam.

Description: 130-item paper-pencil test of computation, problem solving, and concepts. Examiner required. Suitable for group use.

Timed: 50 minutes

Scoring: Hand key

Cost: Test $0.15; manual $0.20; key $0.20

Publisher: Bureau of Educational Measurements

EMPORIA PRIMARY ARITHMETIC TEST
Patricia M. Pease and Merritt W. Sanders

**Child, adolescent
Grades 2-8**

Purpose: Assesses the arithmetic achievement of elementary-school students. Used as a first- or second-semester exam.

Description: 130-item paper-pencil test of basic arithmetic skills. Examiner required. Suitable for group use.

Timed: 20 minutes

Scoring: Hand key

Cost: Test $0.15; manual $0.20; key $0.20

Publisher: Bureau of Educational Measurements

THE ENRIGHT® DIAGNOSTIC INVENTORY OF BASIC ARITHMETIC SKILLS
Brian E. Enright

Child   Grades 1-9   

Purpose: Measures basic arithmetic computation skills and determines individual error patterns for skill-specific corrective instruction. Used for academic placement and to plan remedial instruction programs and establish IEPs for students with special arithmetic needs.

Description: Four sets of multiple-item paper-pencil tests assessing 144 arithmetic skills arranged in 13 computation skill sections: addition, subtraction, multiplication, and division of whole numbers, fractions, and decimals and conversion of fractions. The wide-range placement test (26 items) is available in two equivalent forms, A and B. The skill placement tests, one test for each of the 13 skill sections, are available in two alternate forms, A and B. The four basic facts tests (50 items each) measure basic facts in addition, subtraction, multiplication, and division. The skill tests contain five items for each of the 144 skills assessed. The examiner administers only the skill placement tests indicated by the wide-range placement test or the student's current classroom problems and then administers only the skill tests indicated by the student's performance on the skill placement tests. An instructional objective is listed for each of the 144 skills and the error patterns associated with that skill. Error analysis leads directly to planning and development of remedial instruction. An arithmetic record book, class record sheet, and individual progress reports are

available. A video tape for in-service training of examiners is available. Examiner required. Suitable for group use.

Untimed: Varies

Scoring: Examiner evaluated

Cost: Tester manual with 10 student tests and arithmetic record books $85.00

Publisher: Curriculum Associates, Inc.

ESSENTIAL MATHEMATICS
L.M. Bental

Child, adolescent   
Ages 7-14

Purpose: Assesses mathematics skills. Used to diagnose specific mathematics deficiencies and plan remedial activities.

Description: Multiple-item paper-pencil tests measuring knowledge important in the learning of mathematics. The topics covered are conservations, sets, the four rules, place value, fractions, decimals, time, and length. The tests are not age-normed, and they emphasize the evaluation of specific tasks. The test booklet may be retained for future reference. Examiner required. Not suitable for group use.

BRITISH PUBLISHER

Untimed: 30 minutes

Scoring: Hand key; examiner evaluated

Cost: 10 tests £4.20; manual £2.10 (payment in sterling for all overseas orders)

Publisher: NFER-NELSON Publishing Company Ltd.

GRADED ARITHMETIC-MATHEMATICS TEST, METRIC EDITION
P.E. Vernon and K.M. Miller

Child, adolescent   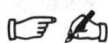
Ages 6-16

Purpose: Measures children's arithmetic and mathematics skills. May be used with the visually impaired.

Description: Multiple-item paper-pencil test measuring achievement in arithmetic and mathematics. The test is available in a Junior Form (ages 6-12) and a Senior Form (ages 11-16). The manual provides relevant technical data and full instruc-

tions for administering the test, including an "oral" version for use with the visually impaired. The answers are clearly presented to facilitate scoring, and advice is given on the acceptability of various alternative forms of response. Norms are provided as mathematics ages (5:0-17:1) and as deviation quotients (for chronological ages 5.3-18 +). Examiner required. Suitable for group use.
BRITISH PUBLISHER

Untimed: 30 minutes

Scoring: Hand key

Cost: Specimen set £2.10; 20 tests (specify form) £2.45; manual £1.35

Publisher: Hodder & Stoughton

GROUP MATHEMATICS TEST: SECOND EDITION
Dennis Young

Child   Ages 6.5-8.10

Purpose: Measures children's mathematical understanding.

Description: Multiple-item paper-pencil test measuring simple mathematical skills and understanding. The item content of this second edition is the same as the first edition. The revised manual provides new norms and slightly revised instructions for administration. Separate tables of quotients are provided to cover a wide range of ability, from infants (ages 6.5-7.10) to first-year juniors (ages 6.5-7.10) to less able pupils up to age 12.10. Examiner required. Suitable for group use.
BRITISH PUBLISHER

Untimed: Not available

Scoring: Examiner evaluated

Cost: Specimen set £1.95; 20 tests (specify form) £2.00; manual £1.35

Publisher: Hodder & Stoughton

INDIVIDUALIZED CRITERION REFERENCED TESTING (ICRT)
Refer to page 400.

INDIVIDUALIZED CRITERION REFERENCED TESTING— MATHEMATICS (ICRT—MATH)
Dale E. Strotman and Margaret T. Steen

Child, adolescent
Grades 1-9

Purpose: Assesses mathematics performance of students. Provides information on skills mastered, skills for review, and skills to learn. Also used in adult basic education.

Description: Multiple-item paper-pencil power tests measuring student knowledge of operations, fractions, measurement, geometry, decimals and percentages, and special topics. The tests are based on a developmental continuum of 384 learning objectives for Grades 1-9. The tests are designed to be taken at each student's instructional level rather than grade level. The tests correlate to more than 115 math programs. Objectives are matched with current curricula and the content of newer textbooks. The results indicate resources for teaching and reinforcing skills, list names of all students who need instruction in each skill, and aid in grouping students according to their specific learning needs. Materials provide for interim testing and recording of progress. A program evaluation report provides criterion-referenced and norm-referenced information for each student, class, building, and district. The report includes scales scores, grade equivalents, percentiles, and NCEs. The testing program is used by administrators and teachers in city-wide instructional management systems, migrant and special education programs, and ECIA-Chapter projects. Examiner required. Suitable for group use.

Untimed: Varies

Scoring: Computer scored

Cost: Computer scoring $1.75 per student; 10 booklets (specify level) $24.00

Publisher: Educational Development Corporation

KEYMATH DIAGNOSTIC ARITHMETIC TEST
Austin Connolly, William Nachtman, and E.M. Pritchett

Child   Grades K-6

Purpose: Diagnoses children's arithmetic skills to identify areas of weakness for remedial instruction.

Description: Three-category verbal test covering content (numeration, fractions, geometry, and symbols), operations (addition, subtraction, multiplication, division, mental computation, and numerical reasoning), and applications (word problems, missing elements, money, measurement, and time). The examiner displays a test plate to the student, asks a test question, and records the student's response on an individual record form. Only those items within the students functional range are administered. Materials include test plates bound into an easel, a manual, and 25 diagnostic records. Grade equivalents, grade percentile ranks, and normal curve equivalents for Grades 2-6 are available. Diagnostic information provided includes total test performance, area performance in content, operations, and applications, subtest performance, and subtest item performance. A KeyMath Metric Supplement to assess metric measurement skills is available. Examiner required. Not suitable for group use.

Untimed: 30-40 minutes

Scoring: Examiner evaluated

Cost: Complete kit $53.50

Publisher: American Guidance Service

KRANER PRESCHOOL MATH INVENTORY (KPMI)
Robert E. Kraner

Child

Purpose: Assesses the math skills of preschool children. Used for planning early math programs.

Description: Multiple item oral response test measuring attainment of criterion-referenced mathematics skills and concepts by preschool children. Areas measured include 7 categories and 77 quantitative

concepts. A receptive age and mastery age are identified in the development of each skill/concept. Examiner required. Not suitable for group use.

Untimed: Varies

Scoring: Examiner evaluated

Cost: Complete program (test manual, 25 scoring forms, classroom record sheet, 5 instructional record forms, 25 math/screen test booklets) $53.00.

Publisher: DLM Teaching Resources

LEICESTER NUMBER TEST
W.E.C. Gillham and K.A. Hesse

Child   Ages 7.1-17.6

Purpose: Measures basic number skills of individual students and class groups. Identifies students needing special help. Indicates areas in which the class as a whole needs special attention.

Description: Multiple-item paper-pencil test assessing a child's understanding of basic concepts of the number system and grasp of the "four rules" of conventional calculation. The test is intended for general screening and should be administered at the beginning of the school year. Norms are provided for ages 7.1-9.0. Examiner required. Suitable for group use.
BRITISH PUBLISHER

Untimed: Not available

Scoring: Examiner evaluated

Cost: Specimen set £3.50; 20 tests £6.20; manual £2.70

Publisher: Hodder & Stoughton

THE MATH DOCTOR (M.D.)
Barbara Signer

Elementary and high-school students

Purpose: Assesses students' mathematical abilities.

Description: Multiple-item computerized test diagnosing mathematics capabilities of students. There are 39 objectives tested in the areas of number concepts, addition, subtraction, multiplication, and division. This test requires students to generate responses to problems. The program provides items appropriate to the ability level of the student and immediate diagnosis of strengths and weaknesses. The test's branching strategy is based on an arithmetic skill hierarchy consistent with the Key Math Diagnostic Test, the Stanford Diagnostic Mathematics Test, and the scope and sequence of elementary mathematics textbooks. Available for Apple II (with language card), Apple II +, Apple IIe, and TRS-80 Models III and IV. Examiner/self-administered. Not suitable for group use.

Untimed: Varies

Scoring: Computer scored

Cost: $40.00 (includes back-up diskette)

Publisher: Modern Education Corporation

MATH TESTS GRADE I/SUB A-STANDARD 10

Purpose: Measures understanding of mathematics. Used for educational evaluation and placement.

Description: 19 separate paper-pencil tests of mathematics achievement and understanding. Particular subtests vary, but generally they include Mechanical, Insight, and Problem Solving. Two alternate forms, A and B, are available for all standards except Grade I/Sub A. Examiner required. Suitable for group use. SOUTH AFRICAN PUBLISHER

Untimed: Not available

Scoring: Hand key; examiner evaluated

Cost: Contact publisher; orders from outside The RSA will be dealt with on merit

Publisher: Human Sciences Research Council

MATHEMATICS 8-12
National Foundation for Educational Research with Alan Brighouse, David Godber, and Peter Patilla

Child   Ages 8-12

Purpose: Assesses progress in the acquisition of mathematical skills and concepts taught in primary and first-year secondary-school programs. Admin-

istered at the end of the school year to measure individual and class achievement in mathematics.

Description: 50-item paper-pencil test measuring academic achievement in mathematics. The test items, many of which incorporate drawings or diagrams, measure four skill areas: understanding, computation, application, and factual recall. The test is available on five levels: Mathematics 8 (first-year junior), Mathematics 9 (second-year junior), Mathematics 10 (third-year junior), Mathematics 11 (fourth-year junior), and Mathematics 12 (first year secondary). The test titles indicate the age ranges for which the tests were designed; for example, Mathematics 9 should be used towards the end of the academic year during which the pupils attain their ninth birthday. An overall standardized score compares each pupil's ability with the national average for the same age and with classmates of differing ages. Consistent use of the series enables progress to be monitored from year to year. Subscores for each of the four skill areas indicate individual strengths and weaknesses. The manual includes a discussion of the background, content, and use of tests; administration and scoring instructions; scoring keys; interpretation guidelines; conversion tables; and technical information. Examiner required. Suitable for group use. BRITISH PUBLISHER

Untimed: Varies

Scoring: Examiner evaluated

Cost: Manual £4.90; 25 test booklets (specify test) £8.00; specimen set (manual, one of each test booklet) £6.35

Publisher: NFER-NELSON Publishing Company Ltd.

MATHEMATICS ATTAINMENT TESTS SERIES

Child, adolescent
Ages 7-13.06

Purpose: Measures understanding of mathematics. Used to identify individual student strengths and weaknesses.

Description: Five paper-pencil tests measuring mathematics attainment: Test A (ages 7-8), Test B (ages 8-10), Test C1 (ages

9-12), Test DE2 (ages 10-11), and Test EF (ages 11-13). Tests A and B are administered orally and are varied in content and style. Tests C1 and DE2 are written tests in which computation is kept to a minimum. Questions cover graphs, simple geometry, base, series and number patterns, fractions, arithmetical processes, and equations. Test EF consists of 60 multiple-choice items measuring number concepts, space operations, geometry, and tabular/graphical representation. Examiner required. Suitable for group use.
BRITISH PUBLISHER

Untimed: 50 minutes per test

Scoring: Hand key; examiner evaluated

Cost: Specimen set primary (pupil forms A, B, C1, DE2, sample manual) £3.20; specimen set secondary (pupil Forms C1, DE2, sample manual) £3.20 (payment in sterling for all overseas orders)

Publisher: NFER-NELSON Publishing Company Ltd.

MATHEMATICS TOPIC TESTS—ELEMENTARY LEVEL

Child, adolescent
Grades 5-9

Purpose: Measures the degree to which students have attained or failed to attain stated mathematics objectives.

Description: Series of criterion-referenced tests focusing on specific topics rather than on the work of one grade level. Each test measures the degree to which students have attained or failed to attain stated educational objectives. The series also measures curricular objectives common to most Canadian courses from Grades 5-9. Tests include Number and Numeration; Addition and Subtraction with Whole Numbers; Multiplication and Division with Whole Numbers; Operations with Fractions; Multiplication and Division with Fractions; Measurement, Graphs, and Geometry; Operations with Decimals; Multiplication and Division with Decimals. Examiner required. Suitable for group use.
CANADIAN PUBLISHER

Timed: Varies

Scoring: Hand key

Cost: Contact publisher

Publisher: Guidance Centre

MICHIGAN PRESCRIPTIVE PROGRAM IN MATH
William E. Lockhart

Adolescent, adult
Grades 6 and over

Purpose: Measures mathematics skills and identifies skill deficits. Used to help students obtain a tenth-grade equivalency and pass the GED test in mathematics.

Description: Multiple-item paper-pencil test assessing the following high school level mathematics skills: addition; subtraction; multiplication; division; fractions; averaging; decimals; changing decimals to percents; simple and compound interest; denominate numbers; reading line, bar, and circle graphs; finding perimeter, area, and volume; square roots; proportions; set theory; laws of operation; Roman numerals; exponents; signs; simple equations; inequalities; sum of angles; coordinate geometry; theorems; graphical solutions; and slope. The test booklet, answer key, and math study materials are reusable; the student response sheet and individual prescription sheet are consumed. Math study materials have allowed students 1.5 to 3.5 math grade gain in 24 clock hours of study. Examiner required. Suitable for group use.

Untimed: Varies

Scoring: Examiner evaluated

Cost: Test book $1.50; 7 response and prescription sheets $2.00; answer key $1.00; math study materials $9.00

Publisher: Ann Arbor Publishers, Inc.

MICROCOMPUTER MANAGED INFORMATION FOR CRITERION REFERENCED OBJECTIVES—MATH (MMICRO-MATH)
Ron Hambleton

Child, adolescent
Grades 1-9

Purpose: Assesses students' mathematics performance. Provides information on skills mastered, skills for review, and skills to learn. Also used in adult basic education.

Description: Multiple-item paper-pencil test measuring student knowledge of operations, fractions, measurement, geometry, decimals and percentages, and special topics. The test is based on the same 348 developmental learning objectives as those for the ICRT-Math Basic + . With this computerized system, diagnostic and objective (mastery) tests are automatically scored in the school with a card or sheet reader recording information onto the software. Reports offer the same comprehensive diagnostic, prescriptive, and grouping information as the ICRT. However, the system does not include the norm-referenced data available from the mainframe computer, nor does it generate three selected correlations per teacher. Correlations may be purchased. Available for Acorn, Apple, Commodore, IBM, and TRS-80 microcomputers. Examiner required. Suitable for group use.

Untimed: Varies

Scoring: Computer scored

Cost: Software $1,595.00; 10 booklets (specify level) $18.00; demonstration program $65.00

Publisher: Educational Development Corporation

MINIMUM ESSENTIALS FOR MODERN MATHEMATICS
Ernest Hayes

Child, adolescent Grades 6-8

Purpose: Measures the mathematical aptitude of children. Used to group students for math instruction.

Description: 55-item paper-pencil test measuring a student's understanding of important basic concepts in modern mathematics. Special symbolization has been avoided to extend the use of the test to classes in modern mathematics and regular mathematics. Percentile ranks, T-scores, deviation scores, and stanines are provided. Examiner required. Suitable for group use.

Timed: 40 minutes

Scoring: Hand key

Cost: Complete set (30 booklets, manuals for administration and interpretation, scoring key, record sheet) $6.95; manual of statistical information sent on request

Publisher: Hayes Educational Tests

MORETON MATHEMATICS TESTS: LEVEL II
R. J. Andrews, R. G. Cochrane, and J. Elkins

Child   Grades 3-5

Purpose: Measures the mathematical abilities of primary-school children.

Description: Multiple-item paper-pencil test consisting of two subtests, Form N and Form P. Form N measures numerical abilities. Form P measures mathematical operations. Metric measurement is used. Australian norms are provided in terms of arithmetic ages, 15-point scale scores, and percentiles for Grades 3, 4, and 5. Examiner required. Suitable for group use.
AUSTRALIAN PUBLISHER

Untimed: Varies

Scoring: Examiner required

Cost: Classroom kit (manual, 40 Form N, 40 Form P) $14.00

Publisher: Teaching and Testing Resources

Information and availability unconfirmed; no publisher response.

MORETON MATHEMATICS TESTS: LEVEL III
J. Elkins, R. J. Andrews, and R. G. Cochrane

Child   Grades 5-7

Purpose: Measures the mathematics abilities of primary-school children.

Description: Multiple-item paper-pencil test measuring mathematical abilities involving numerical operations. Metric measurement is employed. Australian norms are provided in terms of arithmetic ages, 15-point scale scores, and percentiles for Grades 5, 6, and 7. Examiner required. Suitable for group use.
AUSTRALIAN PUBLISHER

Untimed: Varies

Scoring: Examiner evaluated

Cost: Standard kit (manual and 100 tests) $14.00

Publisher: Teaching and Testing Resources

Information and availability unconfirmed; no publisher response.

NATIONAL ACHIEVEMENT TESTS FOR ELEMENTARY SCHOOLS: ARITHMETIC AND MATHEMATICS—ALGEBRA TEST FOR ENGINEERING AND SCIENCE
Refer to page 411.

NATIONAL ACHIEVEMENT TESTS FOR ELEMENTARY SCHOOLS: ARITHMETIC AND MATHEMATICS—AMERICAN NUMERICAL TEST
Refer to page 411.

NATIONAL ACHIEVEMENT TESTS FOR ELEMENTARY SCHOOLS: ARITHMETIC AND MATHEMATICS—ARITHMETIC FUNDAMENTALS
Refer to page 412.

NATIONAL ACHIEVEMENT TESTS FOR ELEMENTARY SCHOOLS: ARITHMETIC AND MATHEMATICS: FUNDAMENTALS AND REASONING (GRADES 3-6)
Refer to page 412.

NATIONAL ACHIEVEMENT TESTS FOR ELEMENTARY SCHOOLS: ARITHMETIC AND MATHEMATICS: FUNDAMENTALS AND REASONING (GRADES 6-8)
Refer to page 412.

NATIONAL ACHIEVEMENT TESTS FOR ELEMENTARY SCHOOLS: ARITHMETIC AND MATHEMATICS—GENERAL MATH
Refer to page 413.

NATIONAL ACHIEVEMENT TESTS FOR ELEMENTARY SCHOOLS: ARITHMETIC AND MATHEMATICS—GENERAL MATHEMATICS
Refer to page 413.

NOTTINGHAM NUMBER TEST
W.E.C. Gillham and K.A. Hesse

Child   Ages 9.1-11

Purpose: Measures children's basic knowledge of arithmetic. Identifies students needing further testing. Groups students according to ability for teaching purposes.

Description: Two multiple-item paper-pencil subtests measuring knowledge and understanding of basic arithmetic. The first test assesses basic number concepts (series and place-value). The second test assesses basic calculation skills (the "four rules" of formal arithmetic). Items of each type are presented in varied order, but are graded for difficulty and are identified by symbols in the scoring column. Separate norms are provided for the two subtests, as well as for the test as a whole. Examiner required. Suitable for group use. BRITISH PUBLISHER

Untimed: Not available

Scoring: Examiner evaluated

Cost: Specimen set £3.50; 20 tests £4.25; manual £2.95

Publisher: Hodder & Stoughton

NUMBER TEST DE
B. Barnard

Child   Ages 10.06-12.06

Purpose: Measures understanding of basic number processes. Used for educational evaluation.

Description: Multiple-item paper-pencil test measuring four basic number processes: addition, subtraction, multiplication, and division. The test is based on the principle that knowledge of these four processes will allow the child to apply them and use them logically. Examiner required. Suitable for group use. BRITISH PUBLISHER

Untimed: 50 minutes

Scoring: Hand key

Cost: 10 tests £3.75; manual £1.85 (payment in sterling for all overseas orders)

Publisher: NFER-NELSON Publishing Company Ltd.

PEABODY MATHEMATICS READINESS TEST (PMRT)
Otto C. Bassler, Morris I. Beers, Lloyd I. Richardson, and Richard L. Thurman

Child   Grades K-1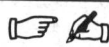

Purpose: Measures the ability of average (ages 4-6) and special education (mental ages 4-6) children to complete first-grade mathematics. Used for diagnosis and placement.

Description: Multiple-item examination assessing the readiness factors of number, containment, size, shape, configuration, and drawing, which have been proven to identify students who later display poor mathematics achievement. The manual provides activities to assist in prescriptive remediation. Examiner required. Suitable for group use.

Timed: 20 minutes

Scoring: Hand key; examiner evaluated

Cost: Starter set (manual, 20 test booklets and performance records, manual) $24.70

Publisher: Scholastic Testing Service, Inc.

PORTLAND PROGNOSTIC TEST FOR MATHEMATICS
Ernest Hayes

Child, adolescent Grades 6.5-9

Purpose: Measures the mathematical aptitude of children. Used to group students for math instruction, measure achievement, and predict success in algebra classes, especially for the more competent math student.

Description: 59-item paper-pencil test provides an inventory of basic arithmetic concepts useful for prognosis and measuring achievement. The test is available on three levels. Grade 9 (Forms A and B), for testing at the end of Grade 8, is designed to predict mathematical success in Grade 9; Grade 8 (Forms A and B), for testing at the end of Grade 7 or the beginning of Grade 8, is designed to predict mathematical success in Grade 8 accelerated mathematics; Grade 7 (Forms A and B), for testing at the end of Grade 6 or the beginning of Grade 7, is the same test administered to Grade 8; however, it has special norms for identifying students who can profit from an accelerated mathematics program in Grade 7. The norms developed include percentile ranks, T-scores, deviation scores, predicted achievement, and stanines. Examiner required. Suitable for group use.

Timed: 40 minutes

Scoring: Hand key

Cost: Complete set (30 booklets, manuals for administration and interpretation, scoring key, record sheet) $6.95; manual of statistical information sent on request

Publisher: Hayes Educational Tests

PROFILE OF MATHEMATICAL SKILLS
Norman France

Child, adolescent Ages 8-15

Purpose: Measures mathematics achievement. Used for diagnosis of specific student strengths and weaknesses.

Description: Multiple-item paper-pencil criterion-referenced tests of mathematics skills. The tests are divided into two levels. Level 1 (ages 8-13) measures addition, subtraction, multiplication, division, operations, measurement and money, and extensions. Level 2 (ages 10-15) measures fractions, decimal fractions and percentages, and diagrams in addition to the areas measured in Level 1. The tests are

administered over the normal course of mathematics lessons. Examiner required. Suitable for group use.
BRITISH PUBLISHER

Untimed: 30 minutes

Scoring: Hand key; examiner evaluated

Cost: Specimen set (Level 1 and Level 2 pupil's booklet profile chart, teacher's book) £5.70 (payment in sterling for all overseas orders)

Publisher: NFER-NELSON Publishing Company Ltd.

PROGRESS TESTS IN MATHS
Roy Hollands

Child   Ages 7-12

Purpose: Assesses mathematics achievement throughout the primary and middle school years. Measures both individual and group performance. Used for program planning and assessment.

Description: Six multiple-item paper-pencil tests measuring children's yearly progress in mathematics. The test items measure achievement of particular skills and subskills in the following mathematical areas: number, measure, shape, and pictorial representations. Each of the six tests corresponds to one year's work in mathematics and is intended for use with a particular age group, ranging from age 7 (Math 1) to age 12 (Math 6). The tests also are suitable for diagnostic use with older students in remedial classes. Tests for the first three years can be read aloud by the teacher to minimize problems caused by the children's limited reading abilities. Test objectives are based on reference to existing math schemes, government and LEA guidelines, and the recommendations of a panel of teachers and advisors. Tests are scored on an A-E grading system. The teacher's manual provides information on the background of the series, objectives, administering the tests, modifying them to suit individual needs, and recording and interpreting the results. Suggestions also are provided for remedial and follow-up work where necessary. A secondary teacher's manual is available for use with tests 5 and 6 only. Examiner required. Suitable for group use.

Untimed: Varies

Scoring: Examiner evaluated

Cost: Evaluation pack (teacher's manual for Levels 1-6, copy of each test) £4.95; secondary teacher's manual with 1 copy each of test 5 and 6 £3.50

Publisher: Macmillan Education

READINESS FOR OPERATIONS (K-3)
Sam Adams and Charles Sauls

Child   Grades K-3

Purpose: Measures student understanding of math concepts that are prerequisite to addition and subtraction. Used to determine readiness for kindergarten mathematics and to assess remedial needs of first- and second-grade students.

Description: 48-item paper-pencil test measuring 16 concepts, including one-to-one correspondence (pictures of objects), one-to-one correspondence (symbols), matching equal sets, matching numerals, matching numerals and names, recognizing numerals, writing numbers, separating subsets, recognizing cardinal numbers, sequencing through 10, writing numerals for set, and basic meaning of addition. The examiner reads aloud the directions for each test item; no reading is required of the examinees. Examiner required. Suitable for group use.

Untimed: 30 minutes

Scoring: Examiner evaluated

Cost: Contact publisher

Publisher: Dr. Charles Sauls

Information and availability unconfirmed; no publisher response.

SEQUENTIAL ASSESSMENT OF MATHEMATICS INVENTORY-INDIVIDUAL ASSESSMENT BATTERY (SAMI)
Fredricka K. Reisman

**Child, adolescent
Grades K-8**

Purpose: Assesses math performance of elementary-school students. Used to provide detailed diagnosis of an individual's

---

strengths and weaknesses and for referral to gifted or remedial classes.

Description: 240-item paper-pencil test measuring math performance in eight content areas: math language, ordinality, number/notation, measurement, geometry, computation, word problems, and math applications. Norms reported include standard scores, percentile ranks, stanines, and grade equivalents. Test kit includes a stimulus manual, a response form, and a teacher record form. Examiner required. Not suitable for group use.

Untimed: 30-60 minutes

Scoring: Hand key

Cost: Complete program $59.00; components available individually

Publisher: The Psychological Corporation

SKILLCORP COMPUTER MANAGEMENT SYSTEM—MATH

Child   Grades K-8

Purpose: Assesses math skill deficiencies. Used to diagnose individual deficiencies in math and prescribe resources for reteaching.

Description: 111 criterion-referenced tests determine math skill deficiencies. A microcomputer prints prescriptions for individual students or groups to reteach the skills not mastered. All skills tested are cross-referenced to major publisher materials. Materials include test administration manual and test cards for each grade level. Examiner required. Suitable for group use.

Timed: Varies, depending on test

Scoring: Hand key; may be computer scored

Cost: Contact publisher

Publisher: Skillcorp Software, Inc.

STANFORD MEASUREMENT SERIES—STANFORD DIAGNOSTIC MATHEMATICS TEST (SDMT): THIRD EDITION
Refer to page 449.

STEENBURGEN DIAGNOSTIC-PRESCRIPTIVE MATH PROGRAM AND QUICK MATH SCREENING TEST
Fran Steenburgen Gelb

Grades 1-6
and older students

Purpose: Determines an elementary school student's exact level of functioning in mathematics. Used to plan programs for children and older remedial students whose math skills are still at the elementary level.

Description: Multiple-item paper-pencil screening test measuring ability in simple addition, subtraction, one-digit carrying, addition of mixed numbers, and long division. The items are arranged in a sequential hierarchy according to the grade level at which each skill is introduced. For example, Level I includes problems appropriate for Grades 1-3, and Level II contains problems for Grades 4-6. Scores can be plotted on a profile sheet that graphically shows a student's progress from pre- to posttest. After the student's strengths and weaknesses are identified, the diagnostic-prescriptive program consisting of 55 reproducible worksheets can be used by the student until skills are mastered. The format of the screening test does not overstimulate hyperactive or distractible children. Examiner required. Suitable for group use.

Untimed: 10 minutes

Scoring: Hand key

Cost: Manual $10.00; 25 Level I test forms, 25 profile sheets $10.00; 25 Level II test forms, 25 profile sheets $10.00

Publisher: Academic Therapy Publications

TEST OF COMPUTATIONAL PROCESSES
Neldon D. Kingston

Child, adolescent
Grades 3-8

Purpose: Determines strengths and weaknesses in mathematics computation. Used with students in Grades 3-8.

Description: Multiple-item paper-pencil test measuring computational skills in seven areas: addition, subtraction, multiplication, and division of whole numbers, fractions, decimals, and knowledge of essential measurement units. The test is norm-referenced. Examiner required. Suitable for group use.

Timed: 30 minutes

Scoring: Examiner evaluated

Cost: Complete kit (25 8-page test booklets, manual) $50.00

Publisher: DLM Teaching Resources

TEST OF EARLY MATHEMATICS ABILITY (TEMA)
Herbert Ginsburg and
Arthur J. Baroody

Child   Ages 4-8

Purpose: Measures the mathematics performance of children. Diagnoses individual strengths and weaknesses. Used to plan instructional programs in mathematics.

Description: 26-item oral-response or paper-pencil test assessing mathematical abilities in two domains: informal mathematics (concepts of relative magnitude, counting, and calculation) and formal mathematics (knowledge of convention number facts, calculation, and base ten concepts). A picture card is used to present test items. Raw scores may be converted to standard scores, percentiles, and age equivalences. Criterion-referenced interpretation leads directly to instructional objectives. Examiner required. Suitable for group use.

Untimed: Varies

Scoring: Examiner evaluated

Cost: Complete kit (manual, 50 record forms, 26 picture cards) $41.00

Publisher: Pro-Ed

TEST OF MATHEMATICAL ABILITIES (TOMA)
Virginia L. Brown and
Elizabeth McEntire

Child, adolescent
Grades 3-10

Purpose: Assesses the mathematical attitudes and aptitudes of students. Used to plan and assess instructional programs in mathematics.

Description: Five paper-pencil subtests assessing knowledge, mastery, and attitudes in two major skill areas: story problems and computation. In addition to measuring the student's abilities, the following broad diagnostic areas are assessed: expressed attitudes toward mathematics, understanding of vocabulary as applied to mathematics, the functional use of mathematics as applied to our general culture, and the relationship between a student's attitudes and abilities and those of his peers. Normative information related to age and IQ, as well as graded mastery expectations for the "400" basic number facts, is provided for students ages 8-17. Scores differentiate diagnostically between students who have problems in mathematics and those who do not. Examiner required. Suitable for group use.

Untimed: Varies

Scoring: Examiner evaluated

Cost: Complete kit (examiner's manual, 25 profile sheets, 25 student worksheets, 25 story problems) $43.00

Publisher: Pro-Ed

TEST OF PERFORMANCE IN COMPUTATIONAL SKILLS (TOPICS)
CTB/McGraw-Hill

Adolescent   Grades 10-12

Purpose: Measures high-school students' proficiency in basic mathematical skills. Used to identify student needs and institute remedial instruction.

Description: 72-item paper-pencil test in two sections measuring a student's ability to apply basic mathematics concepts of

---

life-role situations involving the use of price lists, time cards, deposit slips, maps, and checkbook records. The test is available in Forms A and C. Examiner required. Suitable for group use.

Timed: 50 minutes per section

Scoring: Hand key; may be computer scored

Cost: Specimen set (test book, manual, both a machine-scorable and a hand-scorable answer sheet, class summary sheet, objectives matrix, test reviewer's guide) $8.95

Publisher: CTB/McGraw-Hill

TESTS OF COMPETENCE IN MATHEMATICS
Frances C. Morrison

**Child, adolescent
Grades 4-9**

Purpose: Assesses students' mathematics achievement. Provides information on specific areas of strengths and weaknesses. Used as a pre- or postcourse test.

Description: Three paper-pencil multiple-choice subtests of 50 items each measuring mastery of computational skills, mathematical concepts, and word problems. The material covered includes fractional and decimal knowledge, computational skills, geometry, and metric measurement. Subtest Level 4-5 is intended mainly for use at the end of Grade 4 or the beginning of Grade 5; Level 6-7 is designed for the end of Grade 6 or the beginning of Grade 7; and Level 8-9 is used at the end of Grade 8 or the beginning of Grade 9. Examiner required. Suitable for group use.
CANADIAN PUBLISHER

Timed: 30 minutes per subtest

Scoring: Hand key

Cost: Specimen set, specify level (test booklets, answer sheet, key, manual) $5.25

Publisher: Guidance Centre

WORKING WITH WHOLE NUMBERS
Sam Adams and Leslie Ellis

**Child, adolescent
Grades 4-8**

Purpose: Assesses ability to add, subtract, multiply, and divide. Used to plan remedial approaches for students in Grades 4-8.

Description: 575-item paper-pencil test in two sections measuring mastery of the four basic arithmetic operations using whole numbers. The survey portion measures concepts and is administered by the teacher. The second portion measures ability with facts and is completed independently. Examiner required. Suitable for group use.

Untimed: 45 minutes

Scoring: Examiner evaluated

Cost: Contact publisher

Publisher: Dr. Charles Sauls

Information and availability unconfirmed; no publisher response.

Y' MATHEMATICS SERIES
Dennis Young

Child   Ages 7.5-11.10

Purpose: Measures children's achievement in mathematics. Assesses individual and class progress in the study of mathematics and identifies strengths or weaknesses of curriculum and teaching methods.

Description: Four paper-pencil tests measuring mathematics achievement in four overrlapping stages (Y1, Y2, Y3, and Y4) covering the overall age range from 7.5-11.10 years. Both Y1 (ages 7.5-8.10) and Y2 (ages 8.5-9.10) consist of three sections: orally-presented items, computation, and written problems, a format that helps to identify those students whose mathematical ability is being underestimated because of reading difficulties. An additional table of quotients for Y2 is provided for use with older backward and slow reading children up to age 14.10. Both Y3 (ages 9.5-10.10) and Y4

(ages 10.5-11.10) contain computation and written problems. Examiner required. Suitable for group use.
BRITISH PUBLISHER

Timed: Single class period

Scoring: Examiner evaluated

Cost: Specimen set £3.80; 20 tests (specify form) £2.95; manual (specify level) £1.05

Publisher: Hodder & Stoughton

YARDSTICKS

Child   Ages 6-12

Purpose: Assesses achievement in mathematics. Used for regular measurement of student progress.

Description: Multiple-item paper-pencil test of mathematics skills applicable to the teaching curriculum. The test is divided into six levels: Level 1 (age 6), Level 2 (age 7), Level 3 (age 8), Level 4 (age 9), Level 5 (age 10), and Level 6 (age 11). The test for each level is broken down into teaching objectives for the age group served by the level. There are 5 questions per objective for Levels 1-3, and 10 questions per objective for Levels 4-6. Examiner required. Suitable for group use.
BRITISH PUBLISHER

Untimed: Not available

Scoring: Hand key; examiner evaluated

Cost: Sample kit £11.45; value packs for each level £79.95

Publisher: NFER-NELSON Publishing Company Ltd.

Academic Subjects: Mathematics: Upper Math Skills

ACER MATHEMATICS TESTS

Child, adolescent
Grades K-11

Purpose: Measures achievement in mathematics. Used for diagnosing individual student strengths and weaknesses.

Description: Six sets of multiple-choice and two sets of open-ended paper-pencil tests of basic mathematics skills: addition, subtraction, multiplication, and division. Tests are ACER Class Achievement Test in Mathematics (CATIM), a criterion-referenced test for years 4-5; ACER Class Achievement Test in Mathematics (CATIM), years 6-7; ACER Review and Progress Tests in Mathematics (open-ended); ACER Mathematics Profile Series, measuring Operations at years 4-10 and Space, Measurement, and Number at years 7-10; ACER Mathematics Tests (AM Series); Progressive Achievement Tests in Mathematics—Forms A or B, for years 3-8; Mathematics Evaluation Procedures K-2, years K-4 (open-ended); New Zealand Item Bank: Mathematics, years 3-8. Examiner required. Suitable for group use.
AUSTRALIAN PUBLISHER

Timed: Varies

Scoring: Hand key

Cost: Contact publisher

Publisher: The Australian Council for Educational Research Limited

---

ACER NUMBER TEST
Refer to page 854.

ADMISSIONS EXAMINATIONS: ADMISSIONS AND CREDENTIALING GROUP: DOPPELT MATHEMATICAL REASONING TEST
J.E. Doppelt

Adult
Graduate students

Purpose: Measures mathematical reasoning ability. Assists in the selection of graduate students.

Description: Multiple-item paper-pencil test of mathematical reasoning ability. The test was developed to provide a high-level measure of mathematical skills comparable to the Miller Analogies Test and the Advanced Personnel Test. Examiner required. Suitable for group use.

Timed: 50 minutes

Scoring: Scoring service available

Cost: Contact publisher

Publisher: Admissions and Credentialing Group/The Psychological Corporation

AMERICAN INVITATIONAL MATHEMATICS EXAMINATION (AIME)

Adolescent   Grades 9-12

Purpose: Measures mathematical achievement of high-school students with exceptional mathematical ability. Used to select students with the specific talents necessary for doing well on examinations such as the U.S.A. Mathematical Olympiad (USAMO).

Description: 15-item paper-pencil free-response test measuring mathematics abilities of selected high-school students. No multiple-choice questions are included. All problems can be solved using pre-calculus methods. Only students scoring above a cut-off score announced each fall on the American High School Mathematics Examination (ASHME) are invited to participate in the examination, which in turn serves as the qualifying examination for the USAMO. Participating schools must register each fall with the Regional Examination Coordinators. Examiner required. Suitable for group use.

Timed: 3 hours

Scoring: Scored by M.A.A. Committee on High School Contests

Cost: Contact Dr. Walter E. Mientka at M.A.A. address

Publisher: M.A.A. Committee on High School Examinations

Information and availability unconfirmed; no publisher response.

ANNUAL HIGH SCHOOL MATHEMATICS EXAMINATION (AHSME)

Adolescent   Grades 7-12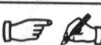

Purpose: Assesses skills and conceptual knowledge of precalculus mathematical students. Designed to provide challeng-

ing problems to create and sustain an interest in mathematics.

Description: 30-item paper-pencil multiple-choice test assessing proficiency in the concepts and skills associated with pre-calculus mathematics with emphasis on intermediate algebra and plane geometry. Participating high schools must register each fall with the Regional Examination Coordinators. Each school makes its own decision as to the number of participants (for official status the minimum number of participants per school is three) although the test is open to all students with the necessary background. The test is administered in the U.S.A., Canada, England, Finland, Belgium, Hungary, Ireland, Israel, Italy, Jamaica, Luxembourg, Australia, Malaysia, and other American and foreign schools abroad. Examiner required. Suitable for group use. Available in Spanish, Braille, and large-print editions.

Timed: 1 hour, 30 minutes

Scoring: Hand key

Cost: Specimen sets of prior examinations $35.00 each

Publisher: M.A.A. Committee on High School Contests

Information and availability unconfirmed; no publisher response.

ARITHMETIC AND MATH SPLIT FORM (FORM M)
Mary Meeker and Robert Meeker

Adolescent, adult
Grades 7 and above

Purpose: Assesses the arithmetic and mathematics skills of intermediate, high-school, and college students.

Description: Multiple-item paper-pencil test assessing potential in arithmetic and mathematics. Discipline-focused test items are selected from the SOI-LA Basic Test. The Basic Test manual is required for administration. Materials are available to train any abilities not developed. Examiner required. Suitable for group use.

Timed: 1 hour

Scoring: Hand key

Cost: Examiner's manual $24.50; test form $1.95

Publisher: Western Psychological Services

AUSTRALIAN ITEM BANK

Child, adolescent
Grades 8-12

Purpose: Assesses achievement in academic subjects. Used for selecting items for classroom and final examinations.

Description: Multiple-item paper-pencil test consisting of mathematical items covering recall, computation, comprehension, application, and analysis. The items may be used for achievement tests, diagnostic tests, to stimulate class discussions, and to evaluate teaching methods. The manual provides basic techniques of test construction. Examiner required. Suitable for group use.
AUSTRALIAN PUBLISHER

Untimed: Varies

Scoring: Hand key

Cost: Contact publisher

Publisher: The Australian Council for Educational Research Limited

---

BASIC SKILLS TEST— MATHEMATICS SECONDARY- FORMS A AND B
IOX Assessment Associates

Adolescent   Grades 8-11

Purpose: Measures minimum competency of high-school students in basic mathematic skills. Also used for program evaluation.

Description: 25-item paper-pencil test examining a student's ability to perform basic calculations and solve everyday problems requiring single arithmetic operations, multiple arithmetic operations, and formulas. This test succeeds the IOX Basic Skills Test—Mathematics-Elementary Level. Examiner required. Suitable for group use.

Untimed: 30-45 minutes

Scoring: Hand key; may be computer scored

Cost: 24 BM-A1 $37.50; 25 BM-B1 $37.50; teacher's guide BM-G1 $3.95; BTM-1 test manual $3.95; 50 answer sheets $6.95

Publisher: IOX Assessment Associates

CHELSEA DIAGNOSTIC MATHEMATICS TESTS
Kathleen Hart, Margaret Brown, Dietmar Kuchemann, Daphne Kerslake, and Graham Ruddock

Child, adolescent
Ages 9-15

Purpose: Assesses student's level of mathematics achievement. Used by teachers for educational program planning and evaluation.

Description: Battery of 10 paper-pencil tests assessing levels of achievement in the following areas: algebra, fractions, graphs, measurement, number operations, place value and decimals, ratio and proportion, reflection and rotation, and vectors. Examiner required. Suitable for group use.
BRITISH PUBLISHER

Untimed: 30-60 minutes

Scoring: Hand key

Cost: Complete kit (10 of each test booklet, teacher's guide, and a set of marking overlays) £74.75

Publisher: NFER-NELSON Publishing Company Ltd.

CHELSEA DIAGNOSTIC MATHEMATICS TESTS: ALGEBRA
Kathleen Hart, Margaret Brown, Dietmar Kuchemann, Daphne Kerslake, and Graham Ruddock

Adolescent   Ages 12-15

Purpose: Assesses algebra abilities of students.

Description: Multiple-item paper-pencil test assessing a broad range of typical secondary school algebra tasks and focusing on different ways children use and interpret letters in generalized arithmetic. Practice items precede the main test to remind children of certain conventions. The test may be used with older children.

One in a series of 10 tests in the Chelsea Diagnostic Mathematics Tests. Examiner required. Suitable for group use.
BRITISH PUBLISHER
Untimed: 30-60 minutes
Scoring: Hand key
Cost: 10 test booklets £5.65
Publisher: NFER-NELSON Publishing Company Ltd.

CHELSEA DIAGNOSTIC MATHEMATICS TESTS: FRACTIONS 1
Kathleen Hart, Margaret Brown, Dietmar Kuchemann, Daphne Kerslake, and Graham Ruddock

Adolescent   Ages 11-13

Purpose: Measure students' ability to solve problems and compute fractions.

Description: Multiple-item paper-pencil test in two parts focusing on labeling fractions, adding and subtracting fractions, and solving problems using fractions. The main test is composed of problems, and a related section consists of fractional computations that mirror the problems. One in a series of 10 tests in the Chelsea Diagnostic Mathematics Tests. Examiner required. Suitable for group use.
BRITISH PUBLISHER
Untimed: 30-60 minutes
Scoring: Hand key
Cost: 10 test booklets £5.65
Publisher: NFER-NELSON Publishing Company Ltd.

CHELSEA DIAGNOSTIC MATHEMATICS TESTS: FRACTIONS 2
Kathleen Hart, Margaret Brown, Dietmar Kuchemann, Daphne Kerslake, and Graham Ruddock

Adolescent   Ages 13-15

Purpose: Measures the ability of children ages 13 + -15 + to solve problems and do computations using fractions.

Description: Multiple-item paper-pencil test focusing on labeling fractions and adding, subtracting, multiplying, and dividing fractions. A related section deals

with computation. One in a series of 10 tests in the Chelsea Diagnostic Mathematics Tests. Examiner required. Suitable for group use.
BRITISH PUBLISHER
Untimed: 30-60 minutes
Scoring: Hand key
Cost: 10 test booklets £5.15
Publisher: NFER-NELSON Publishing Company Ltd.

CHELSEA DIAGNOSTIC MATHEMATICS TESTS: GRAPHS
Kathleen Hart, Margaret Brown, Dietmar Kuchemann, Daphne Kerslake, and Graham Ruddock

Adolescent   Ages 12-15

Purpose: Assesses students' understanding of graphs.

Description: Multiple-item paper-pencil test measuring understanding of bar charts, coordinates, scale, continuous graphs, and simple equations. One in a series of 10 tests in the Chelsea Diagnostic Mathematics Tests. Examiner required. Suitable for group use.
BRITISH PUBLISHER
Untimed: 30-60 minutes
Scoring: Hand key
Cost: 10 test booklets £6.30
Publisher: NFER-NELSON Publishing Company Ltd.

CHELSEA DIAGNOSTIC MATHEMATICS TESTS: MEASUREMENT
Kathleen Hart, Margaret Brown, Dietmar Kuchemann, Daphne Kerslake, and Graham Ruddock

Adolescent   Ages 11-14

Purpose: Assesses students' ability to solve problems related to measurement.

Description: Multiple-item paper-pencil test involving mathematical computations of length, area, and volume. Practice questions describe common terms such as area and perimeter. One in a series of 10 tests in the Chelsea Diagnostic Mathematics Tests. Examiner required. Suitable for group use.

BRITISH PUBLISHER
Untimed: 30-60 minutes
Scoring: Hand key
Cost: 10 test booklets £7.45
Publisher: NFER-NELSON Publishing
Company Ltd.

CHELSEA DIAGNOSTIC MATHEMATICS TESTS: NUMBER OPERATIONS
*Kathleen Hart, Margaret Brown,
Dietmar Kuchemann, Daphne
Kerslake, and Graham Ruddock*

Adolescent   Ages 11-12

Purpose: Assesses conceptual understanding of the four basic number operations applied to whole numbers.

Description: Multiple-item paper-pencil test assessing whether children can recognize where each of the four basic number operations—addition, subtraction, multiplication, division—is applicable. The test also requires children to provide a concrete example of each operation. The test can be used with younger and older students and with students ages 13 + -15 + with lower mathematical abilities. One in a series of 10 tests in the Chelsea Diagnostic Mathematics Tests. Examiner required. Suitable for group use.
BRITISH PUBLISHER
Untimed: 30-60 minutes
Scoring: Hand key
Cost: 10 test booklets £5.15
Publisher: NFER-NELSON Publishing
Company Ltd.

CHELSEA DIAGNOSTIC MATHEMATICS TESTS: PLACE VALUES AND DECIMALS
*Kathleen Hart, Margaret Brown,
Dietmar Kuchemann, Daphne
Kerslake, and Graham Ruddock*

Adolescent   Ages 11-15

Purpose: Assesses students' understanding of the base-10 place value notation system.

Description: Multiple-item paper-pencil test measuring students' understanding of the base-10 place value notation system for

whole numbers and decimals and whether students can use it appropriately. One in a series of 10 tests in the Chelsea Diagnostic Mathematics Tests. Examiner required. Suitable for group use.
BRITISH PUBLISHER
Untimed: 30-60 minutes
Scoring: Hand key
Cost: 10 test booklets £6.30
Publisher: NFER-NELSON Publishing
Company Ltd.

CHELSEA DIAGNOSTIC MATHEMATICS TESTS: RATIO AND PROPORTION
*Kathleen Hart, Margaret Brown,
Dietmar Kuchemann, Daphne
Kerslake, and Graham Ruddock*

Adolescent   Ages 12-15

Purpose: Assesses students' conceptual understanding of ratio and proportion.

Description: Multiple-item paper-pencil test measuring understanding of ratio and proportion through a range of problems of varying complexity. The test also may be used with adults in higher education and some primary-school pupils. One in a series of 10 tests in the Chelsea Diagnostic Mathematics Tests. Examiner required. Suitable for group use.
BRITISH PUBLISHER
Untimed: 30-60 minutes
Scoring: Hand key
Cost: 10 test booklets £5.15
Publisher: NFER-NELSON Publishing
Company Ltd.

CHELSEA DIAGNOSTIC MATHEMATICS TESTS: REFLECTION AND ROTATION
*Kathleen Hart, Margaret Brown,
Dietmar Kuchemann, Daphne
Kerslake, and Graham Ruddock*

Adolescent   Ages 12-14

Purpose: Assesses students' understanding of reflection and rotation.

Description: Multiple-item paper-pencil test covering single reflections, single rotations (using a quarter turn), and combinations of reflections and rotations. The first two parts are preceded by trial items designed to remind students of terms such as "reflection," "mirror line," "rotation," and "quarter turn." One in a series of 10 tests in the Chelsea Diagnostic Mathematics Tests. Examiner required. Suitable for group use. BRITISH PUBLISHER

Untimed: 30-60 minutes

Scoring: Hand key

Cost: 10 test booklets £6.30

Publisher: NFER-NELSON Publishing Company Ltd.

COOPERATIVE MATHEMATICS TESTS
Educational Testing Service

Adolescent   Grades 7-14 [☞ 🖉]

Purpose: Measures achievement in major mathematical content areas ranging from arithmetic to calculus.

Description: Multiple-item test assessing a student's comprehension of basic mathematical concepts, techniques, and unifying principles. The recommended grade levels for each subtest and the concepts it measures are Arithmetic (Grades 7-9), basic concepts without emphasis on commercial applications; Structure of the Number System (Grades 7-8), concepts underlying the structure of the real number system; Algebra (Grades 8-9), concepts and skills underlying quadratic equations, inequalities, number line, and field properties; Algebra II (Grades 9-12), concepts and skills underlying inequalities and absolute values; Geometry Part I (Grades 9-12), concepts in Euclidean geometry; Geometry Part II (Grades 9-12), advanced understanding, proof, spatial reasoning; Trigonometry (Grades 9-14), functional and numerical trigonometry; Algebra III (Grades 9-14), traditional topics and contemporary material, such as inequalities and functional notation; Analytic Geometry (Grades 9-14), suitable for one-semester course or combined analytic geometry-calculus course; Calculus Part I (Grades 9-14), algebraic functions, emphasis on differential calculus; Calculus Part II (Grades 9-14), transcendental functions, emphasis on integral calculus. Separate norms for

college engineering, education, and liberal arts students are available. Subtests may be ordered independently. Examiner required. Suitable for group use.

Timed: 40-80 minutes

Scoring: Hand key; may be computer scored

Cost: 20 tests $12.00 (specify title); 100 answer sheets (specify hand- or machine-scorable) $18.00; manual $7.50; 10 scoring stencils $4.50

Publisher: CTB/McGraw-Hill

EMPORIA STATE ALGEBRA II TEST
Stanley J. Laughlin and Howard P. Schwartz

Adolescent   Grades 10-12 [☞ 🖉]

Purpose: Assesses the algebra aptitude of high-school students. Used as an Algebra II preassessment test and for program evaluation.

Description: 50-item paper-pencil criterion-referenced test of general knowledge for Algebra II courses. Seven goals and 17 objectives are evaluated. Examiner required. Suitable for group use.

Timed: 50 minutes

Scoring: Hand key

Cost: Test $0.15; manual $0.20; key $0.20

Publisher: Bureau of Educational Measurements

NATIONAL ACHIEVEMENT TESTS FOR ELEMENTARY SCHOOLS: ARITHMETIC AND MATHEMATICS—FIRST YEAR-ALGEBRA TEST
Refer to page 412.

NATIONAL ACHIEVEMENT TESTS FOR ELEMENTARY SCHOOLS: ARITHMETIC AND MATHEMATICS—PLANE GEOMETRY, SOLID GEOMETRY, AND PLANE TRIGONOMETRY TESTS
Refer to page 413.

NM CONSUMER MATHEMATICS TEST (NMCMT)
S.P. Klein

Adolescent   Grades 9-12

Purpose: Measures ability to solve consumer problems using basic arithmetic operations. Used for program evaluation and needs assessment.

Description: 20-item paper-pencil multiple-choice test measuring ability to solve problems involving measures and prices, addition, subtraction, multiplication, and division in a consumer context. The test booklets are reusable, and a lay-over stencil is used for scoring. Reliability and norms have been determined from samples of ninth- and twelfth-grade secondary students. Examiner required. Suitable for group use.

Timed: 20 minutes

Scoring: Hand key

Cost: Specimen set $6.00; 35 tests $12.00; 35 answer sheets $4.00; scoring stencil $3.00; manual $3.00

Publisher: Monitor

ORLEANS-HANNA ALGEBRA PROGNOSIS TEST (REVISED)
Refer to page 439.

SENIOR MATHEMATICS TEST

Adolescent   Ages 16-18

Purpose: Assesses basic mathematics skills. Used to allocate students to engineering courses.

Description: 50-item paper-pencil test of basic elementary mathematics needed in any engineering course. The topics covered include common units of measurement, decimals and fractions, averages, percentages, indices, and simple algebra and geometry. Examiner required. Suitable for group use.
BRITISH PUBLISHER

Timed: 45 minutes

Scoring: Not available

Cost: 10 tests £3.75; manual £1.85 (payment in sterling for all overseas orders)

Publisher: NFER-NELSON Publishing Company Ltd.

TEST OF COGNITIVE STYLE IN MATHEMATICS (TCSM)
John B. Bath, Stephen J. Chinn, and Dwight E. Knox

Ages 7-adult

Purpose: Identifies the cognitive-perceptual style of an individual's mathematic problem-solving skills.

Description: Multiple-item paper-pencil test assessing how an individual solves mathematical problems in four areas: mental computation, arithmetic, geometry/visual, and algebra. The results are used to place the individual's problem-solving style on a continuum between two extremes: Gestalt thinker and stimulus bound. Examiner required. Not suitable for group use.

Timed: 20 minutes

Scoring: Examiner evaluated

Cost: Complete kit (manual, test questions, 50 profile record forms, 50 worksheets, 50 observation folders) $54.00

Publisher: Slosson Educational Publications, Inc.

Academic Subjects: Religious Education

BECOMING THE GIFT (BTG)
Merton P. Strommen

Adolescent, adult   Grades 8-12

Purpose: Helps young people express their values, beliefs, and concerns and decide directions for personal growth. Designed for persons with a Christian orientation. Used for one-on-one counseling sessions with a caring adult, group sharing, and individual study and growth.

Description: 176-item paper-pencil survey assessing the attitudes and beliefs of church-oriented high-school students. Subscales include family unity, parental understanding, lack of self-confidence, personal faults, classroom relationships, national issues, God relationship, orientation for change, moral responsibility, meaningful life, religious participation, self-regard, human relations, God awareness, and biblical concepts. Each person receives a computer-analyzed profile and a 64-page self-study guide, which explains the profile, guides the person in interpreting the results, helps identify areas where faith or values need to grow, and provides suggestions for dealing with these areas. Group profiles, which provide a composite description of a youth group while protecting the confidentiality of the individuals, are available. Profiles also are available for subgroups, such as boys, girls, and seniors. Self-administered. Suitable for group use.

Untimed: 45 minutes

Scoring: Computer scored

Cost: Per individual (test booklet, answer sheet, profile, self-study guide, manual) $5.75; group profiles $22.00 each

Publisher: Search Institute

NEW YOUTH RESEARCH SURVEY (NYRS)
Merton P. Strommen

Adolescent, adult   Grades 8-12

Purpose: Provides information on the attitudes and beliefs of church-related youth groups.

Description: 248-item paper-pencil survey assessing the concerns, beliefs, values, and perceptions of members of church-related youth groups. Subscales include family unity, parental understanding, lack of self-confidence, personal faults, classroom relationships, national issues, God relationships, orientation for change, religious participation, moral responsibility, meaningful life, self-regard, human relations, God awareness, biblical concepts, interest in help, youth group vitality, and adult caring. The survey yields computer-analyzed scale scores and response frequencies for the youth group

as a whole. Individual profiles also are available. Norms are available for the following denominations: ecumenical, Lutheran, Southern Baptist, Roman Catholic, and parochial high schools. Self-administered. Suitable for group use.

Untimed: 1-1½ hours

Scoring: Computer scored

Cost: Complete $3.75 per person

Publisher: Search Institute

A PARTIAL INDEX OF MODERNIZATION: MEASUREMENT OF ATTITUDES TOWARD MORALITY
Panos D. Bardis

Adolescent, adult
Grades 10 and above

Purpose: Measures attitudes toward traditional concepts of sin. Used for clinical assessment, counseling, research on religion and morals, and discussions in religion and social science classes.

Description: 10-item paper-pencil test in which the subject rates 10 statements about sin and morality from 0 (least amount of agreement) to 10 (highest amount of agreement). The score equals the sum of the 10 numerical responses. The theoretical range of scores extends from 0 (least modern) to 100 (most modern). Examiner/self-administered. Suitable for group use.

Untimed: 5 minutes

Scoring: Examiner evaluated

Cost: Free

Publisher: Panos D. Bardis

PROFILE OF ADAPTATION TO LIFE—HOLISTIC (PAL-H)
Refer to page 166.

A RELIGION SCALE
Refer to page 84.

STANDARDIZED BIBLE CONTENT TESTS
AABC Commission on Testing and Measurement

Adult

Purpose: Evaluates knowledge of the Bible. Used for college entrance examinations, class assignment, and comparing national and institutional norms.

Description: 150-item paper-pencil multiple-choice test measuring biblical knowledge: people, history, doctrine, geography, and quotations. The test is recommended for institutions of higher education and is available in six equivalent forms, A, B, C, D, E, F. Self-administered. Suitable for group use.
Timed: 45 minutes
Scoring: Hand key
Cost: Test (specify form) $0.75; answer sheet $0.10; scoring key $2.00; manual $5.00
Publisher: American Association of Bible Colleges

STRAIT BIBLICAL KNOWLEDGE TEST
Jim Strait and Merritt W. Sanders

Adolescent, adult
Grades 10 and above

Purpose: Assesses the biblical knowledge of students and adults. Used as a pretest or an end-of-course exam.

Description: 100-item paper-pencil test covering the general content of the Old (Form 1) and New (Form 2) Testaments. Examiner required. Suitable for group use.
Timed: 40 minutes
Scoring: Hand key
Cost: Test $0.15; manual $0.20; key $0.20
Publisher: Bureau of Educational Measurements

THANATOMETER
Panos D. Bardis

Adolescent, adult

Purpose: Measures awareness and acceptance of death.

Description: 20-item paper-pencil Likert-scale test assessing attitudes toward death and dying. Examinee responds by indicating degree of agreement with each item. Self-administered. Suitable for group use.
Untimed: 12 minutes
Scoring: Hand key
Cost: Free
Publisher: Panos D. Bardis

Academic Subjects: Science: General Science

ACER SCIENCE TESTS

Child   Years 7-12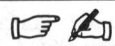

Purpose: Measures achievement in science courses. Used for diagnosis of individual student strengths and weaknesses.

Description: Eight multiple-choice paper-pencil tests of basic science subjects. Tests are Australian Biology Test Item Bank for year 11; Australian Biology Test Item Bank, year 12; ACER Chemistry Item Bank; ACER Physics Unit Tests, years 11 and 12; Tests of Perception of Scientists and Self, a test of science attitudes for years 9-12; Test of Science-Related Attitudes (TOSRA); Understanding in Science Test, a test of science concepts for years 7 and 8; and Test of Enquiry Skills (TOES), years 7 and 8. Examiner required. Suitable for group use.
AUSTRALIAN PUBLISHER
Timed: Varies
Scoring: Hand key
Cost: Contact publisher
Publisher: The Australian Council for Educational Research Limited

ADVANCED HIGH SCHOOL CHEMISTRY TESTS

Adolescent, adult
Grades 10 and above

Purpose: Measures achievement in advanced or honors courses in high-school chemistry. Evaluates student strengths and weaknesses and aids in assigning grades.

Description: 60-item multiple-choice paper-pencil test covering 10 areas of high-school chemistry: atomic structure; chemical bonding; thermodynamics; kinetics; solids, liquids, gases, and solutions; acid-base chemistry; electrochemistry; chemical periodicity; descriptive chemistry and stoichiometry; and laboratory procedures and techniques. Materials include Form 1982-ADV (60 items), 1984-ADV (60 items), 1986-ADV (60 items). The tests are for use only by authorized chemistry teachers and administrators. Examiner required. Suitable for group use.

Timed: Form 1982-ADV 110 minutes; Form 1984-ADV 110 minutes; Form 1986-ADV 110 minutes

Scoring: Hand key

Cost: Specimen set $5.00; 25 tests $15.00; 25 answer sheets $3.00; scoring stencil $1.00

Publisher: Examinations Committee, American Chemical Society

BIOCHEMISTRY TESTS

Adolescent, adult
College students

Purpose: Measures achievement in undergraduate general biochemistry courses. Evaluates prospective graduate students and serves as a comprehensive final examination for undergraduate courses.

Description: 60-item paper-pencil test covering topics in general biochemistry. Forty percent of the items deal with the properties and structure-function relationships of biological molecules, and sixty percent of the questions cover intermediary metabolism and its control, the biochemistry of information macromolecules, and biochemical methods. Materials include Form 1977 and Form 1982. The test is for use only by authorized chemistry teachers and administrators. Examiner required. Suitable for group use.

Timed: Form 1982 120 minutes; Form 1977 120 minutes

Scoring: Hand key

Cost: Specimen set $5.00; 25 tests $18.00; 25 answer sheets $3.00; scoring stencil $1.00

Publisher: Examinations Committee, American Chemical Society

BORMAN-SANDERS ELEMENTARY SCIENCE TEST
Ina M. Borman and
Merritt W. Sanders

Child   Grades 5-6

Purpose: Assesses the general science achievement of elementary-school students. Used as an end-of-first or second-semester exam.

Description: 100-item paper-pencil test of general physical science concepts and facts. Examiner required. Suitable for group use.

Timed: 40 minutes

Scoring: Hand key

Cost: Test $0.15; manual $0.20; key $0.20

Publisher: Bureau of Educational Measurements

BRIEF ORGANIC CHEMISTRY TESTS

Adolescent, adult
College students

Purpose: Measures achievement in undergraduate organic chemistry courses. Evaluates student strengths and weaknesses and aids in assigning grades.

Description: 70-item paper-pencil test measuring topics in organic chemistry, including bonding, isomerism, functional group recognition, IUPAC nomenclature, physical properties, acidity and basicity, characteristic reactions of major functional groups, reaction mechanisms, qualitative organic analysis, applications, lipids, carbohydrates, and proteins. Materials include Forms 1977-B (70 items) and 1984-B (70 items). For use only by authorized chemistry teachers and administrators. Examiner required. Suitable for group use.

Timed: Form 1977-B 90 minutes; Form 1984-B 90 minutes

Scoring: Hand key

Cost: Specimen set $5.00; 25 tests $18.00; 25 answer sheets $3.00; scoring stencils $1.00

Publisher: Examinations Committee, American Chemical Society

BRIEF QUALITATIVE ANALYSIS TEST

Adolescent, adult
College students

Purpose: Measures achievement in undergraduate qualitative analysis courses. Evaluates student strengths and weaknesses and aids in assigning grades.

Description: 35- or 50-item paper-pencil test assessing knowledge of qualitative analysis. Materials include Form 1973-B (50 items) and Form 1977-B (35 items). The test may be administered in combination with any of the General Chemistry tests. For use only by authorized chemistry teachers and administrators. Examiner required. Suitable for group use.

Untimed: 50 minutes

Scoring: Hand key

Cost: Specimen set $5.00; 25 tests $18.00; 25 answer sheets $3.00; scoring stencils $1.00

Publisher: Examinations Committee, American Chemical Society

EMPORIA BIOLOGY TEST
*Ted F. Andrews and
Merritt W. Sanders*

Adolescent, adult

Purpose: Measures knowledge of topics in biological sciences. Used to measure achievement in high-school students.

Description: Paper-pencil multiple-choice test covering the following areas of biology: function of life, interdependence of plants and animals, and structure of plants and their relationship to other organisms as environmental factors. Percentile norms available. Examiner required. Suitable for group use.

Timed: 40 minutes

Scoring: Hand key

Cost: Test $0.15; manual $0.20; key $0.20

Publisher: Bureau of Educational Measurements

EMPORIA CHEMISTRY TEST
A. T. Ericson and Merritt W. Sanders

Adolescent   Grades 10-12

Purpose: Assesses the chemistry achievement of high-school students. Used as an end-of-first- or second-semester exam.

Description: 100-item paper-pencil test of chemistry definitions, formulas, equations, principles, theories, and problems. Examiner required. Suitable for group use.

Timed: 40 minutes

Scoring: Hand key

Cost: Test $0.15; manual $0.20; key $0.20

Publisher: Bureau of Educational Measurements

EMPORIA GENERAL SCIENCE TEST
Donald Cross and Merritt W. Sanders

Adolescent   Grades 10-12

Purpose: Assesses the general science achievement of high-school students. Used as an end-of-first- or second-semester exam.

Description: 90-item paper-pencil test covering a wide variety of topics in general science. Examiner required. Suitable for group use.

Timed: 40 minutes

Scoring: Hand key

Cost: Test $0.15; manual $0.20; key $0.20

Publisher: Bureau of Educational Measurements

EMPORIA PHYSICS TEST
Gerald L. Witten and Merritt W. Sanders

Adolescent   Grades 10-12

Purpose: Assesses high-school students' knowledge of physics. Used as an end-of-first- or second-semester exam.

Description: 90-item paper-pencil test of general physics concepts, such as mechanics, heat, magnetism, electricity, and sound. Examiner required. Suitable for group use.

Timed: 40 minutes

Scoring: Hand key

Cost: Test $0.15; manual $0.20; key $0.20

Publisher: Bureau of Educational Measurements

GENERAL CHEMISTRY TESTS

Adolescent, adult College students

Purpose: Measures achievement in first-year college chemistry courses. Evaluates student strengths and weaknesses and aids in assigning grades.

Description: 80-item paper-pencil test measuring the following chemistry subject areas: states of matter, stoichiometry, carbon chemistry, solutions, acid-based chemistry, equilibria, electrochemistry and redox, thermodynamics and kinetics, descriptive chemistry, special topics, and laboratory skills. Materials include Form 1985, Form 1985-S, Form 1985-B, Form 1983, Form 1983-S, Form 1983-B, Form 1981, Form 1981-S, and Form 1981-B. "Scrambled" forms, with items in different order, and brief forms, which are shortened versions of the tests, are also available. The tests are for use only by authorized chemistry teachers and administrators. Examiner required. Suitable for group use.

Timed: Form 1981 110 minutes; Form 1983 110 minutes; Form 1985 110 minutes; Form 1981-B 55 minutes; Form 1983-B 55 minutes; Form 1985-B 55 minutes

Scoring: Hand key; examiner evaluated; may be machine scored

Cost: Specimen set $5.00; 25 tests $18.00; 25 answer sheets $3.00; scoring stencils $1.00

Publisher: Examinations Committee, American Chemical Society

GENERAL-ORGANIC-BIOLOGICAL CHEMISTRY (FOR ALLIED HEALTH SCIENCES PROGRAM) TESTS

Adolescent, adult College students

Purpose: Measures achievement in courses covering basic materials in general, organic, and biological chemistry. Used as a unit or end-of-semester examination.

Description: 180-item paper-pencil test measuring proficiency in three areas of chemistry: general, organic, and biological. Each subtest is divided into Part A (40 items) and Part B (20 items). Materials include Form 1979 and Form 1985. The test is for use only by authorized chemistry teachers and administrators. Examiner required. Suitable for group use.

Timed: Part A 35 minutes; Part B 20 minutes

Scoring: Hand key

Cost: Specimen set $5.00; 25 tests $18.00; 25 answer sheets $3.00; scoring stencil $1.00

Publisher: Examinations Committee, American Chemical Society

GENERAL SCIENCE TEST

College student

Purpose: Assesses scientific understanding of college entrants and higher.

Description: Multiple-item paper-pencil test in two parts assessing general scientific knowledge and understanding of technical materials. The first part contains questions on general science, and the second part consists of several paragraphs that determine the extent to which the examinee understands technical articles. Norms are available. Examiner required. Suitable for group use. SOUTH AFRICAN PUBLISHER

Timed: 55 minutes

Scoring: Hand key

Cost: (In Rands) reusable booklet 4,60; 25 answer sheets 2,30; scoring key 3,50; manual 9,50

Publisher: Human Sciences Research Council

GRADUATE LEVEL PLACEMENT EXAMINATIONS: ANALYTICAL CHEMISTRY

Adult
Graduate students

Purpose: Measures achievement in college analytical chemistry courses. Used for placement of graduate students.

Description: 35- or 40-item paper-pencil multiple-choice test measuring knowledge of analytical chemistry. Materials include Form 1977-A (35 items), Form 1981-A (40 items), and Form 1985-A (50 items). The tests are for use only by authorized chemistry teachers and administrators. Examiner required. Suitable for group use.

Timed: Form 1985-A 120 minutes; Form 1981-A 90 minutes; Form 1977-A 90 minutes

Scoring: Hand key

Cost: Specimen set $5.00; 25 tests $18.00; 25 answer sheets $3.00; scoring stencils $1.00

Publisher: Examinations Committee, American Chemical Society

GRADUATE LEVEL PLACEMENT EXAMINATIONS: INORGANIC CHEMISTRY

Adult
Graduate students

Purpose: Measures achievement in college inorganic chemistry courses. Used for placement of graduate students.

Description: 60-item paper-pencil multiple-choice test measuring knowledge of inorganic chemistry. Materials include Forms 1976-I, 1981-I, and 1985-I. The test is for use only by authorized chemistry teachers and administrators. Examiner required. Suitable for group use.

Timed: Form 1985-I 120 minutes; Form 1981-I 110 minutes; Form 1976-I 110 minutes

Scoring: Hand key

Cost: Specimen set $5.00; 25 tests $18.00; 25 answer sheets $3.00; scoring stencils $1.00

Publisher: Examinations Committee, American Chemical Society

GRADUATE LEVEL PLACEMENT EXAMINATIONS: ORGANIC CHEMISTRY

Adult
Graduate students

Purpose: Measures achievement in college organic chemistry courses. Used for placement of graduate students.

Description: 70- or 75-item paper-pencil multiple-choice test measuring knowledge of organic chemistry. Materials include Forms 1977-O (75 items), 1981-O (70 items), and 1985-O (70-items). The test is for use only by authorized chemistry teachers and administrators. Examiner required. Suitable for group use.

Timed: Form 1985-O 90-120 minutes; Form 1981-O 90-120 minutes; Form 1977-O 110 minutes

Scoring: Hand key

Cost: Specimen set $5.00; 25 tests $18.00; 25 answer sheets $3.00; scoring stencils $1.00

Publisher: Examinations Committee, American Chemical Society

GRADUATE LEVEL PLACEMENT EXAMINATIONS: PHYSICAL CHEMISTRY

Adult
Graduate students

Purpose: Measures achievement in college physical chemistry courses. Used for placement of graduate students.

Description: 60-item paper-pencil multiple-choice test measuring knowledge of physical chemistry. Materials include Forms 1977-P, 1981-P, and 1986-P. The test is for use only by authorized chemistry teachers and administrators. The number of items and administration time of Form 1986-P is to be announced in July 1986. Examiner required. Suitable for group use.

Timed: Form 1981-P 150-180 minutes; Form 1977-P 120 minutes

Scoring: Hand key

Cost: Specimen set $5.00; 25 tests $18.00; 25 answer sheets $3.00; scoring stencils $1.00

Publisher: Examinations Committee, American Chemical Society

HIGH SCHOOL CHEMISTRY TESTS

Adolescent   Grades 10-12

Purpose: Measures achievement in first-year high-school chemistry courses. Identifies student strengths and weaknesses and aids in assigning grades.

Description: 80-item paper-pencil test measuring understanding of fundamental concepts and application of basic principles in chemistry. Areas tested include introductory concepts, physical concepts, atomic and molecular concepts, and solutions concepts. Materials include Form 1985, Form 1985-S, Form 1983, Form 1983-S, Form 1981-S, and Form 1979-S. The "S" denotes scrambled versions, which contain items in a different order. The test is for use only by authorized chemistry teachers and administrators. Examiner required. Suitable for group use.

Timed: Form 1985 80 minutes; Form 1985-S 80 minutes; Form 1983 80 minutes; Form 1983-S 80 minutes; Form 1981-S 80 minutes; Form 1979-S 80 minutes

Scoring: Hand key

Cost: Specimen set $5.00; 25 tests $15.00; 25 answer sheets $3.00; scoring stencils $1.00

Publisher: Examinations Committee, American Chemical Society

INORGANIC CHEMISTRY TESTS

Adolescent, adult
College students

Purpose: Measures achievement in undergraduate inorganic chemistry courses. Assesses student strengths and weaknesses and assists graduate-level placement of entering students.

Description: 60-item paper-pencil test covering theoretical and descriptive inorganic chemistry. Topics include nomenclature, bonding, structure, reaction mechanisms, coordination chemistry, and thermodynamics of inorganic elements and compounds. Materials include Forms 1976, 1981, and 1985. The test is for use only by authorized chemistry teachers and administrators. Examiner required. Suitable for group use.

Timed: Form 1985 120 minutes; Form 1981 110 minutes; Form 1976 110 minutes

Scoring: Hand key

Cost: Specimen set $5.00; 25 tests $18.00; 25 answer sheets $3.00; scoring stencils $1.00

Publisher: Examinations Committee, American Chemical Society

INSTRUMENTAL DETERMINATIONS (ANALYSIS) TESTS

Adolescent, adult
College students

Purpose: Measures achievement in undergraduate instrumental determinations courses. Evaluates student strengths and weaknesses and aids in assigning grades.

Description: 69- or 75-item paper-pencil test assessing knowledge of instrumental methods. Materials include Form 1971 (69 items) and Form 1981 (75 items). Form 1981 measures spectroscopy, electroanalytical chemistry, separations, instrumentation, thermal, NMR, mass spectroscopy, radioactivity, and choice of method, x-ray, internal standard methods, titration curves, and kinetics. Form 1971 covers electroanalytical chemistry, spectrophotometry, instrumentation, chromatography, choice of method for an analytical situation, NMR, EPR, emission spectroscopy, and kinetics. The tests are for use only by authorized chemistry teachers and administrators. Examiner required. Suitable for group use.

Timed: Form 1981 110 minutes; Form 1971 110 minutes

Scoring: Hand key

Cost: Specimen set $5.00; 25 tests $18.00; 25 answer sheets $3.00; scoring stencils $1.00

Publisher: Examinations Committee, American Chemical Society

MECHANICAL COMPREHENSION TEST A/3

Adolescent

Purpose: Measures mechanical abilities.

Description: Multiple-item paper-pencil test assessing the ability to apply the laws and principles of physics and mechanics. The test is based on the secondary-school syllabus. Examiner required. Suitable for group use.
SOUTH AFRICAN PUBLISHER

Untimed: 30-35 minutes

Scoring: Hand key

Cost: (In Rands) booklet 5,90; 25 answer sheets 3,00; set of keys 9,00; manual 12,00

Publisher: Human Sciences Research Council

NM CONCEPTS OF ECOLOGY TEST—LEVEL 1 (NMCET-1)
S.P. Klein

Child, adolescent
Grades 6-8

Purpose: Measures an individual's understanding of the concepts of ecology from micro to macro systems. Used for program evaluation and needs assessment.

Description: 20-item paper-pencil multiple-choicee test measuring a student's

understanding of natural resources, pollution, plant/animal dependencies, life processes, natural balance, geographic evolution and conservation, and natural adaptation. The test booklets are reusable, and a lay-over stencil is used for scoring. The reliability and norms have been determined from a sample of sixth-grade students. Examiner/self-administered. Suitable for group use.

Timed: 20 minutes

Scoring: Hand key

Cost: 35 tests (specify level) $12.00; 35 answer sheets (specify level) $4.00; scoring stencil $3.00; manual $3.00

Publisher: Monitor

NM CONCEPTS OF ECOLOGY TEST—LEVEL 2 (NMCET-2)
S.P. Klein

Adolescent   Grades 9-12

Purpose: Measures an individual's understanding of the basic concepts of ecology and conservation. Used for program evaluation and needs assessment.

Description: 20-item paper-pencil multiple-choice test measuring student's understanding of life processes, plant/animal dependencies, geographic evolution and conservation, soil conservation, and natural adaptation. The test booklets are reusable, and a lay-over stencil is used for scoring. Reliability and norms have been determined from samples of ninth- and twelfth-grade secondary students. Examiner/self-administered. Suitable for group use.

Timed: 20 minutes

Scoring: Hand key

Cost: Specimen set $6.00; 35 tests (specify level) $12.00; 35 answer sheets (specify level) $4.00; scoring stencil $3.00; manual $3.00

Publisher: Monitor

ORGANIC CHEMISTRY TESTS

Adolescent, adult
College students

Purpose: Measures achievement in undergraduate organic chemistry courses.

Evaluates student strengths and weaknesses and aids in assigning grades.

Description: 70-item paper-pencil test measuring diverse aspects of organic chemistry, including theoretical concepts, acid and basic character of organic compounds, stereochemistry, various reaction types associated with organic molecules, reaction mechanisms, spectroscopic identification of organic structures, and synthetic sequences. Materials include Form 1986, Form 1982, and Form 1978. The test is for use only by authorized chemistry teachers and administrators. Examiner required. Suitable for group use.

Timed: Form 1986 115 minutes; Form 1982 115 minutes; Form 1978 115 minutes

Scoring: Hand key

Cost: Specimen set $5.00; 25 tests $18.00; 25 answer sheets $3.00; scoring stencils $1.00

Publisher: Examinations Committee, American Chemical Society

PHYSICAL CHEMISTRY FOR THE LIFE SCIENCES TEST

Adolescent, adult
College students

Purpose: Measures achievement in undergraduate courses in physical chemistry taught for life science students. Evaluates student strengths and weaknesses and aids in assigning grades.

Description: 50-item paper-pencil test measuring comprehension of principles of physical chemistry. Topic areas include thermodynamics, solutions and equilibria, dynamics, quantum chemistry, and macromolecules. The test is for use only by authorized chemistry teachers and administrators. Examiner required. Suitable for group use.

Timed: 100 minutes

Scoring: Hand key

Cost: Specimen set $5.00; 25 tests $18.00; 25 answer sheets $3.00; scoring stencils $1.00

Publisher: Examinations Committee, American Chemical Society

PHYSICAL CHEMISTRY TESTS

Adult   College students

Purpose: Measures achievement in undergraduate physical chemistry courses. Evaluates student strengths and weaknesses and aids in assigning grades.

Description: Three 45-50-item paper-pencil subtests measuring three aspects of physical chemistry: thermodynamics, chemical dynamics, and quantum chemistry. The subtests may be administered separately. The thermodynamics subtest covers fundamental laws, state functions, criteria for equilibrium, solutions, and electrochemistry. The chemical dynamics subtest covers rate theories, kinetic theory of gases, and transport phenomena. The quantum chemistry subtest covers fundamental laws of quantum mechanics and their applications. Each subtest is divided into Part A (30 items) and Part B (15 items). Three forms are available. Form 1976-I contains only thermodynamics, Form 1981-II covers only chemical dynamics, and Form 1983-III contains only quantum chemistry. The entire physical chemistry sequence, Form 1975, is also available. This 49-item test may be given at the end of the physical chemistry tests and covers chemical thermodynamics, chemical kinetics and transport phenomena, and quantum chemistry and spectroscopy. The test is for use only by authorized chemistry teachers and administrators. Examiner required. Suitable for group use.

Timed: Part A 50 minutes; Part B 40 minutes

Scoring: Hand key

Cost: Specimen set $5.00; 25 tests $18.00; 25 answer sheets $3.00; scoring stencils $1.00

Publisher: Examinations Committee, American Chemical Society

POLYMER CHEMISTRY TEST

Adolescent, adult
College students

Purpose: Measures achievement in upper-level undergraduate and lower-level graduate courses in polymer chemistry.

Evaluates student strengths and weaknesses and aids in placement and admission of graduate students.

Description: 70-item paper-pencil test covering five areas of polymer chemistry: organic, thermo-kinetics, characterization, physical behavior, and general. The test is for use only by authorized chemistry teachers and administrators. Examiner required. Suitable for group use.

Timed: 110 minutes

Scoring: Hand key

Cost: Specimen set $5.00; 25 tests $18.00; 25 answer sheets $3.00; scoring stencils $1.00

Publisher: Examinations Committee, American Chemical Society

QUANTITATIVE ANALYSIS (ANALYTICAL CHEMISTRY) TESTS

Adolescent, adult
College students

Purpose: Measures achievement in undergraduate analytical chemistry courses. Evaluates student strengths and weaknesses and aids in assigning grades.

Description: 50-item paper-pencil test covering the following topics in analytical chemistry: gravimetric, volumetric, spectrophotometric, electrometric analysis, complexity, pH and buffers, solubility, analytical separations, data evaluation, oxidation-reduction, and indicators. The test is for use only by authorized chemistry teachers and administrators. Examiner required. Suitable for group use.

Timed: Form 1982 90 minutes

Scoring: Hand key

Cost: Specimen set $5.00; 25 tests $18.00; 25 answer sheets $3.00; scoring stencil $1.00

Publisher: Examinations Committee, American Chemical Society

SCIENTIFIC KNOWLEDGE AND APTITUDE TEST

Refer to page 444.

TOLEDO CHEMISTRY PLACEMENT EXAMINATION

Adolescent, adult
College students

Purpose: Predicts performance in college chemistry. Used for placement in appropriate chemistry courses.

Description: 60- or 67-item paper-pencil multiple-choice test assessing readiness for college chemistry. Materials include Form 1974 and Form 1981. Form 1981 (60 items) measures three areas: general mathematics, general chemical knowledge, and specific chemical knowledge. Form 1974 (67 items) is arranged in five parts. The test is for use only by authorized chemistry teachers and administrators. Examiner required. Suitable for group use.

Timed: Form 1981 55 minutes; Form 1974 55 minutes

Scoring: Hand key

Cost: Specimen set $5.00; 25 tests $18.00; 25 answer sheets $3.00; scoring stencils $1.00

Publisher: Examinations Committee, American Chemical Society

Academic Subjects: Science: Health Science

EMPORIA ELEMENTARY HEALTH TEST
Gary Adamson and Merritt W. Sanders

Child, adolescent
Grades 6-9

Purpose: Assesses the health achievement of students in Grades 6-8. Used as an end-of-course exam.

Description: 60-item paper-pencil multiple-choice exam measuring knowledge of health attitudes and the rules and principles of healthful living. Two sets of forms are available for each semester. Examiner required. Suitable for group use.

Timed: 30 minutes

Scoring: Hand key

Cost: Test $0.15; manual $0.20; key $0.20

Publisher: Bureau of Educational Measurements

EMPORIA HIGH SCHOOL HEALTH TEST
Ron Blaylock and Merritt W. Sanders

Adolescent   Grades 10-12

Purpose: Assesses the health knowledge of high-school students. Used as an end-of-course exam.

Description: 60-item paper-pencil multiple-choice test measuring knowledge of basic facts and rules fundamental to healthful living and attitudes toward basic health rules. Student is given the test booklet and answer sheet. Examiner required. Suitable for group use.

Timed: 30 minutes

Scoring: Hand key

Cost: Test $0.15; manual $0.20; key $0.20

Publisher: Bureau of Educational Measurements

FAST-TYSON HEALTH KNOWLEDGE TEST FORM C, 1986 REVISION
Charles G. Fast

Adolescent   Grades 12-13

Purpose: Measures discrimination and judgment in matters of personal health. Used to counsel high-school and college students and upgrade their health knowledge and for pre- and posttesting in curriculum studies.

Description: 100-item paper-pencil multiple-choice test assessing a student's knowledge of factors contributing to personal health. Thirteen areas are covered: personal health, exercise, relaxation and sleep, nutrition and diet, consumer health, contemporary health problems, tobacco, alcohol, drugs and narcotics, safety and first aid, communicable and noncommunicable diseases, mental health, and sex and family life. Norms are provided for college freshmen and high-school seniors. Examiner required. Suitable for group use.

Untimed: 40-50 minutes

Scoring: Hand key

Cost: 50 copies (specify form) $60.00; 100 copies (both forms) $110.00

Publisher: Charles G. Fast

HUMAN REPRODUCTION
H. Frederick Kilander and Glenn C. Leach

Adolescent   Grades 10-13

Purpose: Measures high-school and college students' knowledge of the human reproductive system. Used for health and human sexuality courses.

Description: 33-item paper-pencil multiple-choice test assessing knowledge of human reproduction. Self-administered. Suitable for group use.

Timed: 30 minutes

Scoring: Hand key

Cost: Free

Publisher: Glenn C. Leach, Ed.D.

INFORMATION TEST ON DRUGS AND DRUG ABUSE
Glenn C. Leach and H. Frederick Kilander

Adolescent   Grades 10-13

Purpose: Measures high-school and college students' knowledge of drugs and drug abuse. Used for drug abuse counseling.

Description: 30-item paper-pencil multiple-choice test covering legal and illegal drug use. Self-administered. Suitable for group use.

Timed: 30 minutes

Scoring: Hand key

Cost: Free

Publisher: Glenn C. Leach, Ed.D.

KILANDER-LEACH HEALTH KNOWLEDGE
H. Frederick Kilander and Glen C. Leach

Adolescent Grades 10-13

Purpose: Measures high-school and college students' general knowledge of health. Used as a pre- or end-of-course exam in high-school health education classes.

Description: 100-item paper-pencil multiple-choice test measuring health knowledge, including personal health, nutrition, community health, sanitation, communicable diseases, safety, first aid, family living, and mental health. Self-administered; proctor desirable. Suitable for group use.

Untimed: 45-50 minutes

Scoring: Hand key

Cost: 100 booklets $30.00; 35 answer sheets $15.00; guide $1.00

Publisher: Glenn C. Leach, Ed.D.

NATIONAL ACHIEVEMENT TESTS: HEALTH AND SCIENCE TESTS—HEALTH EDUCATION
John S. Shaw, Maurice E. Troyer, and Clifford L. Brownell

Adolescent Grades 7 and above

Purpose: Assesses health knowledge. Used for educational evaluation.

Description: Paper-pencil test of newer phases of health information. The test contains problems with which students in high school and college should be familiar. Two equivalent forms, A and B, are available. Examiner required. Suitable for group use.

Timed: 40 minutes

Scoring: Hand key

Cost: Specimen set (test, manual, key) $4.00; 25 tests $8.75; 25 answer sheets $4.00

Publisher: Psychometric Affiliates

NUTRITION INFORMATION TEST
H. Frederick Kilander and Glenn C. Leach

Adolescent, adult Grades 10 and above

Purpose: Determines nutrition knowledge and attitudes of high-school and college students.

Description: 33-item paper-pencil multiple-choice test covering various aspects of nutrition, including calories, diseases, physical health, and weight control. Self-administered. Suitable for group use.

Untimed: 15 minutes

Scoring: Hand key

Cost: Free

Publisher: Glenn C. Leach, Ed.D.

NUTRITION KNOWLEDGE AND INTEREST QUESTIONNAIRE
G. Darrell Passwater

Child, adolescent Grades 9-12

Purpose: Assesses high-school students' knowledge of nutrition and determines additional knowledge they desire in that area. Used for high-school curriculum planning.

Description: 56-item paper-pencil test consisting of 50 multiple-choice questions and six written-answer items covering six general areas: physical, mental, emotional, social, and economic factors affecting an individual's diet; relationships between nutritional status and disease; interrelationships of diet, activity, and other factors that regulate weight control; distinguishing between food fads and fallacies and those diets based on scientific principles of nutrition; emergency trends in society that influence dietary patterns; and nutritional behaviors that promote health. Examiner required. Suitable for group use.

Untimed: Not available

Scoring: Examiner evaluated

Cost: Complete kit (35 student test book-lets, 35 test answer sheets, teacher's manual/answer key) $14.95; 35 student answer sheets $2.95; teacher's manual/answer key $1.95

Publisher: Teachers College Press

THE OHIO VOCATIONAL ACHIEVEMENT TESTS IN HEALTH OCCUPATIONS EDUCATION: DENTAL ASSISTING

Refer to page 725.

THE OHIO VOCATIONAL ACHIEVEMENT TESTS IN HEALTH OCCUPATIONS EDUCATION: DIVERSIFIED HEALTH OCCUPATION

Refer to page 725.

THE OHIO VOCATIONAL ACHIEVEMENT TESTS IN HEALTH OCCUPATIONS EDUCATION: MEDICAL ASSISTING

Refer to page 725.

SCIENCE TESTS—STANDARD 5 THROUGH STANDARD 8 HIGHER GRADE

Child, adolescent

Purpose: Assesses achievement in science courses. Used for educational evaluation and placement.

Description: Six paper-pencil tests of science knowledge in Standards 5 through 8 Higher Grade. General Science-Standard 5 consists of the following subtests: Measurement of Matter, Heat, Magnetism, and Biology. Physical Science-Standard 6 has three subtests: Matter Classification of Matter, Oxygen, Hydrogen, Carbon Dioxide; Water; and Force, Work, Energy, and Electricity. Physical Science-Standard 7 is very similar to Standard 6. Standard 8 and above measures eight aspects of physical science: light; sound; heat, light, and energy; electricity; atomic structure; chemical reactions; acids, bases, and salts; and chemical reactions

and electricity. Biology tests for Standards 6 and 7 measure some of the following areas: reproduction, growth and development, nutrition, and gaseous exchange during respiration. Examiner required. Suitable for group use.

SOUTH AFRICAN PUBLISHER

Untimed: Not available

Scoring: Hand key; examiner evaluated

Cost: Contact publisher; orders from outside The RSA will be dealt with on merit

Publisher: Human Sciences Research Council

SMOKING AND HEALTH
H. Frederick Kilander

Adolescent, adult
Grades 10-13

Purpose: Assesses an individual's commitment to and knowledge of smoking. Used for analysis of smoking behavior and research.

Description: 33-item paper-pencil multiple-choice and objective test on smoking. Self-administered. Suitable for group use.

Timed: 25 minutes

Scoring: Hand key

Cost: Free

Publisher: Glenn C. Leach, Ed.D.

Academic Subjects: Social Studies

AMERICAN GOVERNMENT TEST

Adolescent   Grades 8-12

Purpose: Evaluates high-school students' understanding of government, with strong emphasis on political action and dynamics of American politics. Used for course testing.

Description: 100 paper-pencil multiple-choice questions in each of six tests. The tests are Fundamentals of Government, Executive Branch, Legislative Branch,

Civil Liberties and American Law, State and Local Government, and a Final Test. Materials include test booklets, answer sheet, manual, and key. Examiner required. Suitable for group use.

Untimed: 50 minutes

Scoring: Hand key

Cost: Single test with answer sheet $0.45; complete set of 6 tests $2.60; 30 additional answer sheets $1.20

Publisher: The Perfection Form Company

Information and availability unconfirmed by publisher.

AMERICAN HISTORY MAP TEST FOLIO

Adolescent **Grades 10-12**

Purpose: Measures high-school students' understanding of American history through map reading skills. Used for teaching or testing.

Description: 100-item paper-pencil multiple-choice test covering knowledge of history, politics, religion, and other areas for each of 21 map titles, including New World Explorations, French and Indian War, World War I, and America and Europe. Questions are posed on basic outline maps that students check to complete the questions. Examiner required. Suitable for group use.

Untimed: Not available

Scoring: Hand key

Cost: Test $1.25; 30 classroom test sets (one set includes 21 map tests-one for each title) $27.95

Publisher: The Perfection Form Company

Information and availability unconfirmed by publisher.

AMERICAN HISTORY TEST

Child, adolescent Grades 7-9

Purpose: Evaluates junior high-school students' knowledge of specific periods of American history. Used as unit tests.

Description: 75 paper-pencil objective questions in separate tests for each of 12 periods from colonial America to post-World War II. Examiner required. Suitable for group use.

Untimed: 50 minutes

Scoring: Hand key

Cost: Test (answer key and sheet) $0.45; complete set $4.75; 30 additional answer sheets $1.20

Publisher: The Perfection Form Company

Information and availability unconfirmed by publisher.

AMERICAN HISTORY TESTS

Adolescent **Grades 10-12**

Purpose: Evaluates senior high-school students' knowledge of specific periods in American history. Used for unit posttests.

Description: 100 paper-pencil multiple-choice questions in each of 13 tests covering American history from the colonial period to post-World War II and the present. Two semester tests and a final exam are included. Examiner required. Suitable for group use.

Untimed: 50 minutes

Scoring: Hand key

Cost: Test (answer sheet and key) $0.45; 13 tests $3.95; 30 additional answer sheets $1.20

Publisher: The Perfection Form Company

Information and availability unconfirmed by publisher.

BASIC ECONOMICS TEST (BET)
John F. Chizmar and Ronald S. Halinski

Child **Grades 4-6**

Purpose: Measures elementary-school students' understanding of economic principles. Used to assess curricular development and to determine the effectiveness of materials and teaching strategies.

Description: 38-item paper-pencil multiple-choice test covering basic economic concepts, economic systems, micro-economics, resource allocation, macroeconomics, and economic institutions. The test is available in two forms, A and B. Examiner required. Suitable for group use.

Timed: 50 minutes

Scoring: Hand key; may be computer scored

Cost: Manual and answer key $3.00; 25 test booklets (specify form) $6.00

Publisher: Joint Council on Economic Education

BLACK HISTORY: A TEST TO CREATE AWARENESS AND AROUSE INTEREST
Gregory C. Coffin, Elsie F. Harley, and Bessie M.L. Rhodes

Child   Grade 5

Purpose: Creates awareness and interest in black history; not intended as a measure of factual knowledge. Used to supplement class studies.

Description: 100-item paper-pencil test intended to create awareness of distortions or omissions of black history in the basic curriculum and history books. May be self-administered. Suitable for group use.

Untimed: 1 hour

Scoring: Hand key

Cost: 30 copies $50.00

Publisher: Coffin Associates

Information and availability unconfirmed; no publisher response.

CASS-SANDERS PSYCHOLOGY TEST
Dall H. Cass and Merritt W. Sanders

Adolescent, adult
Grades 10 and above

Purpose: Assesses the psychology course achievement of high-school and college students. Used as an end-of-course exam.

Description: 125-item paper-pencil test of the basic facts, rules, and principles covered in a beginning psychology course. Examiner required. Suitable for group use.

Timed: 50 minutes

Scoring: Hand key

Cost: Test $0.15; manual $0.20; key $0.20

Publisher: Bureau of Educational Measurements

CPRI QUESTIONNAIRES (Q-71, Q-74, Q-75, Q-76)
Refer to page 686.

===

ECONOMICS TESTS

Adolescent   Grades 10-12

Purpose: Measures high-school students' economic knowledge over a semester course. Used as unit posttests.

Description: 100-item paper-pencil test measuring concepts in economics (price, income, and personal growth), money (banking and insurance), and international trade. A final exam is included. Examiner required. Suitable for group use.

Untimed: Not available

Scoring: Hand key

Cost: Test (answer sheet and key) $0.45; complete set $2.20; 30 additional answer sheets $1.20

Publisher: The Perfection Form Company

Information and availability unconfirmed by publisher.

EMPORIA AMERICAN GOVERNMENT TEST
Bureau of Educational Measurements

Adolescent   Grades 10-12

Purpose: Measures high-school students' understanding of American government. Used as a pretest or end-of-course exam.

Description: 75-item paper-pencil multiple-choice test of the theory and facts of American government. The test also assesses students' ability to apply knowledge to hypothetical problems and situations. Examiner required. Suitable for group use.

Untimed: 50-60 minutes

Scoring: Hand key

Cost: Test $0.15; manual $0.20; key $0.20

Publisher: Bureau of Educational Measurements

EMPORIA AMERICAN HISTORY TEST
Shirley Meares and Merritt W. Sanders

Adolescent   Grades 10-12

Purpose: Assesses high-school students' understanding of American history. Used as an end-of-course exam.

Description: 120-item paper-pencil general survey test of concepts, historical events, vocabulary, and people covered in a one-year American history course. Examiner required. Suitable for group use.

Timed: 40 minutes

Scoring: Hand key

Cost: Test $0.15; manual $0.20; key $0.20

Publisher: Bureau of Educational Measurements

HOLLINGSWORTH-SANDERS GEOGRAPHY TEST
Leon Hollingsworth and Merritt W. Sanders

Child, adolescent Grades 5-7

Purpose: Assesses achievement in geography course work. Used as an end-of-course exam.

Description: 65-item paper-pencil objective test of geographical facts, principles, cause and effect, and map study. Examiner required. Suitable for group use.

Timed: 30 minutes

Scoring: Hand key

Cost: Test $0.15; manual $0.20; key $0.20

Publisher: Bureau of Educational Measurements

HOLLINGSWORTH-SANDERS INTERMEDIATE HISTORY TEST
Leon Hollingsworth and Merritt W. Sanders

Child   Grades 5-6

Purpose: Assesses the history achievement of upper elementary-school students. Used as a first- or second-semester exam.

Description: 55-item paper-pencil test covering historical facts, the application of information, and reasoning. Examiner required. Suitable for group use.

Timed: 30 minutes

Scoring: Hand key

Cost: Test $0.15; manual $0.20; key $0.20

Publisher: Bureau of Educational Measurements

HUMAN LOYALTY EXPRESSIONAIRE
Theodore F. Lentz

Adolescent, adult College student

Purpose: Measures human loyalty and global awareness. Used in peace and global studies courses.

Description: 172-item paper-pencil test in three sections. The subject agrees or disagrees with each statement. Self-administered. Suitable for group use.

Timed: 45 minutes

Scoring: Hand key

Cost: 3 forms of questionnaire, scoring keys, norms $7.00; questionnaires can be reproduced at no further charge

Publisher: Lentz Peace Research Laboratory

INFORMETER: AN INTERNATIONAL TECHNIQUE FOR THE MEASUREMENT OF POLITICAL INFORMATION
Panos D. Bardis

Adolescent Grades 10 and above

Purpose: Measures political knowledge and awareness of local, national, and international affairs. Used for research on political information in the general population and discussion in social sciences classes.

Description: 100-item paper-pencil test in which the subject is asked to list important names, dates, events, and issues in response to specific questions about politics, government, and current events. Examiner/self-administered. Suitable for group use.

Untimed: 15 minutes

Scoring: Examiner evaluated

Cost: Free

Publisher: Panos D. Bardis

IRENOMETER
Refer to page 222.

JUNIOR HIGH SCHOOL TEST OF ECONOMICS
Committee for the Development of a Junior High School Test of Economics

Adolescent   Grades 7-9

Purpose: Tests junior high-school students' understanding of economics. Used to evaluate classroom progress and effectiveness of teaching materials.

Description: 40-item paper-pencil examination of students' knowledge of economic facts and concepts. The concepts tested are scarcity, opportunity costs, supply and demands, GNP, money, prices and inflation, government taxation and spending, economic growth, and government policies to achieve full employment and price stability. Examiner required. Suitable for group use.

Timed: 40 minutes

Scoring: Hand key; may be computer scored

Cost: Manual with answer key $3.00; 25 tests $6.00

Publisher: Joint Council on Economic Education

MEARES-SANDERS JUNIOR HIGH SCHOOL HISTORY TEST
Shirley Meares and Merritt W. Sanders

Adolescent   Grades 7-8

Purpose: Assesses the history achievement of junior high-school students. Used as a first- or second-semester exam.

Description: 100-item paper-pencil test covering historical factual knowledge, the application of information, and reasoning. Examiner required. Suitable for group use.

Timed: 40 minutes

Scoring: Hand key

Cost: Test $0.15; manual $0.20; key $0.20

Publisher: Bureau of Educational Measurements

THE MULTI-ETHNIC AWARENESS SURVEY
Gregory C. Coffin, Nancy S. Coffin, Bessie L. Rhodes, and Robert E. Rhodes

Child, adolescent
Grades 5 and above

Purpose: Creates awareness of and arouses interest in the historical role of seven American ethnic groups: blacks, Asians, Jews, Irish, Italians, Latinos, and Native Americans. The test is used as a supplement to the curriculum, not as a measure of factual knowledge.

Description: 100-item paper-pencil inventory designed to create awareness of the contributions of seven major ethnic groups to America's history. Self-administered. Suitable for group use.

Untimed: 1 hour

Scoring: Hand key

Cost: Complete set $50.00

Publisher: Coffin Associates

Information and availability unconfirmed; no publisher response.

A PARTIAL INDEX OF MODERNIZATION: MEASUREMENT OF ATTITUDES TOWARD MORALITY
Refer to page 306.

PRIMARY TEST OF ECONOMIC UNDERSTANDING
Donald G. Davison and John H. Kilgore

Child   Grades 2-3

Purpose: Reveals a child's understanding of economic concepts typically taught in Grades 2 and 3. Used for diagnosis and to evaluate effectiveness of teaching materials.

Description: 32-item paper-pencil yes-no test. The child must answer both questions correctly to be scored correct. The examiner reads the questions aloud, and the child writes "yes" or "no" for each one. Materials include a test and answer key. Examiner required. Suitable for group use.
Untimed: 40 minutes
Scoring: Hand key
Cost: Manual and answer key $3.00; 25 test booklets $6.00
Publisher: Bureau of Business and Economic Research/University of Iowa

REVISED TEST OF UNDERSTANDING IN COLLEGE ECONOMICS
Phillip Saunders

Adolescent, adult

Purpose: Serves as a measuring instrument for controlled experiments in the teaching of introductory college economics. Used for research and to compare one college course with another.

Description: 90-item paper-pencil examination consisting of three subtests, each in comparable A and B forms. Each form contains 30 questions dealing with recognition and understanding and simple and complex application of macro-, micro-, and hybrid economic principles. The macro test covers the measurement of aggregate economic performance, aggregate supply, productive capacity and growth, income and expenditure approach to aggregate demand and fiscal policy, monetary approach to aggregate demand, policy combination, and practical problems of stabilization. The micro test covers basic economic problems, markets and market failure, externalities, government intervention and regulation, income distribution and government redistribution. The hybrid test covers material from both the macro and micro tests. Examiner required. Suitable for group use.
Timed: 45 minutes
Scoring: Hand key; may be computer scored
Cost: Manual $3.00; 25 test booklets $6.00 (specify form)
Publisher: Joint Council on Economic Education

SANDERS-BULLER WORLD HISTORY TEST
Merritt W. Sanders and Robert Buller

Adolescent   Grades 10-12

Purpose: Assesses the world history knowledge of high-school students. Used as a first- or second-semester exam.

Description: 100-item paper-pencil test of ancient, medieval, and modern history. Examiner required. Suitable for group use.
Timed: 40 minutes
Scoring: Hand key
Cost: Test $0.15; manual $0.20; key $0.20
Publisher: Bureau of Educational Measurements

SARE-SANDERS CONSTITUTION TEST
Harold V. Sare and Merritt W. Sanders

Adolescent   Grades 10-12

Purpose: Assesses high-school student knowledge of the U.S. Constitution. Used as an end-of-first- or second-semester exam.

Description: 125-item paper-pencil test covering the vocabulary, history, and application of the U.S. Constitution. Examiner required. Suitable for group use.

Timed: 40 minutes

Scoring: Hand key

Cost: Test $0.15; manual $0.20; key $0.20

Publisher: Bureau of Educational Measurements

SARE-SANDERS SOCIOLOGY TEST
Harold V. Sare and Merritt W. Sanders

Adolescent   Grades 10-12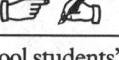

Purpose: Assesses the sociology achievement of high-school students. Used as an end-of-course exam.

Description: 142-item paper-pencil test of customs, folkways, mores, traditions, and social problems. Examiner required. Suitable for group use.

Timed: 40 minutes

Scoring: Hand key

Cost: Test $0.15; manual $0.20; key $0.20

Publisher: Bureau of Educational Measurements

TEST OF ECONOMIC LITERACY (TEL)
John C. Soper

Adolescent   Grades 11-12

Purpose: Measures senior high-school students' knowledge of economic systems and theory. Used to evaluate the quality of instruction and effectiveness of materials used.

Description: 46-item paper-pencil test covering seven content areas: basic economic problems, economic systems, microeconomics, resource allocation and economic distribution, macroeconomics, economic stability and growth, world economy, economic institutions, and concepts for evaluating economic actions and

policies. The test is available in two forms, A and B. Examiner required. Suitable for group use. Available in Spanish.

Untimed: 40 minutes

Scoring: Hand key

Cost: Manual with answer key $3.00; 25 Form A $6.00; 25 Form B $6.00; single copy of Spanish language test $1.00

Publisher: Joint Council on Economic Education

TEST OF UNDERSTANDING IN PERSONAL ECONOMICS
Joint Council on Economic Education

Adolescent   Grades 9-12

Purpose: Measures high-school students' understanding of personal economics, including principles and operations. Used as course review and to determine effectiveness of instruction.

Description: 50-item paper-pencil multiple-choice test of the student's knowledge of economics. Examiner required. Suitable for group use.

Timed: 45 minutes

Scoring: Hand key

Cost: Manual with answer key $3.00; 25 test booklets $6.00

Publisher: Joint Council on Economic Education

A VIOLENCE SCALE
Refer to page 186.

WORLD GOVERNMENT SCALE
Refer to page 696.

WORLD HISTORY MAP TEST FOLIO
Earl Brightwater

Adolescent   Grades 9-12

Purpose: Measures high-school students' understanding of world history through map reading skills. Used as transparencies and unit teaching aids.

Description: 100-item paper-pencil multiple-choice test covering knowledge of history, politics, religion, and other areas for each of 20 map titles including Roman Empire, Europe 1812, and the Far East. Questions are posed in basic outline maps that students check to complete the questions. Examiner required. Suitable for group use.

Untimed: 50 minutes

Scoring: Hand key

Cost: Test (answer sheet and key) $1.25; test set (30 sets of 20 maps) $29.95

Publisher: The Perfection Form Company

Information and availability unconfirmed by publisher.

WORLD HISTORY TEST

Adolescent Grades 8-12

Purpose: Measures high-school students' recall of factual information from specific periods in world history. Used as unit tests.

Description: 100-item paper-pencil test covering each of 16 periods from the earliest civilizations to new imperialism and Russian history. Two semester tests and a final exam are included. Materials include test, answer key, and answer sheets. Examiner required. Suitable for group use.

Untimed: 50 minutes

Scoring: Hand key

Cost: Test (answer sheet and key) $0.45; complete set $6.25; 30 additional answer sheets $1.20

Publisher: The Perfection Form Company

Information and availability unconfirmed by publisher.

ZIMMERMAN-SANDERS SOCIAL STUDIES TEST
John J. Zimmerman and Merritt W. Sanders

Adolescent Grades 7-8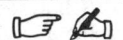

Purpose: Assesses the social studies achievement of junior-high-school students. Used as an end-of-course exam.

Description: 85-item paper-pencil test of basic areas of history, geography, and civics. Examiner required. Suitable for group use.

Timed: 30 minutes

Scoring: Hand key

Cost: Test $0.15; manual $0.20; key $0.20

Publisher: Bureau of Educational Measurements

Academic Achievement and Aptitude

ACADEMIC APTITUDE TEST (AAT)—1974

Adolescent

Purpose: Assesses academic abilities. Used for vocational guidance.

Description: Battery of 10 tests measuring specific academic aptitudes: Nonverbal Reasoning, Verbal Reasoning, English Vocabulary, English Reading Comprehension, Numerical Comprehension, Afrikaans Vocabulary, Afrikaans Reading Comprehension, Squares, Spatial Perception (3D), and Mathematical Proficiency. Examiner required. Suitable for group use.
SOUTH AFRICAN PUBLISHER

Timed: 7 hours

Scoring: Hand key; examiner evaluated

Cost: (In Rands) test booklet 2,40; manual 5,00; demonstration model 3,80; 10 answer sheets 1,00; scoring stencil 3,90; orders from outside The RSA will be dealt with on merit

Publisher: Human Sciences Research Council

ACADEMIC APTITUDE TEST (AAT)—1976

Adolescent, adult

Purpose: Assesses academic abilities at the university level. Used for vocational guidance.

Description: Multiple-item battery of tests measuring 10 specific academic aptitudes: Nonverbal Reasoning, Verbal Reasoning, English Vocabulary, English Reading Comprehension, Numerical Comprehension, Afrikaans Vocabulary, Afrikaans Reading Comprehension, Squares, Spatial Perception (3D), and Mathematical Proficiency. Examiner required. Suitable for group use.
SOUTH AFRICAN PUBLISHER

Timed: 7 hours

Scoring: Hand key; examiner evaluated

Cost: (In Rands) test booklet 2,10; manual 5,50; demonstration model 3,80; 10 answer sheets 1,00; scoring stencil 3,90; orders from outside The RSA will be dealt with on merit

Publisher: Human Sciences Research Council

ACADEMIC INSTRUCTIONAL MEASUREMENT SYSTEM (AIMS)

Child, adolescent
Grades 1-12

Purpose: Assesses mathematics, reading, and language arts skills for students in Grades 1-12. Used for achievement reporting, diagnosis, screening, and progress monitoring in school settings.

Description: 985-item paper-pencil item bank measuring curriculum-referenced, instructionally sequenced objectives. Reading/Language Arts content categories are phonic analysis, structural analysis, vocabulary, life study and reference, literal comprehension, inferential comprehension, critical comprehension, understanding literature, listening, spelling, mechanics, usage, grammar and syntax, proofreading, and composition. Mathematics content categories are numeration, whole numbers: addition, whole numbers: subtraction, whole numbers: multiplication, whole numbers: division, decimals, fractions, ratio/proportion/percent, measurement, geometry, problem solving, graphing/statistics, probability, pre-algebra, and essential life skills. Materials include professionally prepared art and instructions. Test building software allows users to access,

organize, and edit both AIMS and locally developed objectives. Examiner required. Suitable for group use.

Untimed: Not available

Scoring: Machine scored

Cost: Contact publisher

Publisher: The Psychological Corporation

ACADEMIC-TECHNICAL APTITUDE TESTS FOR COLOURED PUPILS IN STANDARDS 6, 7, AND 8 (ATA)

Adolescent

Purpose: Measures the differential aptitudes of pupils in Standards 6-8. Used for vocational and educational guidance.

Description: Multiple-item battery of 10 paper-pencil tests, including verbal reasoning, nonverbal reasoning, computations, spatial perception (2D), mechanical reasoning, language comprehension, spatial perception (3D), comparison, coordination, and writing speed. Stanines and percentile ranks are available for each standard. Examiner required. Suitable for group use.
SOUTH AFRICAN PUBLISHER

Untimed: 4 hours

Scoring: Hand key

Cost: Test booklet $2.40; manual $3.90; scoring stencil (specify I or II) $1.30; 10 answer sheets $0.60

Publisher: Human Sciences Research Council

ACER TESTS OF LEARNING ABILITY (TOLA)

Child, adolescent
Ages 8.6-13.2

Purpose: Measures the language and reasoning aspects of general intellectual ability important for academic success for students ages 8.6-13.2.

Description: Multiple-item paper-pencil test of general academic aptitude is available at two levels: TOLA 4 (Year 4 of schooling or ages 8.6-11.5) and TOLA 6 (Year 6 of schooling or ages 10.3-13.2). Each level contains three separately timed subtests: Verbal Comprehension (vocabulary); General Reasoning (problem solving in a mathematical framework); and Syllogistic Reasoning (verbal analogies). Australian norms are provided in the form of stanines and percentile ranks. Examiner required. Suitable for group use.

AUSTRALIAN PUBLISHER

Timed: 33 minutes

Scoring: Hand key

Cost: Contact publisher

Publisher: The Australian Council for Educational Research Limited

---

ACHIEVEMENT AND SPECIAL ABILITIES TESTING PROGRAMS: ADMISSIONS AND CREDENTIALING MEASUREMENT GROUP
The Psychological Corporation

Adolescent, adult

Purpose: Assesses special abilities and achievements of students and adults. Used for selection and admission of applicants and students to various programs and schools.

Description: Multiple-item multiple-choice paper-pencil tests of special ability and achievement. The Tests for Accounting (high school, college, and professional levels) assess the promise and achievement of prospective accounting students, enrolled accounting students, and graduate accountants. The Proficiency Test in Practical Nursing tests medical-surgical nursing, pharmacology, nutrition, maternal and child care, and general nursing information. The Qualifying Examination Services for Securities and Exchange Organizations is used by the National Association of Securities Dealers, New York Stock Exchange, American Stock Exchange, Pacific Coast Stock Exchange, and Chicago Board of Trade. Examiner required. Suitable for group use.

Timed: Varies, depending on exam

Scoring: Computer scoring service provided

Cost: Contact publisher

Publisher: Admissions and Credentialing Group/The Psychological Corporation

---

ACHIEVEMENT TEST
College Board Achievement Test Development Committees

Adolescent   Grades 10-12

Purpose: Measures high-school students' knowledge of a particular subject and the ability to apply that knowledge in a specified subject area. Used to predict how well the student will do in a college-level course and for admissions selection and course placement.

Description: 14 paper-pencil multiple-choice tests, each one hour in length and containing from 60 to 100 questions each, covering the following areas: English composition (with and without essay), literature, American history and social studies, European history and world cultures, mathematics level I, mathematics level II, French, German, Hebrew, Latin, Spanish, biology, chemistry, and physics. The English composition test includes a 20-minute essay. One point is given for each correct answer, and a fraction of a point is deducted for each wrong answer. Scores are reported on a scale of 200 to 800. Most tests are administered five times a year, and the fee entitles a student to take as many as three tests on one date. The achievement tests, together with the Scholastic Aptitude Test (SAT), are offered through the Admissions Testing Program (ATP) of the College Board. For students with disabilities, the ATP offers special testing arrangements, including extended time administrations of the achievement tests. Examiner required. Suitable for group use.

Timed: 1 hour per test

Scoring: Computer scored

Cost: Contact publisher

Publisher: The College Board

Information and availability unconfirmed by publisher.

ACHIEVEMENT TEST: ENGLISH—ENGLISH COMPOSITION
College Board Achievement Test Development Committees

Adolescent   Grades 10-12

Purpose: Measures high-school students' ability to write clear and effective prose in standard English. Used to predict college performance and by some schools for admissions selection and course placement.

Description: Multiple-item paper-pencil multiple-choice and essay test in two forms. One form is administered only in December and requires the student to answer approximately 70 multiple-choice questions and write a brief essay. The second form, offered at four other times during the year, consists of about 90 multiple-choice questions; no writing is involved. The various types of questions test the student's understanding of the relationship between ideas in a sentence, awareness of tone and meaning of words, sensitivity to wordiness and ambiguity, and knowledge of the structure and idiom of the written English that is acceptable to college teachers. The essay test (administered only in December) is a 20-minute assignment, preceded by a quotation or statement intended to stimulate the writer's thoughts on the subject. It gives the writer an opportunity to demonstrate quality of self-expression. Graded by high-school and college English teachers, the essay comprises one-third of the total English Composition score, which is reported on a 200 to 800 scale. This achievement test, together with the Scholastic Aptitude Test (SAT), is offered through the Admissions Testing Program (ATP) of the College Board. For students with disabilities, the ATP has available special testing arrangements, including extended time administrations of the achievement test. Examiner required. Suitable for group use.

Timed: 1 hour

Scoring: Computer scored

Cost: Contact publisher

Publisher: The College Board

Information and availability unconfirmed by publisher.

ACHIEVEMENT TEST: ENGLISH—LITERATURE
College Board Achievement Test Development Committees

Adolescent   Grades 10-12 👉 ✍

Purpose: Assesses high-school students' understanding and interpretation of works of literature. Used to predict college performance and by some schools for admissions selection and course placement.

Description: 60-item paper-pencil multiple-choice test based on passages drawn from poetry, fiction, drama, and prose written in English from the Renaissance to the present. Some questions ask for analysis or summation of parts of or whole passages; others ask that elements of style (such as rhythm, rhyme, and metaphor) be related to the meaning, mood, or structure of the passage. The student is not expected to have read or studied any of the passages; he is expected to be able to examine them using developed skills. One point is given for each correct answer, and a fraction of a point is deducted for each wrong answer. Scores are reported on a scale of 200 to 800. This achievement test (offered five times a year), together with the Scholastic Aptitude Test (SAT), is offered through the Admissions Testing Program (ATP) of the College Board. For students with disabilities, the ATP has available special testing arrangements, including extended time administrations of the achievement test. Examiner required. Suitable for group use.

Timed: 1 hour

Scoring: Computer scored

Cost: Contact publisher

Publisher: The College Board

Information and availability unconfirmed by publisher.

ACHIEVEMENT TEST: FOREIGN LANGUAGES—FRENCH
College Board Achievement Test Development Committees

Adolescent   Grades 10-12 👉 ✍

Purpose: Measures high-school students' vocabulary mastery, grammatical control, and reading comprehension of French. Used to predict college performance and by some schools for admissions selection and course placement.

Description: Multiple-item paper-pencil multiple-choice test of ability and knowledge in three areas: vocabulary mastery, the knowledge of the meaning of words and idiomatic expressions as they appear in the written and spoken forms of the language; grammatical control, the identification of usage that is structurally correct and appropriate in context; and reading comprehension, the overall meaning of passages in various styles and levels of writing and recall of specific details. One point is given for each correct answer, and a fraction of a point is deducted for each wrong answer. Scores are reported on a scale of 200 to 800. This achievement test (administered five times a year), together with the Scholastic Aptitude Test (SAT), is offered through the Admissions Testing Program (ATP) of the College Board. For students with disabilities, the ATP has available special testing arrangements, including extended time administrations of the achievement test. Examiner required. Suitable for group use.

Timed: 1 hour

Scoring: Computer scored

Cost: Contact publisher

Publisher: The College Board

Information and availability unconfirmed by publisher.

ACHIEVEMENT TEST: FOREIGN LANGUAGES—GERMAN
College Board Achievement Test Development Committees

Adolescent   Grades 10-12 ☞ 🖉

Purpose: Measures high-school students' vocabulary mastery, grammatical control, and reading comprehension of German. Used to predict college performance and by some schools for admissions selection and course placement.

Description: Multiple-item paper-pencil multiple-choice test of ability and knowledge in three areas: vocabulary mastery, the knowledge of the meaning of words and idiomatic expressions as they appear in the written and spoken forms of the language; grammatical control, the identification of usage that is structurally correct and appropriate in context; and reading comprehension, the overall meaning of passages in various styles and levels of writing and recall of specific details.

One point is given for each correct answer, and a fraction of a point is deducted for each wrong answer. Scores are reported on a scale of 200 to 800. This achievement test (administered five times a year), together with the Scholastic Aptitude Test (SAT), is offered through the Admissions Testing Program (ATP) of the College Board. For students with disabilities, the ATP has available special testing arrangements, including extended time administrations of the achievement test. Examiner required. Suitable for group use.

Timed: 1 hour

Scoring: Computer scored

Cost: Contact publisher

Publisher: The College Board

Information and availability unconfirmed by publisher.

ACHIEVEMENT TEST: FOREIGN LANGUAGES—HEBREW
College Board Achievement Test Development Committees

Adolescent   Grades 10-12 ☞ 🖉

Purpose: Measures high-school students' vocabulary mastery, grammatical control, and reading comprehension of Hebrew. Used to predict college performance and by some schools for admissions selection and course placement.

Description: Multiple-item paper-pencil multiple-choice test of ability and knowledge in three areas: vocabulary mastery, the knowledge of the meaning of words and idiomatic expressions as they appear in the written and spoken forms of the language; grammatical control, the identification of usage that is structurally correct and appropriate in context; and reading comprehension, the overall meaning of passages in various styles and levels of writing and recall of specific details. One point is given for each correct answer, and a fraction of a point is deducted for each wrong answer. Scores are reported on a scale of 200 to 800. This achievement test (administered five times a year), together with the Scholastic Aptitude Test (SAT), is offered through the Admissions Testing Program (ATP) of the College Board. For students with disabilities, the ATP has available special testing arrangements, including extended time administrations of the achievement test. Examiner required. Suitable for group use.

Timed: 1 hour

Scoring: Computer scored

Cost: Contact publisher

Publisher: The College Board

Information and availability unconfirmed by publisher.

ACHIEVEMENT TEST: FOREIGN LANGUAGES—LATIN
College Board Achievement Test Development Committees

Adolescent   Grades 10-12

Purpose: Measures high-school students' vocabulary mastery, grammatical control, and reading comprehension of Latin. Used to predict college performance and by some schools for admissions selection and course placement.

Description: Multiple-item paper-pencil multiple-choice test of ability and knowledge in three areas: vocabulary mastery, the knowledge of the meaning of words and idiomatic expressions as they appear in the written and spoken forms of the language; grammatical control, the identification of usage that is structurally correct and appropriate in context; and reading comprehension, the overall meaning of passages in various styles and levels of writing and recall of specific details. One point is given for each correct answer, and a fraction of a point is deducted for each wrong answer. Scores are reported on a scale of 200 to 800. This achievement test (administered five times a year), together with the Scholastic Aptitude Test (SAT), is offered through the Admissions Testing Program (ATP) of the College Board. For students with disabilities, the ATP has available special testing arrangements, including extended time administrations of the achievement test. Examiner required. Suitable for group use.

Timed: 1 hour

Scoring: Computer scored

Cost: Contact publisher

Publisher: The College Board

Information and availability unconfirmed by publisher.

ACHIEVEMENT TEST: FOREIGN LANGUAGES—SPANISH
College Board Achievement Test Development Committees

Adolescent   Grades 10-12

Purpose: Measures high-school students' vocabulary mastery, grammatical control, and reading comprehension of Spanish. Used to predict college performance and by some schools for admissions selection and course placement.

Description: Multiple-item paper-pencil multiple-choice test of ability and knowledge in three areas: vocabulary mastery, the knowledge of the meaning of words and idiomatic expressions as they appear in the written and spoken forms of the language; grammatical control, the identification of usage that is structurally correct and appropriate in context; and reading comprehension, the overall meaning of passages in various styles and levels of writing and recall of specific details. One point is given for each correct answer, and a fraction of a point is deducted for each wrong answer. Scores are reported on a scale of 200 to 800. This achievement test (administered five times a year), together with the Scholastic Aptitude Test (SAT), is offered through the Admissions Testing Program (ATP) of the College Board. For students with disabilities, the ATP has available special testing arrangements, including extended time administrations of the achievement test. Examiner required. Suitable for group use.

Timed: 1 hour

Scoring: Computer scored

Cost: Contact publisher

Publisher: The College Board

Information and availability unconfirmed by publisher.

ACHIEVEMENT TEST: HISTORY AND SOCIAL STUDIES— AMERICAN HISTORY AND SOCIAL STUDIES
College Board Achievement Test Development Committees

Adolescent   Grades 10-12 📖 ✍️

Purpose: Evaluates high-school students' knowledge of American history and social studies. Used to predict college performance and by some schools for admissions selection and course placement.

Description: 100-item paper-pencil multiple-choice test measuring knowledge of 19th- and 20th-century American history in the political, social, economic, diplomatic, intellectual, and cultural fields. The test also covers social studies concepts, methods, and generalizations as they are encountered in the study of history. One point is given for each correct answer, and a fraction of a point is deducted for each wrong answer. Scores are reported on a scale of 200 to 800. This achievement test (administered five times a year), together with the Scholastic Aptitude Test (SAT), is offered through the Admissions Testing Program (ATP) of the College Board. For students with disabilities, the ATP has available special testing arrangements, including extended time administrations of the achievement test. Examiner required. Suitable for group use.
Timed: 1 hour
Scoring: Computer scored
Cost: Contact publisher
Publisher: The College Board
Information and availability unconfirmed by publisher.

ACHIEVEMENT TEST: HISTORY AND SOCIAL STUDIES— EUROPEAN HISTORY AND WORLD CULTURES
College Board Achievement Test Development Committees

Adolescent   Grades 10-12 📖 ✍️

Purpose: Measures high-school students' understanding of the development of Western and non-Western cultures, comprehension of fundamental social science concepts, and the ability to use basic historical techniques. Used to predict college performance and by some schools for admissions selection and course placement.

Description: 100-item paper-pencil multiple-choice test, half dealing with Western Europe and half with other areas. Most of the questions cover the period from the middle of the 15th century to the present, including political and diplomatic history, intellectual and cultural history, and social and economic history. One point is given for each correct answer, and a fraction of a point is deducted for each wrong answer. Scores are reported on a scale of 200 to 800. This achievement test (administered five times a year), together with the Scholastic Aptitude Test (SAT), is offered through the Admissions Testing Program (ATP) of the College Board. For students with disabilities, the ATP has available special testing arrangements, including extended time administrations of the achievement test. Examiner required. Suitable for group use.
Timed: 1 hour
Scoring: Computer scored
Cost: Contact publisher
Publisher: The College Board
Information and availability unconfirmed by publisher.

ACHIEVEMENT TEST: MATHEMATICS—MATHEMATICS LEVEL I
College Board Achievement Test Development Committees

Adolescent   Grades 10-12 📖 ✍️

Purpose: Determines high-school students' level of skill in mathematics typical of three years of college preparatory work. Used to predict college performance and by some schools for admissions selection and course placement.

Description: Broad-range cumulative paper-pencil multiple-choice examination covering algebra, plane Euclidean geometry, coordinate geometry, trigonometry of the right triangle, functions and functional notation for composition and inverse, space perception of simple solids, mathematical reasoning, and the nature of proof. One point is given for each correct answer, and a fraction of a point is deducted for each wrong answer. Scores are reported on a scale of 200 to 800. This achievement test (administered five times a year), together with the Scholastic Aptitude Test (SAT), is offered through the Admissions Testing Program (ATP) of the College Board. For students with disabilities, the ATP has available special testing arrangements, including extended time administrations of the achievement test. Examiner required. Suitable for group use.

Timed: 1 hour

Scoring: Computer scored

Cost: Contact publisher

Publisher: The College Board

Information and availability unconfirmed by publisher.

ACHIEVEMENT TEST: MATHEMATICS—MATHEMATICS LEVEL II
College Board Achievement Test Development Committees

Adolescent   Grades 10-12 🖝 ✍

Purpose: Determines the level of skill of high-school students who have taken college preparatory-level mathematics for 3½ years or more. Used to predict college performance and by some schools for admissions selection and course placement.

Description: Paper-pencil multiple-choice test overlapping the Mathematics Level I test. The questions in the Level II test concentrate on more advanced work, calling for a greater depth of understanding and sophistication and stressing aspects that are prerequisites for calculus. The Level II test is composed of nearly equal parts of algebra, geometry, trigonometry, functions, and a miscellaneous category consisting of such topics as sequences and limits, logic and proof, probability and statistics, and number theory. One point is given for each correct answer, and a fraction of a point is deducted for each wrong answer. Scores are reported on a scale of 200 to 800. This

achievement test (administered five times a year), together with the Scholastic Aptitude Test (SAT), is offered through the Admissions Testing Program (ATP) of the College Board. For students with disabilities, the ATP has available special testing arrangements, including extended time administrations of the achievement test. Examiner required. Suitable for group use.

Timed: 1 hour

Scoring: Computer scored

Cost: Contact publisher

Publisher: The College Board

Information and availability unconfirmed by publisher.

ACHIEVEMENT TEST: SCIENCES—BIOLOGY
College Board Achievement Test Development Committees

Adolescent   Grades 10-12 🖝 ✍

Purpose: Measures high-school students' knowledge of biology and the skills of comprehension, application, analysis, synthesis, and evaluation that have been acquired for using that knowledge. Used to predict college performance and by some schools for admissions selection and course placement.

Description: Multiple-item paper-pencil multiple-choice test covering the following topics: cellular structure and function; organismal reproduction, development, growth, nutrition, structure, and function; genetics; evolution; systematics; ecology; and behavior. Some test questions require interpretation of experimental data, understanding of scientific methods and laboratory techniques, and knowledge of biology history. One point is given for each correct answer, and a fraction of a point is deducted for each wrong answer. Scores are reported on a scale of 200 to 800. This achievement test (administered five times a year), together with the Scholastic Aptitude Test (SAT), is offered through the Admissions Testing Program (ATP) of the College Board. For students with disabilities, the ATP has available special testing arrangements, including extended time administrations of the achievement test. Examiner required. Suitable for group use.

Timed: 1 hour

Scoring: Computer scored

Cost: Contact publisher

Publisher: The College Board

Information and availability unconfirmed by publisher.

ACHIEVEMENT TEST: SCIENCES—CHEMISTRY
College Board Achievement Test Development Committees

Adolescent   Grades 10-12

Purpose: Measures high-school students' knowledge of chemistry and skills in comprehension, application, analysis, synthesis, and evaluation that have been acquired for using that knowledge. Used to predict college performance and by some schools for admissions selection and course placement.

Description: Multiple-item paper-pencil multiple-choice test covering areas such as kinetic-molecular theory and the three states of matter, atomic structure, quantitative relations, chemical bonding and molecular structure, the nature of chemical reactions, interpretation of chemical equilibria and reaction rates, electrochemistry, nuclear chemistry and radiochemistry, physical and chemical properties of the more familiar metals, transition elements, and nonmetals and of the more familiar compounds. One point is given for each correct answer, and a fraction of a point is deducted for each wrong answer. Scores are reported on a scale of 200 to 800. This achievement test (administered five times a year), together with the Scholastic Aptitude Test (SAT), is offered through the Admissions Testing Program (ATP) of the College Board. For students with disabilities, the ATP has available special testing arrangements, including extended time administrations of the achievement test. Examiner required. Suitable for group use.

Timed: 1 hour

Scoring: Computer scored

Cost: Contact publisher

Publisher: The College Board

Information and availability unconfirmed by publisher.

ACHIEVEMENT TEST: SCIENCES—PHYSICS
College Board Achievement Test Development Committees

Adolescent   Grades 10-12

Purpose: Measures high-school students' knowledge of physics and skills in comprehension, application, analysis, synthesis, and evaluation that have been acquired for using that knowledge. Used to predict college performance and by some schools for admissions selection and course placement.

Description: Multiple-item paper-pencil multiple-choice test covering mechanics, electricity and magnetism, geometric optics and waves, heat and kinetic theory, and modern physics. One point is given for each correct answer, and a fraction of a point is deducted for each wrong answer. Scores are reported on a scale of 200 to 800. This achievement test (administered five times a year), together with the Scholastic Aptitude Test (SAT), is offered through the Admissions Testing Program (ATP) of the College Board. For students with disabilities, the ATP has available special testing arrangements, including extended time administrations of the achievement test. Examiner required. Suitable for group use.

Timed: 1 hour

Scoring: Computer scored

Cost: Contact publisher

Publisher: The College Board

Information and availability unconfirmed by publisher.

THE ACT ASSESSMENT
The American College Testing Program

Adolescent, adult
Grades 7 and older

Purpose: Assesses the academic achievement of high school students. The program is a comprehensive system of data collection, processing, and reporting designed to help students and counselors develop post-secondary plans and to help colleges develop instructional programs suited to the needs and characteristics of their applicants.

Description: 219-item paper-pencil test consisting of four separately timed sections: the English usage section is 40 minutes long and consists of 75 items; the mathematics usage section is 50 minutes long and consists of 40 items; the social studies reading section is 35 minutes long and consists of 52 items; the natural sciences reading section is 35 minutes long and consists of 52 items. The student must take all four sections of the test. Also included are a student profile section and an interest inventory. The test is administered five times each year at designated ACT test centers to college-bound students and is also available at certain college campuses under residual testing. Examiner required. Suitable for group use.

Timed: 3 hours, 15 minutes; untimed for handicapped

Scoring: Hand key; may be computer scored

Cost: Basic test fee $10.00, New York $12.00 (includes 3 score reports); additional score reports $2.50 each

Publisher: The American College Testing Program

ACT ASSET PROGRAM
The American College Testing Program

Adult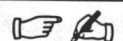

Purpose: Measures academic preparation of entering community college students. Used for academic advising and course placement in 2-year institutions.

Description: Battery of seven paper-pencil tests: Language Usage Skills (64 items/11 minutes), Reading Skills (40 items/20 minutes), Numerical Skills (32 items/18 minutes), Elementary Algebra Skills (25 items/25 minutes), Intermediate Algebra Skills (25 items/25 minutes), College Algebra Skills (25 items/25 minutes), and Advanced Language Usage Skills (45 items/25 minutes). The student generally

must take the first three tests, which cover basic skills; the last four tests, which cover advanced skills, are optional. Scored by Scan-Tron portable scanners, self-scoring answer folders, or immediately computer-scored by NCS. Examiner required. Suitable for group use.

Timed: Varies, depending on test

Scoring: Computer scored; hand key

Cost: Each participant (includes descriptive and follow-up research services) $2.40; reusable test booklet $0.50

Publisher: The American College Testing Program

ACT PROFICIENCY EXAMINATION PROGRAM (ACT PEP)
The American College Testing Program

Adult

Purpose: Assesses college level academic achievement. Used to grant college credit and advanced placement in academic courses to students at over 700 colleges and universities, including the New York Regents College Degree Program.

Description: 49 paper-pencil tests measuring achievement in a wide range of fields: Arts and Sciences (11 tests), Business (18 tests), Education (4 tests), Nursing (16 tests). Most of the tests are objective (125-150 items), some are multiple-choice and essay, and some are entirely essay. College level achievement is measured from introductory to advanced levels of study. There are no restrictions on who may take the tests. The multiple-choice tests are administered nationwide up to six times yearly. Individuals seeking credit should contact their local colleges for information. These tests are known as Regents College Examinations in New York State. Developed by the University of the State of New York, the tests are administered by ACT and accepted by over 700 participating colleges and universities. Examiner required. Suitable for group use.

Timed: 3-7 hours per test

Scoring: Examiner evaluated and computer scored by ACT

Cost: Varies in fee from $40.00-$235.00
Publisher: The American College Testing Program

ACT PROFICIENCY EXAMINATION PROGRAM—ARTS AND SCIENCES: ABNORMAL PSYCHOLOGY
The American College Testing Program

Adult

Purpose: Measures knowledge and understanding of abnormal psychology. Used to grant college credit and/or advanced placement in academic courses.

Description: Paper-pencil multiple-choice test assessing knowledge of the historical background of abnormal psychology, the major conceptualizations in the area, and the nature and description of abnormal disorders as well as their definitions, classification, etiology, and major treatments. The test assumes a familiarity with concepts typically learned in an introductory psychology course. Examiner required. Suitable for group use.
Timed: 3 hours
Scoring: Computer scored by ACT
Cost: Fee $40.00
Publisher: The American College Testing Program

ACT PROFICIENCY EXAMINATION PROGRAM—ARTS AND SCIENCES: AFRO-AMERICAN HISTORY
The American College Testing Program

Adult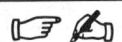

Purpose: Measures knowledge and understanding of the history of Black Americans. Used to grant college credit and advanced placement in academic courses.

Description: Multiple-item paper-pencil multiple-choice test measuring knowledge of facts, events, and themes during the periods 1500-1865 (from the beginning of slavery through the Civil War), 1865-1909 (Reconstruction and its aftermath), and

1909-1968 (beginning of the 20th century through the civil rights era). Individuals seeking credit should contact their local colleges for information. Examiner required. Suitable for group use.
Timed: 3 hours
Scoring: Computer scored by ACT
Cost: Fee $40.00
Publisher: The American College Testing Program

ACT PROFICIENCY EXAMINATION PROGRAM—ARTS AND SCIENCES: AMERICAN HISTORY
The American College Testing Program

Adult

Purpose: Measures knowledge and understanding of American historical facts and events. Used to grant college credit and advanced placement in academic courses.

Description: Multiple-item paper-pencil multiple-choice and essay test measuring knowledge of historical events from the colonial period to the present, and the ability to discuss and interpret their historical significance. Individuals seeking credit should contact their local colleges for information. Administered in February, May, and November only. Examiner required. Suitable for group use.
Timed: 3 hours
Scoring: Examiner evaluated and computer scored by ACT
Cost: Fee $60.00
Publisher: The American College Testing Program

ACT PROFICIENCY EXAMINATION PROGRAM—ARTS AND SCIENCES: ANATOMY AND PHYSIOLOGY
The American College Testing Program

Adult

Purpose: Measures knowledge and understanding of anatomy and physiology. Used to grant college credit and advanced placement in academic courses.

Description: Multiple-item paper-pencil multiple-choice test. Items are based on anatomical terminology and facts, physiological concepts and principles, and the structure and function of body cells, tissues, organs, and systems. Emphasis is placed on systems that maintain, integrate, and control bodily functions. Individuals seeking credit should contact their local colleges for information. Examiner required. Suitable for group use.

Timed: 3 hours

Scoring: Computer scored by ACT

Cost: Fee $40.00

Publisher: The American College Testing Program

ACT PROFICIENCY EXAMINATION PROGRAM—ARTS AND SCIENCES: EARTH SCIENCE
The American College Testing Program

Adult

Purpose: Measures proficiency in the earth sciences: astronomy, geology, meteorology, and oceanography. Used to grant college credit and advanced placement in academic courses.

Description: Multiple-item paper-pencil test consisting of both essay and multiple-choice questions. Items cover astronomy, geology, meteorology, and oceanography and are based upon their interrelationships and mans' interaction with the earth, atmosphere, and the oceans. Students must be able to read charts, manipulate data, and understand the operation of scientific instruments. Individuals seeking credit should contact their local colleges for information. Administered in February, May, and November only. Examiner required. Suitable for group use.

Timed: 3 hours

Scoring: Examiner evaluated and computer scored by ACT

Cost: Fee $60.00

Publisher: The American College Testing Program

ACT PROFICIENCY EXAMINATION PROGRAM—ARTS AND SCIENCES: FOUNDATION OF GERONTOLOGY
The American College Testing Program

Adult

Purpose: Measures knowledge and understanding of the biological, psychological, and social aspects of aging. Used to grant college credit and advanced placement in academic courses.

Description: Multiple-item paper-pencil multiple-choice test. Items are based on material normally taught in a one-semester introductory course in gerontology at the undergraduate level. Measures the ability to describe, understand, and analyze issues pertaining to the functioning and well-being of the elderly. Emphasis is placed on an awareness of the needs and realities involved in both the normal aspects of aging and problems associated with aging. Individuals seeking credit should contact their local colleges for information. Examiner required. Suitable for group use.

Timed: 3 hours

Scoring: Computer scored by ACT

Cost: Fee $40.00

Publisher: The American College Testing Program

ACT PROFICIENCY EXAMINATION PROGRAM—ARTS AND SCIENCES: FRESHMAN ENGLISH
The American College Testing Program

Adult

Purpose: Measures proficiency in English composition and literary criticism. Used to grant college credit and advanced placement in academic courses.

Description: Multiple-item paper-pencil test consisting of both multiple-choice and essay questions. Items are based on specific works of fiction (short story and novel), nonfiction (essay and autobiography), drama, and poetry; literary terminology; the nature and characteristics of the various genres and their relationship to content; and the concepts of prosody. The exam requires the ability to write a good composition. Individuals seeking credit should contact their local colleges for information. Administered in February, May, and November only. Examiner required. Suitable for group use.

Timed: 3 hours

Scoring: Examiner evaluated and computer scored by ACT

Cost: Fee $60.00

Publisher: The American College Testing Program

ACT PROFICIENCY EXAMINATION PROGRAM—ARTS AND SCIENCES: MICROBIOLOGY
The American College Testing Program

Adult

Purpose: Assesses knowledge of microbiology. Used to grant college credit and advanced placement in academic courses.

Description: Paper-pencil multiple-choice test of knowledge and understanding of bacteria, algae, fungi, protozoa, viruses, and their relationships to humans. The test covers such areas as history, morphology, and ultrastructure, metabolism, growth and nutrition, genetics, physiological types, methods of control, and applied and environmental microbiology. Questions are based on material normally taught in a one-semester, introductory course in microbiology at the undergraduate level. Examiner required. Suitable for group use.

Timed: 3 hours

Scoring: Computer scored by ACT

Cost: Fee $40.00

Publisher: The American College Testing Program

ACT PROFICIENCY EXAMINATION PROGRAM—ARTS AND SCIENCES: PHYSICAL GEOLOGY
The American College Testing Program

Adult

Purpose: Measures proficiency in the study of physical geology. Used to grant college credit and advanced placement in academic courses.

Description: Multiple-item paper-pencil multiple-choice test covering material normally taught in introductory undergraduate courses in physical geology. Measures knowledge and understanding of the following areas: the processes which form the earth through geologic time; the structure, composition, and evolution of the earth; and the landforms created by the processes which form the earth. Individuals seeking credit should contact their local colleges for information. Examiner required. Suitable for group use.

Timed: 3 hours

Scoring: Computer scored by ACT

Cost: Fee $40.00

Publisher: The American College Testing Program

ACT PROFICIENCY EXAMINATION PROGRAM—ARTS AND SCIENCES: SHAKESPEARE
The American College Testing Program

Adult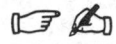

Purpose: Measures knowledge of Shakespeare, his plays, and the historical and literary context in which the plays were written. Used to grant college credit and advanced placement in academic courses.

Description: Multiple-item paper-pencil test consisting of both multiple-choice questions (Part I) and essay questions (Part II). Items are based on specific plays of Shakespeare, their dates, sources, and textual history; the life of Shakespeare; and the conventions and customs of the Elizabethan theater. Individuals seeking credit should contact their local colleges for information. Administered in February, May, and November only. Examiner required. Suitable for group use.

Timed: 3 hours

Scoring: Examiner evaluated and computer scored by ACT

Cost: Fee $60.00

Publisher: The American College Testing Program

ACT PROFICIENCY EXAMINATION PROGRAM—ARTS AND SCIENCES: STATISTICS
The American College Testing Program

Adult

Purpose: Assesses knowledge and understanding of the fundamental concepts of descriptive and inferential statistics. Used to grant college credit and advanced placement in academic courses.

Description: Paper-pencil multiple-choice test of material normally taught in a one-semester, introductory course in mathematical statistics at the undergraduate level. Both the meaning and application of basic ideas are tested. Examiner required. Suitable for group use.

Timed: 3 hours

Scoring: Computer scored by ACT

Cost: Fee $40.00

Publisher: The American College Testing Program

ACT PROFICIENCY EXAMINATION PROGRAM— BUSINESS: ACCOUNTING: LEVEL I
The American College Testing Program

Adult

Purpose: Measures knowledge and understanding of basic accounting concepts, principles, and procedures. Used to grant college credit and advanced placement in academic courses.

Description: Multiple-item paper-pencil multiple-choice test. Measures knowledge

of terms, the ability to apply appropriate techniques in recording, analyzing, and summarizing financial data, and interpreting and reporting financial results. Individuals seeking credit should contact their local colleges for information. Available in February, May, June, and November only. Examiner required. Suitable for group use.

Timed: 3 hours

Scoring: Computer scored by ACT

Cost: Fee $50.00

Publisher: The American College Testing Program

ACT PROFICIENCY EXAMINATION PROGRAM— BUSINESS: ACCOUNTING: LEVEL II
The American College Testing Program

Adult

Purpose: Measures proficiency in financial accounting, cost accounting, and the handling of financial data. Used to grant college credit and advanced placement in academic courses.

Description: Multiple-item paper-pencil test consisting of both essay and multiple-choice questions. Items are based on financial accounting concepts, terminology, and theory as recommended by the American Institute of Certified Public Accountants and the Financial Accounting Standards Board; the solution to financial and cost accounting problems; and the preparation of financial budgets and statements. Individuals seeking credit should contact their local colleges for information. Administered in May and November only. Examiner required. Suitable for group use.

Timed: 3 hours

Scoring: Examiner evaluated and computer scored by ACT

Cost: Fee $125.00

Publisher: The American College Testing Program

ACT PROFICIENCY EXAMINATION PROGRAM—BUSINESS: ACCOUNTING: LEVEL III (AREA I, II, III)

The American College Testing Program

Adult

Purpose: Measures knowledge of accounting based upon business law, federal income taxation, auditing and cost analysis, income concepts, valuation basis, measurements, and other professional issues. Used to grant college credit and advanced placement in academic courses.

Description: Multiple-item paper-pencil essay test in three levels: accounting, auditing, and advanced accounting. Area I measures detailed knowledge of business law, federal income taxation, and the ability to integrate and interpret data. Area II measures knowledge of auditing and cost analysis. Auditing items are based on CPA examinations of financial statements and auditor's reports, as well as on professional ethics and responsibility. Area III includes advanced accounting theory and special problems. Students are awarded credit only if all three examinations are completed successfully. Individuals seeking credit should contact their local colleges for information. Administered in May and November only. Examiner required. Suitable for group use.

Timed: 3 hours per area

Scoring: Examiner evaluated and computer scored by ACT

Cost: Fee per area $125.00

Publisher: The American College Testing Program

ACT PROFICIENCY EXAMINATION PROGRAM—BUSINESS: BUSINESS ENVIRONMENT AND STRATEGY

The American College Testing Program

Adult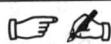

Purpose: Measures knowledge of the concepts and principles of general management decision making and corporate strategy formulation and the ability to apply that knowledge to specific situations. Used to grant college credit and advanced placement in academic courses.

Description: Multiple-item paper-pencil test consisting of both multiple-choice and essay questions. Items are based on the relationship between a manager and his environment, the formulation of corporate policy and strategy, and the integration of facts from these two areas. The essay questions include case incidents which students analyze. Students then choose a particular course of action, demonstrating their ability to integrate a working knowledge of the functional areas of business (accounting, finance, marketing, personnel, and production) and an understanding of the impact of the social, political, and economic environments in which the business operates. Individuals seeking credit should contact their local colleges for information. Administered in February, May, and November only. Examiner required. Suitable for group use.

Timed: 4 hours

Scoring: Examiner evaluated and computer scored by ACT

Cost: Fee $125.00

Publisher: The American College Testing Program

ACT PROFICIENCY EXAMINATION PROGRAM—BUSINESS: FINANCE: LEVEL I

The American College Testing Program

Adult

Purpose: Measures proficiency in the areas of money and banking and corporation finance. Used to grant college credit and advanced placement in academic courses.

Description: Multiple-item paper-pencil multiple-choice test. Items are based on concepts, definitions, and terminology in the areas of money and banking and corporation finance. Questions on money and banking require an analytical as well as a descriptive knowledge of the area, and questions in both areas assume an understanding of the principles of macroeconomics and microeconomics. Students must solve problems requiring simple computations and apply analytic procedures to practical situations. Individuals seeking credit should contact their local colleges for information. Available in February, May, June, and November only. Examiner required. Suitable for group use.

Timed: 3 hours

Scoring: Computer scored by ACT

Cost: Fee $50.00

Publisher: The American College Testing Program

ACT PROFICIENCY EXAMINATION PROGRAM— BUSINESS: FINANCE: LEVEL II
The American College Testing Program

Adult

Purpose: Assesses proficiency in the areas of advanced corporation finance, security analysis and portfolio management, and financial institutions and markets. Used to grant college credit and advanced placement in academic courses.

Description: Multiple-item paper-pencil test consisting of both objective and essay questions. Items are based on financial facts and concepts and their relationships, the analysis of given situations, and the solutions of presented problems. Individuals seeking credit should contact their local colleges for information. Available in May and November only. Examiner required. Suitable for group use.

Timed: 4 hours

Scoring: Examiner evaluated and computer scored by ACT

Cost: Fee $125.00

Publisher: The American College Testing Program

ACT PROFICIENCY EXAMINATION PROGRAM— BUSINESS: FINANCE: LEVEL III
The American College Testing Program

Adult

Purpose: Measures proficiency in financial analysis. Used to grant college credit

and advanced placement in academic courses.

Description: Multiple-item paper-pencil essay test arranged in two parts. Part I covers advanced corporation finance, security analysis, and portfolio management. Part II covers financial institutions and markets. Items for both sections are based on the principles of finance, the interrelationships among the areas of finance, the analytic tools and measures of financial performance, and alternative solutions to financial problems. Individuals seeking credit should contact their local colleges for information. Available in May and November only. Examiner required. Suitable for group use.

Timed: 7 hours

Scoring: Examiner evaluated

Cost: Fee $235.00

Publisher: The American College Testing Program

ACT PROFICIENCY EXAMINATION PROGRAM— BUSINESS: MANAGEMENT OF HUMAN RESOURCES: LEVEL I
The American College Testing Program

Adult

Purpose: Measures proficiency in management of human resources. Used to grant college credit and advanced placement in academic courses.

Description: Multiple-item paper-pencil multiple-choice test. Items are based on facts, terminology, concepts, and theories in the area of human relations as applied to individual and group behavior, organization dynamics, organizational development, functions of management, and the development of management thought. Individuals seeking credit should contact their local colleges for information. Available in February, May, June, and November only. Examiner required. Suitable for group use.

Timed: 3 hours

Scoring: Computer scored by ACT

Cost: Fee $50.00

Publisher: The American College Testing Program

ACT PROFICIENCY EXAMINATION PROGRAM— BUSINESS: MANAGEMENT OF HUMAN RESOURCES: LEVEL II
The American College Testing Program

Adult

Purpose: Measures proficiency in the management of human resources. Used to grant college credit and advanced placement in academic courses.

Description: Multiple-item paper-pencil test consisting of both essay and objective questions. Items are based on factual material applied to given situations in the areas of management theories related to management practice, functions of management, organization dynamics, individual and group behavior, and personnel administration and labor relations. Individuals seeking credit should contact their local colleges for information. Available in May and November only. Examiner required. Suitable for group use.

Timed: 4 hours

Scoring: Examiner evaluated and computer scored by ACT

Cost: Fee $125.00

Publisher: The American College Testing Program

ACT PROFICIENCY EXAMINATION PROGRAM— BUSINESS: MANAGEMENT OF HUMAN RESOURCES: LEVEL III
The American College Testing Program

Adult

Purpose: Measures proficiency in the management of human resources. Used to grant college credit and advanced placement in academic courses.

Description: Multiple-item paper-pencil essay test. Items are based on knowledge of evolution of management thought, functions of management, individual and group behavior, organization dynamics, organizational development, and business policy. A knowledge of content from sup-

porting courses in related areas of business is assumed. Individuals seeking credit should contact their local colleges for information. Available in May and November only. Examiner required. Suitable for group use.

Timed: 7 hours

Scoring: Examiner evaluated

Cost: Fee $235.00

Publisher: The American College Testing Program

ACT PROFICIENCY EXAMINATION PROGRAM— BUSINESS: MARKETING: LEVEL I
The American College Testing Program

Adult

Purpose: Assesses proficiency in the areas of marketing management and analysis, products, pricing, promotion, distribution, and legal and social issues. Used to grant college credit and advanced placement in academic courses.

Description: Multiple-item paper-pencil multiple-choice test, measuring the following aspects of marketing management and analysis: knowledge of marketing terminology, concepts, and trends; comprehension of marketing conditions, strategies, principles, and theories; ability to explain marketing procedures and theories and anticipate their effects; and ability to explain advantages and disadvantages of using various principles and techniques in defined situations. Those seeking credit should contact their local colleges for information. Available in February, May, June, and November only. Examiner required. Suitable for group use.

Timed: 3 hours

Scoring: Computer scored by ACT

Cost: Fee $50.00

Publisher: The American College Testing Program

academic achievement and aptitude

ACT PROFICIENCY EXAMINATION PROGRAM—BUSINESS: MARKETING: LEVEL II

The American College Testing Program

Adult

Purpose: Assesses proficiency in the application of factual material to given situations in the areas of marketing research, consumer behavior, marketing communications, and distribution. Used to grant college credit and advanced placement in academic courses.

Description: Multiple-item multiple-choice and essay test covering the following aspects of marketing: knowledge of terminology, facts, and resources; comprehension of concepts and strategies, including the purposes, conditions, advantages, and limitations of each; ability to explain advantages and disadvantages of using various principles and techniques in defined situations; and ability to apply principles and procedures to specific situations. Individuals seeking credit should contact their local colleges for information. Available in May and November only. Examiner required. Suitable for group use.

Timed: 4 hours

Scoring: Examiner evaluated and computer scored by ACT

Cost: Fee $125.00

Publisher: The American College Testing Program

ACT PROFICIENCY EXAMINATION PROGRAM—BUSINESS: MARKETING: LEVEL III

The American College Testing Program

Adult

Purpose: Measures knowledge of industrial and consumer marketing approaches. Used to grant college credit and advanced placement in academic courses.

Description: Multiple-item paper-pencil essay test consisting of case incidents and case studies which the examinee must analyze and discuss. Items are based on the economic, cultural, psychological, and social characteristics of industrial and consumer markets. The following areas are included: evolution of marketing and marketing policy, management, strategies, and procedures. Individuals seeking credit should contact their local colleges for information. Available in May and November only. Examiner required. Suitable for group use.

Timed: 7 hours

Scoring: Examiner evaluated

Cost: Fee $235.00

Publisher: The American College Testing Program

ACT PROFICIENCY EXAMINATION PROGRAM—BUSINESS: OPERATIONS MANAGEMENT: LEVEL I

The American College Testing Program

Adult

Purpose: Assesses proficiency in the skills required for quantitative operations analysis. Used to grant college credit and advanced placement in academic courses.

Description: Multiple-item paper-pencil multiple-choice test covering the following areas: knowledge of the terminology and basic principles of statistics, mathematics, and operations management; comprehension of analytic procedures and situations in which they apply; uses and interpretations of statistics and graphical data; uses, advantages, and disadvantages of analytic techniques; ability to apply knowledge of descriptive and inferential statistics and probability to the solution of problems requiring simple computation. Individuals seeking credit should contact their local colleges for information. Available in February, May, June, and November only. Examiner required. Suitable for group use.

Timed: 3 hours

Scoring: Computer scored by ACT

Cost: Fee $50.00

Publisher: The American College Testing Program

ACT PROFICIENCY EXAMINATION PROGRAM—BUSINESS: OPERATIONS MANAGEMENT: LEVEL II
The American College Testing Program

Adult

Purpose: Measures proficiency in material covered in intermediate undergraduate courses in operations management and quantitative decision making. Used to grant college credit and advanced placement in academic courses.

Description: Multiple-item paper-pencil test consisting of objective, essay, and computational questions. Items are based on the concepts and techniques of operations management and involve determining the solution to problems typically encountered in the field. Assesses the level of learning expected of a student with a minor concentration in operations management. Individuals seeking credit should contact their local colleges for information. Available in May and November only. Examiner required. Suitable for group use.

Timed: 4 hours

Scoring: Examiner evaluated and computer scored by ACT

Cost: Fee $125.00

Publisher: The American College Testing Program

ACT PROFICIENCY EXAMINATION PROGRAM—BUSINESS: OPERATIONS MANAGEMENT: LEVEL III
The American College Testing Program

Adult

Purpose: Measures proficiency in operations management. Used to grant college credit and advanced placement in academic courses.

Description: Multiple-item paper-pencil test consisting of essay and computational

questions. Items are based on the application of knowledge and concepts to given situations involving such areas as production system design, forecasting methodology, programming and planning, quality control, inventory, management, queing, statistical decision making, and simulation. Individuals seeking credit should contact their local colleges for information. Available in May and November only. Examiner required. Suitable for group use.

Timed: 7 hours

Scoring: Examiner evaluated

Cost: Fee $235.00

Publisher: The American College Testing Program

ACT PROFICIENCY EXAMINATION PROGRAM—EDUCATION: CORRECTIVE AND REMEDIAL INSTRUCTION IN READING
The American College Testing Program

Adult

Purpose: Assesses proficiency in corrective and remedial reading instruction. Used to grant college credit and advanced placement in academic courses.

Description: Multiple-item paper-pencil multiple-choice test. Items are based upon the following aspects of teaching reading from the primary grades through secondary school: planning programs for pupils, parents' role, relationship between the reading teacher and the school support staff, and personal responsibilities of the reading teacher. Individuals seeking credit should contact their local colleges for information. Available in February, May, and November only. Examiner required. Suitable for group use.

Timed: 3 hours

Scoring: Computer scored by ACT

Cost: Fee $40.00

Publisher: The American College Testing Program

ACT PROFICIENCY EXAMINATION PROGRAM— EDUCATION: EDUCATIONAL PSYCHOLOGY
The American College Testing Program

Adult

Purpose: Assesses proficiency in the material covered by introductory college courses in educational psychology or in the psychological foundations of education. Used to grant college credit and advanced placement in academic courses.

Description: Multiple-item paper-pencil multiple-choice test. Covers terminology, concepts, theories, and principles in the following areas: individual growth and development; learning and instruction; the influence of social, cultural, and environmental factors; and measurement. No classroom or tutorial experience is assumed. Individuals seeking credit should contact their local colleges for information. Available in February, May, and November only. Examiner required. Suitable for group use.

Timed: 3 hours

Scoring: Computer scored by ACT

Cost: Fee $40.00

Publisher: The American College Testing Program

ACT PROFICIENCY EXAMINATION PROGRAM— EDUCATION: HISTORY OF AMERICAN EDUCATION
The American College Testing Program

Adult

Purpose: Assesses proficiency in the study of history of American education. Used to grant college credit and advanced placement in academic courses.

Description: Multiple-item paper-pencil test consisting of objective and essay questions. Items are based on the influence of English-European heritage on American education, important events in the development of American education, the influence of those events on contempo-

rary education policy and practice, and the relationships between education and various societal factors. Individuals seeking credit should contact their local colleges for information. Available in February, May, and November only. Examiner required. Suitable for group use.

Timed: 3 hours

Scoring: Examiner evaluated and computer scored by ACT

Cost: Fee $60.00

Publisher: The American College Testing Program

ACT PROFICIENCY EXAMINATION PROGRAM— EDUCATION: READING INSTRUCTION IN THE ELEMENTARY SCHOOL
The American College Testing Program

Adult

Purpose: Assesses proficiency in elementary school reading instruction. Used to grant college credit and advanced placement in academic courses.

Description: Multiple-item paper-pencil multiple-choice test. Items are based on terms, concepts, and methods related to the following areas of reading instruction: assessment, goal setting, materials, methodologies, instructional management, instruction, evaluation, parental role, school support staff, and personal responsibilities of the teacher. Individuals seeking credit should contact their local colleges for information. Available in February, May, and November only. Examiner required. Suitable for group use.

Timed: 3 hours

Scoring: Computer scored by ACT

Cost: Fee $40.00

Publisher: The American College Testing Program

ACT PROFICIENCY EXAMINATION PROGRAM— NURSING: ADULT NURSING

The American College Testing Program

Adult

Purpose: Assesses proficiency in adult nursing care. Used to grant college credit and advanced placement in academic courses.

Description: Multiple-item paper-pencil multiple-choice test. Items are based on material normally taught in an upper-division sequence of courses in medical-surgical nursing or adult nursing at the baccalaureate level. Designed for and standardized at the B.S. degree level. Individuals seeking credit should contact their local colleges for information. Examiner required. Suitable for group use.

Timed: 3 hours

Scoring: Computer scored by ACT

Cost: Fee $40.00

Publisher: The American College Testing Program

ACT PROFICIENCY EXAMINATION PROGRAM— NURSING: COMMONALITIES IN NURSING CARE: AREA A

The American College Testing Program

Adult

Purpose: Assesses proficiency in dealing with basic nursing problems. Used to grant college credit and advanced placement in academic courses.

Description: Multiple-item paper-pencil multiple-choice test. Items are based on common nursing problems and nursing care as they are related to patients' basic health needs. Knowledge and understanding of technical vocabulary, anatomy, physiology, emotional and physical development, and pharmacology is assumed. Designed for and standardized at the A.S. degree level. Those seeking credit should contact their local colleges for information. Examiner required. Suitable for group use.

Timed: 3 hours

Scoring: Computer scored by ACT

Cost: Fee $50.00

Publisher: The American College Testing Program

ACT PROFICIENCY EXAMINATION PROGRAM— NURSING: COMMONALITIES IN NURSING CARE: AREA B

The American College Testing Program

Adult

Purpose: Assesses proficiency in dealing with common nursing problems. Used to grant college credit and advanced placement in academic courses.

Description: Multiple-item paper-pencil multiple-choice test. Items are based on common nursing problems and nursing care as they are related to nutrition, elimination, oxygenation, and fluid and electrolyte balance. Knowledge and understanding of technical vocabulary, anatomy, physiology, emotional and physical development, and pharmacology are assumed. Designed for and standardized at the A.S. degree level. Individuals seeking credit should contact their local colleges for information. Examiner required. Suitable for group use.

Timed: 3 hours

Scoring: Computer scored by ACT

Cost: Fee $50.00

Publisher: The American College Testing Program

ACT PROFICIENCY EXAMINATION PROGRAM— NURSING: DIFFERENCES IN NURSING CARE: AREA A

The American College Testing Program

Adult

Purpose: Assesses proficiency in the nursing care of children and adult patients with common diseases and health care problems, particularly those problems relating to oxygenation and cell growth. Used to grant college credit and advanced placement in academic courses.

Description: Multiple-item paper-pencil multiple-choice test measuring four areas of basic nursing care: knowledge of anatomy, physiology, pathophysiology, physical and emotional development, and psychosocial aspects of acute and long-term health problems; comprehension of the causes, symptoms, and relationships between common and specific manifestations involving oxygenation and cell growth; comprehension of the effects and relative advantages and disadvantages of various treatments; and ability to apply knowledge of differences in nursing care related to oxygenation and cell growth and resulting from specific health problems and the individual's response to clinical situations. Knowledge of anatomy, physiology, pharmacology, and nutrition is assumed. Designed for and standardized at the A.S. degree level. Individuals seeking credit should contact their local colleges for information. Examiner required. Suitable for group use.

Timed: 3 hours

Scoring: Computer scored by ACT

Cost: Fee $50.00

Publisher: The American College Testing Program

ACT PROFICIENCY EXAMINATION PROGRAM— NURSING: DIFFERENCES IN NURSING CARE: AREA B
The American College Testing Program

Adult

Purpose: Assesses proficiency in the nursing care of children and adults with common diseases and health problems, particularly those problems relating to behavioral responses and endocrine/regulatory mechanisms. Used to grant college credit and advanced placement in academic courses.

Description: Multiple-item paper-pencil multiple-choice test measuring four areas of basic nursing care: knowledge of anatomy, physiology, pathophysiology, physical and emotional development, and psychosocial aspects of acute and long-

term health problems; comprehension of the causes, symptoms, and relationships between common and specific manifestations involving behavioral responses and endocrine/regulatory mechanisms; comprehension of the effects and relative advantages and disadvantages of various treatments; and ability to apply knowledge of differences in nursing care related to behavioral responses and endocrine/regulatory mechanisms resulting from specific health problems and the individual's response to clinical settings. Knowledge of anatomy, physiology, pharmacology, and nutrition is assumed. Designed for and standardized at the A.S. degree level. Individuals seeking credit should contact their local colleges for information. Examiner required. Suitable for group use.

Timed: 3 hours

Scoring: Computer scored by ACT

Cost: Fee $50.00

Publisher: The American College Testing Program

ACT PROFICIENCY EXAMINATION PROGRAM— NURSING: DIFFERENCES IN NURSING CARE: AREA C
The American College Testing Program

Adult

Purpose: Assesses proficiency in nursing care of children and adults with diseases and common health problems, particularly those relating to the infectious process, tissue trauma, and neuromuscular dysfunctions. Used to grant college credit and advanced placement in academic courses.

Description: Multiple-item paper-pencil multiple-choice test measuring four areas of basic nursing care: knowledge of anatomy, physiology, pathophysiology, physical and emotional development, and psychosocial aspects of acute and long-term health problems; comprehension of the causes, symptoms, and relationships between common and specific manifestations involving the infectious process, tissue trauma, and neuromuscular dysfunctions; comprehension of the effects and relative advantages and disadvantages of various treatments; and ability to apply knowledge of differences in nursing care related to the infectious process, tissue trauma, and neuromuscular dysfunctions resulting from specific health problems and the individual's response to clinical situations. Knowledge of anatomy, physiology, pharmacology, and nutrition is assumed. Designed for and standardized at the A.S. degree level. Individuals seeking credit should contact their local colleges for information. Examiner required. Suitable for group use.

Timed: 3 hours

Scoring: Computer scored by ACT

Cost: Fee $50.00

Publisher: The American College Testing Program

ACT PROFICIENCY EXAMINATION PROGRAM— NURSING: FUNDAMENTALS OF NURSING
The American College Testing Program

Adult

Purpose: Assesses proficiency in nursing skills and procedures. Used to grant college credit and advanced placement in academic courses.

Description: Multiple-item paper-pencil multiple-choice test measuring terms, facts, and trends and the ability to apply principles and theories to nursing situations. Examination is based on conventional nursing content. Designed for and standardized for the A.S. degree level. Individuals seeking credit should contact their local colleges for information. Examiner required. Suitable for group use.

Timed: 3 hours

Scoring: Computer scored by ACT

Cost: Fee $40.00

Publisher: The American College Testing Program

ACT PROFICIENCY EXAMINATION PROGRAM— NURSING: HEALTH RESTORATION: AREA I
The American College Testing Program

Adult

Purpose: Assesses proficiency in nursing care and intervention aimed at health restoration for individuals, families, and communities. Used to grant college credit and advanced placement in academic courses.

Description: Multiple-item paper-pencil multiple-choice test. Items are based on the interrelationship of the nursing process and changes in the client system (individual, family, community). The nursing process is emphasized as the framework for assisting client adaptation to change in a way that promotes restoration, palliation, habilitation, and rehabilitation. Designed for and standardized at the B.S. degree level. Individuals seeking credit should contact their local colleges for information. Examiner required. Suitable for group use.

Timed: 3 hours

Scoring: Computer scored by ACT

Cost: Fee $50.00

Publisher: The American College Testing Program

ACT PROFICIENCY EXAMINATION PROGRAM— NURSING: HEALTH RESTORATION: AREA II
The American College Testing Program

Adult

Purpose: Assesses proficiency in nursing care and intervention aimed at health restoration of individuals, families, and communities. Used to grant college credit and advanced placement in academic courses.

Description: Multiple-item paper-pencil multiple-choice test. Items are based on the interrelationship between the nursing process and changes in the client system (individual, family, community). The nursing process is emphasized as the framework for assisting client adaptation to change in a way that promotes restoration, palliation, habilitation, and rehabilitation. Designed for and standardized at the B.S. degree level. Individuals seeking credit should contact their local colleges for information. Examiner required. Suitable for group use.

Timed: 3 hours

Scoring: Computer scored by ACT

Cost: Fee $50.00

Publisher: The American College Testing Program

ACT PROFICIENCY EXAMINATION PROGRAM— NURSING: HEALTH SUPPORT: AREA I
The American College Testing Program

Adult

Purpose: Assesses proficiency in health support approaches. Used to grant college credit and advanced placement in academic courses.

Description: Multiple-item paper-pencil multiple-choice test. Items cover the patterns that influence wellness and their interrelationships and potential barriers to wellness: rhythmicity, culture and ethnicity, values, socioeconomic status, and client perception of patterns. The examination emphasizes use of the nursing process to support health of the client throughout the life cycle. Client spectrum includes individuals, families, and communities. Designed for and standardized at the B.S. degree level. Individuals seeking credit should contact their local colleges for information. Examiner required. Suitable for group use.

Timed: 3 hours

Scoring: Computer scored by ACT

Cost: Fee $50.00

Publisher: The American College Testing Program

ACT PROFICIENCY EXAMINATION PROGRAM— NURSING: HEALTH SUPPORT: AREA II
The American College Testing Program

Adult

Purpose: Assesses the use of the nursing process in supporting the health of the client throughout the life cycle. Used to grant college credit and advanced placement in academic courses.

Description: Multiple-item paper-pencil multiple-choice test. Items focus on alterations of developmental, sustenal, activity, or life-space patterns that place the client (individual, family, community) at high risk for major health problems. Emphasis is placed on nursing actions related to prevention, teaching and counseling, screening, and early detection with regard to the need of the clients. Designed for and standardized at the B.S. degree level. Individuals seeking credit should contact their local colleges for information. Examiner required. Suitable for group use.

Timed: 3 hours

Scoring: Computer scored by ACT

Cost: Fee $50.00

Publisher: The American College Testing Program

ACT PROFICIENCY EXAMINATION PROGRAM— NURSING: MATERNAL AND CHILD NURSING: ASSOCIATE DEGREE
The American College Testing Program

Adult

Purpose: Assesses proficiency in maternal and child nursing. Used to grant college credit and advanced placement in academic courses.

Description: Multiple-item paper-pencil multiple-choice test. Items are based on knowledge of facts, trends, and terminology and on the ability to recognize and apply theories of nursing care and principles of interpersonal relationships, nutrition, and pharmacology to a variety of health care situations. The test also assesses the ability to utilize the nursing process (assessment, planning, implementation, and evaluation) as it relates to the nursing care of the family during the childbearing cycle. Designed for and standardized at the A.S. degree level. Individuals seeking credit should contact their local colleges for information. Examiner required. Suitable for group use.

Timed: 3 hours

Scoring: Computer scored by ACT

Cost: Fee $40.00

Publisher: The American College Testing Program

ACT PROFICIENCY EXAMINATION PROGRAM— NURSING: MATERNAL AND CHILD NURSING: BACCALAUREATE DEGREE
The American College Testing Program

Adult

Purpose: Measures proficiency in maternal and child nursing. Used to grant college credit and advanced placement in academic courses.

Description: Multiple-item paper-pencil multiple-choice test. Items are based on the physiology and pathophysiology of maternal and child nursing, the theoretical framework of family functioning, and the application of the nursing process to practical situations. Designed for and standardized at the B.S. degree level. Individuals seeking credit should contact their local colleges for information. Examiner required. Suitable for group use.

Timed: 3 hours

Scoring: Computer scored by ACT

Cost: Fee $40.00

Publisher: The American College Testing Program

ACT PROFICIENCY EXAMINATION PROGRAM—

NURSING: OCCUPATIONAL STRATEGIES IN NURSING
The American College Testing Program

Adult

Purpose: Assesses an individual's knowledge and understanding of the roles and functions of the technical nurse as that individual contributes to the current practice of nursing within the legal limitations placed on the profession. Used to grant college credit and advanced placement in academic courses.

Description: Multiple-item paper-pencil multiple-choice test covering the health team, nursing team, and legal guidelines to nursing practice within both the context of the history and the current framework of the health care delivery system. The test covers knowledge and understanding of how licensure, nursing organizations, and education influence the technical nurse's function, as well as ethical guidelines for nursing practice. Designed for and standardized at the A.S. degree level. Individuals seeking credit should contact their local colleges for information. Examiner required. Suitable for group use.

Timed: 3 hours

Scoring: Computer scored by ACT

Cost: Fee $50.00

Publisher: The American College Testing Program

ACT PROFICIENCY EXAMINATION PROGRAM— NURSING: PROFESSIONAL STRATEGIES IN NURSING
The American College Testing Program

Adult

Purpose: Measures knowledge and understanding of the professional role in nursing. Used to grant college credit and advanced placement in academic courses.

Description: Multiple-item paper-pencil multiple-choice test focused on professional practice and the health care delivery system. Other areas tested include understanding of the development of the profession of nursing, professional organizations, and the evolution of nursing practice and education. Designed for and standardized at the B.S. degree level. Individuals seeking credit should contact their local colleges for information. Examiner required. Suitable for group use.

Timed: 3 hours

Scoring: Computer scored by ACT

Cost: Fee $50.00

Publisher: The American College Testing Program

ACT PROFICIENCY EXAMINATION PROGRAM— NURSING: PSYCHIATRIC/ MENTAL HEALTH NURSING
The American College Testing Program

Adult

Purpose: Assesses proficiency in psychiatric/mental health nursing. Used to grant college credit and advanced placement in academic courses.

Description: Multiple-item paper-pencil multiple-choice test. Items are based on terminology, principles, and dynamics in the areas of personality development, family development, and psychological dysfunctions as they relate to nursing assessment, planning, intervention, and evaluation. Designed for and standardized at the B.S. degree level. Individuals seeking credit should contact their local colleges for information. Examiner required. Suitable for group use.

Timed: 3 hours

Scoring: Computer scored by ACT

Cost: Fee $40.00

Publisher: The American College Testing Program

ADMISSIONS EXAMINATIONS: ADMISSIONS AND CREDENTIALING GROUP
The Psychological Corporation

Adolescent, adult
Grades 10 and above

Purpose: Assesses students' readiness to enter various health and medical schools and colleges. Used for admission and guidance of students seeking to enter posthigh-school studies.

Description: 10 paper-pencil admissions examinations: Allied Health Professions Test (AHPAT), Entrance Examination for Schools of Health Related Technologies (EESRT), Pharmacy College Admissions Test (PCAT), Optometry College Admission Test (OCAT), Veterinary Aptitude Test (VAT), Dental Hygiene Candidate Aptitude Test (DHCAT), Entrance Examination for Schools of Nursing, Entrance Examination for Schools of Practical/Vocational Nursing, Aptitude Test for Allied Health Programs, and Allied Health Entrance Examination. The Admissions and Credentialing Group provides testing services to certification boards, professional registries, and national associations in connection with professional licensing, certification, counseling, admissions, scholarships, and personnel selection. It also offers related consulting services. Applicants must complete and file an application and the appropriate fee by specific deadlines. Results are sent to the applicant and schools or colleges designated by the applicant approximately three to six weeks following the date of testing. Tests are given at designated test centers. For specific content and cost information, contact the publisher. Examiner required. Suitable for group use.

Timed: 4 hours approximately per test

Scoring: Computer scoring service provided

Cost: Contact publisher

Publisher: Admissions and Credentialing Group/The Psychological Corporation

ADMISSIONS EXAMINATIONS: ADMISSIONS AND CREDENTIALING GROUP: ALLIED HEALTH ENTRANCE EXAMINATION
The Psychological Corporation

Adolescent, adult
Grades 10 and above

Purpose: Assesses aptitude and achievement of students seeking admission to short-term assistant and technician educational programs. Used for admissions and selection.

Description: Multiple-item multiple-choice paper-pencil test for applicants to short-term assistant and technician educational programs. See Admissions Examinations: Admissions and Credentialing Group of The Psychological Corporation. Examiner required. Suitable for group use.

Untimed: Not available

Scoring: Scoring service provided by publisher

Cost: Contact publisher

Publisher: Admissions and Credentialing Group/The Psychological Corporation

---

ADMISSIONS EXAMINATIONS: ADMISSIONS AND CREDENTIALING GROUP: ALLIED HEALTH PROFESSIONS ADMISSIONS TEST (AHPAT)
The Psychological Corporation

Adolescent, adult
Grades 10 and above

Purpose: Assesses students' readiness for entering upper division majors in programs leading to baccalaureate and postbaccalaureate degrees in allied health professions. Used for admissions and selection.

Description: Multiple-item multiple-choice paper-pencil test measuring verbal ability, quantitative ability, biology principles and concepts, chemistry principles, including inorganic and organic chemistry, and reading comprehension. See Admissions Examinations: Admissions and Credentialing Group of The Psychological Corporation. Examiner required. Suitable for group use.

Timed: Not available

Scoring: Scoring service provided by publisher

Cost: Contact publisher

Publisher: Admissions and Credentialing Group/The Psychological Corporation

---

ADMISSIONS EXAMINATIONS: ADMISSIONS AND CREDENTIALING GROUP: APTITUDE TEST FOR ALLIED HEALTH PROGRAMS
The Psychological Corporation

Adolescent, adult
Grades 10 and above

Purpose: Assesses aptitude and achievement of students seeking admission to one- and two-year allied health educational programs. Used for admissions and selection.

Description: Multiple-item multiple-choice paper-pencil test designed for students applying to allied health educational programs. See Admissions Examinations: Admissions and Credentialing Group of The Psychological Corporation. Examiner required. Suitable for group use.

Timed: Not available

Scoring: Scoring service provided by publisher

Cost: Contact publisher

Publisher: Admissions and Credentialing Group/The Psychological Corporation

---

ADMISSIONS EXAMINATIONS: ADMISSIONS AND CREDENTIALING GROUP: DOPPELT MATHEMATICAL REASONING TEST
Refer to page 299.

ADMISSIONS EXAMINATIONS: ADMISSIONS AND CREDENTIALING GROUP: ENTRANCE EXAMINATION FOR SCHOOLS OF HEALTH RELATED TECHNOLOGIES (EESRT)
The Psychological Corporation

Adolescent, adult
Grades 10 and above

Purpose: Measures general academic and scientific knowledge with emphasis on the physical sciences for applicants seeking admission to one- or two-year posthigh-school programs in health-related tech-

---

nologies. Used for admissions and selection.

Description: Multiple-item multiple-choice paper-pencil test measuring verbal ability, quantitative ability, science, reading comprehension, and space relations. See Admissions Examinations: Admissions and Credentialing Group of The Psychological Corporation. Examiner required. Suitable for group use.
Timed: Not available
Scoring: Scoring service provided by publisher
Cost: Contact publisher
Publisher: Admissions and Credentialing Group/The Psychological Corporation

ADMISSIONS EXAMINATIONS: ADMISSIONS AND CREDENTIALING GROUP: ENTRANCE EXAMINATION FOR SCHOOLS OF NURSING
The Psychological Corporation

Adolescent, adult
Grades 10 and above

Purpose: Assesses students' readiness for entering a posthigh-school nursing school. Used for admissions and selection.

Description: Multiple-item paper-pencil test designed to assist in the admission and guidance of students entering nursing school. See Admissions Examinations: Admissions and Credentialing Group of The Psychological Corporation. Examiner required. Suitable for group use.
Timed: Not available
Scoring: Scoring service provided by publisher
Cost: Contact publisher
Publisher: Admissions and Credentialing Group/The Psychological Corporation

ADMISSIONS EXAMINATIONS: ADMISSIONS AND CREDENTIALING GROUP: ENTRANCE EXAMINATION FOR SCHOOLS OF PRACTICAL/ VOCATIONAL NURSING
The Psychological Corporation

Adolescent, adult
Grades 10 and above

Purpose: Assesses aptitude and achievement of students seeking admission to

schools of practical or vocational nursing. Used for admissions and selection.

Description: Multiple-item multiple-choice paper-pencil test designed for programs admitting students being prepared to become practical or vocational nurses. See Admissions Examinations: Admissions and Credentialing Group of The Psychological Corporation. Examiner required. Suitable for group use.
Timed: Not available
Scoring: Scoring service provided by publisher
Cost: Contact publisher
Publisher: Admissions and Credentialing Group/The Psychological Corporation

ADMISSIONS EXAMINATIONS: ADMISSIONS AND CREDENTIALING GROUP: MILLER ANALOGIES TEST
W.S. Miller

Adult   College students

Purpose: Assesses information and verbal reasoning ability. Used for admission of students to graduate school.

Description: 100-item paper-pencil test of verbal reasoning ability. Items are multiple-choice analogies. Braille and large-type editions are available. Distribution is restricted, and the test is administered at specified licensed university centers. Examiner required. Suitable for group use.
Timed: 50 minutes
Scoring: Scoring service available
Cost: Contact publisher
Publisher: Admissions and Credentialing Group/The Psychological Corporation

ADMISSIONS EXAMINATIONS: ADMISSIONS AND CREDENTIALING GROUP: OPTOMETRY COLLEGE ADMISSION TEST
The Psychological Corporation

Adolescent, adult
Grades 10 and above

Purpose: Assesses aptitude and achievement of students seeking admission to colleges of optometry. Used for admissions and selection.

Description: Multiple-item multiple-choice paper-pencil test measuring verbal ability, quantitative ability, biology principles and concepts, organic and inorganic chemistry knowledge, physics knowledge with emphasis on light, and study-reading ability. See Admissions Examinations: Admissions and Credentialing Group of The Psychological Corporation. Examiner required. Suitable for group use.
Timed: 3 hours
Scoring: Scoring service provided by publisher
Cost: Contact publisher
Publisher: Admissions and Credentialing Group/The Psychological Corporation

ADMISSIONS EXAMINATIONS: ADMISSIONS AND CREDENTIALING GROUP: PHARMACY COLLEGE ADMISSION TEST (PCAT)
The Psychological Corporation

Adolescent, adult Grades 10 and above

Purpose: Assesses aptitude and achievement of students seeking admission to colleges of pharmacy. Used for admissions and selection.

Description: Multiple-item multiple-choice paper-pencil test designed to assist in the admission and guidance of students seeking admission to pharmacy colleges. The test measures verbal ability, quantitative ability, chemistry knowledge, biology knowledge, and reading comprehension. See Admissions Examinations: Admissions and Credentialing Group of The Psychological Corporation. Examiner required. Suitable for group use.
Timed: 2½ hours
Scoring: Scoring service provided by publisher
Cost: Contact publisher
Publisher: Admissions and Credentialing Group/The Psychological Corporation

ADMISSIONS EXAMINATIONS: ADMISSIONS AND

CREDENTIALING GROUP: VETERINARY APTITUDE TEST (VAT)
The Psychological Corporation

Adolescent, adult Grades 10 and above

Purpose: Assesses aptitude and achievement of students seeking admission to colleges of veterinary medicine. Used for admissions and selection.

Description: Five multiple-item paper-pencil tests measuring abilities related to scholastic performance: reading comprehension, quantitative ability, biology, chemistry, and study reading. In addition, applicant performance on these measures is combined in a total score to provide a single index of scholastic aptitude. See Admissions Examinations: Admissions and Credentialing Group of The Psychological Corporation. Examiner required. Suitable for group use.
Timed: 4 hours
Scoring: Scoring service provided by publisher
Cost: Contact publisher
Publisher: Admissions and Credentialing Group/The Psychological Corporation

ADMISSIONS TESTING PROGRAM (ATP)

Adolescent   Grades 11-12

Purpose: Assists students, high schools, colleges, universities, and scholarship agencies with postsecondary educational planning and decision-making through a battery of aptitude and achievement tests.

Description: The ATP consists of the Scholastic Aptitude Test (SAT), the Test of Standard Written English (TSWE), the Achievement Tests, and the Student Descriptive Questionnaire (SDQ). Closely related to the ATP are the Student Search Service, the Summary Reporting Service, and the Validity Study Service. The SAT, TSWE, and Achievement Tests are described in separate entries. The Student Descriptive Questionnaire, answered by about 91% of all students who take the ATP, provides additional information about and specific characteristics of the student (background, academic record, extracurricular activities, etc.). The Student Search Service helps colleges and scholarship programs identify students with certain characteristics based on the SDQ. Students are included by their response on the SDQ and a search is conducted quarterly for colleges and programs requesting it. Handicapped students may be tested under special arrangements such as extended time administrations, with special editions of the SAT and TSWE (large type, braille, cassette) or with the use of a reader, manual translator, or an amanuensis. Tests for registered students are given at specified times by membership schools. Preenrollment is required. Examiner required. Suitable for group use.

Timed: See specific test

Scoring: Computer scored

Cost: Contact publisher

Publisher: The College Board Publications

Information and availability unconfirmed by publisher.

ADMISSIONS TESTING PROGRAM: PRELIMINARY SCHOLASTIC APTITUDE TEST/ NATIONAL MERIT (PSAT/NM)

Adolescent   Grade 11

Purpose: Assesses high-school students' verbal and mathematical reasoning abilities and evaluates readiness for college-level study. Used as a preview of the Scholastic Aptitude Test and serves as the qualifying test for student competitions conducted by the National Merit Scholarship Corporation: the National Merit Scholarship Program and the National Achievement Scholarship Program for Outstanding Negro Students.

Description: 115-item paper-pencil multiple-choice test measuring verbal and mathematical achievement and aptitude. The verbal section consists of 65 questions of four types: antonyms, sentence completions, analogies, and reading comprehension. The mathematical section consists of 50 questions applying graphic, spatial, numerical, symbolic, and logical techniques at a knowledge level no higher

than elementary algebra and geometry. Special testing arrangements can be made for away-from school testing, for students abroad, and for students with visual and other handicaps. Examiner required. Suitable for group use.

Timed: 1 hour, 40 minutes

Scoring: Computer scored

Cost: $4.25 per student

Publisher: The College Board Publications

Information and availability unconfirmed by publisher.

ADMISSIONS TESTING PROGRAM: SCHOLASTIC APTITUDE TEST (SAT)

Adolescent   Grades 11-12

Purpose: Measures verbal and mathematic reasoning abilities that are related to successful performance in college. Used to supplement secondary-school records and other information in assessing readiness for college-level work.

Description: 135-item paper-pencil multiple-choice test measuring reading comprehension, vocabulary, and mathematical problem-solving ability involving arithmetic reasoning, algebra, and geometry. The test consists of two verbal sections of 85 questions, including 25 antonyms, 20 analogies, 15 sentence completions, and 25 reading questions and two mathematical sections of 50 questions, including approximately two-thirds multiple-choice and one-third quantitative comparison questions. Examiner required. Suitable for group use.

Timed: 2½ hours

Scoring: Computer scored

Cost: Contact publisher

Publisher: The College Board Publications

Information and availability unconfirmed by publisher.

ADMISSIONS TESTING PROGRAM: TEST OF STANDARD WRITTEN ENGLISH (TSWE)

Adolescent   Grades 11-12

Purpose: Evaluates a student's ability to recognize standard written English. Used by colleges to help place students in appropriate freshman English courses.

Description: 50-item paper-pencil multiple-choice test measuring the basic principles of grammar and usage, as well as more complicated writing problems. This test is administered with the Scholastic Aptitude Test. Examiner required. Suitable for group use.

Timed: 30 minutes

Scoring: Computer scored

Cost: Contact publisher

Publisher: The College Board

Information and availability unconfirmed by publisher.

ADULT BASIC LEARNING EXAMINATION (ABLE)
Bjorn Karlsen, Richard Madden, and Eric F. Gardner

Adolescent, adult
Ages 17 and older

Purpose: Measures adult achievement in basic learning.

Description: Multiple-item paper-pencil measure of vocabulary knowledge, reading comprehension, spelling and arithmetic computation, and problem-solving skills. The test is divided into three levels: Level I, yielding scores for Grades 1 to 6; Level II, yielding scores for Grades 3 to 9; and Level III, yielding percentile ranks and stanines for Grades 9 to 12. Because the vocabulary test is dictated, no reading is required. The Arithmetic Problem-Solving test is dictated at Level I. A short screening test, SelectABLE, is available for use in determining the appropriate level of ABLE for each applicant. The test is available in two alternate forms, A and B, at each level. SelectABLE is available in only one form. Examiner required. Suitable for group use.

Untimed: SelectABLE 15 minutes; Levels I and II 2 hours, Level III 3 hours, 25 minutes

Scoring: Hand key; may be machine scored

Cost: Specimen set (test, handbook, group record booklet, key except Level III) $12.50 (specify level); cassettes for Level I and Level III $30.00

Publisher: The Psychological Corporation

AP EXAMINATION: ADVANCED PLACEMENT PROGRAM

Adolescent   Grades 10-12

Purpose: Measures academic achievement in a wide range of fields. Used by participating colleges to grant credit and placement in these fields to more gifted or advanced students and to measure the effectiveness of a school's Advanced Placement (AP) Program.

Description: The AP examinations are a part of the AP Program, which provides course descriptions, examinations, and curricular materials to high schools to allow those students who wish to pursue college-level studies while still in secondary school to receive advanced placement and/or credit upon entering college. The AP Program provides descriptions and examinations on 26 introductory college courses in the following 14 fields: art, biology, chemistry, computer science, English, French, German, government and politics, history, Latin, mathematics, music, physics, and Spanish.
No test is longer than three hours, and some are shorter. All examinations are paper-pencil tests (except for the art portfolios) with an essay or problem-solving section and a multiple-choice section. Using the operational services provided by the Educational Testing Service, the AP Examinations are administered in May by schools throughout the world. Any school may participate; it need only appoint an AP coordinator and order its examinations in time. The current fee for each examination is $53.00. Fee reductions are available for students with acute financial need. In June the examinations are graded on the following 5-point scale: 5 = extremely well qualified, 4 = well qualified, 3 = qualified, 2 = possibly qualified, 1 = no recommendation. In early July, the grades are sent to the students, their designated colleges, and their schools. Booklets on Beginning and

Advanced Placement Course and Grading the Advanced Placement Examination are available in most fields. Films and booklets describing the AP Program as a whole are available also. Examiner required. Suitable for group use.

Timed: 3 hours maximum

Scoring: Computer scored

Cost: Per student $53.00

Publisher: The College Board

AP EXAMINATION: ART— HISTORY OF ART

Adolescent   Grades 10-12 ☞ 🖎

Purpose: Measures academic achievement in the study of art history. Used by participating colleges to grant credit and placement to more gifted or advanced students. Also measures the effectiveness of a school's AP Program in art history.

Description: Multiple-item paper-pencil test arranged in two sections. Section I is a multiple-choice test of the student's acquisition of factual or objective aspects of history of art. Questions in this section test the student's knowledge about the history of Western art from antiquity to the present. Test items include names of artists, schools, movements, chronological periods and specific dates, and the subjects' styles, as well as the techniques of particular works of art. Section II has two parts. Part A is a series of short-answer questions testing the student's familiarity with a wide range of visual types and their historical significance. Test items in this part involve a comparison of related works of art. Section II, Part B is an essay test of the student's ability to deal with style development, treatment of a theme in art, the influence of historical context on works of art, and the influence of style from one given period to another. See AP Examination: Advanced Placement Program for administration time, scoring, and grade reporting. Examiner required. Suitable for group use.

Untimed: 3 hours

Scoring: Computer scored

Cost: Per student $53.00

Publisher: The College Board

AP EXAMINATION: ART—STUDIO ART (DRAWING)

Adolescent   Grades 10-12 ☞ 🖎

Purpose: Evaluates academic achievement in the study of basic drawing skills. Used by participating colleges to grant credit and placement to more gifted or advanced students. Also measures the effectiveness of a school's AP Program in studio art.

Description: Student portfolios are evaluated according to criteria that parallel specialized drawing curricula at college and university levels. Students are asked to show evidence of experience and skill in perceptual and conceptual aspects of drawing. Portfolios are evaluated for quality, concentration (depth), and breadth. For evaluation of quality, students submit four original drawings to be judged in terms of their artistic "success." For evaluation of concentration, students submit up to 20 drawings (slides required) demonstrating in-depth work with a single concept or medium. For evaluation of breadth, students submit 14-20 additional slides to demonstrate exposure to and experience in a wide range of drawing alternatives. Detailed instructions for shipping, sizes of works to be submitted, and acceptable mediums are contained in the course description. See AP Examination: Advanced Placement Program for administration time, scoring, and grade reporting. Examiner required. Suitable for group use.

Untimed: Not available

Scoring: Computer scored

Cost: Per student $53.00

Publisher: The College Board

AP EXAMINATION: ART—STUDIO ART (GENERAL PORTFOLIO)

Adolescent   Grades 10-12 ☞ 🖎

Purpose: Evaluates general academic achievement in the study of studio art. Used by participating colleges to grant credit and placement to more gifted or advanced students. Also measures the effectiveness of a school's AP Program in studio art.

Description: Student portfolios are evaluated for three factors: quality, concentration (depth), and breadth. For evaluation of quality, students submit four original works in their original form to be judged in terms of artistic "success." For evaluation of concentration, students are asked to show evidence of work that reveals an in-depth artistic investigation (accompanied by a written commentary). For evaluation of breadth, students must submit slides of six drawings, as well as slides of six additional works addressing the following six artistic factors: technique, color, design, spatial content, and three-dimensional. Detailed instructions for shipping, size of works to be submitted, and acceptable mediums are included in the course description. See AP Examination: Advanced Placement Program for administration time, scoring, and grade reporting. Examiner required. Suitable for group use.

Untimed: Not available
Scoring: Computer scored
Cost: Per student $53.00
Publisher: The College Board

AP EXAMINATION: BIOLOGY— GENERAL BIOLOGY

Adolescent   Grades 10-12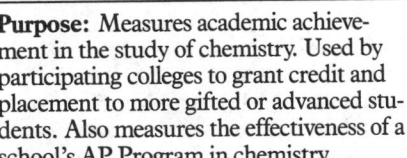

Purpose: Measures academic achievement in the study of biology. Used by participating colleges to grant credit and placement to more gifted or advanced students. Also measures the effectiveness of a school's AP Program in biology.

Description: Multiple-item paper-pencil test consists of a 90-minute multiple-choice section and a 75-minute free-response section. Both sections test the student's knowledge and understanding of the three major subdivisions of biology: molecular and cellular, organismal, and populational. Part of the multiple-choice section includes questions on experimental situations. In the free-response section, three pairs of questions are presented (one pair for each subdivision), and students are required to answer one question from each pair. See AP Examination: Advanced

Placement Program for administration time, scoring, and grade reporting. Examiner required. Suitable for group use.

Untimed: 3 hours maximum
Scoring: Computer scored
Cost: Per student $53.00
Publisher: The College Board

AP EXAMINATION: CHEMISTRY— GENERAL CHEMISTRY

Adolescent   Grades 10-12

Purpose: Measures academic achievement in the study of chemistry. Used by participating colleges to grant credit and placement to more gifted or advanced students. Also measures the effectiveness of a school's AP Program in chemistry.

Description: Multiple-item paper-pencil test in two parts. Part I (105 minutes) is an 85-item multiple-choice test. Part I accounts for 45% of the final grade. Part II (75 minutes) consists of several comprehensive problems and essay topics that allow the student to demonstrate reasoning abilities by the application of chemical principles to problem solving. Part II accounts for 55% of the final grade. Both parts cover the following areas of fundamental chemistry: structure of matter, states of matter, reactions, descriptive chemistry, and laboratory work. Non-programmable hand calculators are allowed. See AP Examination: Advanced Placement Program for administration time, scoring, and grade reporting. Examiner required. Suitable for group use.

Untimed: 3 hours maximum
Scoring: Computer scored
Cost: Per student $53.00
Publisher: The College Board

AP EXAMINATION: COMPUTER SCIENCE

Adolescent   Grades 10-12

Purpose: Measures academic achievement in the study of computer science. Used by participating colleges to grant credit and placement to more gifted or advanced students. Also measures the effectiveness of a school's AP Program in computer science.

Description: Multiple-item paper-pencil test consisting of equally weighted multiple-choice and free-response sections requiring the students to design, write, and document programs and procedures. Both sections include the following topics: programming methodology, features of programming languages, data types and structures, linear data structures, algorithms, and applications of computing. Knowledge of computer systems and social implications of computing are tested in questions on other topics. Details on equipment needed are included in the course guide. See AP Examination: Advanced Placement Program for administration time, scoring, and grade reporting. Examiner required. Suitable for group use.

Untimed: 3 hours maximum

Scoring: Computer scored

Cost: Per student $53.00

Publisher: The College Board

AP EXAMINATION: ENGLISH— ENGLISH LANGUAGE

Adolescent   Grades 10-12   [☞ ✍]

Purpose: Measures academic achievement in the study of English language and composition. Used by participating colleges to grant credit and placement to more gifted or advanced students. Also measures the effectiveness of a school's AP Program in English language and composition.

Description: Multiple-item paper-pencil test arranged in two parts: Part I (60 minutes), which accounts for 40% of the final grade, employs multiple-choice questions testing a student's skill at recasting sentences and analyzing the rhetoric of prose passages. Part II (90 minutes), which accounts for 60% of the final grade, requires students to demonstrate their skill at composition directly by writing several essays of varying lengths in various rhetorical modes. Both parts test abilities to recognize and work with the following factors: kinds and levels of diction, varieties of sentence structures, logical and functional semantic relationships, modes

of discourse, aims of discourse, various rhetorical strategies, and appropriate relationships among author, audience, and subject. See AP Examination: Advanced Placement Program for administration time, scoring, and grade reporting. Examiner required. Suitable for group use.

Untimed: 3 hours maximum

Scoring: Computer scored

Cost: Per student $53.00

Publisher: The College Board

AP EXAMINATION: ENGLISH— ENGLISH LITERATURE

Adolescent   Grades 10-12   [☞ ✍]

Purpose: Measures academic achievement in the study of English literature and composition. Used by participating colleges to grant credit and placement to more gifted or advanced students. Also measures the effectiveness of a school's AP Program in English literature and composition.

Description: Multiple-item paper-pencil test in two parts: Part I (60 minutes), which accounts for 40% of the final grade, employs multiple-choice questions testing the student's reading of selected passages. Part II (90 minutes), which accounts for 60% of the final grade, requires writing as a direct measure of the student's ability to read and interpret literature. Both parts measure the following critical and compositional skills: the use of modes of discourse, the recognition of assumptions underlying various rhetorical strategies, and the awareness of the resources of language (connotation, metaphor, irony, syntax, and tone). See AP Examination: Advanced Placement Program for administration time, scoring, and grade reporting. Examiner required. Suitable for group use.

Untimed: 3 hours maximum

Scoring: Computer scored

Cost: Per student $53.00

Publisher: The College Board

AP EXAMINATION: FRENCH LANGUAGE

Adolescent Grades 10-12 🖙 📝

Purpose: Measures academic achievement in the study of the French language. Used by participating colleges to grant credit and placement to more gifted or advanced students. Also measures the effectiveness of a school's AP Program in French language.

Description: Multiple-item paper-pencil test evaluating level of performance in the use of the French language, both in understanding written and spoken French, and in responding with ease in correct and idiomatic French. Listening and reading skills are tested in the multiple-choice section. Writing and speaking skills are tested in the free-response section. The portion of the examination devoted to each skill accounts for 25% of the final grade. The examination as a whole tests the following objectives: ability to understand spoken French in both formal and conversational situations; the development of an ample vocabulary; and the ability to express ideas accurately and resourcefully, both orally and in writing. Students' oral responses are taped, requiring that all students be familiar with the equipment to be used in the examination. See AP Examination: Advanced Placement Program for administration time, scoring, and grade reporting. Examiner required. Suitable for group use.

Timed: 3 hours maximum

Scoring: Computer scored

Cost: Per student $53.00

Publisher: The College Board

AP EXAMINATION: FRENCH LITERATURE

Adolescent Grades 10-12 🖙 📝

Purpose: Measures academic achievement in the study of French literature and language. Used by participating colleges to grant credit and placement to more gifted or advanced students. Also mea-

sures the effectiveness of a school's AP Program in French literature.

Description: Multiple-item paper-pencil test in two sections. Section I (60 minutes), which accounts for one-third of the final grade, employs multiple-choice questions testing the student's ability to understand and analyze literary prose and poetry in French. Section II (120 minutes), which accounts for two-thirds of the final grade, consists of an essay and literary analysis. The examination as a whole measures understanding of the works of French literature on the reading list provided by the AP Program, the ability to interpret and analyze literary texts, and competence in the use of written French. See AP Examination: Advanced Placement Program for administration time, scoring, and grade reporting. Examiner required. Suitable for group use.

Timed: 3 hours maximum

Scoring: Computer scored

Cost: Per student $53.00

Publisher: The College Board

AP EXAMINATION: GERMAN LANGUAGE

Adolescent Grades 10-12 🖙 📝

Purpose: Measures academic achievement in the study of the German language. Used by participating colleges to grant credit and placement to more gifted or advanced students. Also measures the effectiveness of a school's AP Program in German.

Description: Multiple-item paper-pencil test consists of two sections. Section I (120 minutes), which accounts for two-thirds of the final grade, is a multiple-choice test for listening comprehension and reading skills. Section II (60 minutes), which accounts for one-third of the final grade, is a free-response essay test of writing skills. Speaking ability is not tested. The test evaluates level of performance in the use of the German language. See AP Examination: Advanced Placement Program for administration time, scoring, and grade reporting. Examiner required. Suitable for group use.

Timed: 3 hours maximum

Scoring: Computer scored

Cost: Per student $53.00

Publisher: The College Board

AP EXAMINATION: GOVERNMENT AND POLITICS

Adolescent   Grades 10-12   [☞ ✍]

Purpose: Measures academic achievement in the study of government and politics. Used by participating colleges to grant credit and placement to more gifted or advanced students. Also measures the effectiveness of a school's AP Program in government and politics.

Description: Two 180-minute multiple-item paper-pencil tests: American Government and Politics and Comparative Government and Politics. (Students may take either test or both for a single fee, receiving a separate grade on each.) Each test is divided nearly equally between a multiple-choice section and a free-response section. Each test contributes 50% of the final grade. The topics covered in each test include the concepts and facts commonly covered in cognate introductory college courses. See AP Examination: Advanced Placement Program for administration time, scoring, and grade reporting. Examiner required. Suitable for group use.

Untimed: 3 hours maximum

Scoring: Computer scored

Cost: Per student $53.00

Publisher: The College Board

AP EXAMINATION: HISTORY— AMERICAN HISTORY

Adolescent   Grades 10-12   [☞ ✍]

Purpose: Measures academic achievement in the study of American history. Used by participating colleges to grant credit and placement to more gifted or advanced students. Also measures the effectiveness of a school's AP Program in American history.

Description: Multiple-item paper-pencil test consisting of two equally weighted sections. Section I (75 minutes) employs multiple-choice questions testing the stu-dent's factual knowledge, breadth of preparation, and knowledge-based analytical skills. Section II consists of two parts: Part A (40 minutes), in which students answer a document-based essay question and Part B (50 minutes), in which students answer one of five standard essay questions. The essay questions test the student's mastery of historical interpretation and the ability to express views and knowledge in writing. Both sections cover the period from the earliest colonial settlements to the present (with emphasis on the nineteenth and twentieth centuries) and cover the following topics: political institutions, behavior, public policy, social and economic change, diplomacy, international relations, and cultural and intellectual developments. See AP Examination: Advanced Placement Program for administration time, scoring, and grade reporting. Examiner required. Suitable for group use.

Timed: 3 hours maximum

Scoring: Computer scored

Cost: Per student $53.00

Publisher: The College Board

AP EXAMINATION: HISTORY— EUROPEAN HISTORY

Adolescent   Grades 10-12   [☞ ✍]

Purpose: Measures academic achievement in the study of European history. Used by participating colleges to grant credit and placement to more gifted or advanced students. Also measures the effectiveness of a school's AP Program in European history.

Description: Multiple-item paper-pencil test in two equally weighted sections. Section I (75 minutes) is a multiple-choice test dealing with concepts, major historical facts, and historical analysis. Section II consists of two parts. Part A (45 minutes) is a document-based essay question, and Part B (45 minutes) requires the student to answer one of six standard essay questions. Students are expected to demonstrate a knowledge of basic chronology of major events and trends from approximately 1450 to the 1980s (high Renaissance to present). Test items cover the following historical themes: intellectual-cultural, social-economic, and political-diplomatic. See AP Examination: Advanced Placement Program for administration time, scoring, and grade reporting. Examiner required. Suitable for group use.

Timed: 3 hours maximum
Scoring: Computer scored
Cost: Per student $53.00
Publisher: The College Board

AP EXAMINATION: MATHEMATICS—CALCULUS AB

Adolescent   Grades 10-12 $\mathbb{F}$ 🖎

Purpose: Measures academic achievement in the study of calculus. Used by participating colleges to grant credit and placement to more gifted or advanced students. Also measures the effectiveness of a school's AP Program in calculus.

Description: Multiple-item paper-pencil test in two equally weighted parts: a multiple-choice test of proficiency covering a wide variety of topics and a problem section requiring students to demonstrate their ability to carry out proofs and solve problems involving a more extended chain of reasoning. The topics covered include elementary functions, differential calculus, and integral calculus. The use of specific functions, rather than their theoretical development and basis, is emphasized. Calculus AB level is not generally as difficult as Calculus BC level. See AP Examination: Advanced Placement Program for administration time, scoring, and grade reporting. Examiner required. Suitable for group use.

Timed: 3 hours maximum
Scoring: Computer scored
Cost: Per student $53.00
Publisher: The College Board

AP EXAMINATION: MATHEMATICS—CALCULUS BC

Adolescent   Grades 10-12 $\mathbb{F}$ 🖎

Purpose: Measures academic achievement in the study of calculus. Used by participating colleges to grant credit and placement to more gifted or advanced stu-

dents. Also measures the effectiveness of a school's AP Program in calculus.

Description: Multiple-item paper-pencil test in two equally weighted parts: a multiple-choice test of proficiency covering a wide variety of topics and a problem section requiring students to demonstrate their ability to carry out proofs and solve problems involving a more extended chain of reasoning. The topics covered include elementary functions, differential calculus, integral calculus, sequences and series, and elementary differential equations. Calculus BC level is generally more difficult and involves more theoretical reasoning than Calculus AB level. See AP Examination: Advanced Placement Program for administration time, scoring, and grade reporting. Examiner required. Suitable for group use.

Timed: 3 hours maximum
Scoring: Computer scored
Cost: Per student $53.00
Publisher: The College Board

AP EXAMINATION: MUSIC— LISTENING AND LITERATURE

Adolescent   Grades 10-12 $\mathbb{F}$ 🖎

Purpose: Measures academic achievement in the study of music listening and literature. Used by participating colleges to grant credit and placement to more gifted or advanced students. Also measures the effectiveness of a school's AP Program in music.

Description: Multiple-item paper-pencil test measuring knowledge of musical styles and forms. The test contains 70 minutes of questions specific to music listening and literature and a 40-minute test of the Aural Perception Component (APC). The APC is also a part of the AP Music Theory exam and is taken only once if both tests are taken in the same year. In the specific questions section, multiple-choice and free-response questions (using both aural and visual stimuli) address the structural aspects (70%) and historical and cultural aspects (30%) of music. The APC requires the student to distinguish among various scales, meters, and rythms; identify cadence and texture types; and recognize formal structure and function. See AP Examination: Advanced Placement Program for administration time, scoring, and grade reporting. Examiner required. Suitable for group use.

Timed: 1 hour, 50 minutes

Scoring: Computer scored

Cost: Per student $53.00

Publisher: The College Board

AP EXAMINATION: MUSIC— MUSIC THEORY

Adolescent   Grades 10-12   [☞ 🖉]

Purpose: Measures academic achievement in the study of music theory. Used by participating colleges to grant credit and placement to more gifted or advanced students. Also measures the effectiveness of a school's AP Program in music theory.

Description: Multiple-item paper-pencil test measuring the student's understanding of musical structure and compositional procedures. Three kinds of questions are included: multiple-choice based on recorded music; multiple-choice based not on aural materials, but on general musical knowledge; and free-response questions of various lengths, some of which are based on recorded music. Also included is a 40-minute test of the Aural Perception Component. The APC is also a part of the AP Music Listening and Literature exam and is taken only once if both tests are taken in the same year. The following fundamentals are covered: terminology and notational skills, elementary composition, visual analysis, and aural skills. The Aural Perception Component (APC) requires the student to discriminate among various scales, meters, and rhythms; identify cadence and texture types; and recognize formal structure and function. See AP Examination: Advanced Placement Program for administration time, scoring, and grade reporting. Examiner required. Suitable for group use.

Timed: 3 hours maximum

Scoring: Computer scored

Cost: Per student $53.00

Publisher: The College Board

AP EXAMINATION: PHYSICS B

Adolescent   Grades 10-12   [☞ 🖉]

Purpose: Measures academic achievement in the study of physics as a basis for more advanced work in the life sciences, medicine, geology, and related fields. Used by participating colleges to grant credit and placement to more gifted or advanced students. Also measures the effectiveness of a school's AP Program in physics.

Description: Multiple-item paper-pencil test consisting of two equally weighted sections (90 minutes each): one multiple-choice section and one free-response section. Five general topics are covered: mechanics, kinetic theory and thermodynamics, electricity and magnetism, waves and optics, and modern physics. Calculus is not required. See AP Examination: Advanced Placement Program for administration time, scoring, and grade reporting. Examiner required. Suitable for group use.

Timed: 3 hours maximum

Scoring: Computer scored

Cost: Per student $53.00

Publisher: The College Board

AP EXAMINATION: PHYSICS C

Adolescent   Grades 10-12   [☞ 🖉]

Purpose: Measures academic achievement in the study of physics as a basis for more advanced study in the physical sciences and engineering. Used by participating colleges to grant credit and placement to more gifted or advanced students. Also measures the effectiveness of a school's AP Program in physics.

Description: Paper-pencil test in two parts (90 minutes each): one covering mechanics and one covering electricity and magnetism. Students may take one or both parts. Each part has a separate grade representing roughly one semester of college-level work. The parts are divided equally (in time and scoring weight) between a multiple-choice section and a free-response section. The mechanics part covers kinematics; Newton's Laws of

Motion; work, energy, and power; systems of particles (statics); rotational motion; and oscillations and gravitation. The electricity and magnetism part covers electrostatics, electric current and circuits, capacitance and capacitors, magnetostatics, and electromagnetism. Use of calculus is required (when appropriate) for both parts. See AP Examination: Advanced Placement Program for administration time, scoring, and grade reporting. Examiner required. Suitable for group use.

Timed: 3 hours maximum

Scoring: Computer scored

Cost: Per student $53.00

Publisher: The College Board

AP EXAMINATION: SPANISH— SPANISH LANGUAGE

Adolescent   Grades 10-12   👉 ✍

Purpose: Measures academic achievement in the study of the Spanish language. Used by participating colleges to grant credit and placement to more gifted or advanced students. Also measures the effectiveness of a school's AP Program in Spanish.

Description: Paper-pencil and oral-response test consisting of two sections. Section I (90 minutes) employs multiple-choice questions and tests listening and reading comprehension skills, including mastery of grammatical structure and vocabulary. Section II (75 minutes), a free-response section, tests the active skills of speaking and writing. The portion of the examination devoted to each skill counts for one-fourth of the composite score. The test evaluates general ability to understand written and spoken Spanish and to write and speak easily and idiomatically. Students must be trained in the use of the examination equipment in order to insure that their oral responses are properly recorded. See AP Examination: Advanced Placement Program for administration time, scoring, and grade reporting. Examiner required. Suitable for group use.

Timed: 3 hours maximum

Scoring: Computer scored

Cost: Per student $53.00

Publisher: The College Board

AP EXAMINATION: SPANISH— SPANISH LITERATURE

Adolescent   Grades 10-12   👉 ✍

Purpose: Measures academic achievement in the study of Spanish literature. Used by participating colleges to grant credit and placement to more gifted or advanced students. Also measures the effectiveness of a school's AP Program in Spanish.

Description: Paper-pencil test consisting of two equally weighted parts: a multiple-choice section on aural comprehension, literary analysis, the reading comprehension of passages, and the analysis of two poems and a free-response section on literary interpretation and analysis and skill in writing critical, expository prose in Spanish. Section 2 contains two essays. Each essay deals with two or more of the authors required by the AP Program in Spanish Literature. Students are asked to analyze and discuss, in Spanish, works that they have read (no choice of authors is given). See AP Examination: Advanced Placement Program for administration time, scoring, and grade reporting. Examiner required. Suitable for group use.

Timed: 3 hours maximum

Scoring: Computer scored

Cost: Per student $53.00

Publisher: The College Board

AP EXAMINATION: VERGIL AND CATULLUS-HORACE

Adolescent   Grades 10-12   👉 ✍

Purpose: Measures academic achievement in the study of Latin. Used by participating colleges to grant credit and placement to more gifted or advanced students. Also measures the effectiveness of a school's AP Program in Latin.

Description: Multiple-item paper-pencil test consists of three parts: a multiple-choice section testing students' ability to read and understand Latin poetry at sight and two free-response sections measuring the students' ability to comprehend and interpret the material read in the two specific courses on Vergil and Catullus-Horace. Students may elect to take either or both of the free-response sections (each one represents roughly one semester of college work). Students are expected to be able to translate accurately from Latin into English the poetry they are reading and demonstrate a grasp of the grammatical structures and vocabulary used. Other important factors include stylistic analysis, awareness of political, social, and cultural backgrounds of the works being read, and awareness of the classical influences of later literature. See AP Examination: Advanced Placement Program for administration time, scoring, and grade reporting. Examiner required. Suitable for group use.

Timed: 3 hours maximum

Scoring: Computer scored

Cost: Per student $53.00

Publisher: The College Board

APTITUDE TEST BATTERY FOR PUPILS IN STANDARDS 6 AND 7 (ATB)

Adolescent

Purpose: Measures aptitudes of students in Standards 6 and 7. Used in South Africa for educational placement and for identifying underachievement in black pupils.

Description: Multiple-item paper-pencil battery of 5-item multiple-choice tests for determining academic aptitude and achievement. The core battery of six tests includes English (reading comprehension and vocabulary), spatial perception, non-verbal reasoning, mathematics, Afrikaans (reading comprehension and vocabulary), and verbal reasoning. The supplementary tests are comparison, numerical, and mechanical insight. Stanines are calculated for the third term. Examiner required. Suitable for group use.
SOUTH AFRICAN PUBLISHER

Untimed: 5 hours

Scoring: Hand key; may be machine scored

Cost: Test booklet $3.50; manual $1.60; 10 answer sheets $0.90; scoring stencil $3.70

Publisher: Human Sciences Research Council

APTITUDE TEST FOR ADULTS (AA)—1979

Child, adolescent

Purpose: Assesses scholastic aptitudes. Used for psychoeducational evaluation.

Description: 225-item paper-pencil test measuring nine scholastic aptitudes, including comparison, figural series, calculations, reasoning, mechanical insight, spatial visualization (2-D), classification, spatial visualization (3-D), and spare parts. Examiner required. Suitable for group use.
SOUTH AFRICAN PUBLISHER

Timed: 3½ hours

Scoring: Hand key; examiner evaluated

Cost: (In Rands) test booklet 3,90; manual 9,10; 10 answer sheets 1,20; scoring stencil 3,80; orders from outside The RSA will be dealt with on merit

Publisher: Human Sciences Research Council

APTITUDE TESTS FOR INDIAN SOUTH AFRICANS—JATISA AND SATISA

Child, adolescent

Purpose: Assesses aptitudes of Indian children. Used for vocational guidance.

Description: Multiple-item paper-pencil test batteries measuring scholastic and vocational attitudes. JATISA (Standards 6 to 8) consists of 10 subtests: Verbal Reasoning, Series Completion, Social Insight, Language Usage, Numerical Reasoning, Spatial Perception (2-D), Spatial Perception (3-D), Visual Arts, Clerical Speed and Accuracy, and Mechanical Insight. SATISA (Standards 9 and 10) consists of 11 subtests: Verbal Reasoning, Numerical Reasoning, Spatial Perception (3-D), Series Completion, Mechanical Insight, Classification, Spatial Perception (2-D),

Comparison, Language Usage, Memory, and Filing. Examiner required. Suitable for group use.
SOUTH AFRICAN PUBLISHER
Timed: Junior 3½ hours; Senior 4½ hours
Scoring: Hand key; examiner evaluated
Cost: (In Rands) Junior test plus photos 1,10; manual 9,10; scoring stencil 5,00; 10 answer sheets 0,90; Senior tests A or B 2,10 each; 10 answer sheets I, 0,60; 10 answer sheets II 0,60; manual 6,30; scoring stencils I, II, III, IV 3,40 each; orders from outside The RSA will be dealt with on merit
Publisher: Human Sciences Research Council

APTITUDE TESTS FOR SCHOOL BEGINNERS (ASB)—1974

Child   Ages 5-8

Purpose: Assesses aptitudes of children beginning school. Used for placement, program planning, and prediction of future achievement.

Description: Multiple-item paper-pencil test measuring eight areas important in the early school years: perception, spatial, reasoning, numerical, gestalt, coordination, memory, and verbal comprehension. The test yields a differential aptitude profile rather than IQ-type score. Administration during the first two months of the school year is recommended. Examiner required. Suitable for group use.
SOUTH AFRICAN PUBLISHER
Timed: 7 hours
Scoring: Hand key; examiner evaluated
Cost: (In Rands) 10 tests 3,00; 10 tests of Verbal Comprehension 0,70; scoring key 0,60; manual 5,70; orders from outside The RSA will be dealt with on merit
Publisher: Human Sciences Research Council

APU ARITHMETIC TEST AND APU VOCABULARY TEST
S. J. Closs and Michael Hutchings

Child, adolescent
Ages 11-18

Purpose: Measures children's vocabulary and arithmetic skills. Used in schools and colleges, vocational guidance, industrial selection, and similar situations in which an overall indication of verbal and arithmetical skills is required.

Description: Two paper-pencil tests measuring vocabulary and arithmetic skills. The APU Vocabulary Test contains 75 items culled from newspapers and magazines to ensure that the range of difficulty is realistic and that the scores give a valid indication of understanding of vocabulary in current use. Materials include reusable test booklets and separate answer sheets, which can be scored using a template. Norms are provided for ages 11-17. The APU Arithmetic Test contains 50 items covering the whole range from basic skills to percentages, sets, ratios, and elementary statistics. The test is fully metricated. Scoring employs a specially designed key provided in the manual. Norms are provided for ages 11-18. Examiner required. Suitable for group use.
BRITISH PUBLISHER
Timed: Arithmetic 25 minutes; vocabulary 15 minutes
Scoring: Hand key
Cost: Arithmetic specimen set £1.75; 20 tests £2.95; manual £1.35; vocabulary specimen set 80p; 20 tests £1.90; 20 answer sheets £1.00 plus VAT; template 65p. plus VAT; manual 65p.
Publisher: Hodder & Stoughton

ASSESSMENT OF BASIC COMPETENCIES (ABC)
Jwalla P. Somwaru

Child, adolescent
Grades PreK-9

Purpose: Assesses ability of elementary and intermediate school students to use language, process information, and work mathematics problems. Used to determine level of development for instructional planning and for Chapter I assessment.

Description: Multiple-item multiple-choice and verbal paper-pencil test covering 11 defined test areas in three broad domains. Language skills covers reading, decoding, comprehending expressions, producing expressions, and understanding words. Information Processing covers relating, organizing, and observing. Mathematics Skills covers solving problems, understanding concepts, and knowing numbers and operations. The test is individually administered with the student and examiner on opposite sides of a table. Scoring provides a raw score, level of competence, developmental age, grade equivalent, standard score, and percentile. Since the battery is both criterion- and norm-referenced, two kinds of response forms are included: 1) the diagnostic version, which enables the user to observe performance primarily in terms of clusters of skills and 2) the developmental version, which enables the user to observe performance primarily in terms of developmental level. All items relate to specific objectives that can be placed in an Individualized Education Program. Examiner required. Not suitable for group use.

Timed: 2 hours

Scoring: Hand key; examiner evaluated

Cost: Starter set $414.00

Publisher: Scholastic Testing Service, Inc.

BASIC ACHIEVEMENT SKILLS INDIVIDUAL SCREENER (BASIS)
The Psychological Corporation, Measurement Division Staff

Grades 1-12
Posthigh school

Purpose: Measures achievement in reading, mathematics, and spelling. Assesses individual students' academic strengths and weaknesses with both norm-referenced and criterion-referenced information. Used for program planning and evaluation, academic placement, and establishing IEPs.

Description: Three subtests assessing academic achievement in reading, mathematics, and spelling. Test items are grouped in grade-referenced clusters, which constitute the basic unit of administration. Testing begins at a grade cluster with which the student is expected to have little difficulty and continues until the student fails to reach the criteria for a particular cluster. The clusters range from Readiness through Grade 8 for reading

and mathematics and from Grades 1-8 for spelling. The reading test assesses comprehension of graded passages. The student is required to read the passages aloud and supply the missing words. Comprehension at the lower levels is assessed by word reading and sentence reading, and readiness is measured by letter identification and visual discrimination. The mathematics test consists of a readiness subtest and assesses computation and problem solving above that level. The student works on the computation items directly in the record form. Word problems are dictated by the teacher and require no reading on the part of the student. The spelling test for Grades 1-8 consists of clusters of words that are dictated in sentence contexts. The student writes the words on the record form. An optional writing exercise (average samples provided for Grades 3-8) requires the student to write descriptively for 10 minutes. Samples are scored by comparison with criterion samples for each grade. Criterion-referenced scores for the subtests describe performance in basic skills and suggest grade and textbook placement. Raw scores can be converted to standard scores, age- and grade-based percentile ranks, stanines, grade equivalents, and age equivalents. The manual includes information for administering, scoring, and interpreting the tests. Examiner required. Not suitable for group use.

Untimed: 1 hour

Scoring: Examiner evaluated

Cost: Examiner's kit (manual, content booklet, 2 record forms) $45.00

Publisher: The Psychological Corporation

BASIC EDUCATIONAL SKILLS TEST (BEST)
Ruth Segel and Sandra Golding

Child   Grades 1-5

Purpose: Determines perceptual abilities and reading, writing, and mathematical skills of elementary school children and older remedial students. Used to screen for group placement and program planning.

for group placement and program planning.

Description: 75-item paper-pencil examination consisting of three subtests: Reading, Writing/Spelling, and Mathematics. Materials include a manual, test plates, and recording forms, which correlate performance on each item with relevant perceptual modalities (auditory, visual, vocal, and haptic). Examiner required. Not suitable for group use.

Untimed: 20 minutes per subtest

Scoring: Hand key

Cost: Manual $7.50; test plates $18.00; 25 recording forms $6.00

Publisher: United Educational Services, Inc.

BASIC SKILLS ASSESSMENT PROGRAM (BSAP)
Educational Testing Service

Ages 7-adult

Purpose: Evaluates an individual's ability to apply academic skills to everyday situations. Used to screen students who need special help in basic skills.

Description: 210-item paper-pencil multiple-choice test assessing an individual's ability to apply reading, writing, and mathematics skills to everyday tasks, such as understanding consumer information, reading newspapers, making simple calculations, writing letters, and completing job applications. The program can be used in high schools to judge attainment of minimal proficiency in basic skills before graduation. Examiner required. Suitable for group use.

Timed: 45 minutes

Scoring: Hand key; may be computer scored

Cost: Contact publisher

Publisher: CTB/McGraw-Hill

BOEHM TEST OF BASIC CONCEPTS—REVISED (BOEHM-R)
Ann E. Boehm

Child   Grades K-2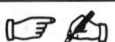

Purpose: Measures children's mastery of basic concepts used in classroom instruc-

tion. Identifies individual children with low level of concept development. Targets specific areas for basic concept remediation.

Description: 50-item paper-pencil multiple-choice picture test of concepts in such contexts as quantity, space, and time. The child responds to oral instructions by marking one of several pictures. Two alternate forms, C and D, measure the same concepts. A new 26-item Applications level for Grades 1 and 2 requires the child to respond to combinations of basic concepts. Examiner required. Suitable for small group use.

Untimed: 30 minutes

Scoring: Hand key

Cost: Examination kit (booklet, directions, manual, class record, parent-teacher conference report, hand key) $15.00; 35 test booklets, directions, class record, key (specify form) $26.00; maual $10.00

Publisher: The Psychological Corporation

THE BRIGANCE® DIAGNOSTIC ASSESSMENT OF BASIC SKILLS— SPANISH EDITION
Albert H. Brigance

Child, adolescent
Grades PreK-9

Purpose: Measures the academic skills of Spanish-speaking students. Distinguishes language barriers from learning disabilities. Used by bilingual, ESL, migrant, and bilingual special educators to identify, develop, implement, and evaluate appropriate academic programs for Spanish-speaking students.

Description: 102 multiple-item paper-pencil or oral-response and direct observation diagnostic tests and 8 multiple-item paper-pencil or oral-response screening forms assessing Spanish-speaking students' abilities in the following areas: readiness, speech, functional word recognition, oral reading, reading comprehension, word analysis, listening, writing and alphabetizing, numbers and computation, and measurement. Directions to the examiner are written in English; directions to the student are

dominant language screening present directions to the student in English and Spanish.

The diagnostic tests identify skills the student has and has not mastered and students who might have learning disabilities and determine individual instructional objectives. The dominant language screening form provides a means of comparing a student's performance in English and Spanish on all of the oral language and literacy diagnostic assessments. Results of the screening are used to place students in appropriate ESL and bilingual programs. The seven grade-level screens assess skills that indicate grade-level competency in Grades K-6. The results are used to place students at their appropriate instructional levels and to identify students who need further evaluation. Individual student record books graphically record at each testing the level of competency the student has achieved. An optional class record book tracks the progress of 35 students. A videotape program for in-service training of examiners is available. Examiner required. Many sections are suitable for group use.

Untimed: Varies

Scoring: Examiner evaluated

Cost: Assessment book, 10 student record books $89.00; class record book $6.95; ABS excerpts are available at no charge

Publisher: Curriculum Associates, Inc.

THE BRIGANCE® DIAGNOSTIC COMPREHENSIVE INVENTORY OF BASIC SKILLS (CIBS)
Albert H. Brigance

Child, adolescent
Grades PreK-9

Purpose: Measures attainment of basic academic skills. Used to screen kindergarten and first-grade students, meet minimal competency requirements, develop IEPs, and determine academic placement.

Description: 203 multiple-item tests assessing skill sequences in the following 22 sections: readiness, speech, word recognition grade placement, oral reading,

reading comprehension, listening, functional word recognition, word analysis, reference skills, graphs and maps, spelling, writing, math grade placement, numbers, number facts, computation of whole numbers, decimals, percents, word problems, metrics, and math vocabulary. Assessment is initiated at the skill level at which the student will be successful and continues until the student's level of achievement for that skill is attained. The following assessment methods may be used to accommodate different situations: parent interview, teacher observation, group or individual, and informal appraisal of student performance in daily work. Two alternate forms, A and B, are available for pre- and posttesting for 51 skill sequences. All skill sequences are referenced to specific instructional objectives and grade level expectations. The comprehensive record book indicates graphically at each testing the level of competency the student has achieved. An optional class record book tracks the progress of 30 students. IEP objective forms are available for readiness, reading, mathematics, and individual use (blank forms). A videotape for in-service training of examiners is available. Examiner required. Many sections are suitable for group use.

Untimed: Varies

Scoring: Examiner evaluated

Cost: Test book, 10 comprehensive record books $99.00; class record book $6.95; 30 IEP objective forms $15.95; CIBS excerpts available at no charge

Publisher: Curriculum Associates, Inc.

THE BRIGANCE® DIAGNOSTIC INVENTORY OF BASIC SKILLS
Albert H. Brigance

Child   Grades K-6

Purpose: Measures students' mastery of basic academic skills. Used for academic placement, mainstreaming students, competency evaluations, and IEP development and evaluation.

Description: 143 paper-pencil or oral-response tests assessing student mastery in readiness, reading, language arts, and math. Test items are arranged in developmental and sequential order. Major skill sections include readiness, word recognition, reading (fluency and level), word analysis, vocabulary, handwriting, grammar and mechanics, spelling, reference skills, math placement, numbers, operations, measurement, and geometry. IEP objectives are included for each of the 143 academic skills assessed. The individual student record book indicates graphically at each testing the level of competency the student has achieved and identifies the student's current instructional goals. An optional class record book monitors the progress of 35 students and forms a comprehensive matrix of individual student's levels. IEP objective forms are available for reading, readiness, mathematics, and individual use (blank form). A videotape program for in-service training of examiners is available. Examiner required. Some sections are suitable for group use.

Untimed: Varies

Scoring: Examiner evaluated

Cost: Assessment book, 10 individual record books $69.95; class record book $5.95; free test excerpts available

Publisher: Curriculum Associates, Inc.

THE BRIGANCE® DIAGNOSTIC INVENTORY OF ESSENTIAL SKILLS
Albert H. Brigance

Child, adolescent
Grades 4-12

Purpose: Measures a student's mastery of skills essential to success as a citizen, consumer, worker, and family member. Used in secondary programs serving students with special needs. Used to develop IEPs.

Description: 186 paper-pencil or oral-response skill assessments measuring minimal academic and vocational competencies in the areas of reading, language arts, and math. The inventory includes rating scales to measure applied skills that cannot be assessed objectively, such as health and attitude, responsibility and self-discipline, job interview preparation, auto safety, and communication. Other practical assessments include sections on food and clothing, money and finance,

travel and transportation, and communication and telephone skills. Test results identify basic skills which have and have not been mastered, areas of strengths and weaknesses in academic and practical skills, and instructional objectives for a specified skill level. Individual record books indicate graphically at each testing the level of competency the student has achieved and the student's current instructional goals. An optional class record book monitors the progress of 15 students and forms a matrix of specific student competencies. IEP objective forms are available for reading, writing and spelling, mathematics, and individual use (blank form). Tests may be administered by teachers, aides, or parent volunteers. A videotape program for in-service training of examiners is available. Examiner required. Some sections are suitable for group use.

Untimed: Varies

Scoring: Examiner evaluated

Cost: Assessment book, 10 individual record books $118.00; class record book $7.50; free test excerpt available

Publisher: Curriculum Associates, Inc.

BRISTOL ACHIEVEMENT TESTS, REVISED EDITION
Alan Brimer, general editor

Child, adolescent
Ages 8-14

Purpose: Measures achievement in basic academic skills. Used for evaluation of student progress and identification of an individual's strengths and weaknesses.

Description: Multiple-item paper-pencil tests measuring achievement in English language, mathematics, and study skills. The English Language Tests measure word meaning, paragraph meaning, sentence organization, organization of ideas, and spelling and punctuation. The Mathematics Tests cover number, reasoning, space, measurement, and arithmetical laws and processes. The Study Skills Tests measure properties, structures, processes, explanations, and interpretation. The tests are available on five levels for individuals ages 8-13. Two parallel forms, A and B, are available. Examiner required. Suitable for group use. BRITISH PUBLISHER

Timed: Varies

Scoring: Hand key; examiner evaluated

Cost: Teacher's set for each area (one each of Forms A and B, 2 marking keys, profile, manual) £9.75 (payment in sterling for all overseas orders)

Publisher: NFER-NELSON Publishing Company Ltd.

CALIFORNIA ACHIEVEMENT TESTS: FORMS C AND D (CAT/C&D)
CTB McGraw-Hill

Child, adolescent
Grades K-12.9

Purpose: Assesses achievement in basic academic skills. Used for making educational decisions leading to improvement in instruction.

Description: Multiple-item paper-pencil tests measuring a student's reading, spelling, language, reference, and mathematics skills. The tests are divided into 10 overlapping levels spanning Kindergarten through Grade 12. Level 10 is a kindergarten readiness instrument derived from Form S, Level A of the Comprehensive Tests of Basic Skills. Levels 11-19 are composed of separate tests that combine to yield the following scores: Total Reading, Spelling, Total Language, Total Mathematics, and Reference Skills. Spelling is not tested at Level 11; reference skills are tested only at Levels 14-19. Two alternate forms, C and D, are available. Levels 10-12 are available only in Form C; Levels 13-19 are available in both forms. Examiner required. Suitable for group use.

Timed: Complete battery 2 hours, 48 minutes or less, depending on level

Scoring: Hand key; may be computer scored

Cost: Multi-level examination kit (Grades K-12) $24.00

Publisher: CTB/McGraw-Hill

CALIFORNIA ACHIEVEMENT TESTS: FORM E AND F

Grades K-12.9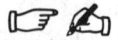

Purpose: Measures students' achievement. Used for evaluating educational programs and for instructional planning.

Description: Multiple-item paper-pencil battery of tests assessing student knowledge of reading, language, spelling, mathematics, study skills, science, and social studies. The battery is available in 11 overlapping levels ranging from Level 10 (Kindergarten) to Level 20 (Grades 10.6-12.9). Two scoring options are offered: the traditional number of correct responses (NCR) and a newer method based on item-response theory (IRT). Computer literacy, consumer economics, and high school end-of-course tests (alegbra, geometry, physics, chemistry, biology, world history, and American history) are also available. Examiner required. Suitable for group use.

Timed: Complete battery, depending on level 2 hours, 48 minutes

Scoring: Hand key; may be computer scored

Cost: Contact publisher

Publisher: CTB/McGraw-Hill

CANADIAN COGNITIVE ABILITIES TEST (CCAT), FORM 3, 1981
E. Wright, R. Thorndike, and Elizabeth P. Hagan

Child, adolescent
Grades K-12

Purpose: Measures students' cognitive development. Used for placement, counseling, and class planning.

Description: Multiple-item paper-pencil tests available in a primary battery (Grades K-3) and a multilevel battery (Grades 3-12). The primary battery (76-90 items) tests the following concepts: relational, multimental, quantitative, and oral. The multilevel battery (240 items) tests the following abilities: verbal (vocabulary, sentence completion, verbal classification, verbal analogies); quan-

titative (relations, number series, equations); and nonverbal (figure classification, analysis, and synthesis). This test is a Canadian adaption of the Cognitive Abilities Test published by Riverside Publishing Company. Examiner required. Suitable for group use.
CANADIAN PUBLISHER
Timed: Multilevel battery 1 hour, 38 minutes
Untimed: Primary battery 54 minutes
Scoring: Hand key; may be computer scored
Cost: Booklet $5.95; 500 answer sheets $92.75; scoring mask $7.30; manual $10.65
Publisher: Nelson Canada

CANADIAN COMPREHENSIVE ASSESSMENT PROGRAM— ACHIEVEMENT SERIES

Child, adolescent Grades PreK-9

Purpose: Evaluates students' achievement levels and development of learning processes and capabilities in the areas of reading, mathematics, and language.

Description: Multiple-item multiple-level paper-pencil test measuring student performance in reading, mathematics, and language. Some levels also measure performance in word attack, study skills, science, and social studies. Levels 4-6 (PreK-Grade 1) assess facility with language, ease in dealing with written symbols, and perception of quantity and applications of that perception. Level 4 contains 96 items divided among 10 subtests; Level 5 contains 96 items in 10 subtests; and Level 6 contains 128 items in 13 subtests. Levels 7 and 8 (Grades 2-3) measure achievement in reading, mathematics, and language. Level 7 contains 9 subtests; Level 8 contains 10 subtests. Two forms, A and B, are available at each level. Levels 9-12 (Grades 4-9) measures achievement in reading, mathematics, language, and study skills. Two forms, A and B, are available at each level, and each level contains 10 subtests. Examiner required. Suitable for group use.
CANADIAN PUBLISHER
Timed: Varies

Scoring: Hand key
Cost: Contact publisher
Publisher: Guidance Centre

CANADIAN TESTS OF BASIC SKILLS: HIGH SCHOOL EDITION (CTBS), FORM 5, 1981
E. King, D. Scannel, et al.

Adolescent   Ages 14-18

Purpose: Assesses high-school students' progress in developing basic educational skills. Used for class planning and counseling.

Description: 233-242-item paper-pencil test of achievement measuring reading comprehension, mathematics, using sources of information, and written expression. The test has a multilevel format with Canadian norms. This test is a Canadian adaption of the Tests of Achievement and Proficiency published by Riverside Publishing Company. Examiner required. Suitable for group use.
CANADIAN PUBLISHER
Timed: 2 hours, 40 minutes
Scoring: Hand key; may be computer scored
Cost: Booklet $5.95; 500 answer sheets $90.90; scoring masks $7.80; teacher's guide $9.90
Publisher: Nelson Canada

CANADIAN TESTS OF BASIC SKILLS: MULTILEVEL EDITION (CTBS), FORMS 5 AND 6, 1981
E. King, A. Hieronymus, et al.

Child, adolescent Ages 8-14

Purpose: Assesses student progress in developing basic educational skills. Used for group placement and curriculum planning.

Description: 350-465-item paper-pencil measure of achievement in vocabulary, reading comprehension, spelling, capitalization, punctuation, usage, visual materials, reference materials, math concepts, math problems, and math computation. The test is timed, scaled to grade, and Canadian normed. One multi-

level, reusable booklet is appropriate for students in Grades 3-8. This test is a Canadian adaption of Iowa Tests of Basic Skills published by Riverside Publishing Company. Examiner required. Suitable for group use.
CANADIAN PUBLISHER
Timed: 4 hours, 40 minutes
Scoring: Hand key; may be computer scored
Cost: Booklet $5.95; 500 answer sheets $90.90; scoring mask $7.80; teacher's guide $9.90
Publisher: Nelson Canada

CANADIAN TESTS OF BASIC SKILLS: PRIMARY BATTERY (CTBS)
E. King, A. N. Hieronymus, et al.

Child   Ages 5-8

Purpose: Assesses students' progress in developing basic educational skills. Used for class grouping and evaluation.

Description: 157-539-item paper-pencil test measuring vocabulary, reading comprehension, spelling, capitalization, punctuation, usage, visual materials, reference materials, mathematic concepts, problems, and computations. The test is scaled to grade. Examiner required. Suitable for group use.
CANADIAN PUBLISHER
Timed: 2 hours, 30 minutes-3 hours, 55 minutes
Scoring: Hand key
Cost: Contact publisher
Publisher: Nelson Canada

CHECK UP TESTS
Betty Kerr, Ronald Deadman, Melvyn Nolan, Redvers Brandling, and Peter Pile

Child   Ages 8-11

Purpose: Measures student progress in core subjects during the last four years of primary school. Used for classroom planning and program assessment.

Description: Six books, each containing 22 multiple-item paper-pencil tests, assessing student abilities in the following subjects: English composition, English language, mathematics, workskills, general knowledge, and science. The English composition, English language, mathematics, and workskills tests are available for three levels: first check ups (ages 8-9), intermediate check ups (ages 9-10), and check ups (ages 10-11). The general knowledge and science tests are available for check ups (ages 10-11) only. Each book includes practice and revision material to build up student confidence, a resource bank of ideas and methods for teaching and testing, and feedback for teachers, showing where teaching is most effective and where extra attention might need to be directed. Each book also is available in a teacher's edition with a complete set of answers. Examiner required. Suitable for group use.
Untimed: One class period
Scoring: Examiner evaluated
Cost: Pupils' books each 99p; teacher's books £3.50
Publisher: Macmillan Education

THE CHILD CENTER OPERATIONAL ASSESSMENT TOOL (OAT)
CHILD Center multidisciplinary team

Child   Special Education   Grades K-6

Purpose: Diagnoses the learning needs of elementary-school children. Identifies students needing further evaluation. Monitors educational progress during the course of the year. Used by both regular and special classroom teachers.

Description: Six subtests assess skills in reading, spelling, math concepts, math operations, language, and behavior. The criterion-referenced tests in reading, spelling, math concepts and math operations present test items in logical sequence, from pre-academic to most complex. The language test assesses underlying learning abilities and identifies modality preferences. The behavior questionnaire identifies the child's profile in the following behavioral areas: learning, coordination, self-esteem, concentration, emotional lability, motor expression, involuntary behavior, and school attitude. Results yield precise instructional skill levels for each child in reading, spelling, and math and identify specific teaching objectives. Parents and aides may administer the test. *How to Use OAT Reading/Spelling Tests* and *The OAT Reading/Spelling Program* are available. Examiner required. Not suitable for group use.

Untimed: Varies

Scoring: Examiner evaluated

Cost: Specimen set (reading test, spelling test, examiner's manual-spelling tests, *How To Use the OAT Reading/Spelling Tests*) $10.00

Publisher: The CHILD Center

COGNITIVE ABILITIES TEST: FORM 3 (COGAT)
Robert L. Thorndike and Elizabeth P. Hagen

Child, adolescent
Grades K-12

Purpose: Assesses verbal, quantitative, and other abstract cognitive skills important for academic success. Used to identify students who need help developing general cognitive skills, aid in the diagnosis of learning disabilities, and plan individualized instructional programs.

Description: Multiple-item paper-pencil test measuring the development of students' cognitive skills. The Primary Battery, available on two levels (Level 1, 76 items, Grades K-1 and Level 2, 90 items, Grades 2-3) measures the following factors: oral vocabulary, relational concepts, multimental concepts, and quantitative concepts. The Multilevel Edition is available in Levels A-H (Grades 3-12). Each level (240 items each) contains a verbal battery assessing vocabulary, sentence completion, verbal classification, and verbal analogies; a quantitative battery assessing quantitative relations, number series, and equation building; and a nonverbal battery measuring figure classification, figure analogies, and figure synthesis. All levels are normed concurrently with the Iowa Tests of Basic Skills and the Tests of Achievement and Proficiency to provide comparisons of

achievement and abilities test scores. Examiner required. Suitable for group use.

Timed: Multilevel Edition 98 minutes

Untimed: Primary Battery 54-56 minutes

Scoring: Hand key; may be computer scored

Cost: 35 Primary Battery machine-scorable test booklets (specify level), examiner's manual $42.00; complete battery test booklet for Multilevel Edition Levels A-H $3.51 each; 35 MRC answer sheets, examiner's manual $16.17 per level; examiner's manual $6.18

Publisher: The Riverside Publishing Company

COGNITIVE ABILITIES TEST: FORM 4
Robert L. Thorndike and Elizabeth P. Hagen

Grades K-12

Purpose: Assesses verbal, quantitative, and other abstract cognitive skills that are important in learning activities. Used to identify students who need help developing general cognitive skills, to aid in the diagnosis of learning disabilities, and to plan individualized instructional programs.

Description: Multiple-item paper-pencil test measuring the development of students' academic skills as an indicator of potential academic success. Level 1 (147 items) for Grades K-1 and Level 2 (172 items) for Grades 2-3 comprise the Primary Battery, which measures the following factors: relational concepts, oral vocabulary, figure classification, verbal classification, quantitative concepts, and matrices. Content of the Primary Battery tests is completely pictorial and does not penalize students with reading weaknesses. Levels A-H (200 items each) comprise the Multilevel Edition for use with Grades 3-12. Each level (A-H) contains a verbal battery assessing verbal classification, sentence completion, and verbal analogies; a quantitative battery assessing quantitative relations, number series, and equation building; and a nonverbal battery measuring figure classification, figure analogies, and figure analysis. All levels are normed concurrently with the Iowa Test of Basic Skills and the Tests of Achievement and Proficiency to provide comparisons of achievement and abilities test scores. Examiner required. Suitable for group use.

Timed: Multilevel edition 32-34 minutes
Untimed: Primary battery 54-56 minutes
Scoring: Hand key; may be computer scored
Cost: 35 Primary Battery MRC machine-scorable test booklets (specify level), manual $42.00; Multilevel Edition complete test booklet for Levels A-H $3.66; 35 MRC answer sheets (specify level), manual $6.15
Publisher: The Riverside Publishing Company

COLLEGE LEVEL EXAMINATION PROGRAM (CLEP)

Adolescent, adult
Grades 12 and above

Purpose: Enables both traditional and nontraditional students to earn college credit by recognizing college-level achievement acquired outside the conventional college classroom. Anyone may take the tests to demonstrate college-level competency, regardless of where or how this knowledge was acquired: through formal study, private reading, employment experience, noncredit courses, adult classes, TV/radio/cassette courses, military/industrial/business training, or advanced work in regular high-school courses.

Description: Five general examinations and 46 subject examinations assessing college-level proficiency in a wide range of fields. The general examinations measure achievement in five basic areas of the liberal arts: English composition, humanities, mathematics, natural sciences, and social sciences and history. The material tested in each area is usually covered in the first two years of college and is often referred to as the general or liberal education requirement. The subject examinations measure achievement in specific college courses and are used to grant exemption from and credit for these courses.

The examinations are not based on a particular syllabus; they stress concepts, principles, relationships, and applications of course material. Constructed to differentiate among several levels of mastery, they contain questions of varying difficulty. All CLEP tests are constructed by committees composed of teachers and scholars from colleges and universities in all parts of the United States.

Test content is based on a curriculum survey prepared by the Educational Testing Service and completed by colleges and universities throughout the country. The survey enables the committees to determine test specifications according to current curriculum standards, textbooks, and methods of teaching. Examinations are administered during the third week of each month at more than 900 test centers located on college and university campuses throughout the country (the General Examination in English Composition with essay is available in June and October only).

Approximately one month after the test date, test scores and a booklet explaining them are sent to the candidates and to colleges, universities, or other recipients specified by the candidates. If the optional essay section of a subject examination is taken, it is sent for grading to the institution receiving the score. Institutions honoring CLEP test scores for credit are listed in "Moving Ahead with CLEP," available free from the publisher. Examiner required. Suitable for group use.

Timed: 1 hour, 30 minutes per test
Scoring: Computer scored
Cost: Contact publisher
Publisher: The College Board
Information and availability unconfirmed by publisher.

COLLEGE LEVEL EXAMINATION PROGRAM (CLEP) AMERICAN HISTORY I: EARLY COLONIZATIONS TO 1877

Adolescent, adult
Grades 12 and above

Purpose: Measures proficiency in the material commonly covered in one-semester introductory college courses on the early period of American history.

Description: 120-item paper-pencil multiple-choice test assessing knowledge and understanding of American history from the Spanish and French colonizations to the end of Reconstruction (1877). Coverage of the colonial period emphasizes the development of the English colonies; the test as a whole emphasizes the period of nationhood. Candidates are expected to describe, characterize, analyze, and explain major historical phenomena in the following categories: political institutions and behavior and public policy, social and economic change, cultural and intellectual developments, and diplomacy and international relations. An optional essay section assesses the ability to present organized, logical historical arguments dealing with the topics covered in the objective section. Examiner required. Suitable for group use.

Timed: 1 hour, 30 minutes

Scoring: Computer scored

Cost: Contact publisher

Publisher: The College Board

Information and availability unconfirmed by publisher.

COLLEGE LEVEL EXAMINATION PROGRAM (CLEP) AMERICAN HISTORY II: 1865 TO THE PRESENT

Adolescent, adult Grades 12 and above

Purpose: Measures college-level competency in the study of American history from 1865 to the present.

Description: 120-item paper-pencil test in two sections covering the period of American history from the end of the Civil War to the present: from 1865 to 1914 and from 1915 to the present. Content coverage emphasizes political institutions and behavior and public policy, social and economic change, cultural and intellectual developments, and diplomacy and international relations. An optional 90-minute essay section also is offered. Examiner required. Suitable for group use.

Timed: 1 hour, 30 minutes; optional essay 1 hour, 30 minutes

Scoring: Computer scored

Cost: Contact publisher

Publisher: The College Board

Information and availability unconfirmed by publisher.

COLLEGE LEVEL EXAMINATION PROGRAM (CLEP) BUSINESS: COMPUTERS AND DATA PROCESSING

Adolescent, adult Grades 12 and above

Purpose: Measures proficiency in the material commonly taught in introductory one-semester college courses in computers and data processing.

Description: 100-item paper-pencil multiple-choice test assessing knowledge and understanding of concepts of computer programming and data processing that are applicable to a variety of programming languages. The test assumes a general knowledge of hardware and software but does not emphasize hardware design or language-specific programming techniques. Arranged in two sections of 50 items each, the test covers hardware, data, software, systems concepts, and miscellaneous historical and state-of-the-art topics. An optional essay section contains five questions dealing in-depth with important topics in computer programming and data processing. Examiner required. Suitable for group use.

Timed: 1 hour, 30 minutes

Scoring: Computer scored

Cost: Contact publisher

Publisher: The College Board

Information and availability unconfirmed by publisher.

COLLEGE LEVEL EXAMINATION PROGRAM (CLEP) BUSINESS: ELEMENTARY COMPUTER PROGRAMMING, FORTRAN IV

Adolescent, adult Grades 12 and above

Purpose: Measures knowledge, understanding, and skill equivalent to that gained from a college-level one-semester course in FORTRAN IV computer programming.

Description: 100-item paper-pencil objective test measuring the elements of FORTRAN IV that are common to most users including constants, variables, arrays, logic expressions, statement functions, and function subprograms; subscripts, GOTO, Data, Dimension, explicit type, Common, and Equivalence; subroutine subprograms; logical and arithmetic IF; Arithmetic expressions and DO; Read and Write. Fifteen percent of the test questions are embedded within program segments. Examiner required. Suitable for group use.

Timed: 1 hour, 30 minutes

Scoring: Computer scored

Cost: Contact publisher

Publisher: The College Board

Information and availability unconfirmed by publisher.

COLLEGE LEVEL EXAMINATION PROGRAM (CLEP) BUSINESS: INTRODUCTION TO MANAGEMENT

Adolescent, adult
Grades 12 and above

Purpose: Measures understanding of the material taught in introductory courses on the essentials of management and organization.

Description: 199-item paper-pencil test assessing knowledge of manpower and human resources, operational aspects of management, functional aspects of management, and miscellaneous aspects of management. The optional essay section contains five questions measuring the ability to relate the concepts of management to current issues and to bring together material drawn from different parts of the subject. Examiner required. Suitable for group use.

Timed: 1 hour, 30 minutes

Scoring: Computer scored

Cost: Contact publisher

Publisher: The College Board

Information and availability unconfirmed by publisher.

COLLEGE LEVEL EXAMINATION PROGRAM (CLEP) BUSINESS: INTRODUCTORY ACCOUNTING

Adolescent, adult
Grades 12 and above

Purpose: Assesses the level of accounting skills expected of a person with one year of college accounting or equivalent on-the-job training.

Description: 80-item paper-pencil objective test measuring proficiency in financial accounting and managerial accounting, including familiarity with accounting concepts and terminology, the ability to prepare and use financial reports issued for internal and external purposes, and the ability to apply accounting techniques to simple problem situations involving computations. An optional essay section tests the candidates' abilities to apply general concepts and procedures to stated problems and to combine material from various areas of accounting. Silent hand calculators are allowed. Examiner required. Suitable for group use.

Timed: 1 hour, 30 minutes

Scoring: Computer scored

Cost: Contact publisher

Publisher: The College Board

Information and availability unconfirmed by publisher.

COLLEGE LEVEL EXAMINATION PROGRAM (CLEP) BUSINESS: INTRODUCTORY BUSINESS LAW

Adolescent, adult
Grades 12 and above

Purpose: Measures knowledge and understanding of the function of contracts in American business law at the introductory undergraduate level.

Description: 100-item paper-pencil objective test assessing six major content categories: history and sources of American law, American legal systems and procedures, contracts, agency and employment, sales, and miscellaneous. An optional essay portion measures the ability to select pertinent material and present it in an organized manner dealing with case materials or business law concepts. Examiner required. Suitable for group use.

Timed: 1 hour, 30 minutes
Scoring: Computer scored
Cost: Contact publisher
Publisher: The College Board
Information and availability unconfirmed by publisher.

COLLEGE LEVEL EXAMINATION PROGRAM (CLEP) BUSINESS: INTRODUCTORY MARKETING

Adolescent, adult
Grades 12 and above

Purpose: Measures proficiency in the material usually covered in introductory one-semester college courses on the fundamentals of marketing.

Description: 100-item paper-pencil multiple-choice test assessing knowledge and understanding of the principles of marketing. Test items concern marketing interactions, marketing functions and institutions, and selected issues and topics related to marketing problems, strategies, and decisions. The test assumes a basic knowledge of demographic and economic trends, wholesaling and retailing institutional structures, and the classification of consumer and industrial goods. Four optional essay questions test the ability to apply marketing principles to basic marketing problems. Candidates who have business experience equivalent to a course in introductory marketing will be well prepared for the exam. Examiner required. Suitable for group use.

Timed: 1 hour, 30 minutes
Scoring: Computer scored
Cost: Contact publisher
Publisher: The College Board
Information and availability unconfirmed by publisher.

COLLEGE LEVEL EXAMINATION PROGRAM (CLEP) BUSINESS: MONEY AND BANKING

Adolescent, adult
Grades 12 and above

Purpose: Measures competency in the basic material covered in a one-semester college-level money and banking course.

Description: 100-item paper-pencil objective test assessing knowledge and understanding of the banking system in the United States. The test is concerned with the use of actual knowledge in new situations and in problem-solving contexts, as well as the analysis and understanding of economic relationships and the basic interpretation of appropriate materials. The material covered includes money and supply, commercial banking, monetary theory, monetary policy implementation, international monetary relations, and problems in monetary policy. The three optional essay questions measure the ability to relate principles to current issues and assimilate various materials learned in the course. Examiner required. Suitable for group use.

Timed: 1 hour, 30 minutes
Scoring: Computer scored
Cost: Contact publisher
Publisher: The College Board
Information and availability unconfirmed by publisher.

COLLEGE LEVEL EXAMINATION PROGRAM (CLEP) DENTAL AUXILIARY EDUCATION: DENTAL MATERIALS

Adolescent, adult
Grades 12 and above

Purpose: Measures proficiency in the material commonly covered in an introductory one-semester course on dental materials for students of dental hygiene or dental assisting (but not for students of dental laboratory technology).

Description: Multiple-item paper-pencil test assessing knowledge and understanding of dental materials and their use in the practice of dentistry, including structure and properties of materials, gypsum products, impression materials, synthetic resins, dental cements, science of metals (including tarnish and corrosion), dental amalgams, direct-filling gold, castings, porcelain, miscellaneous abrasives, tools, and dentifrices. Examiner required. Suitable for group use.

Timed: 1 hour, 30 minutes
Scoring: Computer scored
Cost: Contact publisher
Publisher: The College Board
Information and availability unconfirmed by publisher.

COLLEGE LEVEL EXAMINATION PROGRAM (CLEP) DENTAL AUXILIARY EDUCATION: HEAD, NECK AND ORAL ANATOMY

Adolescent, adult
Grades 12 and above

Purpose: Measures proficiency in the material commonly taught in an introductory one-semester course in head, neck, and oral anatomy for students of dental hygiene, dental assisting, or dental laboratory technology.

Description: Multiple-item paper-pencil test assessing knowledge and understanding of head, neck, and oral anatomy, including osteology, myology, angiology, neurology, orally related structures, oral landmarks, and anthrology. Examiner required. Suitable for group use.
Timed: 1 hour, 30 minutes
Scoring: Computer scored
Cost: Contact publisher
Publisher: The College Board
Information and availability unconfirmed by publisher.

COLLEGE LEVEL EXAMINATION PROGRAM (CLEP) DENTAL AUXILIARY EDUCATION: ORAL RADIOGRAPHY

Adolescent, adult
Grades 12 and above

Purpose: Measures competency in oral radiography.

Description: Multiple-item paper-pencil objective exam assessing knowledge of material usually covered in an introductory course in oral radiography for students of dental hygiene and dental assisting, including X-radiation physics, biological effects, radiation hygiene and safety, technique, film, film processing, mounting and viewing, and radiographic

analysis. The development committee recommends that colleges supplement the exam with a practical test of their own. Examiner required. Suitable for group use.
Timed: 45 minutes
Scoring: Computer scored
Cost: Contact publisher
Publisher: The College Board
Information and availability unconfirmed by publisher.

COLLEGE LEVEL EXAMINATION PROGRAM (CLEP) DENTAL AUXILIARY EDUCATION: TOOTH MORPHOLOGY AND FUNCTION

Adolescent, adult
Grades 12 and above

Purpose: Measures competency in tooth morphology and function.

Description: Paper-pencil objective test assessing knowledge of material usually covered in an introductory course in tooth morphology and function for students of dental hygiene, dental assisting, and dental laboratory technique, including tooth development and eruption, morphology of dentition (primary and secondary), function (interaction), and abnormalities. Examiner required. Suitable for group use.
Timed: 45 minutes
Scoring: Computer scored
Cost: Contact publisher
Publisher: The College Board
Information and availability unconfirmed by publisher.

COLLEGE LEVEL EXAMINATION PROGRAM (CLEP) EDUCATION: EDUCATIONAL PSYCHOLOGY

Adolescent, adult
Grades 12 and above

Purpose: Measures competency in educational psychology at the introductory college-course level.

Description: 100-item paper-pencil objective test assessing knowledge and comprehension of basic information, concepts, and principles pertaining to the psychology of education, including one's ability to integrate various aspects of this content as it applies to teaching situations and problems. The categories covered are theories and theorist, teaching, education, development, motivation, and learning. The optional essay section assesses factors such as accuracy of information, comprehensiveness and relevance of treatment, organization of materials, approach to problems from a psychological frame of reference, and logic and imaginativeness. Examiner required. Suitable for group use.

Timed: 1 hour, 30 minutes
Scoring: Computer scored
Cost: Contact publisher
Publisher: The College Board
Information and availability unconfirmed by publisher.

COLLEGE LEVEL EXAMINATION PROGRAM (CLEP) EDUCATION: HUMAN GROWTH AND DEVELOPMENT

Adolescent, adult
Grades 12 and above

Purpose: Measures knowledge and understanding of the subject matter usually covered in introductory one-semester college courses in human growth and development, child psychology, or child development.

Description: 90-item paper-pencil multiple-choice test assessing proficiency in the field of child development with emphasis on the periods of early and middle childhood. Test items measure three levels of mastery: knowledge of facts, terminology, and theory; understanding of concepts and principles; and ability to apply what has been learned to particular problems or situations. The examination covers theoretical foundations (major views of development), research strategies and methodology, biological aspects of development, perceptual and sensorimotor development, cognitive development, language development, emotional development, personality, intelligence testing, influences of schooling, social development, family relations and child-rearing practices, learning, and atypical

behavior and development. An optional essay section consisting of four questions covers the same material as the objective section and measures the ability to select pertinent material and present it in an organized and logical manner. Examiner required. Suitable for group use.

Timed: 1 hour, 30 minutes
Scoring: Computer scored
Cost: Contact publisher
Publisher: The College Board
Information and availability unconfirmed by publisher.

COLLEGE LEVEL EXAMINATION PROGRAM (CLEP) GENERAL EXAMINATION: ENGLISH COMPOSITION

Adolescent, adult
Grades 12 and above

Purpose: Measures college-level competency in English composition.

Description: Multiple-item paper-pencil test available in two editions: Edition One (130 items) contains two 45-minute objective sections. Edition Two contains one 45-minute, 65-question objective section and one 45-minute essay section. Both editions measure competency in writing expository essays that follow the conventions of standard written English. The exam is concerned with freshman English students' acquired knowledge, not technical vocabulary or imaginative writing. Section One of both editions deals primarily with logical and structural relationships within the sentence. Section Two of Edition One (multiple-choice items) deals with logical arrangement of ideas, use of evidence, and adaptation of language to purpose and audience. Section Two of Edition Two requires an expository essay to demonstrate skill at presenting a point of view, developing a logical argument, and providing supporting evidence. Examiner required. Suitable for group use.

Timed: 1 hour, 30 minutes
Scoring: Computer scored
Cost: Contact publisher
Publisher: The College Board
Information and availability unconfirmed by publisher.

COLLEGE LEVEL EXAMINATION PROGRAM (CLEP) GENERAL EXAMINATION: HUMANITIES

Adolescent, adult
Grades 12 and above

Purpose: Measures college-level knowledge of literature, art, and music.

Description: 150-item paper-pencil objective exam covering drama, poetry, fiction, nonfiction, visual arts, music, performing arts, and architecture. The test measures understanding of cultural interests and humanities subject matter in three ways: recollection or recognition of specific information; comprehension and application of concepts; and analysis and interpretation of various works of art. Examiner required. Suitable for group use.

Timed: 1 hour, 30 minutes

Scoring: Computer scored

Cost: Contact publisher

Publisher: The College Board

Information and availability unconfirmed by publisher.

COLLEGE LEVEL EXAMINATION PROGRAM (CLEP) GENERAL EXAMINATION: MATHEMATICS

Adolescent, adult
Grades 12 and above

Purpose: Measures college-level competency in general mathematics.

Description: 90-item paper-pencil test consisting of two parts. Part A (40 questions) measures facility in arithmetic, elementary algebra, geometry, and data interpretation. The first 25 questions require special directions and involve comparing quantities in two columns. The remaining 15 questions are objective. Part B (50 objective questions) covers sets, logic, real number systems, probability and statistics, and miscellaneous topics. Calculators are not permitted. Examiner required. Suitable for group use.

Timed: 1 hour, 30 minutes

Scoring: Computer scored

Cost: Contact publisher

Publisher: The College Board

Information and availability unconfirmed by publisher.

COLLEGE LEVEL EXAMINATION PROGRAM (CLEP) GENERAL EXAMINATION: NATURAL SCIENCE

Adolescent, adult
Grades 12 and above

Purpose: Measures college-level competency in introductory biological and physical science areas.

Description: 120-item paper-pencil objective test consisting of two 45-minute timed sections—one concerning biological science, the other physical science. The exam should not be considered appropriate as a prerequisite for more advanced study than the subject exams in general biology and general chemistry. Emphasis is placed on the role of science in our contemporary society, the knowledge and application of the basic principles and concepts of science, and the understanding of scientific information and data that may be presented. The content covers origin and evolution of life, cell study, development in organisms, population biology with an emphasis in econogy, atomic and nuclear structure, chemical compounds/molecular structure, thermodynamics, classical mechanics and relativity, electrical and magnetism, the universe, and the Earth. Examiner required. Suitable for group use.

Timed: 1 hour, 30 minutes

Scoring: Computer scored

Cost: Contact publisher

Publisher: The College Board

Information and availability unconfirmed by publisher.

COLLEGE LEVEL EXAMINATION PROGRAM (CLEP) GENERAL EXAMINATION: SOCIAL SCIENCE AND HISTORY

Adolescent, adult
Grades 12 and above

Purpose: Measures the level of knowledge and understanding expected of

Purpose: Measures the level of knowledge and understanding expected of college students meeting a distributional or general education requirement in social sciences and history.

Description: 125-item paper-pencil multiple-choice test addressing a wide range of topics from the social sciences and history, including subject matter from introductory college courses in political science, economics, sociology, social psychology, United States history, Western civilization, and African-Asian civilizations. Test items assess knowledge of terminology, facts, conventions, methodology, concepts, principles, generalizations, and theories in the fields listed above, as well as the ability to apply these abstractions to particulars. Examiner required. Suitable for group use.

Timed: 1 hour, 30 minutes
Scoring: Computer scored
Cost: Contact publisher
Publisher: The College Board
Information and availability unconfirmed by publisher.

COLLEGE LEVEL EXAMINATION PROGRAM (CLEP) HUMANITIES: AMERICAN LITERATURE

Adolescent, adult
Grades 12 and above

Purpose: Measures familiarity with American prose and poetry from colonial time to midtwentieth century.

Description: 110-item paper-pencil test measuring competency level comparable to a one-year college survey course in American literature. Knowledge of critical and historical literacy terms is assumed. The areas covered include the colonial and early national period, the period since World War II, and the periods of religion and early naturalism. The test also covers writers of the Romantic and Modern periods. The remaining questions assess knowledge of content of particular literary works, including their characters, plots, settings, and themes. Some knowledge of historical and social settings, authors and their influence, and relations of literary works and traditions is required. The optional 90-minute essay

section contains three questions, two of which must be answered. The section tests the candidate's ability to make organized statements on American literature that are pertinent and informed. Examiner required. Suitable for group use.

Timed: 1 hour, 30 minutes; optional essay section 1 hour, 30 minutes
Scoring: Computer scored
Cost: Contact publisher
Publisher: The College Board
Information and availability unconfirmed by publisher.

COLLEGE LEVEL EXAMINATION PROGRAM (CLEP) HUMANITIES: ANALYSIS AND INTERPRETATION OF LITERATURE

Adolescent, adult
Grades 12 and above

Purpose: Measures college-level competency equivalent to a one-year undergraduate course in literature.

Description: 100-item paper-pencil objective test assessing the ability to read prose and poetry with understanding and respond to nuances of meaning, tone, mood, imagery, and style. The optional essay section assesses the ability to write well-organized critical essays on given passages of poetry and on general literary questions. Examiner required. Suitable for group use.

Timed: 1 hour, 30 minutes
Scoring: Computer scored
Cost: Contact publisher
Publisher: The College Board
Information and availability unconfirmed by publisher.

COLLEGE LEVEL EXAMINATION PROGRAM (CLEP) HUMANITIES: COLLEGE COMPOSITION

Adolescent, adult
Grades 12 and above

Purpose: Assesses knowledge of the theoretical aspects of writing and the ability to put into practice the principles of standard written English.

Description: 100-item paper-pencil objective test measuring proficiency in English composition, including the sentence, the paragraph and essay, style, logic in writing, library information, and manuscript format and documentation. An optional 90-minute essay section provides three questions, two of which must be answered. Examiner required. Suitable for group use.

Timed: 1 hour, 30 minutes; optional essay section 1 hour, 30 minutes

Scoring: Computer scored

Cost: Contact publisher

Publisher: The College Board

Information and availability unconfirmed by publisher.

COLLEGE LEVEL EXAMINATION PROGRAM (CLEP) HUMANITIES: ENGLISH LITERATURE

Adolescent, adult
Grades 12 and above

Purpose: Measures college-level competency in English literature.

Description: 100-item paper-pencil objective test assessing proficiency in the study of English literature. Knowledge of common literary terms and forms, as well as major authors and texts is assumed. Many items are based on passages and poems. Other areas include literary background, content of major works, chronology, author identification, material patterns, and literary references. The candidate also is asked to analyze elements of form, perceive meanings, and identify tone, mood, and style. The optional 90-minute essay section contains three topics, one of which is required. A second essay must be written on one of the other two topics. Examiner required. Suitable for group use.

Timed: 1 hour, 30 minutes; optional essay 1 hour, 30 minutes

Scoring: Computer scored

Cost: Contact publisher

Publisher: The College Board

Information and availability unconfirmed by publisher.

COLLEGE LEVEL EXAMINATION PROGRAM (CLEP) HUMANITIES: FRESHMAN ENGLISH

Adolescent, adult
Grades 12 and above

Purpose: Measures a candidate's ability to recognize and apply principles of good writing.

Description: 100-item paper-pencil objective test measuring sensitivity in reading and skill in judging and controlling language on the assumption that these abilities are closely related to the ability to write well. One-third of the exam requires the analysis of short passages of prose and poetry, both for comprehension of content and for judgment of structure and style. One-third of the test is devoted to considerations of style and logical development. The final third focuses on clear syntax, correct usage, and correct punctuation. The optional essay section allows a candidate to demonstrate writing skills in three sustained writing tasks. The topics present concrete problems involving personal knowledge and require control and flexibility in the use of language. Examiner required. Suitable for group use.

Timed: 1 hour, 30 minutes; optional essay section 1 hour, 30 minutes

Scoring: Computer scored

Cost: Contact publisher

Publisher: The College Board

Information and availability unconfirmed by publisher.

COLLEGE LEVEL EXAMINATION PROGRAM (CLEP) MATHEMATICS: CALCULUS WITH ELEMENTARY FUNCTIONS

Adolescent, adult
Grades 12 and above

Purpose: Measures skills and concepts usually covered in a one-year college course in calculus with elementary functions.

Description: 45-item paper-pencil objective test assessing a person's intuitive understanding of calculus and experience with its methods and application. Knowledge of preparatory mathematics (algebra, plane and solid geometry, trigonometry, and analytical geometry) is assumed. The topics covered include elementary functions, differential calculus, and integral calculus. Examiner required. Suitable for group use.

Timed: 1 hour, 30 minutes

Scoring: Computer scored

Cost: Contact publisher

Publisher: The College Board

Information and availability unconfirmed by publisher.

COLLEGE LEVEL EXAMINATION PROGRAM (CLEP) MATHEMATICS: COLLEGE ALGEBRA

Adolescent, adult
Grades 12 and above

Purpose: Measures college-level competency equivalent to a one-semester college algebra course.

Description: 80-item paper-pencil objective exam consisting of questions that require the solution of routine or straightforward problems and understanding and application of concepts and skills to situations that may not be familiar. The exam assesses understanding and knowledge of basic algebraic operations: linear equations and inequities and their graphs, quadratic equations and their graphs, functions, exponential and logarithmic functions, and theory of equations. The test also covers sets, the real number system, complex numbers, systems of equations, sequence and series, matrix addition and multiplication, evaluation of determinants, and mathematical induction. Examiner required. Suitable for group use.

Timed: 1 hour, 30 minutes

Scoring: Computer scored

Cost: Contact publisher

Publisher: The College Board

Information and availability unconfirmed by publisher.

COLLEGE LEVEL EXAMINATION PROGRAM (CLEP) MATHEMATICS: COLLEGE ALGEBRA-TRIGONOMETRY

Adolescent, adult
Grades 12 and above

Purpose: Measures college-level competency equivalent to a one-semester course that combines college algebra with trigonometry.

Description: 80-item paper-pencil multiple-choice test consisting of two 40-item sections. One section is devoted entirely to algebra, the other to trigonometry. The test as a whole provides a single score based on the entire 90-minute test. For descriptions of test content, refer to the college algebra and college trigonometry descriptions. Examiner required. Suitable for group use.

Timed: 1 hour, 30 minutes

Scoring: Computer scored

Cost: Contact publisher

Publisher: The College Board

Information and availability unconfirmed by publisher.

COLLEGE LEVEL EXAMINATION PROGRAM (CLEP) MATHEMATICS: STATISTICS

Adolescent, adult
Grades 12 and above

Purpose: Measures college-level competency equivalent to a one-semester course in probabilities and statistics.

Description: 60-item paper-pencil objective test assessing levels of understanding in elementary statistical inference, probabilities, descriptive statistics, random variables, and expected values. Other content categories include sampling and problems related to distributions, combinations, and permutations. The test contains two tables: the normal curve and the student's distribution. The 90-minute optional essay section covers the same general content areas as the multiple-choice test and consists of four questions that may require either computation or discussion or both. Examiner required. Suitable for group use.

Timed: 1 hour, 30 minutes
Scoring: Computer scored
Cost: Contact publisher
Publisher: The College Board
Information and availability unconfirmed by publisher.

COLLEGE LEVEL EXAMINATION PROGRAM (CLEP) MATHEMATICS: TRIGONOMETRY

Adolescent, adult
Grades 12 and above

Purpose: Measures knowledge and ability equivalent to a one-semester college course with primary emphasis on analytical trigonometry.

Description: 80-item paper-pencil objective test assessing academic achievement in analytical trigonometry, including trigonometric functions and their relationships, cofunction relationships, reciprocal relationships, Pythagorean relationships, functions of two angles, functions of double angles, functions of half angles, and identities. Other topics include trigonometric equations and inequalities; graphs of trigonometric function; and trigonometry of the triangle, including the law of sines and cosines, inverse functions, and the trigonometric form of complex numbers. Examiner required. Suitable for group use.

Timed: 1 hour, 30 minutes
Scoring: Computer scored
Cost: Contact publisher
Publisher: The College Board
Information and availability unconfirmed by publisher.

COLLEGE LEVEL EXAMINATION PROGRAM (CLEP) MEDICAL TECHNOLOGY: CLINICAL CHEMISTRY

Adolescent, adult
Grades 12 and above

Purpose: Measures knowledge normally gained in courses offered during the

clinical portion of four-year medical technology programs.

Description: 100-item paper-pencil objective test assessing general chemical principles, general clinical chemistry principles, instrumentation for important techniques, specific analysis of biologic fluids, quality control, clinical pathology, toxicology, biochemistry, physiology, and genetics. Examiner required. Suitable for group use.

Timed: 1 hour, 30 minutes
Scoring: Computer scored
Cost: Contact publisher
Publisher: The College Board
Information and availability unconfirmed by publisher.

COLLEGE LEVEL EXAMINATION PROGRAM (CLEP) MEDICAL TECHNOLOGY: HEMATOLOGY

Adolescent, adult
Grades 12 and above

Purpose: Measures knowledge normally gained in courses offered during the clinical portion of four-year medical technology programs.

Description: 100-item paper-pencil objective test covering development and components of blood, collection of specimens, hemoglobin disorders, and coagulation and hemostasis. Examiner required. Suitable for group use.

Timed: 1 hour, 30 minutes
Scoring: Computer scored
Cost: Contact publisher
Publisher: The College Board
Information and availability unconfirmed by publisher.

COLLEGE LEVEL EXAMINATION PROGRAM (CLEP) MEDICAL TECHNOLOGY: IMMUNOHEMATOLOGY AND BLOOD BANKING

Adolescent, adult
Grades 12 and above

Purpose: Measures knowledge normally gained in courses offered during the clinical portion of four-year medical technology programs.

Description: 100-item paper-pencil objective test covering history and general principles of blood transfusion, the anti-gen-antibody reaction, ABO blood type system, M, K, and P blood types, the Rh system, the Kell and Duffy blood types, the Lewis types, other blood systems, detection of new blood type systems, pretransfusion procedures, leukocyte and platelet groups, blood types in anthropology and forensic pathology, autoimmune acquired hemolytic anemia, principles of blood banking procedures, and serologic tests on donor blood. Examiner required. Suitable for group use.

Timed: 1 hour, 30 minutes

Scoring: Computer scored

Cost: Contact publisher

Publisher: The College Board

Information and availability unconfirmed by publisher.

COLLEGE LEVEL EXAMINATION PROGRAM (CLEP) MEDICAL TECHNOLOGY: MICROBIOLOGY

Adolescent, adult
Grades 12 and above

Purpose: Measures college-level competency normally gained in a one-semester course in microbiology.

Description: 100-item paper-pencil objective test assessing both the knowledge of microbiology and the analytical abilities that are important in the first course. The test covers nature of microorganisms, virology, nutrition and metabolism of bacteria, microbial genetics, control of microorganisms, microbiology of water, microbiology of foods, basis of infectious disease, resistance and immunity, the pathogenic cocci and diseases they cause, gram-negative enteric bacteria, other gram-negative bacteria, gram-positive bacilli, the spirochetes and spirochetal diseases, and soil and nonpathogens. Examiner required. Suitable for group use.

Timed: 1 hour, 30 minutes

Scoring: Computer scored

Cost: Contact publisher

Publisher: The College Board

Information and availability unconfirmed by publisher.

COLLEGE LEVEL EXAMINATION PROGRAM (CLEP) MODERN LANGUAGES: COLLEGE FRENCH LEVELS 1 AND 2

Adolescent, adult
Grades 12 and above

Purpose: Measures knowledge and ability equivalent to that of students who have completed from two to four semesters of college-level French.

Description: Multiple-item paper-pencil test assessing proficiency in the skills typically achieved from the end of the first year through the second year of college-level French. Both levels are incorporated into a single examination measuring knowledge and ability in the following areas: vocabulary mastery, grammatical control, reading comprehension, and listening comprehension. Examiner required. Suitable for group use.

Timed: 1 hour, 30 minutes

Scoring: Computer scored

Cost: Contact publisher

Publisher: The College Board

Information and availability unconfirmed by publisher.

COLLEGE LEVEL EXAMINATION PROGRAM (CLEP) MODERN LANGUAGES: COLLEGE GERMAN LEVELS 1 AND 2

Adolescent, adult
Grades 12 and above

Purpose: Measures knowledge and ability equivalent to that of students who have completed from two to four semesters of college-level German.

Description: Multiple-item paper-pencil test assessing proficiency in the skills typically achieved from the end of the first year through the second year of college-level German. Both levels are incorporated into a single examination measuring knowledge and ability in the following areas: vocabulary mastery, grammatical control, reading comprehension, and listening comprehension. Examiner required. Suitable for group use.

Timed: 1 hour, 30 minutes
Scoring: Computer scored
Cost: Contact publisher
Publisher: The College Board
Information and availability unconfirmed by publisher.

COLLEGE LEVEL EXAMINATION PROGRAM (CLEP) MODERN LANGUAGES: COLLEGE SPANISH LEVELS 1 AND 2

Adolescent, adult
Grades 12 and above

Purpose: Measures knowledge and ability equivalent to that of students who have completed from two to four semesters of college-level Spanish.

Description: Multiple-item paper-pencil test assessing proficiency in the skills typically achieved from the end of the first year through the second year of college-level Spanish. Both levels are incorporated into a single examination measuring knowledge and ability in vocabulary mastery, grammatical control, reading comprehension, and listening comprehension. Examiner required. Suitable for group use.

Timed: 1 hour, 30 minutes
Scoring: Computer scored
Cost: Contact publisher
Publisher: The College Board
Information and availability unconfirmed by publisher.

COLLEGE LEVEL EXAMINATION PROGRAM (CLEP) NURSING: ANATOMY, MICROBIOLOGY, PHYSIOLOGY

Adolescent, adult
Grades 12 and above

Purpose: Measures subject matter knowledge covered during first-year ADN programs. Provides Licensed Practical Nurses and others with an opportunity to gain credit toward the first year of study in an ADN program.

Description: 75-item paper-pencil objective test assessing general proficiency in anatomy, physiology, and microbiology, including basic physiological (food, elimination, sex, and security—integrity of organism) and internal and external environment. Examiner required. Suitable for group use.

Timed: 1 hour, 30 minutes
Scoring: Computer scored
Cost: Contact publisher
Publisher: The College Board
Information and availability unconfirmed by publisher.

COLLEGE LEVEL EXAMINATION PROGRAM (CLEP) NURSING: BEHAVIORAL SCIENCES FOR NURSES

Adolescent, adult
Grades 12 and above

Purpose: Measures knowledge of subject matter covered during first-year ADN programs.

Description: Multiple-item paper-pencil test assessing knowledge of sociology and psychology. Approximately 60 percent of the questions are from the field of sociology. The topics covered are social change, the family, social institutions and their functions, process of socialization norms, mores, social roles, culture, demography, and crime and crime rate. Questions from the field of psychology comprise 35 percent of the test. The topics covered are child development, personality, social psychology, clinical and abnormal psychology, and mental health. Examiner required. Suitable for group use.

Timed: 1 hour, 30 minutes
Scoring: Computer scored
Cost: Contact publisher
Publisher: The College Board
Information and availability unconfirmed by publisher.

COLLEGE LEVEL EXAMINATION PROGRAM (CLEP) NURSING: FUNDAMENTALS OF NURSING

Adolescent, adult
Grades 12 and above

Purpose: Measures subject matter knowledge covered during first-year ADN programs.

Description: Multiple-item paper-pencil test assessing proficiency in the fundamental skills of nursing, including introduction to nursing fundamentals, communication, stress and adaptation, nutrition (fluid and electrolyte balance), rest and comfort, elimination, providing safe environment, observation and assessment, and special therapeutics. Examiner required. Suitable for group use.

Timed: 1 hour, 30 minutes

Scoring: Computer scored

Cost: Contact publisher

Publisher: The College Board

Information and availability unconfirmed by publisher.

COLLEGE LEVEL EXAMINATION PROGRAM (CLEP) NURSING: MEDICAL-SURGICAL NURSING

Adolescent, adult
Grades 12 and above

Purpose: Measures knowledge of subject matter covered during first-year ADN programs.

Description: Multiple-item paper-pencil test covering the areas of study and content presented in the first year of two-year ADN programs, including transport to and from the cells (cardiovascular), exchange of gases (respiratory), immobility (digestive and renal), and aging. Examiner required. Suitable for group use.

Timed: 1 hour, 30 minutes

Scoring: Computer scored

Cost: Contact publisher

Publisher: The College Board

Information and availability unconfirmed by publisher.

COLLEGE LEVEL EXAMINATION PROGRAM (CLEP) SCIENCES: GENERAL BIOLOGY

Adolescent, adult
Grades 12 and above

Purpose: Measures proficiency in the material usually covered in a one-year biology course at the college level.

Description: 120-item paper-pencil multiple-choice test assessing knowledge and understanding in three broad areas of the biological sciences: molecular and cellular, organismal, and populational. Test items measure three levels of proficiency: knowledge of facts, principles, and processes of biology; understanding of the means by which information is collected, how it is interpreted, how one hypothesizes and synthesizes from available information, and how one draws conclusions and makes further predictions; and understanding that science is a human endeavor with social consequences. An optional essay section covers the same material and measures the ability to select pertinent material and present it in an organized and logical manner. Examiner required. Suitable for group use.

Timed: 1 hour, 30 minutes

Scoring: Computer scored

Cost: Contact publisher

Publisher: The College Board

Information and availability unconfirmed by publisher.

COLLEGE LEVEL EXAMINATION PROGRAM (CLEP) SCIENCES: GENERAL CHEMISTRY

Adolescent, adult
Grades 12 and above

Purpose: Determines college-level competency in general chemistry.

Description: 80-item paper-pencil objective test requiring the candidate to demonstrate knowledge of the material that institutes the core topics of introductory college chemistry courses and to interpret and apply this material in ways not necessarily familiar to the candidate. The test measures structure of matter, status of matter, reaction types, equations and stoichiometry, kinetics, equilibrium, thermodynamics, descriptive chemistry, and experimental chemistry. The use of slide rules and calculators is permitted. The content of the optional essays section includes essays, equations, and quantitative problems. Examiner required. Suitable for group use.

Timed: 1 hour, 30 minutes

Scoring: Computer scored

Cost: Contact publisher

Publisher: The College Board

Information and availability unconfirmed by publisher.

COLLEGE LEVEL EXAMINATION PROGRAM (CLEP) SOCIAL SCIENCES: AFRO-AMERICAN HISTORY

**Adolescent, adult
Grades 12 and above**

Purpose: Measures college-level competency in the material covered in a one-semester course in Afro-American History.

Description: 100-item paper-pencil objective test covering the African experience and the relationship of Africa to the discovery of America, the Afro-American experience from colonial America through Reconstruction to about 1900, and the Afro-American experience in the United States from about 1900 to the present. The optional essay section offers a choice of two questions in three broad areas: African background through colonial America, the black experience from the American Revolution through World War I, and the black experience from 1919 to the present. Examiner required. Suitable for group use.

Timed: 1 hour, 30 minutes

Scoring: Computer scored

Cost: Contact publisher

Publisher: The College Board

Information and availability unconfirmed by publisher.

COLLEGE LEVEL EXAMINATION PROGRAM (CLEP) SOCIAL SCIENCES: AMERICAN GOVERNMENT

**Adolescent, adult
Grades 12 and above**

Purpose: Measures college-level competency in the study of American government and politics.

Description: 100-item paper-pencil objective test consisting of two sections of 50 items each. The areas tested include institutions and policy processes; presidency, executive branch and Congress; federal courts and civil liberties; political parties and pressure groups; political beliefs and behavior; and constitutional underpinnings of American democracy. The optional essay section offers a choice of writing on any three of four topics offered. Examiner required. Suitable for group use.

Timed: 1 hour, 30 minutes

Scoring: Computer scored

Cost: Contact publisher

Publisher: The College Board

Information and availability unconfirmed by publisher.

COLLEGE LEVEL EXAMINATION PROGRAM (CLEP) SOCIAL SCIENCES: GENERAL PSYCHOLOGY

**Adolescent, adult
Grades 12 and above**

Purpose: Measures college-level competency in general psychology.

Description: 100-item paper-pencil objective test assessing basic facts, concepts, and principles of general psychology, including physiology and behavior, perceptual and sensory experience, motivation and emotion, learning, cognition, life-span development, personality and adjustment, behavior disorders, social psychology, measurement and statistics, and history and philosophy. An optional essay section is included. Examiner required. Suitable for group use.

Timed: 1 hour, 30 minutes

Scoring: Computer scored

Cost: Contact publisher

Publisher: The College Board

Information and availability unconfirmed by publisher.

COLLEGE LEVEL EXAMINATION PROGRAM (CLEP) SOCIAL SCIENCES: INTRODUCTORY MACROECONOMICS

Adolescent, adult
Grades 12 and above

Purpose: Measures college-level competency in introductory macroeconomics.

Description: 90-item paper-pencil objective test assessing knowledge and understanding of determinants of aggregate demand on the monetary and/or fiscal policies that are appropriate to achieve particular policy objectives, including basic or generic concepts and macroeconomic concepts. A 90-minute optional essay section is offered. Examiner required. Suitable for group use.

Timed: 1 hour, 30 minutes

Scoring: Computer scored

Cost: Contact publisher

Publisher: The College Board

Information and availability unconfirmed by publisher.

COLLEGE LEVEL EXAMINATION PROGRAM (CLEP) SOCIAL SCIENCES: INTRODUCTORY MICROECONOMICS

Adolescent, adult
Grades 12 and above

Purpose: Measures college-level competency in introductory microeconomics.

Description: 90-item paper-pencil objective test requiring students to apply analytical techniques to hypothetical situations and to analyze and evaluate interpretations or criticism of government policies on the basis of simple theoretical models. The test emphasizes analytical capabilities rather than factual understanding of United States institutions and policies. The test covers basic or generic concepts and microeconomic concepts. A

90-minute optional essay section is included. Examiner required. Suitable for group use.

Timed: 1 hour, 30 minutes; optional essay 1 hour, 30 minutes

Scoring: Computer scored

Cost: Contact publisher

Publisher: The College Board

Information and availability unconfirmed by publisher.

COLLEGE LEVEL EXAMINATION PROGRAM (CLEP) WESTERN CIVILIZATION I: ANCIENT NEAR EAST TO 1648

Adolescent, adult
Grades 12 and above

Purpose: Measures college-level competency in the study of Western civilization from the ancient Near East to 1648.

Description: 120-item paper-pencil objective test covering six broad historical periods: ancient Near East, ancient Greece and Hellenistic civilization, ancient Rome, medieval history, the Renaissance and Reformation, and early modern Europe (1560-1648). The optional essay section requires the candidate to write three essays, one from each of three chronological areas. Examiner required. Suitable for group use.

Timed: 1 hour, 30 minutes; optional essay 1 hour, 30 minutes

Scoring: Computer scored

Cost: Contact publisher

Publisher: The College Board

Information and availability unconfirmed by publisher.

COLLEGE LEVEL EXAMINATION PROGRAM (CLEP) WESTERN CIVILIZATION II: 1648 TO THE PRESENT

Adolescent, adult
Grades 12 and above

Purpose: Measures college-level competency in the study of Western civilization from 1648 to the present.

Description: 120-item paper-pencil objective exam covering 12 broad historical periods: absolutism and constitutionalism (1648-1715); competition for empire and economic expansion; the scientific view of the world; the Enlightenment and enlightened despotism; the French revolution and Napoleonic Europe; the Industrial Revolution; political developments, 1815-1848; politics and diplomacy in the age of nationalism (1850-1914); economy, culture and imperialism, 1850-1914; World War I, the Russian Revolution, and postwar Europe (1914-1924); Europe between the Wars; and World War II and contemporary Europe. The exam measures a person's ability to identify the causes and effects of major events in history; to analyze, interpret, and evaluate historical materials; and to reach conclusions. A 90-minute optional essay section is included. Examiner required. Suitable for group use.

Timed: 1 hour, 30 minutes; optional essay 1 hour, 30 minutes

Scoring: Computer scored

Cost: Contact publisher

Publisher: The College Board

Information and availability unconfirmed by publisher.

THE COMMUNITY COLLEGE ASSESSMENT PROGRAM (CCAP)

Adult   Community college enrollees

Purpose: Measures abilities, background, and plans of community college students. Used for advisement and placement in serial English and math classes in community colleges in Washington. Also used as a diagnostic screening device for applicants to selected technical programs.

Description: Paper-pencil test of abilities and achievement predictive of performance in community college subjects. This is a modified version of the Washington Pre-College Test, which is somewhat shorter and designed to measure a broader range of ability. Examiner required. Suitable for group use.

Timed: 2 hours, 15 minutes

Scoring: Machine scored

Cost: Test booklet $2.00; answer sheet $2.00

Publisher: Washington Pre-College Program

COMPREHENSION TEST FOR COLLEGE OF EDUCATION STUDENTS
E.L. Black

Adult

Purpose: Assesses comprehension abilities of students who have not been in school for several years and screens for academic placement.

Description: 60-item paper-pencil multiple-choice test measuring reading comprehension. Test questions are based on eight passages of prose, each with a different kind of subject matter and style of language. The test provides diagnostic information regarding student reading comprehension. Examiner required. Suitable for group use.

CANADIAN PUBLISHER

Untimed: Not available

Scoring: Examiner evaluated

Cost: Specimen set $8.55; 25 booklets $46.39; manual $7.54

Publisher: Institute of Psychological Research, Inc.

Information and availability unconfirmed; no publisher response.

COMPREHENSIVE ASSESSMENT PROGRAM: ACHIEVEMENT SERIES
John W. Wick and Jefferey K. Smith

**Child, adolescent
Ages 4-18**

Purpose: Assesses student achievement in basic academic areas. Used for evaluating individual or group status, planning instructional improvement, monitoring student progress, and evaluating program effectiveness.

Description: Multiple-item paper-pencil test available on 11 test levels. Levels 4-6 (PreK-Grade 1) emphasize children's capabilities to perform given tasks to ascertain their level of development. Levels 7-12 (Grades 2-8) measure achievement in reading, language, and mathematics. Levels 13 and 14 (Grades 9-12) test achievement in reading, language, writing, mathematics, science, and social studies. When combined with the Developing Cognitive Abilities Test, the level of student performance in relation to abilities can be determined. Examiner required. Suitable for group use.

Untimed: Varies with level and test

Scoring: Hand key; may be computer scored

Cost: 35 test booklets $30.35-$41.15 (specify level and machine or hand-scorable); key $1.50 (specify level); manual $7.20

Publisher: American Testronics

COMPREHENSIVE ASSESSMENT PROGRAM: HIGH SCHOOL SUBJECT TESTS
Louis A. Gatta

Adolescent   Grades 9-12

Purpose: Measures student's proficiency in common high-school courses. Also used to analyze instruction and planning.

Description: Multiple-item individual tests for the 15 most commonly taught courses at the secondary level: general mathematics, algebra, geometry, health, consumer education, biology, chemistry, physical science, American history, American government, world geography, world history, language, literature and vocabulary, and writing and mechanics. Examiner required. Suitable for group use.

Timed: 40 minutes

Scoring: Hand key; may be computer scored

Cost: 35 test booklets $25.15; 35 self-score answer sheets $14.45; manual $7.40; directions for administration $3.25; 35 machine-scorable answer sheets (specify subject) 10.25

Publisher: American Testronics

COMPREHENSIVE NURSING ACHIEVEMENT TEST—1985 EDITION (FORM 3015)

Registered nursing students

Purpose: Measures achievement of graduating students in registered nursing programs in a range of knowledge needed by the beginning practitioner. Assesses readiness for the nurse licensure examination.

Description: Approximately 220-item multiple-choice paper-pencil test of a graduating student's knowledge of human functioning, the nursing process, and clinical content. A new edition each year assesses readiness for the registered nurse licensure examination, NCLEX-RN. Questions are presented as case situations drawn from a variety of clinical areas and are written within the nursing process framework. A total standard score and a variety of subscores are reported in the form of individual diagnostic profiles. A copy is provided for the student and another for faculty analysis. Norms are reported for registered nursing students. Examiner required. Suitable for group use.

Untimed: 3½ hours

Scoring: Computer scored

Cost: Test service (test booklets, answer sheets, directions for administration, scoring service) $8.00 per student

Publisher: National League for Nursing

COMPREHENSIVE TESTING PROGRAM (CTP)
Committees of teachers and curriculum specialists

Child, adolescent Grades 1-12

Purpose: Measures the verbal and mathematical skills of students. Used for guidance counseling, the evaluation of student progress, and monitoring the effectiveness of instructional programs.

Description: Multiple-item paper-pencil multiple-choice tests arranged in five levels: Levels 1 and 2 for Grade 1 through early Grade 3; and Levels 3, 4, and 5 for the end of Grade 3 through Grade 12. Levels 1 and 2 (225 items) measure mathematics, reading, word analysis, and writing skills. Levels 3, 4, and 5 (300 items) measure verbal aptitude, quantitative aptitude, reading comprehension, mathematics, the mechanics of writing, vocabulary, and English expression. For Levels 1 and 2, students mark answers in machine-scorable test booklets; Levels 3, 4, and 5 use separate answer sheets. Use is restricted to schools with ERB membership. Examiner required. Suitable for group use.

Untimed: Levels 1 and 2 150 minutes

Timed: Levels 3, 4, and 5 260 minutes

Scoring: Hand key; may be computer scored

Cost: 20 booklets (Levels 1 and 2) $24.00; 20 booklets (Levels 3, 4, and 5) $38.00; manual $5.00

Publisher: Educational Records Bureau

COMPREHENSIVE TESTS OF BASIC SKILLS (FORMS S AND T)

Child, adolescent
Grades K-12.9

Purpose: Assesses reading skills, language acquisition, and mathematics concepts.

Description: Multiple-item paper-pencil test measuring basic academic skills. The test is available in Form S and Form T. Form S contains seven levels: Level A (Grades K-1.3), Level B (Grades K.6-1.9), Level C (Grades 1.6-2.9), Level 1 (Grades 2.5-4.9), Level 2 (Grades 4.5-6.9), Level 3 (Grades 6.5-8.9), and Level 4 (Grades 8.5-12.9). Levels A and B assess reading, language, and mathematics skills. Level C measures reading, language, mathematics, science, and social studies skills. Levels 1-4 assess reading, language, mathematics, social studies, and reference skills. Form T is available only for Levels 1-4. Forms S and T have been superseded by CTBS Forms U and V. Examiner required. Suitable for group use. Available in Spanish (CTBS-Espanol).

Timed: Complete battery 4 hours, 15 minutes, depending on level

Scoring: Hand key; may be computer scored

Cost: Multilevel examination kit $24.00; specimen set (specify level) $8.95

Publisher: CTB/McGraw-Hill

COMPREHENSIVE TESTS OF BASIC SKILLS: FORMS U AND V (CTBS/U AND V)

Child, adolescent
Grades K-12.9

Purpose: Assesses reading skills, language acquisition, and mathematics concepts.

Description: Multiple-item paper-pencil test measuring basic academic skills. The test is available in Forms U and V. Form U contains 10 levels: Level A (Grades K.0-K.9), Level B (Grades K.6-1.6), Level C (Grades 1.0-1.9), Level D (Grades 1.6-2.9), Level E (Grades 2.6-3.9), Level F (Grades 3.6-4.9), Level G (Grades 4.6-6.9), Level H (Grades 6.6-8.9), Level J (Grades 8.6-12.9), and Level K (Grades 11.0-12.9). Level A tests reading and mathematics skills. Levels B and C test reading, language, and mathematics. Levels D and E assess reading, language, mathematics, science, social studies, and spelling. Levels F-K measure reading, language, mathematics, science, social studies, and reference skills. Form V is available only for Levels D-J. Forms U and V replace CTBS Forms S and T. Examiner required. Suitable for group use. Available in Spanish.

Timed: Complete battery 1 hour, 8 minutes-4 hours, 50 minutes

Scoring: Hand key; may be computer scored

Cost: Multi-level examination kit (Grades K-12) $24.00; specimen set (specify level) $14.25

Publisher: CTB/McGraw-Hill

COMPUTER COMPETENCE TESTS

Grades 4-adult

Purpose: Assesses an individual's knowledge of computers. Points out areas of instructional need.

Description: Multiple-item paper-pencil test consisting of five modules: Development and Impact, Computer Operations I, Computer Operations II, Applications I, and Applications II. Teachers can select any or all modules that best match the content of their particular course. The tests are criterion-referenced. National norms are not available. Examiner required. Suitable for group use.

Untimed: 20-25 minutes per module

Scoring: Hand key

Cost: Contact publisher

Publisher: The Psychological Corporation

COOPERATIVE ENGLISH TESTS
Refer to page 243.

COOPERATIVE MATHEMATICS TESTS
Refer to page 304.

CORNELL CLASS REASONING TEST, FORM X
William H. Ennis,
William L. Gardiner,
Richard Morrow, Dieter Paulus,
and Lucille Ringel

Child, adolescent   Grades 1-12

Purpose: Assesses level of logical competence in deductive reasoning. Used for research in school systems.

Description: 72-item paper-pencil measure of class reasoning ability. A supposition is presented in each item, and the subject indicates whether a related statement is true, may be true, or false. Self-administered. Suitable for group use.

Timed: 50 minutes

Scoring: Hand key; may be computer scored

Cost: Test booklet with answer key $0.50

Publisher: Illinois Thinking Project

CORNELL CONDITIONAL REASONING TEST, FORM X
Robert H. Ennis,
William L. Gardiner, John Guzzetta,
Richard Morrow, Dieter Paulus,
and Lucille Ringel

Child, adolescent   Grades 1-12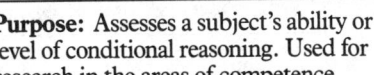

Purpose: Assesses a subject's ability or level of conditional reasoning. Used for research in the areas of competence.

Description: 72-item paper-pencil measure of conditional reasoning. Two conditions or assumptions are presented in each item; the subject then is asked to indicate whether a conclusion based on those assumptions is true, may be true, or false. Self-administered. Suitable for group use.

Timed: 50 minutes

Scoring: Hand key; may be computer scored

Cost: Test booklet with answer key $0.50

Publisher: Illinois Thinking Project

CORNELL CRITICAL THINKING TEST, LEVEL X
Robert H. Ennis and Jason Millman

Child, adolescent
Grades 4-14

Purpose: Assesses an individual's ability to think critically. Used for research, teaching of critical thinking, or admission to positions or areas requiring ability to think critically.

Description: 71-item paper-pencil measure of critical thinking divided into four sections. In the first section, the examinee reads a conclusion and decides which of several premises supports the conclusion. The second section measures the examinee's ability to judge the reliability of information. The third section tests the examinee's ability to judge whether a statement follows from premises. The fourth section involves the identification of assumptions. Level X is somewhat easier than Level Z. Examiner required for Grades 4-6. Suitable for group use.

Timed: 50-62 minutes, depending on grade

Scoring: Computer scored

Cost: Specimen set (tests, manual) $10.00; 10 tests $16.95; 10 machine-scorable answer sheets $4.95

Publisher: Midwest Publications

CORNELL CRITICAL THINKING TEST, LEVEL Z
Robert H. Ennis and Jason Millman

**Adolescent, adult
Grades 13 and above**

Purpose: Assesses an individual's ability to think critically. Used for research, teaching of critical thinking, or admission to positions or areas requiring ability for critical thinking.

Description: 52-item paper-pencil measure of critical thinking divided into seven sections directed at assessing the examinee's ability to decide whether a statement follows from a given premise, detect equivocal arguments, judge reliability of observations and authenticity of sources, judge direction of support for a hypothesis, and find assumptions of various types. Level Z is somewhat more difficult than Level X. Self-administered. Suitable for group use.

Timed: 50 minutes

Scoring: Computer scored

Cost: Specimen set (manual, tests) $10.00; 10 tests $16.95; 10 machine-scorable answer sheets $4.95

Publisher: Midwest Publications

CRITERION TEST OF BASIC SKILLS
Kerth Lundell, William Brown, and James Evans

Child   Grades 1-6

Purpose: Assesses reading and arithmetic skills of elementary school students. Used by teachers for classroom placement.

Description: Multiple-item paper-pencil criterion-referenced test covering reading and arithmetic skills. The Reading subtest measures letter recognition, letter sounding, blending, sequencing, special sounds, and sight words. The Arithmetic subtest measures number and numerical recognition, addition, subtraction, multiplication, and division. After scoring, both portions of the test can be transferred to a graphic profile of each student's strengths and weaknesses. Materials include recording forms, problem sheets, a stimulus cards booklet, and a manual, which contains activities correlated to the skill areas assessed. Examiner required. Suitable for group use.

Untimed: 10-15 minutes

Scoring: Hand key

Cost: Manual $12.00; 25 arithmetic recording forms $7.00; 25 reading recording forms $7.00; 25 math problem sheets $4.00; stimulus cards booklet $6.00

Publisher: Academic Therapy Publications

DENTAL ADMISSION TEST (DAT)
American Dental Association

**Adult
Grades 14 and over**

Purpose: Measures general academic ability, scientific understanding, and perceptual ability of potential dental school students. Required of all candidates for admission to U.S. dental schools.

Description: 290-item paper-pencil competitive examination in four sections: Quantitative Reasoning (50 items); Reading Comprehension (50 items); Natural Sciences, including biology and general and organic chemistry (100 items); and Perceptual Ability (90 items). The test is administered only to individuals who have completed at least one year of college, including courses in natural sciences, although two or more years of college experience are recommended. No books, slide rules, paper, calculators, or other resource materials are permitted in the exam room. Administered biannually in specific cities only. Examiner required (provided through the American Dental Association). Suitable for group use.

Timed: ½ day

Scoring: Computer scored

Cost: Fee $50.00 per person

Publisher: American Dental Association

DETROIT TESTS OF LEARNING APTITUDE
Harry J. Baker

All ages

Purpose: Measures concentration and comprehension skills for professional diagnosis of individual learning disabilities.

Description: 19 category, examiner-led test, covering pictorial and verbal absurdities, pictorial and verbal opposites, oral ommissions, social adjustment, free association, memory for design, number ability, and likenesses and differences. Eight classifications are measured within each category: reasoning and comprehension, practical judgment, verbal ability, time and space relationships, number ability, auditory attentive ability, visual attentive ability, and motor ability. Materials consist of record booklets and forms, examiner's handbook and supplement, book of pictorial materials and a sample packet. The examiner, depending upon the subtest, shows response cards or reads to the pupils and records their responses. Must be administered individually by trained professionals.

Untimed: 35-40 minutes

Scoring: Hand key; examiner evaluated

Cost: 35 record booklets $12.75; examiner's handbook and 8 record forms $9.80; handbook supplement $3.75; pictorial materials $7.50; specimen set $17.95; set of 8 record forms $2.75.

Publisher: Pro-Ed

DETROIT TESTS OF LEARNING APTITUDE (DTLA-2)
Donald D. Hammill

Child, adolescent Ages 6-17

Purpose: Measures general aptitude and discrete abilities of children. Identifies students deficient in general or specific aptitude and serves as a standardized instrument in research.

Description: Multiple-item, oral-response, paper-pencil battery of 11 subtests yielding a detailed profile of a

student's abilities and deficiencies. Subtests include word opposites, sentence imitation, oral directions, word sequences, story construction, design reproduction, object sequences, symbolic relations, conceptual matching, word fragments, and letter sequences. The abilities measured are vocabulary, grammar, following commands, repeating words, storytelling, drawing from memory, order recall, reasoning, relationship knowledge, Gestalt-closure function, and order recall. Nine composite scores of verbal, nonverbal, conceptual, structural, attention enhanced, attention reduced, motor enhanced, and motor reduced aptitudes, and the general intelligence quotient, provide information on linguistic, cognitive, attention, and motor abilities. The test is useful in diagnosing learning disabilities and mental retardation. Examiner required. Not suitable for group use.

Untimed: Varies

Scoring: Computer scored

Cost: Complete kit (25 student response forms, 25 examiner record forms, 25 summary and profile sheets, picture book, examiner's manual, storage box) $79.00

Publisher: Pro-Ed

DETROIT TESTS OF LEARNING APTITUDE—PRIMARY (DTLA-P)
Donald D. Hammill and Brian R. Bryant

Child 3.5-9

Purpose: Measures general and specific aptitudes of children. Identifies deficiencies and serves as a standardized instrument in research.

Description: 130-item oral-response paper-pencil battery yielding eight subtest scores (Verbal Quotient, Nonverbal Quotient, Conceptual Quotient, Structural Quotient, Motor-Enhanced Quotient, Motor-Reduced Quotient, Attention-Enhanced Quotient, Attention-Reduced Quotient) and one total score (General Intelligence Quotient) and providing a detailed profile of a student's abilities and deficiencies. The test is useful with low-functioning school-aged children. Examiner required. Not suitable for group use.

Untimed: 15-40 minutes

Scoring: Computer scored

Cost: Complete kit (examiner's manual, 25 student response forms, 25 profile/ examiner record forms, picture book, storage box) $64.00

Publisher: Pro-Ed

DIAGNOSTIC ABILITIES IN MATH (D.A.M. TEST)
Refer to page 283.

DIAGNOSTIC ACHIEVEMENT BATTERY (DAB)
Phyllis L. Newcomer and Delores Curtis

Child, adolescent Ages 5-14

Purpose: Assesses a child's ability to listen, speak, read, write, and perform simple mathematics operations. Diagnoses learning disabilities.

Description: 10 paper-pencil and oral-response subtests assessing the following five components of a child's verbal and mathematical skills: listening (Listening Comprehension Test and Characteristics Test), speaking (Synonyms Test and Grammar Completion Test), reading (Alphabet/Word Knowledge Test and Reading Comprehension Test), writing (Written Conventions Test and Creative Writing Test), and math (Math Reasoning Test and Math Calculation Test). Results, converted to standard scores, provide a profile of the child's strengths and weaknesses on each of the five components, as well as on the 10 subtests. The components of the test may be administered independently, depending on the needs of the child being tested. Examiner required. The creative writing, writing conventions, and math computation subtests may be administered to small groups; the other subtests must be individually administered.

Untimed: Varies

Scoring: Examiner evaluated; may be computer scored

Cost: Complete kit (manual, 25 student work sheets, 25 profile/answer sheets, picture book, storage box) $57.00

Publisher: Pro-Ed

DIAGNOSTIC SKILLS BATTERY (DSB)
O. F. Anderhalter, STS staff and consultants

Child, adolescent Grades 1-8

Purpose: Evaluates student abilities in reading, mathematics, and language arts. Used for pre- and posttesting.

Description: Multiple-item paper-pencil test battery covering 30-40 objectives for each of the following skills areas: reading, mathematics, and language arts. The battery is based on selected "terminal" objectives from the more detailed Analysis of Skills series. Level 12 covers Grades 1-3 and does not include language arts; Level 34 covers Grades 3-5; Level 56 covers Grades 5-7; and Level 78 covers Grades 7-9. The Standard Scoring Service offers two plans. Plan I reports class lists of norm-referenced scores, and Plan II provides performance profiles, which show both norm- and objective-based information. Both plans provide summary information. Scoring options include normal curve equivalent scores for Chapter I use and an individual skills analysis. The battery is available as a lease/score program or as a school purchase program with STS scoring only. Examiner required. Suitable for group use.

Timed: 2 hours, 40 minutes

Scoring: Hand key; may be computer scored

Cost: Specimen set (specify level and form) $6.00

Publisher: Scholastic Testing Service, Inc.

DIFFERENTIAL APTITUDE TEST BATTERY
Manjula Makerjee

Child, adolescent Ages 11-13

Purpose: Identifies specific areas of students' academic aptitude.

Description: 547-item paper-pencil test consisting of seven subtests measuring aptitude in several academic fields. The subtests include English Knowledge and Comprehension, Clerical Aptitude I (speed), Clerical Aptitude II, Abstract Reasoning, Verbal Reasoning, Mathematics Knowledge and Comprehension, Scientific Aptitude, and Mechanical Comprehension. The scores from the subtests can be used to predict success in various education fields, such as the humanities, science, and commerce. An eighth-grade reading level is required. Examiner required. Suitable for group use.

PUBLISHED IN INDIA

Untimed: Not available

Scoring: Hand key; examiner evaluated

Cost: Contact publisher

Publisher: Manasayan

Information and availability unconfirmed; no publisher response.

DIFFERENTIAL APTITUDE TESTS (DAT): FORMS S AND T
G.K. Bennett, H.G. Seashore, and A.G. Wesman

Adolescent   Grades 8-12

Purpose: Assesses aptitude. Used for educational and vocational guidance in junior and senior high schools.

Description: Multiple-item paper-pencil test of eight abilities: verbal reasoning, numerical ability, abstract reasoning, clerical speed and accuracy, mechanical reasoning, space relations, spelling, and language usage. A ninth score is obtained by summing the verbal reasoning and numerical ability scores. Materials include two alternate forms, S and T. The Career Planning Questionnaire is optional. Forms S and T have been superseded by Forms V and W. Examiner required. Suitable for group use.

Timed: Complete battery 3 hours or longer

Scoring: Hand key; may be machine scored; may be computer scored

Cost: Specimen set, specify Form S or Form T (test, various answer documents, directions, and norms) $14.00; Career Planning Service Information Packet (counselor's manual, questionnaire, glossary, interpretive report) $9.00

Publisher: The Psychological Corporation

DIFFERENTIAL APTITUDE TESTS (DAT): FORMS V AND W
G.K. Bennett, H.G. Seashore, and A.G. Wesman

Adolescent   Grades 8-12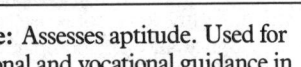

Purpose: Assesses aptitude. Used for educational and vocational guidance in junior and senior high schools.

Description: Multiple-item paper-pencil test of eight abilities: verbal reasoning, numerical ability, abstract reasoning, clerical speed and accuracy, mechanical reasoning, space relations, spelling, and language usage. A ninth score, an index of scholastic ability, is obtained by summing the verbal reasoning and numerical ability scores. Materials include two alternate and equivalent forms, V and W. The Career Planning Questionnaire is optional. Forms V and W supersede Forms S and T. Examiner required. Suitable for group use.

Timed: Complete battery 3 hours or longer

Scoring: Hand key; may be machine scored; may be computer scored

Cost: Specimen set (test, directions, administrator's handbook, MRC and NCS answer documents and sheets NC, list of correct answers, order for scoring service, sample profile forms) $11.00; Career Planning Service Information Packet (counselor's manual, directions, glossary, sample career planning report, explanation of school summary report, MRC answer document with MRC sheet NC, orientation booklet) $8.00.

Publisher: The Psychological Corporation

EDUCATIONAL ABILITIES SCALES

Adolescent   Ages 13-15

Purpose: Assesses abilities important to educational achievement. Used for identifying individual pupil strengths and weaknesses.

Description: Multiple-item battery of five pencil-paper tests covering the following abilities: mechanical, spatial, symbolic, scientific process and inference, and clerical speed and accuracy. The student uses a scraper to scratch away coating from answers; immediate feedback concerning accuracy is provided. Equivalent scores are provided for each ability, allowing comparison between different abilities. Examiner required. Suitable for group use. BRITISH PUBLISHER

Untimed: Not available

Scoring: Examiner evaluated

Cost: Student's book £2.85; 10 answer sheets £8.00; manual £7.50; specimen set £10.50 (payment in sterling for all overseas orders)

Publisher: NFER-NELSON Publishing Company Ltd.

EDUCATIONAL DEVELOPMENT SERIES, REVISED 1984 EDITION
O.F. Anderhalter, R.H. Bauernfeind, Mary E. Greig, George Mallinson, Jacqueline Mallinson, Joseph Papenfuss, and Neil Vail

Child, adolescent Grades K-12

Purpose: Assesses ability, achievement, and career interests of children and adolescents. Used by guidance counselors, teachers, and others for counseling, diagnosis, and construction.

Description: Multiple-item paper-pencil battery of tests in four formats: Complete Battery, Core Achievement Battery, Basic Skills Battery, and Cognitive and Basic Skills Battery. The Complete Battery (Grades 4-12) contains the following eleven subtests: Career Interests and School Plans, School Interests, Non-Ver-

bal Cognitive Skills, Verbal Cognitive Skills, Reference Skills, Reading, Language Arts, Mathematics, Science, and Social Studies. The Core Achievement Battery (Grades 2-12) contains eight subtests: Career Interests and School Plans, School Interests, Reference Skills, Reading, Language Arts, Mathematics, Science, and Social Studies. Skills are assessed with five subtests in the Basic Skills Battery (Grades K-12): Career Interests and School Plans, School Interests, Reading, Language Arts, and Mathematics. The Cognitive and Basic Skills Battery (Grades K-12) contains seven subtests: Career Interests and School Plans, School Interests, Non-Verbal Skills, Verbal Skills, Reading, Language Arts, and Mathematics. The 1984 edition uses a single test level for each grade. Examiner required. Suitable for group use.

Timed: 6 hours or less

Scoring: Hand key; scoring service available

Cost: Specimen set (specify level and form) $10.00

Publisher: Scholastic Testing Service, Inc.

GENERAL ABILITY TESTS: NUMERICAL (GAT NUMERICAL)
Refer to page 893.

GENERAL ABILITY TESTS: PERCEPTUAL (GAT PERCEPTUAL)
Refer to page 893.

GENERAL ABILITY TESTS: VERBAL (GAT VERBAL)
Refer to page 894.

GENERAL EDUCATIONAL PERFORMANCE INDEX
Don F. Seaman and Anna Seaman

Adult

Purpose: Assesses adult students' preparedness to take the General Educational Development (GED) test. Also indicates academic areas in which the student is weak.

Description: 168-item paper-pencil test measuring students' competency in writing, social studies, science, reading, and mathematics. The test is available in two forms, A and B. Examiner required. Suitable for group use.

Timed: 2½-3 hours

Scoring: Hand key

Cost: 25 tests (specify form) $29.25; teacher's set $8.91; 50 answer sheets $11.70

Publisher: Steck-Vaughn Company

GOYER ORGANIZATION OF IDEAS TEST
Robert S. Goyer

Adolescent, adult
Grades 9-adult

Purpose: Measures the ability to organize ideas verbally and to assess an individual's general mental ability. Used to place undergraduates in upper-level courses and to screen students from areas in which they might not succeed.

Description: 30-item paper-pencil multiple-choice test of ability to perceive oral-visual-written stimuli and to analyze and synthesize the ideas selected. The total process applied involves the following identifiable skill categories: component (part-whole) relationships, including dependence-independence, significance-insignificance, and coordination of ideas; sequential relationships, including chronological, cause-to-effect, climax, and topical; material-to-purpose (relevance) relationships, including recognition of central or unifying idea and exclusion of ideas lacking consistency with total group; and transitional (connective) relationships, including use of relational words and phrases based on total pattern of communication. Self-administered. Suitable for group use. Available in Korean.

Untimed: 40-60 minutes

Scoring: Hand key; may be computer scored

Cost: Test booklet $2.00; answer key with normative summary $20.00

Publisher: Robert S. Goyer, Ph.D.

GRADUATE AND MANAGERIAL ASSESSMENT
Psychometric Research Unit,
The Hatfield Polytechnic

Adult

Purpose: Assesses numerical, verbal, and abstract reasoning abilities of adults. Used to select graduate-school candidates and identify management potential of individuals.

Description: Three paper-pencil multiple-choice tests measuring the numerical, verbal, and abstract reasoning abilities of adults. The numerical test, used for recruiting graduates from general disciplines into finance-related occupations, presents realistic problems in commercial context and emphasizes problem-solving strategies rather then computational skills. The verbal test measures the capacity for detached critical appraisal of verbal material and is useful for assessing the ability of general arts graduates to evaluate semi-technical information. The abstract test assesses the flexibility and insight of individuals whose work is analytic, conceptual, and nonroutine. The tests may be used together or separately. Parallel forms are available. Examiner required. Suitable for group use.
BRITISH PUBLISHER

Timed: 30 minutes per test

Scoring: Self-scored

Cost: Specimen set £45.95

Publisher: NFER-NELSON Publishing Company Ltd.

GRADUATE MANAGEMENT ADMISSION TEST (GMAT)

Adult   College graduates

Purpose: Measures verbal and quantitative abilities related to success in graduate management schools. Used for admission to graduate management schools.

Description: Multiple-choice paper-pencil test measuring general verbal and quantitative abilities. It does not measure proficiency in undergraduate business or economics courses. The test is administered four times annually at centers established by the publisher, and registration materials are available at no charge. The test is not available for institutional use. Examiner required. Suitable for group use.

Untimed: 4 hours

Scoring: Computer scored

Cost: Contact publisher

Publisher: Educational Testing Service

GRADUATE RECORD EXAMINATIONS (GRE)

Adult   College graduates

Purpose: Measures the academic abilities and knowledge of graduate school applicants. Used by graduate schools for screening the qualifications of applicants and by organizations for selecting fellowship recipients.

Description: Multiple-item multiple-choice paper-pencil battery of advanced achievement and aptitude tests. The General Test measures verbal, quantitative, and analytical abilities. The Subject Tests are available for the following 17 subjects: biology, chemistry, computer science, economics, education, engineering, French, geology, history, literature in English, mathematics, music, physics, political science, psychology, sociology, and Spanish. The tests are administered on specified dates at centers established by the publisher. Examiner required. Suitable for group use.

Timed: General test 3½ hours; subject tests 2 hours, 50 minutes each

Scoring: Computer scored

Cost: Contact publisher

Publisher: Educational Testing Service

GUIDANCE TEST BATTERY FOR SECONDARY PUPILS (GBS)—1981

Adolescent

Purpose: Measures scholastic achievement. Used for educational guidance.

Description: Paper-pencil test of pupils' proficiency in English, Afrikaans, Mathematics, Nonverbal Reasoning, and Verbal Reasoning. Two forms, A and B, are

available. Examiner required. Suitable for group use. The test publisher notes that this test is "normed on Blacks only."
SOUTH AFRICAN PUBLISHER

Timed: 3½ hours

Scoring: Hand key; examiner evaluated; may be machine scored

Cost: (In Rands) test (A or B) 1,20 each; instructions and norms 1,40; scoring stencil 1,90; 10 answer sheets (machine and hand scoring) 0,70; orders from outside The RSA will be dealt with on merit

Publisher: Human Sciences Research Council

HIGH LEVEL BATTERY B/75

Adult

Purpose: Assesses educational abilities of older students. Used with individuals entering college or higher.

Description: Multiple-item paper-pencil multiple-choice tests of academic abilities. The six tests are Mental Alertness, Language Ability in English and Afrikaans, Reading Comprehension, Vocabulary, Spelling, and Arithmetic. Examiner required. Suitable for group use.
SOUTH AFRICAN PUBLISHER

Timed: 1 hour, 53 minutes

Scoring: Hand key

Cost: (In Rands) booklet 9,75; 25 answer sheets 3,00; key 10,00; manual 12,00

Publisher: National Institute for Personnel Research

IDENTI-FORM: IDENTIFICATION, ASSESSMENT, AND BEYOND
Refer to page 571.

INDIVIDUALIZED CRITERION REFERENCED TESTING (ICRT)

Child

Purpose: Measures student progress and achievement against a specific set of objectives in reading and mathematics. Measures student mastery of specific skills. Used for program planning, instructional management, and program assessment.

Description: 718-item paper-pencil test assessing student skills in math and reading. The reading test (304 objectives) measures skills in the following areas: phonetic analysis, structural analysis, word function skills, and comprehension. Items are arranged in 38 color-coded test booklets divided into eight levels. The mathematics test (384 objectives) measures knowledge of whole number operations, fractions, measurement, geometry, decimals/per cent, and special topics. Items are arranged in 51 test booklets divided into nine levels. The tests measure the students' mastery or lack of mastery for each skill or concept tested. Placement tests and procedures are provided for both reading and math to insure that students are tested at a level compatible with their abilities. These placement tests indicate which five reading tests and which five mathematics tests should be administered for the actual testing. Three computer reports are provided. The student report identifies for each student which skills have been mastered, which skills need review, and which skills should be attempted next. Individual student records are kept in separate student profile folders for reading and mathematics. A teacher report and an administrative report are available. Benchmark tests also are provided for interim assessment of student progress. Objective-by-objective correlations are also provided for more than 275 reading materials and more than 130 mathematics materials. Examiner required. Suitable for group use.

Untimed: Varies

Scoring: Placement tests examiner evaluated; ICRT tests computer scored

Cost: Reading tests $24.00 per level; math tests (Levels 1-5) $24.00 per level; math tests (Level 6 and up) $115.00; sample sets (reading or math) $31.00

Publisher: Educational Development Corporation

INITIAL EVALUATION TESTS IN ENGLISH AND MATHEMATICS

Child, adolescent

Purpose: Measures achievement in English and math. Used for educational evaluation at the beginning of a new standard.

Description: Nine tests measuring achievement in English and mathematics. Initial Evaluation Tests in English are available at Standards 5 and 8. Seven Initial Evaluation Tests in Mathematics are available for Standards 1 to 7. Two alternate forms, A and B, are available for each of the nine tests. Tests should be administered as soon as possible after the beginning of the school year. Examiner required. Suitable for group use.
SOUTH AFRICAN PUBLISHER

Untimed: Not available

Scoring: Hand key; examiner evaluated

Cost: Contact publisher; orders from outside The RSA will be dealt with on merit

Publisher: Human Sciences Research Council

INTERMEDIATE BATTERY B/77

Adult

Purpose: Assesses academic achievement and clerical aptitudes of individuals who have 10-12 years of schooling.

Description: Multiple-item paper-pencil set of seven subtests, six of which are similar to those in the High Level Battery (mental alertness, English, reading comprehension, vocabulary, spelling, and arithmetic). This battery does not include the Afrikaans reading comprehension, vocabulary, and spelling tests. However, it does include a clerical perception test. Examiner required. Suitable for group use.
SOUTH AFRICAN PUBLISHER

Timed: 2 hours, 45 minutes

Scoring: Hand key

Cost: (In Rands) booklet 9,75; 25 answer sheets 3,00; set of keys 10,00; manual 12,00

Publisher: National Institute for Personnel Research

---

academic achievement and aptitude

IOWA TESTS OF BASIC SKILLS, FORMS 7 AND 8 (ITBS)

A.N. Hieronymus, E.F. Lindquist, and H.D. Hoover

Child, adolescent
Grades K-9

Purpose: Assesses the development of students' basic academic skills. Identifies strengths and weaknesses in basic academic skills and evaluates the effectiveness of instructional programs.

Description: Multiple-item paper-pencil tests assessing proficiency in the basic skills required for academic success. The test is available on 10 levels. The Primary Battery (Levels 5-8) is used with students in Grades K-3. The Multilevel Edition (Levels 9-14) is designed for students in Grades 3-9. All 10 levels assess combinations of the following skills: vocabulary, reading, language, spelling, capitalization, punctuation, language usage, work-study, visual materials, reference materials, mathematics concepts, problem solving, and computation. Listening and word analysis are also measured at the primary level. The Primary Battery (Levels 5-6) is available only in a basic battery. The Primary Battery (Levels 7-8) and the Multilevel Edition (Levels 9-14) are available in a basic battery and a complete battery. The ITBS is normed concurrently with the Cognitive Abilities Test for reliable comparisons between attained and expected achievement scores. The Primary Battery uses machine-scorable test booklets, and the Multilevel Edition uses test booklets and separate answer sheets. Examiner required. Suitable for group use.

Timed: Multilevel Edition Basic Battery 244 minutes; Complete Battery 139 minutes

Untimed: Primary Battery 150-235 minutes, depending on form

Scoring: Hand key; may be computer scored

Cost: 25 Primary Battery Level 5 machine-scorable test booklets $5.74; 25 Primary Battery Level 6 machine-scorable test booklets $30.03; 25 Primary Battery Level 7 or 8 complete battery machine-scorable test booklets $6.42 per level; 25 Primary Battery Level 7 or 8 basic battery machine-scorable test booklets, teacher's guide $30.03; Multilevel Edition complete battery $4.02 per level; basic battery $3.00 per level; 35 MRC answer sheets, teacher's guide, $16.17 per level; teacher's guide $6.18

Publisher: The Riverside Publishing Company

IOWA TESTS OF BASIC SKILLS: FORMS G AND H

A.N. Hieronymus and H.D. Hoover

Child, adolescent
Grades K-9

Purpose: Assesses the development of basic academic skills. Identifies individual student's strengths and weaknesses and evaluates the effectiveness of instructional programs.

Description: Multiple-choice paper-pencil test assessing proficiency in the basic skills required for academic success. The Multilevel editions (Grades 3-9) measure the following skill areas at each level: vocabulary, reading, language, work-study, mathematics, science, and social studies. New tests in listening and writing have been added to these forms. Schools can track listening skills through junior high school and offer paper-pencil, generative writing assessments for Grades 3-8. The Early Primary and Primary batteries (Grades K-3.5) include tests in listening, vocabulary, reading (except for Kindergarten), word analysis, language, and mathematics. The Primary Battery (Grades 2-3.5) contains tests in work-study. The test is normed concurrently with the New Cognitive Abilities Test for reliable comparisons between attained and expected achievement scores. The tests are available in a complete battery and a basic battery, depending on level. Examiner required. Suitable for group use.

Timed: Complete Battery 4 hours, 16 minutes; Basic Battery, Multilevel Edition 2 hours, 15 minutes

Untimed: Primary Battery 115-127 minutes

Scoring: Hand key; may be machine scored

Cost: 35 Level 5 machine-scorable test booklets $36.00; 35 Level 6 machine-scorable test booklets $42.00; 35 Level 7 or 8 Complete Battery machine-scorable test booklets $45.00; MRC Basic Battery for Level 7 or 8, teacher's guide $42.00; Multilevel Complete Battery test booklet $3.87; Multilevel Basic Battery test booklet $3.00; 35 MRC answer sheets, teacher's guide (specify level) $15.00; Multilevel Edition teacher's guide $6.15

Publisher: The Riverside Publishing Company

IOWA TESTS OF EDUCATIONAL DEVELOPMENT (ITED): FORMS X7 AND Y7
E. F. Lindquist and Leonard S. Feldt

Adolescent   Grades 9-12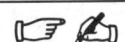

Purpose: Measures adolescent and adult learning skills and abilities and general educational development. Identifies strengths and weaknesses in content skill areas (although not a test of specific curriculum areas or minimal competencies) and monitors educational development.

Description: 357-item paper-pencil achievement test assessing knowledge and application of skills of analysis. The factors measured are recognizing good writing, solving quantitative problems, critically analyzing social issues, understanding nontechnical scientific reports, recognizing sound scientific inquiry methods, using common information sources and tools, and perceiving subtle meanings and moods in literature. The test is available on two levels: Level I for Grades 9-10 and Level II for Grades 11-12. Some items overlap. Examiner required. Suitable for group use.

Timed: 4 hours

Scoring: Hand key; may be computer scored

Cost: Rental and scoring for student $2.80; test booklets scoring $1.90; 25 tests $47.75; review set $5.00

Publisher: Science Research Associates, Inc.

JUNIOR APTITUDE TESTS (JAT)—1974

Child, adolescent

Purpose: Measures scholastic aptitude. Used for educational counseling.

Description: Multiple-item paper-pencil test measuring specific scholastic aptitudes: classification, reasoning, number ability, synonyms, comparison, spatial (2D), spatial (3D), memory (paragraph), memory (words and symbols), and mechanical insight. Examiner required. Suitable for group use. SOUTH AFRICAN PUBLISHER

Untimed: 2 hours, 45 minutes

Scoring: Hand key; examiner evaluated; may be machine scored

Cost: (In Rands) test booklet 0,90; 10 answer sheets (T1-T6), 0,60; 10 answer sheets (T7-T10) 0,60; scoring stencil for 1224 2,20; scoring stencil for 1225 2,90; manual 5,20; 10 machine answer sheets 1,50; orders from outside The RSA will be dealt with on merit

Publisher: Human Sciences Research Council

KAUFMAN TEST OF EDUCATIONAL ACHIEVEMENT (K-TEA)
Alan S. Kaufman and Nadeen L. Kaufman

Child, adolescent
Grades 1-12

Purpose: Assesses educational achievement of students ages 6-18. Used for educational planning by school and clinical psychologists, educational diagnosticians, learning disabilities specialists, remedial reading teachers, counselors, and other specialists.

Description: Multiple-item oral-response paper-pencil test in two forms. The Brief Form measures global achievement in reading, mathematics, and spelling. The 52-item reading subtest assesses decoding of printed words and comprehension. The 52-item mathematics subtest measures basic arithmetic concepts, applications of mathematical principles to real-life situations, numerical reasoning, and simple and advanced computation skills. The 40-item spelling dictation subtest assesses ability using a steeply graded word list. The Comprehensive Form provides a more thorough assessment of achievement through 5 subtests. The 60-item mathematics/applications subtest measures a wide variety of arithmetic concepts and extensive applications of mathematical principles and reasoning skills to real-life situations. The 60-item reading/decoding subtest measures the ability to identify letters and pronounce words of gradually increasing phonetic and nonphonetic difficulty. The 50-item spelling dictation subtest assesses ability using an increasingly difficult word list. The 50-item reading/comprehension subtest assesses literal and inferential comprehension. The 60-item mathematics/computation subtest assesses written computation skills including the four basic operations and more complex computational abilities such as algebra. Examiner required. Not suitable for group use.

Timed: Brief form 15-35 minutes; comprehensive form 30-65 minutes

Scoring: Hand key; computer scoring available in 1987

Cost: Brief Form kit (75 test plates in easel, manual, 25 record booklets, Report to Parents, shelf storage box) $42.50; Comprehensive Form kit (131 test plates in easel, manual, 25 record booklets, Report to Parents, shelf storage box) $74.00

Publisher: American Guidance Service

KUHLMANN ANDERSON TESTS (KA), 8TH EDITION
F. Kuhlmann and Rose Anderson

Child, adolescent
Grades K-12

Purpose: Evaluates students' academic ability and potential. Used for group placement and diagnosing individual learning abilities.

Description: 80- to 130-item paper-pencil test assessing academic potential. The test is available in eight booklets: K (Kindergarten), A (Grade 1), BC (Grades 2-3), CD (Grades 3-4), EF (Grades 5-7), G (Grades

7-9), and H (Grades 9-12). The test yields mental age, deviation IQ, grade percentile rank, IQ percentile rank, stanine, and separate verbal and quantitative grade percentile scores. Norms are based on a large national sampling of socio-economic, ethnic, and social diversity. Only STS answer sheets may be machine-scored. Examiner required. Suitable for group use.

Timed: 50-75 minutes

Scoring: Hand key; may be computer scored

Cost: 20 booklets $11.00-$17.60; 50 answer sheets $11.00

Publisher: Scholastic Testing Service, Inc.

LIFE SKILLS: FORMS 1 AND 2
Kenneth Majer and Dena C. Wadell

Adolescent   Grades 9-12

Purpose: Assesses student and group competency in basic reading and mathematics skills.

Description: Two multiple-item paper-pencil subtests measuring functional competencies in reading and mathematics. The Reading Test includes four objectives measuring the ability to follow directions (labels, signs); three objectives measuring locating and understanding references (phone books, catalogs); five objectives measuring interpretation and use of information (want ads, lease agreements); and two objectives measuring the understanding of forms (taxes, installment purchases). The Mathematics Test objectives require the student to compute basic consumer problems; apply principles of percent, interest, and fractions; identify, estimate, and convert time, currency, and measurements; and interpret graphs, charts, and statistics. The manual includes test administration procedures, scoring, and basic technical data. The technical supplement provides comprehensive information. Two test forms, 1 and 2, are available for pretest-posttest experimental studies. Examiner required. Suitable for group use.

Timed: Reading test 40 minutes; mathematics test 40 minutes

academic achievement and aptitude

Scoring: Examiner evaluated; may be computer scored

Cost: 35 test booklets (specify form) $45.69; 35 self-mark answer sheets $26.13; 35 MRC answer sheets $19.59; manual $3.45; technical supplement $13.98; examination kit (both test booklets, manual) $3.69

Publisher: The Riverside Publishing Company

MARTINEZ ASSESSMENT OF THE BASIC SKILLS
David Martinez

LD students

Purpose: Diagnoses deficiencies in basic academic skills. Used with learning disabled, mildly to moderately retarded, and other academically troubled students.

Description: Multiple-item paper-pencil test consisting of six subtests, each testing proficiency in a different basic skill area. The Diagnostic Counting and Numerals Test covers 14 beginning mathematical skills. The Diagnostic Arithmetic Test identifies computational performance in seven skill areas. The Diagnostic Reading Test assesses prereading skills, symbol-sound correspondences, phonically irregular sight words, sound patterns, silent letters, and related word study skills. The Diagnostic Spelling Test assesses spelling skills in writing letters, words, and sentences. The Diagnostic Primary Language Concepts Test assesses 24 language-concept skills relating to such classroom activities as circling, underlining, and crossing out. The Diagnostic Time Telling Test assesses 14 skill areas with optional assessment of digital clock time available. Individual student performance profiles allow pre-post test comparison. Examiner required. Suitable for group use.

Untimed: Varies

Scoring: Examiner evaluated

Cost: Complete test kit (administration manual, 5 student profile charts, 5 student response and record booklets for each diagnostic test) $69.95

Publisher: ASIEP Education Company

MEASURE OF ACADEMIC PROGRESS (MAP)
Wayne Adams, David Sheslow, and Lynn Erb

Child, adolescent
Grades K-12

Purpose: Determines the approximate grade level at which a student is performing. Identifies students who are operating above or below their expected grade level.

Description: 160-item paper-pencil test containing approximately five items per grade level in each of the following categories: mathematics, spelling, word recognition, and passage comprehension. An informal handwriting checklist and a writing sample (both optional) are provided also. The student must produce, rather than identify, the correct response. Test items are tied to actual content taught at each grade level. Examiner required. Spelling and mathematics suitable for group use.

Untimed: 20-30 minutes

Scoring: Hand key

Cost: Complete kit $35.00; examiner's manual $25.00; 25 record forms $13.00

Publisher: The Psychological Corporation

MEDICAL COLLEGE ADMISSION TEST

Adolescent, adult
Grades 13 and above

Purpose: Assists medical school admission committees in the evaluation of candidates primarily applying to medical school.

Description: One full day of examinations assessing academic achievement and aptitude of medical school applicants. The examinations are administered in four sections: Science Knowledge (presents biology, chemistry, and physics in separate assessment areas as a partial assessment of science achievement), Science Problems (intermingles biology, chemistry, and physics to assess the application of knowledge in solving problems), Skills Analysis: Reading (presents information in reading passages to assess analytical and reasoning skills), and Skills Analysis: Quantitative (assesses analytical and reasoning skills using questions involving quantitative material). The student manual includes test day schedule, a complete practice test, descriptions of the tests, and comprehensive guidelines for preparing for the test. Prerequisite subjects for the science subtests are usually covered in one-year introductory courses in biology, general chemistry, organic chemistry, and physics. The examinations are administered in the spring and fall of each year at centers established and supervised by the American College Testing Program. Examiner required. Suitable for group use.

Timed: 6½ hours

Scoring: Computer scored

Cost: Regular exam (on Saturday) $65.00; Sunday exam $70.00; student manual $7.00 plus postage

Publisher: Association of American Medical Colleges

METROPOLITAN ACHIEVEMENT TEST: 5TH EDITION—SURVEY BATTERY
Irving H. Balow, Roger Farr, Thomas P. Hogan, and George A. Prescott

---

Child, adolescent
Grades K-12.9

Purpose: Assesses school achievement. Used for measuring performance of large groups of students.

Description: Multiple-item paper-pencil tests of school achievement divided into eight levels: Preprimer (Grade K.0-K.5), Primer (Grades K.5-1.4), Primary 1 (Grades 1.5-2.4), Primary 2 (Grades 2.5-3.4), Elementary (Grades 3.5-4.9), Intermediate (Grades 5.0-6.9), Advanced 1 (Grades 7.0-9.9), and Advanced 2 (Grades 10.0-12.9). The Basic Battery for all eight levels consists of tests in reading comprehension, mathematics, and language. The Complete Battery for the Primary 1 through the Advanced 1 levels also include social science and science tests. Materials include two alternate and equivalent forms, JS and KS. The Metro-

politan instructional tests in reading, mathematics, and language provide more in-depth analyses than the Survey Battery. Examiner required. Suitable for group use.

Timed: Varies

Scoring: Hand key; may be machine scored; scoring service available

Cost: Specimen sets, specify level (test, manual) $11.00; the Preprimer set includes a practice test and directions, and the Intermediate and Advanced 1 and 2 sets include a hand-scorable answer document

Publisher: The Psychological Corporation

METROPOLITAN ACHIEVEMENT TESTS: 6TH EDITION—SURVEY BATTERY

Child, adolescent
Grades K-12

Purpose: Assesses school achievement. Used for measuring performances of large groups of students.

Description: Multiple-item paper-pencil tests of school achievement divided into eight levels: Preprimer (Grades K.0-K.9), Primer (Grades K.5-1.9), Primary 1 (Grades 1.5-2.9), Primary 2 (Grades 2.5-3.9), Elementary (Grades 3.5-4.9), Intermediate (Grades 5.0-6.9), Advanced 1 (Grades 7.0-9.9), and Advanced 2 (Grades 10.0-12.9). The Basic Battery for all eight levels consists of tests in reading, mathematics, and language. The Complete Battery for the Primary 1 level through the Advanced 2 level also assesses social science and science. Research skills are measured at the Elementary level through the Advanced 2 level. The Metropolitan Reading, Mathematics, and Language Instructional tests provide more in-depth analyses than the Survey Battery. Examiner required. Suitable for group use.

Timed: Varies according to level

Scoring: Hand key; machine scoring available

Cost: Examination kit $10.00

Publisher: The Psychological Corporation

METROPOLITAN LANGUAGE INSTRUCTIONAL TESTS
Irving H. Balow, Roger Farr, Thomas P. Hogan, and George A. Prescott

**Child, adolescent
Grades K.5-9.9**

Purpose: Assesses basic skill areas in language arts. Used for providing prescriptive information on educational performance of individual pupils.

Description: Multiple-item series of paper-pencil tests measuring major components of language arts skills, including listening comprehension, punctuation and capitalization, usage, grammar and syntax, spelling, and study skills. The test is divided into six levels: Primer (Grades K.5-1.4), Primary 1 (Grades 1.5-2.4), Primary 2 (Grades 2.5-3.4), Elementary (Grades 3.5-4.9), Intermediate (Grades 5.0-6.9), and Advanced 1 (Grades 7.0-9.9). Each level assesses three to six of the above language skills components. This test is one in a series of instructional tests related to the Metropolitan Achievement Test Survey Battery. Examiner required. Suitable for group use.

Timed: Varies

Scoring: Scoring service available

Cost: Specimen sets, specify level (test, manual) $11.00; the Intermediate and Advanced 1 set includes hand-scorable answer document

Publisher: The Psychological Corporation

METROPOLITAN MATHEMATICS INSTRUCTIONAL TESTS
Thomas P. Hogan, Roger Farr, George A. Prescott, and Irving H. Balow

**Child, adolescent
Grades K.5-9.9**

Purpose: Assesses mathematics skills and competence. Used for providing prescriptive information on educational performance of individual pupils.

Description: Multiple-item series of paper-pencil tests measuring major com-
ponents of mathematics skills, including numeration, geometry and measurement, problem solving and operations, whole numbers, laws and properties, fractions and decimals, and graphs and statistics. The test is divided into six levels: Primer (Grades K.5-1.4), Primary 1 (Grades 1.5-2.4), Primary 2 (Grades 2.5-3.4), Elementary (Grades 3.5-4.9), Intermediate (Grades 5.0-6.9), and Advanced 1 (Grades 7.0-9.9). Each level assesses four to seven of the above mathematic skills components. The test is one in a series of instructional tests related to the Metropolitan Achievement Test Survey Battery. Examiner required. Suitable for group use.

Timed: Varies

Scoring: Hand key; may be machine scored; scoring service available

Cost: Specimen set, specify level (test, manual) $11.00; the Intermediate and Advanced 1 sets include a hand-scorable answer document

Publisher: The Psychological Corporation

METROPOLITAN READINESS TESTS: 1986 EDITION (MRT)
Refer to page 482.

MILL HILL VOCABULARY SCALE
J.C. Raven

**Adolescent, adult
Ages 6-adult**

Purpose: Measures an individual's ability to recall information and state it verbally. Used for diagnosis, counseling, and school placement.

Description: Multiple-item paper-pencil vocabulary test consisting of two sets of words. In most common forms of the test, half the words are in multiple-choice format and half are in open-ended format. The scale can be used with an appropriate level of the Progressive Matrices Test. U.S. versions, with U.S. norms, are available. Materials include an expendable test booklet, a specimen set, and a manual. Examiner required. Suitable for group use.

BRITISH PUBLISHER

academic achievement and aptitude

Untimed: 15 minutes

Scoring: Hand key; may be computer scored

Cost: 50 record forms £9.00; Section 5A of manual £3.20

Publisher: H.K. Lewis & Co., Ltd.; distributed in U.S.A. by The Psychological Corporation

---

MINIMUM ESSENTIALS TEST (MET)

William K. Rice, Jr.,
Thomas R. Guskey,
Carole Lachman Perlman,
and Marion F. Rice

Adolescent, adult
Grades 8 and above

Purpose: Measures minimum basic academic skills. Used as a minimum competency test or as a final examination for basic essentials course.

Description: 124-item paper-pencil test of basic skills in reading, language, and mathematics. The test provides information on students' ability to apply basic skills to life situations. An optional writing test requiring students to write a paragraph based on a given cartoon depiction is included. The academic and life skills sections may be used independently. Standards of acceptable performance are determined by local district. Examiner required. Suitable for group use.

Timed: Basic academic skills 45 minutes; basic life skills 45 minutes; writing sample 20 minutes

Scoring: Hand key; may be computer scored

Cost: 35 test booklets $28.50; 35 answer sheets $9.10; manual $4.90; key $1.50; directions for administration $2.40; norms booklet $4.95

Publisher: American Testronics

MISSOURI CRITERION REFERENCED TESTS (CRT)

Child   Grades 2-6

Purpose: Measures the reading and mathematics abilities of students in Grades 2-6.

Description: Multiple-item paper-pencil test assessing students' strengths and weaknesses in reading and mathematics. The tests, based on objectives appropriate to each grade level, are used for diagnosis in the fall and for progress evaluation in the spring. For Chapter 1 evaluation reporting, the tests were equated to the Metropolitan Achievement Tests in reading and mathematics, and percentile scores were developed using the equipercentile method. Forms are available for each grade level. Examiner required. Suitable for group use.

Timed: 2 hours

Scoring: Machine scored

Cost: Contact publisher

Publisher: Missouri Testing and Evaluation Service

MORAY HOUSE TESTS

Child, adolescent
Ages 7.3-14

Purpose: Assesses academic aptitude by measuring mathematic, English language, and verbal reasoning skills.

Description: 15 paper-pencil tests measuring mathematics, English, and verbal reasoning abilities at a number of different levels. Three tests cover mathematical reasoning and arithmetic computation. Achievement is effectively measured whether the children are taught by old or new methods. The MHM (Junior) 2 (ages 8.6-10.6) and the MHM 4, 4a, 7, 9, and 10 (ages 10-12) are standardized tests. The MHM (Advanced) 1 (ages 12-14) is not standardized.

Four tests measure the following English language skills: vocabulary, punctuation, semantics, syntax, and general comprehension of prose and poetry. MHE (Junior) 5 and 6 (ages 8.6-10.6), MHE 41 and 42 (ages 10-12, and MHE (Advanced) 1 and 2 (ages 12-14) are standardized. The MHE (Advanced) 3 and 4 is not standardized.

The eight Verbal Reasoning Tests relate less directly to current attainment and schooling than the English and mathematics tests and as such have a semipredictive function. The MHT (Junior) 2, 4, 6, and 7 (ages 8.6-10.6), the

---

MHT 82, 86, 87, 88, and 89 (ages 10-12), the MHT 12/1 (ages 11-13), the MHT (Advanced) 10 (ages 12-14), and the MHT (Adult) 1 (ages 13.6-17.6) are standardized. The MHT 8/1 (ages 7.3-8.6), MH Vernier 8 (ages 10-12), and MHT (Advanced) 14 (ages 12-14) are not standardized. Normative data are available for all the tests but are derived from smaller samples (usually a single LEA) in the case of the unstandardized tests. The tests are available to schools with the permission of the local Chief Education Officer. Examiner required. Suitable for group use. BRITISH PUBLISHER

Untimed: 45 minutes per test

Scoring: Examiner evaluated

Cost: 20 copies £5.25-£7.75 depending on test; contact publisher for further information

Publisher: Hodder & Stoughton

MULTILEVEL ACADEMIC SKILLS INVENTORY: MATH PROGRAM (MASI)
Kenneth W. Howell,
Stanley H. Zucker,
and Mada Kay Morehead

Child, adolescent
Grades 1-8

Purpose: Assesses student math performance in general and in detail to help teachers and school psychologists plan instructional strategies and refer students to remedial programs.

Description: Multiple-item reuseable paper-pencil test on three levels measuring computation, application of skills with money, time and temperature, problem-solving, metric measurement, addition, subtraction, multiplication, division, fractions, decimals, ratios, percent, and geometry. A Survey Test samples performance over a wide range of objectives. The Placement Test assesses abilities in more detail with a content area, and a Specific Level Test examines subskills in detail. Materials include a manual, diagnostic batteries, survey and placement test booklets, response booklets, and record forms. Examiner required. Suitable for group use.

Untimed: Varies

Scoring: Examiner evaluated

Cost: Complete set $90.00

Publisher: The Psychological Corporation

MULTILEVEL ACADEMIC SKILLS INVENTORY: READING PROGRAM (MASI)
Kenneth W. Howell,
Stanley H. Zucker,
and Mada Kay Morehead

Child, adolescent
Grades 1-8

Purpose: Assesses student reading and language arts performance in general and in detail to help teachers and school psychologists plan instructional strategies and refer students to remedial programs.

Description: Multiple-item reuseable paper-pencil test in three levels measuring decoding, reading comprehension, vocabulary, handwriting, and spelling. A Survey Test samples performance over a wide range of objectives. The Placement Test assesses abilities in more detail with a content area, and a Specific Level Test examines subskills in detail. Materials include a manual, diagnostic batteries, survey and placement test booklets, response booklets, and record forms. Examiner required. Suitable for group use.

Untimed: Varies

Scoring: Examiner evaluated

Cost: Complete set $83.00

Publisher: The Psychological Corporation

MULTILEVEL ACADEMIC SURVEY TEST: CURRICULUM LEVEL TEST (MAST)
Kenneth W. Howell,
Stanley H. Zucker,
and Mada Kay Morehead

Child, adolescent
Grades K-12

Purpose: Identifies students' specific strengths and weaknesses in reading and mathematics skills.

Description: Multiple-item paper-pencil and oral reading test providing teachers with specific recommendations for additional testing, instruction, or progression to higher-level content in reading and mathematics. The reading portion includes oral reading (decoding) and silent reading (vocabulary and comprehension) on eight levels of graded passages. The mathematics portion includes additon, subtraction, multiplication, and division of whole numbers, fractions, decimals, ratios, and proportions. This test complements the normative information obtained from the MAST Grade Level Test. Examiner required. Not suitable for group use.

Untimed: 10-30 minutes per subject

Scoring: Hand key

Cost: Specimen set (examiner's manual, grade level test booklet, curriculum level record form, answer sheet) $30.00

Publisher: The Psychological Corporation

MULTILEVEL ACADEMIC SURVEY TEST: GRADE LEVEL TEST (MAST)
Kenneth W. Howell,
Stanley H. Zucker,
and Mada Kay Morehead

Child, adolescent
Grades K-12

Purpose: Assesses overal grade-level performance in mathematics and reading. Used by teachers, school psychologists, educational diagnosticians, and special education teachers with students in Grades K-12.

Description: Multiple-item paper-pencil test of mathematics and reading performance available in a primary form for Grades K-2 and a short form and extended form for grades 3-12. The test is standardized on a representative national sample and used primarily with students in Grades K-8 and high-school students with performance deficits reflecting inadequate skills. Two types of normed scores are reported: within-group norms and across-group norms. The within-group norms represent one-year age intervals from 5.0-17.0 and separate grade norms

from K-12. Bith age and grade norms tables include standard scores, percentile ranks, stanines, and normal curve equivalents. The across-grade norms are expressed as grade equivalents from K.1-12.9. Examiner required. Suitable for group use.

Untimed: 30 or 60 minutes, depending on form used

Scoring: Self-scored

Cost: Specimen set (examiner's manual, grade level test booklet, curriculum level record form, answer sheet) $30.00

Publisher: The Psychological Corporation

MULTISCORE
The Riverside Publishing Company staff and consultants

Grades 1 and above

Purpose: Measures student proficiency in basic academic skills and the effectiveness of curricula and teaching materials. May be used as a minimum competency examination, as an exit test for measuring end-of-year proficiencies, and as a pretest or posttest for federal programs or other special projects.

Description: Customized paper-pencil multiple-choice test development service providing criterion-referenced assessment of reading, language arts, mathematics, science, social studies, and/or life skills. Educators may create their own customized criterion-referenced test booklets from a pool of over 5,500 items. Catalogs of instructional objectives allow educators to select the objectives most important to their schools. Educators also may choose the number of items (one, two, or three) to be used for testing each objective. Test booklets may be created to test one or more subject areas of one of more grade levels. Reusable test booklets and consumable machine-scorable booklets are available. Examiner required. Suitable for group use.

Untimed: Varies

Scoring: Hand key; may be machine scored; scoring service available

Cost: Examination kit (three Objective Catalogs, sample test booklets, performance objective selection booklet, technical handbook, and MULTISCORE brochure with sample scoring service report) $12.27

Publisher: The Riverside Publishing Company

NATIONAL ACADEMIC APTITUDE TESTS: NON-VERBAL INTELLIGENCE
Andrew Kobal, J. Wayne Wrightstone, and Karl R. Kunze; edited by A. J. MacElroy

Adolescent, adult
Grades 10 and above

Purpose: Assesses mental abilities. Used to indicate aptitude for academic training in such areas as engineering, chemistry, and other sciences.

Description: Three nonverbal paper-pencil tests measuring mental aptitudes. The tests are Nonverbal Test of Spatial Relations, Comprehension of Physical Relations, and Graphic Relations. The test detects the ability to handle nonverbal materials at a high mental level. Items include pictorial and graphic work. Examiner required. Suitable for group use.

Timed: 26 minutes

Scoring: Hand key

Cost: Specimen set $4.00; 25 tests $13.75

Publisher: Psychometric Affiliates

NATIONAL ACADEMIC APTITUDE TESTS—VERBAL INTELLIGENCE
Andrew Kobal, J. Wayne Wrightstone, Karl R. Kunze, edited by A. J. MacElroy

Adolescent, adult
Grades 12 and above

Purpose: Assesses mental aptitudes important in academic and professional work. Used for evaluation of applicants for employment and school programs.

Description: Three verbal paper-pencil tests measuring mental aptitudes. The tests cover general information, academic and general science, mental alertness,

comprehension, judgment, arithmetic reasoning, comprehension of relations, logical selection, analogies, and classification. Norms are provided for Grades 7-12, college students, administrative and executive employees, physicians, lawyers, and other professionals. Examiner required. Suitable for group use.

Timed: 40 minutes

Scoring: Hand key

Cost: Specimen set $4.00; 25 tests $13.75

Publisher: Psychometric Affiliates

NATIONAL ACHIEVEMENT TESTS FOR ELEMENTARY SCHOOLS: ARITHMETIC AND MATHEMATICS—ALGEBRA TEST FOR ENGINEERING AND SCIENCE
A. B. Lonski and edited by John Kinsella

Adolescent, adult

Purpose: Assesses achievement in intermediate algebra. Used for screening students planning to register in an engineering college or technical school.

Description: Paper-pencil test of algebra knowledge. Items represent mistakes made in algebra by college freshmen who failed the subject in engineering and science courses. The test represents minimum essentials for entry into regular freshmen mathematics. Examiner required. Suitable for group use.

Untimed: Not available

Scoring: Hand key

Cost: Specimen set (test, key, manual) $4.00; 25 tests $17.50; 25 answer sheets $3.00

Publisher: Psychometric Affiliates

NATIONAL ACHIEVEMENT TESTS FOR ELEMENTARY SCHOOLS: ARITHMETIC AND MATHEMATICS—AMERICAN NUMERICAL TEST
John J. McCarty

Child

Purpose: Assesses arithmetic and numerical ability. Used for educational evaluation and vocational guidance.

Description: 60-item paper-pencil test arranged in sequences of the four basic arithmetical operations. Items require numerical alertness and adaptation. Two equivalent forms, A and B, are available. Examiner required. Suitable for group use.

Timed: 4 minutes

Scoring: Hand key

Cost: Specimen set (test, key, manual) $4.00; 25 tests $5.00

Publisher: Psychometric Affiliates

NATIONAL ACHIEVEMENT TESTS FOR ELEMENTARY SCHOOLS: ARITHMETIC AND MATHEMATICS—ARITHMETIC FUNDAMENTALS
Robert K. Speer and Samuel Smith

**Child, adolescent
Grades 3-8**

Purpose: Assesses students' achievement in basic arithmetic skills. Used to identify strengths and weaknesses as part of an educational evaluation.

Description: Multiple-item paper-pencil test covering three basic areas of arithmetic skills: speed and accuracy in computation; judgment, speed, and accuracy in comparing computations; and skill and understanding, without special reference to speed. Two equivalent forms, A and B, are available. Examiner required. Suitable for group use.

Timed: 45 minutes

Scoring: Hand key

Cost: Specimen set (test, key, manual) $4.00; 25 tests $5.00

Publisher: Psychometric Affiliates

NATIONAL ACHIEVEMENT TESTS FOR ELEMENTARY SCHOOLS: ARITHMETIC AND MATHEMATICS: FIRST YEAR-ALGEBRA TEST
Ray Webb and Julius H. Hlavaty

Adolescent

Purpose: Assesses achievement in first-year algebra. Used to identify strengths and weaknesses as part of an educational evaluation.

Description: Paper-pencil test measuring pupils' knowledge of first-year algebra. Two equivalent forms, A and B, are available. Examiner required. Suitable for group use.

Timed: 40 minutes

Scoring: Hand key

Cost: Specimen set (test, key, manual) $4.40; 25 tests $6.00; 25 answer sheets $4.50

Publisher: Psychometric Affiliates

NATIONAL ACHIEVEMENT TESTS FOR ELEMENTARY SCHOOLS: ARITHMETIC AND MATHEMATICS: FUNDAMENTALS AND REASONING (GRADES 3-6)
Robert K. Speer and Samuel Smith

Child   Grades 3-6

Purpose: Assesses students' achievement in arithmetic. Used to identify strengths and weaknesses as part of an educational evaluation.

Description: 5-part paper-pencil test of arithmetic reasoning and fundamentals, including computation, arithmetical judgments, problem reading, and problem solving. Special norms for students with high and low IQs are provided. Two equivalent forms, A and B, are available. Examiner required. Suitable for group use.

Timed: 30 minutes per part

Scoring: Hand key

Cost: Specimen set (test, key, manual) $4.00; 25 tests $5.00

Publisher: Psychometric Affiliates

NATIONAL ACHIEVEMENT TESTS FOR ELEMENTARY SCHOOLS: ARITHMETIC AND MATHEMATICS: FUNDAMENTALS AND REASONING (GRADES 6-8)
Robert K. Speer and Samuel Smith

Adolescent   Grades 6-8

Purpose: Assesses students' achievement in arithmetic. Used to identify strengths and weaknesses as part of an educational evaluation.

Description: 5-part paper-pencil test of arithmetic reasoning and fundamentals, including fundamentals, number comparisons, mathematical judgments, problem reading, and problem solving. Special norms for students with high and low IQs are provided. Two equivalent forms, A and B, are available. Examiner required. Suitable for group use.

Timed: 30 minutes per part

Scoring: Hand key

Cost: Specimen set (test, key, manual) $4.00; 25 tests $5.00

Publisher: Psychometric Affiliates

NATIONAL ACHIEVEMENT TESTS FOR ELEMENTARY SCHOOLS: ARITHMETIC AND MATHEMATICS—GENERAL MATH
Stanley J. Lejeune

Child   Grades 4-6

Purpose: Assesses students' achievement in general mathematics. Used to identify strengths and weaknesses as part of an educational evaluation.

Description: Multiple-item paper-pencil power test of student comprehension of 11 major topics in general mathematics: the numeration system; addition, subtraction, multiplication, and division; common fractions; decimal fractions and percentages; measurements; geometry; solving written problems; graphs and scale drawings; set terminology; mathematical structure; and money. Two equivalent forms, A and B, are available. Examiner required. Suitable for group use.

Untimed: Approximately 2-3 class periods

Scoring: Hand key

Cost: Specimen set (test, key, manual) $5.00; 25 tests $9.00; 25 answer sheets $3.50

Publisher: Psychometric Affiliates

NATIONAL ACHIEVEMENT TESTS FOR ELEMENTARY SCHOOLS: ARITHMETIC AND MATHEMATICS—GENERAL MATHEMATICS
Harry Eisner

Adolescent   Grades 7-9

Purpose: Assesses students' achievement in general mathematics. Used to identify strengths and weaknesses as part of an educational evaluation.

Description: Multiple-item paper-pencil test of student's knowledge of essential concepts, skills, and insights that should be developed in junior high-school mathematics. The abilities measured are arithmetic, algebraic, and geometric concepts; applications; problem analysis; and reasoning. Two equivalent forms, A and B, are available. Examiner required. Suitable for group use.

Timed: Section 1 10 minutes; Section 2 15 minutes; Section 3 27 minutes

Scoring: Hand key

Cost: Specimen set (test, key, manual) $4.00; 25 tests $9.00

Publisher: Psychometric Affiliates

NATIONAL ACHIEVEMENT TESTS FOR ELEMENTARY SCHOOLS: ARITHMETIC AND MATHEMATICS—PLANE GEOMETRY, SOLID GEOMETRY, AND PLANE TRIGONOMETRY TESTS
Ray Webb and Julius H. Hlavaty

Adolescent

Purpose: Assesses achievement in geometry and trigonometry. Used to identify strengths and weaknesses as part of an educational evaluation.

Description: Three paper-pencil tests measuring essential concepts, skills, and insight in three content areas: plane geometry, solid geometry, and plane trigonometry. Two equivalent forms, A and B, are available. Examiner required. Suitable for group use.

Timed: 40 minutes

Scoring: Hand key

Cost: Specimen set (test, key, manual) $4.00; 25 tests $8.75; 25 answer sheets $3.50

Publisher: Psychometric Affiliates

NATIONAL ACHIEVEMENT TESTS: ENGLISH, READING, LITERATURE, AND VOCABULARY TESTS—AMERICAN LITERACY TEST
John J. McCarty

Adult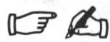

Purpose: Assesses literacy in adults. Used for detecting the functionally illiterate.

Description: 50-item paper-pencil test measuring vocabulary or depth of literacy. Items require knowledge of approximate synonyms. The test discriminates degrees of literacy from the illiterate to the highly sophisticated. Examiner required. Suitable for group use.

Timed: 4 minutes

Scoring: Hand key

Cost: Specimen set (test, manual, key) $4.00; 25 scales $5.00

Publisher: Psychometric Affiliates

NATIONAL ACHIEVEMENT TESTS: ENGLISH, READING, LITERATURE, AND VOCABULARY TESTS—COLLEGE ENGLISH FOR HIGH SCHOOL AND COLLEGE
A.C. Jordon

Adolescent, adult Grades 10 and above

Purpose: Assesses English achievement of high-school and college students. Used for evaluating prospective college students.

Description: Multiple-item paper-pencil test measuring a range of English skills, including the ability to use correct capitalization, punctuate correctly, use proper syntax, determine subject/verb agreement, vary sentence structure, use modifiers correctly, and apply language

principles. Two equivalent forms, A and B, are available. Examiner required. Suitable for group use.

Timed: 45 minutes

Scoring: Hand key

Cost: Specimen set (test, manual, key) $4.00; 25 tests $8.75

Publisher: Psychometric Affiliates

NATIONAL ACHIEVEMENT TESTS: ENGLISH, READING, LITERATURE, AND VOCABULARY TESTS—ENGLISH
Robert K. Speer and Samuel Smith

Adolescent   Grades 7-12

Purpose: Assesses students' achievement in English. Used to identify students' strengths and weaknesses as part of an educational evaluation.

Description: Multiple-item paper-pencil test of knowledge and skill in English, including word usage, punctuation, vocabulary, the ability to select correct, sensible sentences, the ability to identify or express ideas, and the ability to identify or express feelings. The test emphasizes the power of self-expression and judgment. Two equivalent forms, A and B, are available. Examiner required. Suitable for group use.

Timed: 40 minutes

Scoring: Hand key

Cost: Specimen set (test, manual, key) $4.00; 25 tests $26.00

Publisher: Psychometric Affiliates

NATIONAL ACHIEVEMENT TESTS: ENGLISH, READING, LITERATURE, AND VOCABULARY TESTS—READING
Robert K. Speer and Samuel Smith

Adolescent, adult Grades 7 and above

Purpose: Assesses students' reading achievement. Used to identify student strengths and weaknesses as part of an educational evaluation.

Description: Multiple-item paper-pencil test of reading skills important for achievement, including vocabulary, word discrimination, sentence meaning, noting details, and interpreting paragraphs. Two equivalent forms, A and B, are available. Examiner required. Suitable for group use.

Timed: 40 minutes

Scoring: Hand key

Cost: Specimen set (test, manual, key) $5.00; 25 tests $13.75

Publisher: Psychometric Affiliates

NATIONAL ACHIEVEMENT TESTS: ENGLISH, READING, LITERATURE, AND VOCABULARY TESTS—VOCABULARY (GRADES 3-8)
Robert K. Speer and Samuel Smith

Child, adolescent Grades 3-8

Purpose: Assesses the vocabulary knowledge of children. Used as part of an educational evaluation.

Description: Multiple-item paper-pencil test of vocabulary knowledge. For each item, the base word is printed in capital letters in a meaningful sentence. The pupil selects a synonym for the base word from a group of words. The base words are more difficult than the synonyms. Two equivalent forms, A and B, are available. Examiner required. Suitable for group use.

Timed: 15 minutes

Scoring: Hand key

Cost: Specimen set (test, manual, key) $4.00; 25 tests $3.50

Publisher: Psychometric Affiliates

NATIONAL ACHIEVEMENT TESTS: ENGLISH, READING, LITERATURE, AND VOCABULARY TESTS—VOCABULARY (GRADES 7-COLLEGE)
Robert K. Speer and Samuel Smith

Adolescent Grades 7 and above

Purpose: Assesses students' vocabulary knowledge. Used as part of an educational evaluation.

Description: Multiple-item paper-pencil test measuring knowledge and judgment related to word meaning and word discrimination. Two equivalent forms, A and B, are available. Examiner required. Suitable for group use.

Timed: 15 minutes

Scoring: Hand key

Cost: Specimen set (test, manual, key) $4.00; 25 tests $3.50

Publisher: Psychometric Affiliates

NATIONAL EDUCATIONAL DEVELOPMENT TEST (NEDT)
Science Research Associates and T.G. Thurstone

Adolescent Grades 9-10

Purpose: Assesses students' strengths and weaknesses in English, math, social studies, reading, natural sciences, and educational ability. Predicts success on and serves as a practice instrument for college admissions exams.

Description: 209-item paper-pencil test measuring the ability to apply rules and principles of grammar and general English usage, understand mathematical concepts and apply principles in solving quantitative problems, comprehend reading selections, and apply critical reading skills. The test is used only in schools that are designated test centers. Examiner required. Suitable for group use.

Timed: 2 hours, 30 minutes

Scoring: Computer scored

Cost: Test materials and scoring service per student $3.35

Publisher: Science Research Associates, Inc.

THE NATIONAL TESTS OF BASIC SKILLS

PreK-college

Purpose: Measures basic skills taught by schools. Used to test achievement at individual, classroom, school, and district levels.

Description: Series of paper-pencil tests spanning 14 levels from preschool to college. Reading, language, mathematics, social studies, and science skills are measured by up to 11 subscales, depending on the level being tested. Score reporting includes both numerical and narrative material. Evaluations of student ability and attitudes may be obtained by using companion instruments, such as the Developing Cognitive Abilities Test and the School Attitude Measure. Examiner required. Suitable for group use.

Timed: 109-261 minutes depending on level

Scoring: All levels hand key; Levels A-D machine scoring available

Cost: Examination kit (all levels) $45.00

Publisher: American Testronics

THE NATIONAL TESTS OF BASIC SKILLS: LEVEL A COMPLETE BATTERY

Child   Grades K-1

Purpose: Measures instructional objectives schools use to teach basic academic skills. Used to assess achievement at individual, classroom, school, and district levels.

Description: Paper-pencil test of cognitive level in three content areas: prereading, language, and mathematics. The prereading skills measured are sound recognition, letter recognition, alphabet knowledge, and word matching. Language skills are assessed by a listening comprehension test. The mathematics skills assessed include simple counting, recognition of numbers and symbols, addition, subtraction, and dealing with money and time. Examiner required. Suitable for group use.

Timed: 109 minutes

Scoring: Hand key; may be machine scored

Cost: 10 test booklets, examiner's manual $13.75; scoring and reporting services extra

Publisher: American Testronics

THE NATIONAL TESTS OF BASIC SKILLS: LEVEL B COMPLETE BATTERY

Child   Grades K.6-1.5

Purpose: Measures instructional objectives schools use to teach basic academic skills. Used to assess achievement at individual, classroom, school, and district levels.

Description: Paper-pencil test of student growth and development in three areas: reading, language, and mathematics. The three reading skills measured at this level are word attack, vocabulary, and reading comprehension. Language skills include listening comprehension and language expression. Mathematics exercises evaluate skills in simple counting, recognition of numbers and symbols, addition, subtraction, and concepts of dealing with money and time. A mathematics computation subtest is also added at this level. Examiner required. Suitable for group use.

Untimed: Examiner paced

Scoring: Hand key; may be machine scored

Cost: 10 test booklets, examiner's manual $13.75; scoring and reporting services extra

Publisher: American Testronics

THE NATIONAL TESTS OF BASIC SKILLS: LEVEL C COMPLETE BATTERY

Child   Grades 1.0-1.9

Purpose: Measures instructional objectives schools use to teach basic academic skills. Used to assess achievement at individual, classroom, school, and district levels.

Description: Paper-pencil test of student growth and development in five areas: reading, language, mathematics, social studies, and science. Three reading skills measured at this level are word attack, vocabulary, and reading comprehension. Language skills include language expression. Mathematics exercises evaluate skills in simple counting, recognition of numbers and symbols, addition, subtraction, and dealing with money and time. A mathematics computation subtest also is added at this level. Social studies questions reflect knowledge of history, political science, geography, economics, and sociology. Science test questions measure knowledge of earth and space science, life science, physical science, and the scientific method. Examiner required. Suitable for group use.

Untimed: Examiner paced

Scoring: Hand key; may be machine scored

Cost: 10 test booklets, examiner's manual $13.75; scoring and reporting services extra

Publisher: American Testronics

THE NATIONAL TESTS OF BASIC SKILLS: LEVEL D COMPLETE BATTERY

Child   Grades 1.6-2.9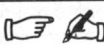

Purpose: Measures instructional objectives schools use to teach basic academic skills. Used to assess achievement at individual, classroom, school, and district levels.

Description: Paper-pencil test of student growth and development in five areas: reading, language, mathematics, social studies, and science. Three reading skills measured at this level are word attack, vocabulary, and reading comprehension. Language skills include language expression, spelling, and language mechanics. Mathematics skills at this level are measured through computation and concepts/applications subtests. Social studies questions reflect knowledge of history, political science, geography, economics, and sociology. Science test questions measure knowledge of earth and space science, life science, physical science, and the scientific method. Evaluations of student ability may be obtained by using the Developing Cognitive Abilities Test. Examiner required. Suitable for group use.

Timed: 193 minutes

Scoring: Hand key; may be machine scored

Cost: 10 test booklets, examiner's manual $13.75; scoring and reporting services extra

Publisher: American Testronics

THE NATIONAL TESTS OF BASIC SKILLS: LEVEL E COMPLETE BATTERY

Child   Grades 2.6-3.9

Purpose: Measures instructional objectives schools use to teach basic academic skills. Used to assess achievement at individual, classroom, school, and district levels.

Description: Paper-pencil test of student growth and development in five areas: reading, language, mathematics, social studies, and science. Reading skills measured at this level are vocabulary and reading comprehension. Language skills include language expression, spelling, language mechanics, and references. Mathematics skills at this level are measured through computation, concepts, and applications subtests. Social studies questions reflect knowledge of history, political science, geography, economics, and sociology. Science test questions measure knowledge of earth and space science, life science, physical science, and the scientific method. Evaluations of student ability may be obtained by using the Developing Cognitive Abilities Test. Examiner required. Suitable for group use.

Timed: 228 minutes

Scoring: Hand key; may be machine scored

Cost: 10 test booklets, examiner's manual $11.95; scoring and reporting services extra

Publisher: American Testronics

THE NATIONAL TESTS OF BASIC SKILLS: LEVEL F COMPLETE BATTERY

Child   Grades 3.6-4.9

Purpose: Measures instructional objectives schools use to teach basic academic skills. Used to assess achievement at individual, classroom, school, and district levels.

Description: Paper-pencil test of student growth and development in five areas: reading, language, mathematics, social studies, and science. Reading skills measured at this level are vocabulary and reading comprehension. Language skills include language expression, spelling, language mechanics, and references. Mathematics skills are measured through computation, concepts, and applications subtests. Social studies questions reflect knowledge of history, political science, geography, economics, and sociology. Science test questions measure knowledge of earth and space science, life science, physical science, and the scientific method. Evaluations of student ability and attitude may be obtained by using the Developing Cognitive Abilities Test and the School Attitude Measure. Examiner required. Suitable for group use.

Timed: 261 minutes

Scoring: Hand key; may be machine scored

Cost: 10 test booklets, examiner's manual $11.95; scoring and reporting services extra

Publisher: American Testronics

THE NATIONAL TESTS OF BASIC SKILLS: LEVEL G COMPLETE BATTERY

Child   Grades 4.6-5.9

Purpose: Measures instructional objectives schools use to teach basic academic skills. Used to assess achievement at individual, classroom, school, and district levels.

Description: Paper-pencil test of student growth and development in five areas: reading, language, mathematics, social studies, and science. Reading skills measured at this level are vocabulary and reading comprehension. Language skills include language expression, spelling, language mechanics, and references. Mathematics skills are measured through computation, concepts, and applications subtests. Social studies questions reflect knowledge of history, political science, geography, economics, and sociology. Sci-

ence test questions measure knowledge of earth and space science, life science, physical science, and the scientific method. Evaluations of student ability may be obtained by using the Developing Cognitive Abilities Test and the School Attitude Measure. Examiner required. Suitable for group use.

Timed: 261 minutes

Scoring: Hand key; may be machine scored

Cost: 10 test booklets, examiner's manual $11.95; scoring and reporting services extra

Publisher: American Testronics

THE NATIONAL TESTS OF BASIC SKILLS: LEVEL H COMPLETE BATTERY

Child, adolescent
Grades 5.6-6.9

Purpose: Measures instructional objectives schools use to teach basic academic skills. Used to assess achievement at individual, classroom, school, and district levels.

Description: Paper-pencil test of student growth and development in five areas: reading, language, mathematics, social studies, and science. Reading skills measured at this level are vocabulary and reading comprehension. Language skills include language expression, spelling, language mechanics, and references. Mathematics skills are measured through computation, concepts, and applications subtests. Social studies questions reflect knowledge of history, political science, geography, economics, and sociology. Science test questions measure knowledge of earth and space science, life science, physical science, and the scientific method. Evaluations of student ability may be obtained by using the Developing Cognitive Abilities Test and the School Attitude Measure. Examiner required. Suitable for group use.

Timed: 261 minutes

Scoring: Hand key; may be machine scored

Cost: 10 test booklets, examiner's manual $11.95; scoring and reporting services extra

Publisher: American Testronics

THE NATIONAL TESTS OF BASIC SKILLS: LEVEL I COMPLETE BATTERY

Child, adolescent
Grades 6.6-7.9

Purpose: Measures instructional objectives schools use to teach basic academic skills. Used to assess achievement at individual, classroom, school, and district levels.

Description: Paper-pencil test of student growth and development in five areas: reading, language, mathematics, social studies, and science. Reading skills measured at this level are vocabulary and reading comprehension. Language skills include language expression, spelling, language mechanics, and references. Mathematics skills are measured through computation, concepts, and applications subtests. Social studies questions reflect knowledge of history, political science, geography, economics, and sociology. Science test questions measure knowledge of earth and space science, life science, physical science, and the scientific method. Evaluations of student ability may be obtained by using the Developing Cognitive Abilities Test and the School Attitude Measure. Examiner required. Suitable for group use.

Timed: 261 minutes

Scoring: Hand key; may be machine scored

Cost: 10 test booklets, examiner's manual $11.95; scoring and reporting services extra

Publisher: American Testronics

THE NATIONAL TESTS OF BASIC SKILLS: LEVEL J COMPLETE BATTERY

Adolescent
Grades 7.6-8.9

Purpose: Measures instructional objectives schools use to teach basic academic

skills. Used to assess achievement at individual, classroom, school, and district levels.

Description: Paper-pencil test of student growth and development in five areas: reading, language, mathematics, social studies, and science. Reading skills measured at this level are vocabulary and reading comprehension. Language skills include language expression, spelling, language mechanics, and references. Mathematics skills are measured through computation, concepts, and applications subtests. Social studies questions reflect knowledge of history, political science, geography, economics, and sociology. Science test questions measure knowledge of earth and space science, life science, physical science, and the scientific method. Evaluations of student ability may be obtained by using the Developing Cognitive Abilities Test and the School Attitude Measure. Examiner required. Suitable for group use.

Timed: 261 minutes

Scoring: Hand key; may be machine scored

Cost: 10 test booklets, examiner's manual $11.95; scoring and reporting services extra

Publisher: American Testronics

THE NATIONAL TESTS OF BASIC SKILLS: LEVEL K COMPLETE BATTERY

Adolescent
Grades 8.6-10.9

Purpose: Measures instructional objectives schools use to teach basic academic skills. Used to assess achievement at individual, classroom, school, and district levels.

Description: Paper-pencil test of student growth and development in five areas: reading, language, mathematics, social studies, and science. Reading skills measured at this level are vocabulary and reading comprehension. Language skills include language expression, spelling, language mechanics, and written expression. Mathematics skills are measured through computation, concepts, and applications subtests. Social studies questions reflect knowledge of history, political science, geography, economics, and sociology. Science test questions measure knowledge of earth and space science, life science, physical science, and the scientific method. Evaluations of student ability may be obtained by using the Developing Cognitive Abilities Test and the School Attitude Measure. Examiner required. Suitable for group use.

Timed: 177 minutes

Scoring: Hand key; may be machine scored

Cost: 10 test booklets, examiner's manual $11.95; scoring and reporting services extra

Publisher: American Testronics

THE NATIONAL TESTS OF BASIC SKILLS: LEVEL L COMPLETE BATTERY

Adolescent
Grades 10.6-12.9

Purpose: Measures instructional objectives schools use to teach basic academic skills. Used to assess achievement at individual, classroom, school, and district levels.

Description: Paper-pencil test of student growth and development in five areas: reading, language, mathematics, social studies, and science. Reading skills measured at this level are vocabulary and reading comprehension. Language skills include language expression, spelling, language mechanics, and written expression. Mathematics skills are measured through computation, concepts, and applications subtests. Social studies questions reflect knowledge of history, political science, geography, economics, and sociology. Science test questions measure knowledge of earth and space science, life science, physical science, and the scientific method. Evaluations of student ability may be obtained by using the Developing Cognitive Abilities Test and the School Attitude Measure. Examiner required. Suitable for group use.

Timed: 177 minutes

Scoring: Hand key; may be machine scored

Cost: 10 test booklets, examiner's manual $11.95; scoring and reporting services extra

Publisher: American Testronics

THE NATIONAL TESTS OF BASIC SKILLS: LEVEL M COMPLETE BATTERY

Adult
Grades 11.6-college

Purpose: Measures instructional objectives schools use to teach basic academic skills. Used to assess achievement at individual, classroom, school, and district levels.

Description: Paper-pencil test of student growth and development in five areas: reading, language, mathematics, social studies, and science. Reading skills measured at this level are vocabulary and reading comprehension. Language skills include language expression, spelling, language mechanics, and written expression. Mathematics skills are measured through computation, concepts, and applications subtests. Social studies questions reflect knowledge of history, political science, geography, economics, and sociology. Science test questions measure knowledge of earth and space science, life science, physical science, and the scientific method. Examiner required. Suitable for group use.

Timed: 177 minutes

Scoring: Hand key; may be machine scored

Cost: 10 test booklets, examiner's manual $11.95; scoring and reporting services extra

Publisher: American Testronics

THE NATIONAL TESTS OF BASIC SKILLS: LEVEL P COMPLETE BATTERY

Child   Grades PreK-K.5

Purpose: Assesses basic preschool skills. Used to measure the cognitive growth of preschool children.

Description: Paper-pencil test of cognitive level in three content areas: prereading, language, and developmental mathematics. Prereading skills measured are visual matching, auditory attention, auditory picture closure, and auditory picture rhymes. Language skills are assessed by combining information, auditory comprehension, silly pictures, visual oddities, and generalizations. Developmental mathematics skills are assessed by requiring the child to choose one of two boxes in which the numbers, concepts, or geometric figures are most alike. Examiner required. Suitable for group use.

Untimed: Examiner paced

Scoring: Hand key

Cost: 10 test booklets, examiner's manual $11.95

Publisher: American Testronics

NEW JERSEY TEST OF REASONING SKILLS
Virginia Shipman

Child, adolescent

Purpose: Measures thinking and language-related reasoning skills.

Description: 50-item paper-pencil multiple-choice test of reasoning ability in 22 skill areas, including converting statements, analogical reasoning, detecting underlying assumptions, detecting ambiguities, distinguishing differences of kind and degree, recognizing dubious authority, contradicting statement, and discerning causal relationships. Examiner/self-administered. Suitable for group use.

Untimed: Varies

Scoring: Computer scored

Cost: Contact publisher

Publisher: Institute for the Advancement of Philosophy for Children

NLN ACHIEVEMENT TESTS FOR PRACTICAL NURSING

Practical nursing students

Purpose: Measures individual student achievement in practical/vocational nursing programs and enables faculty to evaluate specific course or program objectives in terms of nationally accepted objectives in nursing and compare the scores of students in a nursing program with those of students throughout the country.

Description: 7 paper-pencil multiple-choice tests consisting of 80-170 questions each. The following tests are available: Comprehensive Nursing Achievement Test for Practical Nursing Students, Medical-Surgical Nursing for Practical Nursing Students, Maternity Nursing for Practical Nursing Students, Mental Health Concepts for Practical Nursing Students, Nursing of Children for Practical Nursing Students, Pharmacology for Practical Nursing Students, and Three Units of Content (TUC) for Practical Nursing Students. Test items have been developed in cooperation with faculty members throughout the United States, reflecting the objectives and subject-matter content of practical/vocational nursing programs from all geographic areas. All test papers must be returned to NLN Test Service for scoring. Reports on test results are returned to the nursing program within 10 working days after NLN receives the answer sheets. Reports include raw scores and percentiles, item descriptors, a list of omitted or incorrectly answered items for each student, and an additional group analysis when more than 10 students are tested as a group. NLN encourages faculty members to review the tests before ordering them to insure that appropriate subject-matter content areas have been covered. NLN achievement tests may be used in the United States, its territories, and Canada by state- or province-approved programs preparing students for nursing practice; by hospitals and colleges that are approved to provide instruction to students from such programs; and by nurse licensing authorities in the United States and Canada or their agents. Requests for use by any other program are evaluated individually. The tests are available in English only. Examiner required. Suitable for group use.

Untimed: 1½-3 hours per test

Scoring: Computer scored

Cost: Test service (test booklets, answer sheets, directions for administration, scoring service) $3.00-$8.00 per student per test

Publisher: National League for Nursing

NLN ACHIEVEMENT TESTS FOR PRACTICAL NURSING: COMPREHENSIVE NURSING ACHIEVEMENT TEST FOR PRACTICAL NURSING STUDENTS (FORM 3513)

Practical nursing students

Purpose: Measures the full range of knowledge needed by graduating students in practical/vocational nursing programs for beginning practice. Assesses readiness for the nurse licensure examination.

Description: Approximately 170-item paper-pencil multiple-choice test measuring the full range of material presented in programs preparing students for practical nursing. Questions pertain to case situations representative of conditions commonly encountered by the beginning practitioner in health-care settings, including medical-surgical nursing, nursing during childbearing, and nursing of children. The questions call for the application of knowledge in the assessment of client status, planning, intervention in basic nursing situations, evaluating, recording, and reporting. Questions related to growth and development, mental health concepts, basic communication techniques, medication administration and effects, as well as nutrition are integrated. A total score, along with subscores in broad clinical areas, are reported in the form of individual diagnostic profiles. Two copies are provided: one for distribution to students and one for faculty analysis. Norms are provided for practical nursing students. The test should be administered at the end of the program to assess readiness for the nurse licensure examination and for practice. The test is available for faculty review. Examiner required. Suitable for group use.

Untimed: 3 hours

Scoring: Computer scored

Cost: Test service (test booklets, answer sheets, directions for administration, scoring service) $8.00 per student

Publisher: National League for Nursing

NLN ACHIEVEMENT TESTS FOR PRACTICAL NURSING: MATERNITY NURSING FOR PRACTICAL NURSING STUDENTS (FORM 1182)

Practical nursing students

Purpose: Measures the individual achievement of practical/vocational nursing students in maternity nursing and attainment of nationally accepted objectives in nursing.

Description: Approximately 110-item paper-pencil multiple-choice test measuring student knowledge of the objectives of maternity nursing related to nursing measures, including medications, nutrition, and communication. A total score and three subscores (antepartum, intrapartum and postpartum, and neonate) are provided based on a correction-for-guessing formula. Norms are reported for practical nursing students. The test should be administered after completion of the course in maternity nursing. The test is available for faculty review. Examiner required. Suitable for group use.

Untimed: 2 hours

Scoring: Computer scored

Cost: Test service (test booklets, answer sheets, directions for administration, scoring service) $3.00 per student

Publisher: National League for Nursing

NLN ACHIEVEMENT TESTS FOR PRACTICAL NURSING: MEDICAL-SURGICAL NURSING FOR PRACTICAL NURSING STUDENTS (FORM 1982)

Practical nursing students

Purpose: Measures individual achievement of practical/vocational nursing students in medical-surgical nursing and attainment of nationally accepted objectives in nursing.

Description: Approximately 120-item paper-pencil multiple-choice test measuring knowledge and application of the facts and principles related to the care of medical and surgical patients. Questions refer to patient situations and represent a variety of ages and common conditions. Items relating to the practical nurse's role in drug and diet therapy are integrated. A total score and two subscores (medical nursing and surgical nursing) are reported based on a correction-for-guessing formula. Norms are reported for practical nursing students. The test should be administered late in the program. The test is available for faculty review. Examiner required. Suitable for group use.

Untimed: 2 hours

Scoring: Computer scored

Cost: Test service (test booklets, answer sheets, directions for administration, scoring service) $3.00 per student

Publisher: National League for Nursing

NLN ACHIEVEMENT TESTS FOR PRACTICAL NURSING: MENTAL HEALTH CONCEPTS FOR PRACTICAL NURSING STUDENTS (FORM 4415)

Practical nursing students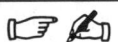

Purpose: Measures practical nursing students' understanding of the principles of mental health and psychiatric nursing and their application to the general practice of practical/vocational nursing.

Description: 102-item paper-pencil test focusing on the mental health and psychiatric nursing concepts applicable to the basic care of persons with physical impairment and mental illness. The test also covers the psychological aspects of children. A total score and two subscores (behaviors/concepts and nursing interventions) are reported. Scores are based on the number of questions answered correctly. Norms for practical nursing students are provided. The test is available for faculty review. This edition of the test replaces Form 0481. Examiner required. Suitable for group use.

Untimed: 2 hours

Scoring: Computer scored

Cost: Test service (test booklets, answer sheets, directions for administration, scoring service) $3.50 per student

Publisher: National League for Nursing

NLN ACHIEVEMENT TESTS FOR PRACTICAL NURSING: NURSING OF CHILDREN FOR PRACTICAL NURSING STUDENTS (FORM 4113)

Practical nursing students

Purpose: Measures individual achievement of practical/vocational nursing students in nursing care of children and attainment of nationally accepted objectives in nursing.

Description: 120-item paper-pencil multiple-choice test measuring achievement of nine objectives arranged in three subscores related to the nursing of children. The questions in Subscore A (normal growth and development) measure knowledge of growth and development in children and nursing measures based on age-related needs, including preventive measures. Items in Subscore B (pathophysiologies and treatments) measure knowledge and recognition of various pathophysiological processes and treatments, including nutrition and expected outcomes. Questions in Subscore C (nursing measures) assess knowledge of nursing measures commonly used in the care of children who are ill, including drug administration and communication skills. Questions about teaching and providing emotional support to family members are included also. A total score is provided in addition to the three subscores. All scores are based on the number of questions answered correctly. Norms are reported for practical nursing students. The test should be administered to students who have completed their major learning experience in the content area of the test. The test is available for faculty review. Examiner required. Suitable for group use.

Untimed: 2 hours

Scoring: Computer scored

Cost: Test service (test booklets, answer sheets, directions for administration, scoring service) $3.00 per student

Publisher: National League for Nursing

NLN ACHIEVEMENT TESTS FOR PRACTICAL NURSING: PHARMACOLOGY FOR PRACTICAL NURSES (FORM 1782)

Practical nursing students

Purpose: Measures individual achievement of practical/vocational nursing students in pharmacology and attainment of nationally accepted objectives in nursing.

Description: Approximately 100-item paper-pencil multiple-choice test measuring general knowledge of pharmacology, chiefly through the interpretation of orders and observations necessary for detecting the effects of common drugs and assessing the basic principles of drug administration. In addition to a total score, two subscores are provided: principles of drug administration, calculations, and other implications for nursing; and effects, therapeutic and other. All scores are based on a correction-for-guessing formula. Norms are reported for practical nursing students. The test should be administered when the program is completed. The test is available for faculty review. Examiner required. Suitable for group use.

Untimed: 1½ hours

Scoring: Computer scored

Cost: Test service (test booklets, answer sheets, directions for administration, scoring service) $3.00 per student

Publisher: National League for Nursing

NLN ACHIEVEMENT TESTS FOR PRACTICAL NURSING: THREE UNITS OF CONTENT (TUC) (FORM 1482)

Practical nursing students

Purpose: Measures individual achievement of practical/vocational nursing students in body structure and function, nursing procedures, and normal nutrition and attainment of nationally accepted objectives in nursing.

Description: Approximately 110-item paper-pencil multiple-choice test measuring achievement in three basic areas of instruction: body structure and function, nursing procedures, and normal nutrition. A total score and scores for each of the three areas are provided based on a correction-for-guessing formula. Norms are reported for practical nursing students. The test should be administered early in the program, after completion of the areas covered by the test. The test is available for faculty review. Examiner required. Suitable for group use.

Untimed: 2 hours

Scoring: Computer scored

Cost: Test service (test booklets, answer sheets, directions for administration, scoring service) $3.50 per student

Publisher: National League for Nursing

NLN ACHIEVEMENT TESTS FOR REGISTERED NURSING

Registered nursing students

Purpose: Appraises individual achievement in all associate degree, baccalaureate, and diploma RN programs. Enables faculty to evaluate specific course or program objectives in terms of nationally accepted objectives in nursing and compare the scores of students in a nursing program with those of students throughout the country.

Description: Paper-pencil multiple-choice tests consisting of approximately 80-215 questions. The following tests are available: Anatomy and Physiology, Basics in Nursing I, Basics in Nursing II, Basics in Nursing III, Chemistry, Comprehensive Nursing Achievement, Diet Therapy and Applied Nutrition, Fundamentals of Drug Therapy, Maternity and Child Nursing, Microbiology, Natural Sciences in Nursing, Normal Nutrition, Nursing Care of Adults with Pathophysiological Disturbances I, Nursing Care of Adults with Pathophysiological Disturbances II, Nursing Care of Adults in Special Care Units, Nursing of Children, Nursing the Childbearing Family, Pharmacology in Clinical Nursing, and Psychiatric Nursing. Test items have been developed in cooperation with faculty members throughout the United States, reflecting the objectives and subject-matter emphases of teachers from all geographic areas. Some achievement tests are designed to be administered at the end of a course; others are administered after the completion of major learning experiences that may include more than one course or toward the end of the program. The timing of administration depends on the individual school's curriculum organization. All test papers must be returned to NLN Test Service for scoring. Reports on test results are returned to the program within 10 working days after NLN receives the answer sheets. Reports include raw scores and percentiles, item descriptors, a list of omitted or incorrectly answered items for each student, and an additional group analysis when more than 10 students are tested as a group. NLN encourages faculty members to review the tests before ordering to insure that appropriate subject-matter content areas have been covered.

NLN achievement tests may be used in the United States, its territories, and Canada by state- or province-approved programs preparing students for nursing practice; by hospitals and colleges approved to provide instruction to students from such programs; and by nurse licensing authorities in the United States and Canada or their agents. Requests for use by any other program are evaluated individually. The tests are available in English only. Examiner required. Suitable for group use.

Untimed: 1½-3½ hours per test

Scoring: Computer scored

Cost: Test service (test booklets, answer sheets, directions for administration, scoring of answer sheets, reporting of test results) $3.00-$8.00 per student per test

Publisher: National League for Nursing

NLN ACHIEVEMENT TESTS FOR REGISTERED NURSING: ANATOMY AND PHYSIOLOGY (FORM 1213)

Nursing students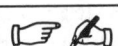

Purpose: Measures individual achievement of registered nursing students in anatomy and physiology and attainment

of nationally accepted objectives in nursing.

Description: Approximately 115-item paper-pencil multiple-choice test measuring knowledge of anatomy and physiology in the following subject-matter areas: cellular metabolism and integumentary system, musculoskeletal system, circulatory system (including lymphatics and fetal circulation), respiratory system, gastrointestinal system, endocrine system, reproductive system, nervous system, special senses, urinary system, and water, electrolyte, and acid-base regulation. A total score and two subscores (anatomy and physiology) are provided based on the number of questions answered correctly. Separate norms are reported for students in associate degree, baccalaureate, and diploma programs. The test is available for faculty review. Examiner required. Suitable for group use.

Untimed: 2 hours

Scoring: Computer scored

Cost: Test kit (test booklets, answer sheets, directions for administration, scoring service) $3.00 per student

Publisher: National League for Nursing

NLN ACHIEVEMENT TESTS FOR REGISTERED NURSING: BASICS IN NURSING I (FORM 0413)

Registered nursing students

Purpose: Measures individual achievement of registered nursing students in the basics of nursing care and attainment of nationally accepted objectives in nursing.

Description: Approximately 80-item paper-pencil multiple-choice test measuring basic knowledge related to fluid balance, medication administration, nursing procedures, and infection control. A total score, a fluid balance and medication administration subscore, and a nursing procedures and infection control subscore are provided based on a correction-for-guessing formula. Separate norms are reported for students in associate degree, baccalaureate, and diploma programs.

The test is available for faculty review. Examiner required. Suitable for group use.

Untimed: 1½ hours

Scoring: Computer scored

Cost: Test service (test booklets, answer sheets, directions for administration, scoring service) $3.00 per student

Publisher: National League for Nursing

NLN ACHIEVEMENT TESTS FOR REGISTERED NURSING: BASICS IN NURSING II (FORM 0423)

Registered nursing students

Purpose: Measures individual achievement of registered nursing students in the basics of nursing care and attainment of nationally accepted objectives in nursing.

Description: Approximately 80-item paper-pencil multiple-choice test measuring basic knowledge related to technical skills, scientific concepts, and assessment. A total score, a technical skills subscore, and an assessment and scientific concepts subscore are provided based on a correction-for-guessing formula. Separate norms are reported for students in associate degree, baccalaureate, and diploma programs. The test is available for faculty review. Examiner required. Suitable for group use.

Untimed: 1½ hours

Scoring: Computer scored

Cost: Test service (test booklets, answer sheets, directions for administration, scoring service) $3.00 per student

Publisher: National League for Nursing

NLN ACHIEVEMENT TESTS FOR REGISTERED NURSING: BASICS IN NURSING III (FORM 0433)

Registered nursing students

Purpose: Measures individual achievement of registered nursing students in the basics of nursing care and attainment of nationally accepted objectives in nursing.

Description: Approximately 70-item paper-pencil multiple-choice test measur-

ing basic knowledge related to the psychosocial aspects of nursing, ethical/legal situations, nutrition, and other items covering basic nursing. A total score, a psychosocial and legal/ethical subscore, and a nutrition and other fundamentals subscore are provided based on a correction-for-guessing formula. Separate norms are reported for students in associate degree, baccalaureate, and diploma programs. The test is available for faculty review. Examiner required. Suitable for group use.

Untimed: 1½ hours

Scoring: Computer scored

Cost: Test service (test booklets, answer sheets, directions for administration, scoring service) $3.00 per student

Publisher: National League for Nursing

NLN ACHIEVEMENT TESTS FOR REGISTERED NURSING: CHEMISTRY (FORM 1013)

Registered nursing students

Purpose: Measures individual achievement of students in registered nursing programs in the principles and concepts of chemistry and attainment of nationally accepted objectives in nursing.

Description: Approximately 120-item paper-pencil multiple-choice test measuring recognition of the concepts and principles of general chemistry that pertain to the health sciences, organic compounds and structures that form the basis for understanding physiological reactions, and concepts and principles of biochemistry as they relate to human functioning. A total score and three subscores (general chemistry, organic chemistry, and biochemistry) are provided based on the number of questions answered correctly. Separate norms are reported for students in associate degree, baccalaureate, and diploma programs. The test is available for faculty review. Examiner required. Suitable for group use.

Untimed: 2 hours

Scoring: Computer scored

Cost: Test service (test booklets, answer sheets, directions for administration, scoring service) $3.25 per student

Publisher: National League for Nursing

NLN ACHIEVEMENT TESTS FOR REGISTERED NURSING: DIET THERAPY AND NUTRITION (FORM 3313)

Registered nursing students

Purpose: Measures individual achievement of registered nursing students in diet therapy and applied nutrition and attainment of nationally accepted objectives in nursing.

Description: Approximately 120-item paper-pencil multiple-choice test measuring knowledge of the facts and principles of nutrition and the ability to apply that knowledge to situations involving patients who have specific nutritional problems. A total score, a facts and principles subscore, and an application of knowledge subscore are provided based on the number of questions answered correctly. Separate norms are reported for students in associate degree, baccalaureate, and diploma programs. The test should be administered at the end of the students' program and is not a substitute for the NLN achievement test in normal nutrition. The sample test is available for faculty review. Examiner required. Suitable for group use.

Untimed: 2 hours

Scoring: Computer scored

Cost: Test service (test booklets, answer sheets, directions for administration, scoring service) $3.00 per student

Publisher: National League for Nursing

NLN ACHIEVEMENT TESTS FOR REGISTERED NURSING: FUNDAMENTALS OF DRUG THERAPY (FORM 1414)

Registered nursing students

Purpose: Measures individual achievement of registered nursing students in

drug therapy and attainment of nationally recognized objectives in nursing.

Description: Approximately 110-item paper-pencil multiple-choice test measuring knowledge of the general principles of drug administration, calculations, and drug effects. A total score and three subscores (calculations, principles of drug administration, and drug effects) are reported based on the number of questions answered correctly. Separate norms are reported for associate degree, baccalaureate, and diploma programs. The test is intended for use relatively early in the program (knowledge of clinical nursing is not required) and is not a substitute for the NLN achievement test in pharmacology in clinical nursing. The test is available for faculty review. Examiner required. Suitable for group use.

Untimed: 2 hours

Scoring: Computer scored

Cost: Test service (test booklets, answer sheets, directions for administration, scoring service) $3.00 per student

Publisher: National League for Nursing

NLN ACHIEVEMENT TESTS FOR REGISTERED NURSING: MATERNITY AND CHILD NURSING (FORM 0513)

Registered nursing students

Purpose: Measures individual achievement of registered nursing students in maternal and child nursing and attainment of nationally recognized objectives in nursing.

Description: Approximately 125-item paper-pencil multiple-choice test measuring understanding of the facts and principles of maternal and child nursing and the ability to apply them. Test items include case situations. Some cases are structured to follow a family over a period of time and require the student to apply principles from both maternal and child nursing to a particular situation. A total score and two subscores (nursing care during the pregnancy cycle and nursing care of children) are provided based on a correction-for-guessing formula. Separate norms are reported for students in associate degree, baccalaureate, and diploma programs. The test should be administered late in the program, after completion of all major areas that contribute to the understanding of maternity and child nursing. It is not a replacement for NLN's separate achievement tests in nursing the childbearing family and nursing of children, which are designed for use relatively early in the program. The test is available for faculty review. Examiner required. Suitable for group use.

Untimed: 2 hours

Scoring: Computer scored

Cost: Test service (test booklets, answer sheets, directions for administration, scoring service) $3.00 per student

Publisher: National League for Nursing

NLN ACHIEVEMENT TESTS FOR REGISTERED NURSING: MICROBIOLOGY (FORM 1113)

Registered nursing students

Purpose: Measures individual achievement of registered nursing students in microbiology as it applies to nursing and attainment of nationally accepted objectives in nursing.

Description: Approximately 115-item paper-pencil multiple-choice test measuring the nursing student's understanding of facts and principles related to the causative microorganisms of infectious diseases. In addition to a total score, subscores are provided for three areas: the basic processes occurring during the cellular activity of microorganisms, the structural and functional differences of the microorganisms, techniques and measures for studying and culturing microorganisms that cause infectious disease; substances developed for immunization, the body's immunological response to foreign substances, and the antimicrobials used in controlling diseases; and the transmission of organisms, the incidence, manifestation, and progression of communicable diseases, as well as methods used to destroy microorganisms. Each score is based on the number of questions answered correctly. Separate norms are provided for students in associ-

ate degree, baccalaureate, and diploma programs. The test is available for faculty review. Examiner required. Suitable for group use.

Untimed: 2 hours

Scoring: Computer scored

Cost: Test service (test booklets, answer booklets, directions for administration, scoring service) $3.00 per student

Publisher: National League for Nursing

NLN ACHIEVEMENT TESTS FOR REGISTERED NURSING: NATURAL SCIENCES IN NURSING (FORM 3213)

Registered nursing students

Purpose: Measures individual achievement of registered nursing students in the natural sciences and attainment of nationally accepted objectives in nursing.

Description: Approximately 110-item paper-pencil multiple-choice test measuring understanding of natural science facts and principles related to patient care. Questions cover the areas of physiology, chemistry, physics, microbiology, and anatomy. A total score, a facts and principles subscore, and an application of knowledge subscore are provided based on the number of questions answered correctly. Separate norms are reported for students in associate degree, baccalaureate, and diploma programs. The test should be administered after students have completed science courses pertaining to the fields listed above. The test is available for faculty review. Examiner required. Suitable for group use.

Untimed: 2 hours

Scoring: Computer scored

Cost: Test service (test booklets, answer sheets, directions for administration, scoring service) $3.25 per student

Publisher: National League for Nursing

NLN ACHIEVEMENT TESTS FOR REGISTERED NURSING: NORMAL NUTRITION (FORM 1313)

Registered nursing students

Purpose: Measures individual achievement of registered nursing students in normal nutrition and attainment of nationally accepted objectives in nursing.

Description: Approximately 110-item paper-pencil multiple-choice test measuring knowledge of the facts and principles of normal nutrition and the ability to apply those principles. Test items cover nutrients, the bodily processes involved in the utilization of nutrients in food, and the role of nutrition in health. A total score, a knowledge and interpretation of information basic to normal nutrition subscore, and an application of knowledge of normal nutrition subscore are provided based on a correction-for-guessing formula. Separate norms are reported for students in associate degree, baccalaureate, and diploma programs. This test should be administered after the student completes initial major learning experience in normal nutrition (knowledge of clinical nursing is not required). The test is available for faculty review. Examiner required. Suitable for group use.

Untimed: 2 hours

Scoring: Computer scored

Cost: Test service (test booklets, answer sheets, directions for administration, scoring service) $3.00 per student

Publisher: National League for Nursing

NLN ACHIEVEMENT TESTS FOR REGISTERED NURSING: NURSING CARE OF ADULTS IN SPECIAL CARE UNITS (FORM 0214)

Registered nursing students

Purpose: Assesses knowledge related to the nursing care of adults with acute physical impairment due to disease or accident. Used with registered nursing students completing this nursing sequence.

Description: Approximately 100-item paper-pencil multiple-choice test measuring knowledge related to the nursing care of adults with acute physical impairment, patients in a rehabilitation unit, and the dying. Emphasis is on pathophysiological conditions and the nursing measures required. Questions on pharmacology,

nutrition, and the psychosocial aspects of patient care are integrated. Questions reflect the steps of the nursing process. A total score and three subscores are reported. Each score is based on the number of questions answered correctly. Separate norms are reported for students in associate degree, baccalaureate, and diploma programs. The test is available for faculty review. Examiner required. Suitable for group use.

Untimed: 2 hours

Scoring: Computer scored

Cost: $3.50 per student tested

Publisher: National League for Nursing

NLN ACHIEVEMENT TESTS FOR REGISTERED NURSING: NURSING CARE OF ADULTS WITH PATHOPHYSIOLOGICAL DISTURBANCES—PARTS I AND II (FORMS 0213 AND 0223)

Registered nursing students

Purpose: Measures individual achievement of registered nursing students in nursing care of adults with pathophysiological disturbances and attainment of nationally accepted objectives in nursing.

Description: Two approximately 130-item paper-pencil multiple-choice tests measuring knowledge of the nursing care of adults with pathophysiological disturbances. Part I (Form 0213) measures knowledge of problems related to deficiencies in providing oxygen or nutrients to cells, difficulty in elimination, and failures in regulation of metabolism. Part II (Form 0223) measures alterations in renal function and reproductive organs, defects in musculoskeletal or neurological functions, sensory defects, and integumentary problems. Most of the questions are presented as case situations and relate to hospitalized patients. The health problems selected reflect those occurring most frequently in the adult population of the United States. The questions emphasize the nursing care demanded by the patient's condition and are written to reflect the nursing process. Questions to measure knowledge of pharmacology and nutrition are integrated.

For each test, a total score and two sets of subscores are reported based on a correction-for-guessing formula. One set of subscores reflects the objectives of the test: pathophysiology, nursing measures, and therapeutic management (including drugs and diet). The second set of subscores reflects the nursing process: assessing, analyzing, and evaluating—steps that require the ability to gather and interpret information about a patient; and planning and implementing—steps that require the ability to select appropriate measures for providing care to a patient. Separate norms are reported for students in associate degree, baccalaureate, and diploma programs. These tests are intended as end-of-course tests after students have completed the major learning experiences in the content described. Tests are available for faculty review. Examiner required. Suitable for group use.

Untimed: Part I 2 hours; Part II 2 hours

Scoring: Computer scored

Cost: Test service, specify Part I or Part II (test booklets, answer sheets, directions for administration, scoring service) $4.00 per student

Publisher: National League for Nursing

NLN ACHIEVEMENT TESTS FOR REGISTERED NURSING: NURSING OF CHILDREN (FORM 0113)

Registered nursing students

Purpose: Measures individual achievement of registered nursing students in nursing care for children and attainment of nationally accepted objectives in nursing.

Description: Approximately 120-item paper-pencil multiple-choice test measuring understanding of facts and principles related to the nursing care of children and the ability to apply those principles. Questions relating to growth and development, teaching, interpersonal relations, nutrition, pharmacology, and the basic

sciences are integrated. A total score and three subscores (care of infants, care of toddlers and preschoolers, and care of school-age children) are provided based on the number of questions answered correctly. Separate norms are reported for students in associate degree, baccalaureate, and diploma programs. The test is available for faculty review. Examiner required. Suitable for group use.

Untimed: 2 hours

Scoring: Computer scored

Cost: Test service (test booklets, answer sheets, directions for administration, scoring service) $3.00 per student

Publisher: National League for Nursing

NLN ACHIEVEMENT TESTS FOR REGISTERED NURSING: NURSING THE CHILDBEARING FAMILY (FORM 0015)

Registered nursing students

Purpose: Assesses knowledge related to nursing the childbearing family. Used with registered nursing students completing the maternity nursing sequence.

Description: 123-item paper-pencil multiple-choice test measuring understanding of the facts and principles related to nursing the childbearing family and the ability to apply them. Questions on nutrition, pharmacology, the basic sciences, and interpersonal relations are integrated. While emphasis is on the normal, questions dealing with common abnormalities of the mother and newborn are included. Questions are written in the framework of the nursing process. A total score and three subscores (antepartal care; intrapartal and postpartal care; and fetal and newborn development and care) are provided. Scores are based on the number of questions answered correctly. Separate norms are reported for students in associate degree, baccalaureate, and diploma programs. The test is available for faculty review. This edition replaces Form 0581. Examiner required. Suitable for group use.

Untimed: 2 hours

Scoring: Computer scored

academic achievement and aptitude

Cost: Test service (test booklet, answer sheets, directions for administration, scoring service) $3.50 per student

Publisher: National League for Nursing

NLN ACHIEVEMENT TESTS FOR REGISTERED NURSING: PHARMACOLOGY IN CLINICAL NURSING (FORM 0982)

Registered nursing students

Purpose: Measures individual achievement of registered nursing students in applied pharmacology and attainment of nationally accepted objectives in nursing.

Description: Approximately 110-item paper-pencil multiple-choice test measuring understanding of facts and principles related to drugs and drug administration, including the actions of pharmacologic agents, untoward effects of drugs and their control, drug administration, and the calculation of dosages. Case situations are drawn from medical-surgical nursing, the nursing of children, obstetric and gynecologic nursing, and psychiatric nursing. A total score is reported based on a correction-for-guessing formula. Separate norms are reported for students in associate degree, baccalaureate, and diploma programs. The test should be administered late in the nursing program, after students have considerable clinical experience. The test is available for faculty review. Examiner required. Suitable for group use.

Untimed: 2 hours

Scoring: Computer scored

Cost: Test service (test booklets, answer sheets, directions for administration, scoring service) $3.00 per student

Publisher: National League for Nursing

NLN ACHIEVEMENT TESTS FOR REGISTERED NURSING: PSYCHIATRIC NURSING (FORM 0314)

Registered nursing students

Purpose: Measures individual achievement of registered nursing students in psychiatric nursing and attainment of nationally accepted objectives in nursing.

Description: Approximately 110-item paper-pencil multiple-choice test measuring knowledge of theory and practice in psychiatric nursing, including patient situations. The therapeutic role of the nurse in the care of patients with mental disorders is emphasized. A total score and two subscores (concept/process and intervention) are reported based on the number of questions answered correctly. Separate norms are reported for students in associate degree, baccalaureate, and diploma programs. The test should be administered after students have completed their major learning experiences in psychiatric nursing. This form is a revision of Form 0781. The test is available for faculty review. Examiner required. Suitable for group use.

Untimed: 2 hours

Scoring: Computer scored

Cost: Test service (test booklets, answer sheets, directions for administration, scoring service) $3.00 per student

Publisher: National League for Nursing

NLN BACCALAUREATE-LEVEL ACHIEVEMENT TESTS FOR REGISTERED NURSING

Registered nursing students

Purpose: Appraises individual achievement of students in baccalaureate-level registered nursing programs and attainment of nationally accepted objectives in nursing.

Description: Seven paper-pencil multiple-choice tests consisting of 80-210 questions. The following tests are available: Applied Natural Sciences, Community Health Nursing, Comprehensive Nursing Achievement Test for Baccalaureate Students, Leadership in Nursing, Medical-Surgical Nursing, Parent-Child Care, and Psychiatric Nursing (nursing care in mental health and mental illness). Test items were developed in cooperation with faculty members throughout the United States, reflecting the objectives and subject-matter content of baccalaureate programs from all geographic areas. All test papers must be returned to NLN Test Service for scoring. Reports on test results are returned to the program within 10 working days after NLN receives the answer sheets. Reports include raw scores and percentiles, item descriptors, a list of omitted and incorrectly answered items for each student, and an additional group analysis when more than 10 students are tested as a group. NLN encourages faculty members to review the tests before ordering to insure that appropriate subject-matter content areas are covered. Examiner required. Suitable for group use.

Untimed: 1½-4 hours per test

Scoring: Computer scored

Cost: Test service (test booklets, answer sheets, directions for administration, scoring service) $3.00-$6.00 per student per test

Publisher: National League for Nursing

NLN BACCALAUREATE-LEVEL ACHIEVEMENT TESTS FOR REGISTERED NURSING: APPLIED NATURAL SCIENCES (FORM 0981)

Registered nursing students

Purpose: Measures individual achievement in the applied natural sciences for students in baccalaureate-level registered nursing programs and attainment of nationally accepted objectives in nursing.

Description: Approximately 110-item paper-pencil multiple-choice test measuring students' ability to apply knowledge of the natural sciences to patient care. The areas covered are physiology, pathophysiology, chemistry, physics, microbiology, and anatomy. The test is arranged in two sections. Section A consists of four-option questions similar to those in other NLN achievement tests. Section B consists of six-option questions measuring students' comprehension of cause-and-effect relationships. Four subscores are provided, but no overall score. Two subscores for Sections A and B are provided in terms of the number of questions answered correctly. The knowledge subscore measures the number of Section B questions in which the student demon-

strated knowledge of only the facts in the paired statements. The application subscore measures the number of Section B questions in which the student knew the correct relationship between the two statements. Norms are provided for students in baccalaureate programs only. The test should be administered toward the end of the program. The test and a fuller description of the questions in Section B are available for faculty review. Examiner required. Suitable for group use.

Untimed: 2 hours

Scoring: Computer scored

Cost: Test service (test booklets, answer sheets, directions for administration, scoring service) $3.00 per student

Publisher: National League for Nursing

NLN BACCALAUREATE-LEVEL ACHIEVEMENT TESTS FOR REGISTERED NURSING: COMMUNITY HEALTH NURSING (FORM 2314)

Registered nursing students

Purpose: Measures individual student achievement in community health nursing in baccalaureate-level registered nursing programs and attainment of nationally recognized objectives in nursing.

Description: Approximately 100-item paper-pencil multiple-choice test measuring students' ability to apply the principles of community health planning and organization of health care services in contemporary society and knowledge of the nursing process as it is applied to the community and to family groups and individuals in community settings. The test is based on an approach to community health nursing that stresses promotion of maximum health with respect for cultural differences and individual values and with recognition of the ethical-legal constraints within which the community health nurse functions. Knowledge basic to nursing practice in any setting, such as communication, nutrition, and pharmacology, is tested within the context of the community settings where nurses practice. A total score and three subscores (human ecology, individual in systems, community health planning/health care system) are provided based on the number of questions answered correctly. Norms are reported for baccalaureate-level students only. The test should be administered to students in baccalaureate programs who have completed a major learning experience in community health nursing. The test is available for faculty review. Examiner required. Suitable for group use.

Untimed: 1½ hours

Scoring: Computer scored

Cost: Test service (test booklets, answer sheets, directions for administration, scoring service) $3.00 per student

Publisher: National League for Nursing

NLN BACCALAUREATE-LEVEL ACHIEVEMENT TESTS FOR REGISTERED NURSING: COMPREHENSIVE NURSING ACHIEVEMENT TEST FOR BACCALAUREATE NURSING STUDENTS (FORM 3113)

Registered nursing students

Purpose: Measures individual achievement of students ready to graduate from baccalaureate-level registered nursing programs and attainment of nationally accepted objectives in nursing.

Description: Approximately 210-item paper-pencil multiple-choice test measuring students' ability to apply knowledge derived from nursing science, as well as from the natural, behavioral, and social sciences. The test focuses on the cumulative results of the educational program rather than on the content of individual clinical components. To accommodate the heterogeneity of baccalaureate nursing curricula, an attempt has been made to construct a test that reflects a number of representative conceptual frameworks. Subscores are reported for each of the following content areas: clients being assessed for health status, including risk factors; clients experiencing a knowledge deficit; clients experiencing maturational or situational crisis; clients experiencing alteration of physiological functioning; clients with dysfunctional

patterns of behavior; and leadership and research process. The six subscores reflect the percentage of questions answered correctly within the diagnostic cluster. The total score, based on the number of questions answered correctly, is a standard score. The score report includes information about individual student performance, as well as group performance. Norms are reported for baccalaureate students. The test should be administered to students about to graduate from a baccalaureate program in registered nursing. The test is available for faculty review. Examiner required. Suitable for group use.

Untimed: 4 hours

Scoring: Computer scored

Cost: Test service (test booklets, answer sheets, directions for administration, scoring services) $6.00 per student

Publisher: National League for Nursing

NLN BACCALAUREATE-LEVEL ACHIEVEMENT TESTS FOR REGISTERED NURSING: LEADERSHIP IN NURSING (FORM 0381)

Registered nursing students

Purpose: Measures individual achievement of leadership skills of students in baccalaureate-level registered nursing programs and attainment of nationally accepted objectives in nursing.

Description: Approximately 80-item paper-pencil multiple-choice test measuring knowledge of general principles and their application in the techniques and skills of nursing leadership. The questions present a variety of clinical situations requiring the judgment and intervention of the nurse as first-line manager. A total score is reported based on a correction-for-guessing formula. Norms are provided for baccalaureate students. The test should be administered to students in baccalaureate programs who have completed a sequence of learning activities introducing the concepts of leadership and management. The test is available for faculty review. Examiner required. Suitable for group use.

Untimed: 1½ hours

Scoring: Computer scored

Cost: Test service (test booklets, answer sheets, directions for administration, scoring service) $3.00 per student

Publisher: National League for Nursing

NLN BACCALAUREATE-LEVEL ACHIEVEMENT TESTS FOR REGISTERED NURSING: MEDICAL-SURGICAL NURSING (FORM 0182)

Registered nursing students

Purpose: Measures individual achievement in medical-surgical nursing for students in baccalaureate-level registered nursing programs and attainment of nationally accepted objectives in nursing.

Description: Approximately 120-item paper-pencil test measuring students' knowledge of facts and principles related to medical-surgical nursing and the ability to apply them to patient care situations. The questions relate to adult patients in a variety of age groups and to situations focusing on the healthy individual, the individual presenting early changes in health status, the individual with acute health problems, and the individual with rehabilitation needs. The situations presented emphasize the nursing care of acutely ill, hospitalized patients. A total score and two subscores are provided: care of healthy patients and patients with early changes in health status; and care of acutely ill patients and patients in need of rehabilitation. All scores are based on a correction-for-guessing formula. Norms are reported for baccalaureate students. The test should be administered after students in baccalaureate programs complete their major learning experience in medical-surgical nursing. The test is available for faculty review. Examiner required. Suitable for group use.

Untimed: 2 hours

Scoring: Computer scored

Cost: Test service (test booklets, answer sheets, directions for administration, scoring service) $3.00 per student

Publisher: National League for Nursing

NLN BACCALAUREATE-LEVEL ACHIEVEMENT TESTS FOR REGISTERED NURSING: NURSING CARE IN MENTAL HEALTH AND MENTAL ILLNESS (FORM 2214)

Registered nursing students

Purpose: Measures individual achievement in psychiatric nursing in baccalaureate-level registered nursing programs and attainment of nationally accepted objectives in nursing.

Description: Approximately 120-item paper-pencil multiple-choice test measuring knowledge of the concepts and principles essential in the care of clients with a variety of mental disorders. The case situations cover a number of different settings, and questions covering primary and tertiary prevention are included. Although the test focuses on the knowledge required for caring for clients with mental disorders, questions covering new approaches to treatment and concepts of a broader nature are integrated. A total score and three subscores (knowledge/concepts, assessing/analyzing/evaluating, planning/implementing) are reported based on the number of questions answered correctly. Norms are reported for baccalaureate students. The test should be administered to students who have completed their major learning experience in psychiatric nursing. The test is available for faculty review. Examiner required. Suitable for group use.

Untimed: 2 hours

Scoring: Computer scored

Cost: Test service (test booklets, answer sheets, directions for administration, scoring service) $3.00 per student

Publisher: National League for Nursing

NLN BACCALAUREATE-LEVEL ACHIEVEMENT TESTS FOR REGISTERED NURSING: PARENT-CHILD CARE (FORM 0882)

Registered nursing students

Purpose: Measures individual achievement in parent-child nursing care in baccalaureate-level registered nursing programs and attainment of nationally accepted objectives in nursing.

Description: Approximately 110-item paper-pencil multiple-choice test measuring knowledge of nursing interventions for individuals during infancy, childhood, and adolescence and for families during the childbearing and childrearing years. In addition to measuring the achievement of learning objectives pertinent to all areas of nursing practice, such as principles of communication, the test measures learning objectives specific to the nursing of parents and children, including psychosocial and physical development of children and parents and normal and unexpected physical changes related to childhood and childbearing. The test presents nursing situations in a variety of inpatient and outpatient settings where parents and children requiring health care are encountered. A total score and two subscores (childbearing, including fetal development and the neonate to one month of age; and care of the child from one month to young adulthood, including family health concepts) are provided based on a correction-for-guessing formula. Norms are reported for baccalaureate students. The test assesses students' knowledge of all steps of the nursing process and should be administered to students in baccalaureate programs who have completed all of the major learning experiences in the content area. The test is available for faculty review. Examiner required. Suitable for group use.

Untimed: 2 hours

Scoring: Computer scored

Cost: Test service (test booklets, answer sheets, directions for administration, scoring service) $3.00 per student

Publisher: National League for Nursing

NLN NURSING MOBILITY PROFILE I

Registered nursing students

Purpose: Evaluates previous learning and experience in order to establish credit and placement in programs preparing individuals for registered nursing practice. Administered to licensed practical nurses.

Description: Approximately 400-item paper-pencil multiple-choice battery assessing three content areas: foundations of nursing (200 items), nursing care during childbearing (100 items), and nursing care of the child (100 items). Book One (foundations of nursing) includes questions related to nursing care to meet basic physiological and psychosocial needs. The first section of Book Two (nursing care during childbearing) includes questions related to nursing care during antepartal, intrapartal, and neonatal periods. The second section of Book Two (nursing care of the child) includes questions related to nursing care of the infant, toddler, preschooler, school-age child, and adolescent. The two test books may be administered separately or together as determined by individual needs. Questions are based on the nursing care of clients in health care settings and are presented in case situations representative of those commonly encountered in nursing practice. Test items are written within the framework of the four steps of the nursing process (assessment, planning, implementation, and evaluation).

To safeguard the security of the examination, the tests may be administered by faculty at individual schools of nursing on uniform test dates selected by NLN Test Service. (Contact NLN Test Service to arrange alternate dates.) The tests should be administered in a one-day session to be scheduled by faculty at participating schools of nursing during the restricted periods.

A total score (decision score) is reported for each of the three content areas. Diagnostic scores are also provided as a supplement to faculty evaluations of students and students' self-assessments of strengths and weaknesses. An information bulletin providing more detailed information about the content, scoring, and administration of the examination is available upon request. Suggested methods for institutional standard setting are available upon request. Examiner required. Suitable for group use.

Timed: Book One 3½ hours; Book Two 3½ hours

Scoring: Computer scored

Cost: Test service, specify book (test booklets, answer sheets, directions for administration, scoring service) $25.00 per student

Publisher: National League for Nursing

NLN NURSING MOBILITY PROFILE II

Registerd nursing students

Purpose: Evaluates previous learning and experience in order to establish credit and placement in nursing education programs. Administered to registered nurses seeking placement in a baccalaureate nursing program.

Description: Approximately 560-item paper-pencil multiple-choice battery assessing four content areas: care of the adult client (220 items), care of the client during childbearing (110 items), care of the child (110 items), and care of the client with mental disorder (120 items). Test books may be administered in any order or combination as determined by individual needs. Book One (care of the adult client) includes content related to the nursing care of individual clients whose delivery of oxygen to the cells is deficient; clients with digestive and metabolic problems and difficulty providing nutrients to the cells; clients with sensorimotor function impairment; and clients with genitourinary or reproductive system dysfunctions. The first section of Book Two (care of the client during childbearing) includes content related to nursing care during the antepartal, intrapartal, postpartal, and neonatal periods. The second section of Book Two (care of the child) includes content related to nursing care of the infant, the toddler and preschooler, and the school-age child and adolescent. Book Three (care of the client with mental disorder) contains content related to nursing care of children and adults with psychological, adjustmental, and organic mental disorders. Most of the questions on the profile are presented in case situations representative of health problems and conditions commonly encountered in nursing practice. The questions relate to the promotion, maintenance, and restoration of health. Items emphasize normal findings, deviations from normal, and treatment modalities, including drugs, nutrition, and nursing interventions.

The tests may be administered by faculty at individual schools of nursing on uniform test dates selected by NLN Test Service to safeguard the security of the examination. Contact NLN Test Service to arrange alternate dates. The tests should be administered in a one and a half day session to be scheduled by faculty at participating schools of nursing during the restricted periods. Standardized scores for each of the four main content areas are reported to faculty for use in making decisions about placement or awarding/denying specific course credits. Subscores for content and nursing process are reported also to provide additional advisory information. Two copies of the performance report are provided: one for student use and a second for faculty use. An information bulletin providing more detailed information about the scoring, content, and administration of the examination is available. Examiner required. Suitable for group use.

Timed: Book One 4 hours; Book Two 4 hours; Book Three 2 hours

Scoring: Computer scored

Cost: Test service, specify book (test booklets, answer sheets, directions for administration, scoring service) $25.00 per student

Publisher: National League for Nursing

NLN NURSING SERVICE TEST: PROFICIENCY IN PHARMACOLOGY FOR NURSING PRACTICE

Nurses

Purpose: Measures basic knowledge of pharmacology required for safe practice. Used with registered and practical nurses to establish educational objectives for in-service training programs designed for new or currently employed nursing staff.

Description: 92-item paper-pencil multiple-choice test measuring knowledge of the principles of drug administration and the effects of commonly used drugs and the ability to carry out simple dosage calculations. Test items emphasize essential knowledge required for safe practice. Raw scores are provided for the total test and three subsections: drug administration, dosage calculations, and drug effects. Examiner required. Suitable for group use.

Untimed: 1½ hours

Scoring: Computer scored

Cost: Test service (test booklet, answer sheet, directions for administration, score reporting) $4.00 per test scored

Publisher: National League for Nursing

NLN PRE-ADMISSION EXAMINATION-PN (PAX-PN)

Nursing program
applicants

Purpose: Measures ability and scholastic achievement in specific content areas that predict academic success in practical nursing programs. Assists in admissions and placement decisions by schools preparing students for practical nursing.

Description: Battery of three paper-pencil multiple-choice tests measuring ability in the following areas: verbal ability, science achievement, and mathematics achievement. The verbal ability test consists of word knowledge and reading comprehension sections. The word knowledge section measures the ability to recognize the meaning of a word as it is used in a sentence. Applicants choose the answer that best completes a statement. The reading section is composed of passages of a scientific or general nature and associated questions suitable for measuring reading comprehension skills. The mathematics test measures the ability to solve computational or word problems involving proportions, ratios, decimals, fractions, percentages, and elementary algebraic concepts. The science test measures knowledge of general principles of chemistry, physics, biology, and health. Most of the questions test knowledge of information from secondary-school gen-

eral science and health classes that has useful applications to practical nursing. Experimental questions are included for test development purposes only and are not scored. The tests, administered as a single battery, are administered at scheduled sessions throughout the country at test sites established by NLN Test Service. Contact NLN if alternate dates are required. The test performance of each applicant is reported in terms of raw scores and percentiles. Percentile norms are based on performance of applicants to practical/vocational nursing programs. A composite score based on a weighted combination of the subscores is also reported. Interpretive material is provided with each report. Examiner required. Suitable for group use.

Timed: 3½ hours

Scoring: Computer scored

Cost: One administration with two score reports (one for applicant and one for designated school of practical nursing) $15.00; additional reports $5.00

Publisher: National League for Nursing

NLN PRE-ADMISSION EXAMINATION-RN (PAX-RN)

Nursing program
applicants

Purpose: Measures ability and academic achievement in specific content areas that predict academic success in programs preparing students for beginning registered nursing practice. Assists schools in making admissions and placement decisions.

Description: Battery of three multiple-item paper-pencil multiple-choice tests measuring ability in the following areas: verbal ability, mathematics achievement, and science achievement. The verbal ability test consists of word knowledge and reading comprehension sections. The word knowledge section measures the ability to recognize the meaning of a word as it is used in a sentence. Applicants choose the answer that best completes a statement. The reading section is composed of passages of a scientific or general nature with associated questions suitable for measuring reading comprehension skills. The mathematics test measures skills in basic arithmetic calculations, as well as elementary algebraic and geometric concepts. Straight computational, as well as reading problems, are included. The science test evaluates knowledge of high-school-level general science, chemistry, physics, and biology, with particular emphasis on areas most applicable to the nursing curriculum. Experimental questions are included for test development purposes only and are not included in scoring.

The test is administered at scheduled sessions throughout the country at test sites established by NLN Test Service. Contact NLN if alternate dates are required. The test performance of each applicant is reported in terms of raw scores and percentiles. Separate percentile norms are provided for applicants to associate degree programs, diploma programs, and all registered nursing programs. A standardized composite score based on a weighted combination of subscores is also reported. Interpretive material is provided with each report. Examiner required. Suitable for group use.

Timed: 3½ hours

Scoring: Computer scored

Cost: One administration with two score reports (one for the applicant and one for a designated school of nursing) $15.00; additional reports $5.00

Publisher: National League for Nursing

NORMAL BATTERY A/76

Adult

Purpose: Assesses academic abilities of older students. Used with college entrants and higher.

Description: Multiple-item paper-pencil battery of six multiple-choice tests: Mental Alertness, Language Ability in English and Afrikaans, Reading Comprehension, Vocabulary, Spelling, and Arithmetic. Norms are available. Examiner required. Suitable for group use.
SOUTH AFRICAN PUBLISHER

Timed: 2 hours

Scoring: Hand key

Cost: (In Rands) booklet 8,80; 25 answer sheets 3,00; set of keys 10,00; manual 12,00

Publisher: National Institute for Personnel Research

NURSING TESTS
Thelma Hunt

Adolescent
Grades 12 and above

Purpose: Measures aptitude for nursing. Used to select applicants for nursing or practical nursing schools or for assistance in guidance and counseling of prenursing students.

Description: Four multiple-choice paper-pencil tests assessing aptitude for nursing: the Nursing Aptitude Test (specialized general ability test), the Arithmetic Test for Prospective Nurses, the General Science Test for Prospective Nurses, and the Interest-Preference Test for Prospective Nurses. The tests may be administered separately or as a complete battery. Norms are available for high-school seniors. Examiner required. Suitable for group use.

Timed: Varies

Scoring: Examiner evaluated

Cost: 25 aptitude tests $6.00; 25 arithmetic tests $3.00; 25 general science tests $4.00; 25 interest-preference tests $5.00; specimen set for all four tests $5.00

Publisher: The Center for Psychological Service

OFFICIAL GED PRACTICE TEST
GED Testing Service of the American Council on Education

Adolescent, adult

Purpose: Determines readiness to take the full-length GED. Alleviates anxiety associated with taking the GED Test.

Description: Multiple-item paper-pencil test paralleling the content, format, and range of difficulty of the full-length GED tests. Five subtests cover the following academic areas: writing skills, social studies, science, reading skills, and mathematics. The answer sheet accommodates responses for all five subtests on

---

both sides of a single sheet and contains a summary profile chart that identifies general strengths and weaknesses in various subject areas. Scoring templates and a detailed teacher's manual are provided in the administrator's set. The test is available in Forms A and B. All forms are statistically equated to a full-length secure GED Test. Audiotapes are available for Forms A and B in English. Examiner required. Suitable for group use. Available in Spanish.

Untimed: Varies

Scoring: Examiner evaluated

Cost: English Form A or B (10 test booklets, 10 answer sheets, 10 information bulletins) $15.95; administrator's set $11.00

Publisher: American Council on Education; distributed by Cambridge

ONTARIO ASSESSMENT INSTRUMENT POOL (OAIP)

Adolescent   Grades 4-13

Purpose: Evaluates student achievement and program effectiveness in Ontario Province Schools. Measures pupils' mastery of predetermined educational objectives. Used as a unit pre- or posttest. May be used with any other educational assessment device.

Description: 20 paper-pencil assessment instruments covering a variety of school subjects in both French and English. The following unit test titles are available: Chemistry I, II, III, and IV, Senior Division (Grades 11-13); English I and II, Intermediate Division (Grades 7-10); Anglais I, Junior Division Writing and Speaking (Grades 4-6); Anglais au cycle, Intermediate I Writing and Speaking (Grades 7-10); French as a Second Language, Junior and Intermediate Divisions (Grades 6-10); Français au cycle moyen I, Savoir écrire, savoir parler (Grades 4-6); Français au cycle intermédiaire I, Savoir écrire, savoir parler (Grades 7-10); Geography, Intermediate Division (Grades 7-10); Géographie (L'amérique du nord) au cycle intermédiaire (Grades 7-10); Geography (Canada) Intermediate Division (Grades 7-10); Géographie (le

Canada) au cycle intermédiare (Grades 7-10); History, Intermediate Division (Grades 7-10); History Part II, Intermediate Division (Grades 7-10); Mathematics, Intermediate Division (Grades 7-10); Mathématique au cycle intermédiaire (Grades 7-10); Physics, Senior Division (Grades 11-13); Physique au cycle superiéur (Grades 11-13).

The Pool will be made available to all teachers in systems within the Ontario province. The materials, which may be used separately or in groups, include test booklets, information sheets, and manuals. Examiner required. Suitable for group use.

CANADIAN PUBLISHER

Untimed: Varies

Scoring: Not available

Cost: $15.00 per pool

Publisher: The Ontario Institute for Studies in Education

ORLEANS-HANNA ALGEBRA PROGNOSIS TEST (REVISED)
*Gerald S. Hanna and
Joseph B. Orleans*

**Adolescent
Grades 7 and above**

Purpose: Identifies students likely to experience difficulties in an algebra course. Used in counseling, selecting, and grouping algebra students.

Description: Multiple-item test of three variables related to the prognosis of success in an algebra course: aptitude, achievement, and interest and motivation. Items include a questionnaire and work samples. Students complete the questionnaire by indicating recent grades and estimating their algebra grade and then complete the 60-item work sample. This test is a revision of the 1968 Orleans-Hanna Algebra Prognosis Test. Examiner required. Suitable for group use.

Timed: 40 minutes

Scoring: Hand key; may be machine scored; computer scoring service available

Cost: 35 tests with manual $30.00; 35 hand-scorable answer documents $10.00; keys $5.00; 35 NCS machine-scorable answer documents $10.00; 35 student report forms $9.00

Publisher: The Psychological Corporation

OTIS-LENNON MENTAL ABILITY TEST
Arthur S. Otis and Roger T. Lennon

**Child, adolescent
Grades K.5-12**

Purpose: Assesses general mental ability or scholastic aptitude.

Description: Multiple-item test covering a broad range of cognitive abilities. The test is divided into six levels: Primary I and II (K-Grade 1), Elementary I and II (Grades 1-6), Intermediate (Grades 7-9), and Advanced (Grades 10-12). No reading is required for the first three levels. Materials include two alternate and equivalent forms, J and K. This test replaces the Otis Quick-Scoring Mental Ability Test. Examiner required. Suitable for group use.

Timed: Varies

Scoring: Hand key; may be machine scored; computer scoring service available

Cost: Examination kit, specify level (test, hand-scoring key, manual, norms, conversion booklet) $7.00

Publisher: The Psychological Corporation

OTIS-LENNON SCHOOL ABILITY TEST (OLSAT)
Arthur S. Otis and Roger T. Lennon

**Child, adolescent
Grades 1-12**

Purpose: Measures abstract thinking and reasoning ability. Used for predicting success in cognitive, school-related activities.

Description: Multiple-item test covering abilities emphasized in school. Items use verbal, figural, and numerical stimuli. The test is divided into five levels: Primary I (Grade 1), Primary II (Grades 2-3), Elementary (Grades 4-5), Intermediate (Grades 6-8), Advanced (Grades 9-12). No

reading is required of pupils in Grades 1, 2, and 3. Materials include two alternate and equivalent forms, R and S. Form R may be used in conjunction with the Metropolitan Achievement Tests: 5th Edition. Examiner required. Suitable for group use.

Timed: Varies

Scoring: Hand key; may be machine scored; computer scoring service available

Cost: Examination kit, specify level (test, manual, parent/teacher report) $7.00

Publisher: The Psychological Corporation

PEABODY INDIVIDUAL ACHIEVEMENT TEST (PIAT)
*Lloyd M. Dunn and
Frederick C. Markwardt, Jr.*

All ages

Purpose: Provides an overview of individual scholastic attainment. Used to screen for areas of weakness requiring more detailed diagnostic testing.

Description: 402-item test of mathematics (84 items), reading recognition (84 items), reading comprehension (66 items), spelling (84 items), and general information (84 items), including science, social studies, fine arts, and sports. Derived scores are grade equivalents, grade percentile ranks, age equivalents, age percentile ranks, and standard scores by age or grade. Materials include two easel kits containing test plates, 25 record sheets, and a manual. Examiner required. Not suitable for group use.

Untimed: 30-50 minutes

Scoring: Examiner evaluated

Cost: Complete kit: regular edition $76.00; special plastic edition $90.75

Publisher: American Guidance Service

PROFICIENCY BATTERIES—JSPB, SPB, APP AND SPT-HT

All ages

Purpose: Assesses achievement in scholastic fields. Used for selection and placement of students and applicants.

Description: Four paper-pencil measures of proficiency in a range of scholastic fields. The JSPB (Standards 5 to 7) measures proficiency in first language (English or Afrikaans), mathematics, natural sciences, geography, history, and second language. The SPB (Standards 8 to 10) measures social sciences, commercial sciences, natural sciences, arithmetic, and home language (English or Afrikaans). APP (first-year university students) tests proficiency in social sciences, commercial sciences, natural sciences, mathematical sciences, and their home language. The SPT-HP (adults whose proficiency is at the higher primary level) measures performance in mathematics, English, and Afrikaans. Examiner required. Suitable for group use.
SOUTH AFRICAN PUBLISHER

Timed: JSPB 2½ hours; SPB 1¾ hours; APB 1¾ hours

Scoring: Hand key; examiner evaluated

Cost: (In Rands) JSPB test 2,00; 10 answer sheets 0,70; scoring stencil 2,40; manual 2,20; SPB test 0,80; 10 answer sheets 0,60; scoring stencil and manual 1,00 each; APB test 0,90; 10 answer sheets 0,60; scoring stencil 1,00; manual 2,40; SPT-HP test 0,50; manual 2,30; scoring stencil 1,50; 10 answer sheets 0,50; orders from outside The RSA will be dealt with on merit

Publisher: Human Sciences Research Council

PROGRESSIVE ACHIEVEMENT TESTS
Warwick Elley, Neil Reid, David Hughes, Cedric Croft, and Peter Jackson

Child, adolescent Ages 7-15

Purpose: Measures school achievement. Used for educational assessment.

Description: Five paper-pencil tests measuring school achievement. The PAT: Reading Vocabulary test consists of multiple-choice items requiring the child to select the best synonym from five alternatives. The PAT: Listening Comprehension test measures the child's ability to understand material presented

orally. The child chooses the best answer from four alternatives presented in multiple-choice format. The PAT: Reading Comprehension test consists of graded reading passages followed by five to seven multiple-choice questions. The PAT: Mathematics test is a 50-item multiple-choice test measuring achievement in knowledge, computation, understanding, and application. The PAT: Study Skills test measures skills in three broad areas: knowledge and use of common reference materials, reading and interpreting graphic and tabular materials, and general reading study skills. Examiner required. Suitable for group use.
NEW ZEALAND PUBLISHER

Timed: 30-40 minutes

Scoring: Hand key; examiner evaluated

Cost: Contact publisher

Publisher: New Zealand Council for Educational Research

PSB APTITUDE FOR PRACTICAL NURSING EXAMINATION

Adult Practical nursing students

Purpose: Measures abilities, skills, knowledge, and attitudes important to successful performance as a practical nurse. Used as an admission test for schools and programs of practical nursing.

Description: Multiple-item paper-pencil battery of five tests assessing areas important for performance as a practical nurse: General Mental Ability, Spelling, the Natural Sciences, Judgment in Practical Nursing Situations, and Personal Adjustment. The battery predicts an individual's readiness for specialized instruction in practical nursing. Examiner required. Suitable for group use.

Timed: 2 hours, 45 minutes

Scoring: Machine scored

Cost: Reusable test booklets $4.00; answer sheets (scoring and reporting service) $4.00

Publisher: Psychological Services Bureau

PSB HEALTH OCCUPATIONS APTITUDE EXAMINATION

Adult   Health occupations students

Purpose: Measures abilities, skills, knowledge, and attitudes important to successful performance in various health care occupations. Used as an admission test for schools and programs in health occupations.

Description: Multiple-item paper-pencil battery of five tests assessing areas important to performance in health care occupations: academic aptitude, spelling, reading comprehension, the natural sciences, and vocational adjustment. The test predicts an individual's readiness for specialized instruction in numerous health care positions, including medical record technician, dental assistant, psychiatric aide, histologic technician, nursing assistant, respiratory therapy technician, and radiologic technologist. Examiner required. Suitable for group use.

Timed: 2 hours

Scoring: Machine scored

Cost: Reusable test booklets $4.00; answer sheets (scoring and reporting service) $4.00

Publisher: Psychological Services Bureau

PSB NURSING SCHOOL APTITUDE EXAMINATION (RN)

Adult   Nursing school candidates

Purpose: Measures abilities, skills, knowledge, and attitudes important to successful performance as a nurse. Used as an admission test for schools and departments of nursing.

Description: Multiple-item paper-pencil battery of five tests assessing areas important for performance as a nurse: academic aptitude, spelling, reading comprehension, information in the natural sciences, and vocational adjustment. The battery predicts readiness for instruction in nursing at the diploma or associate degree levels. Examiner required. Suitable for group use.

Timed: 2 hours, 45 minutes

Scoring: Machine scored

Cost: Reusable test booklets $4.00; answer sheets (scoring and reporting service) $4.00

Publisher: Psychological Services Bureau

PSYCHO-EDUCATIONAL BATTERY (PEB)
Lillie Pope

All ages

Purpose: Identifies learning problems of children and adults. Used to develop individualized teaching plans.

Description: Multiple-item paper-pencil observational instrument measuring the following aspects of a student's functioning: motor performance; sensory and perceptual performance; language cognition and memory; and reading, spelling, and arithmetic skills. The examiner completes the inventory based on observations of the student. Some additional probing by the evaluator may be necessary. Interpretation of the inventory yields a psycho-educational assessment of skills and deficits in young children and all age groups for special needs populations. The subjects should be within a normal range of behavior and gross-motor skills. Two forms are available: Level Y (Grades K-6) and Level O (junior high to adult). The PEB consists of five components: a student recording form; evaluator recording form; a family, social, and medical history; a visual pack; and a teacher's referral form. Examiner required. Not suitable for group use.

Untimed: 1-2 hours

Scoring: Examiner evaluated

Cost: Complete kit (specify Level Y or O) $29.95; part A, recording forms $7.95; part B, evaluator's form $14.95; part C, family, social, and medical history $9.95; part D, visual pack $9.95; part E, teacher's referral form $6.95

Publisher: Book-Lab

academic achievement and aptitude

PUPIL RECORD OF EDUCATIONAL BEHAVIOR (PREB)
Ruth Cheves

Child   Grades PreK-6

Purpose: Evaluates a child's level and pattern of functioning in visual-motor, auditory, language, and mathematical skills. Used for instructional programming.

Description: Multiple-item visual-motor test profiling performance over a range of developmental skills, including gross-motor coordination and fine-motor skills, visual-motor integration, auditory and visual perception, association and generalization, language development, and mathematical concepts. In addition to the guide and record booklets, the materials include a variety of cards (shape, color, picture/word, etc.), jigsaw puzzles, stencils, cubes, pegboard with pegs, whistle, and scissors. Examiner required. Not suitable for group use.

Untimed: Not available

Scoring: Examiner evaluated

Cost: Complete $76.00

Publisher: DLM Teaching Resources

QUICKSCREEN
Refer to page 585.

RICHMOND TESTS OF BASIC SKILLS
A.N. Hieronymus, E.F. Lindquist, and Norman France

**Child, adolescent
Ages 8-14**

Purpose: Assesses child's progress in academic work. Used to diagnose areas of general strengths and weaknesses.

Description: Multiple-item paper-pencil test measuring progress in five areas: vocabulary, reading comprehension, language skills, study skills, and mathematics. The instrument consists of 11 individual tests: Vocabulary, Reading Comprehension, Spelling, Use of Capital Letters, Punctuation, Usage, Map Reading, Reading Graphs and Tables,

Knowledge and Use of Reference Materials, Mathematics Concepts, and Mathematics Problem Solving. The test is available in six levels for children ages 8-14. A 96-page book incorporating all 11 tests for all six levels of difficulty is provided. Examiner required. Suitable for group use.

BRITISH PUBLISHER

Timed: Varies

Scoring: Hand key; computer scoring service available

Cost: 30 pupil books £3.95; 25 answer sheets £4.00; keys (specify level) £5.70; teacher's guide £6.05; table of norms £5.50 (payment in sterling for all overseas orders)

Publisher: NFER-NELSON Publishing Company Ltd.

SCHOLASTIC APTITUDE TEST BATTERIES FOR STANDARDS 2, 3 AND 5-SATB AND JSATB

Child

Purpose: Assesses academic and scholastic aptitudes. Used for psychoeducational counseling.

Description: Multiple-item test batteries measuring a broad range of scholastic aptitudes. SATB (Standards 2 and 3) measures mathematics, nonverbal reasoning ability, and proficiency in English, Afrikaans, and one of seven mother tongues: Northern Sotho, Southern Sotho, Tswanga, Tsonga, Venda, Xhosa, and Zulu. JSATB (Standard 5) assesses abilities in language, mathematics, and verbal and nonverbal reasoning ability. Examiner required. Suitable for group use.

SOUTH AFRICAN PUBLISHER

Timed: SATB 3 hours; JSATB 2½ hours

Scoring: Hand key; examiner evaluated

Cost: (In Rands) SATB test booklet (specify language) 0,60; manual 1,40; 10 answer sheets 1,00; scoring stencil 1,20; JSATB test booklet 2,40; manual 6,70 net; orders from outside The RSA will be dealt with on merit

Publisher: Human Sciences Research Council

SCHOLASTIC PROFICIENCY TEST—HIGHER PRIMARY LEVEL (SPT-HP)

Adult

Purpose: Assesses proficiency in mathematics, English, and Afrikaans. Used in South Africa with adult blacks with an educational level of Standards 2-5 for selection and placement in training programs or occupations.

Description: Multiple-item paper-pencil test of scholastic proficiency in mathematics, English, and Afrikaans. Norms indicate the typical performance of people passing Standards 2-5. The test can be used for selecting and placing adults in training courses or occupations requiring a higher primary scholastic level. Examiner required. Suitable for group use. SOUTH AFRICAN PUBLISHER

Untimed: 3 hours, 15 minutes

Scoring: Hand key

Cost: Test booklet $0.50; manual $2.30; scoring stencil $1.50; 10 answer sheets $0.50

Publisher: Human Sciences Research Council

SCHOOL AND COLLEGE ABILITY TESTS, SERIES III (SCAT III)
Educational Testing Service

Child, adolescent Grades 3.5-12.9

Purpose: Measures a student's basic verbal and quantitative abilities.

Description: 100-item two-part paper-pencil test measuring verbal and mathematical skills. The verbal portion of the test uses verbal analogies to assess a student's understanding of words. The quantitative section uses quantitative comparison items to measure a student's knowledge of basic number operations. The test yields verbal, quantitative, and total raw scores, which may be converted to standard scores, national percentile ranks, and stanines. Forms are available for three levels: Elementary (Grades 3-6), Intermediate (Grades 6-9), and Advanced (Grades 9-12). The SCAT III is a revision

of the SCAT II; the metric system has been incorporated in the SCAT III and racial and ethnic biases have been deleted. Examiner required. Suitable for group use.

Timed: 40 minutes

Scoring: Hand key; may be computer scored

Cost: 35 reusable test books (specify level) $16.80; 100 answer sheets $18.00; scoring stencil $2.50

Publisher: CTB/McGraw-Hill

SCIENTIFIC KNOWLEDGE AND APTITUDE TEST
S. Chatterji

Adolescent   Ages 15-16

Purpose: Measures the scientific knowledge and aptitude of high-school students.

Description: 72-item paper-pencil test assessing scientific knowledge and aptitude. The test may be used with students whose native language is not English but who have been taught in English-language schools. Examiner required. Suitable for group use. PUBLISHED IN INDIA

Timed: 1 hour

Scoring: Hand key; examiner evaluated

Cost: (In Rupees) complete kit (25 booklets, 100 answer sheets, manual, key) Rs90

Publisher: Manasayan

Information and availability unconfirmed; no publisher response.

SECONDARY SCHOOL ADMISSION TEST (SSAT)

Child, adolescent Grades 5-10

Purpose: Measures the abilities of students applying for admission to Grades 6-11 of selective schools. Used by independent schools for student selection.

Description: Multiple-item paper-pencil multiple-choice test measuring verbal and quantitative abilities and reading comprehension. The test consists of four sections: one measuring verbal ability, two measuring mathematical ability, and one measuring reading comprehension. An upper level form is administered to students in Grades 8-10; a lower form is administered to students in Grades 5-7. Scores are normed on the student's grade level at the time of testing. Norms for each grade level are developed annually on the basis of the most recent three-year sample of candidates tested.

The test is administered on specific dates (six Saturdays during the school year and biweekly during the summer) at designated test centers. ETS publishes a *Bulletin of Information for Candidates,* which contains a list of test centers and dates, registration information, and a registration form. The *Bulletin* is mailed to score recipients in August for distribution to candidates, who complete the form and return it with the test fee to ETS. A booklet entitled *Preparing for the SSAT* is available for candidates who want to familiarize themselves with the test. The booklet contains a description of the test, examples and explanations of test questions, a sample test, and instructions for scoring the test and interpreting the scores.

Reading comprehension, verbal, quantitative, and total verbal and quantitative scaled scores, as well as program percentiles, are mailed to score recipients approximately 15 working days after each administration. Each score recipient receives a roster of scores for candidates who designated it as a score recipient, two gummed label reports for each candidate, current program norms, and an interpretive guide explaining how the information can be used. At the time of testing, students may designate up to six score recipients. A report of the candidate's scaled scores and percentiles, along with a booklet for interpreting scores, is sent to parents approximately four days after the reports are sent to the schools. A program for the handicapped permits physically or visually handicapped students to take the test with up to double the amount of testing time per section. Examiner required. Suitable for group use.

Timed: Varies

Scoring: Computer scored; may be hand scored

Cost: Domestic test fee (administration, parents' score report, six designated school reports) $25.00; foreign test fee (including Canada, Puerto Rico, U.S. territories) $45.00

Publisher: Educational Testing Service

SENIOR ACADEMIC-TECHNICAL APTITUDE TESTS FOR COLOUREDS IN STANDARDS 8, 9, AND 10 (SATA)

Adolescent, adult

Purpose: Measures the differential aptitudes of students and young adults with an educational level of Standards 8-10. Used for educational and occupational guidance.

Description: Multiple-item paper-pencil battery of tests in two forms assessing aptitudes. Forms A and B include 10 tests: Verbal Reasoning, Nonverbal Reasoning I (figure series), Nonverbal Reasoning II (dominoes), computations, reading comprehension, spelling and vocabulary, mechanical reasoning, spatial perception (3D), comparison, and price controlling. Form B has an additional filing test. Stanines and percentile ranks are available. Examiner required. Suitable for group use.

SOUTH AFRICAN PUBLISHER

Untimed: 4½ hours

Scoring: Hand key

Cost: Test booklet $1.60; manual $5.80; set of scoring stencils $4.20; 10 answer sheets $1.30

Publisher: Human Sciences Research Council

SENIOR APTITUDE TESTS (SAT)— 1969
F.A. Fouche and N.F. Alberts

Adolescent

Purpose: Measures scholastic aptitude. Used for educational counseling.

Description: Multiple-item paper-pencil test of 12 specific aptitudes: verbal comprehension, calculations, disguised words, comparison, pattern completion, figural series, spatial (2D), spatial (3D), memory (paragraph), memory (symbols), coordination, and writing speed. Examiner required. Suitable for group use. SOUTH AFRICAN PUBLISHER

Timed: 2 hours

Scoring: Hand key; examiner evaluated; may be machine scored

Cost: (In Rands) test booklet 1,90; 10 answer sheets T11-T12 0,40; 10 answer sheets T1-T6, T7-T10 (specify form) 0,70; 10 profile sheets 0,70; scoring stencil (T1-T6) 2,10; scoring stencil (T7-T10) 1,60; manual 5,60; 10 machine answer sheets 1,10; orders from outside The RSA will be dealt with on merit

Publisher: Human Sciences Research Council

SEQUENTIAL TESTS OF EDUCATIONAL PROGRESS (STEP II)

Educational Testing Service

**Adolescent, adult
Grades 13 and above**

Purpose: Measures achievement in language, mathematics, science, and social studies. Used to assess academic mastery, diagnose deficiencies, and plan curriculum.

Description: Multiple-item paper-pencil battery of five tests measuring basic academic achievement. The 65-item English Expression Test assesses the ability to evaluate the correctness and effectiveness of sentences and proficiency in standard written English. The 60-item Reading Test measures the ability to read and comprehend a variety of materials. The 50-item Mathematics Basic Concepts Test measures the ability to recall facts and perform mathematical manipulation, comprehension of mathematical concepts, problem-solving techniques, and numerical operations, such as algebraic relations and statistics. The 50-item Science Test measures knowledge and understanding of fundamental science concepts, comprehension and application of fundamental science concepts, and mastery of science skills. The 85-item Social Studies Test measures student development skills and understanding of social change, the interdependence of indi-

viduals, communities, and societies; the way society directs and regulates the behavior of its members; and the nature of a democratic society. All tests are available in two equivalent forms, A and B. Examiner required. Suitable for group use.

Timed: 40 minutes per test

Scoring: Hand key; may be computer scored

Cost: Contact publisher

Publisher: CTB/McGraw-Hill

SEQUENTIAL TESTS OF EDUCATIONAL PROGRESS (STEP III)

Educational Testing Service

**Child, adolescent
Grades 3.5-12.9**

Purpose: Measures achievement in language, mathematics, science, and social studies. Used to assess individual and group academic mastery and to evaluate curriculum program.

Description: Multiple-item comprehensive testing program consisting of 10 levels: CIRCUS Preprimary and Primary Levels A-D (Grades PreK-3.5) and Intermediate and Advanced Levels E-J (Grades 3.5-12.9). The CIRCUS Preprimary and Primary levels assess prereading, reading, mathematics, and listening skills. Beginning with Grade 2, writing skills are measured. Study skills and social studies and science skills are tested beginning at Grade 3. The program also contains four end-of-course tests in algebra and geometry, biology, chemistry, and physics. Examiner required. Suitable for group use.

Timed: 40 minutes per test

Scoring: Hand key; may be computer scored

Cost: Multi-level specimen set (test booklet for Levels E-J, complete battery answer sheet, directions for administration, test development and content) $14.25; specimen set, Levels A and B (copy of both test books, teacher's edition, user's guide) $20.00; specimen set, Levels C and D (basic assessment tests, user's guide, directions for administration) $8.95

Publisher: CTB/McGraw-Hill

SRA ACHIEVEMENT SERIES FORMS 1-2 (ACH 1-2)
Robert A. Naslund, Louis P. Thorpe, and D. Welty Lefever

Child, adolescent
Grades K-12

Purpose: Assesses students' general scholastic achievement.

Description: Multiple-item paper-pencil academic achievement test assessing reading, math, language, science, and social studies. An optional section on educational ability and reference materials is included. The tests are norm-referenced. Two equivalent forms are available for each test. Examiner required. Suitable for group use.

Timed: 3-5 hours

Scoring: Hand key; may be computer scored

Cost: Forms 1 and 2, Level A: 25 booklets with ability measure $40.50; without ability measure $31.75; 25 practice sheets $2.50; manual $0.85; key for all levels $5.25; 100 profile sheets $13.80

Publisher: Science Research Associates, Inc.

SRA PAC PROGRAM
Robert A. Naslund, Louis P. Thorpe, and D. Welty Lefever

Child, adolescent
Grades 4-10

Purpose: Assesses students' general academic achievement. Used for student screening, grade placement, and scheduling.

Description: Multiple-item paper-pencil test measuring academic achievement in reading, math, language, science, social studies, and knowledge of reference materials. The Educational Ability Series (EAS) and the Kuder General Interest Survey are available optionally. The test is a norm-referenced, shortened version of the SRA Achievement Series. Examiner required. Suitable for group use.

Timed: 3 hours

Scoring: Hand key; may be computer scored

Cost: Contact publisher

Publisher: Science Research Associates, Inc.

SRA SURVEY OF BASIC SKILLS (SBS)

Grades K-12

Purpose: Measures students' achievement. Used by teachers and administrators for program planning and evaluation, teachers to provide remediation, and parents and counselors to understand a student's performance as it relates to others across the country.

Description: Multiple-item paper-pencil battery of tests surveying general academic achievement. The lower battery of tests (Levels 20-23), for Grades K-3, measures basic skills taught in reading (auditory discrimination, letters and sounds, decoding, listening comprehension, vocabulary, comprehension); mathematics (concepts/problem solving and computation); and language arts (mechanics, usage, spelling). The upper battery (Levels 34-37), for Grades 4-12, measures basic skills in reading (vocabulary and comprehension); language arts (mechanics, usage, spelling); mathematics (concepts, computation, problem solving); use of reference materials; social studies; and science. For Level 37, an additional Survey of Applied Skills score is reported, measuring knowledge of consumer economics, health and safety, employment, and community resources. An Education Ability Series also is available for use with the Survey of Basic Skills. The EAS measures vocabulary, arithmetic computation, letter patterns, word differences, and manipulation of forms in space, and provides an estimate of educational ability. Examiner required. Suitable for group use.

Timed: Varies

Scoring: Hand key; may be computer scored; may be machine scored

Cost: 25 machine-scorable test booklets and examiner's manual (SBS with EAS) $40.50-$45.00 depending on level; 25 machine-scorable test booklets (SBS only) $31.75-$36.50 depending on level; 25 practice sheets (required) $2.50 all levels; booklet containing answer keys, norms, and conversion tables $5.25 all levels

Publisher: Science Research Associates, Inc.

STANFORD MEASUREMENT SERIES—STANFORD ACHIEVEMENT TEST: 1ST EDITION (TASK)

*Eric F. Gardner, Robert Callis,
Jack C. Merwin,
and Richard Madden*

Adolescent   Grades 8-13   ☞ ✍

Purpose: Assesses school achievement status of children.

Description: Multiple-item paper-pencil test measuring achievement in three areas: reading, English, and mathematics. The test is divided into three levels: Level I (Grades 8-10), Level II (Grades 10-12), and College Edition (Grade 13). Two alternate and equivalent forms, A and B, are available. TASK scores are related to those of other Stanford batteries (SESAT, Stanford Achievement Test). The test has been superseded by the second edition of TASK. Examiner required. Suitable for group use.

Timed: Total battery 2 hours

Scoring: Hand key; computer scoring service available

Cost: Specimen set, specify level (test, manual) $12.00

Publisher: The Psychological Corporation

STANFORD MEASUREMENT SERIES—STANFORD ACHIEVEMENT TEST: 2ND EDITION (TASK)

*Eric F. Gardner, Robert Callis,
Jack C. Merwin,
and Herbert C. Rudman*

Adolescent   Grades 8-13   ☞ ✍

Purpose: Assesses school achievement status of children.

Description: Multiple-item paper-pencil test covering seven aspects of school achievement. The test is divided into two levels: TASK 1 and TASK 2. Both measure reading comprehension, vocabulary, spelling, language/English, mathematics, science, and social science. Together with the SESAT and the Stanford Achievement Test, the TASK provides continuous assessment throughout the school years. Examiner required. Suitable for group use.

Timed: Total battery 3 hours, 5 minutes

Scoring: Hand key; computer scoring service available

Cost: Specimen set (complete battery book, teacher's directions, norms booklet) $12.00

Publisher: The Psychological Corporation

STANFORD MEASUREMENT SERIES—STANFORD ACHIEVEMENT TEST: 6TH EDITION

*Richard Madden, Eric F. Gardner,
Herbert C. Rudman, Bjorn Karlsen,
and Jack C. Merwin*

Child, adolescent   ☞ ✍
Grades 1.5-9.9

Purpose: Assesses school achievement status of children.

Description: Six-level battery of paper-pencil tests measuring achievement in school. The six levels are Primary Level I, Primary Level II, Primary Level III, Intermediate Level I, Intermediate Level II, and Advanced Level. Primary Level I measures vocabulary, reading comprehension, word study skills, mathematics concepts, mathematics computation, spelling, and listening comprehension. Primary Level II tests mathematics applications, social science, and science, as well as the areas assessed at Primary Level I. Language is added at Primary Level III and Intermediate Levels I and II. The Advanced Level drops the word study skills and listening comprehension subtests. The test has been superseded by the Stanford Achievement Test: 7th Edition. Examiner required. Suitable for group use.

Timed: Varies

Scoring: Hand key; computer scoring service available

Cost: Specimen set, specify level (complete battery, teacher's directions, norms booklet) $12.00; the primary and intermediate levels include a practice test and directions

Publisher: The Psychological Corporation

STANFORD MEASUREMENT SERIES—STANFORD ACHIEVEMENT TEST: 7TH EDITION
Eric F. Gardner, Herbert C. Rudman, Bjorn Karlsen, and Jack C. Merwin

Child, adolescent
Grades 1.5-9.9

Purpose: Assesses school achievement status of children.

Description: Multiple-item paper-pencil test measuring several aspects of school achievement. The test is divided into six levels: Primary 1, Primary 2, Primary 3, Intermediate 1, Intermediate 2, and Advanced. Primary 1 and 2 test nine achievement areas: word study skills, word reading, reading comprehension, vocabulary, listening comprehension, spelling concepts of number, mathematics computation, and environment. Primary 3 and Intermediate 1 and 2 measure the same areas as Primary 1 and 2, as well as language/English, mathematics applications, science, and social science. Word reading and environment are not assessed. The Advanced Level assesses every area except word study skills. Together with the Stanford Early School Achievement Test and the Stanford Test of Academic Skills, the test provides for continuous assessment throughout the school years. Examiner required. Suitable for group use.

Timed: Varies

Scoring: Hand key; computer scoring service available

Cost: Specimen set, specify level (complete battery booklet, teacher's directions, norms booklet) $12.00

Publisher: The Psychological Corporation

STANFORD MEASUREMENT SERIES—STANFORD DIAGNOSTIC MATHEMATICS TEST (SDMT)
Leslie S. Beatty, Richard Madden, Eric F. Gardner, and Bjorn Karlsen

Child, adolescent
Grades 1.5-13

Purpose: Identifies individual pupil needs in the area of mathematics.

Description: Multiple-item paper-pencil test measuring mathematics skill in three areas: number system and numeration, computation, and applications. The test is divided into four levels: red (Grades 1.5-4.5), green (Grades 3.5-6.5), brown (Grades 5.5-8.5), and blue (Grades 7.5-13). Materials include a manual with prescriptive teaching strategies and two alternate and equivalent forms, A and B. The test is linked statistically with the Stanford Achievement Test Series. Examiner required. Suitable for group use.

Timed: Varies

Scoring: Hand key; computer scoring service available

Cost: Specimen set, specify level (test, manual, instructional placement report) $10.00; green, brown, and blue levels also include a hand-scorable answer document

Publisher: The Psychological Corporation

STANFORD MEASUREMENT SERIES—STANFORD DIAGNOSTIC MATHEMATICS TEST (SDMT): THIRD EDITION
Leslie S. Beatty, Eric F. Gardner, and Bjorn Karlsen

Child, adolescent
Grades 1.5-13

Purpose: Identifies individual pupil needs in mathematics.

Description: Multiple-item paper-pencil test covering three mathematics skill areas: number system and numeration, computation, and applications. The test is divided into four levels: red (Grades 1.8-4.8), green (Grades 4.1-6.8), brown (Grades 6.1-8.0), and blue (Grades

8.1-12.8). Materials include manual with prescriptive teaching strategies and two alternate and equivalent forms, G and H. The test is linked statistically with the Stanford Achievement Test Series. Examiner required. Suitable for group use.

Timed: 85-100 minutes, depending on level

Scoring: Hand key; computer scoring available

Cost: Examination kit, specify level (test booklet, manual, instructional placement report, directions for administering, a hand-scorable and MRC answer document for green, brown, and blue levels) $9.00

Publisher: The Psychological Corporation

STANFORD MEASUREMENT SERIES—STANFORD DIAGNOSTIC READING TEST (SDRT)
Bjorn Karlsen, Richard Madden, and Eric F. Gardner

Child, adolescent
Grades 1.5-13

Purpose: Measures major components of the reading process. Used for diagnosing specific pupil needs.

Description: Multiple-item paper-pencil test measuring four aspects of reading: comprehension, decoding, vocabulary, and rate. The test is divided into four levels: red (Grades 1.5-3.5), green (Grades 2.5-5.5), brown (Grades 4.5-9.5), and blue (Grades 9-13). Cutoff scores indicate whether remedial programming is needed. Materials include handbooks with instructional suggestions and instructional materials. Two alternate and equivalent forms, A and B, are available. The test is linked statistically with the Stanford Achievement Test Series. Examiner required. Suitable for group use.

Timed: Varies

Scoring: Hand key; computer scoring service available

Cost: Specimen set, specify level (test, manual, instructional placement report) $10.00; brown and blue levels include answer document

Publisher: The Psychological Corporation

STANFORD MEASUREMENT SERIES—STANFORD DIAGNOSTIC READING TESTS (SDRT): THIRD EDITION
Bjorn Karlsen and Eric F. Gardner

Child, adolescent
Grades 1.5-12.8

Purpose: Measures major components of the reading process. Used for diagnosing specific student needs.

Description: Multiple-item paper-pencil test measuring four aspects of reading: comprehension, vocabulary, decoding, and rate. The test is divided into four levels: red (Grades 1.8-3.8), green (Grades 3.1-5.8), brown (Grades 5.1-8.8), and blue (Grades 8.8-12.8). Cutoff scores indicate the need for remedial programming. Materials include handbooks with instructional suggestions and instructional materials. The test is linked statistically with the Stanford Achievement Test Series. Two alternate and equivalent forms, G and H, are available. Examiner required. Suitable for group use.

Timed: 1 hour, 45 minutes-2 hours, 6 minutes, depending on level

Scoring: Hand key; machine scoring available

Cost: Examination kit, specify level (test booklet, instructional placement report, directions for administering, hand-scorable and MRC answer document for brown and blue levels) $10.00

Publisher: The Psychological Corporation

STANFORD MEASUREMENT SERIES—STANFORD EARLY SCHOOL ACHIEVEMENT TEST: 1ST EDITION (SESAT)
Richard Madden and Eric F. Gardner

Child   Grades K.1-1.8

Purpose: Assesses school achievement of children at the kindergarten and first-grade level.

Description: Multiple-item paper-pencil test measuring children's achievement prior to entry into formal school instruction. The test is divided into two levels: Level I for kindergartners and Level II for first graders. The test covers the following areas at both levels: environment, mathematics, letters and sounds, and aural comprehension. Level II also measures word reading and sentence reading. This first edition has been superseded by the second edition. Examiner required. Suitable for group use. Available in Spanish.

Timed: Level I 1 hour, 30 minutes; Level II 2 hours, 20 minutes

Scoring: Hand key; computer scoring service available

Cost: Specimen set, specify level (test, directions) $11.00

Publisher: The Psychological Corporation

STANFORD MEASUREMENT SERIES—STANFORD EARLY SCHOOL ACHIEVEMENT TEST: 2ND EDITION (SESAT)
Richard Madden, Eric F. Gardner, and Cathy S. Collins

Child   Grades K.0-1.9

Purpose: Assesses school achievement of children at the kindergarten and first-grade level.

Description: Multiple-item paper-pencil test measuring several aspects of school achievement. The test is divided into two levels: SESAT 1 for kindergartners and SESAT 2 for children from midkindergarten through first grade. Both levels assess sounds and letters, word reading, listening to words and stories, mathematics, and environment. SESAT 2 also tests reading comprehension. Together with the Stanford Achievement Test: 7th Edition and the Stanford Test of Academic Skills, the SESAT provides for continuous assessment throughout the school years. Examiner required. Suitable for group use.

Timed: Total battery 2 hours, 25 minutes

Scoring: Hand key; computer scoring service available

Cost: Specimen set, specify level (complete battery book, teacher's directions, norms booklet) $11.00

Publisher: The Psychological Corporation

STECK-VAUGHN PLACEMENT SURVEY FOR ADULT BASIC EDUCATION
Beth Phillips

Adult

Purpose: Determines entry point for students in adult basic education.

Description: Multiple-item paper-pencil test assessing the student's ability in reading, language, and mathematics. The test is available at Level 1 (105 items) and Level 2 (141 items). The student reads a 60-word screening list to determine the proper level. Examiner required. Suitable for group use except the reading portion of Level 1.

Untimed: 45 minutes

Scoring: Hand key

Cost: 25 tests (specify level) $66.00; 50 answer sheets $6.00; teacher's set (manual, scoring template) $6.00

Publisher: Steck-Vaughn Company

STEENBURGEN DIAGNOSTIC-PRESCRIPTIVE MATH PROGRAM AND QUICK MATH SCREENING TEST
Refer to page 296.

STS-HIGH SCHOOL PLACEMENT TEST (HSPT)

Adolescent
Grades 8.3-9.3

Purpose: Measures eighth-graders' ability to read, write, and solve arithmetic problems. Used for high-school placement.

Description: 298-item paper-pencil test measuring verbal cognitive skills (60 items), quantitative cognitive skills (52 items), reading skills (62 items), mathe-

items), reading skills (62 items), mathematics skills (64 items), and language skills (60 items). Optional tests include Mechanical Aptitude, Science, and Catholic Religion. For these closed edition tests, schools may purchase the test materials and hand score them, or they may lease the test materials and use the standard scoring service. The closed edition offers new materials each year, with security insured (no specimen sets are available). One of the optional tests may be selected free-of-charge with the closed edition. The open edition is a reprint of a recent closed edition, for which specimen sets are available. Optional materials available for both editions include student record cards, student score folders, an interpretive manual, and technical reports. Examiner required. Suitable for group use.

Timed: 2½ hours

Scoring: Hand key; may be computer scored

Cost: Specimen set $9.00

Publisher: Scholastic Testing Service, Inc.

SURVEY OF BASIC COMPETENCIES (SBC)
Jwalla P. Somwaru

Child, adolescent Ages 3-15

Purpose: Measures children's ability to read, write, and solve arithmetic problems. Used to identify children with learning problems and screen for further testing with the Assessment of Basic Competencies diagnostic battery and for Chapter I assessment.

Description: 138-item verbal-response paper-pencil test consisting of four subtests: Information Processing (36 items), Language (36 items), Reading (30 items), and Mathematics (36 items). The test is individually administered, with the child and examiner on opposite sides of a desk. The test yields a raw score, developmental age score, grade equivalent score, and operating range (in terms of grade). The starter set includes the manual, a reusable

test, 20 response forms, and a carrying case. Examiner required. Not suitable for group use.

Untimed: 30 minutes

Scoring: Hand key

Cost: Starter set $54.50

Publisher: Scholastic Testing Service, Inc.

THE TEST FOR ENTRANCE INTO TEACHER EDUCATION PROGRAMS (TETEP)

Adult College students

Purpose: Measures abilities and achievement. Used with college students for admission and placement into schools of education in Washington.

Description: Paper-pencil test of abilities and achievement. The subtests include English Usage, Spelling, Reading Comprehension, Applied Mathematics, Vocabulary, and Mathematics Achievement. Test scores are returned to the institution in which the student desires entry into the teacher education program. The TETEP is a modified, shortened form of the Washington Pre-College Test. Examiner required. Suitable for group use.

Timed: 116 minutes

Scoring: Machine scored

Cost: $8.00 per student

Publisher: Washington Pre-College Program

TEST OF COGNITIVE SKILLS (TCS)
CTB/McGraw-Hill

Child, adolescent Grades 2-12

Purpose: Assesses skills important for success in school settings. Used for predicting school achievement and screening students for further evaluation.

Description: Multiple-item paper-pencil test consisting of four subtests (Sequences, Analogies, Memory, Verbal Reasoning) assessing cognitive skills. The Sequences test measures the student's ability to comprehend a rule or principle implicit in a pattern or sequence of figures, letters, or numbers. The Analogies test measures the student's ability to discern concrete or abstract relationships and to classify objects or concepts according to common attributes. The Memory test measures the student's ability to recall previously presented materials. The Verbal Reasoning test measures the student's ability to discern relationships and reason logically. The test is divided into five levels spanning Grades 2-12. The test yields the following scores: number of correct responses, age or grade percentile rank, stanine, scale score, and cognitive skills index. Examiner required. Suitable for group use.

Untimed: 1 hour

Scoring: Hand key; may be computer scored

Cost: Multi-level examination kit (assorted test booklets and answer sheets for different levels, handbook, record sheet) $24.00

Publisher: CTB/McGraw-Hill

TEST OF ENQUIRY SKILLS

Child, adolescent
Grades 7-10

Purpose: Measures achievement. Used as part of an educational evaluation.

Description: Multiple-item paper-pencil test of learning skills for students in Grades 7-10. Materials include a set of masters and a handbook. Examiner required. Suitable for group use.
AUSTRALIAN PUBLISHER

Untimed: 30-40 minutes

Scoring: Examiner evaluated

Cost: Contact publisher

Publisher: The Australian Council for Educational Research Limited

TEST OF SCHOLASTIC ABILITIES (TOSCA)
Neil Reid, Peter Jackson, Alison Gilmore, and Cedric Croft

Child, adolescent
Ages 9-14

Purpose: Measures student's current status in broad language and numerical

reasoning abilities. Used as beginning step in educational assessment.

Description: 70-item paper-pencil test measuring basic scholastic abilities. Both multiple-choice and completion-type items are included. The abilities measured are school-related but do not involve skills taught directly in the classroom. The test is divided into three levels: primary, intermediate, and secondary. Examiner required. Suitable for group use.
NEW ZEALAND PUBLISHER

Timed: 30 minutes

Scoring: Examiner evaluated

Cost: Contact publisher

Publisher: New Zealand Council for Educational Research

TEST ON APPRAISING OBSERVATIONS
Stephen P. Norris and Ruth King

Adult

Purpose: Measures the ability of senior high-school and college students to appraise observations reported by others. Used in critical thinking research and evaluation, classroom instruction and evaluation, and selection and placement of students.

Description: 50-item paper-pencil test consisting of two stories and related items. Each item consists of two observation statements. Examinees decide which statement, if either, is more believable. The test is based on a set of principles for appraising observations related to characteristics of the observer, the observation conditions, and the observation statement. Examiner/self-administered. Suitable for group use.
CANADIAN PUBLISHER

Untimed: 50-60 minutes

Scoring: Hand key

Cost: 35 test forms $35.00; 100 answer sheets $5.00; scoring key $1.00; manual $4.00; technical report of test design $10.00

Publisher: Institute for Educational Research and Development, Memorial University of Newfoundland

TESTS OF ACHIEVEMENT AND PROFICIENCY: FORM G

Dale P. Scannell, Oscar H. Haugh, Alvin H. Schild, and Gilbert Ulmer

Adolescent   Grades 9-12

Purpose: Measures student progress in the basic skills: reading, writing, listening, mathematics, using sources, social studies, and science. Used for evaluation and career planning.

Description: Multiple-item paper-pencil battery asessing student achievement in the basic skills. The test is available in Levels 15-18, which corresponds to the four high-school grades. Each level is available in a basic battery and a complete battery. The Complete Battery contains subtests measuring reading, mathematics, written expression, sources of information, science, social studies, listening, and expository writing. The listening test, new to this form, evaluates students' ability to remember exactly what they hear, to identify word meanings in context, to distinguish between fact and opinion, and to remember main points and important details in a lecture. The optional writing test offers a generative assessment to measure skills in narration in Grade 9, explanation in Grade 10, analysis in Grade 11, and argumentation in Grade 12. The Complete Battery is published in both a multilevel format with all four levels contained in a single test book and in a separate-level format. The multilevel format allows mixed-level testing in the same group. The test is normed concurrently with the New Cognitive Abilities Test for reliable comparisons between attained and anticipated achievement test scores. Examiner required. Suitable for group use.

Timed: Complete Battery 4 hours; Basic Battery 2 hours, 40 minutes

Scoring: Hand key; may be machine scored

Cost: Complete Battery test booklet for Levels 15 (single copy) $3.87; Basic Battery Test Booklet for Levels 15-18 (single copy) $3.00; 35 MRC answer sheets, teacher's guide (specify level) $15.00; two MRC scoring masks (specify level) $9.00

Publisher: The Riverside Publishing Company

TESTS OF ACHIEVEMENT AND PROFICIENCY: FORM T (TAP)

Dale P. Scannell, Oscar M. Haugh, Alvin H. Schild, and Gilbert Ulmer

Adolescent   Grades 9-12

Purpose: Measures student progress in learning such basic skills as reading, writing, mathematics, and science. Used for evaluation and career planning.

Description: Multiple-item paper-pencil battery assessing student achievement in the basic skills. The test is available in Levels 15-18, which correspond to the four high-school grades. Each level is available in a basic battery and a complete battery. The Complete Battery (353-365 items) contains six subtests covering reading comprehension, mathematics, written expression, using sources of information, social studies, and science. The Basic Battery (233-242 items) measures reading, mathematics, writing, and sources of information.

Objective, primarily norm-referenced score information allows students to compare their performances to those of other students in their grade and indicates areas where they have performed the most and least successfully. The test is normed concurrently with the Cognitive Abilities Test for reliable comparisons between attained and anticipated achievement test scores. Examiner required. Suitable for group use.

Timed: Complete Battery 240 minutes; Basic Battery 160 minutes

Scoring: Hand key; may be computer scored

Cost: Complete Battery test booklet for Levels 15-18 (single copy) $4.02; Basic Battery test booklet for Levels 15-18 (single copy) $2.82; 35 MRC answer sheets, teacher's guide, 35 student report folders, materials for machine scoring (specify level) $16.17; two MRC scoring masks (specify level) $9.27

Publisher: The Riverside Publishing Company

TESTS OF ACHIEVEMENT IN BASIC SKILLS (TABS)
EdITS Staff

Child, adolescent
Grades 2-13

Purpose: Evaluates individual student progress in reading, mathematics, and geometry. Used to measure overall class and school achievement growth related to specific academic objectives.

Description: 66-item paper-pencil criterion-referenced tests measuring student achievement in mathematics and reading comprehension. Two parallel forms, 1 and 2, are available at four ability levels: Level A for Grades 2-4, Level B for Grades 4-6, Level C for Grades 7-9, and Level D for Grades 10-13. Test items are arranged in three parts. Part I, Arithmetic Skills, consists of 30 items measuring basic arithmetic skills. Part II, Geometry-Measurement-Application, consists of 25 items measuring basic geometric concepts, arithmetic measurements, and application to practical problems. Part III, Modern Concepts, consists of 11 items measuring modern mathematics concepts. Examiner required. Suitable for group use.

Untimed: Not available

Scoring: Scoring service available

Cost: Contact publisher

Publisher: Educational and Industrial Testing Service

TESTS OF ADULT BASIC EDUCATION (TABE)
CTB/McGraw-Hill

Adult

Purpose: Measures adult proficiency in reading, mathematics, and language. Used by educators to identify individual weaknesses, establish the appropriate level of instruction, and measure growth after instruction.

Description: Multiple-item paper-pencil test measuring an adult's grasp of the reading, mathematics, and language skills required to function in society. The test is available on three levels: Level D, Difficult (Grades 6-9), Level M, Medium (Grades 4-6), and Level E, Easy (Grades 2-4). Levels D and M assess reading (vocabulary and comprehension), mathematics (computation, concepts, and problems), and language (mechanics and expression, spelling skills). Level E assesses only reading and math. A practice exercise is included to reduce anxiety and provide some experience in test-taking procedures. A Locator Test is administered to determine the appropriate test level. Examiner required. Suitable for group use.

Timed: Level D 2 hours, 17 minutes; Level M 2 hours, 29 minutes; Level E 1 hour, 28 minutes

Scoring: Hand key; may be computer scored

Cost: Multilevel examination kit (descriptive brochure, practice exercise and locator test, practice exercise and locator test answer sheet, test books and manuals for all levels, complete battery answer sheet, group record sheet, test reviewer's guide) $8.95

Publisher: CTB/McGraw-Hill

THE 3-R'S TEST
Nancy S. Cole, E. Roger Trent, Dena C. Wadell, Robert L. Thorndike, and Elizabeth P. Hagen

Child, adolescent
Grades K-12

Purpose: Measures achievement in basic reading, language, and mathematics skills.

Description: Three multiple-item paper-pencil batteries assessing academic achievement and ability: the Achievement Edition for Grades K-12 (Levels 6-18), the Achievement/Abilities Edition for Grades 3-12 (Levels 9-18), and the Class-Period Edition for Grades K-12 (Levels 6-18). The Achievement Edition measures reading and mathematics abilities for students in Grades K-2 and reading, mathematics, and language skills for students in Grades 3-12. The Achievement Edition is available in two alternate forms, A and B. The Achievement and Abilities Edition includes the achievement tests in the Achievement Edition as well as tests measuring verbal and quantitative abilities. La Prueba is the Spanish edition of The 3-R's Test, Form A (Levels 6-14). It is designed to determine the degree to which students are literate in Spanish and to assess the achievement of students whose primary language is Spanish. Each level is designed for administration in one or two grades. The Spanish version also measures achievement in science and social studies. Examiner required. Suitable for group use.

Timed: 50-190 minutes depending on edition and grade level

Scoring: Hand key; may be machine scored

Cost: Contact publisher concerning price and availability

Publisher: The Riverside Publishing Company

THE TWO CULTURES TEST
Edgar M. VanVleck

Adolescent, adult

Purpose: Measures general knowledge in science and the humanities. Used primarily by adults for personal information or for class placement.

Description: 100-item paper-pencil multiple-choice test of general knowledge in the two knowledge "cultures" of Western civilization: science (50 questions) and the humanities (50 questions). Information tested is likely to be encountered in high school and college curricula. A good knowledge of English and at least a high-school education are required. Examiner/self-administered. Suitable for group use.

Untimed: 1 hour

Scoring: Self-scored

Cost: Complete kit $6.00

Publisher: Polymath Systems

VERBAL REASONING TESTS SERIES

Child, adolescent
Ages 8-15

Purpose: Measures general scholastic ability. Used for educational evaluation.

Description: Six paper-pencil tests of verbal reasoning. Items include analogies, similarities, opposites, codes, odd-man-out, jumbled sentences, classifications, and syllogisms. The six tests and the ages they are designed for are Verbal Test BC (ages 8-10), Verbal Test CD (ages 9-11), Verbal Test C (ages 9-11), Verbal Test D (ages 10-12), Verbal Test EF (ages 11-13), and Verbal Test GH (ages 13-15). All tests require extensive use of written English and may not be suitable for poor readers. Examiner required. Suitable for group use.

BRITISH PUBLISHER

Timed: Varies

Scoring: Hand key

Cost: Primary specimen set (1 pupil booklet BC, CD, C, D and sample manual) £2.85; Secondary specimen set (1 pupil booklet D, EF, GH and sample manual) £2.25 (payment in sterling for all overseas orders)

Publisher: NFER-NELSON Publishing Company Ltd.

WASHINGTON PRE-COLLEGE PROGRAM

High-school juniors—
college transfer students

Purpose: Measures achievement, abilities, and interests and assesses values, personal background, and career plans. Used with Washington high-school students for admissions, guidance, and placement in colleges in Washington and nearby states. Used by high schools and state agencies for evaluation and policy making.

Description: Paper-pencil test of abilities and achievement. Includes English Usage, Spelling, Reading Comprehension, Mechanical Reasoning, Spatial Ability, Applied Mathematics, Vocabulary, and Mathematics Achievement subtests. The WPC program also includes the Registration Questionnaire, Vocational Interest Inventory (VII), standardized high school records compiled from official transcripts, and exercises for collecting additional career guidance data.

collecting additional career guidance data. Results are returned via a Guidance Report containing test results, high school record summary, 8 interest area scores, overall interest profile analysis, expectancies of success in 36 four-year college fields and 15 two-year training fields, and a summary of personal objectives. Available materials include a career planning guide that integrates the Guidance Report and additional personal data. Examiner required. Suitable for group use.

Timed: 3½ hours

Scoring: Machine scored

Cost: Test booklets, Registration Booklet, Guidance Report, Student Interpretation Guide $13.00 per student

Publisher: Washington Pre-College Program

WESTERN MICHIGAN UNIVERSITY ENGLISH QUALIFYING EXAM (EQE)
Refer to page 247.

WIDE RANGE ACHIEVEMENT TEST—REVISED (WRAT-R)
Sarah Jastak and Gary S. Wilkinson

Ages 5-adult

Purpose: Measures the basic educational skills of word recognition, spelling, and arithmetic, and identifies individuals with learning difficulties. Used for educational placement, measuring school achievement, vocational assessment, and job placement and training.

Description: Three paper-pencil subtests (50-100 items per subtest) assessing coding skills: Reading (recognizing and naming letters and pronouncing printed words); Spelling (copying marks resembling letters, writing name, and printing words); and Arithmetic (counting, reading number symbols, oral and written computation). The test consists of two levels: Level I (ages 5-11) and Level II (ages 12-adult). Optional word lists for both levels of the reading and spelling tests are offered on plastic cards, and a recorded pronunciation of the lists is provided on cassette tape. The tape itself can be used

to administer the spelling section. The test is normed for age rather than grade. For this revised version, norms are based on a national, stratified sample. In conjunction with other tests, such as the Wechsler Scales, WRAT-R is useful for determining personality structure. The test is restricted to educational and psychological professionals. A Large Print edition is available for those who require magnification of reading material. Examiner required. The spelling and arithmetic subtests are suitable for group use. The reading subtest must be individually administered.

Timed: 10 minutes per subtest

Scoring: Examiner evaluated

Cost: Manual $20.00; 25 test forms $8.00

Publisher: Jastak Assessment Systems

WOODCOCK LANGUAGE PROFICIENCY BATTERY (WLPB)
Richard W. Woodcock

Grades PreK and above

Purpose: Measures oral, reading, and written language in either English or Spanish. Used to diagnose learning disabilities in children and adults and for instructional planning.

Description: Multiple-item battery of eight subtests taken from the Woodcock-Johnson Psycho-Educational Battery measuring the following factors: picture vocabulary, antonyms-synonyms, analogies, letter-word identification, word attack, passage comprehension, dictation, and proofing. Within the school-age range, the WLPB-English can be administered to students with English as their second language. If the Spanish form also is given, the overview can include a description of proficiency in each language in each area of skill. Materials, in both forms, include the battery, response booklets, and manual. Examiner required. Not suitable for group use. Available in Spanish.

Untimed: Not available

Scoring: Examiner evaluated

Cost: English form $46.00; Spanish form $50.00

Publisher: DLM Teaching Resources

WOODCOCK-JOHNSON PSYCHO-EDUCATIONAL BATTERY (WJPEB)
Richard W. Woodcock and Mary Bonner Johnson

Grades PreK and above

Purpose: Evaluates individual cognitive ability, scholastic achievement, and interest level. Used to diagnose learning disabilities and for instructional planning, vocational rehabilitation counseling, and research.

Description: 27-test battery in three parts, some paper and pencil. It can be administered in its entirety or as single tests or clusters to meet specific appraisal needs. Part One tests cognitive ability in areas such as picture vocabulary, sentence memory, visual-auditory learning, antonyms-synonyms, and concept formation. Part Two covers letter-word identification, calculation, dictation, proofing, and science. Part Three tests interest levels in reading, mathematics, language, and physical and social fields. Materials include the test books, response booklets, cassette tape, and a technical manual, which also may be ordered separately. Not suitable for group use. Examiner required. Available in Spanish.

Untimed: Varies

Scoring: Examiner evaluated; computer scored

Cost: Complete set $125.00

Publisher: DLM Teaching Resources

WORD AND NUMBER ASSESSMENT INVENTORY (WNAI)
Charles B. Johansson

Adolescent, adult Grades 9 and above

Purpose: Measures individual aptitude for words and numbers. Used for career and school counseling and employment screening.

Description: 80-item paper-pencil multiple-choice test consisting of 50 vocabulary and 30 mathematics items on combined question-answer forms. The scores are compared to those of individuals at sev-

eral educational levels and in a number of occupations. Self-administered. Suitable for group use.

Untimed: 1 hour

Scoring: Computer scored

Cost: Manual $9.75; interpretive report $4.25-$8.50 depending on quantity and scoring method; profile report $2.65-$4.25 depending on quantity and scoring method; 25 answer sheets $8.75

Publisher: National Computer Systems/PAS Division

Education Development and School Readiness

THE ABC INVENTORY
Normand Adair and George Blesch

Child   Ages 3½-6½

Purpose: Assesses the school readiness of preschoolers and provides an index of a child's maturity upon entering school. Identifies children needing further evaluation and assistance. Provides a basis for better parent-teacher understanding.

Description: Oral-response and task-performance test assessing a child's general level of maturity and development. The four sections of the test require the child to draw a man; answer language questions, such as "what has wings" or "tell me the color of grass"; answer cognitive questions, such as "what is ice when it melts" or "how do we hear"; and perform motor activity tasks, such as counting four squares, folding a paper triangle, repeating four digits, and copying a square. Examiner required. Not suitable for group use.

Untimed: 8-9 minutes

Scoring: Examiner evaluated

Cost: 50 inventories, manual $8.00

Publisher: Educational Studies and Development

ACER CHECKLISTS FOR SCHOOL BEGINNERS

Child   Grades PreK-1

Purpose: Measures the school readiness of preschool and kindergarten children. Identifies children in need of further evaluation and developmental assistance.

Description: Multiple-item paper-pencil checklist consisting primarily of single-task activities covering the following areas: social development, motor skills, memory and attention, and language skills. Each item is scored plus or minus, depending on whether the child has displayed the developmental behavior presented in the item. The items may be checked in any order, and most may be evaluated through informal observation. Based on the results of the checklist, the child's behavioral development is assessed to provide a measure of the child's readiness for participation in formal school situations. The checklist is available in two forms: one for teachers and one for parents. Materials include the checklist in its alternate forms, a class record sheet, and a manual. Self-administered by evaluator. Suitable for group use. The parent checklist is available in the following foreign language versions: Arabic, Greek, Italian, Maltese, Serbo-Croatian (Yugoslav), Spanish, and Turkish.
AUSTRALIAN PUBLISHER

Untimed: Varies

Scoring: Examiner evaluated

Cost: Contact publisher

Publisher: The Australian Council for Educational Research Limited

ACER EARLY SCHOOL SERIES

Child   PreK

Purpose: Measures the perceptual, verbal, and numerical skills that are needed by children entering kindergarten. Used for readiness screening and to identify children in need of further evaluation and assistance.

Description: Multiple-item paper-pencil tests of 10 readiness skills: auditory discrimination, recognition of initial consonant sounds, numbers, figure formation, prepositions, pronouns, verb tense, negation, and comprehension. Overall Word Knowledge score is also obtained. Materials include separate administration booklets for each test and the handbook *Early Identification and Intervention.* Examiner required. Suitable for group use.
AUSTRALIAN PUBLISHER

Untimed: Varies

Scoring: Hand key

Cost: Contact publisher

Publisher: The Australian Council for Educational Research Limited

ACHIEVEMENT IDENTIFICATION MEASURE (AIM)
Refer to page 696.

ADAPTIVE BEHAVIOR SCALE FOR INFANTS AND EARLY CHILDHOOD (ABSI)
Henry Leland, Mandana Shoaee, Douglas McElwain, and Rachael Christie

Child   Ages 0-6

Purpose: Describes the adaptive behavior of infants and young children. Aids effective program planning and preschool placement. May be used with the mentally retarded, developmentally disabled, and physically handicapped.

Description: 63-item interview examination covering seven domains and an 80-item review test of potential maladaptive social behavior. The domains measured are adaptive behavior, independent functioning and physical development, communication skills, conceptual skills, play skills, self-direction and personal responsibility, and socialization. The test may be used to detect major psychological problems that may be developing, indications of possible brain damage or other sensory-motor problems, and indications of possible delays in cognitive and communication development. The test is administered by an examiner acting as a third party to a parent, teacher, or other individual who has thorough knowledge of the child. Examiner required. Not suitable for group use.

Untimed: 45 minutes

Scoring: Examiner evaluated

Cost: Specimen set $9.00.

Publisher: The Nisonger Center, Ohio State University

ADELPHI PARENT ADMINISTERED READINESS TEST (A.P.A.R.T.)
Pnina S. Klein

Child   Ages 5.2-6.3

Purpose: Identifies learning disabilities and language problems of preschoolers. Used for counseling and helping parents understand the relationship between ability and academic achievement.

Description: 42-item paper-pencil examination consisting of 10 subtests covering concept formation, letter form recognition, writing ability, knowledge of numbers, visual perception, visual memory, comprehension and memory, auditory sequential memory, recognition of facial expressions of emotion, and creative ability. The parent reads directions to the child, records responses, and scores the test. The test is to be administered 4-6 months before the child enters first grade. Examiner required. Not suitable for group use. May be administered in languages other than English.

Untimed: 20 minutes

Scoring: Hand key; examiner evaluated

Cost: 10 tests $24.95

Publisher: Mafex Associates, Inc.

Information and availability unconfirmed; no publisher response.

ANALYSIS OF READINESS SKILLS
Mary C. Rodriques,
William H. Vogler,
and James F. Wilson

Child   Grades K-1

Purpose: Measures a child's reading and mathematics readiness.

Description: 30-item oral-response test consisting of three subtests (10 items

each): visual perception of letters, letter identification, and mathematics (identification of numerals and counting numerals). The teacher's manual provides directions for administering the tests in English or Spanish and includes norms for both English-speaking and Spanish-speaking children. Examiner required. Suitable for group use.

Untimed: 35 minutes

Scoring: Examiner evaluated

Cost: Test kit (25 test booklets, teacher's manual, scoring key, class record sheet, sample item chart) $17.16

Publisher: The Riverside Publishing Company

ANTON BRENNER DEVELOPMENTAL GESTALT TEST OF SCHOOL READINESS
Anton Brenner

Child   Ages 5-6

Purpose: Assesses a child's readiness for kindergarten or first grade. Used to identify children requiring special attention.

Description: Multiple-item oral-response and task-assessment test using Gestalt and developmental principles to measure children's conceptual and perceptual differentiating abilities. The test provides a quantitative and qualitative evaluation of a child's perceptual-conceptual development and identifies three special groups: early maturing and/or gifted; slowly maturing and/or retarded; and emotionally disturbed. The test is almost "culture free" and can be used with non-English-speaking and culturally deprived children. Examiner required. Not suitable for group use.

Untimed: 5 minutes

Scoring: Hand key; examiner evaluated

Cost: Complete kit (25 booklets, manual, set of test materials) $29.50

Publisher: Western Psychological Services

ASSESSMENT IN NURSERY EDUCATION
Margaret Bate and Marjorie Smith

Child   Ages 3-5

Purpose: Assesses development of children. Used for identifying strengths and weaknesses and for monitoring progress.

Description: Multiple-item observational assessment of five major developmental areas: social skills and social thinking, talking and listening, thinking and doing, manual and tool skills, and physical skills. The child is assessed on his observed and demonstrated ability to perform special tasks. Materials include outlines of model people, pictures and picture story cards, a set of shapes for copying, a set of shapes for cutting out, and guideline patterns for drawing. Videotapes demonstrating assessment are also available. Examiner required. Not suitable for group use.
BRITISH PUBLISHER

Untimed: Varies

Scoring: Examiner evaluated

Cost: Complete kit (1 manual, 1 colour selection booklet, 1 individual record form, 1 set of outlines of model people, 2 pictures, 2 sets of picture story cards, 1 set of shapes for cutting out, guideline patterns for drawing) £31.60; video recordings set in three parts £132.25 (payment in sterling for all overseas orders)

Publisher: NFER-NELSON Publishing Company Ltd.

ATTITUDE TOWARD SCHOOL QUESTIONNAIRE (ASQ)
Refer to page 683.

THE BARBER SCALES OF SELF-REGARD FOR PRESCHOOL CHILDREN
Refer to page 3.

BASIC SCHOOL SKILLS INVENTORY—DIAGNOSTIC (BSSI-D)
Donald D. Hammill and James E. Leigh

Child   Ages 4-6.11

Purpose: Determines the special learning needs of children by pinpointing both the general areas and the specific readiness skills that need remedial attention. Results of this testing-for-teaching-

approach-to-assessment provide practical knowledge for teaching children the items they do not know.

Description: 110-item paper-pencil test enabling the examiner to view a child's performance individually or compared with his peers. The test measures six areas of school performance: daily living skills, spoken language, reading readiness, writing readiness, math readiness, and classroom behavior. A companion test is the Basic School Skills Inventory—Screen. Examiner required. Not suitable for group use.

Untimed: Varies

Scoring: Examiner evaluated

Cost: Complete (examiner's manual, 50 answer sheets, picture cards, storage box) $46.00

Publisher: Pro-Ed

BASIC SCHOOL SKILLS INVENTORY—SCREEN (BSSI-S)
Donald D. Hammill and James E. Leigh

Child   Ages 4-6.11

Purpose: Diagnoses children who are "high risk" for school failure, need more in-depth assessment, and should be referred for further evaluation. Assesses a child's overall readiness for school.

Description: 20-item paper-pencil observational screening device that examines daily living skills, spoken language, reading readiness, writing readiness, math readiness, and classroom behavior. The examiner checks off the answers he knows about the child; further investigation may be needed for some items. A companion test is the Basic School Skills Inventory—Diagnostic. Examiner required. Not suitable for group use.

Untimed: 5-8 minutes

Scoring: Examiner evaluated

Cost: Complete (examiner's manual, 50 answer sheets) $14.00

Publisher: Pro-Ed

BATTELLE DEVELOPMENTAL INVENTORY
DLM Teaching Resources staff

Child   Ages 0-8

Purpose: Evaluates the development of children from infant to primary levels. Screens and diagnoses developmental strengths and weaknesses. Used to establish IEPs and aid in placement and eligibility decisions.

Description: Multiple-item test assessing key developmental skills in five domains: personal-social, adaptive, motor, communications, and cognition. Information is obtained through structured interactions with the child in a controlled setting, observation of the child, and interviews with the child's parents, caregivers, and teachers. Test items contain content and sequence directly compatible with infant and preschool curricula for use in generating IEPs. The test yields standard scores, percentile ranks, and age equivalent scores. The test is administered by a teacher or trained paraprofessional and may be administered to handicapped children using various modifications. Examiner required. Not suitable for group use.

Untimed: Screening examination 10-30 minutes; diagnostic evaluation 1-2 hours

Scoring: Examiner evaluated

Cost: Test kit (15 scoring booklets, 15 screening test booklets, test items, manual) $135.00

Publisher: DLM Teaching Resources

BEHAVIOUR STUDY TECHNIQUE
Refer to page 4.

BIRTH TO THREE DEVELOPMENTAL SCALE
Refer to page 5.

BOEHM TEST OF BASIC CONCEPTS
Ann E. Boehm

Child   Grades K-2

Purpose: Measures children's mastery of basic concepts used in classroom instruction. Identifies children with low level of concept development. Targets specific areas for basic concept remediation.

Description: 50-item paper-pencil multiple-choice picture test of concepts related to quantity, space, and time. The child responds to oral instructions by marking one of several pictures. Materials include two alternate forms, A and B, which measure knowledge of the same concepts. Examiner required. Suitable for group use. Available in Spanish.

Untimed: 15-20 minutes

Scoring: Hand key

Cost: Examination kit (test booklet for each form, English directions, manual, class record, hand key) $5.50; manual $5.00; Spanish directions (Form A or B) $2.00

Publisher: The Psychological Corporation

BOEHM TEST OF BASIC CONCEPTS—PRESCHOOL VERSION
Ann E. Boehm

Child   Ages 3-5

Purpose: Measures young child's knowledge of 26 basic relational concepts. Used for early detection of poor concept understanding that could lead to developmental delay.

Description: 52-item test utilizing a pictorial booklet to display the concepts to be tested. The child responds to oral instructions by pointing to one of several pictures. The examiner records the child's responses on the record form. Each concept is tested twice. Examiner required. Not suitable for group use.

Untimed: 10-15 minutes

Scoring: Hand key

Cost: Contact publisher

Publisher: The Psychological Corporation

BRACKEN BASIC CONCEPT SCALE—DIAGNOSTIC SCALE (BBCS-DIAG)
Bruce A. Bracken

Child   Ages 2½-8

Purpose: Measures a child's ability to acquire concepts such as color, quantity, and time sequence. Used by speech pathologists and school psychologists to screen students for special attention.

Description: 258-item verbal "point-to" test using picture stimuli to evaluate 11 categories of basic concept acquisition, including color, shape, size, quantity, counting, letter identification, direction/position, time/sequence, texture, comparisons, and social/emotional responses. The examiner shows a picture to the child and records the "point-to" response on a diagnostic scale form provided with the test package. The test is influenced by expressive language deficits or physical disabilities. Examiner required. Not suitable for group use.

Untimed: 20-40 minutes

Scoring: Hand key

Cost: Complete program $83.00; examiner's manual $12.00; stimulus manual $59.00; 25 diagnostic record forms $12.00; 12 screening tests (specify Form A or B) $11.00

Publisher: The Psychological Corporation

BRACKEN BASIC CONCEPT SCALE—SCREENING TEST (BBCS-SCREENING)
Bruce A. Bracken

Child   Ages 2½-8

Purpose: Helps identify children whose ability to distinguish concepts is below age-level expections. Used as a guide for further testing.

Description: Two 30-item paper-pencil multiple-choice tests in which two books of picture stimuli assess different concepts of approximately equal difficulty in eight categories of basic concept acquisition.

The test yields a single norm-referenced standard score. Examiner required. Suitable for group use.

Timed: 20-30 minutes

Scoring: Hand key

Cost: $11.00

Publisher: The Psychological Corporation

BRIEF INDEX OF ADAPTIVE BEHAVIOR (BIAB)
R. Steve McCallum, Maurice S. Herrin, Jimmy P. Wheeler, and Jeanette R. Edwards

Child, adolescent   Ages 5-17

Purpose: Evaluates the development of adaptive behavior in children and adolescents. Used for counseling purposes.

Description: 39-item paper-pencil observational inventory assessing three domains of adaptive behavior: independent functioning, socialization, and communication. The inventory is completed and scored by either a parent or teacher. The manual includes a discussion of the test and procedures for administration and scoring. Self-administered. Not suitable for group use.

Untimed: Varies

Scoring: Examiner evaluated

Cost: Starter set (manual, 20 response sheets) $8.00; specimen set $6.00

Publisher: Scholastic Testing Service, Inc.

THE BRIGANCE® DIAGNOSTIC INVENTORY OF EARLY DEVELOPMENT
Albert H. Brigance

Child   Developmental ages 0-7

Purpose: Measures the development of children functioning below the developmental age of seven years. Diagnoses developmental delays and monitors progress over a period of time. Used to develop IEPs.

Description: 200 paper-pencil oral-response and direct-observation skill assessments measuring psychomotor, self-help, communication, general knowledge and comprehension, and academic skill levels. Test items are arranged in developmental sequential order in the following major skill areas: preambulatory, gross motor, fine motor, prespeech, speech and language, general knowledge and comprehension, readiness, basic reading, manuscript writing, and basic math skills. An introductory section outlines how to administer the tests, assess skill levels, record the results, identify specific instructional objectives, and develop IEPs. Results, expressed in terms of developmental ages, are entered into the individual record book, which indicates graphically at each testing the level of competency the individual has achieved. An optional group record book monitors the progress of 15 individuals. Examiner required. Not suitable for group use.

Untimed: Varies

Scoring: Examiner evaluated

Cost: Assessment book, 10 individual developmental record books $79.00; group record book $7.95; free test excerpts available

Publisher: Curriculum Associates, Inc.

THE BRIGANCE® K & 1 SCREEN
Albert H. Brigance

Child   Grades K-1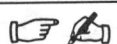

Purpose: Assesses the basic skills necessary for success in Grades K-1. Identifies students needing special service referral, determines appropriate pupil placement, and assists in planning instructional programs and developing IEPs.

Description: Multiple-item paper-pencil oral-response and direct-observation assessments measuring the following basic skills: personal data response, color recognition, picture vocabulary, visual discrimination, visual-motor skills, standing gross-motor skills, draw-a-person (body image), rote counting, identification of body parts, reciting the alphabet, following verbal directions, numeral comprehension, recognizing lowercase letters (uppercase alternate), auditory discrimination, printing personal data, syntax and fluency, and numerals in sequence. Five

optional advanced assessments are included for students scoring 95 percent or above on the basic first-grade assessment: response to picture, articulation of sounds, basic preprimer vocabulary, preprimer/primer oral reading, and basic number skills.

Personal information, assessment results, scoring, testing observations, comparative summary of the screening, and recommendations are all recorded on the pupil data sheet. An optional class summary record folder collects and summarizes data for 30 pupils. Optional forms for teacher rating, parent rating, and examiner observations are available. Separate pupil data sheets and class summary record folders are required. Criterion-referenced results are translated directly into curriculum or program objectives to meet the needs of individual pupils. Test items are cross-referenced to the Brigance Inventory of Basic Skills and the Inventory of Early Development to facilitate further evaluation of skill deficiencies. Examiner required. Not suitable for group use.

Untimed: 12 minutes

Scoring: Examiner evaluated

Cost: Assessment manual $35.95; 30 pupil data sheets, class summary record folder for Grade K $11.95; 30 pupil data sheets, class summary record folder for Grade 1 $12.00

Publisher: Curriculum Associates, Inc.

BRIGANCE® PRESCHOOL SCREEN
Albert H. Brigance

Child

Purpose: Evaluates basic developmental and readiness skills of children. Used for program planning, placement, and special service referrals.

Description: Multiple-item oral-response and task-performance test evaluating basic developmental and readiness skills. Children identify body parts, objects, and colors; demonstrate gross and visual motor skills; match colors; explain the use of objects; repeat sentences; build with blocks; and provide personal data. Number concepts, picture vocabulary, and use of plural s, -ing, prepositions, and irregular plural nouns are tested also. Rating forms and supplementary skill assessments allow for additional observations and extended screening options. Examiner required. Suitable for group use.

Untimed: 12 minutes

Scoring: Examiner evaluated

Cost: SCREEN (with building blocks for tests) $35.90; 30 three-year-old child data forms $11.95; 30 four-year-old child data forms $12.00

Publisher: Curriculum Associates, Inc.

BRITISH PICTURE VOCABULARY SCALES
Refer to page 503.

CALIFORNIA PRESCHOOL SOCIAL COMPETENCY SCALE
Samuel Levine, Freeman F. Elzey, and Mary Lewis

Child   Ages 2.6-5.6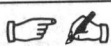

Purpose: Assesses the social competency of preschool children ages 2.6-5.6. Used by teachers for diagnosis, placement, or measurement of the development of young children.

Description: 30-item paper-pencil rating scale providing objective, numerical evaluations of the social competency of preschool children. The items call for specific behaviors (preschool children's interpersonal behavior and the degree to which they assume social responsibility). The manual provides percentile norms for children from high and low occupational levels for four age groups (by sex) from ages 2.6-5.6. Examiner required. Not suitable for group use.

Untimed: Not available

Scoring: Hand key

Cost: Specimen set $2.75; manual $2.25; 25 tests $8.75

Publisher: Consulting Psychologists Press, Inc.

CALLIER-AZUSA SCALE: G-EDITION
Refer to page 5.

CENTRAL INSTITUTE FOR THE DEAF PRESCHOOL PERFORMANCE SCALE (CID PRESCHOOL PERFORMANCE SCALE)
Refer to page 600.

CLYMER-BARRETT READINESS TEST
Theodore Clymer and Thomas C. Barrett

Child   Grades K-1

Purpose: Measures the important skills and background necessary for success in beginning instruction, especially in reading. Identifies students with serious skill deficits. Used at the end of Kindergarten to assess the results of a readiness program and at the beginning of Grade 1 to group students and determine instructional goals.

Description: 116-item paper-pencil multiple-choice test and 24-item observational inventory (completed by the child's classroom teacher) assessing readiness for first-grade instruction. Six tests measure three types of skills: recognizing letters (35 items) and matching words (20 items) measuring visual discrimination, beginning sounds (20 items) and ending sounds (20 items) measuring auditory discrimination, and completing shapes (20 items) and copy-a-sentence (1 item) measuring visual-motor coordination. The tests are administered during three separate periods, one period for each skill area assessed. The first test of visual discrimination (recognizing letters) and the first test of auditory discrimination (beginning sounds) may be administered in a short form for screening purposes. The readiness survey collects teacher observations concerning oral language facility, concept development, listening and thinking skills, social and emotional development, and work habits. All six tests, the readiness survey, and a student summary page are contained in one 16-page booklet and available in equivalent Forms A and B for pre- and posttesting. The test also includes a class record sheet and a manual. The test is a revised version of the

Clymer-Barrett Prereading Battery.
Examiner required. Suitable for group
use.

Untimed: Varies

Scoring: Examiner evaluated

Cost: Contact publisher

Publisher: Chapman, Brook & Kent

COGNITIVE CONTROL BATTERY: THE FRUIT DISTRACTION TEST
Refer to page 578.

COGNITIVE CONTROL BATTERY: THE LEVELING-SHARPENING HOUSE TEST
Refer to page 578.

COGNITIVE CONTROL BATTERY: THE SCATTERED SCANNING TEST
Refer to page 579.

COGNITIVE SKILLS ASSESSMENT BATTERY
Ann E. Boehm and Barbara Slater

Child   Grades PreK-K

Purpose: Assesses preschool and kindergarten children's progress relative to teaching goals in cognitive and physical-motor areas. Used by teachers for curriculum planning and to match classroom goals with cognitive skills.

Description: 64-item verbal test using easel cards to measure orientation towards environment, discrimination of similarities and differences, comprehension and concept formation, coordination, and immediate and delayed memory. The easel is placed between the examiner and the child, and the child is introduced to the task. The examiner goes through the cards asking questions and recording the responses. Materials include an easel and 64 cards, response sheets, manual, eight blocks, watch, and paper and pencils. The test does not provide criteria levels and no total score is obtained. The examiner should be a teacher, learning

disability specialist, or school psychologist. Examiner required. Not suitable for group use. Available in Japanese.

Untimed: 20-25 minutes

Scoring: Examiner evaluated

Cost: Complete kit (card easel, assessor's manual, class record sheet, 30 pupil response sheets) $48.95; manual $3.50

Publisher: Teachers College Press

THE COMMUNICATION SCREEN: A PRESCHOOL SPEECH-LANGUAGE SCREENING TOOL
Refer to page 622.

COMMUNICATIVE EVALUATION CHART
Refer to page 6.

COMPREHENSIVE ASSESSMENT PROGRAM: BEGINNING EDUCATION ASSESSMENT (BEA)

Child   Ages 4-6

Purpose: Assesses children's educational development. Used for screening children for learning problems.

Description: Multiple-item paper-pencil measure of student's cognitive growth with reading-, language-, and mathematics-related tasks. The test consists of three separate but related test levels. All tasks are examiner-paced to reduce anxiety and respond to individual needs. The test may be used with the CAP Achievement Series to provide continuous assessment from prekindergarten through high school. Examiner required. Suitable for group use.

Untimed: Open ended

Scoring: Hand key; may be machine scored; may be computer scored

Cost: 35 hand-scorable test booklets Level 4 $40.28; Levels 5 and 6 $30.35; 35 machine-scorable test booklets Levels 5 and 6 $41.15; manual $7.20; hand key (specify level) $1.50; 35 record forms (specify level) $6.75

Publisher: American Testronics

COMPREHENSIVE IDENTIFICATION PROCESS (CIP)
R. Reid Zehrbach

Child   Ages 2.5-5.5

Purpose: Evaluates the mental and physical development of young children. Used to identify those in need of special medical, psychological, or educational help before entering Kindergarten or the first grade.

Description: Multiple-item verbal response and task-assessment test of eight areas of child development: cognitive-verbal, fine motor, gross motor, speech and expressive language, hearing, vision, social/affective, and medical history. The screening kit contains administrator's and interviewer's manuals, screening booklet, 35 parent interview forms, 35 observation of behavior forms, 35 speech and expressive language forms, 35 record folders, and the materials required for the tasks (blocks, balls, beads, buttons, crayons, etc.). The test can be administered by trained paraprofessionals supervised by professionals in the preschool area. Suggestions for dealing with various cultural and language backgrounds are included. The test helps meet the Child Find requirements of PL94-142. Examiner required. Not suitable for group use. Available in Spanish.

Untimed: 30 minutes

Scoring: Examiner evaluated

Cost: CIP screening kit $84.00

Publisher: Scholastic Testing Service, Inc.

CONCEPT ASSESSMENT KIT— CONSERVATION (CAK)
Marcel L. Goldschmid and Peter M. Bentler

Child   Ages 4-7

Purpose: Assesses the cognitive development of preschool and early school-age children. Used to assess the effect of training based on Piaget's theories.

Description: Multiple-item task-assessment and oral-response test measuring the development of the concept of conservation. Two parallel forms, A and B, measure conservation in terms of two-dimensional space, number, substance, continuous quantity, discontinuous quantity, and weight. Form C measures conservation in terms of area and length. Test items are constructed to assess the child's conservation behavior and comprehension of the principle involved. The items require the child to indicate the presence or absence of conservation and specify the reason for his judgment. CAK is relatively independent of IQ but correlates significantly with school performance. The two parallel forms assess the effect of training, and Form C tests the transfer effects of the training. Norms are provided separately for boys and girls ages 4-7. Examiner required. Not suitable for group use.

Untimed: 15 minutes per form

Scoring: Hand key

Cost: Complete kit (Forms A, B, C, manual) $41.50

Publisher: Educational and Industrial Testing Service

COOPERATIVE PRESCHOOL INVENTORY
Bettye M. Caldwell and Judith H. Freund

Child   Ages 3-6

Purpose: Assesses a child's achievement in areas necessary for school success. Used to screen children entering school and to estimate the degree of disadvantage the child may have.

Description: 64-item oral-response test measuring the child's knowledge of self, ability to follow directions, verbal expressions, basic numerical concepts, and sensory attributes. The test is verbally administered, and the examiner records the child's "right," "wrong," or "don't know" responses. Items necessary for testing are a recording leaflet, blank sheet of paper, three small cars, eight large crayons, one box of checkers, and three cardboard boxes. Examiner required. Not suitable for group use. Available in Spanish.

Untimed: 15 minutes

Scoring: Examiner evaluated

Cost: Directions for administering and scoring $1.00; 20 recording forms $6.25; handbook $3.75

Publisher: CTB/McGraw-Hill

CREATIVITY TESTS FOR CHILDREN (CT)
J.P. Guilford et al.

Child   Grades 4-7

Purpose: Measures creative thinking among children by assessing verbal and nonverbal modes of expression. Used for counseling, group placement, and research.

Description: 10 paper-pencil tests measuring different aspects of divergent production. Both semantic (verbal) and visual-figural abilities are tested in the battery. The tests are Names for Stories, What to Do with It, Similar Meanings, Writing Sentences, Kinds of People, Make Something Out of It, Different Letter Groups, Making Objects, Hidden Letters, and Adding Decorations. It is recommended that the battery as a whole be used. The tests are adaptations of adult forms for the same factors. The manual of interpretations, profile chart, and review set cover the entire battery. The tests, scoring guides, and administratives manuals may be ordered for individual tests. Alternate forms are available. Norms are provided for fourth- and sixth-grade students. The tests are restricted to A.P.A. members. Examiner required. Suitable for group use.

Timed: 1 hour, 40 minutes

Scoring: Examiner evaluated

Cost: Specimen set (tests, scoring guide, manual) $25.00

Publisher: SOI Institute; distributed by M & M Systems

CROFT READINESS ASSESSMENT IN COMPREHENSION KIT (CRAC-KIT)
Marion L. McGuire and Marguerite J. Bumpus

Child

Purpose: Provides diagnostic information about comprehension readiness. Used for planning instruction in deficit areas with special needs, bilingual, and gifted children.

Description: Mulitple-item four-part performance test of 18 comprehension readiness objectives. Six skills (oral language readiness, written language readiness, and pattern readiness: classification, sequence, causation, and comparison) are taught at the concrete, semiabstract, and abstract levels. A box for each skill area contains objects, pictures, and activities for assessing a child's developmental stage in thinking. The kit also includes a teacher's guide, class record charts, and individual reading readiness record cards. Examiner required. Not suitable for group use.

Untimed: Not available

Scoring: Not available

Cost: $199.00

Publisher: Media Materials, Inc.

CTBS READINESS TEST
Refer to page 519.

DABERON SCREENING FOR SCHOOL READINESS
Virginia A. Danzer, Mary Frances Gerber, and Theresa M. Lyons

Handicapped children Ages 4-6

Purpose: Assesses the school readiness of children and other handicapped and difficult to manage children. Used to develop IEPs.

Description: Multiple-item oral-response and task-performance test assessing language skills, knowledge of body parts, color and number concepts, functional use of prepositions, plurals, ability to follow directions, general knowledge, visual perception, gross-motor development, and the ability to categorize. A high percentage of accurate responses indicates school readiness. Innaccurate responses indicate future problem areas, the need for further diagnostic and prognostic study, and information that needs to be taught. The results yield a Learning Readiness Equivalency age score to identify children with learning difficulties. A *Report On Readiness* is provided for parent and teacher discussion. The manual includes information regarding administration and assessment procedures and instructional objectives for writing IEPs. Examiner required. Not suitable for group use.

Untimed: 20-40 minutes

Scoring: Examiner evaluated

Cost: Complete test kit (manual, materials needed for administration, 25 screening forms, 25 *Report On Readiness*, and 5 classroom summary forms) $59.95

Publisher: ASIEP Education Company

THE DALLAS PRE-SCHOOL SCREENING TEST

Child   Ages 3-6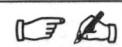

Purpose: Assesses learning disabilities of preschool children. Identifies children in need of special education assistance.

Description: Measures level of development in six learning areas: auditory (listening, discrimination, memory), language (receptive, expressive, communication), motor (gross and fine), visual (drawings, color discrimination, geometric designs), psychological (vocabulary and number concepts), and articulation (phonemes, initial and final positions). Examiner required. Not suitable for group use. Available in Spanish.

Untimed: Not available

Scoring: Hand key; examiner evaluated

Cost: Complete kit (manual, cards, 25 pupil record forms and profile sheets) $27.50

Publisher: Dallas Educational Services

DEGANGI-BERK TEST OF SENSORY INTEGRATION (TSI)
Refer to page 559.

DEVELOPMENTAL ACTIVITIES SCREENING INVENTORY (DASI)
Rebecca R. Fewell and Mary Beth Langley

Child
Ages 6 months-5 years

Purpose: Assesses developmental skills and abilities in infants and young children. Used for early detection of disabilities for determination of remedial teaching.

Description: 55-item paper-pencil and manual-dexterity test measuring academic/cognitive and basic skills/perceptual motor factors. The test may be presented in different sequences in one or two sittings. Instructions are given either visually or verbally. The developmental skills studied include fine-motor manipulation, cause-effect relationships, associations, number concepts, size discriminations, and sequencing. Materials include a kit of manipulative materials, such as cubes, a pegboard and pegs, a form board, beads, rings, an assortment of cards, cups, bowls, and plastic shapes and student response forms. The manual suggests instructional programs that can be used before a comprehensive remedial program is developed. The inventory can be modified for use with the visually or hearing impaired. Examiner required. Not suitable for group use.

Untimed: Not available

Scoring: Examiner evaluated

Cost: Complete $99.00

Publisher: DLM Teaching Resources

DEVELOPMENTAL ACTIVITIES SCREENING INVENTORY-II (DASI-II)
Rebecca R. Fewell and Mary Beth Langley

Child   Ages 1-60 months

Purpose: Detects early developmental disabilities in children.

Description: 67-item oral-response and task-performance test assessing 15 developmental skills categories ranging from sensory intactness, means-end relationships, and causality to memory, seriation, and reasoning. Test items may be administered in different sequences in one or two sittings. Instructions are given either verbally or visually. Each test item includes adaptations for use with visually impaired children. The following stimulus items are included in the test kit: 37 picture cards, 5 set-configuration cards, 2 pairs of numeral cards, 3 pairs of word cards, and 4 shape cards. The manual includes a matrix for identifying the concepts tapped by each test item, simple instructional programs for teaching the specific skills assessed by the test items, and an example of the type of program that might be used for a child assessed with this instrument. The test may be administered by classroom teachers with a minimum of testing experience. Examiner required. Not suitable for group use.

Untimed: Varies

Scoring: Examiner evaluated

Cost: Complete kit (manual, 50 record forms, stimulus items in storage box) $45.00

Publisher: Pro-Ed

DEVELOPMENTAL INDICATORS FOR THE ASSESSMENT OF LEARNING—REVISED (DIAL-R)
Carol D. Mardell-Czudnowski and Dorothea S. Goldenberg

Child   Ages 2-6

Purpose: Assesses a child's developmental level. Identifies potential problem, average, and gifted young children who may have special educational needs.

Description: 24-item oral-response and task-performance test assessing developmental abilities in three skill areas: motor (catching, jumping, hopping and skipping, building, touching fingers, cutting, matching, copying, and writing name); concepts (naming colors, identifying body parts, rote counting, meaningful counting, positioning, identifying concepts, naming letters, sorting chips); and language (articulating, giving personal data, remembering, naming nouns, naming verbs, classifying foods, problem solving, sentence length). The movable plastic dial, which is used to present test items, reduces distractions by presenting only one stimulus at a time. Social and emotional considerations are noted through behavioral observations, and a parent questionnaire is available to collect parent information. The test kit includes plastic dials and stands, blocks, scissors, beanbag, cutting cards, scoresheets, pencil, colored marking pens, and tape. A small

mirror or the child's photograph is used to assist in self-identification. An empirical scoring system based upon national norms is used. The test is administered by a team of paraprofessionals and/or professionals at three stations. Training procedures are available separately. Examiner required. Not suitable for group use.

Untimed: 20-30 minutes

Scoring: Examiner evaluated

Cost: Assessment kit $149.95

Publisher: Childcraft Education Corporation

Information and availability unconfirmed; no publisher response.

THE DEVELOPMENTAL PROFILE II
Gerald D. Alpern, Thomas Boll, and Marsha Shearer

Child   Ages 0-9

Purpose: Evaluates the age-equivalent physical, social, and mental development of normal or handicapped children. Used for counseling, school planning, and research.

Description: 186-item interview test covering five areas: physical, self-help, social, academic, and communication. Developmental age scores are derived by interviewing a parent or through teacher observation. From birth to age 4, the scales are graded by half-year increments. From Ages 5-9, they are graded in yearly increments. The test also provides an IQ equivalency score. Materials include test books, profile and scoring forms, a manual, and step-by-step procedures for administering and interpreting. The test is available on computer diskette. Examiner required. Suitable for group use.

Untimed: 20-40 minutes

Scoring: Examiner evaluated

Cost: Complete set $35.00; manual $18.50; 25 profile and scoring forms $19.50; computer diskette $165.00

Publisher: Western Psychological Services

DEVELOPMENTAL TASKS FOR KINDERGARTEN READINESS (DTKR)
Walter J. Lesiak

Child   Ages 4½-6½

Purpose: Assesses a child's skills and abilities as they relate to performance in kindergarten. Aids curriculum planning by providing school personnel with profiles of children entering kindergarten.

Description: Multiple-item test consisting of 12 subtests utilizing auditory and visual stimuli to assess the following areas: social development, receptive and expressive oral language, visual-motor skills, and cognitive development. The examiner asks questions, arranged in order of difficulty, and/or presents stimulus cards to the child. The child responds, and the examiner records judgments and observations of the response for diagnostic and prescriptive use. Examiner required. Not suitable for group use.

Untimed: 20 minutes

Scoring: Hand key; examiner evaluated

Cost: Complete kit $30.00; manual $7.00; cards $6.00; 25 record booklets $18.50

Publisher: Clinical Psychology Publishing Co., Inc.

DIAL-DEVELOPMENT INDICATORS FOR THE ASSESSMENT OF LEARNING
Carol Mardell and Dorothea S. Goldenberg

Child   Ages 2.5-5.5

Purpose: Assesses a child's general developmental level. Used for screening of potentially delayed children who need professional evaluation.

Description: 28-item multidimensional developmental assessment of abilities in four skill areas: gross motor, fine motor, concepts, and communication. Behavior is reviewed and the child's picture is taken. The test is administered by a team of paraprofessionals and professionals at four stations. The DIAL kit contains plastic dials and stands, blocks, scissors, beanbags, cutting cards, scoresheets, primary pencil, colored marking pens, tape, and clipboard. Supplemental materials include a small mirror or camera, playdough, and a balance beam; these items may be ordered from the publisher. Examiner required. Not suitable for group use.

Untimed: 20-30 minutes

Scoring: Examiner evaluated

Cost: Complete kit (consumable materials for 50 children) $139.95; 50 scoresheets $3.50; 100 cutting cards $3.50

Publisher: Childcraft Education Corporation
Information and availability unconfirmed; no publisher response.

EARLY IDENTIFICATION SCREENING PROGRAM
Office of Continuum Services, Baltimore City Public Schools

Child   Grades K-1

Purpose: Identifies children who lack basic school readiness skills. Used by classroom teachers for program planning and referral purposes.

Description: Multiple-item paper-pencil and oral-response test assessing a child's ability to perform tasks generally required for academic success. Three subtests screen for proficiency levels in auditory, visual, and articulation skills. The Hear-Write Tasks subtest measures auditory discrimination, short-term memory, beginning penmanship, and fine-muscle control. The See-Write Tasks subtest measures visual discrimination, eye-hand coordination, beginning penmanship, and fine-muscle control. The See-Say Tasks subtest measures general information, verbal skills, reading readiness, eye-hand coordination, and articulation skills. Scoring is based on frequency measure, counting the number of correct responses per minute, and the period allowed for each subtest. The tests are administered over a three-day period, one subtest per day. The children being tested within a class or school are ranked according to their performance, identifying those needing further attention. Not suitable for group use. Available in Spanish.

Timed: 20 minutes per child

Scoring: Examiner evaluated

Cost: 15 Kindergarten screening booklets $11.91; 15 first-grade screening booklets $11.91; administration and scoring manual $8.64

Publisher: Modern Curriculum Press, Inc.

EARLY LEARNING ASSESSMENT AND DEVELOPMENT
Audrey Curtis and Mary Wignall

Child

Purpose: Assesses developmental skills and capacities of children in the first years of school. Identifies appropriate remedial activities for children who need to practice and develop certain skills.

Description: Multiple-item task-performance and teacher-observation instrument assessing five developmental areas: motor skills (fine motor and gross motor), perceptual skills (visual, auditory, and tactile perception), communication skills, learning and memory, and emotional and social development. Eleven cards (for sequencing and auditory perception activities) and nine spirit duplicator masters (for individual child profile and visual perception activities) are provided for eliciting activities that allow teachers to observe and pinpoint children's individual developmental abilities. Using guidelines presented in the handbook, teachers can identify and remedy areas of weakness in the first year of infant school, before the child becomes used to failure. The materials also are useful for older children who have specific learning difficulties. Specific remedial suggestions are provided in the handbook. Record sheets are provided to monitor class progress. Examiner required. Not suitable for group use.

Untimed: Varies

Scoring: Examiner evaluated

Cost: Test kit (handbook, 11 cards, 9 spirit duplicating masters, 5 record sheets, ring-binding folder) £19.95

Publisher: Macmillan Education

EARLY SCHOOL INVENTORY
Joanne R. Nurss and Mary E. McGauvran

Child Grades PreK-1

Purpose: Assesses potential school problems for children in kindergarten and first grade.

Description: 82-item checklist for recording observed physical, language, socio-emotional, and cognitive development. The teacher indicates whether the child demonstrates each behavior. The test may be used with the Metropolitan Readiness Test to provide additional information. Examiner required. Not suitable for group use.

Untimed: Open ended

Scoring: Examiner evaluated

Cost: 35 inventories $20.00

Publisher: The Psychological Corporation

EARLY SCREENING INVENTORY (ESI)
Samuel J. Meisels and Martha Stone Wiske

Child Ages 4-6

Purpose: Assesses children's ability to acquire new skills. Designed to identify children who may need further evaluation and special educational services.

Description: Multiple-item task-performance and oral-response screening instrument assessing the development of kindergarten-aged children. The test is divided into four sections. The initial screening items section assesses the child's ability to respond to an unstructured drawing task and fine-motor control. The visual-motor/adaptive section examines fine-motor control, eye-hand coordination, the ability to remember visual sequences, the ability to draw visual forms, and the ability to reproduce three-dimensional structures. The language and cognition section assesses language comprehension and verbal expression, the ability to reason and count, and the ability to remember auditory sequences. The gross-motor/

body awareness section assesses balance, large motor coordination, and the ability to imitate body positions from visual cues. Nonconsumable stimuli for all tests are provided. The manual includes directions for administration, scoring, and interpreting the tests and statistical information. The parent questionnaire provides relevant information about the child's family, medical, and developmental history. Examiner required. Suitable for group use.

Untimed: Varies

Scoring: Examiner evaluated

Cost: Test kit (manual, screening materials, 30 score sheets, 30 parent questionnaires) $39.95

Publisher: Teachers College Press

EDINBURGH PICTURE TEST
*Godfrey Thomson Unit
for Educational Research,
University of Edinburgh*

Child   Ages 6.6-8.0

Purpose: Assesses the nonverbal reasoning abilities of children. Identifies children needing further evaluation. Used to measure achievement in the infant school and to aid in selection procedures.

Description: Multiple-item paper-pencil test consisting of five subscales: doesn't belong, classification, reversed similarities, analogies, and sequences. Each subscale is separately timed with its own instructions and examples. Pictures and shapes are used to present tasks similar to those used in verbal reasoning tests. Items are based on ideas used in the former Moray House Picture Tests, but have been completely redrawn and retested. The manual contains information for administering and scoring the test and details of the test's construction and standardization. Examiner required. Suitable for group use.

Timed: 30-40 minutes

Scoring: Examiner evaluated

Cost: 20 test booklets £4.95; manual £2.50; specimen set £3.50

Publisher: Hodder & Stoughton

THE FIRST GRADE READINESS CHECKLIST
John J. Austin

Child   Kindergarten

Purpose: Evaluates a child's readiness for first-grade work. Used to determine the learning experiences at which the child can be expected to succeed and for school placement.

Description: 54-item paper-pencil yes-no test measuring the subject's comprehension, age and growth, practical skills, attitudes and interests, memory for numbers, and general knowledge. Self-administered by parents or teachers. Suitable for group use.

Untimed: 15 minutes

Scoring: Examiner evaluated

Cost: Parent's kit (condensed version of handbook, 2 each of 4 sample checklists) $7.00; 50 checklists $9.00; manual $8.95

Publisher: Research Concepts

THE FIVE P'S: PARENT PROFESSIONAL PRESCHOOL PERFORMANCE PROFILE
Judith Simon Bloch

Child   Ages 6-60 months

Purpose: Assesses the development of preschoolers (and older children functioning at the preschool level) with behavioral, emotional, or developmental disorders. Used to plan IEPs for emotionally disturbed, schizophrenic, autistic, and language-impaired students.

Description: 453-item paper-pencil observational assessment tool consisting of 13 scales grouped in five developmental areas: routines and self-help skills (classroom adjustment, toileting and hygiene, mealtime behaviors, dressing), motor development (gross-motor/balance/coordination skills, perceptual/fine-motor skills), language (communicative competence, receptive language, expressive language), social development (emerging self, relationships to adults, relationships to children), and cognitive development/skills. Items in each of the 13 scales (26-56 items each) describe developmental skills and interfering behaviors. Items are rated "yes," "no," or "sometimes," according to which behaviors are demonstrated by the child. A parent (or primary caregiver) and teacher simultaneously and independently complete the scales in the fall and spring of each school year, providing a means of ongoing assessment. The test kit also includes IEP forms, a graphic profile sheet, and a Learning Alerts form, which identifies the child's particular style of learning and corresponding methods of intervention. An instructional manual is provided. Not suitable for group use.

Untimed: Varies

Scoring: Examiner evaluated

Cost: Contact publisher

Publisher: Variety Pre-Schooler's Workshop

FROSTIG DEVELOPMENTAL TEST OF VISUAL PERCEPTION
Marianne Frostig and Associates

Child   Grades PreK-3

Purpose: Evaluates children referred for learning difficulties or neurological handicaps by assessing perceptual skills.

Description: 41-item paper-pencil test of five operationally defined perceptual skills: eye-motor coordination, figure-ground, constancy of shape, position in space, and spatial relationships. The test is correlated with reading achievement in a normal first-grade classroom. Materials include 11 demonstration cards showing various shapes and figures. The examiner provides regular and colored pencils and crayons. A blackboard is necessary for group administration. Examiner required. Suitable for group use. Available in Spanish, French, German, Italian, Dutch, Japanese, and Swedish.

Untimed: 30-45 minutes

Scoring: Hand key

Cost: Specimen set (includes test booklet, manual, monograph, demonstration cards, set of score keys) $11.00; 25 tests $19.50

Publisher: Consulting Psychologists Press, Inc.

THE GESELL PRESCHOOL TEST
Gesell Institute

Child   Ages 2½-6

Purpose: Assesses the behavioral, emotional, and physical development of children. Used for screening, early intervention, or diagnosis depending on the qualifications of the examiner. Meets Child Find Requirements of P.L. 94-142.

Description: 13 tests assessing a wide range of developmental factors in preschoolers. The Cube Test measures eye-hand coordination, motor skill, attention span, level of functioning in a structured fine-motor task, and ability to understand and follow directions. The Interview Questions test assesses clarity of speech and accuracy of information. The Pencil and Paper Tests (Name, Numbers, and Copy Form) assess visual perception and neuro-muscular and eye-hand coordination. The Incomplete Man test assesses perceptual functioning by requiring the child to draw additional parts to a partially drawn human figure. The Discriminates Prepositions test measures understanding of words and concepts related to spatial position. The Digit Repetition test assesses the ability to focus attention, hold information, repeat information in order given, and short-term memory. The Picture Vocabulary test assesses verbal intelligence. The Color Forms test measures recognition of similar shapes. The Action Agent test assesses language comprehension. The Three-Hole Formboard test measures form discrimination ability and general adaptability. The Identifying Letters and Numbers test measures academic abilities against standard norms. The Motor test assesses patterns of comprehension, manipulation, and gross-motor activity. The Developmental Schedules section provides behavioral age-level in all areas tested.
The test yields an effective personality profile. Materials include test manual, 50 pre-collated test recording sheets, developmental schedules, Typical Response Cards to help evaluate the Copy Form and Incomplete Man tests, ten cubes, bean bag, picture vocabulary booklet, two-sided chart of letters and numbers, three-

---

hole formboard, color forms, copy forms, non-toxic pellets and bottle, 1-hour cassette tape on school readiness, and complimentary case. Examiner required. Not suitable for group use.

Untimed: 40 minutes

Scoring: Examiner evaluated

Cost: Complete $129.00 (item PS-24)

Publisher: Programs for Education, Inc.

THE GESELL SCHOOL READINESS TEST—COMPLETE BATTERY
Gesell Institute

Child   Ages 4½-9

Purpose: Determines whether a child is ready to begin Kindergarten, assesses a child's readiness for grade promotion (Grades 1-3), and evaluates whether a child has been placed at the proper grade level for his abilities. Used by school psychologists, educators, early childhood specialists, and child development professionals.

Description: Seven subtests measuring the adaptive behavior and visual-perceptual skills necessary for successful performance in Kindergarten to Grade 3. The Cube Test measures eye-hand coordination, motor skills, attention span, and level of functioning in a structured fine-motor task. The Interview Questions test assesses clarity of speech and accuracy of information. The Pencil and Paper Tests (Name, Numbers, and Copy Forms) assess visual perception, neuro-muscular and eye-hand coordination, and general level of maturity. The Incomplete Man test measures perceptual functioning by asking the child to draw additional parts to an incomplete human figure. The Right and Left test measures the ability to name parts of the body, distinguish right from left, and follow single and double commands. The Visual Tests assess understanding of directions, ability to carry out orders, and the ability to hold and recall information. The Animals and Interests test measures verbal abilities while providing clues about the child's tempo, organization of thinking, and capacity to attend.

Materials include pre-collated recording sheets for 50 students; a textbook of administration procedures and background information; Typical Response Cards to help evaluate the Copy Form and Incomplete Man tests; visual stimuli cards, cubes, and cylinders required for the various tests; a sample School Readiness Test (for practice and preparation); and carrying case. Examiner required. Not suitable for group use.

Untimed: 40 minutes

Scoring: Examiner evaluated

Cost: Complete $97.50 (item 145)

Publisher: Programs for Education, Inc.

GOODMAN LOCK BOX
Joan Goodman

Child   PreK

Purpose: Screens preschool children for mental retardation, fine-motor problems, and distractibility/hyperactivity. Used as a nonthreatening warm-up instrument for more extensive preschool screening.

Description: Multiple-task assessment of a preschooler's ability to organize a free-choice situation. The child is presented with a box with 10 locked doors to open and investigate. A toy is behind each door. The manner in which the child removes the toys is observed to determine whether the child is systematic and organized or poorly focused and distractible. The test relies entirely on spontaneous behavior (no questions are asked). It supplements, without duplicating, other intelligence tests. Norms are provided at six-month intervals for normally developing children and at yearly intervals for mentally retarded children. Examiner required. Not suitable for group use.

Timed: 6½ minutes

Scoring: Examiner evaluated

Cost: Complete kit (testing materials, manual, record forms) $312.00

Publisher: Stoelting Company

HARRISON-STROUD READING READINESS PROFILE
Refer to page 527.

HAWAII EARLY LEARNING PROFILE (HELP)
Refer to page 9.

HESS SCHOOL READINESS SCALE (HSRS)
Richard J. Hess

Child   Ages 3.5-7

Purpose: Measures the general mental ability of young children. Used to determine readiness to enter school and to predict classroom success.

Description: 45-item paper-pencil verbal test consisting of 12 subtests: Pictoral Identification, Discrimination of Animal Pictures, Picture Memory, Form Perception and Discrimination, Comprehension and Discrimination, Copying Geometric Forms, Paper Folding, Number Concepts, Digital Memory Span, Opposite Analogies, Comprehension, and Sentence Memory Span. All subtests are presented with verbal instructions. Materials include the manual, a guide for administering, a counting frame, 4"x 4" paper package, triangle paper package, 5½"x 8½" paper package, scoring forms, pencil, and case. Examiner required. Not suitable for group use.
BRITISH PUBLISHER

Timed: 2 hours

Scoring: Hand key; examiner evaluated

Cost: Complete kit $34.95

Publisher: Mafex Associates, Inc.

Information and availability unconfirmed; no publisher response.

HOWELL PREKINDERGARTEN SCREENING TEST
Joseph P. Ryan, Ronald Mead, and Howell Township Schools, Howell, N.J.

Child   Ages 4-5

Purpose: Measures the school readiness of children entering kindergarten. Identifies children with learning disabilities, special talents, and English language deficiencies. Used for academic placement at the kindergarten level.

Description: Battery of oral-response and task-performance subtests assessing 21 critical skills related to school readiness, including shape and letter identification, listening comprehension, visual, motor, and fine coordination, auditory memory, and prereading and math skills. Scoring provides a profile of each child's strengths and weaknesses and identifies children needing special placement: learning disabled, gifted and talented, and E.S.L. programs. Consumable student test booklets are scored according to guidelines provided in the manual. Individual record sheets are included in each test booklet for teacher reference. The test may be administered by teachers, paraprofessionals, or volunteers. Examiner required. Suitable for group use.

Timed: 1 hour (maximum)

Scoring: Examiner evaluated

Cost: 10 student test booklets $17.95; user's guide and technical manual $12.95; specimen set (student test booklet, user's guide) $14.95

Publisher: Book-Lab

HUMANICS NATIONAL CHILD ASSESSMENT FORMS: AGES 0-3 YEARS

Child   Ages 0-3

Purpose: Records children's skills and behaviors. Used by parents and teachers for planning educational and developmental experiences.

Description: 90-item paper-pencil checklist for assessing the development of a child's skills and behaviors in five areas: social-emotional, language, cognitive, gross motor, and fine motor. Items are arranged in developmental sequence. Space is provided for recording observations three times during one year. Examiner required. Not suitable for group use.

Untimed: Varies

Scoring: Examiner evaluated

Cost: $0.75 per form

Publisher: Humanics Limited

HUMANICS NATIONAL CHILD ASSESSMENT FORMS: AGES 3-6 YEARS

Child   Ages 3-6

Purpose: Records children's skills and behaviors. Used by parents and teachers for planning educational activities.

Description: Multiple-item paper-pencil checklist for measuring skills and behaviors of children. Teachers or teacher aides record observations for educational planning. The checklist is useful in helping parents understand their child's growth and development. Examiner required. Not suitable for group use.

Untimed: Varies

Scoring: Examiner evaluated

Cost: $0.75 per form

Publisher: Humanics Limited

ILLINOIS TEST OF PSYCHOLINGUISTIC ABILITIES (ITPA)
Samuel A. Kirk, James J. McCarthy, and Winifred D. Kirk

Child   Ages 2-10

Purpose: Assesses specific psycholinguistic abilities and disabilities in young children; facilitates assessment of a child's abilities for purposes of remediation.

Description: 300-item test evaluating a child's cognitive and perceptual abilities in three areas: communication, psycholinguistic processes, and levels of organization. There are 10 subtests: Auditory Reception, Visual Reception, Auditory Association, Visual Association, Verbal Expression, Manual Expression, Grammatic Closure, Visual Closure, Auditory Sequential Memory, Visual Sequential Memory, Auditory Closure, and Sound Blending. The test kit includes an examiner's manual, Visual Sequential Memory booklet, two picture books, chips and tray for visual sequences, picture strips, objects for the verbal and manual expression test, audio cassette, and carrying case. Examiner required. Not suitable for group use. Available in Spanish (from the author only).

Untimed: 1 hour

Scoring: Hand key

Cost: Kit $110.00; record forms and picture strips $15.75; aids and precautions in administering the ITPA $4.95; Psycholinguistic Learning Disabilities $6.95

Publisher: University of Illinois Press

INFANT RATING SCALE (IRS)
G.A. Lindsay

Child   Ages 5-7½

Purpose: Evaluates a child's developing skills and behavior and provides an overall picture of the child's developmental progress compared with his peer group. Identifies children "at risk" in one or more areas and helps the teacher respond appropriately.

Description: 25-item paper-pencil observational instrument rating a child's strengths and weaknesses on a 5-point scale in the following developmental areas: language, early learning and motor skills, behavior, social integration, and general development. The scale is available on two levels: Level 1 (ages 5-5½) and Level 2 (ages 7-7½). The teacher completes a form for each pupil and enters the ratings on a separate profile/record sheet, providing a broad overview of the child's areas of strength and weakness and a comparison of the child with other children the same age, in terms of subtests and total scores. When Level 2 is used later with the same pupil, the scale forms part of a consecutive monitoring procedure to facilitate the planning of an individualized educational strategy as the child progresses from the Infants to the Junior School. Full statistical details, together with practical illustrations of the uses and interpretations of the IRS, are given in the manual. Self-administered. Suitable for group use.
BRITISH PUBLISHER

Untimed: Not available

Scoring: Examiner evaluated

Cost: Specimen set (Levels 1 and 2) £3.50; manual £2.15

Publisher: Hodder & Stoughton

THE INFANT READING TESTS
M.A. Brimer and B. Raban

Child   Ages 4-6

Purpose: Assesses the reading-related skills of children.

Description: Multiple-item task-performance diagnostic tests measuring reading-related abilities. The three pre-reading tests, used with children who have not begun formal reading instruction, examine linguistic competence, the ability to use printed symbols, recognition of speech sounds, and discrimination of printed shapes. The three reading tests examine word recognition, sentence completion, and reading comprehension skills. Together, the tests yield a profile of maturation and learning. Rather than standardized scores and reading ages, the tests provide a scale ranging from 1-7, derived in the same manner as the new British Ability Scales. A score of two or lower indicates that a child lacks the skill tested. A score of five or higher indicates that a child possesses the required processes. Tests may be administered on separate days. Examiner required. Suitable for group use.
BRITISH PUBLISHER

Untimed: 20 minutes

Scoring: Not available

Cost: Contact publisher

Publisher: Educational Evaluation Enterprises

INFANT SCREENING
*Humberside Local
Education Authority*

Child   Ages 5 and older

Purpose: Identifies children who are "at risk" in terms of educational, social, or emotional failure in their early school years. Diagnoses exact areas where problems exist. Suggests appropriate teaching programs to deal with the problems. Used for in-service training of teachers of young children.

Description: Two multiple-item paper-pencil observational checklists and one multiple-item paper-pencil test assessing developmental areas of ability ranging from visual and auditory discrimination to managing behavior. Checklist 1 is completed for children ages 5 and older; Checklist 2 is completed for children ages 6 and older. The test booklet is administered to children ages 6 and older and is used in conjunction with the second checklist. Individual pupil profiles record children's progress and problems, forming a basis from which decisions about remedial work can be made. The teacher's book explains use of the materials for initial screening and provides ideas for follow-up diagnosis and remediation throughout the infant and lower junior years. Examiner required. Suitable for group use.

Untimed: Varies

Scoring: Examiner evaluated

Cost: 20 Checklist 1 or 2 £2.25; 10 test booklets £2.95; 25 pupil profiles £3.60; teacher's book and 8 diagnostic test cards £7.95

Publisher: Macmillan Education

KAUFMAN DEVELOPMENTAL SCALE (KDS)
Harvey Kaufman

Child

Purpose: Evaluates school readiness, developmental deficits, and all levels of retardation for normal children through age nine and the mentally retarded of all ages. Used in programming accountability.

Description: 270-item task-assessment test consisting of behavioral evaluation items that are actually expandable teaching objectives. The KDS yields a Developmental Age and Developmental Quotient, as well as individual age-scores and quotients for the following areas of behavioral development: gross motor, fine motor, receptive, expressive, personal behavior, and interpersonal behavior. Examiner required. Not suitable for group use.

Untimed: Not available

Scoring: Examiner evaluated

Cost: Complete kit (testing materials, manual, 25 record forms, carrying case) $190.00

Publisher: Stoelting Company

KAUFMAN INFANT AND PRESCHOOL SCALE (KIPS)
Refer to page 11.

KEELE PRE-SCHOOL ASSESSMENT GUIDE
Stephen Tyler

Child   Preschool

Purpose: Assesses child development. Used for identifying strengths and weaknesses and for individual program planning.

Description: Two-part instrument outlining a child's developmental abilities. Section I assesses social behavior, and Section II covers cognition, language, socialization, and physical skills. Performance may be plotted on a circular chart. Examiner required. Not suitable for group use.
BRITISH PUBLISHER

Untimed: Completed in stages over a number of days

Scoring: Examiner evaluated

Cost: 25 record forms £5.60; manual £3.25 (payment in sterling for all overseas orders)

Publisher: NFER-NELSON Publishing Company Ltd.

KENT INFANT DEVELOPMENT SCALE (KID SCALE)
Refer to page 11.

KINDERGARTEN BEHAVIOURAL INDEX
Enid M. Banks

Child   Ages 5½-6

Purpose: Measures behavioral development of children. Identifies children in need of further evaluation and assistance.

Description: Paper-pencil checklist records the behavioral responses of children in the normal kindergarten classroom situation. Test items represent the various areas of development considered relevant to future academic learning. The index may be used as a screening technique to identify children whose present functioning indicates a lack of readiness for formal tasks such as learning to read. It may also be used as a guide to specific remediation requirements. Materials include manual and teaching guide, individual record forms, and class record sheet. Self-administered by evaluator. Suitable for group use.
AUSTRALIAN PUBLISHER

Untimed: Varies

Scoring: Examiner evaluated

Cost: Contact publisher

Publisher: The Australian Council for Educational Research Limited

KINDERGARTEN INVENTORY OF DEVELOPMENTAL SKILLS (KIDS)
State Task Force on Early Childhood Screening

Child   Ages 4-6

Purpose: Assesses the development of children. Used by teachers and screening teams for prekindergarten screening.

Description: Multiple-item response test assessing the number, auditory, paper-pencil, language, visual, and gross-motor skills of prekindergarten children or children entering kindergarten. The 1978 Revised Edition is used with children ages 4.5-6 during the spring or summer preceding kindergarten entrance. The 1980 Alternate Edition is used with children ages 4-6 anytime during the year preceding kindergarten entrance. The screening battery includes an optional parent questionnaire. Examiner required. Not suitable for group use.

Untimed: 35 minutes

Scoring: Hand key

Cost: Specimen set (Pupil Record Sheet, Response Sheets 1 and 2, Parent Questionnaire, administration and scoring manual, instructional guide book, technical report) 1978 Edition $15.00; alternate edition $12.50

Publisher: Missouri Testing and Evaluation Service

KINDERGARTEN LANGUAGE SCREENING TEST (KLST)

Refer to page 630.

KNOX'S CUBE TEST (KCT)
Mark Stone and Benjamin Wright

Child, adolescent

Purpose: Measures children's and adult's short-term memory and attention span, which together constitute the most elementary stage of mental activity. Used to evaluate deaf, language-impaired, and foreign-speaking persons.

Description: Multiple-task assessment of attention span and short-term memory measuring how accurately an individual can repeat simple rhythmic figures tapped out for him by the examiner. Test materials include four cubes attached to a wooden base and a separate tapping block. Directions can be delivered in pantomime. The manual provides procedures and rationale for administering, scoring, and interpreting a comprehensive version of KCT, which incorporates all previous versions. This revision utilizes Rasch measurement procedures to develop an objective psychometric variable, along which both items and persons can be positioned. Examiner required. Not suitable for group use.

Timed: Not available

Scoring: Examiner evaluated

Cost: Both versions complete (testing materials, manual, record forms) $24.50 each

Publisher: Stoelting Company

KOONTZ CHILD DEVELOPMENTAL PROGRAM: TRAINING ACTIVITIES FOR THE FIRST 48 MONTHS
Charles W. Koontz

Child Developmental ages 1-48 months

Purpose: Evaluates the development of normal and retarded children who are functioning at developmental levels of 1-48 months. Used for evaluating and develop-

ing skills. May be modified for use with the hearing- and visually impaired.

Description: 550-item paper-pencil inventory of observable performance items arranged to parallel development in a normal child. A parent, teacher, or therapist checks off the specific behaviors that have been observed in the child's routine activities in order to establish the level of functioning in each of four areas of evaluation (gross motor, fine motor, social, and language). Progress is recorded in relation to performance items, and the training activities are designed to reinforce and develop each skill. The test pages, which are made of cardboard, are organized so that different developmental age levels of each of the four areas appear at the same item. Consequently, an examiner working with a child functioning at different levels in any of the four areas has all the appropriate activities visible simultaneously. Examiner required. Not suitable for group use.

Untimed: Not available

Scoring: Hand key

Cost: Complete kit (50 record cards, manual) $37.50

Publisher: Western Psychological Services

LEXINGTON DEVELOPMENTAL SCALES (LDS)
Child Development Centers of the Bluegrass, Inc. Staff

Child   Ages 2-6

Purpose: Assesses the development of handicapped and nonhandicapped preschool children. Identifies a child's needs and abilities. Used to plan programs and evaluate the effectiveness of classroom and child instruction.

Description: Multiple-item observational inventory assessing development in the following areas: gross and fine motor, language, personal and social, and cognitive. Test items are organized according to developmental area and are listed by age. The results are plotted on an interpretive chart, and age norms are arranged in sequence denoting four continuous stages of development. The LDS Long Form provides an in-depth assessment and requires approximately two hours to administer. The LDS Short Form is a screening tool that takes 30-45 minutes to administer. Examiner required. Not suitable for group use.

Untimed: 30 minutes-2 hours

Scoring: Examiner evaluated

Cost: LDS Long Form manual $6.00; LDS Long Form chart $1.25; LDS Short Form manual $4.00; LDS Short Form chart $1.00

Publisher: Child Development Centers of the Bluegrass, Inc.

Information and availability unconfirmed; no publisher response.

LINGUISTIC AWARENESS IN READING READINESS
Refer to page 530.

THE LOLLIPOP TEST: A DIAGNOSTIC SCREENING TEST OF SCHOOL READINESS
Alex L. Chew

Child   PreK-Grade 1

Purpose: Evaluates the school readiness of preschoolers, kindergartners, and first-graders. Used to plan individualized programs in Grades K-1.

Description: Multiple-item oral-response and task-assessment measuring a preschooler's attainment of the developmental skills necessary for success in Grades K-1. Test items are culture-free. Results identify both deficiencies and strengths for each child tested. The test may be administered before and after preschool programs to assess progress in readiness skills. Examiner required. Suitable for group use.

Untimed: 15-20 minutes

Scoring: Examiner evaluated

Cost: Test kit (manual, 7 cards, 5 booklets) $19.95

Publisher: Humanics Limited

MAXFIELD-BUCHHOLZ SOCIAL MATURITY SCALE FOR BLIND PRE-SCHOOL CHILDREN
Refer to page 601.

MCCARTHY SCALES OF CHILDREN'S ABILITIES
Refer to page 12.

MCCARTHY SCREENING TEST
Dorothea McCarthy

Child   Ages 4-6.5

Purpose: Predicts a child's ability to cope with school work in the early grades. For use in early identification of children at risk for school problems.

Description: Six-task test measuring the following mental abilities: right-left orientation, verbal memory, draw-a-person, numerical memory, conceptual grouping, and leg coordination. Children with learning disabilities or other handicaps perform less well than children without problems. Materials include card for right-left orientation, tape, and blocks. The tasks are taken from the McCarthy Scales of Children's Abilities. Examiner required. Not suitable for group use.

Untimed: 20 minutes

Scoring: Examiner evaluated

Cost: Complete set (all necessary equipment, manual, 25 record forms, 25 drawing booklets, carrying case) $47.50

Publisher: The Psychological Corporation

THE MEASUREMENT OF SELF-CONCEPT IN KINDERGARTEN CHILDREN (MSCKC)
Lucienne Y. Levin and J. Clayton Lafferty

Kindergarten

Purpose: Assesses self-concept of kindergartners by analyzing their drawings.

Description: Multiple-item paper-pencil instrument used by kindergarten teachers for measuring children's self-concept. The objective evaluation system applied to the children's drawings and paintings is a tool for predicting probable academic success and indicating problem areas for correction by curriculum design and alternative teaching methods. The instrument provides a means of comparing a child to his own self rather than to other children. Examiner required. Suitable for group use.

Untimed: 10-20 minutes

Scoring: Hand key

Cost: Complete set (general manual, scoring manual, 100 score sheets) $26.00

Publisher: Research Concepts

MEEKER-CROMWELL BEHAVIOR DEVELOPMENTAL ASSESSMENT
Refer to page 633.

MEETING STREET SCHOOL SCREENING TEST
Peter Hainsworth and Marion Siqueland

Child   Ages 5-7½

Purpose: Identifies kindergartners and first-graders with learning disorders. Used to minimize subsequent learning failure and behavioral upset.

Description: 15-item paper-pencil test containing three subtests (5 items each). The Motor Patterning subtest assesses the ability to hop, skip, move on command, fine-finger dexterity, and ability to imitate the examiner's hand gestures. The Visual-Perceptual subtest assesses copying geometric and letter forms, drawing when commanded, and tapping block patterns in sequence. The Language subtest assesses repetition of short phrases, sentences, and nonsense words; counting forward and backward; sequencing time concepts; and describing an abstract picture. The examiner uses a spiral-bound manual and a record booklet containing a worksheet, scoresheet, behavior rating scale, and performance grid. Normative tables for tests and scores are provided at one-half year levels based on 1966 census figures. Examiner required. Not suitable for group use.

Untimed: 20 minutes

Scoring: Hand key; examiner evaluated

Cost: Manual $12.00; 50 record forms $5.00; 100 record forms $9.00

Publisher: Meeting Street School, Easter Seal Society of Rhode Island, Inc.

METROPOLITAN READINESS TESTS: 1986 EDITION (MRT)
Joanne R. Nurss and Mary E. McGauvran

Child   Grades PreK-1

Purpose: Assesses underlying skills important for early school learning. For use in identifying each individual child's needs.

Description: Multiple-item paper-pencil test of skills important for learning reading and mathematics and for developing language. The test is divided into two levels. Level I yields four scores: Auditory, Visual Area, Language Area, and Pre-Reading Skills Composite. Level II yields scores in Auditory Area, Visual Area, Language Area, Quantitative Area, Pre-Reading Skills Composite, and Battery Composite. The test is also available in a 1976 edition. Examiner required. Suitable for group use.

Timed: Level I 80-90 minutes; Level II 100 minutes

Scoring: Computer scoring service available

Cost: Examination kit, 1986 edition, specify level (test booklet, manual, Parts I and II; parent-teacher report, Early School Inventory-Developmental, Early School Inventory-Preliteracy, class record, practice booklet) $13.00; Examination kit, 1976 edition $11.00

Publisher: The Psychological Corporation

MILLER ASSESSMENT FOR PRESCHOOLERS (MAP)
Refer to page 12.

MINNESOTA CHILD DEVELOPMENT INVENTORY (MCDI)
Refer to page 13.

MINNESOTA PRESCHOOL INVENTORY (MPI)
Harold Ireton and Edward Thwing

Child   Ages 4½-5½

Purpose: Measures a child's readiness for kindergarten. Used by educators, psychologists, physicians, and other professionals to assess the child's current development, readiness skills, social and emotional adjustment, and symptoms.

Description: 150-item paper-pencil inventory completed by the mother. The inventory measures self-help, fine-motor, expressive language, comprehension, memory, letter recognition, number comprehension, immaturity, hyperactivity, behavior problems, emotional problems, motor, language, somatic, and sensory skills. Intended for mothers with a high-school education. Self-administered. Suitable for group use.

Untimed: 15 minutes

Scoring: Hand key

Cost: 25 reusable booklets $14.00; 25 answer sheets $6.00; 25 profile forms $6.00; scoring templates $12.00; manual $12.00

Publisher: Behavior Science Systems, Inc.

THE MINNESOTA PRESCHOOL INVENTORY (MPI) FORM 34
Harold Ireton and Edward Thwing

Child   Ages 3-4

Purpose: Determines childrens' readiness to enter preschool.

Description: Multiple-item paper-pencil inventory used by the mother to review a child's development, adjustment, and symptoms. Materials include Form 34 booklets, answer sheets, Form 34 profile forms and a manual. Examiner required. Not suitable for group use.
CANADIAN PUBLISHER

Untimed: Not available

Scoring: Examiner evaluated

Cost: Specimen set $5.21; 25 Form 34 booklets $17.85; 25 answer sheets $8.95; 25 Form 34 profile forms $8.95; manual $14.88

Publisher: Institute of Psychological Research, Inc.

Information and availability unconfirmed; no publisher response.

MOTOR SKILLS INVENTORY (MSI)
Refer to page 562.

PARENT READINESS EVALUATION OF PRESCHOOLERS (PREP)
A. Edward Ahr

Child   Ages 3.9-5.5

Purpose: Evaluates the verbal and mental abilities of preschool children. Used to assess educational readiness.

Description: 190-item verbal and manual test to ascertain educational readiness in preschoolers by parent. The test aids parents helping their children learn at home by pointing out strengths and weaknesses. Used in conjunction with the handbook *Developing Your Child's Skills and Abilities at Home*. Examiner required. Not suitable for group use.

Untimed: 30 minutes

Scoring: Hand key

Cost: Specimen set $2.50

Publisher: Priority Innovations, Inc.

PEABODY DEVELOPMENTAL MOTOR SCALES AND ACTIVITY CARDS
M. Rhonda Folio and Rebecca R. Fewell

Child   Ages 0-83 months

Purpose: Assesses the motor development of children during the first eight years of life. Identifies children whose gross or fine-motor skills are delayed or abnormal. Used to establish IEPs.

Description: Multiple-item task-performance test consisting of a comprehensive sequence of gross- and fine-motor skills from which the child's relative developmental skill level can be determined. The test may be used to analyze a wide range of skills identified as questionable by prior screening or to diagnose specific characteristics of a motor problem. Norms are provided for each skill category at each level and for the total test. The instructional program components include a tab-indexed card file of 170 gross-motor and 112 fine-motor activities referenced to the items on the test. These activity cards provide an instructional curriculum to fill developmental gaps, strengthen emerging skills, and set objectives for skills not yet attained. Examiner required. May be administered individually or to groups of children using a station-testing procedure.

Untimed: 20-30 minutes

Scoring: Examiner evaluated

Cost: Test kit (manual, 15 scoring booklets, 282 activity cards, cubes, pegboard, pegs, formboard and shapes, bottle, beads and laces, box, dowel and string, etc.) $165.00

Publisher: DLM Teaching Resources

PEABODY MATHEMATICS READINESS TEST (PMRT)
Refer to page 294.

PEDIATRIC EXAMINATION OF EDUCATIONAL READINESS (PEER)
Melvine D. Levine

Child   Ages 4-6

Purpose: Detects high-prevalence low-severity disabilities in young children that are critical to success in school. Used for diagnosis, screening, research, and professional training.

Description: Verbal paper-pencil show-tell measure of six developmental areas: orientation, gross-motor, visual-fine motor, sequential, linguistic, and pre-academic skills. The child is asked to identify pictures and copy some of them with a pencil; tasks are presented to the child using numerous miscellaneous items (keys, tennis balls, blocks) contained in the kit; sentences are provided for language assessment. The examination produces an empirical description of what occurred when a child was asked to perform age-appropriate tasks. The information then can be used to help plan health, education, and developmentally oriented services. Examiner administered. Not suitable for group use.

Untimed: 1 hour

Scoring: Examiner evaluated

Cost: Record forms and stimulus booklet $16.00; examiner's manual $6.50; stimulus booklet $4.00; kit $6.50

Publisher: Educators Publishing Service, Inc.

PRE-ACADEMIC LEARNING INVENTORY (PAL)
Mildred H. Wood and Fay M. Layne

Child   Ages 4½-6

Purpose: Assesses readiness of young children to handle academic tasks. Used to diagnose strengths and weaknesses in order to plan educational and remedial programs.

Description: Multiple-item checklist examination covering nine areas: language development, speech development, concept development, body concept, auditory channel development, visual channel development, visual-motor integration, eye-hand coordination, and gross-motor coordination. Materials include stimulus pictures and cards, record booklets and sheets, eye-hand coordination activity sheets, and parent-child activity leaflets. Scoring is by the checklist method. Examiner required. Not suitable for group use.

Untimed: 30-35 minutes

Scoring: Hand key; examiner evaluated

Cost: Test kit $27.00

Publisher: United Educational Services, Inc.

PRESCHOOL AND EARLY PRIMARY SKILLS SURVEY (PEPSS)

Child   Ages 3-7

Purpose: Measures developmental skills necessary for early school success. Identifies children needing further evaluation.

Description: Four task-performance subtests assessing four developmental skills related to learning ability. The subtests are Picture Recognition (17 items), measuring visual recognition; Picture Relationship (18 items), measuring discrimination and association; Picture

Sequencing (11 items), measuring cognition of picture story sequences; and Form Completion (8 items), measuring perceptual motor skills. Norms are provided for preschool, kindergarten, and first-grade classes. Examiner required. Not suitable for group use.

Untimed: 15-20 minutes

Scoring: Examiner evaluated

Cost: Test kit (10 test booklets, examiner's manual, technical manual, scoring keys) $29.75

Publisher: Stoelting Company

PRESCHOOL AND KINDERGARTEN INTEREST DESCRIPTOR (PRIDE)
Refer to page 571.

PRESCHOOL AND KINDERGARTEN PERFORMANCE PROFILE
Alfred J. DiNola, Bernard Kaminsky, Allen E. Sternfeld

Child   Grades PreK-K

Purpose: Assesses the developmental levels of preschool and kindergarten children.

Description: 50-item paper-pencil inventory of the social, intellectual, and physical development of children in preschool and kindergarten. The items are grouped in 10 areas: interpersonal relations, emotional behavior, safety, communication, basic concepts, perceptual development, imagination and creative expression, self-help, gross-motor skills, and fine-motor skills. Each item is rated on a 7-point scale. The test helps teachers identify students with low developmental levels or possible learning disabilities, indicates strengths and weaknesses, and determines readiness for new learning. Examiner required. Not suitable for group use.

Untimed: Varies

Scoring: Examiner required

Cost: Class kit (Teacher's Manual, record booklet, Progress Report Folder) $5.50

Publisher: Educational Performance Associates

PRESCHOOL EMBEDDED FIGURES TEST (PEFT)
Susan W. Coates

Child   Ages 3-6

Purpose: Assesses individual perceptual processes, including field dependence. Used for counseling and research.

Description: 24-item nonverbal test of cognitive functioning and styles. Items are complex black and white line drawings in which the subject must find an embedded triangle. Materials include plates with complex figures, clear plastic envelopes, and one simple figure. Examiner required. Not suitable for group use.

Timed: 15 minutes

Scoring: Examiner evaluated

Cost: Complete kit (manual, plates, 25 record sheets) $15.75

Publisher: Consulting Psychologists Press, Inc.

PRESCHOOL LANGUAGE ASSESSMENT INSTRUMENT (PLAI)
Refer to page 640.

PRESCHOOL LANGUAGE SCALE (PLS)
Refer to page 640.

PRESCHOOL SCREENING INSTRUMENT
Stephen Paul Cohen

Child   Ages 4-5.3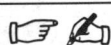

Purpose: Identifies prekindergarten children with learning disabilities. Used to meet P.L. 94-142 screening requirements.

Description: Multiple-item task-assessment test in which the child is told he will be "playing some games" with the examiner, who administers the following subtests: Figure Drawing, Circle Drawing, Tower Building, Cross Drawing, Block Design, Square Drawing, Broad Jumping, Balancing, Ball Throwing, Hopping, Whole Name, Picture Responses, Comprehension, and Oral

Vocabulary. The child's responses are evaluated in seven developmental areas: visual-motor perception, fine-motor development, gross-motor skills, language development, verbal fluency, conceptual skills, and speech and behavioral problems. Examiner required. Not suitable for group use.

Untimed: 5-8 minutes

Scoring: Examiner evaluated

Cost: Complete kit (25 student record books, manual, 16 wooden blocks, picture story card, 6 kindergarten-size pencils) $51.00

Publisher: Stoelting Company

PRESCHOOL SELF-CONCEPT PICTURE TEST (PS-CPT)
Refer to page 703.

PRESCREENING DEVELOPMENTAL QUESTIONNAIRE (PDQ)
William F. Frankenburg, W. VanDoorninck, T. Liddell, and N. Dick

Child
Ages 3 months-6 years

Purpose: Determines whether children can perform certain skills performed by most children their age. Used as an indicator for further testing.

Description: 97-item paper-pencil test administered by the parents, who are given response forms color-coded by age with 10 questions appropriate for each age group. Forms are available for the following age groups: 3-5 months, 6-8 months, 9-12 months, 13-15 months, 16-24 months, 2 years 1 month-2 years 9 months, 3-4 years, 4 years 3 months-4 years 9 months, and 5-6 years. Examiners must have at least a high-school education. Examiner required. Suitable for group use. Available in Spanish and French.

Untimed: 2-5 minutes

Scoring: Hand key

Cost: 100 forms (specify age group) $6.00; directions and interpretive instructions included

Publisher: Ladoca Publishing Foundation
Information and availability unconfirmed; no publisher response.

PRESCRIPTIVE TEACHING SERIES
Sue Martin

Child, adolescent
Grades 1-8

Purpose: Measures individual child development. Used for assessment of child's strengths and weaknesses and for planning educational experiences.

Description: 6-scale test of development in the following areas: visual, visual-motor, motor, auditory, reading and language, and math. The Visual Skills Test is composed of 22 skills with 104 subitems. The Visual-Motor Skills Booklet is composed of 28 items in four areas: body imagery, spatial orientation, visual-motor discrimination, and writing skills. The Motor Skills booklet consists of 166 items. The Auditory Skills Booklet consists of 31 items in several areas: auditory stimuli, speech response to auditory stimuli, oral reading, and phonetic analysis. The Reading and Language Skills booklet is composed of 152 skills, and Math Skills is composed of 315 skills. Examiner required. Not suitable for group use.

Untimed: Each rating period 15 minutes

Scoring: Hand key; examiner evaluated

Cost: Examiner's set (10 copies all booklets, manual) $40.00; 25 Visual Skills, 25 Visual-Motor Skills $13.50 each; 25 Motor Skills, 25 Auditory Skills, 25 Reading and Language Skills $18.00 each; 25 Math Skills $32.00

Publisher: Psychologists and Educators, Inc.

PRIMARY ACADEMIC SENTIMENT SCALE (PASS)
Glen Robbins Thompson

Child   Ages 4.4-7.3

Purpose: Assesses a child's motivation for learning, level of maturity, and parental independence. Used to screen for school readiness and develop academic motivation plans.

Description: 38-item verbal scale yielding two scores: sentiment quotient (interest in academics) and dependency stanine (child's interdependence on parents). The child is shown pictures of various activities and asked to point to a happy, neutral, or sad face, depending on how he feels about the activity. Examiner required. Suitable for group use.

Untimed: 30 minutes

Scoring: Hand key

Cost: Specimen set $4.00; tests $1.50 in quantity, with one manual for every 35 tests

Publisher: Priority Innovations, Inc.

PRIMARY EDUCATION PROGRAM: DIAGNOSTIC TEST FOR CLASSIFICATION/ COMMUNICATION SKILLS (PEP)
*Margaret C. Wang and
Lauren B. Resnick*

Child   Ages 3-6

Purpose: Measures the ability of young children to match, sort, and name things. Used by teachers for individual curriculum planning.

Description: Multiple-item picture-book verbal test of a child's ability to match like objects, discriminate shapes and sizes, name colors and shapes, and handle descriptions of size, length, width, and height. One test is provided for each objective. Materials include a progress chart and a manual. Examiner required. Not suitable for group use.

Untimed: Not available

Scoring: Hand key; examiner evaluated

Cost: Complete kit $27.95

Publisher: Mafex Associates, Inc.

Information and availability unconfirmed; no publisher response.

PRIMARY EDUCATION PROGRAM: DIAGNOSTIC TESTS FOR QUANTIFICATION SKILLS
*Margaret C. Wang and
Lauren B. Resnick*

Child   Ages 3-6

Purpose: Assesses entry-level quantification skills of preschool and primary-grade children. Used for group placement and checking instructional progress.

Description: 8-unit verbal test covering 56 objectives: nine in counting and comprehending one-to-one correspondences to the number 5; nine in counting and comprehending one-to-one correspondences to the number 10; seven in numerals to the number 5; seven in numerals 6-10; seven in comparison of sets; four in seriation and ordinal position; seven in addition and subtraction; and six in adding and subtracting equations. Materials include a manual, progress chart, and handbook with all the necessary instructions. Examiner required. Not suitable for group use.

Untimed: Not available

Scoring: Hand key; examiner evaluated

Cost: Complete kit $22.95

Publisher: Mafex Associates, Inc.

Information and availability unconfirmed; no publisher response.

PRIMARY MENTAL ABILITIES (PMA) READINESS LEVEL, REVISED
*L.L. Thurstone and
Thelma Gwinn Thurstone*

Child   Grades K-1

Purpose: Assesses learning readiness of kindergartners and first-graders. Provides information about level of development compared with other children. Used to plan materials and instruction rates, identify special needs, facilitate grouping, and communicate with parents.

Description: 90-item paper-pencil test measuring auditory discrimination, verbal meaning, perceptual speed, number facility, and spatial relations. Grade-based normative information is available. Examiner required. Suitable for group use.

Untimed: 1 hour

Scoring: Hand key

Cost: Complete set (30 copies each of 4 test booklets and student profile folders, examiner's manual, and user's manual) $30.50

Publisher: Science Research Associates, Inc.

THE PRIMARY VISUAL MOTOR TEST
Refer to page 564.

PSYCHOEDUCATIONAL PROFILE (PEP)
Eric Schopler and Robert J. Reichler

Developmentally disabled children

Purpose: Measures the learning abilities and characteristics of autistic and related developmentally disordered children. Used to establish individualized special education curricula or home programs for developmentally disabled children who were previously regarded as untestable.

Description: Multiple-item task-performance test assessing the learning abilities of autistic and developmentally disabled children. The test results comprise a learning profile reflecting the individual characteristics of the child. This profile is translated into an appropriately individualized special education curriculum or home program according to the teaching strategies described in Volume II of the manual. The test kit includes the following standard materials required for uniform and accurate administration of the test: bubbles, tactile blocks, kaleidoscope, call bell, clay, cat and dog puppets, three-piece geometric formboard, four-piece formboard, three-piece mitten formboard, four-piece kitten puzzle, six-piece cow puzzle, matching item, clapper, whistle, writing booklet and lotto letters, pouch and objects, felt board and nine felt pieces, scissors, blocks and box, number cards, beads and string, function cards, hand bell, category

cards I and II, and language. The following materials are required also but are not provided: mirror, candy, large ball, styrofoam cups, and a wheeled walker. The manual, *Individualized Assessment for Autistic and Developmentally Disabled Children,* is published in two volumes by Pro-Ed. Volume I describes the psychoeducational profile, and Volume II discusses teaching strategies for parents and professionals. Examiner required. Not suitable for group use.

Untimed: Varies

Scoring: Examiner evaluated

Cost: Test kit (standard materials) $200.00; Volume I of manual $29.95; Volume II of manual $19.95

Publisher: Orange Industries

PSYCHOLOGICAL EVALUATION OF CHILDREN'S HUMAN FIGURE DRAWINGS (HFD)
Refer to page 112.

PUPIL RECORD OF EDUCATIONAL BEHAVIOR (PREB)
Refer to page 443.

THE PYRAMID SCALES
Refer to page 604.

REVISED PRE-READING SCREENING PROCEDURES
Beth H. Slingerland

Child   Grades K-1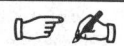

Purpose: Evaluates young children of average to superior intelligence in order to locate individuals with hearing, seeing, or moving difficulties that might indicate a language disability. Used to determine what kinds of special instruction/counseling are needed.

Description: Series of 12 verbal-visual subtests measuring visual perception; visual discrimination; visual recall; visual-motor skills; auditory recall; auditory discrimination; auditory perception; letter knowledge; and language skills, such as vocabulary, enunciation, comprehension or oral directions, oral expression, and recall of new words. The test also evaluates the child's motor coordination, hobbies and interests, attention span, and mental growth.

The test identifies children who are ready for formal instruction in reading, writing, and spelling and are able to learn through conventional methods; children, who while appearing to be ready, reveal indications of a language disability and need immediate multisensory instruction; children who show language confusion or possible developmental lag but whose maturity indicates a need to begin strengthening their language background; children, regardless of age, who are unready to begin reading instruction and who would benefit from more readiness and social development training. Materials consist of a test booklet (including 12 teacher observation/summary sheets and 12 practice pages), teacher's manual (including instructions and detachable answer key), and teacher's cards and chart (two sets of cards and two copies of a wall chart used in the tests). Many of the tests require students to use a pencil for marking. The examiner first explains the directions to the students and then they proceed with the task. Examiner required. Suitable for group use.

Untimed: 2-3 hours

Scoring: Hand key; examiner evaluated

Cost: 12 test booklets $12.00; teacher's manual $5.00; teacher's cards and chart $6.50; specimen set (teacher's manual, test booklet) $5.25

Publisher: Educators Publishing Service, Inc.

REYNELL-ZINKIN DEVELOPMENT SCALES FOR YOUNG VISUALLY HANDICAPPED CHILDREN
Joan Reynell and P. Zinkin

Child

Purpose: Assesses development of blind and partially sighted babies and young children. Used for planning management and early education programs.

Description: Performance test of intellectual development with separate subscales for the following areas: social adaptation,

sensori-motor understanding, exploration of environment, response to sound and verbal comprehension, and expressive language and communication. The assessment yields a profile detailing strong and weak areas. The provided tables allow comparisons to blind, partially sighted, and sighted children. The test is designed for professionals responsible for the assessment and education of the handicapped (doctors, psychologists, and teachers of blind and partially sighted children). The examiner provides toys and other necessary materials. The motor development component of the Reynell-Zinkin scales is currently being completed. Examiner required. Not suitable for group use.

BRITISH PUBLISHER

Untimed: Not available

Scoring: Examiner evaluated

Cost: Specimen set £9.55; 25 record forms £7.30; manual £9.45 (payment in sterling for all overseas orders)

Publisher: NFER-NELSON Publishing Company Ltd.

RILEY PRESCHOOL DEVELOPMENTAL SCREENING INVENTORY
Clara M.D. Riley

Child   Grades PreK-1

Purpose: Measures readiness to attend school and identifies children most likely to need assistance adjusting to normal school situations. Used for counseling and to meet the requirements of P.L. 94-142.

Description: Multiple-item observational test providing a child's developmental age and self-concept and determining serious developmental and maturational problems. The instrument can be administered at the beginning of preschool, kindergarten, or first grade. It was developed and has been used widely in Head Start programs. Suggested cutoff scores are provided. Examiner required. Suitable for group use. Test instructions are in both Spanish and English.

Untimed: 15-20 minutes

Scoring: Examiner evaluated

Cost: Complete kit (25 tests, manual) $15.80

Publisher: Western Psychological Services

ROCKFORD INFANT DEVELOPMENTAL SCALES (RIDES)
Project RHISE

Child Ages 0-4

Purpose: Evaluates the level of a child's skill and behavioral development. Used for initial assessment by special education teachers to guide and objectify their observations of a child.

Description: Multiple-item paper-pencil evaluation of 308 developmental behaviors arranged by age into five skill areas: personal-social/self-help, fine motor/adaptive, receptive language, expressive language, and gross motor. Each behavioral item is determined to be present, emerging, or absent in the child. Test results relate these single items to major developmental patterns and competencies. The format calls for one eight-page booklet per child. An Individual Child Progress Graph on the back page shows progress and allows comparison of levels across developmental areas. The manual contains a section detailing development, use, and interpretation of the test. The entries for all 308 behaviors provide scoring criteria, developmental significance, equipment specifications, and references to further information. An appendix containing master equipment list, skill group listings, notes, and bibliography are included. The Starter Set includes the manual and 20 checklists. Examiner required. Not suitable for group use.

Untimed: Varies

Scoring: Hand key

Cost: Starter set $36.90

Publisher: Scholastic Testing Service, Inc.

S.O.I. LEARNING ABILITIES TEST
Mary Meeker and Robert Meeker

Grades K-adult

Purpose: Measures an individual's learning abilities. Used for cognitive clinical assessment, diagnosis, screening for giftedness, and to identify specific learning deficiencies.

Description: 430-item paper-pencil multiple-choice free-response test. The test measures 26 factors identified by Guilford's Structure-of-Intellect model. The operations of cognition, memory, evaluation, convergent production, and divergent production are applied to figural, symbolic, and semantic content. The test is available in two equivalent forms, A and B, and five shorter forms (gifted-screening, math, reading, primary screening, and reading readiness). The shorter forms use 10-12 subtest factors, printed test forms, and a manual with visual aids for group presentations. Training in administration and usage is required. Examiner required. Suitable for group use in some situations.

Untimed: 2½ hours

Scoring: Hand key

Cost: Contact publisher

Publisher: Western Psychological Services

SANTA CLARA PLUS COMPUTER MANAGEMENT SYSTEM

Child Ages 3½-7

Purpose: Assesses cognitive and affective skills of children. Used for diagnostic and prescriptive mastery of objectives for kindergarten and special education students.

Description: Multiple-test kit assessing 60 cognitive and 12 affective skills (one item per objective). The examiner directs the child to perform an activity, monitors the task, and rates the child's performance. Results are transferred to a profile chart or microcomputer diskette for analysis and prescription. Prescriptive materials are provided. Examiner required. Suitable for group use.

Untimed: Not available

Scoring: Hand key; may be computer scored

Cost: Complete $160.00 and $50.00 per diskette for each additional classroom; package of test cards $4.00

Publisher: Skillcorp Software, Inc.

SCALES OF INDEPENDENT BEHAVIOR
Robert H. Bruininks,
Richard W. Woodcock,
Richard F. Weatherman,
and Bradley K. Hill

All ages

Purpose: Evaluates adaptive behavior and social adjustment from infancy through adult levels. Used in school and institutional settings for determining eligibility for special services, program planning, and individual and program evaluation.

Description: Multiple-item interview guide assessing adjustment in social, behavioral, and adaptive areas. The information gained from the parent, caregiver, or teacher is used to evaluate functional independence and adaptive behavior in motor skills, social and communication skills, personal living skills, and community living skills. A problem behavior scale focuses on more severe problems. This test is structurally and statistically related to the Woodcock-Johnson Psycho-Educational Battery. Because common norms are provided for the two tests, an individual's adaptive behavior may be interpreted in relation to his cognitive ability. The test yields age scores, percentile ranks, standard scores, relative performance index (RPI), expected range of independence, and instructional range. Examiner required. Not suitable for group use.

Untimed: 45-50 minutes

Scoring: Computer scored

Cost: Test kit (test book, interviewer's manual, 15 response booklets) $110.00

Publisher: DLM Teaching Resources

SCHOOL ENTRANCE CHECKLIST
John McLeod

Child   Grades K-1

Purpose: Gathers relevant social data about a child just entering school.

Description: 18-item paper-pencil questionnaire completed by parents or guardians at the time a child enters

school. The questionnaire is recommended for routine survey and screening. The School Entrance Checklist contains the most pertinent questions from the Dyslexia Schedule, but contains only 18 of the Dyslexia Schedule's 89 questions to avoid overwhelming the parent. The School Entrance Checklist may be sent home for the parents to complete and return. Self-administered. Not suitable for group use.

Untimed: 20-30 minutes

Scoring: Examiner evaluated

Cost: 1-100 $0.50 each; 100 or more $0.45 each

Publisher: Educators Publishing Service, Inc.

THE SCHOOL READINESS CHECKLIST
John J. Austin and J. Clayton Lafferty

Child   PreK

Purpose: Determines a child's readiness for kindergarten work. Used to educate parents about learning patterns and to help with preschool clinics and meetings.

Description: 43-item paper-pencil yes-no test measuring the subject's comprehension, age and growth, practical skills, attitudes and interests, memory for numbers, and general knowledge. Materials include booklets with white child or black child illustrations. Self-administered by parents and teachers. Not suitable for group use. Manual available in Spanish.

Untimed: 15 minutes

Scoring: Examiner evaluated

Cost: Specimen set (condensed version of handbook, 2 kindergarten, 2 first grade) $7.00; manual $8.95; 50 checklists $9.00

Publisher: Research Concepts

SCHOOL READINESS SCREENING TEST
Gesell Institute

Child   Ages 4½-5

Purpose: Measures coordination, motor skills, and verbal ability of young children. Used to determine developmental readiness for Kindergarten.

Description: Multiple-task verbal and manual paper-pencil examination containing five subtests measuring predominant adaptive behavior. The Cube Test measures eye-hand coordination, motor skills, attention span, and level of functioning in a structured fine-motor task. The Interview Questions reveal speech clarity and accuracy of information. The Paper and Pencil Tests reveal visual perception, neuro-muscular and eye-hand coordination, and general maturity level. The Incomplete Man test provides clues to perceptual functioning by requiring the child to complete a human figure. The Animals and Interests test assesses verbal abilities and provides clues about a child's tempo, organization of thinking, and capacity to attend.

Materials include pre-collated recording sheets for 50 students; a textbook of administration procedures and background information; cubes, visual stimuli cards, and cylinders required for the various tests; Typical Response Cards to help evaluate the Copy Form and Incomplete Man tests; a sample School Readiness Test (for practice and preparation); and carrying case. Examiner required. Not suitable for group use.

Untimed: 20 minutes

Scoring: Examiner evaluated

Cost: Complete kit $95.50 (item 144)

Publisher: Programs for Education, Inc.

SCHOOL READINESS SURVEY
F.L. Jordan and James Massey

Child   Ages 4-6

Purpose: Assesses a child's understanding of numbers, colors, words, and forms. Used to determine readiness for kindergarten.

Description: 95-item paper-pencil verbal test consisting of eight school readiness subtests: Number Concept, Discrimination of Form, Color Naming, Symbol Matching, Speaking Vocabulary, Listening Vocabulary, General Information, and General Readiness. The test may be administered by parents or an examiner. Parent-administered scores are correlated with teacher-administered scores. Materials include suggestions to parents for developing the child's skill areas. Parents must supply two pencils and a marker. Examiner required. Not suitable for group use.

Untimed: Not available

Scoring: Examiner evaluated

Cost: Manual $1.00; 25 surveys $17.50

Publisher: Consulting Psychologists Press, Inc.

SCHOOL READINESS TEST (SRT)
Oliver F. Anderhalter

Child   Grades K-1

Purpose: Determines individual and group readiness for first grade. Used to identify and diagnose students with skill deficiencies.

Description: Multiple-item paper-pencil verbal test designed for children entering the first grade. The test reveals readiness for formal instruction by assessing seven skill areas: word recognition, identifying letters, visual discrimination, auditory discrimination, comprehension and interpretation, handwriting readiness, and number readiness. The test results which can be used as the basis for placement, show each child at one of six readiness levels. Examiner required. Suitable for group use. Manual available in Spanish.

Timed: 1 hour

Scoring: Hand key; examiner evaluated

Cost: Complete set (35 booklets, manual, scoring key, class record sheet) $21.45

Publisher: Scholastic Testing Service, Inc.

SCHOOL READINESS TESTS FOR BLIND CHILDREN (STBC)

Blind children

Purpose: Assesses cognitive abilities of blind children. Used for determining school readiness.

Description: 7-subtest measure of cognitive skills important to school readiness, including Information Test, Kinesthesis Test, Vocabulary Test, Number Concept Test, Motor Development Test, Memory Test, and Reasoning Test. The examiner may make subjective evaluations of the child's perseverance, readiness to follow instructions, and social adjustment. Examiner required. Not suitable for group use.
SOUTH AFRICAN PUBLISHER

Untimed: 1½ hours

Scoring: Examiner evaluated

Cost: (In Rands) complete kit (10 biographical questionnaires, 10 answer sheets, container, apparatus, manual) 99,70; orders from outside The RSA will be dealt with on merit

Publisher: Human Sciences Research Council

SCREENING TEST FOR THE ASSIGNMENT OF REMEDIAL TREATMENT
A. Edward Ahr

Child   Ages 4.5-6.5

Purpose: Assesses the skill development of children. Identifies children needing evaluation for potential learning difficulties. Also used to evaluate Kindergarten and Grade 1 instructional programs.

Description: 50-item orally administered test assessing the basic skills required for successful performance in Kindergarten and first grade. The test measures the following factors: visual memory, auditory memory, visual-motor coordination, and visual discrimination. Each test item consists of four pictures presented on one page in the test booklet. The examiner instructs the child to look at each page and then asks the child to select the correct answer, copy the pictures, or remember what is pictured (for delayed response) for the pictures presented for each test item. Examiner required. Suitable for group use.

Timed: 45 minutes

Scoring: Hand key

Cost: Specimen set $4.00; test $1.50; manual included with order of 35 tests

Publisher: Priority Innovations, Inc.

SCREENING TEST OF ACADEMIC READINESS (STAR)
A. Edward Ahr

Child   Ages 4-6

Purpose: Measures mental ability and emotional development of young children. Used to determine school readiness.

Description: 50-item paper-pencil test consisting of eight subtests: Picture Vocabulary, Letters, Picture Completion, Copying, Picture Description, Human Figure, Relationships, and Numbers. The examiner asks the child to point to the correct answer or mark it in the answer book. The child's understanding of the world is evaluated by asking him or her to identify objects, copy simple figures, or identify an object among other items in a picture after hearing a description of the object. Examiner required. Suitable for group use.

Untimed: 1 hour

Scoring: Hand key

Cost: Specimen set $4.00; test $1.50; manual included with 35 tests

Publisher: Priority Innovations, Inc.

SENTENCE IMITATION SCREENING TEST (SIST)
Refer to page 645.

SLOSSON ARTICULATION, LANGUAGE TEST WITH PHONOLOGY (SALT-P)
Wilma Jean Tade

Child   Ages 3-5.11

Purpose: Assesses articulation, phonology, and language in children. Used in educational, clinical, private practice, Head-start, and other preschool settings.

Description: Multiple-item oral-response test using stimulus pictures to measure communicative competence in preschool children. The test features a prescreening segment that identifies children in need of further testing. Children recommended for further testing are simultaneously screened for articulation, phonology, and language. The articulation section is composed of 22 initial and 18 final consonant sounds and 10 consonant blends or clusters. The test contains provisions that allow the examinee to demonstrate ability to use selective vowels and dipthongs. Five phonological processes are measured: initial consonant omission, final consonant omission, fronting, stopping, and cluster reduction. The language subscore reflects errors on 31 language barriers. The test yields a single score that indicates communicative competence. The score can be compared to an index of scores denoting normal performance with respect to chronological age. An instructional video is available for examiners and students. Examiner required. Not suitable for group use.

Untimed: 7-10 minutes

Scoring: Examiner evaluated

Cost: Complete kit (manual, test book, 50 scoring forms) $35.00; videotape (½″ VHS) $70.00

Publisher: Slosson Educational Publications, Inc.

SWANSEA EVALUATION PROFILE FOR SCHOOL ENTRANTS
R. Evans, P. Davies, N. Ferguson, and P. Williams

Child   Ages 4.11-5

Purpose: Evaluates mental ability and background of children. Used to identify those needing special education.

Description: Three-section paper-pencil profile evaluating home background and initial adjustment to school. A cognitive test battery measures child development. The test is experimental and is not yet available for classroom use. It is produced in limited quantities for research. Materials include a set of three tests. Examiner required. Not suitable for group use.
CANADIAN PUBLISHER

Timed: Section 1 5 minutes; Section 2 5 minutes; Section 3 30 minutes

Scoring: Examiner evaluated

Cost: Contact publisher

Publisher: Institute of Psychological Research, Inc.

Information and availability unconfirmed; no publisher response.

THE TACTILE TEST OF BASIC CONCEPTS

Visually handicapped children   Grades K-2

Purpose: Assesses the visually handicapped child's mastery of concepts commonly found in preschool and primary-grade instructional materials and essential to understanding oral communications from teachers and fellow pupils. Used with children in Grades K-2 who require braille and other tactile media.

Description: 50-item tactile test of verbal comprehension and conceptual development of visually handicapped children. Five practice cards are provided to familiarize the child with the test task and to determine if he is familiar with the raised outline forms used in the test (circle, square, triangle, rectangle). The test is a tactile analog of the Boehm Test of Basic Concepts, Form A, presented with raised outline forms. A few items consist of simple raised outline drawings. The BTBC test manual is included for use in interpreting the test results. Examiner required. Not suitable for group use.

Untimed: Not available

Scoring: Hand key; examiner evaluated

Cost: Complete set (5 practice cards, 50 test cards, 1 class record form, TTBC test manual, BTBC test manual) $36.75

Publisher: American Printing House for the Blind, Inc.

TEST OF BASIC EXPERIENCES, SECOND EDITION (TOBE/2)
Margaret H. Moss

Child   Grades K-1

Purpose: Measures the degree to which young children have acquired concepts and experiences related to effective school participation. Used for evaluation of school readiness.

Description: Multiple-item battery of paper-pencil tests measuring quantity and quality of children's early learning experiences. The test is divided into two overlapping levels, K and L, covering programs from preschool through first grade. Each level contains a language, mathematics, science, and social studies test. Each test item consists of a verbal stimulus and four pictured responses. As the examiner reads the stimulus aloud, the child responds by marking one of the pictures. Level K can be used in the spring of prekindergarten, the fall and spring of kindergarten, and the fall of first grade. Level L is for use in the spring of kindergarten and the fall and spring of first grade. An Instructional Activities Kit contains materials for teaching concepts and skills. Examiner required. Suitable for group use. Available in Spanish.

Untimed: 45 minutes per test

Scoring: Hand key; may be computer scored

Cost: Specimen set, specify level (machine- and hand-scorable test books, manual, answer key, norms and technical data book, practice test, class evaluation record, test reviewer's guide) $8.95

Publisher: CTB/McGraw-Hill

TEST OF EARLY LEARNING SKILLS (TELS)
Jwalla P. Somwaru

Child   Ages 3.5-5.5

Purpose: Assesses the cognitive skills of preschool and kindergarten children at the beginning of their formal education. Used to evaluate individual strengths and weaknesses and plan instruction.

Description: 54-item verbal-response test consisting of three subtests: Thinking Skills (18 items), Language Skills (18 items), and Number Skills (18 items). The test is individually administered with the child and examiner on opposite sides of a table. The test yields diagnostic information, raw scores, and a developmental age score. The starter set contains a manual, a reusable test, 20 response forms, manipulatives, and a carrying case. Examiner required. Not suitable for group use.

Untimed: 30 minutes

Scoring: Hand key; examiner evaluated

Cost: Starter set $54.50

Publisher: Scholastic Testing Service, Inc.

TEST OF GROUP LEARNING SKILLS
Michael A. Watson

Child   Grades PreK-3

Purpose: Assesses level of general language development and identifies strengths and weaknesses in specific learning skills. Used as a guide for placing prekindergarten through third-grade children into teaching groups.

Description: 139-item paper-pencil test consisting of visual and auditory subtests. The visual subtests are Motor, Memory, Association, and Discrimination Factors. The auditory subtests are Memory, Association, and Discrimination Factors. One subtest measures auditory-visual association. The test package includes a manual, response booklets, a learning profile ditto, test sheets, a cassette for the auditory subtests, and a filmstrip for the visual subtests. A cassette player, projector, screen, stopwatch, chalk and board, pencils, and paper are required. Examiner required. Suitable for group use.

Untimed: 4 hours

Scoring: Hand key; examiner evaluated

Cost: Complete program $49.00; booklet kit $53.00

Publisher: Educational Activities, Inc.

UNIFORM PERFORMANCE ASSESSMENT SYSTEM (UPAS)
Owen R. White, Norris G. Haring, Eugene B. Edgar, James Q. Affleck, and Alice H. Hayden

All ages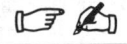

Purpose: Evaluates the social and behavioral development of handicapped individuals. Used by psychologists and special educators to establish IEP objectives and measure progress.

Description: 250-item verbal-response test using stimulus cards to introduce tasks for measuring five categories of performance: preacademic/fine-motor skills, communication skills, social/self-help skills, gross-motor development, and behavior management. The test kit includes stimulus cards, record forms, and a manual. Examiner required. Not suitable for group use.

Untimed: Varies; some subtests timed

Scoring: Examiner evaluated

Cost: Complete $95.00

Publisher: The Psychological Corporation

VALETT DEVELOPMENTAL SURVEY OF BASIC LEARNING ABILITIES
Robert E. Valett

Child   Ages 2-7

Purpose: Assesses the developmental abilities of preschool and early primary children. Aids in formulating individual program plans for special education and remedial teaching.

Description: 233-item paper-pencil verbal test covering a range of developmental abilities, including motor integration and physical development, tactile discrimination, auditory discrimination, visual-motor coordination, visual discrimination, language development and verbal fluency, and conceptual development. Materials include a pupil workbook and a small kit of paper materials. The examiner, who should be a special educator or psychologist, selects items appropriate for the child's developmental level and scale scores are plotted to yield a developmental profile. Examiner required. Not suitable for group use.

Untimed: 50 minutes

Scoring: Examiner evaluated

Cost: Examiner's kit (test materials, scoring booklets, workbooks, manual) $22.50

Publisher: Consulting Psychologists Press, Inc.

VALETT INVENTORY OF CRITICAL THINKING ABILITIES (VICTA)
Robert E. Valett

Ages 4-15 and older exceptional pupils

Purpose: Assesses problem-solving skills and abilities of children and older exceptional pupils with developmental difficulties. Used at the beginning of a diagnostic session to establish rapport with a child.

Description: 100-item verbal-response examination of sensory-perceptual exploration, intuitive organization, concrete relationships, representational concepts, and propositional logic. The test consists of problems dealing with 10 critical thinking abilities: knowledge, analysis, calculation, verbal conceptualization, synthesis, comprehension, application, humor, evaluation, and imagination. A quantitative evaluation of the student's critical thinking ability is provided by determining the percentage of tasks the student passes at each of the five developmental stages and comparing that figure with the child's age. Only items of appropriate difficulty for a child are tested. Examiner required. Not suitable for group use.

Untimed: 40 minutes

Scoring: Examiner evaluated

Cost: Manual $10.00; 50 record forms $14.00

Publisher: Academic Therapy Publications

THE VANE KINDERGARTEN TEST (VKT), 1984 REVISION
Julia R. Vane

Child   Kindergarten

Purpose: Evaluates the academic potential of young children and identifies those for whom remedial help may be necessary.

Description: Three-part multiple-item task-assessment oral-response test assessing eye-hand coordination, vocabulary development, emotional adjustment, and hearing deficiency. In Part I, the child is presented with pictures of three shapes (circle, square, hexagon) and copies them on a sheet of paper. In Part II, the child turns the paper over and draws a picture of a man. In Part III, the child identifies as many words as possible from a list of 12 words arranged in order of difficulty. The words generally are used only by exceptionally bright children. Examiner required. Suitable for group use.

Untimed: 10 minutes

Scoring: Examiner evaluated

Cost: Manual $7.50; 50 record sheets $3.50

Publisher: Clinical Psychology Publishing Company, Inc.

VINELAND ADAPTIVE BEHAVIOR SCALES
Refer to page 215.

VINELAND SOCIAL MATURITY SCALE
Refer to page 19.

VISCO CHILD DEVELOPMENT SCREENING TEST (THE CHILDS TEST)
Susan J. Visco and Carmela R. Visco

Child   Ages 3-7

Purpose: Assesses the development of learning abilities and skills in children. Identifies children with possible learning disabilities who should be referred for diagnostic evaluation.

Description: 118-item task-performance test measuring the basic skills and abilities required in the learning process. The following factors are evaluated: processing functions (visual perceptuomotor, auditory-visual-motor integration, visual vocal, and auditory vocal); abilities (sequencing, language, numerical, syntax, and articulation); and cognition (cognitive efficiency). In addition to the materials included in the kit, a stopwatch, a small table, 2 chairs, a tape for a line, a small cup, and a flight of stairs are required. Examiner required. Not suitable for group use.

Untimed: 25-30 minutes

Scoring: Hand key; examiner evaluated

Cost: Program (overview manual, test administration and scoring manual, 20 individualized record booklets, nine 1-inch cubes, 7 numerical Gestalt cards, 25 labels and functions picture cards, felt strip with 4 buttons, felt strip with 4 button holes $49.00; 10 extra record booklets $11.95; orientation and training sound filmstrip $29.00

Publisher: Educational Activities, Inc.

VOCABULARY COMPREHENSION SCALE (VCS)
Refer to page 240.

WACHS ANALYSIS OF COGNITIVE STRUCTURES
Harry Wachs and Lawrence J. Vaughan

Child   Ages 3-5.11

Purpose: Measures the development of learning ability among young children and suggests activities to stimulate learning growth. Used with the learning disabled and the culturally disadvantaged.

Description: An observational examination in which the examiner watches the child perform tasks based on Piaget's theories of measuring cognitive development in terms of body and sense thinking. The inventory consists of 15 clusters of tasks divided into subtests consisting of a variety of manipulative, visual-sensory, and body movement actions that are grouped into four areas of assessment: identification of objects, object design, graphic design, and general movement. The test is primarily nonverbal and culture free and has been used successfully with children with language deficiencies, mental deficiencies, and hearing deficits. A profile sheet enhances communication with parents. The manual includes a curriculum guide and supplemental diagnostic tasks for more complete analysis. Examiner required. Not suitable for group use.

Untimed: 30-45 minutes

Scoring: Hand key; examiner evaluated

Untimed: 30-45 minutes

Scoring: Hand key; examiner evaluated

Cost: Complete kit (test materials, 10 record books and profile sheets, manual, carrying case) $260.00

Publisher: Western Psychological Services

YELLOW BRICK ROAD (YBR)
Christine Kallstrom

Child   Preschool

Purpose: Identifies functional strengths and weaknesses in preschool children. Used for kindergarten screening and instructional programming.

Description: 24-item paper-pencil motor and vision test specifically designed to follow the Wizard of Oz theme. It is divided into four batteries: motor, visual, auditory, and language, with each battery subdivided into six test units. Materials include the manual, battery booklets for administration and scoring, and the testing materials (manipulatives). The test can be administered individually by an examiner or in a group setting, with volunteers, aides, and parents assisting the examiners.

Untimed: 45 minutes

Scoring: Examiner evaluated

Cost: Complete $52.00

Publisher: DLM Teaching Resources

Intelligence and Related

ACER ADVANCED TEST AL-AQ (SECOND EDITION) AND BL-BQ

**Adolescent, adult
Ages 15 and older**

Purpose: Measures intelligence of students ages 15 and older at secondary and tertiary levels.

Description: Multiple-item paper-pencil intelligence test available in two parallel forms: AL-AQ (Second Edition) and BL-BQ. The L section of both forms deals with linguistic items, and the Q section deals with quantitative items. Norms are presented for upper secondary level and first-year samples from TAFE colleges and Colleges of Advanced Education. Materials iclude expendable booklets for each section (AL, BL, AQ, or BQ), scoring keys for each section, manual, and specimen set. Examiner required. Suitable for group use.
AUSTRALIAN PUBLISHER

Timed: AL, BL 15 minutes; AQ, BQ 20 minutes

Scoring: Hand key; examiner evaluated

Cost: Contact publisher

Publisher: The Australian Council for Educational Research, Limited

ACER ADVANCED TEST B40 (REVISED)

**Adolescent, adult
Ages 15 and older**

Purpose: Measures intelligence of students ages 15 years and older.

Description: Multiple-item paper-pencil test measuring general mental abilities, including both verbal and numerical reasoning. The manual has been revised for this edition, and the test has been standardized. Materials include an expendable booklet, score key, manual, and specimen set. Examiner required. Suitable for group use.
AUSTRALIAN PUBLISHER

Untimed: 1 hour

Scoring: Hand key

Cost: Contact publisher

Publisher: The Australian Council for Educational Research Limited

ACER ADVANCED TEST N

**Adolescent, adult
Ages 15 and older**

Purpose: Measures intelligence of students ages 15 and older.

Description: 76-item paper-pencil test containing both verbal and nonverbal items to measure verbal, numerical, and abstract reasoning abilities. Australian norms are provided. Not available to Australian government schools. Materials

include an eight-page booklet, manual (with key), and specimen set. Examiner required. Suitable for group use.
AUSTRALIAN PUBLISHER
Timed: 1 hour
Scoring: Hand key
Cost: Contact publisher
Publisher: The Australian Council for Educational Research Limited

ACER HIGHER TESTS: WL-WQ, ML-MQ (SECOND EDITION) AND PL-PQ

Adolescent, adult
Ages 13 and older

Purpose: Measures the intelligence of students ages 13 and older.

Description: 72-item paper-pencil test of general mental abilities available in three forms: WL-WQ for students ages 13 and older and parallel forms ML-MQ and PL-PQ for students ages 15 and older. The L section (36 items) of each form has a linguistic bias; the Q section (36 items) is quantitative. Australian norms are provided for both sections separately and for a combined score. Examiner required. Suitable for group use.
AUSTRALIAN PUBLISHER
Timed: Varies
Scoring: Hand key; examiner evaluated
Cost: Contact publisher
Publisher: The Australian Council for Educational Research Limited

ACER INTERMEDIATE TEST F

Child, adolescent
Ages 10-14

Purpose: Measures the intelligence of students ages 10-14.

Description: 80-item pencil-paper test measuring general mental abilities in the following areas: classification, jumbled sentences, number series, synonyms and antonyms, arithmetical and verbal problems, and proverbs. Materials include a four-page booklet, scoring key, manual, and specimen set. Australian norms are provided. Examiner required. Suitable for group use.

AUSTRALIAN PUBLISHER
Timed: 30 minutes
Scoring: Hand key
Cost: Contact publisher
Publisher: The Australian Council for Educational Research Limited

ACER INTERMEDIATE TEST G

Child, adolescent
Ages 10-14

Purpose: Measures intelligence of students ages 10-14.

Description: 75-item paper-pencil test measuring general mental abilities in the following areas: analogies, classifications, synonyms, number and letter series, arithmetical and verbal reasoning questions, and proverbs. Materials include a four-page booklet, scoring key, manual, and specimen set. Australian norms are provided. Not available to Australian government schools. Examiner required. Suitable for group use.
AUSTRALIAN PUBLISHER
Timed: 30 minutes
Scoring: Hand key
Cost: Contact publisher
Publisher: The Australian Council for Educational Research Limited

ACER JUNIOR A TEST

Child Ages 8.6-11.11

Purpose: Measures intelligence of children ages 8.6-11.11.

Description: 75-item paper-pencil test measuring verbal, nonverbal, and quantitative reasoning abilities. Materials include an eight-page booklet, scoring key, manual, and specimen set. Examiner required. Suitable for group use.
AUSTRALIAN PUBLISHER
Timed: 30 minutes
Scoring: Hand key
Cost: Contact publisher
Publisher: The Australian Council for Educational Research Limited

ACER JUNIOR NON-VERBAL TEST
Manual by D. Spearritt

Child   Ages 8.6-12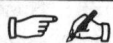

Purpose: Measures intelligence of children ages 8.6-12.

Description: 60-item paper-pencil test measuring general mental abilities using pictorial and diagrammatic analogies and matrices. The four subtests cover time sequences, block series, diagrammatic analogies, and matrices. Australian norms are provided. Materials include a 16-page booklet, scoring key, manual, and specimen set. Examiner required. Suitable for group use.
AUSTRALIAN PUBLISHER

Timed: 34 minutes

Scoring: Hand key

Cost: Contact publisher

Publisher: The Australian Council for Educational Research Limited

AH1 X AND Y GROUP TESTS OF FORMAL REASONING
A. W. Heim, K. P. Watts, and V. Simmonds

Child   Ages 7-11

Purpose: Assesses perceptual or nonverbal reasoning skills. Used for classroom evaluation of poor readers.

Description: Four-subtest multiple-choice paper-pencil measure of nonverbal reasoning. The subtests cover series, likes, analogues, and differents. Items are presented in pictorial or diagrammatic format. Two parallel forms, X and Y, are available. Examiner required. Suitable for group use.
BRITISH PUBLISHER

Timed: 45 minutes

Scoring: Hand key

Cost: AH1 specimen set £14.45; 25 booklets (specify form) £20.20; key £4.75 plus VAT; manual £10.10 (payment in sterling for all overseas orders)

Publisher: NFER-NELSON Publishing Company Ltd.

AH2/AH3 GROUP TESTS OF GENERAL REASONING
A. W. Heim, K. P. Watts, and V. Simmonds

Ages 10-adult

Purpose: Assesses general reasoning ability. Used for evaluating intelligence.

Description: 120-item multiple-choice paper-pencil test consisting of three subtests of 40 items each measuring reasoning ability: Verbal (V), Numerical (N), and Perceptual (P). The Perceptual subtest presents items in diagrammatic and pictorial formats. A profile of the subject, showing areas of strength and weakness, may be constructed. Two parallel forms, AH2 and AH3, are available. The test was developed as an alternative to the AH4 Group Tests of Intelligence. Examiner required. Suitable for group use.
BRITISH PUBLISHER

Timed: Short time 28 minutes; longer time 42 minutes

Scoring: Hand key

Cost: Specimen set £25.25; 25 question books (specify form) £32.85; 25 answer sheets (specify form) £7.30; marking keys £5.35 each; manual £8.80 (payment in sterling for all overseas orders)

Publisher: NFER-NELSON Publishing Company Ltd.

AH4 GROUP TEST OF GENERAL INTELLIGENCE (REGULAR EDITION)
A. W. Heim

Ages 10-adult

Purpose: Measures general intellectual ability. Used for evaluation of children, adults, or selected groups with below-average levels of intelligence.

Description: Multiple-item paper-pencil test measuring general intelligence. The first section tests verbal and numerical skills, and the second section contains items, presented in diagrammatic form, requiring deductive reasoning, the understanding of everyday words, accurate observance of details, and the following of

simple instructions exactly. Although most items are multiple-choice, a few require more extensive answers. Examiner required. Suitable for group use.
BRITISH PUBLISHER

Timed: 10 minutes per part

Scoring: Hand key; computer scoring service available

Cost: Specimen set £8.20; 25 booklets £14.45; 25 answer sheets £3.45 plus VAT; key £3.20 plus VAT; manual £5.75 (payment in sterling for all overseas orders)

Publisher: NFER-NELSON Publishing Company Ltd.

AH5 GROUP TEST OF HIGH GRADE INTELLIGENCE
A. W. Heim

Adolescent, adult
Ages 13-college

Purpose: Assesses general intellectual ability. Used for evaluating subjects of above-average intelligence.

Description: Two-part paper-pencil test measuring intelligence. The first part contains verbal and numerical problems, and the second part contains problems in diagrammatic form. The items, the majority of which are multiple-choice, emphasize deductive reasoning, but they also require accurate observation, attention to detail, and the ability to appreciate shades of meaning. Examiner required. Suitable for group use.
BRITISH PUBLISHER

Timed: 20 minutes per part

Scoring: Hand key

Cost: Specimen set £10.65; 25 booklets £11.45; 25 answer sheets £3.95 plus VAT; key £2.25; manual £8.00 plus VAT (payment in sterling for all overseas orders)

Publisher: NFER-NELSON Publishing Company Ltd.

AH6 GROUP TESTS OF HIGH LEVEL INTELLIGENCE
A. W. Heim, K. P. Watts, and V. Simmonds

Adolescent, adult
Ages 16-college

Purpose: Assesses general learning ability. Used for evaluating above-average subjects.

Description: Two separate paper-pencil tests of general reasoning. The SEM (Scientists, Engineers, and Mathematicians) is used with scientists, engineers, and mathematicians (whether potential or qualified). The AG (Arts and General) is used with historians, linguists, teachers, economists, other candidates in arts courses and management, and applicants for management training positions. Both tests include verbal, numerical, and diagrammatic items, but the proportion of each item type differs. Form AG contains half verbal items, and Form SEM contains equal proportions of the three item types. The test is similar in concept to the AH5 but is suitable for a somewhat higher age range. Examiner required. Suitable for group use.
BRITISH PUBLISHER

Timed: Form AG 35 minutes; Form SEM 40 minutes

Scoring: Hand key

Cost: Specimen set £13.90; 25 AG booklets £12.60; 25 AG answer sheets £4.75; 25 SEM booklets £12.60; 25 SEM answer sheets £4.80 plus VAT; manual £8.80 (payment in sterling for all overseas orders)

Publisher: NFER-NELSON Publishing Company Ltd.

ARLIN TEST OF FORMAL REASONING (ATFR)
Patricia Kennedy Arlin

Child, adolescent
Grades 6-12

Purpose: Assesses student's cognitive abilities. Used by teachers to plan curriculum, modify teaching techniques, and identify gifted students.

Description: 32-item paper-pencil multiple-choice test assessing students' cognitive abilities at one of five levels: concrete, high concrete, transitional, low formal, and high formal reasoning in the application of Piaget's developmental theory. The interpretation of both the total test score and the subtest scores is based on Inhelder and Piaget's description of formal operational thought and the eight schemata associated with that thought (multiplicative compensation, probability, correlations, combinational reasoning, proportional reasoning, forms of conservation beyond direct verification, mechanical equilibrium, and coordination of two or more systems or frames of reference). Two computer scoring packages are available. Package 1 provides an alphabetical pupil list indicating subtest scores, total test scores, and cognitive level designation. Package 2 includes summary item statistics, coefficients of correlations, means, total test statistics, subtest statistics, total test report, number tested, grade, mean, standard deviation, highest and lowest scores, Hoyt reliability, standard error of measurement statistics, and a total test histogram. Individual, class, group, grade level, and school statistics are available for total test, subtest, and items. A sixth-grade reading level is required. Examiner required. Suitable for group use.

Untimed: 1 hour

Scoring: Hand key; may be computer scored

Cost: Test kit (manual, 35 test booklets, 35 answer sheets, template) $42.00

Publisher: Slosson Educational Publications, Inc.

ARTHUR POINT SCALE OF PERFORMANCE TESTS: REVISED FORM II
Grace Arthur

Child, adolescent
Ages 5-15

Purpose: Measures mental abilities of difficult-to-assess children. Used to assess children with reading problems, delayed speech, and hearing impairments and non-English-speaking subjects.

Description: Scale of five tests measuring mental abilities. The scale includes the Knox Cube Test (Arthur Revision); Seguin Formboard Test (Arthur Revision); Arthur Stencil Design Test I; Healy Picture Completion Test II; and Porteus Maze Test (Arthur Modification). Revised Form II supercedes Form I of the Arthur

Point Scales of Performance and is more completely nonlanguage. The test may be used independently or as a supplement to the Arthur Adaptation of the Leiter International Performance Scale. Examiner required. Not suitable for group use.

Untimed: 45-90 minutes

Scoring: Examiner evaluated

Cost: Complete set (all necessary equipment for 5 tests, manual, 100 record forms, carrying case) $295.00

Publisher: The Psychological Corporation

BLOOMER LEARNING TEST (BLT)
Richard H. Bloomer

Child, adolescent
Grades 1.5-11+

Purpose: Determines strengths and weaknesses in learning patterns of individual pupils for purposes of planning remedial or compensatory educational programs. Used with special groups such as the learning disabled, emotionally disturbed, and gifted, as well as with normal students.

Description: 10 multiple-item multiple-choice paper-pencil subtests, each of which may be used alone and in any order. The subtests measure activity, visual and auditory short-term memory, visual apprehension, serial learning, recall, relearning, association, paired associate learning, concept recognition and production, and problem solving. The test also evaluates simple-learning IQ, problem-solving IQ, and full-learning IQ. The 10 subtests are contained in a loose-leaf binder. Scores are calculated on a student record form. Examiner required. Suitable for group use.

Timed: Rate of Responding 8 minutes; Association 5 minutes

Scoring: Hand key; examiner evaluated

Cost: Manual, test stimuli, answer forms, record forms, scoring key $78.00

Publisher: Brador Publications, Inc.

Information and availability unconfirmed; no publisher response.

THE BRITISH ABILITY SCALES, REVISED EDITION
Colin D. Elliott, David J. Murray, and Lea S. Pearson

**Child, adolescent
Ages 2.5-17**

Purpose: Assesses cognitive ability. Used for individual, educational, and clinical evaluations.

Description: 23 scales measuring cognitive ability. The scales are classified along three major dimensions: stimulus presentation mode, response mode, and behavioral characteristics. The behavioral characteristics dimension is divided into speed of information processing and five major areas of processes. Each scale may be administered on its own or in combination with the other scales. A short-form version is available for most of the scales. Examiner required. Suitable for group use.
BRITISH PUBLISHER

Timed: Open ended

Scoring: Examiner evaluated

Cost: Complete set £293.25 (payment in sterling for all overseas orders)

Publisher: NFER-NELSON Publishing Company Ltd.

BRITISH PICTURE VOCABULARY SCALES
Lloyd M. Dunn, Leota M. Dunn, Chris Whetton, and David Pintilie

**Child, adolescent
Ages 2.6-18**

Purpose: Measures receptive vocabulary of children. Used with physically disabled, mentally handicapped, disturbed, retarded, speech-impaired, and learning disabled children.

Description: Multiple-item response test assessing receptive vocabulary of children. Test plates are set up on a stand, and the examiner pronounces a stimulus word from the manual. The subject, looking at the test plate, indicates by nodding or gesturing which picture best indicates the meaning of that word. The results indicate above or below average ability

and problems that may require special attention. The test is used for screening new school entrants or measuring child development in the early years. A short and a long form are available. Examiner required. Not suitable for group use.
BRITISH PUBLISHER

Untimed: Varies

Scoring: Hand key

Cost: Complete set £40.25

Publisher: NFER-NELSON Publishing Company Ltd.

CHILDREN'S ABILITIES SCALES

Child   Ages 11-12½

Purpose: Assesses children's intellectual abilities. Used for describing individual strengths and weaknesses and for identifying learning difficulties.

Description: Battery of paper-pencil tests covering verbal, nonverbal, and spatial abilities. The manual explains the relationship between the tests, allowing the teacher to build a profile of the child's abilities. Examiner required. Suitable for group use.
BRITISH PUBLISHER

Untimed: Not available

Scoring: Hand key; examiner evaluated

Cost: Pupil's book £3.75; 10 answer sheets £2.25; specimen set £12.40 (payment in sterling for all overseas orders)

Publisher: NFER-NELSON Publishing Company Ltd.

COLOURED PROGRESSIVE MATRICES
Refer to page 21.

COLUMBIA MENTAL MATURITY SCALE (CMMS)
Refer to page 21.

COMPOUND SERIES TEST (CST)
Refer to page 891.

COMPREHENSIVE ASSESSMENT PROGRAM DEVELOPING COGNITIVE ABILITIES TEST
Donald L. Beggs and John T. Mouw

Child, adolescent
Grades 2-12

Purpose: Identifies intellectual strengths and weaknesses in groups and individuals. Used to compare learning ability to academic achievement. Identifies students for gifted programs and evaluates curricular alternatives.

Description: 80-item paper-pencil test measuring verbal, quantitative, and spatial abilities. Tests for Grades 3-12 provide information about the individual's skills in application, analysis, synthesis; knowledge; and comprehension. When administered with the Comprehensive Assessment Program: Achievement Series, the test shows the level of student performance in relation to abilities. Examiner required. Suitable for group use.

Timed: 50 minutes

Scoring: Hand key; may be computer scored

Cost: 35 test booklets $20.35-26.80 (specify level and machine or hand-scorable); 35 answer sheets $9.00; directions for administration $2.25; manual $7.15; key $4.35

Publisher: American Testronics

THE CULTURE FAIR SERIES: SCALES 1, 2, 3
Refer to page 21.

ESSENTIAL INTELLIGENCE TESTS
F.J. Schonell and R.H. Adams

Child   Ages 7-12.5

Purpose: Measures general intelligence of children. Also used with older children who have a reading age of at least 7.5.

Description: Two multiple-item paper-pencil tests measuring intelligence. Examiner required. Suitable for group use.

BRITISH PUBLISHER

Untimed: Not available

Scoring: Examiner evaluated

Cost: 20 tests £3.80; manual 65p.

Publisher: Oliver and Boyd; distributed in U.S.A. by Longman, Inc.

EXPRESSIVE ONE-WORD PICTURE VOCABULARY TEST (EOWPVT)
Morrison F. Gardner

Child   Ages 2-12

Purpose: Assesses a child's verbal intelligence. Used to screen for possible speech defects, to evaluate bilingual student fluency in English, and to determine preschool placement.

Description: 110-item verbal test of definitional and interpretational skills. The test consists of 100 pictures presented one at a time to the examinee who names each picture while the examiner records the response. Scoring tables yield deviation IQs, percentiles, and mental age equivalents. Materials include test plates and a set of Spanish recording forms. Examiner required. Not suitable for group use. Available in Spanish.

Untimed: 20 minutes

Scoring: Hand key

Cost: Manual $10.00; test plates $25.00; 25 recording forms (Spanish or English) $7.00

Publisher: Academic Therapy Publications

FULL-RANGE PICTURE VOCABULARY TEST (FRPV)
Refer to page 22.

GENERAL ABILITY BATTERY
Herman J.P. Schubert

Adolescent, adult

Purpose: Measures general mental abilities. Used for scholastic and industrial placement and guidance in high school, college, and industry.

Description: Multiple-item paper-pencil battery of tests assessing general mental abilities in order to predict educational and employment success. The battery yields scores for verbal skills, precise thinking, arithmetic reasoning, and logical analysis. Examiner required. Suitable for group use.

Timed: Varies

Scoring: Hand key

Cost: 25 tests $16.50; specimen set (25 tests, answer key, manual) $35.00

Publisher: Slosson Educational Publications, Inc.

GRIFFITHS MENTAL DEVELOPMENT SCALES
Refer to page 22.

GROUP TEST FOR INDIAN PUPILS—1968

Child, adolescent

Purpose: Measures general mental ability. Used for psychoeducational evaluation.

Description: 6-subtest paper-pencil measure of general mental ability. Three subtests are verbal and three are nonverbal. Tests provide three scores: verbal, nonverbal, and total. The test is divided into three series: Junior, Intermediate, and Senior. Two alternative forms are available for the Junior and Intermediate Series. Examiner required. Suitable for group use.
SOUTH AFRICAN PUBLISHER

Timed: 2 hours

Scoring: Hand key; examiner evaluated

Cost: (In Rands) Junior Form A test booklet 1,70; Junior Form B test booklet 1,40; Intermediate Form A test booklet 1,40; Intermediate Form B 1,70; Senior test booklets 1,40; manual 5,00; scoring stencils-Junior A 2,10; Junior B 2,40; Intermediate A & B 1,80 each; Senior 1,90; orders from outside The RSA will be dealt with on merit

Publisher: Human Sciences Research Council

GROUP TESTS FOR 5/6 AND 7/8 YEAR OLDS—1960

Child   Ages 5-8

Purpose: Assesses intellectual ability. Used for measurement of school readiness.

Description: 6-subtest measure of general intellectual ability. Materials include bilingual (English, Afrikaans) test booklets. The child should be able to handle a pencil and follow instructions without emotional distress. Examiner required. Suitable for group use.
SOUTH AFRICAN PUBLISHER

Untimed: No time limit

Scoring: Hand key; examiner evaluated

Cost: (In Rands) 10 tests for 5/6 1,60; 10 tests for 7/8 1,70; manual 3,10; orders from outside The RSA will be dealt with on merit

Publisher: Human Sciences Research Council

GROUP TESTS—1974
Refer to page 23.

HARDING SKYSCRAPER FORM B-C
Chris Harding

Adult

Purpose: Measures mental abilities at a high level of achievement. Originally developed to serve the selection needs of the International Society for Philosophical Enquiry. Used with candidates in the 140-173 Ability Quotient range, with a ceiling of 181 + .

Description: 40-item paper-pencil test measuring the integration of thinking, creative, and informational abilities to yield a single unified score called the Ability Quotient (A.Q.). Using multiple-choice and short-answer questions for Section B and incomplete analogies (each with four choices) for Section C, the test measures convergent, divergent, and condivergent thinking processes. Examiner required. Suitable for group use.
AUSTRALIAN PUBLISHER

Untimed: 1½-2 hours
Scoring: Scored by publisher
Cost: Test $2.00; scoring $5.00
Publisher: Harding Tests

HARDING W87 TEST
Chris Harding

Adult

Purpose: Measures mental abilities at a high level of achievement. Developed to replace the Harding Skyscraper as the entrance test of the International Society for Philosophical Enquiry (ISPE). Suitable for individuals with Ability Quotient 140-173.

Description: 64-item paper-pencil test measuring the integration of thinking, creative, and informational abilities. The test consists of two parts. Set I (34 items) uses multiple-choice and free-response questions to test verbal, numerical, and logical reasoning abilities. Set II (30 items) provides incomplete word analogies, requiring the subject to choose from 10 possible words to complete the analogy. The test as a whole measures convergent, divergent, and condivergent thinking processes. This test may be obtained only from IPSE, which wishes to control its use. Examiner required. Suitable for group use.
AUSTRALIAN PUBLISHER
Untimed: 3 hours
Scoring: Publisher scored
Cost: Contact publisher
Publisher: Harding Tests

HEALY PICTORIAL COMPLETION TEST I
William Healy

Child

Purpose: Measures mental ability and intelligence based on an individual's apperceptive ability. Used with all ages, primarily with individuals with a child-type mind.

Description: 10-item task-assessment test using a picture board with 10 pieces missing so that the scene is incomplete. The missing pieces are of uniform size and

shape, and the subject must select the 10 correct insets from the 50 choices presented and insert them in their proper places to complete the scene. Errors are rated as logical errors and total errors. Observation of the child's approach to the task provides information about the child's mental control and processes of association. The instrument is particularly useful with defectives and aberrational individuals. This test also is included in the Arthur Point Scale of Performance, Form I. Examiner required. Not suitable for group use.

Timed: 20 minutes
Scoring: Examiner evaluated
Cost: Test, manual, carrying case $87.75
Publisher: Stoelting Company

HENMON-NELSON TESTS OF MENTAL ABILITY
Joseph L. French, Tom A. Lamke, and Martin J. Nelson

Child, adolescent
Grades K-12

Purpose: Measures the general mental abilities of elementary and high-school students.

Description: Battery of multiple-item paper-pencil tests assessing the cognitive abilities of students. The tests are available on four levels designed for use in the following grade ranges: Grades K-2 (Primary Battery), Grades 3-6, Grades 6-9, and Grades 9-12. The Primary Battery consists of three subtests (listening, picture vocabulary, and size and number), which measure nine abilities and require no reading on the part of the students. The tests for Grades 3-12 contain items, arranged in omnibus-cycle form, related to academic success (vocabulary, sentence completion, opposites, general information, verbal analogies, verbal classification, verbal inference, number series, arithmetic reasoning, and figure analogies).
The following scores are available: raw score, Deviation IQ (a standard score by age), age percentile rank and stanine, and grade percentile rank and stanine. Consumable test booklets are available for all levels. Reusable test booklets and MRC

answer cards (for use with scoring service) are available for Grades 3-12 only. The Primary Battery examiner's manual includes directions for administering each test, information about the nature and purposes of the tests, and guidelines for interpreting and using the test results. The examiner's manual for Grades 3-12 includes information for administering, understanding, and using the tests, technical information, and norms tables. Examiner required. Suitable for group use.

Untimed: Grades K-2 25-30 minutes; grades 3-12 30 minutes

Scoring: Examiner evaluated; may be computer scored (Grades 3-12 only)

Cost: 35 Primary Battery test booklets, manual, class record sheet $32.19; 35 test booklets (specify consumable or reusable) for Grades 3-6, 6-9, or 9-12, manual, class record sheet $24.03; 100 MRC answer cards (includes all materials needed to obtain scoring service) $16.59; examiner's manual (Grades K-2 or 3-12) $3.18; 35 class record sheets $8.31

Publisher: The Riverside Publishing Company

INDIVIDUAL SCALE FOR INDIAN SOUTH AFRICANS (ISISA)—1971
R.J. Prinsloo and F.W.O. Heinichen in collaboration with D.J. Swart

Child, adolescent
Ages 8-17

Purpose: Assesses intelligence in Indian pupils. Used for psychological-educational evaluation.

Description: 10-subtest measure of general intellectual ability. Five subtests are verbal; five are nonverbal. Scores obtained include Vocabulary, Comprehension, Similarities, Problems, Memory, Pattern Completion, Blocks, Absurdities, Formboard, and Mazes. The test may be administered in an abbreviated form. The test was adapted for Indians from the New South African Individual Scale. Examiner required. Not suitable for group use.

SOUTH AFRICAN PUBLISHER

Untimed: 1 hour, 20 minutes

Scoring: Hand key; examiner evaluated

Cost: (In Rands) complete specimen set (2 pattern completions, 2 mazes, 2 answer sheets) 63,00; orders from outside The RSA will be dealt with on merit

Publisher: Human Sciences Research Council

INTELLIGENCE TESTS

Child, adolescent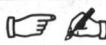

Purpose: Measures general intelligence of secondary-school pupils.

Description: Several tests assessing the reasoning abilities of secondary-school pupils. The Cotswold Tests provide measures of Mental Ability and English Ability for two age levels: 10-12½ years and 8½-9½ years. The Kelvin Tests include infant, reading, and mental tests. The Ryburn Tests are available for two levels: junior and senior. The Cotswold Personality Assessment provides three preference scores (things, people, ideas) and three attitude scores (using one's hands, being with other people, talking about school) for students ages 11-16. The last test of the battery is the Orton Intelligence Test for students ages 9-14 years. Instructions, norms, and a booklet entitled *Spotlight on Reasoning* are available for all tests.

BRITISH PUBLISHER

Timed: Varies

Scoring: Not available

Cost: 20 Cotswold tests (specify title) £1.60; 20 Kelvin tests (specify title £1.60; 20 Ryburn tests (specify junior or senior) £1.60; 100 Cotswold Personality Assessment £7.95; 20 Orton Intelligence tests £1.40; instructions and norms for all tests 20p.

Publisher: Robert Gibson Publisher

Information and availability unconfirmed; no publisher response.

JENKINS INTERMEDIATE NONVERBAL TEST: ACER ADAPTATION
J.W. Jenkins

Child, adolescent
Ages 10-14

Purpose: Measures the intelligence of students ages 10-14.

Description: 80-item paper-pencil test measuring nonverbal reasoning abilities. The diagrammatic test items are divided into five subtests involving classification, serial ordering, and diagrammatic analogies. Materials include a 16-page booklet, scoring key, manual, and specimen set. This test is an Australian adapatation (with Australian norms) of the Scale of Non-Verbal Mental Ability published by the National Foundation for Educational Research in England and Wales. Examiner required. Suitable for group use. AUSTRALIAN PUBLISHER

Timed: 24 minutes

Scoring: Hand key

Cost: Contact publisher

Publisher: The Australian Council for Educational Research Limited

---

KOHS BLOCK DESIGN TEST
S.C. Kohs

Mental ages 3-19

Purpose: Measures intelligence of persons with a mental age of 3-19 years. Used for testing individuals with language and hearing handicaps, the disadvantaged, and non-English-speaking individuals.

Description: Multiple-item task-assessment test consisting of 17 cards containing colored designs and 16 colored blocks that the subject uses to duplicate the designs on the cards. Performance is evaluated for attention, adaptation, and auto-criticism. This test also is included in the Merrill-Palmer and Arthur Performance scales. The complete set includes cubes, cards, manual, and 50 record blanks. Examiner required. Suitable for group use.

Timed: 40 minutes or less

Scoring: Examiner evaluated

Cost: Complete kit $58.50

Publisher: Stoelting Company

LANGDON ADULT INTELLIGENCE TEST
Refer to page 26.

LEITER INTERNATIONAL PERFORMANCE SCALE (ARTHUR ADAPTATION)
Refer to page 26.

LEITER INTERNATIONAL PERFORMANCE SCALE (LIPS)
Refer to page 26.

MATRIX ANALOGIES TEST— EXPANDED FORM (MAT-EF)

Child, adolescent
Ages 5-17

Purpose: Measures nonverbal reasoning ability of students.

Description: 64-item multiple-choice paper-pencil test consisting of abstract designs or matrices from which an element in a progression is missing. The child chooses the missing element from six alternatives. Items are organized in four groups: pattern completion, reasoning by analogy, serial reasoning, and spatial visualization. The test was normed on a large, nationally representative U.S. sample and yields standard scores, percentile ranks, age equivalents for the total score, and item group scores. Since minimal verbal comprehension and response are required, the test is appropriate for assessment of bilingual, gifted, learning-disabled, mentally retarded, hearing and/or language-impaired, and physically disabled persons with limited response capabilities. The test can be administered by psychologists, counselors, school psychologists and diagnosticians, rehabilitation psychologists, and other professionals with proper training and experience in testing. Examiner required. Not suitable for group use.

Untimed: 30 minutes

Scoring: Hand key

Cost: Specimen set (examiner's manual, reusable test booklet, self-scoring answer sheet) $59.00

Publisher: The Psychological Corporation

MATRIX ANALOGIES TEST—SHORT FORM (MAT-SF)
Jack A. Naglieri

Child, adolescent
Ages 5-17.11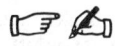

Purpose: Measures nonverbal reasoning abilities of students. Identifies children with learning difficulties or potentially gifted bilingual or educationally disadvantaged students whose school performance may be poor due to limited English language proficiency.

Description: 35-item paper-pencil test consisting of abstract designs with missing elements and matrices containing progressive elements that predict the next element in a progression. Test items are part of the larger MAT—Expanded Form. The test features norms on a large nationally representative U.S. sample and a six-option, multiple-choice format. When used with the Multi-Level Academic Survey Test, this test also may be used to screen for learning-disabled children identified on the basis of an ability-achievement discrepancy. The test yields percentile ranks, stanines by half-year age intervals, and age equivalents from 5.0-17.11. Examiner required. Suitable for group use.

Untimed: 20 minutes

Scoring: Hand key

Cost: Specimen set (examiner's manual, answer sheet, test booklet) $13.50

Publisher: The Psychological Corporation

NEW SOUTH AFRICAN GROUP TEST (NSAGT)—1965

Child, adolescent
Ages 8-17

Purpose: Assesses intellectual ability. Used for psychological and educational evaluation.

Description: 6-subtest measure of general intellectual ability. Three subtests are verbal, and three are nonverbal. The test is available at three levels: Junior, Intermediate, and Senior. Two equivalent forms are available for the Junior and Senior Series. The test is available only to departments of education and private schools or to schools training teachers for the purpose of training and research. Examiner required. Not suitable for group use.

SOUTH AFRICAN PUBLISHER

Timed: 2 hours

Scoring: Hand key; examiner evaluated; may be machine scored

Cost: (In Rands) Form J test 0,30; Form G test 0,60; Form S/T test 0,30; Intermediate manual 1,10; Junior and Senior manual 1,60; scoring stencils (specify form) 0,40 each; 10 answer sheets 0,40; 10 machine answer sheets 1,10; orders from outside The RSA will be dealt with on merit

Publisher: Human Sciences Research Council

NON-LANGUAGE LEARNING TEST
Refer to page 29.

NON-LANGUAGE TEST OF VERBAL INTELLIGENCE
S. Chatterji and Manjula Makerjee

Child   Ages 8-12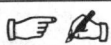

Purpose: Measures verbal intelligence of children using a nonlanguage medium. Used to test groups of children with differing linguistic or cultural backgrounds. Also identifies children whose academic backwardness is due to linguistic difficulty rather than lack of verbal ability.

Description: 62-item paper-pencil multiple-choice test consisting entirely of pictured test items. The test consists of four parts: analogy, classification, opposites, and picture arrangement. The candidates are required to record their answers on a separate answer sheet. The test booklets are reusable. The examiner's manual includes detailed instructions for administration, evaluation, and interpretation of the test. Examiner required. Suitable for group use.

PUBLISHED IN INDIA

Timed: 45 minutes

Scoring: Hand key; examiner evaluated

Cost: Contact publisher

Publisher: Statistical Publishing Society

*Information and availability unconfirmed; no
publisher response.*

NON-READERS INTELLIGENCE TEST (THIRD EDITION) AND ORAL VERBAL INTELLIGENCE TEST
Dennis Young

Child, adolescent
Ages 6.7-14.11

Purpose: Measures intelligence of students whose performance would be underestimated if they were required to read the questions. Used with children suspected of or diagnosed as Educationally Subnormal (ESN). Identifies children needing special educational assistance.

Description: Multiple-item paper-pencil intelligence test orally administered to slow or nonreaders. The test is available in two forms: The Non-Readers Intelligence Test for use with unstreamed children ages 6.7-8.11 and with less able children up to the age of 13.11 and the Oral Verbal Intelligence Test for use with unstreamed children ages 7.6-10.11 and with less able children up to the age of 14.11. The third edition of the Non-Readers Intelligence Test manual offers revised items (replacing words like "pop" which have acquired new meanings) and new norms. The manual for the Oral Verbal Intelligence Test contains details of test construction and full instructions for administering and scoring the test. Both tests employ the same scoring template. Examiner required. Suitable for group use.
BRITISH PUBLISHER

Untimed: Not available

Scoring: Hand key

Cost: NRIT manual £2.10; specimen set £2.95; template £1.75; 20 answer sheets £1.20; OVIT manual £2.15; specimen set £2.45; 20 answer sheets £1.75; template £1.75

Publisher: Hodder & Stoughton

NON-VERBAL ABILITY TESTS (NAT)
H.A.H. Rowe

Child, adolescent
Ages 8-adult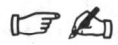

Purpose: Measures general ability of the 'g' type as well as perceptual, conceptual, and attention and concentration skills of individuals ages 8 and older.

Description: Domain-referenced battery of 18 nonverbal paper-pencil tests assessing general and specific abilities. The tests cover matching shapes, matching directions, categorization, picture completion, embedded figures, figure formation, mazes, sequencing, picture arrangement, visual search, simple key tests, complex key tests, code tracking, and visual recall. The tests do not require verbalization, reading, or writing in either the administration or the completion of the largely diagrammatic stimulus materials. The battery yields an ability profile, the level and shape of which can be interpreted for each individual. Materials include test forms, a manual, and a monograph entitled *Language-Free Evaulation of Cognitive Development.* Examiner required. Suitable for group use.
AUSTRALIAN PUBLISHER

Untimed: Varies

Scoring: Hand key; examiner evaluated

Cost: Contact publisher

Publisher: The Australian Council for Educational Research Limited

---

NON-VERBAL REASONING TESTS SERIES

Child, adolescent
Ages 7-15

Purpose: Assesses nonverbal reasoning ability. Used for evaluation of poor readers.

Description: Three paper-pencil tests of basic reasoning using geometric shapes and pictures. All questions appear in pictorial or diagrammatic form. Pictures Test A (ages 7- 8) uses three types of questions in picture form. In the first section, the child chooses the picture different from a set; in the second section, the child chooses one of five alternative patterns to complete a story or pattern; the third section presents analogues in pictorial form. Non-Verbal Test BD (ages 8-11) consists of questions relating to geometric shapes, cyphers, similarities, analogues, and series. Non-Verbal Test DH (ages 10-15) contains two main types of questions. The first requires the child to select one of five small squares that will complete the overall series or pattern contained in a larger square. Other questions are series type. The test may be administered in the full 96-question form or in the shorter 64-question form. Examiner required. Suitable for group use. BRITISH PUBLISHER

Timed: Varies, depending on test

Scoring: Hand key

Cost: 10 picture tests £5.70; manual £1.75; 10 tests BD £5.95; manual £1.80; 10 tests DH £9.50; 10 answer sheets £2.05 plus VAT; manual £2.50 (payment in sterling for all overseas orders)

Publisher: NFER-NELSON Publishing Company Ltd.

NONVERBAL TEST OF COGNITIVE SKILLS (NTCS)
G. Orville Johnson and Herbert F. Boyd

Child   Grades K-7

Purpose: Assesses school-related abilities in children.

Description: Multiple-item nonverbal test in which the examiner uses pantomime to guide the child in the manipulation of blocks, color cubes, dominos, picture stimuli, and Knox cubes to measure the following skills and abilities: reasoning, rote memory, recognition and memory of patterns, visual memory, discrimination, space and spatial relationships, conceptual thinking, recognition of and ability to deal with quantities, quantitative memory, and visual motor perception. Examiner required. Not suitable for group use.

Timed: 25-30 minutes

Scoring: Examiner evaluated

Cost: Test kit $150.00

Publisher: The Psychological Corporation

PEABODY PICTURE VOCABULARY TEST-REVISED (PPVT-R)
Lloyd M. Dunn and Leota M. Dunn

All ages

Purpose: Measures receptive vocabulary for Standard American English, estimates verbal ability, and assesses academic aptitude. Used with English as a Second Language students, mentally retarded and gifted students, and applicants for jobs requiring good aural vocabulary.

Description: 175-item "point-to" response test measuring receptive vocabulary in English. Test items, arranged in order of increasing difficulty, consist of plates of four pictures. Subjects are shown a plate and asked to point to the picture which corresponds to the stimulus word. Only those plates within a subject's ability range are administered. Age-based norms include standard scores, percentile ranks, stanines, and age equivalents. The complete kit includes 175 test plates bound in an easel, manual, 25 individual record forms, and shelf box. Available in two forms, L and M. A special plastic plate edition is available. Examiner required. Not suitable for group use.

Untimed: Not available

Scoring: Examiner evaluated

Cost: Complete kit (Form L or M): regular edition $35.75; special plastic edition $44.00

Publisher: American Guidance Service

PICTORIAL TEST OF INTELLIGENCE
Joseph L. French

Child   Ages 3-8

Purpose: Measures children's general ability. Used for curriculum planning and evaluation.

Description: Multiple-item oral picture test in six sections. The subtests are Picture Vocabulary, Information and Comprehension, Form Discrimination,

Similarities, Size and Number, and Immediate Recall. The examiner presents picture cards on which are represented four possible answers and asks questions of the child. The cards are designed so that the examiner, by observing eye movement, also can determine the response of children who are physically handicapped. Materials include cards, a manual, and record forms. Examiner required. Not suitable for group use.

CANADIAN PUBLISHER

Untimed: 45 minutes

Scoring: Hand key

Cost: Complete test kit (record forms and manual) $190.00; 35 record forms $22.00; manual $22.00

Publisher: Institute of Psychological Research, Inc.

Information and availability unconfirmed; no publisher response.

PROVERBS TEST
Donald R. Gorham

All ages

Purpose: Assesses abstract verbal functioning. Used for individual clinical evaluation, screening, and clinical research.

Description: 12- or 40-item power test measuring verbal comprehension. The subject is required to explain the meanings of proverbs. The 12-item free-answer format allows the subject to respond in his or her own words. A 40-item multiple-choice format is also available. The free-response forms are scored for abstractness and pertinence on a 3-point scale. The multiple-choice form is scored with a hand stencil. Forms I, II, and III are available for free-answer administration. Examiner required. Only the multiple-choice form is suitable for group use.

Untimed: Individual test 10-30 minutes; group multiple-choice test 20-40 minutes

Scoring: Hand key; examiner evaluated

Cost: Complete kit (general manual, clinical manual, 10 each of Forms I, II, III, scoring cards, 10 free-response form booklets, scoring stencils) $13.00; 100 test blanks $18.00; 25 test booklets (specify Form I, II, or III) $8.00; 100 answer sheets $8.00

Publisher: Psychological Test Specialists

QUICK TEST (QT)
Refer to page 30.

QUICK WORD TEST
Edgar F. Borgatta and Raymond J. Corsini

Grades 4-adult

Purpose: Measures verbal intelligence. Used for quick screening purposes in educational and clinical settings.

Description: 50- or 100-item paper-pencil multiple-choice vocabulary test measuring specific aspects of verbal mental ability. Test items consist of a word followed by four response choices. Individuals select the word that has the same meaning as the first word. The test is available for three levels: Elementary (50 items) for Grades 4-6; Level 1 (100 items) for Grades 7-12 and average adult groups; and Level 2 (100 items) for superior students in Grades 11 and 12 and college and professional groups. The vocabulary items for each level are printed on one side of a single test sheet. IBM 1230 and combined IBM 805/Digitek test sheets are available in parallel form Am. Hand and machine scoring stencils are available for all forms. The manual includes directions for administering, scoring, and interpreting the test; comparative data and correlations with raw scores from other verbal intelligence tests; and developmental and normative data. Norms are provided in terms of percentile ranks and stanines for the following groups: Grades 4, 5, and 6 (by grade) for the elementary level; Grades 7-12 (by grade) for Level 1; and college freshmen, adult education groups (by educational level), and various occupational groups for Level 2. Examiner required. Suitable for group use.

Untimed: 15 minutes

Scoring: Hand key; machine scored; computer scored

Cost: Elementary test kit (35 test sheets, answer key, manual, group record sheet) $3.00; Level 1 or 2 test kit (45 test sheets, manual, supplementary report, group record sheet) $6.00; scoring key for Level 1 or 2 $1.00

Publisher: F.E. Peacock Publishers, Inc.

ROSS TEST OF HIGHER COGNITIVE PROCESSES (ROSS TEST)
John D. Ross and Catherine M. Ross

Child   Grades 4-6

Purpose: Assesses abstract and critical thinking skills among gifted and non-gifted intermediate grade students. Used to screen students for special programs and to evaluate program effectiveness.

Description: 105-item paper-pencil multiple-choice test in eight sections, each dealing with a specific level of higher cognitive processes within the areas of analysis, synthesis, and evaluation. Test is taken in two sittings. Responses may be recorded directly in the student test booklet or on an optional answer sheet. Materials include overlays for the scoring of answer sheets and a cassette tape of the test. Examiner required. Suitable for group use.

Timed: First sitting 50 minutes; second sitting 55 minutes

Scoring: Hand key

Cost: Manual $10.00; 10 test booklets $15.00; 25 answer sheets/profile forms $7.00; hand key $4.00; cassette tape test $10.00

Publisher: Academic Therapy Publications

SENIOR SOUTH AFRICAN INDIVIDUAL SCALE (SSAIS)—1964
Refer to page 31.

SILVER DRAWING TEST OF COGNITIVE AND CREATIVE SKILLS
Rawley A. Silver

Ages 6-adult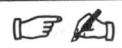

Purpose: Uses drawings to identify children with cognitive or creative strengths that may be overlooked by traditional tests of intelligence and achievement. Used by school psychologists, art therapists, speech and hearing specialists, resource teachers, teachers of art,

rehabilitation counselors, and other professionals.

Description: Three multiple-item paper-pencil subtests assessing the concepts of space, sequential order, and class-inclusion. The predictive drawing subtest assesses the ability to sequence and deal with hypothetical situations. Students are asked to add lines to outline drawings. Responses are scored for ability to show how the objects would appear if filled, tilted, or placed on a slope. The drawing from the observation subtest assesses concepts of space. Students are asked to draw an arrangement of cylinders. Responses are scored for ability to represent left-right, above-below, and front-back relationships. The drawing from the imagination subtest assesses the ability to form associations on the basis of class or function. Students are asked to choose subjects from two arrays of drawings and to create a narrative drawing. Responses are scored for ability to select, combine, and represent. When appropriate, drawings also are scored for projection (emotional content) and language (titles). Drawing ability is not evaluated. Figures and tables are presented for interpretation of scores. Instructions for taking the test may be signed or pantomimed for use with handicapped populations in a variety of cultural settings. Examiner required. Suitable for use with small groups.

Untimed: 15 minutes

Scoring: Examiner evaluated

Cost: Test kit (manual, 10 test booklets, stimulus photograph and stimulus layout sheet for drawing from observation test, classroom record sheets) $35.00

Publisher: Special Child Publications

SLOSSON INTELLIGENCE TEST (SIT)
Refer to page 31.

SOI PRIMARY FORM (FORM P)
SOI Institute Staff

Child   Grades K-3

Purpose: Assesses the learning abilities of young children. Screens for special education or gifted placement. Used for early testing of bilingual and disadvantaged students in order to identify special needs or giftedness.

Description: Eleven subtests evaluating the processing abilities required for success in Grades K-3. Six subtests test processing abilities; the remaining five are diagnostic subtests. The test is designed for screening all students in Grades K-3 before an in-depth testing by a competency team for P.L. 94-142 or gifted placement. The test includes auditory sequencing. Suitable for teacher administration to groups; some subtests are administered individually to students who cannot write. A Spanish form is available.

Untimed: Processing 30 minutes; diagnostic 25 minutes

Scoring: Hand key

Cost: Test form $2.70

Publisher: Western Psychological Services

THE SOUTH AFRICAN INDIVIDUAL SCALE FOR THE BLIND (SAISB)—1979

Child, adolescent
Ages 6-18

Purpose: Measures general intelligence of blind children. Used for psychological and educational evaluations.

Description: 9-subtest measure of general intellectual ability. Five subtests are verbal, and four are nonverbal. Materials include Braillon sheets for the Pattern Completion and Dominos subtests, a form board, and wooden blocks. The test was adapted from the New South African Individual Scale (NSAIS). Examiner required. Not suitable for group use. SOUTH AFRICAN PUBLISHER

Untimed: Not available

Scoring: Hand key; examiner evaluated

Cost: Complete specimen (Pattern Completion, Rubberboard, Subtest 7, 8, 9 Form Board B, manual, vulvalite case, 2 sheets of cellophane paper, 2 general answer sheets; orders from outside The RSA will be dealt with on merit

Publisher: Human Sciences Research Council

THE STANDARD PROGRESSIVE MATRICES (SPM-1956)
Refer to page 32.

STANFORD-BINET INTELLIGENCE SCALE: FORM L-M
Refer to page 33.

THE STANFORD-BINET INTELLIGENCE SCALE, FOURTH EDITION
Refer to page 32.

SYSTEM OF MULTICULTURAL PLURALISTIC ASSESSMENT (SOMPA)
Jane R. Mercer and June F. Lewis

Child   Ages 5-11

Purpose: Assesses cognitive abilities, sensorimotor abilities, and adaptive behavior of children. Used for assessing children of diverse cultural backgrounds.

Description: Multiple-instrument measure covering various aspects of functioning of children from diverse cultural backgrounds. The test has two major components: The Parent Interview and Student Assessment Materials. The Parent Interview is conducted in the home and requires the administration of the Adaptive Behavior Inventory for Children (ABIC), Sociocultural Scales, and Health History Inventories. Student Assessment Materials data are collected in the school and include administration or completion of the following tests and tasks: Physcial Dexterity Tasks, Weight by Height, Visual Acuity, Auditory Acuity, Bender Visual Motor Gestalt Test (sold separately), and the WISC-R or WPPSI (sold separately). The test should be interpreted by a psychologist or a qualified team. Normative data are provided for black, Hispanic, and white children. Examiner required. Not suitable for group use. The Parent Interview is available in Spanish.

Untimed: Parent interview 60 minutes; Student Assessment Materials 20 minutes in addition to time required for the Wechsler and Bender-Gestalt tests

Scoring: Examiner evaluated

Cost: Basic kit (Parent Interview manual, 25 parent interview record forms, ABIC scoring keys, Student Assessment manual, 25 student assessment record forms, 25 profile folders, technical manual) $99.00

Publisher: The Psychological Corporation

TEST OF CONCEPT UTILIZATION (TCU)
Richard L. Crager

Child, adolescent Ages 5-18

Purpose: Measures the ability of children and adolescents to think conceptually. Used by teachers to identify children's conceptual strengths, especially under-achievers and children with learning disabilities.

Description: 50-item oral-response test consisting of 50 pairs of colored pictures of common objects. The child indicates how the objects are alike. Analysis of the responses provides qualitative and quantitative assessments of five areas of conceptual thinking: color, shape, relational function, homogeneous function, and abstract function. Norms are provided for individuals ages 5-18. *The Development of Concepts: A Manual for the Test of Concept Utilization* (104 pages) includes all scoring instructions, standardization, normative data, and chapters on clinical and educational uses of the test. The new (1980) manual, *Concepts in the Classroom: A Manual for the Educational Use of the Test of Conceptual Utilization,* provides instructions for a short scoring procedure. New studies are presented in the revised manual, but it does not include administration instructions or normative data. The original manual is still needed to administer and interpret the test. Examiner required. Not suitable for group use.

Untimed: 10 minutes

Scoring: Hand key

Cost: Complete kit (set of test plates, 5 protocol sheets, 25 scoring booklets, 2 manuals, 25 short-scoring forms) $79.50

Publisher: Western Psychological Services

THE TEST OF NONVERBAL INTELLIGENCE (TONI)
Refer to page 33.

TEST OF PROBLEM SOLVING (TOPS)
Linda Zachman, Carol Jorgensen, Rosemary Huisingh, and Mark Barrett

Child Ages 6-12

Purpose: Assesses the verbal reasoning and problem-solving abilities of children.

Description: Multiple-item oral-response test assessing expressive language skills and problem-solving abilities. Problems are presented with picture stimuli and test thinking skills, such as determining causes, answering negative why questions, determining solutions, avoiding problems, and explaining inferences. The results yield age equivalencies, percentile ranks, standard scores, and standard deviations. Examiner required. Not suitable for group use.

Untimed: Varies

Scoring: Examiner evaluated

Cost: Test kit $58.00

Publisher: LinguiSystems, Inc.

Information and availability unconfirmed; no publisher response.

WECHSLER SCALES: WECHSLER ADULT INTELLIGENCE SCALE (WAIS)
Refer to page 34.

WECHSLER SCALES: WECHSLER ADULT INTELLIGENCE SCALE— REVISED (WAIS-R)
Refer to page 34.

WECHSLER SCALES: WECHSLER INTELLIGENCE SCALE FOR CHILDREN—REVISED (WISC-R)
Refer to page 34.

WECHSLER SCALES: WECHSLER INTELLIGENCE SCALE FOR CHILDREN: 1949 EDITION (WISC)
Refer to page 35.

WECHSLER SCALES: WECHSLER PRESCHOOL AND PRIMARY SCALE OF INTELLIGENCE (WPPSI)
Refer to page 35.

WHIMBEY ANALYTICAL SKILLS INVENTORY (WASI)
Arthur Whimbey

Adolescent, adult
Grades 9 and above

Purpose: Assesses the analytical reasoning ability of high school and college students and adults.

Description: 38-item paper-pencil test assessing analytical reasoning ability and measuring academic aptitude. The test, which is incorporated in Arthur Whimbey and Jack Lochhead's book *Problem Solving and Comprehension* (4th ed.), can be used to indicate a student's potential for college success. After administration, students discuss and compare solutions to test items. A fourth-grade reading level is required. A table is provided to compute IQ. Self-administered. Suitable for group use.

Untimed: 50 minutes

Scoring: Hand key

Cost: Test booklet $1.00; *Problem Solving and Comprehension* (4th ed.) $10.95

Publisher: Lawrence Erlbaum Associates, Inc.

WILLIAMS INTELLIGENCE TEST FOR CHILDREN WITH DEFECTIVE VISION
M. Williams

Child, adolescent
Ages 5-15

Purpose: Assesses intelligence in blind children and those with visual impairments. Used for individual evaluation.

Description: Series of performance tests measuring intelligence. Materials include Braille cards. The test has been standardized on British children whose visual acuity did not amount to more than approximately 6/36 according to the Snellen Chart. Examiner required. Not suitable for group use.
BRITISH PUBLISHER

Untimed: Not available

Scoring: Examiner evaluated

Cost: Complete kit (12 record forms, handbook, 3 Braille cards, set of materials) £107.55 (payment in sterling for all overseas orders)

Publisher: Distributed by NFER-NELSON Publishing Company Ltd.

Reading: Elementary

ANALYTICAL READING INVENTORY, 2ND EDITION
Mary Lynn Woods and Alden J. Moe

Child, adolescent
Grades 1-9

Purpose: Analyzes reading skills to help classroom teachers and reading specialists make remediation decisions.

Description: 170 items of graded word lists and reading passages measuring strengths and weaknesses in word attack and comprehension skills, level of reading achievement, and potential for reading growth. Examiner required. Not suitable for group use.

Untimed: Varies

Scoring: Examiner evaluated

Cost: Complete package (student record summary sheets, qualitative analysis summary sheets, graded word lists, graded reading passages) $9.95
Publisher: Charles E. Merrill Publishing Company

ASSESSING READING DIFFICULTIES: A DIAGNOSTIC AND REMEDIAL APPROACH
Refer to page 606.

BASIC SIGHT WORD TEST
E. W. Dolch

Child

Purpose: Measures children's knowledge of basic sight words—the most commonly used words which cannot be learned from pictures and must be recognized instantly by sight before a child can read with interest and confidence. Identifies children needing remedial work.

Description: 220-item paper-pencil multiple-choice test measuring children's knowledge of basic sight words (service words), such as commonly used pronouns, adjectives, adverbs, prepositions, conjunctions, and common verbs. Each test item consists of four words. The children are asked to circle the word read aloud by their teacher. The 100 sheets printed in primer type on both sides are enough to test 25 children on all the words. All the words should be known by the end of Grade 2. Examiner required. Suitable for group use.
Untimed: Varies
Scoring: Examiner evaluated
Cost: 100 sheets $5.47
Publisher: Garrard Publishing Company
Information and availability unconfirmed; no publisher response.

BASIC SKILLS TEST—READING-ELEMENTARY-FORMS A AND B
IOX Assessment Associates

Child   Grades 5-6

Purpose: Measures student's end-of-elementary school achievement in basic reading skills. Used for determining minimum competency or grade promotion and for program evaluation.

Description: 35-item paper-pencil test measuring a student's ability to comprehend word meaning and syntax; identify sequences, main ideas, and details; and use a dictionary and common reference sources. This test preceeds The IOX Basic Skills Test—Reading-Secondary Level. Examiner required. Suitable for group use.
Untimed: 30-45 minutes
Scoring: Hand key
Cost: 25 BR-A2 tests $37.50; 25 BR-B2 tests $37.50; teacher's guide BR-G2 $3.95; test manual BTM-2 $3.95
Publisher: IOX Assessment Associates

BASIC VISUAL-MOTOR ASSOCIATION TEST
Refer to page 558.

BOTEL READING INVENTORY
Morten Botel

Child

Purpose: Measures elementary-school students' ability to read. Used for academic placement and measuring student progress throughout the school year.

Description: Four paper-pencil and oral-response tests assessing skills in three areas crucial to success in elementary reading and language arts: decoding, word recognition (oral reading ability), and word opposites (reading comprehension). The Decoding Test measures decoding competency at seven levels ranging from the awareness of sounds and letter correspondences to decoding multi-syllabic nonsense words. The seven levels are covered by 12 subtests of 10 items each. All responses are scored according to the following code: correct word, mispronunciation, substitution, or no response. As on all of the tests, the student's highest instructional level is considered to be the first level at which he falls below 80% correct answers. The Spelling Test consists of five graded lists of 20 words each. The words are dictated, and the students are asked to spell them. The Word Recognition Test consists of eight 20-word samples, spanning eight graduated reading levels from preprimer through fourth grade. As the student reads the words, responses are graded as correct word, mispronunciation, substitution, or no response. The Word Opposites Test is a group test consisting of 10 scaled 10-word subtests that progress from first-reader level through senior high school. For each test item, the student is asked to select from four words the one which means the opposite. The Word Opposites Test may be administered both as a reading test and as a listening test. As a reading test, it indicates the student's current reading performance; as a listening test, it indicates the student's reading potential. The reading placement tests yield three levels of reading competency: free reading level, instructional level, and frustration level. The Word Recognition and Word Opposites Tests are available in two forms, A and B, for pre- and posttesting. The administration manual includes information on administering, scoring, and interpreting the test, as well as technical data. Examiner required. Suitable for group use.

Untimed: Varies

Scoring: Examiner evaluated

Cost: Manual $8.64; Decoding Test, 35 Word Recognition Tests (specify form) $6.48 each; 35 Word Opposites Tests (specify form) $7.46 each

Publisher: Modern Curriculum Press, Inc.

BURT WORD READING TEST
Scottish Council for Research in Education

Ages 5 and older

Purpose: Measures word reading skills of children with reading ages 6.4-12.0. Also assesses the reading performance of class groups. Identifies children needing special reading assistance. Used in planning individual and class instructional approaches.

Description: Multiple-item oral-response test measuring word reading skills in which the student reads from a test card that consists of 100 words printed in decreasing size of type and graded in approximate order of difficulty. The student's achievement on the test provides a basis for making decisions about appropriate teaching and reading materials, instructional groupings, etc. This 1974 revised edition offers up-to-date normative data and establishes present-day levels of difficulty of the words. A separate version revised and standardized for use in New Zealand is also available. Norms are provided for both versions for students ages 6-13. Examiner required. Suitable for group use.
BRITISH PUBLISHER

Untimed: 5-10 minutes

Scoring: Examiner evaluated

Cost: 20 tests £2.10; manual £1.50 net c.

Publisher: Hodder & Stoughton

CLYMER-BARRETT READINESS TEST
Refer to page 465.

COMPUTER CROSSROADS
Stuart Paltrowitz and Donna Paltrowitz

Child

Purpose: Diagnoses weaknesses and strengths in reading comprehension skills of children with interest levels of Grades 2-5 and reading levels of Grades 1.8-2.8. Used in school settings.

Description: Computer-administered test of reading comprehension skills, including finding the main idea, sequencing, noting details, predicting outcomes, and inferring. The program allows students to create a story through which they journey with "computer pets," which the students also create. The program provides practice toward remediation and diagnostic information. Examiner required. Not suitable for group use.

Untimed: Varies

Scoring: Computer scored

Cost: Complete kit (3 diskettes, 3 back ups, management, documentation, and reproducible activity masters) $99.95

Publisher: Educational Activities, Inc.

CONCISE WORD READING TESTS
R. J. Andrews

Child   Ages 7-12

Purpose: Measures the word reading skills of primary and lower secondary-school students. Used for class or school surveys and as a basis for grouping children for reading instruction.

Description: Four 20-item oral-response tests measuring the word recognition and word attack skills of children. Each test is suitable for use with more than one age level. Age norms and standardized scores are provided for Australian students. Examiner required. Suitable for group use. AUSTRALIAN PUBLISHER

Untimed: Varies

Scoring: Examiner evaluated

Cost: Basic kit (test materials for 4 forms, 50 record forms with instructions and norms) $10.50

Publisher: Teaching and Testing Resources

Information and availability unconfirmed; no publisher response.

CTBS READINESS TEST

Child   Grades K-1.3

Purpose: Assesses the reading readiness of students.

Description: Multiple-item paper-pencil test assessing whether students possess the skills necessary for beginning reading. The test is organized in skill clusters, and the results indicate instructional priorities for each cluster. The test yields a Reading Readiness Report of Skill Mastery, which indicates student performance on the mathematics and language subtests. Examiner required. Suitable for group use.

Timed: 2 hours, 39 minutes

Scoring: Hand key; may be machine scored

Cost: Specimen set (machine-scorable test booklet, examiner's manual, user's handbook, test reviewer's guide) $8.95

Publisher: CTB/McGraw-Hill

THE DELAWARE COUNTY SILENT READING TESTS: LEVEL 1[2]
Delaware County Reading Council

Child   Grade 1

Purpose: Measures first-graders' ability to read and write. Used to provide reading instruction and as a pretest to diagnose reading strengths and weaknesses and as a posttest of teaching effectiveness.

Description: 20-item paper-pencil multiple-choice and short-answer test covering four major areas: interpretation of ideas, organization of ideas, vocabulary, and structural analysis of words. The examiner distributes the story and test booklets and writes the following words on a chalkboard: "paragraph," "sentences," "word," "underline," "write," "letter," and "number." These words are not usually found in typical second-grade reading materials. The examiner guides the pupils in pronouncing the words and tells them they may ask for help in figuring out which words correspond to the appropriate constructions in the story. Examiner required. Suitable for group use.

Untimed: 45-50 minutes

Scoring: Hand key

Cost: Pupil test $0.10; story booklet $0.15; teacher's guide included with each order of 25; additional teacher guides and answer keys $0.10 each; specimen set $3.50

Publisher: Delaware County Reading Council

DELAWARE COUNTY SILENT READING TESTS: LEVEL 2[1] AND LEVEL 2[2]
Delaware County Reading Council

Child   Grade 2

Purpose: Measures second-graders' ability to read and write. Used to provide reading instruction and as a pretest to diagnose reading strengths and weaknesses and as a posttest of teaching effectiveness.

Description: 20-item paper-pencil multiple-choice and short-answer test covering four major areas: interpretation of ideas, organization of ideas, vocabulary, and structural analysis of words. The examiner distributes the story and test booklets and writes the following words on a chalkboard: "paragraph," "sentence," "question," "underline," "title," and "root." These words usually are not found in typical second-grade reading materials. The examiner guides the pupils in pronouncing the words and tells them they may ask for help in figuring out which words correspond to the appropriate constructions in the story. Examiner required. Suitable for group use.

Untimed: 45-50 minutes

Scoring: Hand key

Cost: Pupil test $0.10; story booklet $0.15; teacher's guide included with each order of 25; additional teacher's guides and answer keys $0.10 each; specimen set $3.50

Publisher: Delaware County Reading Council

THE DELAWARE COUNTY SILENT READING TESTS: LEVEL 3¹ AND LEVEL 3²
Delaware County Reading Council

Child   Grade 3

Purpose: Measures third-graders' ability to read and write. Used to provide reading instruction and as a pretest to diagnose reading strengths and weaknesses and as a posttest of teaching effectiveness.

Description: 20-item paper-pencil multiple-choice and short-answer test covering four major areas: interpretation of ideas, organization of ideas, vocabulary, and structural analysis of words. The examiner distributes the story and test booklets and writes the following words on a chalkboard: "sentences," "opposite," "paragraph," "syllable," "root," and "blank spaces." These words are not usually found in typical third-grade reading materials. The examiner guides the pupils in pronouncing the words and tells them they may ask for help in figuring out

which words correspond to the appropriate constructions in the story. Examiner required. Suitable for group use.

Untimed: 45-50 minutes

Scoring: Hand key

Cost: Pupil test $0.10; story booklet $0.15; teacher's guide included with each order of 25; additional teacher guides and answer keys $0.10 each; specimen set $3.50

Publisher: Delaware County Reading Council

THE DELAWARE COUNTY SILENT READING TESTS: LEVELS 4-8
Delaware County Reading Council

Child, adolescent
Grades 4-8

Purpose: Measures intermediate-grade students' reading achievement and ability to express ideas in writing. Used to evaluate progress and for classroom placement and counseling.

Description: 20-item paper-pencil multiple-choice and short-answer test with separate forms for Grades 4-8. The student answers questions from a story booklet covering four areas: interpretation of ideas (8 items), organization of ideas (2 items), vocabulary (7 items), and structural analysis of words (3 items). Scores are ranked as excellent, good, average, poor, or very poor. Examiner required. Suitable for group use.

Untimed: 45-50 minutes

Scoring: Hand key

Cost: Pupil test $0.10; story booklet $0.15; teacher's guide included with each order of 25; additional teacher guides and answer keys $0.10 each; specimen set $3.50

Publisher: Delaware County Reading Council

DIAGNOSTIC AND ACHIEVEMENT READING TESTS: DART PHONICS TESTING PROGRAM

Child

Purpose: Measures student achievement of phonics skills. Diagnoses specific skills that have not been mastered. Used for instructional placement and planning.

Description: 10 multiple-item paper-pencil multiple-choice test booklets measuring 66 phonics skills. Tests are arranged in three levels: A, B, and C. Test A-1 measures readiness skills and initial and final consonants. Test A-2 measures alphabet letters and initial and final consonants. Test A-3 measures short and long vowels. Test A-4 measures consonant blends and digraphs. Test B-1 measures initial and final consonants, vowels, blends, and digraphs. Test B-2 measures Y as a vowel, soft C and G, mumur diphthongs, and plurals. Test B-3 measures prefixes, root words, irregular double vowels, and diphthongs. Test C-1 measures monosyllabic and polysyllabic words with prefixes, roots, suffixes, long and short vowels, digraphs, diphthongs, and final e. Test C-2 measures synonyms, antonyms, homonyms, and contracted forms. Test C-3 measures syllabication. The tests may be administered in any order. All test booklets are supplied in spirit master form. Test sections are keyed to specific pages in the MCP Phonics Workbooks but may be used with any reading program that employs the decoding approach to word recognition. Examiner required. Suitable for group use.

Untimed: Varies

Scoring: Examiner evaluated

Cost: Complete set of 10 test booklets $53.94

Publisher: Modern Curriculum Press, Inc.

DIAGNOSTIC READING SCALES, REVISED (DRS)
George D. Spache

Child

Purpose: Identifies a student's reading strengths and weaknesses. Used by educators to determine placement and to prescribe instruction.

Description: Multiple-item verbal test consisting of a series of graduated scales containing 3 word-recognition lists, 22 reading selections, and 12 phonics and word analysis tests. The word-recognition list yields a tentative performance level and is used to determine the level at which the student begins the reading selections. The reading selections assess three types of reading levels for the student: an instructional level, measuring oral reading and comprehension; an independent level, measuring silent reading and comprehension; and a potential level, measuring auditory comprehension. The word analysis and phonics tests measure the following skills: recognition of initial and final consonants, consonant digraphs and blends, short and long vowel sounds, vowels with r, vowel diphthongs and digraphs, common syllables and phonograms, initial consonants presented auditorily; auditory discrimination of minimal word pairs; initial consonant substitution; and blending of word parts. Examiner required. Not suitable for group use.

Timed: Not available

Scoring: Examiner evaluated

Cost: Specimen set, 1981 edition (test book, record book, manual, and test reviewer's guide) $14.25

Publisher: CTB/McGraw-Hill

DOMAIN PHONIC TEST KIT
J. McLeod and J. Atkinson

Child

Purpose: Diagnoses reading disabilities due to uncertainty about phonic structures and provides appropriate remedial approaches.

Description: Multiple-item oral-response tests assessing strengths and weaknesses of a student's knowledge of phonic structures. Analysis sheets indicate which of the Domain Phonic Workshop sheets should be used to remedy weaknesses once they are identified. Student progress is monitored in the record book. The manual includes complete instructions for use of the kit and gives examples of typical cases. Examiner required. Not suitable for group use.
BRITISH PUBLISHER

Untimed: Not available

Scoring: Not available

Cost: Complete kit (manual, 2 sets of phonic tests, 5 record books, 5 phonic workshops) £10.95; manual £1.50

Publisher: Oliver and Boyd; distributed in U.S.A. by Longman, Inc.

DOREN DIAGNOSTIC READING TEST OF WORD RECOGNITION SKILLS
Margaret Doren

Child   Grades 1-4

Purpose: Assesses why a child has difficulty reading. Used with groups to identify the level from which reading instruction should proceed.

Description: 12-category paper-pencil measure of word recognition skills in the following areas: letter recognition, beginning sounds, whole word recognition, words within words, speech consonants, ending sounds, blending, rhyming, vowels, discriminate guessing, spelling, and sight words. The examiner reads the directions printed in the manual and encourages the students to follow the same directions in their test booklets. Sample questions are provided at the beginning of each subtest. Scores are graphed on an Individual Skill Profile for each student, and overall class performance is recorded on the Class Composite Record. The test is designed to provide, in a group situation, the detailed diagnosis that otherwise could be obtained only through individual testing. Examiner required. Suitable for group use.

Untimed: 1-3 hours

Scoring: Hand key; examiner evaluated

Cost: Manual $4.00; 25 test booklets $15.50; key $9.50

Publisher: American Guidance Service

DURRELL ANALYSIS OF READING DIFFICULTY: THIRD EDITION
Donald D. Durrell and Jane H. Catterson

Child   Grades 1-6

Purpose: Assesses reading behavior. Used for diagnosis, measurement of pre-

reading skills, and planning remedial programs.

Description: Multiple-item series of tests and situations measuring 10 reading abilities: oral reading, silent reading, listening comprehension, listening vocabulary, word recognition/word analysis, spelling, auditory analysis of words and word elements, pronunciation of word elements, visual memory of words, and prereading phonics abilities. Supplementary paragraphs for oral and silent reading are provided for supplementary testing or retesting. Materials include a spiral-bound booklet containing items to be read and a tachistoscope with accompanying test card. Examiner required. Not suitable for group use.

Untimed: 30-45 minutes

Scoring: Examiner evaluated

Cost: Examiner's kit (5 record booklets, tachistoscope, reading booklet, manual) $35.00

Publisher: The Psychological Corporation

EARLY DETECTION OF READING DIFFICULTIES

Child   Years 1 and 2

Purpose: Assesses reading skills. Used for diagnosing individual reading deficiencies.

Description: Multiple-item test for screening the reading skills of children in Years 1 and 2. Materials include a set of two test booklets and guide and a textbook, *The Patterning of Complex Behavior.* Examiner required. Suitable for group use.
NEW ZEALAND PUBLISHER

Untimed: Not available

Scoring: Not available

Cost: $14.95

Publisher: Heinemann Educational Books Limited; distributed in U.S.A. by Heinemann Educational Books, Inc.

EFFECTIVE READING TESTS
Denis Vincent and
Michael de la Mare with Helen Arnold

Child   Ages 7-12

Purpose: Screens for and monitors reading ability and special needs when used as a progress test. Diagnoses skill strengths and weaknesses and assists in formulating plans for remedial teaching when used as a skills test.

Description: Multiple-item paper-pencil multiple-choice test measuring reading comprehension on four levels. At each level, the test may be administered as a progress test or a skills test. As a progress test, reading comprehension is measured within a "real reading" context. When used as a skills test, reading comprehension is measured, but the results allow analysis of the following skills: using relationships within a text (following the thread of sentences and using context cues); acting upon the text (interpreting or reorganizing the text); employing reading strategies appropriate to the text and purpose (skimming and scanning); making an effective, imaginative, or personal response to reading; critical awareness and evaluation (distinguishing between fact and fiction); and location and selection (using aplphabetical order and reference skills). The student is given a reader and either the progress test or the skills test and answers the test questions using the reader. The test ends when the student has completed all the questions or the questions become too difficult. The skills tests on all four levels begin with a timed skimming and scanning series of questions. Examiner required. Suitable for group use.
BRITISH PUBLISHER

Untimed: Progress tests 45 minutes; skills test 1 hour

Scoring: Progress tests, hand key; skills tests, examiner evaluated

Cost: Readers (six per level) £7.50; progress tests (25 per level) £4.25; skills tests (12 per level) £4.25; teacher's guide £5.95

Publisher: Macmillan Education

EMPORIA ELEMENTARY READING TEST
Marjorie Barnett and
Merritt W. Sanders

Child   Grades 2-3

Purpose: Assesses the general reading achievement of elementary-school students. Used for determining students' actual reading level.

Description: 65-item paper-pencil test of word recognition and sentence and paragraph comprehension. Examiner required. Suitable for group use.
Timed: 25 minutes
Scoring: Hand key
Cost: Test $0.15; manual $0.20; key $0.20
Publisher: Bureau of Educational Measurements

EMPORIA INTERMEDIATE READING TEST
Donald E. Carline, Ed L. Eaton,
and Merritt W. Sanders

Child   Grades 4-6

Purpose: Assesses the general reading achievement of elementary-school students. Used for determining students' actual reading level.

Description: 65-item paper-pencil test of general reading comprehension. Examiner required. Suitable for group use.
Timed: 25 minutes
Scoring: Hand key
Cost: Test $0.15; manual $0.20; key $0.20
Publisher: Bureau of Educational Measurements

EMPORIA JUNIOR HIGH SCHOOL READING TEST
Donald E. Carline,
Stanford S. Studer, Ed L. Eaton,
and Merritt W. Sanders

Adolescent   Grades 7-8

Purpose: Assesses the general reading achievement of junior high-school students. Used for determining students' actual reading level.

Description: 65-item paper-pencil test of general comprehension. Examiner required. Suitable for group use.
Timed: 25 minutes
Scoring: Hand key
Cost: Test $0.15; manual $0.20; key $0.20
Publisher: Bureau of Educational Measurements

EMPORIA PRIMARY READING TEST
*Marjorie Barnett and
Merritt W. Sanders*

Child   Grade 1

Purpose: Assesses the general reading achievement of first-grade students. Used to determine students' actual reading level.

Description: 65-item paper-pencil test of reading achievement and readiness of beginners. Examiner required. Suitable for group use.
Timed: 15 minutes
Scoring: Hand key
Cost: Test $0.15; manual $0.20; key $0.20
Publisher: Bureau of Educational Measurements

THE FLORIDA KINDERGARTEN SCREENING BATTERY
Paul Satz and Jack M. Fletcher

Child   Kindergarten

Purpose: Identifies kindergartners at high risk for later reading difficulties. Permits identification of learning problems prior to the beginning of reading instruction.

Description: Multiple-item battery of five tests screening children for potential reading problems. The battery includes the Peabody Picture Vocabulary Test-Revised, Beery Developmental Test of Visual-Motor Integration, Recognition-Discrimination Test, Finger Localization Test, and Alphabet Recitation. The bat-

tery may be administered by supervised paraprofessionals. Examiner required. Not suitable for group use.
Untimed: 20 minutes
Scoring: Examiner evaluated
Cost: Kit (all five tests, 50 record forms, manual) $115.00
Publisher: Psychological Assessment Resources, Inc.

GAP READING TEST

Child   Ages 7-12

Purpose: Assesses the reading comprehension of students. Used by teachers for planning instruction and checking progress.

Description: 45-item paper-pencil test in two alternate forms (R and B) consisting of several increasingly difficult paragraphs of information. The test uses a modified cloze technique in which students provide the missing words. Teachers can use the test for placement, information on a child's reading and spelling techniques, and retesting. Examiner required. Suitable for group use.
AUSTRALIAN PUBLISHER
Timed: 15 minutes
Scoring: Examiner evaluated
Cost: Complete kit (48 copies of Test R, 48 copies of Test B, manual) $17.50
Publisher: Heinemann Publishers Australia Party Limited

GATES-MCKILLOP-HOROWITZ READING DIAGNOSTIC TESTS
*Arthur I. Gates, Anne S. McKillop,
and Elizabeth C. Horowitz*

Child   Grades 1-6

Purpose: Evaluates children's oral reading, spelling, and writing skills, and diagnoses reading difficulties of older students. Used for class grouping and curriculum planning.

Description: 11-part verbal paper-pencil test measuring oral reading, isolated word recognition, knowledge of word parts, recognizing and blending common word parts, reading words, giving letter sounds, naming letters, identifying vowel sounds, auditory blending and discrimination, and writing through an informal sample. Not all parts need be given to every student. Materials include a test materials booklet containing a tachistoscope (for word flash tests), a pupil record book, and a manual. Examiner required. Not suitable for group use.

Untimed: 1 hour

Scoring: Examiner evaluated

Cost: Test materials (contains tachistoscope) $3.75; 30 pupil record booklets $13.50; manual of directions $1.50; specimen set (test materials, pupil record booklet, manual of directions) $5.25

Publisher: Teachers College Press

GILLINGHAM-CHILDS PHONICS PROFICIENCY SCALES: SERIES I, BASIC READING AND SPELLING; SERIES II, ADVANCED READING
*Sally B. Childs and
Ralph de S. Childs*

Child, adolescent Grades 1-8

Purpose: Evaluates student progress in the mastery of phonic and beginning reading skills to provide teachers with an index of remedial progress.

Description: Multiple-item primarily verbal examination in two series: Basic Reading and Spelling and Advanced Reading. Series I contains 12 scales dealing with basic reading and spelling skills: letter-sound relationships; three-letter words; consonant digraphs and blends; one-syllable words ending with f, l, or s; vowel-consonant-words; syllabication rules; sight words; and suffix rules. The teacher uses the reading booklet for dictation of the spelling words because the reading and spelling words are the same. Series II contains 16 scales measuring advanced reading skills: alternating phonograms; hard and soft sounds of c and g; long vowel sounds; nonsense words; vowel dipthongs and digraphs; words irregular for reading; and more advanced syllabication rules. There is no spelling test in Series II. The teacher should be familiar with the pronunciation of nonsense words. The original version of the scales was developed by Anna Gillingham. The scales have been strengthened in their revised version and should be useful to anyone teaching phonics. Examiner required. Not suitable for group use.

Untimed: 30 minutes-1 hour

Scoring: Examiner evaluated

Cost: Series I $6.50; reading record booklet $3.25; spelling record booklet $4.00; directions for use $0.50; Series II $6.50; record booklet $2.50; directions for use $0.50

Publisher: Educators Publishing Service, Inc.

GILMORE ORAL READING TEST
*John V. Gilmore and
Eunice C. Gilmore*

Child   Grades 1-8

Purpose: Assesses the oral reading abilities of students. Used for program planning and academic placement.

Description: Oral-reading test measuring three aspects of oral reading ability: accuracy, comprehension, and rate. The spiral-bound booklet of reading paragraphs and the manual of directions are needed to administer the test. A separate record blank is needed for each child tested. A five-level classification of accuracy, rate, and comprehension is provided, as well as stanines and grade-equivalents for accuracy and comprehension scores. The test is available in two alternate and equivalent forms, C and D. Examiner required. Not suitable for group use.

Untimed: 15-20 minutes

Scoring: Examiner evaluated

Cost: Examination kit (manual, record blank) $6.00; booklet of reading paragraphs $14.00; 35 record blanks (Form C or D) $24.00; manual $6.00

Publisher: The Psychological Corporation

GROUP DIAGNOSTIC READING APTITUDE AND ACHIEVEMENT TESTS—INTERMEDIATE FORM

Marion Monroe and Eva Edity Sherman

Child   Grades 3-9

Purpose: Measures reading aptitude and achievement. Diagnoses specific skill deficits that may impair reading performance.

Description: 391-item paper-pencil battery consisting of eight achievement tests in the following areas: (paragraph meaning, speed of reading, vowels, consonants, reversals, additions and omissions, arithmetic, and spelling) and seven aptitude tests (visual letter memory, visual form memory, auditory letter memory, auditory orientation and discrimination, copying text, cross-out letters, and vocabulary). The Paragraph Reading Test (28 items; 7 minutes) requires students to read a question, read a paragraph containing the answer to the question, and select the appropriate one-word or short-phrase answer from five given choices. The Speed of Reading Test (45 items; 1½ minutes) requires students to read through a one-page text and indicate comprehension by performing simple game-like tasks, such as "put a dot in this circle" or "cross out the three." The vowels, consonants, reversals, and additions and omissions tests (24 items each; 2 minutes each) measure word discrimination skills by presenting three sentences for each test item, one of which is correct with the other two containing errors appropriate to the test (vowel substitution, consonant substitution, reversals, or additions or omissions). Students underline the correct sentence. The Arithmetic Computation Test (30 items; 5 minutes) measures the ability to add, subtract, multiply, and divide with whole numbers, fractions, and decimals. The Spelling Test (40 minutes; untimed) consists of sentences with blanks provided for missing words. The teacher reads the sentence with the missing word, and the students fill in the blank with the word pronounced by the teacher. In the Visual Letter Memory Test (18 items), the teacher shows the students a card on which a nonsense word is printed. Each card is flashed for five seconds, and students are asked to write as much of the nonsense word from each card as they can remember. In the Visual Form Memory Test (4 items), the teacher flashes cards with simple line-drawing designs for 10 seconds each and then asks the students to draw as much of each card as they can remember. The Auditory Letter Memory Test (16 items) is similar to the visual test, except the teacher spells aloud the letters of some nonsense words for the students to copy down. The Auditory Discrimination and Orientation Test (25 items) requires students to mark a grid of X's in response to aural stimuli dictated by the teacher. The Copying Text Test (1 item; 1½ minutes) measures fine-motor skills by requiring the students to copy a short story as quickly and plainly as they can. In the Crossing-Out Letters Test (60 items; 1 minute), a text of nonsense words is provided in which every other word contains one letter "a." Students are directed to cross out all the a's they can find. The Vocabulary Test (28 items; untimed) provides four pairs of words for each test item. Only one of the pairs of words makes sense; the other three pairs are abstract combinations or obvious malapropisms. The teacher reads each pair aloud, and students are directed to underline the pair that makes the best sense to them. The achievement tests are scored in terms of grade equivalents. The aptitude tests are scored in terms of percentiles by age. The front sheet of the 14-page test booklet provides forms for developing educational and diagnostic profiles and deriving a mental age for each student tested. Examiner required. Suitable for group use.

Timed: 9 timed tests 24 minutes

Untimed: 6 untimed tests varies

Scoring: Examiner evaluated

Cost: Test booklets each $0.25; 22 visual test cards $2.50; set of norms $0.75; directions to the examiner included free of charge

Publisher: C.H. Nevins Printing Company

GROUP PHONICS ANALYSIS
Edward B. Fry

Child   Grades 1-3

Purpose: Determines students' weaknesses and strengths in basic phonics skills. Used as an aid in teacher guidance.

Description: 32-item paper-pencil test measuring the ability to read numbers and letters, hear consonants, alphabetize, recognize vowels, recognize short and long vowel sounds in words, use vowel-sounding rules, and syllabification. Examiner required. Suitable for group use.

Untimed: Varies

Scoring: Self-scored

Cost: 30 tests, manual $10.00

Publisher: Jamestown Publishers

GROUP READING ASSESSMENT
F.A. Spooncer

Child   Ages 7.8-9

Purpose: Measures group achievement of reading ability in the first two years of junior school (ages 7-9). Suitable for less able older juniors and the most backward entrants to secondary schools. Assesses performance of teaching programs at the classroom, school, or district level.

Description: Multiple-item paper-pencil test measuring achievement of reading skills that are taught in the first two years of junior school. Norms, derived from testing of over 3,000 children, are provided to cover reading ages 6.3 -11.7. A table is provided for conversion of raw scores to standardized scores for children ages 7-9. Examiner required. Suitable for group use.
BRITISH PUBLISHER

Untimed: 30 minutes

Scoring: Examiner evaluated

Cost: Specimen set £2.25; 20 tests £2.70; manual £2.10

Publisher: Hodder & Stoughton

GROUP READING TEST: SECOND EDITION
Dennis Young

Child   Ages 7-12.10

Purpose: Assesses children's reading achievement. Identifies children reading significantly above or below their age level.

Description: Multiple-item paper-pencil test of reading achievement available in two parallel forms, A and B, which remain unchanged from the original version. The two forms, along with template scoring methods, facilitate use of the test by one teacher with a full class. The second edition of the manual provides new norms for infants (ages 6.5-7.10), first-year juniors (7.10-8.10), and older, less able pupils up to age 12.10, increasing the accuracy of comparison between children of different ages. Examiner required. Suitable for group use.
BRITISH PUBLISHER

Untimed: Not available

Scoring: Hand key

Cost: Specimen set £1.90; 20 tests (specify form) £1.50; template (specify form) £1.25 plus VAT; manual £1.50

Publisher: Hodder & Stoughton

HARRISON-STROUD READING READINESS PROFILE
M. Lucille Harrison and James B. Stroud

Child   Grades K-1

Purpose: Measures specific abilities and skills that children use in learning to read. Identifies areas in which children may need help before or during initial reading instruction.

Description: Five multiple-item paper-pencil group tests assessing the following prereading skills: symbols, visual discriminations, context, auditory discriminations, and context and auditory clues. An optional sixth test, which is individually administered, identifies in approximately three minutes how well a student knows the names of the capital and lowercase letters. Raw scores are plotted on a chart that determines the percentile rank of each score and identifies the strengths and weaknesses of each student. Examiner required. Suitable for group (12-15 students) use.

Untimed: 80 minutes

Scoring: Examiner evaluated

Cost: Test kit (35 consumable test booklets, manual, class record sheet, letter card, scoring mask) $29.97

Publisher: The Riverside Publishing Company

INDIVIDUAL PHONICS CRITERION TEST
Edward B. Fry

Child   Grades 1-6

Purpose: Determines a student's knowledge of letter sounds. Used to detect reading or speaking deficiencies.

Description: 99-item paper-pencil test containing 99 nonsense words, each of which tests a phoneme-grapheme correspondence. The student reads the nonsense words aloud to the examiner from one copy of the test, and the examiner uses a separate copy for scoring. Each test item matches a chart in *99 Phonics Charts* by Jamestown. Examiner required. Not suitable for group use.

Untimed: Not available

Scoring: Examiner evaluated

Cost: 40 test sheets $10.00

Publisher: Jamestown Publishers

INDIVIDUALIZED CRITERION REFERENCED TESTING (ICRT)
Refer to page 400.

INDIVIDUALIZED CRITERION REFERENCED TESTING— READING (ICRT—READING)
Dale E. Strotman and Margaret T. Steen

Child, adolescent Grades K-8

Purpose: Assesses students' reading abilities. Provides information on skills mastered, skills requiring review, and

skills to learn. Also used in adult basic education.

Description: Multiple-item paper-pencil power test measuring phonetic analysis, structural analysis, word function, and comprehension. The test is based on a developmental continuum of 304 learning objectives for Grades K-8. Objectives are matched with current curricula and the content of newer textbooks. The results indicate resources for teaching and reinforcing skills, list names of students who need instruction in each skill, and aid in grouping students according to their specific learning needs. Materials provide for interim testing and recording of progress. The program evaluation report provides criterion-referenced and norm-referenced information for each class, student, building, and district. The report includes scale scores, grade equivalents, percentiles, and NCEs. The test is used by administrators and teachers in city-wide instructional management systems, migrant and special education programs, and ECIA-Chapter projects. Examiner required. Suitable for group use.

Untimed: Varies

Scoring: Computer scored

Cost: Computer scoring $1.75 per student; 10 booklets (specify level) $24.00

Publisher: Educational Development Corporation

INFORMAL READING COMPREHENSION PLACEMENT TEST
Eunice Insel and Ann Edson

Child   Grades 1-8

Purpose: Measures reading comprehension. Determines students' instructional placement level.

Description: 68-item microcomputer-administered test assessing word comprehension and passage comprehension. The 60-item word comprehension test uses a word analogy format to measure students' knowledge of word meanings and thinking skills. The passage comprehension test consists of a series of eight graded selections and questions ranging in difficulty from the primary level through eighth grade. The level of difficulty for each of these selections was determined by using the Spache, Frye, and Dall Chall readability formulas. Students are placed in an instructional reading range of first through eighth grade in word comprehension and passage comprehension. The test is totally administered, scored, and managed by the microcomputer. A cassette or diskette is available for the Apple II+ and IIe and TRS Models III and IV microcomputers. All diskette programs include backups. Examiner required. Not suitable for group use.

Untimed: Varies

Scoring: Microcomputer scored

Cost: Cassette (specify model) $44.95; 1 diskette (specify model) $49.95

Publisher: Educational Activities, Inc.

THE INSTANT WORDS CRITERION TEST
Edward B. Fry

Child   Grades K-3

Purpose: Determines a student's ability to read the 300 English words which make up 65 percent of all written material. Used as a teaching tool.

Description: 300-word oral test diagnosing knowledge of suffixes and spelling. The student reads each word aloud to the examiner (teacher or parent). The test ends after the student misses five or ten words. These words then are taught as new words. Examiner required. Not suitable for group use.

Untimed: 30 minutes

Scoring: Examiner evaluated

Cost: 40 tests $10.00

Publisher: Jamestown Publishers

JANSKY DIAGNOSTIC BATTERY
Jeannette J. Jansky

Child   Kindergarten

Purpose: Measures the reading readiness of kindergartners. Used for educational planning.

Description: Multiple-item battery of 15 verbal paper-pencil tests measuring reading readiness abilities. The battery is designed for kindergartners identified by the Jansky Screening Index as being at risk for not learning to read. The factors assessed are expressive and receptive language, verbal pattern matching, verbal memory, and graphomotor status. Instructions for administering and scoring are presented in Jansky and Hirsch's *Preventing Reading Failure*, published by Harper and Row. Examiner required. Not suitable for group use.

Untimed: 30 minutes

Scoring: Hand key: examiner evaluated

Cost: Complete kit (35 profile forms, 2 cartoon sequences, 35 nonsense word-matching forms, speech sound discrimination test, pattern tapper, word recognition and spelling cards) $30.00

Publisher: Jeannette J. Jansky

JANSKY SCREENING INDEX
Jeannette J. Jansky

Child   Kindergarten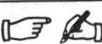

Purpose: Identifies kindergartners who may show signs of failing to read by the time they finish second grade. Used to screen those in need of special educational help.

Description: 5 multiple-item paper-pencil and oral-language tests of basic readiness skills measuring ability in design copying, picture naming, lettering, naming, word matching, and sentence repetition. The Screening Index evolved after research on a preliminary longer battery, the Predictive Index by de Hirsch, Jansky, and Langford. Instructions for administering and scoring are included in *Preventing Reading Failure* by Jansky and de Hirsch, Harper and Row, 1972. Examiner required. Suitable for group use.

Untimed: 20-30 minutes

Scoring: Hand key; examiner evaluated

Cost: Complete kit $20.00

Publisher: Jeannette J. Jansky

LANGUAGE DEVELOPMENT READING EVALUATION PROGRAM
Refer to page 631.

LINGUISTIC AWARENESS IN READING READINESS
John Downing, Douglas Ayers, and Brian Schaefer

Child   **Ages 4-8**   

Purpose: Measures understanding of vocabulary and concepts related to reading and writing. Used for determining reading readiness of children. Also used with older children with reading difficulties.

Description: 75-item paper-pencil test in three parts assessing children's understanding of linguistic concepts. The test, available in two parallel forms, measures how well children recognize activities involved in reading and writing (22 items), their understanding of the uses of reading and writing (23 items), and their understanding of words related to literacy such as "word," "letter," and "sentence" (30 items). Examiner required. Suitable for group use.
BRITISH PUBLISHER

Untimed: 15-20 minutes per part

Scoring: Hand key

Cost: Specimen set (manual, one each of 3 Form A booklets, one each of 3 Form B booklets, one each of 3 record forms) £14.45

Publisher: NFER-NELSON Publishing Company Ltd.

LONDON READING TEST (LRT)

Child   **Ages 10.07-12.04**

Purpose: Assesses reading level and pattern of abilities. Used to identify children needing remedial teaching.

Description: Multiple-item paper-pencil measure of reading abilities. The two alternate forms, A and B, contain three reading passages. Comprehension of the first two passages is tested using the cloze technique, and the third passage asks questions that tap a wide range of comprehension skills. Scores at both an independent and instructional level are obtained. Examiner required. Suitable for group use.
BRITISH PUBLISHER

Untimed: 1 hour

Scoring: Examiner evaluated

Cost: Specimen set £5.35; 25 booklets (specify A or B) £7.55; 25 practice sheets A/B £3.15; manual £5.00 (payment in sterling for all overseas orders)

Publisher: NFER-NELSON Publishing Company Ltd.

THE MACMILLAN DIAGNOSTIC READING PACK
Ted Ames

Child, adolescent   
Reading Ages 5-8

Purpose: Diagnoses children's reading problems. Suggests appropriate remedial programs. Used for in-service teacher training programs.

Description: 16 multiple-item paper-pencil and oral-response test cards presenting tests on specific reading skills and subskills, such as letter-matching and consonant blending. Checklists, for recording student performance on the tests and providing a detailed picture of individual ability, are available for four stages in the development of reading skills: reading ages 5-6, 6-7, 7-8, and 8-9. Together, the test cards and checklists provide a means of observing and testing reading skills from beginning reading to fluency. A teacher's manual provides clear instructions for testing and diagnosis and prescribes source references for further remedial procedures. Examiner required. Suitable for group use.

Untimed: Varies

Scoring: Examiner evaluated

Cost: Test kit (manual, 16 test cards, 10 copies each of 4 checklists) £16.50

Publisher: Macmillan Education

MACMILLAN GRADED WORD READING TEST
The Macmillan Test Unit

Child   **Ages 6-14**   

Purpose: Measures the oral reading abilities of students. Also used for remedial work with older children.

Description: Two parallel tests of 50 words each on one card used by teachers for evaluating oral reading abilities. The tests are graded in difficulty, grouped in five levels, and accompanied by record sheets for marking and analyzing errors. Standardized scores and alternative reading ages are provided. Examiner required. Not suitable for group use. BRITISH PUBLISHER

Untimed: 5 minutes

Scoring: Examiner evaluated

Cost: Complete kit (word card, teacher's manual, 25 record sheets) £12.95

Publisher: Macmillan Education

MACMILLAN GROUP READING TEST
The Macmillan Test Unit

Child   Ages 7-11

Purpose: Assesses word recognition and reading comprehension of children.

Description: 48-item paper-pencil graded reading test in two similiar forms assessing simple word recognition and full reading comprehension. Each form contains five picture-word recognition items and 43 sentence completion items. Standardized scores and alternative reading ages are provided. Examiner required. Suitable for group use. BRITISH PUBLISHER

Untimed: 30 minutes

Scoring: Hand key

Cost: Specimen set (copy Form A, copy Form B, teacher's manual) £3.35

Publisher: Macmillan Education

MICROCOMPUTER MANAGED INFORMATION FOR CRITERION REFERENCED OBJECTIVES— READING (MMICRO—READING)
Ron Hambleton

Child, adolescent   Grades 1-8

Purpose: Assesses students' reading abilities. Provides information on skills mastered, skills requiring review, and skills to learn. Also used in adult basic education.

Description: Multiple-item paper-pencil test measuring phonetic analysis, structural analysis, word function, and comprehension. The test is based on the same 304 developmental learning objectives grouped into four strands as those for the ICRT-Reading: phonetic analysis, structural analysis, word function, and comprehension. With this computerized system, diagnostic and objective (mastery) tests are automatically scored in the school with a card or sheet reader recording information onto the software. Reports offer the same comprehensive diagnostic, prescriptive, and grouping information as the ICRT. However, the system does not include the norm-referenced data available from the mainframe computer, nor does it generate three selected correlations per teacher. Correlations may be purchased. Available for Acorn, Apple, Commodore, IBM, and TRS-80 microcomputers. Examiner required. Suitable for group use.

Untimed: Varies

Scoring: Computer scored

Cost: Software $1,595.00; 10 booklets (specify level) $18.00; demonstration program $65.00

Publisher: Educational Development Corporation

MONROE DIAGNOSTIC READING TEST
Marion Monroe

Child, adolescent   Grades 1-10

Purpose: Assesses reading deficiencies according to chronological and mental age. Used to diagnose special reading difficulties.

Description: 326-item card test comprised of nine analytic subtests. The analytic tests include the Alphabet Repeating and Reading Test; Iota Word Test; B, D, P, Q, U, N Test; Recognition of Orientation; Mirror Reading; Mirror Writing; Number Reversal; Word Discrimination; and Sounding and Handedness. The examiner can immediately tell if a child makes the usual mistakes for his grade-level, or if he makes an excessive amount of a particular type of error. Examiner required. Not suitable for group use.

Timed: 30 minutes

Scoring: Hand key

Cost: Complete set (test cards, 50 record blanks, manual) $24.00

Publisher: C.H. Nevins Printing Company

MONROE READING APTITUDE TESTS
Marion Monroe

Child Grades K-1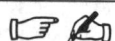

Purpose: Measures essential skills which determine reading ability. Used by schools to determine reading readiness.

Description: Five subtests assessing factors essential to success in reading: visual, auditory, motor control, oral speech and articulation, and language. Scores are presented in percentile terms for each half year. Examiner required. Suitable for group use.

Untimed: 10-15 minutes per subtest

Scoring: Examiner evaluated

Cost: 35 test booklets (teacher's manual, percentile chart, class analysis record, suggestions for special classes) $19.20; test card material $8.05; teacher's manual $1.95; suggestions for special classes $1.50

Publisher: C.H. Nevins Printing Company

NEALE ANALYSIS OF READING ABILITY
M.D. Neale

Child Ages 6-12

Purpose: Assesses reading standard of children.

Description: Test booklet with three parallel forms, each containing reading passages standardized for six different grades. The test is printed in three different size types. Each left-hand page has a drawing that sets the scene for the passage to be read. British equivalent reading ages are provided for each raw score. Materials

include a booklet, a manual, and record sheets for each form. Examiner required. Suitable for group use.

BRITISH PUBLISHER

Untimed: 10-15 minutes

Scoring: Examiner evaluated

Cost: Test booklet £4.95; manual £2.95; record sheets 18 p. each

Publisher: Macmillian Education Ltd.

THE NELSON READING SKILLS TESTS: FORMS 3 AND 4
Gerald S. Hanna, Leo M. Schell, and Robert L. Schreiner

Child Grades 3-9

Purpose: Assesses student achievement and progress in word attack skills, vocabulary, reading comprehension, and reading rate. Diagnoses a student's reading strengths and weaknesses. Used with students in Grades 3-9 to meet Chapter 1 (Title 1) requirements.

Description: Multiple-item paper-pencil test consisting of two subtests: Word Meaning and Reading Comprehension. The Word Meaning test measures three kinds of vocabulary items: words in isolation, words in phrases, and words in sentences. The Reading Comprehension test measures literal, translational, and higher order tasks. The test is available on three levels: Level A (Grades 3-4), Level B (Grades 5-6), and Level C (Grades 7-9). All three levels are available in a single test booklet. Two optional tests are available: the Word Parts test, available at Level A, diagnoses a student's decoding skills, including sound/symbol correspondence, root words, and syllabication; the Reading Rate test, available at Levels B and C, includes a short subtest measuring comprehension of the reading rate passage. Test booklets are available in two parallel forms, 3 and 4. Scores provided for the Word Parts, Word Meanings, and Reading Comprehension tests include raw scores, grade equivalent scores, national percentile ranks, national stanines, and normal curve equivalent scores. Verbal indicators of student performance on the Word Parts subtest are also provided. Words-per-minute and grade equivalent scores are provided for the Reading Rate test. Standardization and other studies are described in the technical manual. Administration and scoring procedures are described in the teacher's manual. Self-marking answer sheets are available for hand scoring; MRC answer sheets are available for machine scoring. Examiner required. Suitable for group use.

Timed: Word Parts 24 minutes; Word Meaning 8 minutes; Reading Comprehension 24 minutes; Reading Rate 3 minutes

Scoring: Hand key; may be machine scored

Cost: 35 test booklets (specify form) $25.53; 35 MRC answer sheets, teacher's manual, 35 student score report folders, materials for machine scoring $17.19; 35 self-marking answer sheets, teacher's manual, 35 student score report folders, 2 class record sheets $23.67; 2 scoring masks $5.34; technical manual $3.78

Publisher: The Riverside Publishing Company

NEW MACMILLAN READING ANALYSIS
Denis Vincent, Michael de la Mare, and Helen Arnold

Child   Ages 7-10

Purpose: Measures oral reading abilities of children ages 7-10 and older remedial students.

Description: Series of six graded oral reading passages in three parallel forms, combined with four-page analysis sheets, for determining oral reading comprehension, analyzing reading strategies, and monitoring progress. The progressively difficult passages allow the instructor to score reading accuracy and compare it with comprehension scores, as well as to classify errors, including reversals, mispronunciations, insertions, omissions, refusals, substitutions, and self-correction. The test also provides a miscues analysis of errors according to their semantic, graphophonic, or syntactic basis and an evaluation of the severity. Norms are expressed as age equivalent ranges. Examiner required. Not suitable for group use.
BRITISH PUBLISHER

Untimed: 15 minutes

Scoring: Examiner evaluated

Cost: Starter pack (Reader, record sheets A, B, and C, manual) £18.00

Publisher: Macmillan Education

THE NEW SUCHER-ALLRED READING PLACEMENT INVENTORY
Floyd Sucher and Ruel A. Allred

Child, adolescent
Grades 1-6

Purpose: Assesses students' independent, instructional, and frustrational reading levels. Used for reading placement, identification of reading difficulties, and general screening for remedial reading.

Description: Multiple-item test measuring in two parts word recognition, oral reading, oral reading comprehension, and silent reading comprehension. In the Word-Recognition Test, which is administered first, the child orally reads a list of words. The teacher assesses word recognition and uses the results to select a starting point for administering the Oral Reading Test. Two forms, A and B, are available. Examiner required. Not suitable for group use.

Untimed: 20 minutes

Scoring: Examiner evaluated

Cost: One form and teacher's manual for class of 35 $17.49; two forms $27.48

Publisher: The Economy Company

THE O'BRIEN VOCABULARY PLACEMENT TEST
Janet O'Brien

Child   Grades 1-6

Purpose: Measures the reading ability of elementary-school students. Used to identify children who have reading deficiencies.

Description: 10-item paper-pencil test in six sections, one for each grade through the sixth. Each test contains a list of words for which the student selects the antonym from four possible choices. The test enables a teacher to find the independent reading level of an entire class in 15

minutes. The test also can be used individually for new students and those in special education classes. Examiner required. Suitable for group use.

Untimed: 15 minutes

Scoring: Hand key

Cost: Diskette $29.95; cassette $24.95

Publisher: Educational Activities, Inc.

ORAL READING CRITERION TEST
Edward B. Fry

Child, adolescent
Grades 1-7

Purpose: Determines students' independent, instructional, and frustration reading ability levels. Used for teacher guidance.

Description: Seven-paragraph paper-pencil test in which the student reads the paragraphs aloud and the examiner records scores. The number of errors indicates the reading level category: independent, instructional, or frustration. A Fry Readability Graph is provided to help the teacher match materials to the student's ability. A minimum first-grade reading level is required. Examiner required. Not suitable for group use.

Untimed: 15-30 minutes

Scoring: Examiner evaluated

Cost: 40 tests $10.00

Publisher: Jamestown Publishers

PERFORMANCE ASSESSMENT IN READING (PAIR)
CTB/McGraw-Hill

Adolescent   Grades 7-9

Purpose: Identifies a student's basic reading skill deficits and the instruction required to correct them. Used by junior high-school reading teachers.

Description: 72-item two-part paper-pencil test consisting of displays such as warning signs, street maps, card catalogs, encyclopedia entries, telephone directories, and bus schedules. Questions are designed to determine vocabulary, com-

prehension, and location/study skills. Examiner required. Suitable for group use.

Untimed: Not available

Scoring: Hand key; may be computer scored

Cost: Specimen set (test book, manual, one hand-scorable and one computer-scorable answer sheet, class summary sheet, test reviewer's guide) $8.95

Publisher: CTB/McGraw-Hill

PREREADING EXPECTANCY SCREENING SCALE (PRESS)
Lawrence C. Hartlage and David G. Lucas

Child   Ages 6-9
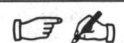

Purpose: Assesses skills important in reading. Used for predicting reading problems for beginning readers.

Description: Multiple-item paper-pencil test measuring a child's recognition of the numbers 1-9 and the following shapes: cross, circle, star, square, and diamond. The scale consists of four subtests: Sequencing, Spatial, Memory, and Letter Identification. Items are read by the teacher. Examiner required. Suitable for group use.

Untimed: 35 minutes

Scoring: Hand key; examiner evaluated

Cost: Specimen set $8.00; 25 tests $13.50; 25 profile sheets (specify boys or girls) $6.00; manual $6.00

Publisher: Psychologists and Educators, Inc.

PRIMARY READING PROFILES
James B. Stroud, A. N. Hieronymus, and Paul McKee

Child   Grades 1-3

Purpose: Measures a child's achievement of primary reading skills.

Description: Five multiple-item paper-pencil tests assessing student progress in the following reading skills: aptitude for reading, auditory association, word recognition, word attack, and reading comprehension. The Word Recognition, Word Attack, and Reading Comprehension tests yield a composite score, which indicates the student's grasp of the reading process. A comparison of the composite score with the student's score on the Aptitude for Reading Test provides a comparison between actual and expected reading performance. The scores on the Auditory Association, Word Attack, and Word Recognition tests often will indicate a reason for the divergence between actual and expected reading ability. The test is available in two levels: Level 1 for late Grade 1 or early Grade 2 and Level 2 for late Grade 2 or early Grade 3. Norms are provided in the form of grade-equivalents and percentile ranks. Examiner required. Suitable for group use.

Untimed: 85 minutes

Scoring: Hand key

Cost: 35 hand-scorable test booklets, manual, scoring masks, class record sheet, 35 profile charts (specify Level 1 or 2) $24.33

Publisher: The Riverside Publishing Company

THE PRIMARY READING TEST
Norman Franck

Child   Ages 6-12

Purpose: Assesses reading comprehension. Used for individual pupil evaluations.

Description: Multiple-item paper-pencil test of reading comprehension. Items involve word recognition and sentence completion. The test is divided into two levels: Level 1 for children ages 6-10 and Level 2 for children ages 7-12. Two alternate forms, 1A and 2A, are available. Examiner required. Suitable for group use.

BRITISH PUBLISHER

Untimed: 20-30 minutes

Scoring: Hand key

Cost: 25 pupils' booklets (specify level) £5.50; teacher's book (scoring keys) £4.35 (payment in sterling for all overseas orders)

Publisher: NFER-NELSON Publishing Company Ltd.

READING CLASSIFICATION TEST
H. J. Williamson and I.L. Bell

Child   Grades 2-6

Purpose: Measures reading skills of Australian children.

Description: Multiple-item test measures and provides ways of evaluating reading performance in Australian children. The packet includes diagnostic information, a pronunciation guide, test cards, a manual, and "links with children's literature." Examiner required. Not suitable for group use.

AUSTRALIAN PUBLISHER

Untimed: Not available

Scoring: Not available

Cost: Complete kit $2.40; 10 individualized record forms $0.40; (Australian currency)

Publisher: Educational Resources

Information and availability unconfirmed; no publisher response.

READING READINESS TEST (FORM RR)
SOI Institute Staff

Child

Purpose: Assesses the reading readiness of young children.

Description: Multiple-item oral-response test assessing abilities relating to reading readiness. The test includes instructions for administration. Examiner required. Suitable for group use (some sections must be individually administered).

Untimed: 1 hour

Scoring: Examiner evaluated

Cost: 5 test forms $10.75

Publisher: Western Psychological Services

READING SKILLS CHECKLISTS

Child, adolescent

Purpose: Measures individual students' growth in reading skills from Kindergarten through junior high school. Used for program planning and parent conferences and as a part of a transferring student's permanent file.

Description: Multiple-item paper-pencil checklist assessing student knowledge and mastery of important reading skills. Items on the list consist of descriptions of reading skills, which the teacher must rate according to the following scale: the skill has not been taught, the skill has been taught but not mastered, the skill has been taught and mastered. Checklists are presented in the form of file-sized folders and are available in three levels: primary, intermediate, and junior high. The checklists are suitable for use with most basal reading programs (phonics or sight-word based). Examiner required. Not suitable for group use.

Untimed: Varies

Scoring: Examiner evaluated

Cost: 30 primary checklists $10.44; 30 intermediate checklists $11.04; 30 junior high checklists $12.27

Publisher: Modern Curriculum Press, Inc.

THE READING SKILLS DIAGNOSTIC TEST III, 3RD REVISION (RSDT III)
Richard H. Bloomer

Child, adolescent
Grades 2-8

Purpose: Measures content, learning processes, and learning capacities necessary for learning how to read. Provides a structure for beginning reading instruction, as well as a model for diagnosis and treatment of early learning difficulties related to reading and writing.

Description: 48 paper-pencil subtests measuring mastery of beginning encoding-decoding and word recognition skills, basic processing skills, and learning processes. The subtests are arranged in four groups of 12 to measure four levels of response strength: reproduction, recognition, visual-oral, and auditory-motor. Each of the four levels measures content (letter knowledge, simple phonic knowledge, sight words, long vowels, consonant digraphs, and vowel dipthongs); basic processing skills (imitation, copying, multiple discrimination, consonant-vowel

blending, and consonant-vowel-consonant blending); and learning capacities (short-term memory for words, short-term memory for letters and stimulus magnitude). Context clues at all four levels of response strength help teachers plan specific instructional and remedial approaches. Subtests and levels are arranged sequentially, and the test is designed to be administered one subtest at a time in a test-teach-test format. Levels 1 and 3 are individually administered; Levels 2 and 4 are group administered. Examiner required.

Untimed: Not available

Scoring: Hand key; examiner evaluated

Cost: Level 1 manual and answer sheets $16.40; Level 2 manual and answer sheets $19.70; Level 3 manual and test stimuli, record forms $25.50; Level 4 manual and answer sheets $21.80

Publisher: Brador Publications, Inc.
Information and availability unconfirmed; no publisher response.

READING TESTS SR-A AND SR-B

Child   Ages 7½-12

Purpose: Measures reading attainment of primary school children. Used for screening and surveying groups of pupils.

Description: Multiple-item paper-pencil tests measuring reading achievement. The items consist of sentence completion tasks. Examiner required. Suitable for group use.
BRITISH PUBLISHER

Timed: 20 minutes per test

Scoring: Examiner evaluated

Cost: 10 SR-A or 10 SR-B £3.20 per set; combined manual £2.50 (payment in sterling for all overseas orders)

Publisher: NFER-NELSON Publishing Company Ltd.

READING YARDSTICKS

Child, adolescent
Grades K-8

Purpose: Assesses students' strengths and weaknesses in reading readiness, reading, and language skills. Used for grouping students for instruction and for helping teachers develop teaching strategies and materials.

Description: Paper-pencil multiple-choice test of reading ability divided into nine levels (6-14) corresponding to Grades K-8. At Level 6 (70 items), students are tested for visual and auditory discrmination, letter and word matching, vocabulary, and comprehension. Levels 7 (105 items) and 8 (135 items) test discrimination and study skills, phonic analysis, vocabulary, and comprehension. Level 8 also tests structural analysis. Levels 9-14 (210 items) test vocabulary, comprehension, structural analysis, and study skills. The test contains from four to nine subtests, depending on the test level. Available materials include a teacher's guide, technical report, and both class and students diagnostic reports. Machine-scorable test booklets are available for Levels 6-9. Answer folders are available for use with the reusable test booklets for Levels 9-14. Examiner required. Suitable for group use.

Untimed: Level 6 110 minutes; Level 7 150 minutes; Level 8 185 minutes; Levels 9-10 210 minutes; Levels 11-14 227 minutes

Scoring: Levels 6-9 machine scored; Levels 9-14 hand key; scoring service available

Cost: Examination kit, specify Levels 6-9, 9-12, or 13-14 (test booklets, directions for administration, teacher's guide, technical report) $3.21

Publisher: The Riverside Publishing Company

ROSWELL-CHALL AUDITORY BLENDING TEST
Florence Roswell and Jeanne Chall

Child   Grades 2-6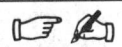

Purpose: Evaluates a child's ability to blend sounds when the sounds are presented orally. Used for classroom and remedial work in elementary and secondary schools.

Description: Multiple-item oral-response test assessing a child's ability to blend sounds auditorily into whole words, whether or not he has learned to associate the sounds with the corresponding letters. The test indicates the facility or difficulty

students will encounter with phonics instruction. Examiner required. Not suitable for group use.

Untimed: 5 minutes

Scoring: Examiner evaluated

Cost: Get-acquainted set (manual, 2 copies of test) $4.50

Publisher: Essay Press

ROSWELL-CHALL DIAGNOSTIC READING TEST OF WORD ANALYSIS SKILLS (REVISED AND EXTENDED)
Florence Roswell and Jeanne Chall

Child   Grades K-4

Purpose: Assesses a child's ability to use fundamental phonic and word recognition skills. Used for diagnostic and prescriptive teaching purposes in classrooms, tutorial work, and reading clinics.

Description: Multiple-item oral-response test containing the following subtests: sight recognition of high frequency words, naming capital and lowercase letters, consonant sounds, consonant blends and digraphs, short vowels, long vowels with e, long vowel combinations, writing and spelling CVC words. Appropriate subtests are indicated for different levels of reading ability. Results yield a comprehensive profile indicating a grade level and classifies skills as mastered, requiring review, or requiring systematic instruction. The test is available in Forms A and B for test-retest purposes. Suitable for use with older students whose phonic and word recognition skills are at a Grade 4 level or below. Examiner required. Not suitable for group use.

Untimed: 10-15 minutes

Scoring: Examiner evaluated

Cost: Get-acquainted set (manual, 2 copies Form A) $4.50

Publisher: Essay Press

SALFORD SENTENCE READING TEST
G.E. Bookbinder

Child   Ages 6-12

Purpose: Measures reading achievement of children with reading ages between 6 and 10.6 years.

Description: Multiple-item oral-response test measuring reading achievement. The test form consists of a test card containing 13 sentences presented in order of increasing difficulty. Testing ceases when the child has completed the sentence in which the sixth reading error is made. The child's reading age can immediately be read off from the test card. Percentile scores for chronological ages 6.1-11.9 are listed separately in the manual. The test is available in three parallel forms, A, B, and C. The test cards are reuseable and are available in sets containing one copy each of the three forms. Examiner required. Not suitable for group use. BRITISH PUBLISHER

Untimed: 2-3 minutes

Scoring: Examiner evaluated

Cost: Specimen test card is available free upon request; test cards Forms A, B, and C £1.80 per set of 3; manual £1.10

Publisher: Hodder & Stoughton

SIPAY WORD ANALYSIS TEST (SWAT)
Edward R. Sipay

Child   Grades 1-2　　

Purpose: Determines a child's strengths and weaknesses in word analysis skills. Used to assess individual progress and program effectiveness.

Description: 17 tests measuring three basic reading skills: visual analysis, phonic analysis, and visual blending. The tests allow for discriminant testing of specific word analysis skills (consonant blends, monosyllabic words, single letters) depending on each student's reading level. The areas the test measure are sequenced according to the level of difficulty. Examiner required. Not suitable for group use.

Untimed: Total time 3-6 hours; 10-20 minutes for each of the tests

Scoring: Examiner evaluated

Cost: SWAT kit (manual, one of each of the 17 mini-manuals, 12 answer sheets and report forms, 756 test cards) $80.00

Publisher: Educators Publishing Service, Inc.

SKILLCORP COMPUTER MANAGEMENT SYSTEM— READING

Child   Grades 1-6　　

Purpose: Assesses reading skill deficiencies. Used to diagnose an individual student's reading base and prescribe resources for reteaching.

Description: 77 tests assessing five strands: phonetic analysis, structural analysis, vocabulary, comprehension, and study skills. All skills tested are cross-referenced to basal and supplementary reading programs. A microcomputer prints prescriptions for individual students or groups to reteach skills not mastered. Materials include a test administration manual and test cards for each grade level. Examiner required. Suitable for group use.

Untimed: Not available

Scoring: Hand key; may be computer scored

Cost: Contact publisher

Publisher: Skillcorp Software, Inc.

SOUTHGATE GROUP READING TESTS
Vera Southgate

Child   Ages 5-9　　

Purpose: Measures children's basic reading skills. Identifies students reading significantly above or below their expected age level.

Description: Two paper-pencil tests of reading ability measure word selection and sentence completion skills. Test 1 is a word selection test suitable for older infants and younger juniors and for older pupils of low reading ability. Norms are provided for ages 5.9-7.9. Test 1 is available in three parallel forms for test-retest purposes. Test 2, a sentence completion test, assesses the second stage of learning to read. It slightly overlaps Test 1, and norms are provided for ages 7.0-9.7. Two parallel forms are intended for simultaneous administration to children seated next to one another. Test 2 is used with average seven- and eight-year-olds and for bright younger children and slower older ones. Examiner required. Suitable for group use.

BRITISH PUBLISHER

Untimed: Not available

Scoring: Examiner evaluated

Cost: Specimen sets £3.25; 20 copies Test 1 (specify form) £2.95; 20 copies Test 2 (specify form) £2.95; Test 1 manual £2.95; Test 2 manual £2.70

Publisher: Hodder & Stoughton

ST. LUCIA GRADED WORD READING TEST
R. J. Andrews

Child, adolescent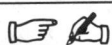

Purpose: Measures the word reading skills of primary and lower secondary-school students. Diagnoses specific skill deficits.

Description: Multiple-item oral-response reading test measuring word recognition skills. The test provides reading ages, as well as diagnostic information on word attack skills and error patterns. Examiner required. Not suitable for group use.

AUSTRALIAN PUBLISHER

Untimed: Varies

Scoring: Examiner evaluated

Cost: Basic kit (manual, test materials, 50 record forms) $11.00

Publisher: Teaching and Testing Resources

Information and availability unconfirmed; no publisher response.

ST. LUCIA READING COMPREHENSION TEST
J. Elkins and R. J. Andrews

Child   Grades 2-4

Purpose: Measures reading comprehension of children in the lower primary school.

Description: Multiple-item paper-pencil cloze-type test measuring the reading ability of students. The test is available in two alternate forms, A and B. Australian norms allow scores to be expressed as

reading ages, percentiles, or 15-point scale scores. Examiner required. Suitable for group use.

AUSTRALIAN PUBLISHER

Untimed: Varies

Scoring: Examiner evaluated

Cost: Basic kit (manual, 25 Form A, 25 Form B) $11.50

Publisher: Teaching and Testing Resources

Information and availability unconfirmed; no publisher response.

TEST OF EARLY READING ABILITY (TERA)
D. Kim Reid, Wayne P. Hresko, and Donald D. Hammill

Child   Ages 3-7.11

Purpose: Determines the actual reading ability (not "readiness") of preschool, kindergarten, and primary level students. Results can be used to document early reading ability.

Description: Multiple-item paper-pencil test examining three areas related to early learning: knowledge of the alphabet, comprehension, and the conventions of reading (e.g., book orientation and format). Examiner required. Not suitable for group use.

Untimed: Not available

Scoring: Hand key

Cost: Complete (manual, 50 picture cards, 50 record forms, storage box) $48.00

Publisher: Pro-Ed

THACKRAY READING READINESS PROFILES
Derek V. Thackray and Lucy Thackray

Child   Ages 4-7

Purpose: Measures reading readiness of reception class children. Diagnoses pre-reading skill deficiencies of older nonreaders. Used to develop individualized prereading skill programs.

Description: Task-assessment and oral-response test measuring reading readiness indicators. Full instructions for interpret-

ing the profiles and suggestions for developing specific reading readiness skills are contained in the manual. Examiner required. Suitable for group use. BRITISH PUBLISHER
Untimed: Not available
Scoring: Examiner evaluated
Cost: Specimen set £3.25; 10 profiles £6.10; manual £2.45
Publisher: Hodder & Stoughton

VISUAL MEMORY SCALE (VMS)
James L. Carroll

Child   Ages 5-6

Purpose: Measures short-term visual memory. Used as an aid in diagnosing reading and spelling problems.

Description: 25-card examiner-led test of a child's ability to recognize patterns. The examiner gives the child a 5-second look at a card containing a complex geometric design and asks him to pick out the same design among four similar designs on a second card. Examiner required. Not suitable for group use.
Timed: Total test 5-7 minutes
Scoring: Hand key
Cost: Set of plates $6.00; manual $3.00; answer blanks $1.50
Publisher: Carroll Publications

VISUAL MEMORY TEST
Joseph M. Wepman, Anne Morency, and Maria Seidl

Child   Ages 5-8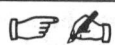

Purpose: Measures a child's ability to remember nonalphabetical, visual forms. Used to identify any perceptual inadequacy that might reduce the ability to learn to read.

Description: 16-item test measuring a child's ability to recall forms unfamiliar to him that cannot readily be named. The examiner shows the child a design on a target page, and the child chooses the design from four designs on a response page. Norms are provided for ages 5, 6, 7, and 8. Adequacy threshold scores indicate the need for additional evaluation. Examiner required. Not suitable for group use.

Untimed: 10-15 minutes
Scoring: Hand key
Cost: Complete kit (1 set of reusable stimulus cards, 25 score sheets, manual) $52.50
Publisher: Western Psychological Services

VISUAL-AURAL DIGIT SPAN TEST (VADS)
Elizabeth M. Koppitz

Child   Ages 5½-12

Purpose: Diagnoses specific problems in reading recognition and spelling for children who can read and write digits. Used to develop individual educational programs for learning-disabled children.

Description: Multiple-item test in which digit sequences on 26 test cards must be reproduced from memory, first orally, then in writing after being presented orally, and then, as a separate series, visually. The test measures auditory, visual, visual-auditory, and auditory-visual integration; sequence and recall of digits; and organization of written material. There are 11 scores, which are interpreted individually. Examiner required. Suitable for group use. Available in Spanish.
Untimed: 10 minutes
Scoring: Examiner evaluated
Cost: Manual $26.50; 100 tests $19.50
Publisher: Grune & Stratton, Inc.

WIDE-SPAN READING TEST
Alan Brimer with Herbert Gross

Child, adolescent Ages 7-15

Purpose: Measures sentence reading skills. Used to identify individual students' abilities.

Description: Multiple-item paper-pencil test of reading skills. Items consist of decoding printed symbols, fitting meanings to groups of sounds, and construing the structural relationship of meaning within the context of a sentence. Two parallel forms, A and B, are available. Examiner required. Suitable for group use.

BRITISH PUBLISHER
Timed: 30 minutes
Scoring: Hand key
Cost: Specimen set (1 pupil booklet A and B, 1 pupil answer sheet, manual) £5.70; introductory set (25 Form A and 25 Form B tests, 50 answer sheets, teacher's manual) £27.00 (payment in sterling for all overseas orders)
Publisher: NFER-NELSON Publishing Company Ltd.

WORD ANALYSIS DIAGNOSTIC TESTS
Selma E. Herr

Child Grades K-3

Purpose: Evaluates the word attack abilities of students in Grades K-3 and of remedial students in Grades K-12. Diagnoses skill deficiencies, assists in placement decisions, and serves as an achievement test.

Description: Multiple-item paper-pencil tests assessing proficiency in word analysis and phonics skills. The tests are arranged in four levels: Level A-1 (administered at the end of the reading readiness period), Level A-2 (Grade 1), Level B (Grade 2), and Level C (Grade 3). All levels may be used with students of any age for appropriate remedial purposes. Each level consists of four to six sections measuring skills appropriate to the student's grade level. Students are provided with a printed form containing familiar objects. Students respond by marking the appropriate symbol for material presented orally by an examiner or tape cassette. Examiner required. Suitable for group use.
Timed: 20-30 minutes per level
Scoring: Hand key
Cost: Comprehensive Teacher's Guide, cassette for each level $52.00
Publisher: Instructional Materials & Equipment Distributors

WORD ANALYSIS DIAGNOSTIC TESTS—LEVEL A-1/READINESS
Selma E. Herr

Child Grades K-1

Purpose: Assesses kindergartners' and first-graders' readiness to begin learning

the printed symbols (letters and groups of letters) used in reading. Diagnoses skill deficiencies, assists in placement decisions, and measures reading readiness.

Description: 40-item paper-pencil test assessing students' readiness to apply printed symbols to phonetic units. Subtests include rhyming words, initial consonant sounds, ending consonant sounds, and digraph sounds. Students are provided with a printed form containing familiar objects. Students respond by marking the appropriate symbol for material presented orally by an examiner or tape cassette. Examiner required. Suitable for group use.
Timed: 20 minutes
Scoring: Hand key
Cost: Class packet (30 tests, teacher's guide/keys, cassette containing test) $16.00
Publisher: Instructional Materials & Equipment Distributors

WORD ANALYSIS DIAGNOSTIC TESTS—LEVEL A-2/GRADE 1
Selma E. Herr

Child Grades 1-2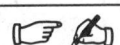

Purpose: Measures word attack skills at the end of the first year of phonics instruction. Used with students at the end of Grade 1, beginning of Grade 2, or remedial students in Grades 3-4 to diagnose skill deficiencies, assist in placement decisions, and measure achievement.

Description: 79-item paper-pencil multiple-choice test assessing proficiency in word attack skills and phonics, including initial and final consonants, consonant digraphs, four consonant blends, short vowel sounds, and rhyming words. Students are provided with a printed form containing familiar objects. Students respond by marking the appropriate symbol for material presented orally by an examiner or tape cassette. Examiner required. Suitable for group use.
Timed: 20 minutes
Scoring: Hand key

Cost: Class packet (30 tests, teacher's guide/keys, cassette containing test) $16.00

Publisher: Instructional Materials & Equipment Distributors

WORD ANALYSIS DIAGNOSTIC TESTS—LEVEL B/GRADE 2
Selma E. Herr

Child   Grades 2-3

Purpose: Measures word attack skills at the end of the second year of phonics instruction. Used with students at the end of Grade 2, the beginning of Grade 3, or remedial students in Grades 4-6 to diagnose skill deficiencies, assist in placement decisions, and measure achievement.

Description: 76-item paper-pencil multiple-choice test assessing proficiency in word attack skills and phonics, including long and short vowel sounds; vowels followed by r; the sounds ou, ow, aw, and all; hard and soft c and g; and the blends and digraphs. The test also assesses the ability to pronounce any phonetically based word, use context clues, and understand the meanings of words. Students are provided with a printed form containing familiar objects. Students respond by marking the appropriate symbol for material presented orally by an examiner or tape cassette. Examiner required. Suitable for group use.

Timed: 20 minutes

Scoring: Hand key

Cost: Class packet (30 tests, teacher's guide/keys, cassette containing test) $16.00

Publisher: Instructional Materials & Equipment Distributors

WORD ANALYSIS DIAGNOSTIC TESTS—LEVEL C/GRADE 3
Selma E. Herr

Child   Grades 3-4

Purpose: Measures word attack skills at the end of Grade 3. Identifies students needing further training in word analysis before entering Grade 4. Used with older students in Grades 5-12 to diagnose reading disabilities related to word attack skills.

Description: 116-item paper-pencil test assessing proficiency in word analysis skills, including vowel sounds, silent letters, syllabications, and structural and phonetic analysis. Students are provided with a printed form containing familiar objects. Students respond by marking the appropriate symbol in response to material presented orally by an examiner or tape cassette. Examiner required. Suitable for group use.

Timed: 30 minutes

Scoring: Hand key

Cost: Class packet (30 tests, teacher's guide/keys, cassette containing test) $16.00

Publisher: Instructional Materials & Equipment Distributors

WORD DISCRIMINATION TEST
Charles B. Huelsman, Jr.

Child   Grades 1.2-8.3

Purpose: Measures ability to recognize words. Identifies children with word-recognition skill deficiencies.

Description: 92-item paper-pencil multiple-choice test measuring how well students use length, internal design, and external configuration in perceiving words. Each test item consists of one word and four groups of letters that are not words. The students must draw a circle around the one word in each row. Grade equivalents are given for all raw scores. Norms are based on 1,299 sets of scores from children in Grades 1-6. Examiner required. Suitable for group use.

Untimed: 15 minutes

Scoring: Hand key; examiner evaluated

Cost: Test $0.15

Publisher: Miami University Alumni Association

Reading: High School and Above

BASIC SKILLS TEST-READING-SECONDARY: FORMS A AND B
IOX Assessment Associates

Adolescent   Grades 8-11

Purpose: Measures high-school minimum competency in the basic reading skills. Used for minimum competency testing and program evaluation.

Description: 30-item paper-pencil test examining student's ability to understand safety warnings, complete forms and applications, use common reference sources, determine main ideas, and use documents to take action. This test succeeds the IOX Basic Skills Test—Reading-Elementary Level. Examiner required. Suitable for group use.

Untimed: 30-45 minutes

Scoring: Hand key

Cost: 25 BR-Al tests $42.50; 25 BR-Bl tests $42.50; teacher's guide BR-Gl $3.95; test manual BTM-1 $3.95; 50 answer sheets $6.95

Publisher: IOX Assessment Associates

BUFFALO READING TEST
Refer to page 798.

CALIFORNIA PHONICS SURVEY
*Grace M. Brown and
Alice B. Cottrell*

**Adolescent, adult
Grades 7 and above**

Purpose: Measures the overall phonic adequacy of a group, class, or school system. Identifies individuals with some degree of phonic disability and determines the degree of impairment.

Description: 5-item oral response test assessing a student's phonic adequacy. Items consist of exercises involving reading and listening that are constructed to reveal the most common reversals, confusions of blends and vowels, and other errors that reflect inability to relate letter combinations to spoken sounds. The student's pattern of errors is interpreted in terms of eight diagnostic categories related to skills necessary for adequate reading, spelling, and language. Four general levels of phonic adequacy are defined by raw scores: adequate phonics, some phonic disability, serious phonic disability, and gross phonic disability. Available in two forms for pre- and post-testing. A single test booklet is used to administer either form. Examiner required. Suitable for group use.

Untimed: 45 minutes

Scoring: Examiner evaluated

Cost: Manual $9.50; 25 test booklets $8.50; 50 answer sheets (profiles on back) $7.00; scoring stencils (diagnostic set; form 1) $8.50; scoring stencils (retest score; form 2) $1.50; cassette tape $10.00

Publisher: Consulting Psychologists Press, Inc.

CLARKE READING SELF-ASSESSMENT SURVEY (SAS)
John H. Clarke and Simon Wittes

Grades 9-adult

Purpose: Measures student language skills prior to beginning the first semester in college. Used for self-assessment and counseling.

Description: Multiple-item paper-pencil instrument diagnosing strengths and weaknesses in reading, conceptualization, and written expression, with suggestions for skill improvement. The test booklet contains instructions for the student, multiple-choice questions, answers, scoring guide, and graphic profile. Self-administered. Suitable for group use.

Untimed: 1 hour

Scoring: Hand key

Cost: 10 surveys $25.00

Publisher: Academic Therapy Publications

DIAGNOSTIC ANALYSIS OF READING ERRORS (DARE)
Jacquelyn Gillespie and Jacqueline Shohet

Adolescent, adult
Ages 12 and older

Purpose: Identifies adolescents and adults with language-related problems, diagnoses learning disabilities, and provides specific data on the visual-auditory coding process for psychoeducational diagnoses. Used to survey school and community populations for educational planning and research.

Description: 46-item paper-pencil multiple-choice test in which the examiner dictates Wide Range Achievement Test Level II spelling items and the individual selects one of four choices as the correct answer. Four measures of visual-auditory transcoding ability are provided: Correct (reading and spelling skills), Sound Substitution (phonic analysis skills), Ommission (word structure analysis), and Reversal (sequencing efficiency). DARE coordinates with WRAT reading and spelling tests in reading improvement programs and attempts to provide a culture-fair measure of English language skills. Scoring yields diagnostic error patterns, age level norms (ages 12-adult), and standard scores. Free computer scoring is available. The test is restricted to educational and psychological professionals. Examiner required. Suitable for group use.

Untimed: 10 minutes

Scoring: Hand key; may be computer scored

Cost: Manual $15.00; 50 answer sheets $10.25

Publisher: Jastak Assessment Systems

EDINBURGH READING TESTS
Godfrey Thomson Unit for Education Research and Moray House College of Education

Child, adolescent
Ages 7-16

Purpose: Measures students' general reading abilities. Diagnoses the reading

strengths and weaknesses of each student and identifies those needing special help. Measures success of teaching methods in classes, schools, or districts.

Description: Paper-pencil tests of reading achievement presented in four stages for four different age groups. Each stage is divided into four or more separately timed subtests designed to assess different areas of reading competence. An overall score for the whole test and a separate score for each subtest are obtained for each child. The subtest scores are plotted on a profile, showing which relatively high or low scores are significant and merit further observation. Stage 1 (ages 7-9) is available in two equivalent forms, A and B, for test-retest programs. Practice items are included in the test forms, which are designed for administration in two sessions of 25 minutes. The profile is printed on the back of each form. Stages 2 (ages 8.6-10.6) and 3 (ages 10.0-12.6) are presented in a single test booklet (test content is the same for both stages). Both tests are designed for administration in three sessions: Practice Test (30-35 minutes), Part I (40 minutes), and Part II (35 minutes). Stage 4 (ages 12-16) is designed for administration in two sessions of 35 minutes. The profile is printed on the back of the test booklet. Examiner required. Suitable for group use.
BRITISH PUBLISHER

Timed: 25-35 minutes for each section

Scoring: Hand key

Cost: Stage 1 specimen set £2.70; stage 2 specimen set £2.40; stage 3 specimen set £5.30; stage 4 specimen set £2.70

Publisher: Hodder & Stoughton

THE MARYLAND-BALTIMORE COUNTY DESIGN FOR BASIC EDUCATION (BCD TEST)
Adult educators under a federal 310 grant

Nonreading adults

Purpose: Measures the skills adults must master to achieve literacy. Used for program planning and placement in adult literacy courses.

Description: 21 oral-response subtests assessing strengths, weaknesses, and deficits in prereading skills. Subtests may be given in any order. The manual includes instructions for administering and scoring the test, as well as criterion-referenced guidelines for interpreting the results. Correlation charts identify appropriate remediation programs for specific pre-reading skill deficits. May be administered by nonspecialists. Examiner required. Not suitable for group use.

Untimed: 10 minutes per subtest

Scoring: Examiner evaluated

Cost: Test $2.75; manual $10.50

Publisher: Cambridge

MINNESOTA SPEED OF READING TEST
Alvia C. Eruich

Adolescent, adult
Grades 12 and above

Purpose: Measures reading speed. Designed for high school seniors, college students, and college graduates.

Description: 38-item paper-pencil test in two forms, A and B, consisting of short paragraphs, each of which contains an "absurd" sentence or phrase that the subject is asked to cross out. The score depends on how many paragraphs are completed correctly within the time limit. Examiner required. Suitable for group use.

Timed: 6 minutes

Scoring: Hand key

Cost: 100 forms $5.00; specimen set $0.35

Publisher: University of Minnesota Press

NELSON-DENNY READING TEST: FORMS E AND F
James I. Brown, J. Michael Bennett, and Gerald S. Hanna

Adolescent, adult
Grades 9 and above

Purpose: Assesses student achievement and progress in vocabulary, comprehension, and reading rate.

Description: 136-item paper-pencil reading survey test in two parts. Part I, the vocabulary test, measures vocabulary

development. Part II, the Comprehension test, assesses comprehension and reading rate. A standard score scale is provided. A special cut-time adult administration of 26 minutes is recommended for extension of graduate class testing. The test is available in two parallel forms, E and F. Examiner required. Suitable for group use.

Timed: 35 minutes

Scoring: Hand key; may be machine scored

Cost: 35 test booklets (specify form) $22.17; 35 MRC answer sheets $15.12; manual $5.13

Publisher: The Riverside Publishing Company

PSB READING COMPREHENSION EXAMINATION

Health occupations
students

Purpose: Measures an individual's ability to understand material he has read. Used to identify students in the health professions who need counseling or remedial assistance.

Description: Multiple-item paper-pencil test sampling essential functional elements of reading comprehension. It is specifically designed for secondary, post-secondary, and professional programs and may be used as an adjunct to PSB tests in practical nursing, health occupations, and nursing. Examiner required. Suitable for group use.

Timed: 30 minutes

Scoring: Machine scored

Cost: Reusable test booklets $4.00; answer sheets (scoring and reporting service) $2.00

Publisher: Psychological Services Bureau

READING PROGRESS SCALE: COLLEGE VERSION
Ronald P. Carver

Adolescent, adult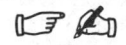

Purpose: Estimates reading level of college students. Particularly appropriate for use with students who do not read well.

Used for academic placement and referral.

Description: 80-item paper-pencil test assessing basic reading abilities. Scoring takes only seconds and provides immediate feedback to community-college students regarding which courses they should take. The test is available in two alternate forms: Form 2C and Form 5C. Examiner required. Suitable for group use.

Timed: 7 minutes

Scoring: Hand key

Cost: Specimen set $1.00; 100 tests $30.00; 1 manual free

Publisher: Revrac Publications, Inc.

READING/EVERYDAY ACTIVITIES IN LIFE (R/EAL)
Marilyn Lichtman

Adolescent, adult
Grades 10 and above

Purpose: Assesses whether an individual is functionally literate. Suitable for blacks, Puerto Ricans, Mexican Americans, rural groups, and other minority groups who have traditionally been singled out by the bias of standardized reading achievement tests, as well as for adults at basic educational levels and children ages 10 and older. Used for diagnostic and evaluative purposes.

Description: 45-item paper-pencil free-response test measuring an individual's ability to read and use language. The test consists of nine reading selections, each representing a general category of daily reading situations encountered by most individuals high-school age and older. The nine passages include a set of road signs, a TV schedule, a set of directions for preparing cheese pizza, a reading on narcotic drugs, a food market ad, an apartment lease or credit agreement, a road map, a want ad, and a job or credit application. Five questions, based on task analyses of the functions required to deal with the reading material, are asked for each selection. A cassette player, headphones (optional), a test booklet, and cassette are used to administer the test to insure that the subject's inability to understand written directions will not

prevent him from understanding what is on the test. The test is available in two equivalent forms, A and B, for pre- and posttesting. Examiner required. Suitable for group use. Available in Spanish.

Untimed: 1 day

Scoring: Examiner evaluated

Cost: Specimen set (cassette, test, manual) $8.00; test booklet $1.00; cassettes $6.00 each; manual $6.50 each

Publisher: Westwood Press, Inc.

SENIOR HIGH ASSESSMENT OF READING PERFORMANCE (SHARP)
CTB/McGraw-Hill

Adolescent
Grades 10-12

Purpose: Measures reading skills necessary for everyday situations. Used as an outcome measure for competency-based reading programs.

Description: 120-item paper-pencil test assessing minimum competencies in reading. The three-section test contains items consisting of 30 displays representing forms and written materials typically encountered in everyday situations. Four multiple-choice items follow each display. Section 1 includes a clothing tab, social security card, telephone directory index, job application form, change of address order, business letter, marriage license application, invitation, directions for hanging wallpaper, and auto loan application. Section 2 includes a charge account agreement, newspaper article, classified newspaper ad, financial agreement card, stop payment request, package label, recipe, selections from a driver's license handbook, an unemployment insurance claim, and four road signs. Section 3 includes a job resume, cash register receipt, area code map, TV review, dictionary entry, magazine article, street and freeway map, highway map, tax form, and bank statement. Form E, a short version of the test, consists of two sections of 40 items each. Examiner required. Suitable for group use.

Timed: Not available

Scoring: Hand key; may be computer scored

Cost: Specimen set (test book, manual, machine-scorable answer sheet, class summary sheet, objective matrix, test reviewer's guide) $8.95

Publisher: CTB/McGraw-Hill

Reading: Multilevel

ACER READING TESTS

Child, adolescent
Grades 1-12

Purpose: Assesses reading skills. Used for diagnosis of individual strengths and weaknesses as part of an educational evaluation.

Description: 10 multiple-choice paper-pencil tests of skills important in reading achievement. Tests are ACER Paragraph Reading Test, a screening test for years 6-8; ACER Primary Reading Survey Tests (Levels AA-BB), years 1 and 2. ACER Primary Reading Survey Tests (Levels A-D), years 3-6; ACER Primary Reading Survey Tests (Level D 1A-1C), a three-part test of reading achievement for year 6; Cooperative Reading Comprehension Test— Form Y, years 11 and above; Cooperative Reading Comprehension Test—L and M, years 8-10; English Skills Assessment, years 11 and 12; Progressive Achievement Tests-Form A or B; and Reading Appraisal Guide. Examiner required. Suitable for group use.

AUSTRALIAN PUBLISHER

Timed: Varies

Scoring: Hand key

Cost: Contact publisher

Publisher: The Australian Council for Educational Research Limited

ASSESSMENT OF READING GROWTH

Grades 2 and above

Purpose: Determines silent reading comprehension. Helps teachers predict how students will perform on statewide and standardized tests.

Description: 36-item paper-pencil test containing literal comprehension and inferential comprehension items that measure vocabulary, references, facts, main idea, organization, inferences, and the ability to read critically. The items, which are classified by skill type, have been screened for cultural fairness and are based on material released from the National Assessment of Educational Progress. The test provides item-by-item average scores of students throughout the nation and total score comparisons for inner city, medium city, and suburban school settings, as well as national averages. The test is available on three levels: Level 9 (Grades 2-4), Level 13 (Grades 6-8), and Level 17 (Grades 10-12, college, adult). Examiner required. Suitable for group use.

Untimed: Not available

Scoring: Hand key

Cost: 30 tests, manual (specify level) $10.00

Publisher: Jamestown Publishers

BASIC WORD VOCABULARY TEST
Harold J. Dupuy

Ages 4-adult

Purpose: Measures an individual's vocabulary size and development.

Description: 123-item paper-pencil multiple-choice test measuring vocabulary in relation to grade level, grade percentile (Grades 3-12 and college), chronological age grade placement, vocabulary age, and vocabulary development quotient (similar to IQ). The number of items to be answered depends on students' grade levels. Examiner required. Suitable for group use.

Untimed: 20 minutes

Scoring: Hand key

Cost: 40 tests, manual $10.00

Publisher: Jamestown Publishers

BIEMILLER TEST OF READING PROCESSES
Andrew Biemiller

Grades 2 and above

Purpose: Determines why a child is reading at a given level of proficiency and identifies strengths and weaknesses of a child's reading abilities.

Description: Multiple-item oral reading test monitoring letter speed, word speed out of context, and word speed in context. The test identifies individual differences in three kinds of reading processes: the ability to recognize print quickly, the ability to identify words quickly, and the ability to use context to facilitate word identification. A stopwatch is required. Examiner required. Not suitable for group use.
CANADIAN PUBLISHER

Untimed: Not available

Scoring: Examiner evaluated

Cost: Examiner kit for 35 (administration booklet, test book, 35 record forms) $16.25

Publisher: Guidance Centre

THE BODER TEST OF READING-SPELLING PATTERNS
Refer to page 462.

CLASSROOM READING INVENTORY, FIFTH EDITION, 1986
Nicholas J. Silvaroli

Child, adolescent
Grades 1 and above

Purpose: Assesses student's specific word-recognition and comprehension skills. Used for planning individual skills-oriented reading programs.

Description: Multiple-item paper-pencil and oral-response inventory measuring reading capabilities. The test is available in four forms: Forms A and B for students in Grades 1-6, Form C for junior high-school students, and Form D for high-school and adult students. Forms A and B consist of three parts: Graded Word Lists, Graded Oral Paragraphs, and Graded Spelling Survey. Forms C and D contain two parts, Graded Word Lists and Graded Oral Paragraphs. The inventory provides information on students' independent, instructional, and frustration reading levels and on their listening capacity levels. The test also provides specific

subskill development information in the areas of word recognition (consonant, vowel, and syllable) and comprehension (literal, inference, and vocabulary). All four forms may be reproduced without the publisher's permission. Examiner required. The Graded Spelling Survey is suitable for group use.

Untimed: 12 minutes

Scoring: Examiner evaluated

Cost: Contact publisher

Publisher: William C. Brown Company Publishers

DIAGNOSTIC SCREENING TEST: READING, THIRD EDITION (DSTR)
Thomas D. Gnagey and Patricia A. Gnagey

Child, adolescent
Grades 1-13

Purpose: Determines reading achievement levels and diagnoses common reading problems by testing word recognition and reading and listening comprehension.

Description: 84-word paper-pencil test yielding two major scores (Word Recognition and Reading Comprehension Grade Equivalents) and eight diagnostic scores that reflect skills in using seven basic word attack skills, as well as sight vocabulary. The student reads a word list and comprehension passages aloud and answers prescribed questions. The examiner then reads a passage aloud and the student answers questions. The test yields a consolidation index which reflects how solid or spotty each skill is. The test is available in two equivalent forms, A and B. Examiner required. Not suitable for group use.

Untimed: 5-10 minutes

Scoring: Hand key

Cost: Manual, 25 Form A, 25 Form B $25.00

Publisher: Slosson Educational Publications, Inc.

DIAGNOSTIC WORD PATTERNS: TESTS 1, 2, AND 3
Evelyn Buckley

Ages 3-adult

Purpose: Assesses basic phonic knowledge. Used to help classroom teachers determine general word attack concepts to review with an entire class and to identify individual students' strengths and weaknesses in order to develop suitable reading programs.

Description: Three verbal paper-pencil 100-word tests, each of which can be used to test spelling and/or word recognition. When used as a spelling test, the words are dictated to the students, who write the words on their answer sheets. When used as a word recognition test, the same words are printed on cards for the students to read aloud. As a spelling test, they can be administered to groups; as a word recognition test they must be administered individually. Test 1 deals with short vowels, nonphonetic words, and consonant digraphs. Test 2 covers vowel and diphthong patterns, suffixes, two-syllable words, and nonphonetic words. Materials include a teacher's manual. Examiner required. Not suitable for group use.

Untimed: 20-45 minutes

Scoring: Examiner evaluated

Cost: Tests 1, 2, 3, teacher's manual $3.85; 50 student charts $3.80; cards for word recognition test $4.40

Publisher: Educators Publishing Service, Inc.

FORMAL READING INVENTORY (FRI)
J. Lee Wiederholt

Child, adolescent Grades 1-12

Purpose: Assesses silent reading comprehension and diagnoses the oral reading miscues of students. Used to develop teaching strategies.

Description: Multiple-item, paper-pencil and oral-response test in four forms assessing reading comprehension and miscues. Each form contains 13 developmentally sequenced passages with five literal, inferential, critical, and affective multiple-choice questions following each story. Form A is used to derive a silent reading quotient. Form B, read orally by the student and marked by the examiner on a separate worksheet, is used to note reading behaviors, including comprehension strategies (meaning similarity), appropriate grammar forms (function similarity), word attack strategies (graphic/phonemic similarity), self-correction strategies, omissions, additions, dialect, and reversals. Form C (silent) and Form D (oral) are used as posttests. Examiner required. The silent reading forms are suitable for group use. The oral reading forms are not suitable for group use.

Untimed: Varies

Scoring: Hand key

Cost: Complete kit (examiner's manual, student book, 50 student record forms, storage box) $52.00

Publisher: Pro-Ed

GAPADOL READING COMPREHENSION TESTS
J. McLeod and J. Anderson

Child, adolescent Ages 7-16

Purpose: Measures reading comprehension. Used for identifying student achievement as part of an educational evaluation.

Description: Multiple-item tests of reading achievement using the cloze technique. The student fills in words omitted from reading passages. The test is useful for placement, information on a child's reading and spelling techniques, and retesting. Available in two alternate forms, G and Y. Examiner required. Suitable for group use.
AUSTRALIAN PUBLISHER

Timed: 15 minutes

Scoring: Examiner evaluated

Cost: $17.50

Publisher: Heinemann Publishers Australia Party Limited

GATES MACGINITIE READING TEST, CANADIAN EDITION (GMRT)
Walter MacGinitie

Child, adolescent
Grades K-12

Purpose: Measures student's reading and vocabulary achievement levels. Used for placement and class planning.

Description: Multiple-item paper-pencil test of vocabulary and reading comprehension. The basic Level R contains 54 items. Levels A-F contain 85-89 items. Examiner required. Suitable for group use.
CANADIAN PUBLISHER
Timed: 55 minutes
Untimed: Level R 65 minutes
Scoring: Hand key; may be computer scored
Cost: 35 booklets $18.85; manual $9.75; key $1.70
Publisher: Nelson Canada

GATES-MACGINITIE READING TESTS, SECOND EDITION
Walter MacGinitie

Child, adolescent
Grades 1-12

Purpose: Measures the reading achievement of students in Grades 1-12. Used to identify students who would benefit from remedial or accelerated programs, evaluate instructional programs, and counsel students and report progress to parents.

Description: Multiple-item paper-pencil test assessing reading comprehension and vocabulary development. The test is available on seven levels: Basic R (Grade 1), A (Grade 1.5-1.9), B (Grade 2), C (grade 3), D (Grades 4-6), E (Grades 7-9), F (Grades 10-12). Each level measures vocabulary and reading comprehension; Basic R also measures letter recognition and letter "sounds." Examiner required. Suitable for group use.
Timed: Levels A-F 55 minutes
Untimed: Level Basic R 65 minutes
Scoring: Hand key; may be computer scored

Cost: 25 machine-scorable test booklets (specify Level R or A, B, C, D), manual $21.48; 35 hand-scorable test booklets (specify level), manual, scoring key $17.97; 35 MRC answer sheets (specify level D, E, or F) $10.65; manual $3.84; MRC scoring templates (specify level D, E, or F) $3.93
Publisher: The Riverside Publishing Company

GRAY ORAL READING TESTS— REVISED (GORT-R)
J. Lee Wiederholt and
Brian R. Bryant

Child, adolescent
Ages 7-17

Purpose: Measures growth in oral reading and diagnoses reading difficulties in students.

Description: Multiple-item oral-response test in two alternate, equivalent forms. The student reads 13 developmentally sequenced passages and responds to five comprehension questions. The passage score, derived from reading rate and errors, is reported in standard scores and percentiles. This new test provides standard scores and percentiles for oral reading comprehension and a system for analyzing miscues in meaning similarity, function similarity, graphic/phenomic similarity, and self-correction. Examiner required. Not suitable for group use.
Untimed: 20-30 minutes
Scoring: Examiner evaluated
Cost: Complete kit (examiner's manual, student book, 25 profile/examiner record forms, storage box) $63.00
Publisher: Pro-Ed

INFORMAL EVALUATION OF ORAL READING
Deborah Edel

All ages

Purpose: Measures reading ability of individuals of all ages. Used to estimate the student's reading level and diagnose specific reading weaknesses. Also used with students learning English as a second language.

Description: Multiple-item oral-response test evaluating reading ability by informally surveying the student's reading performance. Eight reading passages measure the following factors: independent, instructional, frustration, oral comprehension, pattern of reading, type and frequency of reading error, reading style, and behavior. The test may be used at any level of oral-reading ability. Examiner required. Not suitable for group use.

Untimed: 15-35 minutes

Scoring: Examiner evaluated

Cost: Complete set (2 reading booklets, 25 evaluation forms, instructions) $9.95

Publisher: Book-Lab

INFORMAL READING ASSESSMENT
Paul C. Burns and Betty D. Roe

**Child, adolescent
PreK-Grade 12**

Purpose: Measures students' reading performance level. Used by preservice and inservice teachers who have little or no experience with reading assessment.

Description: Multiple-item inventory of oral reading ability consisting of graded word lists and graded reading passages. Two equivalent forms of the graded word lists and four equivalent forms of the graded passages are provided for each level. All forms are presented on reproducible pages. The equivalent forms provide a built-in provision for retesting to assure instructional flexibility. The test package includes a detailed description of how to administer, score, and interpret the inventory, a scoring aid, and record-keeping sheets. Examiner required. Not suitable for group use.

Untimed: Varies

Scoring: Examiner evaluated

Cost: Test kit $16.45

Publisher: Nelson Canada

IOWA SILENT READING TESTS (ISRT)
Roger Farr, coordinating editor

**Adolescent, adult
Grades 6 and above**

Purpose: Assesses ability to read. Used to diagnose student strengths and weaknesses and for implementation of remedial lesson plans.

Description: Multiple-item battery of paper-pencil tests measuring four reading skill areas. The subtests are Vocabulary, Comprehension, Directed Reading (work-study skills), and Reading Efficiency (rate with comprehension). Items in the Directed Reading subtest measure students' ability to use reference sources. The test is divided into three levels: Level 1 for Grades 6-9, Level 2 for Grades 9-community college, and Level 3 for accelerated students in Grades 11 and 12, college students, and professional groups. Level 3 does not include the Directed Reading subtest. Materials include two alternate and equivalent forms, E and F. Examiner required. Suitable for group use.

Timed: Level 1 1 hour, 31 minutes; Level 2 1 hour, 26 minutes; Level 3 56 minutes

Scoring: Hand key; may be machine scored; scoring service available

Cost: Specimen set, specify level (test, MRC answer document, hand-scorable answer document, class record, manual of directions, pupil profile) $8.00

Publisher: The Psychological Corporation

MCCARTHY INDIVIDUALIZED DIAGNOSTIC READING INVENTORY
William G. McCarthy

Grades 2 and over

Purpose: Diagnoses the development of student reading skills so the teacher can screen for reading disabilities and select appropriate instructional materials.

Description: 11 brief reading selections ranked from primer to Grade 12, read by the student to the examiner. Beginning with Part One, the student's skills are quickly measured by the Controlled Vocabulary List and Basal Reader Graded Selections. All reading errors can be marked on the Teacher Administration Booklet. Based on the student's performance in Part 1, the appropriate reading selections are administered for Parts 2, 3,

reading: multilevel

and 4. The factors measured are oral reading, reading comprehension, critical thinking skills, vocabulary, phonics, word recognition, sight vocabulary, and study skills. Hobbies, reading interests, and physcal health also are evaluated. The last part of the test moves into prescription by providing structure to develop a preliminary plan for reading instruction based on the information gained in the inventory. Examiner required. Not suitable for group use.

Untimed: 1-1½ hours

Scoring: Examiner evaluated

Cost: Information booklet $2.40; teacher booklet $6.50; pupil booklet $1.60; 12 individual record forms $4.90

Publisher: Educators Publishing Service, Inc.

METROPOLITAN READING INSTRUCTIONAL TESTS
Roger Farr, George A. Prescott, Irving H. Balow, and Thomas P. Hogan

Child   Grades K.5-9.9

Purpose: Measures reading skills. Used for providing prescriptive information on the educational performance of individual pupils.

Description: Multiple-item series of paper-pencil tests measuring major components of reading skills, including visual discrimination, letter recognition, auditory discrimination, sight vocabulary, phoneme/grapheme: consonants, phoneme/grapheme: vowels, vocabulary in context, word part clues, rate of comprehension, skimming and scanning, and reading comprehension. The test is divided into six levels: Primer (Grades K.5-1.4), Primary 1 (Grades 1.5-2.4), Primary 2 (Grades 2.5-3.4), Elementary (Grades 3.5-4.9), Intermediate (Grades 5.0-6.9), and Advanced 1 (Grades 7.0-9.9). Each level assesses four to seven of the above reading skills components. Materials include two alternate and equivalent forms, JI and KI. The test is one in a series of instructional tests related to the Metropolitan Achievement Tests Survey Battery. Examiner required. Suitable for group use.

Timed: Varies

Scoring: Hand key; may be machine scored; scoring service available

Cost: Specimen sets, specify level (test, manual) $11.00; the Intermediate and Advanced 1 sets include a hand-scorable document

Publisher: The Psychological Corporation

NATIONAL ACHIEVEMENT TESTS: ENGLISH, READING, LITERATURE, AND VOCABULARY TESTS—READING
Refer to page 414.

POPE INVENTORY OF BASIC READING SKILLS
Lillie Pope

Child, adolescent
Grades K-12

Purpose: Evaluates basic reading skills. Appropriate for all students reading below the fourth-grade level. Used to plan reading instruction.

Description: Oral reading, verbal word recognition, and written responses measure 13 basic reading and word recognition skills, including the ability to match symbols with sounds, knowledge of right and left, and knowledge of basic sight words. The student's responses are evaluated and summarized in 12 areas. Examiner required. Not suitable for group use.

Untimed: 15-30 minutes

Scoring: Examiner evaluated

Cost: Complete kit (20 forms) $9.95

Publisher: Book-Lab

PRESCRIPTIVE READING PERFORMANCE TEST (PRPT)
Janet B. Fudala

Child, adolescent
Grades 1-12

Purpose: Assesses an individual's reading level and prereading readiness and diagnoses a student's strengths and weaknesses in word attack skills. Used for reading or learning disabilities programs and to comply with P.L. 94-142.

Description: Multiple-item paper-pencil and oral-response test assessing a student's reading and spelling performance and identifying four groups of readers: normal readers, readers with auditory problems, readers with visual problems, and readers with auditory and visual problems. The student reads words presented on graded word lists. By evaluating words that are in the student's sight vocabulary and words that are not, the examiner documents strengths and weaknesses in the visual and auditory channels and identifies patterns of performance that have characteristic prescriptive educational implications. The manual presents standardization, validity and reliability data, and a number of case studies. Examiner required. Not suitable for group use.

Untimed: 15-20 minutes

Scoring: Hand key

Cost: Complete kit (one reusable set of word lists, 25 record forms, 25 answer sheets, manual) $37.50

Publisher: Western Psychological Services

PRI READING SYSTEMS (PRI/RS)
CTB/McGraw-Hill

Child, adolescent
Grades K-9

Purpose: Assesses reading and language arts skills.

Description: Multiple-item paper-pencil test measuring four language arts skill areas: oral language (language and comprehension), word attack and usage (word analysis, vocabulary, word usage), comprehension (literal, interpretive and critical), and applications (study skills, content area reading). The system is available on five grade levels: Level A (Grades K-1), Level B (Grades 1-2), Level C (Grades 2-3), Level D (Grades 4-6), and Level E (Grades 7-9). It is available in two formats: System 1 and System 2. System 1 uses a graded approach, which assesses skills by grade level. Each skill can be assessed at two levels of specificity: category objectives assessment level and

instructional objectives assessment level. System 2 assesses skills across grade levels. Examiner required. Suitable for group use.

Untimed: Not available

Scoring: Hand key; may be computer scored

Cost: Contact publisher

Publisher: CTB/McGraw-Hill

READING EFFICIENCY TESTS
Lyle L. Miller

Adolescent, adult
Grades 7 and above

Purpose: Measures pre- and posttesting of reading rate, comprehension, and efficiency.

Description: Five tests that include content on history, geography, government, culture, and the people of Brazil, Japan, India, New Zealand, and Switzerland. Each reading test contains 5,000 words, and each line of the test is numbered. Each answer sheet contains 50 items about the content of the reading selection. When the timed test is stopped, each student marks the line on which he was reading and is tested only on the material he has read. Examiner required. Suitable for group use.

Timed: 10 minutes per test

Scoring: Hand key

Cost: 20 booklets $15.00; 20 answer sheets $5.00; specimen set $5.00

Publisher: Developmental Reading Distributors

READING SPLIT FORM (FORM R)
Mary Meeker and Robert Meeker

Adolescent, adult
Grades 7 and above

Purpose: Assesses the reading ability of elementary, intermediate, high-school, and college students.

Description: Multiple-item paper-pencil test measuring reading ability. Discipline-focused test items are selected from the SOI-LA Basic Test. The Basic Test manual is required for administration. Examiner required. Suitable for group use.

Timed: 1 hour

Scoring: Hand key

Cost: Examiner's manual $24.50; test form $1.95

Publisher: Western Psychological Services

READING TEST SERIES

Child, adolescent
Grades 1-12

Purpose: Assesses reading skills. Used to screen students and provide teachers with information regarding the overall reading performance of a class.

Description: Five multiple-item tests measuring reading comprehension. The tests are Reading Test A (ages 6-8), Reading Test AD (ages 8-10), Reading Test BD (ages 7-10), Reading Comprehension Test DE (ages 10-12), and Reading Test EH 1-2 (ages 11-15). Reading Tests A, AD, and BD consist of multiple-choice sentence completion items. Reading Comprehension Test DE (50 items) measures understanding of complex reading passages. Test 1 of Reading Test EH 1-2 consists of 60 sentence completion items. Test 2 contains 35 questions based on comprehension passages. Examiner required. Suitable for group use.
BRITISH PUBLISHER

Timed: Varies

Scoring: Hand key

Cost: Primary specimen set (one each of pupil forms A, AD, BD, DE and sample manual) £2.85; secondary specimen set (one each of pupils forms DE and EH 1-2 and a sample manual) £3.05 (payment in sterling for all overseas orders)

Publisher: NFER-NELSON Publishing Company Ltd.

SLOSSON ORAL READING TEST (SORT)
Richard L. Slosson

Child, adolescent
Grades 1-12

Purpose: Measures the reading ability of and identifies reading handicaps in students.

Description: Oral screening test yielding reading levels from 10 word lists. The test is based upon the ability to pronounce words at various levels of difficulty. Directions for administration and scoring are contained on each score sheet. Form A, a large-print edition, is available for adults and the visually and verbally handicapped. The word lists are identical to those contained in the regular version, but they have been enlarged and printed on cards for ease of presentation. Scoring instructions accommodate adult literacy programs. Examiner required. Not suitable for group use.

Untimed: 3-5 minutes

Scoring: Examiner evaluated

Cost: 50 SORT forms complete with directions and word lists $8.00; 50 Form A and 10 cards with word lists and revised scoring instructions $10.00

Publisher: Slosson Educational Publications, Inc.

SPADAFORE DIAGNOSTIC READING TEST (SDRT)
Gerald J. Spadafore

Child, adolescent, adult

Purpose: Assesses reading skills of students in Grades 1-12 and adults. Used as a screening and diagnostic instrument for academic placement and career guidance counseling.

Description: Four subtests assess word recognition, oral reading and comprehension, silent reading comprehension, and listening comprehension. Criterion-referenced test items are graded for difficulty. Independent, Instructional, and Frustration reading and comprehension levels are designated for performance at each grade level. Test results may be used for screening to determine whether reading problems exist at a student's current grade placement. Administration for screening requires 30 minutes for all four subtests and determines whether reading problems exist at a student's current grade placement. Administration for diagnostic purposes requires 60 minutes for all four subtests and yields a comparison of decoding reading skills. Guidelines are provided for interpreting performance in terms of vocational literacy. The test may be scored as it is administered. Provisions for conducting a detailed error analysis of oral reading are included. Examiner required. Not suitable for group use.

Untimed: Screening 30 minutes; diagnosis 1 hour

Scoring: Examiner evaluated

Cost: Test kit (manual, test plates, 10 test booklets) $45.00

Publisher: Academic Therapy Publications

STANFORD MEASUREMENT SERIES—STANFORD DIAGNOSTIC READING TEST (SDRT)

Refer to page 450.

STANFORD MEASUREMENT SERIES—STANFORD DIAGNOSTIC READING TESTS (SDRT): THIRD EDITION

Refer to page 450.

THE STETSON READING-SPELLING VOCABULARY TEST (RSVT)

Elton Stetson

Grades 1-14

Purpose: Assesses students' reading and spelling abilities. Used for educational placement and planning.

Description: Norm-referenced and criterion-referenced achievement test of reading and of written spelling. The test contains 120 words divided into four subtests arranged in order of difficulty. As a reading test, the subtests may be administered using either the regular method or the cut-time method. In the regular method, the subtests must be administered in order. The student pronounces the 120 words, and the examiner makes one of three marks on the record sheet. In the cut-time method, the examiner instructs the student to begin reading the word list at a more difficult level. To

assess written spelling skills, the examiner dictates the 120 words, and the student writes them on the spelling test form. The spelling test may also be administered using either the regular or cut-time method. The oral reading test is valid for students reading between grade levels 1-9, and the written spelling test (which can be administered to groups) is valid for students in Grades 2-14. Available in two equivalent forms. Examiner required. Not suitable for group use.

Untimed: Reading test 5 minutes; spelling test 30 minutes

Scoring: Hand Key

Cost: Complete program (50 reading tests, student reading chart, 50 spelling tests, training manual) $38.00

Publisher: Modern Education Corporation

TEST OF READING COMPREHENSION (TORC)

Virginia L. Brown,
Donald D. Hammill,
and J. Lee Wiederholt

Child, adolescent
Grades 2-12

Purpose: Assesses students' reading comprehension. Used to diagnose reading problems in terms of current psycholinguistic theories of reading comprehension as a constructive process involving both language and cognition.

Description: Eight paper-pencil subtests measuring aspects of reading comprehension. Three of the subtests (General Vocabulary, Syntactic Similarities, and Paragraph Reading) are combined to determine a basic Comprehension Core, which is expressed as a Reading Comprehension Quotient (RCQ). Three subtests measure students' abilities to read the vocabularies of math, science, and social studies. Subtest #7, Reading the Directions of Schoolwork, is a diagnostic tool for younger or remedial students. The eighth subtest is Sentence Sequences. Scaled scores are provided for each subtest. Examiner required. Not suitable for group use.

Untimed: 1 hour, 45 minutes

Scoring: Hand key

Cost: Complete (manual, 10 student booklets, 50 answer sheets, 50 profile sheets, set of scoring keys, storage box) $68.00

Publisher: Pro-Ed

WOODCOCK READING MASTERY TESTS (WRMT)
Richard W. Woodcock

Child, adolescent
Grades K-12

Purpose: Detects student reading problems. Used for classroom grouping, program evaluation, research, and clinical diagnosis.

Description: 400-item verbal test covering word identification (150 items), word attack (50 items), word comprehension (70 items), and passage comprehension (85 items). The examiner shows the student a test plate and asks a question to which the student responds orally. Only those items within the student's functioning level are administered. The test is available in two alternate forms, A and B. Materials include test plates bound into an easel and 25 response forms. The test is norm- and criterion-referenced. Derived scores are grade equivalents, grade percentile ranks, age equivalents, standard scores and mastery scores. Normal curve equivalents for Chapter I programs are available for Grades 2-6. Examiner required. Not suitable for group use.

Untimed: 30-45 minutes

Scoring: Examiner evaluated; may be computer scored

Cost: Complete kit (Form A or B) $45.75

Publisher: American Guidance Service

Reading: Library Skills

BENNETT LIBRARY USAGE TEST
Alma Bennett and H.E. Schrammel

Adolescent, adult
Grades 10 and above

Purpose: Assesses the library knowledge of high-school and college students. Used as an end-of-course exam.

Description: 130-item paper-pencil test of library knowledge including organization, the Dewey Decimal System, vocabulary, reference books, topical locations, and the *Readers' Guide to Periodical Literature*. Examiner required. Suitable for group use.

Timed: 50 minutes

Scoring: Hand key

Cost: Test $0.15; manual $0.20; key $0.20

Publisher: Bureau of Educational Measurements

DIAGNOSTIC TEST OF LIBRARY SKILLS
Barbara Feldstein and Janet Rawdon

Child, adolescent
Grades 5-9

Purpose: Evaluates student's working knowledge of essential library skills.

Description: 50-item paper-pencil multiple-choice test measuring library skills in the following areas: definitions of library terms, use of the title page, use of the table of contents, use of an index, use of the card catalog, library arrangement, and use of reference materials. The results are recorded on an analytic sheet that indicates areas that require general class or small group attention. Further examination of individual answer sheets indicates specific needs. The test is available in equivalent forms A and B with interchangeable answer key. A bibliography of sources providing instruction and learning experiences for concepts included in this test is provided in the teacher's guide. Examiner required. Suitable for group use.

Untimed: Varies

Scoring: Hand key

Cost: Test kit, specify form (50 test booklets, 100 answer sheets, scoring key, teacher's guide) $26.95

Publisher: Learnco, Inc.

LIBRARY SKILLS TEST
Illinois Association of College and Research Libraries

**Adolescent
Grades 7-college**

Purpose: Assesses students' skills in working with library materials.

Description: Multiple-item paper-pencil test covering current terminology, card catalog, classification systems, filing, parts of a book, indexes, reference tools, and bibliographic forms. The manual includes an answer key, content outline, and norms for Grades 7-12 and college freshmen. The scoring service provides three alphabetical lists and class summary data. Examiner required. Suitable for group use.

Timed: 45 minutes

Scoring: Computer scored

Cost: Test kit (manual, 20 test booklets) $17.60; scoring service $0.80 per student

Publisher: Scholastic Testing Service, Inc.

LIBRARY SKILLS TEST
Wayne DeMouth

Adolescent

Purpose: Measures students' ability to use a library.

Description: 50-item paper-pencil multiple-choice test in four categories. The Dewey Decimal System and Card Catalog test deals with classification numbers and subject areas and mechanics of the card catalog. The Reader's Guide and Periodicals test focuses on format, abbreviations of terms, and subject areas of periodicals used in research. The Reference Materials test concentrates on The Dictionary, World Atlas, and other sources. The Effective Use of Information in Research test includes useful terms, footnote and bibliography styling, and conventions of correct presentation. Materials include spirit master sets and answer keys. Examiner required. Suitable for group use.

Untimed: 50 minutes

Scoring: Hand key

Cost: Spirit master set $5.25

Publisher: The Perfection Form Company

TEST OF LIBRARY/STUDY SKILLS
Irene Gullette and Frances Hatfield

Child, adolescent   Grades 2-12

Purpose: Measures the basic essentials of library/media center skills.

Description: Multiple-item paper-pencil test measuring knowledge of book arrangement, parts of a book, the card catalog, indexes, and reference books. Available in three levels for different age groups: Level I (Grades 2-5), Level II (Grades 4-9), Level III (Grades 8-12). Self-administered. Suitable for group use.

Untimed: 50 minutes per level

Scoring: Hand key

Cost: Complete kit (50 test booklets, 100 answer cards, key) Level 1 $22.00, Level 2 or 3 $25.00

Publisher: Larlin Corporation

Sensorimotor Skills

ADOLESCENT AND ADULT PSYCHOEDUCATIONAL PROFILE (AAPEP)
Refer to page 598.

ANN ARBOR LEARNING INVENTORY AND REMEDIATION PROGRAM
Barbara Meister Vitale and Waneta Bullock

Child   Grades K-7

Purpose: Evaluates the central processing and perceptual skills necessary for reading, writing, and spelling. Identifies learning difficulties and deficits and suggests appropriate remedial strategies. Used to establish IEPs.

Description: Multiple-item task performance oral-response and paper-pencil test measuring the following central processing skills: visual discrimination, visual memory, auditory discrimination, auditory memory, and modality strength (auditory or visual). Also identifies specific visual and auditory perceptual problems, such as rotations, closure, omissions, directionality, and sequencing problems. Test items are presented in order of natural cognitive development, beginning with pictures, proceeding to objects and geometric forms, and finally to letters, words, and phrases. Tasks involve listening, manipulating, showing, matching, visualizing, telling, and writing. In addition to information on central processing skills and perceptual abilities, results also provide objective data on developmental levels for prereading readiness, precomputational skills, kinesthetic and motor skills, and comprehension and critical thinking. Available for three levels: Level A (Grades K-1), Level B (Grades 2-4), and Level 3 (Grades 5-7). Manual provides remedial suggestions for immediate classroom use. Examiner required. Suitable for group use.

Untimed: Varies

Scoring: Examiner evaluated

Cost: Teacher's manual for Level A, B, or C $4.00; student booklet for Level A, B, or C $0.50

Publisher: Ann Arbor Publishers, Inc.

BASIC VISUAL-MOTOR ASSOCIATION TEST
James Battle

Child   Grades 1-9

Purpose: Measures visual short-term memory. Predicts students' skills in reading, spelling, and arithmetic. Used by classroom teachers, resource teachers, school psychologists, and remedial therapists.

Description: 120-item paper-pencil symbol-copying test in two forms assessing the following visual-motor skills: recall of visual symbols, visual sequencing ability, visual association skills, visual-motor ability, visual integrative ability, and symbol-integration skills. Students are asked to copy 60 symbols (uppercase letters) on Form A and 60 symbols (lowercase letters) on Form B. Conversion tables

provide percentile ranks and t-scores derived from raw scores. Examiner required. Suitable for group use in Grades 2-9 and for individual use in Grade 1.

Timed: 3 minutes per form

Scoring: Examiner evaluated

Cost: Test kit (manual, 25 forms A and B, scoring acetate) $19.50; specimen set (manual, sample test form) $12.50

Publisher: Special Child Publications

BENDER VISUAL MOTOR GESTALT TEST
Refer to page 36.

BENDER-PURDUE REFLEX TEST AND TRAINING MANUAL
Miriam Bender

Child   Ages 6-12

Purpose: Determines the presence and/or level of symmetric tonic neck reflex activity in children who are suspected of having learning disabilities. Used to diagnose whether the response interferes with learning and to plan motor-training programs.

Description: Six-task motor performance test in which the child participates in a variety of movement tasks (such as rocking and creeping backward and forward on hands and knees) as the examiner physically resists the student's progress from varying points of leverage. Scoring is based on the number of deviations from a standard, "perfect" posture and pattern of locomotion. Materials include illustrated instructions for a motor-training program and a book of spirit masters for parents' use at home. The test is also available on videotape. Examiner required. Not suitable for group use.

Untimed: 20 minutes

Scoring: Examiner evaluated

Cost: Manual $10.00; 25 recording forms and 12 spirit masters $6.00

Publisher: United Educational Services, Inc.

BENTON REVISED VISUAL RETENTION TEST
Refer to page 37.

BRUININKS-OSERETSKY TEST OF MOTOR PROFICIENCY
Robert H. Bruininks

Child, adolescent
Ages 4¼-14½

Purpose: Determines a child's level of motor proficiency. Used for educational placement, large-group screening, assessing neurological development, and evaluating motor training programs.

Description: 46-item physical performance paper-pencil battery grouped into eight subtests: Running Speed and Agility, Balance, Bilateral Coordination, Strength, Upper-Limb Coordination, Response Speed, Visual-Motor Control, and Upper-Limb Speed and Dexterity. The examiner records the child's performance on given tasks, and the child uses a student booklet for cutting and paper-pencil responses. Two forms are available: the complete battery and a short form. The complete battery yields three scores: Gross Motor Composite (large muscles of the shoulders, trunk, and legs), Fine Motor Composite (small muscles of the fingers, hand, and forearms), and Battery Composite (general motor performance). Subtest and composite scores can be converted to age-based standard scores, percentile ranks, stanines, and age equivalents. The short form of the test includes 14 items from the complete battery to yield a single score of general motor proficiency, which can be converted to an age-based standard score, percentile rank, and stanine. Materials include a manual, 25 individual record forms, a sample of the alternate Short Form, 25 student booklets, and a set of testing equipment, all in a metal case. Examiner required. Not suitable for group use.

Untimed: Short form 15-20 minutes; complete battery 45-60 minutes

Scoring: Examiner evaluated

Cost: Complete battery $215.00

Publisher: American Guidance Service

DEGANGI-BERK TEST OF SENSORY INTEGRATION (TSI)
Georgia A. DeGangi and Ronald A. Berk

Child   Ages 3-5

Purpose: Measures overall sensory integration in preschool children. Screens for young children with delays in sensory, motor, and perceptual skills in order to facilitate intervention programs.

Description: 36-item performance test of three subdomains of sensory integration: postural control, bilateral motor integration, and reflex integration. The examiner rates the child's response to each item on a numerical scale indicating abnormal to normal development. Examiner required. Not suitable for group use.

Untimed: 30 minutes

Scoring: Examiner required

Cost: Complete kit (test materials, 25 star design sheets, 25 protocol booklets, manual, and carrying case) $42.75

Publisher: Western Psychological Services

DENVER HANDWRITING ANALYSIS (DHA)
Peggy L. Anderson

Child   Grades 3-8

Purpose: Assesses the general quality of a student's cursive handwriting and provides detailed information related to handwriting instruction.

Description: Multiple-item paper-pencil test consisting of five areas: near-point copying, writing the alphabet from memory, far-point copying, manuscript-cursive transition, and dictation. Each subtest yields a Mastery Level score that allows intra-individual comparisons to be made across varying task formats. The DHA Scoring Profile includes a subskill analysis section that classifies errors by type and a performance analysis section that yields more general information about spatial organization, speed, slant, and appearance. The manual includes interpretive guidelines, samples of written reports summarizing student performance, and remedial suggestions related to each subtest. Examiner required. Suitable for group use.

Untimed: 20-60 minutes

Scoring: Examiner evaluated

Cost: Test kit (manual and wall chart, 25 record forms, 25 scoring profiles, 50 remedial checklists, in vinyl folder) $30.00

Publisher: Academic Therapy Publications

DEVELOPMENTAL TEST OF VISUAL-MOTOR INTEGRATION (VMI)
Refer to page 40.

EARLY LEARNING ASSESSMENT AND DEVELOPMENT
Refer to page 472.

EARLY SCREENING INVENTORY (ESI)
Refer to page 472.

FOSTER MAZES

Adult

Purpose: Measures nonverbal intelligence.

Description: Task-performance test assessing spatial orientation and spatial reasoning ability. A blindfolded individual must find his way out of a grooved maze pattern using a stylus or pencil. Mazes are presented in the form of grooves etched into 8½ x 11-inch boards, which are available in two equivalent forms, A and B. The manual provides scoring guidelines. Examiner required. Not suitable for group use.

Untimed: Varies

Scoring: Examiner evaluated

Cost: Maze (specify form A or B) $97.50

Publisher: Stoelting Company

FROSTIG MOVEMENT SKILLS TEST BATTERY (EXPERIMENTAL EDITION)
Russel E. Orpet

Child   Ages 6-12

Purpose: Evaluates the development of sensory-motor skills in children. Diagnoses areas of sensory-motor development requiring special attention.

Description: 12-item task-performance test providing scaled scores on five factors: hand-eye coordination, strength, balance, visually guided movement, and flexibility. Norms by sex are provided for normally developing children ages 6-12. The manual provides a rationale for the battery, statistical information, and instructions for administration and scoring. The equipment required for the test can be assembled or built from specifications provided in the manual or purchased in the standard equipment kit, which includes the manual, 50 recording sheets, wooden blocks, block transfer kit, bean bags, floor targets, carpenter's rule, and brackets for walking board. The equipment kit does not include the two 12-foot 2x4's and stopwatch that are required. Examiner required. Suitable for group use.

Untimed: Single child 20 minutes; group of 3 or 4 45 minutes

Scoring: Examiner evaluated

Cost: Standard equipment kit $96.50; manual $5.00; 50 recording sheets $5.25

Publisher: Consulting Psychologists Press, Inc.

GIBSON SPIRAL MAZE
H.B. Gibson

All ages

Purpose: Measures psychomotor performance in both children and adults. Used for screening and clinical diagnosis.

Description: Paper-pencil test measuring psychomotor performance. The test consists of a printed design on a large card that provides a "maze" for the subject to run under timed conditions. Scores of quickness and accuracy are obtained

---

through a standard marking procedure defined in the manual. Characteristic deviations from normal psychomotor performance are used to identify behavioral disturbances, such as maladjustment, delinquency, and mental ill-health. The test is restricted to senior staff members of any recognized medical or educational institution, medical doctors, and BPS and APA members. Examiner required. Not suitable for group use.

BRITISH PUBLISHER

Untimed: Not available

Scoring: Hand key

Cost: Specimen set £1.65; 20 test cards £3.00 plus VAT; manual £1.25

Publisher: Hodder & Stoughton

LATERAL AWARENESS AND DIRECTIONALITY TEST (LAD)
August J. Mauser and Joseph F. Loackavitch

Child, adolescent
Grades 1-12

Purpose: Determines lateral awareness and directional skills of elementary and secondary school children. Used to identify high-risk, medium-risk, and low-risk students for possible program intervention.

Description: 35-illustration paper-pencil test measuring right-left labeling ability at two levels: lateral awareness and directionality. Items range from single to double commands which require either a unilateral, contralateral, or cross diagonal response. Also measured are such spatial concepts as same direction, 180-degree inversion, 90-degree rotation, and person-to-person orientation. Materials consist of test plates, recording forms, a scoring template, and a manual, which includes information on screening, diagnosis, and potential program modification. Examiner required. Suitable for group use.

Untimed: 20 minutes

Scoring: Hand key

Cost: Test kit $32.00

Publisher: United Educational Services, Inc.

LINCOLN-OSERETSKY MOTOR DEVELOPMENT SCALE
William Sloan

Child, adolescent

Purpose: Measures motor development of children. Used to supplement information obtained from other techniques concerning intellectual, social, emotional, and physical development.

Description: 36-item task-assessment of a child's motor development. The areas covered are static coordination, dynamic coordination, speed of movement and asynkinesia (finger dexterity), eye-hand coordination, and gross activity of the hands, arms, legs, and trunk. Both unilateral and bilateral tasks are involved. The test items, arranged in order of difficulty, include walking backwards, crouching on tiptoe, standing on one foot, touching nose, touching fingertips, tapping rhythmically with feet and fingers, jumping over a rope, finger movement, standing heel to toe, close and open hands alternately, making dots, catching a ball, making a ball, winding thread, balancing a rod crosswise, describing circles in the air, tapping, placing coins and matchsticks, jump and turn about, putting matchsticks in a box, winding thread while walking, throwing a ball, sorting matchsticks, drawing lines, cutting circle, putting coins in a box, tracing mazes, balancing on tiptoe, tapping with feet and fingers, jumping and touching heels, tapping feet and describing circles, standing on one foot, jumping and clapping, balancing on tiptoe and opening and closing hands, and balancing a rod vertically. The manual includes a complete analysis of test results obtained from boys and girls ages 6-14 for each item of the scale; percentages passing each item at each age level; correlation of item-scores with age; percentile norms of both sexes, separately and combined; and odd-even reliability for boys and girls. Examiner required. Not suitable for group use.

Untimed: Not available

Scoring: Examiner evaluated

Cost: Complete kit (test materials, 50 record blanks, manual) $105.50

Publisher: Stoelting Company

MEMORY-FOR-DESIGNS TEST (MFD)

Refer to page 50.

MINNESOTA SPATIAL RELATIONS TEST

*American Guidance Service
Test Division*

**Adolescent, adult
Grades 10 and over**

Purpose: Assesses an individual's ability to visualize spatial relations. Used for vocational education, rehabilitation counseling, and personnel selection.

Description: Manual test measuring an individual's accurate perception of relationships and speed in manipulating three-dimensional objects. The test requires four form boards, A-B and C-D paired. Each board has a different arrangement of 58 cutouts, into which blocks of various shapes are fitted. The individual transfers blocks from Board A to the proper places on Board B and then repeats the process with Boards C and D. The kit includes four boards, blocks, two carrying cases, 50 record forms, and a manual. Time scores are converted to standard scores and percentile ranks, and error scores are expressed as a percentile rank. Examiner required. Not suitable for group use.

Timed: 10-20 minutes
Scoring: Examiner evaluated
Cost: Complete $595.00
Publisher: American Guidance Service

MKM PICTURE ARRANGEMENT TEST (PAT)

Leland Michael and James W. King

Child   Grades K-6

Purpose: Measures the extent to which the subject places information and objects in the left-right sequence common to the United States. Useful in diagnosing poor reading skills and learning disabilities related to directionality problems.

Description: Five-item visual-manual sequencing test in which a poem entitled "A Great Gray Elephant" is read to the subject. Five pictures illustrating the poem are placed before the subject in random order, and as the poem is read, the subject is asked to place the pictures in the order in which they occur in the poem. The examiner records the subject's actions. A left-right movement is expected. Examiner required. Not suitable for group use.

Untimed: 3 minutes
Scoring: Examiner evaluated
Cost: Complete (instruction sheet, 5 picture cards, 5 poems) $10.00
Publisher: MKM

MOBILE VOCATIONAL EVALUATION (MVE)

Refer to page 830.

MOTOR SKILLS INVENTORY (MSI)

John Aulenta

Child

Purpose: Evaluates the motor functioning of normal and handicapped preschool and primary-age children. Establishes motor functioning age levels and identifies children needing further evaluation. Used by trained diagnostic personnel as part of a comprehensive psychological or developmental evaluation.

Description: 85-item paper-pencil observational inventory assessing fine-motor (40 items) and gross-motor (45 items) skill development. Test items represent individual motor abilities (e.g., "lifts cup with handle" or "turns single pages in book"), which are scored "plus" or "minus" according to the child's success or failure at performing the described task. Test items for the two areas are presented in order of normal development. Basal and ceiling levels are established using a guideline of five consecutive successes or failures. Examiners are encouraged to utilize information gained from parental report and results of other tests in completing the inventory. Intended for use with children ages six months to seven years, the inventory also may be used with older handicapped children functioning within that developmental age range. Results of the inventory can contribute significantly to the diagnosis of retardation, developmental language delays, learning disability, specific motor deficit, and general or specific developmental immaturities and clarify developmental discrepancies among cognitive, linguistic, social, and motor areas. The manual includes directions for administration and interpretation of results. Self-administered by examiner. Not suitable for group use.

Untimed: 5-15 minutes

Scoring: Examiner evaluated

Cost: Complete test kit (manual, 15 administration booklets) $9.00; manual $5.00; 15 administration booklets $5.00

Publisher: Stoelting Company

MOTOR-FREE VISUAL PERCEPTION TEST (MVPT)
Ronald R. Colarusso and Donald D. Hammill

Ages 4-8 and older individuals

Purpose: Assesses visual perception in children and older individuals who have motor problems. Used for screening, diagnostic, and research purposes, especially with individuals who are learning disabled, motorically impaired, physically handicapped, or mentally retarded.

Description: 36-item point-and-tell test in which the subject is shown a line drawing and asked to match the stimulus by pointing to one of a multiple-choice set of other drawings. Materials consist of test plates and recording forms. Examiner required. Not suitable for group use.

Untimed: 10 minutes

Scoring: Hand key

Cost: Manual $8.00; test plates $22.50; 50 recording forms $6.00

Publisher: Academic Therapy Publications

ONE-HOLE TEST LEVELS I AND II
Gavriel Salvendy and W. Douglas Seymour

Ages 7-96

Purpose: Measures the ability to learn new manipulative tasks. Identifies individuals who are able to learn new skills most rapidly.

Description: Multiple-item task-performance test assessing the ability to learn a new task requiring precise and repetitive manipulations. An apparatus is provided containing a power supply, photocell control, counting module, two recepticles, and a number of pins. The pins are automatically positioned in the recepticle nearest the subject, who grasps the pins one at a time and deposits them in the second recepticle seven inches away. Level I simply records the number of pins deposited per trial. Level II involves the use of stopclocks and other data collection devices to process "grasp" and "position" factors. Both levels can be administered with either 7- or 15-minute trials. Examiner required. Not suitable for group use.

Timed: 8-20 minutes

Scoring: Hand key

Cost: Level I test unit $250.00; Level II test unit $425.00

Publisher: Lafayette Instrument Company, Inc.

PHOTOELECTRIC ROTARY PURSUIT

Adolescent, adult Ages 15 and older

Purpose: Measures general perceptual motor learning across such parameters as handedness, transfer of training, and distribution of practice. Used for vocational evaluation, research, and classroom demonstration of learning principles.

Description: Manual nonverbal test in which the subject uses a rotary pursuit apparatus to follow a moving light around a pattern (square, circle, or triangle). The light moves in either a clockwise or counterclockwise direction at a fixed or variable speed for either a fixed time or a

---

fixed number of revolutions. "On target" time, hits, and total test time are measured. Examiner required. Not suitable for group use.

Untimed: Time not standardized

Scoring: Examiner evaluated

Cost: Photoelectric rotary pursuit $520.00; variable speed photoelectric rotary pursuit $740.00; variable speed photoelectric rotary pursuit with tachometer $785.00; basic accessory package $221.00; intermediate accessory package $579.50; deluxe package $789.00

Publisher: Lafayette Instrument Company, Inc.

THE PREVERBAL ASSESSMENT-INTERVENTION PROFILE (P.A.I.P.)
Refer to page 641.

THE PRIMARY VISUAL MOTOR TEST
Mary R. Haworth

Mental ages 4-8

Purpose: Assesses visual-motor functioning in preschool and primary-grade children. Used as a rough measure of intellectual performance skills in deaf or speech-handicapped children.

Description: Multiple-task nonverbal test in which the examiner presents 16 geometrical and simple representational designs for the child to copy in designated rectangular spaces marked off on the test sheets. The test screens for reading-related difficulties, determines the extent of visual-motor deficiencies in retarded children, and assesses the general level of functioning in deaf or speech-handicapped children. Test data are also available on 130 psychotic children ages 6-12. The test must be administered by persons trained in test administration and interpretation. Suitable for group use. Examiner required.

Untimed: 10-15 minutes

Scoring: Examiner evaluated

Cost: Manual $45.00; test cards $10.50; 100 tests $16.50; 50 scoring forms $24.00

Publisher: Grune & Stratton, Inc.

PURDUE PERCEPTUAL-MOTOR SURVEY (PPMS)
Eugene G. Roach and Newell C. Kephart

Child, adolescent Grades PreK-8

Purpose: Identifies children with perceptual-motor disabilities by tracing a child's development to the point where developmental dysfunction occurs. Assists teachers in developing remedial programs.

Description: 22-item task assessment measuring laterality, directionality, and perceptual-motor matching skills. The walking board and jumping tests measure balance and posture. The body image and differentiation tests include naming 10 parts of the body, imitation of movements, obstacle course, the Krauss-Weber test, and angels in the snow. A chalkboard test for rhythmic writing, ocular control, and form perception measures perceptual-motor matching skills. Examiner required. Not suitable for group use.

Untimed: Varies

Scoring: Examiner evaluated

Cost: Manual $18.00; score forms $20.00

Publisher: The Psychological Corporation

QUICK NEUROLOGICAL SCREENING TEST (QNST)
Refer to page 55.

THE RAIL-WALKING TEST
Refer to page 56.

REACTION TIME TESTING

Ages 5 and older

Purpose: Measures the reaction time component of perceptual motor coordination. Used for psychological research, drug screening, reaction training, and vocational guidance.

Description: Manual nonverbal test in which the subject faces various stimulus presentations and trials incorporated with the stimulus-response device controlled by the examiner, who is seated across the table. The devices vary in resolution, stimulus presentation, and response requirements and test auditory or visual simple reaction time, visual discrimination reaction time, and reaction-movement time. Examiner required. Not suitable for group use.

Untimed: 1-15 minutes

Scoring: Examiner evaluated

Cost: Multi-Choice Reaction Time Apparatus 1/100th second $515.00, with ready signal $620.00, with Digital 1/1000th seconds $1,035.00, with Digital 1/100th seconds and voice activated RT control $1,135.00; Reaction Movement Timer 1/100th second $980.00, Digital 1/1000th second $1,545.00

Publisher: Lafayette Instrument Company, Inc.

RECEPTIVE-EXPRESSIVE OBSERVATION (REO)
Joan M. Smith

Ages 6-adult

Purpose: Assesses simple memory and memory coding across sensory channels: visual-motor, visual-vocal, auditory-vocal, and auditory-motor. Identifies student deficiencies in the perceptual areas addressed.

Description: Multiple-task test assessing performance in labeling, discrimination, sequencing, and short-term memory. Eighteen visual-vocal and 18 visual-motor cards are provided. The examiner reads each item to the subject, and the subject answers with auditory-vocal and auditory-motor responses. Items are increased progressively in length in each of the four cross-channel perceptual areas. Responses are observed and entered on the recording form. Conversion tables are provided for scores. The test manual includes suggestions for remediation. Examiner required. Not suitable for group use.

Untimed: 15 minutes

Scoring: Examiner evaluated

Cost: Test kit (manual, two sets of visual-motor and visual-vocal cards, spirit response form) $45.00

Publisher: Learning Time Products

RILEY MOTOR PROBLEMS INVENTORY
Refer to page 59.

ROEDER MANIPULATIVE APTITUDE TEST
Wesley S. Roeder

Adolescent, adult
Ages 15 and older

Purpose: Assesses eye, hand, and finger coordination. Used to screen employees and trainees for jobs requiring eye-hand coordination, including typing, mechanics, radio/TV repair, machinists, draftsmen, and machine operators.

Description: Task-performance test measuring speed and dexterity in executing certain movements with the hands, arms, and fingers, particularly thrusting and twisting movements. Four tasks are provided using the following materials: one styrene-plexiglass board with T-Bar, four trays containing 10 sockets each, and a supply of rods, caps, washers, and nuts. Part 1 requires the subject to insert and twist a rod into a socket on the board and place a cap on the top of each rod, completing as many assemblies as possible in three minutes. Part 2 involves alternately sliding a washer and nut on each side of the T-bar as quickly as possible for 40 seconds. Part 3 repeats the washer/nut task, using the left hand only. Part 4 repeats the washer/nut task with the right hand only. Examiner required. Suitable for group use (limited only by availability of materials).

Timed: 5 minutes

Scoring: Hand key

Cost: Board and parts $110.00; 50 score sheets $5.00

Publisher: Lafayette Instrument Company, Inc.

SOUTHERN CALIFORNIA MOTOR ACCURACY TEST, REVISED 1980

Refer to page 63.

THE SOUTHERN CALIFORNIA ORDINAL SCALES OF DEVELOPMENT

California State Department of Education: Diagnostic School for the Neurologically Handicapped, Southern California

All ages

Purpose: Assesses all levels of Piagetian development from sensorimotor through formal operations. Used especially with multihandicapped, developmentally delayed, and learning disordered children for comparative assessments, ability-grouping, research, and IEP development.

Description: Six separately bound scales measuring the quality of the child's sensory and information processing in the following areas: cognition, communication, social-affective behavior, practical abilities, fine-motor abilities, and gross-motor abilities. The procedures are easily adapted to meet the needs of each child, and require no special setting. Examiner required. Not suitable for group use.

Untimed: 45-90 minutes per scale

Scoring: Examiner evaluated; hand key

Cost: Scale of Cognition $20.00; Scale of Communication $25.00; Scale of Social-Affective Behavior, Scale of Practical Abilities, Scale of Fine Motor Abilities, Scale of Gross Motor Abilities $18.00 each; complete set $117.00

Publisher: Foreworks Publications

SOUTHERN CALIFORNIA SENSORY INTEGRATION TESTS (SCSIT)

A. Jean Ayers

Child   Ages 4-10

Purpose: Measures an individual's ability to see, touch, and move in a coordinated manner. Used to identify the degree and type of disorder often associated with learning and emotional problems, minimal brain dysfunction, and cerebral palsy.

Description: 17 paper-pencil and task-assessment tests measuring visual, tactile, and kinesthetic perception and several different types of motor performance. The battery includes the following tests: Space Visualization, Figure-Ground Perception, Position in Space, Design Copying, Motor Accuracy (Revised), Kinesthesia, Manual Form Perception, Finger Identification, Graphesthesia, Localization of Tactile Stimuli, Double Tactile Stimuli Perception, Imitation of Postures, Crossing Mid-Line of Body, Bilateral Motor Coordination, Right-Left Discrimination, Standing Balance (Eyes Open), and Standing Balance (Eyes Closed). Materials for the following tests may be ordered separately: Space Visualization, Figure-Ground Perception, Position in Space, Design Copying, Motor Accuracy Test (Revised), Form Perception, and Kinesthesia. The Protocol Booklet is used for recording and calculating the scores for all tests except Motor Accuracy and Design Copying. Additional materials available include a profile of standard scores, manual (revised 1980), carrying case, and 58-page book interpreting the battery. Normative data is provided at 6-month intervals for children ages 4-10. Use of the battery is restricted to qualified personnel. Examiner required. Not suitable for group use.

Untimed: 1½ hours

Scoring: Hand key; examiner evaluated

Cost: Complete set of 17 tests and accompanying material $197.00

Publisher: Western Psychological Services

STANDARDIZED ROAD-MAP TEST OF DIRECTION SENSE

John Money

Ages 7-adult

Purpose: Assesses directional orientation in children and adults. Used as a quick measure of disability and as part of a full neuropyschological battery to evaluate children suspected of underachieving.

Description: With a marker, the student traces a path through a maze consisting of

32 possible turns. Scoring is on the basis of items-correct-to-total. Conversion tables for percentiles are provided for males and females for three age groupings within the 7-18-year-old range. Examiner required. Not suitable for group use.

Untimed: 10 minutes

Scoring: Hand key

Cost: Manual $10.00; 50 test forms $6.00; scoring template $2.00

Publisher: United Educational Services, Inc.

SYSTEM OF MULTICULTURAL PLURALISTIC ASSESSMENT (SOMPA)
Refer to page 514.

TEST OF GROSS MOTOR DEVELOPMENT (TGMD)
Dale A. Ulrich

Child   Ages 3-10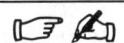

Purpose: Assesses common motor skills of children. Used for educational planning and research and to evaluate existing special education programs.

Description: Multiple-item task-performance test consisting of two subtests. The Locomotor Skills subtest measures the run, gallop, hop, skip, horizontal jump, leap, and slide. The Object Control Skills subtest measures the two-hand strike, stationary bounce, catch, kick, and overhand throw. The examiner records observations in a student record book. Examiner required. Not suitable for group use.

Timed: 15 minutes

Scoring: Examiner evaluated

Cost: Complete kit (examiner's manual, 50 student record books) $36.00

Publisher: Pro-Ed

TEST OF MOTOR IMPAIRMENT— HENDERSON REVISION (TOMI-R)
D.H. Stott, F.A. Moyes, and S.E. Henderson

Child   Ages 5 and older

Purpose: Identifies and describes impairments of gross and fine-motor functioning in children.

Description: Multiple-task test measuring a child's ability to perform tasks requiring manual dexterity, ball skills, and dynamic and static balance. Two separate tasks are provided in each area. The test also assesses factors of attitude and temperament as they influence performance. Materials include manual, record form, and other task aids. Examiner required. Not suitable for group use.

Timed: 35-40 minutes

Scoring: Examiner evaluated

Cost: Complete set $225.00

Publisher: The Psychological Corporation

TEST OF VISUAL-MOTOR SKILLS (TVMS)
Morrison F. Gardner

Child   Ages 2-13

Purpose: Provides an accurate measurement of a child's eye-hand coordination (how a child motorically translates with his hand what he visually perceives). Helps determine whether a child has a neurosensory integration dysfunction. Used by teachers, occupational therapists, psychologists, pediatricians, resource specialists, counselors, and other professionals.

Description: 26 designs in a single test booklet, arranged progressively according to difficulty, assessing a child's eye-hand-motor accuracy, motor control, motor coordination, and/or gestalt interpretation. Examiner required. Suitable for group use.

Untimed: 3-5 minutes

Scoring: Hand key; examiner evaluated

Cost: Kit (manual, 15 test booklets with 26 designs each) $29.00

Publisher: Children's Hospital of San Francisco, Publications Department

---

Special Education: Gifted

CARTOON CONSERVATION SCALES (CCS)

**Child, adolescent
Grades K-6**

Purpose: Assesses students' intellectual development.

Description: Multiple-item paper-pencil neo-Piagetian test identifying gifted or special education students. The scales may be scored in two ways. The first method is based on the simple addition of the correct responses within and across subscales. The second method is based on probability and is used to determine which of the subscales the student actually passed. The test has no cultural or language bias and may be administered in any language to individuals or small groups. Examiner required. Suitable for group use.

Untimed: 20-25 minutes

Scoring: Hand key

Cost: Complete kit $79.00

Publisher: Linguametrics Group

CREATIVITY ASSESSMENT PACKET
Frank E. Williams

**Child, adolescent
Ages 6-18**

Purpose: Measures cognitive and affective factors related to the creative process. Identifies gifted students.

Description: Two multiple-item paper-pencil tests assessing eight general areas of cognitive and affective behavior. The Test of Divergent Thinking measures fluency, flexibility, elaboration, and originality. Test items require semantic transformation, thus combining right-left brain abilities. The Divergent Feelings Test measures curiosity, imagination, complexity, and risk-taking (affective traits measured in a verbal analysis mode also requiring left-right brain synthesis).

A parent-teacher inventory (the Williams scale) asks parents and teachers to rate each child on various manifestations of the eight subscores, providing a means of comparing observed behavior with measured potential. The manual includes directions for administering and scoring the tests, scoring templates, and a list of teaching strategies related to the creative processes measured by the test. On the back of the Test of Divergent Thinking is a pupil assessment matrix for profiling results of all three tests. The tests are available in two alternate forms, A and B. Examiner required. Suitable for group use.

Untimed: Varies

Scoring: Examiner evaluated

Cost: Complete kit (manual, 25 each Form A and B divergent thinking tests, 25 divergent feelings tests, 25 Williams scale booklets) $29.95

Publisher: D.O.K. Publishers, Inc.

CREATIVITY ATTITUDE SURVEY (CAS)
Charles E. Schaefer

Child   Grades 4-6

Purpose: Assesses attitudes important for creative thinking. Used in the evaluation of training programs in creativity.

Description: 32-item paper-pencil test measuring five dimensions associated with creative thinking: confidence in own ideas; appreciation of fantasy; theoretical and aesthetic orientation; openness to impulse expression; and desire for novelty. The items are statements to which the child indicates agreement or disagreement. Examiner required. Suitable for group use.

Untimed: 10 minutes

Scoring: Hand key

Cost: Specimen set $4.50; manual $4.00; 25 tests $13.50

Publisher: Psychologists and Educators, Inc.

CREATIVITY CHECKLIST (CCH)
David L. Johnson

Grades K-graduate school

Purpose: Evaluates creativity in people of all educational levels, in any social setting. Used in school, business, family, free play, and training settings to identify gifted individuals and to evaluate creativity programs.

Description: 8-item paper-pencil questionnaire used by an examiner to record observations of eight categories of the subject's creative behavior. The categories are sensitivity or preference for complexity, fluency, flexibility, resourcefulness, constructional skill, ingenuity or productiveness, independence, and positive self-referencing behavior. The examiner (parent, teacher, counselor) indicates the extent to which he or she has observed (consistently, frequently, occasionally, seldom, never) examples of these characteristics in the individual being evaluated. The sum of the eight items provides a total creativity score. Cut-off points for different levels of creative performance are provided. Examiner required. Suitable for group use.

Untimed: 15 minutes

Scoring: Examiner evaluated

Cost: Complete kit (30 record forms, manual) $9.50

Publisher: Stoelting Company

CREATIVITY TESTS FOR CHILDREN (CT)
Refer to page 468.

EBY ELEMENTARY IDENTIFICATION INSTRUMENT (EEII)
Judy W. Eby

Child, adolescent
Grades K-8

Purpose: Measures academic talent and gifted behavior. Used to select students for gifted programs.

Description: Multiple-item paper-pencil inventories assessing academic performance and classroom behavior in order to identify gifted students. The identification model consists of the following three components: general selection matrix, teacher recommendation form, and unit selection matrix. Together they provide a profile of the child's potential for academically challenging educational experiences. Examiner required. Suitable for group use.

Untimed: Varies

Scoring: Examiner evaluated

Cost: Test kit (manual, 50 general selection matrix forms, 50 teacher recommendation forms, 50 unit selection matrix forms) $20.00

Publisher: Slosson Educational Publications, Inc.

EVALUATING EDUCATIONAL PROGRAMS FOR INTELLECTUALLY GIFTED STUDENTS
Joanne Rand Whitmore

Child, adolescent
Grades K-12

Purpose: Evaluates educational programming for gifted students. Used by administrators, school psychologists, and teachers.

Description: Multiple-item paper-pencil process tool for evaluating whether programs for intellectually gifted students are meeting the students' needs, especially those needs that influence socioemotional and cognitive development. Educators may add their own specific curriculum content-related questions appropriate to the specific areas of giftedness of a particular student or the goals of a particular program. Examiner required. Suitable for group use.

Untimed: Varies

Scoring: Examiner evaluated

Cost: Complete kit $20.00

Publisher: D.O.K. Publishers, Inc.

GIFTED AND TALENTED SCALE

Child   Grades 4-6

Purpose: Assesses abstract and reasoning abilities in gifted children. Can be used to screen for placement.

Description: Paper-pencil multiple-choice test of five categories of abstract and reasoning abilities: numerical reasoning, vocabulary, synonyms and antonyms, similarities, and analogies. The test was normed on students in gifted programs in Grades 4-6. Examiner/self-administered. Suitable for group use.

Untimed: Not available

Scoring: Hand key

Cost: Complete kit (manual, 25 pupil record forms) $50.00

Publisher: Dallas Educational Services

GIFTED AND TALENTED SCREENING FORM (GTSF)
David L. Johnson

**Child, adolescent
Grades K-9**

Purpose: Identifies gifted and talented children. Used in educational, family, and social settings and by school districts initiating formal, federally funded programs.

Description: 24-item paper-pencil inventory measuring the following talent areas: academics, intelligence, creativity, leadership, visual-performing arts, and psychomotor ability. The respondent (parent, teacher, or anyone familiar with the child) is asked to indicate the extent to which he or she has observed (consistently, frequently, occasionally, seldom, never) gifted and talented characteristics in the child being evaluated. Cut-off criterion points are suggested for each of the talent areas. Examiner required. Suitable for group use.

Untimed: 20 minutes

Scoring: Examiner evaluated

Cost: Complete kit (30 record forms, score keys, manual) $14.25

Publisher: Stoelting Company

GROUP INVENTORY FOR FINDING CREATIVE TALENT (GIFT)
Sylvia B. Rimm

Child   Grades K-6

Purpose: Assesses creativity. Used to identify gifted students.

Description: Multiple-item paper-pencil test of interests and attitudes related to creativity. The test yields the following dimension scores: Imagination, Independence, and Many Interests. Validation groups include minorities, urban and suburban students, learning disabled, and gifted students. Examiner required. Suitable for group use.

Untimed: 20-40 minutes

Scoring: Machine scored

Cost: Specimen set $8.00; class set of 30 $35.00 (indicate grade level); scoring included in price

Publisher: Educational Assessment Service, Inc.

GROUP INVENTORY FOR FINDING INTERESTS (GIFFI)
Sylvia B. Rimm and Gary A. Davis

**Child, adolescent
Grades 6-12**

Purpose: Assesses creativity in children. Used to identify gifted children.

Description: Multiple-item paper-pencil test of interests and attitudes related to creativity. The test yields the following dimension scores: Creative Art and Writing, Confidence, Imagination, Challenge-Inventiveness, and Many Interests. Validation groups include minorities, urban and suburban students, learning disabled, and gifted children. Examiner required. Suitable for group use.

Untimed: 20-40 minutes

Scoring: Machine scored

Cost: Specimen set $8.00; class set of 30 $50.00 (indicate grade level); scoring included in price

Publisher: Educational Assessment Service, Inc.

IDENTI-FORM: IDENTIFICATION, ASSESSMENT, AND BEYOND
Patricia Weber and Cathy Battaglia

Adult

Purpose: Assesses students for educational placement. Used by educators primarily to identify gifted students.

Description: Multiple-item prescriptive assessment system incorporating test, performance, and anecdotal data. The system is used for developing individualized educational programs and selecting students for programs for gifted children. Information also can be used for educational planning for students not selected for special programs for the gifted. Examiner required. Suitable for group use.

Untimed: Varies
Scoring: Examiner evaluated
Cost: $19.95
Publisher: D.O.K. Publishers, Inc.

KHATENA-TORRANCE CREATIVE PERCEPTION INVENTORY
Joe Khatena and E. Paul Torrance

Adolescent, adult
Ages 13 and older

Purpose: Identifies creative people and diagnoses their strengths and weaknesses. Used to select individuals for special education programs and job assignments and to evaluate the effects of instruction that includes creative components.

Description: Two 50-item paper-pencil subtests evaluating individual creativity by measuring the following biographical components: What Kind of Person Are You? (WKOPAY) and Something About Myself (SAM). WKOPAY uses 50 pairs of words arranged in forced-choice format and requires the individual to choose from each pair the word that is most true for himself. The word pairs are chosen to represent bipolar characteristics (socially desirable versus undesirable, creative versus noncreative) and to measure the following personality characteristics: acceptance of authority, self-confidence, inquisitiveness, awareness of others, and

disciplined imagination. SAM presents 50 statements and asks the takers to check those that apply to themselves. The statements reflect potential for creativity in three areas (personality traits, use of creative thinking strategies, and creative productions) and measure the following scales: Environmental Sensitivity, Initiative, Self Strength, Intellectuality, Individuality, and Artistry. Together, the two subtests provide a creative index and an individual score for each of the characteristics measured. Examiner required. Suitable for group use.

Untimed: 5-15 minutes
Scoring: Examiner evaluated
Cost: Complete kit (manual, 30 WKOPAY forms, 30 SAM forms, 30 scoring worksheets) $44.50
Publisher: Stoelting Company

LANGDON ADULT INTELLIGENCE TEST
Refer to page 26.

MATRIX ANALOGIES TEST— EXPANDED FORM (MAT-EF)
Refer to page 508.

MATRIX ANALOGIES TEST— SHORT FORM (MAT-SF)
Refer to page 509.

PRESCHOOL AND KINDERGARTEN INTEREST DESCRIPTOR (PRIDE)
Sylvia B. Rimm

Child   Ages 3-6

Purpose: Identifies creatively gifted preschool and kindergarten children. Used for academic placement in gifted programs.

Description: 50-item paper-pencil inventory in which parents assess their child's attitudes and interests by responding "no," "to a small extent," "average," "more than average," or "definitely" to each item. Scores are provided on four dimensions: many interests, independence-perseverance, imagination-playfulness, and originality. All scoring is completed by Educational Assessment Service, Inc. Examiner required. Suitable for group use.

Untimed: 20-35 minutes
Scoring: Computer scored
Cost: Specimen set $6.00
Publisher: Educational Assessment Service, Inc.

SCALES FOR RATING THE BEHAVIORAL CHARACTERISTICS OF SUPERIOR STUDENTS (SRBCSS)

Joseph S. Renzulli, Linda H. Smith, Alan J. White, Carolyn M. Callahan, and Robert K. Hartman

Child, adolescent

Purpose: Assesses the behavioral characteristics related to the objectives of gifted and talented elementary and junior high-school programs. Used to supplement measures of intelligence, achievement, and creativity in selecting students for gifted and talented programs.

Description: 95-item paper-pencil inventory consisting of 10 subscales, each of which assesses a different dimension of behavioral characteristics related to gifted and talented educational objectives. The following 10 dimensions are evaluated: learning, motivation, creativity, leadership, art, music, dramatics, planning, precise communication, and expressive communication. Each scale consists of 4-15 statements describing behaviors attributed to gifted and talented students. The teacher rates each item on a 4-point scale from "seldom" to "almost always," reflecting the degree to which the presence or absence of each characteristic has been observed. The 10 subscales represent 10 distinct sets of behavioral characteristics; therefore, no total score is derived. Only scales relevant to program objectives should be selected for use in a given program. Self-administered by teacher. Suitable for group use.

Untimed: Varies
Scoring: Examiner evaluated
Cost: Test kit $7.95; additional sets of 100 tests $49.95
Publisher: Creative Learning Press, Inc.

SCALES OF CREATIVITY AND LEARNING ENVIRONMENT (SCALE)

Steven W. Slosson

Child, adolescent
Grades 1-12

Purpose: Aids teachers in recognizing gifted attributes and characteristics in students.

Description: 170-item descriptive rating scale composed of the Scale of Gifted Students and the Scale of Divergent/Convergent Thinking. The Scale of Gifted Students assesses attributes and characteristics in the following areas: cognitive (19 items), comprehension (15 items), language (11 items), affective (14 items), behavioral (13 items), problem-solving (21 items), and hobbies and play (12 items). The Scale of Divergent/Convergent Thinking assesses attributes and characteristics in six areas: knowledge (9 items), ability (9 items), task commitment (15 items), synthesis (12 items), creativity (11 items), and evaluation (9 items). Raw scores are converted to ordinal scale scores. Ratings are based on a 5-point Likert scale and month-long observation of student behavior. Examiner required. Not suitable for group use.

Timed: 10 minutes
Scoring: Examiner evaluated
Cost: Complete kit (manual, 25 of each scale in vinyl binder) $33.00
Publisher: Slosson Educational Publications, Inc.

THE SIMILES TEST

Charles E. Schaefer

Child, adolescent

Purpose: Identifies children and adolescents who have creative literary talent. Used in educational programs designed to foster creativity and to study the relationship between creativity, personality, and styles of thought.

Description: 10-item paper-pencil test in which the subject is asked to provide three different endings to each of 10 incomplete simile forms that appeal to a variety of senses and emotions (e.g., "The young girl was as playful as . . ."). Each completion is scored on a 6-point scale for originality. The uniqueness and aptness of a response determines the originality scoring weights. Numerous examples of responses falling within each of the scoring cateogries are provided. Materials include the manual, scoring sheets, and two separate forms. Examiner required. Suitable for group use.

Untimed: 15 minutes

Scoring: Hand key; examiner evaluated

Cost: Examination kit $12.00

Publisher: Research Psychologists Press, Inc.

SOCIAL INTERACTION AND CREATIVITY IN COMMUNICATION SYSTEM (SICCS)
David L. Johnson

Grades 1 and above

Purpose: Evaluates creativity, leadership, and communication skills of students from elementary school through college. Used to identify gifted and talented individuals who might be overlooked due to low academic achievement.

Description: Multiple-item paper-pencil inventory providing a system of observation, recording, encoding, and analysis of creativity, leadership, and communication skills, including appraisal (expressing a conclusion); prescriptive (expression of concern for control); informational (providing information about characteristics); questioning (asking for response from others); self-reference (making reference to one's own characteristics); self-initiated (spontaneous or uninitiated); productivity (listening or reading the setting dialogue); and quantity (number of verbal acts). The system has been used in a variety of educational, business, training, therapeutic, play, organizational, and community settings. It also has been applied by regular classroom and special education teachers to a variety of work/ setting problems. Examiner required. Suitable for group use.

Untimed: Not available

Scoring: Examiner evaluated

Cost: Complete kit $14.25

Publisher: Stoelting Company

SOI PRIMARY FORM (FORM P)
Refer to page 513.

SOI-LEARNING ABILITIES TEST: SCREENING FORM FOR ATYPICAL GIFTED
Mary Meeker

Grades 2-adult

Purpose: Identifies gifted students who do not fit the typical gifted pattern of high semantic and verbal abilities. Used primarily with minority, culturally different populations, and disadvantaged children who do not enter school with expected verbal/language concepts.

Description: 161-item paper-pencil set of 10 subtests selected from the SOI-LA Test, which contains 26 subtests measuring structure of intellect abilities: constancy of objects in space (CFS), understanding abstract information (CSR), auditory attention (MSU— auditory), judging similarities and matching of concepts (EFC), word recognition and speed of reading (NST), psychomotor readiness (NFU), auditory concentration for sequencing (MSS— auditory), judgment of arithmetic similarities (ESC), and symbolic problem solving (NSI). The examiner may begin with any subtest; the test may be given in parts on different days. The test is based on the Structure of Intellect Theory of Human Intelligence. Results reflect students' intellectual abilities rather than knowledge of content. The test is recommended for use when the whole SOI-LA Test cannot be administered. The entire SOI-LA Test should be administered when developing comprehensive educational programs. Examiner required. Suitable for group use.

Timed: 3-10 minutes per subtest

Scoring: Hand key; may be computer scored

Cost: Contact publisher

Publisher: M & M Systems

SOI-LEARNING ABILITIES TEST: SCREENING FORM FOR GIFTED
Mary Meeker

Grades 2-adult

Purpose: Screens for gifted students as potential candidates for gifted educational programs. Identifies children at risk for learning problems and is used to develop educational plans.

Description: 155-item paper-pencil test identifying children from larger populations or groups who show gifted abilities and should be considered for gifted programs. The 12 subtests measure visual closurer (16 items), verbal relations (25 items), visual attending and auditory attention (4 items each), word recognition and speed of reading (27 items), creativity with things (1 item), vocabulary (30 items), understanding extended verbal information (18 items), visual concentration for sequencing and auditory concentration for sequencing (4 items each), symbolic problem solving (21 items), and creativity with words and ideas (1 item). The test is recommended for use when the entire SOI-LA Test cannot be administered. Examiner required. Suitable for group use.

Timed: 3-10 minutes per subtest

Scoring: Hand key

Cost: Test booklet $1.90

Publisher: Western Psychological Services

A SURVEY OF STUDENTS' EDUCATIONAL TALENTS AND SKILLS (ASSETS)
Grand Rapids Public School System

Child   Grades K-6

Purpose: Identifies gifted and talented students in order to individualize study programs and planning and to help parents and teachers discuss students' needs.

Description: 35-item paper-pencil test in three parts: one for the student, one for the parent, and one for the teacher. The students respond to statements as "almost," "sometimes," and "never" and

fill in blanks about their favorite books, hobbies, and activities. Self-administered. Suitable for group use.

Untimed: 40 minutes

Scoring: Computer scored

Cost: Specimen set $5.95; 30 tests specify early (Grades K-3) or later (Grades 4-6) elementary $39.60

Publisher: Learning Publications

TEST OF CREATIVE POTENTIAL (TCP)
R. Hoepfner and J. Hemenway

Grades 2-adult

Purpose: Measures general creative potential. Used for individual and program evaluation and for research.

Description: Multiple-item paper-pencil examination in three separate subtests assessing fluency, flexibility, and elaboration of verbal, symbolic, and figural materials. The Writing Words subtest asks the subject to write many words that mean the same as the given words. The Picture Decoration section requires the takers to elaborately decorate simplified pictures. The License Plate Words subtest asks the subject to make many words that have certain literal qualities. All items are open-ended and restricted only by time. Scoring procedures, reliability estimates, and norms have been developed on samples of subjects ranging from the second- to the twelfth-grade. Suitable for group use.

Timed: 22 minutes

Scoring: Hand key; examiner evaluated; scoring service available

Cost: Specimen set (specify form) $8.00; 35 tests $30.00; manual $4.00; 10 score rosters $3.00; scoring service $2.50 per booklet

Publisher: Monitor

THINKING CREATIVELY IN ACTION AND MOVEMENT (TCAM)
E. Paul Torrance

Child   Ages 3-8

Purpose: Identifies creative children. Used as part of a program to keep alive and further develop promising creative talent among young children.

Description: Nonverbal movement test assessing the creativity of young children, especially preschoolers. The responses are appropriate to the developmental characteristics of the younger child and are physical in nature, although verbal responses are acceptable. A standard scoring service (raw scores and T-scores are entered on scoring worksheets) is available. The manual contains a scoring guide for those who wish to self-score the test. Examiner required. Not suitable for group use.

Timed: 10-30 minutes

Scoring: Hand key; examiner evaluated

Cost: 20 tests $15.75

Publisher: Scholastic Testing Service, Inc.

THINKING CREATIVELY WITH SOUNDS AND WORDS (TCSW)
E. Paul Torrance, Joe Khantena, and Bert F. Cunnington

Grades 3-adult

Purpose: Measures ability to create images for words and sounds. Used to identify gifted and creative individuals and to teach imagery.

Description: Two-test battery assessing creativity by measuring the originality of ideas stimulated by abstract sounds and spoken onomatopoeic words. TCSW is a battery of two tests: Sounds and Images and Onomatopeia and Images. It is available in equivalent forms (A and B) on two levels: Level I (Grades 3-12) and Level II (Adult). Two long-playing records provide the stimuli for each level. The test may be scored by the examiner with the help of the scoring guide included in the manual; the standard scoring service is also available. Examiner required. Suitable for group use.

Timed: 30 minutes per test

Scoring: Hand key; examiner evaluated

Cost: 20 tests $13.20

Publisher: Scholastic Testing Service, Inc.

TORRANCE TESTS OF CREATIVE THINKING (TTCT)
E. Paul Torrance

Grades K-adult

Purpose: Assesses the ability to visualize and transform words, meanings, and patterns. Used to identify gifted, creative individuals.

Description: Multiple-task paper-pencil measure of an individual's creativity assessing four mental characteristics: fluency, flexibility, originality, and elaboration. The test is available in two editions. The Verbal TTCT uses seven word-based exercises. The Figural TTCT uses three picture-based exercises. The Verbal TTCT can be administered orally to students in Kindergarten through Grade 3 and is easily administered and scored. Individuals with psychometric training should interpret the subtest and total scores. "Streamlined" scoring of the figural forms of the overall test is available. This alternative scoring yields norm-referenced measures for fluency, originality, abstractness of titles, elaboration, and resistance to premature closure. It provides an overall Creativity Index and criterion-referenced scores for several creativity indicators. This test is available in two equivalent forms (A and B) for both the verbal and the figural editions. A scoring guide is available in the directions manual. The TTCT standard scoring service and streamlined scoring for figural tests are also available. Examiner required. Suitable for group use.

Timed: Figural TTCT 30 minutes; Verbal TTCT 45 minutes

Scoring: Examiner evaluated

Cost: 20 tests (specify edition and form) $13.20

Publisher: Scholastic Testing Service, Inc.

WATSON-GLASER CRITICAL THINKING APPRAISAL
Goodwin Watson and Edward M. Glaser

Adolescent, adult Grades 9 and above

Purpose: Assesses critical thinking abilities. Used for evaluation of gifted and talented individuals. Used to select candidates for positions in which analytic reasoning is an important part of the job.

Description: 80-item paper-pencil test measuring five aspects of the ability to think critically: inference, recognition of assumptions, deduction, interpretation, and evaluation of arguments. The subject responds to the exercises, which include problems, statements, arguments, and interpretation of material encountered on a daily basis. Two alternate and equivalent forms, A and B, are available. Examiner required. Suitable for group use.

Untimed: 50 minutes

Scoring: Hand key; may be machine scored

Cost: 35 tests $50.00; 35 OPScan answer documents $13.00; key $6.00; manual $7.00; class record $2.00 (specify form for each item ordered)

Publisher: The Psychological Corporation

Special Education: Learning Disabled

ADELPHI PARENT ADMINISTERED READINESS TEST (A.P.A.R.T.)

Refer to page 460.

ANALYTIC LEARNING DISABILITY ASSESSMENT (ALDA)

Thomas D. Gnagey and Patricia D. Gnagey

Child, adolescent
Ages 8-14

Purpose: Measures the skills necessary to read, spell, write, and work with numbers. Aids in the neuropsychological evaluation of learning disabled, educable mentally retarded, and behaviorally disturbed students.

Description: Multiple-item test assessing a student's strengths and weaknessess in 77 skills underlying basic school subjects. The strengths and weaknessess are matched with the student's most appro-

priate learning method for each subject: 11 reading methods, 23 spelling methods, 6 math computation methods, and 8 handwriting methods. The results are transferred to the Recommendation Pamphlet to create an individualized teaching plan providing specific procedures and methods for teachers. Materials include a scoring sheet, student worksheets with tear-out sections, an individualized student learning plan, a teacher recommendation pamphlet, also with tear-out sections, four colored scoring pencils, tape, and a straight-edge ruler in a leather carrying case. The test should not be used unless a learning dysfunction is suspected. Examiner required. Not suitable for group use.

Untimed: 75 minutes

Scoring: Hand key

Cost: Complete kit (test book, manual, scoring straight edge, four colored scoring pencils, tape, chalk, 20 complete testing forms, teaching plan, carrying case) $82.50

Publisher: Slosson Educational Publications, Inc.

ANN ARBOR LEARNING INVENTORY AND REMEDIATION PROGRAM

Refer to page 557.

THE ANSER SYSTEM-AGGREGATE NEUROBEHAVIORAL, STUDENT HEALTH AND EDUCATIONAL REVIEW

Melvin D. Levine

Child, adolescent
Ages 3-18

Purpose: Gathers information from parents and teachers for the educator or clinician who has questions about a child with learning and/or behavioral problems. Used in schools, health-care, and counseling centers to evaluate children with low severity, high prevalence disabilities.

Description: Three separate short-answer paper-pencil questionnaires for parents and school personnel to evaluate three age groups: Form 1 (ages 3-5), Form 2 (ages 6-11), and Form 3 (ages 12 and over). Form 4 is a self-administered student profile to be completed by students ages 9 and older. The parent questionnaire surveys family history, possible pregnancy problems, health problems, functional problems, early development, early educational experience, skills and interests, activity-attention problems, associated behaviors, and associated strengths. The school questionnaire covers the educational program and setting, special facilities available, and the results of previous testing. The self-administered Student Profile asks the student to rate himself on a series of statements in the following categories: fine motor, gross motor, memory, attention, language, general efficiency, visual-spatial processing, sequencing, general academic performance, and social interaction. Examiner required. Not suitable for group use.

Untimed: 30-60 minutes

Scoring: Examiner evaluated

Cost: Interpreter's guide 1 $5.50; specimen set (guide, sample of each form) $5.50

Publisher: Educators Publishing Service, Inc.

AUDITORY POINTING TEST
Janet B. Fudala, LuVern H. Kunze, and John D. Ross

All ages   Grades K-adult

Purpose: Measures short-term memory in children and adults through visual-motor responses. Used for remedial planning, especially with individuals with oral communication problems.

Description: Multiple-item cross-modal test in which the teacher/clinician shows the student 10 different stimulus cards, each of which contains eight simple line drawings (from a total stimulus pool of 32 separate drawings). The child is asked to point to the item mentioned by the examiner. Two forms are provided for test and retest. Scoring is on the basis of items-correct-to-ceiling. Norms are available for students in Grades K-5. The test has not been normed on older students and adults. Materials include recording forms,

summary sheets, set of test cards and plates, and manual. Examiner required. Not suitable for group use.

Untimed: 20 minutes

Scoring: Hand key

Cost: Manual $6.00; 25 recording forms (specify A or B) $6.00; 25 student summary sheets $3.00; set of test cards and plates $7.00

Publisher: United Educational Services, Inc.

BASIC NUMBER DIAGNOSTIC TEST
Refer to page 281.

BENDER-PURDUE REFLEX TEST AND TRAINING MANUAL
Refer to page 558.

BLOOMER LEARNING TEST (BLT)
Refer to page 502.

THE BODER TEST OF READING-SPELLING PATTERNS
Elena Boder and Sylvia Jarrico

All ages

Purpose: Differentiates specific reading disability (developmental dyslexia) from nonspecific reading disability through reading and spelling performance. Used to classify dyslexic readers into one of three subtypes, each with its own prognostic and remedial implications.

Description: 300-item paper-pencil tests of reading and spelling ability. The Reading Test uses 13 graded word lists of 20 words each, half of which are phonetic and half of which are nonphonetic. The words, which are presented flash and untimed, require sight vocabulary and phonic word analysis skills. The Spelling Test uses two individualized spelling lists (10 known words and 10 unknown) based on the student's reading performance. Both the reading and spelling tests tap the central visual and auditory processes required for reading and spelling, making it possible to diagnose developmental dyslexia by the joint analysis of reading and

---

spelling as interdependent functions. The results should be supplemented with testing that uses instructional materials to which the child already has been and will be exposed. Examiner required. Not suitable for group use.

Timed: 30 minutes

Scoring: Examiner evaluated

Cost: Complete kit $55.00

Publisher: Grune & Stratton, Inc.

THE BRIGANCE® DIAGNOSTIC ASSESSMENT OF BASIC SKILLS— SPANISH EDITION
Refer to page 367.

CAREER ASSESSMENT INVENTORIES: FOR THE LEARNING DISABLED (CAI)
Carol Weller and Mary Buchanan

LD students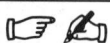

Purpose: Assesses the personality, abilities, and interests of learning-disabled students. Used to help learning-disabled students make intelligent and realistic career choices.

Description: Multiple-item paper-pencil test consisting of three inventories. The Attributes Inventory assesses the examinee's dominant personality characteristics. The Ability Inventory provides a profile of strengths and weaknesses across the auditory, visual, and motor areas. The Interest Inventory determines whether the examinee's career goals are realistic. The inventories are completed by the examiner after observing the examinee. However, the Interest Inventory may be completed by the examinee. Each inventory presents a list of descriptors that are evaluated using a numerical scale. The results are profiled and used to locate appropriate career options in the Job Finder section of the manual. The attributes and interests inventories are keyed to John I. Holland's theory of careers. Examiner required. Suitable for group use.

Untimed: 20-30 minutes

Scoring: Examiner evaluated

Cost: Test kit (manual, 50 attributes/ability inventories, 50 interest inventories) $38.00

Publisher: Academic Therapy Publications

COGNITIVE CONTROL BATTERY: THE FRUIT DISTRACTION TEST
Sebastiano Santostefano

Child, adolescent
Grades PreK-9

Purpose: Predicts the presence of learning disabilities and assesses the role of cognitive dysfunctions in school and adjustment problems.

Description: Verbal measure of an individual's ability to selectively attend even when there is interference from competing stimuli. The child resonds by naming a series of colors presented with and without distractions or contradictions. This test, along with the Leveling-Sharpening House Test and the Scattered Scanning Test, comprise the Cognitive Control Battery. Examiner required. Not suitable for group use.

Untimed: Not available

Scoring: Examiner required

Cost: Complete kit (stimulus materials, 100 record sheets, manual) $60.00

Publisher: Western Psychological Services

COGNITIVE CONTROL BATTERY: THE LEVELING-SHARPENING HOUSE TEST
Sebastiano Santostefano

Child   Grades PreK-5

Purpose: Predicts the presence of learning disabilities and assesses the role of cognitive dysfunctions in school adjustment problems.

Description: 60-item verbal-response measure of the manner in which a child organizes memory images and relates them to current perceptions. Items consist of two-dimensional line drawings of a house printed on separate cards. The child examines each card and describes how the drawing is different, if it is at all, from the previous card. This test, along with the Fruit Distraction Test and the Scattered Scanning Test, comprise the Cognitive Control Battery. Examiner required. Not suitable for group use.

Untimed: Not available

Scoring: Examiner evaluated

Cost: Complete kit (picture book, 100 record sheets, manual) $110.00

Publisher: Western Psychological Services

COGNITIVE CONTROL BATTERY: THE SCATTERED SCANNING TEST
Sebastiano Santostefano

Child, adolescent
Grades PreK-9

Purpose: Predicts the presence of learning disabilities and assesses the role of cognitive dysfunctions in school and adjustment problems.

Description: Paper-pencil test of an individual's preferred way of scanning information (broad vs. narrow). The child scans a display of geometric shapes randomly scattered over a sheet of paper and marks certain ones. This test, along with the Leveling-Sharpening House Test and the Fruit Distraction Test, comprise the Cognitive Control Battery. The test is available in two forms: Form 1 (ages 3-8) and Form 2 (ages 9-adult). Examiner required. Not suitable for group use.

Untimed: Not available

Scoring: Examiner evaluated

Cost: Complete kit (100 Form 1 test sheets, 25 Form 2 test sheets, 1 line measure, 100 record sheets, manual) $83.00

Publisher: Western Psychological Services

THE DEVEREUX ELEMENTARY SCHOOL BEHAVIOR RATING SCALE (DESB-II)
Refer to page 670.

DIAGNOSIS AND REMEDIATION OF HANDWRITING PROBLEMS (DRHP)
Denis H. Stott, Fred A. Moyes, and Sheila E. Henderson

Child, adolescent
Ages 7½-18

Purpose: Evaluates children's handwriting skills. Identifies children with possible learning disabilities. Used in regular classrooms, remedial clinics, and work with individual children.

Description: Multiple-item paper-pencil test assessing handwriting problems. Objective analysis of handwriting faults distinguishes between faults that should yield to regular teaching procedures and those of a more serious nature requiring special treatment. Also measures fine-motor problems due to unknown or suspected neurological dysfunction or associated with stress. The manual includes programs of remediation that can be adapted to the type of fault and ages of the children involved. Examiner required. Suitable for group use.
CANADIAN PUBLISHER

Untimed: 20 minutes

Scoring: Examiner evaluated

Cost: Contact publisher

Publisher: Brook Educational Publishing Ltd., Canada

DIAGNOSTIC ACHIEVEMENT BATTERY (DAB)
Refer to page 396.

DYSLEXIA DETERMINATION TEST (DDT)
John R. Griffin and Howard N. Walton

Child, adolescent
Grades 2-12

Purpose: Evaluates learning disorders in reading, writing, and spelling; differentiates dyslexic patterns from other disorders. Used for diagnostic purposes and to suggest appropriate remedial approaches.

Description: Multiple-item paper-pencil test measuring and evaluating a student's ability to decode and encode the English language. The test identifies seven specific dyslexic patterns and provides suggestions for therapy. The test may be used with students who have normal sensory-perceptual, cognitive, and motor abilities, yet have difficulty reading and writing. Examiner required. Not suitable for group use.

Untimed: 20-25 minutes

Scoring: Examiner evaluated

Cost: Complete kit (examiner's instructional manual; decoding word list booklet; instructional audiocassette; 60 interpretation recording forms; decoding patterns checklists, 30 Form A, 30 Form B; Therapy in Dyslexia and Reading Problems) $66.95

Publisher: Instructional Materials & Equipment Distributors

DYSLEXIA SCHEDULE
John McLeod

Child   Grades K-1

Purpose: Gathers relevant social data from parents or guardians about a child who has been referred to a specialist due to a reading disability.

Description: 89-item paper-pencil questionnaire completed by the parents or guardians before the child visits a clinic. The results provide the clinician with background data to help evaluate characteristics associated with childhood dyslexia before testing begins. Examiner required. Not suitable for group use.

Untimed: 20-30 minutes

Scoring: Examiner evaluated

Cost: 1-24 $1.00 each; 24 or more $0.90 each

Publisher: Educators Publishing Service, Inc.

THE DYSLEXIA SCREENING SURVEY (DSS)
Refer to page 41.

EARLY LEARNING ASSESSMENT AND DEVELOPMENT
Refer to page 472.

ENGLISH PICTURE VOCABULARY TESTS (EPVTS)
Refer to page 250.

EXPRESSIVE ONE-WORD PICTURE VOCABULARY TEST (EOWPVT)
Refer to page 504.

EXPRESSIVE ONE-WORD PICTURE VOCABULARY TEST: UPPER EXTENSION (EOWPVT: UE)
Refer to page 627.

FISHER LANGUAGE SURVEY AND WRITE-TO-LEARN PROGRAM, REVISED 1985
Alyce F. Fisher

Child   Grades 1-8

Purpose: Identifies students needing special education programs due to learning disabilities. Used to teach language processing and to evaluate reading and math skills.

Description: Multiple-item paper-pencil test measuring a student's ability to write sentences dictated by the teacher. The sentences include many samples of short vowels, blends, digraphs, and inconsistently spelled words. The child's responses are evaluated for deficiencies in nine areas: cognition, attention, fine motor, auditory and visual memory, auditory and visual perception, self-image, and integration. Pretests and posttests are provided for students in Grades 2-8. Only one test is administered to first-grade students. The test determines each student's reading and math levels. Examiner required. Suitable for group use.

Untimed: Group 15-30 minutes; individual 5-15 minutes

Scoring: Examiner evaluated

Cost: Complete kit (30 record forms, 10 profile forms, manual) $8.25; manual $8.75

Publisher: Stoelting Company

GORDON DIAGNOSTIC SYSTEM (GSI)
Michael Gordon

Child, adolescent Ages 3-16

Purpose: Assesses attention deficit disorders and impulsivity in children. Used by clinicians, educators, and physicians.

Description: 2-item game-like task test measuring levels of impulsivity, attentiveness, motivation, and concentration without interference of other factors such as intelligence or visual-motor skills. The portable electronic unit measures the ability to delay responding in the presence of feedback (Delay Task) and the ability to maintain attention in the absence of tangible feedback (Vigilance Task). The test provides information on alertness and motivation and insights into a child's problem-solving style, which helps with treatment and educational planning recommendations. Examiner required. Not suitable for group use.

Untimed: 8-9 minutes per task

Scoring: Computer scored

Cost: GDS unit, manual, and record forms $1,295.00

Publisher: Clinical Diagnostics, Inc.

ILLINOIS TEST OF PSYCHOLINGUISTIC ABILITIES (ITPA)
Refer to page 477.

THE INFORMAL WRITING INVENTORY
Gerard Giordano

Grades 3-12, reading handicapped adults

Purpose: Measures a person's ability to communicate by writing. Focuses on formation (handwriting and spelling), grammatical, and communication skills. Enables clinicians or teachers to analyze the abilities of potentially disabled writers.

Description: Paper-pencil inventory utilizing pictures that stimulate students to write. A simple notation system is used to annotate the writing samples and identify the types of writing problems. Errors are summarized on a profile sheet and a communication index is calculated. Based on this information, remedial exercises are suggested. The manual contains information on administering, scoring, and profiling the inventory and its results and information on remedial writing exercises. Examiner required. Not suitable for group use.

Timed: Varies

Scoring: Hand key; examiner evaluated

Cost: Contact publisher

Publisher: Scholastic Testing Service, Inc.

JORDAN LEFT-RIGHT REVERSAL TEST (JLRRT)
Brian T. Jordan

Child   Ages 5-12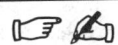

Purpose: Assesses the extent to which a child reverses letters, numbers, and words. Used as a screening device by classroom teachers or as one part of a full diagnostic battery.

Description: Multiple-item paper-pencil examination on two levels. Level 1 tests reversals of capital letters and numerals. Level 2 reveals reversed lowercase letters within words and whole-word reversals within sentences. The manual includes a chapter on remediation techniques and a conversion table to determine developmental age. Examiner required. Suitable for group use.

Untimed: 20 minutes

Scoring: Hand key

Cost: Manual $10.00; 50 test forms $7.00

Publisher: Academic Therapy Publications

JOSEPH PRESCHOOL AND PRIMARY SELF-CONCEPT SCREENING TEST (JPPSST)
Jack Joseph

Child   Ages 3.5-9

Purpose: Measures social-emotional development of children. Used to identify children who may have learning difficulties due to negative self-appraisals and to monitor progress in early childhood programs and special education classes. Used to meet requirements of P.L. 94-142.

Description: 16-item paper-pencil and oral-response test in two parts. First, the child draws his own face on a blank figure of the corresponding sex. Next, the child answers two simple oral-response questions and 13 questions asking the child to select from pairs of pictures the one with which he identifies more closely. The face drawing is evaluated qualitatively, and the 15 questions are scored objectively. The test generates a Global Self-Concept Score based on five dimensions and provides objective high-risk cut-off points. The effects of socially desirable responses are corrected for at upper ranges (ages 5-9). Both quantitative and qualitative indices regarding possible cognitive deficits and experiential or receptive language lags are developed. The manual provides normative data, measures of validity and reliability, item analysis, specific case illustrations, and research considerations. Examiner required. Not suitable for group use.

Untimed: 5-7 minutes

Scoring: Examiner evaluated

Cost: Complete kit (manual, stimulus cards, identify reference drawings, 100 record forms) $60.00

Publisher: Stoelting Company

KAUFMAN TEST OF EDUCATIONAL ACHIEVEMENT (K-TEA)
Refer to page 403.

KERBY LEARNING MODALITY TEST, REVISED 1980
Maude L. Kerby

Child   Ages 5-11

Purpose: Measures the learning abilities of children in terms of visual, auditory, and motor activity skills. Used to identify children with learning disabilities, to plan teaching strategies, and to comply with P.L. 94-142.

Description: Multiple-item paper-pencil test measuring strengths and weaknesses in three primary learning modalities: visual, auditory, and motor activity. The test consists of a variety of classroom work samples in eight subtests: visual and auditory discrimination, visual and auditory closure, visual and auditory memory, and visual and auditory motor coordination. Kits are available for three age levels: kindergarten, age 5; primary, ages 6-8; and intermediate, ages 8-11. Examiner required. Suitable for group use.

Timed: 15 minutes

Scoring: Hand key

Cost: Kindergarten kit (10 test booklets, tape cassette, 10 record sheets, manual) $29.50; primary kit (10 test booklets, scoring keys, tape cassette, 10 record sheets, manual) $37.50; intermediate kit (10 test booklets, 10 answer sheets, scoring keys, tape cassette, 10 record sheets, manual) $39.50; complete kit (kindergarten kit, primary kit, intermediate kit) $98.00

Publisher: Western Psychological Services

LANGUAGE INVENTORY FOR TEACHERS (LIT)
Arlene Cooper and Beverly A. School

Grades PreK-9 and older students

Purpose: Assesses the language ability of students who have difficulties in reading and writing. Used to determine areas of deficiency requiring remedial intervention and to help teachers write comprehensive Individualized Education Programs.

Description: Multiple-item paper-pencil sequence of more than 500 language tasks corresponding to 13 long-range goals, five for spoken language and eight for written language. The tasks are ordered by type and difficulty to correspond to the hierarchical development of language concepts. Testing begins at a point where the examinee is expected to succeed and is discontinued when the examinee has made several errors. The examiner may translate the items the student misses into instructional objectives by following the guidelines in the manual. Examiner required. Not suitable for group use.

Untimed: 30 minutes

Scoring: Hand key

Cost: Manual $12.00; 50 record forms $14.00; specimen set $12.00

Publisher: Academic Therapy Publications

LANGUAGE-STRUCTURED AUDITORY RETENTION SPAN TEST (LARS)
Luis Carlson

Ages 3.7-adult

Purpose: Assesses the ability of children and adults to maintain short-term memory for linguistically significant information. Used to detect the inability to recall when there is an unfamiliar or nonsense word in an otherwise familiar sentence.

Description: 58-item test determining recall of information in a linguistic context when there are two conditions of familiar words, an unfamiliar word, or two nonsense words in the stimuli. The test provides an estimate of the optimum length of an aural message from which a person may profit during a learning experience. Two equivalent forms allow test-retest without learning effect. Examiner required. Not suitable for group use.

Untimed: 12-15 minutes

Scoring: Hand key

Cost: Manual $10.00; 50 test forms (A or B) $14.00

Publisher: Academic Therapy Publications

LEARNING DISABILITY RATING PROCEDURE (LDRP)
Gerald J. Spadafore and Sharon J. Spadafore

Child, adolescent
Grades 1-12

Purpose: Helps evaluate the general mental and social abilities of elementary and secondary school students. Used to determine LD placement.

Description: Multiple-item paper-pencil evaluation in which the examiner rates the examinee on each of 10 indicators ranging from general intelligence and listening comprehension to socially inappropriate behavior and learning motivation. The test provides a basis for discussion during placement meetings as each participant completes the rating form. Total scores are averaged and compared to the criteria which describe each student as a poor, fair, good, or excellent candidate for LD placement. The manual outlines necessary testing and observations which should be made before the meeting. Examiner required. Not suitable for group use.

Untimed: 15 minutes

Scoring: Examiner evaluated

Cost: Test kit (manual, 25 rating forms, in vinyl folder) $18.00

Publisher: Academic Therapy Publications

LEARNING EFFICIENCY TEST (LET)
Raymond E. Webster

Child, adolescent, adult
Ages 6-adult

Purpose: Measures visual and auditory memory characteristics of children and adults. Used to determine deficits that may be related to classroom learning problems and for academic placement, identification of learning-handicapped students, and identification of students' preferred learning style.

Description: Multiple-item paper-pencil norm-referenced measure of visual memory and auditory memory. Two subtests assess both ordered and unordered recall under three conditions: immediate recall, short-term recall, and long-term recall. In the Visual Memory subtest, the examiner shows the examinee nonrhyming letters on stimulus cards. For the Auditory Memory subtest, the examiner reads the letters to the examinee. Sequences to be remembered range in length from two to nine items. The manual includes an interpretation of memory performance and describes remedial activities that can be used to improve learning efficiency. Examiner required. Not suitable for group use.

Untimed: 10-15 minutes

Scoring: Hand key

Cost: Test kit (manual, stimulus cards, 25 record forms, in vinyl folder) $30.50

Publisher: Academic Therapy Publications

THE LEARNING PREDICTOR
Joan M. Smith

Child, adolescent
Grades K-12

Purpose: Assesses potential visual and auditory retention problems of students in Grades K-12.

Description: Multiple-item digit-span test measuring symbol memory functioning. An examiner uses visual and auditory stimuli to seek a written response from students. This screening instrument for learning disabilities helps teachers identify pupils for possible special education referral. Examiner required. Suitable for group use.

Untimed: 10-15 minutes

Scoring: Not available

Cost: $45.00 including postage

Publisher: Learning Time Products

MARTINEZ ASSESSMENT OF THE BASIC SKILLS
Refer to page 405.

MATRIX ANALOGIES TEST— EXPANDED FORM (MAT-EF)
Refer to page 508.

MATRIX ANALOGIES TEST— SHORT FORM (MAT-SF)
Refer to page 509.

MEASUREMENT OF LANGUAGE DEVELOPMENT
Refer to page 633.

MINNESOTA PERCEPTO-DIAGNOSTIC TEST (MPD), 1982 REVISION
Refer to page 50.

MOTOR SKILLS INVENTORY (MSI)
Refer to page 562.

NEW MACMILLAN READING ANALYSIS
Refer to page 533.

THE O'BRIEN VOCABULARY PLACEMENT TEST
Refer to page 533.

THE POLLACK-BRANDEN BATTERY: FOR IDENTIFICATION OF LEARNING DISABILITIES, DYSLEXIA, AND CLASSROOM DYSFUNCTION

Child, adolescent
Ages 6-18

Purpose: Diagnoses students' learning disabilities. Used by clinicians and special education teachers to establish treatment plans or educational programs (IEPs).

Description: Multiple-item paper-pencil battery assessing receptive and expressive language skills. The battery diagnoses and classifies learning disabilities, dyslexia, and other classroom dysfunctions. The test consists of two subbatteries: a clinical battery informing clinicians of weaknesses and strengths in cognitive and emotional areas of development as a basis for a treatment plan and a classroom battery informing the educator of an individualized educational program (IEP) and identifying individual problem areas. Both subbatteries are based on the application of Luria's neuropsychological theories of functional learning systems in the brain. Criterion-referenced scoring and interpretation offers a direct guide to effective remedial approaches. Examiner required. Classroom battery suitable for group use.

Untimed: Varies

Scoring: Examiner evaluated

Cost: Contact publisher

Publisher: Book-Lab

PORTABLE TACTUAL PERFORMANCE TEST (P-TPT)
Refer to page 54.

PRESCRIPTIVE READING PERFORMANCE TEST (PRPT)
Refer to page 552.

PSYCHOEDUCATIONAL PROFILE (PEP)
Refer to page 488.

THE PUPIL RATING SCALE (REVISED): SCREENING FOR LEARNING DISABILITIES
Helmer R. Myklebust

Child   Grades K-6

Purpose: Measures hearing, speech, motor, and social behavior of elementary school children. Used to screen for learning disabilities.

Description: 24-item rating scale covering auditory comprehension, spoken language, orientation, motor coordination, and personal-social behavior. The test provides objective data for language disorders as well as for nonverbal behavior. Teachers must be familiar with the children they are rating. Examiner required. Suitable for group use.

Untimed: 5-10 minutes

Scoring: Examiner evaluated

Cost: Scale and manual $21.50; 50 record forms $13.50

Publisher: Grune & Stratton, Inc.

QUICKSCREEN
Janet B. Fudala

Child   Grades K-2

Purpose: Measures young children's ability to read, write, and use numbers in order to identify students who may have speech, language, or learning problems. Used to implement P.L. 94-142.

Description: Multiple-item paper-pencil verbal test available at three levels: kindergarten, first grade, and second grade. The kindergarten level, which is available in parallel forms A, B, C, and D, consists of four subtests: Name Writing, Figure Copying, Story, and Sentence Repetition. The first-grade level, available in parallel forms A and B, consists of five subtests: Name Writing, Figures, Words, Story, and Sentences. The second-grade level, available in parallel forms A and B, consists of five subtests: Name Writing, Figures, Story, Cognitive, and Sentences. Cutoff scores are provided to identify students with a high or possible risk of potential learning disability so they can be referred for more detailed evaluation. The manual provides evidence of reliability and validity, detailed instructions for administration and scoring, case studies, and recommended materials and tests for subsequent evaluation and remediation. The Score Sheet provides a summary of the entire classroom, and the Scoring Summary Card for the first-grade and second-grade levels summarizes scoring procedures on an easy-to-refer-to card to facilitate scoring. Examiner required. Suitable for group use.

Untimed: 15-25 minutes

Scoring: Hand key

Cost: Complete kindergarten kit $19.85; complete first-grade kit $29.50; complete second-grade kit $29.50; complete kit for all three levels (test booklets, score sheets, templates, a summary card, manual) $75.00

Publisher: Western Psychological Services

READING FREE VOCATIONAL INTEREST INVENTORY (R-FVII)
Refer to page 756.

READING FREE VOCATIONAL INTEREST INVENTORY— REVISED (R-FVII REVISED)
Refer to page 756.

THE REVERSALS FREQUENCY TEST
Richard A. Gardner

**Child, adolescent
Ages 5-15½**

Purpose: Assesses a child's letter and number reversals frequency. Identifies children needing further evaluation for a neurologically based learning disability.

Description: Three multiple-item paper-pencil tests of letter and number reversals frequency. In The Reversals Execution Test, the child writes a specific list of numbers and letters, and the examiner records the number of items written in reversed orientation. The Reversals Recognition Test presents the child with an array of numbers and letters, some of which are correctly oriented and some of which are presented as mirror images. The child places a cross over the reversed items, and the examiner records the number of errors. In the Reversals Matching Test, each item consists of a model number or letter followed by four samples of the same letter or number. One of the four samples is correctly oriented, like the model. The child places a circle around the number or letter that matches the model, and the examiner records the number of errors. Each test is scored separately. Means, standard deviations, and percentile ranks are provided for both normal children and those known to have neurologically based learning disabilities. The manual provides tabulated data, graphs, and theoretical material that enable the examiner to ascertain the significance of a child's score in learning disability assessment. Examiner required. Suitable for group use.

Untimed: Varies

Scoring: Examiner evaluated

Cost: Test $12.00

Publisher: Creative Therapeutics

SCHOOL BEHAVIOR CHECKLIST
Refer to page 677.

SCHOOL PROBLEM SCREENING INVENTORY, FIFTH EDITION
Thomas D. Gnagey

**Child, adolescent
Grades PreK-12**

Purpose: Diagnoses and classifies learning and behavior problems. Used for teacher planning and evaluation and to verify the continued eligibility of previously placed special education students.

Description: 37-item paper-pencil test consisting of 10 empirically derived scales. Six scales assess the following specific diagnostic categories: learning disabilities (visual-motor and auditory-verbal), mental retardation, behavior disorder (over-controlled and under-controlled), and educational handicap. The four less differentiated scales that follow are used to determine the broad problem area in which to initiate further diagnostic evaluation when a child's problem does not fall within the six specific categories listed above: learning disabilities (general nonspecific), general learning skill deficit, behavior disorder (general nonspecific), and general maladjustment. The teacher uses an inventory sheet to rate the student on the 37 characteristics and sums the scores in each of the diagnostic categories to obtain ratings of "not likely," "possible," and "very likely." Examiner required. Not suitable for group use.

Untimed: 7-10 minutes

Scoring: Hand key

Cost: Manual, 20 analysis worksheets $14.00

Publisher: Slosson Educational Publications, Inc.

SEARCH: A SCANNING INSTRUMENT FOR THE IDENTIFICATION OF POTENTIAL LEARNING DISABILITY
Archie A. Silver and Rosa A. Hagin

Child   Ages 5-6

Purpose: Detects learning difficulties and identifies specific skill deficits in children. Used to establish educational objectives for individual students and groups of students.

Description: Multiple-item oral-response and task-performance test consisting of 10 subtests: three tests of visual perception (matching, recall, and visual-motor), two auditory tests (discrimination and sequencing), two intermodal tests (articulation and initial consonants), and three body-image tests (directionality, finger schema, and pencil grip). The total score indicates the degree of each child's vulnerability to learning failure in the early grades. The subtest scores yield a profile of the child's perceptual skills (assets and deficits), which is used in guiding subsequent educational intervention. Specific intervention procedures may be found in the test's companion program TEACH. Test scores are interpreted by means of VABs (vulnerable ranges for each component) and stanines for completion of the student's profile. Two kinds of norms may be used: age norms and local norms. The manual includes age norms ranging from 63-80 months for specific samples, such as inner-city, small-town rural, suburban, and selected independent schools, as well as instructions for computing local norms. The test may be used independently or in conjunction with TEACH. Examiner required. Not suitable for group use.

Untimed: 20 minutes

Scoring: Examiner evaluated

Cost: Complete kit (manual, 30 record blanks, 12 miniature identification toys) $42.50

Publisher: Walker Educational Book Corporation

special education: learning disabled

SLINGERLAND SCREENING TESTS FOR IDENTIFYING CHILDREN WITH SPECIFIC LANGUAGE DISABILITY
Beth H. Slingerland

Child   Grades 1-6

Purpose: Screens elementary-school children for indications of specific language disabilities in reading, spelling, handwriting, and speaking in order to identify those needing special tutoring and further evaluation and to show teachers the strengths and weaknesses of their pupils.

Description: Multiple-item verbal paper-pencil examination containing five subtests evaluating visual-motor coordination and visual memory linked with motor coordination and three subtests evaluating auditory-visual discrimination and auditory memory-to-motor ability. The test is available in four forms, A, B, C for Grades 1-4 and D for Grades 5-6. Form D, which contains a ninth subtest evaluating personal orientation in time and space and the ability to express ideas in writing, helps identify children whose specific language difficulties may have become persistent. All the forms contain separate Echolalia tests and include individual auditory tests to identify students who have difficulty recalling words and pronouncing words correctly or are unable to express their ideas in an organized manner. Examiner required. Suitable for group use.

Untimed: 1½ hours

Scoring: Examiner evaluated

Cost: 12 screening tests (Forms A, B, C) $4.50, 12 Form D $7.00; teacher's manual (Forms A, B, C) $5.50, Form D $4.50; cards and charts (Forms A, B, C) $8.00, Form D $11.00

Publisher: Educators Publishing Service, Inc.

SOUTHGATE GROUP READING TESTS
Refer to page 538.

SPATIAL ORIENTATION MEMORY TEST
Joseph M. Wepman and D. Turaids

Child   Ages 5-9

Purpose: Measures a child's ability to retain and recall the orientation of visually presented forms. Used to identify children facing potential learning difficulties.

Description: Multiple-item response test. The examiner presents a target page with a nonalphabetic design to the child, asking the child to select the same design from the response page, which contains four or five samples of the same design in different rotational positions. Spatial orientation ability prepares the child for individual letter discrimination recall, sequential ordering of letters in words, and related skills essential for reading. Adequacy scores are indicated for ages 5, 6; 7, 8, and 9. The test is available in two forms for retesting. Examiner required. Not suitable for group use.

Untimed: 10-15 minutes

Scoring: Hand key

Cost: Complete kit (reusable test booklet, 25 score sheets, manual) $52.50

Publisher: Western Psychological Services

SPELLMASTER DIAGNOSTIC SPELLING SYSTEM
Refer to page 239.

STUDENT LEARNING PROFILE
Cuyahoga Special Education Service Center

Learning disabled students   Grades K-12

Purpose: Provides an ongoing record of the basic skills and accomplishments of learning-disabled children. Used by teachers, psychologists, counselors, and parents to assess the student's long- and short-term goals.

Description: 871-item paper-pencil examination administered to small groups over a period of 13 school years. The test measures accomplishment in seven major areas: learning style (modality preferences), progress in study skills, language arts, perceptual development, career development, mathematics, and social/coping skills. The examiner partially fills in squares to the left of the performance objectives to signify emergent behaviors and completely fills the squares to signify consistent behaviors. Each entry is color-coded to correspond to the student's level at the time the objective is met: black for Grades K-3, green for Grades 4-6, red for Grades 7-8, and blue for Grades 9-12. Materials are contained in a 30-page spiral-bound book. The profile is designed specifically for use with children with specific learning disabilities, but many of the skills included are part of the regular school curricula. Examiner required. Suitable for group use.

Untimed: Not available

Scoring: Examiner evaluated

Cost: 1 copy $4.85; 6 copies $24.85; 100 copies $2.50

Publisher: Creative Learning Systems, Inc.

SYMBOL DIGIT MODALITIES TEST
Refer to page 64.

TASK ASSESSMENT FOR PRESCRIPTIVE TEACHING (TAPT)
Daniel Hofeditz and Duane Wilke

Ages 6-adult

Purpose: Measures an individual's language and math abilities. Used by special education teachers to evaluate students with learning disabilities, mental impairments, or behavior disorders.

Description: Multiple-item paper-pencil test consisting of 12 mathematics and 11 reading booklets containing all necessary instructions and places for student responses. The mathematics booklets cover the following areas: pre-skills, addition, subtraction, monetary concepts, time concepts, multiplication, division, fractions, decimals, percentages, weights and measures, and practical skills (with calculator). The reading booklets cover the following areas: pre-skills, letters, consonant/symbol sound, vowel/symbol sound, blending skills, academic/instructional words, community/functional words, word structure analysis, question orientation and context, thought expression, and informational resources. The booklets can be kept in a folder as a permanent part of a student's record. Each booklet contains a Student Progress Sheet, which summarizes and graphs performance. The test also provides preprinted objective sheets that help meet the local requirements of Individualized Education Programs (IEPs). Examiner required. Suitable for group use.

Untimed: 20-40 minutes

Scoring: Hand key; examiner evaluated

Cost: Starter set $272.75

Publisher: Scholastic Testing Service, Inc.

TEST LISTENING ACCURACY IN CHILDREN (TLAC)
Merlin J. Mecham and J. Dean Jones

Child   Grades K-5

Purpose: Measures the verbal listening abilities of elementary-school children. Identifies children with listening and other language and learning disorders.

Description: Multiple-item multiple-choice intelligibility type test measuring verbal listening skills. The test is available in two versions. The Individual Version is used with children ages 5-7. The Group-Test Version is used in classrooms of children in Grades 2-5. Both versions are percentile rated and have nominal descriptions. Examiner required. Suitable for group use.

Untimed: Individual version 20 minutes; group version 45 minutes

Scoring: Examiner evaluated; hand key

Cost: Individual version kit (manual, picture plates, cassette plates, score sheets) $25.00; group version kit (manual, filmstrip, tape, key, 35 scoring sheets $25.00; individual and group kits combined $45.00

Publisher: Communication Research Associates, Inc.

TEST OF CONCEPT UTILIZATION (TCU)
Refer to page 515.

VISUAL SKILLS APPRAISAL (VSA)
Refer to page 665.

WELLER-STRAWSER SCALES OF ADAPTIVE BEHAVIOR: FOR THE LEARNING DISABLED (WSSAB)
Carol Weller and Sherri Strawser

Child, adolescent
Grades 1-12

Purpose: Assesses the adaptive behavior of elementary and secondary school learning-disabled students. Used to determine severity of disabilities and to identify areas requiring remedial attention.

Description: Multiple-item paper-pencil norm-referenced scales covering social coping, relationships, pragmatic language, and production. The scales are completed by a teacher or diagnostician following a period of observation of the student. The total score and subtest scores define behavior problems as mild to moderate or moderate to severe. Using the results and following suggestions in the manual, the examiner may develop compensatory teaching techniques to help the student cope with situations in school, home, social, and job environments. Examiner required. Not suitable for group use.

Untimed: 15 minutes

Scoring: Examiner evaluated

Cost: Manual $15.00; 50 forms (specify elementary or secondary) $14.00

Publisher: Academic Therapy Publications

THE WORD TEST
Refer to page 655.

Special Education: Mentally Handicapped

AAMD ADAPTIVE BEHAVIOR SCALE, SCHOOL EDITION (ABS-SE)
Kazuo Nihira, Ray Foster, Max Shellhaas, Henry Leland, Nadine M. Lambert, and Myra Windmiller

Child, adolescent
Ages 3-16

Purpose: Assesses the social and daily living skills of children whose adaptive behavior indicates possible mental retardation, emotional disturbance, or other learning handicaps. Used for screening and instructional planning.

Description: 95-item paper-pencil scale measuring the social and daily living skills and behaviors of children. The instrument, which is completed by the examiner, yields five factor scores and one comparison score. Scores are converted to profiles that are used in diagnostic and placement decisions and in formulating general educational goals. Examiner required. Not suitable for group use.

Untimed: 30 minutes

Scoring: Examiner evaluated

Cost: Starter set (manuals, 2 assessment booklets, 2 instructional profiles, 2 diagnostic profiles, 2 parent guides) $22.75

Publisher: CTB/McGraw-Hill

ABERRANT BEHAVIOR CHECKLIST (ABC)
Refer to page 188.

BALTHAZAR SCALES OF ADAPTIVE BEHAVIOR I: SCALES OF FUNCTIONAL INDEPENDENCE
Earl E. Balthazar

Mentally retarded of all ages

Purpose: Evaluates the self-help skills of the profoundly or severely mentally

retarded. Used to plan and monitor goal-directed remedial programs.

Description: Multiple-item paper-pencil observational inventory assessing the functional independence of profoundly and severely handicapped individuals. Data derived from direct observation of the individual are used to determine objective performance levels, which in turn identify appropriate remedial programs for developing self-help skills. The scoring form includes nighttime supplements. Program effectiveness can be evaluated by readministering the scales. Personnel in residential treatment facilities can be trained within a week to become observers and raters. The inventory is also helpful in explaining the development of self-help skills to families. Examiner required. Not suitable for group use.

Untimed: Varies

Scoring: Examiner evaluated

Cost: Manual set $10.00; 25 scoring forms $9.25

Publisher: Consulting Psychologists Press, Inc.

BALTHAZAR SCALES OF ADAPTIVE BEHAVIOR II: SCALES OF SOCIAL ADAPTATION
Refer to page 190.

BRISTOL SOCIAL ADJUSTMENT GUIDES, AMERICAN EDITION (BSAG)
Refer to page 667.

CAIN-LEVINE SOCIAL COMPETENCY SCALE
Leo F. Cain, Samuel Levine, and Freeman F. Elzey

Child, adolescent
Ages 5-13

Purpose: Measures the social competence of trainable mentally retarded children. Used for diagnosis, placement, planning, and training evaluation.

Description: 44-item scale of four aspects of social competence: self-help, initiative, social skills, and communication. Items are administered and evaluated by interviewing the child's parents. Percentile norms based on mentally retarded children are offered for chronological ages 5-13. The manual includes instructions for use of the scales by teachers and clinicians. Examiner required. Not suitable for group use.

Untimed: Open ended
Scoring: Examiner evaluated
Cost: Manual $6.00; 25 scales $16.00
Publisher: Consulting Psychologists Press, Inc.

CAMELOT BEHAVIORAL CHECKLIST
Ray W. Foster

All ages

Purpose: Evaluates adaptive behavior skills in mentally retarded persons. Used to plan and monitor educational programs for such individuals.

Description: 399-item paper-pencil checklist in 10 categories and 40 subcategories measuring the following skills: self-help, physical development, home, duties, vocational and economic behaviors, independent travel, numerical and communication skills, and social behavior responsibility. The examiner assigns each description a plus or minus value, which is transferred to a profile sheet that records and displays the student's progress and aids in the sequencing of training objectives. The test is of limited use to the severely retarded. Examiner required. Not suitable for group use.

Untimed: 20 minutes
Scoring: Hand key
Cost: Manual $3.50; checklist $0.45 each
Publisher: Camelot Behavioral Systems
Information and availability unconfirmed; no publisher response.

COGNITIVE DIAGNOSTIC BATTERY (CDB)
Stanley R. Kay

All ages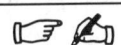

Purpose: Evaluates the nature and degree of intellectual disorders. May be used with intellectually limited, nonverbal,

inattentive, overtly psychotic, or otherwise untestable patients for purposes of diagnostic evaluation and monitoring treatment progress.

Description: Multiple-item nonverbal-response and task-performance tests assessing cognitive deficits due to impaired development versus later regression. Five tests utilize a Piagetian developmental framework to assess early conceptual maturation, higher order concept utilization, egocentric versus socialized thinking, perceptual motor development, attention span, arousal-related cognitive disturbance, and psychomotor rate. Normative data are provided for schizophrenics, mentally retarded psychotics, normal adults, children, and the elderly. The results differentially diagnose mental retardation from psychosis. The manual includes technical data. Examiner required. Not suitable for group use.

Untimed: 10-30 minutes
Scoring: Examiner evaluated
Cost: Test kit (5 subtests, manual, 50 of each scoring form) $44.95
Publisher: Psychological Assessment Resources, Inc.

COMPREHENSIVE LANGUAGE PROGRAM (CLP)
Peoria Association for Retarded Citizens

Mental ages 0-5

Purpose: Evaluates the language and pre-language skills of retarded and handicapped individuals who have language development problems. Used for diagnosis and remediation.

Description: Multiple-item oral-response and task-assessment test covering eight areas of language development: attending, manipulation of objects, mimicking, matching, identifying, labeling, following directions, and word combinations. A checklist records the student's entry-level achievement. The results provide a basis for subsequent instruction. There are 285 detailed lesson plans, designed for use 20 to 30 minutes daily, 5 days a week, covering the eight areas. Record sheets record incremental progress. Examiner required. Not suitable for group use.

Untimed: Varies

Scoring: Hand key

Cost: Starter set $190.00

Publisher: Scholastic Testing Service, Inc.

COMPREHENSIVE TEST OF ADAPTIVE BEHAVIOR
Gary Adams

All ages

Purpose: Aids in the precise evaluation of handicapped individual's adaptive abilities. Used for placement and to determine where an individual stands in relation to others of the same age or handicap. Also helps in establishing the scope and sequence of training.

Description: 527-item paper-pencil inventory of adaptive behavior in six skill categories: self-help, home living, independent living, social, sensory motor, and language concepts/academic skills. The examiner checks off those skills that the individual has mastered based on observation of the individual, parent/guardian report, and formal testing. Because skills are sequenced in the order handicapped individuals acquire them, not in normal developmental order, the test is inappropriate for normally developing individuals. Examiner required. Not suitable for group use.

Untimed: Variable

Scoring: Examiner evaluated

Cost: Complete program $44.00; components available individually

Publisher: The Psychological Corporation

DEVELOPMENTAL ASSESSMENT OF LIFE EXPERIENCES (DALE)
Gertrude A. Barber,
John P. Mannino, and Robert J. Will

All ages

Purpose: Assesses skill development in individuals who have been withdrawn from the mainstream of society for long durations of time at institutions for developmental and/or physical handicaps.

Description: Two 200-item paper-pencil observational inventories assessing two levels of skill development. Level I items describe tasks reflecting the functioning of individuals who are profoundly to severely mentally retarded and measure the following areas of self-help skills: sensory motor, language, self-help, cognition, and socialization. Level II items list behaviors that are of a higher functioning nature and assess the following community living skills: personal hygiene, personal management, communications, residence-home management, and community access. The items describe skills in terms of the ways in which specific tasks are approached or completed and are expressed in positive terminology. The items within each skill area are listed in order of increasing difficulty. Two types of scores are utilized in rating every item on the inventory. A quantitative score indicates the frequency of the response; items are rated responds less than 50%, responds approximately 50%, responds 90% or greater, (N/A) not applicable, (N/O) never observed, or (INCAP.) incapable of responding. Qualitative ratings identify responses for each behavioral item as inappropriate/incorrect, fair approximation with reminders, or excellent approximation with few reminders. Initial evaluation identifies an individual's competencies which can then serve as a basis for determining the skills that need to be expanded or developed. As specific strengths related to a particular task or skill area are observed and identified, they are recorded on pages opposite inventory items set aside for that purpose in the inventory booklets. Each strength-need page corresponds to the items in the inventory on the opposite page. A general strength-need list also is provided. A circular chart is used to provide a graphic illustration of an individual's progress. Although the inventory is designed to be rated quarterly, items on which the individual has achieved competency are graphed immediately on the cumulative circle chart, showing on any given day all of the areas in which an individual has exhibited competency. The manual provides an instructional narrative, which serves as a guide in the use of the system and presents sample copies of pertinent data recording forms. Individual data forms are presented in separate booklets for Levels I and II. A therapist's handbook discussing the assessment of strengths and needs of the individuals being serviced and more effective programming for the therapist in planning goals is available. Examiner required. Not suitable for group use.

Untimed: Varies

Scoring: Examiner evaluated

Cost: Manual $7.80; therapist's handbook $4.00; inventory list, profile fact sheet, and illustrative progress chart (Level I or II) $3.50

Publisher: Barber Center Press Publications

Information and availability unconfirmed; no publisher response.

DEVELOPMENTAL LEARNING PROFILE
Cuyahoga Special Education Service Center

Educable mentally retarded Grades K-12

Purpose: Provides an on-going record of educable mentally retarded children's accomplishment of basic survival skills. Used by teachers, psychologists, counselors, and parents to determine long- and short-term goals.

Description: 1,461-item paper-pencil examination administered to small groups over a period of 13 school years. The test measures accomplishments in seven major curriculum areas: language arts, science, social studies, physical and perceptual development, career development, mathematics, and personal-social development. Performance objectives are sequentially arranged to each final objective to prevent skill development gaps. The examiner partially fills in squares to the left of the performance objectives to signify emergent behaviors and completely fills the squares to signify consistent behaviors. Each entry is color-coded to correspond to the student's level at the time the objective is met: gold for Primary, green for Intermediate, orange for

Junior High, and blue for Senior High. Materials are contained in a 42-page spiral-bound book. The profile is designed specifically for educable mentally retarded children, but many of the skills included are part of the regular school curricula. Examiner required. Suitable for group use.

Untimed: Not available

Scoring: Examiner evaluated

Cost: 1 copy $4.85; 6 copies $24.85

Publisher: Creative Learning Systems, Inc.

THE DEVEREUX CHILD BEHAVIOR RATING SCALE (DCB)
George Spivack and Jules Spotts

Child   Ages 6-12

Purpose: Assesses symptomatic behaviors of children. Used with mentally retarded and emotionally disturbed children for diagnostic and screening procedures, group placement decisions, and assessment of progress in response to specific programs or procedures.

Description: 97-item paper-pencil inventory assessing overt behavior patterns of children. The evaluator (parent or child care worker living with the child) rates each item according to how he feels the subject's behavior compares to the behavior of normal children of the same age. The test yields 17 scores: Distractibility, Poor Self-Care, Pathological Use of Senses, Emotional Detachment, Social Isolation, Poor Coordination and Body Tonus, Incontinence, Messiness-Sloppiness, Inadequate Need for Independence, Unresponsiveness to Stimulation, Proneness to Emotional Upset, Need for Adult Contact, Anxious-Fearful Ideation, "Impulse" Ideation, Inability to Delay, Social Aggression, and Unethical Behavior. Self-administered by evaluator. Not suitable for group use.

Untimed: 10-15 minutes

Scoring: Examiner evaluated

Cost: Examination set (25 scales, manual) $10.50; manual $2.00; 50 scales $0.26 each

Publisher: The Devereux Foundation

FLORIDA INTERNATIONAL DIAGNOSTIC-PRESCRIPTIVE VOCATIONAL COMPETENCY PROFILE

Refer to page 764.

GOODMAN LOCK BOX

Refer to page 475.

GRASSI BASIC COGNITIVE EVALUATION

Refer to page 44.

KAUFMAN INFANT AND PRESCHOOL SCALE (KIPS)

Refer to page 11.

LANGUAGE IMITATION TEST (LIT)

Paul Berry and Peter Mittler

Severely educationally retarded

Purpose: Assesses the speaking abilities of the severely educationally retarded (ESNS). Used by speech therapists and other teachers with special qualifications in language remediation.

Description: Multiple-item oral-response test measuring the linguistic competence of the severely educationally retarded. Evaluation of elicited imitative responses provide a psycholinguistic assessment of the individual's speaking abilities. The test has been used only on a limited basis with mildly handicapped (ESNM) and normal children. The test may be used with other tests of language ability for more complete diagnosis or as part of language remediation programs. Examiner required. Not suitable for group use. BRITISH PUBLISHER

Untimed: Not available

Scoring: Examiner evaluated

Cost: Specimen set (record form, manual) £8.20; 25 record forms £5.70; manual £8.10 (payment in sterling for all overseas orders)

Publisher: NFER-NELSON Publishing Company Ltd.

MARTINEZ ASSESSMENT OF THE BASIC SKILLS

Refer to page 405.

NISONGER QUESTIONNAIRE FOR PARENTS

Refer to page 601.

NON-READERS INTELLIGENCE TEST (THIRD EDITION) AND ORAL VERBAL INTELLIGENCE TEST

Refer to page 510.

READING FREE VOCATIONAL INTEREST INVENTORY (R-FVII)

Refer to page 756.

READING FREE VOCATIONAL INTEREST INVENTORY— REVISED (R-FVII REVISED)

Refer to page 756.

SCHOOL CHILD STRESS SCALE (SCSS)

Refer to page 113.

SEQUENCE RECALL (SEQREC)

Refer to page 61.

SEQUENCED INVENTORY OF COMMUNICATION DEVELOPMENT, REVISED EDITION, 1984

Refer to page 645.

SOCIAL AND PREVOCATIONAL INFORMATION BATTERY (SPIB)

Andrew Halpern, Paul Raffeld, Larry K. Irvin, Robert Link, and Jacqueline D. Beckland

EMR students in junior and senior high school

Purpose: Assesses an educable mentally retarded student's knowledge of skills and competencies important for community adjustment. Used by educators as an evaluative device in programs for EMR students.

Description: 277-item orally administered paper-pencil test consisting of nine subtests (Job Search Skills, Job Related Behavior, Banking, Budgeting, Purchasing, Home Management, Physical Health Care, Hygiene and Grooming, Functional Signs) measuring a student's attainment of five long-range goals of work-study or work experience programs in secondary schools: employability, economic self-sufficiency, family living, personal habits, and communication. The student responds to each item by marking it true-false or by selecting an appropriate picture. Results can be used to place students in the Skills for Independent Living resource kit curriculum. Examiner required. Suitable for use with groups not exceeding 20 students.

Untimed: 15-25 minutes per subtest

Scoring: Hand key; may be computer scored

Cost: Specimen set (both a machine-scorable and hand-scorable test book, manual, answer key, user's guide, class record sheet, test reviewer's guide) $8.95

Publisher: CTB/McGraw-Hill

SOCIAL AND PREVOCATIONAL INFORMATION BATTERY-T (SPIB-T)
Andrew Halpern, Paul Raffeld, Larry K. Irvin, Robert Link, and Jacqueline D. Beckland

TMR students in junior and senior high school

Purpose: Assesses a mild to moderately mentally retarded student's knowledge of skills and competencies important for community adjustment. Used by educators to evaluate students and programs.

Description: 291-item orally administered paper-pencil test consisting of nine subtests (Job Search Skills, Job Related Behavior, Banking, Budgeting, Purchasing, Home Management, Physical Health Care, Hygiene and Grooming, Functional Signs) measuring a student's attainment of five long-range goals of work-study or work experience programs in secondary

schools: employability, economic self-sufficiency, family living, personal habits, and communication. The results can be used to place students in the Skills for Independent Living resource kit curriculum. Examiner required. Suitable for use with groups not exceeding 20 students.

Untimed: 15-25 minutes per subtest

Scoring: Hand key

Cost: Specimen set (hand-scorable test book, pretest, manual, answer key, technical summary) $8.95

Publisher: CTB/McGraw-Hill

SOCIO-SEXUAL KNOWLEDGE AND ATTITUDES TEST (SSKAT)
Refer to page 100.

T.M.R. PERFORMANCE PROFILE FOR THE SEVERELY AND MODERATELY RETARDED
Alfred J. DiNola, Bernard Kaminsky, and Allen E. Sternfeld

Mentally retarded individuals

Purpose: Assesses the adaptive behavior of severely and moderately retarded individuals. Used by teachers for curriculum planning.

Description: 240-item paper-pencil inventory assessing six areas of behavior: social, self-care and safety, communication, basic knowledge, practical skills, and body usage and health. Individual performance is measured against specific developmental items on a 5-point rating scale. Examiner required. Not suitable for group use.

Untimed: Varies

Scoring: Examiner evaluated

Cost: Class kit (teacher's manual, 10 record booklets, and 10 yearly comparative charts) $20.00

Publisher: Educational Performance Associates

T.M.R. SCHOOL COMPETENCY SCALES
Samuel Levine, Freeman F. Elzey, Paul Thormahlen, and Leo F. Cain

Child, adolescent
Ages 5 and older

Purpose: Assesses students' adaptive skills in trainable mentally retarded (T.M.R.) classroom settings. Used to evaluate strengths and weaknesses and to measure progress.

Description: 91- or 103-item paper-pencil rating scale measuring five school competence skill areas: perceptual-motor, initiative-responsibility, cognition, personal-social, and language. Items are rated on a 4-point scale by the classroom teacher. Materials include separate scales for each of five age groups: 5-7, 8-10, 11-13, 14-16, and 17 and older. Scales are published in two forms: one for the two younger age groups (91 items), and one for the three older age groups (103 items). Examiner required. Not suitable for group use.

Untimed: Not available

Scoring: Examiner evaluated

Cost: Specimen set $6.25; manual $4.00; 25 scales $30.00 (specify form)

Publisher: Consulting Psychologists Press, Inc.

TARC ASSESSMENT SYSTEM FOR SEVERELY HANDICAPPED CHILDREN
Wayne Sailor and Bonnie Jean Mix

Severely handicapped
children

Purpose: Measures the self-help, motor communication, and social skills of severely handicapped children. Used to evaluate rehabilitation programs and to assess the effectiveness of specific instruction.

Description: Multiple-item observational examination in which the examiner spends several weeks observing a child's behavior in group situations, then uses an assessment inventory to score specific behaviors. The scores are transferred to a profile display sheet that relates behavior to both the child and a standard sample, pointing out undeveloped and strong skills. The examiner must have professional training. Examiner required. Not suitable for group use.

Untimed: Open ended

Scoring: Examiner evaluated

Cost: Manual, 10 assessment sheets $10.00

Publisher: Pro-Ed

VALETT DEVELOPMENTAL SURVEY OF BASIC LEARNING ABILITIES
Refer to page 496.

VALETT INVENTORY OF CRITICAL THINKING ABILITIES (VICTA)
Refer to page 496.

VCWS 17—PRE-VOCATIONAL READINESS BATTERY
Refer to page 734.

VOCATIONAL ADAPTATION RATING SCALES (VARS)
Robert G. Malgady, Peter R. Barcher, John Davis, and George Towner

Mentally retarded

Purpose: Measures problem behaviors among mentally retarded adolescents and adults in vocational settings. Used for curriculum development, Individualized Education Programs (IEPs) placement, and evaluating readiness for mainstreaming.

Description: 133-item paper-pencil inventory measuring the kind of maladaptive behavior likely to occur in vocational settings, such as sheltered workshops, job facilities, or vocational training programs. The examiner (a teacher, nurse, parent, or other adult familiar with the individual) uses a scale ranging from "never" to "regularly" to indicate the frequency with which the individual displays the behavior described in the statement. Six scales are measured: Verbal Manners,

Communication Skills, Attendance and Punctuality, Interpersonal Behavior, Respect for Property, Rules and Regulations, and Grooming and Personal Hygiene. All six scales and the total score are profiled for both frequency and severity (a useful indicator of potential job impairment) in deciles and T-scores. Examiner required. Suitable for group use.

Untimed: 20-30 minutes

Scoring: Hand key

Cost: Complete kit (25 booklets, manual) $25.00

Publisher: Western Psychological Services

VOCATIONAL INFORMATION AND EVALUATION WORK SAMPLES (VIEWS)
Refer to page 759.

VOCATIONAL INTEREST AND SOPHISTICATION ASSESSMENT (VISA)
J.J. Parnicky, H. Kahn, and A.D. Burdett

Adolescent, adult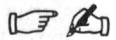

Purpose: Determines the vocational interests and job information of mildly retarded adolescents and young adults. Used for counseling, training projections, and job placement.

Description: Verbal, picture book examination. The book for men evaluates aptitudes for work in garages, laundries, food service, maintenance, farm/grounds, materials handling, and industry. The book for women evaluates interests in business/clerical, housekeeping, food service, laundry, and sewing. Examiner required. Not suitable for group use.

Untimed: 30-45 minutes

Scoring: Examiner evaluated

Cost: Specimen set $15.00; manual $4.00; male picture book $5.00; female picture book $4.00; 50 inquiry forms $5.00; 25 male or female response forms $2.00; 25 male or female profile forms $3.00

Publisher: The Nisonger Center, Ohio State University

VOCATIONAL INTEREST, TEMPERAMENT, AND APTITUDE SYSTEM (VITAS)

ERM adults

Purpose: Assesses aptitudes, vocational interests, and work-related temperaments of disadvantaged and educably mentally retarded persons. Used for vocational guidance.

Description: Performance test of vocational aptitudes consisting of work samples in 21 areas: nuts, bolts, and washers assembly; packing matchbooks; tile sorting and weighing; collating material samples; verifying numbers; pressing linens; budget book assembly; nail and screw sorting; pipe assembly; filing by letters; lock assembly; circuit board inspection; calculating; message taking; bank teller; proofreading; payroll computation; census interviewing; spot welding; laboratory assistant; and drafting. The assessment process includes orientation, assessment, a motivational group session, feedback, and an interest interview. The test requires less than a sixth-grade reading level. Individually packaged hardware is provided for all work samples. Examiner required. Suitable for group use (10 persons per week).

Untimed: 2½ days

Scoring: Examiner evaluated

Cost: Contact publisher

Publisher: Vocational Research Institute—J.E.V.S.

WASHER VISUAL ACUITY SCREENING TECHNIQUE (WVAST)
Refer to page 666.

WIDE RANGE EMPLOYABILITY SAMPLE TEST (WREST)
Refer to page 769.

Y.E.M.R. PERFORMANCE PROFILE FOR THE YOUNG MODERATELY AND MILDLY RETARDED

Alfred J. DiNola, Bernard Kaminsky, and Allen E. Sternfeld

Mentally retarded children

Purpose: Assesses the adaptive behavior of moderately and mildly retarded children. Used by teachers for planning and reporting.

Description: 100-item paper-pencil inventory of 10 areas of behavior: social, self-help, safety, communication, motor skills, manipulative skills, perceptual and intellectual development, academics, imagination and creative expression, and emotional behavior. The profile can be used for educational planning and for reporting strengths and needs to parents. Examiner required. Not suitable for group use.

Untimed: Varies

Scoring: Examiner evaluated

Cost: Class kit (teacher's manual, 15 record booklets, and 15 yearly comparative charts) $25.00

Publisher: Educational Performance Associates

Special Education: Physically Handicapped: Auditory, Orthopedic, and Visual

ADOLESCENT AND ADULT PSYCHOEDUCATIONAL PROFILE (AAPEP)

Gary B. Mesibov, Eric Schopler, and Bruce Schaffer

Handicapped adolescents and adults

Purpose: Measures the learning abilities and characteristics of severely handi-capped adolescents and adults. Used by service providers, teachers, and parents for preparing and maintaining autistic and developmentally handicapped individuals in community-based programs. Used with individuals previously regarded as untestable.

Description: Multiple-item task-performance test assessing the learning abilities of autistic and developmentally handicapped individuals. The test results comprise a profile reflecting the individual characteristics of the person. The profile is translated into an appropriately individualized set of goals and objectives for each individual. The test kit includes the following standard materials required for uniform administration of the test: nerf ball and basket, checkers and board, pinball game, radio and battery, empty box, playing cards, tape of typical workshop sounds, five magic markers, work box, 100 pencils, erasers, target board with balls, magazine, catalog, pad of paper, pen, wooden block, metal plate, nut and bolt, box sorting tray, green buttons, three wing nuts, five bolts, seven washers, five nuts, five sandwich bags, 10 dominoes, sewing block and lace, screwdriver, wrench, 4-piece shape board, survival signs, comic book, paperback book, movie ticket, price signs, December calendar, #1, #2, and #3 cards, color jig, four color chips, written instruction cards, alphabet cards, five jig cards, schedule, five paper clips, clock, pill bottles, tops, 20 markers, and manual. The following materials are required also but not included in the kit: nickels, dimes, quarters, $1 bill, $5 bill, pennies, package of nabs and soda, candy bar, stopwatch, typewriter, and tape recorder. Examiner required. Not suitable for group use.

Untimed: Varies

Scoring: Examiner evaluated

Cost: Test kit (standard materials, manual) $225.00

Publisher: Orange Industries

BEHAVIOR ASSESSMENT BATTERY: SECOND EDITION

Chris Kiernan and Malcolm Jones

Handicapped children and adults

Purpose: Assesses handicapped individuals' ability to function in their environment.

Description: Battery of tests providing a range of assessment procedures for use with profoundly handicapped individuals. The tests, which are presented in book form, identify an individual's developmental strengths and weaknesses and may be used as a basis for effective educational planning. Each section consists of a set of items aimed at certain criterion behaviors. Successful completion of the items is an indication of the person's ability to function adequately in his environment. This revision includes a chapter on the use and interpretation of the battery and material on sign language. Examiner required. Not suitable for group use. BRITISH PUBLISHER

Untimed: Varies

Scoring: Examiner evaluated

Cost: Book of procedures £12.60

Publisher: NFER-NELSON Publishing Company Ltd.

THE BLIND LEARNING APTITUDE TEST (BLAT)
T. Ernest Newland

Child, adolescent
Ages 6-16

Purpose: Evaluates the academic aptitude of blind children.

Description: 61-item nonverbal test of tactile discrimination involving patterned dots and lines on 61 embossed plastic pages. The examiner guides the child's hand over the pages, and the child describes what he feels. Materials include a 39-page examiner's manual, testing book, embossed pages, and 30 record forms. Examiner required. Not suitable for group use.

Untimed: 20-45 minutes

Scoring: Hand key

Cost: Complete $50.00; manual $7.50

Publisher: University of Illinois Press

THE BODY IMAGE OF BLIND CHILDREN
*Bryant J. Cratty and
Theresa A. Sams*

Blind children   Ages 5-15

Purpose: Evaluates the extent to which a blind child is able to identify his body

parts and respond to requests for various types of movements.

Description: Multiple-item oral-response and task-performance assessment procedure measuring the body image of blind children in the following areas: body parts, body planes, body movements, laterality, and directionality. The manual includes norms for comparison among various subpopulations of blind children, suggested applications, interpretive guidelines, and a discussion of body-image training for blind children. Examiner required. Not suitable for group use.

Untimed: Varies

Scoring: Examiner evaluated

Cost: Manual $4.50

Publisher: The American Foundation for the Blind

Information and availability unconfirmed; no publisher response.

CAROLINA PICTURE VOCABULARY TEST
*Thomas L. Layton and
David W. Holmes*

Child   Ages 4-11.5

Purpose: Determines the receptive sign vocabulary level of deaf and hearing-impaired children and of hearing children who communicate manually.

Description: 130-item test assessing the receptive sign vocabulary of deaf and hearing-impaired children. The test is contained in an easel format. The examinee responds to a word signed by the examiner by pointing to one of four pictures. Examiner required. Not suitable for group use.

Timed: 10-15 minutes

Scoring: Hand key

Cost: Complete program $68.50

Publisher: Modern Education Corporation

CENTRAL INSTITUTE FOR THE DEAF PRESCHOOL PERFORMANCE SCALE (CID PRESCHOOL PERFORMANCE SCALE)
Ann E. Geers and Helen S. Lane

Hearing and language-impaired preschoolers

Purpose: Measures intellectual potential using completely nonverbal testing procedures. Predicts school achievement in hearing-impaired and language-impaired preschoolers.

Description: Multiple-item task-performance test assessing the intellectual abilities of preschoolers without requiring a single spoken word from either the examiner or the child (optional verbal clues are provided for use with children who do hear). Six subtests assess intellectual abilities in the following areas: manual planning (block building, Montessori cylinders, and two-figure formboard); manual dexterity (buttons and Wallin pegs); form perception (Decroly pictures, Seguin formboard); perceptual/motor skills (Knox cube, drawing, and paper folding); preschool skills (color sorting and counting sticks); and part/whole relations (Manikin and Stutsman puzzles). Test materials were selected from existing mental tests for children ages 2-5 to obtain a broad, clinical picture of the child's ability and a numerical rating (Deviation IQ) that would correlate with a Stanford-Binet IQ. The test is an adaptation of the early Randall's Island Performance Series. Examiner required. Not suitable for group use.

Untimed: Varies

Scoring: Examiner evaluated

Cost: Complete kit (manual, record forms, manipulatives for subtests) $395.00; manual $4.50; 30 record forms $10.50

Publisher: Stoelting Company

COLUMBIA MENTAL MATURITY SCALE (CMMS)
Refer to page 21.

DEVELOPMENTAL ASSESSMENT OF LIFE EXPERIENCES (DALE)
Refer to page 592.

FULL-RANGE PICTURE VOCABULARY TEST (FRPV)
Refer to page 22.

HISKEY-NEBRASKA TEST OF LEARNING APTITUDE
Marshall S. Hiskey

Child, adolescent
Ages 2½-18½

Purpose: Evaluates learning potential of deaf children and those with hearing, speech, or language handicaps.

Description: Battery of 12 subtests measuring visual-motor coordination, sequential memory, visual retention or stimuli in a series, visual discrimination and matching, and awareness of environment. The tests are Bead Patterns, Memory for Color, Picture Identification, Picture Association, Paper Folding Patterns, Visual Attention Span, Block Patterns, Completion of Drawings, Memory for Digits, Puzzle Block Picture Analogies, and Spatial Reasoning. The scales are nonverbal and have norms for evaluating either hearing or deaf children. Examiner required. Not suitable for group use.

Untimed: 50-60 minutes

Scoring: Examiner evaluated

Cost: Complete set $104.00

Publisher: The Hiskey-Nebraska Test

MARTIN DEVELOPMENTAL ABILITY TEST FOR THE BLIND
William T. Martin

Child, adolescent
Ages 0-16

Purpose: Measures developmental level of blind or blind-retarded children.

Description: Paper-pencil checklist of basic functional performance measuring factors. The test is scored on seven subscales: Basic Developmental Skills, Body

Imagery-Spatial Orientation, Psycho-motor, Math and Problem Solving, Analogies, General Information, and Rote Memory-Recall. The test is administered with several manipulative items. Materials include separate test forms for each sub-scale and a manual. Examiner required. Not suitable for group use.
CANADIAN PUBLISHER

Untimed: Not available

Scoring: Hand key

Cost: Complete test kit $202.62; 25 test forms (specify subtest name) $20.26; replacement manual $20.26

Publisher: Institute of Psychological Research, Inc.

Information and availability unconfirmed; no publisher response.

MAXFIELD-BUCHHOLZ SOCIAL MATURITY SCALE FOR BLIND PRE-SCHOOL CHILDREN
Kathryn E. Maxfield and Sandra Buchholz

Blind children   Ages 0-8

Purpose: Measures the social maturity of blind children.

Description: Multiple-item paper-pencil observational inventory and parent-inter-view guide assessing the developmental skills and social maturity of blind infants and preschool children. The examiner's ratings are based on personal observations in the home setting and supplemented by parent interview. This scale is an adaption of the Vineland Social Maturity Scale. Examiner required. Not suitable for group use.

Untimed: Varies

Scoring: Examiner evaluated

Cost: 25 record blanks $2.00; manual $5.00

Publisher: The American Foundation for the Blind

Information and availability unconfirmed; no publisher response.

THE MOSSFORD ASSESSMENT CHART OF THE PHYSICALLY HANDICAPPED
Janet Whitehouse

Handicapped individuals   Ages 14-18

Purpose: Evaluates the daily living skills of handicapped children. Used in schools, hospitals, and residential and assessment centers for the physically handicapped and by social workers making placement or employment decisions.

Description: Multiple-item paper-pencil checklist of daily living skills relevant to adolescents with mild to severe degrees of physical handicap. Items cover mobility, dressing, manipulative skills, personal hygiene, health, communicating, reading, writing, mathematics, financial and domestic skills, and leisure activities. Results are presented on a pie-chart, depicting the skills that are being learned, those already mastered, and those that may have been overlooked entirely. The chart enables annual comparisons of pro-gress to be made and forms a visual record of the child's progress. Examiner required. Not suitable for group use.
BRITISH PUBLISHER

Untimed: Varies

Scoring: Examiner evaluated

Cost: Manual £7.55; 10 record forms £5.65; transparency of chart £6.90

Publisher: NFER-NELSON Publishing Company Ltd.

NISONGER QUESTIONNAIRE FOR PARENTS
W. Loadman, F.A. Benson, and Douglas McElwain

Handicapped children

Purpose: Gathers preliminary informa-tion on a handicapped child from the perspective of the parents.

Description: Multiple item paper-pencil questionnaire consisting of nontechnical questions concerning the status of a hand-icapped child. Parents complete the form, which emphasizes current rather than historical information. A pocket is provided on the form for the child's picture. Self-administered. Suitable for group use.

Untimed: Varies

Scoring: Examiner evaluated

Cost: 20 questionnaires $20.00; user's guide $0.75; specimen set (user's guide, one questionnaire) $3.00

Publisher: The Nisonger Center, Ohio State University

PAIRED WORD MEMORY TASK (PAIRMEM)
Refer to page 52.

PICTORIAL TEST OF INTELLIGENCE
Refer to page 511.

RECEPTIVE ONE-WORD PICTURE VOCABULARY TEST (ROWPVT)
Refer to page 239.

TARC ASSESSMENT SYSTEM FOR SEVERELY HANDICAPPED CHILDREN
Refer to page 596.

TEST OF SYNTACTIC ABILITIES
Refer to page 652.

VCWS 18—CONCEPTUAL UNDERSTANDING THROUGH BLIND EVALUATION (CUBE)

Blind adults

Purpose: Measures the perceptive abilities that help a person compensate for visual handicaps. Used with the congenitally and adventitiously blind.

Description: Performance-based battery of six tests assessing a person's perceptual skills in meeting the basic needs of judgment, mobility, orientation, discrimination, and balance. The subtests are Tactual Perception, Mobility/Discrimination Skills, Spatial Organization and Memory, Assembly and Packaging, and Audile Perception. Administration of the

tests varies according to the factors being assessed: mobility or job skills. Examiner required. Not suitable for group use.

Timed: Not available

Scoring: Examiner evaluated

Cost: $2,600.00

Publisher: Valpar International Corporation

VINELAND ADAPTIVE BEHAVIOR SCALES
Refer to page 215.

WILLIAMS INTELLIGENCE TEST FOR CHILDREN WITH DEFECTIVE VISION
Refer to page 516.

Special Education: Special Education

ADOLESCENT AND ADULT PSYCHOEDUCATIONAL PROFILE (AAPEP)
Refer to page 598.

BARCLAY CLASSROOM ASSESSMENT SYSTEM (BCAS)
Refer to page 697.

BATTELLE DEVELOPMENTAL INVENTORY
Refer to page 462.

THE BEHAVIOR EVALUATION SCALE (BES)
Refer to page 666.

BENCH MARK MEASURES
Refer to page 248.

BESSEMER SCREENING TEST
Evelyn V. Jones and Gary L. Sapp

Child, adolescent
Ages 7-14

Purpose: Identifies children who may require special education services. Used to screen the learning disabled, emotionally disturbed, mentally retarded, and academically gifted.

Description: Five paper-pencil subtests requiring the student to write his own name, produce a human figure drawing, read words or symbols, reproduce abstract designs, and perform mathematic computations. The subtests are arranged in order of increasing difficulty and are similar to tasks the student would encounter in a regular classroom. Examiner required. Suitable for group use.

Timed: Maximum 15 minutes

Scoring: Examiner evaluated

Cost: Complete kit (15 student booklets, 30 scoring sheets, manual) $13.00

Publisher: Stoelting Company

THE BRIGANCE® DIAGNOSTIC INVENTORY OF ESSENTIAL SKILLS
Refer to page 369.

BRISTOL SOCIAL ADJUSTMENT GUIDES, BRITISH EDITION (BSAG)
Refer to page 668.

CAREER ADAPTIVE BEHAVIOR INVENTORY (CAB)
Refer to page 735.

CARTOON CONSERVATION SCALES (CCS)
Refer to page 568.

THE CHILD CENTER OPERATIONAL ASSESSMENT TOOL (OAT)
Refer to page 372.

DABERON SCREENING FOR SCHOOL READINESS
Refer to page 468.

DEVELOPMENTAL ASSESSMENT FOR THE SEVERELY HANDICAPPED (DASH)
Mary K. Dykes

Child   Developmental
        ages 0-8

Purpose: Assesses the development of severely handicapped individuals functioning between the developmental ages of birth to eight years. Used to establish IEPs.

Description: Five multiple-item paper-pencil observational scales assessing development in the following domains: sensory-motor, language, preacademic, activities of daily living, and social-emotional. The five Pinpoint Scales are sensitive to small changes in skill performance. The skills assessed are identified as either present, emerging, task-resistive, nonrelevant, or unknown. Examiner required. Not suitable for group use.

Untimed: Varies

Scoring: Examiner evaluated

Cost: Complete kit (manual, 5 each of 5 pinpoint scales, 25 daily plan sheets, 25 comprehensive program records, 25 individualized education plans) $85.00

Publisher: Exceptional Resources, Inc.

DIAGNOSTIC SCREENING TEST: ACHIEVEMENT (DSTA)
Thomas D. Gnagey and Patricia A. Gnagey

Child, adolescent
Grades K-14

Purpose: Measures basic knowledge of science, social studies, and literature and the arts to help determine a course of study for special education students.

Description: 108-item multiple-choice paper-pencil test measuring a student's conceptual level in science, social studies, and literature and the arts. Scores are obtained for practical knowledge and estimated mental age. The manual discusses subtest pattern analysis of student motivation, cultural versus organic retardation, cultural deprivation, reading and study skill problems, and possession of practical versus formal knowledge. The examiner explains the procedure to individuals or groups and reads the test if the students have poor reading skills. Examiner required. Suitable for group use.

Untimed: 5-10 minutes

Scoring: Hand key

Cost: Manual and 50 test forms $27.00

Publisher: Slosson Educational Publications, Inc.

THE DYSINTEGRAL LEARNING CHECKLIST
Refer to page 40.

EFFECTIVE READING TESTS
Refer to page 523.

EXPLORE THE WORLD OF WORK (E-WOW)
Refer to page 743.

FLORIDA INTERNATIONAL DIAGNOSTIC-PRESCRIPTIVE VOCATIONAL COMPETENCY PROFILE
Refer to page 764.

KAUFMAN ASSESSMENT BATTERY FOR CHILDREN (K-ABC)
Refer to page 25.

KAUFMAN TEST OF EDUCATIONAL ACHIEVEMENT (K-TEA)
Refer to page 403.

KHATENA-TORRANCE CREATIVE PERCEPTION INVENTORY
Refer to page 571.

THE LEARNING PREDICTOR
Refer to page 584.

PERFORMANCE ASSESSMENT OF SYNTAX: ELICITED AND SPONTANEOUS (PASES)
Refer to page 637.

THE POLLACK-BRANDEN BATTERY: FOR IDENTIFICATION OF LEARNING DISABILITIES, DYSLEXIA, AND CLASSROOM DYSFUNCTION
Refer to page 584.

THE PYRAMID SCALES
John D. Cone

Ages birth-78

Purpose: Assesses adaptive behavior in moderately to severely handicapped persons of all ages. Used to plan appropriate intervention programs, monitor changes in adaptive functioning over long periods of time, and establish relevant training priorities.

Description: 20 multiple-item paper-pencil scales assessing a handicapped individual's adaptive functioning skills. The scales are completed by the examiner using one or all of the following three modes: interview with the handicapped individual, interview with an informant, direct observation. The 20 skills areas assessed are arranged in three scale categories: sensory, primary, and secondary. Sensory scales assess tactile, auditory, and visual responsiveness skills. Items in this category are appropriate for very young and/or low-functioning individuals. Primary scales assess nine basic skills: gross motor, eating, fine motor, toileting, dressing, social interaction, washing and grooming, and receptive and expressive language. Secondary scales assess eight skills appropriate for older, higher-functioning individuals: recreation and leisure, writing, domestic behavior, reading, vocational, time, numbers, and money. Items in the scale were selected from and curriculum-referenced to such sources as the Brigance Inventory, the

Behavior Characteristics Progression (BCP), the Learning Accomplishment Profile (LAP), and the Uniform Performance Assessment System (UPAS). Tables are provided in the manual showing correlations between the scores of this test and those of other measures of adaptive ability. The test formerly was known as The West Virginia Assessment and Tracking System. Examiner required. Not suitable for group use.

Untimed: Varies

Scoring: Examiner evaluated

Cost: Complete kit (manual, 50 answer sheets, storage box) $32.00

Publisher: Pro-Ed

RECEPTIVE ONE-WORD PICTURE VOCABULARY TEST (ROWPVT)
Refer to page 239.

SCALES OF INDEPENDENT BEHAVIOR
Refer to page 491.

SCREENING TEST OF ADOLESCENT LANGUAGE (STAL)
Refer to page 644.

SOI PRIMARY FORM (FORM P)
Refer to page 513.

THE SOUTHERN CALIFORNIA ORDINAL SCALES OF DEVELOPMENT
Refer to page 566.

SPELLMASTER DIAGNOSTIC SPELLING SYSTEM
Refer to page 239.

SURVIVAL SKILLS PROFILE
Cuyahoga Special Education Service Center

Emotionally disturbed students   Grades K-12

Purpose: Provides an ongoing record of emotionally disturbed children's accomplishment of social survival skills. Used by teachers, psychologists, counselors, and parents for planning short- and long-term goals.

Description: 412-item paper-pencil examination administered to small groups over a period of 13 school years. Measures skills related directly to daily living (telling time, using maps and calendars, and nutritional knowledge) and those related to personal development (handling criticism, controlling aggression). The examiner marks squares to the left of the performance objectives with a slash to indicate emergent behavior or with an X to indicate mastery. Materials are contained in a spiral-bound 24-page booklet. Because the profile is designed for use with emotionally disturbed children, care should be taken to establish guidelines in the recording of behaviors to avoid observer subjectivity. The test may be used in conjunction with either the Developmental Learning Profile or the Student Learning Profile. Examiner required. Suitable for group use.

Untimed: Not available

Scoring: Examiner evaluated

Cost: 1 copy $4.85; 6 copies $24.85; 100 copies $2.50 each

Publisher: Creative Learning Systems, Inc.

TEST FOR EXAMINING EXPRESSIVE MORPHOLOGY (TEEM)
Refer to page 648.

THE TEST OF PRACTICAL KNOWLEDGE (TPK)
J. Lee Wiederholt and Stephen C. Larsen

Adolescent   Grades 8-12

Purpose: Identifies high-school students who are less knowledgeable than their peers about important daily living skills. Determines particular strengths and weaknesses. Used to document student's progress in special programs.

Description: Paper-pencil test consisting of three subtests: Personal Knowledge (relating to information needed to deal independently with day-to-day living), Social Knowledge (relating to social interactions, community services, and leisure activities), and Occupational Knowledge (relating to information needed to operate successfully in job situations). Examiner required. Suitable for group use.

Untimed: 35-40 minutes

Scoring: Hand key

Cost: Complete set (examiner's manual, 25 student booklets, 50 profile sheets, scoring stencil, storage box) $46.00

Publisher: Pro-Ed

TESTS FOR EVERYDAY LIVING (TEL)
Andrew Halpern, Larry K. Irvin, and Janet T. Landman

**Child, adolescent
Grades 7-12**

Purpose: Measures low-functioning students' knowledge of skills necessary for performing everyday activities. Also used by educators as a curriculum guide.

Description: 245-item orally administered multiple-choice paper-pencil test consisting of seven subtests: Job Search Skills, Job Related Behavior, Health Care, Home Management, Purchasing Habits, Banking, and Budget. A few performance items require reading skill. Results can be used to place students in the Skills for Independent Living resource kit curriculum. The test may be used at the junior high-school level with regular, remedial, and learning-disabled students. At the senior high-school level, it is most effective when used with average or low-functioning students. Examiner required. Suitable for use with groups not exceeding 20 students.

Untimed: Not available

Scoring: Hand key

Cost: Specimen set (test book, manual, answer key, technical report) $8.95

Publisher: CTB/McGraw-Hill

Speech, Hearing, and Visual (Sensory): Auditory

ADVANCED TESTS OF CENTRAL AUDITORY ABILITIES
Arthur Flowers

Grades 2 and above

Purpose: Measures central auditory abilities of low-achieving children and adults. Screens for general hearing-perception problems and isolates specific auditory phonemic identification deficiencies.

Description: 56-item two-part verbal test measuring auditory closure and figure-ground (ability to listen selectively against background noise). Part I (28 items) deals with competing messages. Part II (28 items) assesses low-pass filtered speech. All the items and examiner instructions are on audiotape. The examiner plays the tape, and the individual responds verbally. This test is the same as the Flowers-Costello test except that this test is suitable for adults, as well as children. Examiner required. Not suitable for group use.

Untimed: 8-10 minutes

Scoring: Examiner evaluated

Cost: Tape, 12 booklets $59.50

Publisher: Perceptual Learning Systems
Information and availability unconfirmed; no publisher response.

ASSESSING READING DIFFICULTIES: A DIAGNOSTIC AND REMEDIAL APPROACH
Lynette Bradley

Child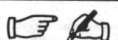

Purpose: Identifies children whose reading difficulties are the result of poor auditory organization and children who

---

are likely to encounter future reading and spelling problems.

Description: Multiple-item paper-pencil test assessing the problems of children who are making little or no progress towards learning to read. Test items are based on extensive longitudinal research that proved the close relationship between the inability to rhyme or identify rhyming words and reading failure. A section for recording teacher observations is included. The manual provides full details for administering the schedule and interpreting the results. Guidelines for appropriate remedial action are provided also. Examiner required. Not suitable for group use.

Untimed: Varies

Scoring: Examiner evaluated

Cost: Manual £3.75; 25 test sheets £2.75

Publisher: Macmillan Education

AUDITORY DISCRIMINATION TEST
Joseph M. Wepman

Child   Ages 5-8

Purpose: Measures the auditory discrimination ability of children. Used to identify specific auditory learning disabilities for possible remediation.

Description: Oral-response test in which the examiner verbally presents pairs of words to the child, and the child is asked to discriminate between them. The test predicts articulatory speech defects and certain remedial reading problems and has complete phonetic and phonemic balance. Available in two equivalent forms for retesting and measuring therapy progress. Examiner required. Not suitable for group use.

Untimed: 10-15 minutes

Scoring: Hand key

Cost: Complete kit (100 each of forms 1 and 2, manual) $47.50

Publisher: Western Psychological Services

AUDITORY DISCRIMINATION TEST, REVISED (1973) VERSION
Joseph M. Wepman

Child   Ages 5-8

Purpose: Measures the auditory discrimination ability of children ages 5-8. Used to identify specific auditory learning disabilities for possible remediation.

Description: Oral-response test in which children are verbally presented pairs of words and asked to discriminate between them. The test predicts articulatory speech defects and certain remedial reading problems. The 1973 revision is identical to the 1958 edition except for scoring. In the 1973 version, scoring is based on a correct score rather than on the "error" basis of the original edition. The new manual contains standardization tables for children ages 5-8, a 5-point rating scale, an interpretation section discussing how the test results may be used, reports on research using the test, and selected references. Examiner required. Not suitable for group use.

Untimed: 10-15 minutes

Scoring: Hand key

Cost: Complete kit (100 each of form 1A and 2A, manual) $49.50

Publisher: Western Psychological Services

AUDITORY INTEGRATIVE ABILITIES TEST (AIAT)
Carole Grote

Child   Ages 6-9

Purpose: Diagnoses auditory perceptual disorders as they relate to language-based learning disabilities in children. Used in conjunction with other tests to develop a remedial program.

Description: 30-item paper-pencil test consisting of three subtests. The auditory-motor subtest requires the student to clap his hands to sound patterns. The auditory-graphic subtest requires the student to chart sound patterns on index cards. The auditory-verbal subtest requires the student to orally reproduce sound patterns. A cassette tape, included with the material, is used to administer the test. The student uses score sheets to record his responses. Since the tasks involved may be new and unfamiliar, some pretest training is recommended and provided for in the manual. Examiner required. Suitable for group use.

Untimed: Not available

Scoring: Hand key

Cost: Program (cassette tape, 25 individual scoring sheets, index cards, examiner's manual) $14.50; 25 additional score sheets $3.30

Publisher: Educational Activities, Inc.

AUDITORY MEMORY SPAN TEST
Joseph M. Wepman and Anne Morency

Child   Ages 5-8

Purpose: Measures the ability of children ages 5-8 to retain and recall words as auditory units, an essential capacity for learning how to speak and read accurately. Used to identify specific auditory learning disabilities.

Description: Oral-response test assessing the development of a child's ability to retain and recall familiar, isolated words received aurally. The test items are based on the most frequently used words in the spoken vocabulary of five-year-old children. Norms are provided for children ages 5, 6, 7, and 8. Available in two equivalent forms, 1 and 2. Examiner required. Not suitable for group use.

Untimed: 5-10 minutes

Scoring: Hand key

Cost: Complete kit (includes 100 each of Forms 1 and 2, manual) $47.50

Publisher: Western Psychological Services

AUDITORY POINTING TEST
Refer to page 577.

AUDITORY SEQUENTIAL MEMORY TEST
Joseph M. Wepman and Anne Morency

Child   Ages 5-8

Purpose: Measures the ability of children ages 5-8 to remember and repeat what they have just heard. Used to diagnose specific auditory learning disabilities.

Description: Oral-response test assessing a child's ability to repeat from immediate memory an increasing series of digits in the exact order of their verbal presentation. The test is useful for determining a child's readiness for learning to read and speak with accuracy and is also a determinant of spelling and arithmetic achievement. Norms are provided for children ages 5, 6, 7, and 8. Available in two equivalent forms, 1 and 2. Examiner required. Not suitable for group use.

Untimed: 5 minutes

Scoring: Hand key

Cost: Complete kit (100 each of Forms 1 and 2, manual) $47.50

Publisher: Western Psychological Services

CARROW AUDITORY-VISUAL ABILITIES TEST (CAVAT)
Refer to page 656.

DENVER AUDIOMETRIC SCREENING TEST (DAST)
Amelia F. Drumwright

Ages 3 and older

Purpose: Detects children with hearing deficiencies. Used to screen for 25dB loss. Those who fail the test are referred for additional examination.

Description: Function test in which a trained examiner creates a tone with an audiometer and checks the child's response. The child indicates whether he can hear the tone at different decibel levels. Examiner and audiometer required. Not suitable for group use.

Untimed: 5-10 minutes

Scoring: Examiner evaluated

Cost: 25 tests $1.75; manual $6.50
Publisher: Ladoca Publishing
Foundation
Information and availability unconfirmed; no
publisher response.

EVALUATING COMMUNICATIVE COMPETENCE: A FUNCTIONAL PRAGMATIC PROCEDURE
Refer to page 626.

FLOWERS AUDITORY TEST OF SELECTIVE ATTENTION (FATSA)
Arthur Flowers

Child   Grades 1-6

Purpose: Determines a child's ability to understand what is being said. Measures auditory attention deficit. Used as a screening tool for possible remedial work.

Description: 35-item paper-pencil test consisting of three practice items and 32 test items measuring central hearing function and selective attention skills. The child is given a directive on tape and then marks one of seven "Simon Says..." statements most appropriate to the recorded directive. An auditory deficit score is obtained, and remedial instruction is planned. Examiner required. Suitable for group use.

Untimed: 23 minutes
Scoring: Hand key
Cost: Complete kit (includes 12 booklets) $69.96
Publisher: Perceptual Learning Systems
Information and availability unconfirmed; no
publisher response.

FLOWERS-COSTELLO TESTS OF CENTRAL AUDITORY ABILITY
Arthur Flowers and
Mary Rose Costello

Child   Grades K-6

Purpose: Identifies kindergartners and first-graders who have hearing-perception problems and establishes probabilities for future reading success. For low-achieving elementary school students, it measures central auditory abilities in order to isolate

specific auditory phonemic identification deficiencies.

Description: 48-item two-part verbal test measuring auditory closure and figure-ground (ability to listen selectively against background noise). Part I (24 items) deals with low-pass filtered speech. Part II (24 items) assesses how the child handles competing messages. All the items and examiner instructions are on audiotape. The examiner plays the tape, and the taker responds verbally. For kindergarten students, pictures are shown, a statement (i.e., "We put a shoe on our...") is made, pictures are shown, and the child points to the object not mentioned. The test is designed for low-achieving children whose CAA scores suggest a specific learning disability that may interfere with the child's progress. Examiner required. Not suitable for group use.

Untimed: 15 minutes
Scoring: Examiner evaluated
Cost: Basic kit $89.50; 30 test score sheets $3.50
Publisher: Perceptual Learning Systems
Information and availability unconfirmed; no
publisher response.

GOCHNOUR IDIOM SCREENING TEST (GIST)
Refer to page 628.

GOLDMAN-FRISTOE-WOODCOCK AUDITORY SKILLS TEST BATTERY
Ronald Goldman, Macalyne Fristoe,
and Richard W. Woodcock

All ages

Purpose: Diagnoses an individual's ability to hear clearly under difficult conditions. Used for instructional planning.

Description: Twelve subtests measure auditory selective attention, diagnostic auditory discrimination, auditory memory, and sound-symbol skills. The examiner presents a test plate to the subject and records the subject's response. The Auditory Selective Attention Test assesses the ability to attend under increasingly difficult listening conditions.

The Diagnostic Auditory Discrimination Test—Part I assesses the individual's ability to discriminate between specific speech sounds that are frequently confused. The Diagnostic Auditory Discrimination Test—Part II is used with individuals who experience difficulty with speech-sound discrimination in Part I. The Auditory Memory Tests assess three aspects of auditory memory performance: recognition memory, memory for content, and memory for sequence. The Sound Symbol Tests assess several abilities underlying the development of written language skills. Scores derived are age equivalents, age-based percentile ranks, standard scores, and stanines. Materials include four manuals, 25 response forms in each of the five easels (diagnostic auditory discrimination tests are in two easels), test plates bound into five easels, one test tape per easel, 25 battery profile forms, and a technical manual. Examiner required. Not suitable for group use.

Untimed: 15 minutes per subtest

Scoring: Examiner evaluated

Cost: Complete test battery (5 easel-kits) $204.75

Publisher: American Guidance Service

THE HEARING MEASUREMENT SCALE
William G. Noble

Hearing-impaired individuals

Purpose: Measures degree of hearing impairment as reported by the hearing-impaired individual.

Description: Multiple-item interview or paper-pencil self-report questionnaire assessing the degree to which an individual's hearing is impaired. The scale yields eight scores: Speech Hearing, Hearing for Nonspeech Sounds, Spatial Localization, Emotional Response to Hearing Impairment, Speech Distortion, Tinnitus, Personal Opinion of Hearing, and Total. Self-administered. Paper-pencil version suitable for group use.

Untimed: Varies

Scoring: Examiner evaluated

Cost: Test kit (manual, 50 questionnaires, transparent scoring matrix) $17.50

Publisher: University of New England (Australia)

THE HOLLIEN-THOMPSON GROUP HEARING TEST
Harry Hollien and Carl Thompson

Child   Ages 5-8

Purpose: Identifies children suffering from a loss of hearing. Used by educators to screen groups of children to determine which children need further individual testing.

Description: Multiple-item hearing discrimination test consisting of a 45-page test booklet or original designs in two equated forms for group testing of up to 40 children. Norms for each age group are available. Materials consist of manual, guide, cue sheet for administration, scoring template, poster, and pack of 50 test forms. Examiner required. Suitable for group use.
CANADIAN PUBLISHER

Untimed: 1-2 minutes

Scoring: Hand key; examiner evaluated

Cost: Complete kit $50.00; 50 additional test forms $8.00

Publisher: Institute of Psychological Research, Inc.

Information and availability unconfirmed; no publisher response.

INVENTORY OF PERCEPTUAL SKILLS (IPS)
Refer to page 658.

LANGUAGE-STRUCTURED AUDITORY RETENTION SPAN TEST (LARS)
Refer to page 583.

THE LEARNING PREDICTOR
Refer to page 584.

LINDAMOOD AUDITORY CONCEPTUALIZATION TEST (LAC)

Charles H. Lindamood and Patricia C. Lindamood

All ages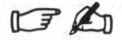

Purpose: Measures an individual's ability to discriminate one speech sound from another and to perceive the number, order, and sameness or difference of speech sounds in sequences. Used to diagnose auditory-conceptual dysfunctions and to determine the need for remedial training.

Description: 40-item verbal response test in which the subject arranges colored blocks (each symbolizing one speech sound) in a row to represent a sound pattern spoken by the examiner. The color of the blocks indicates sameness or difference with a repeated sound symbolized by the same color block and a different sound by a different color. Materials include the manual, cassette, 24 wooden blocks in six colors, test forms, and examiner's cue sheets. A separate product, "Auditory Discrimination in Depth," provides a training program. The LAC, which is not appropriate for deaf subjects, is to be administered individually by an examiner. Not suitable for group use. Available in Spanish.

Untimed: Not available

Scoring: Examiner evaluated

Cost: Complete set $25.00

Publisher: DLM Teaching Resources

NON-LANGUAGE MULTI-MENTAL TEST

Refer to page 29.

OLIPHANT AUDITORY DISCRIMINATION MEMORY TEST

Genevive Oliphant

Child, adolescent Grades 1-8

Purpose: Evaluates the ability of grade-school students to hear and discriminate sounds and words. Used to identify stu-

dents needing further testing and to diagnose the relationship between perceptual problems and learning disabilities.

Description: 20-item paper-pencil test measuring how well students discriminate sounds and remember what they hear. Each item presents the student with two words, which are either alike or minimally different. The examiner then presents a third word, and the student is asked to decide whether that word is the same as the first or second word or whether all three words are the same. The words are all single-syllable in a consonant-vowel-consonant format. Examiner required. Suitable for group use.

Untimed: 30-45 minutes

Scoring: Examiner evaluated

Cost: Complete kit (12 tests, 2 sheets of teacher directions) $3.30

Publisher: Educators Publishing Service, Inc.

SCREENING TEST FOR AUDITORY PERCEPTION (STAP)

Geraldine M. Kimmel and Jack Wahl

Child Grades 1-6 and re- medial students

Purpose: Assesses weaknesses in five areas of auditory perception in elementary school and remedial students. Used to identify those who are performing below grade or age level.

Description: Series of multiple-item paper-pencil subtests measuring ability to discriminate among long versus short vowels, single versus blend initial consonants, rhyming versus nonrhyming words, same versus different rhythmic patterns, and same versus different words. Abnormal limits indicating a student's need for remedial attention or further testing are provided. Materials include suggested remedial activities for each of the five skill areas tapped. Available on cassette tape for uniform administration. Examiner required. Suitable for group use.

Untimed: 45 minutes

Scoring: Hand key

Cost: Manual $7.50; 50 record forms $5.00

Publisher: Academic Therapy Publications

A SCREENING TEST FOR IDENTIFYING CENTRAL AUDITORY DISORDERS (SCAN)
Robert W. Keith

Child

Purpose: Identifies central auditory disorders in children.

Description: Multiple-item standardized response test consisting of four subtests of auditory abilities. In the Filtered Words subtest, the child hears words in which high frequency sounds have been filtered. In the Auditory Figure Ground subtest, the child hears words with background noise. In the Auditory Fusion subtest, the child hears words that consist of low and high pass filtered bands presented to both ears separately, then split and presented to different ears simultaneously. In the Competing Words subtest, the child hears a different word in each ear simultaneously. Examiner required. Not suitable for group use.

Untimed: 15 minutes

Scoring: Not available

Cost: Contact publisher

Publisher: The Psychological Corporation

SEQUENCED INVENTORY OF COMMUNICATION DEVELOPMENT, REVISED EDITION, 1984
Refer to page 645.

SHORT TERM AUDITORY RETRIEVAL AND STORAGE TEST (STARS)
Arthur Flowers

Child   Grades 1-6

Purpose: Identifies a child's short-term ability to remember and use what is heard. Used as a guide to possible remedial help.

Description: 55-item paper-pencil test used to isolate auditory retrieval and storage problems. The examiner plays a tape recording, and the child listens and marks the appropriate pictures in the test booklet. A low score indicates a problem and need for a remedial program. Examiner required. Suitable for group use.

Untimed: 16 minutes

Scoring: Examiner evaluated

Cost: Complete set $69.50

Publisher: Perceptual Learning Systems

Information and availability unconfirmed; no publisher response.

SMITH-JOHNSON NONVERBAL PERFORMANCE SCALE
Refer to page 17.

STYCAR HEARING TESTS
Mary D. Sheridan

Child
Ages 6 months-7 years

Purpose: Assesses child's capacity to hear with comprehension in commonplace situations. Used for preliminary screening of very young or mentally handicapped children.

Description: Multiple-item series of simple clinical auditory screening tests. The child responds to toys and pictures. Materials include a manual, vocabulary cards, toy blocks, rattle, plane, boat, cars, and dolls. The tests are available to medical doctors, speech therapists, and teachers of the deaf, blind, and physically handicapped. Examiner required. Not suitable for group use.
BRITISH PUBLISHER

Untimed: Not available

Scoring: Examiner evaluated

Cost: Complete kit (toys, coloured square card, 5 picture vocabulary cards, children's cutlery set, 25 record forms, manual) £68.95 (payment in sterling for all overseas orders)

Publisher: NFER-NELSON Publishing Company Ltd.

TEST FOR AUDITORY COMPREHENSION OF LANGUAGE—1985 REVISED EDITION (TACL-R)
Elizabeth Carrow-Woolfolk

Ages 3-adult

Purpose: Measures auditory comprehension of children. Also used with adults.

Description: Multiple-item response test assessing auditory understanding of word classes and relations, grammatical morphemes, and elaborated sentence constructions. The test requires no oral response. This revised edition provides high reliability and validity, a more efficient scoring system, and a variety of normative comparisons. The test yields percentile ranks, standard scores, and age equivalents. Examiner required. Not suitable for group use.

Untimed: 10-20 minutes

Scoring: Examiner evaluated; may be computer scored

Cost: Complete kit (test book, manual, record forms) $95.00

Publisher: DLM Teaching Resources

TEST FOR AUDITORY FIGURE-GROUND DISCRIMINATION (TAFD)—1981

Child Ages 5-10

Purpose: Measures ability to attend to one sound and to perceive it in relation to, but separate from, competing sounds. Used for educational evaluation.

Description: 7-subtest measure of auditory perception of specific sounds against a variety of background sounds (e.g., a bicycle bell against traffic noise or speech against background music). The child responds verbally to tape-recorded stimuli. Materials include a cassette tape recording of the TAFD. Available to professional personnel attached to education departments and others who can document their expertise. Examiner required. Not suitable for group use.

SOUTH AFRICAN PUBLISHER

Timed: 1 hour

Scoring: Examiner evaluated

Cost: Contact publisher; all orders from outside The RSA will be dealt with on merit

Publisher: Human Sciences Research Council

TEST OF AUDITORY COMPREHENSION (TAC)
Los Angeles County Schools

Hearing-impaired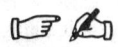
Ages 4-17

Purpose: Assesses comprehension in hearing-impaired children. Used for academic placement and instructional planning.

Description: Ten subtests measuring auditory comprehension. The subtests begin with simple auditory discrimination tasks and conclude by assessing the child's understanding of complex stories given with a competing message background. The child responds to recorded messages by pointing to one of several pictures. The test results produce a profile of the child's performance on a continuum of auditory tasks, provide a basis for instruction, and allow comparison of results by age, degree of hearing loss, and type of placement. Administration requires the child's usual amplification, a quiet room, and a program-stop or cassette player. Norms are provided for individuals ages 4-17 with moderate or profound hearing losses. The test is directly correlated to a curriculum and training program and also may be used to assess auditory processing of the learning disabled. Examiner required. Not suitable for group use.

Untimed: 30 minutes

Scoring: Examiner evaluated; hand key

Cost: Test, manual $75.00

Publisher: Foreworks Publications

TEST OF AUDITORY-PERCEPTUAL SKILLS (TAP)
Morrison F. Gardner

Child Ages 4-12

Purpose: Assesses the auditory functions of children. Used by psychologists, speech pathologists, language specialists, learning specialists, diagnosticians, and other professionals.

Description: Multiple-item response test consisting of six subtests measuring auditory discrimination, auditory sequential memory, auditory word memory, auditory interpreting directions, auditory processing, and hyperactivity. The test is used for diagnosing auditory perceptual difficulties, imperceptions of auditory modality, language problems, and learning problems. Examiner required. Not suitable for group use.

Untimed: 10-15 minutes

Scoring: Hand key

Cost: Test kit (manual, 35 test booklets) $46.50

Publisher: Children's Hospital of San Francisco, Publications Department

TESTING-TEACHING MODULE OF AUDITORY DISCRIMINATION (TTMAD)
Victoria Risko

Child   Grades K-6

Purpose: Determines auditory discrimination in elementary school children and increases proficiency in those skills. Used in developmental, corrective, or remedial programs which focus on auditory discrimination and blending.

Description: Multiple-item paper-pencil verbal assessment in two sections. Section 1 is a 125-item diagnostic instrument consisting of subtests in six areas: initial and final consonants, initial and final blends and diagraphs, vowels and vowel combinations. The second section is a series of 450 games and activities to increase proficiency. When skill deficiencies are detected by diagnostic testing, the examiner refers to the teaching activities in the manual. The games and activities, which correspond directly to each skill assessed, are coded by whether they are appropriate for individualized or group instruction or both. Individual item analysis sheets are provided. Examiner required. Suitable for group use.

Untimed: 20-30 minutes

Scoring: Examiner evaluated

Cost: Complete kit $13.50

Publisher: United Educational Services, Inc.

TIP AND DIP TESTS FOR THE HEARING OF SPEECH BY YOUNG CHILDREN
Bruce M. Siegenthaler and George S. Haspiel

Child   Ages 3-12

Purpose: Measures hearing threshold and speech discrimination. Used to evaluate hearing loss with and without amplification and for medical therapy.

Description: Multiple-item two-test battery. The threshold of Hearing Test (TIP) (25 items) measures hearing threshold by identification of pictures. The test booklet, available in Forms A and B, contains five pictures per page of objects with names that do not sound alike (blocks, doll, tree, watch). The examiner names an object and the child points to the appropriate picture. The Discrimination of Speech Test (DIP) uses 48 sets of pictures. The names of the pictured items sound similar (bear, pear). The child points to the item described by the examiner. The test may be administered to individuals older than age 12 when other word tests have not obtained satisfactory responses. The TIP test obtains a threshold of speech hearing score, and DIP yields a discrimination score. The test must be administered by a trained audiologist in a sound room. Examiner required. Not suitable for group use.

Untimed: TIP 5 minutes; DIP 7 minutes

Scoring: Hand key

Cost: Complete (picture book with 2 sections, scoring form, response sheets, manual) $15.00 plus postage and handling

Publisher: Speech and Hearing Clinic

TREE/BEE TEST OF AUDITORY DISCRIMINATION (TREE/BEE TEST)
Janet B. Fudala

Ages 3-adult

Purpose: Measures auditory discrimination abilities in children and adults. Used as a basis for further testing and remediation.

Description: Multiple-item oral response test in which the examinees are shown stimulus pictures and point to or mark the proper picture as the examiner says the word or phrase (e.g., a tree, a bee, or a key). Four equivalent forms are provided for test-retest situations. There are two sets of stimulus pictures and two sets of stimulus items, which can be mixed. A flip-flop book is available for individual administration. No reading or writing is required of the examinee. The test has been normed for children ages 3-9, but not for older children or adults. Examiner required. Suitable for group use.

Untimed: 10 minutes

Scoring: Hand key

Cost: Test kit $31.50

Publisher: United Educational Services, Inc.

WICHITA AUDITORY FUSION TEST (WAFT)
Robert L. McCroskey

Ages 3-30

Purpose: Assesses temporal integrity of the auditory system at the brainstem level. Used by academic specialists, speech-language clinicians, and audiologists.

Description: Response test evaluating how a listener responds to variations in frequency, intensity, and temporal patterns that comprise the speech signal. The examinee wears earphones, listens to a series of tone pairs, and signals whether one or two tones occur as each pair is presented. Impaired temporal functions indicate communication problems. Specialists use the test for identifying auditory age and underlying neural transmission differences that can have an adverse effect on educational progress. The test is available in four forms: screening test, full test, expanded version, and short form. A standard cassette audio playback system is adequate for administering the test. Examiner required. Not suitable for group use.

Untimed: Varies

Scoring: Hand key

Cost: Contact publisher

Publisher: Modern Education Corporation

WICHITA AUDITORY PROCESSING TEST (WAPT)
Robert L. McCroskey

Preschool-elementary-school students

Purpose: Assesses auditory processing abilities of preschool and elementary students. Identifies communicative and educational problems and suggests remedial procedures.

Description: 40-item response test yielding information about subtle auditory disorders contributing to verbal and learning problems. A picture association task is used to measure auditory language comprehension. The test consists of four sets of 10 sentences recorded at four different speaking rates ranging from faster-than-normal to slower-than-normal speech. The examinee listens to the sentences and touches pictures on multiple-choice picture response plates that match the sentence. Norms are provided for normal children and those with speech-language problems, including reading disorders, articulation disorders, language and learning disabilities, mental-retardation, and poor academic achievement. Examiner required. Not suitable for group use.

Untimed: Not available

Scoring: Not available

Cost: Complete kit $68.00

Publisher: Modern Education Corporation

WRITTEN LANGUAGE SYNTAX TEST
Refer to page 254.

Speech, Hearing, and Visual (Sensory): Speech and Language

ADOLESCENT LANGUAGE SCREENING TEST (ALST)
Denise L. Morgan and
Arthur M. Guilford

Adolescent   Ages 11-17

Purpose: Assesses speech and language proficiency of adolescents. Used by speech-language pathologists and other professionals in clinics, hospitals, universities, schools, and private practice.

Description: Multiple-item oral-response screening test consisting of seven sub-tests—pragmatics, receptive vocabulary, concepts, expressive vocabulary (naming to confrontation, naming to description, and use of lexical items), sentence formulation, morphology, and phonology—in three areas: use, content, and form. The test outlines the language dimensions on which extension testing should focus. Examiner required. Not suitable for group use.

Untimed: 10-15 minutes

Scoring: Examiner evaluated

Cost: Complete kit $55.00

Publisher: Modern Education Corporation

ARIZONA ARTICULATION PROFICIENCY SCALE: REVISED
Janet Barker Fudala

Child   Ages 3-12

Purpose: Measures the speaking abilities of children ages 3-12. Used to identify children requiring speech therapy.

Description: 48-item oral-response measure of articulation performance in which the child responds to pictures and sentences presented on 48 stimulus cards. The examiner records all errors in the protocol booklet. A sentence test is pro-vided as an alternative for use with older children. Scores provided include total articulatory proficiency and percentage of improvement. Norms are provided for children ages 3-12. A Survey Form is available for compiling an abbreviated articulation record of 10 children on a single sheet. Examiner required. Suitable for group use.

Untimed: 10-15 minutes

Scoring: Hand key

Cost: Kit (set of reusable picture test cards, 25 protocol booklets, 10 survey forms, manual) $45.00

Publisher: Western Psychological Services

ARTICULATION SCREENING ASSESSMENT (ASA)
Jean Gilliam de Gaetano

Preschool and elementary-school children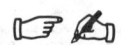

Purpose: Identifies the sounds that a student has not mastered and determines whether articulation errors occur in isolated words or elicited speech. Used to determine the need for additional testing or therapy.

Description: Multiple-item three-part articulation screening device. In Section I, the student is required to name isolated pictures which contain the indicated sound in various positions. Section II uses the pictures in Section I in sequential action to elicit free-flowing speech. The third section is for children who are capable of reading the sentences. All three sections or only one or two sections may be used by the examiner. A unique feature of the test is the double use of the vowel being tested in each picture. Two different forms are used to record sound substitution, omissions, distortions, and exact verbal responses. Examiner required. Not suitable for group use.

Untimed: Varies

Scoring: Examiner evaluated

Cost: Complete Kit $32.00

Publisher: Modern Education Corporation

ASSESSMENT OF CHILDREN'S LANGUAGE COMPREHENSION (ACLC)

Rochana Foster, Jane J. Giddan, and Joel Stark

Child   Ages 3-6.5

Purpose: Identifies receptive language difficulties in young children in order to provide guidelines for remediation of language disorders.

Description: 41-item verbal test of language comprehension measuring understanding of core vocabulary and combination of language elements. Each of the 41 spiral-bound stimulus cards is presented to the child, who points to an appropriate picture in response to a word or phrase from the examiner. A 17-item ACLC Group Form has been developed for classroom screening. Examiner required. Not suitable for group use. Available in Spanish.

Timed: 10-15 minutes

Scoring: Examiner evaluated

Cost: Complete kit $22.00 (includes card set, manual, pad of recording sheets)

Publisher: Consulting Psychologists Press, Inc.

ASSESSMENT OF FLUENCY IN SCHOOL-AGE CHILDREN (AFSC)

Julia Thompson

Child, adolescent
Grades K-12

Purpose: Evaluates speech deficiencies. Used to assess individuals who stutter and for therapy and school programs.

Description: 37-item paper-pencil test measuring expressive language, physiological components, oral motor and breath control, and self-awareness of disfluencies. Materials include a tape recorder, picture stimulus watch, test form, and resource guide. The test must be administered by a speech pathologist. Examiner required. Not suitable for group use.

Untimed: 45 minutes

Scoring: Examiner evaluated

Cost: Complete set (resource guide, 32 assessment forms, 32 parent interview forms, 32 teacher evaluation forms, 32 dismissal forms, carrying case) $32.50

Publisher: The Interstate Printers and Publishers, Inc.

THE ASSESSMENT OF PHONOLOGICAL PROCESSES

Barbara Williams Hodson

Child   Ages 3-8

Purpose: Evaluates the ability of children with severe speech disorders to use phonetics. Used for early childhood intervention and placement.

Description: 55-item test measuring spontaneous utterances naming three-dimensional stimuli. The examiner records speech deviations using narrow phonetic transcription. Materials include recording, analysis, summary, and screening forms. Examiner required. Not suitable for group use.

Untimed: 20 minutes

Scoring: Examiner evaluated; may be computer scored

Cost: Complete kit (manual, 48 recording forms, 48 analysis sheets, 48 analysis summary sheets, 96 screening forms) $28.95

Publisher: The Interstate Printers & Publishers, Inc.

AUSTIN SPANISH ARTICULATION TEST

Elizabeth Carrow-Woolfolk

Child   Ages 3-12

Purpose: Identifies articulation problems in Spanish-speaking children.

Description: 59-item verbal test in which the examiner reads an incomplete sentence and the child completes it. The manual contains reliability and validity data and gives specific instructions for administering and scoring. The examiner must be experienced in articulation testing and have a working knowledge of Spanish. Not suitable for group use.

Untimed: 25 minutes

Scoring: Examiner evaluated

Cost: Complete $19.00

Publisher: DLM Teaching Resources

BANKSON LANGUAGE SCREENING TEST (BLST)
Nicholas W. Bankson

Child   Ages 4-8

Purpose: Assesses the language development of children. Identifies children needing further evaluation. Used to plan language intervention programs.

Description: Multiple-item oral-response test measuring the development of expressive language behavior and related auditory and visual perception skills. Picture stimuli are used to present test items based on a model that includes the morphological, syntactic, and semantic aspects of language necessary for linguistic performance. The results determine appropriate areas for follow-up diagnostic assessment and identify initial language areas in need of remediation. Examiner required. Not suitable for group use.

Untimed: Varies

Scoring: Examiner evaluated

Cost: Complete kit $32.00; manual $21.00; 25 scoring sheets $13.00

Publisher: Pro-Ed

BASIC INVENTORY OF NATURAL LANGUAGE (BINL)
CHECpoint Systems, Inc.

Child, adolescent
Grades K-12

Purpose: Measures students' language proficiency. Used in bilingual, ESL, language development, and speech and language remediation programs.

Description: Oral-response test in which each test item consists of a color photograph that is used to elicit language samples from the students. The language samples are transcribed and analyzed at three levels: word class (determiner, noun, verb, adjective, adverb, preposition, etc.); type of phrase employed (noun phrase, verb phrase, prepositional phrase, gerund phrase, etc.); and sentence type (simple sentence, compound sentence,

compound/complex sentence, etc.). Four BINL kits are available. Forms A and B are elementary kits for use with Grades K-6. Forms C and D are secondary kits for use with Grades 7-12. The kits include an instructions manual, 20 full-color photographs on heavy posterboard, 400 individual oral scoring sheets, class profile cards, sorting envelopes to prepare the tests for machine scoring, and materials for teaching the prescription activities included in the instructions manual. Three BINL computer scoring programs are available. BINL I scoring is available from the publisher. The reports from this program include individual scores, class and grade level, graphs of student placement, and classification of students into four categories: Non, Limited, Functional, and Proficient. The program is available in English, Spanish, and 24 other languages. BINL II SDS (Same Day Scoring) and BINL II LPS (Language Profile Scoring) are available for the Apple IIe and IIc computers only. Use is limited by licensing to one machine per program. BINL II SDS is an on-site program in which language samples may be entered and holistically scored by up to three persons. The following scores are obtained: Listening Comprehension, Fluency, Vocabulary, Pronunciation, and Grammar. A detailed report and a summary report are available. The BINL II SDS diskettes may be sent to the publisher for scoring by the BINL II LPS, a language analysis program that produces a detailed profile of the language sample produced during the test. The profile shows variety of vocabulary, sentence length, total words, total unique words, number of nouns, verbs, modals, prepositions, complexity level of each sentence, and average complexity level for the sample. The profiles are used as data for planning lessons for oral language development and remediation. Examiner required. Not suitable for group use.

Untimed: Varies

Scoring: Computer scored

Cost: BINL kit A, B, C, or D $59.00 each

Publisher: CHECpoint Systems, Inc.

BASIC LANGUAGE CONCEPTS TEST (BLCT)
Siegfried Engelmann, Dorothy Ross, and Virginia Bingham

Child   Ages 4-6.5

Purpose: Assesses the language competence of children ages 4-6.5 and older language-deficient children. Used by teachers, special educators, speech-language pathologists, school psychologists, or supervised nonprofessionals to diagnose specific skill deficiencies, to serve as a basis for developing IEPs, and to obtain baseline measures against which to evaluate progress.

Description: Multiple-item three-part oral-response test assessing receptive and expressive deficiencies, the representational character of language, and the recognition of sequence and pattern in language. Part I (32 items) measures receptive language skills; Part II (35 items) measures expressive language skills; Part III assesses analogy skills. Results provide diagnostic information for the teacher/clinician to distinguish between children with language disorders and disadvantaged children who develop more slowly and to set goals for individual education programs. Examiner required. Not suitable for group use.

Untimed: 15 minutes

Scoring: Hand key

Cost: Test kit (includes manual, 40 test forms) $29.95

Publisher: C.C. Publications, Inc.

BILINGUAL SYNTAX MEASURE (BSM)
Refer to page 260.

BOSTON DIAGNOSTIC APHASIA EXAMINATION
Refer to page 38.

BRACKEN BASIC CONCEPT SCALE—DIAGNOSTIC SCALE (BBCS-DIAG)
Refer to page 463.

BRACKEN BASIC CONCEPT SCALE—SCREENING TEST (BBCS-SCREENING)
Refer to page 463.

THE BZOCH-LEAGUE RECEPTIVE-EXPRESSIVE EMERGENT LANGUAGE SCALE (REEL)
Refer to page 5.

CAMBRIDGE KINDERGARTEN SCREENING TEST
Ann M. Shahzade

Child   Kindergarten

Purpose: Measures the speech and language abilities of kindergartners. Identifies children needing further evaluation or observation.

Description: Multiple-item oral-response and task-performance test screening all major areas of speech and language. The various subtests are administered by means of realistic, full-color photographs of common objects and with the use of 10 wooden color cubes. The test may be administered by a speech pathologist, classroom teacher, aide, or volunteer. Step-by-step directions for administering the test are provided in the spiral-bound testing book. The screener's manual contains instructions for administering, scoring, and record keeping. Examiner required. Suitable for screening groups of children.

Untimed: 10-20 minutes

Scoring: Examiner evaluated

Cost: Test kit (testing book, manual, wooden color cubes, vinyl carrying case) $40.00

Publisher: DLM Teaching Resources

CARROW AUDITORY-VISUAL ABILITIES TEST (CAVAT)
Refer to page 656.

CARROW ELICITED LANGUAGES INVENTORY (CELI)
Elizabeth Carrow-Woolfolk

Child   Ages 3-7.11

Purpose: Measures the productive control of grammar in young children and diagnoses expressive language delays and disorders. Used to obtain data on a child's grammatical structure.

Description: 52-item test of oral stimuli based on the technique of eliciting imitation of a sequence of sentences that include basic construction types and specific grammatical morphemes. The stimuli (51 sentences and one phrase) are presented by the examiner. The child's responses are recorded and transcribed from the tape onto a scoring/analysis form, which provides a format for analyzing errors of substitution, addition, omission, transposition, and reversal. A separate verb protocol sheet provides for analyzing production of verb forms. Materials include the test manual, a training guide with practice exercises, the analysis forms, and a cassette or reel training tape. The test is not appropriate for nonverbal subjects. Examiner required. Not suitable for group use.

Untimed: 5 minutes

Scoring: Examiner evaluated

Cost: Complete $53.00

Publisher: DLM Teaching Resources

CHILD LANGUAGE ABILITY MEASURES (CLAM)
Albert Mehrabian and
Christy Floynihan

Child   Ages 2-7

Purpose: Measures the language production and language comprehension abilities of children. Identifies linguistic abilities and difficulties. Used by educators, speech-language pathologists, testers, and child psychologists to plan language development programs.

Description: Six multiple-item oral-response and nonverbal task-performance tests measuring a child's expressive and receptive language abilities, including vocabulary comprehension, grammar comprehension, inflection production, grammar imitation, "grammar formedness" judgment, and grammar equivalence judgment. The tests assess a child's knowledge of syntactic, semantic, and phonological rules and do not confound measurement of language development with intellectual skills such as memory span, knowledge of real world facts, or ability to form abstract relationships. Administration procedures contain built-in safeguards against tester bias (such as encouraging one child more than another). The six tests may be administered separately or together, depending on the needs of the child in question (a selected pair of tests is usually sufficient to obtain a reliable and valid measure of a child's language skills). Norms are provided to calculate standardized scores for each test and for combinations of tests. In addition, norms are included to provide the age level corresponding to a child's language skills. The manual (for all six tests) includes details regarding the construction of the tests, statistics on item selection and test reliabilities, appropriate age ranges for each test, and scoring procedures and norms. Two administration books are available. Sample answer sheets are provided at the end of each test administration booklet and can be copied by the examiner for use in recording children's answers during testing. Examiner required. Not suitable for group use.

Untimed: 15 minutes per test

Scoring: Examiner evaluated

Cost: Manual $12.00; test administration booklets $20.00 each

Publisher: Albert Mehrabian

CLARK-MADISON TEST OF ORAL LANGUAGE
John B. Clark and
Charles L. Madison

Child   Ages 4-8.11

Purpose: Evaluates the expressive capacity of children. Diagnoses language disorders.

Description: Multiple-item oral response test utilizing a nonimitative elicitation technique and assessing responses in seven categories: syntax, modifiers, determiners, prepositions, verbs, pronouns, and inflections. Ninety-seven targets are elicited in the context of a 66-sentence communicative exchange. The test is cross-referenced to create specific multiple-response eliciting probes. Examiner required. Not suitable for group use.

Untimed: 10-20 minutes

Scoring: Examiner evaluated

Cost: Test kit (includes manual, 40 test forms) $59.95

Publisher: C.C. Publications, Inc.

CLINICAL ARTICULATION PROFILE (CAP)
Judith A. Hurvitz and Donna Rilla

Child

Purpose: Measures articulation pattern of young children with moderate to severe articulation disorders.

Description: Multiple-item paper-pencil inventory measuring the articulation abilities of children with articulation disorders. Children imitate words and other sounds while the examiner records responses on the form. The profile helps document progress during therapy, develop individual education programs, and report to parents and teachers. Examiner required. Not suitable for group use.

Untimed: Varies

Scoring: Examiner evaluated

Cost: 100 forms $20.00

Publisher: Modern Education Corporation

CLINICAL EVALUATION OF LANGUAGE FUNCTIONS— DIAGNOSTIC BATTERY (CELF)
Eleanor Semel and Elisabeth H. Wiig

Child, adolescent
Grades K-12

Purpose: Builds a complete picture of a student's language abilities and disabilities. Used to diagnose language difficulties and make decisions about remediation and intervention.

Description: 11-category verbal test measuring language processing and production, including phrase and sentence imitation, phrase completion, serial recall, phoneme recall production, abstraction, formulation of attributes, syntax and morphology, semantics, memory, and word finding and retrieval. Examiner required. Not suitable for group use.

Untimed: 1-2 hours

Scoring: Examiner evaluated

Cost: Complete battery $120.00

Publisher: The Psychological Corporation

CLINICAL EVALUATION OF LANGUAGE FUNCTIONS— ELEMENTARY AND ADVANCED LEVEL SCREENING (CELF)
Eleanor Semel and Elisabeth H. Wiig

Child, adolescent
Grades K-12

Purpose: Evaluates a student's language processing and production abilities. Used to help teachers and school psychologists identify students with language problems.

Description: Multiple-item verbal-visual test measuring phrase and sentence imitation, phrase completion, serial recall, antonyms, phoneme recall production, abstraction, and formulation of attributes. The Grades K-5 version contains 42 items in a "Simon Says" format, and the Grades 6-12 test contains 52 items in a card-game format. Materials include audiotapes, picture stimulus manuals, and score forms. Examiner required. K-5 version suitable for group use.

Untimed: 20 minutes

Scoring: Examiner evaluated

Cost: Elementary package $29.00; advanced level package $29.00

Publisher: The Psychological Corporation

CLINICAL PROBES OF ARTICULATION CONSISTENCY (C-PAC)
Wayne Secord

Ages 4 and older

Purpose: Provides an in-depth picture of how well an individual speaks and articulates specific sounds; used for planning and evaluating speech therapy.

Description: Verbal response test of 25 illustrated stories, adult-level reading passages, and duplicating-master articulation probes to elicit responses and check for articulation of target sounds. Specific sounds are assessed in a wide range of contexts: consonants in isolated words, clusters, sentences, and conversational speech; vowels and dipthongs in single words and minimal contrast pairs; and vocalic "R" sounds. Examiner evaluated. Not suitable for group use.

Untimed: 10 minutes per probe

Scoring: Examiner evaluated

Cost: Complete program $59.00; story manual $19.00; spirit masters $21.00; manual $19.00; sounds handbook $10.00

Publisher: The Psychological Corporation

COARTICULATION ASSESSMENT IN MEANINGFUL LANGUAGE (CAML)
Kathryn W. Kenney and Elizabeth M. Prather

Child   Ages 2½-5½

Purpose: Assesses the articulation ability of children. Used for articulation therapy and early childhood education.

Description: 33-item oral-response test using stimulus pictures to assess a child's ability to produce the sounds R, S, L, SH, F, CH, K, and T in meaningful words and word strings. Each consonant appears in eight phonetic contexts: as they precede and follow a bilabial-, alveolar, and velar-stop and a fricative. The test helps determine developmental delays. Examiner required. Not suitable for group use.

Untimed: 6-20 minutes

Scoring: Hand key

Cost: Complete kit $24.95

Publisher: Communication Skill Builders, Inc.

THE COGNITIVE, LINGUISTIC AND SOCIAL-COMMUNICATIVE SCALES (CLASS)
Dennis C. Tanner and Wendy M. Lamb

Child   PreK

Purpose: Measures language skills in preschool children. Also assesses difficult-to-test populations, severely handicapped, and very young children. Used by speech pathologists, pediatricians, or early childhood educators.

Description: Multiple-item interview tool assessing development of basic concepts, use and understanding of English grammar, and communicative effectiveness. The interviewer presents examples of developmental milestones to the parent, who indicates whether the child displays the behavior. The test indicates specific language delays, and therapy goals for individual education plans can be written from the response forms. Examiner required. Not suitable for group use.

Untimed: Varies

Scoring: Examiner evaluated

Cost: Contact publisher

Publisher: Modern Education Corporation

THE COMMUNICATION SCREEN: A PRESCHOOL SPEECH-LANGUAGE SCREENING TOOL
Nancy Striffler and Sharon Willig

Child   Language age 2.10-5.9 years

Purpose: Assesses the speech and language development of children. Identifies children needing further evaluation. Used as a screening instrument by nursery school and Head Start teachers, health care personnel, and paraprofessionals who do not have specialized skills in the speech and language area.

Description: Multiple-item oral-response test measuring a child's development of speech, language comprehension, language expression, verbal imitation, and recall of digits (to tap short-term auditory memory and sequencing and temporal ordering abilities). A laminated picture sheet is used to administer the test. Responses are recorded on the test forms, which are available in three levels: 3-year screen (ages 2.10-3.9), 4-year screen (ages 3.10-4.9), and 5-year screen (ages 4.10-5.9). The manual includes a description of the test, administration and scoring instructions, and interpretive information. Examiner required. Suitable for group use.

Untimed: 5 minutes

Scoring: Examiner evaluated

Cost: Test kit (manual, 25 each of 3-year, 4-year, and 5-year screen test forms, laminated picture sheet) $12.95

Publisher: Communication Skill Builders, Inc.

COMMUNICATIVE ABILITIES IN DAILY LIVING (CADL)
Audrey L. Holland

Aphasic adults

Purpose: Assesses the functional communication skills of aphasic adults. Used for planning treatment programs.

Description: Multiple-item oral-response test assessing functional communication disorders. Descriptive data are provided in 10 categories: reading/writing/calculating, speech acts, content utilization, role playing, sequential relationships, social conventions, divergences, nonverbal symbols, deixis (movement-related communicative behavior), and humor, metaphor, and absurdity. The test employs both traditional (usual examiner roles) and nontraditional (role playing) methods. Examiner required. Not suitable for group use.

Untimed: Not available

Scoring: Examiner evaluated

Cost: Complete kit (administration booklet, scoring kit, audiotape cassette, storage box) $79.00

Publisher: Pro-Ed

COMPREHENSIVE SCREENING TOOL FOR DETERMINING OPTIMAL COMMUNICATION MODE (CST)
Linda I. House and Brenda S. Rogerson

Developmental ages 6 months-adult

Purpose: Assesses the communication mode of children and adults. Used by speech and language pathologists.

Description: Multiple-item battery of response tests used by clinicians for systematically and objectively determining what the examinee's potential is for use of an augmentative system, its mode, and code. The test also helps determine whether augmentative communication is needed to support or substitute for vocal communication. Three subtests assess oral skills, manual skills, and pictographic skills. The Oral Skills Battery consists of three subtests addressing the following areas: prespeech and oral awareness, prearticulatory and articulatory skills, and auditory awareness. The Manual Skills Battery covers prerequisite skills for manual training, movement patterning, and cognitive correlates for manual communication. The Pictographic Skills Battery assesses prerequisites for visual training, attending behaviors and accuracy of movement, and cognitive correlates for pictographic skills. Scoring is completed on a 5-point scale. Examiner required. Not suitable for group use.

Untimed: Varies

Scoring: Examiner evaluated

Cost: Complete kit $53.00

Publisher: United Educational Services, Inc.

COMPUTER MANAGED ARTICULATION DIAGNOSIS
James L. Fitch

Language age 4-adult

Purpose: Assesses the articulation skills of individuals with a language age of 4-

---

adult. Used for preparing individual education programs.

Description: 46-item oral-response test analyzing articulation errors. Using an elicited sentence format for nonreaders or stimulus sentences on the screen, examiners can test single phonemes, blends, or both, as well as stimulatability. Each sound is presented in pre- and postvocalic position, and no consonants are abutting the consonants tested. A computer-generated, four-page analysis of error patterns by distinctive feature is available in 5 minutes. Examiner required. Not suitable for group use.

Untimed: 5 minutes

Scoring: Computer scored

Cost: Complete kit (20-page manual, 1 diskette and 1 backup, storage folder) $59.95

Publisher: Communication Skill Builders, Inc.

COMPUTER MANAGED SCREENING TEST
James L. Fitch

Child Ages 3-8

Purpose: Assesses articulation, expressive and receptive language, voice, and fluency in children. Used for language development and early childhood education.

Description: 32-item oral-response test using manipulative objects to assess children's language abilities. The examiner reads instructions displayed on a computer screen and keys the child's responses. The program runs on Apple II +, IIe, and IIc computers with DOS 3.3, 48K RAM, disk drive, and a compatible printer. Examiner required. Not suitable for group use.

Untimed: 2½-4 minutes

Scoring: Not available

Cost: Complete kit $79.95

Publisher: Communication Skill Builders, Inc.

A DEEP TEST OF ARTICULATION: PICTURE FORM
Eugene T. McDonald

Child Grades K-4

Purpose: Assesses a child's ability to produce sounds in various phonetic combinations. Useful for planning therapy.

Description: Verbal test measuring a child's articulatory proficiency by assessing 13 sounds. Each sound is tested by 60 items. The examiner places two sets of picture cards mounted side by side before the child. The child names the two pictures, and the examiner determines if the sounds made by the child were correct. A trained examiner is required. Not suitable for group use.

Untimed: 15-20 minutes

Scoring: Examiner evaluated

Cost: Test kit (instructions, sample cards) $17.95

Publisher: Communication Skill Builders, Inc.

A DEEP TEST OF ARTICULATION: SENTENCE FORM
Eugene T. McDonald

Grades 3 and above

Purpose: Assesses a child's ability to produce sounds in a sentence. Used to determine for which sounds the child needs remedial work.

Description: Multiple-item verbal test measuring a child's articulatory proficiency. The examiner flips the pages of a booklet, and the child reads sentences containing sound combinations. A trained examiner is required. Not suitable for group use.

Untimed: Not available

Scoring: Examiner evaluated

Cost: Test kit (test booklet, instructions) $13.95

Publisher: Communication Skill Builders, Inc.

DENVER ARTICULATION SCREENING EXAM (DASE)
Amelia F. Drumwright

Child   Ages 2.5-7

Purpose: Detects speech articulation problems in children. Screens for more sophisticated testing.

Description: 22-picture test measuring a child's intelligibility (does not assess language ability, vocabulary, school readiness, or intelligence). The examiner shows the pictures, displayed on eleven cards, to the child, says a word, and the child repeats it. The test is not recommended for shy or younger children. Examiner required. Not suitable for group use.

Untimed: 5 minutes

Scoring: Examiner evaluated

Cost: 25 tests $1.75; manual $6.50; picture cards $1.25

Publisher: Ladoca Publishing Foundation

Information and availability unconfirmed; no publisher response.

DEVELOPMENTAL ARTICULATION PROFILE (DAP)
Dennis C. Tanner,
Kathryn E. Mahoney,
and Gale Derrick

Child   Ages 3-7.3

Purpose: Assesses children's articulation abilities.

Description: Multiple-item inventory providing speech pathologists with a method for rapidly examining articulation errors relative to frequency of occurrence and approximate developmental ages for each phoneme. The form can be used in schools, clinical settings, and private practice for counseling parents and planning individual education programs. Examiner required. Not suitable for group use.

Untimed: Varies

Scoring: Examiner evaluated

Cost: $15.00

Publisher: Modern Education Corporation

DIAGNOSTIC AND ACHIEVEMENT READING TESTS: DART PHONICS TESTING PROGRAM
Refer to page 520.

DIAGNOSTIC SCREENING TEST: LANGUAGE, SECOND EDITION (DSTL)
Refer to page 248.

THE EARLY LANGUAGE MILESTONE SCALE (ELM SCALE)
James Coplan

Ages 0-36 months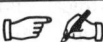

Purpose: Assesses language development in children from birth-36 months. Used by physicians, nurses, teachers, psychologists, speech pathologists, and infant development specialists.

Description: 41-item paper-pencil screening instrument detecting language-impaired children at young ages. The test contains three subscales: auditory expressive, auditory receptive, and visual. The scale is norm-referenced, and percentile values for the expected age of emergence for each item are provided. The test is sensitive to causes of speech or language delay, including mental retardation, hearing loss, dysarthria, and communicative disorders but does not yield a specific developmental diagnosis. Materials include recording sheet, drinking cup, spoon, crayon, rubber ball, and wooden cube. Examiner required. Not suitable for group use.

Untimed: 1-3 minutes

Scoring: Examiner evaluated

Cost: Complete program $55.00

Publisher: Modern Education Corporation

EVALUATING ACQUIRED SKILLS IN COMMUNICATION (EASIC)
Anita Marcott Riley

Ages 4-adult

Purpose: Assesses the language abilities of individuals with a language age of 3 months-8 years and an interest level age of 4-20 years. Used for planning speech-language therapy programs for severely language-impaired clients.

Description: Multiple-item oral-response test consisting of five inventories assessing an individual's abilities in semantics, syntax, morphology, and pragmatics. The examiner uses picture stimuli to elicit spontaneous, cued, imitated, manipulated, noncompliant, or incorrect responses. The test helps determine emerging communication skills, including before meaningful speech; understanding of simple noun labels, action verbs, and basic concepts; emerging modes of communication; understanding of more complex language functions; and use of more complex communication. The test includes goals for individual education prescriptions. It is used with autistic, mentally-impaired, developmentally delayed, and preschool language-delayed children and adolescents. Examiner required. Not suitable for group use.

Untimed: Not available

Scoring: Hand key

Cost: Complete kit $69.95

Publisher: Communication Skill Builders, Inc.

EVALUATING COMMUNICATIVE COMPETENCE: A FUNCTIONAL PRAGMATIC PROCEDURE
Charlann S. Simon

**Child, adolescent
Ages 9-17**

Purpose: Appraises the auditory and expressive language skills of language-learning-impaired children and adolescents.

Description: 21 informal communication tasks assessing a student's auditory and expressive language skills. An examiner observes the child's language processing abilities, metalinguistic skills, and functional uses of language. The student demonstrates his speaking and listening abilities by performing tasks involving comprehension of directions, giving directions, creative storytelling, maintenance of tense in storytelling, stating similarities and differences, barrier games,

expression, and justification of an opinion. For each task, the manual provides a description (including the materials needed to perform the task), rationale, directions for clinical administration, and analytical procedures for interpreting the student's language behaviors. Required stimulus materials, recordkeeping forms, and reproducible materials needed for test administration are included in the test kit. Examiner required. Not suitable for group use.

Untimed: Varies

Scoring: Examiner evaluated

Cost: Test kit (manual, 6 blocks, 12 cards, 3-ring binder) $49.95

Publisher: Communication Skill Builders, Inc.

EXAMINING FOR APHASIA: SECOND EDITION
Jon Eisenson

Adolescent, adult

Purpose: Assesses language functioning of aphasics.

Description: Multiple-item procedure for systematically exploring language functioning in aphasics. Materials include a manual detailing issues in the assessment of aphasics and fourteen plates of stimulus materials in black and white. The examiner assembles other common objects required for the examination. Examiner required. Not suitable for group use.

Untimed: 30-120 minutes

Scoring: Examiner evaluated

Cost: Complete set (manual, 25 record forms) $39.00

Publisher: The Psychological Corporation

EXPRESSIVE ONE-WORD PICTURE VOCABULARY TEST (EOWPVT)
Refer to page 504.

EXPRESSIVE ONE-WORD PICTURE VOCABULARY TEST: UPPER EXTENSION (EOWPVT: UE)
Morrison F. Gardner

Adolescent   Ages 12-15

Purpose: Assesses the expressive vocabulary of students ages 12-15 as a measure of verbal intelligence. Used to detect speech defects and learning disabilities.

Description: Multiple-item oral-response test in which the student demonstrates his ability to understand and use words by naming pictures that range from simple objects to representations of abstract concepts. Each test item consists of one picture stimulus that requires a single-word answer. Test results yield mental ages, percentiles, stanines, and deviation IQ scores which allow for the comparison of expressive language skills to other measures of receptive language, the detection of speech defects, the identification of learning disorders related to hearing loss and imperceptions of the auditory modality, the assessment of auditory-visual association ability, and the evaluation of a bilingual student's English/Spanish fluency. Examiner required. Suitable for use with small groups that respond in writing. Available in Spanish.

Untimed: 5-10 minutes

Scoring: Examiner evaluated

Cost: Test kit (manual, test plates, 25 English record forms, in vinyl folder) $38.00

Publisher: Academic Therapy Publications

FLETCHER TIME-BY-COUNT TEST OF DIADOCHOKINETIC SYLLABLE RATE
Samuel G. Fletcher

Child, adolescent Ages 6-13

Purpose: Assesses oral motor coordination.

Description: Multiple-item test assessing oral motor coordination, which may reflect residual impairment of speech

structure or function. The test provides a method for recording diadochokinetic syllable rate and comparing results to norms by age for children ages 6-13. Examiner required. Not suitable for group use.

Untimed: Not available

Scoring: Hand key

Cost: 3 pads of 50-page forms $11.95

Publisher: C.C. Publications, Inc.

FLUHARTY PRESCHOOL SPEECH AND LANGUAGE SCREENING TEST
Nancy Buono Fluharty

Child   Ages 2-6

Purpose: Evaluates the language performance of preschoolers. Identifies children with delayed or abnormal language development.

Description: Multiple-item oral-response test assessing vocabulary, articulation, and receptive and expressive language performance. Picture stimuli (8⅜" X 5" cards) are used to elicit language samples. Cut-off scores are provided for each age level of each area screened. Examiner required. Not suitable for group use.

Untimed: Varies

Scoring: Examiner evaluated

Cost: Complete program (10 picture cards, 2 pads of 50 response forms, guide) $25.00

Publisher: DLM Teaching Resources

FRENCHAY DYSARTHRIA ASSESSMENT
P. Enderby

Adolescent, adult Ages 12 and older

Purpose: Assesses dysarthria—speech impairment due to neuromuscular disorders—due to such conditions as cerebral palsy, Parkinson's disease, head injury, and stroke. Used by speech therapists, doctors, psychiatrists, and clinical psychologists to select and monitor appropriate treatment programs.

Description: 29-item task-performance and behavioral-observation test measuring speech impairment due to neuromuscular disorders. The test items cover reflex, respiration, lips, jaw, palate, laryngeal, tongue, intelligibility, influencing factors (sight, teeth, language, mood, posture), rate, and sensation. The results are recorded graphically on multicopy forms using a 9-point rating scale. Examiner required. Not suitable for group use. BRITISH PUBLISHER

Untimed: Varies

Scoring: Examiner evaluated

Cost: Contact publisher

Publisher: College Hill Press; co-published in the United Kingdom and Western Europe by NFER-NELSON Publishing Company Ltd.; distributed in Canada by Phonic Ear Ltd.; distributed worldwide by Taylor and Francis Ltd.

FULLERTON LANGUAGE TEST FOR ADOLESCENTS (EXPERIMENTAL EDITION)
Arden R. Thorum

Ages 11-adult

Purpose: Measures receptive and expressive language skills. Identifies language-impaired adolescents.

Description: 142-item verbal test of eight functions important in the acquisition and effective use of language skills: auditory synthesis, morphology competency, oral commands, convergent production, divergent production, syllabication, grammatic competency, and idioms. Each function is scored according to three language performance levels: competency, instruction, or frustration. Materials include a set of stimulus items. Examiner required. Not suitable for group use.

Untimed: 45 minutes

Scoring: Hand key; examiner evaluated

Cost: Examiner's kit $23.00 (includes stimulus items, 25 scoring forms and profiles, manual)

Publisher: Consulting Psychologists Press, Inc.

GOCHNOUR IDIOM SCREENING TEST (GIST)
Elizabeth A. Gochnour

Deaf adolescents and adults

Purpose: Measures a deaf person's knowledge of the English language. Used by speech pathologists, audiologists, and vocational counselors for program planning.

Description: 20-idiom multiple-choice pencil-paper test measuring comprehension of idioms by deaf persons. The examiner demonstrates how to mark the test. Separate instructions are provided for oral- and manual-communicating subjects. Examiner required. Suitable for group use.

Untimed: 10 minutes

Scoring: Examiner evaluated; may be computer scored

Cost: Complete $4.90; manual $1.95; 20 test booklets $2.95

Publisher: The Interstate Printers and Publishers, Inc.

GOLDMAN-FRISTOE TEST OF ARTICULATION
Ronald Goldman and Macalyne Fristoe

Child, adolescent Ages 2-16

Purpose: Assesses an individual's ability to speak clearly. Used as a basis for remedial planning.

Description: Three verbal subtests of articulation of major speech sounds in the initial, medial, and final positions; articulatory skills used in connected speech; and articulation of sounds known to be difficult for the student. In the Sounds-in-Words subtest, the student names the pictures of 35 familiar objects. In the Sounds-in-Sentences subtest, the student retells two stories the examiner has just read. In the Stimulability subtest, the examiner tests the student on the sounds misarticulated in the Sounds-in-Words subtest. Percentile ranks are provided by age for the Sounds-in-Words and Stimulability subtests. However, the interpretation of the test lies more in knowing which sounds the individual produces incorrectly and the type of mis-production than in an overall quantitative score that shows performance in relation to that of other individuals. Materials include test plates in an easel, 50 response forms, and a manual. No reading is required. The picture format enables the examiner to use the test with retarded or easily distractible children. Examiner required. Not suitable for group use.

Untimed: Sounds-In-Words subtest 15 minutes; varies for other two subtests

Scoring: Examiner evaluated

Cost: Complete test kit $47.50

Publisher: American Guidance Service

INTERPERSONAL LANGUAGE SKILLS ASSESSMENT— PRELIMINARY VERSION
*Carolyn M. Blagden and
Nancy L. McConnell*

**Child, adolescent
Ages 8-14**

Purpose: Determines how effectively students use language to participate in social situations. Identifies students with inadequate communication skills and pinpoints specific communication behavior problems.

Description: Multiple-item paper-pencil observational inventory assessing a student's pragmatic use of the linguistic social skills necessary for successful interpersonal interactions. The student being tested is observed interacting in a group with two or three of his peers, and his interpersonal language skills are assessed according to percentage of utterances by age that are either negative; inadequate semantically, syntactically, mor-phologically or prosodically; or statements of advice, deprecation, infor-mation, justification, requesting, support, commanding, accusation, and prompting. One to four students may be evaluated simultaneously. The results identify students with inadequate communication skills. Norms are provided for students ages 8-14. Examiner required. Suitable for group use.

Untimed: Varies

Scoring: Examiner evaluated

Cost: Test kit (manual, 100 transcript forms, 20 test forms) $48.00

Publisher: LinguiSystems, Inc.

Information and availability unconfirmed; no publisher response.

INVENTORY OF LANGUAGE ABILITIES
*Esther H. Minskoff,
Douglas E. Wiseman,
J. Gerald Minskoff*

Grades PreK-2

Purpose: Assesses language abilities of preschool and early primary-school children. Used by teachers and educational specialists for identifying language learn-ing disabilities. Also used in bilingual or ESL programs.

Description: 132-item paper-pencil inventory based on the Illinois Test of Psy-cholinguistic Abilities and used to screen language disabilities. The test covers auditory reception, visual memory, gram-matic closure, visual closure, and auditory closure and sound blending. The 11 checklists each contain 12 social and academic behaviors observable by a teacher. If more than 50% of the behav-iors in a category are checked, a possible learning disability in that area is indi-cated. Examiner required. Not suitable for group use.

Untimed: Varies

Scoring: Examiner evaluated

Cost: 25 record booklets $15.00

Publisher: Educational Performance Associates

THE JOLIET 3-MINUTE SPEECH AND LANGUAGE SCREEN (JMSLS)
*Mary C. Kinzler and
Constance Cowing Johnson*

Child   Grades K-5

Purpose: Measures the speech and lan-guage development of school-age children. Identifies children with speech and language disorders. Used to screen large numbers of children.

Description: Multiple-item individually administered oral-response test assessing receptive vocabulary, expressive syntax, voice, fluency, and phonological competence. Line drawings are used to elicit receptive vocabulary. Sentences are used to identify expressive syntax, morphology, and phonological competence. Norms are provided for Grades K, 2, and 5. Examiner required. Suitable for group use.

Untimed: 3 minutes

Scoring: Examiner evaluated

Cost: Test kit (manual, 20 vocabulary plates, 2 scoring sheets) $21.95

Publisher: Communication Skill Builders, Inc.

THE KHAN-LEWIS PHONOLOGICAL ANALYSIS (KLPA)
Linda Khan and Nancy Lewis

Child   Ages 2-5

Purpose: Assesses the phonological processes of children ages 2-5. Also used with older children with articulation problems. Used by speech language pathologists with training in phonetic transcription.

Description: Multiple-item paper-pencil assessment identifying specific phoneme errors and determining speech simplification patterns. This test is used following administration of the Sounds-in-Words subtest of the Goldman-Fristoe Test of Articulation. The examiner completes the KLPA analysis form, which lists over 1,200 sound changes occuring when responses to the Sounds-in-Words subtest are mispronounced. Norms are based on a representative national sample of children ages 2-5 years, 11 months. Scores include an index of individual usage for each of the 12 developmental phonological processes; a percentage-of-occurrence score for each of three nondevelopmental phonological processes; an index of overall phonological process usage expressed as a percentile rank, a speech simplification rating, and an age equivalent; and an inventory of phonemes the child pro-

duces, which may be used for developing treatment programs. Examiner required. Not suitable for group use.

Untimed: 15-40 minutes

Scoring: Hand key

Cost: Complete kit (manual, 25 analysis forms in folder) $33.50

Publisher: American Guidance Service

KINDERGARTEN LANGUAGE SCREENING TEST (KLST)
Sharon V. Gauthier and Charles L. Madison

Child   Kindergarten

Purpose: Tests receptive and expressive language competency and assesses language deficits that may cause kindergartners to fail academically.

Description: Multiple-item oral response test identifying children for further diagnostic testing for language deficits that may accelerate academic failure. The examiner assesses expressive and receptive language competence through identification of name, age, colors, body parts, number concepts, commands, sentence repetition, and spontaneous speech. The test is based on the verbal language abilities considered average for children of kindergarten age. Examiner required. Not suitable for group use.

Untimed: 4-5 minutes

Scoring: Examiner evaluated

Cost: Portfolio (including manual, 40 test forms) $29.95

Publisher: C.C. Publications, Inc.

LANGUAGE ASSESSMENT SCALES (LAS)

Child, adolescent Grades K-12

Purpose: Assesses students' oral language abilities.

Description: Multiple-item paper-pencil test available in two parallel forms (A and B), two levels (Level 1 for Grades K-5 and Level II for Grades 6-12 +), and two formats (multi-copy scoresheets and student test booklets). The Multi-Copy Scoresheets (MSC) for the SCAN-TRON

Optical Readers format consists of two parts. Part 1 is hand or machine-scoreable and administered with reusable cue pictures for testing or placement. Part II is a separate tearoff sheet for the teacher and provides specific assignments for language arts activities, an individual student academic profile and performance record, and a five-level checklist for placement based on communicative competence and linguistic proficiency. Examiner required. Not suitable for group use. Available in Spanish.

Untimed: Short form 10 minutes; long form 20 minutes

Scoring: Hand key; may be machine scored

Cost: Complete kit $63.95

Publisher: Linguametrics Group

LANGUAGE DEVELOPMENT READING EVALUATION PROGRAM
Rosemary Courtney, Mimi Garry, Clayton Graves, Margaret Hughes, and John McInnes

Child   Grades 1-7

Purpose: Measures students' language development and reading abilities. Used for both diagnostic and achievement testing. Intended for use with the Language Development Reading Program.

Description: 17 multiple-item and oral-response tests covering 22 levels of language and reading abilities. The assessment instruments include informal diagnostic tests, informal oral tests, and end-of-level written tests, including Evaluation Resource Books for Grade 1 (Levels 2-6), Grade 2 (Levels 7-10), and Grade 3 (Levels 11-14); Backpacks and Bumblebees for Grades 3-4 (Level 15); Rowboats and Rollerskates for Grade 4 (Level 16); Driftwood and Dandelions for Grades 4-5 (Level 17); Hockey Cards and Hopscotch for Grade 5 (Level 18); Northern Lights and Fireflies for Grades 5-6 (Level 19); Kites and Cartwheels for Grade 6 (Level 20); Sleeping Bags and Flying Machines for Grades 6-7 (Level 21); and Toboggans and Turtlenecks for Grade 7 (Level 22). The tests are presented in duplicating-master format and

include follow-up strategies for teachers. Examiner required. Some tests are suitable for group use.

Untimed: Varies

Scoring: Examiner evaluated

Cost: Evaluation Resource Book (Grade 1, 2, or 3) $31.95; all other tests (Levels 15-22) each $16.95

Publisher: Nelson Canada

LANGUAGE FACILITY TEST
John T. Dailey

Child, adolescent
Ages 3-15

Purpose: Evaluates how well children ages 3-15 speak in the language or dialect in which they were reared. Assesses gains in language ability. Used for bilingual, early and special education programs, as well as programs for the deaf and physically or mentally handicapped.

Description: 12-item oral response test in which children are asked to tell stories about or describe each of three pictures in four forms. Responses are assigned scores on a nine-point scale according to detailed scoring criteria and examples at each level. The scores measure how well children use the language or dialect to which they have been exposed in the home or school environment. Provides a measure of language facility which is relatively independent of vocabulary, information, pronunciation, and grammar. Norms are available for ages 3 to 15. Normative data also are reported for many subgroups, such as the mentally retarded, deaf, physically handicapped, poor readers, and children with behavior problems. Not suitable for adults with better-than-average language facility. The test kit includes 12 picture plates, test administrator's manual, Spanish supplement to the manual, and Manual Supplement II (Selected Dissertations and other Reports). The test can be administered in Spanish, sign language, or other languages or dialects. Examiner required. Not suitable for group use.

Untimed: 10 minutes

Scoring: Examiner evaluated

Cost: Complete kit $22.50; 100 answer booklets $12.00

Publisher: The Allington Corporation

LANGUAGE IMITATION TEST (LIT)
Refer to page 594.

LANGUAGE INVENTORY FOR TEACHERS (LIT)
Refer to page 582.

LANGUAGE PROFICIENCY TEST (LPT)
Joan E. Gerald and Gloria Weinstock

Grades 9-adult

Purpose: Evaluates an individual's ability to use the English language, especially those individuals whose lack of skill prevents them from succeeding at work or school. Used to identify competency levels and to detect specific deficiencies of ESL students.

Description: Multiple-item paper-pencil criterion-referenced test in three major sections: aural/oral, reading, and writing. The test covers nine areas of language functioning, including an optional translation section for ESL students. Each section was designed with subtests of increasing difficulty to provide scores indicating the most appropriate levels of instruction for the student. Scores for each subtest are converted to a percentage and plotted on a profile chart that indicates the level of proficiency. Materials are appropriate in content for the mature student who has low-level skills. Most of the nine subtests can be group administered; the two which measure low-level functioning require individual administration and are optional for native English students. Examiner required.

Untimed: 1½ hours

Scoring: Hand key

Cost: Manual $8.00; 10 test booklets $15.00

Publisher: Academic Therapy Publications

LANGUAGE SAMPLING AND ANALYSIS (LSA)
Merlin J. Mecham and J. Dean Jones

Child, adolescent
Ages 2-14

Purpose: Assesses the speaking ability of children. Identifies changes in a child's language performance and assesses the effectiveness of professional intervention.

Description: 51-item oral-response test measuring the following language domains: mean-length-of utterance, fluency in language production, diversity of vocabulary and lexical categories, diversity of grammatical morphemes, and completeness of grammatical constructions. The manual specifies stimulus and eliciting materials for each test item. The picture stimulus book from the Utah Test of Language Development (UTLD) Kit is used. Responses from the child are tape recorded and later analyzed for the number of responses meeting specified criteria. The administrator must be familiar with language sampling and analysis procedures. The test kit includes 50 language sample data sheets, 25 summary analysis sheets, and the manual. The test may be used with the Utah Test of Language Development for an extended analysis of a child's language structure. Examiner required. Not suitable for group use.

Untimed: 90 minutes

Scoring: Examiner evaluated

Cost: Complete kit (50 language sample data sheets, 25 summary analysis sheets, manual) $20.00; UTLD and LSA kit $50.00

Publisher: Communication Research Associates, Inc.

"LET'S TALK" INVENTORY FOR ADOLESCENTS
Elisabeth H. Wiig

Adolescent
Grades 9 and above

Purpose: Evaluates students' ability to communicate by talking; used by speech pathologists, special educators, and psychologists to identify and diagnose students who have social communication problems.

Description: 40-item verbal test in which the examiner gives the description and context of a picture and asks the student to formulate appropriate speech acts for the context, thereby probing four communication functions: ritualizing, informing, controlling, and feeling. Scoring reflects the register and appropriateness of the speech acts formulated. "Drop back" items are included. Subsequent use provides data on progress as a result of intervention. The test may be followed by the instructional program "Let's Talk": Developing Prosocial Communication Skills. Examiner required. Not suitable for group use.
Timed: 30-45 minutes
Scoring: Examiner evaluated
Cost: Complete kit $59.00
Publisher: The Psychological Corporation

THE LISTENING FOR MEANING TEST
Refer to page 252.

MEASUREMENT OF LANGUAGE DEVELOPMENT
Carol Melnick

Child   Ages 3.0-7.11

Purpose: Measures progress of therapy programs for language-impaired children, including presentence level children. Used with language-delayed (with normal intelligence), mentally retarded, hearing-impaired, and emotionally disturbed children to assess effects of language intervention programs.

Description: 186-item "point-to" and oral-response test covering eight subtasks: primary verbs, personal pronouns, negatives, indefinite pronouns, interrogative reversals, who-questions, secondary verbs, and conjunctions. The items consist of familiar objects and situations pictured in the stimulus book. The examiner describes the stimulus pictures and asks the child to point to the one that has been described. The examiner then describes pictures and asks the child to

describe them in his own words. The responses are evaluated for both receptive and expressive language, mean length of utterance, word order, and semantic relations. The complete test kit includes a manual, receptive-expressive picture plates, and 25 record forms. Examiner required. Not suitable for group use.
Untimed: Not available
Scoring: Examiner evaluated
Cost: Complete kit $49.50
Publisher: Stoelting Company

MEEKER-CROMWELL BEHAVIOR DEVELOPMENTAL ASSESSMENT

Ages 2-adult

Purpose: Measures the language development of severely impaired individuals. Used for instructional planning and placement.

Description: Multiple-item behavioral observation inventory assessing the functional development of language skills in severely impaired individuals. The inventory consists of a list of language behaviors arranged in chronological developmental order. A person who knows the student well rates him on a 5-point scale for each behavioral item. The test contains a normal rating paralleled by a delayed or deficient scale; students are rated on both scales (one per student). The point at which training should begin is determined by the first score of "5" and will identify the age at which the student is functioning. Examiner required. Not suitable for group use.
Untimed: Varies
Scoring: Examiner evaluated
Cost: Test form $1.25
Publisher: M & M Systems

MERRILL LANGUAGE SCREENING TEST (MLST)
Myrna Mumm, Wayne Secord, and Katherine Dykstra

Child   Grades K-1

Purpose: Detects potential language problems in young children by indicating language competencies in comparison to peer performance. Used by teachers and school psychologists to screen groups of children.

Description: Six picture stimulus cards, a manual, and an audiocassette are used to elicit responses from children in order to assess receptive and expressive language skills in five areas: production of complete sentences, utterance length, verb-tense agreement, elaboration, and communication competence. The optional Articulation Screening Inventory can be used to test 16 phonemes. The components are available individually. Examiner required. Suitable for group use.

Untimed: 5 minutes

Scoring: Examiner evaluated

Cost: Complete kit $54.00.

Publisher: The Psychological Corporation

MILLER-YODER LANGUAGE COMPREHENSION TEST (MY)
Jon F. Miller and David Yoder

**Child   Developmental
          ages 4-8**

Purpose: Assesses language comprehension of children whose developmental ages are 4-8. Used by speech clinicians.

Description: Picture-book test assessing children's understanding of short, simple sentences in a variety of grammatical structures. The test helps determine similarity of language comprehension in same-age peers and comprehension difficulties. The test is designed for normal, developmentally delayed, and mentally retarded children between the developmental ages of 4-8. Three sets of picture plates provide selection for different populations. Examiner required. Not suitable for group use.

Untimed: 10-30 minutes

Scoring: Hand key

Cost: Complete kit (examiner's manual, 25 scoring forms, picture book) $49.00; response forms $19.00

Publisher: Pro-Ed

MINNESOTA TEST FOR DIFFERENTIAL DIAGNOSIS OF APHASIA
Mildred Schuell

Adult

Purpose: Assesses language disturbance due to brain damage; aids in classifying patients and determining prognosis.

Description: The subject responds to questions and cards presented by the examiner, who then evaluates disturbances in hearing, seeing, and reading; speech and language; visuomotor and writing; and disturbances of numerical relationships and arithmetic processes. The test may be administered over several sessions, depending on patient's fatigue. Examiner required. Not suitable for group use.

Untimed: Open ended

Scoring: Hand key; examiner evaluated

Cost: Manual $2.00; Differential Diagnosis of Aphasia with the Minnesota test $7.95

Publisher: University of Minnesota Press

MULTILEVEL INFORMAL LANGUAGE INVENTORY (MILI)
Candace L. Goldsworthy

**Child, adolescent
Grades K-6**

Purpose: Assesses the speaking abilities of children. Used to identify students with language problems and provide learning disabilities specialists with informal measures for intervention.

Description: Verbal test assessing three levels of speech (spontaneous evoked, indirect imitation, and receptive) and eight oral language functions (verbs, nouns, modification, interrogatives, negations, combining prepositions, adverbs and prepositions, associative language). Using the manual and picture stimuli provided in the test kit, specific types of responses are obtained. Survey scenes elicit short, spontaneous language samples; survey stories elicit more complex language forms through storytelling and paraphrasing; and specific probes focus on key syntactic constructions. Examiner required. Not suitable for group use.

Untimed: Varies

Scoring: Examiner evaluated

Cost: Complete $58.00; 12 record forms $12.00; picture manual $39.00; examiner's manual $16.00

Publisher: The Psychological Corporation

NEW ENGLAND PANTOMIME TESTS: ASSESSMENT OF NONVERBAL COMMUNICATION
Robert J. Duffy and Joseph R. Duffy

Adolescent, adult

Purpose: Assesses the gestural expressive and receptive abilities of language-disordered clients. Used as a standardized measure of therapy effectiveness.

Description: Multiple-item test diagnosing communication disorders common to aphasics and other brain-injured adults and adolescents. The program consists of four distinct pantomime tests: Pantomime Recognition Test (forms A and B), a nonverbal test assessing an individual's ability to recognize pantomime acts associated with common pictured objects; Pantomime Expression Test, evaluating the simple pantomimic performance of aphasic individuals, and Pantomime Referential Abilities Test, measuring the communicative effectiveness of a client on a simple pantomimic referential task. Results help clinicians determine appropriate treatment. Examiner required. Not suitable for group use.

Untimed: Varies

Scoring: Examiner evaluated

Cost: Test kit (picture plates; tests; normative data; scoring procedures) $64.95

Publisher: C.C. Publications, Inc.

NORTHWESTERN SYNTAX SCREENING TEST (NSST)
Laura L. Lee

Child   Ages 3-7

Purpose: Measures a child's syntactic development. Used to identify deficient children needing further evaluation.

Description: Screening test in which the child is asked to respond to short verbal statements by picking out a picture that the statement best describes or by repeating an appropriate statement pertaining to the picture. Receptive and expressive language abilities are evaluated. Examiner required. Not suitable for group use.

Untimed: 15-25 minutes

Scoring: Examiner evaluated

Cost: Test, 100 answer forms $19.95

Publisher: Northwestern University Press

Information and availability unconfirmed; no publisher response.

ORAL LANGUAGE EVALUATION (OLE)
Refer to page 267.

ORAL LANGUAGE SENTENCE IMITATION DIAGNOSTIC INVENTORY—FORMAT REVISED (OLSIDI-F)
Linda Zachman, Rosemary Huisingh, Carol Jorgensen, and Mark Barrett

Child   Ages 5-7

Purpose: Analyzes the syntactical, morphological, and grammatical errors of children. Used by clinicians to identify targets for intervention and to monitor changes in a child's language performance.

Description: 270-item sentence-imitation test consisting of 27 subtests of 10 sentences each. Designed as a follow-up to the OLSIST-F, each subtest covers one of the 27 syntactical, morphological, and grammatic structures tested on the OLSIST-F. Only those subtests indicated by the results of the OLSIST-F are administered. Performances are scored in percentages. This revised format presents all 27 subtests and the diagnostic profile on one form. Examiner required. Not suitable for group use.

Untimed: Varies

Scoring: Examiner evaluated

Cost: Test kit (20 test forms, instruction manual, statistical manual) $23.00

Publisher: LinguiSystems, Inc.

Information and availability unconfirmed; no publisher response.

ORAL LANGUAGE SENTENCE IMITATION SCREENING TEST— FORMAT REVISED (OLSIST-F)
Linda Zachman, Rosemary Huisingh, Carol Jorgensen, and Mark Barrett

Child   Ages 3-7

Purpose: Evaluates a child's use of language structures. Used by speech-language pathologists.

Description: 18-22-item sentence-imitation test assessing syntax, morphology, and grammar at three stages of linguistic development. Stage III (ages 3-4) assesses 18 linguistic structures with sentence length ranging from 4-9 morphemes. Stage IV (ages 4-5) assesses 22 linguistic structures with sentence length ranging from 5-11 morphemes. Stage V (ages 5-7) assesses 23 linguistic structures with sentence length ranging from 6-13 morphemes. One protocol for each stage combines the 20-sentence test form and score sheet. Examiner required. Not suitable for group use.

Untimed: 5 minutes

Scoring: Examiner evaluated

Cost: Test kit (50 protocols each for Stages III, IV, and V, instruction manual, statistical manual) $30.00

Publisher: LinguiSystems, Inc.

Information and availability unconfirmed; no publisher response.

ORAL SPEECH MECHANISM SCREENING EXAMINATION (OSME)
Kenneth O. St. Louis and Dennis M. Ruscello

All ages

Purpose: Examines the oral speech mechanisms of children and adults. Used by speech pathologists for diagnosis and therapy.

Description: Descriptive tool for examining structure and function of the lips,

tongue, jaw, teeth, hard palate, soft palate, and pharynx; breathing behavior; and diadochokinesis rates. Examiner required. Not suitable for group use.

Untimed: 5-10 minutes

Scoring: Examiner evaluated

Cost: Complete kit (examiner's manual, 50 scoring forms) $16.00

Publisher: Pro-Ed

PARENTAL DIAGNOSTIC QUESTIONNAIRE (PDQ), REVISED EDITION
Dennis C. Tanner

Adult

Purpose: Reports parental observations of a child's stuttering behavior and assesses parental attitudes and reactions toward stuttering. Used by speech pathologists for evaluation, prevention, and treatment of child stuttering and for counseling parents.

Description: 81-item paper-pencil inventory in three sections reporting parent observation of a child's speech behaviors, parent attitudes regarding the behaviors, and parent reactions to a child's dysfluent speech. In addition to its use for evaluating child stuttering and counseling parents, the test can be used with teachers, guardians, and others who are significant in the child's communicative environment. The revised edition provides normalized data from parents of nonstuttering children. Self-administered. Suitable for group use.

Untimed: Varies

Scoring: Examiner evaluated

Cost: Complete kit (instructions, 25 questionnaires, profiles, normative data, worksheets) $28.75

Publisher: Modern Education Corporation

THE PATTERNED ELICITATION SYNTAX TEST (PEST)
Edna Carter Young and Joseph J. Perachio

Child   Language age 3-7.5 years

Purpose: Determines whether a child's expressive grammatical skills are age appropriate. Identifies children needing further evaluation.

Description: Multiple-item oral-response test using the delayed imitation technique to assess a child's use of 44 syntactic structures. The child listens to three consecutive modeled sentences with a common syntactic pattern but varying vocabulary while looking simultaneously at corresponding line illustrations. The child then repeats the sentences with the aid of the drawings. The first two sentences serve as carriers. The third sentence, which is most distant from the examiner's model, is used in scoring. In addition to determining the child's language age, criterion-referenced interpretation of the child's responses provides an in-depth analysis of the child's use of grammatical structures. The manual includes stimulus pictures, a demonstration page, normative data, and instructions for administration and scoring. The response form is used to record the child's utterances, the assessment form includes grammatical analysis, and the individual data form is used for recordkeeping. Examiner required. Not suitable for group use.

Untimed: 20 minutes

Scoring: Examiner evaluated

Cost: Test kit (stimulus pictures, demonstration page, normative data, instructions, response sheets, assessment sheets, individual data form) $19.95

Publisher: Communication Skill Builders, Inc.

PERFORMANCE ASSESSMENT OF SYNTAX: ELICITED AND SPONTANEOUS (PASES)
Lila Coughran

Child   Ages 3-8

Purpose: Assesses a child's ability to produce key syntactic structures. May be used with young, severely impaired children or children with short attention spans.

Description: Multiple-item oral-response test measuring the 11 most frequently exhibited errors in children's syntax: articles, personal pronouns, possessive

pronouns, adjectives, verbs (is/are and present progressive), verbs (has/have), verbs (past tense, regular, and irregular), plurality, negation, interrogation, and conjunctions. The child's spontaneous use of language is assessed when possible, but in the event of failure, stimulus items are provided for eliciting appropriate responses. The criterion-referenced nature of the test allows specific subtests rather than the entire battery to be administered. The test may be used with language-impaired and normally developing children functioning within the 3-8 year age-range. Examiner required. Not suitable for group use.

Untimed: Varies

Scoring: Examiner evaluated

Cost: Complete kit (manual, stimulus items, easel binder, 10 response forms) $80.00

Publisher: Exceptional Resources, Inc.

PHONEMIC SYNTHESIS: BLENDING SOUNDS INTO WORDS
Jack Katz and Cornelia Harmon

Child, adolescent
Grades 1-4

Purpose: Identifies phonemic synthesis difficulties.

Description: Multiple-item response test and instructional package for diagnosing and remediating speech problems, including discrimination, sequencing, and/or blending. Although the program was designed for children in Grades 1-4, it can be used with slow learners in Grades 5-12. The package includes the test, 15 progressively more difficult lessons, 9 audiocassette tapes, a 52-page picture book, and 12 picture cards. Examiner required. Not suitable for group use.

Untimed: Varies

Scoring: Not available

Cost: Complete package $85.00

Publisher: DLM Teaching Resources

PHONOLOGICAL ASSESSMENT OF CHILD SPEECH
Pamela Grunwell

Child

Purpose: Assesses sound system of children. Used by clinicians and therapists to diagnose problems and develop treatment programs.

Description: Multiple-item oral-response test providing a comprehensive assessment of children's speech. The detailed phonological analysis aids clinicians in obtaining a representative sample of a child's speech, recording the sample in analyzable form, analyzing data obtained, interpreting the analysis, and designing effective treatment programs. The test compares a child's sound system to that of an adults' and with a normal developmental stage. The test provides a diagnostic indication of the type and severity of speech problems. Examiner required. Not suitable for group use.
BRITISH PUBLISHER

Untimed: Not available

Scoring: Examiner evaluated

Cost: Manual, cards £18.35

Publisher: NFER-NELSON Publishing Company Ltd.

PHOTO ARTICULATION TEST (PAT)
K. Pendergast, S. Dickey, J. Selmar, and A. Soder

Child   Ages 3-11

Purpose: Measures articulation skills. Used for screening and analysis in schools and clinics and for therapy.

Description: 72 color photographs arranged with nine pictures on each of eight sheets to measure articulation of consonants, consonant blends, vowels, and diphthongs. The test categorizes defective sounds as tongue, lip, or vowel sounds. The subject names the items in the color photographs as the examiner points to the pictures and records responses on the recording sheet. Materials include a supplementary test words list. Examiner required. Not suitable for group use.

Untimed: 5 minutes

Scoring: Examiner evaluated

Cost: Complete $35.00; 96 recording sheets $3.50; photo articulation cards $8.50

Publisher: The Interstate Printers & Publishers, Inc.

PICTURE ARTICULATION AND SCREENING TEST (PALST)
Word Making Productions

Child   Grades PreK-6

Purpose: Screens articulation and language skills of children. Identifies children needing further evaluation and assistance.

Description: 13-item oral-response test assessing strengths and weaknesses in articulation. Each test item consists of a picture card showing an activity or scene, such as an Indian shooting an arrow at a rabbit or a child brushing his teeth. The child is asked to describe each card. The examiner evaluates the responses based on the completeness of the child's articulation. Six sounds are emphasized: sh, r, th, s, l, and t. Examiner required. Suitable for group use.

Untimed: 2-3 minutes

Scoring: Examiner evaluated

Cost: Complete kit (test, recording forms) $18.95

Publisher: Word Making Productions

Information and availability unconfirmed; no publisher response.

PICTURE SPONDEE THRESHOLD TEST
Paul Waryas and Gail Gudmundsen

Child, handicapped individuals

Purpose: Measures speech reception of individuals unable to give oral responses.

Description: Multiple-item response test providing information on the speech reception thresholds of very young children and individuals who are physically handicapped, mentally retarded, or have dialectic differences or other handicapping conditions. Examiner required. Not suitable for group use.

Timed: 30 minutes

Scoring: Examiner evaluated

Cost: Complete kit (2 sets of 25 picture cards, manual) $38.00

Publisher: DLM Teaching Resources

PORCH INDEX OF COMMUNICATIVE ABILITY (PICA)
Bruce E. Porch

Adolescent, adult
Ages 13 and older

Purpose: Evaluates the ability of aphasic individuals to communicate with other people. Useful for diagnosis and therapy.

Description: 180-item paper-pencil verbal test covering nine modalities of communication: writing, copying, reading, pantomime, verbal, auditory, visual, gestural, and graphic. The test measures changes in functioning due to time, treatment, and surgery. Items are scored for accuracy, responsiveness, completeness, promptness, and efficiency. Materials include 10 pairs of test objects, plastic stimulus cards, and graphic test sheets. A fiber-tip pen is required for the graphic items. The test is not recommended for children under age 12. Examiner required. Not suitable for group use.

Untimed: 30-60 minutes

Scoring: Examiner evaluated

Cost: Complete kit for 25 subjects $130.00 (test items and sheets, stimulus cards, manuals, profiles, carrying case)

Publisher: Consulting Psychologists Press, Inc.

PORCH INDEX OF COMMUNICATIVE ABILITY IN CHILDREN (PICAC)
Bruce E. Porch

Child   Ages 3-12

Purpose: Assesses a child's communicative behavior. Used for diagnosis, prognosis, and treatment planning.

Description: Battery of paper-pencil verbal tests measuring three modalities of communication: gestural, verbal, and graphic. Visual and auditory level scores are obtained also. The test documents changes in a child's processing ability over time. Items are scored for accuracy, responsiveness, completeness, promptness, and efficiency. The Basic Battery tests preschool children ages 3-6. The Advanced Battery is administered to children ages 6-12. Materials include 10 pairs of test objects, plastic stimulus cards, and graphic test sheets. A black-tip pen is required for graphic items. Examiner required. Not suitable for group use.

Untimed: 30-60 minutes

Scoring: Examiner evaluated

Cost: Deluxe test kit for 25 subjects $130.00; economy test kit for 25 subjects (no carrying case) $110.00

Publisher: Consulting Psychologists Press, Inc.

PRACTICAL ARTICULATION KIT: GAME CARDS AND SCREENING TEST
Martha M. McDonough

Child   Grades K-8

Purpose: Assesses an individual's ability to produce consonant and blend sounds in initial, medial, and final positions in words.

Description: Multiple-item oral-response test with 81 illustration cards used for screening, as a game for language building, and as a tool for auditory training or building sequential memory skills. Results are used for goal setting or for determining need for further assessment. Examiner required. The games are suitable for group use. The test is not suitable for group use.

Untimed: Varies

Scoring: Examiner evaluated

Cost: Complete $10.50; 64 screening test sheets $2.50

Publisher: The Interstate Printers & Publishers, Inc.

PRAGMATICS SCREENING TEST
Philip M. Prinz and
Frederick F. Weiner

Child Ages 3.5-8.5

Purpose: Evaluates the communication skills of children. Used with children who may have language delays.

Description: Multiple-item response test made up of three gamelike tasks: Absurd Requests, Ghost Trick, and Referential Communication. The standardized test covers pragmatic skills, including maintaining a topic; returning to a topic; formulating speech acts (e.g., making statements or requests); modifying a request in terms of politeness; narrating a story; revising a directive when the listener appears not to understand; and establishing a referent for a listener. Examiner required. Not suitable for group use.

Untimed: 15 minutes

Scoring: Not available

Cost: Contact publisher

Publisher: The Psychological Corporation

PRE-LAS
S. Duncan and E. De Avila

Child Ages 4-6

Purpose: Assesses children's oral-language abilities.

Description: Multiple-item response test measuring the expressive and receptive language skills of preschool and kindergarten children. The six subtests are What's in the House (lexical), Choose a Picture (sentence comprehension), Simon Says (following instructions), Say What You Hear (sentence imitation/morphemes), Let's Tell Stories (story retelling), and Finishing Stories (sentence completion/clauses). Results are used for educational planning. Materials include colored cue pictures and an audio cassette. Examiner required. Not suitable for group use.

Untimed: 15 minutes

Scoring: Hand key

Cost: Examiner's kit $63.95

Publisher: Linguametrics Group

PRESCHOOL LANGUAGE ASSESSMENT INSTRUMENT (PLAI)
Marion Blank, Susan A. Rose,
and Laura J. Berlin

Child Ages 3-6

Purpose: Evaluates preschoolers' thinking and verbal reasoning skills. Used to make placement, remediation, and therapy decisions.

Description: Multiple-item oral-response test assessing how well a preschooler understands and uses classroom language to solve problems encountered in the academic world. Picture stimuli are used to present test items assessing four levels of thinking in developmental order. Level I assesses naming abilities, matching abilities, remembering relevant information, and imitating abilities. Level II assesses defining by function, describing a scene, recalling information, defining by attributes, attending to multiple attributes, and identifying differences. Level III assesses predicting, associating by function, assuming a role, following directions, identifying similarities, exclusion, defining words, and sequencing and event telling. Level IV assesses predicting, justifying decisions, determining causes, determining solutions, and explaining inferences. The test results provide means, percentile ranks, and standard deviations for children ages 3-6. Examiner required. Not suitable for group use.

Untimed: Varies

Scoring: Examiner evaluated

Cost: Test kit (hard-cover examiner's manual and therapy guide, picture stimuli book, 100 test forms) $78.50

Publisher: Grune & Stratton, Inc.

PRESCHOOL LANGUAGE SCALE (PLS)
Irla Lee Zimmerman,
Violette G. Steiner,
and Robert Evatt Pond

Child Ages 0-7

Purpose: Provides a system for assessment, diagnosis, and remediation of early developmental language problems in young children.

Description: Verbal-visual test in which a picture book and program manual are used by an examiner to administer auditory and verbal language tasks. The scale measures receptive and expressive language abilities separately for more accurate diagnosis. Examiner required. Not suitable for group use. Available in Spanish.

Untimed: 20 minutes

Scoring: Examiner evaluated

Cost: Complete $45.00

Publisher: The Psychological Corporation

THE PREVERBAL ASSESSMENT-INTERVENTION PROFILE (P.A.I.P.)
Patricia Connard

All ages

Purpose: Assesses communication and motor performance of students and adults whose communication performance is between the developmental range of 0-9 months. Diagnoses communication needs and evaluates prelinguistic behavior of preverbal individuals.

Description: Multiple-item three-stage observational procedure for observing and reporting performance in a natural environment. The test assesses the sensori-motor domains of auditory, visual, vocal/oral, and motor in a manner that yields an individualized preverbal/motor assessment profile. The examiner records information supplied by parents, caregivers, and teachers; observes behaviors during eating, bathing, dressing, and playing; and presents structured tasks using spoons, mirrors, lights, spinning and pull toys, etc. The test, used primarily with severely retarded, profoundly retarded, or multihandicapped individuals, can be adapted for stroke patients. Examiner required. Not suitable for group use.

Untimed: Not available

Scoring: Examiner evaluated

Cost: Complete kit $44.90

Publisher: ASIEP Education Company

PSYCHOLINGUISTIC RATING SCALE (PRS)
Kenneth L. Hobby

Child, adolescent
Grades K-8.9

Purpose: Measures psycholinguistic behaviors relevant to classroom performance of students. Used to screen students for special attention under P.L. 94-142.

Description: Multiple-item paper-pencil inventory in a which teacher familiar with the child uses a 5-point scale ranging from "seldom" to "frequently" to respond to statements about the frequency of classroom behaviors. The scale is available on four levels: readiness (Grades K-1.4), elementary (Grades 1.5-2.9), intermediate (Grades 3.0-5.9), and advanced (Grades 6.0-8.9). The readiness, elementary, and intermediate levels include the following 10 subscales containing 4-5 items each: auditory reception, auditory association, auditory memory, auditory closure, verbal expression, visual reception, visual association, visual memory, visual closure, and manual expression. The Advanced Level does not include the visual closure or manual expression subscales. The scales are based on the same theoretical structure as the Illinois Test of Psycholinguistic Abilities (ITPA). Scoring yields subscores and a total score. Norms are provided for each of the four levels. Not suitable for group use.

Untimed: 5 minutes

Scoring: Hand key

Cost: Complete kit (25 booklets for each level, manual) $45.00

Publisher: Western Psychological Services

THE PUPIL RATING SCALE (REVISED): SCREENING FOR LEARNING DISABILITIES
Refer to page 585.

QUEENSLAND UNIVERSITY APHASIA AND LANGUAGE TEST (QUALT)

Children, impaired adults

Purpose: Meaures language deficiencies in children up to 10 years of age and in

---

aphasic or mentally retarded adults. Used for clinical diagnosis.

Description: Multiple-item paper-pencil and oral response battery measuring deficiencies in the following areas of language usage: oral expression, auditory comprehension, reading, and writing. Three parallel forms (I, II, and III) are available for retesting. Materials include complete set of materials for Forms I, II, and III, a handbook, and the record form. Examiner required. Not suitable for group use. AUSTRALIAN PUBLISHER

Untimed: Varies

Scoring: Examiner evaluated

Cost: Contact publisher

Publisher: The Australian Council for Educational Research Limited

---

A READING READINESS TEST: REVERSAL TESTS (BILINGUAL)
Ake W. Edfeldt

Child   Grade 1

Purpose: Measures degree of speech reversal tendencies in young children before they learn to read. Used by educators and speech therapists to predict reading problems in first grade.

Description: Oral-response test based on research into the cause and effect of word transposition tendencies of children. The test was developed to diagnose and prevent these difficulties. A child who is scored either as "control case" or as "not yet ready to read" is not considered ready to master reading and, therefore, should postpone instruction. Examiner required. Not suitable for group use. CANADIAN PUBLISHER

Untimed: Not available

Scoring: Hand key; examiner evaluated

Cost: Specimen set $5.00; 25 tests $12.00; manual $4.50

Publisher: Institute of Psychological Research, Inc.

Information and availability unconfirmed; no publisher response.

REVISED PRE-READING SCREENING PROCEDURES
Refer to page 488.

REYNELL DEVELOPMENTAL LANGUAGE SCALES—SECOND REVISON
Refer to page 16.

RHODE ISLAND TEST OF LANGUAGE STRUCTURE (RITLS)
Elizabeth Engen and Trygg Engen

Ages 3-20

Purpose: Measures English language development in hearing children ages 3-6 or hearing-impaired children and adults ages 3-20. Used for educational planning.

Description: 100-item multiple-choice verification test assessing understanding of language structure (syntax). The test presents 20 sentence types, both simple and complex. The test is used for educational planning, such as determination of school readiness, bilingual programming, and language introduction procedures. It can also be used where language development is a concern, including mental retardation, learning disability, and bilingual programs. Examiner required. Not suitable for group use.

Timed: 30 minutes

Scoring: Hand key

Cost: Complete kit (test booklet, 10 analysis sheets, 10 response sheets, manual, storage box) $56.00

Publisher: Pro-Ed

RILEY ARTICULATION AND LANGUAGE TEST: REVISED
Glyndon D. Riley

Child   Grades K-2

Purpose: Measures the language proficiency of young children. Used to identify children most in need of speech therapy.

Description: Oral-response screening test consisting of three subtests (Language Proficiency and Intelligibility, Articulation Function, and Language Function) measuring phonemic similarity, stimulability, number of defective sounds, error consistency, frequency of occurrence, and developmental expectancy. The test yields an objective articulation loss score and standardized language loss and language function scores. Examiner required. Not suitable for group use.

Untimed: 2-3 minutes

Scoring: Hand key

Cost: Complete kit (25 tests, manual) $15.90

Publisher: Western Psychological Services

ROSWELL-CHALL AUDITORY BLENDING TEST
Refer to page 537.

SCREENING DEEP TEST OF ARTICULATION
Eugene T. McDonald

Child   Grades K-3

Purpose: Assesses a child's ability to produce commonly misarticulated consonant sounds. Used to determine whether a child needs further testing.

Description: 90-item verbal test assessing a child's ability to produce nine consonant sounds in a variety of phonetic contexts. The examiner displays pairs of pictures to elicit the child's production of bisyllables. Selected consonants occur in different consonant types (single, abutting, in compounds) and in a variety of contexts requiring overlapping articulatory movements. A trained examiner is required. Not suitable for group use.

Untimed: 5 minutes

Scoring: Hand key; examiner evaluated

Cost: 50 individual record sheets $3.95; 50 teacher report forms $3.95

Publisher: Communication Skill Builders, Inc.

SCREENING KIT OF LANGUAGE DEVELOPMENT (SKOLD)
Lynn S. Bliss and Doris V. Allen

Child   Ages 2-5

Purpose: Assesses language disorders and delays in young children. Used by speech-language pathologist paraprofessionals in day care and by health care/nursing and preschool specialists.

Description: 135-item oral-response test measuring language development in children speaking either Black English or Standard English. Picture stimuli are used to assess vocabulary, comprehension, story completion, individual and paired sentence repetition with pictures, individual sentence repetition without pictures, and comprehension of commands. The test consists of six subtests, three for Black English and three for Standard English, in each of the following age ranges: 30-36 months, 37-42 months, and 43-48 months. Norms are provided for speakers of Black and Standard English. The manual includes guidelines for administration and scoring and appendices covering normal language development, disordered language, and the linguistic characteristics of Black English. Examiner required. Not suitable for group use.

Untimed: 15 minutes

Scoring: Examiner evaluated

Cost: Test kit (manual, stimulus book, set of either Black or Standard English scoring forms) $49.95

Publisher: Slosson Educational Publications, Inc.

SCREENING SPEECH ARTICULATION TEST (SSAT)
Merlin J. Mecham, J. Lorin Jex, and J. Dean Jones

Child   Grades PreK-2

Purpose: Identifies children who have significant articulation problems. Used as a screening instrument in Head Start, early education, and early elementary classes; not intended for diagnostic use.

Description: 47-item test in which a child is shown pictures designed to elicit specific phonemes. The child is asked to name what he sees in the picture. Some prompting is allowed. The phonemes are tested in initial, medial, and final word positions. Phonemes produced erroneously are recorded to types of errors on a score sheet. Examiner required. Not suitable for group use.

Untimed: 15 minutes

Scoring: Examiner evaluated

Cost: Complete kit (manual/picture plates, 25 score sheets) $4.50

Publisher: Communication Research Associates, Inc.

SCREENING TEST FOR DEVELOPMENTAL APRAXIA OF SPEECH
Robert W. Blakeley

Child   Ages 4-12

Purpose: Assists in the differential diagnosis of developmental apraxia of speech.

Description: Multiple-item test diagnosing the developmental apraxia of speech through eight subtests. The subtests are Expressive Language Discrepancy, Vowels and Dipthongs, Oral Motor Movement, Verbal Sequencing, Motorically Complex Words, Articulation, Transpositions, and Prosody. The testing results of 169 children of normal intelligence with multiple articulation errors are reported. Examiner required. Not suitable for group use.

Untimed: 10 minutes

Scoring: Examiner evaluated

Cost: Test kit (manual, 40 test forms) $47.95

Publisher: C.C. Publications, Inc.

SCREENING TEST OF ADOLESCENT LANGUAGE (STAL)
Elizabeth M. Prather,
Sheila Van Ausdal Breecher,
Marimyn Lee Stafford,
and Elizabeth Matthews Wallace

Adolescent
Grades 6 and above

Purpose: Assesses linguistic development and identifies junior and senior high-school students needing further testing. Used with large populations of students in public school settings by speech-language pathologists, classroom teachers, school counselors and psychologists, and teachers of special education.

Description: 23-item oral-response screening instrument consisting of four subtests assessing language skills often associated with learning/language dis-

abilities. The Vocabulary subtest (12 items) assesses comprehension of word meaning, substitution of a synonym in a grammatically correct form, and word finding and retrieval competencies. The Auditory Memory Span subtest (3 items) requires repetition of a sentence in its original syntactical form and measures the aspect of memory span associated with related semantic and syntactic stimuli. The Language Processing subtest (5 items) requires the student to decode a message and use language for reasoning and problem solving. The Proverb Explanation subtest (3 items) assesses paraphrasing and cognitive skills needed for verbal clarity. Standard instructions are given at the beginning of each subtest, and the student's oral responses are recorded and evaluated in accordance with the instructions included in the manual. Cut-off scores based on normative studies of sixth- and ninth-grade students identify students needing further testing. Examiner required. Suitable for group use.

Untimed: 7 minutes

Scoring: Examiner evaluated

Cost: Complete kit (manual, 50 test forms, laminated cards summarizing administration and scoring procedures) $30.00

Publisher: University of Washington Press

SENTENCE COMPREHENSION TEST-SCT-(EXPERIMENTAL EDITION)

Child   Ages 3-5

Purpose: Assesses a young child's ability to use receptive language. Used for remediation by teachers, psychologists, and speech therapists.

Description: Multiple-item "point-to" test measuring sentence comprehension. The examiner shows the child a series of sets of drawings, each with four black and white drawings offering a choice in grammatical interpretation when accompanied by the examiner's target sentence. The child answers by pointing to the picture of his choice. Materials include a reuseable

picture booklet, score sheets, and a manual. Examiner required. Not suitable for group use.
CANADIAN PUBLISHER
Untimed: 20 minutes
Scoring: Examiner evaluated
Cost: Contact publisher
Publisher: Institute of Psychological Research, Inc.
Information and availability unconfirmed; no publisher response.

SENTENCE IMITATION SCREENING TEST (SIST)
Merlin J. Mecham and J. Dean Jones

Child   Ages 3-6

Purpose: Identifies children who have problems handling syntactic transformational rules. Used to screen Head Start and early education classes for students who need more extended diagnostic testing.

Description: 90-item oral-response test in three sets of 30 items each measuring the following factors: production (initiation) of syntactic transformational rules, language processing, short-term memory span, and verbal imitative performance. The examiner reads the stimulus sentences and the child repeats them. The child's responses are tape recorded and analyzed later for specified types of errors. The test kit includes a manual (with stimulus sentences) and 50 score sheets. Examiner required. Not suitable for group use.
Untimed: 5-10 minutes
Scoring: Examiner evaluated
Cost: Manual, 50 score sheets $10.50
Publisher: Communication Research Associates, Inc.

SEQUENCED INVENTORY OF COMMUNICATION DEVELOPMENT, REVISED EDITION, 1984
Dona Lea Hedrick,
Elizabeth M. Prather,
and Annette R. Tobin

Child   Ages 4 months-
**   4 years**

Purpose: Evaluates the communication abilities of normal and retarded children functioning between the ages of four months and four years. Used for remedial programming by speech-language pathologists, audiologists, psychologists, and teachers trained in speech and language assessment techniques.

Description: 210-item inventory assessing and diagnosing language disorders in young children. The receptive language section (92 items) includes behavioral items that test sound and speech discrimination and awareness and understanding. The expressive language section (118 items) includes three types of expressive behaviors (imitating, initiating, and responding) and measures verbal output for length, grammatic and syntactic structure, and articulation. The resulting Communication Profile provides guidelines for developing remedial programs for young children with language disorders, mental retardation, specific language problems, and hearing or visual impairments. Some items have been adapted from the REP Scale, the Denver Development Scale, and the Illinois Test of Adaptive Abilities. The test kit includes over 100 objects used as stimuli for test items. Examiner required. Not suitable for group use.
Untimed: Varies
Scoring: Examiner evaluated
Cost: Complete kit (manual, 50 receptive test booklets, 50 expressive test booklets, stimulus objects, plastic carrying case) $175.00
Publisher: University of Washington Press

SKLAR APHASIA SCALE: REVISED 1983
Maurice Sklar

Adult

Purpose: Diagnoses speech and language disorders resulting from brain damage. Used to plan therapy programs and to measure progress.

Description: Multiple-item oral-response test of speech and language disorders resulting from brain damage. The test quantifies disturbances in four areas:

auditory verbal comprehension, reading comprehension, oral expression, and graphic production. Responses are evaluated in each of the four areas for extent of damage and potential responsiveness to therapy. A Total Impairment Score is provided. Examiner required. Not suitable for group use.

Untimed: 10-15 minutes

Scoring: Hand key

Cost: Kit (25 protocol booklets, manual, 1 set test materials) $45.00

Publisher: Western Psychological Services

SLINGERLAND SCREENING TESTS FOR IDENTIFYING CHILDREN WITH SPECIFIC LANGUAGE DISABILITY
Refer to page 587.

SLOSSON ARTICULATION, LANGUAGE TEST WITH PHONOLOGY (SALT-P)
Refer to page 493.

SMITH-JOHNSON NONVERBAL PERFORMANCE SCALE
Refer to page 17.

SPECIFIC LANGUAGE DISABILITY TESTS
Neva Malcomesius

Adolescent   Grades 6-8

Purpose: Screens entire classroom groups or individual students and identifies those who show specific language disability. Used to help design remedial programs and indicate the need for further testing.

Description: 10 paper-pencil subtests identifying perceptual language problems through analysis of written performance. Subtests I-V evaluate visual perception: visual discrimination, visual memory, and visual-motor coordination. Subtests VI-X evaluate auditory perception: auditory discrimination, auditory memory, auditory-motor coordination, and comprehension. All tests check handwriting

and the ability to follow directions. Materials include the subtests, teacher's manual, test booklet, and cards and charts. Examiner required. Suitable for group use.

Untimed: 30-45 minutes

Scoring: Examiner evaluated

Cost: 12 tests $6.00; charts and cards $8.00; teacher's manual $1.50

Publisher: Educators Publishing Service, Inc.

SPEECH-EASE SCREENING INVENTORY (K-1)
Speech-Ease (Teryl Pigott, Jane Barry, Barbara Hughes, Debra Eastin, Patricia Titus, Harriett Stensel, Kathleen Metcalf, and Belinda Porter)

Child   Grades K-1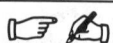

Purpose: Assesses the articulation and language development of children. Used to identify students needing speech-language services.

Description: Multiple-item response test evaluating the speech and language development of children. The basic section assesses articulation, language association, auditory recall, expressive vocabulary, and concept development. An optional section includes additional auditory items, a section on similarities and differences, a language sample, and a section on linguistic relationships. Examiner required. Not suitable for group use.

Untimed: 7-10 minutes

Scoring: Examiner evaluated

Cost: Complete $24.95; 96 scoring forms $3.75; 48 kindergarten summary sheets $2.50; 48 first-grade summary sheets $2.50

Publisher: The Interstate Printers & Publishers, Inc.

STYCAR LANGUAGE TEST
Mary D. Sheridan

Child   Ages 1-7

Purpose: Assesses language development. Used for differential diagnosis and management of speech disorders in young children and mentally retarded individuals.

Description: Multiple-item series of clinical testing procedures for assessing language and speech skills. The test is divided into three overlapping procedures: The Common Objects Test (ages 1-2), The Miniature Toys Test (ages 21 months-4 years), and the Picture Book Test (ages 2½-7). The tests do not provide pass/fail results. Descriptive recording and rating on a 3- to 5-point scale is recommended. The test is available to speech therapists, medical doctors, and specialist language teachers. Examiner required. Not suitable for group use. BRITISH PUBLISHER

Untimed: 30 minutes

Scoring: Examiner evaluated

Cost: Complete kit (picture card booklet, common objects test, miniature toys, manual) £94.30 (payment in sterling for all overseas orders)

Publisher: NFER-NELSON Publishing Company Ltd.

SYMBOLIC PLAY TEST— EXPERIMENTAL EDITION (SPT)
Marianne Lowe and Anthony Costello

Child   Ages 1-3

Purpose: Assesses the conditions necessary for meaningful language development. Used for evaluating the language potentialities of very young children.

Description: Multiple-item test measuring early concept formation and symbolization. The examiner presents objects to the child and rates meaningful responses and connections that the child makes as expressed in spontaneous nonverbal play activities. Materials include a set of toys. A videotape for the SPT is available. The test is for use by all speech therapists completing training in 1973 or later and medical doctors with a course in developmental pediatrics. Speech therapists completing training before 1973 must have undergone further training in this type of testing. Examiner required. Not suitable for group use. BRITISH PUBLISHER

Untimed: 10-15 minutes

Scoring: Examiner evaluated

Cost: Complete kit (25 record forms, set of toys, manual), £71.90; (payment in sterling for all overseas orders)

Publisher: NFER-NELSON Publishing Company Ltd.

TANNER ECLECTIC STUTTERING THERAPY PROGRAM (TEST)
Dennis C. Tanner

Ages 12-adult

Purpose: Diagnoses stuttering in individuals and provides approaches to therapy. Designed for clinicians with limited experience in adolescent and adult stuttering therapy.

Description: 4-part diagnostic and theraputic approach for working with adolescents and adults who stutter. The first step in the program is behavior modification of visible features of stuttering followed by modification of the audible symptoms of stuttering. The next step is systematic desensitization of the anxiety and associated negative emotion occurring before, during, and after stuttering. The fourth part of the program is transactional analysis counseling and instruction for the personality and interpersonal communication variables associated with stuttering. Examiner required. Not suitable for group use.

Untimed: Varies

Scoring: Examiner evaluated

Cost: Complete kit (manual, test forms, tapes) $60.00

Publisher: Modern Education Corporation

TEMPLE UNIVERSITY SHORT SYNTAX INVENTORY (TUSSI)
Adele Gerber and Henry Goehl

Mental ages 5-7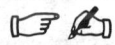

Purpose: Assesses patterns of syntax and morphology in individuals with a mental age of 5-7 and in older language-delayed individuals. Used for creating therapy goals and in writing individual preschool programs and individual education plans.

Description: Multiple-item test analyzing basic sentence elements and morphemes for both initiated and elicited responses. The test contains a broad range of evaluation items and compares language knowledge and use. The test also can be used with individuals who are mentally, emotionally, or physically handicapped. Examiner required. Not suitable for group use.

Untimed: 10-15 minutes

Scoring: Examiner evaluated

Cost: Complete kit (manual, TUSSI-2, 4 multi-picture boards, and 32 picture cards) $34.95

Publisher: Slosson Educational Publications, Inc.

TEST FOR EXAMINING EXPRESSIVE MORPHOLOGY (TEEM)
Kenneth G. Shipley, Terry A. Stone, and Marlene B. Sue

Child, adolescent

Purpose: Assesses the expressive morpheme development of children (language age 3-8 years; interest level 3-16 years), measures general language level, and monitors student progress. Used in language remediation, hearing-impaired, early childhood, special education, and speech therapy classes.

Description: 54-item oral-response sentence-completion test assessing the allomorphic variations of six major morphemes: present progressives, plurals, possessives, past tenses, third-person singulars, and derived adjectives. The examiner presents each stimulus picture while reading the stimulus phrase, and the child completes the phrase while viewing the picture. Results identify specific morphemes and allomorphic variations requiring stimulation or instruction. The manual includes administration and scoring instructions and technical data. Examiner required. Not suitable for group use.

Untimed: 7 minutes

Scoring: Examiner evaluated

Cost: Test kit (manual, 25 scoring forms, test book) $21.95

Publisher: Communication Skill Builders, Inc.

TEST FOR ORAL LANGUAGE PRODUCTION (TOLP)

Child   Ages 4.5-10.5

Purpose: Measures oral language ability. Used for educational evaluation.

Description: Multiple-item verbal test of 16 aspects of language production covering productivity, syntactic complexity, correctness, fluency, and content. Materials include stimulus materials that the subject responds to orally. The TOLP is available only to professional personnel attached to education departments and others with sufficient knowledge of sentence analysis to score the test. Examiner required. Not suitable for group use. SOUTH AFRICAN PUBLISHER

Untimed: 30 minutes-1 hour, 30 minutes

Scoring: Hand key; examiner evaluated

Cost: (In Rands) stimulus material 5,40; manual 13,80; 10 scoring sheets 2,20; orders from outside The RSA will be dealt with on merit

Publisher: Human Sciences Research Council

TEST LISTENING ACCURACY IN CHILDREN (TLAC)
Refer to page 589.

TEST OF ADOLESCENT LANGUAGE (TOAL)
Donald D. Hammill,
Virginia L. Brown,
Stephen C. Larsen,
and J. Lee Wiederholt

Adolescent   Grades 6-12

Purpose: Assesses students' language abilities. Identifies problems in both spoken and written language and specifies areas where intervention is needed. Used to conduct research and make comparisons between language and cognitive abilities.

Description: Eight paper-pencil and oral-response tests measuring a broad spectrum of language abilities. The subtests measure vocabulary (semantics) and grammar (syntax) in listening, speaking, reading, and writing. The sum of the subtest scores yields an Adolescent Language Quotient (ALQ). The test yields composite scores for the following 10 areas: listening, speaking, reading, writing, spoken language, written language, vocabulary, grammar, receptive language, and expressive language. Examiner required. Not suitable for group use.

Untimed: 1 hour, 45 minutes

Scoring: Hand key

Cost: Complete (examiner's manual, 10 student booklets, 50 student answer sheets, 50 profile sheets, storage box) $72.00

Publisher: Pro-Ed

TEST OF ARTICULATION PERFORMANCE—DIAGNOSTIC (TAP-D)
Brian R. Bryant and Deborah L. Bryant

Child   Ages 3-8

Purpose: Assesses a child's articulatory strengths and weaknesses. Used for educational planning and diagnostic evaluation.

Description: 82-item oral-response test assessing the following components of a child's articulatory performance: isolated words (phonetic inventory, percent correct, error analysis of substitutions, omissions, and distortions), distinctive features (place, manner, and voicing), selective deep test (adjacent sounds), continuous speech (key phonemes in sentences), stimulability (syllables, words, and sentences), and verbal communication scales (parent, teacher, and student). Picture stimuli are used to elicit responses. The examiner selects the components needed to provide a comprehensive analysis of the child's articulatory performance. The test kit includes the Verbal Communication Scales as a measure of the child's practical use of language. Examiner required. Not suitable for group use.

Untimed: Varies

Scoring: Examiner evaluated

Cost: Complete kit (manual, 82 picture cards, 25 profile forms, complete VCS, storage box) $74.00

Publisher: Pro-Ed

TEST OF ARTICULATION PERFORMANCE—SCREEN (TAPS-S)
Brian R. Bryant and Deborah L. Bryant

Child   Ages 3-8

Purpose: Identifies children with articulation problems who need further evaluation. Used where large numbers of children must be screened in a short period of time.

Description: 31-item oral-response test assessing the articulation performance of children. Picture stimuli are used to elicit both spontaneous and imitative production. Quotients, percentiles, and age equivalents are available for children ages 3 years to 8 years 11 months. Examiner required. Individually administered; suitable for use with large groups.

Untimed: 3-5 minutes

Scoring: Examiner evaluated

Cost: Complete kit (manual, picture book, 50 answer sheets, storage box) $41.00

Publisher: Pro-Ed

TEST OF EARLY LANGUAGE DEVELOPMENT (TELD)
Wayne P. Hresko, D. Kim Reid, and Donald D. Hammill

Child   Ages 3-7.11

Purpose: Measures content and form in the spoken language abilities of children.

Description: 38-item test using a variety of semantic and syntactic tasks to assess different aspects of receptive/expressive language. Examiner required. Not suitable for group use.

Untimed: 15 minutes

Scoring: Hand key

Cost: Complete kit (manual, 11 picture cards, 50 record forms) $33.00
Publisher: Pro-Ed

TEST OF LANGUAGE COMPETENCE (TLC)
Elisabeth H. Wiig

Child, adolescent
Ages 9-19

Purpose: Measures language competence of students.

Description: Multiple-item response test for diagnosing language disabilities by assessing language strategies rather than language skill. The Recreating Sentences subtest examines the ability to perceive the nature of a communication and recreate a semantically, syntactically, and pragmatically appropriate sentence. The Understanding Metaphoric Expressions subtest has students interpret an expression and select another one with the same meaning. The Understanding Ambiguous Sentences subtest evaluates the ability to recognize and interpret alternative meanings of lexical and structural ambiguities. The Making Inferences subtests has students identify permissible inferences based on causal relationships or chains. The test's features include norm-referenced scores, extension teaching and testing formats for each subtest, and individual education program guidelines. Examiner required. Not suitable for group use.
Untimed: 1 hour
Scoring: Not available
Cost: Complete program (administration manual, technical manual, stimulus manual, record forms) $78.00
Publisher: The Psychological Corporation

TEST OF LANGUAGE DEVELOPMENT (TOLD INTERMEDIATE)
Donald D. Hammill and Phyllis L. Newcomer

Child   Ages 8.5-12.11

Purpose: Assesses the speaking abilities of children. Identifies children with language problems.

Description: 160-item oral-response test consisting of five subtests measuring different aspects of spoken language. The Generals (25 items) and Characteristics (50 items) subtests assess the understanding and meaningful use of spoken words. The Sentence Combining (20 items), Word Ordering (25 items), and Grammatic Comprehension (40 items) subtests assess different aspects of grammar. Test results are reported in terms of standard scores, percentiles, age equivalents, and quotients. By combining various subtest scores, it is possible to diagnose a child's abilities in relation to specific language skills, including overall spoken language, listening (receptive language), speaking (expressive language), semantics (the meaning of words), and syntax (grammar). Examiner required. Suitable for group use.
Untimed: 40 minutes
Scoring: Hand key; may be computer scored
Cost: Complete (examiner's manual, 50 answer sheets, storage box) $36.00
Publisher: Pro-Ed

TEST OF LANGUAGE DEVELOPMENT (TOLD-PRIMARY)
Phyllis L. Newcomer and Donald D. Hammill

Child   Ages 4-8.11

Purpose: Assesses the speaking abilities of children. Used as a language achievement test and to identify children with language problems, including mental retardation, learning disabilities, reading disabilities, speech delays, and articulation problems.

Description: 170-item oral-response test consisting of seven subtests measuring different components of spoken language. The Picture Vocabulary (25 items) and Oral Vocabulary (20 items) subtests assess the understanding and meaningful use of spoken words. The Grammatic Understanding (25 items), Sentence Imitation (30 items), and Grammatic Completion (30 items) subtests assess different aspects of grammar. The Word Articulation (20 items) and Word Discrimination (20 items) subtests are supplemental tests measuring the ability to pronounce words correctly and distinguish between words that sound familiar. Test results are reported in terms of standard scores, percentiles, age equivalents, and quotients. By combining various subtest scores, it is possible to diagnose a child's abilities in relation to specific language skills, including overall spoken language, listening (receptive language), speaking (expressive language), semantics (the meaning of words), and syntax (grammar). Examiner required. Not suitable for group use.

Untimed: 40 minutes

Scoring: Hand key; may be computer scored

Cost: Complete (examiner's manual, picture plates, 50 answer sheets, storage box) $65.00

Publisher: Pro-Ed

TEST OF MINIMAL ARTICULATION COMPETENCE (T-MAC)
Wayne Secord

Ages 5-adult

Purpose: Assesses the severity of individual speech disorders. Used to identify children needing therapy, monitor speech development against age expectations, and target the most trainable phonemes for remediation.

Description: Multiple-item verbal-response test using one of the following procedures: picture identification, sentence reading, or sentence repetition. The test provides a flexible format for obtaining a diagnostic measure of articulation performance on 24 consonant phonemes, frequently occurring "s", "r", and "l" blends, 12 vowels, 4 diphthongs, and variations of vocalic "r." The test kit includes a manual and 25 record forms. Examiner required. Not suitable for group use.

Untimed: 10 minutes

Scoring: Examiner evaluated

Cost: 25 record forms $11.00; manual $25.00; test kit $35.00

Publisher: The Psychological Corporation

TEST OF ORAL STRUCTURES AND FUNCTIONS (TOSF)
Gary J. Vitali

Ages 7-adult

Purpose: Assesses oral structures, nonverbal oral functioning, and verbal oral functioning. Used by speech pathologists for screening, differential diagnosis, caseload management decisions, and pre- and posttreatment assessment.

Description: Multiple-item paper-pencil and oral-response test assessing oral structures and motor integrity during verbal and nonverbal oral functioning and establishing the nature of structural, neurological, or functional disorders. The test is composed of five subtests: Speech Survey, Verbal Oral Functioning, Nonverbal Motor Functioning, Orofacial Structures, and History/Behavioral Survey. The Speech Survey assesses spontaneous or elicited speech in the areas of articulation, rate/prosody, fluency, and voice. The Verbal Oral Functioning subtest assesses the integrity of oral-nasal resonance balance during imitated and spontaneous speech and articulatory precision and rate/prosody during tests which control for performance loading effects, syllable position effects, voicing, manner of articulation, and placement of articulation. The Nonverbal Motor Functioning subtest assesses volitional and automatic oral functioning during essentially static and sequenced activities controlled for general anatomic site of functioning. The Orofacial Structures subtest is an observational survey of intra-oral and orofacial structures at rest. The History/Behavioral Survey is a questionnaire addressing the presence of historical information and behaviors often occurring with disorders of oral structures and functions. Descriptive information and expected subtest performance is given for dysarthria, apraxia, Broca's aphasia, velopharyngeal incompetence-insufficiency, and functional disorders. Examiner required. Not suitable for group use.

Timed: 20 minutes

Scoring: Examiner evaluated

Cost: Complete kit (manual, 25 test booklets, finger cots, tongue blades, balloons, oroscope penlight) $55.00
Publisher: Slosson Educational Publications, Inc.

TEST OF PRAGMATIC SKILLS
Brian B. Shulman

Child   Ages 3-8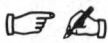

Purpose: Assesses the functional communication abilities of children. Used with language-disordered, learning-disabled, and mentally handicapped children.

Description: Series of four guided play interactions utilizing manipulative objects to assess how a child uses conversation. The test provides information on 10 categories of verbal and nonverbal communication intentions, including naming/labeling, reasoning, requesting, denying, and others. The test contains a Language Sampling Supplement for use when the child successfully passes the conversation intent portion of the test. The supplement assesses how the child uses conversational intent to organize discourse. Examiner required. Not suitable for group use.
Untimed: Not available
Scoring: Hand key
Cost: Complete kit $49.95
Publisher: Communication Skill Builders, Inc.

TEST OF SYNTACTIC ABILITIES
Stephen P. Quigley,
Marjorie W. Steinkamp,
Desmond J. Power,
and Barry W. Jones

Child, adolescent
Ages 10-19

Purpose: Measures the difficulties that profoundly, prelingually deaf students may experience in comprehending and using the syntactic structure of standard English. Used for clinical diagnosis and placement in special education programs.

Description: 20 tests measuring an individual's skill in using nine major syntactic structures: negation, conjunction, determiners, question formation, verb

processes, pronominalization, relativization, complementation, and nominalization. A screening test containing items selected from the diagnostic battery is available in two parallel forms to provide a profile of strengths and weaknesses on individual structures and to determine need for further testing or instruction. The test has been standardized on deaf children but it may also be suitable for diagnostic and normative evaluation of individuals with language problems resulting from other causes. Examiner required. Not suitable for group use.
Untimed: Not available
Scoring: Examiner evaluated
Cost: Contact publisher
Publisher: DORMAC, Inc.

THE TOKEN TEST FOR CHILDREN
Frank DiSimoni

Child   Ages 3-12.5

Purpose: Measures functional listening ability in children and identifies receptive language dysfunction. Used in language therapy.

Description: 20-item test in which the child arranges wooden tokens in response to the examiner's oral directions. In addition to the tokens, the materials include the manual and scoring forms. The results can be used to indicate a need for further testing of lexicon and syntax or to rule out language impairment in a child with reading difficulties. Materials include the tokens, manual, and scoring forms. The test is not appropriate for deaf subjects. Examiner required. Not suitable for group use.
Untimed: 8 minutes
Scoring: Examiner evaluated
Cost: Complete $25.00
Publisher: DLM Teaching Resources

TONGUE THRUST
Donald L. Rampp and
Mary Pannbacker

Child

Purpose: Diagnoses tongue thrust and provides a treatment program.

Description: Multiple-item paper-pencil checklist for determining a tongue-thrust articulation problem and lesson plans for a six-week home treatment program. The program requires less than four hours of professional time, and lesson plans can be used by parent or client. Examiner required. Not suitable for group use.

Untimed: Varies

Scoring: Examiner evaluated

Cost: Contact publisher

Publisher: Modern Education Corporation

UTAH TEST OF LANGUAGE DEVELOPMENT
Merlin J. Mecham and J. Dean Jones

Child, adolescent Ages 2-14

Purpose: Identifies children with language-learning disabilities who may need further assistance.

Description: 51-item task-assessment oral-response test measuring the following factors: receptive semantic language, expressive semantic language, receptive sequential language, and expressive sequential language. Test items are arranged in developmental order. The examiner begins testing at or just below a child's expected level of ability and works down until eight consecutive correct answers are obtained, whereupon he works upward from the starting point. When eight consecutive incorrect answers are obtained, the test is discontinued. Items are scored as correct (plus) or incorrect (minus). The total score is the total number of pluses. The test kit includes a manual, line-drawing plates, booklet, object kit, and 25 score sheets in a vinyl carrying case. Restricted to persons trained in psychological or educational testing. Examiner required. Not suitable for group use.

Untimed: 20-30 minutes

Scoring: Examiner evaluated

Cost: Complete kit $40.00; 25 extra score sheets $3.95

Publisher: Communication Research Associates, Inc.

THE VANE-L SCALE
Julia R. Vane

Child   Ages 2-6

Purpose: Measures the language acquisition of children. Used for clinical assessment and diagnosis and to help parents teach their children concepts that will prepare them for school.

Description: 35-item task-assessment test measuring vocabulary, visual and auditory memory, and language concepts. The examiner asks the child to perform tasks expected of children in the child's age range, such as "put your hands on your head," and to repeat a number of sentences. Factors measured include receptive and expressive language, auditory-verbal and auditory-motor memory, and right- or left-handedness. Standardized scoring procedures are provided. Examiner required (supervision by a psychologist is suggested). Not suitable for group use.

Untimed: 10 minutes

Scoring: Examiner evaluated

Cost: Manual $5.00; 50 record sheets $3.50

Publisher: Clinical Psychology Publishing Co., Inc.

VERBAL COMMUNICATION SCALES (VCS)
Brian R. Bryant and Deborah L. Bryant

Child   Ages 3-8

Purpose: Evaluates a child's use of language at home and school. Used in conjunction with interviews in ecological assessments of spoken language skills.

Description: Three scales assessing the attitudes of parents, teachers, and the student concerning the student's use of language. The parent and teacher scales (25 items each) consist of statements about the child's practical application of spoken language. Each statement is rated on a numerical scale. On the Student Scale (20 items), the examiner asks questions requiring a yes or no response from the child. Norms for the parent and teacher scales are provided for children ages 3 years to 8 years 11 months. Student Scale norms are provided for children ages 5 years to 8 years 11 months. Examiner required. Not suitable for group use.

Untimed: Varies

Scoring: Examiner evaluated

Cost: Complete kit (examiner's fact sheet, 25 teacher scales, 25 parent scales, 25 student scales) $19.00

Publisher: Pro-Ed

WEISS COMPREHENSIVE ARTICULATION TEST (WCAT)
Curtis E. Weiss

Child   Ages 2.5-7

Purpose: Determines articulation disorders or delays in young children and identifies misarticulation patterns and other problems. Used in articulation therapy.

Description: Multiple-item test in two forms: an easel-stand flip book of 85 pictures for subjects who cannot read and a card with 38 sentences for those who can. With the pictures, the child supplies the missing word in a sentence spoken by the examiner; with the sentences, the child does the reading. Materials include the picture cards and sentence card, a manual, and response forms. The test is not appropriate for nonverbal subjects and can be individually administered only by an examiner.

Untimed: Not available

Scoring: Examiner evaluated

Cost: Complete $31.00

Publisher: DLM Teaching Resources

WEISS INTELLIGIBILITY TEST
Curtis E. Weiss

Child, adolescent

Purpose: Quantifies intelligibility of isolated words, contextual speech, and overall intelligibility of children and adolescents. Provides a method for determining which factors most influence intelligibility.

Description: Two-part test using tape-recorded samples of isolated words and contextual speech to provide an intelligibility score in percentage form. The score indicates the severity of the communication problem and provides baseline data at the beginning of treatment. The manual contains instructions, stimulus materials, and forms for recording and scoring data. Examiner required. Not suitable for group use.

Untimed: 10-15 minutes

Scoring: Examiner evaluated

Cost: Test kit (manual, 40 test forms) $29.95

Publisher: C.C. Publications, Inc.

WESSEX REVISED PORTAGE LANGUAGE CHECKLIST
Mollie White and Kathy East

Child   Ages 0-4

Purpose: Assesses receptive and expressive language development of children. Used by teachers and speech therapists with developmentally delayed and mentally handicapped children for educational planning.

Description: Multiple-item oral-response test measuring the language development of children. The checklist is a revision and extension of the language section of the original Portage Checklist. Complex language behaviors have been broken down into smaller component steps, and new language objectives relating to use of language during play have been added. The revision consists of two components: a 4-level checklist representing years or stages and a set of 25 double-sided cards providing teaching strategies. Examiner required. Not suitable for group use. BRITISH PUBLISHER

Untimed: Not available

Scoring: Examiner evaluated

Cost: Language checklist, manual £11.35; activity cards £8.80

Publisher: NFER-NELSON Publishing Company Ltd.

THE WESTERN APHASIA BATTERY (WAB)
Refer to page 68.

WORD DISCRIMINATION
John W. Black

Adults

Purpose: Assesses the ability to articulate words and provides exercises to improve articulation.

Description: Multiple-item multiple-choice test for diagnosing articulation problems and improving articulation. The test provides a relative score for listening and for speaking and eight exercises for improving intelligibility. The test is an updated version of the Multiple-Choice Intelligibility Test and has been extended to persons with speech-language impairments and those using English as a second language. It can be used with up to 24 people divided into two equal teams. Examiner/self-administered. Suitable for group use.

Untimed: 15-18 minutes
Scoring: Self-scored
Cost: $5.75
Publisher: The Interstate Printers & Publishers, Inc.

THE WORD TEST
Carol Jorgensen, Mark Barrett,
Rosemary Huisingh,
and Linda Zachman

Child   Ages 7-12

Purpose: Assesses students' expressive vocabulary and understanding of semantics. Used with language-disabled, learning-disabled, mentally disabled, and other exceptional children as a basis for planning therapy programs.

Description: Multiple-item oral-response subtests assessing vocabulary in six contexts: associations, synonyms, semantic absurdities, antonyms, definitions, and multiple definitions. All tasks are presented auditorially; no reading or pictures are involved. The vocabulary of the test items is related to school curricula. The test results yield age equivalencies, percentile ranks, and standard scores for students ages 7-12. Ceilings and demonstration items are provided. Examiner required. Not suitable for group use.

Untimed: 30 minutes
Scoring: Examiner evaluated
Cost: Test kit (manual, 20 test forms) $36.00
Publisher: LinguiSystems, Inc.
Information and availability unconfirmed; no publisher response.

WRITTEN LANGUAGE SYNTAX TEST
Refer to page 254.

Speech, Hearing, and Visual (Sensory): Visual

ALLEN PICTURE TESTS
Henry F. Allen

Child   Ages 3½-6

Purpose: Measures visual acuity of children. Used in Headstart programs, Kindergarten and the primary grades, and pediatricians' offices to identify children needing further diagnosis and assistance.

Description: Four test slides and a vision tester measuring preschoolers' visual acuity. Slides measure $20/100$, $20/50$, $20/40$, and $20/30$ levels of acuity for both right and left eyes. A training card is used to familiarize the child with the names of the objects used on the test cards (jeep, birthday cake, telephone, and man on a horse). The test is an alternative to the Michigan Pre-School Acuity Tests. Examiner required. Not suitable for group use.

Untimed: 3-5 minutes
Scoring: Hand key; examiner evaluated
Cost: Slide for Vision Tester II $32.50
Publisher: Titmus Optical, Inc.

ANXIETY SCALE FOR THE BLIND
Refer to page 119.

AO PSEUDO-ISOCHROMATIC COLOR TEST

All ages

Purpose: Assesses color perception.

Description: 15-plate test determines red-green vision deficiency. The test utilizes a demonstration plate to explain the numerical plate design. Subject must be able to read. Examiner required. Not suitable for group use.

Untimed: 5 minutes

Scoring: Examiner evaluated

Cost: 15 plates $15.00

Publisher: Richmond Products

BIEGER TEST OF VISUAL DISCRIMINATION
Elaine Bieger

All ages

Purpose: Measures visual discrimination abilities using letters and words.

Description: 112-item paper-pencil multiple-choice test consisting of seven subtests measuring levels of mastery in the following areas: larger and lesser contrasts in letters and words, orientation reversal in letters and words, and sequence reversals in words. The test may be administered independently or in conjunction with the Visual Discrimination of Words Training Program. Following the format of the test, the training program starts with contrasting words and systematically progresses to words with almost identical features. The whole word and parts of the word are presented to provide systematic experiences relating parts of the word and the gestalt simultaneously. The individual is taught to scan words that are simultaneously positioned further and further apart. The test is available in two forms, A and B. Examiner required. Suitable for group use.

Untimed: 5 minutes per subtest; 35 minutes total

Scoring: Examiner evaluated

Cost: Complete kit (manual, test record forms, workbook) $20.50; manual (for both test and training program) $5.50; 30 record forms (15 of each form) $9.75; training program workbook $6.50

Publisher: Stoelting Company

CARROW AUDITORY-VISUAL ABILITIES TEST (CAVAT)
Elizabeth Carrow-Woolfolk

Child   Ages 4-10

Purpose: Measures auditory and visual perceptual, motor, and memory skills in children. Used to identify language/learning problems, analyze sources of auditory and/or visual difficulties and for instructional programming.

Description: Multiple-item set of two paper-pencil verbal-visual batteries containing 14 subtests. They allow comparison of individual performances in auditory and visual abilities by providing data on interrelationships among discrimination, memory, and motor skills. In the Visual Abilities battery, the categories are visual discrimination matching, visual discrimination memory, visual-motor copying, visual-motor memory, and motor speed. In the Auditory Abilities battery, the categories are picture memory, picture sequence selection, digits forward, digits backward, sentence repetition, word repetition, auditory blending, auditory discrimination in quiet, and auditory discrimination in noise. Materials include test books, response/scoring booklets, cassette, manual, and an entry test for determining which subtests or battery to administer. The Visual battery is not appropriate for blind subjects; the auditory is not appropriate for the deaf. Examiner required. Not suitable for group use.

Timed: Motor speed subtest 1 hour

Scoring: Examiner evaluated

Cost: Complete $85.00

Publisher: DLM Teaching Resources

CITY UNIVERSITY COLOR VISION TEST
Robert Fletcher

All ages

Purpose: Diagnoses all types of color deficiencies, including the blue/yellow range. Used to assess the depth and degree of color deficiencies.

Description: 10-item paper-pencil test assessing color deficiencies in children and adults. Four color standards are arranged in a diamond form around a central standard. One of the outer spots is a match or near match to the central one for a color normal. The other three standards are matches for protan, deutan, and tritan defectives. Examiner required. Not suitable for group use.

Untimed: 5 minutes

Scoring: Hand key; examiner evaluated

Cost: Complete kit (two-ring binder, instructions, scoring key, black cards, record charts) $148.00

Publisher: Keeler Instruments, Inc.

Information and availability unconfirmed; no publisher response.

DENVER EYE SCREENING TEST (DEST)
William F. Frankenburg, J. Goldstein, and A. Barker

Child   Ages 6 months-7 years

Purpose: Helps evaluate vision problems in children to determine if a child needs specialized testing.

Description: Performance test in which the examiner shows seven picture cards and asks the child to name the picture at 15 feet. For children age six months to two years-five months, the examiner uses an "E" card and a spinning toy to attract the child's attention and examines its eyes to see if they track; first one eye is tested, then the other. Materials consist of picture cards, cord, toy, plastic occluder, and "E" card. A flashlight is required. Examiner required. Not suitable for group use.

Untimed: 10 minutes

Scoring: Examiner evaluated

Cost: Complete kit $9.00; manual $6.50; 25 test forms $1.75

Publisher: Ladoca Publishing Foundation

Information and availability unconfirmed; no publisher response.

DEVELOPMENTAL VISION TEST
SOI Institute Staff

Child

Purpose: Assesses 10 visual functions of young children. Used by teachers, nurses, and health service personnel to screen all students before vision problems cause academic problems.

Description: Screening instrument for detecting vision problems that may affect learning. The nine subtests are taken from the basic SOI Learning Abilities test, and the SOI-LA manual is used for administration. Scoring is keyed to the *Developmental Vision Guide* for complete interpretation. The test includes a vision checklist. Computer analysis is available. Examiner required. Suitable for group use.

Untimed: Varies

Scoring: Examiner evaluated; may be computer scored

Cost: Test form $2.00

Publisher: M & M Systems

DVORINE COLOR VISION TEST
Israel Dvorine

All ages

Purpose: Identifies individuals with defective color vision. Used for screening for color blindness in schools and industrial settings.

Description: 15-item test for determining the type and degree of color vision defect. The subject reads numbers or traces paths consisting of multicolored dots presented against a background of contrasting dots. Materials include 15 plates and 8 auxiliary plates for verification. Examiner required. Not suitable for group use.

Untimed: 2-3 minutes

Scoring: Examiner evaluated

Cost: Booklet of color plates $125.00; 35 record forms $12.50

Publisher: The Psychological Corporation

ERROR DETECTION IN TEXTS (DETECT)

Refer to page 41.

FARNSWORTH DICHOTOMOUS TEST FOR COLOR BLINDNESS
Dean Farnsworth

Adolescent, adult

Purpose: Assesses color blindness. Used for screening applicants for jobs requiring color vision.

Description: One-task test of color vision in which the applicant arranges colored caps according to color on a hinged rack. The pattern of responses is compared to that of normal subjects. Materials include a hinged rack with one permanently mounted reference color cap and fifteen movable color caps. Examiner required. Not suitable for group use.

Untimed: 5 minutes

Scoring: Hand key; examiner evaluated

Cost: Complete set (caps, rack, manual, 100 analysis sheets) $298.00; manual $17.00; 100 analysis sheets $20.00

Publisher: The Psychological Corporation

FARNSWORTH-MUNSELL 100 HUE TEST

Refer to page 806.

HAPTIC INTELLIGENCE SCALE

Refer to page 23.

HILL PERFORMANCE TEST OF SELECTED POSITIONED CONCEPTS
Everett Hill

Child   Ages 6-10

Purpose: Measures the development of spatial concepts in visually impaired children. Used by teachers and mobility specialists to diagnose visually impaired children.

Description: 72-item task-assessment of basic spatial concepts such as front, back, left, and right. The development of these positional concepts is tested through performance on four types of tasks: identifying body relationships, demonstrating positional concepts of body parts to one another, demonstrating positional concepts of body parts to other objects, and forming object-to-object relationships. The test may be used as a criterion-referenced instrument to identify individual strengths and weaknesses in the area of spatial concepts or as a norm-referenced test. Examiner required. Not suitable for group use.

Untimed: Not available

Scoring: Examiner evaluated

Cost: Complete kit (20 record forms, manual) $16.00

Publisher: Stoelting Company

INVENTORY OF PERCEPTUAL SKILLS (IPS)
Donald R. O'Dell

Child

Purpose: Assesses visual and auditory perceptual skills and provides the structure for individual remedial programs. Aids in instructional planning for students at all age levels and in the development of IEPs.

Description: 79-item oral-response and task-performance test assessing perceptual skills in the following areas: visual discrimination, visual memory, object recognition, visual-motor coordination, auditory discrimination, auditory memory, auditory sequencing, and auditory blending. Once scored and recorded on the student profile (included in the student record booklet), a graphic comparison can be made of all of the subtests. A score below the mean on any subtest indicates a weakness in that area. The test may be administered by teachers, aides, or specialists without special training. The teacher's manual contains many educational activities in visual and auditory perception. Games, exercises, and activities provide the teacher with a variety of approaches and materials to use with the student. The student workbook includes 18 exercises to improve the areas in need of remediation. Examiner required. Not suitable for group use.

Untimed: Varies

Scoring: Examiner evaluated

Cost: Complete set (manual, student workbook, 10 student record booklets, stimulus cards) $16.25; manual $3.25; student workbook $1.75; 10 student record booklets $10.00; stimulus cards $2.25

Publisher: Stoelting Company

ISHIHARA'S TEST FOR COLOUR BLINDNESS
Shinobu Ishihara

All ages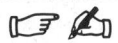

Purpose: Determines whether a patient has normal color vision. Used for school and employee screening.

Description: 24-item visual identification test measuring normal color perception. Each test item consists of a plate of pseudo-isochromatic colors with a number or pattern on each plate. The patient is asked to read the number or trace the pattern on each plate. Children who do not know numbers may trace the numbers. The test identifies both protan and deutan type color deficiencies with an indication of whether they are strong or mild. Test materials include a 24-page book of color plates, an informational guide, and a scoring key. Not limited to English language administration. Examiner required. Suitable for group use.

Untimed: 1 minute or less

Scoring: Hand key; examiner evaluated

Cost: Complete $63.00

Publisher: Kanehara & Co. Ltd., Japan; distributed in the U.S.A. by Titmus Optical, Inc.

KERBY LEARNING MODALITY TEST, REVISED 1980
Refer to page 582.

MICHIGAN PRE-SCHOOL ACUITY AND BINOCULARITY TEST

Child   Ages 3½-6

Purpose: Measures acuity and screens for binocular vision of children in Headstart, preschool programs, and primary grades. Identifies children needing further evaluation. Used with both handicapped and normally developing children.

Description: Vision tester and four slides comprise two tests: one for visual acuity and one for binocular vision. The test for visual acuity consists of three slides and four training cards. The child is familiarized with the task of determining "which way the table legs point" using the training cards and then takes the test using the vision tester. The Acuity Test measures both right eye and left eye acuity. The Standard Test is $^{20}/_{30}$ on a pass/fail basis. The following levels are also available: $^{20}/_{20}$, $^{20}/_{40}$, $^{20}/_{50}$, and $^{20}/_{70}$. The Binocularity Test consists of one slide and uses the "which way do the table legs point" task. It identifies children with cublyopia, suppression, and other binocularity problems. The tests are used by pediatricians, family physicians, medical specialists, and school screening programs for purposes of screening and referral. Examiner required. Not suitable for group use.

Untimed: Acuity 5 minutes; binocularity 2 minutes

Scoring: Hand key; examiner evaluated

Cost: Complete (3 acuity slides, 1 binocularity slide, manual, accessories) $135.00

Publisher: Titmus Optical, Inc.

MKM BINOCULAR PRESCHOOL TEST
Leland Michael and James W. King

Child   PreK

Purpose: Helps evaluate the near-point visual performance of preschool and other nonreading children. Used to demonstrate how learning lenses can improve performance and to monitor progress of visual therapy cases.

Description: One-card visual-verbal test. The card, used with a stereoscope, contains an array of geometric symbols. Some symbols are presented to both eyes and others are presented to the right or left eye alone. If the child has good binocular performance, the symbols will be read in the proper sequence without undue hesitation. A child's tendency to see double might suppress the vision of one eye, thus omitting the symbols presented to that eye. Binocular problems then can be identified. A stereoscope is needed. Examiner required. Not suitable for group use.

Untimed: 2-3 minutes

Scoring: Examiner evaluated

Cost: Complete (50 score sheets, instructions, cards) $10.00

Publisher: MKM

MKM MONOCULAR AND BINOCULAR READING TEST
Leland Michael and James W. King

Child   Grades 1-2

Purpose: Helps identify children with reading problems related to subtle differences in the vision of one eye or the other. Used to demonstrate how learning lenses can improve performance and to monitor progress of visual therapy cases.

Description: Six-card visual-verbal test. The cards are divided into two sets. The first set contains 110 words known by most children by the end of the first grade; the second set contains an additional 110 words children are expected to know by the end of the second grade. Each set contains three cards. The child reads the first card with the left eye alone. The second card presents the same words in reverse order for the right eye alone. The examiner records errors and time on a score sheet, determining which errors were common to both eyes and which were made with the right or left eye alone. Word reversals, improper vowel sounds, and other errors are expected to be about the same for each eye, but if the time for one eye exceeds the other by twenty percent or more, a binocular visual problem should be suspected. The third card contains the same words as the first two

cards. Some words are presented to both eyes and others are presented just to the right or left eye alone. A stereoscope is needed. Examiner administered. Not suitable for group use.

Untimed: 5-10 minutes

Scoring: Examiner evaluated

Cost: Complete (cards, score pads) $30.00; 50 additional score pads $3.50

Publisher: MKM

MOTOR-FREE VISUAL PERCEPTION TEST (MVPT)
Refer to page 563.

PEEK-A-BOO TEST
Pat Hill

Child   Ages 3-7

Purpose: Determines vision impairment in normal and retarded children not yet able to read.

Description: Eight-target set that presents nonlanguage tests in six areas: acuity, vertical and lateral eye coordination, fusion, depth perception, and color discrimination. The cards, which are modern illustrations of familiar objects, are shown one at a time in the Telebinocular (refer to the Visual Survey Telebinocular). The examiner asks specific questions and records answers on a corresponding record form, which is ordered separately. Examiner required. Not suitable for group use.

Timed: 5 minutes

Scoring: Hand key

Cost: Complete $54.00; contact publisher for record forms price

Publisher: Keystone View, Division of Mast Development Company

---

PRG INTEREST INVENTORY
Refer to page 756.

PROFESSIONAL VISION TESTER

Ages 5 and older

Purpose: Measures an individual's visual performance. Used to detect vision deficiencies.

Description: 11-test nonverbal battery. The tests measures phoria-vertical and lateral at near and far distances (4 tests), acuity of right and left eyes at near and far distances (6 tests), and stereopsis and color discrimination (1 test). Materials include a precision stereoscopic instrument equipped with adjustable viewing aperture height, constant illumination, and a revolving drum to hold test slides. All controls are on the right side of the machine and require a minimum number of manipulations. Questions are simple and direct, and the routine can be learned with minimal training. Examiner required. Not suitable for group use.

Untimed: 10 minutes
Scoring: Hand key
Cost: Instrument $1,095.00
Publisher: Lafayette Instrument Company, Inc.

PSEUDOISOCHROMATIC PLATES

Grades PreK-adult

Purpose: Tests for protanoid and deuteranoid types of red-green color blindness. Used for perceptual screening, vision testing, and drivers' tests.

Description: 15-item oral-response test assessing red-green color perception. Plates consisting of patterns of colored dots revealing numbers are held 30 inches in front of the subject, who is given approximately two seconds to call out the number formed by the pattern on each plate. Materials consist of a single booklet of color plates containing a demonstration plate and 14 number plates. Examiner required. Not suitable for group use.

Untimed: 3 minutes
Scoring: Hand key
Cost: Plates $95.00
Publisher: Lafayette Instrument Company, Inc.

RANDOT STEREOPSIS TEST

All ages

Purpose: Determines whether a patient has stereo-depth perception and/or binocular vision. Screens children and adults for further evaluation and treatment.

Description: Two stereo vectographs (dot patterns on a homogeneous background) and polaroid glasses are used to measure children's stereo depth perception and gross depth perception. More definitive tests are included for adult patients. Wearing the polaroid glasses, the patient views the vectographs and picks out the characters formed by the dot patterns. The test is not practical with very young children and provides no monocular clues. Examiner required. Suitable for group use.

Untimed: 10-15 minutes
Scoring: Hand key; examiner evaluated
Cost: Complete $69.00
Publisher: Titmus Optical, Inc./Stereo Optical Co.

REACTION TIME MEASURE OF VISUAL FIELD (REACT)
Refer to page 56.

REYNELL-ZINKIN DEVELOPMENT SCALES FOR YOUNG VISUALLY HANDICAPPED CHILDREN
Refer to page 489.

ROUGHNESS DISCRIMINATION TEST
Carson Y. Nolan and June E. Morris

Visually handicapped children   Grade 1

Purpose: Predicts readiness to learn to read braille for visually handicapped first-grade students.

Description: 69-item test assessing tactual discrimination. Each item consists of a stimulus card containing four pieces of mounted sandpaper. The child is asked to identify which of the pieces feels different from the other three. Two practice cards are provided. The complete test kit includes 71 stimulus cards, test manual, and 25 self-scoring answer sheets. Examiner required. Not suitable for group use.

Untimed: 15 minutes
Scoring: Hand key; examiner evaluated
Cost: Complete kit $152.39
Publisher: American Printing House for the Blind, Inc.

SEARCHING FOR SHAPES (SEARCH)
Refer to page 60.

SINGLE AND DOUBLE SIMULTANEOUS STIMULATION (SDSST)
Refer to page 62.

SLOAN ACHROMATOPSIA TEST
Refer to page 226.

THE SOUTH AFRICAN INDIVIDUAL SCALE FOR THE BLIND (SAISB)—1979
Refer to page 514.

SOUTHERN CALIFORNIA POSTROTARY NYSTAGMUS TEST
A. Jean Ayres

Child   Ages 5-9

Purpose: Evaluates the normalcy of the duration of nystagmus (involuntary rapid movement of the eyeball) following rotation in children. Used to identify disorders of the inner ear.

Description: Test used to evaluate vestibular-system disorders. The child being evaluated is placed on the Nystagmus Rotation Board and passively rotated first to the left and then to the right. At the end of both the left and the right rotations, the duration of nystagmus is observed and recorded. Norms are presented by sex for children ages 5-9. Examiner required. Not suitable for group use.

Timed: 5 minutes

Scoring: Hand key; examiner evaluated
Cost: Complete kit (100 record sheets, Angle Guide Card, board, manual) $95.00
Publisher: Western Psychological Services

SPEEDED READING OF WORD LISTS (SRWL)
Refer to page 63.

STEREO FLY STEREOPSIS TEST

All ages

Purpose: Determines whether a patient has stereo depth perception and/or binocular vision. Screens children and adults for further evaluation and treatment. Used with very young children to determine binocular vision.

Description: Two stereo vectographs (dot patterns on a homogeneous background) and polaroid glasses are used to measure children's stereo depth perception and gross depth perception. More definitive tests are included for adult patients. Wearing the polaroid glasses, the patient views the vectographs and picks out the characters formed by the dot patterns. The test contains a picture of a large housefly, which is particularly effective with very young children. Used as a screening aid but not for diagnosis. Examiner required. Suitable for group use.

Untimed: 5-10 minutes
Scoring: Hand key; examiner evaluated
Cost: Complete $69.00
Publisher: Titmus Optical, Inc./Stereo Optical Co.

STYCAR VISION TESTS
Mary D. Sheridan

**Child   Ages 6 months-
          7 years**

Purpose: Assesses vision in children. Used for evaluating very young and handicapped children.

Description: Multiple-item three-performance test of vision. The Stycar Vision Test (ages 2-7) uses toys and laminated cards and charts. The Graded Balls Test (ages 6 months-2 years) assesses the visual competence of motorically impaired children and those with language difficulties. Use of a reversible occluder is recommended. The Panda Test is used with children with severe visual or other handicaps. The tests are available to medical doctors and teachers of the blind. Examiner required. Not suitable for group use. BRITISH PUBLISHER

Untimed: Not available

Scoring: Examiner evaluated

Cost: Complete kit (miniature toys, distant vision cards, 5-letter booklet, 7-letter booklet, Near Vision card, 3 key cards, graded balls, 25 record forms, manual) £109.25; Panda Test set of cards £12.60; Panda Test set of plastic letters £16.45 (payment in sterling for all overseas orders)

Publisher: NFER-NELSON Publishing Company Ltd.

TEST OF VISUAL-PERCEPTUAL SKILLS (NON-MOTOR) (TVPS)
Morrison F. Gardner

Child   Ages 4-12

Purpose: Measures visual-perceptual skills of children. Used by psychologists, counselors, physicians, learning specialists, social workers, remedial therapists, diagnosticians, and other professionals.

Description: 112-item response test consisting of seven 16-item subtests measuring visual discrimination, memory, spatial relationships, form constancy, sequential memory, figure-ground, and closure. Items in each subtest are increasingly difficult. The child is asked to remember or match a given stimulus with an array of stimuli. Conversion tables are provided for raw scores into scaled scores, percentile ranks, perceptual age, and perceptual quotient; and the relationship of percentile ranks to standard scores is shown. The test can be used worldwide since it is neither culturally bound nor language-oriented. The test has no motor component. Examiner required. Not suitable for group use.

Untimed: 7-15 minutes

Scoring: Hand key

Cost: Complete battery (administration manual, set of test plates, 25 recording forms) $55.00

Publisher: Special Child Publications

TITMUS II VISION TESTER: PEDIATRIC MODEL

Child   Grades PreK-6

Purpose: Screens visual skills of preschool, Head Start, and primary grade students. Identifies students with visual deficits that may affect their performance in school.

Description: Vision tester with eight test slides screening the visual abilities of young children. Preschool children are tested for acuity far, right eye, left eye, and binocularity. Primary-grade students are tested for acuity far, right eye, left eye, hyperopia, heterophorias, and color vision. Test materials include the vision tester with 8 slides, a training manual, record forms, and a lens unit. Examiner required. Not suitable for group use.

Untimed: 3-5 minutes

Scoring: Hand key; examiner evaluated

Cost: Complete $1,195.00

Publisher: Titmus Optical, Inc.

TITMUS II VISION TESTER: PROFESSIONAL MODEL

All ages

Purpose: Screens visual skills of preschool, primary, and secondary students and adults. Identifies individuals with visual deficiencies.

Description: Vision tester with eight slides screening visual skills. Preschool children are tested for acuity far, right eye, left eye, and binocularity. Primary-grade students are tested for acuity far, right eye, left eye, hyperopia, heterophorias, and color vision. Secondary-grade students and adults are tested for acuity far and near, right eye, left eye, both eyes, vertical and lateral heterophorias, and color vision. Test materials include eight slides and vision tester, a training manual, record forms, and a lens unit. Examiner required. Not suitable for group use.

Untimed: 3-5 minutes

Scoring: Hand key; examiner evaluated

Cost: Complete $1,195.00.

Publisher: Titmus Optical, Inc.

VISION TESTING OF YOUNG CHILDREN

**Child
Ages 30 months-PreK**

Purpose: Tests vision in young children.

Description: Eight colorful plastic alphabet letters used for assessing vision in young children. These symbols replace the usual linear chart of letters used with school-age children and adults and sustain cooperation of young children as follows: over 30% cooperate at age 30 months, 65% at 33 months, and 85% at 36 months. Examiner required. Not suitable for group use.
BRITISH PUBLISHER

Untimed: Not available

Scoring: Examiner evaluated

Cost: £3.40

Publisher: The Test Agency Ltd.

VISUAL DISCRIMINATION TEST
Joseph M. Wepman, Anne Morency, and Maria Seidl

Child   Ages 5-8

Purpose: Measures children's ability to discriminate visually between similar forms. Used to measure the skills necessary for learning to read.

Description: 20-item test in which the child responds by pointing to which of four nonalphabetic forms is the same as the example. No verbal responses are required. Separate norms are provided for ages 5, 6, 7, and 8. Adequacy threshold scores are provided to indicate the need for referral. Materials include a 24-page test booklet of original designs, a complete administration and scoring manual, and score sheets marked specifically for the test. Examiner required. Not suitable for group use.

Untimed: 10-15 minutes

Scoring: Hand key

Cost: Complete kit (1 set of reusable stimulus cards, 25 score sheets, manual) $50.00

Publisher: Western Psychological Services

VISUAL FUNCTIONING ASSESSMENT TOOL (VFAT)
Kathleen Costello, Patricia Pinkney, and Wendy Scheffero

All ages

Purpose: Assesses visual functioning in the educational setting. Used to instruct low-vision individuals of all ages and levels, including the severely handicapped, and to help establish IEPs.

Description: Observation test using common classroom materials to assess the following areas of visual functioning: appearance of eyes, basic responses, fixation tracking, saccadic movement, scanning, visual accuity, visual field, depth perception, eye-hand and eye-foot coordination, visual imitation and memory, visual discrimination, visual perception, and concepts of self and others in space, pictures, visual environment, and mobility. It is not necessary to administer the entire VFAT to every student. Specific appropriate areas may be used independently. The test is designed to be administered by an eye specialist or a teacher of the visually impaired. Examiner required. Not suitable for group use.

Untimed: Not available

Scoring: Examiner evaluated

Cost: Complete kit (recording forms, manual) $41.50

Publisher: Stoelting Company

VISUAL SCANNING (SCAN)
Refer to page 67.

VISUAL SKILLS APPRAISAL (VSA)

Regina G. Richards and
Gary S. Oppenheim
in consultation with G. N. Getman

Child   Grades K-4

Purpose: Assesses visual skills of students in Grades K-4. Used by teachers who may not have specialized training in visual skills assessment for identifying visual inefficiencies that affect school performance.

Description: Multiple-item task performance test assessing pursuit, scanning, alignment, and locating movements; eye-hand coordination; and fixation unity. The test identifies students who should be referred for a comprehensive visual examination. The test is self-contained and does not require the use of other equipment. The manual includes many visual training techniques keyed to each subtest. Examiner required. Not suitable for group use.

Untimed: 10-15 minutes

Scoring: Hand key

Cost: Test kit (manual, stimulus cards, 25 design completion forms, 25 red/green trail forms, 25 score sheets, red/green glasses) $35.50

Publisher: Academic Therapy Publications

VISUAL SKILLS TEST

Grades 1-adult

Purpose: Screens basic visual skills as a basis for further optometric examination and diagnosis. Used primarily by optometrists.

Description: 10 cards for use in a standard biopter provide preliminary screening of a patient's visual skills. The cards measure acuity (far and near); right eye; left eye; both eyes; vertical and lateral heterophorias, far; lateral heterophorias, far; lateral heterophorias, near; central fusion, far and near; color perception, and stereopsis. The test will not stand up under constant use, as in school or industrial screening programs. Examiner required. Not suitable for group use.

Untimed: 10-15 minutes

Scoring: Hand key; examiner evaluated

Cost: Complete $45.00

Publisher: Titmus Optical, Inc./Stereo Optical Co.

VISUAL SKILLS TEST SET #5100

Ages 8-adult

Purpose: Determines basic visual patterns, binocular acceptance of prescriptions, and need for orthoptic training. Used for vision screening of school children.

Description: Vision test using 15 stereo targets to screen the following visual skills: phorias, fusion readiness, binocular visual efficiency at near and far points, stereopsis, and color discrimination. Cards are shown to the child one at a time in the telebinocular (refer to the Visual Survey Telebinocular), specific questions are asked, and answers are recorded on a corresponding form, which is ordered separately. The test may be too difficult for young children and slow learners. Examiner required. Not suitable for group use.

Untimed: 5 minutes

Scoring: Hand key

Cost: Complete $91.00

Publisher: Keystone View, Division of Mast Development Company

VISUAL SURVEY TELEBINOCULAR (VISION SCREENING TELEBINOCULAR)

Ages 3-adult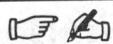

Purpose: Measures near- and far-point vision. Used for remediation screening.

Description: Vision test using a general purpose telebinocular equipped with the same lens system as the opthalmic telebinocular, as well as occluder paddles, adjustable viewing head height, and built-in internal slide illumination. During testing, target slides are placed in the instrument, and the individual is asked specific questions about each card. For slide description, refer to the Visual Skills

Test Set. The telebinocular can accommodate the Plus Lens attachment. Examiner required. Not suitable for group use.

Untimed: 5 minutes

Scoring: Hand key

Cost: Complete $640.00

Publisher: Keystone View, Division of Mast Development Company

WASHER VISUAL ACUITY SCREENING TECHNIQUE (WVAST)
Rhonda Wiczer Washer

Mentally handicapped

Purpose: Measures the visual abilities of severely handicapped (mental age 2.6 years to adult), low-functioning, and very young children. Used for screening groups of children to identify those with possible visual impairments.

Description: Multiple-item vision test screening both near and far-point acuity. The testing procedure omits as many perceptual, motor, and verbal skills as possible. A conditioning process is outlined for familiarizing individuals with the symbols, matching skills, and eye occlusion used in the screening. The test may be administered by trained volunteers. Examiner required. Suitable for screening groups of children.

Untimed: Varies

Scoring: Examiner evaluated

Cost: Starter set (manual, symbol cards, stimulus cards, occluders, near-point panel, 20 screening records) $49.00

Publisher: Scholastic Testing Service, Inc.

Student Evaluation and Counseling: Behavior Problems and Counseling Tools

ADOLESCENT-COPING ORIENTATION FOR PROBLEM EXPERIENCES (A-COPE)
Refer to page 116.

ANALYSIS OF COPING STYLE (ACS)
Herbert F. Boyd and
G. Orville Johnson

Child, adolescent
Grades K-12

Purpose: Identifies students with behavior problems so teachers, counselors, or school pyschologists can screen children for further testing, plan counseling approaches, or intervention procedures.

Description: 20-item paper-pencil test in which the examiner presents pictures of school situations (with peers and adults) and the students choose one of six possible responses. The responses are analyzed for patterns of coping styles: externalized attack, internalized attack, avoidance, or denial. The test discriminates between normal and disturbed populations. Two versions are available: one for elementary-school children and one for high-school students. Materials include picture stimuli (sheets or overhead transparencies), response forms, and manual. Examiner required. Suitable for group use.

Untimed: 10-20 minutes

Scoring: Hand key

Cost: 25 individual record forms $9.00; 100 group response forms $9.00; elementary transparencies $24.00; secondary transparencies $19.95; manual $24.00

Publisher: The Psychological Corporation

THE BEHAVIOR EVALUATION SCALE (BES)
Stephen B. McCarney,
James E. Leigh,
and Jane A. Combleet

Child, adolescent
Grades 1-12

Purpose: Assesses the behavioral problems of students. Used by school personnel to make decisions about eligibility, placement, and programming for students with behavior problems.

Description: Multiple-item paper-pencil observational inventory assessing the behavioral problems of students regardless of primary handicapping conditions. The instrument may be used with students who have learning disabilities, mental retardation, physical handicaps, or other handicapping conditions. Examiner/self-administered. Not suitable for group use.

Untimed: Varies

Scoring: Examiner evaluated

Cost: Complete kit (manual, 50 student record forms, sample data collection form) $40.00

Publisher: Pro-Ed

BEHAVIOR RATING PROFILE (BRP)
Linda L. Brown and Donald D. Hammill

Child, adolescent Grades 1-12

Purpose: Identifies elementary and secondary students thought to have behavior problems and the settings in which those problems seem prominent. Also identifies individuals who have differing perceptions about the behavior of a student.

Description: Multiple-item paper-pencil battery consisting of six independent, individually normed measures: three Student Rating Scales (Home, School, and Peer); Parent Rating Scale, Teacher Rating Scale, and the Sociogram. May be used with disturbed and learning disabled students. Examiner required. Not suitable for group use.

Untimed: Varies

Scoring: Hand key

Cost: Complete kit (examiner's manual; 50 each of teacher, parent, and student rating forms; 50 profile sheets; storage box) $72.00

Publisher: Pro-Ed

BEHAVIOUR PROBLEMS: A SYSTEM OF MANAGEMENT
Peter Galvin and Richard Singleton

Child, adolescent

Purpose: Assesses and monitors the behavior of problem children. Used in the classroom by specialist and nonspecialist teachers.

Description: Three paper-pencil record forms providing a framework for assessing and monitoring the classroom behavior of up to eight children over a six-month period. The Behaviour Checklist enables the teacher to identify and describe inappropriate behaviors, note specific problems, and select two priority behaviors on which future work will concentrate. The Daily Record Sheet provides a record of observed classroom behavior and notes details concerning priority behaviors (frequency, duration), positive behaviors, and other significant items. The observations help assess the success of the long-term program. The Monthly Progress Chart records information about the child (age, IQ, reading age) and provides a systematic account of the behavior management strategies adopted. The manual explains the rationale behind the system and includes guidelines for the system's use and references to books on appropriate remedial programs. Examiner required. Suitable for group use.
BRITISH PUBLISHER

Untimed: Varies

Scoring: Examiner evaluated

Cost: Complete set (manual, set of 3 record forms) £17.85

Publisher: NFER-NELSON Publishing Company Ltd.

BRISTOL SOCIAL ADJUSTMENT GUIDES, AMERICAN EDITION (BSAG)
D.H. Stott

Child, adolescent Ages 5-16

Purpose: Diagnoses the nature and extent of behavioral disturbances and social adjustment in children. Used by teachers and school psychologists.

Description: Multiple-item paper-pencil observational instrument consisting of short phrases describing a child's behavior. The phrases that apply to the child being evaluated are underlined by an adult familiar with the child. The guides are concerned with observable behavior rather than with inferences based on projective techniques or the child's self-assessment. An overall assessment of maladjustment, subscores for five core syndromes (unforthcomingness, withdrawal, depression, inconsequence, hostility), and four additional associated groupings (peer-maladaptiveness, nonsyndromic overreaction, nonsyndromic underreaction, and neurological symptoms are provided). The test is available in separate forms for boys and girls. Separate norms based on students from city, county, and church schools are provided for boys and girls. Examiner required. Suitable for group use.

Untimed: 10-15 minutes

Scoring: Hand key

Cost: Specimen set (includes manual, all forms) $5.50; 25 rating scales (specify boy or girl form) $7.50; 25 diagnostic forms (specify boy or girl form) $4.00; scoring key $9.00; manual $2.50

Publisher: Educational and Industrial Testing Service

BRISTOL SOCIAL ADJUSTMENT GUIDES, BRITISH EDITION (BSAG)
D.H. Stott

Child, adolescent
Ages 5-15

Purpose: Evaluates the behavior patterns of children and adolescents. Identifies maladjusted and disturbed children needing further testing and assistance. Used for clinical diagnosis.

Description: Paper-pencil checklist consisting of statements about a child's habits of response to his environment. The checklist should be filled out by a teacher, social worker, or other adult familiar with the child's behavior. The inventory provides the clinician with a picture of the child's day-to-day behavior and a system for interpreting that behavior by means of diagnostic forms. Separate guides are provided for the child in the school (boys and girls), in the family, or in residential care. Development of the guides, theoretical implications, and related studies are described in the manual. Self-administered by the evaluator under supervision of a psychologist. Not suitable for group use.
BRITISH PUBLISHER

Untimed: Open ended

Scoring: Examiner evaluated

Cost: Specimen set £5.10 plus VAT; manual £4.95 net c.

Publisher: Hodder & Stoughton

BUTTONS: A PROJECTIVE TEST FOR PRE-ADOLESCENTS AND ADOLESCENTS
Esther P. Rothman and Pearl H. Berkowitz

Child, adolescent

Purpose: Identifies acting-out, maladjusted, and disturbed students. Used to identify emotionally and behaviorally disturbed children.

Description: Multiple-item oral-response projective test consisting of an eight-page booklet containing 12 cartoon strips depicting animals in school situations. The last frame in each strip contains an animal with a blank "balloon"; the child supplies the words for that "balloon." Examiner required. Not suitable for group use.

Untimed: 15-20 minutes

Scoring: Examiner evaluated

Cost: Complete kit (25 tests, 25 protocol booklets, manual) $29.50

Publisher: Western Psychological Services

CHILD BEHAVIOR CHECKLIST AND REVISED CHILD BEHAVIOR PROFILE
Refer to page 103.

CHILD OBSERVATION GUIDE
Mark Stone

Child, adolescent

Purpose: Evaluates a child's behavior. Used in diagnosis of behavior problems.

Description: Multiple-item rating scale measuring 10 aspects of behavior: appearance, motor ability, orientation, activity level, attention, speech/language, cognitive functioning, emotional state, peer interaction, and adult interaction. The manual contains recommendations regarding child observation principles. Examiner required. Not suitable for group use.

Untimed: Observation time

Scoring: Examiner evaluated

Cost: Specimen set $6.00; 25 forms $18.00; manual $4.00

Publisher: Psychologists and Educators, Inc.

CHILDREN'S ADAPTIVE BEHAVIOR SCALE
Refer to page 105.

CHILDREN'S VERSION/FAMILY ENVIRONMENT SCALE (CV/FES)
Refer to page 71.

A CLASS PLAY
E.M. Bower

Child   Grades 3-7

Purpose: Evaluates the peer perceptions and self-images of children. Identifies children with low self-images and children whose self-image does not correspond to the perceptions of their peers. Used by classroom teachers to identify children needing further assistance or evaluation.

Description: 50-item paper-pencil test consisting of two sections. Section I (20 items) contains descriptions of 20 hypothetical roles in a play, with instructions directing each student to choose the classmate who would be most suitable and natural in each of the roles. Odd-numbered items present positive roles such as "a class president" or "a very fair person who plays games fairly," and even-numbered items present negative roles such as "a bully who picks on smaller boys and girls." Section II (30 items) consists of multiple-choice questions in which students are presented with four of the roles from the play (two positive and two negative) with instructions such as "Which of these four roles would a teacher pick for you to play?" Students are asked to indicate the roles they would pick for themselves, as well as the roles their peers or teacher would (or would not) pick for

them to play. Scoring for both sections consists of computing the proportion of positive and negative perceptions for each child within each of the two sections. A comparison of the students' peer-perceptions (the score from Section I) with their self-perceptions (the score from Section II) indicates the congruence or incongruence between the students' perceptions of themselves and the way they are perceived by others. Examiner required. Suitable for group use.

Untimed: Varies

Scoring: Examiner evaluated

Cost: Contact publisher

Publisher: Charles C. Thomas, Publisher

DECISION MAKING ORGANIZER (DMO)
Anna Miller-Tiedeman and Patricia Elenz-Martin

Adolescent, adult
Grades 10 and above

Purpose: Diagnoses decision-making problems of high-school and college students. Used for counseling and guidance.

Description: 36-item paper-pencil multiple-choice test measuring self-understanding; educational, career, and vocational plans; time use; and barriers to decision making. The subjects are presented with questions and asked to check from five responses those that apply to them (more than one response may be checked for each question). Self-administered. Suitable for group use.

Timed: 10 minutes

Scoring: Examiner evaluated

Cost: Starter set (manual, 20 organizers) $14.85

Publisher: Scholastic Testing Service, Inc.

DEMOS D (DROPOUT) SCALE
George D. Demos

Adolescent   Grades 7-12

Purpose: Identifies students who are probable school drop-outs. Used for preventive counseling.

Description: 29-item paper-pencil questionnaire measuring attitudes in four areas: toward teachers, toward education, influences by peers or parents, and school behavior. The questionnaire yields a total score and basic area scores, which are converted to probabilities of dropping out of school. A fifth-grade reading level is required. Self-administered. Suitable for group use.

Untimed: 15-20 minutes

Scoring: Hand key

Cost: Complete kit (25 forms, manual) $14.75

Publisher: Western Psychological Services

THE DEVEREUX ADOLESCENT BEHAVIOR RATING SCALE
George Spivack, Peter Haimes, and Jules Spotts

Adolescent   Ages 13-18

Purpose: Assesses the behavior symptoms of normal and emotionally disturbed adolescents. Used for diagnostic and screening procedures, group placement decisions, and assessment of progress in response to specific programs or procedures.

Description: 84-item paper-pencil test assessing symptomatic behaviors of adolescents. The evaluator (someone living with the youth) rates each item according to how he feels the subject's behavior compares with the behavior of normal children of the same age. The test yields 12 factor scores (Unethical Behavior, Defiant-Resistive, Domineering-Sadistic, Heterosexual Interest, Hyperactive Expansive, Poor Emotional Control, Need Approval and Dependency, Emotional Distance, Physical Inferiority-Timidity, Schizoid Withdrawal, Bizarre Speech and Cognition, Bizarre Action), 3 cluster scores (Inability to Delay, Paranoid Thought, Anxious Self-Blame), and 11 item scores (Persecution, Plotting, Bodily Concern, External Influences, Compulsive Acts, Avoids Competition, Withdrawn, Socialization, Peer Dominance, Physical Coordination, Distraction). Self-administered by evaluator. Not suitable for group use.

Untimed: 10-15 minutes

Scoring: Examiner evaluated

Cost: Examination set (25 scales, manual) $10.50; manual $2.00; 50 scales at $0.26 each

Publisher: The Devereux Foundation

THE DEVEREUX ELEMENTARY SCHOOL BEHAVIOR RATING SCALE (DESB-II)
George Spivack and Marshall Swift

Child   Ages 6-12

Purpose: Assesses overt classroom behaviors at the elementary-school level. Diagnoses problem behaviors that interfere with classroom performance. Used for screening procedures, group placement decisions, and assessment of progress in response to specific programs or procedures.

Description: 52-item paper-pencil inventory assessing the symptomatic classroom behavior patterns of children. The classroom teacher rates each item according to how he feels the subject's behavior compares to the behavior of normal children his age. The test yields 11 factor scores (Classroom Disturbance, Impatience, Disrespect-Defiance, External Blame, Achievement Anxiety, External Reliance, Comprehension, Inattentiveness-Withdrawn, Irrelevant-Responsiveness, Creative Initiative, Need for Closeness to the Teacher) and 3 item scores (Unable to Change, Quits Easily, Slow Work). Self-administered by teacher. Not suitable for group use.

Untimed: 10-15 minutes

Scoring: Examiner evaluated

Cost: Examination set $10.50 each (25 scales, manual) $10.50; manual $2.00; 50 scales at $0.26 each

Publisher: The Devereux Foundation

DIMENSIONS OF SELF-CONCEPT (DOSC)
William B. Michael and Robert A. Smith

**Child, adolescent
Grades 4-12**

Purpose: Identifies students who might have difficulty with schoolwork due to low self-esteem and diagnoses factors contributing to low self-esteem.

Description: Multiple-item paper-pencil questionnaire assessing level of aspiration, anxiety, academic interest and satisfaction, leadership and initiative, and identification vs. alienation. Form E is available for Grades 4-6; Form F for Grades 7-12. Percentile ranks are presented for Grades 4-6, 7-9, and 10-12. Examiner required. Suitable for group use.

Untimed: Form E 20-40 minutes; Form F 15-35 minutes

Scoring: Machine scored by publisher

Cost: 25 test forms $7.50; manual $2.50; specimen set $5.25

Publisher: Educational and Industrial Testing Service

EDUCATION APPERCEPTION TEST
Jack M. Thompson and Robert A. Sones

Child, adolescent
Grades PreK-8

Purpose: Assesses students' attitudes toward school and education. Used to work with acting-out and problem children, including some adolescents.

Description: 72-item oral-response test in which the examiner uses 18 photographs depicting children in school and school-related activities to evoke responses in four major areas: reaction to authority, reaction toward learning, peer relationships, and home attitude toward school. Responses to each photograph include "What took place before?," "What is going on now?," "What feelings are involved?," and "What is the outcome?" The test is a projective instrument and yields no scores. Examiner required. Not suitable for group use.

Untimed: 20-30 minutes

Scoring: Examiner evaluated

Cost: Complete set (pictures, manual) $29.50

Publisher: Western Psychological Services

GORDON DIAGNOSTIC SYSTEM (GSI)
Refer to page 581.

HAHNEMANN ELEMENTARY SCHOOL BEHAVIOR RATING SCALE (HESB)
George Spivack and Marshall Swift

Elementary-school
students

Purpose: Assesses classroom behavior relevant to academic achievement and behavioral adjustment during the elementary school years. Used in education, research, and counseling.

Description: 60-item teacher rating instrument consisting of 14 scales: originality, independent learning, involvement, productive with peers, intellectual dependency, failure anxiety, unreflectiveness, irrelevant talk, social over-involvement, negative feelings, holding back/withdrawn, critical/competitive, blaming, and approach to teacher. Of the 14 behavioral factors, 4 tap positive coping behaviors and 10 tap negative coping behaviors. The scale is based on factor analytic studies of normal and deviant children in regular, special, and open classrooms. Factors relate to academic achievement and controlling for I.Q. Norms are provided. Examiner required. Not suitable for group use.

Untimed: 15 minutes

Scoring: Examiner evaluated

Cost: Manual $8.00; 50 scales $0.30 each

Publisher: George Spivack and Marshall Swift

HAHNEMANN HIGH SCHOOL BEHAVIOR RATING SCALE (HHSB)
George Spivack and Marshall Swift

High-school students

Purpose: Assesses classroom behaviors that abet positive coping in the classroom and behaviors that indicate poor coping. Used in education, research, and counseling.

Description: 45-item teacher rating scale consisting of 13 scales: reasoning ability, originality, verbal interaction, rapport with teacher, anxious producer, general anxiety, quiet-withdrawn, poor work habits, lack intellectual independence, dogmatic-inflexible, verbal negativism, disturbance-restless, and expressed inability. The scale has been used to predict adjustment in young adulthood and as an outcome measure for educational and therapeutic interventions. The scale is based on analytic studies of normal and deviant children. Norms are provided. Examiner required. Not suitable for group use.

Untimed: 10 minutes

Scoring: Examiner evaluated

Cost: Manual $8.00; 50 scales $0.30 each

Publisher: George Spivack and Marshall Swift

HOME INDEX
Harrison G. Gough

Grades 6 and above

Purpose: Gathers information from junior-high and high-school students concerning their home backgrounds and socioeconomic status. Used to forecast educational achievement and gather biographical data on delinquents and children with behavioral problems.

Description: 22-item paper-pencil true-false inventory assessing students' home and family backgrounds. The inventory measures four categories: social status of family, ownership and material status, socio-civic involvement, and cultural-aesthetic involvement. Scores are provided for each of the categories, as well as a total score reflecting overall socioeconomic status. To encourage accuracy, students are told prior to filling out the inventory that all information will be confidential. College students must be asked to report on their family life at the time they were in junior and senior high-school. The norms provided are based on 4,381 junior and senior high-school students in a nationwide sample. Test users are furnished with copies of the manual and a test from which they can make copies. Self-administered. Suitable for group use.

Untimed: 10 minutes

Scoring: Hand key

Cost: Free

Publisher: Harrison G. Gough/Institute of Personality Assessment and Research

---

INFERRED SELF-CONCEPT SCALE
E.L. McDaniel

Child   Grades 1-6

Purpose: Evaluates the self-concept of children based on their behavior in school.

Description: 30-item paper-pencil inventory evaluating a child's self-concept. Based on observation of the child, a teacher or counselor familiar with the child rates him on a 5-point scale ranging from "never" to "always." With the aid of standardized scoring and interpretation, the child's self-concept is assessed based on this behavior profile. Administered by a teacher or counselor familiar with the child. Examiner required. Suitable for group use.

Untimed: 15-20 minutes

Scoring: Hand key

Cost: Complete kit (100 scales, manual) $18.00

Publisher: Western Psychological Services

LEARNING STYLE IDENTIFICATION SCALE (LSIS)
Paul J. Malcom, William C. Lutz, Mary A. Gerken, and Gary M. Hoeltke

Child

Purpose: Assesses the manner in which students prefer to learn. Used with low-functioning, average, and gifted students for academic planning.

Description: 24-item paper-pencil observational inventory assessing classroom behaviors related to students' preferred learning styles. The scale measures the extent to which a student relies on internal sources of information (feelings, beliefs, and attitudes) and external sources of information (other people, events, and social institutions). It also identifies five learning styles based on the student's preferred manner of reacting to situations and solving problems. The handbook contains directions for administering, scoring, and profiling the scale; teaching guidelines, techniques, and activities for each learning style; data on test development, reliability, and validity; factor analyses; and rating differences by grade and sex. Examiner required. Suitable for group use.

Untimed: 15 minutes

Scoring: Examiner evaluated

Cost: Contact publisher

Publisher: CTB/McGraw-Hill

LEWIS COUNSELING INVENTORY
Refer to page 148.

LIFE ADJUSTMENT INVENTORY
Ronald C. Doll and
J. Wayne Wrightstone

Adolescent   Grades 9-12

Purpose: Measures general adjustment to high-school curriculum. Used for curriculum surveys and diagnosis of maladjusted pupils for individual guidance.

Description: Multiple-item paper-pencil test of general adjustment to the high-school curriculum. The test measures the feeling of needing additional experiences in 13 specific areas, such as consumer education; religion, morals, and ethics; family living; vocational orientation and preparation; reading and study skills; and citizenship education. The test conforms with the United States Office of Education's Life Adjustment Program. Examiner required. Suitable for group use.

Untimed: 25 minutes

Scoring: Hand key

Cost: Specimen set $5.00; 25 inventories $8.75

Publisher: Psychometric Affiliates

LIGHT'S RETENTION SCALE (LRS)
H. Wayne Light

Child, adolescent
Grades 1-12

Purpose: Determines whether an elementary or secondary school student would benefit from grade retention. Used for counseling and to guide parents and school staff.

Description: 19-category paper-pencil scale pinpointing such areas of concern as age, emotional and behavior problems, motivation, absenteeism, and presence of learning disabilities. Each factor is evaluated on a 5-point scale, and the total score is reduced to several "retention candidacy" categories that indicate whether the student is likely to benefit from retention. Materials include the Parent Guide to Grade Retention, a statement of factors to consider when deciding whether to retain a child. Examiner required. Not suitable for group use.

Untimed: 10-15 minutes

Scoring: Examiner evaluated

Cost: Manual $8.50; 50 recording forms $14.00; 50 parent guides $14.00

Publisher: Academic Therapy Publications

MERRILL-DEMOS DD SCALE (MDDD)
Merrill J. Weijola and
George D. Demos

Child, adolescent
Grades 3-9

Purpose: Identifies potential or actual drug abuse and delinquent behavior on the part of children in Grades 3-9. Used to counsel such children and their parents.

Description: Multiple-item paper-pencil attitude scale measuring understanding and acceptance of teachers, police, school, and community in order to identify children needing guidance or counseling. Formerly known as the TPSC scale, the MDDD norms are available for total score and each of the four subscales for both males and females at the primary (Grades 3-6) and secondary (Grades 6-9) levels. The test is restricted to A.P.A. members. Examiner required. Suitable for group use.

Untimed: 30 minutes

Scoring: Examiner evaluated

Cost: 25 tests $8.50; manual $2.50; 25 profile charts $3.50

Publisher: Sheridan Psychological Services, Inc.

MISSOURI COMPREHENSIVE STUDENT NEEDS SURVEY

Adolescent   Grades 8-12

Purpose: Identifies the needs of high-school students so that guidance programs can be developed for individual students and groups of students with common needs.

Description: Multiple-item paper-pencil inventory providing information on the needs of students. Students rank 16 common needs on a scale of 1 (high) to 5 (low). Four reports are issued: classroom roster, individual student profile, group data (ranking of needs by category form), and group data (ranking of needs by item form). Self-administered. Suitable for group use.

Untimed: 1 hour

Scoring: Computer scored

Cost: Survey instrument $0.20; scoring service $0.24

Publisher: Missouri Testing and Evaluation Service

MULTIDIMENSIONAL PERSONALITY QUESTIONNAIRE (MPQ)
Refer to page 155.

NORMATIVE ADAPTIVE BEHAVIOR CHECKLIST (NABC)
Gary Adams

Ages 0-21 years

Purpose: Assesses an individual's level of behavioral development; provides a norm-referenced evaluation of skills and abilities and identifies individuals needing more comprehensive evaluation. Used for evaluation and placement in special programs and rounding out psychoeducational files.

Description: 120-item paper-pencil checklist (to be filled out by the parent) of adaptive behavior skills in six categories: self-help skills, home living skills, independent living skills, social skills, sensory-motor skills, language concepts/academic skills. The examiner checks off the skills the individual has mastered. Most of the checklist can be completed from memory; some interviews may be needed. The test may be administered by a classroom teacher or school psychologist. Examiner required. Not suitable for group use.

Untimed: 30 minutes

Scoring: Examiner evaluated

Cost: Complete program $18.00; components available individually

Publisher: The Psychological Corporation

PHSF RELATIONS QUESTIONNAIRE—1970
F.A. Fouche and P.E. Grobbelaar

Child, adolescent

Purpose: Assesses adjustment level of high-school students. Used for counseling and guidance.

Description: Paper-pencil questionnaire of 12 aspects of personal adjustment, including self-confidence, self-esteem, self-control, nervousness, health, family influences, personal freedom, sociability-G, sociability-S, moral sense, formal relations, and a desirability scale. Examiner required. Suitable for group use.

SOUTH AFRICAN PUBLISHER

Untimed: 30 minutes

Scoring: Hand key; examiner evaluated; may be machine scored

Cost: (In Rands) test booklet 0,40; 10 answer sheets 0,60; 10 answer sheets (machine-3881) 1,10; scoring stencil 1, 1,20; scoring stencil 2, 1,20; manual 1,50; annexure to manual 1,80; appendix to manual 2,70; orders from outside The RSA will be dealt with on merit

Publisher: Human Sciences Research Council

PORTEOUS PROBLEM CHECKLIST
M. Porteous

Adolescent   Ages 11-17

Purpose: Assesses social, emotional, and personal problems of adolescents. Used by teachers, counselors, educational psychologists, and youth workers.

Description: 68-item paper-pencil screening and diagnostic test in nine sets assessing the degree and focus of young people's concerns. Using colloquial language, the tests center on problems related to parents, peers, employment, authority, symptoms, boy-girl, oppression, delinquency, and image. Examiner required. Suitable for group use. BRITISH PUBLISHER

Untimed: 20-30 minutes

Scoring: Hand key

Cost: 25 questionnaires £5.70; manual £10.30

Publisher: NFER-NELSON Publishing Company Ltd.

THE PORTLAND PROBLEM BEHAVIOR CHECKLIST—REVISED (PPBC-R)
Steven Waksman

Child, adolescent
Grades K-12

Purpose: Identifies problem behaviors of students. Used by teachers, mental health personnel, counselors, childcare workers for evaluation, referral, or planning individual education programs or intervention programs.

Description: 29-item paper-pencil rating scale used by the examiner to identify conduct, academic, anxiety, peer, and personal problems of individual students. The results provide information for research and program evaluation, counseling or diagnostic services, parent conferences, and screening programs. Examiner required. Not suitable for group use.

Untimed: 5-10 minutes

Scoring: Examiner evaluated

Cost: Complete kit $39.95

Publisher: ASIEP Education Company

PRE-MOD
Joseph Kaplan and Sandy Kent

Handicapped students

Purpose: Diagnoses behavior problems and prescribes appropriate interventions. Used by teachers or specialists working with mildly to moderately handicapped children; also used by teachers of normal and slow learners in the regular classroom. Used to establish IEPs in the affective domain and social skills areas.

Description: Multiple-item computer-administered assessment instrument diagnosing the underlying causes of 10 of the most common behavior problems found in the classroom, including physical aggression, abusive-provocative language, noncompliance, and hyperactive-impulsive and withdrawn behavior. The program presents the teacher with a list of the 10 behaviors, from which the individual student's basic problems are identified. For each behavior identified, the program provides a socially appropriate behavior that is incompatible with the student's maladaptive behavior. The teacher then is presented with a list of prerequisite skills, knowledge, and attitudes necessary for the student to engage in the socially appropriate behavior. The teacher then identifies the prerequisites the student lacks and is provided with corresponding performance objectives and suggested interventions for each prerequisite the student lacks. Additional assessments are provided for determining the status of the prerequisites. The accompanying operator's manual is written in plain English. The program may be used independently or in conjunction with the textbook *Beyond Behavior Modification* (Kaplan, 1983) as an instructional aid in teaching behavior management strategies. Self-administered. Not suitable for group use.

Untimed: Varies

Scoring: Computer scored

Cost: Software package for Apple II+ or IIe microcomputers (diskette, backup diskette, user's manual, 10 test sheets) $99.95
Publisher: ASIEP Education Company

PRIMARY SELF-CONCEPT INVENTORY
Douglas G. Muller and Robert Leonetti

Child   Grades PreK-6

Purpose: Evaluates social, personal, and intellectual self-concepts of elementary school children. Used to assess the role of self-concept in behavior problems for remedial work.

Description: 20-item paper-pencil verbal test in which the subject marks pictures to indicate feelings about himself in response to a description read aloud by the examiner. Materials include the manual and booklets. Examiner required. Suitable for group use. Available in Spanish.
Untimed: Not available
Scoring: Examiner evaluated
Cost: Complete $13.50
Publisher: DLM Teaching Resources

PUPIL BEHAVIOR RATING SCALE (PBRS)
Nadine M. Lambert, Eli M. Bower, and Carolyn S. Hartsough

Child, adolescent   Grades K-7

Purpose: Assesses students' classroom behavior and interpersonal skills. Identifies students who are potentially educationally handicapped or gifted. Used to organize and manage appropriate instructional programs.

Description: Three multiple-item paper-pencil and oral-response rating scales measuring student effectiveness in nonintellectual or affective areas. The three scales include one teacher-observation screening instrument, one peer-rating instrument, and one self-rating instrument.
The teacher-observation scale assesses three underlying dimensions of affective behavior: classroom adaptation, interpersonal skills, and intrapersonal behavior. These measures are obtained by using an interval scale of 11 observable attributes. The 11 scales are contained in the rating book; student scores are entered on the group record chart.
Peer and self-rating are available for two levels: Grades K-3 and Grades 3-7. The peer-rating instrument for Grades K-3 is the Who Could This Be Game. The game consists of 20 scenes of school situations, portraying both positive (or neutral) situations and situations that indicate potentially dysfunctional behavior. Students are asked individually to select a classmate for each situation. By tallying responses, a measure of how each student is perceived by the class is obtained. The self-rating instrument for Grades K-3 is the picture game (separate forms for boys and girls). Seventy-two scenes depicting home, school, and play situations are presented. Students circle a happy face next to the scenes they see as happy and a sad face next to the scenes they see as sad. A tally of sad and happy responses determines a child's self-rating. Results from the Who Could This Be Game and the Picture Game are entered on the group record chart for peer and self-ratings.
Peer and self-ratings for Grades 3-7 are presented in the School Play test book. Part I of the play consists of 14 roles for which students choose classmates who they think could best play them. By tallying responses, a measure of how each student is perceived by the class is obtained. Part II elicits from the students responses concerning the roles they would or would not choose for themselves and the roles for which they think they would or would not be chosen by classmates and the teacher. Scores for both parts of the school play are entered on the group record chart for peer and self-ratings. The class screening summary chart combines scores of teacher, peer, and self-ratings. The pupil record folder provides space for recording the scores of the teacher, peer, and self-ratings, data from other achievement tests, and other essential information related to the writing of IEPs. The manual includes information on administering and scoring the scales, interpreting results, and prescribing appropriate instructional intervention.

Administered by a classroom teacher. The teacher-observation scale is self-administered. The peer and self-ratings for Grades K-3 are individually administered, and the peer and self-ratings for Grades 3-7 are group administered.

Untimed: Varies

Scoring: Examiner evaluated

Cost: Manual $10.00; rating book $10.00; 20 group record charts $4.00; Who Could This Be Game (32 recording forms and 1 group record chart) $15.00; Picture Game (16 each boys and girls forms and 2 group record charts) $33.00; School Play (32 test books and 1 group record chart) $28.00; 20 class screening summary charts $5.50; 32 pupil record folders $25.75; technical bulletin $9.00

Publisher: CTB/McGraw-Hill

THE REVISED BEHAVIOR PROBLEM CHECKLIST (RBPC)
Herbert C. Quay and Donald R. Peterson

Child, adolescent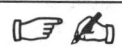

Purpose: Assesses the nature of problem behavior. Used in educational, mental health, pediatric, and correctional settings as well as for research purposes.

Description: 85-item paper-pencil observational inventory consisting of statements about problem behaviors commonly seen in children and adolescents. Each item on the inventory is rated by a knowledgeable observer (parent, teacher, child care worker, correctional staff member). Scores are provided for six subscales: conduct disorder, socialized aggression, attention problems-immaturity, anxiety-withdrawal, psychotic behavior, and motor excess. The Interim Manual, continuously updated, provides a description of the test's development, data on reliability and validity, and means and standard deviations from various normal and clinical samples. Examiner required. Not suitable for group use.

Untimed: 15 minutes

Scoring: Hand key

Cost: Test kit (interim manual, 50 tests, scoring stencil) $20.00

Publisher: Herbert C. Quay

SCALE FOR THE IDENTIFICATION OF SCHOOL PHOBIA (SIS)
Jerome H. Want

Child, adolescent

Purpose: Identifies school-phobic students from other chronically absent students.

Description: 24-item paper-pencil behavior rating scale consisting of two profiles: the School Phobia Profile and the School Truancy Profile. Each profile is completed and scored by the examiner in response to interviews with the student, parents, and other school personnel. Criterion-referenced evaluation of the two profiles identifies school-phobic behavior from school-truant behavior. Intervention strategies are provided in the manual. Examiner required. Not suitable for group use.

Untimed: Varies

Scoring: Examiner evaluated

Cost: Test kit (manual, 25 record forms, in vinyl folder) $18.50

Publisher: Academic Therapy Publications

SCHOOL BEHAVIOR CHECKLIST
Lovick C. Miller

Child, adolescent Ages 4-13

Purpose: Measures a child's classroom behaviors. Used to provide mental health workers with information about school behavior that might indicate psychopathological disorders.

Description: Multiple-item paper-pencil inventory consisting of true-false questions and 11 global judgments describing the child's classroom behavior. The teacher completes the questionnaire, which provides an objective and standardized evaluation of classroom behavior in the following areas: need achievement, aggression, anxiety, cognitive or academic deficit, hostile isolation, and extraversion. The inventory is available in two forms: Form A1 for children ages 4-6 and Form A2 for children ages 7-13. Form A1 measures three additional areas: normal irritability, school disturbance, and total disability. Form A2 measures one additional area: total disability. Norms are provided by sex and age for Form A and by sex for Form A2. Examiner required. Not suitable for group use.

Untimed: 8-10 minutes

Scoring: Hand key

Cost: Complete kit for both age groups $67.50; Kit A1 (10 reusable checklists, 100 answer sheets, 1 set scoring templates, manual) $35.00; Kit A2 (same materials as Kit A1) $35.00

Publisher: Western Psychological Services

SCHOOL ENVIRONMENT PREFERENCE SURVEY
Leonard V. Gordon

Child, adolescent Grades 1-12

Purpose: Measures work role socialization as it occurs in the traditional school setting. Used for academic and disciplinary student counseling, vocational counseling, and instructional planning.

Description: 24-item paper-pencil test measuring a student's levels of commitment to the set of attitudes, values, and behaviors necessary for employment and that are fostered and rewarded in most school settings. The scales measured are structured role orientation, self-subordination, traditionalism, rule conformity, and uncriticalness. High and low scores have differential behavioral implications. Norms are provided for high-school level. Examiner required. Suitable for group use.

Untimed: 10-15 minutes

Scoring: Hand key; may be computer scored

Cost: Specimen set $5.00; 25 forms $6.50; keys $10.00; manual $2.50

Publisher: Educational and Industrial Testing Service

THE SCHOOL PLAY
E.M. Bower

Child   Grades 3-7

Purpose: Evaluates the peer perceptions and self-images of children. Identifies children with low self-images and children whose self-image does not correspond to the perceptions of their peers. Used by classroom teachers to identify children needing further assistance or evaluation.

Description: 38-item paper-pencil peer-rating instrument in two sections. Section I (14 items) contains descriptions of 14 hypothetical roles in a play and instructions directing each student to choose the classmate who would be most suitable and natural in each of the roles. In Section II (24 items), students answer multiple-choice questions eliciting how the students see themselves in relation to each role. This test is the 1980 revision of A Class Play and is contained in *Early Identification of Emotionally Handicapped Children in School*, 3rd Edition. Examiner required. Suitable for group use.

Untimed: Varies

Scoring: Examiner evaluated

Cost: *Early Identification of Emotionally Handicapped Children in School*, 3rd Edition, 1982 $26.75

Publisher: Charles C. Thomas, Publisher

THE SELF-PERCEPTION INVENTORY (SPI)
Anthony T. Soares and Louise M. Soares

Grades 1-adult

Purpose: Assesses how an individual sees himself, how he thinks others see him, and how others do see him. Used to determine the need for counseling and as a counseling tool.

Description: Multiple-item paper-pencil test in four categories: students (10 forms), adults (11 forms), nurses (6 forms), and teachers (9 forms). The student forms are self-concept—how the individual sees self; reflected self-classmates—how the individual thinks classmates see him;

reflected self-teachers—how the individual thinks teachers see him; reflected self-parents—how the individual thinks parents see him; ideal concept—the kind of person the individual would like to be; perceptions of others—other males rate the individual; others rate female individuals; student-self—how the individual sees self as a student; perceptions of others-student-self—how others see the individual as a student (male and female). The adult, nursing, and teacher forms are similar. Students are measured against 20 pairs of bipolar traits; adults, nurses, and teachers are measured against 36 pairs of traits. The subject rates the subject on each pair of traits by marking appropriately within a four-space scale. Examiner required. Suitable for group use. Available in French, Italian, and Spanish.

Untimed: 5-10 minutes per scale

Scoring: Hand key

Cost: Specimen set (indicate level) $6.00

Publisher: SOARES Associates

SELF PROFILE Q-SORT (SPQS)
Alan J. Politte

**Child, adolescent
Grades 2 and above**

Purpose: Assesses student's feelings toward self. Used for elementary-school counseling.

Description: 63-item test of self-perception in which the child indicates whether or not each item describes his feelings. The test is administered orally to younger children; older children may read the items themselves. Examiner required. Suitable for group use.

Untimed: 10 minutes

Scoring: Examiner evaluated

Cost: Specimen set $4.00; 25 forms $6.00

Publisher: Psychologists and Educators, Inc.

SLOSSON POST-OBSERVATIONAL TESTING SCREEN (SPOTS)
*Steven W. Slosson and
Theodore A. Callisto*

All ages

Purpose: Assesses an individual's physical appearance, behavior, and feelings during the administration of the Slosson Intelligence Test (SIT) and other individually administered intelligence tests.

Description: Two observational inventories and one structured interview guide assessing an individual's physical and behavioral problems and attitudes and feelings while being tested. The examiner uses the Visual Scanning For Physical Observations inventory to record information regarding physical properties, such as organic deficits, movements and gestures, and appearance and dress, that may handicap the individual's effective functioning. The Behavior Profile assesses the individual's observed behaviors during a one-to-one testing situation. Seven factors affecting performance levels are measured: outward behavior, relationship with examiner, recall, affective tone, attitude, work habits, and expression. The Post Test Questionnaire provides the examiner with a format for an oral question and answer session regarding the individual's anxiety, health levels, ability to concentrate, and time constraints. The examiner records the individual's direct responses in the space provided on the questionnaire. All three forms are used in conjunction with the Slosson Intelligence Test and other individually administered intelligence tests. Examiner required. Not suitable for group use.

Untimed: Varies

Scoring: Examiner evaluated

Cost: Test kit (forms for SIT and other tests, 50 Visual Scanning for Physical Observations forms, 50 Behavior Profiles, 50 Post-Test Questionnaires) $28.00

Publisher: Slosson Educational Publications, Inc.

SLOSSON PRE-OBSERVATIONAL RECORD SCREEN (SPORS)
Steven W. Slosson

All ages

Purpose: Assesses health factors and cognitive, affective, and behavioral problem areas that may adversely affect performance on standard intelligence tests.

Description: Three multiple-item paper-pencil checklists assessing psychological, medical, and behavioral problems prior to intelligence testing. The Psychological and Medical Profile assesses eight areas of an individual's past medical history: adaptive behavior deficits, developmental ability/disability, medication regimentation, mobility, seizure disorder, expressive language, and receptive language. The Chronic Health Checklist assesses the interplay between physical problems (overall "wellness") and their effect on learning. The Profile of Behavioral Correlations (to optimal independent functioning) measures development in the following behavioral areas: cognitive, receptive language, expressive language, conversational tone, affective, behavioral, attentive listening, and social. The behavior profile assesses the impact of physical health problems, birth defects, organic and functional disorders, neurochemical and hormonal imbalances, lack of environmental support, peer and adult pressures, and overly critical judgments on testing performance. The checklists are completed by the examiner using past medical records, school files, or the parents' or guardians' knowledge. The information should be gathered prior to the testing session so that the examiner can better understand the individual's past performance levels. Examiner required. Not suitable for group use.

Untimed: Varies

Scoring: Examiner evaluated

Cost: Test kit (individual record forms for SIT and other tests, 50 Psychological and Medical Profile forms, 50 Chronic Health Checklist forms, and 50 Profiles of Behavioral Correlation forms) $24.00

Publisher: Slosson Educational Publications, Inc.

SOCIAL TRANSLATIONS (SIST)
*Maureen O'Sullivan and
J.P. Guilford*

**Adolescent, adult
Grades 10 and above**

Purpose: Measures individual ability to understand behavioral change and psychological relationships. Used for counseling and research.

Description: Paper-pencil multiple-choice completely verbal measure of the

"cognition of behavioral transformations" and to a lesser degree the factor of "cognition of behavioral relations," the ability to appreciate what kind of psychological relation occurs between two people who are communicating with each other. Norms are provided for tenth-grade and college students. The test is restricted to A.P.A. members. Examiner required. Suitable for group use.

Timed: 8 minutes

Scoring: Hand key

Cost: 25 tests $10.00; manual $3.50; 25 answer sheets $3.50; scoring key $2.00

Publisher: Sheridan Psychological Services, Inc.

SOCIAL-EMOTIONAL DIMENSION SCALE (SEDS)
*Jerry B. Hutton and
Timothy G. Roberts*

**Child, adolescent
Ages 5.5-18.5**

Purpose: Identifies students who may have behavior problems. Used by teachers, counselors, and psychologists.

Description: 32-item test assessing inappropriate behaviors of students, including physical/fear reaction, depressive reaction, avoidance of peer interaction, avoidance of teacher interaction, and aggressive interaction. The test provides percentiles and standard scores. Examiner required. Not suitable for group use.

Timed: Not available

Scoring: Examiner evaluated

Cost: Complete kit (examiner's manual, 50 profile/record sheets, storage box) $34.00

Publisher: Pro-Ed

STOGDILL BEHAVIOR CARDS

Child

Purpose: Assesses the attitudes of a delinquent child toward his past behavior and experiences. Used for initial screening of juvenile delinquents.

Description: Multiple-item interview guide covering a wide range of delinquent behaviors and background information.

Low-pressure questions deal with specific acts and observable behavior, not subjective feelings. The format provides a child with an opportunity to talk objectively about his problems and helps the examiner understand the child's attitudes toward his delinquencies. Examiner required. Not suitable for group use.

Untimed: 15-20 minutes

Scoring: Examiner evaluated

Cost: Test kit (150 cards, 100 record blanks, manual) $18.00

Publisher: Stoelting Company

STRESS RESPONSE SCALE
Louis A. Chandler

Child, adolescent
Ages 5-14

Purpose: Assesses the emotional status of children ages 5-14 with nonorganic and mild to moderate emotional problems. Used in schools and clinics for screening and diagnosis.

Description: 40-item paper-pencil inventory indicating the maladaptive coping efforts of children. Adults rate children on a 6-point scale. The test is based on a model which predicts five behavior styles: acting out, overactive, passive-aggressive, repressed, and dependent. Test results may be profiled to suggest the child's preferred response pattern. The test should not be used with the mentally retarded, psychoneurologically learning disabled, or severely emotionally handicapped. Examiner required. Not suitable for group use.

Untimed: Varies

Scoring: Hand key; may be computer scored

Cost: Sample kit (manual, set of forms) $15.00

Publisher: Louis A. Chandler, Ph.D.

STUDENT DEVELOPMENTAL TASK INVENTORY: REVISED SECOND EDITION (SDTI-2)
Refer to page 707.

TASKS OF EMOTIONAL DEVELOPMENT TEST (TED)
Haskel Cohen and Geraldine Weil

Child, adolescent
Ages 6-18

Purpose: Detects potential child behavior problems. Used to determine reasons for student learning difficulties.

Description: Multiple-item oral-response projective test consisting of 49 photographs of children, each designed to represent a selected task of emotional development. The test measures 13 factors: socialization, aggression, trust, academic learning, conscience of property of others, identification with same-sex parent, separation from mother figure, acceptance of limits from adults, acceptance of siblings, acceptance of affection between parents, attitudes toward orderliness/cleanliness, positive self-concept, and positive heterosexual socialization. Responses are rated in five dimensions: perception, outcome, affect, motivation, and spontaneity. Four sets of photographs are provided: 12 photographs each for boys and girls ages 6-11 and 13 photographs each for boys and girls ages 12-18. Each set provides essentially the same stimuli with variations for age and sex. The test kit includes 49 photo cards and a manual containing instructions and rating scales for each photo. The book *Tasks of Emotional Development,* which discusses construction of the test and rating scales and includes sample stories scored according to the rating scales is available also. Examiner required. Not suitable for group use.

Untimed: Not available

Scoring: Examiner evaluated

Cost: Complete set $35.00; textbook $18.00

Publisher: T.E.D. Associates

TEST ANXIETY INVENTORY (RESEARCH EDITION) (TAI)
Charles D. Spielberger

Adolescent, adult
Grades 10 and above

Purpose: Measures individual differences in test-taking anxiety. Used for research.

Description: 20-item paper-pencil test of two major components of test anxiety: worry and emotionality. Respondents report how frequently they experience specific anxiety symptoms in examination situations. Similar in structure and concept to the T-Anxiety scale of the State-Trait Anxiety Inventory. May be self-administered. Suitable for group use.

Untimed: 5-10 minutes

Scoring: Hand key

Cost: Manual $4.50; key $1.00; 25 expendable tests $3.25

Publisher: Consulting Psychologists Press, Inc.

TEST OF EARLY SOCIOEMOTIONAL DEVELOPMENT (TOESD)
Wayne P. Hresko and Linda Brown

Child   Ages 3-7.11

Purpose: Evaluates the behavior of children. Identifies children with behavior problems and the setting in which the problems most often occur.

Description: Four multiple-item paper-pencil components assessing problem behaviors in children. The 30-item student rating scale is completed by the student; the 34-item parent rating scale is completed by the parent(s); and the 36-item teacher rating scale is completed by the teacher or other professionals who interact with the child in a school setting. A sociogram provides information about peer perceptions of the child being evaluated. Results discriminate among normal, behavior-disordered, learning-disabled, and mentally retarded children. All four components yield percentile ranks and standard scores. This instrument is a downward extension of the Behavior Rating Profile (BRP) and resembles the BRP in both form and content. Examiner required. Suitable for group use.

Untimed: Varies

Scoring: Examiner evaluated

Cost: Complete kit (manual, 50 student rating forms, 50 parent rating forms, 50 teacher rating forms, storage box) $49.00

Publisher: Pro-Ed

THERAPY ATTITUDE INVENTORY (TAI)
Refer to page 85.

WALKER PROBLEM BEHAVIOR IDENTIFICATION CHECKLIST, REVISED 1983
Hill M. Walker

Child   Grades PreK-6

Purpose: Identifies children with behavior problems. Used to evaluate children for counseling and possible referral.

Description: 50-item paper-pencil true-false inventory consisting of behavior statements that are applied to the child being rated. The checklist can be completed by anyone familiar with the child, although it is used primarily by teachers. The test provides a Total Score, a cut-off score for classifying children as disturbed, and scores for the following five scales: Acting-Out, Withdrawal, Distractibility, Disturbed Peer Relations, and Immaturity. Examiner required. Suitable for group use.

Untimed: 5 minutes

Scoring: Hand key

Cost: Complete kit (pad of 200 checklists—100 each male and female, manual) $35.00

Publisher: Western Psychological Services

Student Evaluation and Counseling: Student Attitudes

ARLIN-HILLS ATTITUDE SURVEYS
Marshall Arlin and David Hills

Child, adolescent Grades K-12

Purpose: Assesses student attitudes. Used for research on student attitudes.

Description: Four 15-item paper-pencil questionnaires measuring student attitudes in the following areas: attitude toward teachers, attitude toward learning, attitude toward language, and attitude toward arithmetic. Items are presented in a cartoon format. Because group results are used, the four instruments may be distributed at random to students within a classroom. Each instrument is divided into three levels: Primary for Grades K-3, Elementary for Grades 4-6, and High School for Grades 7-12. Computer scoring is recommended for groups. Examiner required. Suitable for group use.

Untimed: 5-10 minutes

Scoring: Hand key; may be computer scored

Cost: Contact publisher

Publisher: Psychologists and Educators, Inc.

ATTITUDE TOWARD SCHOOL QUESTIONNAIRE (ASQ)
G.P. Strickland, R. Hoepfner, and S.P. Klein

Child   Grades K-3

Purpose: Assesses children's attitudes toward school. Used to evaluate affective programs and for research on young children's attitudes toward school.

Description: 15-item paper-pencil test measuring attitudes toward school, school work, show-and-tell activities, reading, math, authority, peers, and playing. Children view cartoons depicting school situations while English narrations are read. The children then are asked how they feel about each situation and respond by circling a happy, neutral, or unhappy face. Reading and number skills are not required because each item is on a separate page that is colored rather than numbered. The child needs to know only the five basic colors in order to follow along, and teachers can insure that all students are working on the same item. The people in the cartoons are racially ambiguous so children of various racial groups can equally identify with the figures. The girls' form and the boys' form feature same-sex main characters. Examiner required. Suitable for group use.

Timed: 20 minutes

Scoring: Hand key

Cost: Specimen set $10.00; 20 questionnaires (10 female, 10 male) $28.00; manual $5.00

Publisher: Monitor

CANADIAN COMPREHENSIVE ASSESSMENT PROGRAM: SCHOOL ATTITUDE MEASURE (SAM)

Child, adolescent
Grades 4-9

Purpose: Evaluates students' affective responses to their school experience. Used for program development, individual education planning, selection and placement of students for particular programs, guidance planning, and developing instructional standards and objectives.

Description: Multidimensional self-report survey instrument developed to evaluate students' affective responses to their school experience and to establish students' self-perception as competent learners. The instrument's three levels provide information on five attitude levels: motivation for schooling, academic self-concept, reference-based, student's sense of control over performance, and student's instructional mastery. Examiner required. Suitable for group use.
CANADIAN PUBLISHER

Timed: Varies

Scoring: Machine scored

Cost: Review kit $12.25

Publisher: Guidance Centre

CANFIELD LEARNING STYLES INVENTORY (CLS)
Albert A. Canfield

Adolescent, adult

Purpose: Identifies an individual's preferred learning methods. Identifies individuals with little or no interest in independent or unstructured learning situations. Used in conjunction with the Canfield Instructional Style Inventory to maximize teaching and learning efficiency.

Description: 30-item paper-pencil forced-rank inventory measuring individual learning needs (interacting with others, goal setting, competition, friendly relations with instructor, independence in study, classroom authority); preferred mediums (listening, reading, viewing pictures, graphs, slides, or direct experience); and areas of interest (numeric concepts, qualitative concepts, working with inanimate things and people). The inventory also indicates student perceptions as to how they will perform in the learning situation and identifies learning problems associated with either traditional or innovative teaching methods. The test is available in two forms: Form S-A for use with most adults and Form E for use with persons whose reading level is as low as the fifth grade. The test booklets are reusable. Separate norms are available for males and females. Self-administered. Suitable for group use.

Untimed: 30 minutes

Scoring: Self-scored

Cost: Starter set (25 test booklets, 50 answer sheets, profiles, manual) $62.95; specimen set (includes manual) $19.95; manual $12.00

Publisher: Humanics Media

CHAPIN SOCIAL INSIGHT TEST
F. Stuart Chapin

High school students, adult

Purpose: Measures the social insight of high school and college students and adults.

Description: 25-item paper-pencil test assessing an individual's ability to diagnose a situation involving human interaction. Individuals with this ability recognize the dynamics underlying a described behavior or choose the wisest course of action to resolve a difficulty. The test was devised in 1942, first published in 1968, and currently is distributed with a reprint summarizing recent validation studies. Available until present supply is exhausted. Examiner required. Suitable for group use.

Untimed: Not available

Scoring: Hand key

Cost: 25 test booklets $7.50; 50 response booklets $10.00; manual $3.50

Publisher: Consulting Psychologists Press, Inc.

THE CLASSROOM ENVIRONMENT INDEX (CEI)
George Stern and Associates

Grades 5 and above

Purpose: Measures the psychological environment of a classroom (Grades 5-12 and certain college classes) in terms of the need-press paradigm of human behavior as conceptualized by Henry Murray. Used for research and teacher development purposes.

Description: 300-item paper-pencil true-false inventory assessing the environment of a classroom in terms of 30 press scales reflecting the 30 basic need scales established on the Stern Activities Index (AI). The test items refer to classroom environment, teacher personality, teaching style, creativity, and other facets of the teaching-learning process. Scores are provided for six first-order dimensions (humanistic intellectual climate, group intellectual life, achievement standards, personal dignity, orderliness, and science) and two second-order dimensions (development press and control press). The questionnaire is designed so that it can be divided into two parts, requiring each student to answer only half of the 300 questions. Item content has been kept as similar as possible to that of the other Syracuse Indexes (especially the High School Characteristics Index). A number of revisions make the instrument applicable to the individual classroom rather than to the institution as a whole. Analysis differentiates between classrooms, subjects, grades, and educational levels. Self-administered. Suitable for group use.

Untimed: 40 minutes

Scoring: Examiner evaluated; may be computer scored

Cost: Test booklet $0.50; answer sheet $0.10; profile form $0.10; technical manual $7.50; prices for computer scoring and analysis available on request

Publisher: Evaluation Research Associates

CLASSROOM SOCIOMETRIC ANALYSIS KIT
E. Myers

**Child, adolescent
Grades 3-12**

Purpose: Measures students' attitudes of social acceptance or rejection based on the expressed preferences of their classmates. Used by classroom teachers.

Description: Multiple-item paper-pencil test assessing the sociometric aspect of classroom dynamics. The test is available in two forms, A and B. Form A contains one work and one play question already printed on the pupil questionnaires. In Form B, the sociometric questions are blank to allow the teacher to develop his own questions and print them on the questionnaire. A manual is available. Examiner required. Suitable for group use.

Untimed: Not available

Scoring: Examiner evaluated

Cost: Contact publisher

Publisher: Educational Research Council of America

Information and availability unconfirmed; no publisher response.

THE COLLEGE CHARACTERISTICS INDEX (CCI)
George Stern and Associates

College student

Purpose: Measures the perceived press found in college environments in terms of the need-press paradigm of human behavior as conceptualized by Henry Murray. Used for student survey and research purposes.

Description: 300-item (long form) or 92-item (short form) paper-pencil true-false inventory assessing the atmosphere of a college in terms of 30 press scales reflecting the 30 basic need scales established on the Stern Activities Index (AI). The test items refer to curriculum, teaching and classroom activities, rules, regulations, policies, student organizations, activities, interests, features of the campus, services and facilities, and relationships among students and faculty. The long form provides scores on the 30 basic press scales (10 items per scale), 11 first-order dimensions (aspiration level, intellectual climate, student dignity, academic climate, academic achievement, self-expression, group life, academic organization, social form, play-work, and vocational climate) and three second-order dimensions (intellectual climate, non-intellectual climate, and impulse control). The short form provides scores on 11 first-order dimensions and three second-order dimensions. Self-administered. Suitable for group use.

Untimed: Long form 40 minutes; short form 20 minutes

Scoring: Examiner evaluated; may be computer scored

Cost: Test booklet $0.50; answer sheet $0.10; profile form $0.10; technical manual $7.50; prices for computer scoring and analysis available on request

Publisher: Evaluation Research Associates

COMPREHENSIVE ASSESSMENT PROGRAM: SCHOOL ATTITUDE MEASURE
Lawrence J. Dolan and Marci Morrow Enos

**Child, adolescent
Grades 4-12**

Purpose: Evaluates students' views of their academic environment and of themselves as competent students.

Description: Multiple-item measure of five affective dimensions of the student: motivation for schooling; academic self-concept, performance-based; academic self-concept, reference-based; sense of control over performance; and sense of instructional mastery. The test is available on three levels: Grades 4-6, Grades 7-8, and Grades 9-12. Items may be read to young students provided no interpretive comment is made. National and local percentile ranks are provided. Examiner required. Suitable for group use. Available in Spanish.

Untimed: Not available

Scoring: Computer scored

Cost: 3 pupil booklets (specify level) $24.60; 35 answer sheets $$9.10; manual $7.20; 35 profiles $6.75

Publisher: American Testronics

CONSERVATISM-RADICALISM OPINIONAIRE (C-R)
Theodore F. Lentz and colleagues

Adolescent, adult
Grades 13 and above

Purpose: Measures character and disposition along conservatism-radicalism dimension. Used in college and adult courses in political psychology and political science.

Description: 60-item paper-pencil test measuring the conservative-radical attitudes of the subject, who is asked to agree or disagree with each statement by marking it plus or minus. Self-administered. Suitable for group use.

Untimed: 30 minutes

Scoring: Hand key

Cost: Manual, sample of opinionaire $1.00; discount available upon request for quantities

Publisher: Lentz Peace Research Laboratory

COUNSELING SERVICES ASSESSMENT BLANK (CSAB)
James C. Hurst and Richard G. Weigel

College student

Purpose: Assesses client reaction to counseling services. Used in the evaluation of counseling centers.

Description: Paper-pencil test providing client assessment and feedback about counseling services. Materials include a manual providing information about the use and interpretation of results of the CSAB. Examiner/self-administered. Suitable for group use.

Untimed: Not available

Scoring: Not available

Cost: 100 test blanks $14.00; manual $15.00

Publisher: Rocky Mountain Behavioral Science Institute, Inc.

CPRI QUESTIONNAIRES (Q-71, Q-74, Q-75, Q-76)
William Eckhardt

Adolescent, adult
Grades 10 and above

Purpose: Measures personality, ideology, and philosophy. Used by high schools, colleges, churches, and civic clubs.

Description: 240-item paper-pencil test in four sections covering the following categories: conformity, nationalism, responsibility, religiosity, impulsivity, bureaucracy, neuroticism, militarism, misanthropy, morality, discipline, capitalism, humanism, egoism, authoritarianism, fatalism, justice, imperialism, and mysticism. The person rates each item on a 5-point scale ranging from "strongly disagree" to "strongly agree." Self-administered. Suitable for group use. Available in Spanish, German, Hindi, Dutch, Belgian, Urdu, and Bengali.

Untimed: 15-30 minutes

Scoring: Hand key

Cost: Manual (including background and interpretive material), 4 questionnaires, answer sheets, scoring instructions, norms $5.00; questionnaires and answer sheets may be reproduced at no further charge

Publisher: Lentz Peace Research Laboratory

CULTURE-FREE SELF-ESTEEM INVENTORIES
Refer to page 195.

EVALUATED DISPOSITION TOWARD THE ENVIRONMENT (EDEN)
Norman J. Milchus

Adolescent   Grades 7-13

Purpose: Assesses the strength of a student's environmental values. Used for self-insight and program evaluation.

Description: 70-item paired-comparison test measuring the following values: aesthetic, experiential, knowledge-seeking, responsible, prudent (conservation ethic), active, and practical. Students pick one of the pair of activities they prefer. The test uses a 5-point Likert-type scale. Examiner required. Suitable for group use.

Untimed: 30-40 minutes

Scoring: Computer scored

Cost: Specimen set $3.25; 20 inventory booklets $22.00; 20 response sheets $3.25; computer scoring $1.00 (minimum $60.00)

Publisher: Person-O-Metrics, Inc.

THE HIGH SCHOOL CHARACTERISTICS INDEX (HSCI) AND THE ELEMENTARY AND SECONDARY SCHOOL INDEX (ESI)
George Stern and Associates

Child, adolescent

Purpose: Measures the psychological characteristics of the academic environments of elementary and secondary schools in terms of the need-press paradigm of human behavior as conceptualized by Henry Murray. Used for student survey and research purposes.

Description: 300-item (HSCI) and 61-item (ESI) paper-pencil true-false inventories assessing the atmosphere of elementary and secondary schools along 30 basic press scales reflecting the 30 basic need scales established on the Stern Activities Index (AI). Both scales provide seven first-order scores (intellectual climate, expressiveness, group social life, personal dignity/supportiveness, achievement standards, orderliness/control, and peer group dominance) and three second-order dimensions (development press, orderliness/control, and peer group dominance). The 300-item HSCI contains 10 items for each of the press scales, which are identical in name and parallel in meaning to those used for the College Characteristics Index. Factor analysis was used to develop the ESI, which is essentially a short form of the HSCI. In addition to its use for secondary schools, the ESI can be used at the elementary level down to Grade 4. The HSCI should not be used below the secondary-school level. Self-administered. Suitable for group use.

Untimed: HSCI 40 minutes; ESI 15 minutes

Scoring: Examiner evaluated; may be computer scored

Cost: Test booklet $0.50; answer sheet $0.10; profile form $0.10; technical manual $7.50; prices for computer scoring and analysis available on request

Publisher: Evaluation Research Associates

THE INTEREST-A-LYZER
Joseph S. Renzulli

Child, adolescent

Purpose: Examines the present and potential interests of upper-elementary and junior high-school students. Used as a basis for group discussions and in-depth counseling.

Description: Multiple-item paper-pencil instrument consisting of a series of open-ended questions structured to highlight general patterns of interest. Items cover mathematical, historical, political, scientific, artistic, and technical interest areas. Examiner required. Suitable for group use.

Untimed: Varies

Scoring: Examiner evaluated

Cost: 100 questionnaires $24.95

Publisher: Creative Learning Press, Inc.

INTERPERSONAL STYLE INVENTORY—(ISI)
Refer to page 144.

IRENOMETER
Refer to page 222.

KATZ-ZALK OPINION QUESTIONNAIRE
Phyllis Katz and Sue Rosenberg Zalk

Child   Grades 1-6

Purpose: Measures racial attitudes in children. Used in research to assess change in attitudes.

Description: 55-item paper-pencil test measuring the racial attitudes of children.

The test contains 38 race-related questions and 17 buffer items to provide a measure of gender attitudes. The child is shown a slide of two or four children interacting and is asked to mark the box under the child credited with a positive or negative act or attribute. Although the test only assesses attitudes towards blacks and whites, it could be adapted to other groups. Examiner required. Suitable for group use.

Untimed: 30-60 minutes

Scoring: Hand key

Cost: Booklet $1.00; slides $75.00; prices on large orders are less

Publisher: Sue Rosenberg Zalk and Phyllis Katz

LEADERSHIP SKILLS INVENTORY
*Frances A. Karnes and
Jane C. Chauvin*

**Child, adolescent
Grades 4-12**

Purpose: Assesses leadership abilities of students. Used by students, teachers, consultants, curriculum planners, and teacher-trainers.

Description: Multiple-item paper-pencil inventory assessing fundamentals of leadership, written and oral communication, group dynamics, problem-solving, personal development, decision-making, and planning abilities. The results help students understand and develop leadership abilities. The inventory may be used for pre- and postevaluation. An activities manual is included. Self-administered. Suitable for group use.

Untimed: Varies

Scoring: Self-scored

Cost: Complete kit $19.95

Publisher: D.O.K. Publishers, Inc.

LEARNING STYLE IDENTIFICATION SCALE (LSIS)
Refer to page 672.

LEARNING STYLE INVENTORY (LSI)
*Rita Dunn, Kenneth Dunn,
and Gary E. Price*

Child, adolescent   Grades 3-12

Purpose: Identifies students' preferred learning environments. Used for designing instructional environments and counseling.

Description: 104-item paper-pencil Likert-scale test assessing the conditions under which students prefer to learn. Individual preferences are measured in the following areas: immediate environment (sound, heat, light, and design), emotionality (motivation, responsibility, persistence, and structure), sociological needs (self-oriented, peer-oriented, adult-oriented, or combined ways), and physical needs (perceptual preferences, time of day, food intake, and mobility). Test items consist of statements about how people like to learn. Students indicate whether they agree or disagree with each item. Results identify student preferences and indicate the degree to which a student's responses are consistent. Suggested strategies for instructional and environmental alternatives are provided to complement the student's revealed learning style. The test is available on two levels: Grades 3-9 and Grades 6-12. Computerized results are available in three forms: individual profile (raw scores for each of the 22 areas, standard scores, and a plot for each score in each area), group summary (identifies students with significantly high or low scores and groups individuals with similar preferences), and a subscale summary. Self-administered. Suitable for group use.

Untimed: 30 minutes

Scoring: Computer scored

Cost: Specimen set (manual, research report, inventory booklet, answer sheet) $12.00

Publisher: Price Systems, Inc.

LEARNING STYLES INVENTORY (LSI)
*Joseph S. Renzulli and
Linda H. Smith*

Child   Grades 4-12

Purpose: Assesses the methods through which students prefer to learn. Used to

---

assist teachers in individualizing the instructional process.

Description: 65-item paper-pencil inventory assessing student attitudes toward nine modes of instruction: projects, drill and recitation, peer teaching, discussion, teaching games, independent study, programmed instruction, lecture, and stimulation. Various classrom learning experiences associated with these nine teaching/learning style approaches are described, and students use a 5-point scale ranging from "very unpleasant" to "very pleasant" to indicate their reaction to each activity. A teacher form is included with each set of student materials. Teachers respond to items that parallel those on the student form in terms of how frequently each activity occurs in the classroom. The resulting profile of instructional styles can be compared to individual student preferences and serve to facilitate a closer match between how teachers instruct and the styles to which students respond most favorably. Examiner required. Suitable for group use.

Untimed: Varies

Scoring: Computer scored

Cost: Class set (30 student forms, teacher form, computer scoring) $20.50; manual $7.95; specimen set (manual, teacher form, student form) $8.50

Publisher: Creative Learning Press, Inc.

THE MAJOR-MINOR-FINDER
Arthur Cutler, Francis Ferry, Robert Kauk, and Robert Robinett

---

**Adolescent, adult
Grades 10 and above**

Purpose: Assesses an individual's aptitudes and interests and identifies appropriate college major choices. Used in college orientation courses at the upper high-school and college level.

Description: Multiple-item paper-pencil or computer-administered college major exploration instrument matching student aptitudes and interests with 99 college majors. The test includes information concerning jobs related to 99 college majors, skills and interests required of the 99 majors, and college majors most com-

patible with educational goals and career interests. Reusable assessment booklets are used in conjunction with consumable insert answer folders for paper-pencil administration. Microcomputer programs are available for TRS-80 Models I and III, Commodore PET/CBM, Commodore 64, Apple II+ and IIe, IBM Personal Computer, and Franklin Ace 1000. Software packages include instructions, printed inventories, and additional information. An optional introductory filmstrip is available. A supplement, the *College-Major Handbook,* includes further data on each college major, a definition of the major, courses required, aptitudes most needed, job activities associated with the major, chances for employment in jobs associated with the major, related career opportunities, and where to write for further information. The paper-pencil version may be self-administered. Suitable for group use.

Untimed: Varies

Scoring: Self-scored; may be computer scored

Cost: Reusable test booklet, answer folder $1.45; additional answer folders $0.25; manual $2.00; *College-Major Handbook* $4.00; diskettes $59.95; filmstrip $32.95

Publisher: CFKR Career Materials, Inc.

MASTER ATTITUDE SCALES
H.H. Remmers

**Child, adolescent
and above**

Purpose: Measures attitudes toward a wide range of areas. Used for research.

Description: Nine paper-pencil tests providing formats for assessing attitudes toward the following areas: practice, school subjects, vocations, institutions, defined groups of people, proposed social actions, homemaking activities, individual and group morale, and the high school. Each scale provides a general format for attitudes in that area and leaves the final topic up to the individual examiner. For example, The Scale to Measure Attitudes Toward Any School Subject provides a form that will generally evaluate any academic course, with space

---

provided for the examiner to designate which particular course is to be evaluated. Examiner required. Suitable for group use.

Untimed: 5-10 minutes

Scoring: Examiner evaluated

Cost: Contact publisher

Publisher: Purdue Research Foundation/ University Book Store

MINNESOTA SCHOOL ATTITUDE SURVEY (MSAS)
Andrew Ahlgren

Child, adolescent
Grades 1-12

Purpose: Measures students' feelings and attitudes toward a range of school experiences. Identifies problems and suggests changes.

Description: Multiple-item paper-pencil survey in two forms: a lower form for Grades 1-3 and an upper form for Grades 4-12. Each form has two parts. Part 1 assesses affective reactions to academic subjects, school personnel, self-expression, peers, and various learning modes and situations. Part 2 assesses feelings of support, pressure, motivation, acceptance/exclusion, cooperation/competition, and self-worth. The survey provides information on the impact of instructional programs and school climate on attitudes and feelings, helps with understanding of learning patterns and behavior, and indicates problem areas. No printed score reports are available. A microcomputer display package is available for Apple II, II +, and IIe with 48K memory, DOS 3.3, and a single disk drive. Color monitor and an Apple Silentype or graphics printer with a Grappler Plus interface also is required. Examiner required. Suitable for group use.

Untimed: 30-40 minutes

Scoring: Computer scoring by publisher only

Cost: Complete kit (scoring, general manual, instructions for administrators per 25 answer sheets) $1.50 per student; $170.00 per diskette for microcomputer display of results

Publisher: Science Research Associates, Inc.

MOTIVATION ANALYSIS TEST (MAT)
Refer to page 925.

MY BOOK OF THINGS AND STUFF: AN INTEREST QUESTIONNAIRE FOR YOUNG CHILDREN
Ann McGeevy

Child   Ages 6-11

Purpose: Assesses the interests of young children.

Description: Multiple-item paper-pencil questionnaire including over 40 illustrated items focusing on the special interests and learning styles of students. The book also includes a teacher's section, an interest profile sheet, sample pages from a journal, and bibliographies of interest-centered books and magazines for children. All questionnaire pages are perforated and prepared on blackline masters so that copies can be made for an entire class. Examiner required. Suitable for group use.

Untimed: Varies

Scoring: Examiner evaluated

Cost: Questionnaire booklet $12.95

Publisher: Creative Learning Press, Inc.

NEW YOUTH RESEARCH SURVEY (NYRS)
Refer to page 306.

PURDUE STUDENT-TEACHER OPINIONAIRE—FORM B (PSTO)
Refer to page 777.

QUALITY OF SCHOOL LIFE SCALE (QSL)
Joyce L. Epstein with
James M. McPartland

Child, adolescent
Grades 4-12

Purpose: Assesses student's feelings about the school environment. Used to study and evaluate the social, task, and authority structures of schools and classrooms.

Description: Multiple-item paper-pencil test measuring student's school satisfaction, commitment to classwork, and reactions to teachers. Subscores are provided for each area. The technical manual summarizes research on the scale, provides reliability and validity data, and item-to-scale and item-to-test correlations. The scale is intended for use with local norms or in a criterion-referenced framework. Examiner required. Suitable for group use.

Untimed: 20 minutes

Scoring: Hand key

Cost: Test kit (35 questionnaire folders, manual, scoring key) $11.13

Publisher: The Riverside Publishing Company

QUEST: A LIFE CHOICE INVENTORY
Norman J. Milchus, D. Rodwell, and O. Mumey

Child, adolescent   Grades 9-12

Purpose: Measures the impact of value clarification in career education, substance abuse prevention, and positive group mental health programs on high-school students. Used to provide an overall assessment of school climate.

Description: 40-item paper-pencil Likert-type scale test measuring needs recognition, value clarification, adaptive autonomy, perception of reality, and self-worth. Self-administered. Suitable for group use.

Untimed: 30 minutes

Scoring: Computer scored

Cost: Specimen set $3.00; computer scoring $1.25 each (minimum $75.00)

Publisher: Person-O-Metrics, Inc.

A SCALE TO MEASURE ATTITUDES TOWARD DISABLED PERSONS
H.E. Yuker and J.R. Block

Students, adults

Purpose: Assesses attitudes toward disabled persons. Used to evaluate

mainstreaming in the schools, hiring of disabled persons, and methods of changing attitudes toward the disabled. Used with teachers, employers, counselors, physicians, and students who interact with disabled individuals.

Description: Multiple-item paper-pencil inventory assessing the attitudes of either disabled or nondisabled persons toward disabled persons. The inventory is available in three forms. Self-administered. Suitable for group use. Available in Chinese, Japanese, Hebrew, and Spanish.

Untimed: 10 minutes

Scoring: Examiner evaluated

Cost: Free

Publisher: H.E. Yuker

SCHOOL INTEREST INVENTORY
William C. Cottle

Adolescent   Grades 7-12

Purpose: Assesses an adolescent's school-related attitudes and interests. Identifies potential school dropouts. Used for counseling and program planning.

Description: 150-item paper-pencil inventory surveying student attitudes and interests in order to identify students with a high potential for dropping out of school. Weighted and unweighted scores may be obtained for males and females by using the appropriate scoring mask. The manual contains information about the development of the test, validity studies used to develop the scale, scoring, interpretation, and use. Examiner required. Suitable for group use.

Untimed: 20 minutes

Scoring: Hand key

Cost: 100 test booklets $43.68; manual $3.03; 2 scoring masks $4.41

Publisher: The Riverside Publishing Company

SELF-ESTEEM QUESTIONNAIRE (SEQ-3)
Refer to page 210.

STUDENT ATTITUDE INVENTORY
D.S. Anderson and J.S. Western

Adolescent

Purpose: Measures tertiary students' attitudes toward school and assesses the impact of academic environment on these attitudes. Used for student guidance and counseling.

Description: 57-item paper-pencil test in which students indicate their agreement or disagreement, on a 5-point scale, with statements concerning the following dimensions: academic activities, intellectual interests, political-economic liberalism, social liberalism, pragmatism, dogmatism, and cynicism. Australian norms are provided. Materials include the inventory, set of three scoring keys, monograph "Inventory to Measure Students' Attitudes," and specimen set. Self-administered. Suitable for group use. AUSTRALIAN PUBLISHER

Untimed: 15 minutes

Scoring: Hand key; examiner evaluated

Cost: Contact publisher

Publisher: The Australian Council for Educational Research Limited

STUDENT DEVELOPMENTAL TASK INVENTORY: REVISED SECOND EDITION (SDTI-2)
Refer to page 707.

STUDENT EVALUATION SCALE (SES)
William T. Martin and Sue Martin

Ages 6-21

Purpose: Assesses attitudes and behaviors of elementary- and secondary-school children. Used to evaluate educational and social-emotional responses to school.

Description: 52-item paper-pencil test of two areas of student attitudes: educational response and social-emotional response. Items are rated by teachers or guidance personnel after observing students for a two- to three-week period. The rating scale ranges from 0-never to 3-always. Self-administered. Suitable for group use.

Untimed: 5 minutes

Scoring: Examiner evaluated

Cost: Specimen set (includes manual) $4.50; 25 rating and profile forms $6.00

Publisher: Psychologists and Educators, Inc.

STUDENT OPINION INVENTORY
National Study of School Evaluation Staff

Child, adolescent

Purpose: Assesses students' opinions of their school and its programs. Provides students with an opportunity to make direct recommendations. Used by school personnel as part of a complete school evaluation program.

Description: 46-item paper-pencil opinion survey consisting of two parts. Part A contains 34 multiple-choice items assessing students' attitudes toward various aspects of the school. Part B contains 12 open-ended questions constructed for students to make direct recommendations for school improvement. The manual describes the development of the instrument, provides instructions for administering the inventory, and includes single copies of both Parts A and B. The inventory may be administered independently as a measure of student attitudes and morale or in conjunction with the Teacher Opinion Inventory, the Parent Opinion Inventory, or as a part of a complete school evaluation program. Self-administered. Suitable for group use.

Untimed: Varies

Scoring: Examiner evaluated

Cost: 50 copies Part A $5.00; 50 copies of Part B $3.00; manual $2.00

Publisher: National Study of School Evaluation

STUDENT ORIENTATIONS SURVEY (S.O.S.)
Barry R. Morstain

Adolescent, adult

Purpose: Assesses students' attitudes toward educational policies. Used for research on orientations toward philosophies, purposes, and processes related to a college education.

Description: 80-item paper-pencil measure of 10 aspects of student orientations toward college: achievement, assignment learning, assessment, affiliation, affirmation, inquiry, independent study, interaction, informal association, and involvement. Items are statements that are rated on a modified Likert scale. Self-administered. Suitable for group use. Available in Spanish.

Untimed: 20 minutes

Scoring: Computer scored

Cost: S.O.S. OpScan form scoring (researcher receives an overall group printout and a scored data deck) $0.50

Publisher: Barry R. Morstain, Ph.D.

Information and availability unconfirmed; no publisher response.

STUDENT PROFILE AND ASSESSMENT RECORD (SPAR)
Theodore K. Miller and Roger B. Winston, Jr.

College student   Ages 17-23

Purpose: Assesses perceptions of entering college students. Used by academic advisors, counselors, residence hall staff, and others.

Description: Multiple-item paper-pencil comprehensive self-assessment tool providing information in six categories: general (home address, marital status, disabilities, need for financial assistance, emergency contact person); academic (perceptions of subjects, decision about major, noncredit academic interests and long-range plans, instructional approach preference, academic strengths and weaknesses); career; health and wellness; activities and organizations; and special concerns and other considerations. The SPAR folder has space for recording the student's test profile, high school academic record, and other pertinent information, including educational goals and objectives. The instrument is useful in the initial phases of orientation. It is recommended for use in conjunction with

the Student Developmental Task Inventory. Self-administered. Not suitable for group use.

Untimed: Varies

Scoring: Self-scored

Cost: 50 folders $20.00

Publisher: Student Development Associates, Inc.

STUDENT REACTION TO COLLEGE: TWO YEAR COLLEGE EDITION (SRC/2)
Research staff of Educational Testing Service

Adolescent, adult
College students

Purpose: Assesses the needs and concerns of students enrolled in two-year colleges. Used in institutional self-assessment for developing programs and services for students.

Description: 150-item paper-pencil test assessing four dimensions of student concerns: processes of instruction, program planning, administrative affairs, and out-of-class activities. These four dimensions are divided further into such areas as content of courses, appropriateness of course work to occupational goals, satisfaction with teaching procedures, student-faculty relations, educational and occupational decisions, effectiveness of advisers and counselors, registration, regulations, availability of classes, housing, employment, financial aid, and satisfaction with campus environment. The test is distributed to a random sample of students. Self-administered. Suitable for group use.

Untimed: 50 minutes

Scoring: Computer scored

Cost: Booklet $0.65; processing $1.75

Publisher: Educational Testing Service

SUBSUMED ABILITIES TEST—A MEASURE OF LEARNING EFFICIENCY (SAT)
Martin M. Bruce

Adolescent, adult
Grades 6 and above

Purpose: Measures, nonverbally, the subject's ability and willingness to learn; used for student placement, vocational counseling, and job selection.

Description: 60-item paper-pencil test consisting of 30 pairs of items, each of which is composed of four similar line drawings. The student matches one pair with another, allowing the examiner to construct a Potential Abilities Score and a Demonstrated Abilities Score based on the student's ability to conceptualize, form abstractions, and recognize the abstractions in new situations. Designed for individuals with at least a sixth grade education. Examiner required. May be self-administered. Suitable for group use.

Timed: 30 minutes

Scoring: Hand key

Cost: Package of tests $28.50; manual $6.15; package of scoring key-tabulation sheets $10.50

Publisher: Martin M. Bruce, Ph.D., Publishers

SURVEY OF SCHOOL ATTITUDES (SSA)
Thomas P. Hogan

Child, adolescent
Grades 1-8

Purpose: Assesses children's reaction to major areas of school curriculum. Used for determining instructional presentation in curriculum programs.

Description: Multiple-item paper-pencil test of reactions to four areas of school curriculum: reading and language arts, mathematics, science, and social studies. Each area is represented by 15 activities characteristic of the curriculum. Students indicate whether they like, dislike, or feel neutral toward each activity. The test is divided into two levels: Primary (Grades 1-3) and Intermediate (Grades 4-8). The primary-level items are dictated by the teacher. The intermediate-level items are sentence stems read by the student. Two alternate and equivalent forms, A and B, are available. Examiner required. Suitable for group use.

Untimed: Primary 40 minutes in two sittings; Intermediate 30 minutes

Scoring: Hand key; scoring service available

Cost: Specimen set (test booklets, manual for each level) $7.50; 25 tests $24.00; keys $5.00; 35 hand-scorable answer documents for Intermediate level $7.00; 35 MRC machine-scorable tests for Primary level $33.00; 100 MRC machine-scorable tests for Intermediate level $17.50

Publisher: The Psychological Corporation

TLC-LEARNING PREFERENCE INVENTORY KIT

Students

Purpose: Assesses the manner in which students prefer to learn. Used for classroom planning and management.

Description: 144-item paper-pencil inventory assessing individual student preferences for perception and judgment and providing insights into students' attitudes toward things and ideas in their world. The test items and assessment procedures are based on Jung's Theory of Psychological Type. One adult Learning Style Inventory is included to allow teachers to compare their own preferred learning style with their preferred teaching style. The manual includes guidelines for collecting student data and scoring, analyzing, and plotting student learning styles; guidelines for classroom planning and management based on test results; and sample lesson plans outlining how to use each of the four learning styles for maximum learning. Examiner required. Suitable for group use.

Untimed: Varies

Scoring: Examiner evaluated

Cost: Test kit (manual, 30 student inventories and scoring sheets, 30 student diagnostic folders, student learning behavior checklist, adult learning style inventory, teaching style inventory) $59.00

Publisher: Mafex Associates, Inc.

Information and availability unconfirmed; no publisher response.

TLC-LEARNING STYLE INVENTORY

Adult

Purpose: Assesses the manner in which an individual prefers to learn. Used for adult self-assessments.

Description: Multiple-item paper-pencil test measuring individual preferences for how information is collected and judgments are made about its significance. The test items and scoring procedures are based on Jung's Theory of Personality Type. The words/terms that individuals select to describe their learning styles correspond to the four distinct styles of learning. Self-administered. Suitable for group use.

Untimed: Varies

Scoring: Self-scored

Cost: Six inventories $21.00

Publisher: Mafex Associates, Inc.

Information and availability unconfirmed; no publisher response.

UNIVERSITY RESIDENCE ENVIRONMENT SCALE (URES)
Rudolf H. Moos and Marvin S. Gerst

College students, adult

Purpose: Assesses the social environment of university residence halls and dormitories.

Description: 100-item paper-pencil true-false test of 10 dimensions of the social climate of college dormitories: involvement, emotional support, independence, traditional social orientation, competition, academic achievement, intellectuality, order and organization, student influence, and innovation. Materials include the Real Form (Form R), which measures current perceptions of a residence; the 40-item Short Form (Form S); the Expectations Form (Form E), which measures expectations of a new residence; and the Ideal Form (Form I), which measures conceptions of an ideal residence hall environment. Forms I and E are not in published form, but items and instructions appear in the Appendix of the

URES manual. One in a series of nine Social Climate scales. Examiner required. Suitable for group use.

Untimed: Not available

Scoring: Hand key; examiner evaluated

Cost: 25 reusable tests $4.75; 50 answer sheets $3.50; 50 profiles $3.50; key $1.50; manual $4.00

Publisher: Consulting Psychologists Press, Inc.

VALUES INVENTORY FOR CHILDREN (VIC)
Joan S. Guilford, Willa Gupta, and Lisbeth Goldberg

Child   Grades 1-4

Purpose: Measures values of children. Used to assess their relations to other children, parents, and authority figures.

Description: 47-item paper-pencil test measuring seven independent value dimensions: asocial, social conformity, "me first," sociability, academic, masculinity, and adult closeness. Stimuli for all test items are pictorial. The answer sheets may be used at a third-grade level and above. Items for all seven scales are included in a single test booklet, which is available in two forms: B for boys and G for girls. One scoring key is required for each sex. Profile charts are available for plotting centile rank by grade level and sex. Norms are provided for Grades 1, 2, 3, and 4. The manual of interpretations and administration manual are necessary. The test is restricted to A.P.A. members. Examiner required. Suitable for group use.

Untimed: 30 minutes

Scoring: Hand key

Cost: 25 tests $25.00 (specify sex); 25 answer sheets $3.50; 25 scoring sheets $3.50; 25 profile charts $3.50; 50 answer sheets are required if entire test is to be used

Publisher: Sheridan Psychological Services, Inc.

WORLD GOVERNMENT SCALE
Panos D. Bardis

Adolescent, adult

Purpose: Measures attitudes and beliefs concerning world government and the possible effects world government might have on society. Used for discussion and educational purposes.

Description: 6-item paper-pencil inventory in which individuals rate six statements about world government and its effects on society on a 5-point scale from 0 (strongly disagree) to 4 (strongly agree). All statements express positive attitudes toward world government. The score equals the sum of the six numerical responses. The theoretical range extends from 0 (complete rejection of the concept of world government) to 24 (complete acceptance). Self-administered. Suitable for group use.

Untimed: Varies

Scoring: Self-scored

Cost: Free

Publisher: Panos D. Bardis

Student Evaluation and Counseling: Student Personality Factors

AAMD ADAPTIVE BEHAVIOR SCALE, SCHOOL EDITION (ABS-SE)
Refer to page 590.

ACHIEVEMENT IDENTIFICATION MEASURE (AIM)
Sylvia B. Rimm

Grades K-12

Purpose: Identifies characteristics contributing to underachievement in students. Used by teachers and parents for communication and intervention.

Description: 77-item paper-pencil inventory in which parents assess their child's characteristics in six areas (competition, responsibility, control, achievement, communication, respect) by responding "no," "to a small extent," "average," "more than average," or "definitely" to each item. The test distinguishes between achievers and underachievers. Parents receive a computer-scored report with a manual that explains the meaning of the scores. Self-administered. Suitable for group use.

Untimed: 20 minutes

Scoring: Computer scored

Cost: Class set of 30 tests and computer scoring $70.00

Publisher: Educational Assessment Service, Inc.

ADAPTIVE BEHAVIOR INVENTORY OF CHILDREN (ABIC)
Refer to page 69.

THE ADJECTIVE CHECK LIST (ACL)
Refer to page 114.

THE ADJUSTMENT INVENTORY: STUDENT FORM
Hugh M. Bell

Adolescent

Purpose: Measures the personal and social adjustment of high-school and college students.

Description: Multiple-item paper-pencil self-report inventory assessing six scales of adjustment: home adjustment, health adjustment, submissiveness (formerly social adjustment), emotionality (formerly emotional adjustment), hostility, and masculinity-femininity. Norms are provided for high-school and college students. Self-administered. Suitable for group use.

Untimed: 25 minutes

Scoring: Hand key

Cost: Manual $4.50; 25 reusable test booklets $5.25; 50 answer sheets (includes profile) $9.75; scoring stencils $8.50

Publisher: Consulting Psychologists Press, Inc.

ADOLESCENT ALIENATION INDEX (AAI)
Refer to page 115.

ADOLESCENT EMOTIONAL FACTORS INVENTORY
Refer to page 116.

THE AFFECTIVE PERCEPTION INVENTORY (API)
*Anthony T. Soares and
Louise M. Soares*

Grades 1-12, college

Purpose: Assesses a student's feelings about self regarding general school experiences and specific curriculum areas. Used by educators, sociologists, counselors, and psychologists interested in subject's view of academic world.

Description: Multiple-item paper-pencil test for four levels: primary (Grades 1-3), intermediate (Grades 4-8), advanced (Grades 9-12), and college. Each level is comprised of nine scales: Self as a Person, Student Self, English, Math, Science, Social Sciences, The Arts, Physical Education, and School. Other scales include Humanities Perceptions and Foreign Language Perceptions. The student rates self by marking perceptions in the appropriate space on a scale for the various traits. The examiner may need to read the test to young children. Examiner required. Suitable for group use. Available in Spanish, Italian, and French.

Untimed: 30 minutes

Scoring: Hand key

Cost: Specimen set (indicate level) $6.00

Publisher: SOARES Associates

BARCLAY CLASSROOM ASSESSMENT SYSTEM (BCAS)
James R. Barclay

Child   Grades 3-6

Purpose: Evaluates children in Grades 3-6 in relation to their classroom situations, their peers, and their teachers. Used by educators and counselors to identify gifted children and children with

learning disabilities, plan Individualized Educational Plans, and to facilitate compliance with P.L. 94-142.

Description: Multiple-entry paper-pencil screening procedure identifying children who are at high-risk for learning-related problems. An Evaluation Booklet is used by the examiner to collect information from the teacher and each child in a class. The results provide a comprehensive report for each child based on sophisticated computer processing of the data gained from the child, classroom peers, and the teacher (who provides demographic information and responds to a brief adjective checklist for each child). The computer report provides the following information for each child: factor scores for task-order achievement, control-predictability, reserved-internal, physical-activity, sociability-affiliation, and enterprising-dominance; a narrative report of the child's self-estimates of his self-competency skills, vocational awareness, reinforcers, and attitude toward school; peer and teacher estimates; suspected difficulties with problem analysis; general intervention direction; and prescriptions. When stanine scores for standardized tests are provided by the teacher, additional relationships between psychosocial variables and academic achievement can be obtained. Examiner required. Suitable for group use.

Untimed: 30-45 minutes

Scoring: Computer scored

Cost: Introductory kit for 36 students (includes computer processing) $135.00

Publisher: Western Psychological Services

BASIC LIVING SKILLS SCALE

Child   Grades 3-6

Purpose: Assesses basic skills necessary for daily living.

Description: Paper-pencil test of six categories of basic living skills: self-concept, interpersonal relations, responsibility, decision making, study skills, and career planning. Materials include pupil task books to assist in skill improvement and strategies handbooks for facilitators. Examiner/self-administered. Suitable for group use.

Untimed: Not available

Scoring: Hand key; may be machine scored; scoring service available

Cost: Complete kit (manual, 35 pupil record forms and profile sheets) $30.80

Publisher: Dallas Educational Services

BECOMING THE GIFT (BTG)
Refer to page 305.

BEHAVIORAL ACADEMIC SELF-ESTEEM (BASE)
Stanley Coopersmith and Ragnar Gilberts

Child, adolescent
Grades PreK-8

Purpose: Measures academic self-esteem. Used for counseling and research.

Description: 16-item paper-pencil test consisting of a behavioral rating scale assessing five factors related to self-esteem: student initiative, social attention, success/failure, social attraction, and self-confidence. The test may be used by teachers, parents, and other professionals who can observe the child directly. May be used in conjunction with The Coopersmith Self-Esteem Inventory. Self-administered. Suitable for group use.

Untimed: 5 minutes

Scoring: Hand key; examiner evaluated

Cost: 25 rating scales $5.00; manual $7.50

Publisher: Consulting Psychologists Press, Inc.

CALIFORNIA LIFE GOALS EVALUATION SCHEDULES
Milton E. Hahn

Adult

Purpose: Differentiates "life goals" from "interests" by identifying significant motivational forces in normal individuals ages 15 and older. Used for career planning, adjusting to aging or retirement,

evoking insights in areas of psychological normality, and college counseling.

Description: 150-item paper-pencil test measuring 10 life goals: esteem, profit, fame, leadership, power, security, social service, interesting experiences, self-expression, and independence. Using a 5-point acceptance or rejection scale, the subject responds to "debatable" statements. Norms are presented based on age, sex, occupation, familial relationships, and projected academic studies. Self-administered. Suitable for group use.

Untimed: 20-30 minutes

Scoring: Hand key

Cost: Complete kit (100 profile forms, manual, 25 reusable test booklets, key, 100 answer sheets) $57.50

Publisher: Western Psychological Services

CANFIELD LEARNING STYLES INVENTORY (CLS)
Refer to page 683.

CHILD & ADOLESCENT ADJUSTMENT PROFILE (CAAP)
Refer to page 102.

CHILD BEHAVIOR RATING SCALE
Refer to page 104.

CHILDREN'S ADAPTIVE BEHAVIOR SCALE
Bert O. Richmond and Richard H. Kicklighter

Child Ages 5-11

Purpose: Assesses the adaptive behavior of children. Used to plan remediation programs.

Description: Multiple-item paper-pencil observational inventory covering five areas of adaptive behavior: language development, independent functioning, family role performance, economic vocational activity, and socialization. A teacher or school psychologist completes the inventory based on direct observation of the child and evaluates the results according to guidelines presented in the manual. Self-administered. Suitable for group use.

Untimed: Varies

Scoring: Examiner evaluated

Cost: Test kit (manual, picture book, 5 record forms) $19.95

Publisher: Humanics Limited

CHILDREN'S PERSONALITY QUESTIONNAIRE (CPQ)
Refer to page 106.

CHILDREN'S VERSION/FAMILY ENVIRONMENT SCALE (CV/FES)
Refer to page 71.

A CLASS PLAY
Refer to page 669.

COMPREHENSIVE PERSONAL ASSESSMENT SYSTEM: ADJECTIVE SELF-DESCRIPTION (ASD)
Refer to page 127.

COMPREHENSIVE PERSONAL ASSESSMENT SYSTEM: DIRECTED IMAGINATION (DI)
Refer to page 127.

COMPREHENSIVE PERSONAL ASSESSMENT SYSTEM: ONE-WORD SENTENCE COMPLETION
Refer to page 127.

COMPREHENSIVE PERSONAL ASSESSMENT SYSTEM: SELF-REPORT INVENTORY (SRI)
Refer to page 127.

COOPERSMITH SELF-ESTEEM INVENTORIES (CSEI)
Refer to page 194.

THE COPING INVENTORY
Shirley Zeitlin

Grades PreK-12

Purpose: Assesses the behavior patterns and skills that are resources a person uses to meet personal needs and to adapt to the demands of his environment. Provides information about level of effectiveness, general coping style, and specific resources and vulnerabilities.

Description: 48-item paper-pencil inventory in two categories: Coping with Self and Coping with Environment. The items in each category are divided into three dimensions that describe coping style: productive, active, and flexible. The Adaptive Behavior Summary is used to describe how effectively a person copes, and Behavior Lists are used to identify strengths and weaknesses in a person's coping actions. The inventory is available in two forms: Observation (ages 3-16) and Self-Rated (adolescent and adults). The manuals for each level contain instructions for rating, scoring, and implementing the results. Examiner required. The Self-Rated form is suitable for group use.

Timed: Varies

Scoring: Hand key; examiner evaluated

Cost: Starter set (manual, 20 forms) $25.00; self-rated specimen set $9.00; observation specimen set $14.00

Publisher: Scholastic Testing Service, Inc.

DESCRIBING PERSONALITY
Union College
Character Research Project

Child, adolescent
Grades PreK-12

Purpose: Determines unique personality characteristics in children. Used to aid parent-child and teacher-child relationships.

Description: Paper-pencil projective test measuring eight personality factors: outstanding characteristics, activities and interests, coaching-school, social relationships, emotional security, imagination and curiosity, vocational interests, and home and family. The test is designed for eight age levels and separate male and female forms are available. Parents are required to respond for the preschool age level. Individual descriptions are modified to fit the person being described. The test may be used with junior and senior high-school students to increase self-understanding. Examiner required. Suitable for group use.

Untimed: 20-30 minutes

Scoring: Examiner evaluated

Cost: Each form $0.25 (specify age and sex); sample set of 16 $3.00

Publisher: Union College, Character Research Project

Information and availability unconfirmed; no publisher response.

EARLY SCHOOL PERSONALITY QUESTIONNAIRE (ESPQ)
Refer to page 108.

EGO STATE INVENTORY
Refer to page 133.

FAMILY PRE-COUNSELING INVENTORY PROGRAM
Refer to page 76.

FROST SELF-DESCRIPTION QUESTIONNAIRE
Refer to page 108.

"GETTING ALONG"—A SITUATION-RESPONSE TEST FOR GRADES 7, 8, 9
Trudys Lawrence

Adolescent   Grades 7-9

Purpose: Evaluates students' emotional health. Used to identify pupils with poor self-image, poor social adjustment, and inadequate adjustment in meeting the demands of daily living.

Description: 45-item paper-pencil multiple-choice test containing 45 illustrated situation-response items divided into three sections: Getting Along With One's Self, Getting Along With Others, and Getting Along In One's Environment. Two equivalent forms, A and B, are available. Examiner/self-administered. Suitable for group use.

Untimed: 45 minutes

Scoring: Hand key

Cost: Classroom test set (30 tests A or B or 15 of each form, teacher's manual, scoring key, 30 answer sheets) $4.00; test (specify form) $0.15; manual $0.20; scoring key $0.10; answer sheets $0.01 each

Publisher: Trudys Lawrence, Ph.D.

GUILFORD-ZIMMERMAN TEMPERAMENT SURVEY (GZTS)
Refer to page 139.

HIGH SCHOOL PERSONALITY QUESTIONNAIRE (HSPQ)
Refer to page 140.

INCOMPLETE SENTENCES TASK
Refer to page 143.

INSTITUTE OF CHILD STUDY SECURITY TEST—ELEMENTARY FORM
Michael F. Grapko

Child, adolescent
Grades 4-8

Purpose: Measures child's personal security and behavior patterns. Provides teachers with a better understanding of children and recognition of the kind of direction and encouragement children need to develop sound mental health habits.

Description: The test is presented in story form *(The Story of Jimmy)* and deals with significant areas of the child's life. The test is based on Dr W.E. Blatz's theory of security. Examiner required. Suitable for group use.
CANADIAN PUBLISHER

Untimed: 25 minutes

Scoring: Hand key

Cost: Specimen set (manual, scoring form, test) $5.25

Publisher: Guidance Centre

INSTITUTE OF CHILD STUDY SECURITY TEST—PRIMARY FORM
Michael F. Grapko

Child   Grades 1-3

Purpose: Measures child's personal security and behavior patterns. Provides teachers with a better understanding of children and recognition of the kind of direction and encouragement children need to develop sound mental health habits.

Description: The test is presented in story form *(The Story of Timmy)* and deals with significant areas of the child's life. A consistency score and a security scale are provided, indicating the child's consistency in mode of response to a variety of life situations and his pattern of security development. Examiner required. Suitable for group use.
CANADIAN PUBLISHER

Timed: 20 minutes

Scoring: Hand key

Cost: Specimen set (manual, scoring form, test) $4.50

Publisher: Guidance Centre

INTERMEDIATE PERSONALITY QUESTIONNAIRE FOR INDIAN PUPILS (IPQI)—1974

Child, adolescent

Purpose: Assesses personality. Used for guidance of children with social and emotional problems. Used in vocational guidance.

Description: Multiple-item paper-pencil measure of 10 aspects of personality, including social extraversion, verbal intelligence, emotional stability, adventuresomeness, creativity, dominance, perserverance, relaxedness, spirit of enterprise, and environment relatedness. Examiner required. Suitable for group use.
SOUTH AFRICAN PUBLISHER

Untimed: 30-45 minutes

Scoring: Hand key

Cost: (In Rands) test booklet 2,00; manual 1,10; scoring stencil 0,20; 10 answer sheets 1,00; orders from outside The RSA will be dealt with on merit

Publisher: Human Sciences Research Council

IPAT ANXIETY SCALE (OR SELF-ANALYSIS FORM)
Refer to page 145.

JESNESS BEHAVIOR CHECK LIST
Refer to page 147.

LEADERSHIP ABILITY EVALUATION
Refer to page 956.

LUTHER HOSPITAL SENTENCE COMPLETIONS (LHSC)
John R. Thurston

Adolescent, adult

Purpose: Evaluates attitudes and emotional reactions of nursing students and nursing school applicants. Used to predict probable success or failure in nursing school.

Description: 90-item paper-pencil incomplete sentence test measuring six attitudes related to nursing school performance: nursing, self, home and family, responsibility, academics, and others-love-marriage. Materials include a self-directing test booklet, answer sheet, and scoring key. A comprehensive manual covering this and other NRA tests is available also. The test is most relevant to 18-20-year-old female applicants. Self-administered. Suitable for group use.

Untimed: 30 minutes

Scoring: Hand key; scoring service available

Cost: Specimen set $5.00; 25 tests $10.00; manual $15.00

Publisher: Nursing Research Associates

MARTINEK-ZAICHKOWSKY SELF-CONCEPT SCALE FOR CHILDREN (MZSCS)
Thomas J. Martinek and Leonard D. Zaichkowsky

Child, adolescent
Grades 1-8

Purpose: Measures the global self-concept of children, identifies children with low self-esteem, and evaluates the impact of the educational process on a child's self-perception. May be used with non-English speaking children. Used for research and referral.

Description: 25-item paper-pencil forced-choice format test measuring physical, behavioral, and emotional aspects of a child's self-confidence. Five factors are covered: satisfaction and happiness; home and family relationships and circumstances; ability in games, recreation, and sports; personality traits and emotional tendencies; and behavioral and social characteristics in school. Each test item consists of a page in the test booklet that presents the child with a pair of pictures representing positive and negative roles. The child circles the picture he considers to be most like himself. The test requires little or no reading ability and is culture-free. Examiner required. Suitable for group use.

Untimed: 10-15 minutes

Scoring: Hand key; examiner evaluated

Cost: Specimen set $9.00; 25 tests $32.00; manual $6.00

Publisher: Psychologists and Educators, Inc.

MILLON ADOLESCENT PERSONALITY INVENTORY (MAPI)
Refer to page 152.

MOONEY PROBLEM CHECKLIST
Refer to page 155.

NEUROTICISM SCALE QUESTIONNAIRE (NSQ)
Refer to page 158.

NEW YOUTH RESEARCH SURVEY (NYRS)
Refer to page 306.

NURSE ATTITUDES INVENTORY (NAI)
John R. Thurston

Adolescent, adult

Purpose: Evaluates attitudes and emotional reactions of nursing students and nursing school applicants. Used to predict probable success or failure in nursing school.

Description: 70-item paper-pencil multiple-choice test in two forms evaluating six attitudes related to nursing school performance: nursing, self, home and family, responsibility, academics, and others-love-marriage. The scales evaluate positive and negative attitudes. Materials include a self-directing test booklet, answer sheet, and scoring key. A comprehensive manual covering this and other NRA tests is available. The test is most relevant to 18-20-year-old female applicants. Self-administered. Suitable for group use.

Untimed: 30 minutes

Scoring: Hand key; examiner evaluated; scoring service available

Cost: Specimen set (excluding key) $10.00; 50 answer sheets $5.00; scoring key $15.00; manual $15.00; scoring service $5.00 per test

Publisher: Nursing Research Associates

NURSING SENTENCE COMPLETIONS (NSC)
John R. Thurston

Adolescent, adult

Purpose: Evaluates attitudes and emotions of nursing students and applicants to nursing school. Used to predict probable success or failure in nursing school.

Description: 40-item paper-pencil incomplete sentence test measuring six attitudes related to nursing school performance: nursing, self, home and family, responsibility, academics, and others-love-marriage. Materials consist of a self-directing test booklet and a scoring key. A comprehensive manual covering this and other NRA tests is available also. The test is most relevant for 18-20-year-old female applicants and can be scored with the Nursing Education Scale. Examiner/self-administered. Suitable for group use.

Untimed: 20 minutes

Scoring: Hand key; scoring service available

Cost: Specimen set $10.00; 25 tests $10.00; comprehensive manual $15.00; scoring service $5.00 per test

Publisher: Nursing Research Associates

THE PERSONAL AUDIT
Refer to page 932.

PERSONALITY DESCRIPTIONS
Refer to page 207.

PERSONALITY RATING SCALE
Refer to page 111.

POLITTE SENTENCE COMPLETION TEST (PSCT)
Alan J. Politte

Child, adolescent
Grades 1-12

Purpose: Evaluates personality traits and adjustment of children. Used to assess personality in the educational, counseling, and clinical areas.

Description: 35-item paper-pencil free-response projective test measuring personality. Students are told that the test is a "questionnaire" or an "exercise" in which they are to read the stems and then complete the sentence. The test serves as a screening device through which the examiner can gain further insight into the thinking processes of the student and not as an instrument which provides a "score" or normative reference for the student. Persons without training in clinical psychology should use the test as an aid in interview or counseling settings. Clinically trained psychologists can base their interpretations from a psycho-analytic, social, behavioral, or similar approach. The test is available in two forms: Elementary for Grades 1-6 and Secondary for Grades 7-12. Examiner/self-administered. Suitable for group use.

Untimed: 15 minutes

Scoring: Examiner evaluated

Cost: Specimen set $4.00; 25 tests (manual included; specify form) $7.50

Publisher: Psychologists and Educators, Inc.

THE PRESCHOOL BEHAVIOR QUESTIONNAIRE
Refer to page 112.

PRESCHOOL SELF-CONCEPT PICTURE TEST (PS-CPT)
Rosestelle B. Woolner

Child   Ages 4-5

Purpose: Assesses a preschooler's opinions of himself in terms of how he perceives himself to be and the way he would like to be. Used to design curriculums that enhance a preschooler's self-concept.

Description: 20-item oral-response test measuring a preschooler's opinion of himself in regard to 10 pairs of bipolar characteristics: dirty/clean, active/passive, aggressive/nonaggressive, afraid/unafraid, strong/weak, acceptance/rejection, unhappy/happy, group rejection/group acceptance, sharing/nonsharing, and dependence/independence. A set of 10 picture plates presents drawings of children representing each of the bipolar characteristics. The child is shown the plates and asked to indicate the drawing with which he identifies and the drawing with which he would like to identify. Variances between the two responses provide the teacher with an opportunity to help the child reduce the degree of difference between the way he sees himself and the way he would like to see himself. Retesting reveals progress in this direction. Available in four forms for Caucasian and Negro boys and girls. Examiner required. Not suitable for group use.

Untimed: 15 minutes

Scoring: Hand key

Cost: Complete (4 subtests, manual, 25 score sheets) $15.00 plus postage and handling

Publisher: Rosestelle B. Woolner, Ed.D.

PSYCHOEPISTEMOLOGICAL PROFILE (PEP)
J.R. Royce and L.P. Mos

Adolescent, adult

Purpose: Evaluates an individual's epistemological hierarchy (approach to reality). Used with high-school students and adults.

Description: 90-item paper-pencil test assessing the psychological processes and criterion for truth that determine an individual's particular world view. The test identifies and quantifies three basic epistemic styles (a major personality integrator or higher order personality factor that determines an individual's basic approach to reality): rationalism (30 items), empiricism (30 items), and metaphorism (30 items). Test items consist of value statements, which the individual rates on a 5-point scale ranging from "complete agreement" to "complete disagreement." The test yields independent scores for each of the three epistemic styles. The highest of the three scores indicates the individual's dominant epistemology. Norms are provided by sex for a junior-college population. Self-administered. Suitable for group use. Available in French (with separate norms). CANADIAN PUBLISHER

Untimed: 20-30 minutes

Scoring: Examiner evaluated; may be machine scored

Cost: Manual, test $10.00

Publisher: Center for Advanced Study in Theoretical Psychology/University of Alberta

PSYCHOLOGICAL DISTRESS INVENTORY (PDI)

College students

Purpose: Measures life stress in college students. Used as a screening device for students seeking psychological services from counseling centers.

Description: 50-item paper-pencil or computer measurement of depression, anxiety, somatic discomfort, and stress in college students requesting psychological services from counseling centers. Students rate life events occurring in the past 12 months on a 5-point, Likert-type scale indicating stressfulness or aversiveness of the event. The results are used for deciding if more extensive psychological evaluation is needed. Self-administered. Suitable for group use.

Untimed: 10-20 minutes

Scoring: Hand key; may be computer scored

Cost: Computer version $275.00

Publisher: Applied Innovations, Inc.

QUALITY OF SCHOOL LIFE SCALE (QSL)
Refer to page 690.

RESIDENT ASSISTANT STRESS INVENTORY
Gary L. Dickson

College students

Purpose: Identifies the type and level of stress experienced by residence-hall personnel. Used by professional housing officers to individualize in-service education of residence-hall personnel.

Description: Multiple-item paper-pencil inventory measuring six categories of stress experienced by resident assistants: emotional resiliency, facilitative leadership, counseling skills, environmental adjustment, confrontive skills, and values development. The *Manual and Inservice Education Guide*, which is divided into two parts, one for the practitioner and one for the researcher, contains 50 stress situations, directions for scoring and interpretation, suggestions for in-service training, annotated references, and recommendations for research. Examiner required. Suitable for group use.

Untimed: Varies

Scoring: Examiner evaluated

Cost: Specimen set (inventory, score sheet, profile form, contract form, research form, *Manual and Inservice Education Guide*) $5.00
Publisher: Andrews University Press

ROGERS PERSONAL ADJUSTMENT INVENTORY—UK REVISION
Refer to page 113.

SCALES FOR RATING THE BEHAVIORAL CHARACTERISTICS OF SUPERIOR STUDENTS (SRBCSS)
Refer to page 572.

SCAMIN: A SELF-CONCEPT AND MOTIVATION INVENTORY: EARLY ELEMENTARY
Norman J. Milchus,
George A. Farrah, and William Reitz

Child   Grades 1-3

Purpose: Measures self-concept and assesses the motivation inventory of students.

Description: 24-item test in which items are responded to on a machine-scorable scale of five sad to happy faces to ascertain the child's self-concept strength and to develop a motivational inventory. Examiner required. Suitable for group use.
Untimed: 25 minutes
Scoring: Hand key; may be computer scored
Cost: Specimen set $7.00; manual $1.25; key $4.00
Publisher: Person-O-Metrics, Inc.

SCAMIN: A SELF-CONCEPT AND MOTIVATION INVENTORY: LATER ELEMENTARY
Norman J. Milchus,
George A. Farrah, and William Reitz

Child   Grades 3-6

Purpose: Measures self-concept and assesses the motivational inventory of students.

Description: 48-item paper-pencil test measuring achievement needs, achievement investment, role expectations, and self-adequacy. The examiner reads the items to the class. Examiner required. Suitable for group use.
Untimed: 30 minutes
Scoring: Hand key; may be computer scored
Cost: Specimen set $7.00; manual $1.25; key $4.00
Publisher: Person-O-Metrics, Inc.

SCAMIN: A SELF-CONCEPT AND MOTIVATION INVENTORY: PRESCHOOL/KINDERGARTEN
Norman J. Milchus,
George A. Farrah, and William Reitz

Child   Grades PreK-K

Purpose: Measures self-concept and assesses the motivation of preschool and kindergarten children.

Description: 24-item test using three sad to happy face responses to evaluate self-concept strength. Examiner required. Suitable for group use.
Untimed: 30 minutes
Scoring: Hand key; may be computer scored
Cost: Specimen set $7.00; manual $1.25; key $4.00
Publisher: Person-O-Metrics, Inc.

SCAMIN: A SELF-CONCEPT AND MOTIVATION INVENTORY: SECONDARY FORM
Norman J. Milchus,
George A. Farrah, and William Reitz

Adolescent   Grades 7-12

Purpose: Determines an individual's self-concept and motivation in an academic context.

Description: 64-item paper-pencil test measuring achievement needs, achievement investment, role expectation, and self-adequacy. Four levels of the test, each with a different number of items and administration time, are available. Examiner required. Suitable for group use. Available in Spanish.

Untimed: 30-40 minutes

Scoring: Hand key; may be computer scored

Cost: Specimen set $7.00; manual $1.25; key $4.00

Publisher: Person-O-Metrics, Inc.

SCHOOL MOTIVATION ANALYSIS TEST (SMAT)
Refer to page 173.

THE SCHOOL PLAY
Refer to page 678.

SCHOOL SOCIAL SKILLS RATING SCALE (S³ RATING SCALE)
Laura Brown, Donald Black, and John Downs

Child, adolescent

Purpose: Identifies strengths and deficits in school-related social behaviors of elementary and high-school students.

Description: 40-item paper-pencil criterion-referenced inventory assessing student social skills needed for success in school and employment. Using a 6-point Likert scale and month-long observation of student behavior, teachers rate students on adult relations (12 items), peer relations (16 items), school rules (6 items), and classroom behaviors (6 items). The test can be used for social skills instruction, discussion of student behavior with parents and other school personnel, and development and monitoring of social behavior goals for individual education plans. The test can be used with residential, special education, and regular education students. Examiner required. Not suitable for group use.

Untimed: 10 minutes

Scoring: Examiner evaluated

Cost: Complete kit (S3 manual, SSS-2 in vinyl binder) $25.00

Publisher: Slosson Educational Publications, Inc.

SELF-CONCEPT SCALE

Adolescent   Grades 7-12

Purpose: Assesses self-concept in students.

Description: Paper-pencil test of five areas of student self-concept: decision-making skills, interpersonal relations, responsibility, study skills, and career planning. Materials include pupil task books to assist in skill development and a strategies handbook providing pupil activities for facilitators. Examiner/self-administered. Suitable for group use.

Untimed: Not available

Scoring: Hand key; may be machine scored; scoring service available

Cost: Complete kit (manual, 35 pupil record forms and profile sheets) $30.80

Publisher: Dallas Educational Services

SELF-OBSERVATION SCALES
Refer to page 211.

SENTENCE COMPLETION TEST
Refer to page 177.

SOCIAL BEHAVIOR ASSESSMENT (SBA)
T.M. Stephens

Child   Grades K-8

Purpose: Assesses the school-related social skills of students. Used in research and education to diagnose behavior deficits, provide classification and descriptive information on social behaviors, and select students who need social skills training.

Description: 136-item teacher-rated observation tool assessing school-related social skills and containing 30 subcategories arranged under four behavior categories: environmental, interpersonal, task related, and self-related. Using observation or recall, teachers rate each student on each item (0 = not observed or applicable, 1 = at acceptable level, 2 = lower than acceptable level, 3 = never exhibited). Examiner required. Suitable for group use.

Untimed: 22 minutes

Scoring: Examiner evaluated

Cost: Packet of 25, with prescriptions $5.00; without prescriptions $6.50

Publisher: Cedars Press

SOCIAL INTELLIGENCE TEST
*F.A. Moss, Thelma Hunt,
and K. Omwake*

**Adolescent, adult
Grades 10 and above**

Purpose: Assesses basic social perceptions and judgments of students.

Description: Multiple-item paper-pencil test measuring five factors: judgment in social situations, recognition of mental state of speaker, observation of human behavior, memory for names and faces, and sense of humor. Percentile norms are provided for high-school, college, and adult populations. Three editions are available: Second Edition (Long Form); Shortened Edition (omits Memory for Names and Faces factor); and Special Edition (contains only Judgment in Social Situations and Observation of Human Behavior). A complete specimen set contains all three forms. Examiner required. Suitable for group use.

Timed: 50 minutes

Scoring: Hand key

Cost: Specimen set $5.00

Publisher: The Center for Psychological Service

STUDENT DEVELOPMENTAL TASK INVENTORY: REVISED SECOND EDITION (SDTI-2)
*Roger B. Winston, Jr.,
Theodore K. Miller,
and Judith S. Prince*

College student   Ages 17-23

Purpose: Assesses the personal growth and development of college students according to constructs formulated by Arthur W. Chickering as reported in *Education and Identity.* Used for general guidance counseling with college students.

Description: 140-item paper-pencil true-false test assessing behaviors and feelings that reflect the personal growth and development of college students. The inventory identifies the accomplishment of three developmental tasks (each of which is defined by three subtasks): developing autonomy (emotional, instrumental, and interdependence); developing purpose in life (appropriate educational plans, mature career plans, and mature lifestyles); and developing mature interpersonal relationships (intimate relationships with the opposite sex, relationships with peers, and tolerance). Eight of the subtasks contain 16 items; the ninth subtask contains 12 items. Each item is a statement describing behavior or reports of feelings representative of a level of development within the specified subtask. Students indicate whether the statement is an accurate (true) or inaccurate (false) self-description. Scoring guidelines emphasize self-understanding, planning, and goal setting. The scoring procedure (using the SDTI-2 Data Sheet) is designed to stimulate the students to plan for and assume responsibility for their own intentional development. May be used in conjunction with the Student Profile and Assessment Record (SPAR). Self-administered. Suitable for group use.

Untimed: 20-30 minutes

Scoring: Self-scored

Cost: Test booklet $0.75; answer sheet $0.35; 100 data sheets $5.00; manual $6.00; specimen set (includes SPAR material and manual) $7.00

Publisher: Student Development Associates, Inc.

STUDY OF VALUES
*Gordon W. Allport, Phillip E. Vernon,
and Gardner Lindzey*

**Adolescent, adult
Grades 10 and above**

Purpose: Measures the relative prominence of an individual's basic interests or personality motives. Used for educational planning, vocational planning and guidance, personnel selection, and research.

Description: 45-item paper-pencil test measuring six values: theoretical, economic, aesthetic, social, political, and religious. The test is designed primarily for use with college students or adults with some college education. It should be used only when the interpretation is supervised and guided by individuals who have had considerable experience in psychological testing and personality theory. Self-administered. Suitable for group use.

Untimed: 20 minutes

Scoring: Hand key

Cost: 35 hand-scorable test booklets, manual $18.57

Publisher: The Riverside Publishing Company

SUINN TEST ANXIETY BEHAVIOR SCALE (STABS)

Adolescent, adult
Grades 7 and above

Purpose: Measures a person's anxiety regarding academic testing situations. Used for screening and diagnostic purposes and research on test anxiety and as a tool in developing anxiety hierarchies for desensitization therapy.

Description: 50-item paper-pencil test assessing the level of a person's test anxiety. Test items refer to experiences related to academic testing that may cause fear or apprehension. The subject rates his anxiety concerning each test item on a 5-point scale ranging from "not at all" to "very much." Norms are available for college students, adult nonstudents, and males and females. Use is restricted to APA membership guidelines. Self-administered. Suitable for group use.

Untimed: 20 minutes

Scoring: Hand key

Cost: 100 scales $45.00

Publisher: Rocky Mountain Behavioral Science Institute, Inc.

TEST ANXIETY PROFILE (TAP)
E.R. Oetting and C.W. Cole

Adolescent, adult
Grades 10 and above

Purpose: Measures a person's anxieties regarding academic testing situations.

Used for screening and counseling purposes.

Description: 77-item paper-pencil test assessing a person's feelings and thoughts in regard to six academic testing situations: multiple-choice exams, math exams, essay exams, unannounced tests, talking in front of a class, and tests with time limits. Each test item consists of a pair of bipolar adjectives separated by a 7-point Likert scale. The subject rates himself on each pair of adjectives according to his thoughts or feelings in each of the testing situations. Two anxiety scores are derived for each testing situations: Feelings of Anxiety (FA) and Thought Interference (TI). Use is restricted to APA membership guidelines. Self-administered. Suitable for group use.

Untimed: 10-15 minutes

Scoring: Hand key; examiner evaluated

Cost: 100 tests $60.00; manual $15.00

Publisher: Rocky Mountain Behavioral Science Institute, Inc.

THE TEST OF SOCIAL INSIGHT: YOUTH EDITION AND ADULT EDITION
Refer to page 213.

THE WAKSMAN SOCIAL SKILLS RATING SCALE (WSSRS)
Steven Waksman

Child, adolescent
Grades K-12

Purpose: Assesses social skills deficits of students. Used by teachers and clinicians for selecting students for social skills training or special counseling programs and for evaluating the effectiveness of those programs.

Description: 21-item rating scale identifying specific social skill deficits in children and adolescents by surveying aggressive and passive domains. The examiner rates the behavior of the "targeted" student or students on a scale ranging from 0 (never) to 3 (usually). The assessment permits clinicians to compare the students with a normative sample for identification or classification purposes and to set criteria for social skills training, counseling, and program evaluation. Examiner required. Not suitable for group use.

Untimed: 5-10 minutes

Scoring: Examiner evaluated

Cost: Complete kit $29.95

Publisher: ASIEP Education Company

Student Evaluation and Counseling: Study Skills Attitudes

CAI STUDY SKILLS TEST
William F. Brown

Adolescent, adult
Grades 11 and above

Purpose: Measures a student's knowledge of efficient study skills and effective academic attitudes. Used to identify students who need help and, when used as a posttest, students who fail to learn adequate skills.

Description: 200-item paper-pencil or computer-administered true-false test of student's knowledge in 10 areas: managing time, improving memory, taking lecture notes, reading texts, taking exams, writing themes and reports, giving oral reports, improving scholastic motivation, improving interpersonal relations, and improving concentration. The test also is available on a computer diskette for Apple II and IBM-PC computers. Self-administered. Suitable for group use.

Untimed: 50 minutes

Scoring: Hand key

Cost: Test $0.85; 100 tests $75.00; answer sheet $0.35; 250 answer sheets $75.00; hand key stencil $5.00; direction manual $3.50; computer disk $200.00

Publisher: WFB Enterprises

CANADIAN COMPREHENSIVE ASSESSMENT PROGRAM: DEVELOPING COGNITIVE ABILITIES TEST (DCAT)

Child, adolescent
Grades 2-9

Purpose: Measures learning characteristics of students.

Description: Multiple-item test measuring students' learning characteristics. Items involve both a content area and a cognitive level. Student performance is evaluated in three content areas: verbal ability, quantitative ability, and spatial ability. Information is provided on the five cognitive levels of Bloom's taxonomy: knowledge, comprehension, application, analysis, and synthesis. Examiner required. Suitable for group use.
CANADIAN PUBLISHER

Timed: Varies

Scoring: Hand key

Cost: Review kit $15.00

Publisher: Guidance Centre

CORNELL LEARNING AND STUDY SKILLS INVENTORY
Walter Pauk and Russell Cassel

Adolescent, adult
Grades 7-12, college

Purpose: Assesses skills important to effective learning in high school and college. Used for educational counseling.

Description: 120-item paper-pencil test of study skills yielding scores in seven areas: goal orientation, activity structure, scholarly skills, lecture mastery, textbook mastery, examination mastery, self mastery, and study efficiency. Twenty-two of the items are included in a Reading Validity Index, which determines whether the student has responded thoughtfully. Two forms, the College Form and the Secondary School Form, are available. College Form items are answered on a 5-point ordinal scale ranging from seldom to always. The Secondary School Form items are written in a true-false format. Self-administered. Suitable for group use.

Untimed: 30-45 minutes

Scoring: Hand key

Cost: Specimen set $8.00; 25 tests $18.00; 25 answer sheets, 25 profile sheets $6.00 each; keys $6.00; manual $6.00 (specify Secondary or College form)

Publisher: Psychologists and Educators, Inc.

EFFECTIVE STUDY TEST (EST)
William F. Brown

Adolescent, adult
Grades 9-college

Purpose: Identifies students needing counseling for their study skills and habits. Used to monitor student progress in response to counseling and instruction intended to improve study methods.

Description: 125-item paper-pencil or computer-administered true-false test assessing students' knowledge of effective study methods. The test contains five subscales: reading behavior, reading orientation, study organization, writing behavior, and examination behavior. The test yields a total score for study effectiveness. Use is restricted to professional educators. The test is available on computer diskette for use with the Apple II computer. Self-administered. Suitable for group use. Available in Spanish.

Untimed: 35-45 minutes

Scoring: Hand key

Cost: Reusable test booklet $0.30; 200 test booklets $55.00; answer sheet $0.12; 500 answer sheets $55.00; scoring stencil $0.70; direction manual $0.70; computer diskette $200.00

Publisher: Effective Study Materials; distributed by The American College Testing Program

---

HOW A CHILD LEARNS
Thomas D. Gnagey

Adult

Purpose: Evaluates a student's learning style in order to plan an individualized teaching program.

Description: 3-category paper-pencil test evaluating how a student listens, sees, talks, and moves, and what they remember. The teacher, using the manual and outlines provided, observes the student's regular activities and enters responses according to directions. The observations are analysed in terms of the students' abilities and are used to write a prescriptive teaching plan. The instrument is useful in teacher-training, student teaching, and in-service training programs. Examiner required. Not suitable for group use.

Untimed: 30-60 minutes

Scoring: Examiner evaluated

Cost: Training manual, 20 forms $10.00

Publisher: Slosson Educational Publications, Inc.

LEARNING PREFERENCE INVENTORY (1978)
Harvey F. Silver and J. Robert Hanson

Purpose: Identifies the learning preferences or styles of students. Used by educators for diagnosing student learning styles, curriculum planning, and selection of appropriate teaching strategies.

Description: 144-item paper-pencil inventory assessing an individual's learning preferences. The instrument is based on Jung's *Theory of Psychological Type* and indicates how an individual perceives (through sensing or intuition), makes judgments (through thinking or feeling), and processes data (through introversion or extroversion). Teachers receive learning style profiles on each student and the class. The inventory was developed with inner-city, urban, and suburban students. Examiner/self-administered. Suitable for group use.

Untimed: 30 minutes

Scoring: Hand key; may be computer scored

Cost: $2.50 per copy; computer-scorable copy (includes full diagnostic printout and class plot) $5.00

Publisher: Hanson, Silver, Strong and Associates, Inc.

LEARNING STYLE INVENTORY (1979)
*Harvey F. Silver and
J. Robert Hanson*

Students, adults

Purpose: Identifies learning styles of students and adults.

Description: 80-item paper-pencil self-assessment tool for identifying learning preferences. The inventory includes behaviors for four different learning styles: sensing-thinkers (factual; memory-based mastery learning); sensing-feelers (involvement and motivation for learning); intuitive thinkers (understanding, critical and conceptual thinking); and intuitive feelers (creative, innovative synthesizing-type thinking). The instrument includes detailed descriptions of the four styles. Individuals draw their own profiles. Results can help teachers understand their own and their students' learning styles. Self-administered. Suitable for group use.

Untimed: 30 minutes

Scoring: Self-scored

Cost: $3.50 per copy

Publisher: Hanson, Silver, Strong and Associates, Inc.

STUDY ATTITUDES AND METHODS SURVEY (SAMS)
William B. Michael, Joan J. Michael, and Wayne S. Zimmerman

**Adolescent, adult
Grades 7 and above**

Purpose: Diagnoses habits and attitudes which may be preventing junior high-school, high-school and college students from achieving full academic potential. Used in the classroom and for school-wide screening to identify students most likely to benefit from individual counseling.

Description: Multiple-item paper-pencil inventory assessing dimensions of a motivational, noncognitive nature that relate to school achievement and contribute to a student's performance beyond those measured by traditional ability tests. The student's profile can provide the requisite

insights and guidelines for study habit improvement. Norms are provided for high-school and college level. Examiner required. Suitable for group use.

Untimed: 20-30 minutes

Scoring: Hand key; may be computer scored

Cost: Specimen set (manual, all forms) $5.00; 25 reusable test booklets $10.50; 50 answer sheets $6.25; 50 profile sheets (specify high school or college) $6.00; keys $10.00; manual $2.50

Publisher: Educational and Industrial Testing Service

STUDY HABITS EVALUATION AND INSTRUCTION KIT
Peter Jackson, Neil Reid, and Cedric Croft

Child, adolescent   Ages 14-17

Purpose: Measures and provides instruction on study habits. Used for educational guidance.

Description: Two-part paper-pencil test measuring study habits. Part 1, the Inventory of Study Habits, assists pupils in measuring study habits. The second part, consisting of self-instructional booklets, allows students to work on improving study habits in seven areas: study environment, study time, study organization, reading skills, notetaking skills, exam preparation, and exam technique. Self-administered. Suitable for group use.
NEW ZEALAND PUBLISHER

Untimed: 45 minutes

Scoring: Hand key; examiner evaluated

Cost: Contact publisher

Publisher: New Zealand Council for Educational Research

STUDY SKILLS COUNSELING EVALUATION
George D. Demos

**Adolescent, adult
Grades 10 and above**

Purpose: Evaluates the study habits and attitudes of high-school and college students.

Description: 50-item paper-pencil questionnaire in which students use a scale ranging from "very often" to "very seldom" to rate themselves on time distribution, study conditions, taking notes, examinations, and habits and attitudes. The questionnaire contains "critical items" that differentiate between B and C students. Self-administered. Suitable for group use.

Untimed: 10-20 minutes

Scoring: Hand key

Cost: Complete kit (25 forms, manual) $14.50

Publisher: Western Psychological Services

STUDY SKILLS SURVEYS (SSS)
William F. Brown

Adolescent   Grades 9-13

Purpose: Identifies study skill problems likely to hinder academic achievement. Used to counsel students about effective study habits and attitudes.

Description: 60-item paper-pencil "yes-no" test containing three scales designed to evaluate organization, study techniques, and study motivation. The test helps students recognize and change poor study habits. The test is available on computer diskette for Apple II or IBM-PC computers. Self-administered. Suitable for group use. Available in Spanish.

Untimed: 15-20 minutes

Scoring: Hand key

Cost: Reusable test booklet $0.30; 200 test booklets $55.00; answer sheet $0.12; student workbook $0.20; 200 student workbooks $35.00; directions manual $0.35; computer disk $200.00

Publisher: Effective Study Materials; distributed by The American College Testing Program

SURVEY OF STUDY HABITS AND ATTITUDES
W.F. Brown and W.H. Holtzman

Adolescent, adult
Grades 7-college

Purpose: Identifies students whose study habits and attitudes may prevent them

from taking advantage of educational alternatives. Used for educational counseling and predicting academic success and as a diagnostic and teaching aid.

Description: 100-item paper-pencil test measuring four basic aspects of study habits and attitudes: delay avoidance, work methods, teacher approval, and education acceptance. Students rate themselves according to their own habits and attitudes. The test yields a Study Habits subtotal, a Study Attitude subtotal, and total study Orientation scores. Two forms, Form H (Grades 7-12) and Form C (college students), are available. Self-administered. Suitable for group use. Available in Spanish.

Untimed: 20-25 minutes

Scoring: Hand key; may be machine scored

Cost: Examination kit (survey, IBM 805 answer document, key, manual) $4.50; 25 surveys $13.00; 50 IBM 805 answer documents $12.00; manual and keys $8.00

Publisher: The Psychological Corporation

WRENN STUDY HABITS INVENTORY
C. Gilbert Wrenn

Adolescent, adult
Grades 10 and above

Purpose: Identifies student study habits and attitudes. Used for academic counseling.

Description: 28-item paper-pencil test of habits and attitudes by which high and low scholarship students are distinguished. A negative item score means response is closer to response given by low scholarship students. Self-administered. Suitable for group use.

Untimed: 10-20 minutes

Scoring: Hand key

Cost: Specimen set (test, manual, key) $1.50

Publisher: Consulting Psychologists Press, Inc.

Student Evaluation and Counseling: Vocational Guidance: Achievement and Aptitude

ACADEMIC-TECHNICAL APTITUDE TESTS—ATA AND SATA

Child, adolescent

Purpose: Assesses differential job aptitudes. Used for vocational and educational guidance.

Description: Multiple-item paper-pencil batteries measuring occupational aptitudes. The ATA battery (for pupils in Standards 6, 7, and 8) consists of 10 tests: Verbal Reasoning, Nonverbal Reasoning, Computations, Spatial Perceptions (2-D), Mechanical Reasoning, Language Comprehension, Spatial Perception (3-D), Comparison, Coordination, and Writing Speed. SATA (for pupils in Standards 8, 9, and 10) is available in two forms, A and B. Form A consists of the following 10 tests: Verbal Reasoning, Nonverbal Reasoning I: Figure Series, Nonverbal Reasoning II: Dominoes, Computations, Reading Comprehension, Spelling and Vocabulary, Mechanical Reasoning, Spatial Perception (3-D), Comparison, and Price Controlling. Form B has one additional subtest, Filing. Examiner required. Suitable for group use.
SOUTH AFRICAN PUBLISHER

Timed: ATA 4 hours; SATA 4½ hours
Scoring: Hand key; examiner evaluated
Cost: (In Rands) ATA test 0,70; manual 3,90; scoring stencils I, II 1,30 each; 10 answer sheets I 0,60; 10 answer sheets II 0,50; SATA test (specify A or B) 1,60; manual 5,80; scoring stencils I, II (specify A or B) 2,10 each; 10 answer sheets I, II 1,30 each; orders from outside The RSA will be dealt with on merit
Publisher: Human Sciences Research Council

THE APPLIED KNOWLEDGE TEST (AKT)
M.A. Brimer

Adolescent   Ages 14-18

Purpose: Measures the ability to use knowledge of mathematics, English, science, and spatial relationships. Used for vocational guidance.

Description: Multiple-item paper-pencil measures of a student's competence in the four employment-related subject areas of mathematics, English, science, and spatial relationships. Results can be used to validate interest scores from the Occupational Interest Rating Scale (OIRS). Examiner/self-administered. Suitable for group use.
BRITISH PUBLISHER

Untimed: 60 minutes
Scoring: Hand key
Cost: Contact publisher
Publisher: Educational Evaluation Enterprises

ARMED SERVICES VOCATIONAL APTITUDE BATTERY (ASVAB)
Department of Defense

Adolescent, adult
Grades 10 and over

Purpose: Evaluates high school students' vocational interests and aptitudes. Used for counseling and by the military services to identify eligible graduates for possible recruitment.

Description: 334-item paper-pencil test of aptitudes in various vocational and technical fields. Factors measured include electronics, mechanical comprehension, general science, automotive and shop information, numerical operations, coding speed, word knowledge, arithmetic, reasoning, paragraph comprehension, and mathematics knowledge. Indicates ability in the following areas: verbal, math, academic, mechanical and crafts, business and clerical, electronics and electrical, and health, social, and technologies. A military service recruiter will assist each school in administering the test and the U.S. Military Entrance Processing Command (USMEPCOM) provides the examiner. Individual test results are delivered to school counselors and copies of the scores are given to the recruiting services. Examiner required. Suitable for group use.

Timed: 3 hours

Scoring: Computer scored

Cost: No charge to schools for administration, materials, and scoring

Publisher: U.S. Department of Defense

BALL APTITUDE BATTERY
Refer to page 796.

BUSINESS ENGLISH TEST (BET)
John T. Dailey

Adolescent, adult
Grades 9 and above

Purpose: Assesses knowledge and potential in business English skills. Used in career counseling and vocational guidance settings.

Description: 111-item paper-pencil test measuring an individual's business English skills. The BET yields a single score, but subscores in spelling, punctuation, capitalization, and grammar can be obtained by using the BET scoring mask. The Spatial Visualization Test (SVT) is no longer published. However, for those who already have SVT booklets, combined BET/SVT answer sheets are available. Together the Technical and Scholastic Test (TST) and the BET make up the Dailey Vocational Tests. The examiner's manual includes information for administering, scoring, and interpreting all three tests. The individual profile sheet and group report form also are designed for use with all the tests. Examiner required. Suitable for group use.

Timed: 30 minutes

Scoring: Hand key

Cost: 35 test booklets $16.26; examiner's manual $3.72; 100 answer sheets $19.86

Publisher: The Riverside Publishing Company

CAREER AND VOCATIONAL FORM OF THE SOI-LA BASIC TEST

Adolescent, adult

Purpose: Measures cognitive abilities patterned to predict career and vocational options.

Description: Multiple-item paper-pencil test measuring 24 cognitive abilities patterned to predict career and vocational options. The test consists of subtests taken from the SOI-LA Basic Test. The MSI subtest has been replaced with a test of MMI. Instructions are included with each form for self-administration. The scoring keys and instructions in the Basic Test manual apply. Career and vocational choices are listed on an accompanying sheet for selection. A *Career and Vocation Choice Guide* is included. Materials are available for training any low abilities required for a desired occupation. Computer analysis is available. Self-administered. Suitable for group use.

Timed: 3-5 minutes per test

Scoring: Hand key; may be computer scored

Cost: Examiner's manual $22.00; test form $2.25

Publisher: M & M Systems

COMMERCIAL TESTS—1962

Adolescent   Ages 13-15

Purpose: Assesses abilities important in commercial fields. Used for vocational guidance.

Description: Multiple-item paper-pencil test battery consisting of six tests of commercial abilities: Arithmetic Part I and II, Comparison, Synonyms, Alphabetizing, and Spelling and Punctuation. Two alternate and equivalent forms, A and B, are available. Examiner required. Suitable for group use.
SOUTH AFRICAN PUBLISHER

Untimed: 1 hour

Scoring: Hand key; examiner evaluated

Cost: (In Rands) test booklet (specify form A or B) 0,30; 10 answer sheets (specify form) 0,40; scoring key (specify A or B) 1,10 each; manual 0,80; orders from outside The RSA will be dealt with on merit

Publisher: Human Sciences Research Council

COMPUTER APTITUDE, LITERACY, AND INTEREST PROFILE (CALIP)
Mary S. Poplin, David E. Drew, and Robert S. Gable

Ages 12-60

Purpose: Assesses computer-related abilities of children and adults. Used by school vocational counselors, school psychologists, administrators, and junior and senior high-school and college instructors. Also used in business and industry to make personnel decisions.

Description: Multiple-item paper-pencil test consisting of six subtests: estimation, graphic patterns, logical structures, series, computer interest, and computer literacy. The test measures computer programming aptitudes; computer use aptitudes, including systems analysis, graphics, and repair; and computer literacy, interest, and experience. Examiner/self-administered. Not suitable for group use.

Untimed: 45 minutes

Scoring: Hand key

Cost: Complete kit (examiner's manual, 50 answer sheets, 10 test booklets, storage box) $48.00

Publisher: Pro-Ed

DAILEY VOCATIONAL TESTS
John T. Dailey

Adolescent, adult
Grades 9 and above

Purpose: Assesses knowledge and potential in electrical, mechanical, and scholastic ability and business English skills. Used in career counseling.

Description: 150-item paper-pencil Technical and Scholastic Test (TST) and 111-item paper-pencil Business English Test

(BET) measuring vocational aptitude for trade, technical, and business careers. The TST yields scores for seven subtests: electricity, electronics, mechanical information, physical sciences, arithmetic reasoning, algebra, and vocabulary. The BET yields a single score, but subscores in spelling, punctuation, capitalization, and grammar can be obtained for local interpretation by using the BET scoring mask. The Spatial Visualization Test (SVT) is no longer published. However, for those who already have the SVT booklets, combined BET/SVT answer sheets are available. The examiner's manual includes information for administering, scoring, and interpreting all three tests. The individual profile sheet and the group report form also are designed for use with all the tests. Examiner required. Suitable for group use.

Timed: TST 65 minutes; BET 30 minutes

Scoring: Hand key

Cost: 35 TST test booklets $29.24; 35 BET test booklets $16.26; 100 answer sheets (specify test) $19.86

Publisher: The Riverside Publishing Company

DIFFERENTIAL APTITUDE TESTS (DAT): FORMS S AND T
Refer to page 397.

DIFFERENTIAL APTITUDE TESTS (DAT): FORMS V AND W
Refer to page 397.

INTUITIVE MECHANICS (WEIGHTS AND PULLEYS)
Refer to page 977.

MINNESOTA ENGINEERING ANALOGIES TEST
M.D. Dunnette

Engineering and graduate
school applicants

Purpose: Measures engineering achievement and mathematical reasoning ability. Used for selection and placement of engineers and admission of graduate students.

Description: Multiple-item paper-pencil test of engineering skills and potential. Items are multiple-choice analogies. Examiner required. Suitable for group use.

Timed: 45 minutes

Scoring: Scoring service available

Cost: Contact publisher

Publisher: Admissions and Credentialing Group/The Psychological Corporation

MISSOURI APTITUDE AND CAREER INFORMATION INVENTORY (MACII)
Refer to page 752.

NIIP ENGINEERING SELECTION TEST BATTERY: ENGINEERING ARITHMETIC TEST EA4

Ages 15-adult

Purpose: Identifies engineering-related abilities of students. Used in counseling for selecting courses, apprenticeships, and occupations.

Description: Multiple-item paper-pencil test identifying candidates for engineering-related courses, apprenticeships, and occupations. One in a series of five tests in the NIIP Engineering Selection Battery. Examiner required. Suitable for group use.
BRITISH PUBLISHER

Timed: 22 minutes

Scoring: Hand key

Cost: 10 test booklets £4.90; marking key £2.25; instruction card £1.45

Publisher: NFER-NELSON Publishing Company Ltd.

NIIP ENGINEERING SELECTION TEST BATTERY: GROUP TEST 82

**Adolescent, adult
Ages 15-adult**

Purpose: Assesses the conceptual ability to rotate and turn over two-dimensional shapes. Used for selecting job applicants in engineering-related fields.

Description: Multiple-item four-part paper-pencil test assessing candidate's ability to rotate and turn over two-dimensional shapes in the mind's eye. The test booklet is reusable. One in a series of five tests in the NIIP Engineering Selection Battery. Examiner required. Suitable for group use.
BRITISH PUBLISHER

Timed: 30 minutes

Scoring: Hand key

Cost: 10 test booklets £11.10; 10 answer sheets £2.60; marking key £1.45; instruction card £1.45

Publisher: NFER-NELSON Publishing Company Ltd.

NIIP ENGINEERING SELECTION TEST BATTERY: GROUP TESTS 70 AND 70B

**Adolescent, adult
Ages 15-adult**

Purpose: Measures general intelligence of applicants for apprentice, managerial, supervisory, skilled, and clerical positions in engineering-related fields.

Description: Two paper-pencil tests assessing general intelligence through nonverbal questions. Each test contains three subtests: Coding, Matrices, and Series. Because the tests are not precisely parallel, separate norms are provided. One in a series of five tests in the NIIP Engineering Selection Battery. Examiner required. Suitable for group use.
BRITISH PUBLISHER

Timed: 30 minutes

Scoring: Hand key

Cost: 10 test booklets and answer sheets Part I £3.75; 10 test booklets Parts II and III £6.75; instruction card £1.45; marking key Part I £2.60; marking key Parts II and III £1.70; manual £4.80

Publisher: NFER-NELSON Publishing Company Ltd.

NIIP ENGINEERING SELECTION TEST BATTERY: GROUP TESTS 90A AND 90B

**Adolescent, adult
Ages 15-adult**

Purpose: Assesses the verbal abilities of adults with a fair level of educational achievement. Used for evaluating applicants for apprentice, management, supervisory, and skilled technical posts.

Description: Two paper-pencil tests of intelligence and verbal aptitude used for evaluating applicants for higher-level positions in engineering-related fields. One in a series of five tests in the NIIP Engineering Selection Battery. Examiner required. Suitable for group use.
BRITISH PUBLISHER

Timed: 30 minutes

Scoring: Hand key

Cost: 10 test booklets £6.30; marking key £1.70; instruction card £1.45; manual £2.25

Publisher: NFER-NELSON Publishing Company Ltd.

NIIP ENGINEERING SELECTION TEST BATTERY: VINCENT MECHANICAL DIAGRAMS TEST (REVISED)

Adolescent, adult
Ages 15-adult

Purpose: Assesses individual's ability to understand the concepts of cog, pulley, and lever systems.

Description: Multiple-item paper-pencil test using diagrams for assessing the mechanical understanding of candidates for positions in engineering-related fields. One in a series of five tests in the NIIP Engineering Selection Battery. Examiner required. Suitable for group use.
BRITISH PUBLISHER

Timed: 15 minutes

Scoring: Hand key

Cost: 10 test booklets £10.90; 10 answer sheets £2.25; marking key £3.30; instruction card £1.45

Publisher: NFER-NELSON Publishing Company Ltd.

NIIP TESTS—ENGINEERING SELECTION TEST BATTERY

Adult

Purpose: Assesses general intellectual ability and specific skills. Used for selecting student, professional, and industrial engineering applicants.

Description: Battery of paper-pencil tests measuring general and specific intellectual abilities. The manual provides administration details and scoring procedure for tests GT82, GT90A/B, GT^{70}/$_{70}$B, EA4, and VMD (1979 revision). Group Test 90A (GT90A) is a 4-part test of general intelligence and verbal aptitude for adults of above-average educational attainment. Group Test 90B (GT90B) is an alternative to GT90A, containing similar but different items. Group Test 70 (GT70) is a 3-part general intelligence test for use with groups of above average educational attainment. Group Test 70B (GT70B) is a similar but alternative test to GT70. Engineering Arithmetic Test 4 (EA4) is a metricated test. Group Test 82 (GT82) is a 4-part test measuring comprehension of shapes and spatial relationships. The Vincents Mechanical Diagrams Test-1979 Revision contains four subtests containing mechanical problems. Examiner required. Suitable for group use.
BRITISH PUBLISHER

Timed: Varies, depending on test

Scoring: Hand key

Cost: Contact publisher

Publisher: NFER-NELSON Publishing Company Ltd.

THE OHIO VOCATIONAL ACHIEVEMENT TEST PROGRAM

Adolescent   Grades 9-12

Purpose: Measures high-school students' abilities and understanding of specific vocational areas. Used to evaluate teaching objectives and materials and for counseling and program supervision.

Description: Tests junior and senior vocational high-school students in 11 vocational areas. The program is part of a test battery package that includes the California Short Form Test of Academic Aptitude (SFTAA). The complete battery, to be administered on any three consecutive days during the first three weeks of March in Ohio (non-Ohio at all times), reveals the correlation of student academic aptitude and vocational achievement. The test measures students' ability to solve problems, analyze data, use abstractions in specific situations, and assemble parts to form a complete structure. The test also assesses student knowledge of principles and specifics. The test booklets are controlled and must be returned after use. Examiner required. Suitable for group use.

Timed: SFTAA 1 hour; Parts I and II 2 hours each

Scoring: Computer scored

Cost: Testing loan service (test booklets, answer sheets, scoring service) Ohio students $1.25 each; out-of-state students $2.50 each for March administration, $3.50 at other times

Publisher: Instructional Materials Laboratory, The Ohio State University

---

THE OHIO VOCATIONAL ACHIEVEMENT TEST PROGRAM: CALIFORNIA SHORT FORM TEST OF ACADEMIC APTITUDE, LEVEL 5 (SFTAA)

Adolescent   Grades 9-12

Purpose: Helps evaluate student comprehension of word and idea relationships. Used as a part of the Ohio Vocational Education Achievement Test battery in high-school vocational programs to evaluate achievement and provide motivation.

Description: 85-item paper-pencil multiple-choice test in two parts. The Language section contains a 25-item test of word meaning, verbal comprehension, and word relationships and a 20-item memory test based on a story read to students. The Non-Language section consists of a 20-item analogies test of literal or symbolic relationships and a 20-item sequence test of numerical and geometric patterns. Each test is timed separately. They precede the Ohio Vocational Achievement Tests, which complete the battery package. The battery is administered on any three consecutive days during the first three weeks of March in Ohio (non-Ohio at all times). The test booklet, answer document, and

instruction booklet are controlled items to be returned after use. Examiner required. Suitable for group use.

Timed: 1 hour, including demographic data coding

Scoring: Computer scored

Cost: Testing loan service (test booklets, answer sheets, scoring service) is included as a part of the Ohio Vocational Achievement Testing Program

Publisher: CTB/McGraw-Hill

THE OHIO VOCATIONAL ACHIEVEMENT TESTS IN AGRICULTURAL EDUCATION: AGRICULTURAL BUSINESS

Adolescent   Grades 9-12

Purpose: Evaluates and diagnoses achievement for instructional improvement in agricultural business. May be used for vocational guidance in an overall program.

Description: 300-item paper-pencil test in two parts. Part I (146 items) covers agricultural careers, human relations, office procedures, agricultural service—animals, and advertising and promotions. Part II (162 items) covers agricultural services—plants, sales, marketing and storage, and money management. Examiner required. Suitable for group use.

Timed: 2 hours per part

Scoring: Computer scored

Cost: Testing loan service (test booklets, answer sheets, scoring service) Ohio students $1.25 each; out-of-state students $2.50 each for March administration, $3.50 at other times

Publisher: Instructional Materials Laboratory, The Ohio State University

---

THE OHIO VOCATIONAL ACHIEVEMENT TESTS IN AGRICULTURAL EDUCATION: AGRICULTURAL MECHANIC

Adolescent   Grades 9-12

Purpose: Evaluates and diagnoses achievement for instructional improvement in agricultural mechanics. May be used for vocational guidance in an overall program.

Description: 343-item paper-pencil multiple-choice test in two parts. Part I (167 items) covers engine service and repair, carburetion systems, diesel engines, cooling systems, hydraulic systems, brakes and steering, and equipment assembly. Part II (176 items) covers charging systems and accessories, cranking systems, ignition systems, power trains and transmissions, metal fabrication and refinishing, heating, ventilation and air conditioning, and personal development. Examiner required. Suitable for group use.

Timed: 2 hours per part

Scoring: Computer scored

Cost: Testing loan service (test booklets, answer sheets, scoring service) Ohio students $1.25 each; out-of-state students $2.50 each for March administration, $3.50 at other times

Publisher: Instructional Materials Laboratory, The Ohio State University

THE OHIO VOCATIONAL ACHIEVEMENT TESTS IN AGRICULTURAL EDUCATION: FARM MANAGEMENT

Adolescent   Grades 9-12

Purpose: Evaluates and diagnoses achievement for instructional improvement in farm management. May be used for vocational guidance in an overall program.

Description: 304-item paper-pencil multiple-choice test in two parts. Part I (137 items) covers plan and work supervision, farm record analysis, buildings and structures, finance operations, and inventory. Part II (167 items) covers planning crop enterprises, marketing products, planning livestock enterprises, equipment and machinery, general management duties, and employment procedures. Examiner required. Suitable for group use.

Timed: 2 hours per part

Scoring: Computer scored

Cost: Testing loan service (test booklets, answer sheets, scoring service) Ohio students $1.25 each; out-of-state students $2.50 each for March administration, $3.50 at other times

Publisher: Instructional Materials Laboratory, The Ohio State University

THE OHIO VOCATIONAL ACHIEVEMENT TESTS IN AGRICULTURAL EDUCATION: HORTICULTURE

Adolescent   Grades 9-12

Purpose: Evaluates and diagnoses achievement for instructional improvement in horticulture. May be used for vocational guidance in an overall program.

Description: 363-item paper-pencil multiple-choice test in two parts. Part I (179 items) covers soil and plant science, greenhouse operations, interior plantscape services, landscape services, and turf services. Part II (184 items) covers retail floriculture, nursery, garden center, fruit and vegetable, production, equipment and mechanics, and personal development. Examiner required. Suitable for group use.

Timed: 2 hours per part

Scoring: Computer scored

Cost: Testing loan service (test booklets, answer sheets, scoring service) Ohio students $1.25 each; out-of-state students $2.50 each for March administration, $3.50 at other times

Publisher: Instructional Materials Laboratory, The Ohio State University

THE OHIO VOCATIONAL ACHIEVEMENT TESTS IN AGRICULTURAL EDUCATION: PRODUCTION AGRICULTURE

Adolescent   Grades 9-12

Purpose: Evaluates and diagnoses achievement for instructional improvement in production agriculture. May be used for vocational guidance in an overall program.

Description: 353-item paper-pencil multiple-choice test in two parts. Part I (177

items) covers beef production, sheep production, soybean production, crop chemical application, and agriculture instruction. Part II (176 items) covers operator equipment maintenance, dairy production, corn production, swine production, forage production, and employment procedures. Examiner required. Suitable for group use.

Timed: 2 hours per part

Scoring: Computer scored

Cost: Testing loan service (test booklets, answer sheets, scoring service) Ohio students $1.25 each; out-of-state students $2.50 each for March administration, $3.50 at other times

Publisher: Instructional Materials Laboratory, The Ohio State University

---

THE OHIO VOCATIONAL ACHIEVEMENT TESTS IN BUSINESS AND OFFICE EDUCATION: ACCOUNTING/ COMPUTING CLERK

Adolescent   Grades 9-12

Purpose: Evaluates and diagnoses achievement for instructional improvement in accounting/computing clerk area. May be used for vocational guidance in an overall program.

Description: 321-item paper-pencil multiple-choice test in two parts. Part I (159 items) covers sales and receivables, payroll records, maintaining inventory records and files, completing the accounting cycle, and worksheet information. Part II (162 items) covers processing purchases and payables, specialized accounting and office functions, cash receipts and payments, mechanical and electronic data accounting, and employment procedures. Examiner required. Suitable for group use.

Timed: 2 hours per part

Scoring: Computer scored

Cost: Testing loan service (test booklets, answer sheets, scoring service) Ohio students $1.25 each; out-of-state students $2.50 each for March administration, $3.50 at other times

Publisher: Instructional Materials Laboratory, The Ohio State University

---

THE OHIO VOCATIONAL ACHIEVEMENT TESTS IN BUSINESS AND OFFICE EDUCATION: CLERK-STENOGRAPHER

Adolescent   Grades 9-12

Purpose: Evaluates and diagnoses achievement for instructional improvement in clerk-stenographer area. May be used for vocational guidance in an overall program.

Description: 278-item paper-pencil multiple-choice test in two parts. Part I (159 items) covers dictation, correspondence, and financial records. Part II (119 items) covers communications, copy reproduction, record management, and personal development-employment. Examiner required. Suitable for group use.

Timed: 2 hours per part

Scoring: Computer scored

Cost: Testing loan service (test booklets, answer sheets, scoring service) Ohio students $1.25 each; out-of-state students $2.50 each for March administration, $3.50 at other times

Publisher: Instructional Materials Laboratory, The Ohio State University

---

THE OHIO VOCATIONAL ACHIEVEMENT TESTS IN BUSINESS AND OFFICE EDUCATION: CLERK TYPIST

Adolescent   Grades 9-12

Purpose: Evaluates and diagnoses achievement for instructional improvement in clerk typing programs. May be used for vocational guidance in an overall program.

Description: 332-item paper-pencil multiple-choice test in two parts. Part I (164 items) covers letters, envelopes, and memos; filing; proofreading and editing; mail procedures; and employment procedures and human relations. Part II (168 items) covers reports, manuscripts and forms, accounting/calculating, telephone and receptionist, machine transcription/

word processing, and reprographics. Examiner required. Suitable for group use.

Timed: 2 hours per part

Scoring: Computer scored

Cost: Testing loan service (test booklets, answer sheets, scoring service) Ohio students $1.25 each; out-of-state students $2.50 each for March administration, $3.50 at other times

Publisher: Instructional Materials Laboratory, The Ohio State University

THE OHIO VOCATIONAL ACHIEVEMENT TESTS IN BUSINESS AND OFFICE EDUCATION: DATA PROCESSING

Adolescent   Grades 9-12

Purpose: Evaluates and diagnoses achievement for instructional improvement in data processing. May be used for vocational guidance in an overall program.

Description: 346-item paper-pencil multiple-choice test in two parts. Part I (166 items) covers computer systems, clerical procedures, programming languages, human relations, and automated electronic data processing equipment. Part II (180 items) covers flow charting, data entry, operations, business math-accounting, and employment procedures. Examiner required. Suitable for group use.

Timed: 2 hours per part

Scoring: Computer scored

Cost: Testing loan service (test booklets, answer sheets, scoring service) Ohio students $1.25 each; out-of-state students $2.50 each for March administration, $3.50 at other times

Publisher: Instructional Materials Laboratory, The Ohio State University

THE OHIO VOCATIONAL ACHIEVEMENT TESTS IN BUSINESS AND OFFICE EDUCATION: GENERAL OFFICE CLERK

Adolescent   Grades 9-12

Purpose: Evaluates and diagnoses achievement for instructional improvement in general office area. May be used for vocational guidance in an overall program.

Description: 392-item paper-pencil multiple-choice test in two parts. Part I (200 items) covers reception, telephone, and electronic communications; financial records; preparing typewritten copy; and records management. Part II (192 items) covers reprographics, mailing, and shipping; accounting functions; information processing and transcription; composition and editing; and personal development and human relations. Examiner required. Suitable for group use.

Timed: 2 hours per part

Scoring: Computer scored

Cost: Testing loan service (test booklets, answer sheets, scoring service) Ohio students $1.25 each; out-of-state students $2.50 each for March administration, $3.50 at other times

Publisher: Instructional Materials Laboratory, The Ohio State University

THE OHIO VOCATIONAL ACHIEVEMENT TESTS IN BUSINESS AND OFFICE EDUCATION: WORD PROCESSING

Adolescent   Grades 9-12

Purpose: Evaluates and diagnoses achievement for instructional improvement in word processing. May by used for vocational guidance in an overall program.

Description: 345-item paper-pencil multiple-choice test in two parts. Part I (170 items) covers typing and transcription, reprographics, word processing concepts and procedures, business transactions, and proofreading and editing. Part II (175 items) covers automated word processing equipment, receptionist duties, composition and dictation, records management, and employment procedures. Examiner required. Suitable for group use.

Timed: 2 hours per part

Scoring: Computer scored

Cost: Testing loan service (test booklets, answer sheets, scoring service) Ohio students $1.25 each; out-of-state students $2.50 each for March administration, $3.50 at other times

Publisher: Instructional Materials Laboratory, The Ohio State University

THE OHIO VOCATIONAL ACHIEVEMENT TESTS IN CONSTRUCTION TRADES: BUILDING MAINTENANCE

Adolescent   Grades 9-12

Purpose: Evaluates and diagnoses achievement for instructional improvement in building maintenanace. May be used for vocational guidance in an overall program.

Description: 325-item paper-pencil multiple-choice test in two parts. Part I (164 items) covers carpentry, masonry, electrical, heating and air conditioning, and painting and decorating. Part II (161 items) covers plumbing, welding, flooring, custodial, grounds and landscape, and personal development. Examiner required. Suitable for group use.

Timed: 2 hours per part

Scoring: Computer scored

Cost: Testing loan service (test booklets, answer sheets, scoring service) Ohio students $1.25 each; out-of-state students $2.50 each for March administration, $3.50 at other times

Publisher: Instructional Materials Laboratory, The Ohio State University

THE OHIO VOCATIONAL ACHIEVEMENT TESTS IN CONSTRUCTION TRADES: CARPENTRY

Adolescent   Grades 9-12

Purpose: Evaluates and diagnoses achievement for instructional improvement in carpentry. May be used for vocational guidance in an overall program.

Description: 325-item paper-pencil multiple-choice test in two parts. Part I (159 items) covers blueprint reading, surveying, foundations, floor framing, wall and

ceiling framing, insulation, and mathematics and estimating. Part II (166 items) covers roof framing, roofing, exterior finish, and interior finish. Examiner required. Suitable for group use.

Timed: 2 hours per part

Scoring: Computer scored

Cost: Testing loan service (test booklets, answer sheets, scoring service) Ohio students $1.25 each; out-of-state students $2.50 each for March administration, $3.50 at other times

Publisher: Instructional Materials Laboratory, The Ohio State University

THE OHIO VOCATIONAL ACHIEVEMENT TESTS IN CONSTRUCTION TRADES: CONSTRUCTION ELECTRICITY

Adolescent   Grades 9-12

Purpose: Evaluates and diagnoses achievement for instructional improvement in construction electricity. May be used for vocational guidance in an overall program.

Description: 317-item paper-pencil multiple-choice test in two parts. Part I (158 items) covers basic electricity, National Electric Code, planning and layout, rough-in wiring, and finish wiring. Part II (159 items) covers safety, service entrance, motors and controls, low voltage systems, electricians' mathematics, and tools and personal development. Examiner required. Suitable for group use.

Timed: 2 hours per part

Scoring: Computer scored

Cost: Testing loan service (test booklets, answer sheets, scoring service) Ohio students $1.25 each; out-of-state students $2.50 each for March administration, $3.50 at other times

Publisher: Instructional Materials Laboratory, The Ohio State University

THE OHIO VOCATIONAL ACHIEVEMENT TESTS IN CONSTRUCTION TRADES: HEATING, AIR CONDITIONING, AND REFRIGERATION

Adolescent   Grades 9-12

Purpose: Evaluates and diagnoses achievement for instructional improvement in heating, air conditioning, and refrigeration. May be used for vocational guidance in an overall program.

Description: 359-item paper-pencil multiple-choice test in two parts. Part I (183 items) covers installing heating systems, installing refrigeration and air conditioning equipment, and troubleshooting refrigeration and air conditioning equipment. Part II (176 items) covers service and repair of refrigeration and air conditioning equipment-mechanical; service and repair of refrigeration and air conditioning equipment-electrical; troubleshooting, service, and repair of oil heating systems; troubleshooting, service, and repair alternate heating systems; and personal development. Examiner required. Suitable for group use.

Timed: 2 hours per part

Scoring: Computer scored

Cost: Testing loan service (test booklets, answer sheets, scoring service) Ohio students $1.25 each; out-of-state students $2.50 each for March administration, $3.50 at other times

Publisher: Instructional Materials Laboratory, The Ohio State University

THE OHIO VOCATIONAL ACHIEVEMENT TESTS IN CONSTRUCTION TRADES: MASONRY

Adolescent   Grades 9-12

Purpose: Evaluates and diagnoses achievement for instructional improvement in masonry. May be used for vocational guidance in an overall program.

Description: 299-item paper-pencil multiple-choice test in two parts. Part I (154 items) covers job-site and material preparation, laying brick and block to a line, laying brick and block with a plumb rule, fireplaces and chimneys, and arches. Part II (145 items) covers miscellaneous masonry construction, concrete masonry, surveying, mathematics and blueprint reading, and personal development. Examiner required. Suitable for group use.

Timed: 2 hours per part

Scoring: Computer scored

Cost: Testing loan service (test booklets, answer sheets, scoring service) Ohio students $1.25 each; out-of-state students $2.50 each for March administration, $3.50 at other times

Publisher: Instructional Materials Laboratory, The Ohio State University

THE OHIO VOCATIONAL ACHIEVEMENT TESTS IN ELECTRONICS: COMMUNICATION PRODUCTS ELECTRONICS

Adolescent   Grades 9-12

Purpose: Evaluates and diagnoses achievement for instructional improvement in industrial electronics. May be used for vocational guidance in an overall program.

Description: 338-item paper-pencil multiple-choice test in two parts. Part I (176 items) covers personal development, DC electronics, AC electronics, active electronic devices, electronic circuitry, and electronic test equipment. Part II (162 items) covers audio systems, radio receivers, TV receiver systems, transmitter systems, antenna and transmission systems, and digital logic systems. Examiner required. Suitable for group use.

Timed: 2 hours per part

Scoring: Computer scored

Cost: Testing loan service (test booklets, answer sheets, scoring service) Ohio students $1.25 each; out-of-state students $2.50 each for March administration, $3.50 at other times

Publisher: Instructional Materials Laboratory, The Ohio State University

THE OHIO VOCATIONAL ACHIEVEMENT TESTS IN ELECTRONICS: INDUSTRIAL ELECTRONICS

Adolescent   Grades 9-12

Purpose: Evaluates and diagnoses achievement for instructional improvement in industrial electronics. May be used for vocational guidance in an overall program.

Description: 326-item paper-pencil multiple-choice test in two parts. Part I (168 items) covers personal development; selling, installing, and testing equipment; fabricating circuits and enclosures; DC electronics; AC electronics; semiconductors; and test equipment. Part II (158 items) covers analog electronic equipment, digital logic, digital electronic circuits, troubleshooting and analysis, special electronic devices, and electromechanical devices. Examiner required. Suitable for group use.

Timed: 2 hours per part

Scoring: Computer scored

Cost: Testing loan service (test booklets, answer sheets, scoring service) Ohio students $1.25 each; out-of-state students $2.50 each for March administration, $3.50 at other times

Publisher: Instructional Materials Laboratory, The Ohio State University

---

THE OHIO VOCATIONAL ACHIEVEMENT TESTS IN GRAPHICS COMMUNICATION: COMMERICAL ART

Adolescent   Grades 9-12   ☞ ✍

Purpose: Evaluates and diagnoses achievement for instructional improvement in commercial art. May be used for vocational guidance in an overall program.

Description: 311-item paper-pencil multiple-choice test in two parts. Part I (153 items) covers drawing, design, illustration, technique, and color. Part II (158 items) covers drafting, mechanical, photography, layout, and typography. Examiner required. Suitable for group use.

Timed: 2 hours per part

Scoring: Computer scored

Cost: Testing loan service (test booklets, answer sheets, scoring service) Ohio students $1.25 each; out-of-state students $2.50 each for March administration, $3.50 at other times

Publisher: Instructional Materials Laboratory, The Ohio State University

---

THE OHIO VOCATIONAL ACHIEVEMENT TESTS IN GRAPHICS COMMUNICATION: DRAFTING

Adolescent   Grades 9-12   ☞ ✍

Purpose: Evaluates and diagnoses achievement for instructional improvement in drafting. May be used for vocational guidance in an overall program.

Description: 347-item paper-pencil multiple-choice test in two parts. Part I (171 items) covers geometric shapes and construction, orthographic and auxiliary projection, pictorial drawing, sectional views, production/working drawings, fastening methods, and industrial materials and processes. Part II (176 items) covers dimensions and tolerances, intersections and developments, mechanics, architectural drawings, structural and civil drawings, electrical and electronic drawings, and personal development. Examiner required. Suitable for group use.

Timed: 2 hours per part

Scoring: Computer scored

Cost: Testing loan service (test booklets, answer sheets, scoring service) Ohio students $1.25 each; out-of-state students $2.50 each for March administration, $3.50 at other times

Publisher: Instructional Materials Laboratory, The Ohio State University

---

THE OHIO VOCATIONAL ACHIEVEMENT TESTS IN GRAPHICS COMMUNICATION: LITHOGRAPHIC PRINTING

Adolescent   Grades 9-12   ☞ ✍

Purpose: Evaluates and diagnoses achievement for instructional improvement in lithographic printing. May be used for vocational guidance in an overall program.

Description: Multiple-item paper-pencil multiple-choice test in two parts. Part I covers layout and design, composing, paste up, proofing, camera and film processing, and personal development. Part

II covers platemaking and proofs, offset presses, stripping, and finishing operations. Examiner required. Suitable for group use.

Timed: 2 hours per part

Scoring: Computer scored

Cost: Testing loan service (test booklets, answer sheets, scoring service) Ohio students $1.25 each; out-of-state students $2.50 each for March administration, $3.50 at other times

Publisher: Instructional Materials Laboratory, The Ohio State University

THE OHIO VOCATIONAL ACHIEVEMENT TESTS IN HEALTH OCCUPATIONS EDUCATION: DENTAL ASSISTING

Adolescent   Grades 9-12   ☞ ✍

Purpose: Evaluates and diagnoses achievement for instructional improvement in dental assistance. May be used for vocational guidance in an overall program.

Description: 344-item paper-pencil multiple-choice test in two parts. Part I (167 items) covers anatomy, microbiology and sterilization, dental emergencies and pharmacology, dental laboratory, restorative and impression materials, preventive dentistry, and ethics and personal development. Part II (177 items) covers radiology, dental office management, chairside assisting—basic, chairside assisting—prosthetics, chairside assisting—oral surgery and pathology, chairside assisting—other specialties, and expanded duties. Examiner required. Suitable for group use.

Timed: 2 hours per part

Scoring: Computer scored

Cost: Testing loan service (test booklets, answer sheets, scoring service) Ohio students $1.25 each; out-of-state students $2.50 each for March administration, $3.50 at other times

Publisher: Instructional Materials Laboratory, The Ohio State University

THE OHIO VOCATIONAL ACHIEVEMENT TESTS IN HEALTH OCCUPATIONS EDUCATION: DIVERSIFIED HEALTH OCCUPATION

Adolescent   Grades 9-12   ☞ ✍

Purpose: Evaluates and diagnoses achievement for instructional improvement in health occupation areas. May be used for vocational guidance in an overall program.

Description: Multiple-item paper-pencil multiple-choice test in two parts. Part I covers anatomy and physiology, asepsis and sterilization, vital signs, acute care nursing, and ward clerk. Part II covers emergency first aid; long-term care nursing; home health aide; medical assisting and laboratory; dental assisting; and personal development, employment skills, and ethics. Examiner required. Suitable for group use.

Timed: 2 hours per part

Scoring: Computer scored

Cost: Testing loan service (test booklets, answer sheets, scoring service) Ohio students $1.25 each; out-of-state students $2.50 each for March administration, $3.50 at other times

Publisher: Instructional Materials Laboratory, The Ohio State University

THE OHIO VOCATIONAL ACHIEVEMENT TESTS IN HEALTH OCCUPATIONS EDUCATION: MEDICAL ASSISTING

Adolescent   Grades 9-12   ☞ ✍

Purpose: Evaluates and diagnoses achievement for instructional improvement in medical assistance. May be used for vocational guidance in an overall program.

Description: 339-item paper-pencil multiple-choice test in two parts. Part I (170 items) covers personal development, body systems, clinical skills, medications, and medical office skills. Part II (169 items) covers sterilization, laboratory skills, E.K.G., X-ray, diet and nutrition, first aid, medical terminology, and medical office computation. Examiner required. Suitable for group use.

Timed: 2 hours per part

Scoring: Computer scored

Cost: Testing loan service (test booklets, answer sheets, scoring service) Ohio students $1.25 each; out-of-state students $2.50 each for March administration, $3.50 at other times

Publisher: Instructional Materials Laboratory, The Ohio State University

THE OHIO VOCATIONAL ACHIEVEMENT TESTS IN HOME ECONOMICS EDUCATION: CHILD CARE SERVICES

Adolescent   Grades 9-12

Purpose: Evaluates and diagnoses achievement for instructional improvement in child care programs. May be used for vocational guidance in an overall program.

Description: 360-item paper-pencil multiple-choice test in two parts. Part I (182 items) covers managing the center, maintaining facilities and supplies, program planning, conducting routine activities, and infant/toddler instruction. Part II (178 items) covers preschool instruction, elementary school instruction, exceptional children instruction, and personal development. Examiner required. Suitable for group use.

Timed: 2 hours per part

Scoring: Computer scored

Cost: Testing loan service (test booklets, answer sheets, scoring service) Ohio students $1.25 each; out-of-state students $2.50 each for March administration, $3.50 at other times

Publisher: Instructional Materials Laboratory, The Ohio State University

THE OHIO VOCATIONAL ACHIEVEMENT TESTS IN HOME ECONOMICS EDUCATION: COMMUNITY AND HOME SERVICES

Adolescent   Grades 9-12

Purpose: Evaluates and diagnoses achievement for instructional improve-

ment in community and home services. May be used for vocational guidance in an overall program.

Description: 354-item paper-pencil multiple-choice test in two parts. Part I (179 items) covers personal care for patient; vital signs; lifting, moving, and transporting patients; special care; infant and child care; and food service. Part II (175 items) covers care of cleaning equipment; care of furnishings; care of resilient and masonry floors; care of draperies, upholstery, and carpeting; room care; care of restrooms; care of public areas; laundry service; and careers and employment. Examiner required. Suitable for group use.

Timed: 2 hours per part

Scoring: Computer scored

Cost: Testing loan service (test booklets, answer sheets, scoring service) Ohio students $1.25 each; out-of-state students $2.50 each for March administration, $3.50 at other times

Publisher: Instructional Materials Laboratory, The Ohio State University

THE OHIO VOCATIONAL ACHIEVEMENT TESTS IN HOME ECONOMICS EDUCATION: FABRIC SERVICE

Adolescent   Grades 9-12

Purpose: Evaluates and diagnoses achievement for instructional improvement in fabric services. May be used for vocational guidance in an overall program.

Description: 391-item paper-pencil multiple-choice test in two parts. Part I (184 items) covers alteration specialist, custom dressmaker, custom tailor, fabric coordinator, fashion coordinator, power machine operator, and dry cleaner. Part II (187 items) covers interior design specialist, drapery consultant, drapery maker, drapery installer, slipcover maker, upholsterer, refinisher, and careers and employment. Examiner required. Suitable for group use.

Timed: 2 hours per part

Scoring: Computer scored

Cost: Testing loan service (test booklets, answer sheets, scoring service) Ohio students $1.25 each; out-of-state students $2.50 each for March administration, $3.50 at other times

Publisher: Instructional Materials Laboratory, The Ohio State University

THE OHIO VOCATIONAL ACHIEVEMENT TESTS IN HOME ECONOMICS EDUCATION: FOOD SERVICES

Adolescent   Grades 9-12 ☞ ✍

Purpose: Evaluates and diagnoses achievement for instructional improvement in food services. May be used for vocational guidance in an overall program.

Description: 376-item paper-pencil multiple-choice test in two parts. Part I (185 items) covers baker, cook-chef, pantry worker, caterer, and dietary aide. Part II (191 items) covers dining-room service, cafeteria line, sanitation and safety, storeroom operations, and careers and employment. Examiner required. Suitable for group use.

Timed: 2 hours per part

Scoring: Computer scored

Cost: Testing loan service (test booklets, answer sheets, scoring service) Ohio students $1.25 each; out-of-state students $2.50 each for March administration, $3.50 at other times

Publisher: Instructional Materials Laboratory, The Ohio State University

THE OHIO VOCATIONAL ACHIEVEMENT TESTS IN MARKETING EDUCATION: APPAREL AND ACCESSORIES

Adolescent   Grades 9-12 ☞ ✍

Purpose: Evaluates and diagnoses achievement for instructional improvement in apparel and accessories. May be used for vocational guidance in an overall program.

Description: 346-item paper-pencil multiple-choice test in two parts. Part I (174 items) covers cashiering, merchandise display, sales, stockkeeping and inventory

control, and first-line management. Part II (172 items) covers product knowledge, receiving and marking merchandise, support functions, customer services, and obtaining employment. Examiner required. Suitable for group use.

Timed: 2 hours per part

Scoring: Computer scored

Cost: Testing loan service (test booklets, answer sheets, scoring service) Ohio students $1.25 each; out-of-state students $2.50 each for March administration, $3.50 at other times

Publisher: Instructional Materials Laboratory, The Ohio State University

THE OHIO VOCATIONAL ACHIEVEMENT TESTS IN MARKETING EDUCATION: FOOD MARKETING

Adolescent   Grades 9-12 ☞ ✍

Purpose: Evaluates and diagnoses achievement for instructional improvement in food marketing. May be used for vocational guidance in an overall program.

Description: 387-item paper-pencil multiple-choice test in two parts. Part I (187 items) covers receiving and storing, operations, front end operations, product and service technology, selling, and advertising. Part II (200 items) covers display/merchandising; communications; human relations; economics, marketing, and entrepreneurship; and personal development. Examiner required. Suitable for group use.

Timed: 2 hours per part

Scoring: Computer scored

Cost: Testing loan service (test booklets, answer sheets, scoring service) Ohio students $1.25 each; out-of-state students $2.50 each for March administration, $3.50 at other times

Publisher: Instructional Materials Laboratory, The Ohio State University

THE OHIO VOCATIONAL ACHIEVEMENT TESTS IN MARKETING EDUCATION: FOOD SERVICE PERSONNEL

Adolescent   Grades 9-12

Purpose: Evaluates and diagnoses achievement for instructional improvement in food service. May be used for vocational guidance in an overall program.

Description: 316-item paper-pencil multiple-choice test in two parts. Part I (154 items) covers restaurant management, inventory and purchasing procedures, business principles, waiter-waitressing, and cashiering. Part II (162 items) covers employment procedures, human relations, communications, selling principles, advertising, product-service information, and safety and housekeeping. Examiner required. Suitable for group use.

Timed: 2 hours per part

Scoring: Computer scored

Cost: Testing loan service (test booklets, answer sheets, scoring service) Ohio students $1.25 each; out-of-state students $2.50 each for March administration, $3.50 at other times

Publisher: Instructional Materials Laboratory, The Ohio State University

---

THE OHIO VOCATIONAL ACHIEVEMENT TESTS IN MARKETING EDUCATION: GENERAL MERCHANDISING

Adolescent   Grades 9-12

Purpose: Evaluates and diagnoses achievement for instructional improvement in general merchandising. May be used for vocational guidance in an overall program.

Description: 352-item paper-pencil multiple-choice test in two parts. Part I (188 items) covers employment procedures, human relations, business principles, communications, and financial transactions. Part II (164 items) covers selling, marketing, cashiering, inventory procedures, housekeeping and security,

advertising and display, and product and service technology. Examiner required. Suitable for group use.

Timed: 2 hours per part

Scoring: Computer scored

Cost: Testing loan service (test booklets, answer sheets, scoring service) Ohio students $1.25 each; out-of-state students $2.50 each for March administration, $3.50 at other times

Publisher: Instructional Materials Laboratory, The Ohio State University

---

THE OHIO VOCATIONAL ACHIEVEMENT TESTS IN METAL TRADES: MACHINE TRADES

Adolescent   Grades 9-12

Purpose: Evaluates and diagnoses achievement for instructional improvement in machine trades. May be used for vocational guidance in an overall program.

Description: Multiple-item paper-pencil multiple-choice test in two parts. Part I covers benchwork, inspection and measuring instruments, drilling machines, turning machines, and saws and special operations. Part II covers milling, layout and blueprint, abrasive machining, heat treating and applied science, N.C./C.N.C., and personal development. Examiner required. Suitable for group use.

Timed: 2 hours per part

Scoring: Computer scored

Cost: Testing loan service (test booklets, answer sheets, scoring service) Ohio students $1.25 each; out-of-state students $2.50 each for March administration, $3.50 at other times

Publisher: Instructional Materials Laboratory, The Ohio State University

---

THE OHIO VOCATIONAL ACHIEVEMENT TESTS IN METAL TRADES: WELDING

Adolescent   Grades 9-12

Purpose: Evaluates and diagnoses achievement for instructional improvement in welding. May be used for vocational guidance in an overall program.

Description: 393-item paper-pencil multiple-choice test in two parts. Part I (200 items) covers oxyfuel welding, shielded metal arc welding, fabrication and assembly, and personal development. Part II (193 items) covers gas tungsten arc welding, gas metal arc welding, specialized welding process (resistance, plasma, and submerged arc). Examiner required. Suitable for group use.

Timed: 2 hours per part

Scoring: Computer scored

Cost: Testing loan service (test booklets, answer sheets, scoring service) Ohio students $1.25 each; out-of-state students $2.50 each for March administration, $3.50 at other times

Publisher: Instructional Materials Laboratory, The Ohio State University

THE OHIO VOCATIONAL ACHIEVEMENT TESTS IN PERSONAL SERVICES: COSMETOLOGY

Adolescent   Grades 9-12

Purpose: Evaluates and diagnoses achievement for instructional improvement in cosmetology. May be used for vocational guidance in an overall program.

Description: 338-item paper-pencil multiple-choice test in two parts. Part I (173 items) covers sanitation, scalp care, manicure, hair shaping, hair styling, and facials. Part II (165 items) covers permanent waving, hair coloring, applied science, and shop management and mathematics. Examiner required. Suitable for group use.

Timed: 2 hours per part

Scoring: Computer scored

Cost: Testing loan service (test booklets, answer sheets, scoring service) Ohio students $1.25 each; out-of-state students $2.50 each for March administration, $3.50 at other times

Publisher: Instructional Materials Laboratory, The Ohio State University

THE OHIO VOCATIONAL ACHIEVEMENT TESTS IN TRADE AND INDUSTRIAL EDUCATION: AUTOMOTIVE—AUTO BODY MECHANIC

Adolescent   Grades 9-12

Purpose: Evaluates and diagnoses achievement for instructional improvement in auto body mechanics. May be used for vocational guidance in an overall program.

Description: 393-item paper-pencil multiple-choice test in two parts. Part I (197 items) covers welding, repair and straightening, patch and fill, fiberglass and plastic repair, panel replacement, reconditioning, and refinishing. Part II (196 items) covers trim, hardware, and glass; frame and unit body repair; suspension systems; engine cooling systems; heating and air conditioning; electrical systems; and personal development and shop management. Examiner required. Suitable for group use.

Timed: 2 hours per part

Scoring: Computer scored

Cost: Testing loan service (test booklets, answer sheets, scoring service) Ohio students $1.25 each; out-of-state students $2.50 each for March administration, $3.50 at other times

Publisher: Instructional Materials Laboratory, The Ohio State University

THE OHIO VOCATIONAL ACHIEVEMENT TESTS IN TRADE AND INDUSTRIAL EDUCATION: AUTOMOTIVE—AUTOMOTIVE MECHANICS

Adolescent   Grades 9-12

Purpose: Evaluates and diagnoses achievement for instructional improvement in automotive mechanics. May be used for vocational guidance in an overall program.

Description: 364-item paper-pencil multiple-choice test in two parts. Part I (169 items) covers lubrication and preventive maintenance; engine service and repair, cooling systems, fuel and exhaust systems, ignition systems, and personal development. Part II (181 items) covers charging systems; accessory systems; transmissions and drive line; emission systems; brake systems; steering and suspension systems; and heating, ventilation, and air conditioning systems. Examiner required. Suitable for group use.

Timed: 2 hours per part

Scoring: Computer scored

Cost: Testing loan service (test booklets, answer sheets, scoring service) Ohio students $1.25 each; out-of-state students $2.50 each for March administration, $3.50 at other times

Publisher: Instructional Materials Laboratory, The Ohio State University

---

THE OHIO VOCATIONAL ACHIEVEMENT TESTS IN TRADE AND INDUSTRIAL EDUCATION: AUTOMOTIVE—DIESEL MECHANIC

Adolescent   Grades 9-12

Purpose: Evaluates and diagnoses achievement for instructional improvement in industrial electronics. May be used for vocational guidance in an overall program.

Description: 332-item paper-pencil multiple-choice test in two parts. Part I (168 items) covers engine service and repair, fuel systems, intake systems, charging and cranking systems, electrical and ignition systems, and hydraulic systems. Part II (164 items) covers cooling systems, drive line, steering systems, suspension systems, brake systems, heating and air conditioning systems, lubrication and preventive maintenance, and service management. Examiner required. Suitable for group use.

Timed: 2 hours per part

Scoring: Computer scored

Cost: Testing loan service (test booklets, answer sheets, scoring service) Ohio students $1.25 each; out-of-state students $2.50 each for March administration, $3.50 at other times

Publisher: Instructional Materials Laboratory, The Ohio State University

THE OHIO VOCATIONAL ACHIEVEMENT TESTS IN TRADE AND INDUSTRIAL EDUCATION: AUTOMOTIVE—SMALL ENGINE REPAIR

Adolescent   Grades 9-12

Purpose: Evaluates and diagnoses achievement for instructional improvement in small engine repair. May be used for vocational guidance in an overall program.

Description: 332-item paper-pencil multiple-choice test in two parts. Part I (170 items) covers tools and fasteners, fuel and exhaust systems, cooling and lubrication systems, short block and governor systems, charging and electrical systems, starting systems, and mechanics' mathematics. Part II (162 items) covers ignition systems, valve train systems, troubleshooting, lawn and garden equipment, motorcycle equipment, marine equipment, snowmobile equipment, and business and shop operations. Examiner required. Suitable for group use.

Timed: 2 hours per part

Scoring: Computer scored

Cost: Testing loan service (test booklets, answer sheets, scoring service) Ohio students $1.25 each; out-of-state students $2.50 each for March administration, $3.50 at other times

Publisher: Instructional Materials Laboratory, The Ohio State University

---

PHOENIX ABILITY SURVEY SYSTEM (PASS)
Refer to page 835.

RIVERMEAD PERCEPTUAL ASSESSMENT BATTERY
Refer to page 59.

STUDENT OCCUPATIONAL COMPETENCY ACHIEVEMENT TESTING (SOCAT)
Refer to page 272.

STUDENT OCCUPATIONAL COMPETENCY ACHIEVEMENT TESTING: ACCOUNTING/ BOOKKEEPING
Refer to page 272.

STUDENT OCCUPATIONAL COMPETENCY ACHIEVEMENT TESTING: AGRICULTURE MECHANICS
Refer to page 272.

STUDENT OCCUPATIONAL COMPETENCY ACHIEVEMENT TESTING: AUTO BODY
Refer to page 273.

STUDENT OCCUPATIONAL COMPETENCY ACHIEVEMENT TESTING: AUTO MECHANICS
Refer to page 273.

STUDENT OCCUPATIONAL COMPETENCY ACHIEVEMENT TESTING: CARPENTRY
Refer to page 273.

STUDENT OCCUPATIONAL COMPETENCY ACHIEVEMENT TESTING: COMMERCIAL FOODS
Refer to page 274.

STUDENT OCCUPATIONAL COMPETENCY ACHIEVEMENT TESTING: COMPUTER PROGRAMMING
Refer to page 274.

STUDENT OCCUPATIONAL COMPETENCY ACHIEVEMENT TESTING: CONSTRUCTION ELECTRICITY
Refer to page 274.

STUDENT OCCUPATIONAL COMPETENCY ACHIEVEMENT TESTING: CONSTRUCTION MASONRY
Refer to page 274.

STUDENT OCCUPATIONAL COMPETENCY ACHIEVEMENT TESTING: DRAFTING
Refer to page 275.

STUDENT OCCUPATIONAL COMPETENCY ACHIEVEMENT TESTING: ELECTRONICS
Refer to page 275.

STUDENT OCCUPATIONAL COMPETENCY ACHIEVEMENT TESTING: GENERAL MERCHANDISING
Refer to page 275.

STUDENT OCCUPATIONAL COMPETENCY ACHIEVEMENT TESTING: GENERAL OFFICE
Refer to page 276.

STUDENT OCCUPATIONAL COMPETENCY ACHIEVEMENT TESTING: GRAPHIC ARTS
Refer to page 276.

STUDENT OCCUPATIONAL COMPETENCY ACHIEVEMENT TESTING: HEATING AND AIR CONDITIONING
Refer to page 276.

STUDENT OCCUPATIONAL COMPETENCY ACHIEVEMENT TESTING: HOME ENTERTAINMENT EQUIPMENT REPAIR
Refer to page 277.

STUDENT OCCUPATIONAL COMPETENCY ACHIEVEMENT TESTING: HORTICULTURE
Refer to page 277.

STUDENT OCCUPATIONAL COMPETENCY ACHIEVEMENT TESTING: INDUSTRIAL ELECTRICITY
Refer to page 277.

STUDENT OCCUPATIONAL COMPETENCY ACHIEVEMENT TESTING: INDUSTRIAL ELECTRONICS
Refer to page 277.

STUDENT OCCUPATIONAL COMPETENCY ACHIEVEMENT TESTING: MACHINE TRADES
Refer to page 278.

STUDENT OCCUPATIONAL COMPETENCY ACHIEVEMENT TESTING: PLUMBING
Refer to page 278.

STUDENT OCCUPATIONAL COMPETENCY ACHIEVEMENT TESTING: PRACTICAL NURSING
Refer to page 278.

STUDENT OCCUPATIONAL COMPETENCY ACHIEVEMENT TESTING: REFRIGERATION
Refer to page 279.

STUDENT OCCUPATIONAL COMPETENCY ACHIEVEMENT TESTING: SEWN PRODUCTS
Refer to page 279.

STUDENT OCCUPATIONAL COMPETENCY ACHIEVEMENT TESTING: SMALL ENGINE REPAIR
Refer to page 279.

STUDENT OCCUPATIONAL COMPETENCY ACHIEVEMENT TESTING: WELDING
Refer to page 280.

TECHNICAL AND SCHOLASTIC TEST (TST)
John T. Dailey

Adolescent, adult
Grades 9 and above

Purpose: Assesses knowledge and potential in electrical, mechanical, and scholastic skills. Used in career counseling and vocational guidance settings.

Description: 150-item paper-pencil test measuring knowledge and abilities that relate to success in trade, technical, and business careers. The TST includes items that yield scores for seven subtests: electricity, electronics, mechanical information, physical sciences, arithimetic reasoning, algebra, and vocabulary. The examiner's manual provides information for administering, scoring, and interpreting both the TST and the BET. Together, the Business English Test (BET) and the TST make up the Dailey Vocational Tests. The individual report profile sheet and group report form are designed for use with both tests. Examiner required. Suitable for group use.

Timed: 65 minutes

Scoring: Hand key

Cost: 35 test booklets $29.24; examiner's manual $3.72; 100 answer sheets $19.86

Publisher: The Riverside Publishing Company

TECHNICAL TESTS—1962

Adolescent   Ages 13-15

Purpose: Measures technical abilities. Used for vocational guidance.

Description: Multiple-item paper-pencil test battery consisting of six subtests of technical abilities: Arithmetic Part I and II, Mechanical Insight, Form Perception Part I and II, and a Tool Test. Materials

include a bilingual test booklet (English, Afrikaans). Examiner required. Suitable for group use.
SOUTH AFRICAN PUBLISHER

Untimed: 1½ hours

Scoring: Hand key; examiner evaluated

Cost: (In Rands) test 0,40; 10 answer sheets 0,50; key 0,60; manual 0,70; orders from outside The RSA will be dealt with on merit

Publisher: Human Sciences Research Council

TRADE APTITUDE TEST (TRAT)—1982

Adolescent, adult

Purpose: Assesses aptitudes of adult blacks for training in trades. Used for screening prospective trade-school students.

Description: 16-subtest paper-pencil measure of skills important to trade training, including skill, coordination, patterns, spare parts, classification, assembling, calculations, inspection, graphs, mechanical insight, mathematics, spatial perception (2-D), vocabulary, figure series, woordeskat, and spatial perception (3-D). Examiner required. Suitable for group use.
SOUTH AFRICAN PUBLISHER

Untimed: 4 hours, 45 minutes

Scoring: Hand key; examiner evaluated; may be machine scored

Cost: (In Rands) test booklet 3,00; manual 9,80; 10 answer sheets 1,00 (specify hand key or machine score); scoring stencil for answer sheet 2,00; scoring stencil for machine answer sheets 3,70, 2,40; orders from outside The RSA will be dealt with on merit

Publisher: Human Sciences Research Council

VCWS 1—SMALL TOOLS (MECHANICAL)
Refer to page 985.

VCWS 2—SIZE DISCRIMINATION
Refer to page 985.

VCWS 3—NUMERICAL SORTING
Refer to page 849.

VCWS 4—UPPER EXTREMITY RANGE OF MOTION
Refer to page 985.

VCWS 5—CLERICAL COMPREHENSION AND APTITUDE
Refer to page 876.

VCWS 6—INDEPENDENT PROBLEM SOLVING
Refer to page 849.

VCWS 7—MULTI-LEVEL SORTING
Refer to page 986.

VCWS 8—SIMULATED ASSEMBLY
Refer to page 986.

VCWS 10—TRI-LEVEL MEASUREMENT
Refer to page 849.

VCWS 11—EYE-HAND-FOOT COORDINATION
Refer to page 987.

VCWS 12—SOLDERING AND INSPECTION (ELECTRONIC)
Refer to page 850.

VCWS 13—MONEY HANDLING
Refer to page 850.

VCWS 14—INTEGRATED PEER PERFORMANCE
Refer to page 947.

VCWS 17—PRE-VOCATIONAL READINESS BATTERY

Adult   ☞ ✍

Purpose: Measures an individual's ability to function independently. May be used with mentally retarded individuals to determine whether the individual requires a sheltered environment or can function independently.

Description: Assessment and training tool containing five subtests: Developmental Assessment, Workshop Evaluation, Vocational Interest Screening, Interpersonal/Social Skills, and Independent Living Skills. The developmental assessment subtest contains functional nonmedical measures of physical and mental abilities. The workshop evaluation is a simulated assembly process designed to determine if the examinee is appropriately placed in a work or training setting. The vocational interest screening subtest, presented in an audiovisual format, identifies job interests. The interpersonal/social skills subtest identifies barriers to employment or independent living. The independent living skills subtest measures skill and knowledge in transportation, money handling, grooming, and living environment. The tasks in each subtest vary in difficulty from very simple recognition of rooms to more complex processes relating to work. The test is designed in such a way that a lack of language or reading skills does not present a barrier to evaluation. The test should not be administered to individuals with severe impairment of the upper extremities. Examiner required. Not suitable for group use.

Timed: Not available

Scoring: Examiner evaluated

Cost: $3,680.00

Publisher: Valpar International Corporation

VCWS 18—CONCEPTUAL UNDERSTANDING THROUGH BLIND EVALUATION (CUBE)
Refer to page 602.

VCWS 19—DYNAMIC PHYSICAL CAPACITIES

Adult   ☞ ✍

Purpose: Measures the Physical Demands factor of the Worker Qualifications Profile of the D.O.T. Evaluates an individual's endurance and strength. May be used in post-injury cases.

Description: Objective measure of functional capacity in terms of strength. The exercise measures each of the strength levels represented in the Physical Demands factor of the Worker Qualifications Profile of the D.O.T.: sedentary, light, medium, heavy, and very heavy. The examinee, who assumes the role of a shipping and receiving clerk, handles materials varying in weight from 5 pounds to 115 pounds. The examinee begins with exercises on the sedentary level and gradually moves through the range of strengths until his capacity is reached. The test may be discontinued at any time. The test should be administered only to individuals who are able to walk, are free of visual handicaps, and who have use of their upper extremities. Examiner required. Not suitable for group use.

Timed: Not available

Scoring: Examiner evaluated

Cost: $1,395.00

Publisher: Valpar International Corporation

WORK SAMPLES
Refer to page 854.

Student Evaluation and Counseling: Vocational Guidance: Interests and Attitudes

ARMED SERVICES-CIVILIAN INTEREST SURVEY (ASCVIS)

Refer to page 713.

ASSESSMENT OF CAREER DECISION MAKING (ACDM)

Vincent A. Harren and Jacqueline N. Buck

Adolescent, adult
Grades 9 and above

Purpose: Assesses the factors involved in the career decision making of high-school, community college, and college students.

Description: 94-item paper-pencil true-false test based on Harren's model of career decision making. It assesses a student's decision-making style, satisfaction with and adjustment to school, and progress in the selection of a college major and in formulating occupational plans. A special counselor's report and a group summary report are provided for each student. Self-administered. Suitable for group use.

Untimed: 10-15 minutes

Scoring: Computer scored

Cost: Complete kit (manual, two ACDM answer sheets including scoring service) $32.00

Publisher: Western Psychological Services

CANADIAN OCCUPATIONAL INTEREST INVENTORY (COII)

Refer to page 735.

CAREER ADAPTIVE BEHAVIOR INVENTORY (CAB)

Thomas P. Lombardi

Developmentally delayed
students   Ages 3-15

Purpose: Assesses the behavior of developmentally disabled students in relation to career planning. Determines readiness for placement in prevocational or vocational education courses. Used to monitor student progress in vocational education courses.

Description: 120-item paper-pencil observational inventory assessing 12 specific behaviors in each of 10 areas: academics, communication, interests, leisure time, motor, responsibility, self-concept, self-help, socialization, and task performance. A parent, teacher, or clinician rates the student's level of ability on a 5-point scale for each behavior. Results are charted on a graphic profile of strengths and weaknesses. The CAB Activity Book provides 360 teaching ideas keyed to the behaviors assessed. Examiner required. Not suitable for group use.

Untimed: Varies

Scoring: Examiner evaluated

Cost: Test kit (activity book, manual, 25 rating forms) $23.50

Publisher: Special Child Publications

CAREER AND VOCATIONAL INTEREST INVENTORY

Adolescent, adult

Purpose: Measures an individual's career and vocational interests. Used to assist high-school students and adults in making educational and/or career decisions.

Description: Multiple-item paper-pencil or computer-administered inventory assessing over 30 basic vocational interest scales and providing scores on the six Holland theme scales. Narrative statements, as well as a list of occupations that match the subject's interests, are presented. Examiner required. Suitable for group use.

Untimed: Varies

Scoring: Computer scored

Cost: Contact publisher
Publisher: Integrated Professional Systems, Inc.

CAREER ASSESSMENT INVENTORY (CAI)
Charles B. Johansson

Adolescent, adult
Grades 8 and above

Purpose: Evaluates career goals of high-school students who want immediate, noncollege-graduate business or technical training. Used for employment decisions, vocational rehabilitation, and self-employment.

Description: 305-item paper-pencil test in a five-response Likert format. The inventory covers six general occupational themes (Holland's RIASEC), 22 basic occupational interest scales, and 91 occupational scales. Self-administered. Suitable for group use. Available in French and Spanish.

Untimed: 20-35 minutes
Scoring: Computer scored by NCS
Cost: Manual $12.75; narrative report $4.50-$8.25 depending on quantity and scoring method; profile report $2.45-$3.95 depending on quantity and scoring method; 25 answer sheets (for scoring via Arion II or Microtest) $8.75
Publisher: National Computer Systems/ PAS Division

CAREER DECISION SCALE (2ND EDITION)
Refer to page 890.

CAREER DIRECTIONS INVENTORY
Douglas N. Jackson

Adolescent, adult

Purpose: Helps evaluate career interests of high-school and college students and adults. Used for educational and vocational planning and counseling.

Description: 100-item paper-pencil inventory consisting of a triad of statements for each item, describing job-related activities. The examinee marks the most and least preferred activities. Computer scoring yields a sex-fair profile of 15 basic interest scales. The pattern of these interests is compared to the interest patterns shown by individuals in a wide variety of occupations. This new test evolved from the Jackson Vocational Interest Survey; the content and vocabulary are easier and more emphasis is placed on activities involved in nonprofessional occupations. Examiner required. Suitable for group use.

Untimed: 30-45 minutes
Scoring: Computer scored by publisher
Cost: Examination kit (manual, sample report, question and answer document, computerized scoring for one individual) $10.00
Publisher: Research Psychologists Press, Inc.

CAREER EXPLORATION PROFILE (CEP)
Gary Harr

High-school students, adults

Purpose: Assesses career-related attitudes, interests, and abilities of high-school students and adults. Used in career exploration, counseling, and training.

Description: Computer-administered tool assessing attitudes, interests, and abilities. The instrument may be used in either an INTERACTIVE mode (using self-estimated aptitudes) or a BATCH mode (based on objective test scores). As many as 50 profiles may be generated in one run. The CEP is compatible with Holland interest code categories and allows direct integration of aptitude and interest data and Holland code type categories and worker trait groups. Materials include a user's manual and masters for transparencies used in interpreting results. Self-administered. Not suitable for group use.

Untimed: Not available
Scoring: Computer scored
Cost: $175.00
Publisher: Precision People, Inc.

CAREER EXPLORATION SERIES (CES)

Arthur Cutler, Francis Ferry,
Robert Kauk, and Robert Robinett

Adolescent, adult

Purpose: Assesses an individual's job-related interests and identifies appropriate vocational choices. Used in vocational education programs.

Description: Six multiple-item paper-pencil or computer-administered inventories matching job interests with job characteristics in the following fields: AG-O (agriculture, conservation, forestry); BIZ-O (business, sales, management, clerical); CER-O (consumer/home econ-related fields); DAC-O (design, performing arts, communication); IND-O (industrial, mechanics, construction); and SCI-O (scientific, mathematical, health). Each of the inventories includes reusable booklets for self-assessment and self-scoring of job matches; answer insert folders that give job information for exploration and decision making; matching of job interests with the job characteristics of selected jobs in each field; listings of 300-500 related job titles in each field; and job duties, pay range, and outlook of job titles within each occupational field. Microcomputer programs are available for TRS-80 Models I and III, Commodore PET/CBM, Commodore 64, Apple II + and IIe, IBM Personal Computer, and Franklin Ace 1000. Software packages include instructions, printed inventories, and additional information. An introductory filmstrip is also available. The paper-pencil version may be self-administered. Suitable for group use.

Untimed: Varies

Scoring: Self-scored; may be computer scored

Cost: Class set (materials for 35 students) $45.00; additional answer folders to use with reusable booklets $0.25; diskettes (complete series) $249.95; filmstrip $32.95

Publisher: CFKR Career Materials, Inc.

CAREER GUIDANCE INVENTORY

James E. Oliver

Adolescent   Grades 7-13

Purpose: Measures comparative strength of interests in 25 trades, services, and technologies. Used to counsel noncollege bound students.

Description: 240-item paper-pencil test covering 14 engineering-related trades and eleven others: carpentry, masonry, mechanical repair, painting and decorating, plumbing-pipefitting, printing, tool and die making, sheet metal and welding, drafting and design technology, mechanical engineering technology, and industrial production. Students rate their interest in each area on a scale from 1 (very low) to 20 (very high). Examiner required. Suitable for group use.

Untimed: 1 hour, 30 minutes

Scoring: Hand key

Cost: Specimen set $3.00; booklet $1.25; manual $1.00; 25 self-scoring answer sheets and profiles $20.00

Publisher: Educational Guidance, Inc.

CAREER INTEREST TEST (CIT)

Refer to page 902.

CAREER MATURITY INVENTORY (CMI)

John O. Crites

Adolescent   Grades 6-12

Purpose: Measures a student's maturity with respect to attitudes and competencies regarding career decisions. Used by vocational counselors and educators in planning programs.

Description: Two paper-pencil inventories assessing attitudes and competencies important for mature career decision-making. The Attitude Scale measures the student's maturity with respect to feelings, subjective reactions, and dispositions toward making a career choice. The Competency Test contains five subtests measuring competencies that are important in making career decisions. See the individual descriptions of the

CMI: Attitude Scale and the CMI: Competence Test. Examiner required. Suitable for group use.

Untimed: 3 hours, 5 minutes

Scoring: Hand key; may be computer scored

Cost: Specimen set (Attitude Scale book, Competence Test book, manual, theory and research handbook, computer-scorable answer sheet, maturity profile, and test reviewer's guide) $8.95

Publisher: CTB/McGraw-Hill

CAREER MATURITY INVENTORY: ATTITUDE SCALE

Adolescent   Grades 6-12

Purpose: Measures a student's maturity with respect to attitudes and competencies regarding career decisions. Used by vocational counselors and educators in planning programs.

Description: Multiple-item paper-pencil test measuring a student's maturity with respect to feelings, subjective reactions, and dispositions toward making a career choice. The test is available in two forms: Screening Form A-2 and Counseling Form B-1. The screening form provides an overall measure and is used for screening or survey purposes. The counseling form provides scores for five variables: decisiveness, involvement, independence, orientation, and compromise. Examiner required. Suitable for group use.

Untimed: Screening form 25 minutes; counseling form 35 minutes

Scoring: Hand key; may be computer scored

Cost: 35 test books, manual, key (specify form) $26.25

Publisher: CTB/McGraw-Hill

CAREER MATURITY INVENTORY: COMPETENCE TEST

Adolescent   Grades 6-12

Purpose: Measures a student's maturity with respect to attitudes and competencies regarding career decisions. Used by vocational counselors and educators in planning programs.

Description: Multiple-item paper-pencil test containing five subtests: Self-Appraisal, Occupational Information, Goal Selection, Planning, and Problem Solving. Each test item presents a hypothetical situation, and the student must choose one of five answer choices. Examiner required. Suitable for group use.

Untimed: 25 minutes per subtest

Scoring: Hand key; may be computer scored

Cost: 35 test books, manual, key $43.40

Publisher: CTB/McGraw-Hill

CAREER ORIENTATION PLACEMENT AND EVALUATION SURVEY (COPES)

Adolescent, adult
Grades 8 and above

Purpose: Measures personal values related to the type of work an individual chooses and the satisfactions derived from the occupation. Used for career evaluation and guidance and to supplement other types of information used in industrial or educational counseling situations in which the goal is improved self-awareness.

Description: Multiple-item paper-pencil inventory measuring the following eight value dimensions related to career evaluation and selection: investigative, practical, independent, leadership, orderliness, recognition, aesthetic, and social. The COPES value dimensions are based on theoretical and factor analytic research. Norms are provided for high-school and college levels. Self-administered. Suitable for group use.

Untimed: 30 minutes

Scoring: Hand key; may be computer scored

Cost: Specimen set (manual, all forms) $2.75

Publisher: Educational and Industrial Testing Service

CAREER PROBLEM CHECKLIST
Tony Crowley

Adolescent   Ages 14-17

Purpose: Identifies the problems secondary-school and college students may experience when making career plans. Used by careers teachers, officers, and counselors in lessons, interviews, and careers programs.

Description: 100-item 4-page paper-pencil questionnaire identifying the problems individual students or groups of students may experience in career planning. Students identify the kinds of problems they are experiencing from the 100 examples listed. Items cover information about school, home, getting information about jobs, starting work, applying for a job, and decision making. The test is used to identify the instructional needs of individuals and groups of students, provide structure in guidance interviews, help form discussion groups in structured careers lessons, and plan and monitor the effects of careers programs. Examiner required. Suitable for group use. BRITISH PUBLISHER

Untimed: Varies

Scoring: Examiner evaluated

Cost: Manual £5.15; checklists £6.30

Publisher: NFER-NELSON Publishing Company Ltd.

CAREER SURVEY

**Adolescent, adult
Grades 7 and above**

Purpose: Measures interests of people in careers. Used in guidance and vocational counseling.

Description: 132-item paper-pencil Likert-scale test covering 12 areas of career interest: accommodating/entertaining, humanitarian/caretaking, plant/animal/caretaking, mechanical, business detail, sales, numerical, communications/promotion, science/technology, artistic expression, educational/social, and medical. The interest scales were built around a two-dimensional model: people-things and data-ideas. Also included is a 40-item ability survey measuring verbal and non-verbal reasoning ability. Explanatory material for the client is available in the orientation booklet and the career planning booklet. Examiner/self-administered. Suitable for group use.

Timed: Ability scales 24 minutes total

Untimed: Interest scales 20-25 minutes

Scoring: Machine scored

Cost: 35 test booklets, 35 orientation booklets, directions for administration $23.00; scoring and reporting services extra

Publisher: American Testronics

CHATTERJI'S NON-LANGUAGE PREFERENCE (CNPR)
S. Chatterji

**Child, adolescent
Ages 10-16**

Purpose: Determines individual areas of interest for students. Used for educational counseling, vocational guidance, and career planning.

Description: 150-item multiple-choice paper-pencil test assessing interest in 10 broad interest areas: fine arts, literary work, scientific, medical, agricultural, technical, craft, outdoor, sports, and household work. Each test item consists of a three-choice question presented with stick-figure drawings. The nonlanguage presentation is suitable for use with non-English speaking students. The manual provides information on administering, scoring, and interpreting the test. Examiner required. Suitable for group use. PUBLISHED IN INDIA

Untimed: 45 minutes

Scoring: Hand key; examiner evaluated

Cost: (In Rupees) specimen set Rs.45; complete kit (25 booklets, 100 answer sheets, 100 profile charts, scoring stencils, manual) Rs.180-00

Publisher: Manasayan

Information and availability unconfirmed; no publisher response.

COPSYSTEM CAREER OCCUPATIONAL PREFERENCE SYSTEM
Robert R. Knapp and Lila F. Knapp

**Adolescent, adult
Grades 7 and above**

Purpose: Measures the interests, abilities, and work values of junior high, high-school, and college students. Used for occupational and career planning and guidance.

Description: The COPSystem consists of three measuring instruments, COPS Interest Inventory, CAPS Ability Battery, and COPES Values Survey, which may be combined and analyzed in two distinct manners. The three (or any two) instruments may be adminstered and then interpreted on the Comprehensive Career Guide; or they may be interpreted separately and then summarized on the Summary Guide. The Comprehensive Career Guides and the separate Self-Interpretation Profile and Guides contain brief descriptions of the 14 clusters. For career and educational planning, sample occupations are presented separately for the 14 clusters. In addition, suggested activities for obtaining experience, college majors and school courses related to the clusters, a decision-making worksheet for career exploration, and a 4-year program planning guide and courses are provided. All instruments are related to the following COPSystem Career Clusters: science, professional and skilled; technology, professional and skilled; consumer economics; outdoor; business, professional and skilled; clerical; communication; arts, professional and skilled; and service, professional and skilled. Self-administered. Suitable for group use.

Untimed: Not available

Scoring: Examiner evaluated

Cost: Specimen set $9.25

Publisher: Educational and Industrial Testing Service

COPSYSTEM INTEREST INVENTORY (COPS)
Robert R. Knapp and Lila Knapp

**Adolescent, adult
Grades 7 and above**

Purpose: Measures job activity interests related to occupational clusters appropriate for college- and vocationally oriented individuals. Used for academic counseling, career planning, and vocational guidance.

Description: Multiple-item paper-pencil inventory measuring interests related to both professional and skilled positions in science, technology, business, arts, and service and to occupations in communication, consumer economics, clerical, and outdoor fields. Each cluster is keyed to curriculum choice and major sources of detailed job information, including the "Dictionary of Occupational Titles," VIEW, and the "Occupational Outlook Handbook." On-site scoring provides immediate feedback of results. Percentile norms are presented separately for high-school and college levels. Self-administered. Suitable for group use. Available in a Spanish and a Canadian version.

Untimed: 30-40 minutes

Scoring: Hand key; may be computer scored

Cost: Specimen set (all forms, technical manual) $6.25; 25 expendable self-scoring test booklets $8.75; 25 self-interpretation guides and profile sheets $8.50; 25 machine-scoring booklets and answer sheets $9.00; 14 hand-scoring keys $10.00; examiner's manual $1.50; technical manual $5.50

Publisher: Educational and Industrial Testing Service

COPSYSTEM INTEREST INVENTORY FORM R (COPS-R)
Lila F. Knapp and Robert R. Knapp

Adolescent   Grades 6-12

Purpose: Measures job activity interests related to occupational clusters. Used for academic counseling, career planning, and vocational guidance.

Description: Multiple-item paper-pencil inventory measuring interests related to both professional and skilled positions in science, technology, business, arts, and service and to occupations in communication, consumer economics, clerical, and outdoor fields. COPS Form R is parallel to the COPS Interest Inventory but uses simpler language and a single norms profile. Items are written at a sixth-grade reading level, and the whole unit is presented in a programmed booklet. The instrument may be used with CAPS and COPES as a part of the Summary COPSystem (COPS-R should be the last test administered in this series). A self-scoring form and a machine-scoring form for processing and scoring by EdITS are available. Percentile norms are provided at the high-school level. Self-administered. Suitable for group use.

Untimed: 20 minutes

Scoring: Hand key; may be computer scored

Cost: Specimen set (manual, all forms) $3.25; 25 self-scoring forms (includes self-scoring booklet and self-interpretation guide) $17.25; 25 machine-scoring booklets and answer sheets $9.00; examiner's manual $1.25

Publisher: Educational and Industrial Testing Service

COPSYSTEM INTERMEDIATE INVENTORY (COPS II)
Lila F. Knapp and Robert R. Knapp

Adolescent   Grades 6-7

Purpose: Measures the career-related interests of students in Grades 6-7. Used for academic counseling and guidance.

Description: Multiple-item paper-pencil inventory providing a rating of student's job-related interests based to a large extent on knowledge of school activities. COPS II extends interest measurement to younger students and to older students with reading or language difficulties or for whom motivational considerations are of special concern. Items are written at a fourth-grade reading level. Self-administered. Suitable for group use.

Untimed: Response 20-30 minutes; scoring 15-20 minutes

Scoring: Self-scored

Cost: Specimen set (includes manual) $2.50; 25 self-scoring forms (combined self-scoring booklet and self-interpretation guide) $18.25; set of 14 COPSystem occupational cluster charts with COPSystem II cartoons $38.50; 25 pocket-size cluster charts $5.00

Publisher: Educational and Industrial Testing Service

COPSYSTEM PROFESSIONAL LEVEL INTEREST INVENTORY (COPS-P)
Lisa Knapp-Lee, Lila Knapp, and Robert R. Knapp

Adolescent, adult
Grades 7 and above

Purpose: Measures the career-related interests of professionally minded high-school and college students. Used for college major and occupational selection and orientation.

Description: Multiple-item paper-pencil inventory measuring interests related to professional level occupations in the following career clusters: physical science, medical life science, civil engineering, electrical engineering, mechanical engineering, agribusiness, nature, business management, finance, computation, written communication, oral communication, design, performing arts, social service, and instructional service. Separate percentile norms are provided for high-school and college levels. Self-administered. Suitable for group use.

Untimed: 30-40 minutes

Scoring: Hand key; may be computer scored

Cost: Specimen set $6.00; 25 expendable self-scoring test booklets $8.75; 25 self-interpretation guides and profile sheets $8.50; 25 machine-scoring booklets and answer sheets $9.00

Publisher: Educational and Industrial Testing Service

THE DECISION MAKING INVENTORY
Refer to page 913.

DF OPINION SURVEY: AN INVENTORY OF DYNAMIC FACTORS (DFOS)
J.P. Guilford, Paul R. Christensen, and Nicholas A. Bond, Jr.

Adolescent, adult
Grades 10 and above

Purpose: Measures general motivational factors. May be used for personnel selection, counseling, and guidance.

Description: Multiple-item paper-pencil inventory measuring 10 general motivational factors that were found in an analysis of interest variables: need for attention, liking for thinking, adventure vs. security, self-reliance vs. dependence, aesthetic appreciation, cultural conformity, need for freedom, realistic thinking, need for precision, and need for diversion. The factors have general implications for personality and are related to broad vocational interests. Norms are provided for high-school and college students. The test is restricted to A.P.A. members. Examiner required. Suitable for group use.

Untimed: 45 minutes

Scoring: Hand key; may be computer scored

Cost: 25 tests $17.00; 25 answer sheets $5.50; 25 profile charts $4.00; manual $2.00; scoring set $9.00

Publisher: Sheridan Psychological Services, Inc.

DOLE VOCATIONAL SENTENCE COMPLETION BLANK
Arthur A. Dole

Adolescent   Grades 7-12

Purpose: Evaluates an individual's career-related interests and abilities. Used with high-school students for educational and vocational counseling, rehabilitation, diagnosis, or therapy.

Description: 21-item paper-pencil projective inventory assessing a student's concerns, emphases, and preferences concerning future vocational choices. Test items consist of sentence stems to be completed in the student's own words. Results yield 29 scores, including Problems, Achievement, Independence, Satisfaction, Material Possessions, Vocation, Effectiveness, Recognition From Others, Relaxation, Intellectual Qualities, Activity, Relationships with Other People, Recreation, Outdoor Activities, Mechanical Interest, Computational Interest, Scientific Interest, Persuasive Influence, Artistic Interest, Literary Interest, Musical Activities, Social Service, Clerical Interests, Domestic Interests, Academic Interests, Armed Forces, and Homemaking Interests (household arts). Scores also

are available for nine optional categories: Peace of Mind, Security, Value, Obligation, Health, Religion, Social Studies, Negative Academic, and Unclassifiable. The test supplements and amplifies, in the student's own words, the results of standardized inventories such as the Kuder or Strong. Examiner required. Suitable for group use.

Untimed: 20 minutes

Scoring: Examiner evaluated

Cost: Test kit (manual, 30 record forms, 30 individual score profiles) $16.25

Publisher: Stoelting Company

EDUCATIONAL DEVELOPMENT SERIES, REVISED 1984 EDITION
Refer to page 398.

EDUCATIONAL INTEREST INVENTORY
James E. Oliver

**Adolescent, adult
Grades 10 and above**

Purpose: Measures comparative strength of interests in 22 major areas of study leading to B.A. degrees in colleges and universities. Used for educational guidance counseling and career planning.

Description: 250-item paper-pencil inventory consisting of forced-choice pairs of statements related to interests in fine arts, applied arts, physical and biological science, and social science. The inventory measures interests in the following major areas of study: music, art, communication, education, business administration, engineering, industrial arts, agriculture, nursing, library arts, home economics, botony, zoology, physics, chemistry, geology, earth science, history, political science, sociology, psychology, and economics. Self-administered. Suitable for group use.

Untimed: 1 hour, 30 minutes

Scoring: Self-scored

Cost: Specimen set $3.00; booklet $1.25; manual $1.00; 25 self-scoring answer sheets and profiles $20.00

Publisher: Educational Guidance, Inc.

EMPLOYABILITY ATTITUDES
Refer to page 915.

EXPERIENCE EXPLORATION
W. Price Ewens

Adolescent, adult
Grades 8 and above

Purpose: Identifies possible job alternatives by evaluating a person's work experience and interests. Used for career planning, vocational guidance, and student counseling.

Description: 200-item paper-pencil inventory assessing an individual's abilities and interests in 10 occupational areas: outdoor, mechanical, computation, scientific, persuasive, artistic, literary, musical, social service, and clerical. The test also includes a 19-item values checklist, which identifies the individual's most and least important occupational values, including living in a small town/big town, working with hands/ideas, working at a desk/physical activity, and working under supervision/unsupervised. Self-administered. Suitable for group use.

Untimed: 45 minutes
Scoring: Examiner evaluated
Cost: 35 survey booklets $17.50; 35 student experience sheets $17.50; interpretative wall chart $5.50; manual $6.50
Publisher: Chronicle Guidance Publications

EXPLORE THE WORLD OF WORK (E-WOW)
Arthur Cutler, Francis Ferry, Robert Kauk, and Robert Robinett

Child   Grades 4-6

Purpose: Measures vocational interests for students in Grades 4-6, special education students at any level, and students who read at the third- to fifth-grade level. Used for early introduction to vocational education.

Description: 36-item paper-pencil rating inventory assessing students' interests in 36 job activities in the following job clus-

ters: business-office-sales, industry-mechanics-transportation-construction, art-communication-design, health-education-social service, forestry-agriculture-natural resources, and scientific-technical-health. Thirty-six pictures with brief captions identify the job activities. Students use colored pencils or crayons to color the drawings green (like), yellow (not sure), or red (don't like). Six activities are listed for each of the six job clusters. After indicating preferred job activities within the clusters, students then select preferred job titles and explore one job in-depth by following an exploration process outlined in the folder (including a visit to workers on the job). For further job research, two copies of the JOB-O Dictionary are included with each class set. The test also may be used with *Exploring Careers*, a junior edition of the *Occupational Outlook Handbook*. A computer version is available. Self-administered. Suitable for group use.

Untimed: Varies
Scoring: Hand key
Cost: Class set (35 folders, 2 JOB-O Dictionaries, and user's guide) $16.00; individual folders $0.40; Exploring Careers $12.00; diskettes $79.95
Publisher: CFKR Career Materials, Inc.

FORER VOCATIONAL SURVEY: MEN-WOMEN
Bertram R. Forer

Adolescent, adult

Purpose: Evaluates attitudes and goals related to work situations among adolescents and adults; useful for career planning, vocational guidance, and employee selection and placement.

Description: 80-item paper-pencil multiple-choice test in which the subject completes structured sentence stems measuring three areas of occupational activity: reactions to specified situations, causes of feelings and actions, and vocational goals. Results reveal interpersonal behavior, attitudes toward work, supervision, authority, people, and work dynamics. Self-administered. Suitable for group use.

Untimed: 20-30 minutes
Scoring: Examiner evaluated

Cost: Complete kit (25 men and 25 women forms, 50 record forms, manual) $37.50

Publisher: Western Psychological Services

G-S-Z INTEREST INVENTORY (GSZ)
J.P. Guilford, Edwin S. Shneidman, and Wayne S. Zimmerman

Adolescent, adult
Grades 10 and above

Purpose: Measures individual traits and interests. Used for occupational and academic guidance and to select appropriate leisure time activities.

Description: Multiple-item paper-pencil measure of nine general interest categories. Two traits are scored for special interests within each of the following categories: artistic, linguistic, scientific, mechanical, outdoor, business-political, social activity, personal assistance, and office work. The traits have been selected on the basis of the best evidence available concerning basic and pertinent values or interests common to occupational and professional levels. Vocational interests are distinguished from avocational interests. Norms are provided for high-school and college students. The test is restricted to A.P.A. members. Examiner required. Suitable for group use.

Untimed: 50 minutes

Scoring: Examiner evaluated

Cost: 25 tests $12.00; 25 answer sheets $4.00; 25 profile charts (essential for evaluation) $5.00; manual $1.75

Publisher: Sheridan Psychological Services, Inc.

GEIST PICTURE INTEREST INVENTORY
Harold Geist

Adolescent, adult
Grades 8 and above

Purpose: Identifies an individual's vocational and avocational interests. Used for vocational guidance and placement, especially with culture-limited and educationally deprived individuals.

Description: Multiple-item paper-pencil multiple-choice test requiring minimal language skills. The subject circles one of three pictures depicting vocational and avocational scenes he prefers. Occupational norms are provided for Grades 8-12, college, and adult. A Motivation Questionnaire can be administered separately to explore motivations behind occupational choices. Examiner/self-administered. Suitable for group use.

Untimed: 20-30 minutes

Scoring: Hand key

Cost: Complete kit (10 male and 10 female tests, 10 male and 10 female motivation questionnaires, manual) $35.00

Publisher: Western Psychological Services

GORDON OCCUPATIONAL CHECK LIST II
Leonard V. Gordon

Adolescent, adult
Grades 8 and above

Purpose: Identifies areas of job interest. Used for counseling of noncollege-bound high-school students.

Description: Multiple-item paper-pencil test of six broad vocational interest categories: business, arts, outdoors, technical-mechanical, technical-industrial, and service. The categories are further divided into the area and work group classifications used in the Department of Labor's Guide for Occupational Exploration. Examiner required. Suitable for group use.

Untimed: 20-25 minutes

Scoring: Examiner evaluated

Cost: 35 check lists, manual, 35 Job Title supplements $28.00; manual $7.50

Publisher: The Psychological Corporation

GUILFORD-ZIMMERMAN INTEREST INVENTORY (GZII)
Joan S. Guilford and Wayne S. Zimmerman

Adolescent   Grade 13

Purpose: Measures broad areas of interest as an aid to vocational guidance.

Description: Multiple-item paper-pencil test measuring 10 interest areas: mechanical, natural, aesthetic, service, clerical, mercantile, leadership, literary, scientific, and creative. The inventory is based on factor analytic findings providing 10 extremely homogeneous scales that comprehensively cover the 10 interest factors. Unique features include the inclusion of an independent scale of Creative Interest, the provision for expression of intensity of interest, and ease of scoring. Norms are provided for college freshmen. The test is restricted to A.P.A. members. Examiner required. Suitable for group use.

Untimed: 20 minutes

Scoring: Hand key; may be computer scored

Cost: 25 tests $12.00; 25 answer sheets $4.00; manual $2.00; scoring set $5.00; 25 profile charts $4.00

Publisher: Sheridan Psychological Services, Inc.

HACKMAN-GAITHER INTEREST INVENTORY
Roy Hackman and James W. Gaither

Adolescent, adult
Grades 7 and above

Purpose: Determines vocational interests and preferences. Used as a guide to administering aptitude tests and for assessing the handicapped.

Description: 200-item paper-pencil test covering business, sales, scientific and technical, artistic, health and welfare, business clerical, mechanical, service, and outdoor activities. Subjects use a 4-item scale ranging from "like very much" to "do not like at all" to mark their answers. Self-administered. Suitable for group use.

Untimed: 30-45 minutes

Scoring: Hand key

Cost: 20 booklets $35.00; 20 answer sheets $10.00; 20 profile sheets $10.00; manual $10.00; specimen set $15.00

Publisher: Psychological Service Center of Philadelphia

HALL OCCUPATIONAL ORIENTATION INVENTORY (HALL)
*Lacy G. Hall and
Randolph B. Tarrier*

Grades 3 and above

Purpose: Emphasizes the many possibilities for the student's future and encourages the broadening of the student's perceptions of potentials and priorities. Used for career planning and vocational guidance.

Description: Multiple-item paper-pencil test based on the personality-need theory inspired by Abraham Maslow and adapted by Anne Roe to the area of occupational choice. The inventory assesses psychological needs, which are correlated to worker traits and job characteristics identified by the U.S. Department of Labor. The inventory focuses on 22 job and personality characteristics: creativity, independence, risk, information-knowledge, belongingness, security, aspiration, esteem, self-actualization, personal satisfaction, routine-dependence, data-orientation, things orientation, people orientation, location concern, aptitude concern, monetary concern, physical abilities concern, environment concern, co-worker concern, qualifications concern, time concern, and defensiveness.
The inventory is available in three levels. Intermediate HALL (Grades 3-7) is a shorter inventory with school-focused items designed to complement awareness/development programs. The Young Adult/College HALL (high-school and college students and professionals) focuses on jobs and occupations. Adult Basic HALL (reading-handicapped adults) is a shorter inventory with a world-of-work orientation and controlled readability levels. Separate inventory booklets, interpretive folders, and response sheets are available for each of the three levels. A counselor's manual, the HALL Career Education Reader, a videotape training film, and the STS scoring service are also available. Self-administered. Suitable for group use.

Timed: 30-40 minutes

Scoring: Hand key; examiner evaluated; may be computer scored

Cost: 20 inventory booklets $15.50; 20 interpretive folders $9.00; 20 response sheets $9.00

Publisher: Scholastic Testing Service, Inc.

THE HARRINGTON-O'SHEA CAREER DECISION-MAKING SYSTEM (CDM)
Thomas F. Harrington and Arthur J. O'Shea

Adolescent, adult
Grades 7 and over

Purpose: Evaluates the interests and abilities of high school and college students and adults. Used with students to guide study for future occupations and with adults to identify new careers and skills.

Description: Multiple-item short-answer examination in which an individual records information about occupational choices, school subject preferences, job values, abilities, and plans for further education or training. The survey includes a list of 120 work activity items. The responses contribute to one of six interest scales: Crafts, Science, Arts, Social, Business, and Clerical. Raw scores on the highest two interest scales are used to identify three or four career clusters for exploration. A Career Clusters Chart shows typical jobs in each cluster, as well as related school subjects and abilities. Occupational outlook and training requirements are given for each job listed. The jobs are keyed to the Dictionary of Occupational Titles. The test is available in three editions. In the self-scored edition, the student records information in a survey booklet, and an interpretive folder shows the student how to compare the career cluster with the self-reported information. The self-scored edition is available in Spanish. The machine-scored edition reports results in a profile report or in a detailed 12-page individualized narrative report, and the student and examiner arrange a counseling session to discuss appropriate careers. Machine-scored users can also order a Group Summary Report, which compiles responses by sex within grade or counselor group.

Up to 10 locally- developed questions can be included in this report. Interpretation is via the raw scores used to find appropriate career clusters. Optional percentile rank norms are available for Grades 7-12 and college freshmen. The microcomputer edition can be used with the TRS-80 Model III, TRS-80 Model 4, Apple II +, and Apple IIe. The student types responses directly into the computer. Results are presented both on the screen and on a print-out. The Interpretive Folder explains the career clusters. When a printer is not available, results can be transferred from the screen to the folder. The Interpretive Report, which includes the Summary Profile and Exploring Your Career Clusters, is included with the microcomputer edition. Seventh-grade reading level required. An audiocassette is available for students whose reading ability may interfere with completion of the questions. Self-administered. Suitable for group use.

Untimed: 30-40 minutes

Scoring: Self-scored, machine-scored, or computer scored

Cost: Specimen set (includes self-scored survey booklet, interpretive folder, machine-scored survey booklet) $3.00; contact publisher for price of microcomputer edition

Publisher: American Guidance Service

HIGH SCHOOL CAREER-COURSE PLANNER
Arthur Cutler, Francis Ferry, Robert Kauk, and Robert Robinett

Adolescent

Purpose: Evaluates career interests of junior high and high-school students. Used to develop a course plan that is consistent with self-assessed career goals.

Description: 6-item paper-pencil test measuring interests in the following six occupational areas: working with tools, working with people, creating new things, solving problems, and doing physical work. Students rate each area on a 3-point scale from one (high interest) to three (low interest). A profile of the six ratings is compared with similar profiles from the following 16 occupational clusters: industrial production, clerical, computer, banking-insurance-administrative, service (food, personal, protective), education, sales, construction, transportation, scientific-technical, mechanics-repairers, health, social scientists-social service, performing arts-communications-design, agriculture-forestry-conservation, and mining petroleum. Related job titles, suggested course work, and job entry requirements are included for each of the 16 occupational clusters, providing a basis for developing course plans. For further job research, each class set includes two copies of the JOB-O Dictionary. A computer version is available. Self-administered. Suitable for group use.

Untimed: Varies

Scoring: Hand key

Cost: Class set (35 folders, 2 JOB-O Dictionaries, user's guide) $16.00; individual folders $0.40; diskettes $79.95

Publisher: CFKR Career Materials, Inc.

HIGH SCHOOL INTEREST QUESTIONNAIRE (HSIQ)—1973

Adolescent   Grades 10-12

Purpose: Measures vocational interests of black students. Used for vocational guidance.

Description: 200-item paper-pencil test of eight interest areas: language, performing arts, fine arts, social, science, technical, business, and office work. The pupil responds like, indifferent, or dislike to each item. Examiner required. Suitable for group use.
SOUTH AFRICAN PUBLISHER

Untimed: 45-60 minutes

Scoring: Hand key; examiner evaluated

Cost: (In Rands) questionnaire 0,30; manual 3,20; 10 answer sheets 0,50; orders from outside The RSA will be dealt with on merit

Publisher: Human Sciences Research Council

HOW WELL DO YOU KNOW YOUR INTERESTS
Thomas N. Jenkins

Adolescent, adult
Grades 10 and above

Purpose: Assesses attitudes toward work activities. Used for vocational guidance.

Description: Multiple-item paper-pencil test measuring interests in 10 vocational areas: business, mechanical, outdoor, service, research, visual art, amusement, literacy, music, and general work attitudes. Items are rated on a 6-point scale ranging from "like tremendously" to "dislike tremendously." Examiner required. Suitable for group use.

Untimed: 10 minutes

Scoring: Hand key

Cost: Complete kit (3 test booklets of each edition and manual) $9.00; 25 tests (specify secondary, college, or personnel) $18.00; keys $6.00; handbook of interpretations $6.00; manual $6.00

Publisher: Psychologists and Educators, Inc.

INDIVIDUAL CAREER EXPLORATION (ICE)
Anna Miller-Tiedeman in consultation with Anne Roe

Child, adolescent   Grades 3-12

Purpose: Identifies career areas of interest to students.

Description: Multiple-item paper-pencil inventory designed to help students focus on future occupations in relation to their current interests, experiences, abilities, and ambitions in the following areas: service, business contact, organization, technology, outdoor, science, general culture, and arts and entertainment. It is based on the Roe theory of occupations. Two forms are available: Verbal ICE (Grades 8-12) and Picture ICE (Grades 3-7). Picture ICE also may be used with special education classes. Self-administered. Suitable for group use.

Timed: 2 hours

Scoring: Self-scored; hand key

Cost: Starter set (20 inventory booklets, 20 classification of occupation by group and level for Picture Form, 20 job trends, 60 job information checklists, manual of directions, technical supplement) $48.75

Publisher: Scholastic Testing Service, Inc.

INTEREST DETERMINATION AND ASSESSMENT SYSTEM (IDEAS)
Charles B. Johansson

Adolescent   Grades 6-12

Purpose: Measures career-related interests of junior high and high-school students. Used in career planning and occupational exploration at the junior high and high-school level.

Description: 112-item paper-pencil multiple-choice inventory assessing a range of career interests. Test items present five response choices. The areas covered are mechanical/fixing, electronics, nature/outdoors, science/numbers, writing, arts/crafts, social service, child care, medical service, business, sales, office practices, and food service. The test is scored on a 7-point Likert-type scale and is sold in a self-contained package that can be scored and interpreted by the student. A sixth-grade reading level is required. Self-administered. Suitable for group use.

Untimed: 30-40 minutes

Scoring: Hand key

Cost: Manual $4.75; 25 booklets $23.00

Publisher: National Computer Systems/PAS Division

INTEREST QUESTIONNAIRE FOR INDIAN SOUTH AFRICANS (IQISA)—1969
S. Oosthuizen

Adolescent

Purpose: Assesses interests of Indian pupils. Used for vocational guidance.

Description: 210-item paper-pencil measure of seven categories of interests: language, art, social service, science, mechanical, business, and office work.

The subject responds like, indifferent, or dislike for each item. Examiner required. Suitable for group use. SOUTH AFRICAN PUBLISHER

Untimed: 2 hours

Scoring: Hand key; examiner evaluated

Cost: (In Rands) questionnaire 1,50; manual 1,40; 10 answer sheets 0,40; orders from outside The RSA will be dealt with on merit

Publisher: Human Sciences Research Council

INVENTORY OF RELIGIOUS ACTIVITIES AND INTERESTS
Sam C. Webb and Richard A. Hunt

Adolescent, adult
Grades 10 and above

Purpose: Measures interest in church-related careers, self-rated abilities, and career values. Form M is used in the candidacy program of the United Methodist Church as a counseling guide.

Description: 240-item paper-pencil inventory of interest in 10 church career areas: counselor, administrator, teacher, scholar, evangelist, spiritual guide, preacher, reformer, priest, and musician. Form M also measures background, family influence values, and self-rated abilities. Examiner required. Suitable for group use.

Untimed: 45 minutes

Scoring: Hand key; may be computer scored

Cost: Specimen set $6.00; Form A hand scoring stencil set $5.00; Form M computer scoring $2.00 per answer sheet

Publisher: Datascan

INVENTORY OF VOCATIONAL INTERESTS
Andrew Kobal, J. Wayne Wrightstone, Karl R. Kunze, edited by Andrew J. MacElroy

Adolescent, adult
Grades 10 and above

Purpose: Assesses vocational interests. Used for vocational guidance.

Description: 25-subject paper-pencil test of occupational interests. Each of the 25 topics contains 10 responses. The test, which provides insight into both major and minor interests, measures academic, artistic, mechanical, business and economic, and farm-agricultural areas. Materials include an inventory and occupation index arranged by vocational categories in the manual. Examiner required. Suitable for group use.

Timed: 35 minutes

Scoring: Examiner evaluated

Cost: Specimen set $4.00; 25 tests $5.00; 25 answer sheets $5.00

Publisher: Psychometric Affiliates

JACKSON VOCATIONAL INTEREST SURVEY (JVIS)
Douglas N. Jackson

Adolescent, adult
Grades 10 and above

Purpose: Helps evaluate career interests of high-school and college students. Used for educational and vocational planning and counseling and for personnel placement.

Description: 289-item paper-pencil inventory consisting of paired statements covering 10 occupational themes: expressive, logical, inquiring, practical, assertive, socialized, helping, conventional, enterprising, and communicative. The subject marks one of two responses. Scoring yields a sex-fair profile of 34 basic career clusters. A seventh-grade reading level is required. Examiner required. Suitable for group use. Available in French.

Untimed: 45-60 minutes

Scoring: Hand key; may be computer scored

Cost: Examination kit $16.00; manual $10.50; 25 test booklets $17.25; 25 answer sheets and key $4.25; 25 profiles $4.25

Publisher: Research Psychologists Press, Inc.

JIIG-CAL OCCUPATIONAL INTERESTS GUIDE AND APU OCCUPATIONAL INTEREST GUIDE
S. J. Closs

Adolescent, adult
Ages 14-adult

Purpose: Evaluates personal interests of adults and adolescents and relates those interests to career orientations. Used by teachers and counselors for career planning and guidance with individuals at all levels of ability.

Description: Multiple-item paper-pencil inventory measuring six broad types of interests related to a number of identified career orientations. The test may be used as a conventional interest test or as part of the JIIG-CAL System for Computer Assisted Career Guidance. The system is a set of interlinked computer programs operating on a file of job information, retrieving from it those jobs that best match details the pupil supplies about his interests, qualifications, health, likes/dislikes, etc. The Jobfile is not a vacancy file but contains coded and descriptive information on the most common jobs. The system provides both students and counselors with ideas (in the form of relevant job titles) and information about each job in the form of a brief description about what the job involves, required skills, qualifications, and other relevant features. The information is supplemented by references to related careers publications for further information. Restriction code (C) applies. Examiner/self-administered. Suitable for group use.
BRITISH PUBLISHER

Untimed: Not available

Scoring: Hand key; may be computer scored

Cost: Specimen set (templates not included) £17.00

Publisher: Hodder & Stoughton

JOB MATCHING II
Refer to page 904.

JOB-O
Arthur Cutler, Francis Ferry,
Robert Kauk, and Robert Robinett

Adolescent, adult
Grades 7 and above

Purpose: Assesses an individual's aspirations and interests and identifies appropriate career and occupational choices. Used in career counseling and vocational guidance.

Description: Multiple-item paper-pencil or computer-administered career exploration instrument assessing nine variables related to educational aspirations, occupational interests, and interpersonal and physical characteristics of occupations. The *Dictionary of Occupational Titles,* the *Occupational Outlook Handbook,* and Dr. William B. Schutz's FIRO-B provide the theoretical basis relating test responses to current labor statistics, trends, and predictions for 120 job titles. The reusable assessment booklet contains complete directions and guides the student in recording responses in the consumable answer folder. The folder displays information on the number of people employed, job outlook, training requirements, and job clusters for the 120 job titles. The JOB-O Dictionary contains precise definitions of all job titles, related job titles, and unusual jobs and indicates which characteristics are related to each job. The manual includes information on development and rationale and instructions for administration and use. Computer programs are available for TRS-80 Models I and III, Commodore PET/CBM, Commodore 64, Apple II + and IIe, IBM Personal Computer, and Franklin Ace 1000. An optional introductory filmstrip is also available. The paper-pencil version may be self-administered. Suitable for group use.

Untimed: Varies

Scoring: Hand key; may be computer scored

Cost: Reusable test booklet, answer folder $1.45; additional answer folders $0.25; manual $2.00; JOB-O dictionary $1.75; filmstrip $32.95; diskettes $59.95

Publisher: CFKR Career Materials, Inc.

JOBMATCH
Refer to page 904.

JUNG PERSONALITY QUESTIONNAIRE (JPQ)—1982

All ages

Purpose: Assesses personality. Assists in vocational guidance.

Description: Multiple-item paper-pencil test of personality based on the theory of Carl Gustav Jung. The personality factors measured are extraversion, introversion, thought, feeling, sensation, intuition, judgment, and perception. Examiner required. Suitable for group use. SOUTH AFRICAN PUBLISHER

Untimed: Not available

Scoring: Hand key; examiner evaluated; may be machine scored

Cost: (In Rands) test booklet 1,00; 10 answer sheets (machine-3881) 0,90; scoring stencil 4,10; orders from outside The RSA will be dealt with on merit

Publisher: Human Sciences Research Council

KUDER GENERAL INTEREST SURVEY, FORM E
Frederic Kuder

Adolescent   Grades 6-12

Purpose: Assesses students' preferences for various activities related to occupational interest areas. Used with students in Grades 6-12 to guide educational planning toward future employment.

Description: 168-item paper-pencil test measuring preferences in 10 occupational interest areas: outdoor, mechanical, scientific, computational, persuasive, artistic, literary, musical, social science, and clerical. Scoring and profile construction can be done by the student. A sixth-grade reading level is required. Self-administered. Suitable for group use.

Untimed: 30-40 minutes

Scoring: Hand key; may be machine scored

Cost: Complete set (materials and scoring for 25 students, machine-scored version) $57.50; complete set (25 booklets and answer pads, hand-scored version) $31.25; specimen set either version $6.50; no charge for general manual if requested when ordering

Publisher: Science Research Associates, Inc.

KUDER OCCUPATIONAL INTEREST SURVEY, FORM DD (KOIS), REVISED
Refer to page 827.

KUDER PREFERENCE RECORD, VOCATIONAL, FORM CP
Frederic Kuder

Adolescent, adult
Grades 9 and above

Purpose: Evaluates occupational interests of students and adults. Used for vocational counseling and employee screening and placement.

Description: 168-item paper-pencil test measuring interests in 10 occupational areas: outdoor, mechanical, scientific, computational, persuasive, artistic, literary, musical, social science, and clerical. The subject uses a pin to indicate a "most liked" and "least liked" activity for each group of three activities. A high-school reading level is required. Self-administered. Suitable for group use.

Untimed: 30-40 minutes

Scoring: Hand key

Cost: Specimen set $6.75; 25 booklets $36.75; no charge for manual if requested when ordering

Publisher: Science Research Associates, Inc.

LEISURE ACTIVITIES BLANK (LAB)
George E. McKechnie

Adult

Purpose: Assesses an individual's past and future leisure and recreation activities. Used for research and counseling.

Description: 120-item paper-pencil test of recreational time use. Items are a list of recreational activities. Respondents indicate the extent of past participation and expected future participation in each activity. The test yields six past factor scores: mechanics, crafts, intellectual, slow living, sports, and glamour sports; eight future factor scores: adventure, mechanics, crafts, easy living, intellectual, ego-recognition, slow-living, and clean living; and two validity scales. Self-administered. Suitable for group use.

Untimed: 15-20 minutes

Scoring: Hand key

Cost: Manual $5.50; 25 tests $4.25; 25 profiles $3.75; scoring stencils $20.00

Publisher: Consulting Psychologists Press, Inc.

LIVING SKILLS
Refer to page 828.

MILWAUKEE ACADEMIC INTEREST INVENTORY
Andrew R. Baggaley

Adolescent, adult
Grades 12-14

Purpose: Measures academic study interests. Used to help college-bound high-school seniors and college freshmen and sophomores select college majors.

Description: 150-item paper-pencil test comparing a student's academic interests with those of typical students in specified fields. Scores provide stanine ranking for six major areas: physical science (physics, chemistry, mathematics, engineering); healing occupations (medicine, medical technology, pharmacy); behavioral science (psychology, sociology, anthropology, social work); economics (economics, commerce); humanities-social studies (political science, history, philosophy, languages, journalism); and elementary education. Items are designed to minimize response patterns adapted to social desirability rather than to the student's real feelings. Self-administered. Suitable for group use.

Untimed: 20 minutes

Scoring: Hand key

Cost: Complete kit (10 reusable tests, 100 answer sheets, manual, key) $35.00

Publisher: Western Psychological Services

MISSOURI APTITUDE AND CAREER INFORMATION INVENTORY (MACII)

**Adolescent
Grades 9.5-12**

Purpose: Assesses the verbal and quantitative aptitudes and career interests of students.

Description: Multiple-item paper-pencil test combining Form X of the School and College Ability Test—Series III (SCAT III) with a career information inventory. The SCAT III portion measures a student's understanding of words and their relationship through verbal analogies and of fundamental number operations through quantitative comparisons. The career inventory indicates occupational preferences using a list of 250 occupations, interests, and future plans. Examiner/self-administered. Suitable for group use.

Timed: 80 minutes

Scoring: Computer scored

Cost: Answer sheets $0.15; test booklet rental $0.12; scoring service $0.35

Publisher: Missouri Testing and Evaluation Service

---

19 FIELD INTEREST INVENTORY (19 FII)—1970
F.A. Fouche and N.F. Alberts

Adolescent, adult

Purpose: Assesses vocational interests of high-school students. Used for vocational guidance.

Description: Paper-pencil measure of 19 broad areas of vocational interest: fine arts, performing arts, language, historical, service, social work, sociability, public speaking, law, creative thought, science, practical-male, practical-female, numerical, business, clerical, travel, nature, and sport. Scores on two aspects

of interests, work-hobby and active-passive, also are obtained. Examiner required. Suitable for group use.
SOUTH AFRICAN PUBLISHER

Untimed: 45 minutes

Scoring: Hand key; examiner evaluated; may be machine scored

Cost: (In Rands) test booklet 1,00; manual 5,20; 10 answer sheets 0,90; 10 machine answer sheets 1,30; student norms 2,80; orders from outside The RSA will be dealt with on merit

Publisher: Human Sciences Research Council

NM ATTITUDE TOWARD WORK TEST (NMATWT)
C.C. Healy and S.P. Klein

Adolescent   Grades 9-12

Purpose: Measures individual appreciation of the personal and social significance of work. Used for career counseling and program evaluation.

Description: 25-item paper-pencil multiple-choice test evaluating attitudes toward preparing for an occupation; the feeling that work contributes to self-confidence, self-esteem, and self-actualization; the belief that work leads to many benefits, such as security, interpersonal contacts, friends, and things money can buy; acceptance of the desirability of the interdependence of people, of people all "pulling together"; and the belief in the value of work for our society. Reliability and norms have been determined from samples of ninth- and twelfth-grade secondary students. Examiner required. Suitable for group use.

Timed: 15 minutes

Scoring: Hand key

Cost: Specimen set $6.00; 35 tests $12.00; 35 answer sheets $4.00; scoring stencil $3.00; manual $4.00

Publisher: Monitor

OCC-U-SORT
Lawrence K. Jones

**Adolescent, adult
Grades 7 and above**

Purpose: Helps an individual clarify his interests and values in order to make career decisions. Used by education counselors.

Description: Self-administered career intervention instrument utilizing a deck of 60 cards, each of which contains the name of an occupation, to identify and clarify an individual's thoughts about an occupation. The subject sorts the cards, choosing the 12 occupations he considers most appropriate for himself. Each occupation is coded, using John Holland's six interest categories, according to the interest category it primarily and secondarily represents. Each interest category receives a numerical score based on the number of times it was a primary or secondary code among the 12 occupations the individual chose. The three categories with the highest scores form the individual's interest code, which the individual uses to explore occupations in the Guide to Occupations. Card sets are available in three different levels based on the educational background of the subject. Self-administered. Suitable for group use.

Untimed: Not available

Scoring: Self-scored; examiner evaluated

Cost: Specimen set (manual, booklet, Guide to Occupations, four sort cards, poster) $8.95

Publisher: CTB/McGraw-Hill

OCCUPATIONAL APTITUDE SURVEY AND INTEREST SCHEDULE—APTITUDE SURVEY (OASIS-AS)
Randall M. Parker

Adolescent   Grades 8-12

Purpose: Evaluates a high-school student's aptitude for various occupations. Used for occupational guidance and counseling.

Description: Multiple-item paper-pencil survey measuring general, verbal, numerical, spatial, perceptual, and manual abilities. A companion test to the Interest Schedule, scores for both surveys are keyed directly to the Dictionary of Occupational Titles, Guide for Occupational Exploration, and the Worker Trait Group Guide. Examiner required. Suitable for group use.

Untimed: 30 minutes

Scoring: Examiner evaluated

Cost: Complete set (examiner's manual, 25 test booklets, 50 answer sheets, 50 profile sheets, storage box) $49.00

Publisher: Pro-Ed

OCCUPATIONAL APTITUDE SURVEY AND INTEREST SCHEDULE—INTEREST SCHEDULE (OASIS-IS)
Randall M. Parker

Adolescent   Grades 8-12

Purpose: Evaluates a high school student's areas of interest, as related to various occupations. Used for occupational guidance and counseling.

Description: Paper-pencil self-rating scale measuring the following interest areas: artistic, scientific, nature, protective, mechanical, industrial, business detail, selling, accommodating, humanitarian, leading/influencing, and physical performing. A companion test is the Aptitude Survey. Scores for both surveys are keyed directly to the Dictionary of Occupational Titles, Guide for Occupational Exploration, and the Worker Trait Group Guide. Examiner required. Suitable for group use.

Untimed: 30 minutes

Scoring: Examiner evaluated; may be computer scored

Cost: Complete set (examiner's manual, 25 test booklets, 50 answer sheets, 50 profile sheets, storage box) $51.00

Publisher: Pro-Ed

THE OCCUPATIONAL INTEREST RATING SCALE (OIRS)
M.A. Brimer

Adolescent   Ages 14-18

Purpose: Identifies the vocational interests of adolescents. Used for vocational counseling.

Description: Multiple-item paper-pencil instrument using a two-way classification system for determining vocational interests. Seven occupational areas (business, technical, care, aesthetic, scientific, numerical, and field) and five directions of involvement (persuasive, operational, empathic, making, and intellectual) are covered in the inventory. The test provides two forms in the same booklet for examining the stability of interest. Used with the Applied Knowledge Tests (AKT), expressed interests can be matched with performance in the cognitive domain. This test minimizes the need to know specific terminology and uses a sample-free item analysis system and test-free ability scale scoring system. Each area and direction of involvement is measured on a scale of 0-10 based on techniques adopted for the new British Intelligence Scale. Strengths of interests between areas and between persons can be compared. Self-administered. Suitable for group use.

BRITISH PUBLISHER

Untimed: Varies

Scoring: Not available

Cost: Contact publisher

Publisher: Educational Evaluation Enterprises

OHIO VOCATIONAL INTEREST SURVEY (OVIS)
*Ayres G. D'Costa,
David W. Winefordner,
John G. Odgers, and
Paul B. Koons, Jr.*

Adolescent   Grades 8-13

Purpose: Assesses occupational and vocational interests. Used to assist students with educational and vocational plans.

Description: 280-item paper-pencil test of job-related interests. Items are work activities to which the student indicates his degree of interest. Materials include a Student Information Questionnaire, which gathers background information about the student's plans, preferences, and interests. This test has been superceded by 1981 OVIS II. Examiner required. Suitable for group use.

Timed: 60-90 minutes

Scoring: Scoring service available

Cost: Specimen set (test, MRC answer document directions, sample MRC reporting forms) $6.50

Publisher: The Psychological Corporation

OHIO VOCATIONAL INTEREST SURVEY: SECOND EDITION (OVIS II)

**Adolescent, adult
Grades 7 and above**

Purpose: Assesses occupational and vocational interests. Used for educational and vocational counseling.

Description: 253-item paper-pencil test of job-related interests. Items are job activities to which the student responds on a 5-point scale ranging from "like very much" to "dislike very much." Used in conjunction with the Dictionary of Occupational Titles, OVIS II classifies occupations according to three elements: data, people, and things. Materials include a Career Planner Workbook, Handbook for Exploring Careers, and filmstrips to aid counselors in administering and interpreting the test. OVIS II supersedes the 1969 OVIS. A microcomputer version is available. Examiner required. Suitable for group use.

Untimed: 45 minutes

Scoring: Hand key; may be machine scored; scoring service available

Cost: 35 tests $32.00; 35 hand-scorable answer documents $28.00; 35 MRC machine-scorable answer documents $16.00; 35 NCS machine-scorable answer documents $16.00; basic scoring service $2.10 per pupil

Publisher: The Psychological Corporation

THE ORIENTATION INVENTORY (ORI)
Bernard M. Bass

**Adolescent, adult
Grades 10 and above**

Purpose: Measures attitudes toward achievement and rewards. Used for personnel assessment, high-school and college vocational counseling, and group research.

Description: 27-item paper-pencil forced-choice test of three types of orientation toward satisfaction and rewards: self-orientation, interaction-orientation, and task-orientation. Results help to predict an individual's success and performance in various types of work. The inventory is based on Bass's theory of interpersonal behavior in organizations. Examiner required. Suitable for group use.

Untimed: 10-15 minutes

Scoring: Hand key

Cost: Specimen set (manual, key, tests) $5.00

Publisher: Consulting Psychologists Press, Inc.

PERSONAL QUESTIONNAIRE/ OCCUPATIONAL VALUES
Educational and Industrial Test Services, Ltd. Staff

Child, adolescent

Purpose: Provides comprehensive details of a person's background. Used for vocational and educational guidance and to supplement interviews.

Description: Multiple-item paper-pencil questionnaire covering the following areas: physical, educational (formal and informal), home and family, social, hobbies, occupational attitudes, occupational achievements (adult form only), occupational checklist, and occupational values. The Occupational Values form is a scale measuring eight important factors in the work situation which indicate the individual's attitude toward various aspects of job security or achievement and risk. The Personal Questionnaire also is available in a juvenile version. Self-administered. Suitable for group use.
BRITISH PUBLISHER

Untimed: Not available

Scoring: Examiner evaluated

Cost: Contact publisher

Publisher: Educational and Industrial Test Services Ltd.

PICTURE VOCATIONAL INTEREST QUESTIONNAIRE FOR ADULTS (PVI)—1981

Adolescent, adult

Purpose: Assesses vocational interests. Used for vocational guidance.

Description: 110-item measure of interest in 11 areas: clerical work, advanced engineering trades, lower engineering trades, woodwork, painting trades, building, domestic work, food preparation, agriculture, tailoring, and leatherwork. The subject indicates preference, dislike, or neutral for each item. Examiner required. Suitable for group use.
SOUTH AFRICAN PUBLISHER

Untimed: 30-45 minutes

Scoring: Hand key; examiner evaluated

Cost: (In Rands) manual 7,00; questionnaire 2,30; 10 answer sheets 1,20; orders from outside The RSA will be dealt with on merit

Publisher: Human Sciences Research Council

PLANNING CAREER GOALS (PCG)
American Institutes for Research

Adolescent   Grades 8-12

Purpose: Provides information to help students make career plans. Used by guidance and counseling personnel.

Description: 906-item paper-pencil test consisting of an Interest Inventory (300 items), Information Measures (240 items), and Ability Measures (366 items). The Interest Inventory consists of three sections: occupations, occupational activities, and current activities. The student indicates his interest in each of 12 career groups by rating job titles, job activities, or job-related youth activities on a 5-point scale. The items contained in Information Measures sample the student's knowledge of various occupations. The items contained in Ability Measures evaluate the student in 10 areas: reading comprehension, mathematics, abstract reasoning, creativity, mechanical reasoning, English, quantitative reasoning, vocabulary, visualization, and computation. A Life and

Career Plans Survey is used to determine the student's present educational and career plans. Examiner required. Suitable for group use.

Untimed: Not available

Scoring: Hand key; may be computer scored

Cost: Examination kit (Ability Measure, Interest Inventory, Information Measure, answer booklet, handbook, student guide, test reviewer's guide) $7.25

Publisher: CTB/McGraw-Hill

PRG INTEREST INVENTORY

Visually handicapped individuals

Purpose: Measures the vocational/occupational interests of visually handicapped individuals.

Description: 150-item paper-pencil questionnaire assessing interests in the following 10 areas: mechanical, computational, scientific, persuasive, artistic, literary, musical, social service, clerical, and outdoor. The questionnaire and answer sheet are presented in large-print format. Examiner required. Suitable for group use.

Untimed: Varies

Scoring: Examiner evaluated

Cost: Test kit (test booklet, 10 answer sheets, instructions for administration and scoring) $10.00

Publisher: Associated Services for the Blind

READING FREE VOCATIONAL INTEREST INVENTORY (R-FVII)
Ralph L. Becker

Adolescent, adult Ages 13 and older

Purpose: Measures vocational preferences of mentally retarded, developmentally disabled, and learning-disabled persons in job areas that are realistically within the individuals' capabilities. Used for job placement, education, and training.

Description: Multiple-item paper-pencil forced-choice test measuring 11 vocational

interest clusters: automotive, building trades, clerical, animal care, food service, patient care, horticulture, housekeeping, personal service, laundry, and materials handling. The test contains 55 groups of three items each. Each triad requires the subject to circle one of three activities (presented in picture form) which most represents the individual's personal job preference. No reading is required. The test is designed especially for persons with language or reading problems. Materials include test booklets, manual, score sheet, and individual profile sheet of job interests. Self-administered. Suitable for group use.

Untimed: 10-20 minutes

Scoring: Hand key

Cost: 20 test booklets $24.00; manual $8.30; sample set (10 tests, manual) $19.85

Publisher: Elbern Publications

READING FREE VOCATIONAL INTEREST INVENTORY— REVISED (R-FVII REVISED)
Ralph Leonard Becker

Adolescent, adult Ages 13 and older

Purpose: Measures vocational preferences of mentally retarded, learning disabled, and disadvantaged persons in job areas that are realistically within the individuals' capabilities. Used for vocational guidance counseling and for selection of prospective job trainees.

Description: 165-item paper-pencil multiple-choice test measuring the vocational preferences of the educable mentally retarded (EMR), learning disabled (LD), and adult trainable mentally retarded (TMR). The test items consist of 55 sets of three drawings each, depicting job tasks from the unskilled, semiskilled, and skilled levels. Each artist-drawn picture is typical of the kind and type of job in which EMR, LD, and TMR individuals are known to be proficient and productive. From the three alternatives in each set, individuals select the one picture or job task they most prefer. Scores are obtained for 11 vocational interest clusters: automotive, building trades, clerical, animal care, food service, patient care, horticulture, housekeeping, personal service, laundry service, and materials handling. A single test booklet is used for both males and females in compliance with federal Title IX requirements. Test booklets include a detachable scoring sheet and individual profile sheet. For each interest cluster a list of appropriate job titles is suggested for individuals who score high in each occupational category. The revised edition includes updated norms and drawings which have been modified to avoid persons appearing in stereotypic occupational roles. Examiner required. Suitable for group use.

Untimed: 20 minutes or less

Scoring: Examiner evaluated

Cost: Contact publisher

Publisher: Elbern Publications

ROTHWELL-MILLER INTEREST BLANK
J.W. Rothwell and K.M. Miller

Adolescent, adult

Purpose: Assesses the vocational interests of secondary-school students and adults. Used for vocational and educational guidance.

Description: Multiple-item paper-pencil test in which the subject ranks representative titles in order of preference in 12 occupational areas: outdoor, mechanical, computational, scientific, persuasive, aesthetic, literary, musical, social services, clerical, practical, and medical. The pattern of scores indicates the relative strengths of a person's interests and may be compared with extensive norm tables provided in the manual. Separate male and female test forms are available, and a unisex version is to be ready soon. Examiner required. Suitable for group use.
BRITISH PUBLISHER

Untimed: 20 minutes

Scoring: Examiner evaluated

Cost: Contact publisher

Publisher: NFER-NELSON Publishing Company Ltd.

SAFRAN STUDENTS INTEREST INVENTORY (THIRD EDITION), 1985
C. Safran

Adolescent   Grades 5-12

Purpose: Assesses occupational interests of students.

Description: Multiple-item three-part paper-pencil inventory determining the relationship of students' interests and occupational characteristics. Section 1 requires students to choose one alternative from 168 pairs of occupational alternatives categorized in the areas of economic, technical, outdoor, service, humane, artistic, and scientific preferences. Section II measures school subject interests, and Section III contains a self-rated Levels of Ability Chart (academic, mechanical, social, and clerical). Student interests are referenced to the Canadian Classification and Dictionary of Occupations (CCDO) and the Student Guidance Information System (SGIS). The inventory is available on two levels: Level 1 (Grades 5-9) and Level 2 (Grades 8-12). Reading levels are matched to the grades indicated for test levels. For remedial and special education students in Grades 8-9, the Level 1 instrument should be used. This new edition includes occupational selections relevant to a student's world. Examiner/self-administered. Suitable for group use.
CANADIAN PUBLISHER

Untimed: 40 minutes

Scoring: Hand key

Cost: Specimen set (test booklets Levels 1 and 2, student manual, counselor's manual) $8.50; 35 student booklets $25.95

Publisher: Nelson Canada

THE SELF-DIRECTED SEARCH, 1985 REVISION (SDS)
Refer to page 907.

THE SELF-DIRECTED SEARCH, CANADIAN EDITION
John L. Holland

**Adolescent, adult
Grades 7 and above**

Purpose: Stimulates students' involvement in an active exploration of the world of work through self-evaluation of abilities and interests.

Description: Multiple-item paper-pencil career-search tool encourages student involvement in vocational guidance. The assessment booklet is a self-evaluation of interests and abilities. The Occupations Finder is designed to stimulate active exploration of career possibilities. The Occupations Finder of this Canadian edition contains job titles and numbers from the Canadian Classification and Dictionary of Occupations (CCDO) but retains the Holland's coding system. The SDS can be used at home or in schools. Self-administered. Suitable for group use.
CANADIAN PUBLISHER

Timed: Varies

Scoring: Self-scored

Cost: Specimen set (test booklet, test booklet Form E, Occupations Finder, Jobs Finder Form E, Counselor's Guide, and Understanding Yourself and Your Career) $4.00

Publisher: Guidance Centre

SIX-FACTOR AUTOMATED VOCATIONAL ASSESSMENT SYSTEM (SAVAS)
Bruce Duthie

Adolescent, adult

Purpose: Assesses client interest patterns and matches them to occupations in the *Occupational Outlook Handbook*. Used by counselors and clients.

Description: Vocational guidance system matching client interest patterns with 180 occupations listed in the *Occupational Outlook Handbook*. The client completes the Six-Factor Vocational Interest Inventory—a forced-choice test using an ipsative procedure for determining the occupational code—or other interest tests using the six factors of Holland's vocational theory. The six factors represented are realistic, investigative, artistic, social, enterprising, and conventional. All 180 occupations in the system are arranged in order based on their similarity to the client's interest profile from the results of the Six-Factor Vocational Interest Inventory. The Report classifies occupations from very similar to very dissimilar

compared to the client's interest pattern. The general, verbal, and numerical ability needed for each occuption, a three-letter interest code, educational level, salary range, job outlook in the 1990s, and the page number for each occupation in the Occupational Outlook Handbook are in the printout. Examiner/self-administered. Suitable for group use.

Untimed: Varies

Scoring: Computer scored

Cost: Software, manual $195.00

Publisher: Pacific Psychological

THEOLOGICAL SCHOOL INVENTORY (TSI)
Richard A. Hunt, Fred R. King, and James Dittes

Adult

Purpose: Provides information about background, perceptions of the ministry as a career, motivation for ministry, and interest in specific areas of professional ministry.

Description: 165-item paper-pencil inventory consisting of the following scales: Call Concept, Special Leading, Natural Leading, Acceptance, Intellectual Concern, Self-Fulfillment, Leadership, Evangelical Outreach, Social Concern, Service to Persons, Definiteness, and Flexibility. When computer scored, the inventory yields a summary of group results in addition to individual profiles. Self-administered. Suitable for group use.

Untimed: 40-50 minutes

Scoring: Hand key; may be computer scored

Cost: Specimen set (manual, test booklet, guide to interpretation) $15.00; computer scoring $2.00 per individual

Publisher: Ministry Inventories

VOC-TECH QUICK SCREENER

Adolescent, adult

Purpose: Assesses career aptitudes, interests, and training plans of high-school students and adults. Used with individuals not planning to attend 4-year college.

Description: Multiple-item paper-pencil test surveying 400 traditional and non-traditional careers demanding high-tech literacy to extreme physical activity. The inventory consists of 14 vocational-technical job clusters based upon the latest information in the Occupational Outlook Handbook and other sources. This screening tool helps match career goals with jobs and identify job options and training programs. A computer version is available. Self-administered. Suitable for group use.

Untimed: Varies

Scoring: Self-scored; may be computer scored

Cost: VTQS individual folders $0.50; class set of 35 $16.00; Occupational Outlook Hnadbook $10.00

Publisher: CFKR Career Materials, Inc.

VOCATIONAL ADAPTATION RATING SCALES (VARS)
Refer to page 596.

===

VOCATIONAL APPERCEPTION TEST: ADVANCED FORM (VAT:ADV)
R.B. Ammons, M.N. Butler, and S.A. Herzig

**Adolescent, adult
Grades 10 and above**

Purpose: Assesses vocational interests and attitudes. Used for vocational guidance and research on development of occupational interests.

Description: 8- or 10-item projective measure of occupational attitudes. Items are cards, 8 for males and 10 for females, showing persons engaged in common occupations. Subjects are asked to tell a story about each picture. Responses are rated for general preference for occupation, areas of concern to the individual, reason for entering occupation, and outcomes. Materials include a set of plates and a manual. Examiner required. Not suitable for group use.

Untimed: 25-40 minutes

Scoring: Examiner evaluated

Cost: Plates, manual $14.50

Publisher: Psychological Test Specialists

VOCATIONAL INFORMATION AND EVALUATION WORK SAMPLES (VIEWS)

Adult

Purpose: Assesses vocational interests and abilities of the mentally retarded. Used for vocational guidance.

Description: Multiple-item performance tests of abilities consisting of 16 work samples. The tasks performed include sorting, cutting, collating, assembling, weighing, tying, measuring, using hand tools, tending a drill press, and electric machine feeding. The assessment process includes client orientation, demonstration by the examiner, training, and timed assessment. Observation of the client helps distinguish between learning and performance and provides information about learning, quality of work, and productivity. The test requires no reading ability. Examiner required. Suitable for small group use.

Untimed: 4-5 days

Scoring: Examiner evaluated

Cost: Contact publisher

Publisher: Vocational Research Institute—J.E.V.S.

VOCATIONAL INTEREST INVENTORY (VII)
Patricia W. Lunneborg

**Adolescent, adult
Grades 11 and above**

Purpose: Measures high-school students' interests in a number of vocational areas. Used for vocational and educational guidance.

Description: 112-item paper-pencil inventory measuring the relative strengths of students' interests in eight occupational areas: service, business contact, organization, technical, outdoor, science, general culture, and arts and entertainment. Each item is a forced-choice statement which pulls interests apart. Two copies of a narrative report are provided for each student. The report includes a profile of scores by percentile; a summary of percentiles and T-scores for each scale; an analysis and discussion of all scores at or above the 75th percentile; a college majors profile, which compares a student's scores with the mean scores of college majors who took the VII when they were in high school; and a discussion of nontraditional areas for exploration for students who scored between the 50th and 75th percentiles in an area that, in the past, has been considered nontraditional for his or her sex (test items are controlled for sex bias and mixed-sex norms are used). An 8-page *Guide to Interpretation* describes the types of people typical of each of the eight interest groups and gives examples of jobs typical of each group for five levels of education and training: on-the-job training, technical school, community college, bachelors degree, and post-graduate degree. Self-administered. Suitable for group use.

Untimed: 20 minutes

Scoring: Computer scored

Cost: Complete kit (2 tests with computer processing, manual) $28.50

Publisher: Western Psychological Services

VOCATIONAL INTEREST QUESTIONNAIRE FOR PUPILS IN STANDARDS 6-10 (VIQ)—1974

Adolescent

Purpose: Assesses vocational interests. Used for vocational and study guidance.

Description: Paper-pencil test of 10 fields of vocational interest, including technical, outdoor, social service, natural sciences, office work (clerical), office work (numerical), music, art, commerce, and language. Examiner required. Suitable for group use.
SOUTH AFRICAN PUBLISHER

Untimed: 1 hour-1 hour, 30 minutes

Scoring: Hand key; examiner evaluated; may be machine scored

Cost: (In Rands) questionnaire 0,80; manual 2,75; 10 answer sheets 0,20; 10 machine answer sheets 0,80; orders from outside The RSA will be dealt with on merit

Publisher: Human Sciences Research Council

VOCATIONAL INTEREST, EXPERIENCE & SKILL ASSESSMENT (VIESA)
The American College Testing Program

Adolescent, adult
Grades 8 and above

Purpose: Summarizes high school students' and adults' career interests and experiences. Used for career counseling.

Description: 129-item paper-pencil questionnaire measuring career-related interests, experiences, and skills in terms of work tasks involving data, ideas, people, and things. The test is designed to help students expand their self-awareness and to identify career options. A World-of-Work Map is used to relate information concerning 500 occupations employing over 95% of the U.S. labor force. A 16-page "Career Guidebook" is used for the test, and an eight-page "Job Family Charts" is provided to identify occupational options. The test is available on two levels: Level I (Grades 8-10) and Level II (Grades 11-adult). Self-administered. Suitable for group use.

Untimed: 45 minutes

Scoring: Self-scored

Cost: Participant material $0.95; specimen set $4.50

Publisher: The American College Testing Program

VOCATIONAL INTEREST, EXPERIENCE, AND SKILL ASSESSMENT (VIESA), CANADIAN EDITION, 1985
ACT Career Planning Services

Purpose: Measures vocational interests, experiences, and skills of individuals. Used by educators and professionals in

career counseling with individuals and for group programs.

Description: Multiple-item two-part paper-pencil assessment providing career counseling information. Individuals link personal characteristics determined using the Career Guidebook to more than 500 occupations on a World of Work Map that shows how occupations relate to each other. The Job Family Charts list occupations according to typical preparation level, including high-school courses, post high-school preparation, and college majors. Occupations are referenced to the Canadian Classification and Dictionary of Occupation (CCDO) and the Student Guidance Information Sytem (SGIS). The test is available on two levels: Level 1 (Grades 8-10) and Level 2 (Grades 11-adult). A seventh-grade reading level is required. Examiner/self-administered. Suitable for group use.

CANADIAN PUBLISHER

Untimed: 40-45 minutes

Scoring: Hand key

Cost: Examination kit Level 1 and 2 $9.90; 25 student booklets $37.45

Publisher: Nelson Canada

WIDE RANGE INTEREST-OPINION TEST (WRIOT)
Joseph F. Jastak and Sarah Jastak

Ages 5-adult

Purpose: Provides information about vocational interests (without language requirements). Assesses levels of self-projected ability, aspiration level, and social conformity. Used in vocational and career planning and counseling and employee selection and placement and to coordinate instruction/therapy plans with interest/attitude patterns.

Description: 150-item paper-pencil test measuring an individual's occupational motivation according to his likes and dislikes. The test booklet contains 150 pages with three pictures on each page. Each picture shows an individual or group performing a specific job. The subject must select the picture he likes the most and the picture he likes the least for each page. The results are presented on a report form that graphically shows an individual's

strength of interest in 18 interest and 8 attitude clusters (normed on seven age groups from ages 5-adult, separately for males and females). The occupational range is from unskilled labor to the highest levels of training. The test may be used with the educationally and culturally disadvantaged, the learning disabled, the mentally retarded, and the deaf. The picture titles can be read to the blind. Individual administration is necessary for those unable to complete a separate answer sheet. A 35mm film strip (used instead of picture book), and supplementary job title lists are available. Personal computer software is available for scoring and reporting of results. Examiner required. Suitable for group use (except where noted).

Untimed: 40 minutes

Scoring: Hand key; may be computer scored

Cost: Manual $24.50; 50 test forms $10.50; 50 report forms $10.50; key $35.95; film strip $85.00; job title list $39.95

Publisher: Jastak Assessment Systems

WORK ASPECT PREFERENCE SCALE
Refer to page 949.

WORK VALUES INVENTORY
Donald E. Super

**Adolescent, adult
Grades 7 and above**

Purpose: Measures values that are particularly important for determining an individual's vocational satisfaction and success. Used for career counseling and vocational guidance.

Description: 45-item paper-pencil inventory measuring 15 values related to vocational satisfaction and success: intellectual stimulation, job achievement, way of life, economic returns, altruism, creativity, relationships with associates, job security, prestige, management of others, variety, aesthetics, independence, supervisory relations, and physical surroundings. Students rate 45 statements pertaining to work values, and the strength of each value is determined from the weighted ratings. Norms are provided by sex for junior and senior high-school students. Examiner required. Suitable for group use.

Untimed: 15 minutes

Scoring: Hand key; may be computer scored

Cost: Test kit (100 MRC machine-scorable test booklets, manual, materials needed to obtain scoring services) $62.64

Publisher: The Riverside Publishing Company; distributed in Canada by Nelson Canada

Student Evaluation and Counseling: Vocational Guidance: Occupational Knowledge and Skills

CAREER ABILITY PLACEMENT SURVEY (CAPS)
Lila F. Knapp and Robert R. Knapp

Adolescent, adult
Grades 7 and above

Purpose: Measures abilities keyed to entry requirements for the majority of jobs in each of the 14 COPSystem Career Clusters. Used with students for career and vocational guidance and academic counseling.

Description: Eight paper-pencil subtests measuring career-related abilities. The tests are Mechanical Reasoning, Spatial Relations, Verbal Reasoning, Numerical Ability, Language Usage, Word Knowledge, Perceptual Speed and Accuracy, and Manual Speed and Dexterity. A cassette tape of recorded instructions is provided. Examiner/self-administered. Suitable for group use.

Timed: 51 minutes

Scoring: Hand key; may be computer scored

Cost: Specimen set (one copy of each test, manual) $6.50

Publisher: Educational and Industrial Testing Service

CAREER AWARENESS INVENTORY (CAI)
La Verna M. Fadale

Child, adolescent
Grades 3-12

Purpose: Helps students assess how much they know about careers and their own career choices. Used for group discussion and as a pre- and posttest for career awareness.

Description: Multiple-item multiple-choice paper-pencil test covers seven areas of career knowledge: related occupations, contact with occupations, job characteristics, functions of occupations, grouping of occupations, work locations of occupations, and self-assessment of career awareness. The Elementary CAI may be used with pupils in Grades 3-6, and the Advanced CAI may be used with pupils in Grades 7-12. The inventory was developed under the sponsorship of the Cornell Institute for Research and Development in Occupational Education. Examiner/self-administered. Suitable for group use.

Timed: 60-90 minutes

Scoring: Hand key; examiner evaluated; may be computer scored

Cost: Complete kit (20 reusable booklets, manual, class record sheet) $22.75; 50 answer sheets $11.00

Publisher: Scholastic Testing Service, Inc.

CAREER DEVELOPMENT INVENTORY (COLLEGE AND UNIVERSITY FORM)
Donald E. Super,
Albert S. Thompson,
Richard H. Lindeman,
Jean P. Jordaan, and Roger A. Myers

College students

Purpose: Assesses knowledge and attitudes about career choices. Used with college and university students for guidance and for designing and evaluating career counseling programs.

Description: Multiple-item paper-pencil inventory for determining knowledge and attitudes of college and university students regarding careers. Students respond on computer-scored answer sheets. The User's Manual contains information on development, use, and interpretation of the test, as well as case studies and norms. The Technical Manual contains statistical and research information. Test booklets are reusable. Also available in a high-school version. Examiner required. Suitable for group use.

Untimed: 55-65 minutes

Scoring: Computer scored

Cost: 25 test booklets $17.00; user's manual $11.00; technical manual $13.50; 10 answer sheets $24.00

Publisher: Consulting Psychologists Press, Inc.

CAREER DEVELOPMENT INVENTORY (SCHOOL FORM)
Donald E. Super,
Albert S. Thompson,
Richard H. Lindeman,
Jean P. Jordaan, and Roger A. Myers

Adolescent   Grades 10-12

Purpose: Assesses individual attitudes, knowledge, and skills related to vocational decisions. Used in career counseling courses.

Description: 120-item paper-pencil test covering eight dimensions of vocational decision-making: career planning, career exploration, decision-making, world-of-work information, knowledge of preferred occupational group, career development attitudes, career development knowledge and skills, and career orientation total. May be administered in one 65-minute session or two—one 40-minute and one 25-minute—sessions. Examiner required. Suitable for group use.

Untimed: 55-65 minutes

Scoring: Computer scored

Cost: Specimen set (includes test booklet, answer sheet, manual) $12.50; computer scoring $2.00 each

Publisher: Consulting Psychologists Press, Inc.

CAREER PATH STRATEGY
Jeffery Siegel

Adolescent, adult
Ages 16 and older

Purpose: Evaluates a person's career potential. Used to develop career guidance programs, recommend career choices or changes, and monitor progress toward career goals.

Description: 75-item paper-pencil interview guide assessing an individual's career strategies. The guide examines the following factors: mental ability; vocational interests; personality testing; ideal career and ideal life-style; personal background data, such as educational and employment history; cultural, geographic, and economic opportunities and limitations; preliminary career decisions; and strategies for achieving career goals. The program includes homework assignments and forms for reassessment and follow-up. The clinician completes the inventory during the counseling session, evaluates the results, and makes appropriate suggestions. Examiner required. Not suitable for group use.

Untimed: 30 minutes

Scoring: Examiner evaluated

Cost: 50 strategy forms $15.00

Publisher: The Wilmington Press

Information and availability unconfirmed; no publisher response.

CAREER PLANNING PROGRAM (CPP)
The American College
Testing Program

Adolescent, adult
Grades 8 and above

Purpose: Evaluates an individual's career-related abilities, interests, and experiences. Used for vocational counseling and course placement.

Description: 436-item paper-pencil test on two levels designed to help the examinee identify and explore personally relevant occupations and educational programs. Six factors are measured in each of three areas: career-related abilities, interests, and experiences. Level I is used with students in Grades 8-10, and Level II is suitable for use with high school juniors and seniors and adults. Examiner required. Suitable for group use.

Timed: 2½ hours

Scoring: Computer scored by ACT

Cost: Student set (consumable materials with scoring, 2-page report of results, and interpretive booklet for one participant) $4.00; reusable test booklet $0.50; group summary report $40.00

Publisher: The American College Testing Program

FLANAGAN APTITUDE CLASSIFICATION TESTS (FACT)
Refer to page 806.

FLORIDA INTERNATIONAL DIAGNOSTIC-PRESCRIPTIVE VOCATIONAL COMPETENCY PROFILE
Howard Rosenberg and Dennis G. Tesolowski

Adolescent, adult　　　　　

Purpose: Evaluates vocational behaviors related to work adjustment, job readiness, and employability. Used with mentally retarded, specific learning-disabled, seriously emotionally disturbed, and economically disadvantaged adolescents and adults.

Description: 70-item paper-pencil rating scale assessing an individual's development in terms of job readiness and employability. The test contains the following subscales: vocational self-help skills, social-emotional adjustment, work attitudes-responsibility, cognitive-learning ability, perceptual-motor skills, and general work habits. Performance on each of the test items is assessed on a 5-point rating scale representing five developmental levels of vocational competency. The profile assists in the selection of training

programs and determines an individual's present vocational functional level. The profile is used in special education classes, work-study programs, and vocational education classes, as well as in sheltered workshops, work activities centers, rehabilitation facilities, adult education classes, and vocational schools. Self-administered by examiner. Not suitable for group use.

Untimed: Varies

Scoring: Examiner evaluated

Cost: Test kit (manual, 10 record forms, 10 individualized vocational prescription forms) $27.00

Publisher: Stoelting Company

JOB AWARENESS INVENTORY
Teen Makowski

Adolescent　Ages 15-17　　　

Purpose: Evaluates student understanding of common occupations. Used as a prevocational test for special needs students, especially those who are slow or nonreaders.

Description: 100-item paper-pencil test measuring knowledge of the world of work, occupations, abilities, general information, and interview procedures. Materials include two forms, A and B; test booklet; and manual. The test may be read to students. Examiner required. Suitable for group use.

Untimed: Not available

Scoring: Hand key

Cost: Class set for 10 students $32.95; 20 students $55.95

Publisher: Mafex Associates, Inc.

Information and availability unconfirmed; no publisher response.

JOB SEARCH ASSESSMENT

Adolescent, adult　　　　　

Purpose: Assesses an individual's understanding of the processes involved in successfully seeking and getting a job. Used for guidance and counseling and in conjunction with job search training programs.

Description: 80-item multiple-choice A-V format instrument assessing the following 20 areas related to job seeking: identifying skills, tasks, and qualities; writing resumes; clarifying values; setting goals; applying grammatical rules; completing application forms; planning the job search; making cold calls; establishing referral/support networks; knowledge of employee responsibility; communicating with others; dealing with employment agencies; the interview; cold canvassing for potential employment; using newspapers and the Yellow Pages; spelling words correctly; knowledge of legal and illegal items; taking employment tests; writing letters in response to want ads; and using interpersonal skills on the job. Items are presented by means of four characters as they face relevant job search situations. Responses are recorded in a booklet for computer scoring or on a card for on-site scoring. Pre- and post-assessment options are available for use with Prep's Job Search or other related curriculum. Examiner/self-administered. Suitable for group use.

Untimed: 2 hours

Scoring: Computer scored on-site or by publisher

Cost: Contact publisher

Publisher: Prep, Inc.

JOB TRAINING ASSESSMENT PROGRAM (JOBTAP)

Adult

Purpose: Assesses the general knowledge and job-related skills of youths and adults. Used with displaced, unskilled, unemployed, or entry-level workers for career planning and placement.

Description: Multiple-item battery of guidance tests and inventories yielding information on an individual's job search skills, general job knowledge, interest, work experience, and verbal, numerical, spatial, and basic work skills. Two of these assessments include Job Finder Tests—Book 1 containing the Basic Work Skills Test (45 minutes) and the Inspection/Visualization Test (20 minutes) and Job Finder Tests—Book 2 containing the Training and Work Manuals Test, Work

Rules and Procedures Test, Follow-the-Rule Basic Arithmetic Test, and Follow-the-Rule Arithmetic Test. Results from these assessments (phase 1 of the program) are presented in three client information reports and two administrator information reports used for planning (phase 2) and implementation (phase 3). Examiner/self-administered. Suitable for group use.

Untimed: Complete test 1½ hours

Scoring: Computer scored

Cost: Contact publisher

Publisher: Educational Testing Service

KNOWLEDGE OF OCCUPATIONS TEST
Leroy G. Baruth

Adolescent Grades 10-12

Purpose: Assesses high-school students' knowledge of occupations. Used for vocational guidance.

Description: 96-item multiple-choice paper-pencil measure of what students know about occupations. Item content was drawn from sources including the *Occupational Outlook Handbook* and *The Encyclopedia of Career and Vocational Guidance*. Examiner required. Suitable for group use.

Timed: 40 minutes

Scoring: Hand key; may be machine scored

Cost: Specimen set $8.00; 25 tests $18.00; 25 profile sheets, 25 answer sheets $7.50 each; key $2.50; manual $6.00

Publisher: Psychologists and Educators, Inc.

MESA

Adolescent, adult

Purpose: Provides baseline data for the development of an individual's education, training, or employment plan or for more extensive vocational evaluation. May be used with individuals contemplating entering the labor market for the first time or changing fields of work.

Description: Multiple-item computer-administered test measuring 21 factors of the Worker Qualifications Profile as defined in the D.O.T. of the U.S. Department of Labor. The test consists of the following six subtests: Hardware Exercises, which measures the ability to use tools, machine-tending, instruction following, finger dexterity, problem solving, and assembly; Computer Exercises, which screens vision, size-color-shape discrimination, eye-hand coordination, and academic skills; Perceptual Screening, which assesses spatial aptitudes; Talking/Persuasive Screening, which measures the ability to communicate verbally; Physical Capacities and Mobility, which measures dynamic strength; and Vocational/Interest Awareness, which consists of two exercises assessing vocational interests and knowledge of the world of work. The test may be used with Apple and IBM computers. Examiner/self-administered. Suitable for group use.

Timed: 4½ hours

Scoring: Hand key; examiner evaluated; computer scored

Cost: 1 station and Apple computer $7,325.00; 1 station and IBM computer $8,925.00

Publisher: Valpar International Corporation

MESA SHORT FORM

Adolescent, adult

Purpose: Provides baseline data for the development of an individual's education, training, or employment plan or for more extensive vocational evaluation. May be used with individuals contemplating entering the labor market for the first time or changing fields of work.

Description: Multiple-item computer-administered test containing the following two subtests: Hardware Exercises, which measures the ability to use tools, machine tending, instruction following, finger dexterity, problem solving, and assembly; and Computer Exercises, which screens vision, size-color-shape discrimination, eye-hand coordination, memory, reasoning, eye-hand-foot coordination, and academic skills. Computer-generated

reports are available. The test is a shortened version of MESA. Examiner/self-administered. Suitable for group use.

Timed: 1½ hours

Scoring: Hand key; examiner evaluated; computer scored

Cost: $2,650.00

Publisher: Valpar International Corporation

NM CAREER DEVELOPMENT TEST (NMCDT)
C.C. Healy and S.P. Klein

Adolescent   Grades 9-12

Purpose: Measures an individual's knowledge of what is required to hold a job and to advance in an occupation. Used for career counseling and program evaluation.

Description: 25-item paper-pencil multiple-choice test measuring student's feelings about whether success or failure is a function of one's own actions rather than luck. It also measures knowledge of how to conduct oneself properly on the job and of factors that influence advancement in a chosen field or occupation. The test booklets are reusable, and a lay-over stencil is used for scoring. Reliability and norms have been determined from samples of ninth- and twelfth-grade secondary students. Examiner required. Suitable for group use.

Timed: 20 minutes

Scoring: Hand key

Cost: Specimen set $6.00; 35 tests $12.00; 35 answer sheets $4.00; scoring stencil $3.00; manual $4.00

Publisher: Monitor

NM CAREER ORIENTED ACTIVITIES CHECKLIST (NMCOAC)
C.C. Healy and S.P. Klein

Adolescent   Grades 9-12

Purpose: Evaluates an individual's experience in consulting sources of information necessary to plan a career. Used for vocational counseling and planning.

Description: 25-item multiple-choice paper-pencil test evaluating a student's experience in consulting various sources of information about occupations; acting to provide information about occupations the student is considering; obtaining the high-school training needed for occupations being considered; and making definite plans regarding what will be done upon graduation. The test is designed for twelfth-graders, but has been employed successfully to ninth-graders. Test booklets are reusable, and a lay-over stencil is used for scoring. Reliability and norms have been determined from samples of ninth- and twelfth-grade students. Examiner required. Suitable for group use.

Timed: 20 minutes

Scoring: Hand key

Cost: Specimen set $6.00; 35 tests $12.00; 35 answer sheets $4.00; scoring stencils $5.00; manual $4.00

Publisher: Monitor

NM CAREER PLANNING TEST (NMCPT)
C.C. Healy and S.P. Klein

Adolescent   Grades 9-12   ☞ ✍

Purpose: Measures an individual's ability to make appropriate decisions about preparing for and selecting an occupation. Used for career counseling and program evaluation.

Description: 20-item paper-pencil multiple-choice test measuring student knowledge of informational sources to consult to obtain knowledge about various occupations and of what actions should be taken in order to make a decision related to selecting and preparing for an occupation. Test booklets for the two equivalent forms, A and B, are reusable. A lay-over stencil is used for scoring. Reliability and norms for both forms of this test have been determined from samples of ninth- and twelfth-grade secondary students. Examiner required. Suitable for group use.

Timed: 20 minutes

Scoring: Hand key

Cost: Specimen set $6.00; 35 tests (specify form) $12.00; 35 answer sheets (specify form) $4.00; scoring stencil (specify form) $3.00; manual $4.00

Publisher: Monitor

NM JOB APPLICATION PROCEDURES TEST (NMJAPT)
C.C. Healy and S.P. Klein

Adolescent   Grades 9-12   ☞ ✍

Purpose: Assesses an individual's knowledge of how to apply for a job. Used for career counseling and program evaluation.

Description: 20-item paper-pencil multiple-choice test of student ability to make inquiries, read advertisements, and use employment agencies. It also measures the ability to complete a job application form satisfactorily and knowledge of how to conduct oneself during an interview. The test booklets are reusable, and a lay-over stencil is used for scoring. Reliability and norms have been determined from samples of ninth- and twelfth-grade secondary students. Examiner required. Suitable for group use.

Timed: 20 minutes

Scoring: Hand key

Cost: Specimen set $6.00; 35 tests $12.00; 35 answer sheets $4.00; scoring stencil $3.00; manual $4.00

Publisher: Monitor

NM KNOWLEDGE OF OCCUPATIONS TEST (NMKOOT)
C.C. Healy and S.P. Klein

Adolescent   Grades 9-12   ✍

Purpose: Measures an individual's knowledge of the characteristics and requirements of various occupations. Used for vocational counseling and program evaluation.

Description: 25-item multiple-choice paper-pencil test measuring a student's knowledge of job characteristics (hours of work, pay, work environment, tasks, and demand) and of job and personal requirements (training, abilities, and interests). The test booklets are reusable, and a lay-over stencil is used for scoring. Reliability and norms have been determined from samples of ninth- and twelfth-grade secondary students. Self-administered. Suitable for group use.

Timed: 20 minutes

Scoring: Hand key

Cost: Specimen set $6.00; 35 tests $12.00; 35 answer sheets $4.00; scoring stencil $3.00; manual $4.00

Publisher: Monitor

PROGRAM FOR ASSESSING YOUTH EMPLOYMENT SKILLS (PAYES)
Educational Testing Service

Adolescent

Purpose: Measures the attitudes, knowledge, and interests of students preparing for entry-level employment. Used by program directors, counselors, and teachers working with dropouts, potential dropouts, and disadvantaged youth in government training programs, skill centers, vocational high schools, ABE centers, and correctional institutions.

Description: Three orally administered paper-pencil tests assessing attitudes, knowledge, and interests related to entry-level employment. Test Booklet I measures attitudes toward job-holding skills (supervisor's requests, appropriate dress, punctuality), attitudes toward supervision by authority figures (judge, supervisor, teacher, police officer, and parent), and self-confidence in social and employment situations. Measurements are made by assessing responses to multiple-choice questions based on statements, real-life situations, and scenes. Test Booklet II provides cognitive measures, including job knowledge (understanding of education required, salary, task performed, location of work, working hours, and tools), job seeking skills (interpretation of newspaper want ads and job application forms), and practical job-related reasoning in situations that require following directions. Test Booklet III measures seven vocational interest clusters (aesthetic, business, clerical, outdoor, service, science, technical). Respondents indicate their degree of interest in specific job tasks that are described verbally and pic-

tured. Students mark answers directly in test booklets. Examiner required. Suitable for group use.

Untimed: Varies

Scoring: Examiner evaluated

Cost: Complete set (10 each of Test Booklets I, II, and III, score sheets) $53.30; user's guide $2.70; administrators' manual $4.80; technical manual $5.90

Publisher: Cambridge

SPACE RELATIONS (PAPER PUZZLES)
Refer to page 840.

SPACE THINKING (FLAGS)
Refer to page 840.

SWEET'S TECHNICAL INFORMATION TEST (STIT)
R. Sweet

Adolescent   Ages 14-17

Purpose: Measures the technical knowledge of students ages 14-17. Used in counseling settings to assess suitability for technical and practical occupations at trade and subprofessional levels.

Description: 55-item paper-pencil multiple-choice test measuring three areas of technical knowledge: mechanics, electricity, and electronics, and woodwork and general tool use. Items are of four main types: identification, use, operation, and component. The test is designed to measure the type of technical information which might be acquired through an interest in the three areas, rather than as a measure of mechanical aptitude. Australian norms are provided for males and females separately. Materials include a reusable test booklet, answer sheet, scoring key, manual, and specimen set. Not available to NSW purchasers. Examiner evaluated. Suitable for group use.
AUSTRALIAN PUBLISHER

Timed: 20 minutes

Scoring: Hand key; examiner evaluated

Cost: Contact publisher

Publisher: The Australian Council for Educational Research Limited

vocational guidance: occupational knowledge and skills

UNIVERSAL SKILLS SURVEY
Refer to page 849.

VCWS 15—ELECTRICAL CIRCUITRY AND PRINT READING
Refer to page 851.

VCWS 16—DRAFTING
Refer to page 851.

WEBER ADVANCED SPATIAL PERCEPTION TEST (WASP)
P.G. Weber

Adolescent, adult
Ages 13½ and older

Purpose: Measures spatial perception abilities of individuals ages 13½ and older. Used in counseling to assess an individual's suitability for technical and practical occupations at trade and sub-professional levels.

Description: Four paper-pencil subtests measuring spatial abilities in four dimensions. The Form Recognition Test measures the ability to identify a stimulus figure which is combined with other figures similar in shape. The Pattern Perception Test requires the examinee to draw a line around those crosses in a complex pattern which correspond to crosses in a simpler given pattern; the Shape Analysis Test requires the examinee to indicate which of five small shapes are used to compose a larger shape. In the Reflected Figure Test, the examinee draws a given figure upside down. Australian norms are provided. Materials include a reusable test booklet for the Form Recognition Test, a separate answer booklet containing an answer sheet for a Form Recognition Test and questions and answer space for the remaining tests, a set of score keys, a manual, and specimen set. Examiner required. Suitable for group use.
AUSTRALIAN PUBLISHER
Timed: 45 minutes

Scoring: Hand key; examiner evaluated
Cost: Contact publisher
Publisher: The Australian Council for Educational Research Limited

WIDE RANGE EMPLOYABILITY SAMPLE TEST (WREST)
Joseph F. Jastak and Sarah Jastak

Adolescent, adult
Ages 16-adult

Purpose: Measures a person's ability to work at routine manual tasks. Assists in diagnosis of mental retardation and determines the feasibility of competitive employment of the severely handicapped. Used for placement in sheltered workshop or daily activities programs.

Description: 10-item test in which individuals complete simple manual tasks, including folding, stapling, packaging, measuring, assembling, tag stringing, gluing, collating, and color or shade and pattern matching. Each of the tasks is carefully taught prior to testing. The tasks measure "horizontal" achievement (the capacity to do the routine operations involved in all jobs regardless of level). Persons with average or above-average scores on WREST are not mentally retarded, even if their scores on "vertical" achievement or intelligence tests rate them as retarded. Scored for speed and accuracy, the results are expressed in scaled scores for each item. Standard scores are provided for total production quantity and quality and for a combined technical productivity rating. Norms are provided for three populations: general, sheltered workshop, and industrial. Examiner required. Not suitable for group use.
Timed: 1 hour
Scoring: Examiner evaluated
Cost: Complete $750.00; specimen set $28.00
Publisher: Jastak Assessment Systems

WORK APTITUDE PROFILE AND PRACTICE SET (WAPPS)
Refer to page 853.

Teacher Evaluation: Student Opinion of Teachers

ACADEMIC ADVISING INVENTORY
Roger B. Winston, Jr. and Janet A. Sandor

College student

Purpose: Assesses undergraduate academic advising programs. Used with college students.

Description: Multiple-item paper-pencil inventory for evaluating advising programs from a theoretical perspective, making comparisons across institutions, and using in different advising delivery systems including college departments and campus-wide advising centers. The inventory has five parts. The Developmental-Prescriptive Advising Scale and Subscales, Part I (14 items) allow the student to describe the nature of the advising relationship and the quality of activities in which the student and advisor engage. In the Advisor-Advisee Activities (30 items), Part II, students report the frequency of advising activities during an academic year. Part II is composed of five scales: Exploring Institutional Policies, Academic Majors and Courses, Personal Development and Interpersonal Relationships, Teaching Personal Skills, and Registration and Scheduling Classes. In Part III, Satisfaction with Advising, students answer five questions related to their satisfaction with advice during the academic year. Demographic information on the student is requested in Part IV. Part V is made up of optional locally generated items. Self-administered. Suitable for group use.

Untimed: 20 minutes
Scoring: Machine scored
Cost: 50 reusable test forms $17.50; manual $5.50
Publisher: Student Development Associates, Inc.

CLASS ACTIVITIES QUESTIONNAIRE (CAQ)
Refer to page 775.

CLASSROOM ENVIRONMENT SCALE (CES)
Rudolf H. Moos and Edison J. Trickett

Adolescent   Grades 7-12

Purpose: Assesses the teaching atmosphere of junior and senior high-school classrooms in order to evaluate the effects of course content, teaching methods, teacher personality, and class composition.

Description: 90-item paper-pencil test measuring nine dimensions of classroom atmosphere: involvement, affiliation, teacher support, task orientation, competition, order and organization, rule clarity, teacher control, and innovation. These dimensions are grouped into four sets: relationship, personal development, system maintenance, and system change. Materials include four forms: The Real Form (Form R), which measures current perceptions of classroom atmosphere; the Ideal Form (Form I), which measures conceptions of the ideal classroom atmosphere; the Expectations Form (Form E), which measures expectations about a new classroom; and a 36-item Short Form (Form S). Forms I and E are not published, although reworded instructions and items are listed in the manual. Examiner required. Suitable for group use.

Untimed: Not available
Scoring: Examiner evaluated
Cost: Specimen set $7.00; manual $5.00; key $1.50
Publisher: Consulting Psychologists Press, Inc.

COMPREHENSIVE PERSONAL ASSESSMENT SYSTEM: STUDENT EVALUATION OF TEACHING II (SET II)
Donald J. Veldman and Robert F. Peck

Child   Grades 1-3

Purpose: Used for primary student evaluation of teacher behavior.

Description: Three-card choice test in which the child is shown a card and is presented with a statement. If the child agrees with the statement, the card is put in a mailbox; if the child disagrees, the card is put in a wastebasket. A cardboard wastebasket and a mailbox are included in the kit with the cards. Examiner required. Not suitable for group use.

Untimed: 15-20 minutes

Scoring: Hand key

Cost: 100 forms $10.00; manual $1.50

Publisher: Research and Development Center for Teacher Education

---

COUNSELOR FEEDBACK QUESTIONNAIRE

Adolescent   Grades 6-8

Purpose: Provides student feedback of counselor effectiveness.

Description: 17-item paper-pencil survey providing student feedback of counselor effectiveness. Items 1-15 are statements concerning the counselor, which the student rates on a 5-point scale ranging from strongly agree to strongly disagree. The items cover the following areas: availability, concern, trustworthiness, communication skills, and follow-up. Items 16 and 17 are free-response questions. Completed questionnaires are returned to the Office of Public and Professional Services for analysis. A leader feedback report is developed and sent to the counselor on whom the feedback was gathered. All responses and feedback are confidential unless the person evaluated authorizes release of the information. It is also possible to gather feedback for comparisons of effectiveness over time. Examiner required. Suitable for group use.

Untimed: Varies

Scoring: Evaluated by publisher

Cost: $0.80 per instrument (including scoring and reporting services)

Publisher: Office of Public and Professional Services, College of Education, Western Michigan University

---

DIAGNOSTIC TEACHER-RATING SCALE
Sister Mary Amatora

Adolescent, adult
Grades 7 and above

Purpose: Measures students' perceptions of their teachers. Used to analyze and improve student-teacher relations.

Description: 56-item inventory consisting of two scales. The Area Scale (7 items) consists of a list of attributes related to effective teaching and good student-teacher relations. Students rate their teacher for each attribute on a 5-point scale from "worst" to "best." The Diagnostic Checklist (49 items) consists of true-false statements assessing seven factors: liking for teacher; ability to explain; kindness, friendliness, and understanding; fairness in grading; discipline; amount of work required; and liking for lessons. The checklist is available in two similar forms, A and B. Examiner required. Suitable for group use.

Untimed: Not available

Scoring: Hand key; examiner evaluated

Cost: Specimen set $1.50; complete kit (35 record sheets for scale, checklist, manual) $5.95

Publisher: Employers' Tests & Services Associates

ENDEAVOR INSTRUCTIONAL RATING SYSTEM
Peter W. Fry

Adolescent, adult
College students

Purpose: Measures teacher effectiveness at the college and university level.

Description: 7-item paper-pencil measure of the instructor's organizational, communication, and interpersonal skills and the difficulty of the course. A brief rating form is distributed to each student, and the students respond to each item. The test requires advanced planning and is limited to classes with five or more students. The publisher no longer provides a scoring service. Self-administered. Suitable for group use.

Untimed: 5-7 minutes
Scoring: Not available
Cost: Contact publisher
Publisher: Endeavor Information Systems, Inc.

MCCORMICK AFFECTIVE ASSESSMENT TECHNIQUE (MAAT)
Ronald R. McCormick

College student, adult

Purpose: Measures student commitment to instructor-determined topical objectives. Used in professional skills training programs typically offered by business colleges and other college-level classroom settings. May be used to assess the learning needs of business professionals and others.

Description: Multiple-item paper-pencil questionnaire assessing taxonomic affective reactions to instructor-determined topical goals and objectives in higher education classroom instruction. This assessment technique operationalizes the *Affective Domain Handbook* for use in higher education. The affective domain instructional objective is to move the students towards commitment to the instructor-determined cognitive goals and objectives. The three levels of affective-domain categories surveyed are Level I, receiving; Level II, responding; and Level III, valuing. Simple awareness is the lowest, and commitment is the highest of the nine affective domain subcategories measured. The instructor designs the questionnaire by constructing three sub-topic stimulus word items for each instructional topic. Students respond to these subtopic items in a sentence-completion format by selecting affective-domain word stems that best describe their relationship to the instructor-determined subtopic item. Any number of subtopic items may be used, but 15 sub-topic items surveying 5 course topics is optimum. Scoring keys are provided for tabulation and grouping of questionnaire scores into three affective domain categories and nine subcategories. Interpretive guidelines are provided. Three forms of the questionnaire, which may be

reproduced for classroom use, are included in the manual. Examiner required. Suitable for group use. Also may be self-administered for survey use.
Untimed: 20 minutes for a 15-item questionnaire
Scoring: Examiner evaluated
Cost: Manual, 3 reproducible questionnaire forms $25.00
Publisher: Dr. R.R. McCormick & Associates

THE PURDUE INSTRUCTOR PERFORMANCE INDICATOR
H.H. Remmers and J.H. Snedeker

**Adolescent, adult
College students**

Purpose: Measures professor's effectiveness as perceived by students. Used for course evaluation.

Description: Multiple-item forced-choice paper-pencil measure of student ratings of professor's effectiveness. The rater chooses from among four alternatives in each of 12 blocks. All phrases in each block are socially acceptable; half discriminate between effective and ineffective teachers. Materials include two forms, A and B. Self-administered. Suitable for group use.
Untimed: 10-15 minutes
Scoring: Hand key
Cost: Contact publisher
Publisher: Purdue Research Foundation/ University Book Store

THE PURDUE RATING SCALE FOR INSTRUCTION
H.H. Remmers and D.N. Elliott

**Adolescent, adult
College students**

Purpose: Measures student perceptions of professors and the classroom teaching situation. Used for research and course evaluation.

Description: Multiple-item paper-pencil test of student perceptions of 10 characteristics of professors and 14 aspects of the classroom teaching situation. Self-administered. Suitable for group use.

Untimed: 5-10 minutes
Scoring: Machine scorable; may be computer scored
Cost: Contact publisher
Publisher: Purdue Research Foundation/ University Book Store

THE PURDUE TEACHER EVALUATION SCALE (PTES)
Ralph R. Bentley and Allan R. Starry

Adolescent   Grades 7-12 ☞ 🖎

Purpose: Measures student opinions of teachers. Used to provide teachers with information for a program of self-improvement and development.

Description: Multiple-item paper-pencil measure of six dimensions of student attitudes toward teachers: ability to motivate students, ability to control students, subject matter orientation of teacher, student-teacher communication, teaching methods and procedures, and fairness of teacher. Examiner required. Suitable for group use.
Untimed: 20 minutes
Scoring: Hand key; may be computer scored
Cost: Contact publisher
Publisher: Purdue Research Foundation/ University Book Store

STUDENT INSTRUCTIONAL REPORT (SIR)
Research Staff of Educational Testing Service

Adolescent, adult College students ☞ 🖎

Purpose: Measures teacher performance. Used for instructional improvement, administrative decisions, and student course selection.

Description: 39-item paper-pencil test assessing six aspects of teacher performance: course organization and planning; faculty/student interaction; communication; course difficulty and workload; textbooks and readings; and tests and exams. The instrument is administered to students during regular class sessions.

Examiner required. Suitable for group use. Available in French (for Canadian universities) and Spanish.
Untimed: 50 minutes
Scoring: Computer scored
Cost: First 20,000 forms $0.18 each, processing first 5,000 forms $0.35 each
Publisher: Educational Testing Service

STUDENT OPINION INVENTORY
Refer to page 692.

TEACHER FEEDBACK QUESTIONNAIRE

Adolescent   Grades 6-12 ☞ 🖎

Purpose: Evaluates students perceptions of their classroom teacher. Used primarily for self-improvement.

Description: 27-item paper-pencil inventory assessing how students perceive important characteristics of their teacher. Students rate items 1-25 on a 5-point scale ranging from strongly agree to strongly disagree. The items cover the following areas: knowledge of subject, fairness, control, attitude toward students, variety in teaching procedures, encouragement of student participation, and sense of humor. Items 26-27 are free-response questions. Completed questionnaires are returned to the Office of Public and Professional Services for analysis. A teacher feedback report is developed and sent to the teacher on whom the student feedback was gathered. Student responses and feedback sent to the teacher are confidential unless the teacher authorizes release of the information. It is also possible to gather feedback for comparisons of effectiveness over time. The test kit includes instructions to the examiner (temporary substitute teacher), a teacher ID form, and a questionnaire. Examiner required. Suitable for group use.
Untimed: 15-20 minutes
Scoring: Evaluated by publisher
Cost: $0.80 per instrument (including scoring and reporting services)
Publisher: Office of Public and Professional Services, College of Education, Western Michigan University

THINKING ABOUT MY SCHOOL
Joanne Rand Whitmore

Child   Grades 4-6

Purpose: Measures perceptions of the school environment and feelings about the school held by students in Grades 4-6.

Description: 47-item paper-pencil questionnaire measuring students' perceptions of their school. The test is used to increase teachers' understanding of pupils as a group and as individuals, stimulate classroom analysis of problems and discussions of attitudes and behavior at school, and provide student government leaders or other groups with information to study school problems. Examiner required. Suitable for group use.

Untimed: Varies

Scoring: Examiner evaluated

Cost: Complete kit $19.95

Publisher: D.O.K. Publishers, Inc.

THE WILSON TEACHER-APPRAISAL SCALE
Howard Wilson

Adolescent, adult   Grades 7-16

Purpose: Allows teachers to see how they are perceived by their students. Used at the close of an academic term, often in conjunction with A Self-Appraisal Scale for Teachers, to aid in the professional development of classroom instructors.

Description: 16-item paper-pencil rating scale allowing students to rate the performance of their classroom instructors. Students rate the teacher as a person and as an instructor compared to other instructors. Course content and assignments are also rated. The scale is purchased and supplied by the institution and voluntarily used by teachers as a tool to increase their effectiveness. Self-administered. Suitable for group use.

Untimed: 5 minutes

Scoring: Examiner evaluated

Cost: 50 scales $2.50

Publisher: Administrative Research Associates

Teacher Evaluation: Teacher Attitudes

ADMINISTRATOR FEEDBACK QUESTIONNAIRE

Adult

Purpose: Evaluates the image of an administrator held by groups such as teachers, parents, service personnel, or board members. Used for administrator appraisal and self-improvement.

Description: 28-item paper-pencil survey measuring reactions of relevant groups of people concerning the effectiveness of an administrator. These groups are usually teachers, but may be other administrators or noncertified personnel. Items 1-26 are statements about the administrator's abilities which must be rated on a 5-point scale from strongly agree to strongly disagree. Items 27 and 28 are free-response questions concerning the administrator's strengths and weaknesses. Completed questionnaires are returned to the Office of Public and Professional Services for analysis. A leader feedback report is developed and sent to the administrator on whom the feedback was gathered. Group responses and the feedback sent to the administrator are confidential unless the person evaluated authorizes release of the information to a superordinate. It is also possible to gather feedback for comparisons of effectiveness over time. The test kit includes instructions for using the questionnaire, an administrator ID form, and a questionnaire. Examiner required. Suitable for group use.

Untimed: Varies

Scoring: Evaluated by publisher

Cost: $0.80 per instrument (including scoring and reporting services)

Publisher: Office of Public and Professional Services, College of Education, Western Michigan Unversity

CANFIELD INSTRUCTIONAL STYLES INVENTORY (CIS)
Albert A. Canfield and Judith S. Canfield

Adult

Purpose: Identifies a teacher's preferred instructional methods. Used in conjunction with the Learning Styles Inventory to maximize teaching and learning efficiency.

Description: 25-item paper-pencil forced-rank inventory assessing a teacher's preferences concerning learning environments, instructional modalities, and topical interests. The inventory also measures how much responsibility the instructor will assume for student learning (instead of measuring performance expectancy), identifies areas where instructional training would be most beneficial, provides information to help instructors interpret classroom problems and student reactions, and measures the same dimensions as the Canfield Learning Styles Inventory to allow for one-to-one comparison between the two inventories. The test booklets are reusable. Separate norms are provided for male and female instructors. Self-administered. Suitable for group use.

Untimed: 25-40 minutes

Scoring: Self-scored

Cost: Starter set (15 test booklets, 25 answer sheets, 25 profile sheets, guide) $32.95; specimen set (includes manual) $12.95

Publisher: Humanics Media

CHANGE AGENT QUESTIONNAIRE (CAQ)
Refer to page 911.

CLASS ACTIVITIES QUESTIONNAIRE (CAQ)
Joe M. Steele

Adolescent, adult

Purpose: Assesses the instructional climate of upper-elementary and high-school classrooms. Enables teachers to determine whether goals and expectations are clearly defined in the classroom. Assesses affective factors, such as openness, independence, divergence, and emphasis on grades.

Description: 30-item paper-pencil questionnaire assessing five dimensions of instructional climate in the classroom: lower thought processes, higher thought processes, classroom focus, classroom climate, and student opinions. Items 1-27 assess cognitive emphasis and classroom conditions by asking students to rate statements about their classroom experiences on a 4-point scale ranging from "strongly agree" to "strongly disagree." Items 28-30 allow the students to describe in their own words what they perceive to be the strengths and weaknesses of their class. Teachers complete the questionnaire twice, once to indicate what they intend to emphasize in the classroom and a second time to indicate what they predict the students as a group will say. Computer scoring compares the teacher's responses to those provided by the students. Examiner required. Suitable for group use.

Untimed: 20-30 minutes

Scoring: Computer scored

Cost: Test kit (30 student forms, two teacher forms, manual, and computer analysis) $20.95

Publisher: Creative Learning Press, Inc.

EARLY CHILDHOOD ENVIRONMENT RATING SCALE
Thelma Harms and Richard M. Clifford

Adult

Purpose: Evaluates the adequacy of preschool child care settings. Used to assess class daycare, headstart, nursery school, and kindergarten programs.

Description: 37-item paper-pencil test in which the examiner rates child-care environments in terms of use of space, materials and experiences to enhance child development, and daily schedule and level of supervision provided. A room-by-room evaluation covers routines for the personal care of the children, room furnishing and display, language-reasoning experiences, fine- and gross-motor activities, creative activities, social development activities, and adult needs. Materials include a rating scale book and a scoring sheet. Examiner required. Not suitable for group use.

Untimed: Not available

Scoring: Examiner evaluated

Cost: Rating scale $7.95; 30 additional scoring sheets $5.95

Publisher: Teachers College Press

EDUCATIONAL VALUES (VAL-ED)
Will Schutz

Adult

Purpose: Assesses an individual's attitudes towards education. Used to evaluate the working relationships of students, teachers, administrators, or community members.

Description: Multiple-item paper-pencil survey of values regarding interpersonal relationships in school settings. The factors included relate to "inclusion, control, and affection" at both the feeling and the behavioral levels and to the purpose and importance of education. Examiner/self-administered. Suitable for group use.

Untimed: Not available

Scoring: Hand key

Cost: Specimen set (including keys) $2.75

Publisher: Consulting Psychologists Press, Inc.

EMPATHY INVENTORY (EI)
John R. Thurston

Adult

Purpose: Measures ability of nursing faculty, counselors, and others to empathize with nursing students. Used for self-evaluation.

Description: 75-item paper-pencil test with a dual-choice format providing interested individuals an opportunity to check their empathic ability. Materials include a self-directing booklet, answer sheet, and scoring key. A comprehensive manual covering this and other NRA tests is available. Self-administered. Suitable for group use.

Untimed: 30 minutes

Scoring: Hand key; scoring service available

Cost: Specimen set (excluding scoring, key) $10.00; 50 answer sheets $5.00; scoring key $5.00; comprehensive manual $15.00; scoring service $2.00 per test

Publisher: Nursing Research Associates

ILLINOIS TESTS IN THE TEACHING OF ENGLISH
William H. Evans and Paul H. Jacobs

Adult Teachers

Purpose: Measures high-school English teachers' achievement of professionally established objectives relating to knowledge and attitudes about the English language and literature and how subjects should be taught. Used by schools and colleges for teacher-training evaluation.

Description: Four paper-pencil competency tests concerning the teaching of the English language and literature: Knowledge of Language, Attitude and Knowledge in Written Composition, Knowledge of Literature, and Knowledge of the Teaching of English. Each test is criterion-referenced, and the battery as a whole is based on criteria developed in the form of guidelines and standards by educational specialists and practicing teachers in cooperation with more than 20 universities and colleges. Examiner required. Suitable for group use.

Untimed: Not available

Scoring: Hand key; may be computer scored

Cost: 1-10 individual tests $1.00 each; 11-50 copies $0.55 each; 8 keys $12.00; 50 OpScan answer sheets $3.00; individual manuals $2.00 each

Publisher: Southern Illinois University Press

OPINIONS TOWARD ADOLESCENTS (OTA SCALE)
William T. Martin

Adolescent, adult Grades 5-7

Purpose: Evaluates attitudes and personality factors that may help or inhibit interpersonal relationships between adults and adolescents. Used to screen persons who will be working with adolescents and to educate current staff members.

Description: 89-item paper-pencil inventory examining bipolar attitudes on the following subscales: conservative-liberal, permissive-punitive, morally accepting-morally restrictive, democratic-authoritarian, trust-mistrust, acceptance-prejudice, misunderstanding-understanding, and sincerity-skepticism (a validity scale reflecting test-taking attitude). Norms are provided for various adult and college groups. A fifth- to seventh-grade reading level is required. Self-administered. Suitable for group use.

Untimed: 20 minutes

Scoring: Hand key

Cost: Examiner's set (manual, keys, 25 test books, 25 answer sheets, 25 profile sheets) $32.00; 25 tests $13.50; 25 profile sheets $7.50; 25 answer sheets $6.00; keys $6.00; manual $4.00

Publisher: Psychologists and Educators, Inc.

PERFORMANCE LEVELS OF A SCHOOL PROGRAM SURVEY (PLSPS)
Frank E. Williams

Adult

Purpose: Evaluates teacher and administrator perceptions of the value of a classroom, a building, or a district program. Used to insure compliance with federal, state, and local guidelines concerning the quality and content of academic programs.

Description: Multiple-item paper-pencil inventory evaluating the following eight areas of multiple abilities that are specifically defined in federal, state, and local guidelines: general intellectual, specific academics, leadership, creative productive thinking, psychomotor, visual performing arts, affective, and vocational career. The inventory pinpoints those areas receiving insufficient emphasis. Self-administered. Suitable for group use.

Untimed: Varies

Scoring: Self-scored

Cost: Test kit (survey materials for 30 participants) $14.95

Publisher: D.O.K. Publishers, Inc.

PURDUE STUDENT-TEACHER OPINIONAIRE—FORM B (PSTO)
Ralph R. Bentley and JoAnn Price

Adult

Purpose: Measures student-teacher morale. Used for providing schools with feedback about student-teachers' experiences.

Description: Multiple-item paper-pencil measure of nine aspects of student-teacher morale: rapport with supervising teacher, student-teacher rapport with principal, rapport with university supervisor, teaching as a profession, school facilities, professional preparation, rapport with students, rapport with other teachers and student-teacher load. Examiner required. Suitable for group use.

Untimed: 20-30 minutes

Scoring: Hand key; may be computer scored

Cost: Contact publisher

Publisher: Purdue Research Foundation/ University Book Store

THE PURDUE TEACHER OPINIONAIRE (PTO)
Ralph R. Bentley and Averno M. Rempel

Adult

Purpose: Assesses teacher opinions of the school environment. Used for studying teacher morale.

Description: Multiple-item paper-pencil measure of 10 teacher morale factors: teacher rapport with principal, satisfaction with teaching, rapport among teachers, teacher salary, teacher load, curriculum issues, teacher status, community support of education, school facilities and services, and community pressures. Materials include a PTO Supplement with two new factors: teacher rapport with school board and superintendent. Examiner required. Suitable for group use.

Untimed: 20-30 minutes

Scoring: Hand key; may be computer scored

Cost: Opinionaire $1.50

Publisher: Purdue Research Foundation/ University Book Store

RUCKER-GABLE EDUCATIONAL PROGRAMMING SCALE
Chauncy N. Rucker and Robert K. Gable

Adult   Teachers

Purpose: Assesses the ability of teachers to measure the attitudes of handicapped children.

Description: 30-item paper-pencil test measuring a teacher's attitude toward and knowledge of appropriate placement for handicapped children on the basis of a brief description of the student's handicap. The student handicap range includes mildly, moderately, and severely handicapped; mentally retarded, emotionally disturbed, and learning disabled; and total disability. Self-administered by examiner. Suitable for group use. Available in Spanish and Chinese.

Untimed: 20-30 minutes

Scoring: Computer scored

Cost: Specimen set $10.00; manual $9.00; scoring service $40.00

Publisher: Rucker-Gable Associates

A SELF-APPRAISAL SCALE FOR TEACHERS
Howard Wilson

Adult   Teachers

Purpose: Allows teachers to self-appraise their classroom performance. Often used in conjunction with the Wilson Teacher-Appraisal Scale at the close of an academic term to aid in the professional development of classroom instructors.

Description: 102-item paper-pencil inventory allowing instructors to rate themselves in six areas: teacher as a person, teacher as a specialist and educator, relations with students, course content, classroom performance, and feelings about how students perceive them. Each item in the scale reflects a characteristic of competency as related to teaching methods. Teachers rate themselves for each item on a 5-point scale from "high" to "low," circling items of particular importance. The scale is often purchased and supplied by the educational institution and voluntarily used by teachers as a tool to increase their classroom effectiveness. Self-administered. Suitable for group use.

Untimed: 20 minutes

Scoring: Self-scored

Cost: Scale $1.50

Publisher: Administrative Research Associates

STAGES OF CONCERN QUESTIONNAIRE (SOCQ)
Gene E. Hall, Archie A. George, and William L. Rutherford

Adult

Purpose: Assesses faculty concerns regarding the implementation of educational innovations. Used to monitor and evaluate programs implementing educational innovations.

Description: 35-item paper-pencil questionnaire assessing attitudes toward specific educational innovations. Each item is rated on a 7-point scale according to the individual teacher's stage of concern: 0-awareness; 1-informational; 2-personal; 3-management; 4-consequences; 5-collaboration; and 6-refocusing. Self-administered. Suitable for group use. Available in Flemish, Hebrew, and Spanish. The translations have new norms and confirming factor analyses.

Untimed: 15 minutes

Scoring: Hand key; examiner evaluated; may be computer scored

Cost: Manual (includes master copy of questionnaire) $4.00

Publisher: The Research and Development Center for Teacher Education

A TEACHER ATTITUDE INVENTORY (TAI): IDENTIFYING TEACHER POSITIONS IN RELATION TO EDUCATIONAL ISSUES AND DECISIONS
Joanne Rand Whitmore

Adult

Purpose: Identifies teacher attitudes regarding philosophical issues and contrasting educational practices.

Description: Multiple-item paper-pencil questionnaire used by district administrators, principals, and teachers for determining attitudes toward educational practices. The responses help in planning in-service professional growth programs, faculty discussions, team teaching, and classroom setting for gifted students. This tool also is useful for evaluation, research, and determining teaching styles. Self-administered. Suitable for group use.

Untimed: Varies
Scoring: Examiner evaluated
Cost: Complete kit $19.95
Publisher: D.O.K. Publishers, Inc.

TEACHER OPINION INVENTORY
*National Study of
School Evaluation Staff*

Adult   Classroom teachers

Purpose: Assesses teachers' opinions of their school and its programs. Provides an opportunity for direct faculty recommendations. Used by school personnel to make decisions regarding program development, policy formulation, administrative organization, faculty development, and community relations.

Description: 72-item paper-pencil opinion survey consisting of two parts. Part A contains 64 multiple-choice items assessing teacher opinion of various aspects of the school. Part B contains eight open-ended questions constructed for teachers to make recommendations for school improvement. The manual describes the development of the instrument, provides instructions for administering the inventory, and contains a single copy of both Parts A and B. The inventory may be administered independently or in conjunction with the Parent Opinion Inventory, the Student Opinion Inventory, or as part of a complete school evaluation program. Self-administered. Suitable for group use. Available in Spanish.

Untimed: Varies
Scoring: Examiner evaluated
Cost: 25 copies Part A $3.00; 25 copies of Part B $2.00; manual $2.00
Publisher: National Study of School Evaluation

TEACHER OPINIONAIRE ON DEMOCRACY
Enola Ledbetter

Adult

Purpose: Assesses teacher's attitudes about what is and is not wise in the way children are treated in school. Used for teacher surveys and college instruction.

Description: 65-item paper-pencil test measuring the "democraticness" of a teacher's philosophy, defined as the extent to which the teacher purports to respect the personality and purpose of the pupil. The teacher is asked to agree or disagree with each statement by marking it plus or minus. Self-administered. Suitable for group use.

Untimed: 30 minutes
Scoring: Hand key
Cost: Manual, sample opinionaire $1.00
Publisher: Lentz Peace Research Laboratory

TEACHING STYLE INVENTORY
*J. Robert Hanson and
Harvey F. Silver*

Adult   Teachers

Purpose: Identifies preferred teaching styles.

Description: 40-item paper-pencil diagnostic tool yielding a teaching style profile. Individuals rank their preferences for 10 categories of behavior: classroom atmosphere, teaching techniques, planning, preferred qualities of students, teacher/student interaction, classroom management, appropriate behaviors, teaching behavior, evaluation, and educational goals. Results help teachers understand their styles of teaching. Administrators can use the information for helping teachers vary their teaching styles to meet the needs of different learning styles. The instrument includes detailed descriptions of four basic teaching styles. Self-administered. Suitable for group use.

Untimed: 30 minutes
Scoring: Self-scored
Cost: $3.50 per copy
Publisher: Hanson, Silver, Strong and Associates, Inc.

TROUBLE-SHOOTING CHECKLIST (TSC) FOR HIGHER EDUCATIONAL SETTINGS
B.A. Manning

Adult

Purpose: Measures organizational variables that predict an educational institution's potential for successfully adopting innovations. Identifies areas of acceptance and resistance. Used by personnel involved in implementing innovations in higher educational settings.

Description: 100-item paper-pencil questionnaire assessing an institution's potential for adopting innovations along the following five scales: organizational climate, organizational staff, communications, innovative experience, and students. The scores on the five scales provide a profile of an institution's particular strengths and weaknesses with respect to the adoption process. Self-administered. Suitable for group use.

Untimed: Varies
Scoring: Examiner evaluated
Cost: Instrument and manual $2.50
Publisher: Distributed by ERIC Document Reproduction Service

TROUBLE-SHOOTING CHECKLIST (TSC) FOR SCHOOL-BASED SETTINGS
B.A. Manning

Adult

Purpose: Measures organizational variables that predict a school's potential for

successfully adopting and implementing educational innovations. Identifies areas of acceptance and resistance. Used by school personnel involved in implementing educational innovations.

Description: Multiple-item paper-pencil checklist assessing a school's potential for adopting innovations along the following seven scales: communication patterns, innovative experience, school-based staff, central administration, relations with the community, organizational climate, and students. The scores on the seven scales provide a profile of a school's particular strengths and weaknesses with respect to the adoption process. Self-administered. Suitable for group use.

Untimed: Varies
Scoring: Examiner evaluated
Cost: Instrument and manual $2.50
Publisher: Distributed by ERIC Document Reproduction Service

Miscellaneous

CHANGE FACILITATOR STAGES OF CONCERN QUESTIONNAIRE (CFSOCQ)
William L. Rutherford, Gene E. Hall, and Archie A. George

Adult

Purpose: Assesses stages of concern of group discussion leaders (change facilitators) when they are involved in facilitating educational changes. Used for training and monitoring the progress of change facilitators.

Description: 35-item paper-pencil questionnaire measuring seven stages of concern: awareness, information, personal, management, consequence, collaboration, and refocusing. All scales are assessed in relation to the generic role of being a change facilitator. The test is normed for educational settings only. The test may be mailed to the respondent. Self-administered. Suitable for group use. Available in Dutch and Flemish.

Untimed: 15 minutes
Scoring: Hand key; examiner evaluated; may be computer scored

Cost: Manual (master copy of question-naire) $5.00

Publisher: The Research and Development Center for Teacher Education

COMMUNITY COLLEGE GOALS INVENTORY (CCGI)
*Research staff of
Educational Testing Service*

**Adolescent, adult
College students**

Purpose: Assesses the educational goals of community colleges. Used to establish priorities and to provide direction to present and future planning.

Description: 90-item paper-pencil test assessing the educational goals of community colleges. The 20 goal areas are divided into two types, outcome goals and process goals. The outcome goals are academic development, intellectual orientation, individual personal development, humanism/altruism, cultural/aesthetic awareness, traditional religiousness, vocational preparation, advanced training, research, meeting local needs, public service, social egalitarianism, and social criticism/activism. The process goals are freedom, democratic governance, community, intellectual/aesthetic environment, innovation, off-campus learning, and accountability/efficiency. The inventory is distributed to a random sample of students, faculty, and administrators at community colleges. Materials include space for 20 additional locally written goals. Self-administered. Suitable for group use.

Untimed: 45 minutes

Scoring: Computer scored

Cost: Booklet $0.65; processing $1.75

Publisher: Educational Testing Service

COUNTRY SCHOOL EXAMINATIONS
*Michigan Department of
Public Instruction*

All ages

Purpose: Compares current elementary-school examinations of basic skills and competency with similar tests given in the early 20th century. Used to develop student, parent, and community appreciation for early standards of educational achievement.

Description: Paper-pencil collection of six reprints from historic educational achievement tests given in the early 1900s in a one-room schoolhouse in Michigan. One is the State of Michigan Examination Questions of 1921 for a city teachers' examination, and three are the State of Michigan Examination Questions used in 1919, 1920, and 1921 for eighth-grade graduation. The other two are the Michigan Winter Term Examination of 1913 and the Michigan Fall Term Examination of 1914, for Grades 1-8. Self-administered. Suitable for group use.

Untimed: 45 minutes

Scoring: Examiner evaluated

Cost: Specimen set (includes all examinations) $8.95; 25 individual test booklets $8.75

Publisher: Research Concepts

EDUCATIONAL GOAL ATTAINMENT TESTS
*Bruce W. Tuckman and
Alberto P.S. Montare*

Adolescent   Grades 7-12

Purpose: Assesses a broad range of cognitive and affective educational goals common to many communities. Used to assess and revise a school system's instructional program.

Description: 1,430-item paper-pencil battery of 10 tests designed to assess school and district needs rather than individual student performance. Three types of test items are used: knowledge items, measuring information that a student has acquired and retained; attitude items, measuring a student's orientation or feelings as reflected by his inclination to agree or disagree with a given attitude statement; and behavior items, indicating how students will behave (these items describe a behavior and ask the student to indicate whether and to what degree he performs this behavior). Each student takes one subtest; retesting may be performed by administering different subtests to the student. Examiner required. Suitable for group use. Available in Spanish.

Timed: 1 hour, 40 minutes

Scoring: Hand key; scoring service available

Cost: Test booklet $0.60; answer sheet $0.05; manual $0.60; no charge for Information Booklet and Handbook for Test Administrators

Publisher: Phi Delta Kappa

EDUCATIONAL GOAL ATTAINMENT TESTS: ARTS AND LEISURE
Bruce W. Tuckman and Alberto P.S. Montare

Adolescent   Grades 7-12

Purpose: Assesses knowledge, attitudes, and behavior related to hobbies, leisure activities, music, art, and literature. Used for curriculum planning in the arts and leisure area.

Description: 150-item test assessing the arts and leisure programs of a community-school program and indicating areas needing improvement or growth. Eight areas are evaluated: knowledge related to hobbies and leisure activities, attitudes toward outdoor pastimes, attitudes toward indoor pastimes, behavior in hobbies and leisure, knowledge of music, knowledge of art and literature, attitude toward value of aesthetics, and behavior of creative expression. Examiner required. Suitable for group use.

Timed: 1 hour, 40 minutes

Scoring: Hand key; scoring service available

Cost: Test booklet $0.60; answer sheet $0.05; manual $0.60; no charge for Information Booklet and Handbook for Test Administrators

Publisher: Phi Delta Kappa

EDUCATIONAL GOAL ATTAINMENT TESTS: CAREERS
Bruce W. Tuckman and Alberto P.S. Montare

Adolescent   Grades 7-12

Purpose: Assesses knowledge, attitudes, and behavior related to careers. Used for curriculum planning in career development and vocational areas.

Description: 139-item paper-pencil test assessing the careers programs of a community school and indicating areas needing improvement. Eight areas are evaluated: knowledge of trades, knowledge of business, attitudes toward good workmanship, behavior related to jobs, knowledge of career information sources, knowledge of job opportunity, attitude of career maturity, behavior of career, and self-awareness. Examiner required. Suitable for group use. Available in Spanish.

Timed: 1 hour, 40 minutes

Scoring: Hand key; scoring service available

Cost: Test booklet $0.60; answer sheet $0.05; manual $0.60; no charge for Information Booklet and Handbook for Test Administrators

Publisher: Phi Delta Kappa

EDUCATIONAL GOAL ATTAINMENT TESTS: CIVICS
Bruce W. Tuckman and Alberto P.S. Montare

Adolescent   Grades 7-12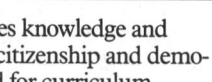

Purpose: Assesses knowledge and attitudes toward citizenship and democratic ideas. Used for curriculum planning in civics.

Description: 172-item paper-pencil test assessing the civics programs of a community school and indicating areas needing improvement. Eight areas are evaluated: knowledge of civic rights, knowledge of civic responsibilities, attitude toward productive citizenship, attitude toward respect for property, knowledge of rights and privileges, knowledge of American heritage, behavior of loyalty to country, and behavior of patriotism. Examiner required. Suitable for group use. Available in Spanish.

Timed: 1 hour, 40 minutes

Scoring: Hand key; scoring service available

Cost: Test booklet $0.60; answer sheet $0.05; manual $0.60; no charge for Information Booklet and Handbook for Test Administrators
Publisher: Phi Delta Kappa

EDUCATIONAL GOAL ATTAINMENT TESTS: ENGLISH LANGUAGE
Bruce W. Tuckman and Alberto P.S. Montare

Adolescent   Grades 7-12

Purpose: Assesses language art skills. Used for curriculum development in English.

Description: 127-item paper-pencil test assessing the English Language program of a community school and indicating areas needing improvement. Three areas are evaluated: knowledge of word meaning; knowledge of language mechanics; and knowledge of reading comprehension. Examiner required. Suitable for group use.
Timed: 1 hour, 40 minutes
Scoring: Hand key; scoring service available
Cost: Test booklet $0.60; answer sheet $0.05; manual $0.60; no charge for Information Booklet and Handbook for Test Administrators
Publisher: Phi Delta Kappa

EDUCATIONAL GOAL ATTAINMENT TESTS: GENERAL KNOWLEDGE
Bruce W. Tuckman and Alberto P.S. Montare

Adolescent   Grades 7-12

Purpose: Assesses general knowledge of math, science, current and historical events, and culture. Used for general curriculum planning.

Description: 126-item paper-pencil test assessing the general knowledge of students in a community school. Five areas are evaluated: math, science, current and historical events, family in culture, and culture in general. Examiner required. Suitable for group use. Available in Spanish.

Timed: 1 hour, 40 minutes
Scoring: Hand key; scoring service available
Cost: Test booklet $0.60; answer sheet $0.05; manual $0.60; no charge for Information Booklet and Handbook for Test Administrators
Publisher: Phi Delta Kappa

EDUCATIONAL GOAL ATTAINMENT TESTS: HUMAN RELATIONS
Bruce W. Tuckman and Alberto P.S. Montare

Adolescent   Grades 7-12

Purpose: Assesses knowledge, attitudes, and behavior related to cultures and change. Used for curriculum planning in human relations programs.

Description: 152-item paper-pencil test assessing the human relations programs of a community school. Nine areas are evaluated: knowledge of others, knowledge of group process, attitudes of tolerance toward others, attitude toward human relations, behavior of positive human relations, knowledge related to change, attitude of tolerance of ambiguity, attitude of internal control, and behavior of nonconformity. Examiner required. Suitable for group use.
Timed: 1 hour, 40 minutes
Scoring: Hand key; scoring service available
Cost: Test booklet $0.60; answer sheet $0.05; manual $0.60; no charge for Information Booklet and Handbook for Test Administrators
Publisher: Phi Delta Kappa

EDUCATIONAL GOAL ATTAINMENT TESTS: LATIN AMERICA
Bruce W. Tuckman and Alberto P.S. Montare

Adolescent   Grades 7-12

Purpose: Assesses knowledge of the Puerto Rican culture and Spanish language arts skills. Used for Latin American curriculum planning.

Description: 123-item paper-pencil test assessing understanding of Latin American culture and foreign language programs of a community school and indicating areas needing improvement. The test is written half in English and half in Spanish to test facility in the language. Four areas are evaluated: knowledge of history and culture; knowledge of people, places, and arts; knowledge of language mechanics; and knowledge of vocabulary reading comprehension. Examiner required. Suitable for group use.

Timed: 1 hour, 40 minutes

Scoring: Hand key; scoring service available

Cost: Test booklet $0.60; answer sheet $0.05; manual $0.60; no charge for Information Booklet and Handbook for Test Administrators

Publisher: Phi Delta Kappa

EDUCATIONAL GOAL ATTAINMENT TESTS: LIFE SKILLS
Bruce W. Tuckman and Alberto P.S. Montare

Adolescent   Grades 7-12   [☞ ✍]

Purpose: Assesses knowledge, attitudes, and behavior toward family and resource-management and health practices. Used for curriculum planning for life skills classes.

Description: 181-item paper-pencil test assessing the life skills programs of a community school. Ten areas are evaluated: knowledge of family management, attitudes toward family management, behavior of family management, knowledge of personal economics, knowledge of environment, behavior of resource management, knowledge of health practices, attitudes toward health practices, behavior of personal hygiene, and behavior of exercise and diet. Examiner required. Suitable for group use. Available in Spanish.

Timed: 1 hour, 40 minutes

Scoring: Hand key; scoring service available

Cost: Test booklet $0.60; answer sheet $0.05; manual $0.60; no charge for Information Booklet and Handbook for Test Administrators

Publisher: Phi Delta Kappa

EDUCATIONAL GOAL ATTAINMENT TESTS: REASONING
Bruce W. Tuckman and Alberto P.S. Montare

Adolescent   Grades 7-12   [☞ ✍]

Purpose: Assesses the ability to use logical and scientific reasoning. Used to assess the need for development of logical reasoning within a curriculum.

Description: 49-item paper-pencil test assessing the "reasoning developmental programs" of a community school and indicating areas needing improvement. The two areas measured are knowledge of scientific methods and problem-solving skills. Examiner required. Suitable for group use.

Timed: 1 hour, 40 minutes

Scoring: Hand key; scoring service available

Cost: Test booklet $0.60; answer sheet $0.05; manual $0.60; no charge for Information Booklet and Handbook for Test Administrators

Publisher: Phi Delta Kappa

EDUCATIONAL GOAL ATTAINMENT TESTS: SELF TEST
Bruce W. Tuckman and Alberto P.S. Montare

Adolescent   Grades 7-12   [☞ ✍]

Purpose: Assesses a student's attitudes towards himself and his values and the way in which his behavior reflects those values. Used to enhance a curriculum to develop student pride in work, feelings of self-worth, good character, and self-respect.

Description: 208-item paper-pencil test assessing the self-development programs of a community school and indicating areas needing improvement. Ten areas are evaluated: attitudes toward one's achievements, attitudes of self-awareness, attitudes of self-worth, attitudes of moral values, attitudes of character, behaving ethically, behaving with self-discipline, attitudes of curiosity, attitudes toward learning, and behavior of self-improvement. Examiner required. Suitable for group use.

Timed: 1 hour, 40 minutes

Scoring: Hand key; scoring service available

Cost: Test booklet $0.60; answer sheet $0.05; manual $0.60; no charge for Information Booklet and Handbook for Test Administrators

Publisher: Phi Delta Kappa

EFFECTIVE SCHOOL BATTERY (ESB)
Gary D. Gottfredson

Adolescent   Grades 7-12

Purpose: Assesses the school environment of middle, junior, and senior high schools. Used by administrators, board members, and teachers to identify excellence, diagnose problems, plan and develop programs, monitor progress, and research specific aspects of the school.

Description: Multiple-item paper-pencil survey used with students and teachers for determining perceptions about school climate and characteristics of students and teachers in the school. Results describe 34 specific aspects of school climate and student and teacher characteristics. Four profiles that describe the school and can be used to compare any school to other schools are produced. Examiner required. Suitable for group use.

Untimed: 50 minutes

Scoring: Computer scored

Cost: Specimen kit (coordinator's manual, survey administrator's instructions, one each of student and teacher survey booklets, answer sheets) $5.00; user's manual $15.00

Publisher: Psychological Assessment Resources, Inc.

INSTITUTIONAL FUNCTIONING INVENTORY
Research staff at Educational Testing Services and Earl J. McGrath

Adult

Purpose: Evaluates functioning of educational institutions. Used in self-studies for accreditation, planning, and research.

Description: 132-item test assessing 11 dimensions of institutional functioning: intellectual-aesthetic extracurriculum, freedom, human diversity, concern for undergraduate learning, democratic governance, meeting local needs, self-study and planning, concern for advanced knowledge, concern for innovation, and institutional esprit. The inventory is distributed to a random sample of college community members, including the faculty, administration, and students. Self-administered. Suitable for group use. Available in French for Canadian institutions.

Untimed: 45 minutes

Scoring: Computer scored

Cost: Reusable faculty booklet $0.50; reusable student booklets $0.35; answer sheet $0.10 each

Publisher: Educational Testing Service

INSTITUTIONAL GOALS INVENTORY (IGI)
Research staff of Educational Testing Service

Adolescent, adult
College students

Purpose: Assesses the educational goals of educational institutions. Used to establish priorities and to provide direction to present and future planning.

Description: 90-item paper-pencil test assessing the educational goals of educational institutions. The 20 goal areas are divided into two types, outcome goals and process goals. The outcome goals are academic development, intellectual orientation, individual personal development, humanism/altruism, cultural/ aesthetic awareness, traditional religiousness, vocational preparation, advanced training, research, meeting local needs, public service, social egalitarianism, and social criticism/activism. The process goals are freedom, democratic governance, community, intellectual/aesthetic environment, innovation, off-campus learning, and accountability/efficiency. The inventory is distributed to a random sample of students, faculty, and administrators at educational institutions. Materials include space for 20 additional locally written goals. Self-administered. Suitable for group use. Available in French (for Canadian universities) and Spanish.

Untimed: 45 minutes

Scoring: Computer scored

Cost: Booklet $0.65; processing $1.75

Publisher: Educational Testing Service

LIGHT'S RETENTION SCALE (LRS)
Refer to page 673.

NUTRITION ACHIEVEMENT TESTS 1, 2, AND 3

Child   Grades K-6

Purpose: Evaluates the nutrition education needs and achievements of elementary-school children.

Description: Multiple-item paper-pencil test measuring knowledge of basic nutrition facts that are generally included in primary school nutrition education programs. Separate tests are included for Grades K-2, 3-4, and 5-6. The effectiveness of nutrition education programs is determined by measuring gains from pretest to posttest. The manual includes directions for administration, guidelines for interpretation of test scores, mean scores achieved by nationwide sample, difficulty level, and reliability statistics. The test forms are provided in the form of reproducible masters. Examiner required. Suitable for group use.

Untimed: Varies

Scoring: Examiner evaluated

Cost: Contact local Dairy Council, among which prices vary. If not served locally, available for $5.00 from publisher

Publisher: The National Dairy Council

PARENT OPINION INVENTORY
National Study of School Evaluation Staff

Adult

Purpose: Evaluates parents' opinions of their children's school and its programs. Provides an opportunity for parents to make direct recommendations. Used by school personnel to make decisions regarding program development, policy formulation, administrative organization, faculty development, and community relations.

Description: 58-item paper-pencil opinion survey consisting of two parts. Part A contains 53 multiple-choice items assessing parent opinion of various aspects of the school. Part B contains five open-ended items constructed for parents to make recommendations for school improvement. The manual describes the development of the instrument, provides instructions for administering the inventory, and contains a single copy of both Parts A and B. The inventory may be administered independently or in conjunction with the Student Opinion Survey, the Teacher Opinion Survey, or as part of a complete school evaluation program. Self-administered. Suitable for group use. Available in Spanish.

Untimed: Varies

Scoring: Examiner evaluated

Cost: 25 copies Part A $3.00; 25 copies Part B $2.00; manual $2.00

Publisher: National Study of School Evaluation

SCHOOL PRINCIPAL JOB FUNCTIONS INVENTORY (SP-JFI)
Melany E. Baehr, Frances M. Burns, R. Bruce McPherson, and Columbus Salley

Adult

Purpose: Assesses the relative importance of functions performed in a particular type of principalship and the principal's ability to perform the functions. Used to clarify a school principal's job responsibilities and to diagnose individual and group training needs.

Description: Multiple-item paper-pencil inventory assessing the relative importance of 17 basic functions for overall successful performance in a given principalship: personal handling of student adjustment problems, organizations and extracurricular activities, individual student development, utilization of specialized staff, evaluation of teacher performance, collegial contacts, racial and ethnic group problems, troubleshooting and problem solving, community involvement and support, dealing with gangs, curriculum development, instructional materials, staffing, working with unions, working with central office, safety regulations, and fiscal control. Items are rated by the incumbent principal. The inventory also may be used to have incumbents rate their relative ability to perform these functions. Separate forms are available for rating the importance of various functions and for self-rating of the incumbent's abilities. Examiner required. Suitable for group use.

Untimed: 40-60 minutes

Scoring: Hand key; may be computer scored

Cost: Specimen set $10.00; 25 test booklets $13.75

Publisher: London House Press

SCHOOL SUPERINTENDENT JOB FUNCTIONS INVENTORY (SS-JFI)
Columbus Salley and
Melany E. Baehr

Adult

Purpose: Assesses the relative importance of functions performed in a particular school superintendency. Used to clarify job descriptions and to resolve possible differences between the superintendent's view of job priorities and the expectations of such groups as school boards, principals, and community or political leaders.

Description: Multiple-item paper-pencil inventory assessing the relative impor-

tance of 17 basic functions for overall success in a given superintendency. Items are rated by the incumbent superintendent. The inventory also may be used to have incumbents assess their relative ability to perform the functions. Separate forms are available for rating the importance of various functions and for self-rating of the incumbent's abilities. Examiner required. Suitable for group use.

Untimed: 45-60 minutes

Scoring: Hand key; may be computer scored

Cost: Specimen set $10.00; 25 test booklets $13.75

Publisher: London House Press

SMALL COLLEGE GOALS INVENTORY (SCGI)
Research staff of
Educational Testing Service

Adolescent, adult
College students

Purpose: Assesses the educational goals of small colleges. Used to establish priorities and to provide direction for present and future planning.

Description: 90-item paper-pencil test assessing the educational goals of small colleges. The 20 goal areas are divided into two types, outcome goals and process goals. The outcome goals are academic development, intellectual orientation, individual personal development, humanism/altruism, cultural/aesthetic awareness, traditional religiousness, vocational preparation, advanced training, research, meeting local needs, public service, social egalitarianism, and social criticism/activism. The process goals are freedom, democratic governance, community, intellectual/aesthetic environment, innovation, off-campus learning, and accountability/efficiency. The inventory is distributed to a random sample of students, faculty, and administrators. Materials include space for 20 additional locally written goals. Self-administered. Suitable for group use.

Untimed: 45 minutes

Scoring: Computer scored

Cost: Booklets $0.65; processing $1.75

Publisher: Educational Testing Service

STUDENT REACTIONS TO COLLEGE: FOUR YEAR COLLEGE EDITION (SRC/4)
*Research staff of
Educational Testing Service*

**Adolescent, adult
College students**

Purpose: Assesses the needs and concerns of students enrolled in four-year colleges. Used in institutional self-assessment for developing programs and services for students.

Description: 150-item paper-pencil test assessing four dimensions of student concerns: processes of instruction, program planning, administrative affairs, and out-of-class activities. These four dimensions are divided further into such areas as content of courses, appropriateness of course work to occupational goals, satisfaction with teaching procedures, student-faculty relations, educational and occupational decisions, effectiveness of advisors and counselors, registration, regulations, availability of classes, housing, employment, financial aid, and satisfaction with campus environment. The test is distributed to random samples of students. Self-administered. Suitable for group use.

Untimed: 50 minutes

Scoring: Computer scored

Cost: Booklet $0.65; processing $1.75

Publisher: Educational Testing Service

UNIVERSITY RESIDENCE ENVIRONMENT SCALE (URES)
Refer to page 695.

WHAT I USUALLY EAT
Iowa State University

Child   Grades 3-6

Purpose: Assesses the eating habits of elementary-school children. Used in conjunction with nutrition education programs and to assess student diets across large numbers of classrooms, schools, or school districts.

Description: Multiple-item computer-administered survey assessing children's eating habits. The program asks students what they usually have for breakfast, lunch, supper, and snacks. As students answer, the computer generates color graphics of the food identified to assure the accuracy of the responses and to maintain student interest. The program then analyzes the meals and snacks selected in terms of the basic food groups and provides students, teachers, and administrators with the results. Group and classroom profiles of food choice behaviors are also provided. The survey may be used with students in higher grades who are reviewing food groups and daily eating patterns. The survey may be administered before nutrition units to motivate student interest, to identify individual and class needs, and to give baseline data for evaluating students' progress. The survey may also be administered during the nutrition unit to reinforce lessons on food choices, meal patterns, and food groups. Administering the survey after nutrition units provides students with feedback and review, measures learning, and pinpoints concepts in need of additional reinforcement. Educational researchers can use the program to obtain hard-to-get food behavior data from students in Grades 3 and above. The software is programmed in color, with sound cues, for use with either Apple II + , IIc, IIe, or IIe enhanced with at least 48K; single disk drive (second disk drive optional); any television monitor compatible with the computer; and printer (optional). The software package includes two floppy disks, master copies of two student handouts for duplication, and a manual describing administration and use of the program. Examiner required. Individually administered on the computer; suitable for use with groups of children.

Untimed: Varies

Scoring: Computer scored

Cost: Contact local Dairy Council, among which prices vary. If not served locally, available for $30.00 from publisher

Publisher: The National Dairy Council

Driving and Safety Education

HOW TO DRIVE
American Automobile Association

Adolescent, adult
Ages 16 and older

Purpose: Measures students' knowledge of many aspects of the safe operation of an automobile. Used by driver education teachers and driver improvement program directors.

Description: 178 multiple-choice items in 12 paper-pencil tests accompanying the book *How to Drive* published by the American Automobile Association. Each test consists of 12 to 20 items and covers one chapter of the book. The chapters are "Driving Laws and Controls," "Car Control, Skills and Habits," "Basic Maneuvers," "Driving an Automobile with a Manual Shift," "Vision and Perception," "Management of Time and Space," "Interacting with Other Users," "Adverse Driving Conditions and Emergencies," "Keeping Fit to Drive," "Consumer's Guide to Trouble-Free and Economical Driving," "Driving with a Trailer," and "Collisions and Insurance." Self-administered. Suitable for group use.

Untimed: 20 minutes per chapter

Scoring: Hand key; examiner evaluated

Cost: 24 test booklets $10.00; 100 answer sheets $2.75

Publisher: American Automobile Association

SAFE DRIVER ATTITUDE TEST (SDAT)
Russell L. Carey, Dawn Bashara, and Harry Schmadeke

Adult

Purpose: Measures attitudes of drivers, including handicapped and learning disabled adolescents, toward certain driving situations.

Description: 19-item paper-pencil multiple-choice test measuring drivers' attitudes toward certain driving situations. The test is designed to reflect such attitudes as self-centeredness, egoism, cautiousness, rashness, and general acceptance of and compliance with the law. In each of two filmstrips, actual and model simulation of driving dilemmas are shown, followed by three illustrative, narrated alternatives. Students view the filmstrips at separate sittings and enter responses on an answer sheet. Examiner required. Suitable for group use.

Untimed: 10-11 minutes

Scoring: Hand key

Cost: Program (2 full-color filmstrips, cassette, teacher's guide, ditto for student answers and profiles) $49.00

Publisher: Educational Activities, Inc.

THEORY TESTS FOR LICENSES

Adult

Purpose: Assesses knowledge of driving skills. Used for issuance of driver's and learner's licenses.

Description: Multiple-item paper-pencil measures of vehicle driver's knowledge of the rules of the road, road traffic signs, and vehicle controls. The test also covers relevant portions of the Road Traffic Ordinances of the Provinces. Three equivalent forms are available. These tests are available only to licensing authorities with the power to issue learner's and driver's licenses and who have examiners with certificates of competency issued by the HSRC. Examiner required. Suitable for group use.
SOUTH AFRICAN PUBLISHER

Untimed: Driver's 45 minutes; learner's 1 hour

Scoring: Hand key; examiner evaluated

Cost: (In Rands) driver's test 1,48; scoring stencils 0,54; instructions 0,19; 10 answer sheets 0,21; manual 1,00 net; learner's test 1,70; scoring stencils 0,54; instructions 0,21; 10 answer sheets 0,21; manual 1,00; orders from outside The RSA will be dealt with on merit

Publisher: Human Sciences Research Council

WILSON DRIVER SELECTION TEST
Clark L. Wilson

Adult

Purpose: Evaluates ability to perceive speed and spatial relationships. Used by driver selection and evaluation companies and schools to screen personnel in order to reduce the risk of operator-caused accidents.

Description: 6-category paper-pencil nonverbal test measuring visual attention, depth visualization, recognition of simple and complex details, eye-hand coordination, and steadiness. The booklet includes norms for males and females, as well as items on the subject's accident record and personal history. Examiner required. Suitable for group use.

Timed: 26 minutes

Scoring: Hand key

Cost: Manual $7.25; key $1.10; package of tests $29.50

Publisher: Martin M. Bruce, Ph.D., Publishers

Business and Industry

The tests described in the Business section generally are used for personnel selection, evaluation, development, and promotion.

In addition, the reader is encouraged to consult the Psychology and Education sections for other assessment instruments that may be of value in the area of business.

Business and Industry Section

Aptitude and Skills Screening

ADULT BASIC LEARNING EXAMINATION (ABLE)
Refer to page 355.

ADVANCED TEST BATTERY (ATB)
Saville & Holdsworth Ltd. Staff

Adult

Purpose: Evaluates verbal, numerical, and spatial reasoning at the very top range of ability. Used in the selection, development, and guidance of personnel at the graduate level or in management positions.

Description: Seven paper-pencil multiple-choice tests measuring verbal, numerical, and diagramming skills. The five main tests are arranged in two levels. Level 1 is somewhat easier and consists of three aptitude tests: Verbal Concepts (VA1), Number Series (NA2), and Diagramming (DA5). Level 2 has a higher perceived relevance (face validity) and consists of two tests in which skills are applied in context: Verbal Critical Reasoning (VA3) and Numerical Critical Reasoning (NA4). These five tests can be administered in various combinations to suit a number of contexts. For some applications, the Technical Test Battery Diagrammatic Reasoning Test (DT8) and the TTB Spatial Reasoning Test (ST7) are used with the ATB tests. The tests are suitable from the good "O" level standard to the top end of the graduate population. Examiner required. Suitable for group use.
BRITISH PUBLISHER

Timed: 15-35 minutes per test

Scoring: Hand key; examiner evaluated; may be computer scored

Cost: Complete (10 Level 1 booklets, 10 Level 2 booklets, keys, administration cards, 50 profile charts, 25 score sheets, 25 testing logs) $993.50

Publisher: Saville & Holdsworth Ltd.

ADVANCED TEST BATTERY: DIAGRAMMATIC REASONING (ATB:DT8)
Saville & Holdsworth Ltd. Staff

Adult

Purpose: Measures diagrammatical reasoning ability. Used for selection and placement for technical occupations and jobs involving systems design, flow charting, and engineering fault diagnosis.

Description: 40-item paper-pencil multiple-choice test requiring the candidate to discover logical rules governing sequences occurring in rows of three related symbols and diagrams and choose a fourth related symbol from the selections in the answer booklet. The test is suitable for individuals from the CSE to GCE "A" level and above. Examiner required. Suitable for group use.
BRITISH PUBLISHER

Timed: 15 minutes

Scoring: Hand key; examiner evaluated; may be computer scored

Cost: 10 question booklets $36.00; 50 answer sheets $36.00; key $9.50; administration card $9.50

Publisher: Saville & Holdsworth Ltd.

ADVANCED TEST BATTERY: DIAGRAMMING (ATB:DA5)
Saville & Holdsworth Ltd. Staff

Adult

Purpose: Measures logical analysis by assessing the ability to follow complex instructions within a given command system in order to arrive at a solution. Used to select personnel for computer programming, data processing, engineering, chemical processing, and related industries.

Description: 50-item paper-pencil multiple-choice test measuring diagramming skills. Each item consists of a column of figures or symbols within boxes, each of which has a command attached. The actual instruction conveyed by each command (represented by coded symbols) is explained on a separate card. The task is to carry out the commands in order to arrive at a new column of figures. The commands involve inverting figures, omitting figures, exchanging figures, or changing the complete order of figures in a specified way. The initial items are simple, but the complexity steadily increases. The diagrams provide a nonverbal task similar to flow-charting. The test is suitable for individuals from the GCE "O" level upwards. Examiner required. Suitable for group use.

BRITISH PUBLISHER

Timed: 20 minutes

Scoring: Hand key; examiner evaluated; may be computer scored

Cost: 10 question booklets $77.00; 10 command cards $50.50; 50 answer sheets $63.00; key $12.50; administration card $12.50

Publisher: Saville & Holdsworth Ltd.

ADVANCED TEST BATTERY: NUMBER SERIES (ATB:NA2)
Saville & Holdsworth Ltd. Staff

Adult

Purpose: Measures the ability to reason with numbers at a high degree of difficulty. Used in selection and development of management staff and graduate recruitment.

Description: 30-item paper-pencil multiple-choice test in which each item consists of a number series with one missing number. The candidates must select from five possible answers the one which completes the series. The test emphasizes developing appropriate strategies and the recognition of relationships between numbers rather than long calculations. The test is suitable for individuals from the GCE "A" level upwards. Examiner required. Suitable for group use.

BRITISH PUBLISHER

Timed: 15 minutes

Scoring: Hand key; examiner evaluated; may be computer scored

Cost: 10 question booklets $53.50; 50 answer sheets $63.00; key $12.50; administration card $12.50

Publisher: Saville & Holdsworth Ltd.

ADVANCED TEST BATTERY: NUMERICAL CRITICAL REASONING (ATB:NA4)
Saville & Holdsworth Ltd. Staff

Adult

Purpose: Measures the ability to make correct inferences from numerical or statistical data. Used for selection and placement for jobs involving control systems, selection and development of management staff, and graduate recruitment.

Description: 40-item paper-pencil multiple-choice test consisting of a series of statistical tables and a number of inferences made from each of them. For each item, the candidates must select the correct inference from five possible answers. The data used in the tables sample production costs, exchange rates, and results from a market research survey. The test has a high degree of apparent relevance to management decision making. The test is suitable for individuals from the GCE "A" level upwards. Examiner required. Suitable for group use.

BRITISH PUBLISHER

Timed: 35 minutes

Scoring: Hand key; examiner evaluated; may be computer scored

Cost: 10 question booklets $77.00; 10 data cards $50.50; 50 answer sheets $63.00; key $12.50; administration card $12.50

Publisher: Saville & Holdsworth Ltd.

ADVANCED TEST BATTERY: SPATIAL REASONING (ATB:ST7)
Saville & Holdsworth Ltd. Staff

Adult

Purpose: Measures ability to visualize and manipulate shapes in three dimensions given a two-dimensional drawing.

Used in selection and development of advanced personnel, such as engineers, designers, architects, and draftsmen.

Description: 40-item paper-pencil multiple-choice test consisting of a series of folded-out cubes and perspective drawings of assembled cubes. Subjects must identify the assembled cubes that could be made from the folded-out cube, each face of which has a different pattern. The test is suitable for individuals from the GCE "O" level to degree. Examiner required. Suitable for group use.
BRITISH PUBLISHER
Timed: 20 minutes
Scoring: Hand key; examiner evaluated; may be computer scored
Cost: 10 question booklets $36.00; 50 answer sheets $36.00; key $9.50; administration card $9.50
Publisher: Saville & Holdsworth Ltd.

ADVANCED TEST BATTERY: VERBAL CONCEPTS (ATB:VA1)
Saville & Holdsworth Ltd. Staff

Adult

Purpose: Measures general verbal skills at an advanced level. Used in selection and development of management, senior specialist staff, and graduate entrants.

Description: 40-item paper-pencil multiple-choice test measuring knowledge of the meanings of words and the relationships between them. Candidates are required to identify the relationship between a pair of words and select, from five possible words, the one which relates in the same way to a third given word. The vocabulary used is general and nonspecialist, but the range of relationships is very diverse. The test is suitable for individuals from the GCE "A" level upwards. Examiner required. Suitable for group use.
BRITISH PUBLISHER
Timed: 15 minutes
Scoring: Hand key; examiner evaluated; may be computer scored
Cost: 10 question booklets $53.50; 50 answer sheets $63.00; key $12.50; administration card $12.50
Publisher: Saville & Holdsworth Ltd.

ADVANCED TEST BATTERY: VERBAL CRITICAL REASONING (ATB-VA3)
Saville & Holdsworth Ltd. Staff

Adult

Purpose: Measures the ability to evaluate the logic of various kinds of arguments. Used for management selection and graduate recruitment.

Description: 60-item paper-pencil multiple-choice test consisting of argumentative passages and a number of statements that might be made in connection with each of them. The statements must be evaluated in terms of whether they, their opposite, or neither, logically follow from the passage in question. The passages sample a wide range of material from politics to medicine, all of which could be on the agenda of a management meeting. The test has a high degree of apparent relevance to the assessment of managerial skills. The test is suitable for individuals from the GCE "A" level upwards. Examiner required. Suitable for group use.
BRITISH PUBLISHER
Timed: 30 minutes
Scoring: Hand key; examiner evaluated; may be computer scored
Cost: 10 question booklets $77.00; 50 answer sheets $63.00; key $12.50; administration card $12.50
Publisher: Saville & Holdsworth Ltd.

APTICOM

Adult

Purpose: Assesses aptitudes, interests, and work-related math and language skills. Used for vocational guidance and counseling.

Description: Multiple-item aptitude battery measuring general learning ability, verbal aptitude, numerical aptitude, spatial aptitude, form perception, clerical perception, motor coordination, finger dexterity, manual dexterity, and eye-hand-foot coordination. The Interest Inventory assesses preference for U.S. Department of Labor interest areas. The Educational

Skills Development Battery assesses math and language achievement levels as defined by the U.S. Department of Labor. Tests are presented via panels mounted on APTICOM, a portable computerized desk-top console. APTICOM times and scores tests and generates score and recommendation reports when interfaced with a printer. Examiner required. Suitable for use with groups of four using optional master control.

Timed: Aptitude 29 minutes; interest 10 minutes; educational skills development battery 25 minutes

Scoring: Computer scored

Cost: Contact publisher

Publisher: Vocational Research Institute—J.E.V.S.

ARITHMETIC FUNDAMENTALS
Richardson, Bellows, Henry and Company, Inc.

Adult

Purpose: Assesses the ability to perform arithmetic calculations quickly and accurately. Used with applicants to hourly and clerical positions.

Description: 42-item paper-pencil test of arithmetic skills. Items are arranged in order of difficulty progressing from simple addition through subtraction, multiplication, and division of whole numbers to handling fractions and decimals. Individuals are provided with printed symbols and verbal instructions indicating which operation to perform on each problem. The test is available in two forms, I and II. The booklet contains space for figuring problems, and answers are recorded in the margins. Norms are available for male clerical and sales applicants, mechanical and operating applicants, and mechanical and operating employees. Norms also are available for female applicants for nurses' training, student nurses, and clerical applicants. Examiner required. Suitable for group use.

Timed: 20 minutes

Scoring: Hand key

Cost: 1-24 packages $18.00; score key $3.00; manual $2.00

Publisher: Richardson, Bellows, Henry and Company, Inc.

BALL APTITUDE BATTERY
Yong H. Sung and Rene V. Davis

Adolescent, adult
High school juniors-adult

Purpose: Measures aptitude for a wide variety of occupational and industrial jobs. Used for employee selection, classification, and placement and for individual career planning.

Description: Standardized battery of 14 multiple-item paper-pencil and task-performance tests evaluating aptitude based on an individual's performance on selected work samples. The battery consists of the following tests: Clerical (240 items; 5 minutes), in which the individual identifies as quickly as possible all pairs of identical numbers from two columns of numbers; Idea Fluency (4 items; 8 minutes), in which the individual generates as many alternative uses as possible for a given object; Inductive Reasoning (30 items; 8 minutes), in which the individual identifies three pictures in each series of six pictures that have a common theme among them; Word Association (100 items; 8 minutes), in which the individual writes a word associated with the given stimulus word; Writing Speed (15 lines; 1 minute), in which the individual writes the given sentence as fast and as many times as possible during the allotted time; Paper Folding (24 items; 10 minutes), in which the individual identifies from among five choices the result when a sheet of paper is folded in the manner shown and one or two holes are punched through the paper; Vocabulary (80 items; 22 minutes), in which the individual selects from five choices the word most equivalent in meaning to the test word; Ideaphoria (1 item; 10 minutes), in which the individual generates and writes as many ideas as possible about or in response to a novel situation; Numerical Computation (40 items; 13 minutes), in which the individual performs simple arithmetic computations as quickly as possible; Numerical Reasoning (40 items; 20 minutes), in which the individual identifies the pattern in a series of numbers and gives the next number that extends the series according to the pattern; Finger Dexterity (2 trials each hand; 6 minutes), in which the individual places three small pins into holes on a board as rapidly as possible; Grip Test (3 trials each hand; 6 minutes), in which the individual squeezes the dynamometer as hard as possible; Analytical Reasoning (18 items; 5-13 minutes), in which the individual arranges five, six, or seven words (printed on chips) on a diagram-board in the most logical order; and Shape Assembly (6 items; 15-35 minutes), in which the individual assembles a disassembled wooden geometric shape.

Items are arranged in ascending order of difficulty for every test except Ideaphoria, Finger Dexterity, and Grip. The administration time for each test was chosen at the point at which 95% of the individuals taking the test were able to complete all the items. The order of administration of the tests is designed to minimize test anxiety and maximize test motivation. A short break should be taken after the first hour of testing. Reliability, validity, and normative data are provided in the manuals. Examiner required. All tests except Grip, Analytical Reasoning, and Shape Assembly are suitable for group use. For operational reasons, the group tests are administered after the individual tests.

Timed: 3-3½ hours

Scoring: Scoring and computer analysis available only through the publisher

Cost: 10 sets of paper-pencil tests $100.00; cassette tape for Word Association $25.00; manual $5.00; scoring service $10.00; computer analysis $10.00; contact publisher for the cost of apparatus tests and purchase of subtests

Publisher: The Ball Foundation

BASIC OCCUPATIONAL LITERACY TEST (BOLT)
U.S. Employment Service

Adult

Purpose: Measures basic reading and arithmetic skills of educationally disad-

vantaged adults. Used for occupational training and counseling.

Description: Multiple-item paper-pencil test consisting of four reading and arithmetic subtests. The reading section assesses vocabulary and comprehension at four levels of difficulty: advanced, high intermediate, basic intermediate, and fundamental. The arithmetic section assesses computation and reasoning at advanced, intermediate, and fundamental levels. The examiner determines the appropriate testing level for each individual using the BOLT Wide Range Scale and the individual's reported years of education. Three alternate forms, A, B, and C, are available for each subtest at each level of difficulty except the advanced level. Two alternate forms, A and B, are available for the advanced level. Raw scores can be converted to standard scores and General Educational Development GED levels. Materials include the test booklet and manuals. Examiner required. Suitable for group use.

Timed: Each reading test 15 minutes; each arithmetic test 30 minutes

Scoring: Hand key

Cost: Available only through State Employment Service Agencies

Publisher: U.S. Department of Labor

BASIC OCCUPATIONAL LITERACY TEST (BOLT): WIDE RANGE SCALE

Adult

Purpose: Measures individual's reading and arithmetic abilities. Used as a pretest to determine whether the individual should be given the General Aptitude Test Battery or the Non-Reading Aptitude Test Battery as a preliminary to taking the Basic Occupational Literacy Test. Used for employment counseling.

Description: 16-item paper-pencil examination consisting of a reading subtest and an arithmetic subtest (8 items each). Examiner required. Suitable for group use.

Untimed: 15 minutes

Scoring: Hand key

Cost: Available through State Employment Service Agencies only
Publisher: U.S. Department of Labor

BRUCE VOCABULARY INVENTORY
Refer to page 890.

BUFFALO READING TEST
Mazie Earle Wagner

Adolescent, adult

Purpose: Measures the reading abilities of high-school and college students and adults. Used for personnel selection and for identifying persons who need remedial training.

Description: Multiple-item paper-pencil test measuring reading speed and reading comprehension. The test is used to select employees who read rapidly and with understanding and to identify persons who need remedial training. The test yields a total score. Examiner required. Suitable for group use.
Timed: 30 minutes
Scoring: Examiner evaluated
Cost: 25 tests $16.00; specimen set (25 tests, manual) $31.00
Publisher: Herman J.P. Schubert

CHEMICAL COMPREHENSION
Richardson, Bellows, Henry and Company, Inc.

Adult

Purpose: Assesses understanding of concepts related to chemistry. Used with applicants to operation, craft, and lab technician positions.

Description: 50-item paper-pencil multiple-choice test measuring general knowledge of chemistry. Content could be learned in school, but persons without formal training in chemistry can achieve high scores. Answers are marked in the test booklet. The test is helpful to applicants choosing between process or mechanical positions in industry. Norms are available for male process and laboratory applicants, process workers, and mechanical workers. Norms also are avail-

able for female student nurses and nurses' training applicants. The test is available in two forms, S and T. Examiner required. Suitable for group use.
Timed: 30 minutes
Scoring: Hand key
Cost: 1-24 packages $18.00; score key $4.00; manual $2.00
Publisher: Richardson, Bellows, Henry and Company, Inc.

CLASSIFICATION TEST BATTERY (CTB)

Adult

Purpose: Evaluates general thinking and adaptability skills of illiterate and semi-literate applicants for unskilled and semiskilled jobs.

Description: Four apparatus tests measuring nonverbal reasoning and spatial ability. The battery contains the Pattern Reproduction Test, Circles Test, Forms Series Test (Mines Version), and Colored Peg Board. The battery was devised as a unit and can be used only as described in the manual. Pretest instructions are available in any of nine African languages and English. The test itself is administered by a silent film. The test is administered at centers established by firms employing the publisher's consultation and training services; use is restricted to competent persons properly registered with the South African Medical and Dental Council. Examiner required. Suitable for group use.
SOUTH AFRICAN PUBLISHER
Untimed: Not available
Scoring: Examiner evaluated
Cost: Contact publisher
Publisher: National Institute for Personnel Research

COLOR MATCHING APTITUDE TEST
Intersociety Council

Adult

Purpose: Measures color perception for vocational placement. Used to screen for positions in paint factories and coatings industries, such as varnishes, paints, and lacquers.

Description: 48-item task-performance test measuring the ability to discriminate between various shades of color. One set of 48 color chips is mounted on an easel. An identical set is in a dispenser on the easel. The subject must match the color chips in the dispenser with those on the easel. Materials include two sets of chips, a scoring card, and scoring key. Examiner required. Not suitable for group use.

Untimed: 45 minutes-1 hour

Scoring: Hand key

Cost: Complete kit (2 sets of 48 chips, scoring card, key) $400.00

Publisher: Federation of Societies for Coating Technologies

COMPREHENSIVE ABILITY BATTERY (CAB)
A. Ralph Hakstian and Raymond B. Cattell

Adolescent, adult
Grades 10 and above

Purpose: Measures a variety of abilities important in industrial settings for individuals high-school age and older. Used in career and vocational counseling and employee selection and placement.

Description: 20 paper-pencil subtests each measuring a single primary ability factor related to performance in industrial settings. The tests in the battery may be used individually or in combination. The subtests are grouped and presented in four test booklets (CAB-1, 2, 3/4, and 5). CAB-1 contains Verbal Ability, Numerical Ability, Spatial Ability, and Perceptual Completion. CAB-2 contains Clerical Speed and Accuracy, Reasoning, Hidden Shapes, Rote Memory, and Mechanical Ability. CAB-3/4 contains Meaningful Memory, Memory Span, Spelling, Auditory Ability, and Esthetic Judgment. CAB-5 contains Organizing Ideas, Production of Ideas, Verbal Fluency, Originality, Tracking, and Drawing. Percentile norms are provided for males, females, and combined for each test at the high-school level. Additional norms for college students, convicts, and general population adults are provided for selected tests. Examiner required. Suitable for group use.

Timed: 5-7 minutes per subtest

Scoring: Hand key

Cost: Specimen set (4 test booklets, answer and profile sheets for all tests, manual) $15.85; 10 CAB-1, CAB-2, or CAB-3/4 test booklets $13.75; 10 CAB-5 test booklets $15.80; 50 answer sheets $8.00

Publisher: Institute for Personality and Ability Testing, Inc.

CRITICAL REASONING TEST BATTERY (CRTB)
Saville & Holdsworth Ltd. Staff

Adult

Purpose: Measures skills of evaluation and reasoning among individuals of average and above average ability (GCE "O" level and above). Used in the selection and development of "A" level entrants and supervisory and junior management personnel. Also used for guidance and placement of students sixth form and above.

Description: Three paper-pencil multiple-choice tests measuring the following skills: verbal evaluation, interpreting data, and diagrammatic reasoning. The Verbal Evaluation Test (VC1) is a 60-item test measuring the ability to understand and evaluate the logic of various types of arguments. The Interpreting Data Test (NC2) is a 40-item test measuring the ability to make correct decisions or inferences from numerical or statistical data, presented as tables or diagrams. The Diagrammatic Series Test (DC3) is a 40-item test measuring the ability to reason with diagrams and requires the candidate to discover logical rules governing sequences of symbols and diagrams. Together, these tests provide information on important abilities related to junior management. Examiner required. Suitable for group use.
BRITISH PUBLISHER

Timed: 20-30 minutes per test

Scoring: Hand key; examiner evaluated; may be computer scored

Cost: Complete (question booklets, answer sheets, key, data cards, profile charts, test logs) $504.00

Publisher: Saville & Holdsworth Ltd.

DENTAL ASSISTANT TEST
Mary Meeker and Robert Meeker

Adult

Purpose: Measures the aptitude and ability of prospective dental assistants. Used for selection of dental assistants.

Description: Multiple-item paper-pencil screening instrument assessing the abilities and aptitudes of prospective dental assistants. The criterion-referenced test items were developed in conjunction with practicing dental groups. Scoring keys and a criteria graph for selection are available separately. Examiner required. Suitable for group use.

Untimed: Varies

Scoring: Hand key

Cost: Test form $2.00; scoring key $12.00

Publisher: M & M Systems

DVORINE COLOR VISION TEST
Refer to page 657.

ELECTRICAL AND ELECTRONICS TEST
J.D. Morgan

Adolescent, adult
Ages 15 and older

Purpose: Assesses knowledge and ability in electrical and electronics fields.

Description: 30-item paper-pencil test for determining knowledge of fundamental laws, symbols, and definitions related to electricity and electronics. The test emphasizes the ability to use knowledge in practical situations. Examiner required. Suitable for group use. BRITISH PUBLISHER

Timed: 15 minutes

Scoring: Hand key

Cost: Specimen set (test booklet, answer key, manual) £9.30

Publisher: The Test Agency Ltd.

EMPLOYEE APTITUDE SURVEY TEST #1—VERBAL COMPREHENSION (EAS #1)
G. Grimsley, F.L. Ruch,
N.D. Warren, and J.S. Ford

Adult

Purpose: Measures ability to use and understand the relationships between words. Used for selection and placement of executives, secretaries, professional personnel, and high-level office workers. Also used in career counseling.

Description: 30-item paper-pencil multiple-choice test measuring word-relationship recognition, reading speed, and ability to understand instructions. Each item consists of a word followed by a list of four other words from which the examinee must select the one meaning the same or about the same as the first word. The test is available in two equivalent forms. Examiner required. Suitable for group use. Available in Polish and German.

Timed: 5 minutes

Scoring: Hand key; may be computer scored

Cost: 25 tests $14.00

Publisher: Psychological Services, Inc.

EMPLOYEE APTITUDE SURVEY TEST #2—NUMERICAL ABILITY (EAS #2)
G. Grimsley, F.L. Ruch,
and N.D. Warren

Adult

Purpose: Measures basic mathematical skill. Used for selection and placement of executives, supervisors, engineers, accountants, sales, and clerical workers.

Description: 75-item paper-pencil multiple-choice test arranged in three 25-item parts assessing addition, subtraction, multiplication, and division skills. Part I covers whole numbers, Part II decimal fractions, and Part III common fractions. The test is available in two equivalent forms. Examiner required. Suitable for group use. Available in Spanish, French, German, Polish, Farsee, and Indonesian.

Timed: 10 minutes

Scoring: Hand key; may be computer scored

Cost: 25 tests $14.00

Publisher: Psychological Services, Inc.

EMPLOYEE APTITUDE SURVEY TEST #3—VISUAL PURSUIT (EAS #3)
G. Grimsley, F.L. Ruch,
N.D. Warren, and J.S. Ford

Adult

Purpose: Measures speed and accuracy in visually tracing lines through complex designs. Used with drafters, design engineers, technicians, and related workers. Used in employee selection and career counseling.

Description: 30-item paper-pencil multiple-choice test consisting of a maze of lines that weave their way from their starting points (numbered 1 to 30) on the right-hand side of the page to a column of boxes on the left. The task is to identify for each starting point the box on the left at which the line ends. Examinees are encouraged to trace with their eyes, not their pencils. The test is available in two equivalent forms. Examiner required. Suitable for group use. Available in Spanish, Polish, French, German, and Indonesian.

Timed: 10 minutes

Scoring: Hand key; may be computer scored

Cost: 25 tests $14.00

Publisher: Psychological Services, Inc.

EMPLOYEE APTITUDE SURVEY TEST #4—VISUAL SPEED AND ACCURACY (EAS #4)
G. Grimsley, F.L. Ruch,
and N.D. Warren

Adult

Purpose: Measures ability to see details quickly and accurately. Used to select bookkeepers, accountants, general office clerks, stenographers, and machine operators. Used in career planning.

Description: 90-item paper-pencil multiple-choice test in which each item consists of two series of numbers and symbols that the subject must compare and determine whether they are "the same" or "different." The test may be administered to sales supervisors and executives with the expectations that their scores will be above the average for other groups. The test is available in two equivalent forms. Examiner required. Suitable for group use. Available in Spanish, Polish, French, German, and Indonesian.

Timed: 5 minutes

Scoring: Hand key; may be computer scored

Cost: 25 tests $14.00

Publisher: Psychological Services, Inc.

EMPLOYEE APTITUDE SURVEY TEST #5—SPACE VISUALIZATION (EAS #5)
G. Grimsley, F.L. Ruch,
N.D. Warren, and J.S. Ford

Adult

Purpose: Measures ability to visualize and manipulate objects in three dimensions on a two-dimensional drawing. Used to select employees for jobs requiring mechanical aptitude, such as drafters, engineers, and technicians. Also used in career planning.

Description: 50-item paper-pencil multiple-choice test consisting of 10 perspective line-drawings of stacks of blocks. The blocks are all the same size and rectangular in shape so that they appear to stack neatly and distinctly. Five blocks in each stack are lettered. The subjects must look at each lettered block and determine how many other blocks in the stack the lettered block touches. The test is available in two equivalent forms. Examiner required. Suitable for group use. Available in Spanish, Polish, German, and Indonesian.

Timed: 5 minutes

Scoring: Hand key; may be computer scored

Cost: 25 tests $14.00

Publisher: Psychological Services, Inc.

EMPLOYEE APTITUDE SURVEY TEST #6—NUMERICAL REASONING (EAS #6)
G. Grimsley, F.L. Ruch, N.D. Warren, and J.S. Ford

Adult

Purpose: Measures ability to analyze and find relationships within a series of numbers and predicts trainability for technical, supervisory, and executive positions. Used for employee selection and career counseling.

Description: 20-item paper-pencil multiple-choice test in which each item consists of a series of seven numbers followed by a question mark where the next number of the series should be. Examinees must determine the pattern of each series and select (from five choices) the number which correctly fills the blank. Logic and deduction, rather than computation, are emphasized. The test is available in two equivalent forms. Examiner required. Suitable for group use. Available in Spanish, Polish, French, German, Farsee, and Indonesian.

Timed: 5 minutes

Scoring: Hand key; may be computer scored

Cost: 25 tests $14.00

Publisher: Psychological Services, Inc.

EMPLOYEE APTITUDE SURVEY TEST #7—VERBAL REASONING (EAS #7)
G. Grimsley, F.L. Ruch, N.D. Warren, and J.S. Ford

Adult

Purpose: Measures ability to analyze information and draw valid conclusions from that information. Used to select employees for jobs requiring the ability to organize, evaluate, and use information, such as administrative and technical decision making, supervisory, scientific, and accounting abilities. Used in career counseling.

Description: 30-item paper-pencil multiple-choice test consisting of six lists of facts (one-sentence statements) with five possible conclusions for each list of facts. The subject reads each list of facts and then looks at each conclusion and decides whether it is definitely true, definitely false, or unknown from the given facts. The test is available in two equivalent forms. Examiner required. Suitable for group use. Available in Spanish, Polish, French, and German.

Timed: 5 minutes

Scoring: Hand key; may be computer scored

Cost: 25 tests $14.00

Publisher: Psychological Services, Inc.

EMPLOYEE APTITUDE SURVEY TEST #8—WORD FLUENCY (EAS #8)
G. Grimsley, F.L. Ruch, N.D. Warren, and J.S. Ford

Adult

Purpose: Measures flexibility in language. Used to select salespersons, journalists, representatives, writers, receptionists, secretaries, and executives. Used in career planning.

Description: Open-ended paper-pencil test measuring word fluency by determining how many words beginning with one specific letter, given at the beginning of the test, a person can produce in a 5-minute test period (75 answer spaces are provided). Examiner required. Suitable for group use.

Timed: 5 minutes

Scoring: Hand key; may be computer scored

Cost: 25 tests $14.00

Publisher: Psychological Services, Inc.

EMPLOYEE APTITUDE SURVEY TEST #9—MANUAL SPEED AND ACCURACY (EAS #9)
G. Grimsley, F.L. Ruch, N.D. Warren, and J.S. Ford

Adult

Purpose: Measures ability to make fine-finger movements rapidly and accurately. Used to select clerical workers, machine operators, technicians, repair personnel, and employees for jobs involving precision and repetitive tasks. Also used in career planning.

Description: Multiple-item paper-pencil test consisting of a straightforward array of evenly spaced lines of 750 small circles. The applicant must place a pencil dot in as many of the circles as possible in five minutes. Examiner required. Suitable for group use. Available in Spanish, Polish, and Indonesian.

Timed: 5 minutes

Scoring: Hand key; may be computer scored

Cost: 25 tests $14.00

Publisher: Psychological Services, Inc.

EMPLOYEE APTITUDE SURVEY TEST #10—SYMBOLIC REASONING (EAS #10)
G. Grimsley, F.L. Ruch, N.D. Warren, and J.S. Ford

Adult

Purpose: Measures ability to manipulate abstract symbols and use them to make valid decisions. Evaluates high levels of reasoning required for science and technology, troubleshooters, data programmers, accountants, and engineers. Used in career planning.

Description: 30-item paper-pencil multiple-choice test consisting of a list of abstract symbols (and their coded meanings) used to establish relationships in the pattern of "A" to "B" to "C." Given the statement, the examinee must decide whether a proposed relationship between "A" and "C" is true, false, or unknown from the given statement. The test is available in two equivalent forms. Examiner required. Suitable for group use. Available in Spanish, Polish, French, German, and Indonesian.

Timed: 5 minutes

Scoring: Hand key; may be computer scored

Cost: 25 tests $14.00

Publisher: Psychological Services, Inc.

EMPLOYMENT BARRIER IDENTIFICATION SCALE (EBIS)
John M. McKee

Adolescent, adult
Ages 15-adult

Purpose: Measures an unemployed individual's ability to gain and retain employment. Identifies areas and skills in which the job seeker may need training and assesses employment training programs. Used with JTPA participants and rehabilitational clients as well as the general unemployed population.

Description: 19-item paper-pencil test evaluating an individual's employability. The topics covered include job skills, education, environmental support, and personal survival skills. The test may be presented as an oral interview for use with illiterate examinees. Examiner required. Suitable for group use (except when orally presented).

Untimed: 30 minutes

Scoring: Hand key

Cost: Complete kit (includes 25 scales and manual) $30.00

Publisher: Behavior Science Press

ENGLISH LANGUAGE ACHIEVEMENT TEST

Adolescent, adult
Grades 12 and above

Purpose: Measures achievement of basic English language skills. Suitable for use with matriculants and higher. Used in employee selection and placement.

Description: Multiple-item paper-pencil test assessing English language abilities in spelling, comprehension, and vocabulary. Norms are based on a group of matriculants. The test is restricted to competent persons properly registered with the South African Medical and Dental Council. Examiner required. Suitable for group use. Afrikaans version available.
SOUTH AFRICAN PUBLISHER

Timed: 19 minutes

Scoring: Hand key; examiner evaluated

Cost: Contact publisher
Publisher: National Institute for Personnel Research

ETSA TESTS
George A. W. Stouffer, Jr.,
and S. Trevor Hadley

Adolescent, adult
Grades 10 and above

Purpose: Measures general and specific job aptitudes. Used for employee selection, placement, promotion, and measurement of training progress.

Description: Eight paper-pencil aptitude tests measuring general mental ability, office arithmetic, general clerical ability, stenographic skills, mechanical familiarity, mechanical knowledge, sales aptitude, and personal adjustment. The General Mental Ability and Personal Adjustment indexes may be combined with one of the specific skills tests to give comprehensive information about an applicant. The test is available only to qualified test users, such as personnel managers, counselors, psychologists, and educators. Examiner required. Suitable for group use.
Timed: Varies
Scoring: Hand key; examiner evaluated
Cost: Complete sample set (Test 1-A through 8-A with manual, keys) $15.00; sample set (one test) $5.00
Publisher: Employers' Tests & Services Associates

ETSA TESTS 1-A—GENERAL MENTAL ABILITY
George A. W. Stouffer, Jr.,
and S. Trevor Hadley

Adolescent, adult
Grades 10 and above

Purpose: Measures general intelligence and learning ability. Used for employee selection, placement, and promotion.

Description: 75-item paper-pencil test of general learning ability consisting of both verbal and nonverbal items. The test may be used in conjunction with ETSA 8-A, Personal Adjustment Index, and any

ETSA test measuring a specific skill area. Examiner required. Suitable for group use.
Untimed: 45 minutes
Scoring: Hand key; examiner evaluated; scoring service available
Cost: 10 tests with key $12.00; manual $3.50; handbook $5.00
Publisher: Employers' Tests & Services Associates

ETSA TESTS 2-A—OFFICE ARITHMETIC TEST
George A. W. Stouffer, Jr.,
and S. Trevor Hadley

Adolescent, adult
Grades 10 and above

Purpose: Measures ability to use office arithmetic. Used for employee selection, placement, and promotion.

Description: 50-item paper-pencil test assessing arithmetic skills used in office work. The areas tested include whole number computation, mixed number computation, written problems, reading tables, reading graphs, and advanced office computation. The test is one in a series of ETSA tests. Examiner required. Suitable for group use.
Timed: 40 minutes
Scoring: Hand key; examiner evaluated; scoring service available
Cost: 10 tests with key $12.00; manual $3.50; handbook $5.00
Publisher: Employers' Tests & Services Associates

ETSA TESTS 3-A—GENERAL CLERICAL ABILITY TEST
George A. W. Stouffer, Jr.,
and S. Trevor Hadley

Adolescent, adult
Grades 10 and above

Purpose: Measures general skills required of clerks in routine office work. Used for employee selection, placement, and promotion.

Description: 131-item paper-pencil test assessing general clerical skills. The items include alphabetizing, checking lists of numbers and names, spelling, office vocabulary, and basic information. Speed and accuracy are emphasized. The test is one in a series of ETSA tests. Examiner required. Suitable for group use.

Timed: 20 minutes

Scoring: Hand key; examiner evaluated; scoring service available

Cost: 10 tests with key $12.00; manual $3.50; handbook $5.00

Publisher: Employers' Tests & Services Associates

ETSA TESTS 4-A— STENOGRAPHIC SKILLS TEST
George A. W. Stauffer, Jr., and S. Trevor Hadley

**Adolescent, adult
Grades 10 and above**

Purpose: Measures typing, shorthand, and general skills required of secretaries and stenographers. Used for employee selection, placement, and promotion.

Description: 120-item paper-pencil test measuring four basic office skills: spelling, filing, grammar, and general office information. Materials include supplemental performance evaluations of typing and shorthand, either or both of which may be used with the basic scale. The test is one in a series of ETSA tests. Examiner required. Suitable for group use.

Untimed: 45 minutes; Typing Test Supplement 5 minutes; Shorthand Test 18 minutes

Scoring: Hand key; examiner evaluated; scoring service available

Cost: 10 tests with key $12.00; manual $3.50; handbook $5.00

Publisher: Employers' Tests & Services Associates

ETSA TESTS 5-A—MECHANICAL FAMILIARITY
George A. W. Stauffer, Jr., and S. Trevor Hadley

**Adolescent, adult
Grades 10 and above**

Purpose: Measures ability to recognize common tools and instruments. Used for

employee selection, placement, and promotion.

Description: 50-item paper-pencil non-verbal test of background in mechanical activities. The items are commonly used tools, which the applicant identifies. The test is one in a series of ETSA tests. Examiner required. Suitable for group use.

Untimed: 1 hour

Scoring: Hand key; examiner evaluated; scoring service available

Cost: 10 tests with key $12.00; manual $3.50; handbook $5.00

Publisher: Employers' Tests & Services Associates

ETSA TESTS 6-A—MECHANICAL KNOWLEDGE
George A. W. Stauffer, Jr., and S. Trevor Hadley

**Adolescent, adult
Grades 10 and above**

Purpose: Measures mechanical insight and understanding. Used for employee selection, placement, and promotion.

Description: 121-item paper-pencil test assessing six areas of mechanical knowledge. The test discriminates between novices, journeymen, and experts. The test is one in a series of ETSA tests. Examiner required. Suitable for group use.

Untimed: 1 hour, 30 minutes

Scoring: Hand key; examiner evaluated; scoring service available

Cost: 10 tests with key $12.00; manual $3.50; handbook $5.00

Publisher: Employers' Tests & Services Associates

ETSA TESTS 7-A—SALES APTITUDE
George A. W. Stauffer, Jr., and S. Trevor Hadley

**Adolescent, adult
Grades 10 and above**

Purpose: Measures abilities and skills required for effective selling. Used for employee selection, placement, and promotion.

Description: 100-item paper-pencil test assessing seven aspects of sales aptitude: sales judgment, interest in selling, personality factors, identification of self with selling occupation, level of aspiration, insight into human nature, and awareness of sales approach. The test is one in a series of ETSA tests. Examiner required. Suitable for group use.

Untimed: 1 hour

Scoring: Hand key; examiner evaluated; scoring service available

Cost: 10 tests with key $12.00; manual $3.50; handbook $5.00

Publisher: Employers' Tests & Services Associates

ETSA TESTS 8-A—PERSONAL ADJUSTMENT INDEX
George A. W. Stauffer, Jr., and S. Trevor Hadley

Adolescent, adult
Grades 10 and above

Purpose: Measures personality traits for all types of jobs. Used for employee selection, placement, and promotion.

Description: 105-item paper-pencil test measuring seven components of personal adjustment: community spirit, attitude toward cooperation with employer, attitude toward health, attitude toward authority, lack of nervous tendencies, leadership, and job stability. The test may be used in conjunction with ETSA 1-A, General Mental Ability, and any ETSA test measuring a specific skill area. Examiner required. Suitable for group use.

Untimed: 1 hour

Scoring: Hand key; examiner evaluated; scoring service available

Cost: 10 tests with key $12.00; manual $3.50; handbook $5.00

Publisher: Employers' Tests & Services Associates

FARNSWORTH DICHOTOMOUS TEST FOR COLOR BLINDNESS
Refer to page 658.

FARNSWORTH-MUNSELL 100 HUE TEST
Munsell Color

Ages 6-adult

Purpose: Determines color vision anomalies and color aptitude. Used to screen workers in such fields as electronics where color determination is a part of the job.

Description: Manual-visual apparatus test consisting of four trays each containing a segment of 85 color reference disks recessed in individual black plastic caps. The subject is asked to place color caps in true order, with the results posted on score sheets to yield numerical and graphic results. Material consists of the trays, a wooden carrying case, instruction manual, and 100 score sheets. Examiner required. Not suitable for group use.

Untimed: 10 minutes

Scoring: Hand key

Cost: Complete (4 trays, wooden carrying case, instruction manual, 100 score sheets) $390.00

Publisher: Munsell Color

FLANAGAN APTITUDE CLASSIFICATION TESTS (FACT)
John C. Flanagan

Adolescent, adult

Purpose: Assesses skills necessary for the successful completion of particular occupational tasks. Used for vocational counseling, curriculum planning, and selection and placement of employees.

Description: Battery of 19 multiple-item paper-pencil aptitude tests designed to help the subject understand his abilities relative to others in the total population and in specific occupations. The Inspection test measures the ability to spot flaws or imperfections in a series of articles quickly and accurately. The mechanics test measures the ability to understand mechanical principles and analyze mechanical movements. The Tables test measures the ability to read tables and charts quickly and accurately. The Reasoning test measures the ability to understand basic mathematical concepts and translate ideas and operations into brief mathematical notations. The Vocabulary test measures the ability to select the right word to convey an idea and knowledge of words in such fields as literature, fine arts, and music. The Assembly test measures the ability to visualize the appearance of an object assembled from a number of separate parts. The Judgment and Comprehension test measures the ability to read with understanding, reason logically, and use good judgment in practical situations. The Components test measures the ability to locate and identify important parts of a whole. The Planning test measures the ability to plan, organize, and schedule. The Arithmetic test measures the ability to work quickly and accurately with numbers in addition, subtraction, multiplication, and division problems. The Ingenuity test measures the creative or inventive skills and ability to devise ingenious procedures, equipment, or presentations. The Scales test measures the ability to read scales, graphs, and charts quickly and accurately. The Expression test measures the feeling for and knowledge of correct English in writing and talking. The Precision test measures the ability to perform precision work with small objects and speed and accuracy in making appropriate finger movements with one or both hands. The Alertness test measures the ability to perceive a dangerous situation and identify the specific action that is needed. The Coordination test measures the ability to coordinate hand and arm movements in a smooth and accurate manner. The Patterns test measures the ability to perceive and reproduce simple pattern outlines in a precise and accurate way. The Coding test measures the ability to code typical office information quickly and accurately. The Memory test measures the ability to learn and recall the classification or identifying symbols for various materials or groups of items.

Each test is printed as a separate non-reuseable booklet and may be administered singly or in combination. The FACT battery differs from the FIT battery in that the tests are generally lower level and have longer time limits. Self-administered. Suitable for group use.

Timed: 5-40 minutes per test

Scoring: Hand key

Cost: 25 test booklets (specify test) $35.00; reasoning manual $10.00; ingenuity manual $10.00; examiner's manual $10.00

Publisher: Science Research Associates, Inc.

FLANAGAN INDUSTRIAL TESTS (FIT)
John C. Flanagan

Adult

Purpose: Predicts success for given job elements in adults. Used for employee screening, hiring, and placement in a wide variety of jobs.

Description: Battery of 18 paper-pencil tests designed for use with adults in personnel selection programs. The Arithmetic (Ar) test measures the ability to work quickly and accurately with numbers. The Assembly (As) test measures the ability to visualize the appearance of an object assembled from a number of separate parts. The Components (Com) test measures the ability to locate and identify important parts of a whole, which involves the ability to change visual patterns. The Coordination (Co) test measures the ability to coordinate hand and arm movements smoothly and accurately. The Electronics (El) test measures the ability to understand electrical and electronic principles and to analyze diagrams of electrical circuits. The Expression (Ex) test measures the feeling for and knowledge of correct English in writing and talking. The Ingenuity (Ing) test measures the creative or inventive skills and the ability to devise ingenious procedures, equipment, or presentations. The Inspection (Ins) test measures the ability to spot flaws or imperfections in a series of articles quickly and accurately. The Judgment and Comprehension test measures the ability to read with understanding, reason logically, and use good judgment in interpreting materials. The Mathematics and Reasoning (M-R) test measures the ability to understand basic math concepts and translate ideas and operations into brief mathematical notations. The Mechanics (Me) test measures the ability to understand mechanical principles and to analyze mechanical movements. The Memory (Mem) test measures the ability to learn and recall a term associated with an unfamiliar one. The Patterns (Pat) test measures the ability to perceive and reproduce simple pattern outlines precisely and accurately. The Planning (Pl) test measures the ability to plan, organize, and schedule. The Precision (Pre) test measures the ability to perform precision work with small objects and speed and accuracy in making appropriate finger movements. The Scales (Sc) test measures the ability to read scales, graphs, and charts quickly and accurately. The Tables (Ta) test measures the ability to choose the right word to convey an idea and knowledge of words used in business and government matters.

Each test is printed as a separate booklet and may be administered singly or in combination. Self-administered. Suitable for group use.

Timed: 5-15 minutes per test

Scoring: Hand key (except for Coordination and Precision tests)

Cost: 25 test booklets (specify test) $24.00; scoring stencil $10.00; Inspection scoring stencil $20.00

Publisher: Science Research Associates, Inc.

FOOT OPERATED HINGED BOX WORK TASK UNIT
Refer to page 976.

GENERAL APTITUDE SERIES (GAS)
Saville & Holdsworth Ltd. Staff

Adult

Purpose: Assesses a wide range of general abilities. Used in the counseling and placement of general managerial personnel, the measurement of abilities in cases of job dissatisfaction, personnel transfers, occupational counseling, and occupational research.

Description: Seven paper-pencil multiple-choice tests measuring verbal, numerical, spatial, mechanical, diagram-

matic, clerical, and diagramming skills. The tests include Verbal Concepts (VA1), Number Series (NA2), Spatial Recognition (ST9), Mechanical Comprehension (MT4), Diagrammatic Reasoning (DT8), Classification (CP4), and Diagramming (DA5). The battery provides a high degree of relevance to occupational work in relation to the amount of testing time required. Examiner required. Suitable for group use.

BRITISH PUBLISHER

Timed: 1 hour, 42 minutes

Scoring: Hand key; examiner evaluated; may be computer scored

Cost: Complete (tests, score sheets, manual, keys) $800.00

Publisher: Saville & Holdsworth Ltd.

GENERAL APTITUDE TEST BATTERY (GATB)
U.S. Employment Service

Adolescent, adult

Purpose: Measures vocational aptitudes of literate individuals who need help choosing an occupation. Used for counseling.

Description: 434-item paper-pencil test consisting of 284 multiple-choice questions, 150 dichotomous choice (same-different) questions, and two dexterity form boards. Twelve subtests measure nine vocational aptitudes: General Learning Ability, Verbal, Numerical, Spatial, Form Perception, Clerical Perception, Motor Coordination, Finger Dexterity, and Manual Dexterity. Raw scores are converted to aptitude scores by use of conversion tables. Occupational Aptitude Patterns (OAP) indicate the aptitude requirements for groups of occupations. There are 66 OAPs covering 97% of all non-supervisory occupations. The GATB is scored in terms of OAPs. A letter grade of "H", "M", or "L" is assigned for each OAP. Results of the battery indicate the individual's likelihood of success in the various occupations. Use in the United States must be authorized by State Employment Service Agencies and in Canada by the Canadian Employment and Immigration Commission. Examiner required. Suitable for group use. Available in Spanish and French.

Timed: Varies

Scoring: Hand key; may be computer scored

Cost: Available from State Employment Service Agencies only

Publisher: U.S. Department of Labor

GOTTSCHALDT FIGURES TEST

Adult

Purpose: Measures visual perception and analytical ability. Used with job applicants with at least 10 years of education for purposes of employee screening and selection.

Description: Multiple-item paper-pencil test requiring the applicant to find given embedded figures in more complex diagrams. The test is restricted to competent persons properly registered with the South African Medical and Dental Council. Examiner required. Suitable for group use. Afrikaans version available. SOUTH AFRICAN PUBLISHER

Timed: 20 minutes

Scoring: Hand key

Cost: Contact publisher

Publisher: National Institute for Personnel Research

GUILFORD-ZIMMERMAN APTITUDE SURVEY (GZAS)
*J. P. Guilford and
Wayne S. Zimmerman*

**Adolescent, adult
Grades 10 and above**

Purpose: Measures mental abilities. Used as a test of aptitude for many areas of employment and academic pursuit.

Description: Six paper-pencil tests measuring abilities in the areas of verbal and abstract intelligence, numerical facility, and perception. The aptitudes fit into the Structure-of-Intellect categories. Code letters after the GZAS test name indicate the category to which the test belongs. The battery includes the following six tests: Verbal Comprehension, General Reasoning, Numerical Operations, Perceptual Speed, Spatial Orientation, and Spatial Visualization. The tests may be used singly or in combination depending on the needs of the situation. The score on each test has a definite meaning. Examiner required. The test is restricted to A.P.A. members. Suitable for group use.

Timed: 1 hour, 33 minutes

Scoring: Hand key; may be computer scored

Cost: 25 tests $9.00-$16.00; manual $5.00; 25 answer sheets $4.00; 25 profile charts $4.00; scoring stencils $5.50

Publisher: Sheridan Psychological Services, Inc.

GUILFORD-ZIMMERMAN APTITUDE SURVEY: GENERAL REASONING (GZAS:GR)
*J. P. Guilford and
Wayne S. Zimmerman*

**Adolescent, adult
Grades 10 and above**

Purpose: Evaluates reasoning abilities through arithmetic-reasoning items. Used as an aptitude test for a variety of problem-solving tasks.

Description: Multiple-item paper-pencil test consisting of arithmetic-reasoning items graded in difficulty. Numerical computation is kept to a minimum, removing most of the numerical-facility component from the measure. The results yield C-scale, centile, and T-scale norms for college groups. The manual, answer sheets, profile charts, and scoring stencils must be ordered separately. The test is restricted to A.P.A. members. Examiner required. Suitable for group use.

Timed: 35 minutes

Scoring: Hand key; may be computer scored

Cost: 25 tests $10.00; 25 answer sheets $3.50; manual $4.00; hand key $4.50

Publisher: Sheridan Psychological Services, Inc.

GUILFORD-ZIMMERMAN APTITUDE SURVEY: NUMERICAL OPERATIONS (GZAS:NO)
J.P. Guilford and
Wayne S. Zimmerman

Adolescent, adult
Grades 10 and above

Purpose: Measures ability to work with numbers. Used with accountants, salespersons, and many types of clerical workers.

Description: Multiple-item paper-pencil multiple-choice test including simple problems of addition, subtraction, and multiplication. The results yield C-scale, centile, and T-scale norms for college groups. Manual, profile charts, and scoring keys must each be ordered separately. The test is restricted to A.P.A. members. Examiner required. Suitable for group use.

Timed: 8 minutes

Scoring: Hand key; may be computer scored

Cost: 25 tests $7.50; manual $4.00; hand key $4.00

Publisher: Sheridan Psychological Services, Inc.

GUILFORD-ZIMMERMAN APTITUDE SURVEY: PERCEPTUAL SPEED (GZAS:PS)
J.P. Guilford and
Wayne S. Zimmerman

Adolescent, adult
Grades 10 and above

Purpose: Measures ability to compare details quickly and accurately. Used to select inspectors, clerks, and machine operators.

Description: Multiple-item paper-pencil multiple-choice test measuring speed and accuracy in comparing visual details. The test evaluates judgment of identity or difference. The skill assessed is evaluation of "figural units." The results yield C-scale, centile, and T-scale norms for college groups. The manual, profile charts, and scoring keys must be ordered separately.

The test is restricted to A.P.A. members. Examiner required. Suitable for group use.

Timed: 5 minutes

Scoring: Hand key; may be computer scored

Cost: 25 tests $7.50; manual $4.00; hand key $4.00

Publisher: Sheridan Psychological Services, Inc.

GUILFORD-ZIMMERMAN APTITUDE SURVEY: SPATIAL ORIENTATION (GZAS:SO)
J.P. Guilford and
Wayne S. Zimmerman

Adolescent, adult
Grades 10 and above

Purpose: Measures ability to perceive spatial arrangements. Relevant to the operation of machines in which there is a choice of direction of movement in response to signals.

Description: Paper-pencil multiple-choice test measuring the cognition of figural systems. The results yield C-scale, centile, and T-scale norms for college groups. The manual, answer sheets, profile charts, and scoring stencils must be ordered separately. The test is restricted to A.P.A. members. Examiner required. Suitable for group use.

Timed: 10 minutes

Scoring: Hand key; may be computer scored

Cost: 25 tests $14.00; 25 answer sheets $3.50; manual $4.00; hand key $4.50

Publisher: Sheridan Psychological Services, Inc.

GUILFORD-ZIMMERMAN APTITUDE SURVEY: SPATIAL VISUALIZATION (GZAS:SV)
J.P. Guilford and
Wayne S. Zimmerman

Adolescent, adult
Grades 10 and above

Purpose: Measures the ability to mentally manipulate ideas visually. Used to screen engineers, architects, and draftsmen. May be used for situations involving work with mechanical devices.

Description: Multiple-item paper-pencil multiple-choice test measuring the "cognition of figural transformations." The results yield C-scale, centile, and T-scale norms for college groups. The manual, answer sheets, profile charts, and scoring stencils must be ordered separately. The test is restricted to A.P.A. members. Examiner required. Suitable for group use.

Timed: 10 minutes

Scoring: Hand key; may be computer scored

Cost: 25 tests $14.00; 25 answer sheets $3.50; manual $4.00; hand key $4.50

Publisher: Sheridan Psychological Services, Inc.

GUILFORD-ZIMMERMAN APTITUDE SURVEY: VERBAL COMPREHENSION (GZAS:VC)
J. P. Guilford and Wayne S. Zimmerman

Adolescent, adult Grades 10 and above

Purpose: Measures verbal comprehension. Assesses academic aptitude and suitability for fields in which reading ability is an important factor.

Description: 72-item paper-pencil multiple-choice test measuring verbal comprehension. Test items are constructed to maintain a uniform level of difficulty for all alternative responses to each item; therefore, the chance of arriving at correct answers simply by eliminating the more familiar wrong answers may be minimized. The results yield C-scale, centile, and T-scale norms for college groups. The manual, answer sheets, profile charts, and scoring stencils must be ordered separately. The test is restricted to A.P.A. members. Examiner required. Suitable for group use.

Timed: 25 minutes

Scoring: Hand key; may be computer scored

Cost: 25 tests $10.00; 25 answer sheets $3.50; manual $4.00; hand key $4.50

Publisher: Sheridan Psychological Services, Inc.

HAND DYNAMOMETER (DYNAMOMETER GRIP STRENGTH TEST)

Ages 5-55

Purpose: Measures general body strength and provides an index of right versus left handedness. Used for vocational evaluation, employee screening, and fitness evaluation.

Description: Task-performance test measuring grip strength. A millimeter rule and grip dynamometer with adjustable stirrup are adjusted until the inside scale equals half the distance from where the subject's thumb joins the hand to the end of the fingers. The subject then squeezes with full strength, which is measured by the dynamometer. Examiner required. Not suitable for group use.

Untimed: 1 minute

Scoring: Hand key

Cost: Model 78010 and 78011 $155.00

Publisher: Lafayette Instrument Company, Inc.

HINGED BOX WORK TASK UNIT
Refer to page 976.

INDEX CARD WORK TASK UNIT
Refer to page 977.

INDUSTRIAL READING TEST (IRT)

Adolescent, adult Grades 10 and above

Purpose: Measures reading comprehension. Used for selecting job applicants and screening trainees for vocational or technical programs.

Description: 38-item paper-pencil test of reading comprehension covering nine reading passages of graded difficulty. Some passages are sections of technical manuals; others take the form of company

---

memoranda. Materials include two forms, A and B. Sales of Form A are restricted to business and industry. Form B available to both schools and businesses. Examiner required. Suitable for group use.

Timed: 40 minutes

Scoring: Hand key; may be machine scored locally

Cost: Specimen set (test, IBM 805/OpScan answer document, manual) $12.00; 25 tests (specify form) $24.00; 50 IBM 805/OpScan answer documents $15.00, keys (specify form) $6.00; manual $10.00

Publisher: The Psychological Corporation

I.P.I. APTITUDE—INTELLIGENCE TEST SERIES: BLOCKS
Industrial Psychology, Inc.

Adult

Purpose: Measures aptitude to visualize objects on the basis of three-dimensional cues. Used to screen applicants for mechanical and technical jobs.

Description: 32-item paper-pencil test of spatial relations and quantitative ability. Examiner required. Suitable for group use. Available in French and Spanish.

Timed: 5 minutes

Scoring: Hand key

Cost: 20 tests $17.00

Publisher: Industrial Psychology, Inc.

I.P.I. APTITUDE—INTELLIGENCE TEST SERIES: DEXTERITY
Industrial Psychology, Inc.

Adult

Purpose: Determines ability to rapidly perform routine motor tasks involving eye-hand coordination. Used to screen applicants for mechanical and technical jobs.

Description: Three one-minute paper-pencil subtests (maze, checks, dots) in which the subject demonstrates his ability to perform routine motor tasks. Examiner required. Suitable for group use. Available in French and Spanish.

Timed: 3 minutes

Scoring: Hand key

Cost: 20 tests $17.00

Publisher: Industrial Psychology, Inc.

I.P.I. APTITUDE—INTELLIGENCE TEST SERIES: DIMENSION
Industrial Psychology, Inc.

Adult

Purpose: Evaluates ability to visualize objects when seen from different angles. Used to screen applicants for mechanical and technical jobs.

Description: 48-item paper-pencil test measuring spatial relations at a high level. Examiner required. Suitable for group use. Available in French and Spanish.

Timed: 5 minutes

Scoring: Hand key

Cost: 20 tests $17.00

Publisher: Industrial Psychology, Inc.

I.P.I. APTITUDE—INTELLIGENCE TEST SERIES: FACTORY TERMS
Industrial Psychology, Inc.

Adult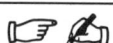

Purpose: Determines ability to understand the words and information used in factory and mechanical settings. Used to screen applicants for mechanical and technical jobs.

Description: 54-item paper-pencil test measuring comprehension of high-level mechanical, engineering, and factory information. Examiner required. Suitable for group use.

Timed: 10 minutes

Scoring: Hand key

Cost: 20 tests $17.00

Publisher: Industrial Psychology, Inc.

I.P.I. APTITUDE—INTELLIGENCE TEST SERIES: FLUENCY
Industrial Psychology, Inc.

Adult

Purpose: Assesses aptitude to use words with ease. Used to screen applicants for clerical, sales, and supervisory jobs.

Description: Three two-minute paper-pencil subtests measuring the ability to write or talk without mentally blocking or searching for the right word. Examiner required. Suitable for group use. Available in French and Spanish.

Timed: 6 minutes

Scoring: Hand key

Cost: 20 tests $17.00

Publisher: Industrial Psychology, Inc.

I.P.I. APTITUDE—INTELLIGENCE TEST SERIES: JUDGMENT
Industrial Psychology, Inc.

Adult

Purpose: Evaluates an individual's ability to solve difficult problems. Used to screen applicants for clerical, sales, and supervisory positions.

Description: 54-item paper-pencil test measuring aptitude to think logically, plan, and deal with abstract relations. Examiner required. Suitable for group use. Available in French and Spanish.

Timed: 6 minutes

Scoring: Hand key

Cost: 20 tests $17.00

Publisher: Industrial Psychology, Inc.

I.P.I. APTITUDE—INTELLIGENCE TEST SERIES: MEMORY
Industrial Psychology, Inc.

Adult

Purpose: Determines ability to remember visual, verbal, and numerical materials. Used to screen applicants for clerical, sales, and supervisory jobs.

Description: Three two-minute paper-pencil subtests demonstrating aptitude to recognize and recall associations such as names, faces, numbers, and prices. Examiner required. Suitable for group use. Available in French and Spanish.

Timed: 6 minutes

Scoring: Hand key

Cost: 20 tests $30.00

Publisher: Industrial Psychology, Inc.

I.P.I. APTITUDE—INTELLIGENCE TEST SERIES: MOTOR
Industrial Psychology, Inc.

Adult

Purpose: Measures adults' ability to coordinate eye and hand movements in a specific motor task. Used to screen applicants for mechanical and technical jobs.

Description: 3-item test measuring the ability to coordinate eye and hand movements in a specific motor task. The examination consists of three trials of the same task. The examiner reviews instructions and sample questions with the subjects, sets the timer, and begins the test. The same procedure is repeated two more times. The test requires a special motor apparatus for administration. Examiner required. Suitable for group use only if more than one apparatus is available. Available in French and Spanish.

Timed: 6 minutes

Scoring: Hand key

Cost: 20 tests $17.00; motor board $125.00

Publisher: Industrial Psychology, Inc.

I.P.I. APTITUDE—INTELLIGENCE TEST SERIES: NUMBERS
Industrial Psychology, Inc.

Adult

Purpose: Measures ability to work rapidly and accurately with numbers. Used to screen applicants for clerical, mechanical, sales, technical, and supervisory positions.

Description: Multiple-item paper-pencil test measuring aptitude for working with number systems, such as files, codes, symbols, and standard procedures. Examiner required. Suitable for group use.

Timed: 6 minutes

Scoring: Hand key

Cost: 20 tests $17.00

Publisher: Industrial Psychology, Inc.

I.P.I. APTITUDE—INTELLIGENCE TEST SERIES: OFFICE TERMS
Industrial Psychology, Inc.

Adult

Purpose: Measures ability to understand special terms used in business and industry. Used to screen applicants for clerical, sales, and supervisory jobs.

Description: 54-item paper-pencil test measuring comprehension of information of an office or business nature and general mental ability. It also indicates over-qualification for routine, repetitive assignments. Examiner required. Suitable for group use. Available in French and Spanish.

Timed: 5 minutes
Scoring: Hand key
Cost: 20 tests $17.00
Publisher: Industrial Psychology, Inc.

I.P.I. APTITUDE—INTELLIGENCE TEST SERIES: PARTS
Industrial Psychology, Inc.

Adult

Purpose: Assesses ability to see the whole in relation to its parts. Used to screen applicants for clerical, mechanical, technical, sales, and supervisory positions.

Description: 48-item paper-pencil test measuring aptitude for visualizing size, shape, and spatial relations of objects in two and three dimensions. The test reveals the subject's sense of layout and organization. Examiner required. Suitable for group use. Available in French and Spanish.

Timed: 6 minutes
Scoring: Hand key
Cost: 20 tests $17.00
Publisher: Industrial Psychology, Inc.

I.P.I. APTITUDE—INTELLIGENCE TEST SERIES: PERCEPTION
Industrial Psychology, Inc.

Adult

Purpose: Measures ability to perceive differences in written words and num-

bers. Used to screen applicants for clerical, sales, and supervisory jobs.

Description: 54-item paper-pencil test measuring the ability to rapidly scan and locate details in words and numbers and to recognize likenesses and differences. Examiner required. Suitable for group use. Available in French and Spanish.

Timed: 6 minutes
Scoring: Hand key
Cost: 20 tests $17.00
Publisher: Industrial Psychology, Inc.

I.P.I. APTITUDE—INTELLIGENCE TEST SERIES: PRECISION
Industrial Psychology, Inc.

Adult

Purpose: Determines ability to perceive details in pictures. Used by employers to screen applicants for technical and mechanical jobs with inspection duties.

Description: 48-item paper-pencil test using pictures to test the ability to identify objects and rapidly recognize differences and likenesses. Examiner required. Suitable for group use. Available in French and Spanish.

Timed: 5 minutes
Scoring: Hand key
Cost: 20 tests $17.00
Publisher: Industrial Psychology, Inc.

I.P.I. APTITUDE—INTELLIGENCE TEST SERIES: SALES TERMS
Industrial Psychology, Inc.

Adult

Purpose: Measures ability to understand words and information related to sales. Used to assist employers in screening applicants for positions in clerical, sales, and supervisory jobs.

Description: 54-item paper-pencil test measuring comprehension of sales-related information. The test indicates whether a person is overqualified for routine or repetitive assignments. Examiner required. Suitable for group use. Available in French and Spanish.

Timed: 5 minutes

Scoring: Hand key

Cost: 20 tests $17.00

Publisher: Industrial Psychology, Inc.

I.P.I. APTITUDE—INTELLIGENCE TEST SERIES: TOOLS
Industrial Psychology, Inc.

Adult

Purpose: Evaluates comprehension of simple tools and mechanical equipment. Used to screen applicants for mechanical and technical jobs.

Description: 48-item paper-pencil test measuring the ability to recognize pictures of common tools, equipment, and machines. The test does not require the ability to read or write. Examiner required. Suitable for group use. Available in French and Spanish.

Timed: 5 minutes

Scoring: Hand key

Cost: 20 tests $17.00

Publisher: Industrial Psychology, Inc.

I.P.I. EMPLOYEE APTITUDE SERIES: CONTACT PERSONALITY FACTOR (CPF)
IPI Staff, Raymond B. Cattell, J.E. King, and A.K. Schuettler

Adult

Purpose: Determines contact versus non-contact factor in personality. Used for screening, placement, and promotion of employees.

Description: 40-item paper-pencil personality test measuring extroversion versus introversion. Examiner required. Suitable for group use. Available in French and Spanish.

Timed: 10 minutes

Scoring: Hand key

Cost: 20 tests $17.00

Publisher: Industrial Psychology, Inc.

I.P.I. EMPLOYEE APTITUDE SERIES: NEUROTIC PERSONALITY FACTOR (NPF)
IPI Staff, Raymond B. Cattell, J.E. King, and A.K. Schuettler

Adult

Purpose: Measures emotional balance and/or the lack of neurotic tendencies in personality. Used to screen applicants for a variety of positions and to place and promote employees.

Description: 40-item paper-pencil test measuring an individual's general stability and emotional balance. Examiner required. Suitable for group use. Available in French and Spanish.

Timed: 10 minutes

Scoring: Hand key

Cost: 20 tests $17.00

Publisher: Industrial Psychology, Inc.

I.P.I. EMPLOYEE APTITUDE SERIES: SIXTEEN PERSONALITY FACTOR (16PF) TEST
IPI Staff, Raymond B. Cattell, J.E. King, and A.K. Schuettler

Adult

Purpose: Measures 16 basic factors of personality. Used to screen applicants for a variety of positions.

Description: 102-item paper-pencil test measuring the following traits: bright, mature, dominant, enthusiastic, participating, consistent, adventurous, tough-minded, trustful, conventional, sophisticated, self-confident, liberal, self-sufficient, controlled, and stable. Examiner required. Suitable for group use. Available in French and Spanish.

Timed: 20 minutes

Scoring: Hand key

Cost: 20 tests $30.00

Publisher: Industrial Psychology, Inc.

I.P.I. JOB TEST FIELD SERIES: CONTACT CLERK
Industrial Psychology, Inc.

Adult

Purpose: Assesses skills and personality of applicants for public relations positions. Used to screen for complaint, information, receptionist, and reservation positions.

Description: Multiple-item paper-pencil battery of four aptitude and one personality test. The tests are Memory, Fluency, Sales Terms, Perception, and Contact Personality Factor. For individual test descriptions, see the I.P.I. Aptitude-Intelligence Test Series. Examiner required. Suitable for group use. Available in French and Spanish.

Timed: 45 minutes

Scoring: Hand key

Cost: Complete instruction kits $15.00; test package $8.00; aptitude instruction kits $10.00; aptitude test packages $6.00

Publisher: Industrial Psychology, Inc.

I.P.I. JOB TEST FIELD SERIES: DENTAL OFFICE ASSISTANT
Industrial Psychology, Inc.

Adult

Purpose: Assesses skills of applicants for dental office assistants. Used to screen assistants who will work chairside, perform light secretarial duties, and work with patients and the dentist.

Description: Multiple-item paper-pencil battery of four aptitude and two personality tests. The tests are Office Terms, Numbers, Judgment, Perception, Neurotic Personality Factor, and Contact Personality Factor. For individual test descriptions, see the I.P.I. Aptitude-Intelligence Test Series. Examiner required. Suitable for group use. Available in French and Spanish.

Timed: 60 minutes

Scoring: Hand key

Cost: Instruction kits $10.00; test packages $6.00

Publisher: Industrial Psychology, Inc.

I.P.I. JOB TEST FIELD SERIES: DENTAL TECHNICIAN
Industrial Psychology, Inc.

Adult

Purpose: Assesses skills of applicants for the position of dental technician. Used to screen laboratory workers in four classification levels: cast metal, denture, crown and bridge, and porcelain and acrylic.

Description: Multiple-item paper-pencil battery of two aptitude and two personality tests. The tests are Dexterity, Dimension, Neurotic Personality Factor, and Contact Personality Factor. For individual test descriptions, see the I.P.I. Aptitude-Intelligence Test Series. Examiner required. Suitable for group use. Available in French and Spanish.

Timed: 25 minutes

Scoring: Hand key

Cost: Instruction kits $10.00; test packages $6.00

Publisher: Industrial Psychology, Inc.

I.P.I. JOB TEST FIELD SERIES: DESIGNER
Industrial Psychology, Inc.

Adult

Purpose: Assesses skills and personality of applicants for designer positions. Used to screen for artists, architects, draftsmen, layout men, and photographers.

Description: Multiple-item paper-pencil battery of six aptitude and three personality tests. The tests are Sales Terms, Precision, Parts, Blocks, Dimension, Dexterity, 16 Personality Factors, Neurotic Personality Factor, and Contact Personality Factor. For individual test descriptions, see the I.P.I. Aptitude-Intelligence Test Series. Examiner required. Suitable for group use. Available in French and Spanish.

Timed: 75 minutes

Scoring: Hand key

Cost: Complete kit $15.00; test packages $8.00 each; aptitude kit $10.00; aptitude test packages $6.00 each

Publisher: Industrial Psychology, Inc.

I.P.I. JOB TEST FIELD SERIES: ENGINEER
Industrial Psychology, Inc.

Adult

Purpose: Assesses skills and personality of applicants seeking various engineering positions. Used to screen for automotive, chemical, electrical, mechanical, and production engineering.

Description: Multiple-item paper-pencil battery of seven aptitude and three personality tests. The tests are Office Terms, Factory Terms, Tools, Numbers, Judgment, Precision, Dimension, 16 Personality Factors, Neurotic Personality Factor, and Contact Personality Factor. For individual test descriptions, see the I.P.I. Aptitude-Intelligence Test Series. Examiner required. Suitable for group use. Available in French and Spanish.

Timed: 90 minutes

Scoring: Hand key

Cost: Complete kit $15.00; test packages $8.00 each; aptitude kits $10.00; aptitude test packages $6.00 each

Publisher: Industrial Psychology, Inc.

I.P.I. JOB TEST FIELD SERIES: FACTORY MACHINE OPERATOR
Industrial Psychology, Inc.

Adult

Purpose: Assesses skills and personality of applicants for various factory machine-oriented positions. Used to screen for cutter, dental lab, lathe, press, sewing, and welder jobs.

Description: Multiple-item paper-pencil battery of five aptitude and two personality tests. The tests are Motor, Precision, Tools, Blocks, Dexterity, Neurotic Personality Factor, and Contact Personality Factor. For individual test descriptions, see the I.P.I. Aptitude-Intelligence Test Series. Examiner required. Suitable for group use. Available in French and Spanish.

Timed: 45 minutes

Scoring: Hand key

Cost: Complete kit $15.00; test packages $8.00 each; aptitude kit $10.00; aptitude test packages $6.00 each

Publisher: Industrial Psychology, Inc.

I.P.I. JOB TEST FIELD SERIES: FACTORY SUPERVISOR
Industrial Psychology, Inc.

Adult

Purpose: Assesses skills and personality for supervisory positions in a factory setting. Used to evaluate the achievement and personality of maintenance and production people, foremen, and superintendents.

Description: Multiple-item paper-pencil battery of eight aptitude and three personality tests. The tests are Office Terms, Factory Terms, Tools, Numbers, Judgment, Fluency, Memory, Parts, 16 Personality Factors, Neurotic Personality Factor, and Contact Personality Factor. For individual test descriptions, see the I.P.I. Aptitude-Intelligence Test Series. Examiner required. Suitable for group use. Available in French and Spanish.

Timed: 120 minutes

Scoring: Hand key

Cost: Complete kit $15.00; test packages $8.00 each; aptitude kit $10.00; aptitude test packages $6.00 each

Publisher: Industrial Psychology, Inc.

I.P.I. JOB TEST FIELD SERIES: GENERAL CLERK
Industrial Psychology, Inc.

Adult

Purpose: Assesses skills of applicants for general clerical positions. Used to evaluate typing, filing, billing, transcribing, sorting, writing, and phone answering skills.

Description: Multiple-item paper-pencil battery of seven aptitude tests. The tests are Office Terms, Numbers, Perception, Judgment, Fluency, Memory, and Parts. For individual test descriptions, see the I.P.I. Aptitude-Intelligence Test Series. Examiner required. Suitable for group use. Available in French and Spanish.

Timed: 40 minutes

Scoring: Hand key

Cost: Aptitude instruction kit $10.00; aptitude test packages $6.00

Publisher: Industrial Psychology, Inc.

I.P.I. JOB TEST FIELD SERIES: INSPECTOR
Industrial Psychology, Inc.

Adult

Purpose: Assesses skills and personality of applicants for inspector-oriented positions. Used to evaluate checking, classifying, examining, grading, pairing, scaling, and sorting skills.

Description: Multiple-item paper-pencil battery of five aptitude and two personality tests. The tests are Tools, Precision, Dimension, Parts, Blocks, Neurotic Personality Factor, and Contact Personality Factor. For individual test descriptions, see the I.P.I. Aptitude-Intelligence Test Series. Examiner required. Suitable for group use. Available in French and Spanish.

Timed: 60 minutes

Scoring: Hand key

Cost: Complete kit $15.00; test packages $8.00 each; aptitude kit $10.00; aptitude test packages $6.00 each

Publisher: Industrial Psychology, Inc.

I.P.I. JOB TEST FIELD SERIES: INSTRUCTOR
Industrial Psychology, Inc.

Adult

Purpose: Assesses skills and personality of applicants for various teaching positions. Used to screen for counselors, instructors, safety directors, teachers, and training directors.

Description: Multiple-item paper-pencil battery of six aptitude and three personality tests. The tests are Fluency, Sales Terms, Parts, Memory, Judgment, Perception, 16 Personality Factors, Neurotic Personality Factor, and Contact Personality Factor. For individual test descriptions, see the I.P.I. Aptitude-Intel-

ligence Test Series. Examiner required. Suitable for group use. Available in French and Spanish.

Timed: 90 minutes

Scoring: Hand key

Cost: Complete kit $15.00; test packages $8.00 each; aptitude kit $10.00; aptitude test packages $6.00 each

Publisher: Industrial Psychology, Inc.

I.P.I. JOB TEST FIELD SERIES: JUNIOR CLERK
Industrial Psychology, Inc.

Adult

Purpose: Assesses skills and personality of entry-level clerical applicants. Used to evaluate checking, coding, indexing, mailing, shipping, sorting, and stocking skills.

Description: Multiple-item paper-pencil battery of one untimed personality test and three timed aptitude tests. The tests are Perception, Office Terms, Numbers, and Contact Personality Factor. For individual test descriptions, see the I.P.I. Aptitude-Intelligence Test Series. Examiner required. Suitable for group use. Available in French and Spanish.

Timed: 45 minutes

Scoring: Hand key

Cost: Complete kit $15.00; test packages $8.00 each; aptitude kit $10.00; aptitude test packages $6.00 each

Publisher: Industrial Psychology, Inc.

I.P.I. JOB TEST FIELD SERIES: NUMBERS CLERK
Industrial Psychology, Inc.

Adult

Purpose: Assesses skills and personality of applicants seeking numerically oriented positions. Used to screen for accounting, billing, insurance, inventory, payroll, and statistical positions.

Description: Multiple-item paper-pencil battery of four aptitude and two personality tests. The tests are Numbers, Perception, Office Terms, Judgment, Neurotic Personality Factor, and Contact Personality Factor. For individual test descriptions, see the I.P.I. Aptitude-Intelligence Test Series. Examiner required. Suitable for group use. Available in French and Spanish.

Timed: 45 minutes

Scoring: Hand key

Cost: Complete kit $15.00; test packages $8.00 each; aptitude kit $10.00; aptitude test packages $6.00 each

Publisher: Industrial Psychology, Inc.

I.P.I. JOB TEST FIELD SERIES: OFFICE MACHINE OPERATOR
Industrial Psychology, Inc.

Adult

Purpose: Assesses skills and personality of applicants for positions utilizing office machines. Used to screen for accounting, billing, IBM, keypunch, and typist positions.

Description: Multiple-item paper-pencil battery of four aptitude and two personality tests. The tests are Office Terms, Perception, Judgment, Parts, Dexterity, Neurotic Personality Factor, and Contact Personality Factor. For individual test descriptions, see the I.P.I. Aptitude-Intelligence Test Series. Examiner required. Suitable for group use. Available in French and Spanish.

Timed: 45 minutes

Scoring: Hand key

Cost: Complete kit $15.00; test packages $8.00 each; aptitude kit $10.00; aptitude test packages $6.00 each

Publisher: Industrial Psychology, Inc.

I.P.I. JOB TEST FIELD SERIES: OFFICE SUPERVISOR
Industrial Psychology, Inc.

Adult

Purpose: Assesses skills and personality of applicants for supervisory positions in an office setting. Used to screen for the positions of administrator, controller, department head, and vice-president.

Description: Multiple-item paper-pencil battery of seven aptitude and three personality tests. The tests are Office Terms, Numbers, Perception, Judgment, Flu-

ency, Memory, Parts, 16 Personality Factors, Neurotic Personality Factor, and Contact Personality Factor. For individual test descriptions, see the I.P.I. Aptitude-Intelligence Test Series. Examiner required. Suitable for group use. Available in French and Spanish.

Timed: 120 minutes

Scoring: Hand key

Cost: Complete kit $15.00; test packages $8.00 each; aptitude kit $10.00; aptitude test packages $6.00 each

Publisher: Industrial Psychology, Inc.

I.P.I. JOB TEST FIELD SERIES: OFFICE TECHNICAL
Industrial Psychology, Inc.

Adult

Purpose: Assesses skills and personality of applicants for various office technical positions. Used to evaluate the achievement and personality of accountants, estimators, methods clerks, statisticians, and time-study experts.

Description: Multiple-item paper-pencil battery of six aptitude and three personality tests. The tests are Office Terms, Numbers, Perception, Parts, Memory, Judgment, 16 Personality Factors, Neurotic Personality Factor, and Contact Personality Factor. For individual test descriptions, see the I.P.I. Aptitude-Intelligence Test Series. Examiner required. Suitable for group use. Available in French and Spanish.

Timed: 90 minutes

Scoring: Hand key

Cost: Complete kit $15.00; test packages $8.00 each; aptitude kit $10.00; aptitude test packages $6.00 each

Publisher: Industrial Psychology, Inc.

I.P.I. JOB TEST FIELD SERIES: OPTOMETRIC ASSISTANT
Industrial Psychology, Inc.

Adult

Purpose: Assesses skills and personality of applicants for positions of optometric assistant. Used to screen individuals who will act as a support person for optometrists, working with the practitioner and patients and performing reception and light secretarial duties.

Description: Multiple-item paper-pencil battery of five aptitude and two personality tests. The tests are Office Terms, Numbers, Perception, Judgment, Fluency, Neurotic Personality Factor, and Contact Personality Factor. For individual test descriptions, see the I.P.I. Aptitude-Intelligence Test Series. Examiner required. Suitable for group use. Available in French and Spanish.

Timed: 45 minutes

Scoring: Hand key

Cost: Instruction kits $10.00; test packages $6.00

Publisher: Industrial Psychology, Inc.

I.P.I. JOB TEST FIELD SERIES: SALES CLERK
Industrial Psychology, Inc.

Adult

Purpose: Assesses skills and personality of applicants for low-level sales positions. Used to screen for department store, post office, teller, ticketer, and waitress positions.

Description: Multiple-item paper-pencil battery of one personality and five aptitude tests. The tests are Sales Terms, Numbers, Perception, Fluency, Memory, and Contact Personality Factor. For individual test descriptions, see the I.P.I. Aptitude-Intelligence Test Series. Examiner required. Suitable for group use. Available in French and Spanish.

Timed: 45 minutes

Scoring: Hand key

Cost: Complete kit $15.00; test packages $8.00 each; aptitude kit $10.00; aptitude test packages $6.00 each

Publisher: Industrial Psychology, Inc.

I.P.I. JOB TEST FIELD SERIES: SALES ENGINEER
Industrial Psychology, Inc.

Adult

Purpose: Assesses skills and personality of applicants for technically oriented sales positions. Used to screen for claims work,

adjusting, purchasing, technical sales, and underwriting.

Description: Paper-pencil battery of six aptitude and three personality tests. The tests are Sales Terms, Numbers, Judgment, Fluency, Memory, Parts, 16 Personality Factors, Neurotic Personality Factor, and Contact Personality Factor. For individual test descriptions, see the I.P.I. Aptitude-Intelligence Test Series. Examiner required. Suitable for group use. Available in French and Spanish.

Timed: 75 minutes

Scoring: Hand key

Cost: Complete kit $15.00; test packages $8.00 each; aptitude kit $10.00; aptitude test packages $6.00 each

Publisher: Industrial Psychology, Inc.

I.P.I. JOB TEST FIELD SERIES: SALES PERSON
Industrial Psychology, Inc.

Adult

Purpose: Assesses skills of applicants for various sales positions. Used to screen for agent, demonstrator, insurance, retail, wholesale, and route sales positions.

Description: Multiple-item paper-pencil battery of five aptitude and two personality tests. The tests are Sales Terms, Numbers, Perception, Fluency, Memory, 16 Personality Factors, and Contact Personality Factor. For individual test descriptions, see the I.P.I. Aptitude-Intelligence Test Series. Examiner required. Suitable for group use. Available in French and Spanish.

Timed: 75 minutes

Scoring: Hand key

Cost: Complete kit $15.00; test packages $8.00 each; aptitude kit $10.00; aptitude test packages $6.00 each

Publisher: Industrial Psychology, Inc.

I.P.I. JOB TEST FIELD SERIES: SALES SUPERVISOR
Industrial Psychology, Inc.

Adult

Purpose: Assesses skills and personality of applicants for supervisory positions in the sales field. Used to screen for advertising, credit, merchandise, service, and store sales positions.

Description: Multiple-item paper-pencil battery of seven aptitude and three personality tests. The tests are Sales Terms, Numbers, Perception, Parts, Fluency, Judgment, Memory, 16 Personality Factors, Neurotic Personality Factor, and Contact Personality Factor. For individual test descriptions, see the I.P.I. Aptitude-Intelligence Test Series. Examiner required. Suitable for group use. Available in French and Spanish.

Timed: 120 minutes

Scoring: Hand key

Cost: Complete kit $15.00; test packages $8.00 each; aptitude kit $10.00; aptitude test packages $6.00 each

Publisher: Industrial Psychology, Inc.

I.P.I. JOB TEST FIELD SERIES: SCIENTIST
Industrial Psychology, Inc.

Adult

Purpose: Assesses skills and personality of applicants for various positions in the field of science. Used to screen for biologists, chemists, economists, physicists, and positions in the inventory and research fields.

Description: Multiple-item paper-pencil battery of seven aptitude and three personality tests. The tests are Factory Terms, Office Terms, Numbers, Judgment, Precision, Dimension, Dexterity, 16 Personality Factors, Neurotic Personality Factor, and Contact Personality Factor. For individual test descriptions, see the I.P.I. Aptitude-Intelligence Test Series. Examiner required. Suitable for group use. Available in French and Spanish.

Timed: 90 minutes

Scoring: Hand key

Cost: Complete kit $15.00; test packages $8.00 each; aptitude kit $10.00; aptitude test packages $6.00 each

Publisher: Industrial Psychology, Inc.

I.P.I. JOB TEST FIELD SERIES: SECRETARY
Industrial Psychology, Inc.

Adult

Purpose: Assesses skills of applicants for secretarial positions. Used to screen for stenographers, executive, legal, private, and social secretaries.

Description: Multiple-item paper-pencil battery of six aptitude and three personality tests. The tests are Sales Terms, Perception, Judgment, Parts, Fluency, Memory, and 16 Personality Factor. For individual test descriptions, see the I.P.I. Aptitude-Intelligence Test Series. Examiner required. Suitable for group use. Available in French and Spanish.

Timed: 75 minutes

Scoring: Hand key

Cost: Complete kit $15.00; test packages $8.00 each; aptitude kit $10.00; aptitude test packages $6.00 each

Publisher: Industrial Psychology, Inc.

I.P.I. JOB TEST FIELD SERIES: SEMI-SKILLED WORKER
Industrial Psychology, Inc.

Adult

Purpose: Assesses skills and personality of applicants for semi-skilled mechanical positions. Used to screen for assembler, construction, helper, and production positions.

Description: Multiple-item paper-pencil battery of four aptitude and two personality tests. The tests are Precision, Motor, Blocks, Tools, Neurotic Personality Factor, and Contact Personality Factor. For individual test descriptions, see the I.P.I. Aptitude-Intelligence Test Series. Examiner required. Suitable for group use. Available in French and Spanish.

Timed: 75 minutes

Scoring: Hand key

Cost: Complete kit $15.00; test packages $8.00 each; aptitude kit $10.00; aptitude test packages $6.00 each

Publisher: Industrial Psychology, Inc.

I.P.I. JOB TEST FIELD SERIES: SENIOR CLERK
Industrial Psychology, Inc.

Adult

Purpose: Assesses skills and personality of applicants for high-level clerical or administrative positions. Used to screen for administrative, bookkeeping, correspondence, cost, and production positions.

Description: Multiple-item paper-pencil battery of five aptitude and two personality tests. The tests are Office Terms, Perception, Numbers, Judgment, Fluency, 16 Personality Factors, and Contact Personality Factor. For individual test descriptions, see the I.P.I. Aptitude-Intelligence Test Series. Examiner required. Suitable for group use. Available in French and Spanish.

Timed: 60 minutes

Scoring: Hand key

Cost: Complete kit $15.00; test packages $8.00 each; aptitude kit $10.00; aptitude test packages $6.00 each

Publisher: Industrial Psychology, Inc.

I.P.I. JOB TEST FIELD SERIES: SKILLED WORKER
Industrial Psychology, Inc.

Adult

Purpose: Assesses skills of applicants for various skilled worker positions. Used to screen for linemen, machinists, maintenance workers, mechanics, and toolmakers.

Description: Multiple-item paper-pencil battery of seven aptitude and two personality tests. The tests are Office Terms, Factory Terms, Tools, Numbers, Precision, Motor, Blocks, 16 Personality Factors, and Neurotic Personality Factor. For individual test descriptions, see the I.P.I. Aptitude-Intelligence Test Series. Examiner required. Suitable for group use. Available in French and Spanish.

Timed: 75 minutes

Scoring: Hand key

Cost: Complete kit $15.00; test packages $8.00 each; aptitude kit $10.00; aptitude test packages $6.00 each

Publisher: Industrial Psychology, Inc.

I.P.I. JOB TEST FIELD SERIES: UNSKILLED WORKER
Industrial Psychology, Inc.

Adult

Purpose: Assesses skills and personality of applicants for low-level mechanical jobs. Used to screen janitors, laborers, loaders, material handlers, packers, and truckers.

Description: Multiple-item paper-pencil battery of one personality and three aptitude tests. The tests are Tools, Precision, Motor, and Neurotic Personality Factor. For individual test descriptions, see the I.P.I. Aptitude-Intelligence Test Series. Examiner required. Suitable for group use. Available in French and Spanish.

Timed: 30 minutes

Scoring: Hand key

Cost: Complete kit $15.00; test packages $8.00 each; aptitude kit $10.00; aptitude test packages $6.00 each

Publisher: Industrial Psychology, Inc.

I.P.I. JOB TEST FIELD SERIES: VEHICLE OPERATOR
Industrial Psychology, Inc.

Adult

Purpose: Assesses skills and personality of applicants for various vehicle operator positions. Used to screen for crane, elevator, motorman, taxi, teamster, tractor, and truck-driving positions.

Description: Multiple-item paper-pencil battery of five aptitude and two personality tests. The tests are Tools, Precision, Dimension, Dexterity, Motor, Neurotic Personality Factor, and Contact Personality Factor. For individual test descriptions, see the I.P.I. Aptitude-Intelligence Test Series. Examiner required. Suitable for group use. Available in French and Spanish.

Timed: 45 minutes

Scoring: Hand key

Cost: Complete kit $15.00; test packages $8.00 each; aptitude kit $10.00; aptitude test packages $6.00 each

Publisher: Industrial Psychology, Inc.

I.P.I. JOB TEST FIELD SERIES: WRITER
Industrial Psychology, Inc.

Adult

Purpose: Assesses skills and personality of applicants for writing positions. Used to screen for advertising, author, copywriter, critic, editor, journalist, and public relations positions.

Description: Multiple-item paper-pencil battery of six aptitude and three personality tests. The tests are Sales Terms, Perception, Judgment, Fluency, Memory, Parts, 16 Personality Factors, Neurotic Personality Factor, and Contact Personality Factor. For individual test descriptions, see the I.P.I. Aptitude-Intelligence Test Series. Examiner required. Suitable for group use. Available in French and Spanish.

Timed: 90 minutes

Scoring: Hand key

Cost: Complete kit $15.00; test packages $8.00 each; aptitude kit $10.00; aptitude test packages $6.00 each

Publisher: Industrial Psychology, Inc.

J.E.V.S. WORK SAMPLES: IN-DEPTH VOCATIONAL ASSESSMENT FOR SPECIAL NEEDS GROUPS

Adult

Purpose: Assesses aptitudes, vocational interests, and work-related behaviors. Used for vocational guidance with individuals for whom paper-pencil tests are inappropriate.

Description: Multiple-item performance measure of worker traits. The test consists of 28 work samples: nut, bolt, and washer assembly; rubber stamping; washer threading; budget book assembly; sign making; tile sorting; nut packing; collating leather samples; grommet assem-

bly; union assembly; belt assembly; ladder assembly; metal square fabrication; hardware assembly; telephone assembly; lock assembly; filing by numbers; proofreading; filing by letters; nail and screw sorting; adding machine; payroll computation; computing postage; resistor reading; pipe assembly; blouse making; vest making; and condensing principle. The assessment process includes a group orientation session, instructions, and the examiner's observations of the subject's interest and work-related behaviors. Individually packaged hardware is included for the work samples. Examiner required. Suitable for use with groups of up to 15 with the standard hardware.

Timed: 5-7 days

Scoring: Examiner evaluated

Cost: Contact publisher

Publisher: Vocational Research Institute—J.E.V.S.

JOB EFFECTIVENESS PREDICTION SYSTEM (JEPS)
Personnel Decisions Research Institute for Life Office Management Association

Adult

Purpose: Measures a variety of skills required for a wide range of clerical and technical/professional positions. Used for selection and placement of entry-level employees in life and property/casualty insurance companies.

Description: 11 multiple-item paper-pencil tests measuring verbal, mathematical, and clerical skills. The tests are Numerical Ability-1, Numerical Ability-2, Mathematical Skill, Spelling, Language Usage, Reading Comprehension-1, Reading Comprehension-2, Verbal Comprehension, Filing, Coding and Converting, and Comparing and Checking. Not all of the tests are required for each selection decision. In many cases, two, three, or four of the tests used in combination will predict potential job performance accurately. Each of the 11 tests is independent. The tests were developed following the Uniform Guidelines on Employee Selection Procedures during a

5-year study in over 100 insurance companies. Batteries have been developed for each entry-level position in each JEPS member company. Use is restricted to insurance companies. Examiner required. Suitable for group use.

Timed: Varies, depending on subtest

Scoring: Hand key

Cost: Test $0.35-$0.70 per applicant, depending on number of subtests and volume ordered

Publisher: Life Office Management Association

JOB EFFECTIVENESS PREDICTION SYSTEM: CODING AND CONVERTING (JEPS: TEST CODE K)
Personnel Decisions Research Institute for Life
Office Management Association

Adult

Purpose: Measures the ability to quickly and accurately use conversion tables and coding guides. Used for selection and placement of entry-level clerical and technical/professional employees in life and property/casualty insurance companies.

Description: 85-item paper-pencil multiple-choice test in three sections measuring the ability to use conversion tables and coding guides. In the first section, the examinee uses a table that converts monthly premiums to annual premiums in order to indicate the correct annual premium for 20 monthly premiums. In the second section, the examinee uses a table of letter codes for annual premiums to indicate the correct letter code for 25 annual premiums. In the third section, the examinee uses both tables to indicate the correct code for 40 monthly premiums. Use is restricted to insurance companies. Examiner required. Suitable for group use.

Timed: 8 minutes

Scoring: Hand key

Cost: Test $0.60-$0.70 per applicant, depending on volume ordered

Publisher: Life Office Management Association

JOB EFFECTIVENESS PREDICTION SYSTEM: COMPARING AND CHECKING (JEPS: TEST CODE L)
Personnel Decisions Research Institute for Life
Office Management Association

Adult

Purpose: Measures ability to compare numbers and words and detect the differences. Used for selection and placement of entry-level clerical and technical/professional employees in life and property/casualty insurance companies.

Description: 40-item paper-pencil multiple-choice test measuring the ability to compare words and numbers and detect differences. The examinee is presented with correct lists of words and numbers (names, addresses, dollar amounts, etc.) and lists to be checked. The subjects are asked to count the number of errors per line. Use is restricted to insurance companies. Examiner required. Suitable for group use.

Timed: 7 minutes

Scoring: Hand key

Cost: Test $0.45-$0.55 per applicant, depending on volume ordered

Publisher: Life Office Management Association

JOB EFFECTIVENESS PREDICTION SYSTEM: FILING (JEPS: TEST CODE J)
Personnel Decisions Research Institute for Life
Office Management Association

Adult

Purpose: Measures general filing skills. Used for selection and placement of entry-level clerical and technical/professional employees in life and property/casualty insurance companies.

Description: 60-item paper-pencil multiple-choice test measuring the ability to file materials according to given instructions. The examinee is presented with existing files with numbered slots between entries and lists of entries to be filed. The examinee indicates the number of the slot into which each of the entries should be filed. Use is restricted to insurance companies. Examiner required. Suitable for group use.

Timed: 5 minutes

Scoring: Hand key

Cost: Test $0.60-$0.70 per applicant depending on volume ordered

Publisher: Life Office Management Association

JOB EFFECTIVENESS PREDICTION SYSTEM: LANGUAGE USAGE (JEPS: TEST CODE E)
Personnel Decisions Research Institute for Life Office Management Association

---

Adult

Purpose: Measures proper usage of the English language. Used for selection and placement of entry-level clerical and technical/professional employees in life and property/casualty insurance companies.

Description: 94-item paper-pencil test measuring knowledge of grammar, punctuation, capitalization, and formation of plurals. The subject indicates whether there are any errors in a reading selection that is divided into two parts. Use is restricted to insurance companies. Examiner required. Suitable for group use.

Timed: 12 minutes

Scoring: Hand key

Cost: Test $0.35-$0.40 per applicant, depending on volume ordered

Publisher: Life Office Management Association

JOB EFFECTIVENESS PREDICTION SYSTEM: MATHEMATICAL SKILL (JEPS: TEST CODE C)
Personnel Decisions Research Institute for Life Office Management Association

---

Adult

Purpose: Measures the ability to work with mathematical relationships and formulas. Used for selection and placement

---

of entry-level clerical and technical/professional employees in life and property/casualty insurance companies.

Description: 23-item paper-pencil multiple-choice test measuring skill in solving and manipulating mathematical relationships and formulas. One section involves solving formulas, and the other requires selecting the appropriate formula to use for problem solving. Use is restricted to insurance companies. Examiner required. Suitable for group use.

Timed: 20 minutes

Scoring: Hand key

Cost: Test $0.45-$0.50 per applicant, depending on volume ordered

Publisher: Life Office Management Association

JOB EFFECTIVENESS PREDICTION SYSTEM: NUMERICAL ABILITY-1 (JEPS: TEST CODE A)
Personnel Decisions Research Institute for Life Office Management Association

---

Adult

Purpose: Measures the ability to add, subtract, multiply, and divide. Used for selection and placement of entry-level clerical and technical/professional employees in life and property/casualty insurance companies.

Description: 50-item paper-pencil multiple-choice test measuring the ability to perform basic arithmetic operations, including the addition, subtraction, multiplication, and division of whole numbers, fractions, decimals, and percentages. Use is restricted to insurance companies. Examiner required. Suitable for group use.

Timed: 8 minutes

Scoring: Hand key

Cost: Test $0.40-$0.50 per applicant, depending on volume ordered

Publisher: Life Office Management Association

JOB EFFECTIVENESS PREDICTION SYSTEM: NUMERICAL ABILITY-2 (JEPS: TEST CODE B)

Personnel Decisions Research Institute for Life Office Management Association

Adult

Purpose: Measures the ability to perform operations with decimals and percentages. Used for selection and placement of entry-level clerical and technical/professional employees in life and property/casualty insurance companies.

Description: 50-item paper-pencil test with multiple-choice and true-false test section measuring numerical ability. Problems require the subject to perform operations with percentages, round off decimal numbers, and approximate correct answers. Use is restricted to insurance companies. Examiner required. Suitable for group use.

Timed: 15 minutes

Scoring: Hand key

Cost: Test $0.40-$0.50 per applicant, depending on volume ordered

Publisher: Life Office Management Association

JOB EFFECTIVENESS PREDICTION SYSTEM: READING COMPREHENSION 1 (JEPS: TEST CODE F)

Personnel Decisions Research Institute for Life Office Management Association

Adult

Purpose: Measures the ability to understand written instructions. Used for selection and placement of entry-level clerical and technical/professional employees in life and property/casualty insurance companies.

Description: 30-item paper-pencil multiple-choice test measuring the ability to understand written directions, definitions, and procedures. The subject reads several passages and answers questions about each passage. Use is restricted to insurance companies. Examiner required. Suitable for group use.

Timed: 30 minutes

Scoring: Hand key

Cost: Test $0.65-$0.70 per applicant, depending on volume ordered

Publisher: Life Office Management Association

JOB EFFECTIVENESS PREDICTION SYSTEM: READING COMPREHENSION-2 (JEPS: TEST CODE G)

Personnel Decisions Research Institute for Life Office Management Association

Adult

Purpose: Measures level of general reading comprehension. Used for selection and placement of entry-level clerical and technical/professional employees in life and property/casualty insurance companies.

Description: 35-item paper-pencil multiple-choice test measuring reading comprehension at approximately a Grades 11-13 reading level. The subject reads several reading passages and answers questions about each passage. Use is restricted to insurance companies. Examiner required. Suitable for group use.

Timed: 30 minutes

Scoring: Hand key

Cost: Test $0.65-$0.70 per applicant, depending on volume ordered

Publisher: Life Office Management Association

JOB EFFECTIVENESS PREDICTION SYSTEM: SPELLING (JEPS: TEST CODE D)

Personnel Decisions Research Institute for Life Office Management Association

Adult

Purpose: Measures the ability to recognize whether words are correctly spelled. Used for selection and placement of entry-level clerical and technical/professional employees in life and property/casualty insurance companies.

Description: 85-item paper-pencil test consisting of a list of words. The examinee indicates whether each word is spelled correctly. Use is restricted to insurance companies. Examiner required. Suitable for group use.

Timed: 7 minutes

Scoring: Hand key

Cost: Test $0.35-$0.40 per applicant, depending on volume ordered

Publisher: Life Office Management Association

JOB EFFECTIVENESS PREDICTION SYSTEM: VERBAL COMPREHENSION (JEPS: TEST CODE H)
Personnel Decisions Research Institute for Life Office Management Association

Adult

Purpose: Measures general word knowledge. Used for selection and placement of entry-level clerical and technical/professional employees in life and property/casualty insurance companies.

Description: 35-item paper-pencil multiple-choice test measuring vocabulary and word knowledge. The words tested are general vocabulary words rather than words from specialized or esoteric vocabularies. Use is restricted to insurance companies. Examiner required. Suitable for group use.

Timed: 6 minutes

Scoring: Hand key

Cost: Test $0.35-$0.40 per applicant, depending on volume ordered

Publisher: Life Office Management Association

JOB PERFORMANCE SCALES SET: PRIMARY RATING #2
Refer to page 919.

JOB SEARCH ASSESSMENT
Refer to page 764.

JOB TRAINING ASSESSMENT PROGRAM (JOBTAP)
Refer to page 765.

KUDER OCCUPATIONAL INTEREST SURVEY, FORM DD (KOIS), REVISED
Frederic Kuder

Adolescent, adult
Grades 11 and above

Purpose: Measures how an individual's interests compare with those of satisfied workers in a number of occupational fields or students in various college majors. Used with high-school and college students and adults for career planning, vocational guidance, and academic counseling.

Description: 100-item paper-pencil inventory assessing the subject's interests in a number of areas related to occupational fields and college majors. Test items consist of a list of three activities. The subject indicates for each item which activity he likes the most and which he likes the least. The test reports comparison to the subject's norm group by sex in 10 vocational areas and compares the subject's interests with those of satisfied workers in approximately 100 specific occupational groups and satisfied students in approximately 40 college major groups. The Report Form lists scores on occupational and college major scales separately, in rank order for each student. All respondents receive scores on all scales, including some nontraditional occupations for men and women. A general manual provides technical data regarding reliability, validity, scoring, interpretation, and compliance with Title IX regulations. Optional interpretive guides include an interpretive audiocassette, Expanding Your Future (a guide to help subjects interpret and use their scores), and Counseling with the Kuder Occupational Interest Survey, Form DD (a handbook for counselors). A sixth-grade reading level is required. Self-administered. Suitable for group use.

Timed: 30-40 minutes

Scoring: Computer scored

Cost: Materials and scoring for 20 persons $70.00; audiocassette $15.95; Expanding Your Future $11.50; Counseling with KOIS $5.00; no charge for general manual if requested when ordering

Publisher: Science Research Associates, Inc.

LICENSURE, CERTIFICATION, REGISTRATION, AND QUALIFYING EXAMINATIONS: ADMISSIONS AND CREDENTIALING GROUP
The Psychological Corporation

Adult

Purpose: Assesses skills and competence of professionals in various areas. Used by local, state, and national organizations and agencies for licensing, certifying, registering, and qualifying members of their respective occupations.

Description: Multiple-item paper-pencil tests used to establish credentials attesting to the skill and competence of those professionals meeting or exceeding minimum standards. Some of the programs administered by the Admissions and Credentialing Group are the Certifying Examination for Surgical Technologists for the Association of Surgical Technologists; the Certification Examination for Rehabilitation Nursing for the Association of Rehabilitation Nurses; the Registration Examination for Electroencephalographic Technologists for the American Board of Registration of Electroencephalographic Technologists; and the Certification Examination for Professional Marketing Communicators for the Business/Professional Advertising Association.
Tests are administered in designated test centers. Applicants must complete and file an application and the appropriate fee by specific deadlines. For specific content and cost information, contact the publisher or the relevant association. Examiner required. Suitable for group use.

Timed: Approximately 4 hours per test

Scoring: Computer scoring service provided

Cost: Contact publisher
Publisher: Admissions and Credentialing Group/The Psychological Corporation

LIGONDE EQUIVALENCE TEST
Paultre Ligonde

Adult

Purpose: Measures grade-level ability of adults who have been out of school 20-30 years. Used when determination of school grade level is relevant to employment qualifications and for placement in adult education programs.

Description: Multiple-item paper-pencil test assessing the grade level of adults who have been out of school several years. Scoring is based on what students from a particular grade level should retain in terms of verbal and numerical skills. The test is used to select employees for positions requiring verbal communication or clerical skills, to determine school levels for trade or labor unions, and to issue competency cards. The test was normed on 3,000 French and English Canadians who left school 20-30 years ago. The test is available in two forms, GE and HE. Both include questions on knowledge of the second language. Examiner required. Suitable for group use.
CANADIAN PUBLISHER

Timed: 15 minutes
Scoring: Hand key
Cost: Specimen key $3.00
Publisher: Institute of Psychological Research, Inc.
Information and availability unconfirmed; no publisher response.

LIVING SKILLS

Adolescent, adult

Purpose: Measures functional literacy.

Description: Self-pace A-V format assessment addressing five basic skills— reading, writing, speaking/listening, computation, and problem solving—as each touches upon five different functional knowledge areas: government and law, occupational knowledge, health, community resources, and consumer education. Response items are woven into a series of 18 high-interest adventures involving fictional people of varying ethnic, sex, and race characteristics. The action stops and the individual is asked to respond to a question that is an outgrowth of the story line. The computer-scored report provides individual and group performance scales for each of the skills and knowledge areas. The results also place the individual in one of three Adult Performance Levels derived by the USOE Adult Functional Competency Study. The results include prescriptions for improvement. Examiner/self-administered. Not suitable for group use.

Untimed: Varies according to ability

Scoring: Computer scored on-site or by publisher

Cost: Contact publisher

Publisher: Prep, Inc.

MATHEMATICAL ACHIEVEMENT TEST

Adult

Purpose: Measures general skills of algebra, geometry, and mathematics at the secondary-school level. Used in employee selection for clerical and technical positions.

Description: Multiple-item paper-pencil achievement test assessing the extent to which the subject can apply the principles of algebra, geometry, and general mathematics as taught in secondary schools. Norms are based on a group of matriculated boys and girls. The test is restricted to competent persons properly registered with the South African Medical and Dental Council. Examiner required. Suitable for group use. Afrikaans version available. SOUTH AFRICAN PUBLISHER

Timed: 23 minutes

Scoring: Hand key; examiner evaluated

Cost: Contact publisher

Publisher: National Institute for Personnel Research

MECHANICAL ABILITY TEST
J.R. Morrisby

Ages 11-adult

Purpose: Measures natural mechanical aptitude, not learned knowledge, in adults. Used to predict potential in most areas of engineering, especially electrical and mechanical; assembly work; carpentry; and building trades.

Description: 35-item paper-pencil test in which each item consists of an illustrated mechanical principle and a question with five alternative answers. A knowledge of theoretical physics is not required since the test is not intended to measure the level of mechanical knowledge the subject has attained. Materials include the booklet, manual, specimen set, answer sheets, and scoring key. The test is restricted to examiners who provide evidence of adequate training and practical experience in the use of such tests. Examiner required. Suitable for group use.
BRITISH PUBLISHER

Timed: 15 minutes

Scoring: Hand key; examiner evaluated; may be computer scored

Cost: Contact publisher

Publisher: Educational and Industrial Test Services Ltd.

MEEKER BEHAVIOR CORRELATES FOR MANAGEMENT MATCHING OF TEAMS
Refer to page 922.

MESA
Refer to page 765.

MESA SHORT FORM
Refer to page 766.

MINNESOTA ENGINEERING ANALOGIES TEST
Refer to page 715.

MOBILE VOCATIONAL EVALUATION (MVE)
Edward J. Hester

Adolescent, adult

Purpose: Measures vocationally related abilities. Used as a basis for identifying specific jobs which fit an individual's abilities and special needs. Used for home applications and as a service of several small workshops or multicampus school systems.

Description: Multiple-test battery assessing the following factors of an individual's ability: finger dexterity, wrist finger speed, arm hand steadiness, manual dexterity, two-arm coordination, two-hand coordination, perceptual accuracy, special perception, aiming, reaction time, abstract reasoning, verbal reasoning, numerical reasoning, reading arithmetic, leadership-structure, and following directions. The battery yields 19 ability factor scores, as well as the 17 personal characteristics. Ability factors and personal characteristics are computer analyzed to identify appropriate jobs. The data base contains a computer analysis of over 700 jobs taken from the current Dictionary of Occupational Titles (DOT) published by the United States Department of Labor. The computer printout provides scaled scores and a listing of up to 100 jobs that are realistic opportunities for the individual, arranged in order from those which are most feasible to those which are least feasible. All components are contained in a single carrying case weighing less than 30 pounds. All electronic components are battery powered. The tests may be administered by nonprofessional personnel such as clerks and assistants. Examiner required. Eighty-five percent of the testing may be accomplished in a group setting.

Untimed: 4-5 hours

Scoring: Computer scored

Cost: Contact publisher

Publisher: Lafayette Instrument Company, Inc.

MULTIFUNCTIONAL WORK TASK UNIT
Refer to page 979.

NON-READING APTITUDE BATTERY (NATB)
U.S. Employment Service

Adult

Purpose: Measures vocational aptitudes of individuals with a low level of literacy skills. Used for vocational counseling and employment screening.

Description: 14 subtests measuring the following nine aptitudes to help individuals with low reading skills choose an occupation: general learning ability, verbal ability, numerical ability, spatial aptitude, form perception, clerical perception, motor coordination, finger dexterity, and manual dexterity. The aptitudes are tested through procedures that involve neither reading nor writing. The subject's performance is interpreted according to the Occupational Aptitude Patterns (OAPs). The subject's scores are compared to those of successful individuals in various occupations. High, medium, or low probability of success in different employment settings is estimated for the individual. Materials consist of test booklets in which all answers are marked, a pegboard for place and turn tests, and a finger dexterity board. Use in the United States must be authorized by State Employment Service Agencies and in Canada by the Canadian Employment and Immigration Commission. Examiner required. Suitable for group use.

Timed: Varies

Scoring: Hand key

Cost: Available through State Employment Service Agencies only

Publisher: U.S. Department of Labor

NORMAL, INTERMEDIATE AND HIGH LEVEL BATTERIES

Adult

Purpose: Measures mental abilities and verbal skills related to many clerical and technical positions. Suitable for matriculants and higher.

Description: Three batteries of paper-pencil tests measuring three levels of mental and verbal abilities. The Normal Battery, used with standards 6-10 and job applicants with 8-11 years of education, contains five tests covering mental alertness, reading comprehension, vocabulary, spelling, and computation. The Intermediate Battery, used with standards 7-10 and job applicants with 9-12 years of education, contains seven tests covering mental alertness, arithmetical problems, computation, spot-the-error, reading comprehension, vocabulary, and spelling. The High Level Battery, used with a wide range of groups at matric and higher levels, contains six tests covering mental alertness, arithmetical problems, reading comprehension (English, Afrikaans) and vocabulary (English, Afrikaans). Norms are provided for all three batteries for their appropriate levels. The test is restricted to competent persons properly registered with the South African medical and Dental Council. Examiner required. Suitable for group use. Afrikaans version available.
SOUTH AFRICAN PUBLISHER

Timed: Normal 120 minutes; Intermediate 165 minutes; High Level 117 minutes

Scoring: Hand key; examiner evaluated

Cost: Contact publisher

Publisher: National Institute for Personnel Research

ONE MINUTE PER-FLU-DEX TESTS
F.J. Holmes

Adult

Purpose: Measures abilities desired in factory and office jobs. Used for evaluation of job applicants.

Description: Seven paper-pencil tests measuring office and industrial skills. The tests are Per-Symb, measuring symbol number substitution; Per-Verb, measuring letter perception and counting; Per-Numb, measuring number perception and counting; Flu-Verb, measuring word completion and verbal fluency; Flu-Num, measuring arithmetical computa-

tion; Dex-Man, measuring manual speed of movement; and Dex-Aim, measuring aiming accuracy and speed. Materials include profile-guidance sheets. Each test may be purchased and used separately. Examiner required. Suitable for group use.

Timed: 1 minute per test

Scoring: Hand key

Cost: Specimen set $5.00; 25 tests (specify test) $2.75; 25 profiles $2.75

Publisher: Psychometric Affiliates

PERSONNEL TEST BATTERY (PTB)
Saville & Holdsworth Ltd.

Adult

Purpose: Evaluates skills relevant to any job that requires the quick and accurate routine use of numbers, words, and other symbols. Assesses skills required for clerks, bookkeepers, typists, data processors, salespersons, nurses, and others.

Description: Six paper-pencil multiple-choice aptitude tests arranged in two levels. Both levels assess language proficiency, numeracy, and perceptual accuracy. Level 1 measures these abilities in terms of basic skills and comprehension and includes the following tests: Verbal Usage (VP1), Numerical Computation (NP2), and Checking (CP3). Level 2 measures similar skills at a more advanced level involving higher order reasoning and includes the following tests: Verbal Meaning (VP5), Numerical Reasoning (NP6), and Classification (CP4). Together, the tests cover a wide range of abilities for persons with no formal educational background through the GCE "O" level and "A" level. Two optional tests measuring basic clerical checking skills are available: Basic Checking (CP7) and Audio Checking (CP8). The combination of PTB tests administered will depend on the specific job and its context. Examiner required. Suitable for group use.
BRITISH PUBLISHER

Timed: 71 minutes complete battery; 7-10 minutes per test

Scoring: Hand key; may be computer scored

Cost: Complete (question booklets, keys, administration cards, profile charts, score sheets, test logs) $829.50

Publisher: Saville & Holdsworth Ltd.

PERSONNEL TEST BATTERY: AUDIO CHECKING (PTB:CP8)
Saville & Holdsworth Ltd.

Adult

Purpose: Tests an individual's ability to receive and check information that is presented orally. Used to select clerical staff who must process information presented orally as in telesales or airline/hotel bookings.

Description: 60-item paper-pencil multiple-choice test in which the task is to listen to a string of numbers or letters presented on an audiotape and select the identical string from the five choices presented in the question booklet. There are three subtests covering letters, numbers, and letters and numbers mixed. The test is suitable for individuals with minimal educational qualifications to the GCE "A" level. Examiner required. Suitable for group use.
BRITISH PUBLISHER

Timed: 10 minutes

Scoring: Hand key; examiner evaluated; may be computer scored

Cost: Audio cassette $35.00; 50 answer sheets $46.20; key $9.50; 10 booklets $46.50; administration card $9.50

Publisher: Saville & Holdsworth Ltd.

PERSONNEL TEST BATTERY: BASIC CHECKING (PTB:CP7)
Saville & Holdsworth Ltd.

Adult

Purpose: Tests for speed and accuracy in checking a variety of materials at a very basic level. Used for selection of clerical and general staff concerned with simple routine checking.

Description: 80-item paper-pencil multiple-choice test consisting of two subtests. One involves checking a list of numbers, and the other involves checking a list of letters. In each list, a series of strings of numbers or letters is presented. These are

compared with another page from which the identical string must be selected (from five choices). The test is suitable for individuals with minimal educational qualifications to GCE "A" level. Examiner required. Suitable for group use.
BRITISH PUBLISHER

Timed: 10 minutes

Scoring: Hand key; examiner evaluated; may be computer scored

Cost: 10 question booklets $46.50; 50 answer sheets $46.20; key $9.50; administration card $9.50

Publisher: Saville & Holdsworth Ltd.

PERSONNEL TEST BATTERY: CHECKING (PTB:CP3)
Saville & Holdsworth Ltd.

Adult

Purpose: Measures ability to perceive and check a variety of material quickly and accurately. Used for personnel selection of office, sales, or general staff positions.

Description: 40-item paper-pencil proof-reading test in which two lists of information about hotels are presented. One list is handwritten and the other is printed. The material contained in the lists includes names, numbers, and symbols. The candidates must compare the two lists and note any errors in accordance with a given code (designed to represent a real clerical task). The test is suitable for individuals with minimal educational qualifications to GCE "A" level. Examiner required. Suitable for group use.
BRITISH PUBLISHER

Timed: 7 minutes

Scoring: Hand key; examiner evaluated; may be computer scored

Cost: 10 question booklets $46.50; 50 answer sheets $46.50; key $9.50; administration card $9.50

Publisher: Saville & Holdsworth Ltd.

PERSONNEL TEST BATTERY: CLASSIFICATION (PTB:CP4)
Saville & Holdsworth Ltd.

Adult

Purpose: Measures the ability to perceive and classify material in accordance with a set of instructions. Used for personnel decisions when data handling, filing, or the following of instructions are important.

Description: 60-item paper-pencil test representing a real clerical task in which a number of sales order forms must be filed. The candidate classifies each order and then records the order in coded form. Some orders ("account sales") must be filed alphabetically and others ("cash sales") must be classified under seven categories of goods purchased. The test is suitable for individuals from GCE "O" level to GCE "A" level. Examiner required. Suitable for group use. BRITISH PUBLISHER

Timed: 7 minutes

Scoring: Hand key; examiner evaluated; may be computer scored

Cost: 10 question booklets $46.50; 50 answer sheets $46.50; key $9.50; administration card $9.50

Publisher: Saville & Holdsworth Ltd.

PERSONNEL TEST BATTERY: NUMERICAL COMPUTATION (PTB:NP2)
Saville & Holdsworth Ltd.

Adult

Purpose: Measures ability to work with numbers. Used for selection of clerical, sales, and general staff.

Description: 30-item paper-pencil multiple-choice test measuring the understanding of relationships between numbers and operations, as well as quick and accurate calculation. In each item, one number has been omitted from an equation. The examinee must select (from five choices) the number that will correctly complete the equation. Simple fractions and decimals are used, and some problems are expressed in £s, but more

complex notation or operations are deliberately omitted. The test is suitable for individuals with minimal educational qualifications to GCE "O" level. Examiner required. Suitable for group use. BRITISH PUBLISHER

Timed: 7 minutes

Scoring: Hand key; examiner evaluated; may be computer scored

Cost: 10 question booklets $40.50; 50 answer sheets $46.50; key $9.50; administration card $9.50

Publisher: Saville & Holdsworth Ltd.

PERSONNEL TEST BATTERY: NUMERICAL REASONING (PTB:NP6)
Saville & Holdsworth Ltd.

Adult

Purpose: Measures simple numerical reasoning skills. Used to select clerical, sales, or general staff.

Description: 30-item paper-pencil multiple-choice test consisting of word problems with numerical answers. Some calculation is involved, but understanding, reasoning, and recognizing shortcut methods is emphasized. The problems cover basic arithmetic operations, simple percentages, fractions, decimals, and graphs. The questions are all given a commercial slant and involve working out sale or purchase prices, profit margins, markups, change, weights, times, and areas. The test is suitable for individuals from GCE "O" to GCE "A" level. Examiner required. Suitable for group use. BRITISH PUBLISHER

Timed: 10 minutes

Scoring: Hand key; examiner evaluated; may be computer scored

Cost: 10 question booklets $46.50; 50 answer sheets $46.50; key $9.50; administration card $9.50

Publisher: Saville & Holdsworth Ltd.

PERSONNEL TEST BATTERY: VERBAL MEANING (PTB:VP5)
Saville & Holdsworth Ltd.

Adult

Purpose: Assesses an individual's knowledge of the meaning of words and the relationships between them. Used for selection with any job in which verbal communication skills are important.

Description: 30-item paper-pencil multiple-choice test requiring the candidate to identify the relationship (same or opposite) between one pair of words and to select (from five choices) the word which relates in the same way to a third given word. The vocabulary used is non-specialist, everyday language. VP5 is more difficult than VP1 of the same battery. The test is suitable for individuals from the ACE "O" level to GCE "A" level. Examiner required. Suitable for group use.
BRITISH PUBLISHER

Timed: 10 minutes

Scoring: Hand key; examiner evaluated; may be computer scored

Cost: 10 question booklets $46.50; 50 answer sheets $46.50; key $9.50; administration card $9.50

Publisher: Saville & Holdsworth Ltd.

PERSONNEL TEST BATTERY: VERBAL USAGE (PTB:VP1)
Saville & Holdsworth Ltd.

Adult

Purpose: Measures ability for spelling, grammar, and choice of words. Used in job placement involving the receipt, processing, or drafting of correspondence.

Description: 30-item paper-pencil multiple-choice test in which each item consists of a sentence from which two words have been omitted. The candidate must choose (from five choices) the correct pair of words to complete the sentence. The sentences consist of words and phrases commonly found in commercial correspondence. The test is suitable for individuals with minimal educational qualifications to GCE "O" level. Examiner required. Suitable for group use.
BRITISH PUBLISHER

Timed: 10 minutes

Scoring: Hand key; examiner evaluated; may be computer scored

Cost: 10 question booklets $46.50; 50 answer sheets $46.50; key $9.50; administration card $9.50

Publisher: Saville & Holdsworth Ltd.

PERSONNEL TESTS FOR INDUSTRY (PTI)
A. G. Wesman and J.E. Doppelt

Adult

Purpose: Assesses general ability. Used to select workers for skilled positions in industrial settings.

Description: Multiple-item multiple-choice paper-pencil tests covering two dimensions of general ability: verbal and numerical competence. Some items involve problem solving. Two equivalent forms and tapes for administering the test are available. Examiner required. Suitable for group use.

Timed: Verbal 5 minutes; numerical 20 minutes

Scoring: Hand key

Cost: Specimen set (both forms of Verbal and Numerical booklets, manual) $11.00; 25 tests, manual, key (specify Verbal or Numerical, Form A or B) $21.00

Publisher: The Psychological Corporation

PERSONNEL TESTS FOR INDUSTRY—ORAL DIRECTIONS TEST (PTI-ODT)
C.R. Langmuir

Adult

Purpose: Measures ability to understand and follow oral directions. Used in the selection of applicants with a limited education and/or knowledge of English.

Description: Multiple-item paper-pencil test covering the ability to follow oral directions. The applicant responds to instructions dictated on tape by marking the answer document. Two equivalent forms, S and T, are available. Examiner required. Suitable for group use. Form S is available in a Spanish-American edition.

Timed: 15 minutes

Scoring: Hand key

Cost: Complete set (recording, manual, script, key, 100 answer documents) $65.00; reel-to-reel tape version $65.00; cassette tape version $65.00; record version $65.00

Publisher: The Psychological Corporation

PHOENIX ABILITY SURVEY SYSTEM (PASS)
Edward J. Hester

Adolescent, adult

Purpose: Measures vocationally related abilities. Used as a basis for identifying specific jobs that fit an individual's abilities and special needs. Used for on-sight applications.

Description: Multiple-test battery measuring 30 ability factors and 21 personal characteristics related to a person's vocational aptitudes and interests. The specific ability factors measured include three measures of unilateral motor functions, six measures of bilateral motor functions, four measures of perceptual factors, four factors of perceptual motor coordination, five factors of intelligence, two factors of achievement, two factors of strength, and four factors of people/relationships abilities. The data base used in the computer analysis consists of over 2,000 jobs taken from the current Dictionary of Occupational Titles (DOT) published by the United States Department of Labor. The jobs in the data base range from physician to laborer, representing virtually every industrial and occupational group in America. A typical computer printout is up to six pages long and includes physical limitations, working conditions, people relationships and individual test scores, ability scores profile sheet, and several job title listings that are realistic for the individual, arranged in order from those which are most feasible to those which are least feasible. The battery may be used to augment job sample testing systems such as Valpar, Singer, JEVS, or VIEWS. Examiner required. Eighty-five percent of the testing may be accomplished in a group setting.

Untimed: Varies

Scoring: Computer scored

Cost: Contact publisher

Publisher: Lafayette Instrument Company, Inc.

PRESS TEST
Refer to page 966.

PROGRAM FOR ASSESSING YOUTH EMPLOYMENT SKILLS (PAYES)
Refer to page 768.

PROGRAMMER APTITUDE SERIES: LEVEL 1 (PAS-1)
Saville & Holdsworth Ltd.

Adult

Purpose: Measures aptitudes for the very diverse range of activities and levels of skills required for programmer jobs. Used for entry-level data processing staff selections.

Description: Five paper-pencil multiple-choice tests measuring the acquisition of skills involved in most business programming functions. The tests include Advanced Testing Battery (ATB), Diagramming (DA5), ATB Verbal Concepts (VA1), ATB Number Series (NA2), Personnel Test Battery (PTB), Basic Checking (CP7), Technical Test Battery (TTB), and Spatial Recognition (ST9). The test provides a good overview of diagramming, verbal, numerical, clerical, and spatial abilities. Examiner required. Suitable for group use.
BRITISH PUBLISHER

Timed: Complete battery 1 hour, 15 minutes

Scoring: Hand key; examiner evaluated; may be computer scored

Cost: Complete (test booklets, 50 answer sheets, keys, profiles, manual) $787.50

Publisher: Saville & Holdsworth Ltd.

PROGRAMMER APTITUDE SERIES: LEVEL 2 (PAS-2)
Saville & Holdsworth Ltd.

Adult

Purpose: Measures aptitudes for the very diverse range of activities and levels of skills required for programmer jobs at an intermediate level. Used for intermediate data processing staff selections.

Description: Five paper-pencil multiple-choice tests measuring the acquisition of skills that are involved in most business programming functions, but at a higher level of difficulty than the basic level. The tests include ATB Diagramming (DA5), ATB Verbal Critical Reasoning (VA3), ATB Number Series (NA2), PTB Basic Checking (CP7), and TTB Spatial Reasoning (ST7). This combination of tests is useful where more "top" is required, for example when dealing with good GCE "O" and "A" level applicants. Examiner required. Suitable for group use. BRITISH PUBLISHER

Timed: 1 hour, 35 minutes

Scoring: Hand key; examiner evaluated; may be computer scored

Cost: Complete (test booklets, 50 answer sheets, keys, profiles, manual) $787.50

Publisher: Saville & Holdsworth Ltd.

PROGRAMMER APTITUDE SERIES: LEVEL 3 (PAS-3)
Saville & Holdsworth Ltd.

Adult

Purpose: Measures aptitudes for the very diverse range of activities and levels of skills required for data processing staff selection at higher levels, including graduates.

Description: Five paper-pencil multiple-choice tests measuring the acquisition of skills involved in most business programming functions by higher staff members and graduates. The tests include ATB Verbal Concepts (VA1), ATB Number Series (NA2), ATB Verbal Critical Reasoning (VA3), ATB Numerical Critical

Reasoning (NA4), and TTB Diagrammatic Reasoning (DT8). Examiner required. Suitable for group use. BRITISH PUBLISHER

Timed: Complete battery 1 hour, 35 minutes

Scoring: Hand key; examiner evaluated; may be computer scored

Cost: Complete (test booklets, 50 answer sheets, keys, profiles, manual) $808.50

Publisher: Saville & Holdsworth Ltd.

PSB READING COMPREHENSION EXAMINATION
Refer to page 545.

PURDUE BLUEPRINT READING TEST
H. F. Owen and J. N. Arnold

Adolescent, adult

Purpose: Assesses ability to read standard blueprints. Used for applicant and student selection.

Description: Multiple-item paper-pencil test of knowledge of fundamental principles of reading blueprints. Sale is restricted to companies employing qualified personnel administrators and to psychologists using the test for instruction or vocational guidance. Examiner required. Suitable for group use.

Untimed: Not available

Scoring: Hand key

Cost: Specimen set $1.00; 25 tests, manual, key $6.00

Publisher: Purdue Research Foundation/ University Book Store

PURDUE INTERVIEW AIDS
C. H. Lawshe

Adult

Purpose: Measures skill in reading working drawings, micrometers, and standard scales. Used to evaluate qualifications of job applicants.

Description: Three verbal tests of specific skills: Can You Read a Working Drawing?, Can You Read a Micrometer?, and Can You Read a Scale? The tests are administered as part of the interview. Sale is restricted to companies employing qualified personnel administrators and to psychologists using tests for instruction or vocational guidance. Examiner required. Not suitable for group use.

Untimed: Not available

Scoring: Examiner evaluated

Cost: Specimen set (3 aids, instruction sheet) $1.00; 25 tests, instruction sheet (specify test) $4.50

Publisher: Purdue Research Foundation/ University Book Store

PURDUE TRADE INFORMATION TESTS

Adolescent, adult

Purpose: Assesses knowledge of various trades. Used for selection of applicants.

Description: Four paper-pencil tests of knowledge of the following trades or positions: welding, carpentry, sheet metal workers, and engine lathe operators. Sale is restricted to companies employing qualified personnel administrators and to psychologists using the tests for instructional or vocational guidance. Examiner required. Suitable for group use.

Untimed: Not available

Scoring: Hand key

Cost: Specimen set (specify test) $1.00; 25 tests, manual, scoring key (specify test) $6.00

Publisher: Purdue Research Foundation/ University Book Store

THE RBH ARITHMETIC REASONING TEST
Richardson, Bellows, Henry and Company, Inc.

Adult

Purpose: Assesses an individual's ability to solve problems using basic arithmetical operations. Used with technical and professional employees, sales employees, clerical employees, and mechanical and operating personnel.

Description: 25-item test assessing an individual's ability to solve arithmetic problems covering the following areas:

determination of selling price, distribution of costs, discounting, production rates, wage and salary rates, payments, overtime procedures, deductions, tax operations, dividend and profit determinations, percentages, and proportions. Examinees mark their answers directly in the test book in boxes placed next to the problem. Space for figuring the problems is provided. The score is the number of items answered correctly. The test is available in two forms, I and II. Examiner required. Suitable for group use.

Timed: 15 minutes

Scoring: Hand key

Cost: 1-24 packages $18.00; score key $3.00; manual $6.00

Publisher: Richardson, Bellows, Henry and Company, Inc.

READING COMPREHENSION
Richardson, Bellows, Henry and Company, Inc.

Adult

Purpose: Measures reading comprehension of applicants to industrial positions.

Description: Multiple-item paper-pencil test assessing the ability to comprehend reading material related to business and industry. The test contains six articles taken from training and safety manuals and publicity releases. Each article is followed by several questions that test the examinee's understanding of the article. The test is not intended to measure critical thinking. For males, the test has been used almost exclusively with industrial employees and applicants. With a maximum score of 40, examinees average about 30 with a standard deviation of seven. The test also has been used with females in nurses' training and clerical jobs. Examiner required. Suitable for group use.

Timed: 20 minutes

Scoring: Hand key

Cost: 1-24 packages $22.00; score key $2.00; manual $2.00

Publisher: Richardson, Bellows, Henry and Company, Inc.

REVOLVING ASSEMBLY TABLE
Refer to page 982.

THE SHAPES ANALYSIS TEST
*Alice Heim, K.P. Watts,
and V. Simmonds*

**Adolescent, adult
Ages 13 and older**

Purpose: Assesses subjects' ability to mentally manipulate different shapes and sizes of geometric figures. Used for screening for job placement or training.

Description: 36-item paper-pencil multiple-choice test of spatial perception. Each item is comprised of several figures. The subject must visualize how each figure will appear if turned over or around, estimate area, and assess spatial relations. Six items are presented cyclically in order of increasing difficulty. Eighteen items are two-dimensional figures, and the rest are three-dimensional figures. Examiner required. Suitable for group use. BRITISH PUBLISHER

Timed: 25 minutes

Scoring: Hand key; examiner evaluated; scoring service available

Cost: Booklet $2.50; answer sheet $1.50; manual $8.00

Publisher: The Test Agency Ltd.

SHAPES TEST
J.R. Morrisby

Ages 11-adult

Purpose: Measures spatial-perceptual ability. Used in occupations such as design work, drafting, and die-making, which involve diagrammatic representation of real objects and systems.

Description: 60-item paper-pencil multiple-choice instrument following the principle of spatial tests in which the subject is required to manipulate figures mentally in three dimensions. Materials include the booklet and manual, specimen set, answer sheets, and the scoring key. The test is restricted to examiners who provide evidence of adequate training and practical experience in the use of such tests. Examiner required. Suitable for group use. BRITISH PUBLISHER

Timed: 10 minutes

Scoring: Hand key; may be computer scored

Cost: Contact publisher

Publisher: Educational and Industrial Test Services Ltd.

SHOP ARITHMETIC TEST
Richardson, Bellows, Henry and Company, Inc.

Adult

Purpose: Assesses arithmetic reasoning abilities. Used with applicants for operations and craft positions and engineering aides.

Description: 20-item paper-pencil test of mathematical abilities related to industrial situations. Content includes simple arithmetic operations (fractions and decimal fractions form the upper limit) involved in figuring sums or remainders on problems of weight or length; computing measures of distance, area, or volume; and analyzing operations data from tables. Illustrations and diagrams are provided to define and illustrate some problems. Space is provided in the test booklet for figuring problems, and answers are recorded in the margin. The test is available in two forms. Form I was normed on male managers and executives, technical and engineering supervisors, industrial foremen and supervisors, and mechanical and operating employees and applicants. Form II, which is slightly easier than Form I, was normed on male industrial applicants and mechanical and operating employees. Examiner required. Suitable for group use.

Timed: 15 minutes

Scoring: Hand key

Cost: 1-24 packages $19.00; score key $3.00; manual $2.00

Publisher: Richardson, Bellows, Henry and Company, Inc.

SKILLS AND ATTRIBUTES INVENTORY
Melany E. Baehr

Adult ☞ 🖎

Purpose: Assesses the relative importance of skill and attribute factors necessary for successful job performance and the degree to which the incumbent possesses the skills and attributes. Used for job selection, placement, diagnosis of training needs, and systematic job and self-analysis.

Description: 96-item paper-pencil test measuring general functioning, intelligence, visual activity, visual coordination skills, physical coordination, mechanical skills, graphic clerical skills, general clerical skills, leadership ability, tolerance in interpersonal relations, organization identification, conscientiousness and reliability, efficiency under stress, and solitary work. Each item is rated on importance to the job, on a 6-point scale ranging from "little or none" to "outstanding." The test also may be used to assess the incumbent's strength in the relative skills and attributes. Basic reading skills are required. Examiner required. Suitable for group use.

Untimed: 45 minutes

Scoring: Hand key; may be computer scored

Cost: Specimen set $10.00; 15 tests $13.75

Publisher: London House Press

SMELL IDENTIFICATION TEST™
Richard L. Doty

All ages 🖎

Purpose: Provides an accurate straightforward quantitative measure of an individual's ability to smell without the use of chemicals or complex odorant presentation equipment. Designed for use in industrial, academic, or medical settings. Applications include screening of industrial smell and taste panels, evaluation of industrial exposure to air-borne chemicals, medical examinations, longitudinal tracking of smell loss or return, and legal determinations of smell function.

Description: Consists of four booklets containing 10 odorants each, one odorant per page. The stimuli are embedded in "scratch n sniff" crystals located on brown strips positioned at the bottom of each page. The individual completes a multiple-choice question for each of the 40 odorant items. The test can detect most malingerers and is sensitive to numerous subject variables, including smoking habits, age, gender, and a number of medical conditions. Total test score is the sum of the number of items correct out of the 40 total. Norms provide percentile values for men and women in 5-year age categories from 5 years of age to 100 years of age and specific function classifications (i.e., normosmia, microsmia or hyposmia, anosmia, probable malingering). Scores also correlate with levels of specific neurotransmitter metabolites in cerebral spinal fluid.

The Pocket Smell Test™, designed for use by medical practitioners and consisting of items selected from the Smell Identification Test arranged in a pocket-sized folded card with instructions, is available. It allows gross olfactory screening. Olfactory abnormalities discovered by this test should be fully characterized using the 40-item Smell Identification Test. Scoring is pass/fail.

Japanese, French, and German versions of both tests are under development. Self-administered by reasonably literate persons ages 10 to 70. Should be administered by a test administrator to persons ages 10 and younger or 70 and older. Not suitable for group use.

Untimed: 10-15 minutes

Scoring: Examiner evaluated

Cost: Test and manual (minimum order of 5) $19.95; Pocket Smell Test (minimum order of 100) $1.25 each plus shipping

Publisher: Sensonics, Inc.

SOI-LA: DENTAL RECEPTIONIST TEST
Mary Meeker and Robert Meeker

Adult ☞ 🖎

Purpose: Measures the abilities and aptitudes of prospective dental receptionists. Used for selection of dental receptionists.

Description: Multiple-item paper-pencil screening instrument assessing the abilities and aptitudes of prospective dental receptionists. The criterion-referenced test items were developed in conjunction with practicing dental groups. Scoring keys and a criteria graph for selection are available separately. Self-interpreted. Examiner required. Suitable for group use.

Untimed: 1 hour

Scoring: Hand key; may be machine scored

Cost: Test form $2.00; scoring key $12.00

Publisher: M & M Systems

SPACE RELATIONS (PAPER PUZZLES)
L.L. Thurstone and T.E. Jeffrey

Adult

Purpose: Assesses the ability to visually select a combination of flat pieces that, together, will cover a given two-dimensional space. Used in vocational counseling or selection.

Description: Multiple-item paper-pencil test of mechanical interest and ability identifying individuals with high mechanical interest and ability. Examiner required. Suitable for group use.

Timed: 9 minutes

Scoring: Hand key

Cost: Specimen set $8.00; 25 test booklets $11.25

Publisher: London House Press

SPACE THINKING (FLAGS)
L.L. Thurstone and T.E. Jeffrey

Adolescent, adult

Purpose: Assesses the ability to visually select a combination of flat pieces that, together, will cover a given two-dimensional space.

Description: 21-item paper-pencil test measuring ability to visualize a rigid configuration in which there is no internal movement when it is moved into different

positions. Each item has six responses. Examiner required. Suitable for group use.

Timed: 5 minutes

Scoring: Hand key

Cost: Specimen set $8.00; 25 tests $11.25

Publisher: London House Press

SPECIFIC APTITUDE TEST BATTERY (SATB)
U.S. Employment Service

Adult

Purpose: Measures aptitude for specific occupations. Used to select untrained or inexperienced applicants for referrals to specific jobs or occupational training.

Description: Multiple-item paper-pencil test reflecting the aptitude requirements for specific occupations against which an individual's scores can be matched. Two to four of SATB's aptitude test batteries are derived from the General Aptitude Test Battery (GATB). The SATB score matching process is the same as that for the Occupational Aptitudes Patterns (OAPs). Examiner required. Suitable for group use. Available in Spanish.

Timed: Not available

Scoring: Hand key

Cost: Available through State Employment Service Agencies only

Publisher: U.S. Department of Labor

SRA READING-ARITHMETIC INDEX
SRA Industrial
Test Development Staff

Adolescent, adult
Ages 14 and older

Purpose: Assesses general reading and computational achievement. Used for entry-level positions and training programs where basic skills of applicants are often too low to be reliably evaluated by typical selection tests.

Description: Two paper-pencil tests measuring reading skills (picture-word association, word decoding, and comprehension of phrases, sentences, and paragraphs) and arithmetic skills (addi-

tion and subtraction, multiplication and division, fractional operations, and decimals and percentages). The score reflects the highest developmental level passed. Examiner required. Suitable for group use.
Untimed: 25 minutes per index
Scoring: Self-scored
Cost: 25 test booklets (specify form) $20.00; examiner's manual $10.00
Publisher: Science Research Associates, Inc.

SRA VERBAL FORM
*L.L. Thurstone and
Thelma Gwinn Thurstone*

Adult

Purpose: Measures an individual's overall adaptability and flexibility in comprehending and following instructions and in adjusting to alternating types of problems on the job. Used in both school and industry for selection and placement.

Description: Paper-pencil short-answer test of general mental abilities. The test measures both linguistic (vocabulary) and quantitative (arithmetic) factors. Items of both types are interspersed with a time limit. The test is similar to the Thurstone Test of Mental Alertness but has a time limit of 15, rather than 20, minutes. Two equivalent forms are available. Examiner required. Suitable for group use.
Timed: 15 minutes
Scoring: Hand key
Cost: 25 test booklets $28.00; examiner's manual $10.00
Publisher: Science Research Associates, Inc.

STUDENT OCCUPATIONAL COMPETENCY ACHIEVEMENT TESTING (SOCAT)
Refer to page 272.

STUDENT OCCUPATIONAL COMPETENCY ACHIEVEMENT TESTING: ACCOUNTING/ BOOKKEEPING
Refer to page 272.

STUDENT OCCUPATIONAL COMPETENCY ACHIEVEMENT TESTING: AGRICULTURE MECHANICS
Refer to page 272.

STUDENT OCCUPATIONAL COMPETENCY ACHIEVEMENT TESTING: AUTO BODY
Refer to page 273.

STUDENT OCCUPATIONAL COMPETENCY ACHIEVEMENT TESTING: AUTO MECHANICS
Refer to page 273.

STUDENT OCCUPATIONAL COMPETENCY ACHIEVEMENT TESTING: CARPENTRY
Refer to page 273.

STUDENT OCCUPATIONAL COMPETENCY ACHIEVEMENT TESTING: COMMERCIAL FOODS
Refer to page 274.

STUDENT OCCUPATIONAL COMPETENCY ACHIEVEMENT TESTING: COMPUTER PROGRAMMING
Refer to page 274.

STUDENT OCCUPATIONAL COMPETENCY ACHIEVEMENT TESTING: CONSTRUCTION ELECTRICITY
Refer to page 274.

STUDENT OCCUPATIONAL COMPETENCY ACHIEVEMENT TESTING: CONSTRUCTION MASONRY
Refer to page 274.

SYSTEM FOR TESTING AND EVALUATION OF POTENTIAL (STEP)
Melany E. Baehr

Adult

Purpose: Estimates potential for successful performance (PSP) in present and future positions. Used for hiring, training, and promotion decisions at all levels of skill from first-line supervisors to vice-president officer level.

Description: Two paper-pencil batteries, the Managerial and Professional Job Functions Inventory (MP-JFI) and the Managerial and Professional Test Battery, assessing an individual's potential for success in present and future positions. The MP-JFI is a standardized and quantified job analysis procedure providing a common grid for the description of higher-level positions with respect to 16 factorially determined dimensions or generic job functions. Composite job profiles and norms have been developed for the 12 key positions based upon a national sample of incumbents. The MP Test Battery is a systematic and quantified procedure providing measures of individuals' abilities, skills, and attributes over a wide range of behavior. The test battery has been specifically developed and validated for managers and other high-level personnel. Composite profiles and normative data have been developed for each of the 12 key positions based upon a national sample.
The key positions include line personnel (first-line supervisors, middle managers, general managers, vice presidents); professionals (nonmanagement professionals, managers of one type of professional, managers of different types of professionals, vice presidents); sales personnel (sales representatives, district managers, regional and general managers, vice presidents); technical specialists (first-level specialists, managers of one type of specialist, managers of different types of specialists, vice presidents). Used together and anchored to the 12 key positions as reference points, these instruments provide information about the position (the relative importance of the functions to be performed) and the individual (the level of job skill or competency in the important job functions—the areas of strengths and weaknesses as revealed by the MP Test Battery—and estimates of potential for successful performance (PSP) in present and possible future positions). Examiner required. Suitable for group use.

Timed: 3-4 hours for entire battery

Scoring: Mail scoring or ITAC (Immediate Telephone Analysis by Computer)

Cost: Contact publisher; $150-$250 per test depending on volume ordered

Publisher: London House Press

TECHNICAL AND SCIENTIFIC INFORMATION TEST AND TECHNICAL READING COMPREHENSION TEST A/9

Adult

Purpose: Assesses scientific and technical understanding of people with little or no schooling in scientific or technical areas. Used for predicting job success in these fields after training.

Description: Multiple-item paper-pencil tests of general scientific knowledge and the ability to comprehend technical information. The two tests should be given together and sequentially. The first is a list of questions on general scientific information likely to be known by individuals who have had little or no formal scientific training. The second test consists of five paragraphs assessing whether a person with little or no formal schooling in technical subjects can comprehend articles of a technical nature. The tests predict job success after technical and scientific training. Norms are available. Examiner required. Suitable for group use.
SOUTH AFRICAN PUBLISHER

Timed: 30 minutes

Scoring: Hand key

Cost: Reusable booklet $2.00; 25 answer sheets $2.30; scoring keys $3.50; manual $9.50

Publisher: Human Sciences Research Council

TECHNICAL AND SCIENTIFIC INFORMATION TEST, TECHNICAL READING COMPREHENSION TEST AND GENERAL SCIENCE TEST

Adolescent, adult

Purpose: Measures technical and scientific knowledge and technical reading comprehension. Used with matriculated students in standards 7-9.

Description: The General Science Test consists of two paper-pencil subtests: The Technical and Scientific Information Test, which contains informational questions over general science topics and The Technical Reading Comprehension Test, which contains a number of paragraphs with questions to determine the extent to which articles of a technical nature can be understood. The two tests are administered in separate booklets. The tests are restricted to competent persons properly registered with the South African Medical and Dental Council. Examiner required. Suitable for group use. Available in Afrikaans.

SOUTH AFRICAN PUBLISHER

Untimed: Not available

Scoring: Hand key; examiner evaluated

Cost: Contact publisher

Publisher: National Institute for Personnel Research

TECHNICAL TEST BATTERY (TTB)
Saville & Holdsworth Ltd.

Adult

Purpose: Measures comprehension and reasoning skills. Used as a test of aptitude for a wide range of apprentice, technical, and technologist categories.

Description: Eight paper-pencil multiple-choice aptitude tests arranged in two levels of four scales each. Level One is intended for craft apprentice, operator, foreman, and similar occupations. The Level One scales, measuring comprehension skills, are Verbal Comprehension (VT1), Numerical Computation (NT2), Visual Estimation (ET3), and Mechanical

Comprehension (MT4). Level One's range extends from those with no formal educational qualifications through CSE and GCE "O" level.

Level Two overlaps Level One but is more extensive and difficult. The test is suitable for technician, HNC/HND, supervisory, technologist, technical sales, and some degree-level candidates. The following Level Two scales measure higher order reasoning skills: Verbal Reasoning (VT5), Numerical Reasoning (NT6), Spatial Reasoning (ST7), and Diagrammatic Reasoning (DT8). The range for Level Two extends from good CSE to GCE "O" and "A" level up to degree. Also available is an optional Spatial Recognition test (ST9) designed to measure spatial ability through complete shape recognition. Examiner required. Suitable for group use.

BRITISH PUBLISHER

Timed: Complete battery 1 hour, 50 minutes

Scoring: Hand key; examiner evaluated; may be computer scored

Cost: Complete (10 question booklets for Level 1 and 20 for Level 2, set of keys, set of administration cards, 50 profile charts, 25 score sheets, 25 test logs) $865.50

Publisher: Saville & Holdsworth Ltd.

TECHNICAL TEST BATTERY: DIAGRAMMATIC REASONING (TTB:DT8)
Saville & Holdsworth Ltd. Staff

Adult

Purpose: Measures diagrammatical reasoning ability. Used for personnel selection for technical occupations and jobs involving systems design, flow charting, and similar skills.

Description: 40-item paper-pencil multiple-choice test consisting of a series of abstract designs in logical sequences. Respondents must select, from five choices, the design which completes the logical sequence. Candidates must think logically and flexibly. The range extends from CSE to GCE "A" level and above. Examiner required. Suitable for group use.

BRITISH PUBLISHER

Timed: 15 minutes

Scoring: Hand key; examiner evaluated; may be computer scored

Cost: 10 question booklets $36.00; key $9.50; administration card $9.50

Publisher: Saville & Holdsworth Ltd.

TECHNICAL TEST BATTERY: MECHANICAL COMPREHENSION (TTB:MT4)
Saville & Holdsworth Ltd. Staff

Adult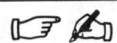

Purpose: Measures understanding of basic mechanical principles. Used in selection and development of craftsmen and technicians.

Description: 40-item paper-pencil multiple-choice test measuring knowledge of the classic mechanical elements, such as gears, pulleys, and levers, and a wide range of domestic and leisure applications of physics and mechanics, from electric ovens to billiard balls. Each item consists of a three-choice question about a technical drawing. The drawings are presented in technical workshop style without demanding any specific pre-knowledge to interpret them. The range extends from minimal educational qualifications to the GCE "A" level. Examiner required. Suitable for group use. BRITISH PUBLISHER

Timed: 15 minutes

Scoring: Hand key; examiner evaluated; may be computer scored

Cost: 10 question booklets $36.00; key $9.50; administration card $9.50

Publisher: Saville & Holdsworth Ltd.

TECHNICAL TEST BATTERY: NUMERICAL COMPUTATION (TTB:NT2)
Saville & Holdsworth Ltd. Staff

Adult

Purpose: Measures basic ability to work with numbers. Used for craft apprentice selection.

Description: 40-item paper-pencil multiple-choice test assessing the understanding of mathematical rela-

---

tionships and operations and the ability to calculate quickly and accurately. In each item, one number or operation has been omitted from an equation. The examinee must select the missing element from five possible answers. Fractions, decimals, and percentages are included, but more complex notations or operations are omitted deliberately (NT2 is slightly more advanced than NP2 in this respect). The range extends from minimal educational qualifications to the GCE "A" level. Examiner required. Suitable for group use.
BRITISH PUBLISHER

Timed: 10 minutes

Scoring: Hand key; examiner evaluated; may be computer scored

Cost: 10 question booklets $36.00; key $9.50; administration card $9.50

Publisher: Saville & Holdsworth Ltd.

TECHNICAL TEST BATTERY: NUMERICAL REASONING (TTB:NT6)
Saville & Holdsworth Ltd. Staff

Adult

Purpose: Measures simple numerical reasoning skills. Used in the selection and development of technical staff, including apprentices.

Description: 30-item paper-pencil multiple-choice test consisting of short word problems with numerical answers. Some calculation is involved, but the emphasis is on understanding, reasoning, and recognizing shortcut methods. The problems cover the basic arithmetic operations, percentages, fractions, decimals, angles, graphs, simple technical drawings, metric lengths, areas, and volumes. The questions are all given a technical slant, dealing with materials, output, production methods, etc. The range extends from GCE "O" level to GCE "A" level. Examiner required. Suitable for group use.
BRITISH PUBLISHER

Timed: 10 minutes

Scoring: Hand key; examiner evaluated; may be computer scored

---

Cost: 10 question booklets $36.00; key $9.50; administration card $9.50

Publisher: Saville & Holdsworth Ltd.

TECHNICAL TEST BATTERY: SPATIAL REASONING (TTB:ST7)
Saville & Holdsworth Ltd. Staff

Adult

Purpose: Measures ability to visualize and manipulate shapes in three dimensions when given a two-dimensional drawing. Used in selection and development work with many technical occupations.

Description: 40-item paper-pencil multiple-choice test consisting of a series of folded-out cubes and perspective drawings of assembled cubes. The respondents must identify the assembled cubes which could be made from the folded-out cube, each face of which has a different pattern. The range extends from GCE "O" level to degree. Examiner required. Suitable for group use. BRITISH PUBLISHER

Timed: 20 minutes

Scoring: Hand key; examiner evaluated; may be computer scored

Cost: 10 question booklets $36.00; key $9.50; administration card $9.50

Publisher: Saville & Holdsworth Ltd.

TECHNICAL TEST BATTERY: SPATIAL RECOGNITION (TTB:ST9)
Saville & Holdsworth Ltd. Staff

Adult

Purpose: Measures generalized spatial ability. Used for apprentice, programmer, or operator selection.

Description: 40-item paper-pencil multiple-choice test measuring the ability to recognize shapes in two dimensions. A series of shapes is presented. For each one, the identical shape must be selected from five choices. The emphasis is on the recognition of a complete shape when rotated rather than the more specific angle or length estimation required in ET3. ST9 requires less complex spatial skills than those measured in ST7. The range

extends from CSE to GCE "A" level. Examiner required. Suitable for group use. BRITISH PUBLISHER

Timed: 15 minutes

Scoring: Hand key; examiner evaluated; may be computer scored

Cost: 10 question booklets $36.00; key $9.50; administration card $9.50

Publisher: Saville & Holdsworth Ltd.

TECHNICAL TEST BATTERY: VERBAL COMPREHENSION (TTB:VT1)
Saville & Holdsworth Ltd. Staff

Adult

Purpose: Measures vocabulary and basic word skills in a technical context. Used in selecting and counseling apprentices in engineering and other industries.

Description: 40-item paper-pencil multiple-choice test assessing basic verbal skills, including sentence completion, same and opposite words, analogies, etc. The language deliberately has been chosen to reflect the comprehension requirements of technical occupations and crafts. The range extends from minimal educational qualifications to GCE "O" level. Examiner required. Suitable for group use. BRITISH PUBLISHER

Timed: 10 minutes

Scoring: Hand key; examiner evaluated; may be computer scored

Cost: 10 question booklets $36.00; key $9.50; administration card $9.50

Publisher: Saville & Holdsworth Ltd.

TECHNICAL TEST BATTERY: VERBAL REASONING (TTB:VT5)
Saville & Holdsworth Ltd. Staff

Adult

Purpose: Measures a high order of verbal skills. Used for technical selection and development from craft apprentice level upwards.

Description: 35-item paper-pencil multiple-choice test concerning the meaning of words and the relationships between

them. Respondents must identify the relationship between one pair of words and then select (from five possible words) the one which relates in the same way to a third given word. The vocabulary used has a scientific and technical bias. The range extends from GCE "O" level to "A" level. Examiner required. Suitable for group use.
BRITISH PUBLISHER

Timed: 10 minutes

Scoring: Hand key; examiner evaluated; may be computer scored

Cost: 10 question booklets $36.00; key $9.50; administration card $9.50

Publisher: Saville & Holdsworth Ltd.

TECHNICAL TEST BATTERY: VISUAL ESTIMATION (TTB:ET3)
Saville & Holdsworth Ltd. Staff

Adult

Purpose: Measures important elements of spatial perception relating to craft and design operations. Used for selection and development of all technical grades, especially craft and operator levels.

Description: 40-item paper-pencil multiple-choice test involving the estimation of lengths, angles, and shapes. In each item, the respondent must select the two figures from a set of five which are identical in form, although in many cases they are rotated on the page. Of the eight tests in the TTB, this is the most independent, suggesting that it measures a special aptitude, relatively free from overlap with general intellectual capacity. The range extends from minimal educational qualifications to GCE "A" level. Examiner required. Suitable for group use.
BRITISH PUBLISHER

Timed: 10 minutes

Scoring: Hand key; examiner evaluated; may be computer scored

Cost: 10 question booklets $36.00; key $9.50; administration card $9.50

Publisher: Saville & Holdsworth Ltd.

TEST A/8: ARITHMETIC

Adolescent, adult

Purpose: Measures general arithmetic ability. Used with technical college students and applicants for clerical and trade positions with 8-12 years of education for employee selection and placement.

Description: Multiple-item paper-pencil test measuring general arithmetic ability. Norms are available for technical college students and matriculated males. The test is restricted to competent persons properly registered with the South African Medical and Dental Council. Examiner required. Suitable for group use. Available in English and Afrikaans.
SOUTH AFRICAN PUBLISHER

Timed: Matriculants 30 minutes; nonmatriculants 40 minutes

Scoring: Hand key; examiner evaluated

Cost: Contact publisher

Publisher: National Institute for Personnel Research

TEST OF ENGLISH FOR INTERNATIONAL COMMUNICATION (TOEIC)

Adult nonnative speakers of English

Purpose: Measures English language proficiency required in business, commerce, and industry. Used as a basis for employee selection and placement and for decisions concerning assignment, placement, and achievement in company-sponsored English-language programs. Used with nonnative speakers of English.

Description: 200-item paper-pencil multiple-choice test of English language skills. Part I contains 100 listening comprehension items administered via audiotape. Part II contains 100 reading items. Total test scale scores range from 10-990; scale subscores for Parts I and II range from 5-495. The scores are correlated to direct measures of listening, speaking, reading, and writing, as well as to indirect measures. The test is used by multinational corporations, language schools, government agencies, public and private organizations for, among other uses, hiring, assignment to overseas posts requiring communication skills in English, assignment to or promotion within departments where English is desirable, identification of employees who know English well enough to benefit from training programs abroad, and determination of the effectiveness of English-language training programs. The test is currently offered in Japan, Korea, Taiwan, Hong Kong P.R.C., Indonesia, Thailand, Mexico, Central America, Europe, and the Middle East. The test also is available from the TOEIC Program Office, ETS, in the form of an off-the-shelf International Corporate Program (ICP). Application to take the test is made through national and regional offices, where available. An audio cassette player is required. Examiner required. Suitable for group use.

Timed: 2½ hours

Scoring: Hand key; may be computer scored

Cost: Contact publisher

Publisher: Educational Testing Service

THURSTONE TEST OF MENTAL ALERTNESS
Refer to page 900.

TITMUS II VISION TESTER: AEROMEDICAL MODEL

Adult

Purpose: Screens visual abilities of people involved in aviation. Used to insure that employees meet minimum standards established by the Federal Aviation Administration.

Description: Six slides in a vision tester measure the following factors: acuity far (right eye, left eye, both eyes); vertical and lateral heterophorias; color vision; and acuity near (right eye, left eye, both eyes). The test is approved by the FAA for aeromedical use. Materials include the tester, 5 slides, a training manual, and record forms. Examiner required. Not suitable for group use.

Untimed: 5-10 minutes

Scoring: Hand key; examiner evaluated

Cost: Complete $1,195.00

Publisher: Titmus Optical, Inc.

TITMUS II VISION TESTER: OCCUPATIONAL MODEL FOR INDUSTRY AND COMMERCE

Adult

Purpose: Identifies common vision problems that could result in employee accidents and production inefficiencies.

Description: Vision screening instrument using eight test slides including binocularity, acuity (both eyes), acuity (right eye), acuity (left eye), stereo depth, color perception, vertical phoria, and lateral phoria. Equipment includes a job standards manual providing vision standards specific to particular jobs. New features are a microdigital remote control unit and a photoelectric sensor, which promotes correct head positioning. Optional equipment includes a fiber optics perimeter system for testing peripheral vision and a feature for testing intermediate distance vision (See Vision Tester: Intermediate Test Lenses). Examiner required. Not suitable for group use.

Untimed: 5 minutes

Scoring: Hand key; examiner evaluated

Cost: $1,195.00

Publisher: Titmus Optical, Inc.

UNDERSTANDING COMMUNICATION
T.G. Thurstone

Adult

Purpose: Measures comprehension of verbal material in short sentences and phrases. Used for industrial screening and selection of skilled occupational groups that need to understand written material and communications.

Description: 40-item paper-pencil single-score test measuring vocabulary and reading speed. Basic reading skills are required. Examiner required. Suitable for group use.

Timed: 15 minutes

Scoring: Hand key

Cost: Specimen set $8.00; 25 test booklets $8.75
Publisher: London House Press

UNIVERSAL SKILLS SURVEY

Adolescent, adult

Purpose: Analyzes the generic skills possessed by individuals, required by jobs, or taught in training programs. Used for counseling, career pathing, and job placement and training analysis.

Description: Paper-pencil survey instrument analyzing 1,451 skills divided into 21 skill categories. Three survey books and three response booklets are available for data collection: one each for individuals, jobs, and training. Responses are completed by the individuals, job incumbant or first line supervisor, or the instructor. The skill proficiency level, skill frequency, and essential skills are recorded. Where relevant, additional data are recorded on the work environment. Other reports available include composites, core skills analysis, and comparisons of base data. Examiner/self-administered. Suitable for group use.
Untimed: Individual 3 hours; job training 2 hours
Scoring: Computer scored
Cost: Contact publisher
Publisher: Prep, Inc.

VCWS 3—NUMERICAL SORTING

Adult

Purpose: Measures an individual's ability to perform work tasks requiring sequential sorting of a combined numerical/alphabetical problem. Provides insight into spatial and form perception, accuracy, and attention to detail in transferring data. May be used with hearing-impaired and visually impaired individuals.

Description: Manual test measuring the ability to sort, file, and categorize objects using a numerical code. The individual must transfer 42 of 56 numerically ordered white plastic chips inserted into correspondingly marked slots in Board I to the appropriate slots in Board II. After the chip placements on Board II are scored, the individual transfers the chips back to Board I. Work activities related to the test include examining, grading, and sorting; keeping records and receipts; recording or transmitting verbal or coded information; and posting verbal or numerical data on stock lists. The test should not be used with individuals with severe impairment of the upper extremities. Examiner required. Not suitable for group use.
Timed: Not available
Scoring: Examiner evaluated
Cost: $785.00
Publisher: Valpar International Corporation

VCWS 6—INDEPENDENT PROBLEM SOLVING

Adult

Purpose: Measures the ability to perform work tasks requiring visual comparison and proper selection of abstract designs. May be used with institutionally retarded and hearing-impaired individuals.

Description: Manual test measuring a person's ability to perform work tasks requiring a visual comparison of colored shapes. Work activities relating to the test are characterized by emphasis on decision-making and instruction-following abilities. The test should not be used with individuals with severe impairment of the upper extremities or severe visual impairment. Examiner required. Not suitable for group use.
Timed: Not available
Scoring: Examiner evaluated
Cost: $895.00
Publisher: Valpar International Corporation

VCWS 10—TRI-LEVEL MEASUREMENT

Adult

Purpose: Measures an individual's ability to perform inspecting and measuring tasks ranging from the very simple to the very precise. Measures ability to use independent judgment in following sequences of operations, selecting proper instruments, and assuming responsibility for attaining prescribed qualitative standards.

Description: Manual test measuring a person's ability to perform very simple to very precise inspection and measurement tasks. The individual must sort 61 incorrectly or correctly machined parts into nine inspection bins. The seven inspection tasks involved are visual and size discrimination, comparison (using jigs), and measurement with a ruler, micrometer, and vernier caliper. Performance indicates the ability to succeed in jobs requiring varying degrees of measurement and inspection skills and decision-making abilities. The test should not be administered to individuals with severe impairment of the upper extremities. Examiner required. Not suitable for group use.

Untimed: Not available

Scoring: Examiner evaluated

Cost: $1,165.00

Publisher: Valpar International Corporation

VCWS 12—SOLDERING AND INSPECTION (ELECTRONIC)

Adult

Purpose: Measures an individual's ability to acquire and apply basic soldering techniques to tasks requiring varying degrees of precision. Provides insight into the ability to follow sequential instructions and acquire new tool use skills. May be used with hearing-impaired and visually impaired individuals.

Description: Manual test measuring an individual's ability to acquire and apply basic skills necessary to perform soldering tasks. The examinee uses wire cutters, wire strippers, needlenose pliers, a soldering iron, and a solder to perform exercises involving the use of the tools in precision solder tasks. Exercises include work with both wires and circuit board assemblies. Performance indicates the individual's degree of ability to become a successful worker in jobs related to electronic assembly and soldering. Work activities related to the test include fabricating, processing, or repairing materials and examining and

measuring for the purpose of grading and sorting. Examiner required. Not suitable for group use.

Timed: Not available

Scoring: Examiner evaluated

Cost: $975.00

Publisher: Valpar International Corporation

VCWS 13—MONEY HANDLING

Adult

Purpose: Measures ability to acquire and comprehend basic principles relating to monetary transactions.

Description: Manual and paper-pencil test measuring an individual's skill in dealing with monetary concepts ranging from basic money recognition to consumer economics. In Level 1 of Section A, the examinee identifies coins, states the value of coins, and makes simple change. Level 2 of Section A contains questions that relate to banking and money, credit, loans, and simple economics. Section B utilizes an electronic display board on which various denominations of coins and bills are pictured. The examinee selects a problem on the board and then turns knobs to show the amount of change he should receive in such a transaction. In Section C, which is in paper-pencil format, the examinee answers economics questions pertaining to the law of supply and demand, interest rates, and insurance and profit. Performance indicates an individual's degree of ability to perform activities of daily living and to succeed in occupations in which the handling of money and monetary transactions are important. The test should not be administered to individuals with severe impairment of the upper extremities or to the visually impaired. Examiner required. Not suitable for group use.

Timed: Not available

Scoring: Examiner evaluated

Cost: $945.00

Publisher: Valpar International Corporation

VCWS 15—ELECTRICAL CIRCUITRY AND PRINT READING

Adult

Purpose: Measures the ability to understand, comprehend, and apply the principles and functions of electrical circuitry through the modality of electronic components. Provides insight into potential without basing performance exclusively on prior knowledge.

Description: Measures the ability to understand and apply principles and functions of electrical circuits. The examinee performs various exercises in three areas: testing for circuit continuity using probes; testing and repairing circuits using probes, wires, and pliers; and reading an electrical schematic print and inserting wires, diodes, and two types of resistors as specified by the print. The examinee is given trays containing various electrical components and appropriate tools. The various electrical circuits to be tested range from very simple to complex. The examinee tests each circuit, records malfunctions and, if necessary, repairs nonfunctioning circuits. No previous experience with electrical or electronic principles is required. The results indicate potential for success in an entry-level position in fields that require electrical circuitry and print reading skills. The test relates to work activities such as repairing materials, dexterous use of the hands, inspecting products, and selecting appropriate tools and materials. The test should not be used with individuals with severe impairment of the upper extremities, severe visual impairment, or severe coordination problems. Examiner required. Not suitable for group use.

Timed: Not available
Scoring: Examiner evaluated
Cost: $940.00
Publisher: Valpar International Corporation

VCWS 16—DRAFTING

Adult

Purpose: Measures an individual's potential to compete in an entry-level position requiring basic drafting and print reading skills. Provides insight into the ability to visualize abstract problems and to acquire new tool use skills.

Description: Manual test measuring the potential to compete in an entry-level position requiring basic drafting skills. The examinee performs a series of exercises measuring his ability to measure objects accurately in inches and centimeters; learn the use of drafting tools such as a T square, compass, circle template, and triangles; and read blueprints. The examinee must produce three view drawings of three wooden blocks. Each subtest screens the examinee in terms of his ability to cope successfully with the next subtest. The test is designed to accommodate a range of needs within the drafting industry from minimal expertise to sophisticated high-level performance. Work activities related to the test include simple measuring, line perception exercises, determining scaled dimensions, drawing schematics and diagrams, freehand drawing, and interpreting blueprints. The test should not be administered to individuals with severe impairment of the upper extremities, severe visual impairment, or severe coordination problems. Examiner required. Not suitable for group use.

Timed: Not available
Scoring: Examiner evaluated
Cost: $900.00
Publisher: Valpar International Corporation

VCWS 19—DYNAMIC PHYSICAL CAPACITIES
Refer to page 734.

VISION TESTER: INTERMEDIATE TEST LENSES

Adult

Purpose: Identifies vision problems in the intermediate range that could cause eyestrain, particularly for VDT and other machine operators.

Description: Five lens units for use with the Titmus II Vision Tester. The lens units screen visual acuity of the intermediate range of 20-40 inches, the working distance of VDT and other machine operators. Examiner required. Not suitable for group use.

Untimed: 5 minutes

Scoring: Hand key; examiner evaluated

Cost: Complete set (5 lens units) $162.00

Publisher: Titmus Optical, Inc.

WESMAN PERSONNEL CLASSIFICATION TEST
A.G. Wesman

Adult

Purpose: Assesses general mental ability. Used for selection of employees for sales, supervisory, and managerial positions.

Description: Multiple-item paper-pencil test of two major aspects of mental ability: verbal and numerical. The verbal items are analogies. The numerical items test basic math skills and understanding of quantitative relationships. Three forms, A, B, and C, are available. The verbal part of Form C is somewhat more difficult than the verbal parts of Forms A and B. Examiner required. Suitable for group use.

Timed: Verbal 18 minutes; Numerical 10 minutes

Scoring: Hand key

Cost: Specimen set (one each of materials for all 3 forms, keys not included) $10.00; 25 tests, manual, booklet, key (specify form) $21.00

Publisher: The Psychological Corporation

WESTERN MICHIGAN UNIVERSITY ENGLISH USAGE-ORIENTATION FORM (EUO)
Bernadine P. Carlson

Adolescent, adult
College students

Purpose: Measures level of English language skills. Used for pre- and posttesting in business and technical seminars in effective writing.

Description: 75-item paper-pencil multiple-choice test consisting of three parts. Part I (30 items) includes three subtests:

Grammatical errors, Spelling, and Diction. Part II (30 items) consists of two subtests: Punctuation for Meaning and Sentence Structure. Part III (15 items) consists of two subtests: Reading Comprehension and Rhetorical Style Evaluation. Examiner required. Suitable for group use.

Timed: 45 minutes

Scoring: Hand key; may be computer scored

Cost: Contact publisher

Publisher: Bernadine P. Carlson

WIDE RANGE ACHIEVEMENT TEST—REVISED (WRAT-R)
Refer to page 457.

WOLFE STAFF SELECTOR TEST KITS

Adult

Purpose: Evaluates intellectual abilities and interpersonal skills of candidates for a wide range of positions.

Description: Multiple-item paper-pencil tests available in four formats. The Comprehensive format is a battery of 15-17 tests measuring a wide range of personality and intellectual attributes of potential middle- and senior-level personnel. This battery yields a six-page analytical report comparing performance with ideal levels for each trait. The Screening format is a battery of 10-14 tests measuring personality and intellectual attributes of junior- and intermediate-level job candidates and providing a three-page report. The Priority Response format is a battery of 4-8 tests of intellectual and personality attributes allowing telephone reporting of results within minutes of test-taking. The Scored by Client format is a booklet of 3-7 subtests for screening large numbers of applicants. Tests are graded on-site. The test kits are appropriate for sales representatives, managers and supervisors, clerks, procedures and business systems analysts, bookkeepers and accountants, secretaries and word processing operators, and any other position which has a job description. Examiner/self administered. Suitable for group use. Custom tests are available in English and French. CANADIAN PUBLISHER

Timed/Untimed: Varies

Scoring: Computer scored

Cost: $25.00-$349.00 per candidate depending on format chosen

Publisher: Wolfe Personnel Testing and Training Systems, Inc.

THE WONDERLIC PERSONNEL TEST
E. F. Wonderlic

Adult

Purpose: Measures level of mental ability in business and industrial situations. Used for selection and placement of business personnel and for vocational guidance.

Description: 50-item paper-pencil test measuring general learning ability in verbal, spatial, and numerical reasoning. The test is used to predict an individual's ability to adjust to complex and rapidly changing job requirements and complete complex job training. The test also measures potential turnover and dissatisfaction on routinized or simple labor intensive jobs. Test items include analogies, analysis of geometric figures, arithmetic problems, disarranged sentences, sentence parallelism with proverbs, similarities, logic, definitions, judgment, direction following, and others. Materials include eight equivalent test forms for employer use; four equivalent forms for personnel agency use; four equivalent forms for scholastic use; and one form for the visually handicapped. Examiner required. Suitable for group use. Available in Spanish and French.

Timed: 12 minutes; may also be administered untimed

Scoring: Hand key

Cost: Introductory package (20 Form I, 20 Form II) $42.00; 25 forms $22.50

Publisher: E. F. Wonderlic Personnel Test, Inc.

WORD FLUENCY
Human Resources Center, The University of Chicago

Adult

Purpose: Determines the speed of relevant verbal associations and individual's ability to produce appropriate words rapidly. Used for vocational counseling and personnel selection in fields requiring communication skills, such as supervision, management, and sales.

Description: 80-item paper-pencil test measuring verbal comprehension and vocabulary. Examiner required. Suitable for group use. May be verbally administered in any language.

Timed: 10 minutes

Scoring: Hand key

Cost: Specimen set $8.00; 25 test booklets $8.75

Publisher: London House Press

WORK APTITUDE PROFILE AND PRACTICE SET (WAPPS)

Ages 15 and older

Purpose: Designed for use by teachers, career officers, and employers for career counseling and to provide experience in taking tests. Provides school dropouts with practice taking tests like those they may encounter when applying for jobs. Also provides a profile of work aptitude across six relevant job-related skills. Not used for selection.

Description: Six tests measure the following work-related skills: basic reading and comprehension, recognizing shapes in two dimensions, basic arithmetic, understanding simple mechanical and physical principles, the ability to pick out errors in written material, and reasoning with diagrams. The range of difficulty covers school leavers (15-17 +) with minimal qualifications through to those with GCE "O" levels (attained or expected). The WAPPS provides experience with the most common types of test problems and answering formats, of being in a selection

test environment, and of listening to and following test instructions. Examiner required. Suitable for group use.
BRITISH PUBLISHER

Timed: Total 1 hour

Scoring: Hand key

Cost: Contact Macmillan Education

Publisher: Saville & Holdsworth Ltd. and Macmillan Education

WORK SAMPLES

Adolescent, adult

Purpose: Assesses aptitude and provides career exploration in 27 job simulations relating to the 16 USOE clusters.

Description: Multiple-item and multiple-task test in A-V format assessing hands-on aptitude for 27 job areas: drafting, clerical/office, metal construction, sales, wood construction, food preparation, medical services, travel services, barbering/cosmetology, small engine, masonry, electrical, police science, electronics, automotive, commercial art, nutrition, bookkeeping, fire science, extraction technology, clothing and textiles, real estate, communication services, refrigeration, computer technology, solar technology, and machine trades. Each work sample is administered and scored independently. The samples have no predetermined order of administration, and there is no requirement concerning the number of samples that should be administered. A-V instructions, industry trends, entry level salaries, and task demonstrations are given prior to evaluation. The examiner records behavioral and performance observations, and the client rates himself on interest, difficulty, and performance. The work samples may be used in conjunction with Job Matching. The reading level, where reading is required, is related to specific tasks. Norms are based on industrial standards. Examiner required. Not suitable for group use.

Untimed: 2 hours per work sample

Scoring: Examiner evaluated

Cost: Contact publisher
Publisher: Prep, Inc.

Clerical

ACER NUMBER TEST

Adolescent, adult
Ages 13.6 and older

Purpose: Measures addition and multiplication skills. Used for employee selection for clerical positions and occupational guidance.

Description: Multiple-item paper-pencil test measuring speed and accuracy in addition and multiplication. The first part contains items involving the addition of three 2-digit numbers; the second part involves the multiplication of two digits by one digit. Items in each part are of nearly equal difficulty. In addition to age norms, data is presented for university, senior technical college, and national service trainee groups. The latter provides the basis for tentative occupational norms. Materials include a four-page expendable test booklet, scoring key, manual, and specimen set. Examiner required. Suitable for group use.
AUSTRALIAN PUBLISHER

Timed: Part I 5 minutes; Part II 5 minutes; instructions 5 minutes
Scoring: Hand key
Cost: Contact publisher
Publisher: The Australian Council for Educational Research Limited

---

ACER SHORT CLERICAL TEST (FORMS C, D, AND E)

Adolescent, adult
Ages 15 and older

Purpose: Measures the basic skills of checking and arithmetic as a test of clerical aptitude. Useful for employee selection for jobs in accountancy, general clerical work, and business machine operating.

Description: Multiple-item paper-pencil test measuring an individual's ability to perceive, remember, and check written or printed material (both verbal and numerical), and to perform arithmetic operations. The test is available in 3 forms: Forms C and D are used for personnel selection and Form E for guidance and counseling in business training colleges. Australian norms are provided. British norms are available for Form C in British Supplement of Norms for Tests Used in Clerical Selection. Examiner required. Suitable for group use. AUSTRALIAN PUBLISHER

Timed: 5 minutes per part

Scoring: Hand key

Cost: Contact publisher

Publisher: The Australian Council for Educational Research Limited

ACER SPEED AND ACCURACY TESTS-FORM A

Adolescent, adult
Ages 13.6 and older

Purpose: Measures the checking skills of individuals ages 13 and older. Useful in the selection of clerical personnel.

Description: Multiple-item paper-pencil test measuring the ability to perceive, retain, and check relatively familiar material in the form of printed numbers and names while working in a limited amount of time. The test contains two sections: name checking and number checking. Australian norms are available for school, university, adult, and some occupational groups. British normative data are available in *British Supplement of Norms for Tests Used in Clerical Selection*. Examiner required. Suitable for group use. AUSTRALIAN PUBLISHER

Timed: 6 minutes per part

Scoring: Hand key

Cost: Contact publisher

Publisher: The Australian Council for Educational Research Limited

AUTOMATED OFFICE BATTERY (AOB)
Refer to page 877.

AUTOMATED OFFICE BATTERY: NUMERICAL ESTIMATION (AOB: NE-1)
Saville & Holdsworth Ltd. Staff

Ages 16-adult

Purpose: Measures the ability to estimate the answers to a variety of numerical calculations.

Description: 50-item paper-pencil multiple-choice test assessing the ability to quickly estimate the answers to calculations. Candidates are presented with calculations requiring addition, subtraction, multiplication, division, and percentages. Candidates are required to estimate the order of magnitude of the solution and choose the correct one from five alternatives. Candidates are discouraged against making precise calculations, and the time constraint encourages estimation. One of three tests in the Automated Office Battery. Examiner required. Suitable for group use. BRITISH PUBLISHER

Timed: 10 minutes

Scoring: Hand key; may be computer scored

Cost: 10 reusable test booklets $210.00; 50 answer sheets $105.00; administration card $10.50; scoring key $21.00

Publisher: Saville & Holdsworth Ltd.

BLOX TEST (PERCEPTUAL BATTERY)

Adolescent, adult

Purpose: Measures visual perception. Used with subjects with 10-12 years of education for purposes of employee selection and placement in a variety of clerical and technical positions.

Description: Multiple-item paper-pencil test measuring spatial relations and visualization. The subject must analyze given geometric figures and then find them in a series as seen from another angle. The test popularly is known as the Perceptual Battery and is restricted to competent persons properly registered with the

South African Medical and Dental Council. Examiner required. Suitable for group use. Afrikaans version available. SOUTH AFRICAN PUBLISHER
Timed: 30 minutes
Scoring: Hand key; examiner evaluated
Cost: Contact publisher
Publisher: National Institute for Personnel Research

THE CANDIDATE PROFILE RECORD
Richardson, Bellows, Henry and Company, Inc.

Adult

Purpose: Assesses background characteristics related to success in office positions.

Description: Multiple-item paper-pencil questionnaire designed to predict an individual's potential for success in teller and customer service positions, processing and verifying positions, and secretarial and clerical positions. The autobiographical test, which was designed to be nondiscriminatory, covers an individual's early development influences, academic history and accomplishments, self-esteem and description, work history, and work-related values and attitudes. Normative, reliability, and validity data are contained in the manual. Self-administered. Suitable for group use.
Untimed: Varies
Scoring: Self-scored
Cost: Contact publisher
Publisher: Richardson, Bellows, Henry and Company, Inc.

CLERICAL APTITUDE TESTS
Andrew Kobal, J. Wayne Wrightstone, and Andrew J. MacElroy

Adolescent, adult Grades 7 and above

Purpose: Assesses aptitude for clerical work. Used for screening job applicants.

Description: Three-part paper-pencil test measuring clerical aptitudes, including business practice; number checking;

and date, name, and address checking. Scores correlate with job success. Examiner required. Suitable for group use.
Timed: 40 minutes
Scoring: Hand key
Cost: Specimen set $4.00; 25 tests $8.75
Publisher: Psychometric Affiliates

CLERICAL SELECTION BATTERY

Adult

Purpose: Identifies applicants with good potential for long-term success as clerical employees.

Description: Battery of three paper-pencil testing instruments providing a complete picture of the applicant's background, abilities, and aptitudes. Biographical Data, a specially-constructed, 75-item version of the Personal Background Inventory, measures work history, educational experiences, drive, leadership, financial responsibility, and health. Self-Assessment, a specially-constructed, 55-item version of the Skills and Attributes Inventory, assesses the applicant's ability in a wide variety of areas as compared to others of similar age, education, and work experience. Cognitive Ability measures applicant's cognitive abilities in four short tests measuring mathematical ability, including simple computation and error recognition, name and number comparison (an ability necessary for many clerical tasks, such as proofreading and credit card verification), number sequence, and verbal comprehension and verbal reasoning. Examiner required. Suitable for group use.
Timed/Untimed: Total battery 50 minutes
Scoring: ITAC (Immediate Test Analysis by Computer) and mail scoring
Cost: $8-$15, depending on volume ordered
Publisher: London House Press

CLERICAL SKILLS SERIES
Martin M. Bruce

Adult

Purpose: Assesses the language, physical coordination, and mathematical abilities necessary for various clerical jobs. Used for screening prospective employees, measuring student skills, and evaluating current employees.

Description: 10-category paper-pencil test series covering alphabetizing, filing, arithmetic, clerical speed and accuracy, coding, eye-hand accuracy, grammar and punctuation, spelling, vocabulary, and word fluency. The series consists of 10 short tests, six of which are timed. The tests may be administered separately or as a unit and can be scored and interpreted independently. Examiner required. Suitable for group use.

Timed: 2-8 minutes per section

Scoring: Hand key

Cost: Specimen set $16.50; manual $7.50; package of profile sheets $10.50; key $1.10

Publisher: Martin M. Bruce, Ph.D., Publishers

CLERICAL SKILLS TEST
U.S. Employment Service

Adult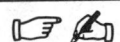

Purpose: Assesses the clerical skills required to perform a variety of occupational tasks. Used for job placement.

Description: Six paper-pencil performance subtests measuring the subject's ability to type from plain copy, take dictation, spell, type statistics, and spell medical and legal terms. Only those subtests that relate to significant job skill needs should be administered. A skilled worker will score higher than an unskilled worker. Norm tables are used to convert raw scores to deciles based on representative samples of experienced workers. Materials required include a typewriter, typing paper, and pencils. Examiner required. Suitable for group use.

Timed: Varies

Scoring: Hand key

Cost: Available through State Employment Service Agencies only

Publisher: U.S. Department of Labor

CLERICAL TASK INVENTORY— FORM C
C.H. Lawshe

Adult

Purpose: Assesses tasks performed by clerical and office personnel. Used for job evaluation of clerical positions and redesigning clerical jobs.

Description: 163-item standardized check list of frequently performed tasks clustered into 13 performance domains such as performing mathematical computations and understanding printed/written communication. The rater checks the tasks frequently performed in the clerical position of interest. Self-administered. Suitable for group use.

Untimed: Not available

Scoring: Examiner evaluated; may be machine scored

Cost: 10 inventories $15.00

Publisher: Purdue Research Foundation/University Book Store

CLERICAL TEST 1
E.I.T.S. Staff

Adult

Purpose: Measures speed and accuracy of basic skills in routine clerical and office occupations that require the employee to check information, especially printed material. Used to screen persons for office work and for positions such as checking clerks, checkout operators, and data checkers.

Description: 140-item paper-pencil test divided in two parts: number checking and name checking. The examinee must determine if two sets of numbers, or two names, are exactly the same or different. A minimal level of reasoning, measuring conceptual speed, or mental alertness is required. The use of number words has increased the discrimination of Part 1 and, similarly, in Part 2, the inclusion of random letters and words has the same effect. Materials include booklets, a scoring key, specimen set, and manual. Tests in arithmetic and language usage also are

---

available as part of this clerical series. Examiner required. Suitable for group use.

BRITISH PUBLISHER

Timed: 7 minutes

Scoring: Hand key; may be computer scored

Cost: Contact publisher

Publisher: Educational and Industrial Test Services Ltd.

CLERICAL TEST 2
E.I.T.S. Staff

Adult

Purpose: Assesses individual skill in ordinary arithmetic processes and the ability to apply this skill to everyday problems. Used to screen for a variety of clerical occupations, such as data checking, routine accounts and shop work.

Description: 50-item paper-pencil two-part test. Part 1 consists of 32 computations in addition, subtraction, multiplication, and division, arranged in order of difficulty. Part 2 consists of 18 arithmetic problems, expressed verbally. Materials include booklets, a scoring key, specimen set, and manual. Tests in speed and accuracy, spelling, grammar, and language usage also are available as part of this clerical series. Examiner required. Suitable for group use.

BRITISH PUBLISHER

Timed: 14 minutes

Scoring: Hand key; examiner evaluated; may be computer scored

Cost: Contact publisher

Publisher: Educational and Industrial Test Services Ltd.

CLERICAL TEST 3
E.I.T.S. Staff

Adult

Purpose: Evaluates a person's ability in spelling, grammar, and language usage. Used to screen for most office jobs, especially those involving the processing of information.

Description: 91-item paper-pencil test in three parts. Part 1 is a 60-word spelling test, in which the subject indicates if a given word is spelled correctly or incorrectly. Part 2 consists of 30 short sentences, in which the subject identifies a word which makes the grammar incorrect. Part 3 is a short business letter, in which the subject marks the errors and rewrites the letter. Materials include booklets, a scoring key, specimen set, and manual. Tests in speed and accuracy and in arithmetic also are available as part of this clerical series. Examiner required. Suitable for group use.

BRITISH PUBLISHER

Timed: 15 ½ minutes

Scoring: Hand key; examiner evaluated; may be computer scored

Cost: Contact publisher

Publisher: Educational and Industrial Test Services Ltd.

CLERICAL TESTS, SERIES N
Stevens, Thurow and Associates

Adult

Purpose: Measures ability to think and to use words and numbers accurately. Used to screen candidates for clerical positions, such as payroll, accounting, receiving, inventory control, warehousing, and filing.

Description: 206-item battery of five paper-pencil tests assessing detail and numerical skills. The Mental Abilities—Inventory II (50 items) is a multiple-choice and free-response measure of general mental ability. Inventory E (96 items) requires subjects to decide whether the pair of words or numbers in each item are the same or different. In Inventory F (30 items), subjects copy a list of 4- to 10-digit numbers in order and in the properly numbered spaces provided on the back of the sheet on which the list is printed. Inventory G (80 items) is a free-response test of basic addition and multiplication skills. Inventory H (30 items) requires examinees to copy a list of names in order and in the properly numbered spaces provided on the back of the sheet on which the list is printed. Examiner required. Suitable for group use.

Timed: 33 minutes

Scoring: Hand key

Cost: 5-test battery with application form and rating chart (pkg. of 10) $20.00; manual of instructions, including scoring keys $2.00

Publisher: Stevens, Thurow and Associates

CLERICAL TESTS, SERIES V
Stevens, Thurow and Associates

Adult

Purpose: Measures ability to use and spell words and to type accurately. Used to screen candidates for clerical positions, such as secretaries, typists, clerks, dictaphone operators, and stenographers.

Description: 233-item battery of four paper-pencil tests and one test of typing ability. Mental Abilities—Inventory II is a 50-item multiple-choice and free-response test of general mental abilities. Inventory A is a 30-item test in which subjects evaluate grammatical correctness of sentences. Inventory B is a 100-item test in which the subjects decide whether words are spelled correctly. Inventory C is a 52-item test in which subjects choose one of five words nearest in meaning to the capitalized word in a phrase. Inventory D is a 10-minute test measuring speed and accuracy in typing a standard business letter from provided copy. Examiner required. Suitable for group use.

Timed: 45 minutes

Untimed: Inventory C

Scoring: Hand key

Cost: 5-test battery with application form and rating chart $20.00; manual of instructions, including scoring keys $2.00

Publisher: Stevens, Thurow and Associates

CURTIS VERBAL-CLERICAL SKILLS TESTS
James W. Curtis

Adolescent, adult
Ages 16 and older

Purpose: Assesses clerical and verbal abilities. Used to evaluate job applicants.

Description: Four multiple-item paper-pencil tests of clerical abilities. The tests are Computation, measuring practical arithmetic; Checking, measuring perceptual speed and accuracy; Comprehension, measuring reading vocabulary; and Capacity, measuring logical reasoning ability. Examiner required. Suitable for group use.

Timed: 2 minutes per test

Scoring: Hand key

Cost: Specimen set $5.00; 25 tests (specify form) $4.00

Publisher: Psychometric Affiliates

DICTATION TEST
Richardson, Bellows, Henry and Company, Inc.

Adult

Purpose: Provides a quick screening of an individual's dictation abilities.

Description: Manual test assessing an individual's dictation speed and accuracy in which the examiner dictates a business letter to the examinee. The examiner adjusts his dictation speed to the examinee's pace. The examiner dictates only words; the examinee must supply appropriate punctuation, capitalization, and spelling. After the letter is dictated, the examiner notes the amount of time that elapsed from the beginning to the end of the dictation. The examinee then reads the notes back to the examiner, who marks errors of interpretation and estimates the examinee's dictation speed. The test yields an estimate of dictation speed accurate to within five words per minute. The following materials are required: a test folder to be used by both the examiner and examinee, two sharp pencils for the examinee, and a stopwatch for the examiner. Examiner required. Not suitable for group use.

Untimed: 5 minutes

Scoring: Hand key

Cost: 1-24 packages $19.00; score key $2.00; manual $2.00

Publisher: Richardson, Bellows, Henry and Company, Inc.

---

clerical

ESV CLERICAL WORKER
McCann Associates, Inc.

Adult

Purpose: Assesses candidate's ability to learn to become a competent clerical worker. Used by employers for job screening.

Description: 100-item criterion-validated paper-pencil multiple-choice test covering memorization, information ordering, number facility, timesharing, problem solving, dealing with people, deductive reasoning, and verbal comprehension. Materials include test booklets, answer sheets, identification sheets, envelopes, candidate study guides, and complete monitoring instructions. The publisher scores answer sheets and provides a comprehensive report that includes total test and subtest means and standard deviations, norms, reliabilities, and candidate evaluations. The test is available on a rental basis only to personnel directors, civil service commissions, or qualified municipal or employment officials. A security agreement is required. Examiner required. Suitable for group use.

Timed: 3 hours

Scoring: Computer scored by publisher

Cost: Contact publisher

Publisher: McCann Associates, Inc.

ETSA TESTS 2-A—OFFICE ARITHMETIC TEST
Refer to page 804.

ETSA TESTS 3-A—GENERAL CLERICAL ABILITY TEST
Refer to page 804.

ETSA TESTS 4-A— STENOGRAPHIC SKILLS TEST
Refer to page 805.

GENERAL CLERICAL TEST (GCT)

Adult

Purpose: Assesses clerical aptitude. Used for selecting applicants and evaluating clerical employees for promotion.

Description: Multiple-item paper-pencil test of three types of abilities needed for clerical jobs: clerical speed and accuracy, numerical ability, and verbal ability. The clerical subtest involves finding errors by comparing copy with the original and using an alphabetical file. The numerical subtest requires the applicant to solve arithmetic problems, find numerical errors, and solve numerical word problems. The verbal subtest involves correcting spelling errors, answering questions about reading passages, understanding word meanings, and correcting grammatical errors. The test also is published in two partial booklets. Booklet A contains the clerical and numerical subtests, and Booklet B contains the verbal subtest. Materials include optional tapes for test administration. Examiner required. Suitable for group use.

Timed: 46 minutes

Scoring: Hand key

Cost: Specimen set (test booklet for complete battery, manual) $7.00; 25 test booklets, manual, key $40.00; 25 test booklet A $25.00; 25 test booklet B $25.00

Publisher: The Psychological Corporation

GUILFORD-ZIMMERMAN APTITUDE SURVEY: NUMERICAL OPERATIONS (GZAS:NO)
Refer to page 810.

GUILFORD-ZIMMERMAN APTITUDE SURVEY: PERCEPTUAL SPEED (GZAS:PS)
Refer to page 810.

THE HARVARD BANK TELLER PROFICIENCY TEST
Steven Stanard

Adult

Purpose: Measures a person's aptitude and skills for work as a bank teller. Used to screen tellers at banks and savings and loans.

Description: 6-section paper-pencil test measuring accuracy, speed, customer relations, judgment, numerical ability, initiative, and communicative skills. Examiner required. Suitable for group use.

Timed: 30 minutes

Scoring: Computer scored

Cost: Complete (includes test and computer report) $35.00 per person

Publisher: Wolfe Personnel Testing and Training Systems, Inc.

HAY APTITUDE TEST BATTERY
Edward N. Hay

Adult

Purpose: Identifies job applicants with the greatest aptitude for handling clerical detail and working with numbers. Used to select personnel for office and clerical positions, trainee positions requiring innate perceptual skills, and positions requiring quick recognition of numbers.

Description: Four paper-pencil tests assessing clerical and numerical aptitude. Tests include "The Warm-Up" (unscored), the Hay Number Perception Test (NP), the Hay Name Finding Test (NF), and the Hay Number Series Completion Test (NS). The battery predicts aptitude for a variety of positions, including accounting, bookkeeping, typing, filing, keypunch, proofreading, general office, shipping, mail workers, warehouse workers, stockroom workers, and printing personnel. Optional cassette tapes are available for administration of the tests. Examiner required. Suitable for group use. Available in French and Spanish.

Timed: 13 minutes total

Scoring: Hand key

Cost: 25 of each form $69.00; cassettes $24.00 each

Publisher: E.F. Wonderlic Personnel Test, Inc.

HAY APTITUDE TEST BATTERY: NAME FINDING
Edward N. Hay

Adult

Purpose: Measures ability to check and verify names quickly and accurately. Used to select office and clerical personnel.

Description: 32-item paper-pencil multiple-choice test assessing the ability to read names and hold them in memory long enough to accurately identify them from four similarly spelled names on the back of the same sheet. The task is similar to many clerical tasks, including making bookkeeping entries or typing invoices or checks. The test may be administered via optional cassette tape. Examiner required. Suitable for group use. Available in French and Spanish.

Timed: 4 minutes

Scoring: Hand key

Cost: 25 forms $22.00

Publisher: E.F. Wonderlic Personnel Test, Inc.

HAY APTITUDE TEST BATTERY: NUMBER PERCEPTION
Edward N. Hay

Adult

Purpose: Measures ability to check pairs of numbers and identify those which are the same. Used to select office and clerical personnel.

Description: 200-item paper-pencil test measuring speed and accuracy of numerical checking. Each test item consists of a pair of numbers that the applicant decides are the same or different. Items are designed to include the most common clerical errors. The test may be administered via optional cassette tape. Examiner required. Suitable for group use. Available in French and Spanish.

Timed: 4 minutes

Scoring: Hand key

Cost: 25 forms $21.00
Publisher: E.F. Wonderlic Personnel Test, Inc.

HAY APTITUDE TEST BATTERY: NUMBER SERIES COMPLETION
Edward N. Hay

Adult

Purpose: Measures the ability to deduce the pattern in a series of six numbers and provide the seventh and eighth numbers in the series. Used to select office and clerical personnel.

Description: 30-item paper-pencil test assessing numerical reasoning abilities. Each item presents a series of six numbers (1-3 digits) related by an unknown pattern. Applicants must provide the next two numbers in the series. Good clerks can find the additional numbers more readily than poor ones. May be administered and timed via optional cassette tape. Examiner required. Suitable for group use. Available in French and Spanish.
Timed: 4 minutes
Scoring: Hand key
Cost: 25 forms $21.00
Publisher: E.F. Wonderlic Personnel Test, Inc.

HAY APTITUDE TEST BATTERY: WARM-UP
Edward N. Hay

Adult

Purpose: Introduces job applicants to the testing procedures of the Hay Aptitude Test Battery.

Description: 20-item unscored paper-pencil test providing a warm-up for the Hay Aptitude tests. The exercise is intended to quiet nervous applicants and to familiarize applicants with the format of the other tests. The warm-up may be administered and timed via optional cassette tape. Examiner required. Suitable for group use. Available in French and Spanish.
Timed: 1 minute
Scoring: Hand key

Cost: 25 forms $15.00
Publisher: E.F. Wonderlic Personnel Test, Inc.

I.P.I. APTITUDE—INTELLIGENCE TEST SERIES: FLUENCY
Refer to page 812.

I.P.I. APTITUDE—INTELLIGENCE TEST SERIES: MEMORY
Refer to page 813.

I.P.I. APTITUDE—INTELLIGENCE TEST SERIES: NUMBERS
Refer to page 813.

I.P.I. APTITUDE—INTELLIGENCE TEST SERIES: PERCEPTION
Refer to page 814.

I.P.I. JOB TEST FIELD SERIES: GENERAL CLERK
Refer to page 817.

I.P.I. JOB TEST FIELD SERIES: JUNIOR CLERK
Refer to page 818.

I.P.I. JOB TEST FIELD SERIES: NUMBERS CLERK
Refer to page 818.

I.P.I. JOB TEST FIELD SERIES: SECRETARY
Refer to page 821.

I.P.I. JOB TEST FIELD SERIES: SENIOR CLERK
Refer to page 822.

INTERMEDIATE BATTERY B/77
Refer to page 401.

IPMA CLERICAL SERIES TESTS: 361.1 CLERICAL SKILLS SERIES

Adult

Purpose: Assesses language and filing abilities related to clerical positions.

Description: 150-item paper-pencil test covering punctuation (30 items), vocabulary (24 items), filing (40 items), reading (16 items), grammar (20 items), and spelling (20 items). The test is one of a series developed from job analysis of public service positions, and all material is drawn directly from work samples. The Job Test Content Matching and Weighing Tool allows user agencies to assemble job-relevant examinations for their own purposes. Examiner required. Suitable for group use.

Timed: 54 minutes

Scoring: Hand key; may be machine scored

Cost: 1-50 test booklets (rental): IPMA agency members $6.25 each; nonmembers $7.75 each

Publisher: International Personnel Management Association

IPMA CLERICAL SERIES TESTS: 362.1 CLERICAL SKILLS SERIES

Adult

Purpose: Assesses the language, coding, and numerical skills related to clerical positions.

Description: 130-item paper-pencil test covering name and number checking (30 items), vocabulary (24 items), reading (16 items), numerical skills (24 items), and coding (36 items). The test is one of a series developed from job analysis of public service positions, and all material is drawn directly from work samples. The Job Test Content Matching and Weighing Tool allows user agencies to assemble job-relevant examinations for their own purposes. Examiner required. Suitable for group use.

Timed: 57 minutes

Scoring: Hand key; may be machine scored

Cost: 1-50 test booklets (rental): IPMA agency members $6.25 each; nonmembers $7.75 each

Publisher: International Personnel Management Association

IPMA CLERICAL SERIES TESTS: 363.1 CLERICAL SKILLS SERIES

Adult

Purpose: Assesses language, filing, and coding skills related to clerical positions.

Description: 130-item paper-pencil test covering name and number checking (30 items), vocabulary (24 items), filing (40 items), and coding (36 items). The test is one of a series developed from job analysis of public service positions, and all material is drawn directly from work samples. The Job Test Content Matching and Weighing Tool allows user agencies to assemble job-relevant examinations for their own purposes. Examiner required. Suitable for group use.

Timed: 42 minutes

Scoring: Hand key; may be machine scored

Cost: 1-50 test booklets (rental): IPMA agency members $6.25 each; nonmembers $7.75 each

Publisher: International Personnel Management Association

IPMA CLERICAL SERIES TESTS: 364.1 ORAL INSTRUCTION AND FORMS COMPLETION

Adult

Purpose: Assesses the ability to follow directions. Used with applicants for clerical positions.

Description: 2-part test measuring the ability to follow directions. In Part I(20 items), candidates respond to taped oral instructions which coordinate with booklets from IPMA Clerical Series Tests 361.1, 362.1, or 363.1 (or may be used separately with a special answer sheet). In Part II, a free-response format, the candidate completes two simulated forms. The test is one of a series developed from job analysis of public service positions, and all material is drawn directly from work samples.

The Job Test Content Matching and Weighing Tool allows user agencies to assemble job-relevant examinations for their own purposes. Examiner required. Suitable for group use.

Timed: Part I 6 minutes; Part II 6 minutes

Scoring: Hand key

Cost: 1-50 test booklets (rental): IPMA agency members $6.25 each; nonmembers $7.75 each

Publisher: International Personnel Management Association

IPMA CLERICAL SERIES TESTS: 365.1 TYPING TEST

Adult

Purpose: Assesses the typing ability and speed of candidates for clerical positions.

Description: 5-minute typing performance test consisting of two forms of a single paragraph to be repeated within time limits. A direction sheet and typing form are included for each applicant. The test is one of a series developed from job analysis of public service positions, and all material is drawn directly from work samples. The Job Test Content Matching and Weighing Tool allows user agencies to assemble job-relevant examinations for their own purposes. Examiner required. Suitable for group use.

Timed: 5 minutes

Scoring: Hand key

Cost: 1-50 test booklets (rental): IPMA agency members $6.25 each; nonmembers $7.75 each

Publisher: International Personnel Management Association

IPMA CLERICAL SERIES TESTS: DICTATION/TRANSCRIPTION TEST

Adult

Purpose: Assesses the stenographic ability of candidates for clerical positions.

Description: 6-minute performance test consisting of two taped 3-minute letter dictations. The applicant takes dictation at 80 words per minute in an agency-sup-

plied stenographic notebook. Dictation is typed on a typing form that is provided. The test is one of a series developed from job analysis of public service positions, and all material is drawn directly from work samples. The Job Test Content Matching and Weighing Tool allows user agencies to assemble job-relevant examinations for their own purposes. Examiner required. Suitable for group use.

Timed: 6 minutes

Scoring: Hand key

Cost: 1-50 test booklets (rental): IPMA agency members $6.25 each; nonmembers $7.75 each

Publisher: International Personnel Management Association

JOB EFFECTIVENESS PREDICTION SYSTEM (JEPS)
Refer to page 823.

JOB EFFECTIVENESS PREDICTION SYSTEM: CODING AND CONVERTING (JEPS: TEST CODE K)
Refer to page 824.

JOB EFFECTIVENESS PREDICTION SYSTEM: COMPARING AND CHECKING (JEPS: TEST CODE L)
Refer to page 824.

JOB EFFECTIVENESS PREDICTION SYSTEM: FILING (JEPS: TEST CODE J)
Refer to page 824.

JOB EFFECTIVENESS PREDICTION SYSTEM: LANGUAGE USAGE (JEPS: TEST CODE E)
Refer to page 825.

JOB EFFECTIVENESS PREDICTION SYSTEM: MATHEMATICAL SKILL (JEPS: TEST CODE C)
Refer to page 825.

JOB EFFECTIVENESS PREDICTION SYSTEM: NUMERICAL ABILITY-1 (JEPS: TEST CODE A)

Refer to page 825.

JOB EFFECTIVENESS PREDICTION SYSTEM: NUMERICAL ABILITY-2 (JEPS: TEST CODE B)

Refer to page 826.

JOB EFFECTIVENESS PREDICTION SYSTEM: READING COMPREHENSION 1 (JEPS: TEST CODE F)

Refer to page 826.

JOB EFFECTIVENESS PREDICTION SYSTEM: READING COMPREHENSION-2 (JEPS: TEST CODE G)

Refer to page 826.

JOB EFFECTIVENESS PREDICTION SYSTEM: SPELLING (JEPS: TEST CODE D)

Refer to page 826.

JOB EFFECTIVENESS PREDICTION SYSTEM: VERBAL COMPREHENSION (JEPS: TEST CODE H)

Refer to page 827.

LANGUAGE SKILLS, FORM G

Richardson, Bellows, Henry and Company, Inc.

Adult

Purpose: Measures word meaning, spelling, hyphenation, and punctuation skills. Used with applicants to clerical positions.

Description: 84-item paper-pencil test assessing the ability of clerical personnel to handle job-related tasks. A portion of the test is multiple-choice. Another portion consists of brief paragraphs containing no punctuation within the sentences. Key words in the sentences are underlined at points where punctuation may be needed. The examinee chooses from among two to four punctuation marks. All answers are marked in the test booklet. Examiner required. Suitable for group use.

Timed: 25 minutes

Scoring: Hand key

Cost: 1-24 packages $19.00; score key $5.00; manual $2.00

Publisher: Richardson, Bellows, Henry and Company, Inc.

MATHEMATICAL ACHIEVEMENT TEST

Refer to page 829.

MINNESOTA CLERICAL TEST (MCT)

D.M. Andrew, D.G. Peterson, and H.P. Longstaff

Adult

Purpose: Measures ability to see differences or errors in pairs of names and pairs of numbers. Used to select clerical applicants.

Description: Multiple-item paper-pencil test of speed and accuracy of visual perception. Items are pairs of names and numbers. The applicant checks each pair that is identical. The test predicts performance in numerous jobs, including adding-machine operators, clerical employees, key machine operators, and filing and cataloging personnel. Materials include optional tapes for test administration. Examiner required. Suitable for group use.

Timed: 15 minutes

Scoring: Hand key

Cost: Specimen set (test, manual) $9.00; 25 tests, manual, key $21.00; key $6.00; manual $7.00

Publisher: The Psychological Corporation

NATIONAL BUSINESS COMPETENCY TESTS AND ENTRANCE TEST

Refer to page 231.

NATIONAL BUSINESS COMPETENCY TESTS: ACCOUNTING PROCEDURES TEST (TRIAL EDITION)

Refer to page 231.

NATIONAL BUSINESS COMPETENCY TESTS: OFFICE PROCEDURES

Refer to page 231.

NATIONAL BUSINESS COMPETENCY TESTS: SECRETARIAL PROCEDURES TEST

Refer to page 232.

NATIONAL BUSINESS COMPETENCY TESTS: TYPEWRITING

Refer to page 232.

NATIONAL BUSINESS ENTRANCE TESTS—STENOGRAPHIC TEST

Refer to page 233.

OFFICE SKILLS ACHIEVEMENT TEST

Paul L. Mellenbruch

**Adolescent, adult
Grades 10 and above**

Purpose: Assesses clerical skills. Used for educational and vocational guidance and for screening applicants for employment.

Description: Multiple-item paper-pencil test measuring several important office and clerical skills, including business letter writing, English usage, checking, filing, simple arithmetic, and following written instructions. The test was developed in office work situations, using clerical employees. Examiner required. Suitable for group use.

Timed: 20 minutes

Scoring: Hand key

Cost: Specimen set (test, manual, key) $5.00; 25 tests $8.75

Publisher: Psychometric Affiliates

OFFICE SKILLS TESTS
Science Research Associates, Inc.

Adult

Purpose: Assesses clerical ability of entry-level job applicants. Used for employee selection and placement.

Description: 12 short tests comprising five batteries suitable for screening clerks, accounting clerks, typists, secretary/stenographers, library assistants, and other office personnel. The Tests are Checking, Coding, Filing, Forms Completion, Grammar, Numerical Skills, Oral Directions, Punctuation, Reading Comprehension, Spelling, Typing, and Vocabulary. Each test is available in two equivalent forms. Norms are provided for timed and untimed tests. Examiner required. Suitable for group use.

Untimed: 3 to 10 minutes per test

Scoring: Hand key

Cost: Kit (5 copies of each test, answer stencils, file folders, audiocassette for Oral Directions test, 2 manuals, normative data) $170.00; 25 test booklets (specify test) $23.00; scoring stencils $8.25 each; oral directions cassette $30.00; examiner's manual $10.00

Publisher: Science Research Associates, Inc.

PERCEPTUAL SPEED (IDENTICAL FORMS)
L.L. Thurstone and T.E. Jeffrey

Adult

Purpose: Measures ability to identify rapidly the similarities and differences in visual configurations. Used to select clerical personnel or workers in occupations that require rapid perception of inaccuracies in written materials and diagrams.

Description: 140-item paper-pencil test of perceptual skill. The subject selects the figure among five choices that appears to be most similar to the illustration. Examiner required. Suitable for group use.

Timed: 5 minutes

Scoring: Hand key

Cost: Specimen set $8.00; 25 test booklets $11.25

Publisher: London House Press

PSI BASIC SKILLS TESTS FOR BUSINESS, INDUSTRY, AND GOVERNMENT: CLASSIFYING (BST #11)
W.W. Ruch, A.N. Shub,
S.M. Moinat, and D.A. Dye

Adult

Purpose: Measures ability to place information into predetermined categories. Used to select clerical and office workers.

Description: 48-item paper-pencil multiple-choice test presenting four sets of codes: time and motion study codes, building visitor codes, employee identification codes, and benefits booklet contents. Each set contains 12 items that must be properly categorized. The items have a high degree of apparent relevancy to clerical duties. Examiner required. Suitable for group use.

Timed: 5 minutes

Scoring: Hand key; may be computer scored

Cost: 25 tests $0.50 each

Publisher: Psychological Services, Inc.

PSI BASIC SKILLS TESTS FOR BUSINESS, INDUSTRY, AND GOVERNMENT: CODING (BST #12)
W.W. Ruch, A.N. Shub,
S.M. Moinat, and D.A. Dye

Adult

Purpose: Measures ability to code information according to a prescribed system. Used to select clerical and office workers.

Description: 18-item paper-pencil multiple-choice test in which the subjects are given systems for coding information (each system codes four categories of related information). For each test item, the subject must code the given information into the four coded categories. The coding systems and the information to be coded have a high degree of apparent relevancy to actual clerical duties. Examiner required. Suitable for group use.

Timed: 5 minutes

Scoring: Hand key; may be computer scored

Cost: 25 tests $17.50

Publisher: Psychological Services, Inc.

PSI BASIC SKILLS TESTS FOR BUSINESS, INDUSTRY, AND GOVERNMENT: COMPUTATION (BST #4)
W.W. Ruch, A.N. Shub,
S.M. Moinat, and D.A. Dye

Adult

Purpose: Measures ability to solve arithmetic problems. Used to select clerical and office workers.

Description: 40-item paper-pencil multiple-choice test measuring the ability to add, subtract, multiply, and divide, using whole numbers, fractions, and decimals. Examiner required. Suitable for group use.

Timed: 5 minutes

Scoring: Hand key; may be computer scored

Cost: 25 tests $17.50

Publisher: Psychological Services, Inc.

PSI BASIC SKILLS TESTS FOR BUSINESS, INDUSTRY, AND GOVERNMENT: DECISION MAKING (BST #6)
W.W. Ruch, A.N. Shub,
S.M. Moinat, and D.A. Dye

Adult

Purpose: Measures ability to read a set of procedures and apply them to new situations. Used to select clerical and office workers.

Description: 20-item paper-pencil multiple-choice test in which sets of procedures (related to clerical or office duties) are described and a set of action codes for implementing the procedures. The examinee is presented with a number of problems in which he must decide the course of action for each item and mark the appropriate answer code. Examiner required. Suitable for group use.

Timed: 5 minutes

---

clerical

Scoring: Hand key; may be computer scored
Cost: 25 tests $17.50
Publisher: Psychological Services, Inc.

PSI BASIC SKILLS TESTS FOR BUSINESS, INDUSTRY, AND GOVERNMENT: FILING NAMES (BST #13)
*W.W. Ruch, A.N. Shub,
S.M. Moinat, and D.A. Dye*

Adult

Purpose: Measures ability to file simple entries alphabetically. Used to select clerical and office workers.

Description: 50-item paper-pencil multiple-choice test in which the subject is presented with a name, followed by a list of four other names (alphabetically arranged). The subject "files" the given name at the beginning, between two of the names, or at the end of the list. Examiner required. Suitable for group use.
Timed: 1½ minutes
Scoring: Hand key; may be computer scored
Cost: 25 tests $17.50
Publisher: Psychological Services, Inc.

PSI BASIC SKILLS TESTS FOR BUSINESS, INDUSTRY, AND GOVERNMENT: FILING NUMBERS (BST #14)
*W.W. Ruch, A.N. Shub,
S.M. Moinat, and D.A. Dye*

Adult

Purpose: Measures ability to file numbers in numerical order. Used to select clerical and office workers.

Description: 75-item paper-pencil multiple-choice test in which each test item consists of a 6-digit number to be filed numerically in a list of four other 6-digit numbers (already arranged in numerical order). Examiner required. Suitable for group use.
Timed: 2 minutes
Scoring: Hand key; may be computer scored

Cost: 25 tests $17.50
Publisher: Psychological Services, Inc.

PSI BASIC SKILLS TESTS FOR BUSINESS, INDUSTRY, AND GOVERNMENT: FOLLOWING ORAL DIRECTIONS (BST #7)
*W.W. Ruch, A.N. Shub,
S.M. Moinat, and D.A. Dye*

Adult

Purpose: Measures ability to listen to information and instructions presented orally and answer questions about what is heard. Used to select clerical and office workers.

Description: 24-item paper-pencil multiple-choice test in which the subjects listen to a 6½ minute prerecorded cassette tape and then answer questions about the content of the tape. The tape is played only once (no rewinding or stopping of the tape is allowed), and subjects are encouraged to take written notes during the playing of the tape. The content of the tape has a high degree of apparent relevancy to clerical and office duties. Examiner required. Suitable for group use.
Timed: 5 minutes
Scoring: Hand key; may be computer scored
Cost: 25 tests $17.50
Publisher: Psychological Services, Inc.

PSI BASIC SKILLS TESTS FOR BUSINESS, INDUSTRY, AND GOVERNMENT: FOLLOWING WRITTEN DIRECTIONS (BST #8)
*W.W. Ruch, A.N. Shub,
S.M. Moinat, and D.A. Dye*

Adult

Purpose: Measures ability to read, understand, and apply sets of written instructions. Used to select clerical and office workers.

Description: 36-item paper-pencil multiple-choice test requiring examinees to read sets of rules and apply them to a number of case examples. The rules and case examples have a high degree of apparent relevancy to clerical and office duties. Examiner required. Suitable for group use.

Timed: 5 minutes

Scoring: Hand key; may be computer scored

Cost: 25 tests $17.50

Publisher: Psychological Services, Inc.

PSI BASIC SKILLS TESTS FOR BUSINESS, INDUSTRY, AND GOVERNMENT: FORMS CHECKING (BST #9)
W.W. Ruch, A.N. Shub,
S.M. Moinat, and D.A. Dye

Adult

Purpose: Measures ability to verify the accuracy of completed forms. Used to select clerical and office workers.

Description: 42-item paper-pencil true-false test in which the examinee verifies the accuracy of information in clerical forms apparently filled out using information in written paragraphs. The examinee must check a number of the entries on each form against the information in the paragraphs to determine whether the entries are correct or incorrect. Examiner required. Suitable for group use.

Timed: 5 minutes

Scoring: Hand key; may be computer scored

Cost: 25 tests $17.50

Publisher: Psychological Services, Inc.

PSI BASIC SKILLS TESTS FOR BUSINESS, INDUSTRY, AND GOVERNMENT: LANGUAGE SKILLS (BST #1)
W.W. Ruch, A.N. Shub,
S.M. Moinat, and D.A. Dye

Adult

Purpose: Measures ability to recognize correct spelling, punctuation, capitalization, grammar, and usage. Used to select clerical and office workers.

Description: 25-item paper-pencil multiple-choice test in which each test item consists of one sentence, part of which is underlined. The underlined section may contain errors in spelling, punctuation, capitalization, grammar, or usage. The examinee must select one of three possible changes for the underlined section or indicate that no change is necessary. Examiner required. Suitable for group use.

Timed: 5 minutes

Scoring: Hand key; may be computer scored

Cost: 25 tests $17.50

Publisher: Psychological Services, Inc.

PSI BASIC SKILLS TESTS FOR BUSINESS, INDUSTRY, AND GOVERNMENT: MEMORY (BST #16)
W.W. Ruch, A.N. Shub,
S.M. Moinat, and D.A. Dye

Adult

Purpose: Measures ability to recall names and categories after being allowed a short period of time to study a chart in which the information is listed. Used to select clerical and office workers.

Description: 25-item paper-pencil multiple-choice test in which applicants are given five minutes to study a reference list and five minutes to recall the information on the list. The reference list presents the names of five building supply companies in each of five categories: plumbing, heating, lighting, roofing, and flooring. The applicant must recall for each of the 25 companies the category in which it was listed. Examiner required. Suitable for group use.

Timed: 5 minutes

Scoring: Hand key; may be computer scored

Cost: 25 tests $17.50

Publisher: Psychological Services, Inc.

PSI BASIC SKILLS TESTS FOR BUSINESS, INDUSTRY, AND GOVERNMENT: PROBLEM SOLVING (BST #5)
W.W. Ruch, A.N. Shub,
S.M. Moinat, and D.A. Dye

Adult

Purpose: Measures the ability to solve "story" problems requiring the application of arithmetic operations. Used to select clerical and office workers.

Description: 24-item paper-pencil multiple-choice test in which each item is a short word problem requiring a numerical answer. The test emphasizes determining the arithmetic problem contained in the "story," rather than lengthy computations. Examiner required. Suitable for group use.

Timed: 10 minutes

Scoring: Hand key; may be computer scored

Cost: 25 tests $17.50

Publisher: Psychological Services, Inc.

PSI BASIC SKILLS TESTS FOR BUSINESS, INDUSTRY, AND GOVERNMENT: READING COMPREHENSION (BST #2)
W.W. Ruch, A.N. Shub, S.M. Moinat, and D.A. Dye

Adult

Purpose: Measures basic reading comprehension. Used to select clerical and office workers.

Description: 23-item paper-pencil multiple-choice test measuring the ability to read short passages and answer literal and inferential questions about them. Examiner required. Suitable for group use.

Timed: 10 minutes

Scoring: Hand key; may be computer scored

Cost: 25 tests $17.50

Publisher: Psychological Services, Inc.

PSI BASIC SKILLS TESTS FOR BUSINESS, INDUSTRY, AND GOVERNMENT: REASONING (BST #10)
W.W. Ruch, A.N. Shub, S.M. Moinat, and D.A. Dye

Adult

Purpose: Measures ability to analyze factual information and draw valid logical conclusions from that information. Used to select clerical and office workers.

Description: 30-item paper-pencil multiple-choice test consisting of six lists of facts (one-sentence statements), with five possible conclusions for each list of facts. The examinee must read each list of facts and decide whether each conclusion is definitely true, definitely false, or unknown from the given facts. Examiner required. Suitable for group use.

Timed: 5 minutes

Scoring: Hand key; may be computer scored

Cost: 25 tests $17.50

Publisher: Psychological Services, Inc.

PSI BASIC SKILLS TESTS FOR BUSINESS, INDUSTRY, AND GOVERNMENT: TYPING: PRACTICE COPY (BST #17)
W.W. Ruch, A.N. Shub, S.M. Moinat, and D.A. Dye

Adult

Purpose: Unscored warm-up exercise that familiarizes subject with the typewriter he will be using during testing. May be administered prior to any of the three BST typing tests.

Description: Unscored typing exercise in which the subjects become familiar with the location of all the typewriter keys, including the margin release and backspace, and make all the necessary machine adjustments. Practice copy is typed double-space with a 5-space paragraph indentation and 60-character lines. Examiner required. Suitable for group use.

Timed: 2 minutes

Scoring: Unscored

Cost: 25 tests $17.50

Publisher: Psychological Services, Inc.

PSI BASIC SKILLS TESTS FOR BUSINESS, INDUSTRY, AND GOVERNMENT: TYPING: REVISED COPY (BST #19)
W.W. Ruch, A.N. Shub, S.M. Moinat, and D.A. Dye

Adult

Purpose: Measures ability to type from printed copy with handwritten corrections. Used to select clerical and office workers.

Description: Typing proficiency test in which examinees are given 5 minutes to type as much of the revised copy as possible, making the indicated changes and corrections as they type. The typed copy must be double-spaced 60-character lines with 5-space paragraph indentations and 10-space tab settings for headings. The typed revised copy is scored for accuracy, speed, and how correctly the handwritten changes are made in the final typed copy. Examiner required. Suitable for group use.

Timed: 5 minutes

Scoring: Hand key

Cost: 25 tests $17.50

Publisher: Psychological Services, Inc.

PSI BASIC SKILLS TESTS FOR BUSINESS, INDUSTRY, AND GOVERNMENT: TYPING: STRAIGHT COPY (BST #18)
W.W. Ruch, A.N. Shub,
S.M. Moinat, and D.A. Dye

Adult

Purpose: Measures ability to type straight copy, word-for-word with no revisions, with speed and accuracy. Used to select clerical and office workers.

Description: Typing proficiency test in which applicants are given 5 minutes to type as much of a given passage as possible. The applicant types the passage line-for-line exactly as it is printed. The typed copy must be double-spaced 60-character lines with 5-space paragraph indentations. The applicant is given time to make machine adjustments before the test begins. The typed copy is scored for speed and accuracy. Examiner required. Suitable for group use.

Timed: 5 minutes

Scoring: Hand key

Cost: 25 tests $17.50

Publisher: Psychological Services, Inc.

PSI BASIC SKILLS TESTS FOR BUSINESS, INDUSTRY, AND GOVERNMENT: TYPING: TABLES (BST #20)
W.W. Ruch, A.N. Shub,
S.M. Moinat, and D.A. Dye

Adult

Purpose: Measures ability to set up and type tables according to specific directions. Used to select clerical and office workers.

Description: Typing proficiency test in which examinees are given seven minutes to type as much of three given tables as possible. The copy and directions for each of the three tables is given in handwritten form. The test requires extensive use of a tabulator; each table has its own specified settings. The final copy is scored on speed, accuracy, and skill at correctly following the handwritten instructions. Examiner required. Suitable for group use.

Timed: 7 minutes

Scoring: Hand key

Cost: 25 tests $17.50

Publisher: Psychological Services, Inc.

PSI BASIC SKILLS TESTS FOR BUSINESS, INDUSTRY, AND GOVERNMENT: VISUAL SPEED AND ACCURACY (BST #15)
W.W. Ruch, A.N. Shub,
S.M. Moinat, and D.A. Dye

Adult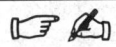

Purpose: Measures ability to see details quickly and accurately. Used to select clerical and office workers.

Description: 150-item paper-pencil multiple-choice test in which each test item consists of two series of numbers and symbols. The examinee compares the numbers or symbols and determines whether they are the same or different. Examiner required. Suitable for group use.

Timed: 5 minutes

Scoring: Hand key; may be computer scored

Cost: 25 tests $17.50

Publisher: Psychological Services, Inc.

PSI BASIC SKILLS TESTS FOR BUSINESS, INDUSTRY, AND GOVERNMENT: VOCABULARY (BST #3)
W.W. Ruch, A.N. Shub, S.M. Moinat, and D.A. Dye

Adult

Purpose: Measures the ability to recognize the correct meaning of words. Used to select clerical and office workers.

Description: 45-item paper-pencil multiple-choice test in which each item consists of a sentence with one word underlined, followed by four words. The examinee must select the word meaning the same or about the same as the word that is underlined in the sentence. Examiner required. Suitable for group use.

Timed: 5 minutes

Scoring: Hand key; may be computer scored

Cost: 25 tests $17.50

Publisher: Psychological Services, Inc.

PURDUE CLERICAL ADAPTABILITY TEST (REVISED)

Adolescent, adult

Purpose: Assesses clerical abilities. Used to select clerical and office personnel.

Description: Multiple-item paper-pencil measure of six aspects of clerical work: spelling, arithmetic computation, checking of names and numbers, word meaning, copying, and arithmetic reasoning. Sale is restricted to companies employing qualified personnel administrators and to psychologists using tests for instruction or vocational guidance. Examiner required. Suitable for group use.

Untimed: Not available

Scoring: Hand key

Cost: Specimen set $1.00; 25 tests, manual, key $9.50

Publisher: Purdue Research Foundation/ University Book Store

THE RBH CLASSIFYING TEST
Richardson, Bellows, Henry and Company, Inc.

Adult

Purpose: Measures the ability to classify material with speed and accuracy. Used with applicants for clerical positions.

Description: Multiple-item paper-pencil test assessing the ability to quickly and accurately classify information covering several different variables. The individual is presented with nine basic problems. Thirty situations are provided for each problem. In the first series of 30 items, the individual must quickly classify material in terms of three restrictions—shipping point, fragility, and value. In the second series, the shipping point is complicated, fragility status is reversed, and weight is the third alternative. In the third set, relationships are further complicated, so attention to instructions is essential. Series 4, 5, and 6 and series 7, 8, and 9 are not more difficult than the first series, but there is an overall pressure to complete as many items as possible. The test yields a speed score, an accuracy score, and a right-wrong score. Male norms are available for marketing trainees, administrative and sales clerks, warehousemen, dispatchers, and laboratory testing personnel. Female norms are available for a variety of clerical applicants and employees. The test is available in two forms, I and II. Examiner required. Suitable for group use.

Timed: 10 minutes

Scoring: Hand key

Cost: 1-24 packages $18.00; score key $2.00; manual $2.00

Publisher: Richardson, Bellows, Henry and Company, Inc.

SEASHORE-BENNETT STENOGRAPHIC PROFICIENCY TEST
G.K. Bennett and H.G. Seashore

Adult

Purpose: Measures stenographic skills. Used for selection and promotion of stenographers.

Description: Five-task test measuring the ability to type dictated commercial letters. Five letters are contained in each form: two are short and slow, two are medium in both length and dictation speed, and one is long and fast. Two parallel, alternate forms, B-1 and B-2, are available. Dictation is available on record, tape, and cassette. The test is sold only to personnel departments of business and industrial firms for the testing of applicants and employees. The test is not sold to schools or employment agencies. Examiner required. Suitable for group use.

Timed: Dictation 15 minutes; Transcription 30 minutes

Scoring: Examiner evaluated

Cost: Complete set (recordings for both forms, manual, script, 100 summary charts, record version $65.00; reel-to-reel tape version $65.00; cassette tape version $65.00

Publisher: The Psychological Corporation

SHORT EMPLOYMENT TESTS
G.K. Bennett and Marjorie Gelink

Adult

Purpose: Measures job skills. Used in applicant and employee selection.

Description: Three paper-pencil tests measuring skills related to performance, particularly in clerical jobs. The tests are SET-Verbal (V), SET-Numerical (N), and SET-Clerical Aptitude (CA). They predict performance in a wide variety of jobs, including bank tellers, accounting clerks, hospital clerical workers, and airline reservation agents. The tests may be used individually or in combination. Four equivalent forms are available. Tapes are available for test administration. The test is sold only to personnel departments of business and industrial firms for testing applicants and employees. The tests are not sold to schools or employment agencies. Form 1 is restricted to member banks of the American Banker's Association (ABA). Examiner required. Suitable for group use.

Timed: 5 minutes per test

Scoring: Hand key

Cost: 25 test booklets, manual, key (specify test) $25.00

Publisher: The Psychological Corporation

SHORT TESTS OF CLERICAL ABILITY (STCA)
Jean Maier Palormo

Adult

Purpose: Assesses aptitudes and abilities important to the successful completion of typical office tasks. Used for selection and placement in office job classifications, such as secretary-stenographer, office clerk, and specialized clerk (accounting, statistical, and billing).

Description: Multiple-item paper-pencil battery consisting of seven tests. The battery includes arithmetic skills, business vocabulary, checking accuracy, coding, oral and written directions, filing, and language (grammar and mechanics). The test is norm referenced, including minority groups. Examiner required. Suitable for group use.

Untimed: 3-6 minutes per test

Scoring: Hand key

Cost: 25 test booklets (specify test) $25.00; scoring stencils (specify test) $8.75; examiner's manual $10.00

Publisher: Science Research Associates, Inc.

SRA CLERICAL APTITUDES
Richardson, Bellows, Henry & Co., Inc., New York

Adult

Purpose: Assesses general aptitudes necessary for clerical work. Used in employee screening and placing.

Description: Three paper-pencil tests measuring office vocabulary, office arithmetic, and office checking. The tests indicate the ability to learn tasks usually performed in various clerical jobs. The office vocabulary test (48 items) measures command of basic vocabulary and verbal relations. The arithmetic test (24 items) requires application of basic math processes to the solution of practical problems. The checking test (144 items) measures the ability to perceive details easily and rapidly. Examiner required. Suitable for group use.

Timed: 25 minutes

Scoring: Hand key

Cost: 25 reuseable test booklets $86.00; 25 answer sheets $18.00; 100 profile sheets $20.00; examiner's manual $10.00

Publisher: Science Research Associates, Inc.

SRA TYPING 5
Steven J. Stanard and LaVonne Macaitis

Adult

Purpose: Measures a person's ability to type a particular kind of assignment. Used with a variety of typing positions requiring different skills.

Description: Task-assessment consisting of three forms measuring typing speed and accuracy. Typing Speed, Form A, consists of a letter with approximately 215 words measuring key-stroking speed and accuracy. Business Letter, Form B, measures the ability to set up a business letter and type it quickly and accurately for the more experienced typist. Numerical, Form C, contains approximately 115 words and 40 numbers and measures speed and accuracy in typing complex material containing words, symbols, and numbers in columns with headings. Examiner required. Suitable for group use.

Timed: 5 minutes per test (after practice time)

Scoring: Hand key

Cost: 25 test booklets (specify test) $24.00; 25 practice sheets $9.00; examiner's manual $10.00

Publisher: Science Research Associates, Inc.

SRA TYPING SKILLS TEST
Marion W. Richardson and Ruth A. Pedersen

Adult

Purpose: Assesses typing skills. Used by teachers and managers to evaluate the skills of students, typists, clerical help, and job applicants.

Description: Test of typing speed and accuracy consisting of a business letter approximately 225 words in length to be typed as often as possible in an accurately timed 10-minute period. The test is scored according to International Typewriting Contest Rules. The test is available in three equivalent forms: one for hiring, one for upgrading, and one properly spaced for electric typewriters. Examiner required. Suitable for group use.

Timed: 10 minutes (after practice time)

Scoring: Hand key

Cost: Contact publisher

Publisher: Science Research Associates, Inc.

STENOGRAPHIC TEST
E. F. Wonderlic & Associates, Inc.

Adult

Purpose: Measures speed and accuracy in taking shorthand notes. Used to select and place stenographers.

Description: 26-item paper-pencil test assessing shorthand-stenographic skills. Items consist of 100-word letters of various "syllable densities" dictated at speeds ranging from 40-160 words per minute. The Vari-Speed Guide quickly determines an applicant's approximate level of skill. From this point, successively more difficult and faster letters are dictated until the applicant's best performance is determined. The test may be administered via an optional cassette tape, which includes all 26 letters dictated at their proper rate, warm-up exercises, and directions. Examiner required. Suitable for group use.

Timed: Varies

Scoring: Hand key

Cost: Complete $96.00; individual tapes (text not included) $24.00; printed text $23.00

Publisher: E.F. Wonderlic Personnel Test, Inc.

TEST A/8: ARITHMETIC
Refer to page 847.

TYPING TEST
E.F. Wonderlic Personnel Test, Inc.

Adult

Purpose: Assesses typing speed and accuracy. Used to select entry-level typists and keypunch operators.

Description: Multiple-item typing performance test consisting of four forms. Letter Forms A and B measure typing speed in copying straight printed material. Random Numbers Form 2 is used to screen typists who will be asked to do significant amounts of typing for accounting, address files, and computer input. Random Letters Form K, which requires no verbal knowledge, is used to screen typists involved in keypunch and other operations using letter codes. The test may be administered with an optional cassette tape. Examiner required. Suitable for group use.

Timed: 5 minutes

Scoring: Hand key

Cost: Reusable complete package $32.00; cassette tape $24.00

Publisher: E.F. Wonderlic Personnel Test, Inc.

TYPING TEST
Richardson, Bellows, Henry and Company, Inc.

Adult

Purpose: Provides a quick screening of an individual's typing ability. Used to estimate the typing skills of applicants for general clerical or clerk-typist positions.

Description: Manual test measuring an individual's typing speed and accuracy in which the examinee is presented with a double-spaced letter to type. After reading the test directions, adjusting the machine settings, and typing the practice copy, the examinee types the test letter exactly as it appears. If the examinee completes the letter before the allotted time expires, he begins retyping the letter. The test yields a words-per-minute score and an accuracy score. A more comprehensive test should be used for promoting present personnel or hiring secretarial or stenographic applicants. The following materials are required: one test folder and one typewriter for each examinee and a timing device for the examiner. Examiner required. Suitable for group use.

Timed: 5 minutes

Scoring: Hand key

Cost: 1-24 packages $19.00; score key $2.00; manual $2.00

Publisher: Richardson, Bellows, Henry and Company, Inc.

TYPING TEST FOR BUSINESS (TTB)
J.E. Doppelt, A.D. Hartman, and F.B. Krawchick

Adult

Purpose: Assesses typing skills. Used to test applicants for typist, keypunch operator, secretarial, and other positions in which typing skill is necessary.

Description: Test of five kinds of typing used in business: straight copy, letters, revised manuscript, numbers, and tables. The warm-up practice copy is administered first. The practice copy and straight copy tests may be given as a quick screening test. Two alternate forms, A and B and AR and BR, are available. The test is sold only to personnel departments of business and industrial firms for the testing of applicants and employees. It is not sold to schools or employment agencies. Examiner required. Suitable for group use.

Timed: Varies

Scoring: Hand key

Cost: Examination kit (test booklet for each test, both forms, manual) $20.00; 25 practice copy tests $11.00; 25 straight copy tests $20.00; 25 letters tests $20.00; 25 revised manuscript tests $20.00; 25 numbers tests $20.00; 25 tables tests $20.00 (specify form for all materials ordered)

Publisher: The Psychological Corporation

VCWS 5—CLERICAL COMPREHENSION AND APTITUDE

Adult

Purpose: Measures basic clerical aptitude and the ability to perform a variety of answering, mail sorting, alphabetical filing, bookkeeping, and typing tasks, and to communicate effectively both verbally and in writing. Also used as a screening device for entry-level general clerical jobs. May be used with hearing-impaired and visually impaired individuals.

Description: Manual test featuring three separate work samples measuring an individual's ability to perform a variety of clerical tasks and his ability to learn the tasks. The test begins with mail sorting and simultaneous phone answering. A tape plays a series of phone conversations at prerecorded intervals requiring the individual to stop the mail sorting in order to take the phone message. The individual also must complete an alphabetical filing task. In the second section of the test, the individual must use a 10-key adding machine to perform three exercises emphasizing accurate recording of numerical data and basic math skills. In the typing section, the typewriter has been modified to measure a person's typing coordination skills regardless of his previous exposure to typing. Work activities related to the test include classifying, filing, and sorting correspondence; recording verbal and written information; preparing numerical records with the aid of an adding machine; and transcribing using a typewriter. The test should not be used with individuals with severe impairment of the upper extremities. Examiner required. Not suitable for group use.

Timed: Not available

Scoring: Examiner evaluated

Cost: $1,775.00

Publisher: Valpar International Corporation

WOLFE CLERICAL STAFF SELECTOR

Adult

Purpose: Evaluates candidates of all levels of experience for clerical positions.

Description: Multiple-item paper-pencil set of four subtests in three formats for assessing problem-solving and logical abilities, numerical skills, attention to detail, and emotional stability. The tests are used for filling inventory control, order desk, filing, accounting, and other clerical positions. The three speed subtests are timed. See the description of the Wolfe Staff Selector Test Kits for further information. The Comprehensive format is not available for this test. Examiner required. Suitable for group use. Available in French.

CANADIAN PUBLISHER

Timed/Untimed: 30 minutes

Scoring: Hand key or computer scored depending on format chosen

Cost: $35.00 per person

Publisher: Wolfe Personnel Testing and Training Systems, Inc.

WOLFE SECRETARIAL STAFF SELECTOR

Adult

Purpose: Evaluates candidates of all levels of experience for secretarial positions.

Description: Multiple-item paper-pencil set of seven timed subtests and two optional subtests available in three formats for assessing attention to detail, alphabetizing and filing skills, grammar and punctuation, spelling and vocabulary, manual dexterity, logical and problem-solving abilities, numerical skills, desire for people contact (optional), and emotional stability (optional). The tests are used for selecting senior clerks, secretaries, administrative assistants, and word processing operators. See the description of the Wolfe Staff Selector Test Kits for further information. The Comprehensive format is not available for this test. Examiner required. Suitable for group use. Available in French.

CANADIAN PUBLISHER

Timed/Untimed: 75 minutes

Scoring: Hand key or computer scored depending on format chosen

Cost: $35.00 each

Publisher: Wolfe Personnel Testing and Training Systems, Inc.

Computer

ADVANCED TEST BATTERY: DIAGRAMMATIC REASONING (ATB:DT8)

Refer to page 793.

ADVANCED TEST BATTERY: DIAGRAMMING (ATB:DA5)

Refer to page 793.

APTITUDE ASSESSMENT BATTERY: PROGRAMMING (AABP)
Jack M. Wolfe

Adult

Purpose: Determines a person's aptitude for computer programming. May be used to select job candidates, as a guide for training programs, and for revealing work habits and task preferences.

Description: Five-problem paper-pencil tests measuring ability to draw deductions, understand complicated instructions, interpret intricate specifications, reason, desk-check, debug, and document and annotate work. Examiner required. Suitable for group use. Available in French, Spanish, and braille. CANADIAN PUBLISHER
Untimed: 2 hours
Scoring: Scoring service provided
Cost: Complete (test, evaluation) $90.00
Publisher: Wolfe Personnel Testing and Training Systems, Inc.

AUTOMATED OFFICE BATTERY (AOB)
Saville & Holdsworth Ltd. Staff

Ages 16-adult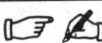

Purpose: Measures job-related skills required in the modern automated office. Assesses the ability to estimate using numerical data to check data on VDU screens and printout and to follow coded instructions. Used with individuals ages 16 and older for selection and career development.

Description: 130-item paper-pencil set of three tests measuring three abilities highly relevant to the needs of the modern electronic office. They are the ability to estimate numerically (where machines will make precise calculations), to check the accurate recording of new data onto VDU screens and printouts (where the information has been reordered and supplemented); and to follow instructions that have been coded into machine-oriented language. The tests include realistic representation, of computer display terminals and printouts. The item content is suitable for international use. The tests are restricted to qualified users and are not available to educational institutions. Examiner required. Suitable for group use.
BRITISH PUBLISHER
Timed: 10-18 minutes per test
Scoring: Hand key; may be computer scored
Cost: See descriptions for individual AOB tests
Publisher: Saville & Holdsworth Ltd.

AUTOMATED OFFICE BATTERY: CODED INSTRUCTIONS (CI-3)
Saville & Holdsworth Ltd. Staff

Ages 16-adult

Purpose: Measures the ability to understand and follow instructions coded into machine-oriented language.

Description: 40-item paper-pencil test assessing the ability to understand and follow coded instructions. Candidates are presented with instructions on how to enter and retrieve information from a machine. They must understand the instructions in the text and decide on the appropriate course of action for each question. The content is office based and relates to new technology within the office environment, particularly to the kinds of instructions that an individual must follow when operating computer systems and word processors. One of three tests in the Automated Office Battery. Examiner required. Suitable for group use.
BRITISH PUBLISHER

Timed: 18 minutes

Scoring: Hand key; may be computer scored

Cost: 10 reusable test booklets $210.00; 50 answer sheets $105.00; administration card $10.50; scoring key $21.00

Publisher: Saville & Holdsworth Ltd.

AUTOMATED OFFICE BATTERY: COMPUTER CHECKING (AOB: CC-2)
Saville & Holdsworth Ltd. Staff

Ages 16-adult

Purpose: Measures the abilities of scanning, reasoning, and checking documentation against VDU or printer output, by comparing input.

Description: 40-item paper-pencil test assessing the ability to check computerized information against typed copy. The candidate must identify quickly and accurately whether the information has been correctly transferred to a facing representation of a VDU screen or a page of computer printout. The information may have been reordered and added to other information during input to the computer. To complete the checking task, the candidate must find the relevant data, understand its new representation and then make the final check on its correct transfer. One of three tests in the Automated Office Battery. Examiner required. Suitable for group use.

BRITISH PUBLISHER

Timed: 12 minutes

Scoring: Hand key; may be computer scored

Cost: 10 reusable test booklets $210.00; 50 answer sheets $105.00; administration card $10.50; scoring key $21.00

Publisher: Saville & Holdsworth Ltd.

BUSINESS ANALYST SKILLS EVALUATION (BUSAN)

Adult

Purpose: Evaluates aptitude and potential for positions in business systems analysis, procedures analysis, and user department/EDP department interface. Used with candidates with prior business

experience. No previous data processing knowledge or experience is required.

Description: Multiple-item paper-pencil test in two groups of subtests used for evaluating candidates for positions such as business analyst, procedures analyst, business systems analyst, and user/EDP department interface. Section 1 subtests measure analytical ability, flow charting, deductive reasoning, procedures and systems analysis, and development of departmental user reports and subsystems. Section 2 subtests measure horizontal interpersonal relationship abilities, people contact desired, emotional stability, stress tolerance, group participation skills, consistency, dominance, adventurousness, maturity, enthusiasm, tough-mindedness, practicality, sophistication, self-sufficiency, leadership potential, drive and initiative, verbal communication skills, and memory. Section 1 and two subtests in Section 2 are timed. Results are available by mail or telephone. A Scored by Client form is available. Examiner required. Suitable for group use.

CANADIAN PUBLISHER

Timed: 1 hour, 45 minutes

Scoring: Hand key; may be computer scored

Cost: Contact publisher

Publisher: Wolfe Personnel Testing and Training Systems, Inc.

COMPUTER OPERATOR APTITUDE BATTERY (COAB)
A. Joanne Holloway

Adult

Purpose: Helps predict job performance of computer operators. Used by data processing managers and personnel directors to select applicants for computer operator positions.

Description: Paper-pencil test predicting success as a computer programmer. The test consists of three separately timed subtests: Sequence Recognition, Format Checking, and Logical Thinking. Examiner required. Suitable for group use.

Timed: 45 minutes

Scoring: Hand key

Cost: 5 reuseable test booklets $85.00; 25 answer sheets $52.00; examiner's manual $10.00

Publisher: Science Research Associates, Inc.

COMPUTER PROGRAMMER APTITUDE BATTERY (CPAB)
Jean Maier Palormo

Adult

Purpose: Measures potential for success in the computer programming field. Used by data processing managers and personnel directors to identify people with the aptitude for computer programming.

Description: Five separately timed paper-pencil tests measuring verbal meaning, reasoning, letter series, number ability, and diagramming (problem analysis and logical solution). Examiner required. Suitable for group use.

Timed: 1 hour, 15 minutes

Scoring: Hand key

Cost: 5 reuseable test booklets $85.00; 25 answer sheets $52.00; examiner's manual $10.00

Publisher: Science Research Associates, Inc.

CRITICAL REASONING TEST BATTERY: DIAGRAMMATIC SERIES (CRTB: DC3)
Refer to page 951.

FOGEL WP OPERATOR TEST
Max Fogel

Adult

Purpose: Measures aptitudes and personality dimensions that predict an individual's success as a word processor operator. Used for employee selection and placement.

Description: Multiple-item paper-pencil test assessing an applicant's potential for success as a word processor operator. The test measures problem solving (the ability to assess information and to make decisions based upon the information and general analytical skills), vocabulary, proofreading, figural transformations,

mechanical-spatial relationships, and personality (including attitudes toward machinery and equipment). Examiner required. Suitable for group use.

Untimed: 45 minutes

Scoring: Examiner evaluated; scoring service available

Cost: Corporate kit (50 test booklets, complete answer key, interpretive manual) $2,000.00; 10 test booklets (includes partial key) $425.00; scoring service per test $20.00

Publisher: Association of Information Systems Professionals

I.P.I. JOB TEST FIELD SERIES: COMPUTER PROGRAMMER
Industrial Psychology, Inc.

Adult

Purpose: Assesses skills and aptitudes of applicants for entry-level computer programmer positions. Used for employee selection and placement.

Description: Multiple-item paper-pencil battery of five aptitude tests measuring skills that predict success as an entry-level computer programmer. The tests include Office Terms (54 items), measuring the ability to understand special terms used in business and industry; Numbers (54 items), measuring aptitude for working quickly and accurately with numbers; Judgment (54 items), measuring aptitude for logical thinking, planning, and dealing with abstract relations; Parts (48 items), measuring aptitude for visualizing size, shape, and spatial relations of objects in two or three dimensions; and Perception (54 items), measuring the ability to rapidly scan and locate details and errors in words and numbers and to recognize likenesses and differences. Examiner required. Suitable for group use. All tests available in French.

Timed: 6 minutes per test

Scoring: Hand key

Cost: Instruction kit $10.00; test packages $6.00 each

Publisher: Industrial Psychology, Inc.

PROGRAMMER ANALYST APTITUDE TEST (PAAT)

Adult

Purpose: Evaluates aptitude and potential for computer programming and business analysis positions. Used for pre-screening entry-level candidates with no prior experience, computer trainees, computer science graduates, and experienced applicants.

Description: 6-item paper-pencil test assessing logical ability, skill in interpreting business specifications, potential for translating business problems into symbolic logic, and ability to follow complex business procedures and analyze them to supply specific requirements. Examiner required. Suitable for group use. CANADIAN PUBLISHER

Timed: 1½ hours

Scoring: Hand key; may be computer scored

Cost: Contact publisher

Publisher: Wolfe Personnel Testing and Training Systems, Inc.

PROGRAMMER APTITUDE COMPETENCE TEST SYSTEM (PACTS)
C.A. Haverly and Pete Seiner

Adult

Purpose: Measures an individual's ability to write good computer programs, regardless of experience. Used for job screening.

Description: Multiple-item test of 4-6 problems with up to 20 total problems possible. The subject is given an instruction book which describes a general computer programming language for a hypothetical computer, to study for 30-50 minutes. The subject then is given a book of problems, with difficulty based on programming experience. Completed programs are evaluated by computer scoring on correctness, efficiency, compactness, problem difficulty, and completion time. Materials include the computer installation, manual, and problems. Examiner required. Suitable for group use.

Untimed: 2-3 hours

Scoring: Computer scored

Cost: Computer installation $8,200.00; PACTS is available on service basis: $100.00 per test for the first five tests; $80.00 per test for additional five tests

Publisher: Haverly Systems, Inc.

Information and availability unconfirmed; no publisher response.

STRUCTURED ANALYSIS AND DESIGN CONCEPTS PROFICIENCY TEST (WWSAD)

Adult

Purpose: Evaluates knowledge of structured analysis, design methodology, and commonly used tools and techniques. Used with candidates for EDP systems analyst/designer positions.

Description: Multiple-item paper-pencil test measuring the ability to use data flow diagrams and knowledge of system development methodology, structured analysis process, structured analysis tools, structure charts, and coupling, cohesion, control, and packaging. The test is used for determining the technical proficiency of experienced programmers, staff expertise, and structured analysis and design training needs. It also is used for evaluating structured analysis and design training effectiveness, conducting skills inventory analysis, and identifying promotable employees. Scores are determined by categorizing different types of errors and deducting different point values for the errors, varying with the severity of error. Examiner required. Suitable for group use. CANADIAN PUBLISHER

Timed: 35 minutes

Scoring: Hand key; may be computer scored

Cost: Contact publisher

Publisher: Wolfe Personnel Testing and Training Systems, Inc.

SYSTEMS ANALYST APTITUDE TEST (SAAT)
Jack M. Wolfe

Adult

Purpose: Measures a person's aptitude for business systems design. Used for hiring, training, and promotion of computer analysts and programmers.

Description: Single-item (case study) test evaluating interpretation of specifications, ability to plan a logical procedure, recognition of alternative solutions, clarity of explanation, quality of organization, attention to detail, and effectiveness and efficiency of design. Available in French. Examiner required. Suitable for group use.
CANADIAN PUBLISHER

Untimed: 3 hours

Scoring: Scoring service provided

Cost: Complete (test, computer report) $250.00 per person

Publisher: Wolfe Personnel Testing and Training Systems, Inc.

SYSTEMS PROGRAMMING APTITUDE TEST (SPAT)
Jack M. Wolfe

Adult

Purpose: Measures a person's aptitude for systems and software programming. May be used for hiring, training, and promotion decisions at all levels of skill.

Description: Five-part paper-pencil test measuring accuracy, reasoning, and ability to deal with complex relationships and skills in deductive, interpretive, and analytic reasoning. Examiner required. Suitable for group use.
CANADIAN PUBLISHER

Untimed: 3 hours

Scoring: Scoring service provided

Cost: Complete (test, computer report) $200.00

Publisher: Wolfe Personnel Testing and Training Systems, Inc.

W-APT PROGRAMMING APTITUDE TEST

Adult

Purpose: Measures aptitude and potential for applications programming. Used for screening entry-level candidates, computer trainees, and computer science graduates and for prescreening experienced applicants.

Description: 5-item paper-pencil test assessing logical ability, interpretation of intricate specifications, ability to follow instructions precisely, attention to detail, accuracy, and problem solving using reasoning with symbols. Available in a microcomputer version. Examiner required. Suitable for group use. Available in French.
CANADIAN PUBLISHER

Untimed: 1 hour

Scoring: Hand key; may be computer scored

Cost: $15.00 per person

Publisher: Wolfe Personnel Testing and Training Systems, Inc.

WOLFE COMPUTER OPERATOR APTITUDE TEST (WCOAT)
Jack M. Wolfe

Adult

Purpose: Evaluates the aptitude of computer operators at all experience levels.

Description: Generalized aptitude test measuring manual dexterity and the ability to solve problems logically, follow procedural logic, and precisely follow all instructions and rules. Examiner required. Suitable for group use. Available in French.
CANADIAN PUBLISHER

Timed: 2 hours

Scoring: Scoring service provided

Cost: Complete (test, computer report) $55.00 per person

Publisher: Wolfe Personnel Testing and Training Systems, Inc.

WOLFE DATA ENTRY OPERATOR APTITUDE TEST (WDEOAT)
S. Berke

Adult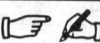

Purpose: Determines a person's aptitude for work as a data entry operator or terminal operator. May be used for hiring or training purposes.

Description: Six-item multiple-part paper-pencil test measuring manual dexterity, coding, accuracy, numerical skills, editing, and work speed. Examiner required. Suitable for group use. CANADIAN PUBLISHER
Timed: 30 minutes
Scoring: Scoring service provided
Cost: Complete (test, computer report) $15.00 per person
Publisher: Wolfe Personnel Testing and Training Systems, Inc.

WOLFE PROGRAMMING APTITUDE TEST (WPAT)
Jack M. Wolfe

Adult

Purpose: Determines a person's aptitude for computer programming. Used as a screening instrument.

Description: 10-problem paper-pencil test. A 64-page booklet with answers is provided so that respondents can score their own tests. Self-administered. Suitable for group use. CANADIAN PUBLISHER
Untimed: 1 hour
Scoring: Hand key; scored by candidate
Cost: $50.00 each
Publisher: Wolfe Personnel Testing and Training Systems, Inc.

WOLFE PROGRAMMING LANGUAGE TEST: COBOL (WCOBL)
Jack M. Wolfe

Adult

Purpose: Assesses a person's knowledge of COBOL. Used for screening experienced programmers.

Description: 47-item paper-pencil test measuring speed of work and evaluating coding skills, documentation, and knowledge of COBOL. Suitable for junior and intermediate programmers with detailed knowledge of the COBOL manual. Examiner required. Suitable for group use.
CANADIAN PUBLISHER
Timed: 2 hours
Scoring: Scoring service provided
Cost: Complete (test, computer report) $40.00 per person
Publisher: Wolfe Personnel Testing and Training Systems, Inc.

WOLFE SCREENING TEST FOR PROGRAMMING APTITUDE (WPT)
Jack M. Wolfe

Adult

Purpose: Measures a person's aptitude for computer programming. Used by schools and placement agencies.

Description: Three-part paper-pencil test measuring attention to detail, ability to solve problems, and ability to interpret specifications. Examiner required. Suitable for group use. Available in French. CANADIAN PUBLISHER
Timed: 40 minutes
Scoring: Hand key; examiner evaluated
Cost: 1-9 test booklets and key $12.50 each
Publisher: Wolfe Personnel Testing and Training Systems, Inc.

WOLFE-SPENCE PROGRAMMING APTITUDE TEST (WSPAT)
Jack M. Wolfe and R. J. Spence

Adult

Purpose: Screens entry-level candidates for computer programming work. May be used for hiring or selecting candidates for training classes.

Description: 8-item paper-pencil test measuring a person's logical capabilities and ability to interpret intricate specifications. Candidates passing the test should

be given the AABP test prior to making hiring decisions. Examiner required. Suitable for group use.
CANADIAN PUBLISHER
Timed: 2 hours
Scoring: Scoring service provided
Cost: Complete (test, computer report) $40.00 per person
Publisher: Wolfe Personnel Testing and Training Systems, Inc.

WOLFE-WINROW CICS/VS COMMAND LEVEL PROFICIENCY TEST (WWCICS)
B. W. Winrow

Adult

Purpose: Measures a person's knowledge of IBM CICS/VS Command Level. Used for hiring, training, and promoting applications programmers and software specialists.

Description: Five-part paper-pencil test measuring general knowledge of CICS/VS concepts, facilities and commands, and the ability to code CICS/VS commands from specifications and debug and test in a CICS/VS environment. The test also includes an optional measure of specific knowledge of Basic Mapping Support and related commands. Examiner required. Suitable for group use.
CANADIAN PUBLISHER
Timed: 30 minutes
Scoring: Scoring service provided
Cost: Complete (detailed report) $40.00
Publisher: Wolfe Personnel Testing and Training Systems, Inc.

WOLFE-WINROW DOS/VS JCL PROFICIENCY TEST
B. W. Winrow

Adult

Purpose: Measures a person's knowledge of DOS, DOS/VS, or DOS/VSE JCL language. May be used for hiring, training, and promoting purposes.

Description: Five-part paper-pencil test measuring the ability to identify common JCL errors, code, overwrite catalogued procedures, and specific knowledge of

JCL parameters. Suitable for examining computer operators, DOS JCL analysts, and applications programmers at all experience levels. Examiner required. Suitable for group use.
CANADIAN PUBLISHER
Timed: 30 minutes
Scoring: Scoring service provided
Cost: Complete (test, computer report) $40.00 per person
Publisher: Wolfe Personnel Testing and Training Systems, Inc.

WOLFE-WINROW OS JCL PROFICIENCY TEST
B. W. Winrow

Adult

Purpose: Measures a person's knowledge of IBM OS/JCL language. Used for hiring, promoting, and training computer operators, analysts, and programmers.

Description: Five-part paper-pencil test measuring general knowledge of JCL statements and parameters and understanding of JCL parameters, catalogued procedures, symbolic parameters, GDGs, and overriding JCL. The test also assesses the ability to identify OS/JCL errors and code OS/JCL. Examiner required. Suitable for group use.
CANADIAN PUBLISHER
Timed: 30 minutes
Scoring: Scoring service provided
Cost: Complete (test, computer report) $40.00 per person
Publisher: Wolfe Personnel Testing and Training Systems, Inc.

WOLFE-WINROW STRUCTURED COBOL
B. W. Winrow

Adult

Purpose: Assesses a person's knowledge of structured COBOL. Used for hiring, evaluating existing staff, evaluating training needs and effectiveness, and promotion.

Description: Five-question paper-pencil test measuring the ability to identify structured programming tools for

COBOL, use concepts such as table look-up and debugging aids, define storage attributes and code PICTURE clauses for COBOL, code from specifications, and understand arithmetic operations and programming efficiencies. Examiner required. Suitable for group use.
CANADIAN PUBLISHER

Timed: 30 minutes

Scoring: Scoring service provided

Cost: Complete (includes report) $40.00 per person

Publisher: Wolfe Personnel Testing and Training Systems, Inc.

WOLFE-WINROW TSO/SPF PROFICIENCY TEST (WWTSO)
B. W. Winrow

Adult

Purpose: Assesses a person's knowledge of IBM TSO/SPE. Used for hiring, training, and promoting programmers and software specialists.

Description: Five-part paper-pencil test evaluating an applicant's knowledge of TSO/SPE features and commands. Examiner required. Suitable for group use.
CANADIAN PUBLISHER

Timed: 30 minutes

Scoring: Scoring service provided

Cost: Complete (test, detailed report) $55.00

Publisher: Wolfe Personnel Testing and Training Systems, Inc.

WORD PROCESSING APTITUDE BATTERY (WPAB)
Saville & Holdsworth Ltd. Staff

Adult

Purpose: Measures a wide range of skills and abilities related to word processing occupations. Used for personnel screening with individuals who have no educational qualifications and those with degrees.

Description: 186-item paper-pencil test of word processing skills and abilities. The battery includes five tests: Verbal Skills (WP1), Checking Skills (WP2), Written Instructions (WP3), Coded Infor-

mation (WP4), and Numerical Computation (WP5). The first three tests are used for jobs involving the basic functions of creating documents, editing, filing, and moving blocks of text. WP5 is used when the job also requires form design, reformatting, justification, and figure work. The whole battery is used for advanced word processing work, including calculations, keyboard programming, and lists and record processing. Examiner required. Suitable for group use.
BRITISH PUBLISHER

Timed: Complete battery 57 minutes

Scoring: Hand key; may be computer scored

Cost: Manual and user's guide $105.00; 10 test booklets (includes all 5 tests) $168.00; 5 administration cards $63.00; 5 scoring keys $84.00; 10 answer sheets and profile chart $63.00; 10 group score sheets $4.20; annual license $220.50

Publisher: Saville & Holdsworth Ltd.

WORD PROCESSING APTITUDE BATTERY: CHECKING SKILLS (WP2)
Saville & Holdsworth Ltd. Staff

Adult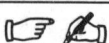

Purpose: Measures ability to check written information. Used in personnel screening and development for word processor operators.

Description: 50-item paper-pencil test measuring the ability to check written information quickly and accurately. Proofreading ability from one set of text to another is measured by having candidates code errors such as omissions and transpositions according to a set of rules. One of five tests in the Word Processing Aptitude Battery. The test is used with WP1 and WP3 to screen for jobs involving creating documents, editing, filing, and moving blocks of text. Examiner required. Suitable for group use.
BRITISH PUBLISHER

Timed: 10 minutes

Scoring: Hand key; may be computer scored

Cost: Manual and user's guide $105.00; 10 test booklets (includes all 5 tests) $168.00; 5 administration cards $63.00; 5 scoring keys $84.00; 10 answer sheets and profile chart $63.00; 10 group score sheets $4.20; annual license $220.50

Publisher: Saville & Holdsworth Ltd.

WORD PROCESSING APTITUDE BATTERY: CODED INFORMATION (WP4)
Saville & Holdsworth Ltd. Staff

Adult

Purpose: Measures reasoning ability using symbols. Used in personnel screening and development for word processing operators.

Description: 35-item paper-pencil test measuring the ability to reason logically and flexibly with information and instructions presented in symbols. The candidate is presented with a row of letters in boxes with symbols attached, which indicate how the letters must be altered. The candidate chooses the correct response from five alternatives. One of five tests in the Word Processing Aptitude Battery. Examiner required. Suitable for group use.
BRITISH PUBLISHER

Timed: 15 minutes

Scoring: Hand key; may be computer scored

Cost: Manual and user's guide $105.00; 10 test booklets (includes all 5 tests) $168.00; 5 administration cards $63.00; 5 scoring keys $84.00; 10 answer sheets and profile chart $63.00; 10 group score sheets $4.20; annual license $220.50

Publisher: Saville & Holdsworth Ltd.

WORD PROCESSING APTITUDE BATTERY: NUMERICAL COMPUTATION (WP5)
Saville & Holdsworth Ltd. Staff

Adult

Purpose: Measures basic mathematics abilities. Used in personnel screening and development for word processor operators.

Description: 35-item paper-pencil test assessing mathematics computation skills and the ability to recognize and understand simple number relationships. The test emphasizes straightforward computation. Candidates select the correct number to complete a sequence or equation from five options. The test is useful for positions requiring complex tabular work and calculations. One of five tests in the Word Processing Aptitude Battery. Examiner required. Suitable for group use.
BRITISH PUBLISHER

Timed: 10 minutes

Scoring: Hand key; may be computer scored

Cost: Manual and user's guide $105.00; 10 test booklets (includes all 5 tests) $168.00; 5 administration cards $63.00; 5 scoring keys $84.00; 10 answer sheets and profile chart $63.00; 10 group score sheets $4.20; annual license $220.50

Publisher: Saville & Holdsworth Ltd.

WORD PROCESSING APTITUDE BATTERY: VERBAL SKILLS (WP1)
Saville & Holdsworth Ltd. Staff

Adult

Purpose: Measures basic language arts skills. Used in personnel screening and development for word processor operators.

Description: 30-item paper-pencil test of word meaning, spelling, and grammar. Emphasis is on vocabulary skills that word processor operators would need for everyday work. For each question, candidates choose a pair of words from five alternatives to correctly complete a sentence. One of five tests in the Word Processing Aptitude Battery. The test is used with WP2 and WP3 to screen for jobs involving creating documents, editing, filing, and moving blocks of text. Examiner required. Suitable for group use.
BRITISH PUBLISHER

Timed: 10 minutes

Scoring: Hand key; may be computer scored

Cost: Manual and user's guide $105.00; 10 test booklets (includes all 5 tests) $168.00; 5 administration cards $63.00; 5 scoring keys $84.00; 10 answer sheets and profile chart $63.00; 10 group score sheets $4.20; annual license $220.50

Publisher: Saville & Holdsworth Ltd.

WORD PROCESSING APTITUDE BATTERY: WRITTEN INSTRUCTIONS (WP3)
Saville & Holdsworth Ltd. Staff

Adult

Purpose: Measures ability to understand and follow complex written instructions. Used in personnel screening and development for word processor operators.

Description: 36-item paper-pencil test of ability to follow complex written directions. The candidate is presented with office-type procedures in a written passage and must retrieve the relevant information to select the correct procedure in each of three cases from five alternatives. One of five tests in the Word Processing Aptitude Battery. The test is used with WP1 and WP2 to screen for jobs involving creating documents, editing, filing, and moving blocks of text. Examiner required. Suitable for group use.

BRITISH PUBLISHER

Timed: 12 minutes

Scoring: Hand key; may be computer scored

Cost: Manual and user's guide $105.00; 10 test booklets (includes all 5 tests) $168.00; 5 administration cards $63.00; 5 scoring keys $84.00; 10 answer sheets and profile chart $63.00; 10 group score sheets $4.20; annual license $220.50

Publisher: Saville & Holdsworth Ltd.

THE WORD PROCESSING OPERATOR ASSESSMENT BATTERY
S. Berke

Adult

Purpose: Determines a person's suitability for work as a word processor operator. Used to supplement interviews,

reference checking, and machine tests in the hiring process.

Description: 5-item paper-pencil test measuring attention to detail, ability to solve problems, manual dexterity, numerical skill, alphabetizing, filing, and coding. Examiner required. Suitable for group use. Available in French.

Timed: 30 minutes

Scoring: Scoring service provided

Cost: Complete (test kit and evaluation) $55.00

Publisher: Wolfe Personnel Testing and Training Systems, Inc.

WORD PROCESSING TEST (WPT)

Job applicants and employees

Purpose: Measures ability to input and edit both text and tables on a word processing machine. Used as a selection or promotion tool with job applicants or current employees.

Description: Computer-administered measure of speed and accuracy of word processing performance. The test assesses an individual's ability to operate actual word processing equipment used on the job. Materials include a manual, test booklet, edit disk containing original documents that the examinee must edit according to instructions given in the test booklet, and a personal scoring record. Two alternate forms, A and B, are available. Form A is sold only to personnel departments of businesses and industries. Examiner required. Not suitable for group use.

Untimed: 25-35 minutes

Scoring: Hand key

Cost: Complete set (5 test booklets, manual, 10 personal scoring records, scoring keys, edit disk) $295.00

Publisher: The Psychological Corporation

WORD PROCESSOR ASSESSMENT BATTERY (WPAB)

Adult

Purpose: Measures abilities related to success in word-processing occupations. Used in business and education for selection and placement.

Description: Multiple-item paper-pencil and task-performance test in three parts assessing machine aptitude, typing speed and accuracy, and machine transcription abilities. Part I tests understanding of word processing equipment functions, including data storage, file creation, manipulation, and others. Part II tests the ability to type a business letter from typed copy with handwritten corrections and insertions. Part III tests the ability to accurately transcribe dictated material and produce a letter with correct spelling, punctuation, and format. Examiner required. Suitable for group use.

Timed: 76 minutes

Scoring: Hand key

Cost: 10 test booklets $60.00; manual $25.00; dictation cassette for Part III $25.00

Publisher: Science Research Associates, Inc.

Engineering

ADVANCED TEST BATTERY: DIAGRAMMING (ATB:DA5)
Refer to page 793.

ADVANCED TEST BATTERY: SPATIAL REASONING (ATB:ST7)
Refer to page 794.

CLOSURE FLEXIBILITY (CONCEALED FIGURES)
Refer to page 975.

ELECTRICAL SOPHISTICATION TEST
Stanley Ciesla

Adult

Purpose: Assesses electrical knowledge. Used to evaluate job applicants.

Description: Multiple-item paper-pencil test of sophistication of electrical knowledge. The test discriminates between persons with electrical know-how and those with none and between electrical engineers and other types of engineers. Examiner required. Suitable for group use.

Untimed: 10 minutes

Scoring: Hand key

Cost: Specimen set $4.00; 25 tests $4.00

Publisher: Psychometric Affiliates

ENGINEER PERFORMANCE DESCRIPTION FORM (EPDF)
John C. South

Adult

Purpose: Evaluates on-the-job performance of nonsupervisory engineers who have less than five years professional experience. Used to counsel and develop junior engineering staff and to assess training programs.

Description: Multiple-item paper-pencil observational forced-choice rating scale. Six performance factors are measured: communication, relating to others, administrative ability, motivation, technical knowledge ability, and self-sufficiency. The supervisory manual contains instructions for using and completing the scale, with guidelines for interpreting the results. Ratings for each of the six factors and an index of overall performance are provided. Percentiles are provided for overall scores. Ratings are completed by the supervisor. Examiner required. Suitable for group use.

Untimed: 20-45 minutes

Scoring: Hand key; scoring service available

Cost: Test $0.75; scoring service $2.00 per scale; manual $10.00

Publisher: John C. South

GUILFORD-ZIMMERMAN APTITUDE SURVEY: SPATIAL VISUALIZATION (GZAS:SV)
Refer to page 810.

I.P.I. APTITUDE—INTELLIGENCE TEST SERIES: DIMENSION
Refer to page 812.

I.P.I. JOB TEST FIELD SERIES: ENGINEER
Refer to page 817.

INDIVIDUAL QUALIFICATION FORM
Morris I. Stein

Adult

Purpose: Determines a profile of the type of individual needed for a specific job in technical industries and research and development (R & D) organizations. Used to improve placement procedures of scientists, engineers, and research personnel.

Description: 30-item paper-pencil questionnaire elicits an accurate statement from the supervisor of a job's requirements, opportunities, and limitations. The items are specified in terms of role requirements in order to facilitate the screening of job applicants. The test is restricted to R & D personnel. Self-administered by supervisor or administrator. Suitable for group use.

Untimed: 20 minutes

Scoring: Examiner evaluated

Cost: $2.50 each

Publisher: Morris I. Stein

Information and availability unconfirmed; no publisher response.

MINNESOTA ENGINEERING ANALOGIES TEST
Refer to page 715.

NIIP ENGINEERING SELECTION TEST BATTERY: ENGINEERING ARITHMETIC TEST EA4
Refer to page 716.

NIIP ENGINEERING SELECTION TEST BATTERY: GROUP TEST 82
Refer to page 716.

NIIP ENGINEERING SELECTION TEST BATTERY: GROUP TESTS 70 AND 70B
Refer to page 716.

NIIP ENGINEERING SELECTION TEST BATTERY: GROUP TESTS 90A AND 90B
Refer to page 716.

NIIP ENGINEERING SELECTION TEST BATTERY: VINCENT MECHANICAL DIAGRAMS TEST (REVISED)
Refer to page 717.

NIIP TESTS—ENGINEERING SELECTION TEST BATTERY
Refer to page 717.

NON-VERBAL REASONING
Richardson, Bellows, Henry and Company, Inc.

Adult

Purpose: Assesses nonverbal reasoning (spatial analysis) abilities. Used with applicants to technical and engineering positions.

Description: 45-item paper-pencil test of nonverbal reasoning. Each test item consists of 10 figures, the first 4 of which are alike. Applicants select two of the last six figures which are like the first four. A variety of elements are tested, including squareness, angle bisection, differential shading, number relationships, and arrangement relationships. Examinees must be able to read numbers. The test has been used successfully with applicants with low educational levels and with technical and managerial personnel with high educational levels. Norms are available for male technical and professional employees, managers and executives, mechanical and operating employees and applicants, and sales employees and applicants. Norms are also available for female applicants for production jobs. The test is available in a long and a short form. Examiner required. Suitable for group use.

Timed: 15 minutes

Scoring: Hand key

Cost: Long form 1-24 packages $19.00; Short form 1-24 packages $18.00; score key $3.00; manual $2.00

Publisher: Richardson, Bellows, Henry and Company, Inc.

PRIMARY MECHANICAL ABILITY TEST
Refer to page 981.

PURDUE BLUEPRINT READING TEST
Refer to page 836.

PURDUE CREATIVITY TEST
Douglas Harris and C.H. Lawshe

Adult

Purpose: Measures creativity in engineering. Used to identify engineers with capacity for production of new ideas.

Description: Multiple-item paper-pencil test measuring creative potential in design production, research, and development. The tests yield three scores: fluency, flexibility and total creativity. Materials include two equivalent forms, G and H. The test is restricted to companies with qualified personnel administrators and to psychologists using tests for instruction or vocational guidance. Examiner required. Suitable for group use.

Untimed: Not available

Scoring: Hand key

Cost: Specimen set (forms G and H, manual) $1.00; 25 tests (specify form), manual $11.00

Publisher: Purdue Research Foundation/ University Book Store

RESEARCH PERSONNEL REVIEW FORM
Morris I. Stein

Adult

Purpose: Evaluates the performance of personnel in research and development organizations. Measures strengths and weaknesses of scientists and engineers in this field.

Description: 120-item paper-pencil questionnaire assesses a scientist's or engineer's work in terms of quantity, quality, and creativity. The test items cover administrative, employee, social, scientific, and professional factors involved in the individual's performance. Self-administered by the individual being reviewed. Suitable for group use.

Untimed: 30 minutes

Scoring: Examiner evaluated

Cost: $2.50 per copy

Publisher: Morris I. Stein

Information and availability unconfirmed; no publisher response.

SURVEYS OF RESEARCH ENVIRONMENTS
Morris I. Stein

Adult

Purpose: Obtains information from scientists and engineers concerning their job situations and the demands being placed upon them. Evaluates morale and identifies problem areas in research and development (R & D) organizations.

Description: 189-item paper-pencil inventory requiring research and administrative personnel to evaluate the organization and factors that lead to success and creativity on the job. The items are presented in terms of the role requirements of scientific, professional, administrative, and social relations employees. Self-administered. The test is restricted to R & D organizations. Suitable for group use.

Untimed: 45 minutes
Scoring: Examiner evaluated
Cost: $2.50 per copy
Publisher: Morris I. Stein

Information and availability unconfirmed; no publisher response.

Intelligence and Related

ADAPTABILITY TEST
Joseph Tiffin and C.H. Lawshe

Adult

Purpose: Measures mental adaptability and alertness. Distinguishes between people who should be placed in jobs requiring more learning ability and those who should be in more simple or routine jobs.

Description: 70-item paper-pencil test consisting primarily of verbal items. The test predicts success in a variety of business and industrial situations. The test is available in two forms, A and B. Examiner required. Suitable for group use.

Timed: 15 minutes
Scoring: Hand key
Cost: 25 test booklets (specify form) $26.50; examiner's manual $10.00
Publisher: Science Research Associates, Inc.

ADVANCED PERSONNEL TEST
W.S. Miller

Adult

Purpose: Assesses verbal reasoning ability. Used for employee selection in business, industry, and government.

Description: Multiple-item paper-pencil test of verbal reasoning ability. This business test is comparable to the Miller Analogies Test. Examiner required. Suitable for group use.

Untimed: Not available
Scoring: Scoring service available

Cost: Contact publisher
Publisher: Admissions and Credentialing Group/The Psychological Corporation

BRUCE VOCABULARY INVENTORY
Martin M. Bruce

Adult

Purpose: Determines how a subject's vocabulary compares to the vocabulary of individuals employed in various business occupations.

Description: 100-item paper-pencil multiple-choice test in which the subject matches one of four alternative words with a key vocabulary word. Measures the ability to recognize and comprehend vocabulary words. The underlying assumption of the test is that the larger the vocabulary, the higher a person's IQ. The subject's score can be compared to the scores of executives, middle-managers, white collar workers, engineers, blue collar workers, and the total employed population. Self-administered. Suitable for group use.

Untimed: 15-20 minutes
Scoring: Hand key
Cost: Package of tests $25.75; manual $3.15; hand key $1.00; IBM scoring stencils $3.50; IBM answer sheets $10.50
Publisher: Martin M. Bruce, Ph.D., Publishers

CAREER DECISION SCALE (2ND EDITION)
Samuel H. Osipow,
Clarke G. Carney, Jane Winer,
Barbara Yanico,
and Maryanne Koschir

Adolescent
Grades 9-college

Purpose: Identifies barriers preventing an individual from making career decisions. Used as a basis for career counseling, to monitor the effectiveness of career counseling programs, and for research on career indecisiveness.

Description: 18-item paper-pencil inventory assessing a limited number of circumstances which cause problems in reaching and implementing educational and career decisions. Each item describes a separate reason for career indecisiveness. Individuals rate each item on a 4-point scale from one ("not like me") to four ("like me") to indicate the extent to which each item describes their personal situation. The manual includes data regarding validity and reliability and norms for various age and grade levels. Examiner required. Suitable for group use.

Untimed: 10-15 minutes
Scoring: Examiner evaluated
Cost: 25 scale booklets $7.00; manual $7.00
Publisher: Marathon Consulting and Press

CLOSURE SPEED (GESTALT COMPLETION)
L.L. Thurstone and T.E. Jeffrey

Adult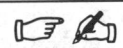

Purpose: Evaluates visual and space perception skills, ideational fluency, and creativity of adults. Used for evaluation of perceptual skills.

Description: 24-item paper-pencil test measuring the subject's ability to construct a total picture from incomplete or ambiguous material. Basic writing skills are required. Examiner required. Suitable for group use.
Timed: 3 minutes
Scoring: Hand key
Cost: Specimen set $8.00; 25 test booklets $11.25
Publisher: London House Press

COMPOUND SERIES TEST (CST)
J.R. Morrisby

Ages 6-adult

Purpose: Assesses general intelligence by measuring the capacity to learn through the systematic analysis of a problem. Used in industry for personnel selection, placement, and promotion.

Description: 60-item paper-pencil test requiring persistence, concentration, and directed effort in order to solve problems.

Each item presents a pattern drawn as a string of beads varying in size, shape, and color. The subject indicates which two beads from a choice of eight continue the pattern. The same type of item, increasing in difficulty and complexity, is used throughout, thereby measuring the ability to direct and control the investment of intellectual effort. Because the test does not depend on such acquired skills as the use of words or numbers, it is suitable for use with educationally and socially disadvantaged subjects. In addition, the colors are arranged so that colorblind subjects can distinguish them. If the CST is used in screening for higher-level occupations, it should be supplemented by other tests, such as the full Differential Test Battery of E.I.T.S. The CST is restricted to examiners who provide evidence of adequate training and practical experience in the use of such tests. Examiner required. Suitable for group use.
BRITISH PUBLISHER
Timed: 20-30 minutes
Scoring: Hand key; examiner evaluated; may be computer scored
Cost: Contact publisher
Publisher: Educational and Industrial Test Services Ltd.

CONCEPT ATTAINMENT TEST
J.M. Schepers

Adolescent, adult

Purpose: Measures conceptual and rational mental abilities of science and technical graduates. Used for employee screening and selection.

Description: Multiple-item paper-pencil test measuring the ability to attain concepts through the use of rational strategies of thought. The test consists of 10 problems in which solutions can be obtained only provided a well-defined and logical strategy is followed consistently. Norms are provided for science graduates. The test is restricted to competent persons properly registered with the South African Medical and Dental Council. Examiner required. Suitable for group use. Afrikaans version available.
SOUTH AFRICAN PUBLISHER
Timed: 50 minutes

Scoring: Hand key; examiner evaluated
Cost: Contact publisher
Publisher: National Institute for Personnel Research

THE CULTURE FAIR SERIES: SCALES 1, 2, 3
Refer to page 504.

DAP QUALITY SCALE (DRAW-A-PERSON)
Herman J.P. Schubert

Adolescent, adult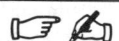

Purpose: Measures intelligence and motivation. Used for personnel selection.

Description: Paper-pencil free-response test assessing nonverbal intelligence in which the individual is asked to draw a picture of a person. The drawing is scored according to objective guidelines. The overall quality score contributes to the prediction of available intelligence and motivation. Examiner required. Suitable for group use.
Untimed: Varies
Scoring: Examiner evaluated
Cost: Test kit $17.50
Publisher: Herman J.P. Schubert

DEDUCTIVE REASONING TEST

Adolescent, adult

Purpose: Measures logical thinking abilities. Used with matriculants and higher for purposes of employee screening and selection for a wide variety of technical positions.

Description: Multiple-item paper-pencil test based on formal syllogisms. Each syllogism contains either factual, contrafactual, or nonsense premises. The test provides a measure of the ability to deduce logically correct conclusions from the information contained in the premises. The test is restricted to competent persons properly registered with the South African Medical and Dental Council. Examiner required. Suitable for group use. Afrikaans version available.
SOUTH AFRICAN PUBLISHER

Timed: 40 minutes
Scoring: Hand key; examiner evaluated
Cost: Contact publisher
Publisher: National Institute for Personnel Research

EMPLOYEE APTITUDE SURVEY TEST #10—SYMBOLIC REASONING (EAS #10)
Refer to page 803.

FIGURE CLASSIFICATION TEST

Adolescent, adult

Purpose: Measures abstract reasoning ability. Used with examinees with seven to nine years of education for purposes of employee selection and placement.

Description: Multiple-item paper-pencil test measuring conceptual reasoning ability by requiring the examinee to analyze sets of figures and deduce the basic relationships that divide each set into two groups. The relationships are indicated by uniformity, symmetry, inversion, repetition, and series. The test is restricted to competent persons properly registered with the South African Medical and Dental Council. Examiner required. Suitable for group use. Afrikaans version available.
SOUTH AFRICAN PUBLISHER
Timed: 1 hour
Scoring: Hand key; examiner evaluated
Cost: Contact publisher
Publisher: National Institute for Personnel Research

FORM SERIES TEST A

Adolescent, adult

Purpose: Measures nonverbal reasoning ability. Used with groups of individuals with six years or less of education for purposes of employee selection and placement.

Description: Multiple-item apparatus test measuring nonverbal reasoning ability using a board printed with a series of patterns made up of forms of different sizes, shapes, and colors. Each pattern must be continued by inferring from the given series of shapes and colors what the next two must be. The test is restricted to competent persons properly registered with the South African Medical and Dental Council. Examiner required. Suitable for group use. Afrikaans version available. SOUTH AFRICAN PUBLISHER

Timed: 25 minutes

Scoring: Hand key; examiner evaluated

Cost: Contact publisher

Publisher: National Institute for Personnel Research

GENERAL ABILITY BATTERY
Refer to page 504.

GENERAL ABILITY TESTS: NUMERICAL (GAT NUMERICAL)
J.R. Morrisby

Ages 11 and older

Purpose: Measures numerical intelligence. Used for personnel selection in most occupations, especially those in which numerical concepts are involved and the ability to think quantitatively is at a premium. Also used as a predictor of academic success.

Description: Multiple-item paper-pencil test in three parts. Part 1 requires the subject to indicate whether simple addition and multiplication calculations, worked out, are correct or incorrect. Part 2 consists of a number series in which the degree of computation required is reduced, but the dependence on the subject's ability to see numerical relationships is increased. In Part 3, the subject completes matrixes with one element missing. The computational requirement in Part 3 is small, but the requirement to see into numerical relationships is at a maximum. The mental functions involved in each subtest are arranged to give a progression throughout the test, from a loading of speed of apprehension in Part 1 to a heavy loading of insight or intuitive power in Part 3. Materials include booklets, scoring keys, the specimen set, and the manual. Tests of verbal intelligence and of nonverbal, or perceptual intelligence, also are available in this three-part GAT series. The series has been constructed as a

matched trio to provide differential assessment of the main areas of mental ability, but any one test may be used alone. The GAT is restricted to examiners who provide evidence of adequate training and practical experience in the use of such tests. Examiner required. Suitable for group use. BRITISH PUBLISHER

Timed: 35 minutes

Scoring: Hand key; examiner evaluated; may be computer scored

Cost: Contact publisher

Publisher: Educational and Industrial Test Service Ltd.

GENERAL ABILITY TESTS: PERCEPTUAL (GAT PERCEPTUAL)
J.R. Morrisby

Ages 11 and older

Purpose: Measures nonverbal, perceptual intelligence. Used for personnel selection in most occupations, especially engineering, design, and scientific work which deals with real objects rather than verbal or numerical concepts.

Description: Multiple-item paper-pencil multiple-choice test in three categories. Part 1 requires the subject to determine which meaningless figures shown are identical with a given example. In Part 2, the subject classifies four of six figures shown in each item and indicates the two that do not belong. In Part 3, the subject selects a pair of figures analogous with a given pair, to test insight into relationships between perceptual forms. The mental functions involved in each subtest are arranged to give a progression throughout the test, from a loading of speed of apprehension in Part 1 to a heavy loading of insight or intuitive power in Part 3. Materials include booklets, scoring keys, the specimen set, and the manual. Tests of verbal intelligence and numerical intelligence also are available in this three-part GAT series. The series has been constructed as a matched trio to provide differential assessment of the main areas of mental ability, but any one test may be used alone. The GAT is restricted to examiners who provide evidence of

adequate training and practical experience in the use of such tests. Examiner required. Suitable for group use.
BRITISH PUBLISHER

Timed: 27 minutes

Scoring: Hand key; examiner evaluated; may be computer scored

Cost: Contact publisher

Publisher: Educational and Industrial Test Service Ltd.

GENERAL ABILITY TESTS: VERBAL (GAT VERBAL)
J.R. Morrisby

Ages 11 and older

Purpose: Measures verbal intelligence. Used for selection in most occupations in which a good level of communicating skill is required or written work is emphasized. Also used as a predictor of academic success.

Description: Multiple-item paper-pencil multiple-choice instrument consisting of three separately timed subtests. Part 1 requires the subject to indicate whether pairs of words are synonyms or antonyms. Part 2 consists of word classification in which the vocabulary requirement is somewhat reduced but dependence on insight into relationships between verbal concepts is increased. In Part 3, the subject makes up pairs of words analogous with a given pair. The demands on vocabulary are low but demands on insight into verbal relationships are at a maximum. The mental functions involved in each subtest are arranged to give a progression throughout the test, from a loading of speed of apprehension in Part 1 to a heavy loading of insight or intuitive power in Part 3. Materials include booklets, scoring keys, the specimen set, and the manual. Tests of numerical intelligence and nonverbal, or perceptual intelligence, also are available in this three-part GAT series. The series has been constructed as a matched trio to provide differential assessment of the main areas of mental ability, but any one test may be used alone. The GAT is restricted to examiners who provide evidence of adequate train-

ing and practical experience in the use of such tests. Examiner required. Suitable for group use.
BRITISH PUBLISHER

Timed: 35 minutes

Scoring: Hand key; examiner evaluated; may be computer scored

Cost: Contact publisher

Publisher: Educational and Industrial Test Service Ltd.

GUILFORD-ZIMMERMAN APTITUDE SURVEY (GZAS)
Refer to page 809.

GUILFORD-ZIMMERMAN APTITUDE SURVEY: GENERAL REASONING (GZAS:GR)
Refer to page 809.

GUILFORD-ZIMMERMAN APTITUDE SURVEY: VERBAL COMPREHENSION (GZAS:VC)
Refer to page 811.

HUMAN INFORMATION PROCESSING SURVEY: HIP SURVEY
E. Paul Torrance, William Taggart, and Barbara Taggart

Adult

Purpose: Assesses the manner in which an individual processes information. Used as a training tool in human resource development programs and for research purposes.

Description: Multiple-item paper-pencil inventory assessing an individual's processing preference: left hemisphere, right hemisphere, integrated, or mixed. The results provide a description of a person's overall approach and specific tactics in problem solving and decision making. The manual outlines applications of the survey and its use in a one-day workshop. A research edition is available. Examiner required. Suitable for group use.

Untimed: Varies

Scoring: Examiner evaluated

Cost: Professional edition starter set (manual, 10 survey forms, 10 profile forms) $34.95

Publisher: Scholastic Testing Service, Inc.

LEARNING ABILITY PROFILE (LAP)
Margarita Henning

Adult

Purpose: Assesses a person's ability to learn. May be used to determine the potential for job success.

Description: 80-item paper-pencil test measuring overall learning ability, flexibility, frustration level, problem-solving ability, and decisiveness. Examiner required. Suitable for group use. Available in French.
CANADIAN PUBLISHER

Untimed: 1 hour

Scoring: Hand key; examiner evaluated

Cost: Complete set (2 test booklets, answer sheets, manual) $100.00

Publisher: Wolfe Personnel Testing and Training Systems, Inc.

MD5 MENTAL ABILITY TEST
D. Mackenzie Davey

Adult

Purpose: Assesses a wide range of educational and ability levels of adults. Used for staff selection, placement, and counseling.

Description: 57-item paper-pencil test used with adults, including supervisors and managers, for measuring mental ability. The test involves finding missing letters, numbers, or words. Norms exist for several managerial groups, and the test is correlated with other mental ability tests. Examiner/self-administered. Suitable for group use.
BRITISH PUBLISHER

Untimed: 15 minutes

Scoring: Hand key

Cost: Specimen set (test booklet, answer key, and manual) £5.45

Publisher: The Test Agency Ltd.

MENTAL ABILITIES— INVENTORY II
Jack Harris Hazlehurst

Adolescent, adult

Purpose: Measures the mental ability of individuals ages 16 and older exclusive of educational level. Used for employee selection and placement.

Description: 50-item paper-pencil multiple-choice and free-response test measuring an individual's ability to solve problems involving word meanings and verbally constructed conceptual relations and requiring the manipulation of number relationships. The problems included are designed to sample the creative, reproductive, and relational aspects of imagination. Examiner required. Suitable for group use.

Timed: 15 minutes

Scoring: Hand key

Cost: 25 tests $6.00; monograph of instructions and critical statistical evaluation, scoring key $2.00

Publisher: Stevens, Thurow and Associates

MENTAL ALERTNESS— ADVANCED AND INTERMEDIATE

Adult

Purpose: Measures general intelligence for purposes of employee screening and selection. Used with matriculants and higher and individuals with 10-12 years of schooling.

Description: Two paper-pencil tests measuring general intelligence, mainly verbal, at two levels of education. The High Level Battery test is suitable for matriculants and higher. The Intermediate Battery is for candidates with 10-12 years of education. Both tests are available in two parallel forms. Norms are provided for each test. The tests are restricted to competent persons properly registered with the South African Medical and Dental Council. Examiner required. Suitable for group use. Afrikaans version available.
SOUTH AFRICAN PUBLISHER

Timed: 35 minutes each

Scoring: Hand key; examiner evaluated

Cost: Contact publisher

Publisher: National Institute for Personnel Research

MORRISBY DIFFERENTIAL TEST BATTERY (DTB)
J.R. Morrisby

**Adolescent, adult
Ages 13 and older**

Purpose: Evaluates a person's intellectual structure and basic personality characteristics. Used to predict the likelihood of success in a large number of occupations and modes of behavior in a variety of situations.

Description: Paper-pencil battery of 12 intelligence and personality tests designed to provide a total assessment of an individual, as well as meaningful single test scores. The four intelligence tests are the Compound Series Test, a measure of basic intellectual power, and the general ability tests: Verbal, Numerical, and Perceptual. The Shapes Test and Mechanical Ability Test provide measures of spatial and mechanical ability to show the subject's level of practicality and analysis and overview abilities. The six speed tests-Conceptual Speed, Perseveration, Word Fluency, Ideational Fluency, Motor Speed, and Motor Skill—measure abilities, tendency toward understanding, and qualities such as leadership, confidence, flexibility, resistance to change, speed of awareness, personal commitment, tenacity, and initiative. Materials include one-time test forms, reusable booklets, a manual, and scoring keys. A scoring service, interpretation service, and grading service are also available. The battery is restricted to examiners who provide evidence of adequate training and practical experience in the use of such tests. Examiner required. Suitable for group use.
BRITISH PUBLISHER

Untimed: 3 hours, 10 minutes

Scoring: Examiner evaluated; may be computer scored

Cost: Contact publisher

Publisher: Educational and Industrial Test Services Ltd.

MULTIDIMENSIONAL APTITUDE BATTERY—FORM L
Refer to page 28.

NON-VERBAL REASONING
Raymond J. Corsini

Adult

Purpose: Assesses logical reasoning ability in nonverbal situations. Used for industrial job screening and selection and for vocational counseling.

Description: 44-item paper-pencil test measuring the capacity to reason logically. The subject studies one picture and then selects from among four others the one which best compliments the first picture. Examiner required. Suitable for group use.

Untimed: 20 minutes

Scoring: Hand key; may be machine scored

Cost: Specimen set $8.00; 25 test booklets $11.25

Publisher: London House Press

PATTERN RELATIONS TEST

Adult

Purpose: Measures inductive reasoning abilities. Used with university level and graduate job applicants for a variety of science and technical positions.

Description: Multiple-item paper-pencil test measuring the ability to recognize associated concepts that fit sets of data and the consequent forming and testing of hypotheses. The test is similar to Raven's Progressive Matrices. Norms have been established on scientific research workers with degrees and first-year engineering students. The test is restricted to competent persons properly registered with the South African Medical and Dental Council. Examiner required. Suitable for group use. Afrikaans version available.
SOUTH AFRICAN PUBLISHER

Timed: 50 minutes each

Scoring: Hand key; examiner evaluated

Cost: Contact publisher
Publisher: National Institute for Personnel Research

PERFORMANCE EFFICIENCY TEST (PET)
Thomas Rex Long

Adult

Purpose: Measures the ability to use intellectual potential for satisfactory performance in any job situation. Used for employee screening and placement.

Description: Multiple-item oral-response test assessing intellectual ability. Applicants read color names or identify colors from three stimulus cards. Card A contains four color names, printed in black, in random order. Card B contains four colors, printed in quarter-inch squares. Card C contains color names, printed in colors different from what the word reads. The number of incorrect answers identifies applicants least likely to compete successfully. The format suggests nothing regarding the psychological variables being measured and, consequently, is nonthreatening to the subject. Because subjects are unaware of what constitutes an acceptable time score, "faking" is no problem. Examiner required. Not suitable for group use.

Untimed: 5-6 minutes
Scoring: Examiner evaluated
Cost: Complete set (manual, three stimulus cards) $7.25
Publisher: Stoelting Company

PROFESSIONAL EMPLOYMENT TEST

Adult

Purpose: Measures three cognitive abilities—verbal comprehension, quantitative problem solving, and reasoning—important for successful performance in many professional occupations. Used to select professional, technical, and managerial personnel.

Description: 40-item paper-pencil multiple-choice test measuring the ability to understand and interpret complex information, determine the appropriate mathematical procedures to solve problems, and analyze and evaluate information to arrive at correct conclusions. The test includes four item types: reading comprehension (the examinee reads a paragraph and selects the alternative that best reflects the content of the paragraph), quantitative reasoning (the examinee reviews a word problem and applies the appropriate mathematical procedures in order to select the correct answer), tabular completion (the examinee, using simple arithmetic, determines the value of missing entries in numerical tables), inference (the examinee determines whether conclusions to given sets of premises that are accepted as true are justified). The test is available in two alternate forms. For test security purposes, the test is available for lease only. Examiner required. Suitable for group use.

Timed: 1 hour, 10 minutes
Scoring: Hand key; may be computer scored
Cost: $5.00 per test administration
Publisher: Psychological Services, Inc.

PURDUE NON-LANGUAGE PERSONNEL TEST
Joseph Tiffin

Adolescent, adult

Purpose: Assesses general mental ability. Used for evaluation of applicants who cannot be fairly tested using verbal tests.

Description: Multiple-item paper-pencil nonverbal measure of intelligence. Items consist entirely of geometric forms. Materials include two forms, A-S and B-S. Sale is restricted to companies employing qualified personnel administrators and to psychologists using tests for instruction or vocational guidance. Examiner required. Suitable for group use.

Untimed: Not available
Scoring: Hand key
Cost: Specimen set (Form A-S, Form B-S, manual, keys) $1.00; 25 tests, manual, key (specify form) $7.50
Publisher: Purdue Research Foundation/ University Book Store

THE RBH TEST OF LEARNING ABILITY, FORMS ST AND STR
Richardson, Bellows, Henry and Company, Inc.

Adult

Purpose: Assesses general abilities. Used for screening, selection, placement, and upgrading of personnel.

Description: 108-item paper-pencil multiple-choice test assessing general ability and intelligence. Examinees must choose the correct answer for each problem from four alternatives. Answers are recorded in the test booklet. This test is a compilation of two shorter forms (S and T) and provides a "floor" low enough to accommodate all but the illiterate and mentally deficient and a "ceiling" high enough for individuals with upper levels of education or ability. The test is organized so that each three consecutive items contains a block-counting, vocabulary, and arithmetic item. Each series of items is more difficult than the preceding series. The three types of items can be scored separately. Two forms, ST and STR, are available. Reading and understanding directions is considered a part of the administration time of the ST form; it is not considered part of the STR form. Normative data are available for male technical and professional employees, managers and executives, clerical employees, sales employees and applicants, mechanical and operating employees and applicants, and industrial foremen and supervisors. Examiner required. Suitable for group use.

Timed: 25 minutes

Scoring: Hand key

Cost: 1-24 packages $22.00; score key $3.00; manual $2.00

Publisher: Richardson, Bellows, Henry and Company, Inc.

REVISED BETA EXAMINATION-SECOND EDITION (BETA-II)
D.E. Kellogg and N.W. Morton

Adult

Purpose: Measures mental ability of non-reading applicants. Used for testing applicants in settings with large numbers of unskilled workers.

Description: Six separately timed paper-pencil tests of mental ability, including mazes, coding, paper formboards, picture completion, clerical checking, and picture absurdities. Directions are given orally to the applicant. Examiner required. Suitable for group use. Available in Spanish.

Untimed: 30 minutes

Scoring: Hand key

Cost: Specimen set (test, demonstration booklet, manual) $11.00; 25 tests, demonstration booklet, manual, key $31.00

Publisher: The Psychological Corporation

SCOTT MENTAL ALERTNESS TEST

Adult

Purpose: Measures general mental alertness. Used for employee selection and vocational guidance counseling.

Description: Multiple-item paper-pencil test assessing arithmetic reasoning, quickness and accuracy of judgment, clearness of perception, degree of comprehension, and ability to follow instructions. The time limits are so short that the most alert person cannot make a perfect score, yet the test is easy enough to permit the less mentally alert to make an appreciable score. Test items are as free as possible from the influence of formal schooling, and no difficult words are used. Examiner required. Suitable for group use.

Timed: 20 minutes

Scoring: Examiner evaluated

Cost: Test kit (50 test booklets, manual) $19.75

Publisher: Stoelting Company

SHIP DESTINATION TEST (SD)
Paul R. Christensen and J.P. Guilford

Adolescent, adult
Grades 10 and above

Purpose: Measures general reasoning ability among high-school and college students and adults. Used for job selection when arithmetic reasoning is important.

Description: 48-item paper-pencil multiple-choice test measuring the cognition of semantic systems by means of a well-disguised arithmetic-reasoning test. The test items are steeply graded in complexity and difficulty. Nine practice problems are included. The test emphasizes problem solving that involves recognizing interrelationships of variables or elements rather than numerical computation. Test materials consist of answer sheets and reusable test booklets. Norms are provided for college groups. The test is restricted to A.P.A. membership or equivalent. Examiner required. Suitable for group use.

Timed: 15 minutes

Scoring: Hand key; may be computer scored

Cost: 25 tests $8.00; 25 answer sheets $4.00; manual $1.00; hand key $2.50

Publisher: Sheridan Psychological Services, Inc.

SRA NONVERBAL FORM
Robert N. McMurry and
Joseph E. King

Adult

Purpose: Assesses general learning ability. Measures learning potential of individuals who have difficulty reading or understanding the English language. Used with adults with a high-school education or less and for employee selection and placement.

Description: 60-item paper-pencil test consisting of five drawings, each measuring recognition of differences. Examiner required. Suitable for group use.

Timed: 10 minutes

Scoring: Hand key

Cost: 25 test booklets $35.00; examiner's manual $10.00

Publisher: Science Research Associates, Inc.

SRA PICTORIAL REASONING TEST (PRT)
Robert N. McMurry and
Phyllis D. Arnold

Adolescent, adult

Purpose: Measures general reasoning ability of students, especially older non-

readers. Used with individuals with a high-school education or less, for predicting job success, and as a basic screening test for entry-level jobs.

Description: 80-item paper-pencil pictorial test measuring aspects of learning ability. The test is culturally unbiased and does not require previously learned reading skills. Examiner required. Suitable for group use.

Timed: 15 minutes (may also be given untimed)

Scoring: Hand key

Cost: 25 test booklets $32.00; examiner's manual $10.00

Publisher: Science Research Associates, Inc.

TEST OF LEARNING ABILITY, FORMS S, T, DS-12, AND DT-12
Richardson, Bellows, Henry and
Company, Inc.

Adult

Purpose: Assesses general abilities. Used for screening, selection, placement, and upgrading of personnel.

Description: 54-item paper-pencil multiple-choice test assessing general ability or intelligence. The test is organized so that each three consecutive items contain a block-counting, vocabulary, and arithmetic item. Each series of items is more difficult than the preceding series. The three types of items can be scored separately. The test is available in four forms: S, T, DS-12, and DT-12. Reading and understanding of the test directions are considered part of the administration time of Forms S and T. Forms DS-12 and DT-12 differ from Forms S and T in that the time spent reading and understanding directions is not included in the administration time of the test. Normative data are available for male sales employees and applicants, clerical employees and applicants, service station dealers and applicants, industrial supervisors and applicants, and industrial employees and applicants. Norms are also available for female statistical, accounting, and supply clerks; secretarial and stenographic personnel; miscellaneous or unspecified clerical applicants and employees; and file and record clerks and office applicants and employees. Examiner required. Suitable for group use.

Timed: 15 minutes

Scoring: Hand key

Cost: 1-24 packages $19.00; score key $3.00; manual $8.00

Publisher: Richardson, Bellows, Henry and Company, Inc.

THURSTONE TEST OF MENTAL ALERTNESS
L.L. Thurstone and
Thelma Gwinn Thurstone

Adult

Purpose: Measures an individual's capacity to acquire new knowledge and skills and to use what they have learned in problem solving. Measures individual differences in ability to learn and perform mental tasks of varying types and complexity. Used for employee selection and vocational counseling.

Description: 126-item paper-pencil test measuring linguistic (vocabulary) and quantitative (arithmetic) factors. Average educational opportunities and familiarity with the English language are a requisite. Two equivalent forms are available. Examiner required. Suitable for group use.

Timed: 20 minutes

Scoring: Hand key

Cost: 25 test booklets $37.50; examiner's manual $10.00

Publisher: Science Research Associates, Inc.

TIME PERCEPTION INVENTORY (TPI)

Adult

Purpose: Measures the difference between physical and mental presence. Helps employees understand how much of their time is wasted due to mental preoccupations. Identifies an individual's particular preoccupations and evaluates their causes and debilitating nature.

Description: Multiple-item paper-pencil inventory measuring an individual's ten-dencies to focus attention on the past, future, or present. Percentile comparison on perceived time effectiveness (typically related to an individual's motivation to improve) is provided. All scales provide opportunities to consider positive and negative aspects of thinking in a particular time reference. Group patterns can be identified through a simple show of hands. The test booklet provides interpretations of scales and implications of scores on scales. Recommendations for additional reading are included. Normative data are available. Self-administered. Suitable for group use.

Untimed: 10 minutes

Scoring: Self-scored

Cost: Demonstration kit (30 inventories, manual) $45.95; specimen set (includes manual) $9.95

Publisher: Humanics Media

VERBAL REASONING
Raymond J. Corsini and
Richard Renck

Adult

Purpose: Assesses individual capacity to reason logically as indicated by solutions to verbal problems. Used for industrial job selection and vocational counseling.

Description: 36-item paper-pencil test of mental reasoning consisting of 12 statements with three questions each. A knowledge of basic English is required. Examiner required. Suitable for group use.

Timed: 15 minutes

Scoring: Hand key

Cost: Specimen set $8.00; 25 tests $8.75

Publisher: London House Press

WATSON-GLASER CRITICAL THINKING APPRAISAL
Refer to page 575.

WESTERN PERSONNEL TESTS (WPT)
Robert L. Gunn and Morse P. Manson

Adult

Purpose: Measures general intelligence. Used for personnel screening.

Description: Multiple-item paper-pencil test providing a quick measure of general intelligence. Available in four equivalent forms: A, B, C, and D. Norms are provided for the general population and for professional, college, clerical, skilled and unskilled populations. Examiner required. Suitable for group use. Form A is available in Spanish.

Timed: 5 minutes

Scoring: Hand key; may be computer scored

Cost: Kit (100 tests—25 each form, manual, key) $39.50

Publisher: Western Psychological Services

THE WONDERLIC PERSONNEL TEST
Refer to page 853.

Interests

ADULT CAREER CONCERNS INVENTORY (ACCI)
Donald E. Super,
Albert S. Thompson,
and Richard H. Lindeman

Adult

Purpose: Measures career and life stages of adults. Used in counseling and research.

Description: Multiple-item paper-pencil measurement of Donald Super's theory of life stages (Exploration, Establishment, Maintenance, Disengagment) and a special Career Change Status Scale. Counselors can use the inventory for assessing a client's career stage and growth. Researchers may use it for assess-

ing how life stage impacts productivity, creativity, turnover, etc. Self-administered. Suitable for group use.

Untimed: 30 minutes

Scoring: Hand key; may be computer scored

Cost: 25 reusable tests $5.00; 50 answer sheets $13.50

Publisher: Consulting Psychologists Press, Inc.

ARMED SERVICES-CIVILIAN INTEREST SURVEY (ASCVIS)
Robert Kauk

Adolescent, adult

Purpose: Assesses an individual's interests in high-tech occupational fields and identifies armed forces and related civilian jobs that match those interests. Used by career counselors with clients who want technical training that might be offered by the armed services.

Description: 6-page multiple-item paper-pencil or computer-administered inventory assessing levels of interest within high-tech occupational clusters. The test identifies appropriate occupational choices and shows how the armed services can be a source of immediate employment and basic and advanced technical training that can be utilized in either a military or civilian career. A career profile is developed for making tentative career decisions, including selection of an educational plan—either civilian or military—to reach career goals (a two-path plan is explained, step by step). The individual is free to take the completed career profile to a recruiter or civilian counselor to make the training connection. Self-administered. Suitable for group use.

Untimed: Varies

Scoring: Self-scored; may be computer scored

Cost: Class set (materials for 35 students, user's guide) $15.00; diskette $79.95

Publisher: CFKR Career Materials, Inc.

CANADIAN OCCUPATIONAL INTEREST INVENTORY (COII)
G. Booth and Luc Begin

High-school student, adult

Purpose: Identifies an individual's attitudes toward occupationally related activities.

Description: 70-item paper-pencil measure of attitudes as they relate occupationally to activities. Interests and activities are measured by the following bipolar factors: things vs. people, business contact vs. scientific, routine vs. creative, social vs. solitary, and prestige vs. production. The test relates to the computer guidance program CHOICES. An IBM microcomputer program is available for administration and scoring. Examiner required. Suitable for group use. Available in French.

Untimed: 40 minutes

Scoring: Hand key

Cost: 25 booklets $25.30; manual $10.50; 500 sheets and charts $95.90; key $4.00

Publisher: Nelson Canada

CAREER AND VOCATIONAL INTEREST INVENTORY
Refer to page 735.

CAREER DIRECTIONS INVENTORY
Refer to page 736.

CAREER EXPLORATION PROFILE (CEP)
Refer to page 736.

CAREER EXPLORATION SERIES (CES)
Refer to page 737.

CAREER INTEREST TEST (CIT)
Educational and Industrial Test Services Ltd. Staff

Adolescent, adult

Purpose: Determines the vocational interests of young people and adults. Used for vocational and educational guidance.

Description: Multiple-item paper-pencil forced-choice test. The score reveals the subject's interests in or aversions to occupations in these six catagories of interests: outdoor-physical, scientific-theoretical, social service, aesthetic-literary, commercial-clerical, and practical technical. Materials include booklets, a scoring key, a specimen set, and a manual. Examiner required. Suitable for group use.

BRITISH PUBLISHER

Untimed: 20 minutes

Scoring: Examiner evaluated

Cost: Contact publisher

Publisher: Educational and Industrial Test Services Ltd.

CAREER SURVEY
Refer to page 739.

CORRECTIONAL OFFICERS' INTEREST BLANK (COIB)
Harrison G. Gough

Adult

Purpose: Measures an individual's potential for correctional work. Used for screening and placement.

Description: 40-item paper-pencil interest and attitude scale identifying applicants and officers of both sexes who possess the temperament and personal qualities required for work in correctional agencies and institutions. Sale is restricted to state and federal correctional agencies and penal institutions. Examiner required. Suitable for group use.

Untimed: 10 minutes

Scoring: Hand key

Cost: 50 test booklets $17.50; manual $7.50; hand scoring stencils $16.00

Publisher: Consulting Psychologists Press, Inc.

CURTIS INTEREST SCALE
James W. Curtis

**Adolescent, adult
Grades 10 and above**

Purpose: Assesses individual vocational interest patterns. Used for vocational guidance, screening, and selection.

Description: 55-item paper-pencil test of vocational interests in 10 occupational areas: applied arts, business, computation, direct sales, entertainment, farming, interpersonal, mechanics, production, and science. The test yields an estimate of "level of responsibility." Self-administered. Suitable for group use.

Untimed: 10 minutes

Scoring: Examiner evaluated; scoring service available

Cost: Specimen set (test, manual, profile sheet) $4.00; 25 scales $7.00; 25 profiles $4.00

Publisher: Psychometric Affiliates

EXPERIENCE EXPLORATION
Refer to page 743.

FORER VOCATIONAL SURVEY: MEN-WOMEN
Refer to page 743.

GENERAL OCCUPATIONAL INTEREST INVENTORY
Saville & Holdsworth Ltd.

Adult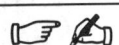

Purpose: Collects information about job-related interests among school dropouts and adults with education up to the "O" level. Used for counseling, vocational guidance, career planning, redundancy, and retirement counseling, as well as for selection and placement decisions.

Description: Multiple-item paper-pencil inventory requiring respondents to state their liking for activities that are related to specific occupations relevant to this level, including child care workers, waiter/waitress, sales representative, security officers, chargehand, secretary, farmer, graphic designer, dressmaker, maintenance electrician, and plumber. Scores are grouped for 18 main categories: medical, welfare, personal services, selling goods, selling services, supervision, clerical, office equipment, control, leisure, art and design, crafts, plants, animals, transport, construction, electrical, and mechanical. Evaluation of the scores for the 18 groups provides derived scores that indicate specific interests. Examiner required. Suitable for group use. BRITISH PUBLISHER

Untimed: 35 minutes

Scoring: Hand key; examiner evaluated; may be computer scored

Cost: 10 booklets $25.50; manual and guide $44.00; key $11.50; administration card $11.50; computer disk (50 administrations) $367.50

Publisher: Saville & Holdsworth Ltd.

HACKMAN-GAITHER INTEREST INVENTORY
Refer to page 745.

THE INTEREST CHECK LIST (ICL)

Adult

Purpose: Determines an individual's employment interests. Used as a guide to vocational counseling and self-assessment.

Description: 210-item paper-pencil checklist of sample tasks that have been keyed to the work groups listed in the Guide for Occupational Exploration. The applicant's likes and dislikes are evaluated, leading to an understanding of why the applicants are interested in the subjects indicated. The test may be used with individuals who have no firmly stated interests or who are not aware of the variety of existing occupations. Self-administered. Suitable for group use. Available in Spanish.

Untimed: 20 minutes

Scoring: Hand key

Cost: Available through State Employment Service Agencies only

Publisher: U.S. Department of Labor

INVENTORY OF VOCATIONAL INTERESTS

Refer to page 748.

JACKSON VOCATIONAL INTEREST SURVEY (JVIS)

Refer to page 749.

JIIG-CAL OCCUPATIONAL INTERESTS GUIDE AND APU OCCUPATIONAL INTEREST GUIDE

Refer to page 749.

JOB MATCHING II

Adolescent, adult

Purpose: Assesses career preferences and experience. Used for career exploration and to match individuals to job families, local jobs, and training programs at the semiskilled, skilled, technical, and professional levels.

Description: 200-item A-V or paper-pencil survey assessing an individual's preferences and experience. The individual responds to 200 pictures with descriptions or narration depicting activities as examples of 20 dimensions of work. Responses are recorded in a booklet for computer scoring or on cards for on-site scoring. A generated profile across the 20 dimensions of work describes the individual's approach/avoid pattern as numerical indicators related to preferences and experience. The profiles can be used to identify the most appropriate match between the individual and local jobs or training programs because the survey also is used to profile local job requirements and training programs. National job bank matches are standard. Local job and training program bank matches are optional. Examiner/self-administered. Suitable for group use.

Timed: 1½ hours

Scoring: Computer scored on-site or by publisher

Cost: Contact publisher

Publisher: Prep, Inc.

JOB TRAINING ASSESSMENT PROGRAM (JOBTAP)

Refer to page 765.

JOB-O

Refer to page 750.

JOBMATCH

Industrial Training Unit (ITRU) in association with the Manpower Services Commission

---

Adolescent, adult

Purpose: Identifies jobs or job areas that nonacademic secondary and college students would find most compatible with their personal job-related likes and dislikes. Used by LEA careers advisors, in training and personnel departments of large companies, and for use in schemes organized under the (British) Government's New Training Initiative.

Description: 49-item paper-pencil or computer-administered questionnaire assessing personal preferences related to four basic aspects of employment: physical environment, social environment, work content, and work method. In the paper-pencil version, students respond on self-profiling answer sheets to items presented in the six-page questionnaire. These profiles are then compared to the 40 profile stencils provided in the *Jobmatch Profiles Book* to identify jobs or job areas which should be of interest to the students. Profiles in the *Jobmatch Profiles Book* are based on workers' responses to a Job Disposition Questionnaire assessing the likes and dislikes of individuals actually working in the 40 jobs covered by the system. Each of these jobs is discussed in further detail in the *Job Facts Book*, which provides illustrated descriptions of each job (including basic information, qualifications required, and a list of the likes and dislikes of persons who work in it), a list

of appropriate books and pamphlets, useful addresses, and a glossary of employment terms.
The teacher's guide provides notes on administration and scoring procedures and research background, as well as guidelines for extending the range of the questionnaire by relating jobs not covered directly by the system to those which are. Two computer versions are available. The Interactive Computer Version computer administers the questions and scores the answers, leaving students to follow up on the results with the *Job Facts Book*. The Scoring and Matching Computer Version is designed for group use where individual computer time is not available. Students answer questions using an answer sheet, and the computer matches the profiles of their responses with the profiles of the 40 jobs. Both programs are suitable for use with the Commodore PET (32K), RML 380Z, and the BBC Micro. The paper-pencil version is self-administered and self-scored. Both the paper-pencil version and the Scoring and Matching Computer Version are suitable for group use.

Untimed: Varies

Scoring: Self-scored; may be computer scored

Cost: Complete pack (5 questionnaires, 20 answer sheets, the *Jobmatch Profiles Book*, the *Job Facts Book*, and teacher's guide) £24.00; contact publisher concerning cost and availability of software

Publisher: Macmillan Education

KUDER PREFERENCE RECORD, VOCATIONAL, FORM CP
Refer to page 751.

LIFE STYLE QUESTIONNAIRE
James Barrett

Adolescent, adult
Ages 15 and older

Purpose: Provides insight regarding interests, attitudes, and behaviors of people about to begin work or already working. Used for vocational guidance, counseling, and management development.

Description: 132-item paper-pencil test for self-assessment of vocational interests and attitudes. Items are statements about work activities. Scores are provided on thirteen scales: six dealing with general motivation, five examining consistency of outlook with interests, and two estimating the degree of certainty about questionnaire responses. The test booklet contains instructions on how to respond to test items. Self-administered. Suitable for group use.
BRITISH PUBLISHER

Timed: 20 minutes

Scoring: Hand key; scoring service available

Cost: Booklet $4.00; answer sheet and graphs set $1.50; manual $13.50

Publisher: The Test Agency

LIMRA CAREER PROFILE SYSTEM
Refer to page 1001.

MINNESOTA IMPORTANCE QUESTIONNAIRE (MIQ)

Adult

Purpose: Measures vocational needs and relates them to occupational reinforcers. Assesses need-reinforcer correspondence as a supplement to standard measures of occupational interests and abilities.

Description: Multiple-item paper-pencil inventory assessing vocational needs in terms of preferred occupational reinforcers. The Paired Form (190 paired comparison and 20 absolute judgment items) presents pairs of vocational needs statements, and the examinee indicates the more important need in each pair. The Ranked Form (42 items) presents vocational need statements in groups of five, and the individual ranks the five needs in each group according to their importance. Both forms measure the following need dimensions: ability utilization, achievement, activity, advancement, authority, company policies and practices, compensation, co-workers, creativity, independence, moral values, recognition, responsibility, security, social service, social status, supervision-human relations, supervision-technical, variety, and working conditions. A computer-generated profile and interpretation are provided for each examinee. They include scores on each dimension (Ranked Form also includes an Autonomy Scale) in the form of a profile, correspondence of examinee's need pattern to Occupational Reinforcer Patterns (ORPs), lists (50 each) of occupations with the ORPs most similar and least similar to the examinee's MIQ profile, predictions of job satisfaction for each occupation listed, references for further information, a validity score, and an error factor for each score. An optional extended report lists MIQ-ORP correspondence for 187 occupations. A technical manual discusses development, reliability, validity, normative data, and interpretations of sample MIQ profiles. Self-administered with clinical supervision. Suitable for group use. The test is a Level B instrument, as defined by the APA. Prospective users must establish qualifications with their initial order. Available in Spanish and French.

Untimed: Varies

Scoring: Computer scored

Cost: 10-99 booklets (specify form) $0.65; 10-499 answer sheets (specify form) $0.10; computer scoring $2.50 per report

Publisher: Vocational Psychology Research, University of Minnesota

---

MULTIDIMENSIONAL PERSONALITY QUESTIONNAIRE (MPQ)
Refer to page 155.

MY VOCATIONAL SITUATION
Refer to page 925.

PAPI SYSTEM
Refer to page 928.

PAPI SYSTEM: RATING OF JOB REQUIREMENTS—FORM D REVISED
Refer to page 931.

PERSONNEL REACTION BLANK
Harrison G. Gough

Adult

Purpose: Measures a dependability-conscientiousness factor among rank-and-file workers. Used by personnel officers for selecting new employees.

Description: 70-item paper-pencil test assessing interests and attitudes related to dependability and conscientiousness. The test is used with rank-and-file workers and is not recommended for management personnel. A manual explains the meaning of high and low scores. The test is restricted, and scoring keys are sold only to registered users. Self-administered. Suitable for group use.

Untimed: 10-15 minutes

Scoring: Hand key

Cost: Specimen set (manual, test booklet, special order form) $12.50

Publisher: Consulting Psychologists Press, Inc.

PRG INTEREST INVENTORY
Refer to page 756.

THE SALIENCE INVENTORY (RESEARCH EDITION)
Donald E. Super and Dorothy D. Nevill

Adult

Purpose: Measures an individual's orientation to life roles. Used in counseling and research related to life roles and careers.

Description: Multiple-item paper-pencil inventory assessing the relative importance of five major life roles: student, worker, homemaker, leisurite, and citizen. The inventory measures an individual in relation to Super's Life-Career Rainbow model and was part of the *Work Importance Study*. International life-role distributions are available. For counselors, the inventory indicates a client's orientation to life roles, readiness for career decisions, and exposure to work and occupations. Examiner required. Suitable for group use.

Untimed: 30 minutes

Scoring: Hand key; scoring service available

Cost: 25 booklets $16.50; 50 answer sheets $14.50

Publisher: Consulting Psychologists Press, Inc.

SELF-DESCRIPTION INVENTORY (SDI)
Charles B. Johansson

Adolescent, adult
Grades 9-adult

Purpose: Evaluates an individual's personal attitudes and vocational interests. Used for personnel selection and vocational needs assessment.

Description: 200-item paper-pencil inventory covering 11 personal description and six vocational scales. The personal scales include the following factors: cautious/adventurous, nonscientific/analytical, tense/relaxed, insecure/confident, conventional/imaginative, impatient/patient, unconcerned/altruistic, reserved/outgoing, softspoken/forceful, lackadaisical/industrious, and unorganized/orderly. The vocational scales cover the following factors: realistic, investigative, artistic, social, enterprising, and conventional. Self-administered. Suitable for group use.

Untimed: 15-20 minutes

Scoring: Computer scored

Cost: Contact publisher

Publisher: National Computer Systems/ PAS Division

THE SELF-DIRECTED SEARCH, 1985 REVISION (SDS)
John L. Holland

Adolescent, adult   Ages 15-70

Purpose: Assesses the abilities and interests of adolescents and adults. Used for career planning and guidance.

Description: Multiple-item paper-pencil test in two forms yielding six interest scores (Realistic, Investigative, Artistic, Social, Enterprising, and Conventional) and a three-letter occupational code used for exploring occupational possibilities.

The Occupations Finder in this revised version contains over 1,100 occupational titles. Directions have been revised to increase self-understanding and vocational exploration. Form E, which yields a two-letter code, is available for individuals with a fourth-grade reading level. A computer version is available also. Self-administered. Suitable for group use. Available in Spanish and Vietnamese.

Untimed: 30-45 minutes

Scoring: Self-scored; may be computer scored

Cost: Professional kit (manual, 25 booklets and Occupations Finders, 10 You and Your Career booklets) $44.00; 50 uses computer version $150.00

Publisher: Psychological Assessment Resources, Inc.

SIX-FACTOR AUTOMATED VOCATIONAL ASSESSMENT SYSTEM (SAVAS)
Refer to page 758.

STRONG-CAMPBELL INTEREST INVENTORY (SCII)
E.K. Strong, Jr., Jo-Ida C. Hansen, and David P. Campbell

Adolescent, adult
Grades 8 and above

Purpose: Measures occupational interests in a wide range of career areas. Used to make long-range curricular and occupational choices and for employee placement, career guidance, career development, and vocational rehabilitation placement.

Description: 325-item paper-pencil multiple-choice test requiring the examinee to respond either "like," "indifferent," or "dislike" to items covering a broad range of familiar occupational tasks and day-to-day activities. General topics include occupations, school subjects, activities, leisure activities, types of people, preference between two activities, and "your characteristics." Responses are then analyzed by computer to yield a profile that presents scores on a number of scales and offers interpretive advice. Specifically, the respondent is scored on six general occupational themes (based on Holland's RIASEC themes), 23 basic interest scales (measuring strength and consistency of specific interest areas), and 207 occupational scales (reflecting degree of similarity between respondent and people employed in particular occupations). The scoring services also provide 11 additional nonoccupational and administrative indexes as a further guide to interpreting the results. Computer scoring is required and is available from a number of sources (test results are available on-site using microcomputer scoring). Self-administered. Suitable for group use. Available in Spanish.

Untimed: 25-30 minutes

Scoring: Computer scored

Cost: Profile only $2.15-$3.35, depending on quantity; profile and interpretation $3.60-$5.60, depending on quantity; scoring via microcomputer: profile only $1.55-$2.00, profile and narrative $3.10-$4.00

Publisher: Stanford University Press; distributed exclusively by Consulting Psychologists Press, Inc.

U.S. EMPLOYMENT SERVICE (USES) INTEREST INVENTORY
U.S. Employment Service

Adult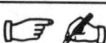

Purpose: Measures an individual's general occupational interests. Used in vocational counseling.

Description: 162-item paper-pencil examination measuring 12 interest areas listed in the USES Guide for Occupational Exploration: artistic, scientific, plants and animals, protective, mechanical, industrial, business retail, selling, accommodating, humanitarian, leading-influencing, and physical performance. Available only to State Employment Services or to organizations that have approval from such services. Examiner required. Suitable for group use.

Untimed: 20 minutes

Scoring: Hand key; may be computer scored

Cost: Available only through State Employment Service Agencies

Publisher: U.S. Department of Labor

THE VALUES SCALE (RESEARCH EDITION)
Donald E. Super and Dorothy D. Nevill

Adult

Purpose: Measures intrinsic and extrinsic life-career values.

Description: Multiple-item paper-pencil inventory measuring intrinsic and extrinsic life-career values and many cultural perspectives of adults. The scale was developed as part of the international *Work Importance Study* and has international norms. Examiner required. Suitable for group use.

Untimed: 30-45 minutes

Scoring: Hand key; computer scoring service available

Cost: 25 booklets $13.50; 50 answer sheets $14.50

Publisher: Consulting Psychologists Press, Inc.

VOC-TECH QUICK SCREENER
Refer to page 758.

VOCATIONAL INTEREST, EXPERIENCE, AND SKILL ASSESSMENT (VIESA), CANADIAN EDITION, 1985
Refer to page 760.

VOCATIONAL PREFERENCE INVENTORY, 1985 REVISION (VPI)
John L. Holland

**Adolescent, adult
Grades 10 and above**

Purpose: Assesses personality using occupational item content. Developed for high-school students and adults for vocational exploration.

Description: Multiple-item paper-pencil test yielding a profile based on 11 dimensions of personality: realistic, investigative, scientific, conventional, enterprising, artistic, self-control, masculinity, femininity, status, infrequency, and acquiescence. Items are all occupational titles and the subjects indicate which they like or dislike. This revision contains new items and answer sheet and stencil revisions. A computer version is available. Examiner/self-administered. Suitable for group use.

Untimed: 15-30 minutes

Scoring: Hand key; may be computer scored

Cost: Professional kit (manual, 25 test booklets, 50 answer sheets, 50 profile forms, scoring key) $24.95; 50 uses computer version $125.00

Publisher: Psychological Assessment Resources, Inc.

WIDE RANGE INTEREST-OPINION TEST (WRIOT)
Refer to page 761.

WORK INTEREST INDEX
Melany E. Baehr, Richard Renck, and R.K. Burns

Adult

Purpose: Measures an individual's interest in 12 vocational areas and flexibility of interest and vocational aspiration. Used for industrial job screening and selection and vocational counseling.

Description: 96-item paper-pencil pictorial examination of the following factors: professional and technical, social and verbal, authority and prestige, artistic and interpretative, artistic and stylized, artistic and creative, technical and scientific, clerical and routine, business contact and structured, personal service and persuasive, mechanical and productive, control of massive equipment. The test booklet consists of a series of pictures which the subject marks with "L" for "like" or "D" for "dislike." Self-administered. Suitable for group use.

Untimed: 15-20 minutes

Scoring: Hand key; may be computer scored

Cost: Specimen set $8.00; 25 test booklets $11.25

Publisher: London House Press

THE WORLD OF WORK INVENTORY
Robert E. Ripley, original author and Karen Hudson, revision

Adolescent, adult   Ages 13-65

Purpose: Measures temperaments and aptitudes related to career and vocational interests. Used for employee selection, career counseling, vocational rehabilitation, and adult/career education classes.

Description: 518-item paper-pencil or computer-administered inventory. The 98 multiple-choice items assess the following achievement-aptitude areas: abstractions, spatial-form, verbal, mechanical, electrical, and clerical. The 420 rating items (subject responds "like," "dislike," or "neutral") assess 12 job-related temperament factors and interests in 17 professional and industrial career areas. A cassette tape is available for instruction of examiners. The inventory is available on an IBM-PC compatible disk. Self-administered. Suitable for group use. Available in Spanish.

Untimed: Paper-pencil administration 2 hours, 15 minutes; computer administration 1½ hours

Scoring: Computer scored

Cost: Reusable test booklet $5.00; single answer sheet $10.00; interpretation manual $19.95; computer service included with cost of answer sheets; a non-profit price schedule is available; discounts for multiple orders are available

Publisher: World of Work, Inc.

Interpersonal Skills and Attitudes

ADULT PERSONALITY INVENTORY
Refer to page 117.

ALIENATION INDEX SURVEY (AI SURVEY)

Adult

Purpose: Assesses work-related attitudes of job applicants. Identifies individuals with alienated attitudes that reduce performance and cause poor morale. Used for applicant screening and employee selection.

Description: Multiple-item paper-pencil preemployment survey assessing the attitudes of job applicants toward employers, supervisors, co-workers, work, pay, and benefits. The survey identifies applicants with alienated attitudes in these areas who have a high potential for becoming problem employees. The survey is administered, scored, and interpreted in-house for immediate use by personnel/human relations/security specialists by license to Psychological Systems Corporation. The survey is also available as part of the PASS Booklet (which includes the Trustworthiness Attitude Survey and the Emotional Stability Survey) or PASS-II Booklet (along with Trustworthiness Attitude Survey) for more complete applicant assessment. Examiner required. Suitable for group use.

Untimed: 8-12 minutes

Scoring: Examiner evaluated

Cost: Contact publisher

Publisher: Psychological Systems Corporation

Information and availability unconfirmed; no publisher response.

BANK PERSONNEL SELECTION INVENTORY (BPSI)

Adult

Purpose: Identifies banking job applicants who might engage in theft or counter-productive behavior in the workplace.

Description: 108-item paper-pencil test examining behavior that could result in theft, violence, or drug abuse on the job. A distortion scale is included. Basic literacy is required. Self-administered. Suitable for group use.

Untimed: 30-40 minutes

Scoring: Computer scored by phone

Cost: $8.50-$14.50 depending on volume ordered

Publisher: London House Press

BIOGRAPHICAL INDEX
Willard A. Kerr

Adult

Purpose: Quantifies background data. Used for predicting success in managerial and sales positions and in recruitment programs for general business.

Description: Multiple-item paper-pencil measure of personal background information. The instrument yields five scores: stability, drive to excel, human relations, financial status, and personal adjustment. Three middle scores provide an estimate of basic energy level. The instrument predicts the annual salary increment of executives. Examiner required. Suitable for group use.

Untimed: Not available

Scoring: Hand key

Cost: Specimen set $5.00; 25 indices $8.75; 25 answer sheets $5.00

Publisher: Psychometric Affiliates

THE BIPOLAR PSYCHOLOGICAL INVENTORY (BPI)
Refer to page 121.

BUSINESS JUDGMENT TEST
Martin M. Bruce

Adult

Purpose: Evaluates the subject's sense of "good business judgment" and "social intelligence" in business-related situations. Used for employee selection and training.

Description: 25-item paper-pencil multiple-choice test in which the subject selects one of four ways to complete a stem statement, allowing the examiner to gauge the subject's sense of socially accepted and desirable ways to behave in business relationships. The score suggests the degree to which the subject agrees with the general opinion of businessmen as to the proper way to handle various relationships. Self-administered. Suitable for group use.

Untimed: 10-15 minutes

Scoring: Hand key

Cost: Manual $6.15; key $1.10; package of tests $25.75

Publisher: Martin M. Bruce, Ph.D., Publishers

CANFIELD LEARNING STYLES INVENTORY (CLS)
Refer to page 683.

CAREER DECISION SCALE (2ND EDITION)
Refer to page 890.

THE CAREER SUITABILITY PROFILE
Christopher P. Harding

Adult

Purpose: Measures fundamental personality characteristics which control career interests, abilities, and the capacity to perform. Used for recruiting, screening candidates, organization design, succession planning, training and assistance, reassignment, and management review.

Description: 70-item multiple-choice test based on 10 personality factors defined by Christopher Harding to characterize an individual's personality structure. The test determines which factors most control an individual's performance potential in his work and personal life, his suitability for various career fields, his outlook for achievement and fulfillment in his most appropriate career area(s), and the type of business in which he will function most effectively. An individual's results are classified into one of several hundred possible profile patterns. The Career Suitability Profile Report provides a personalized 30-page description of the profile, what each element means, what the combination of one's qualities mean, and what the individual may do to enhance his own performance. Although the report is computer generated, it is studied by a skilled professional before it is sent to the individual tested. Arrangements may be made for the examinee and a trained professional to discuss the results. In addition to the report, each profile is accompanied by two numerical indexes: the Success Outlook (a measure of individuation, the ability to achieve on one's own and to feel fulfillment in work) and the Productivity Index (a measure of organizational fit, the capability to function effectively as a team player). Self-administered. Suitable for group use.

Untimed: 10 minutes

Scoring: Computer scored

Cost: Per person $250.00 for test and report

Publisher: Management Strategies, Inc.

CHANGE AGENT QUESTIONNAIRE (CAQ)
Jay Hall and Martha S. Williams

Adult

Purpose: Evaluates attitudes toward change. Used in programs on the dynamics of change with teachers, trainers, managers, members of the clergy, politicians, probation officers, counselors, and social workers—individuals whose role is to bring about positive changes in organizations, institutions, or individuals.

Description: Multiple-item paper-pencil self-report inventory assessing an individual's philosophies, strategies, and approaches concerning the concept of change. The inventory measures basic assumptions regarding the process and duration of change, particularly change which is brought about through the efforts of change agents (individuals who effect change by actively influencing the thoughts and behaviors of others). The inventory yields five scores, which are profiled according to a grid format based on the work of Herbert Kelman concerning change agents. Self-administered. Suitable for group use.

Untimed: Varies

Scoring: Self-scored

Cost: Individual instrument $4.50

Publisher: Teleometrics International

Information and availability unconfirmed; no publisher response.

CHOOSING A CAREER
E.I.T.S. Staff

Adolescent, adult

Purpose: Evaluates individual attitudes towards work. Used for vocational and educational guidance.

Description: Multiple-item paper-pencil supplement to the Rothwell-Miller Interest Blank. The subject is asked to rank a series of statements in order of their importance, thereby determining the subject's attitudes towards five factors: rewards, interests, security, pride and recognition, and autonomy. Norms are given in the manual. Examiner required. Suitable for group use.
BRITISH PUBLISHER

Untimed: 10 minutes

Scoring: Examiner evaluated

Cost: Contact publisher

Publisher: Educational and Industrial Test Services Ltd.

CLAYBURY SELECTION BATTERY
Refer to page 125.

COMMUNICATING EMPATHY
Refer to page 950.

COMREY PERSONALITY SCALES (CPS)
Refer to page 128.

CONFLICT MANAGEMENT SURVEY (CMS)
Jay Hall

Adult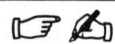

Purpose: Assesses the manner in which group members interpret the meaning of conflict and, consequently, the manner in which they handle it. Used in labor-management sessions, community relations laboratories, and programs on the dynamics of conflict to identify constructive outcomes to conflict.

Description: Multiple-item paper-pencil self-report inventory assessing an individual's reaction to, and consequent handling of, interpersonal, group, and intergroup conflict. Analysis employs a grid format measuring two dimensions: concern for personal goals and concern for relationships. The survey identifies five styles of conflict management: win-lose, yield-lose, lose-leave, compromise, and synergistic. Normative data and conversion tables are provided for transforming raw scores on the five styles into a fivefold conflict management profile. These profiles provide a basis for establishing constructive conflict-handling behavior. Examiner required. Suitable for group use.

Untimed: Varies

Scoring: Examiner evaluated

Cost: Individual instrument $4.50

Publisher: Teleometrics International

Information and availability unconfirmed; no publisher response.

A CREATIVITY MEASURE—THE SRT SCALE
William C. Kosinar

Adolescent, adult
Grades 10 and above

Purpose: Assesses level of creativity. Used for career guidance with youths and to select research and scientific personnel.

Description: Multiple-item forced-choice paper-pencil test of creativity. The manual provides norms on scientific personnel, National Science Talent Search winners, college students, and high-school students. Examiner required. Suitable for group use.

Untimed: 5 minutes

Scoring: Examiner evaluated

Cost: Specimen set $4.00; 25 tests $4.50

Publisher: Psychometric Affiliates

CULTURE SHOCK INVENTORY (CSI)
W.J. Reddin

Adult

Purpose: Assesses an individual's susceptibility to cultural shock. Used to acquaint those who expect to work outside their own culture with potentially difficult areas.

Description: Multiple-item paper-pencil test consisting of scales assessing Western ethnocentrism, cross-cultural experience, cognitive flex, behavioral flex, cultural knowledge (specific and general), customs acceptance, and interpersonal sensitivity. The test may be used with managers, spouses, and older children and in colleges. Self-administered. Suitable for group use.
CANADIAN PUBLISHER

Untimed: 20-30 minutes

Scoring: Hand key

Cost: Test kit (10 test copies, fact sheet, user's guide) $40.00

Publisher: Organizational Tests (Canada) Ltd.

CURTIS COMPLETION FORM
Refer to page 130.

CUSTOMER REACTION SURVEY (CRS)
Refer to page 1000.

D.I.S.C. PERSONALITY PROFILE SYSTEM

Adult

Purpose: Assesses behavior related to a job and personality of applicants. Used for matching candidates with positions.

Description: Multiple-item paper-pencil test in two parts for assessing and matching job applicants with positions. The Job Analysis portion enables the user to develop a structure profile of the behaviors required for the job. The Personality Profile Assessment produces a personality profile of the applicant, which the user interprets for job placement. Examiner/self-administered. Suitable for group use.
BRITISH PUBLISHER

Untimed: Not available

Scoring: Self-scored

Cost: Job analysis form £3.20; Personality Profile form £3.20

Publisher: NFER-NELSON Publishing Company Ltd.

THE DECISION MAKING INVENTORY
Richard Johnson, William Coscarelli, and JaDean Johnson

Adolescent, adult

Purpose: Identifies an individual's preferred decision-making style. Used in career counseling, marriage therapy, task groups, and instructional programs.

Description: 20-item paper-pencil one-page instrument assessing an individual's preferred style of making decisions. Individuals rate a series of statements concerning steps in the decision-making process on a 6-point scale ranging from "never" to "always" to indicate the degree to which each item is true for themselves. Scoring and interpretation is based on Johnson's theory which suggests that information can be gathered in a systematic or spontaneous manner and this information is analyzed either externally or internally. The manual describes the theory in detail, as well as the development of the scale, scoring procedures, and examples of its use in counseling and task groups. Examiner required. Suitable for group use.

Untimed: Varies

Scoring: Examiner evaluated

Cost: 30 inventories $7.00; manual $10.00; scoring grid (set of 2) $1.00

Publisher: Marathon Consulting and Press

DEROGATIS STRESS PROFILE (DSP)
Refer to page 131.

DF OPINION SURVEY: AN INVENTORY OF DYNAMIC FACTORS (DFOS)
Refer to page 741.

THE EDINBURGH QUESTIONNAIRES (1982 EDITION)
John Raven

Adult

Purpose: Identifies factors related to the job satisfaction and motivation of employees and job applicants. Used to monitor and evaluate staff placement, guidance, and development programs.

Description: Multiple-item paper-pencil set of three questionnaires for evaluating and improving manpower and educational policies and identifying sources of job dissatisfaction and motivation. The Quality of Working Life questionnaire assesses an individual's satisfaction with the working environment. The Important Activities questionnaire assesses the way an individual wants to behave at work, the competencies an individual wishes to exercise, and the goals an individual wishes to achieve. The Consequences questionnaire assesses self-image and individual perceptions related to a particular task. The questionnaires may be used together or separately. Examiner/self-administered. Suitable for group use.
BRITISH PUBLISHER

Untimed: Not available

Scoring: Hand key

Cost: Specimen set (manual, 10 each of 3 forms) £19.25

Publisher: NFER-NELSON Publishing Company Ltd.

EMOTIONAL STABILITY SURVEY (ES SURVEY)

Adult

Purpose: Measures the emotional stability of applicants for sensitive positions. Used for applicant screening and employee selection.

Description: Multiple-item paper-pencil preemployment survey measuring emotional stability and control. The survey is highly job related for police and security positions. The self-report questionnaire format requires no interpretive analysis. In addition to the standard scoring template, a critical factor score template also is provided to identify false positive scores indicating attempts to bias answers. The survey was developed according to guidelines established by the EEOC and reviewed by FEPC and EEOC examiners. It may be administered, scored, and interpreted in-house by personnel/human resource/security specialists by license to Psychological Systems Corporation. The survey is also available as part of the PASS Booklet (which includes the Trustworthiness Attitude Survey and the Alienation Index Survey) for more complete applicant assessment. Examiner required. Suitable for group use.

Untimed: 5-10 minutes

Scoring: Hand key

Cost: Contact publisher

Publisher: Psychological Systems Corporation

Information and availability unconfirmed; no publisher response.

THE EMPATHY TEST
W.A. Kerr and B.J. Speroff

Adolescent, adult
Grades 10 and above

Purpose: Measures empathic ability. Used to select managerial and supervisory personnel and graduate students.

Description: Multiple-item paper-pencil test measuring the ability to put oneself in another person's position, establish rapport, and anticipate another person's reactions, feelings, and behavior. Empathy is measured as a variable unrelated to intelligence and most other attitudes. Three forms—Form A, blue collar emphasis; Form B, white collar emphasis; and Form C, Canadian emphasis—are available. Examiner required. Suitable for group use.

Timed: 15 minutes

Scoring: Examiner evaluated

Cost: Specimen set $4.00; 25 tests (specify form) $3.50

Publisher: Psychometric Affiliates

EMPLOYABILITY ATTITUDES

Adolescent, adult

Purpose: Assesses an individual's behavioral attitude in job-seeking and job-keeping situations and compares the attitudes with employers' expectations with regard to hiring, firing, or promoting.

Description: Multiple-item instrument in A-V format assessing 13 job-seeking and 23 job-keeping attitudes by means of 18 illustrated behavioral incidents. Incidents are presented in the form of adventures involving fictional characters of various ethnic backgrounds, races, and sex. The questions are narrated and shown on the A-V screen following each incident. Examinees respond as if they were the character involved. Responses are recorded on a response booklet or card. A generated report includes 36 attitudes and definitions; employers' hiring, firing, and promotion expectations; comparison of individuals' attitude levels to employers' expected levels and a prescription in the form of objectives that are needed to close the gaps. Curricular activities, goals, and objectives are prescribed to improve attitudes at levels of awareness, confidence, and automatic behavior. Curriculum, Learning Contracts, Learning Activity Maps, and Progress Charts are included in the Job Seeking and Job Keeping Curriculum

Packages. An instructor's guide is also available. Examiner/self-administered. Suitable for group use.

Untimed: 3 hours

Scoring: Hand key; may be computer scored

Cost: Contact publisher

Publisher: Prep, Inc.

EMPLOYEE ATTITUDE INVENTORY
London House Press

Adult

Purpose: Identifies employees who might steal or engage in costly counterproductive acts in the workplace. Used in investigative and organizational assessment of honesty and as a guide for in-house promotions.

Description: 179-item paper-pencil test measuring theft admissions, attitudes, and suspicions; drug-abuse tendencies; and job dissatisfaction and burnout. A validity scale is included. Although the test is self-administered, it may be given orally to illiterates. Suitable for group use.

Untimed: 30 minutes

Scoring: Computer scored

Cost: Complete $12.00

Publisher: London House Press

ETSA TESTS 8-A—PERSONAL ADJUSTMENT INDEX
Refer to page 806.

EXPERIENCE AND BACKGROUND QUESTIONNAIRE (EBQ)
Melany E. Baehr

Adult

Purpose: Evaluates an individual's past performance and experience in eight dimensions of quantified personal background data. Used for selection and placement of personnel in entry-level and first-line supervisory positions in public and private institutions.

Description: 71-item paper-pencil multiple-choice questionnaire assessing the following factorially determined background areas: group participation and school achievement, mobility, financial experience and responsibility, family responsibility, job and personal stability, parental family adjustment, and general health. Different combinations of scores are used in validated selection test batteries for transit bus operators, municipal police officers, and industrial supervisors. Basic adult reading skills are required. Self-administered. Suitable for group use.

Untimed: 15-20 minutes

Scoring: Hand key; may be computer scored

Cost: Specimen set $10.00; test booklets $17.50

Publisher: London House Press

FAMOUS SAYINGS (FS)
Bernard M. Bass

Adolescent, adult
Grades 10 and above

Purpose: Assesses personality. Used for industrial and professional screening and for research in social psychology.

Description: 131-item paper-pencil test of four vocationally important aspects of personality, including hostility, fear of failure, social acquiescence, and acceptance of conventional mores. Items are general statements consisting mainly of famous sayings, proverbs, and adages. Instructions are read aloud by the examiner while the subjects read along silently. The subjects indicate whether they agree or disagree with the statements or are uncertain. Examiner required. Suitable for group use.

Untimed: 15-30 minutes

Scoring: Hand key; examiner evaluated

Cost: Complete kit (general manual, 50 Form 1 test blanks, scoring stencil Form 1) $13.00; 50 test blanks $10.00; general manual $3.00

Publisher: Psychological Test Specialists

GIANNETTI ON-LINE PSYCHOSOCIAL HISTORY (GOLPH)
Refer to page 137.

GROUP ENCOUNTER SURVEY (GES)
Jay Hall and Martha S. Williams

Adult

Purpose: Assesses attitudes that affect an individual's ability to participate in group decision-making processes. Used in training programs aimed at improving group decision-making dynamics.

Description: Multiple-item paper-pencil self-report inventory assessing previously formed assumptions about the group decision-making process that determine an individual's effectiveness in such situations. The survey measures concerns about the quality of the group decision and about the other members' commitment to the decision. A decision-making grid is used to identify for the individual a personal style of group interaction. Dominant group styles, leadership preference, conflict resolution, intergroup relations, and feelings about groups per se are portrayed. Normative data are provided. Examiner required. Suitable for group use.

Untimed: Varies

Scoring: Examiner evaluated

Cost: Individual instrument $4.50

Publisher: Teleometrics International
Information and availability unconfirmed; no publisher response.

GROUP ENVIRONMENT SCALE (GES)
Refer to page 138.

HOGAN PERSONALITY INVENTORY
Refer to page 141.

HOGAN PERSONNEL SELECTION SERIES
Robert Hogan and Joyce Hogan

College student, adult

Purpose: Assesses aspects of personality related to job performance. Used for employee selection and placement.

Description: Four paper-pencil batteries, each consisting of 20-90 true-false items. The Primary Performance Battery indicates conscientiousness, honesty, dependability, even-tempered disposition, and tendency toward insubordination, theft, alcohol and substance abuse, illness, and worker compensation claims. The Clerical Performancy Battery predicts success in occupations requiring close attention to details, following instructions, and the ability to communicate effectively. The Sales Performance Battery predicts success in occupations requiring initiative, persistence, and the ability to influence others. The Managerial Performance Battery predicts success in occupations requiring leadership, planning, and the ability to motivate others. Scores are provided on four scales for each of the four batteries: Validity, Service Orientation, Reliability, and Stress Tolerance. The clerical, sales, and managerial batteries each include one additional scale designed to predict success in the relevant class of occupations. Items are presented at an eighth-grade reading level. Norms are provided for college students and adults. Examiner required. Suitable for group use.

Untimed: 5-20 minutes

Scoring: Hand key

Cost: Specimen set (specify inventory) $11.00

Publisher: National Computer Systems/PAS Division

HOW SUPERVISE?
Refer to page 954.

HUMAN FACTORS PERSONNEL SELECTION INVENTORY (HFPSI)

Adult

Purpose: Identifies job applicants who might engage in counterproductive or unsafe behavior in the workplace.

Description: Multiple-item paper-pencil test examining behavior that could result in theft, violence, drug abuse, or accidents on the job. A distortion scale is

included. Basic literacy is required. Self-administered. Suitable for group use. Available in Spanish.

Untimed: 30-40 minutes

Scoring: Computer scored by phone or by microprocessor on-site

Cost: Complete $8.50-$13.50 depending on volume

Publisher: London House Press; distributed by St. Paul Companies

---

INDUSTRIAL SENTENCE COMPLETION FORM
Martin M. Bruce

Adolescent, adult

Purpose: Aids in assessing personal adjustment and attitudes. Used for personnel evaluation and employee selection in business and industry and for clinical assessment.

Description: 50-item paper-pencil projective test of personal adjustment and attitudes. The individual completes 50 sentence items. There is no separate manual or key. Examiner/Self-administered. Suitable for group and individual use.

Untimed: Varies

Scoring: Examiner evaluated

Cost: 20 tests $25.75

Publisher: Martin M. Bruce, Ph.D., Publishers

INTERPERSONAL COMMUNICATION INVENTORY (ICI)
Millard J. Bienvenu

Adolescent, adult
Ages 15 and older

Purpose: Evaluates interpersonal communication skills. Used in counseling and teaching communication skills.

Description: 40-item paper-pencil multiple-choice test measuring the following communication skills: self-disclosure, expression of feelings, listening skills, nonverbal communication, acceptance of feelings, and confrontation. Materials include a questionnaire, answer sheet, and manual. Self-administered. Suitable for group use.

Untimed: 15 minutes

Scoring: Hand key; examiner evaluated

Cost: Test $0.35 each; guide $2.50

Publisher: Counseling and Self-Improvement Programs/Millard Bienvenu, Ph.D.

Information and availability unconfirmed; no publisher response.

INVENTORY OF INDIVIDUALLY-PERCEIVED GROUP COHESIVENESS
David L. Johnson

Adolescent, adult
Grades 10 and above

Purpose: Measures an individual's sense of cooperation in group activities. Used for counseling in school, business, family, training, research, organizational, and community settings.

Description: 20-item paper-pencil inventory of an individual's perception of cooperation, control, and task influence processes operating in a group and resulting in some degree of cohesiveness. The questionnaire may be used before and after group sessions. Self-administered. Suitable for group use.

Untimed: 15 minutes

Scoring: Self-scored

Cost: Complete kit (30 record forms, 3 feedback sheets, manual) $14.50

Publisher: Stoelting Company

I.P.I. EMPLOYEE APTITUDE SERIES: CONTACT PERSONALITY FACTOR (CPF)
Refer to page 815.

I.P.I. EMPLOYEE APTITUDE SERIES: NEUROTIC PERSONALITY FACTOR (NPF)
Refer to page 815.

I.P.I. EMPLOYEE APTITUDE SERIES: SIXTEEN PERSONALITY FACTOR (16PF)
Refer to page 815.

JENKINS ACTIVITY SURVEY (JAS)
Refer to page 203.

JOB ATTITUDE SCALE (JAS)
Shoukry Saleh

Adult

Purpose: Evaluates an employee's job preferences and attitudes. Used in business and industry to evaluate programs and individual orientations toward the workplace.

Description: 120-item long form and 60-item short form paper-pencil forced-choice test of attitudes towards 16 qualities: praise and recognition, growth in skills, creative work, responsibility, advancement, achievement, salary, security, personnel policies, competent supervision, relations-peers, relations-subordinant, relations-supervisor, working conditions, status, and family needs. The long form yields one general score. The short form yields an intrinsic score. Self-administered. Suitable for group use. Available in French.

Untimed: 30 minutes

Scoring: Hand key

Cost: Specimen set (manual, test sheet key) $8.00; 100 tests $20.00

Publisher: Shoukry Saleh

JOB PERFORMANCE SCALES SET

Adult

Purpose: Rates employee performance and attitudes. Used by supervisors for employee reviews.

Description: Multiple-item set of three paper-pencil evaluations including Primary Rating #1, Primary Rating #2, and a Rater's Performance Summary used for preemployment screening and for determining promotions, training needs, transfers, discipline, special consideration, and termination. Each evaluation rates an employee in a slightly different manner, and the combination provides a comprehensive measure of the employee's assets and value to his company. Examiner required. Not suitable for group use.

Untimed: 5 minutes
Scoring: Examiner evaluated
Cost: 25 copies $14.50
Publisher: E.F. Wonderlic Personnel Test, Inc.

JOB PERFORMANCE SCALES SET: PRIMARY RATING #1

Adult

Purpose: Assesses employee performance and attitudes. Used by supervisors for employee reviews.

Description: 35-item paper-pencil scale used by supervisors to rate employees' knowledge of the job, work volume, judgment, accuracy, learning ability, initiative, cooperativeness, and compatibility. Twenty-eight job-function items and seven attitude items make up the scale, which is one part of a three-part set. Examiner required. Not suitable for group use.
Untimed: 5 minutes
Scoring: Examiner evaluated
Cost: 25 copies $14.50
Publisher: E.F. Wonderlic Personnel Test, Inc.

JOB PERFORMANCE SCALES SET: PRIMARY RATING #2

Adult

Purpose: Assesses job-related conceptual abilities, attitudes, and behaviors of employees. Used by supervisors for employee reviews.

Description: 21-item paper-pencil scale used by supervisors to rate employees' abilities to learn the job, solve problems, communicate effectively, plan, make decisions, adapt, and follow instructions. Employees are also rated on attitude, dependability, punctuality, neatness, personality, and drive. From 1-25 points are awarded for each of the 13 job-function items and seven attitude items. Examiner required. Not suitable for group use.
Untimed: 5 minutes
Scoring: Examiner evaluated
Cost: 25 copies $14.50
Publisher: E.F. Wonderlic Personnel Test, Inc.

JOB PERFORMANCE SCALES SET: RATER'S SUMMARY

Adult

Purpose: Ranks employees in order of competence. Used by supervisors for employee reviews.

Description: Multiple-item paper-pencil scale used by supervisors for comparing and ranking employees in the following categories: general ability to learn and perform the job, general attitude toward the job, and total ranking—combination of productivity and attitude. This is the third of a set of three scales. Examiner required. Not suitable for group use.

Untimed: 10-20 minutes

Scoring: Examiner evaluated

Cost: 25 copies $14.50

Publisher: E.F. Wonderlic Personnel Test, Inc.

JOB SENSITIVITY INVENTORY (JSI)

Adult

Purpose: Assesses the opportunity for employees to engage in counterproductive behaviors. Both organizational security procedures and the incumbent's ability to perform counterproductive behaviors are assessed, showing the sensitivity of the job to employee counterproductivity.

Description: 120-item paper-pencil test measuring work area and personnel security practices; theft of property, equipment, or merchandise; theft of cash, credit, or information; alcohol and drug use on the job; violence; and opportunity for accidents. An overall score is provided for the analyzed position's sensitivity to counterproductive behaviors. Factor scores also are provided for assessing sensitivity in the several areas. Basic literacy is required. Security, management, and job incumbents can all complete the inventory. Examiner required. Suitable for group use.

Untimed: 45 minutes

Scoring: Computer scoring by publisher

Cost: $8.00-$13.00 depending on volume ordered
Publisher: London House Press

KIPNIS-SCHMIDT PROFILES OF ORGANIZATIONAL INFLUENCE STRATEGIES: INFLUENCING YOUR CO-WORKERS (POIS: FORM C)
David Kipnis and Stuart M. Schmidt

Adult

Purpose: Assesses which strategies a person uses in attempting to influence co-workers. Used for organizational communication assessment, organizational and human resources development, team building, and managerial training.

Description: 27-item paper-pencil test describing various influence tactics that a subject rates twice on a 6-point scale ranging from 1 (never) to 6 (almost always). The subject first rates the tactic on how frequently one uses it when first trying to influence a co-worker and then rates it on how frequently the tactic is used in a second attempt when the co-worker resists cooperating. Self-administered. Suitable for group use.
Untimed: 20-25 minutes
Scoring: Hand key
Cost: Complete set (materials for 10 participants) $45.00
Publisher: University Associates, Inc.
Information and availability unconfirmed; no publisher response.

KIPNIS-SCHMIDT PROFILES OF ORGANIZATIONAL INFLUENCE STRATEGIES: INFLUENCING YOUR MANAGER (POIS: FORM M)
David Kipnis and Stuart M. Schmidt

Adult

Purpose: Assesses which strategies a person uses in attempting to influence his manager. Used for organizational communication assessment, organization and human resource development, team building, and managerial training.

Description: 27-item paper-pencil test describing various influence tactics that a subject rates twice on a 6-point scale from 1 (never) to 6 (almost always). The subject first rates the tactic on how frequently one uses it when first trying to influence a manager and then how frequently the tactic is used in a second attempt when the manager resists cooperating. Self-administered. Suitable for group use.
Untimed: 20-25 minutes
Scoring: Hand key
Cost: Complete set (materials for 10 participants) $45.00
Publisher: University Associates, Inc.
Information and availability unconfirmed; no publisher response.

KIPNIS-SCHMIDT PROFILES OF ORGANIZATIONAL INFLUENCE STRATEGIES: INFLUENCING YOUR SUBORDINATES (POIS: FORM S)
David Kipnis and Stuart M. Schmidt

Adult

Purpose: Assesses which strategies a person uses in attempting to influence subordinates. Used for organizational communication assessment, organization and human resource development, team building, and managerial training.

Description: 33-item paper-pencil test describing various influence tactics that a subject rates twice on a 6-point scale from 1 (never) to 6 (almost always). The subject first rates each tactic on how frequently one uses it when first trying to influence a subordinate and then on how frequently the tactic is used in a second attempt when the subordinate resists cooperating. Self-administered. Suitable for group use.
Untimed: 25-30 minutes
Scoring: Hand key
Cost: Complete set (materials for 10 participants) $45.00
Publisher: University Associates, Inc.
Information and availability unconfirmed; no publisher response.

THE LAKE ST. CLAIR INCIDENT
Albert A. Canfield

Adult

Purpose: Examines individual and group decision-making processes. Used to improve decision-making, communication skills, and teamwork.

Description: Multiple-item paper-pencil test requiring a team of three to seven individuals to work together to solve a hypothetical problem situation involving cold weather and cold water survival. Participants are provided with considerable information on the subject, maps, charts, drawings, and a list of 15 items available for them to use in their struggle for survival. The team must reach a decision on what action to take and the relative importance of the 15 items. Three different decision-making processes are required: independent, consultive, and participative/consensual. Scoring procedure uses Coast Guard officer decisions and rankings as "expert" opinions. Scores are provided for three types of decision-making processes: autocratic, consultive, and consensual. Data are produced on which to evaluate the decision-making process and individual and team behaviors and compare the performance of different teams. A two-color test booklet includes a table for recording the results of up to 12 teams. The manual includes situation analysis, Coast Guard opinions and rationales, information on hypothermia, and averages of scores from other teams. Self-administered (teams must cooperate to get team performance scores). Suitable for group use.

Untimed: 1½-2 hours

Scoring: Self-scored

Cost: Demonstration kit (30 test booklets, manual) $45.95; specimen set (includes manual) $9.95

Publisher: Humanics Media

LEADERSHIP APPRAISAL SURVEY (LAS)
Jay Hall

Adult

Purpose: Evaluates a leader's behavior from the associates' point of view. Used for assessment and development purposes with nonmanagement supervisory personnel, campus and community groups, volunteer organizations, and administrative personnel.

Description: Multiple-item paper-pencil inventory assessing a leader's impact on and stimulus value for the group from the associates' point of view. The inventory identifies blindspots, pinpoints strengths and weaknesses, and confirms the way leadership practices come across to associates. The inventory yields analyses of overall leadership style, including four components of leadership: philosophy, planning, implementation, and evaluation. The inventory may be administered in conjunction with the Styles of Leadership Survey (SLS) to provide a comparison of the associates' ratings with the leaders self-ratings on the SLS. Normative data are provided. Examiner required. Suitable for group use.

Untimed: Varies

Scoring: Examiner evaluated

Cost: Individual instrument $4.50

Publisher: Teleometrics International

Information and availability unconfirmed; no publisher response.

MANAGEMENT APPRAISAL SURVEY (MAS)
Refer to page 958.

MANAGEMENT BURNOUT SCALE
John W. Jones and Donald M. Moretti

Adult

Purpose: Assesses burnout or work stress among managerial-level employees.

Description: Multiple-item paper-pencil test assessing burnout or work stress through four types of factors: cognitive reactions, affective reactions, behavioral reactions, and psychophysiological reactions. Self-administered. Suitable for group use.

Untimed: 10 minutes

Scoring: Hand key; may be computer scored

Cost: 25 tests $10.00; specimen set (interpretation manual, validation studies) $5.00

Publisher: London House Press

MANAGEMENT OF MOTIVES INDEX (MMI)

Refer to page 960.

MANAGEMENT RELATIONS SURVEY (MRS)

Refer to page 961.

MANAGEMENT TRANSACTIONS AUDIT (MTA)

Refer to page 961.

MANSON EVALUATION

Morse P. Manson

Adult

Purpose: Identifies maladjusted individuals. Used for personnel screening, diagnosis, therapy, and research.

Description: Multiple-item paper-pencil measure of seven personality characteristics: anxiety, depressive fluctuations, emotional sensitivity, resentfulness, incompleteness, aloneness, and interpersonal relations. The instrument identifies three types of maladjusted individuals: alcoholics, inadequates, and immature. Norms are provided for men and women. Examiner required. Suitable for group use.

Untimed: 5-10 minutes

Scoring: Hand key

Cost: Kit (25 tests, manual, key) $18.00

Publisher: Western Psychological Services

MASLACH BURNOUT INVENTORY (MBI)

Refer to page 204.

MAUDSLEY PERSONALITY INVENTORY (MPI)

Refer to page 150.

MCCORMICK JOB PERFORMANCE MEASUREMENT "RATE-$-SCALE" (RATE-$-SCALE)

Ronald R. McCormick

Adult

Purpose: Measures employee performance in terms of the dollar value of a successfully completed job. Used for employee compensation, training, promotion, and recruitment. Used in all industries and public agencies which have professional personnel office staff.

Description: Multiple-item paper-pencil inventory assessing four areas of employee performance: responsibility, attitude, time in labor grade, and efficiency. The employee's supervisor completes the form, which provides a rating scale in terms of the critical tasks and duties that the employee performs for pay. Comparisons of employee job performance are based upon the dollar value of the successful performance of a fully qualified worker. Local validation is required since employee job performance ratings are based upon the individual firm's compensation schedule. Results of employee evaluations can be entered readily into a computer for the detailed analysis required for rating form validation and payroll cost projections. Self-administered. Suitable for group use.

Untimed: 5 minutes

Scoring: Examiner evaluated

Cost: 25 rating forms $7.50

Publisher: Dr. R.R. McCormick and Associates

MEASURE OF ACHIEVING TENDENCY

Refer to page 151.

MEEKER BEHAVIOR CORRELATES FOR MANAGEMENT MATCHING OF TEAMS

Adult

Purpose: Assesses the abilities and attitudes of current and prospective employees. Used for employee selection and placement.

Description: Multiple-item self-report paper-pencil rating scale consisting of a three-way evaluation survey to be completed by supervisors, personnel directors, and prospective employees. The scale assesses major dimensions of intellectual abilities found to be correlates of personality characteristics and identifies team patterns. Self-administered. Suitable for group use.

Untimed: 20 minutes

Scoring: Examiner evaluated

Cost: 10 survey forms $20.00

Publisher: M & M Systems

MEYER-KENDALL ASSESSMENT SURVEY (MKAS)
*Henry D. Meyer and
Edward L. Kendall*

Adult

Purpose: Surveys work-related personality and interpersonal functioning for use in personnel assessment.

Description: 105 dichotomous-item paper-pencil test of 10 aspects of personal functioning relevant to performance at work. The scales are dominance, attention to detail, psychosomatic tendencies, independence, extroversion, anxiety, determination, people concern, stability, and achievement motivation. Scores are also obtained for two broad-band scales: Assertive Drive and Self-Assurance. An optional feature of the MKAS is the Pre-Assessment Worksheet, which determines the profile of an "ideal" applicant for a position. Examiner/self-administered. Suitable for group use.

Untimed: 15 minutes

Scoring: Computer scored

Cost: Manual $24.50; MKAS Assessment Sheets (includes scoring and reports) $35.00 each; MKAS Pre-Assessment Sheets (includes scoring and report) $7.50 each

Publisher: Western Psychological Services

THE MINER SENTENCE COMPLETION SCALE: FORM H
John B. Miner

Adult

Purpose: Measures an individual's hierarchic (bureaucratic) motivation. Used for employee counseling and development and organizational assessment.

Description: Multiple-item paper-pencil free-response or multiple-choice sentence completion test measuring an individual's motivation in terms of motivational patterns which fit the hierarchic (bureaucratic) organizational form. Both forms (free-response version or multiple-choice version offering six alternatives for each stem) measure the following subscales: authority figures, competitive games, competitive situations, assertive role, imposing wishes, standing out from the group, and routine administrative functions. The basic scoring guide (for use with the free-response version) discusses categorizing the responses, the subscales, supervisory jobs, total scores, and the sample scoring sheet. A supplementary scoring guide describing the scoring of the multiple-choice version and variations in scoring the free-response version is available. Examiner required. Suitable for group use.

Untimed: Varies

Scoring: Examiner evaluated

Cost: 50 scales (specify free-response or multiple-choice version) $15.00; basic scoring guide (64 pages) $5.00; supplementary scoring guide (15 pages) $2.50

Publisher: Organizational Measurement Systems Press

THE MINER SENTENCE COMPLETION SCALE: FORM P
John B. Miner

Adult

Purpose: Measures an individual's professional (specialized) motivation. Used for employee counseling and development and organizational assessment.

Description: Multiple-item paper-pencil free-response sentence completion test measuring an individual's motivation in terms of motivational patterns that fit the professional (specialized) organizational form. The test measures the following subscales: acquiring knowledge, independent action, accepting status, providing help, and professional commitment. Each test item consists of a sentence stem that the individual completes in his own words. The scoring guide discusses categorizing the responses, the subscales, actual scoring, reliability, normative data, use of Form P, and bibliographic notes. Examiner required. Suitable for group use.

Untimed: Varies

Scoring: Examiner evaluated

Cost: 50 scales $15.00; scoring guide $5.00

Publisher: Organizational Measurement Systems Press

MINNESOTA JOB DESCRIPTION QUESTIONNAIRE (MJDQ)

Adult

Purpose: Evaluates an employee's or supervisor's perception of the reinforcer characteristics of an occupation. Used for research purposes only.

Description: 42-item paper-pencil test covering ability utilization, achievement, activity, advancement, authority, company policies and practices, compensation, coworkers, creativity, independence, moral values, recognition, responsibility, security, social service, social status, supervision-technical, supervision-human relations, variety, and working conditions. On the first 21 items, subjects rate groups of five statements from one to five according to how well each statement describes their jobs. The test also may be used for obtaining a subject's perception of jobs in terms of expected or perceived reinforcer patterns. Form E (for employees) includes the 20-item short form of the Minnesota Satisfaction Questionnaire. Form S is available for supervisors. Self-administered. Suitable for group use.

Untimed: Open ended

Scoring: Computer scored

Cost: Form S $0.50 each; Form E $0.55 each; minimum order of 20 copies

Publisher: Vocational Psychology Research, University of Minnesota

---

MINNESOTA SATISFACTION QUESTIONNAIRE (MSQ)

Adult

Purpose: Evaluates employees' satisfaction with their jobs. Used for occupational and social research.

Description: 100-item paper-pencil questionnaire consisting of statements about various aspects of an individual's job. The individual rates each statement on a 5-point scale ranging from "very dissatisfied" to "very satisfied." Twenty scales of five items each measure the following factors: ability utilization, achievement, activity, advancement, authority, company policies and practices, compensation, coworkers, creativity, independence, moral values, recognition, responsibility, security, social science, social status, supervision-human relations, supervision-technical, variety, and working conditions. An optional 20-item General Satisfaction scale is also available. The alternative Short Form MSQ consists of one item from each of the 20 scales and yields the following scores: Intrinsic, Extrinsic, and General Satisfaction. The manual includes descriptions of the development and scoring of both forms, reliability and validity data, and norms. Prospective users must establish their qualifications with their initial order. Examiner required. Suitable for group use.

Untimed: Varies

Scoring: Hand key; may be computer scored

Cost: Specimen set (photocopy of manual, single copies of long form, long form 1967 revision, short form) $10.00

Publisher: Vocational Psychology Research, University of Minnesota

MINNESOTA SATISFACTORINESS SCALE (MSS)

Adult

Purpose: Measures an employee's satisfactoriness on a job. Used as a research instrument.

Description: 28-item paper-pencil inventory assessing an employee's behavior on the job. The employee's supervisor completes the form. Scores are provided for five scales: Performance, Conformance, Dependability, Personal Adjustment, and General Satisfactoriness. Additional data analysis are also available. The manual includes information on development and scoring of the test, reliability and validity data, and norms. Prospective users must establish their qualifications with their initial order. Self-administered by supervisor. Suitable for group use.

Untimed: Varies

Scoring: Hand key; may be computer scored

Cost: 30-499 copies $0.20 each; minimum order of 30 copies

Publisher: Vocational Psychology Research, University of Minnesota

MORRISBY DIFFERENTIAL TEST BATTERY (DTB)
Refer to page 896.

MOTIVATION ANALYSIS TEST (MAT)
Arthur B. Sweney,
Raymond B. Cattell, John L. Horn,
and IPAT Staff

Adolescent, adult
Grades 10 and above

Purpose: Measures motivational patterns in high-school seniors and adults. Used in a variety of counseling situations in education and business.

Description: 208-item paper-pencil multiple-choice test providing 10 measures of comfort, social, and achievement needs. Five are basic drives: caution, sex, self-assertion, aggressiveness, and self-indul-

gence. Five are interests that develop and mature through learning experience: career, affection, dependency, responsibility, and self-fulfillment. For each of the 10 interest areas, scores measure drive or need level, satisfaction level, degree of conflict, and total motivational strength. Standard scores are provided for men and women together. Self-administered. Suitable for group use.

Untimed: 50-60 minutes

Scoring: Hand key; may be computer scored

Cost: MAT professional examination kit $22.50; 25 test booklets $22.25; 50 machine-scorable answer sheets $10.50; 50 hand-scorable answer sheets $8.00; 50 profile sheets $6.50; 4 scoring keys $9.25; manual $11.50; individual scoring report certificates $2.50-$16.00

Publisher: Institute for Personality and Ability Testing, Inc.

MY VOCATIONAL SITUATION
John L. Holland, Denise Daiger,
and Paul G. Power

Adult

Purpose: Assesses the problems that may be troubling an individual seeking help with career decisions. Used in career counseling and guidance.

Description: Two-page multiple-item paper-pencil questionnaire determining which of three difficulties may be troubling an individual in need of career counseling: lack of vocational identity, lack of information or training, or environmental or personal barriers. The questionnaire is completed by the individual just prior to the counseling interview and may be tabulated by the counselor at a glance. Responses may offer clues for the interview itself and treatments relevant to each individual's need. The manual discusses development of the diagnostic scheme and reports statistical properties of the three variables. Self-administered. Suitable for group use.

Untimed: 5-10 minutes

Scoring: Examiner evaluated

Cost: 25 questionnaires $4.50; specimen kit (manual and sample questionnaire) $1.00

Publisher: Consulting Psychologists Press, Inc.

MYERS-BRIGGS TYPE INDICATOR (MBTI)
Refer to page 157.

OBSERVATIONAL ASSESSMENTS OF TEMPERAMENT
Melany E. Baehr

Adult

Purpose: Measures an individual's insight into his own behavior and representation to others. Used for career counseling and guidance. Predictive of performance in higher-level specialized and managerial positions.

Description: Paper-pencil test assessing three behavior factors that have been shown to be the most effective in predicting significant aspects of performance in higher-level positions: reserved/cautious vs. extroversive/impulsive, emotionally controlled vs. emotionally responsive, dependent/group oriented vs. self-reliant/individually oriented. Self-administered. Suitable for group use.

Timed/Untimed: 10 minutes

Scoring: Hand key

Cost: 25 tests $13.75

Publisher: London House Press

OCCUPATIONAL ENVIRONMENT SCALES: FORM E-2
Samuel H. Osipow and Arnold R. Spokane

Adult

Purpose: Measures different kinds of stresses people experience in their work, regardless of occupational field or level of employment. Used to redesign jobs to reduce stress and to plan counseling programs aimed at reducing on-the-job stress.

Description: 60-item paper-pencil inventory assessing six aspects of work environment related to role-related stress

that workers often encounter in their work environments: responsibility for others, role ambiguity, role insufficiency, role overload, boundary roles, and stresses induced by the physical environment. The test items consist of statements about work-related stress. Individuals rate each statement on a 5-point scale ranging from one (rarely or never) to five (most of the time) to indicate the degree to which each statement applies to their own work environment.

Scores are yielded for each of the six scales (10 items per scale). The manual includes the theoretical basis for the scales, information on reliability and validity, normative data procedures for scoring and interpretation, and potential applications. The inventory may be administered in conjunction with the Personal Strain Questionnaire and the Personal Resources Questionnaire for a more complete assessment of work environment and stress (all three tests share a common manual and profile form). Self-administered. Suitable for group use.

Untimed: Varies

Scoring: Examiner evaluated

Cost: 10 inventories $4.00; manual $11.00; 10 profiles $3.00; 10 interpretive flyers $3.00

Publisher: Marathon Consulting and Press

OCCUPATIONAL PERSONALITY QUESTIONNAIRES (OPQ)
Saville & Holdsworth Ltd. Staff

Adult

Purpose: Assesses personality characteristics relevant to job success. Used in personnel selection, placement, counseling, and development.

Description: Multiple-item paper-pencil or computer-administered questionnaires divided in four levels measuring personality traits on a scale of 1 (low) to 10 (high). Concept, the most detailed level, measures 30 traits. Other levels measure 14, 8, and 5 traits with progressively broader scale definitions. Research and development was sponsored by 53 major British

industries. Only one of the four levels should be used. Examiner/self-administered. Suitable for group use.
BRITISH PUBLISHER
Untimed: Varies
Scoring: Hand key; may be machine scored
Cost: See individual OPQ descriptions
Publisher: Saville & Holdsworth Ltd.

OPINIONS TOWARD ADOLESCENTS (OTA SCALE)
Refer to page 776.

===

OPQ CONCEPT MODEL
Saville & Holdsworth Ltd. Staff

Adult

Purpose: Assesses 30 work-relevant personality characteristics used in personnel selection, placement, counseling, and development.

Description: Three multiple-item paper-pencil questionnaires measuring 30 personality traits covering relationships with people (persuasive, outgoing, democratic), thinking style (practical, conceptual, conscientious, and feelings and emotions (worrying, critical, competitive.) Examiner/self-administered. Suitable for group use.
BRITISH PUBLISHER
Untimed: Varies
Scoring: Hand key; may be machine scored
Cost: 5 booklets $73.50-$105.00; 25 answer sheets $52.50-$105.00; 25 profile charts $26.25
Publisher: Saville & Holdsworth Ltd.

OPQ FACTOR MODEL
Saville & Holdsworth Ltd. Staff

Adult

Purpose: Assesses 14 work-relevant personality characteristics. Used in personnel selection, placement, counseling, and development.

Description: Two multiple-item paper-pencil or computer-administered questionnaires measuring 14 personality

characteristics, which are factorially derived from the OPQ Concept Model questionnaires. The personality traits assessed include influence, social confidence, conservative, anxious, and decisive. Examiner/self-administered. Suitable for group use.
BRITISH PUBLISHER
Untimed: Varies
Scoring: Hand key; may be machine scored
Cost: 5 booklets $63.00; 25 answer sheets $52.50; 25 profile charts $26.25; scoring key $37.80
Publisher: Saville & Holdsworth Ltd.

OPQ OCTAGON MODEL
Saville & Holdsworth Ltd. Staff

Adult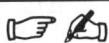

Purpose: Provides a rapid assessment of eight work-relevant personality characteristics. Used in personnel selection, placement, counseling, and development.

Description: Two multiple-item paper-pencil or computer-administered questionnaires measuring eight personality characteristics: assertive, empathy, gregarious, abstract, methodical, anxious, self-controlled, and vigorous. This questionnaire was factorially derived from more detailed OPQ questionnaires. Examiner/self-administered. Suitable for group use.
BRITISH PUBLISHER
Untimed: Varies
Scoring: Hand key; may be machine scored
Cost: 5 booklets $52.50; 25 answer sheets $52.50; 25 profile charts $26.25; scoring key $33.60-$37.80
Publisher: Saville & Holdsworth Ltd.

OPQ PENTAGON MODEL
Saville & Holdsworth Ltd. Staff

Adult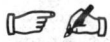

Purpose: Provides an evaluation of five work-related, broadly defined personality factors. Used in personnel selection, placement, counseling, and development.

Description: Two multiple-item paper-pencil or computer-administered questionnaires measuring the five personality factors: extroversion, abstract, methodical, emotional, and vigorous. The questionnaires currently are being used in team role research. Examiner/self-administered. Suitable for group use.
BRITISH PUBLISHER

Untimed: Varies

Scoring: Hand key; may be machine scored

Cost: 5 booklets $52.50; 25 answer sheets $52.50; 25 profile charts $26.25; scoring key $33.60

Publisher: Saville & Holdsworth Ltd.

THE ORGANIZATIONAL CLIMATE INDEX (OCI)
George Stern and Associates

Adult

Purpose: Measures the psychological climate of institutionalized work settings in terms of the need-press paradigm of human behavior as conceptualized by Henry Murray. Used in schools and colleges, industrial settings, and in conjunction with Peace Corps training programs for employee survey and research purposes.

Description: 300-item (long form) or 80-item (short form) paper-pencil true-false inventory assessing institutional work environments along 30 basic press scales reflecting the 30 basic need scales established on the Stern Activities Index (SAI). Both forms provide scores for six first-order dimensions and two second-order dimensions. Slightly different factor structures have been developed for school and college work environments. Analysis of school work environments yields first-order scores for intellectual climate, achievement standards, personal dignity, organizational effectiveness, orderliness, and impulse control and second-order scores for development and task effectiveness. Analysis of college work environments yields first-order scores for achievement standards, intellectual climate, practicalness, supportiveness, orderliness, and impulse control and second-order scores for development and

control. Factor structures, reliabilities, and norms also have been established for industrial, school district, and Peace Corps settings. Self-administered. Suitable for group use.

Untimed: Long form 40 minutes; short form 20 minutes

Scoring: Examiner evaluated; may be computer scored

Cost: Test booklet $0.50; answer sheet $0.10; profile form $0.10; technical manual $7.50; prices for computer scoring and analysis are available on request

Publisher: Evaluation Research Associates

PAPI SYSTEM
M.M. Kostick

Adult

Purpose: Measures employees' work preferences, assesses behavioral job requirements as seen from several perspectives, and evaluates workers' self-images. Explores areas managers need to be aware of in order to motivate, develop, and manage others more effectively. Used to establish in-service training objectives.

Description: Seven multiple-item paper-pencil inventories assisting in the development and management of staff. The inventories are the PA Preference Inventory (90 items measuring work preferences); three questionnaires rating behavioral job requirements from three perspectives (incumbent's view, supervisor's view, and subordinate's view); an ideal job requirements questionnaire; and two personal image questionnaires ("how I see you," and "how I see myself"). Employees complete one or more of the questionnaires, depending upon the objectives to be reached. The responses may be scored manually without being sent for specialist interpretation. Computerized scoring for norm building also is available. Individuals can be trained to interpret the PAPI System questionnaires during a short intensive training program. Personnel staff and selected managers are trained in the use of the system by experienced consultants. Companies without the facilities or personnel to use the system for themselves may be serviced by the PA Management Consultant Staff or its distributors. Other consultants may be trained and licensed to use the system with their own clients. Licensing with PA Consulting, Inc. or its distributors is required for purchase of all instruments in the system. Examiner required. Suitable for group use. Available in Arabic, Danish, Dutch, French, German, Italian, Norwegian, Portuguese, Spanish, and Swedish.

Untimed: 5-15 minutes per questionnaire

Scoring: Examiner evaluated; may be computer scored

Cost: PA license for organizations $4,000.00; PA license for consultants $2,000.00; see individual listings for prices of components

Publisher: PA Consulting Services, Inc.

Information and availability unconfirmed; no publisher response.

PAPI SYSTEM: HOW I SEE MYSELF
M.M. Kostick

Adult

Purpose: Measures an employee's self-image in terms of work-related needs and roles. Used to establish in-service training objectives.

Description: 20-item paper-pencil rating scale assessing an individual's work-related self-image along the following subscales: work direction, work style, activity, leadership, followership, social nature, and temperament. The test items consist of statements about needs (motivations) and roles (behavior). Individuals indicate the strength of the needs and the ease of playing the roles by rating each item on a 10-point scale ranging from 0 (exceptionally low) to 9 (exceptionally high). The subscales correlate directly with those of the PA Preference Inventory and the other components of the PAPI System. The test may be administered separately or in conjunction with other PAPI System components. The test is available only to organizations and consultants licensed with PA Consulting Services, Inc. or its distributors. Examiner required. Suitable for group use.

Available in Arabic, Danish, Dutch, French, German, Italian, Norwegian, Portuguese, Spanish, and Swedish.

Untimed: 5 minutes

Scoring: Examiner evaluated

Cost: 100 questionnaires $120.00

Publisher: PA Consulting Services, Inc.

Information and availability unconfirmed; no publisher response.

PAPI SYSTEM: HOW I SEE YOU
M.M. Kostick

Adult

Purpose: Measures an individual's perception of a fellow employee in terms of work-related needs and roles. Used to establish in-service training objectives.

Description: 20-item paper-pencil rating scale assessing an individual's perception of a co-worker along the following subscales: work direction, work style, activity, leadership, followership, social nature, and temperament. The test items consist of statements about needs (motivations) and roles (behavior). Individuals evaluate their co-workers (peer, subordinate, or supervisor) by rating each item on a 10-point scale ranging from 0 (exceptionally low) to 9 (exceptionally high) to indicate the strength of the needs and the ease of playing the roles. The subscales correlate directly with those of the PA Preference Inventory and the other components of the PAPI System. The test may be administered independently or in conjunction with other PAPI System components. The test is available only to organizations and consultants licensed with PA Consulting Services, Inc. or its distributors. Examiner required. Suitable for group use. Available in Arabic, Danish, Dutch, French, German, Italian, Norwegian, Portuguese, Spanish, and Swedish.

Untimed: 5 minutes

Scoring: Examiner evaluated

Cost: 100 questionnaires $120.00.

Publisher: PA Consulting Services, Inc.

Information and availability unconfirmed; no publisher response.

PAPI SYSTEM: PA PREFERENCE INVENTORY
M.M. Kostick

Adult

Purpose: Assesses an individual's work preferences in terms of needs and behavioral roles. Used to establish in-service training objectives.

Description: 90-item paper-pencil two-choice test measuring an individual's needs and preferred roles along the following subscales: work direction, work style, activity, leadership, followership, social nature, and temperament. Each item consists of a pair of simple descriptive statements. The individual selects the one statement from each pair which most accurately describes himself. The responses are tallied according to subscales and plotted on a circular profile chart. The subscales correlate directly to those of the other PAPI System components. The test may be administered independently or in conjunction with other components of the PAPI System. The test is available only to organizations and consultants licensed with PA Consulting Services, Inc. or its distributors. Examiner required. Suitable for group use. Available in Arabic, Danish, Dutch, French, German, Italian, Norwegian, Portuguese, Spanish, and Swedish.

Untimed: 15 minutes

Scoring: Examiner evaluated

Cost: Reusable test booklet $50.00; non-reusable test booklet $12.00; 100 answer sheets $192.00; 100 profile sheets $60.00

Publisher: PA Consulting Services, Inc.

Information and availability unconfirmed; no publisher response.

PAPI SYSTEM: RATING OF JOB REQUIREMENTS—FORM A REVISED
M.M. Kostick

Adult

Purpose: Evaluates the requirements of a particular job from the incumbent job holder's point of view. Used to establish in-service training objectives.

Description: 20-item paper-pencil multiple-choice questionnaire assessing the manner in which an incumbent job holder would describe the requirements of his job in terms of work-related needs (motivations) and behavioral roles. The test measures the following subscales: work direction, work style, activity, leadership, followership, social nature, and temperament. Each item consists of nine statements describing possible job requirements (the statements for each item represent a continuum between two bipolar extremes, such as adaptable/routine-oriented and leadership/subordinate). The incumbents circle the number of the statement which best describes the requirements of their job and cross out the numbers of any statements which are definitely uncharacteristic. The subscales correlate directly with those of other PAPI System components. The test may be administered independently or in conjunction with other PAPI System components. The test is available only to organizations and consultants licensed by PA Consulting Services, Inc. or its distributors. Examiner required. Suitable for group use. Available in Arabic, Danish, Dutch, French, German, Italian, Norwegian, Portuguese, Spanish, and Swedish.

Untimed: 15 minutes

Scoring: Examiner evaluated

Cost: 100 questionnaires $132.00

Publisher: PA Consulting Services, Inc.

Information and availability unconfirmed; no publisher response.

PAPI SYSTEM: RATING OF JOB REQUIREMENTS—FORM B REVISED
M.M. Kostick

Adult

Purpose: Evaluates the requirements for a subordinate's job from the supervisor's point of view. Used to establish in-service training objectives.

Description: 20-item paper-pencil multiple-choice questionnaire assessing the manner in which a supervisor would describe the job requirements of a subordinate in terms of work-related needs (motivations) and behavioral roles. The test measures the following subscales: work direction, work style, activity, leadership, followership, social nature, and temperament. Each item consists of nine statements describing possible job requirements. The statements for each item represents a continuum between two bipolar extremes, such as adaptable/routine-oriented and leadership/subordinate. The supervisor circles the number of the statement which best describes the requirements of the subordinate's job and crosses out the numbers of any statements which are definitely uncharacteristic. The subscales correlate directly with those of the other PAPI System components. The test may be administered independently or in conjunction with other components of the PAPI System. The test is available only to organizations and consultants licensed with PA Consulting Services, Inc. or its distributors. Examiner required. Suitable for group use. Available in Arabic, Danish, Dutch, French, German, Italian, Norwegian, Portuguese, Spanish, and Swedish.

Untimed: 15 minutes

Scoring: Examiner evaluated

Cost: 100 questionnaires $132.00

Publisher: PA Consulting Services, Inc.

Information and availability unconfirmed; no publisher response.

PAPI SYSTEM: RATING OF JOB REQUIREMENTS—FORM C REVISED
M.M. Kostick

Adult

Purpose: Evaluates the requirements for a boss' job from the subordinate's point of view. Used to establish in-service training objectives.

Description: 20-item paper-pencil multiple-choice questionnaire assessing the manner in which a subordinate would describe the job requirements of a supervisor in terms of work-related needs (motivations) and behavioral roles. The test measures the following subscales: work direction, work style, activity, leadership, followership, social nature, and temperament. Each item consists of nine

statements describing possible job requirements. The statements for each item represent a continuum between two bipolar extremes, such as adaptable/routine-oriented and leadership/subordinate. The subordinate circles the number of the statement which best describes the requirements of the supervisor's job and crosses out the numbers of any statements which are definitely not characteristic. The subscales correlate directly with those of the other PAPI System components. The test may be administered separately or in conjunction with other components of the PAPI System. Available only to organizations and consultants licensed with PA Consulting Services, Inc. or its distributors. Examiner required. Suitable for group use. Available in Arabic, Danish, Dutch, French, German, Italian, Norwegian, Portuguese, Spanish, and Swedish.

Untimed: 15 minutes

Scoring: Examiner evaluated

Cost: 100 questionnaires $132.00

Publisher: PA Consulting Services, Inc.

Information and availability unconfirmed; no publisher response.

PAPI SYSTEM: RATING OF JOB REQUIREMENTS—FORM D REVISED
M.M. Kostick

Adult

Purpose: Evaluates the job requirements an individual would select to describe the ideal job. Used to establish in-service training objectives.

Description: 20-item paper-pencil multiple-choice questionnaire assessing the manner in which an individual would describe the requirements for an ideal job in terms of work-related needs (motivations) and behavioral roles. The test measures the following subscales: work direction, work style, activity, leadership, followership, social nature, and temperament. Each item consists of nine statements describing possible job requirements. The statements for each item represent a continuum between two bipolar extremes, such as adaptable/routine-oriented and leadership/subordinate.

The individual circles the number of the statement which best describes the requirements of an ideal job and crosses out the numbers of any statements which are definitely undesirable or uncharacteristic. The subscales correlate directly with those of the other PAPI System components. The test may be administered independently or in conjunction with other components of the PAPI System. The test is available only to organizations and consultants licensed with PA Consulting Services, Inc. or its distributors. Examiner required. Suitable for group use. Available in Arabic, Danish, Dutch, French, German, Italian, Norwegian, Portuguese, Spanish, and Swedish.

Untimed: 15 minutes

Scoring: Examiner evaluated

Cost: 100 questionnaires $132.00

Publisher: PA Consulting Services, Inc.

Information and availability unconfirmed; no publisher response.

THE PERSONAL AUDIT
Clifford R. Edams and William M. Lepley

Adolescent, adult
Grades 7 and above

Purpose: Assesses an individual's personality as a factor of how well that person will perform in school or industry. Also used for clinical diagnosis of maladjustment.

Description: 450-item paper-pencil objective personality test. Nine scales of 50 items each measure relatively independent components of personality: seriousness-impulsiveness, firmness-indecision, tranquility-irritability, frankness-evasion, stability-instability, tolerance-intolerance, steadiness-emotionality, persistence-fluctuation, and contentment-worry. The test acquaints teachers with personality characteristics of students, is an aid to vocational and educational counseling, and provides an index of employees' job satisfaction and success in terms of their personal adjustment. Two forms are available. Form LL is used with adults with the equivalent of a grammar-school education and senior high-school students. Form SS, composed of the first six scales of Form LL, is used with junior high-school students or where administration time is limited. Self-administered. Suitable for group use.

Untimed: Form LL 40-50 minutes; Form SS 30-40 minutes

Scoring: Hand key

Cost: 25 test booklets Form LL $44.00; 25 test booklets Form SS $37.00; examiner's manual $10.00

Publisher: Science Research Associates, Inc.

PERSONAL DATA FORM
Morris I. Stein

Adult

Purpose: Assesses job applicants in terms of the roles required as scientists, professional, administrators, and employees involved in social relations. Used to place individuals in positions in which they can work creatively and productively.

Description: 80-item paper-pencil questionnaire serves as a job application form for technical and administrative positions with research and development organizations. The test items elicit information concerning the applicant's self-concept, abilities, and self-perception in terms of the roles required by the job for which he is applying. Self-administered. Suitable for group use.

Untimed: 30 minutes

Scoring: Examiner evaluated

Cost: $2.50 per copy

Publisher: Morris I. Stein

Information and availability unconfirmed; no publisher response.

PERSONAL OUTLOOK INVENTORY (POI)

Adult

Purpose: Predicts probability of employee theft. Used for screening job candidates.

Description: 37-item paper-pencil screening test assessing job candidates' potential to steal cash or merchandise. Individuals are less likely to fake test results because of the nonloaded questions. The test complies with legal regulations. The evaluation can be used for rank ordering of applicants and placing high-risk applicants in positions with less opportunity to steal. Examiner required. Suitable for group use. CANADIAN PUBLISHER

Untimed: Varies

Scoring: Computer scored

Cost: $11.00-$18.00 each

Publisher: Wolfe Personnel Testing and Training Systems, Inc.

PERSONAL QUESTIONNAIRE/ OCCUPATIONAL VALUES
Refer to page 755.

PERSONAL REACTION INDEX (PRI)
Jay Hall

Adult

Purpose: Measures the degree to which employees feel they are encouraged to participate in the decision-making process. Used in programs evaluating job satisfaction at all occupational levels and in management training and development programs.

Description: Multiple-item paper-pencil inventory assessing the attitudes of subordinates toward the decision structure which governs their work. Measures the amount of influence subordinates feel they have in making work-related decisions and their consequent satisfaction with and commitment to those decisions. The resulting information provides information concerning the manager's use or lack of use of the participative ethic with subordinates. Normative data are provided. Examiner required. Suitable for group use.

Untimed: Varies

Scoring: Examiner evaluated

Cost: Individual survey $2.00

Publisher: Teleometrics International

Information and availability unconfirmed; no publisher response.

PERSONAL RELATIONS SURVEY (PRS)
Refer to page 965.

PERSONAL RESOURCES QUESTIONNAIRE: FORM E-2
Samuel H. Osipow and Arnold R. Spokane

Adult

Purpose: Measures the extent to which resources are available to people to counteract the effects of occupational stress. Used in conjunction with counseling programs aimed at reducing occupational stress.

Description: 40-item paper-pencil inventory assessing the potential individuals have for dealing effectively with work stress. The inventory measures the following four dimensions: recreation, self-care, rational/coping behaviors, and social support system. Scores are yielded for each of the four scales (10 items per scale). Test items describe activities or feelings which help to relieve stress. Individuals rate each statement on a scale from one ("rarely or never") to five ("most of the time") to indicate the degree to which each item describes their own activities or feelings. The manual includes the theoretical basis for the scales, information on reliability and validity, normative data procedures for administration and scoring, and potential applications. The inventory may be administered in conjunction with the Occupational Environment Scales and the Personal Strain Questionnaire for a more complete assessment of work environment and stress (all three tests share a common manual and profile form). Self-administered. Suitable for group use.

Untimed: Varies

Scoring: Examiner evaluated

Cost: 10 inventories $4.00; manual $11.00; 10 profiles $3.00; 10 interpretive flyers $3.00

Publisher: Marathon Consulting and Press

THE PERSONAL SKILLS MAP (PSM)
Darwin B. Nelson and Gary R. Low

Adolescent, adult

Purpose: Evaluates self-perceived skill levels key to personal and career effectiveness. Used for counseling and to plan individual and group intervention strategies.

Description: 300-item paper-pencil test evaluating two intrapersonal skills: self-esteem and growth motivation; three interpersonal skills: assertion, interpersonal awareness, and empathy; and six career/life skills: drive strength, decision-making, time management, sales orientation, commitment ethic, and stress management. There are three response categories: most descriptive, sometimes descriptive, and least descriptive. There are no right or wrong answers. The test is designed to benefit the person using it, not for screening purposes. An adolescent and an adult form are available. Self-administered. Suitable for group use.

Untimed: 1 hour

Scoring: Computer scored; self-scored version available

Cost: Booklet $5.00 (specify form); manual $20.00; specimen set $75.00

Publisher: Institute for the Development of Human Resources

Information and availability unconfirmed; no publisher response.

PERSONAL STRAIN QUESTIONNAIRE: FORM E-2
Samuel H. Osipow and Arnold R. Spokane

Adult

Purpose: Measures different kinds of strains people experience in their lives, which may be the result of occupational stress. Used in conjunction with counseling programs aimed at reducing occupational stress.

Description: 40-item paper-pencil inventory assessing four dimensions of occupational stress: vocational (productivity and work attitudes), psychological (adjustment and/or mood disruptions), interpersonal (disruption in interpersonal relations), and physical (self-care habits and health). The test items describe behaviors and attitudes that may be symptomatic of personal stress. Individuals rate each statement on a 5-point scale ranging from one ("rarely or never") to five ("most of the time") to indicate the degree to which each item describes their own behaviors or attitudes. Scores are yielded for each of the four scales (10 items per scale). The manual includes the theoretical basis for the scales, information on reliability and validity, normative data procedures for scoring and interpretation, and potential applications. The test may be administered in conjunction with the Personal Resources Questionnaire and the Occupational Environment Scales for a more complete assessment of work environment and stress (all three tests share a common manual and profile form). Self-administered. Suitable for group use.

Untimed: Varies

Scoring: Examiner evaluated

Cost: 10 inventories $4.00; manual $11.00; 10 profiles $3.00; 10 interpretive flyers $3.00

Publisher: Marathon Consulting and Press

PERSONALITY RESEARCH FORM (PRF)
Refer to page 207.

PERSONNEL SELECTION INVENTORY (PSI)
London House Press

Adult

Purpose: Identifies job applicants who might engage in theft or counterproductive behavior in the workplace.

Description: Multiple-item paper-pencil test measuring dishonesty, violence, drug abuse, emotional instability, and safety consciousness. A distortion scale is included. Several versions of the test are included. Basic literacy is required. Self-administered. Suitable for group use. Available in Spanish.

Untimed: 30-40 minutes
Scoring: Computer scored by phone or by on-site personal computer
Cost: Complete $7.00-$15.00 depending on volume ordered
Publisher: London House Press

PICTURE PERSONALITY TEST FOR INDIAN SOUTH AFRICANS (PPT-ISA)
Refer to page 165.

PICTURE SITUATION TEST

Adult males

Purpose: Measures an individual's response to aggression-provoking stimuli within an everyday context. Used for personnel screening and placement and clinical research on aggression.

Description: 20-item paper-pencil test measuring the type of aggression an individual displays and the effect it is likely to have on the interpersonal situation in which aggression appears. The test items consist of partially structured pictures depicting aggression-provoking situations. The individual must complete the situation by giving his own responses. Responses are scored for type of aggression (direct, denial) and effect of response (constructive, destructive). A method for standardized scoring is provided. The test is restricted to competent persons properly registered with the South African Medical and Dental Council. Examiner required. Suitable for group use. Afrikaans version available.
SOUTH AFRICAN PUBLISHER
Untimed: No time limit
Scoring: Hand key; examiner evaluated
Cost: Contact publisher
Publisher: National Institute for Personnel Research

POSITION ANALYSIS QUESTIONNAIRE (PAQ)
Ernest J. McCormick, P.R. Jeanneret, and Robert C. Meacham

Adult

Purpose: Analyzes jobs in terms of job elements that reflect directly or infer the

basic human behaviors involved, regardless of their specific technological areas or functions. Used with jobs at all levels, including managerial, supervisory staff, professional, technical, skilled public contact, office, production and operation, service, and semiskilled.

Description: 187-item paper-pencil job analysis rating scale in which the examiner/analyst indicates the degree of involvement of each of the elements listed using appropriate rating scales such as importance, frequency, etc. The job elements are organized so that they provide a logical analysis of the jobs structure. Six broad areas are assessed: information input, mental processes, work output, relationships with other persons, job context, and other job characteristics. Examples of specific job elements are the use of written materials, the level of decision making, the use of mechanical devices, working in a hazardous environment, and working at a specified pace. Analysis of the questionnaire is in terms of job dimensions (clusters of related elements). The results are used as the basis for job aptitude requirements, deriving "point" values for jobs that in turn can be used to establish compensation rates, and classifying jobs into clusters which have statistically similar profiles. Also available on an experimental basis is the Job Activity Preference Questionnaire (JAPQ), which measures an individual's career interests in terms of the PAQ job dimensions. Self-administered by analyst, personnel staff, job supervisors, and in some cases the workers themselves. Suitable for group use.
Untimed: Not available
Scoring: Examiner evaluated; computer processing available
Cost: Complete kit (PAQ, record form, technical manual, job analysis manual, users manual, binder) $27.00; computer processing from PAQ services $1.60 to $100.00 based on processing option
Publisher: Purdue Research Foundation/University Book Store

POWER PERCEPTION PROFILES: SELF/OTHER
Paul Hersey and Walter E. Natemeyer

Adult

Purpose: Evaluates the manner in which an individual uses power as the basis for asserting leadership. Used for leadership and management training, HRD, and team building.

Description: 21-item paper-pencil test measuring an individual's choice of seven power bases: coercion, connection, expert, information, legitimate, referent, and reward. Two separate forms are available: Perception of Self and Perception of Other. The individual uses the Perception of Self form to answer questions about himself. A person acting as observer completes the Perception of Other form. The two individuals chart and compare scores, drawing a profile of the results for discussion. Materials include profiles, scoring, and interpretation. Self-administered. Suitable for group use.

Untimed: Not available

Scoring: Hand key

Cost: 10-99 forms (specify form) $2.95 each

Publisher: Center for Leadership Studies

PROBLEM-SOLVING DECISION-MAKING STYLE INVENTORY: SELF/OTHER
Refer to page 966.

PROCESS DIAGNOSTIC (PD)
Jay Hall

Adult

Purpose: Assesses interpersonal group dynamics. Used in training programs aimed at raising a group's awareness of its own internal processes.

Description: Multiple-item paper-pencil inventory assessing the internal processes of a group. A matrix format and scoring wheel are used to identify behavioral cluster scores for individual group members. Group members receive individual assessments of the dynamics underlying their behavior and of their impact on the group. Diagnostic information also is provided concerning the group's climate resulting from the problem-solving, "flight," or "fight" behaviors of its members. Several hours are required to initiate in-depth, free-wheeling interchange. Trained pro-

cess specialists or outside consultants are not required. Examiner required. Suitable for group use.

Untimed: Several hours

Scoring: Examiner evaluated

Cost: Individual instrument $4.50

Publisher: Teleometrics International

Information and availability unconfirmed; no publisher response.

PRODUCTIVITY ENVIRONMENTAL PREFERENCE SURVEY (PEPS)
Rita Dunn, Kenneth Dunn, and Gary E. Price

Adult

Purpose: Assesses the manner in which adults prefer to function, learn, concentrate, and perform in their occupational or educational activities. Used for employee placement and counseling and office design and lay-out.

Description: 100-item paper-pencil Likert-scale inventory measuring the following environmental factors related to educational or occupational activities: immediate environment (sound, temperature, light, and design), emotionality (motivation, responsibility, persistence, and structure), sociological needs (self-oriented, peer-oriented, authority-oriented, and combined ways), and physical needs (perceptual preferences, time of day, intake, and mobility). Test items consist of statements about the ways people like to work or study. Respondents are asked to indicate whether they agree or disagree with each statement. Computerized results are available in three forms: individual profile (raw scores for each of the 20 areas, standard scores, and a plot for each score in each area), group summary (identifies individuals with significantly high or low scores and groups individuals with similar preferences), and subscale summary. Results provide a basis for supervisor- or instructor-individual interaction in the ways that permit each person to concentrate best. In addition, the results allow instructors or supervisors to group individuals or design work settings based on similarity among productivity elements. Self-administered. Suitable for group use.

Untimed: 20-30 minutes

Scoring: Computer scored

Cost: Specimen set (manual, answer sheet) $11.00

Publisher: Price Systems, Inc.

PROGRAM FOR ASSESSING YOUTH EMPLOYMENT SKILLS (PAYES)

Refer to page 768.

THE PURDUE HANDICAP PROBLEMS INVENTORY
H.H. Remmers and G.N. Wright

Adult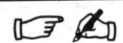

Purpose: Measures self-perceived problems of the handicapped adult. Used for counseling and research.

Description: Paper-pencil self-report of perceived problems in four areas: social, family, vocational, and personal. Examiner required. Suitable for group use.

Untimed: 25-35 minutes

Scoring: Hand key; may be machine scored

Cost: Contact publisher

Publisher: Purdue Research Foundation/ University Book Store

RAHIM ORGANIZATIONAL CONFLICT INVENTORIES: EXPERIMENTAL EDITION (ROCI)
Afzalur Rahim

Adult

Purpose: Measures conflict experienced within an organization and assesses varying styles of handling the conflict.

Description: 105-item paper-pencil self-report inventory in two parts assessing the types of conflict and the various styles of handling conflict found within an organization. Part I contains 21 items assessing three dimensions or types of organizational conflict: intrapersonal, intergroup, and intragroup. Part II consists of three 28-item forms assessing conflict with one's boss (Form A), with one's subordinates (Form B), and with one's peers (Form C). Five styles of handling interpersonal conflict are identified: integrating, obliging, dominating, avoiding, and compromising. Both parts use a 5-point Likert scale. Limited norms are provided for college students and managerial groups. Examiner required. Suitable for group use.

Untimed: 45 minutes

Scoring: Examiner evaluated

Cost: 25 ROCI-I inventories $8.50; 25 ROCI-II inventories (includes 25 each of Forms A, B, C) $11.50; manual $10.00

Publisher: Consulting Psychologists Press, Inc.

REACTION TO EVERYDAY SITUATIONS TEST
Sheena M.A. Waterhouse

Adolescent, adult Ages 16 and older

Purpose: Measures general anxiety shown by individuals in their day-to-day lives. Used for employee selection and screening and clinical research.

Description: 50-item paper-pencil questionnaire measuring the general anxiety shown by examinees in everyday situations. Each test item relates to a particular situation in which anxiety might be displayed. The test is restricted to competent persons properly registered with the South African Medical and Dental Council. Examiner required. Suitable for group use. Afrikaans version available.
SOUTH AFRICAN PUBLISHER

Untimed: No time limit

Scoring: Hand key

Cost: Contact publisher

Publisher: National Institute for Personnel Research

REID REPORT

Adult

Purpose: Evaluates the honesty of job applicants. Identifies individuals most likely to steal at work if given the opportunity. Does not discriminate on the basis of sex, race, or age.

Description: Multiple-item paper-pencil questionnaire consisting of three sections. The first section contains 90 yes-no questions measuring the applicant's attitudes toward theft and the punishment of theft. The second section contains a detailed biographical data blank covering previous employment, education, and social history, including drug and alcohol abuse and excessive gambling as they relate to a need to steal. The third section is an admissions list of previous thefts and other misconduct, including convictions. Based on the score from Section One and the evaluation of the bio-data and admission-of-theft questions, the applicant is recommended or not recommended for employment. Results are available by phone or mail. Examiner required. Suitable for group use. Available in Spanish, Portuguese, Italian, Polish, and French.

Untimed: 45 minutes

Scoring: Computer scored

Cost: $7.00-$12.00 each, depending on volume ordered

Publisher: Reid Psychological Systems

REID SURVEY

Adult

Purpose: Evaluates the honesty of current employees. Identifies employees most likely to be responsible for thefts within the company. Used to screen employees for promotion to sensitive positions. Does not discriminate on the basis of sex, race, or age.

Description: Multiple-item paper-pencil questionnaire consisting of two sections. The first section contains 90 yes-no questions measuring the employee's attitudes toward theft and the punishment of theft. The second section contains questions about recent job history and knowledge and opinions about in-company theft both by the responding employee and by others. Examiner required. Suitable for group use. Available in Spanish, Portuguese, and French.

Untimed: 45 minutes

Scoring: Computer scored

Cost: $11.00-$15.00 each, depending on volume ordered

Publisher: Reid Psychological Systems

REID SURVEY (RETAIL)

Adult

Purpose: Evaluates the honesty of current employees. Identifies employees most likely to be responsible for thefts within the company. Emphasizes theft in retail establishments. Used to screen employees for promotion to sensitive positions. Does not discriminate on the basis of sex, race, or age.

Description: Multiple-item paper-pencil questionnaire consisting of two sections. The first section contains 90 yes-no questions measuring the employee's attitudes toward theft and the punishment of theft. The second section contains 75 objective questions dealing with the employee's attitude toward the company and the employee's knowledge about or opinions concerning the honesty of others in the company, including questions about thefts or other defalcatory behaviors. Examiner required. Suitable fo group use. Available in Spanish, Portuguese, and French.

Untimed: 45 minutes

Scoring: Computer scored

Cost: $11.00-$15.00 each, depending on volume ordered

Publisher: Reid Psychological Systems

RELATIONSHIP PROFILE (EGOGRAM™)
Refer to page 84.

SALES RELATIONS SURVEY (SRS)
Refer to page 1004.

SALES TRANSACTION AUDIT (STA)
Refer to page 1004.

A SCALE TO MEASURE ATTITUDES TOWARD DISABLED PERSONS
Refer to page 691.

THE SCHUTZ MEASURES: ELEMENT F-FEELINGS

Refer to page 174.

THE SCHUTZ MEASURES: ELEMENT J—JOB (JOB HOLDER, CO-WORKER)
Will Schutz

Adult

Purpose: Measures perceptions of personal and interpersonal aspects of a job. Used for analysis of personal growth, job clarification, career planning, and training and development.

Description: 54-item paper-pencil test containing forms for "job or job holder" and "co-workers." For personal feedback, the job holder and co-worker(s) complete the forms and compare results. For job definition, the forms are evaluated by persons evaluating or planning the job. The factors measured include expressed-received and perceived-wanted aspects of the behavioral dimensions of inclusion, control, and openness and the feelings dimensions of significance, competence, and likeability. Self-administered. Suitable for group use.

Untimed: 15-20 minutes

Scoring: Hand key

Cost: Complete set (material for 10 participants) $30.00; trainer's package (manual and each of 5 instruments) $50.00

Publisher: University Associates, Inc.
Information and availability unconfirmed; no publisher response.

THE SCHUTZ MEASURES: ELEMENT R—RELATIONSHIPS
Refer to page 174.

SECURITY, APTITUDE, FITNESS EVALUATION (SAFE)
John Taccarino, Ph.D.

Adult   Ages 16 and older

Purpose: Assesses characteristics of satisfactory employment that would reduce internal theft and increase productivity. Used in hiring for nonmanagement positions, such as store clerk, warehouse worker, truck driver, hotel clerk, janitor, custodian, and bank teller.

Description: Three-part pre-employment screening test assessing six characteristics essential to satisfactory employment: honesty (applicant's likeliness to steal), dependability (punctuality and tardiness), socialization (behavior toward co-workers and customers), credibility, numerical ability, and language skills. Separate scores corresponding to the rankings of high-risk, low-risk, or caution-risk with respect to employment are provided for each characteristic. Examiner required. Suitable for group use.

Untimed: 30 minutes

Scoring: Computer scored (computer is pre-programmed, hand-held, and automatically provides separate scores for all six subtests in less than 3 minutes)

Cost: Introductory kit (computer, 25 test booklets, manual) $200.00

Publisher: SAFE, Inc.

SELF-ACTUALIZATION INVENTORY (SAI)
W.J. Reddin

Adult

Purpose: Measures the degree to which an individual's needs are fulfilled. Used to compare responses of managers and their subordinates.

Description: Paper-pencil test covering the following needs: physical, security, relationships, respect, independence, and self-actualization. Self-administered. Suitable for group use.
CANADIAN PUBLISHER

Untimed: 20-30 minutes

Scoring: Hand key

Cost: Test kit (10 test copies, fact sheet, user's guide) $40.00

Publisher: Organizational Tests (Canada) Ltd.

SIXTEEN PERSONALITY FACTOR QUESTIONNAIRE
Refer to page 179.

SPECTRUM
Larry A. Braskamp and
Martin L. Maehr

Adult

Purpose: Evaluates the opportunities for fulfillment that individuals perceive in their present jobs, motivates workers by determining personal values and incentives, and assesses organizational culture and employee commitment. Used in organizational development.

Description: 200 Likert-scale items measuring four aspects of the worker, job, and organization: accomplishment, recognition, power, and affiliation. Three types of reports are available. The Type I report gives employees feedback about individual incentives, personal values, and job opportunities. The Type II report provides supervisors with insights into their own management style and the impact their personal styles have on the people they supervise. The group report for executive planners provides feedback on organizational culture, degree of employee commitment, and areas of job satisfaction. Examiner/self-administered. Suitable for group use.

Untimed: 1 hour

Scoring: Computer scored

Cost: Introductory kit (manual, sample group report, survey booklet, processing fees for two reports) $30.00

Publisher: MetriTech, Inc.

STAFF BURNOUT SCALE FOR HEALTH PROFESSIONALS
John W. Jones

Adult

Purpose: Assesses burnout or work stress among health-care professionals.

Description: Multiple-item paper-pencil test assessing burnout or work stress through four types of factors: cognitive reactions, affective reactions, behavioral reactions, and psychophysiological reactions. Self-administered. Suitable for group use.

Untimed: 10 minutes

Scoring: Hand key; may be computer scored

Cost: 25 tests $10.00; specimen set (interpretation manual, validation studies) $5.00

Publisher: London House Press

STAFF BURNOUT SCALE FOR POLICE AND SECURITY PERSONNEL
John W. Jones

Adult

Purpose: Assesses burnout or work stress among police and security personnel.

Description: Multiple-item paper-pencil test assessing burnout or work stress through four types of factors: cognitive reactions, affective reactions, behavioral reactions, and psychophysiological reactions. Self-administered. Suitable for group use.

Untimed: 10 minutes

Scoring: hand key; may be computer scored

Cost: 25 tests $10.00; specimen set (interpretation manual, validation studies) $5.00

Publisher: London House Press

THE STANTON CASE REVIEW
Carl S. Klump

Adolescent, adult

Purpose: Assesses an individual's ability to identify persons responsible for an incident. Used with adolescents and adults.

Description: Multiple-item paper-pencil investigative questionnaire assessing an individual's ability to identify a person's degree of responsibility for an incident. The review begins with a description of an incident, such as a theft, and requests individuals to voluntarily complete a questionnaire. Individuals then complete a personal history, respond to questions about the incident, and rate the company. Written explanations are compared with explanations given by others in similar investigations resulting in a finding of similarity to guilty or innocent explanations. Examiner required. Suitable for group use.

Untimed: Not available

Scoring: Examiner evaluated

Cost: Booklet and evaluation $35.00

Publisher: The Stanton Corporation

THE STANTON INVENTORY
Carl S. Klump

Adult

Purpose: Assesses problems of theft and management weaknesses in businesses. Used for identification of responsible parties.

Description: 96-item paper-pencil questionnaire assessing company dishonesty, morale, personal attitudes and general company, and information. The questionnaire assists in identifying problem areas, i.e., management weaknesses and theft. The test is analyzed by a Stanton staff criminologist. Examiner required. Suitable for group use.

Untimed: Not available

Scoring: Examiner evaluated

Cost: 1-99 inventory sheets and evaluation $25.00 each

Publisher: The Stanton Corporation

THE STANTON SURVEY
Carl S. Klump

Adult

Purpose: Measures attitudes toward honesty. Used for screening and evaluating job applicants.

Description: Multiple-item paper-pencil test measuring attitudes toward honesty divided into two major sections. The first section includes one page of biographical items covering educational and vocational history and social habits. The second part consists of 84 multiple-choice questions about attitudes toward honesty and about actual events involving honest and dishonest behaviors. Toll-free phone analysis is available. Examiner required. Suitable for group use.

Untimed: Not available

Scoring: Hand key; may be computer scored

Cost: 1-499 hand scorable surveys $8.00 each; 1-99 phone-in or computer-scored surveys $12.00 each

Publisher: The Stanton Corporation

THE STANTON SURVEY PHASE II
Carl S. Klump

Adult

Purpose: Measures attitudes toward honesty. Used for screening and evaluating job applicants.

Description: Paper-pencil test divided into two parts. The first part consists of 36 agree-disagree items covering attitudes toward honesty and actual events involving honest and dishonest behaviors. The second part consists of multiple-choice and short-answer items probing social habits, such as drinking, gambling, and drug use. The test is similar to The Stanton Survey but omits personal history and biographical information. Examiner required. Suitable for group use.

Untimed: Not available

Scoring: Hand key; may be computer scored

Cost: $7.00 per booklet, including evaluation

Publisher: The Stanton Corporation

STRESS EVALUATION INVENTORY (SEI)
Raymond W. Kulhavy and Samuel E. Krug

Adult

Purpose: Evaluates the stress that individuals are experiencing in their lives, identifies probable sources of stress, and suggests methods of controlling or preventing stress. Used in conjunction with stress management programs in business, health care, education, government, and private counseling settings.

Description: 30-item paper-pencil multiple-choice inventory administered in conjunction with Form A of the 16 Personality Factor Questionnaire as a part of the Individualized Stress Management Program. The SEI provides indices of perceived stress in three areas of an individual's life (job, family, and personal). Diagnostic data from the 16 PF yields personality and life-style information that is used to identify sources of the individual's stress. Each individual receives a book-length, computer-based report, which includes indices of job, family, and personal stress and an overall "distress" level; a discussion of stress and its symptoms; and a variety of work sheets, exercises, and educational materials addressing the types of stress reported by each individual. The first three chapters of this report are the same for all individuals; chapters 4-10 vary according to individual needs.

A one-page computer-based professional summary accompanies each report and includes a profile of the stresses reported by the individual and a brief explanation of the factors that determined which chapters and exercises would be included in the individual's report. Computer reports for the 16PF may be ordered at additional costs. A group profile summary also is provided for groups of 10 or more. Materials for the Individualized Stress Management Program (including the SEI) are available only to qualified program coordinators. Attendance at one of IPAT's training seminars is the preferred method of qualification. Supplementary materials available to program coordinators include a training manual, prepared presentations (slides, overhead transparencies, and audiotapes), a demonstration workbook, and brochures. Examiner required. Suitable for group use.

Untimed: Varies

Scoring: Computer scored

Cost: Assessment materials, computer scoring, and preparation of the individual's report $30.00 per person; for further cost information contact the publisher's Individualized Stress Management Program Coordinator

Publisher: Institute for Personality and Ability Testing, Inc.

STYLES OF LEADERSHIP SURVEY (SLS)
Jay Hall and Martha S. Williams

Adult

Purpose: Assesses leadership styles in terms of "concern for people" and "concern for purpose." Used with nonmanagement supervisory personnel, campus and community groups, volunteer organizations, and administrative personnel.

Description: Multiple-item paper-pencil self-report inventory assessing leadership behavior in terms of the Blake-Mouton model of management behavior. The Blake-Mouton managerial grid is an extension of Likert's production-morale theory and measures two dimensions of leadership behavior: concerns for people and concerns for purpose. The inventory yields analyses of overall leadership style, including four components of leadership: philosophy, planning, implementation, and evaluation. Normative data are provided. The inventory may be administered in conjunction with the Leadership Appraisal Survey for a more complete assessment of leadership styles and effectiveness. Self-administered. Suitable for group use.

Untimed: Varies

Scoring: Self-scored

Cost: Individual instrument $4.50

Publisher: Teleometrics International

Information and availability unconfirmed; no publisher response.

SUPERVISORY COMMUNICATION RELATIONS TEST (SCOM)
Refer to page 969.

SUPERVISORY HUMAN RELATIONS TEST (SHR)
Refer to page 969.

SUPERVISORY INVENTORY ON COMMUNICATION (SIC)
Donald L. Kirkpatrick

Adult

Purpose: Measures knowledge of proper supervisory use of communication procedures within an organization. Used in conjunction with training programs aimed at improving the communication effectiveness of supervisors.

Description: 80-item paper-pencil two-choice test assessing knowledge and understanding of communication philosophy, principles, and methods for supervisors. Each test item describes an action or belief concerned with on-the-job communication. Individuals indicate whether they agree or disagree with each statement. Test results identify topics which should be emphasized in training programs, serve as a tool for conference discussions, measure the effectiveness of training programs, provide information for on-the-job coaching, and assist in the selection of supervisory personnel. The manual includes a discussion of the inventory's development, normative data, research data, and interpretive guidelines. The answer booklet includes the rationale behind all correct answers. Self-administered. Suitable for group use.

Untimed: 20 minutes

Scoring: Self-scored

Cost: 20 tests and answer booklets $20.00; instructor's manual $1.00

Publisher: Donald L. Kirkpatrick

SUPERVISORY INVENTORY ON HUMAN RELATIONS (SIHR)
Donald L. Kirkpatrick

Adult

Purpose: Measures knowledge of basic human relations principles involved in effective supervisory job performance. Used in conjunction with management training programs aimed at increasing knowledge and improving attitudes in dealing with people.

Description: 80-item paper-pencil two-choice test measuring the extent to which supervisors understand and accept the principles, facts, and techniques of human relations in management. Test items cover human relations issues in the following areas: the supervisor's role in management, understanding and motivating employees, developing positive employee attitudes, problem solving techniques, and principles of learning and training. Individuals indicate whether they agree or disagree with the statement about beliefs or behaviors presented in each test item. The answer booklet provides a rationale for each correct answer. Test results identify topics which should be emphasized in training programs, serve as a tool for conference discussions, measure the effectiveness of training programs, provide information for on-the-job coaching, and assist in the selection of supervisory personnel. The manual includes norms for foremen and plant supervisors, office supervisors, and middle and top management; a discussion of validity and reliability, interpretive guidelines, and an answer key providing the rationale behind all correct answers. Self-administered. Suitable for group use.

Untimed: 15 minutes

Scoring: Self-scored

Cost: 20 tests and answer booklets $20.00; instructor's manual $1.00

Publisher: Donald L. Kirkpatrick

SUPERVISORY PRACTICES INVENTORY (SPI)
Refer to page 971.

SURVEY OF INTERPERSONAL VALUES
Refer to page 183.

SURVEY OF PERSONAL VALUES
Leonard V. Gordon

Adolescent, adult
Grades 10 and above

Purpose: Measures the critical values that help an individual determine coping ability with everyday problems. Used for employee screening and placement, vocational guidance, and counseling.

Description: 30-item paper-pencil test consisting of forced-choice triads of value statements. The subject indicates which statement he personally finds most important in each triad. Six values are measured: practical mindedness, achievement, variety, decisiveness, orderliness, and goal orientation. Self-administered. Suitable for group use.

Untimed: 15 minutes

Scoring: Hand key

Cost: 25 test booklets $31.00; scoring stencil $5.50; examiner's manual $10.00

Publisher: Science Research Associates, Inc.

SURVEY PROGRAM FOR BUSINESS AND INDUSTRY

Adult

Purpose: Assesses employee attitudes and perceptions concerning critical job-related issues. Provides information useful for enhancing organization effectiveness and monitoring responses to organizational changes.

Description: Paper-pencil attitude assessment questionnaire available in four versions, one for each of the following employee groups: managers, professionals, outside sales representatives, and general employees. All surveys measure the following areas of common interest: organization identification, job satisfaction, pay, benefits, supervisory leadership and administrative practices, work associates, general administrative effectiveness, work organization, work efficiency, performance, and personal development and communication effectiveness. In addition, each survey contains factors that focus on areas of specific interest to the various target groups (e.g., sales training). The surveys can be customized to meet special needs. Demographic classifications are chosen by the client organization according to its interest. Results of the survey are presented in easy-to-read numerical and graphic displays, with breakdowns for each category and item. Group comparisons are tailored to client needs, and comparisons to national norms are available. Frequent users of the program are able to create company specific norms

and/or conduct longitudinal studies with previous survey results. Examiner required. Suitable for group use.

Untimed: 30 minutes

Scoring: Computer scored

Cost: Contact publisher; $6.50-$14.00 per survey depending on volume ordered and the degree of customization

Publisher: London House Press

SURVEY PROGRAM FOR HEALTH CARE

Adult

Purpose: Assesses employee attitudes and perceptions concerning critical job-related issues. Provides information useful for enhancing organization effectiveness and monitoring responses to organizational change.

Description: Paper-pencil attitude assessment questionnaire available in five versions, one for each of the following employee groups: registered nurses, physicians, paraprofessionals, nonmedical professionals, and general health care personnel. All surveys measure the following areas of common interest: organization identification, job satisfaction, material rewards, supervisory leadership and administrative practices, performance and personal development, work organization, work efficiency, and communication. In addition, each survey contains factors that focus on areas of specific interest to the various target groups (e.g., professional role issues, intergroup relationships). The surveys can be customized to meet special needs. Demographic classifications are chosen by the client organization according to their interest. Results of the survey are presented in easy-to-read numerical and graphic displays, with breakdowns for each category and item. Group comparisons are tailored to client need, and comparisons to national norms are available. Frequent users of the program are able to create organization-specific norms and/or conduct longitudinal studies with previous survey results. Examiner required. Suitable for group use.

Untimed: 30 minutes

Scoring: Computer scored

Cost: Contact publisher; $6.50-$14.00 per survey depending on volume ordered and the degree of customization
Publisher: London House Press

TAV SELECTION SYSTEM
R.R. Morman

Adult

Purpose: Measures the normal interpersonal reactions toward, away from, and versus people. Used as an occupational selection tool and a counseling aid.

Description: Multiple-item paper-pencil test consisting of seven subtests: Personal Data, Proverbs and Sayings, Preferences, Sales Reactions, Judgments, Adjective Check List, and Mental Agility. Predictive validity scores are provided for a number of typical professions: traffic officers, teachers, salesmen, nurses, and others. Self-administered. Suitable for group use.
Timed: 3 hours
Scoring: Hand key
Cost: Contact publisher
Publisher: TAV Selection System

TEAM EFFECTIVENESS SURVEY (TES)
Jay Hall

Adult

Purpose: Assesses team functioning and identifies individuals who are primarily responsible for the team's style of functioning. Used for employee training and development and discussion purposes.

Description: Multiple-item paper-pencil inventory assessing team functioning on the exposure and feedback dimensions inherent in the Johari Window model of interpersonal relations. Each team member rates self and others on items related to both dimensions. The resulting individual and team profiles serve as immediate feedback to confirm or deny self-ratings and furnish an overview of team functioning. Defensive versus supportive climate scores also are obtained. Examiner required. Suitable for group use.

Untimed: Varies
Scoring: Examiner evaluated
Cost: Individual instrument $4.50
Publisher: Teleometrics International
Information and availability unconfirmed; no publisher response.

TEMPERAMENT AND VALUES INVENTORY (TVI)
Charles B. Johansson

Adolescent, adult
Grades 9 and above

Purpose: Measures an individual's attitudes and work values. Used for career development, personnel counseling, and training needs assessment.

Description: 230-item paper-pencil test containing 133 true-false statements and 97 5-point scale items. The test covers seven bipolar temperament scales: Routine-Flexible, Quiet-Active, Attentive-Distractible, Serious-Cheerful, Consistent-Changeable, Reserved-Sociable, and Reticent-Persuasive. The test also contains seven reward value scales: Social Recognition, Managerial Sales Benefits, Leadership, Social Service, Task Specificity, Philosophical Curiosity, and Work Independence. Self-administered. Suitable for group use.
Untimed: 20-30 minutes
Scoring: Computer scored
Cost: Manual $9.75; interpretive report $4.25-$8.50 depending on quantity and scoring method; profile report $2.65-$4.25 depending on quantity and scoring mehod; 25 answer sheets $8.50
Publisher: National Computer Systems/ PAS Division

TEMPERAMENT INVENTORY TESTS
Refer to page 184.

TEST OF WORK COMPETENCY AND STABILITY
A. Gaston Leblanc

Adult   Ages 21-67

Purpose: Measures stress levels in motor coordination and mental concentration.

Used to evaluate psychological capacity for work performance.

Description: Multiple-item paper-pencil interview and manual dexterity test of six factors related to work competency in industry, including work stability, assertiveness, persistence and concentration, psychomotor steadiness, capacity, and stress tolerance. Scores screen workers and provide information for rehabilitation. The materials are provided in a set that includes a manual, interview questionnaire sheets, mirror tracing patterns, tapping patterns (a tremometer and tapping apparatus with 24-volt impulse counter), and record blanks. Examiner required. Not suitable for group use. Available in French.
CANADIAN PUBLISHER

Untimed: Varies

Scoring: Hand key

Cost: Complete set $150.00; 25 record blanks $4.80; 25 interview sheets $4.80; 25 mirror tracing patterns $2.80; 25 tapping patterns $2.80; mirror tracing apparatus $24.00; manual $8.00

Publisher: Institute of Psychological Research, Inc.

Information and availability unconfirmed; no publisher response.

THURSTONE TEMPERAMENT SCHEDULE
L.L. Thurstone and Thelma Gwinn Thurstone

Adult

Purpose: Evaluates permanent aspects of personality and how normal, well-adjusted people differ from one another. Used by managers to determine employee suitability for particular jobs.

Description: 140-item paper-pencil questionnaire assessing seven areas of temperament: active, vigorous, impulsive, dominant, stable, sociable, and reflective. The questionnaire is limited to use by individuals with advanced training in personality instruments. Self-administered. Suitable for group use.

Untimed: 15-20 minutes

Scoring: Hand key

Cost: 25 booklets $18.50; examiner's manual $1.60

Publisher: Science Research Associates, Inc.

TIME PROBLEMS INVENTORY (TPRI)
Albert A. Canfield

Adult

Purpose: Evaluates an individual's time-use problems. Identifies personal and internal causes of time-use problems. Used for group discussions and to assess organizational time-use problems.

Description: Multiple-item paper-pencil inventory measuring the comparative level of an individual's time-use problems in four areas: priority setting, planning, task clarification, and self-discipline. Questions are largely work-related, representing time problems encountered in any organization, but scores may be related to time-use problems in all aspects of daily living. Interpretation focuses on internal causes of time-use problems and may be used to identify time-use problems common to members of any organization. Scoring provides information for the discussion of internal and external factors related to ineffective time use. Self-administered. Suitable for group use.

Untimed: 30 minutes

Scoring: Self-scored

Cost: Demonstration kit (30 test booklets, manual) $45.95; specimen set (includes manual) $9.95

Publisher: Humanics Media

TIME USE ANALYSIS (TUA)

Adult

Purpose: Evaluates a person's time use habits. Provides a basis for discussions of time quality versus time quantity.

Description: Multiple-item paper-pencil test assessing how individuals feel about how their time is being spent in eight aspects of life: at work, asleep, on personal hygiene, taking care of personal/family business, in community and church activities, with family or home members, in education and development, and on recreational and hobby activities. Test booklets contain a discussion of the implications of the results and the general findings. The test produces an awareness of common areas in which most people express some level of dissatisfaction with their time use and helps individuals differentiate between time efficiency and time effectiveness and stimulates concerns for improvement in both areas. Norms are provided for comparing levels of dissatisfaction among groups of supervisors and managers. Self-administered. Suitable for group use.

Untimed: 20 minutes

Scoring: Self-scored

Cost: Demonstration kit (30 test booklets, manual) $45.95; specimen set (includes manual) $9.95

Publisher: Humanics Media

TRAIT EVALUATION INDEX
Alan R. Nelson

Adult

Purpose: Assesses adult personality traits. Used for job placement and career counseling.

Description: 125-item paper-pencil two-choice test measuring 24 personality dimensions, including social orientation, elation, self-control, sincerity, compliance, ambition, dynamism, caution, propriety, and intellectual orientation. Materials consist of a manual and academic and industrial-business profile sheets. Available in German. Self-administered. Suitable for group use.

Untimed: 30-40 minutes

Scoring: Hand key

Cost: 25 tests $25.75; manual $7.25; 24 IBM scoring stencils $14.50; 25 profile sheets $10.50

Publisher: Martin M. Bruce, Ph.D., Publishers

TRIADAL EQUATED PERSONALITY INVENTORY
Refer to page 186.

TRUSTWORTHINESS ATTITUDE SURVEY (T.A. SURVEY)
Alan Strand and Robert W. Cormack

Adult

Purpose: Measures attitudes and personality characteristics related to trustworthiness. Used to screen applicants for jobs involving security, money, and product handling.

Description: 118-item paper-pencil multiple-choice and short-answer test measuring attitudes and beliefs. The test must be administered by a qualified, licensed company or government agency examiner. Examiner required. Suitable for group use.

Untimed: 20-30 minutes

Scoring: Hand key

Cost: Specimen set free; 25 tests $6.00; scoring templates leased yearly $60.00

Publisher: Psychological Systems Corporation

Information and availability unconfirmed; no publisher response.

VCWS 14—INTEGRATED PEER PERFORMANCE

Adult

Purpose: Measures an individual's instruction-following ability and color discrimination skills. Stimulates interaction among workers.

Description: Manual test measuring an individual's ability to follow instructions and discriminate between colors. The test emphasizes the ability to interact effectively with both peers and supervisors and the ability to work as a team member in order to complete a task. Three or four examinees are seated and given colored assembly pieces and an assembly pattern booklet. The examiner places assembly boards on the table and moves them from worker to worker every 20 seconds. Each examinee performs his portion of the assembly and then waits for the next assembly board. As each assembly board is completed, the examiner inspects each board and informs the appropriate examinee(s) of any errors that have been made.

The test allows the examiner to observe and actuarily score universal worker characteristics that relate to human interaction and behavior. The test should not be administered to individuals with severe impairment of the upper extremities or severe visual impairment. Examiner required. Suitable for group use.

Timed: Not available

Scoring: Examiner evaluated

Cost: $1,795.00

Publisher: Valpar International Corporation

VOCATIONAL OPINION INDEX
ARBOR, Inc.

Adult

Purpose: Assesses perceptions and motivations affecting the ability to get and hold a job. Used in counseling, skills training, and general diagnosis of work expectations.

Description: 42-item paper-pencil test measuring an individual's attractions to work, perceived losses associated with work, and possible barriers to employment. The respondent uses 5-point rating scales to indicate agreement or disagreement with statements concerning what might happen in the workplace and about problems which might make it difficult for some people to keep a job. The test is not to be used primarily as a screening device. Examiner required. Suitable for group use. Available in Spanish.

Untimed: 20 minutes

Scoring: Hand key; examiner evaluated; may be computer scored

Cost: 1-100 booklets $0.70 each; scoring manual $5.00

Publisher: ARBOR, Inc.

WARD ATMOSPHERE SCALE (WAS)
Rudolf H. Moos

Adolescent, adult

Purpose: Assesses the social environments of hospital-based psychiatric treatment programs. Used to evaluate organizational effectiveness.

Description: 100-item paper-pencil true-false test covering 10 aspects of social environment and yielding 10 scores: involvement, support, spontaneity, autonomy, practical orientation, personal problem orientation, anger and aggression, order and organization, program clarity, and staff control. Three "treatment outcome" scales may be used: Dropout, Release Rate, and Community Tenure. Materials include the Real Form (Form R), which measures perceptions of a current program; the 40-item Short Form (Form S); the Ideal Form (Form I), which measures conceptions of an ideal program; and the Expectations Form (Form E), which measures expectations of a new program. Forms I and E are not published, but items and instructions appear in the Appendix of the WAS manual. One in a series of nine Social Climate scales. Examiner required. Suitable for group use.

Untimed: 20 minutes

Scoring: Hand key; examiner evaluated

Cost: 25 reusable tests $4.75; 50 answer sheets $3.50; 50 profiles $3.50; key $1.50; manual $8.00

Publisher: Consulting Psychologists Press, Inc.

THE WHISLER STRATEGY TEST
Lawrence Whisler

Adult

Purpose: Assesses strategy used in approaching problems. Used to evaluate applicants for employment.

Description: Multiple-item paper-pencil measure of seven aspects of strategy: solutions, speed, boldness, caution, hypercaution, and net strategy. The test detects both risk-takers and risk-avoiders and evaluates the subject with respect to the wisdom of his strategy. Examiner required. Suitable for group use.

Timed: 25 minutes

Scoring: Hand key

Cost: Specimen set $5.00; 25 tests $5.00; 25 answer sheets $5.00

Publisher: Psychometric Affiliates

WORK ASPECT PREFERENCE SCALE
R. Pryor

**Adolescent, adult
Grades 10 and above**

Purpose: Measures work qualities that individuals consider important. Used in career counseling, vocational rehabilitation, the study of personal and work values, and research on career development and worker satisfaction.

Description: 52-item paper-pencil inventory assessing an individual's work values along 13 scales: altruism, co-workers, creativity, detachment, independence, life style, management, money, physical activity, prestige, security, self-development, and surroundings. Answer sheets are scored by hand or machine. Examiner required. Suitable for group use.

Untimed: 10-20 minutes

Scoring: Hand key; may be machine scored

Cost: Contact publisher

Publisher: The Australian Council for Educational Research Limited

WORK ATTITUDES QUESTIONNAIRE
M.S. Doty and N.E. Betz

Adult

Purpose: Measures an individual's commitment to work and the degree to which such commitment is psychologically healthy or unhealthy. Used for research purposes and to identify "workaholics."

Description: 45-item paper-pencil questionnaire consisting of two scales: one assessing high versus low commitments to work (23 items) and the second assessing the degree to which work attitudes are psychologically healthy or unhealthy (22 items). Test items consist of statements regarding work or career orientation or the role which work plays in the larger scheme of life. Individuals rate each item on a 5-point scale ranging from one ("strongly disagree") to five ("strongly agree") to indicate the degree to which the statement expresses their personal beliefs. Results differentiate the "workaholic" or the Type A personality from the highly committed worker who, although strongly committed to and involved in his work, manages at the same time to lead a balanced psychologically healthy life. The manual includes procedures for administration and scoring, interpretive guidelines, information on the development of the scales, data on reliability and validity, and normative data. Examiner required. Suitable for group use.

Untimed: Varies

Scoring: Examiner evaluated

Cost: 25 questionnaires $5.00; manual $4.95

Publisher: Marathon Consulting and Press

WORK ENVIRONMENT SCALE (WES)
Paul Insel and Rudolf H. Moos

Adult

Purpose: Evaluates the social climate of work units. Used to assess correlates of productivity, worker satisfaction, quality assurance programs, work stressors, individual adaptation, and supervisory methods.

Description: 90-item paper-pencil measure of 10 dimensions of work social environments: involvement, peer cohesion, supervisor support, autonomy, task orientation, work pressure, clarity, control, innovation, and physical comfort. These dimensions are grouped into three sets: relationships, personal growth, and system maintenance and change. Three forms are available: the Real Form (Form R), which measures perceptions of existing work environments; the Ideal Form (Form I), which measures conceptions of ideal work environments; and the Expectations Form (Form E), which measures expectations about work settings. Forms I and E are not published although items and instructions will be provided upon request. Examiner required. Suitable for group use.

Untimed: 20 minutes

Scoring: Hand key

Cost: Specimen set $8.50; manual $6.75; key $1.50

Publisher: Consulting Psychologists Press, Inc.

WORK MOTIVATION INVENTORY (WMI)
Jay Hall and Martha S. Williams

Adult

Purpose: Assesses the work-related needs and motivations of both managers and subordinates. Used for employee training and development and as a basis for discussion.

Description: Multiple-item paper-pencil self-report inventory assessing work-related needs actually experienced by an individual. The inventory yields five scores, which provide a personal motivational profile according to the five need systems established in Maslow's need-hierarchy concept. The inventory may be administered in conjunction with the Management of Motives Index (MMI) in two ways. When used as a subordinate instrument and compared to the manager's MMI profile, discrepancies are identified between what an employee feels is important and what the manager offers in the way of motivational support. When completed by the manager and the results compared with scores on the MMI, areas are indicated in which the manager's own needs may be influencing motivational methods used to meet the needs of others. Normative data are provided. Examiner required. Suitable for group use.

Untimed: Varies

Scoring: Examiner evaluated

Cost: Individual instrument $4.50

Publisher: Teleometrics International

Information and availability unconfirmed; no publisher response.

WORK VALUES INVENTORY
Refer to page 761.

Management and Supervision

ADVANCED TEST BATTERY (ATB)
Refer to page 793.

ADVANCED TEST BATTERY: NUMBER SERIES (ATB:NA2)
Refer to page 794.

ADVANCED TEST BATTERY: NUMERICAL CRITICAL REASONING (ATB:NA4)
Refer to page 794.

ADVANCED TEST BATTERY: VERBAL CONCEPTS (ATB:VA1)
Refer to page 795.

ADVANCED TEST BATTERY: VERBAL CRITICAL REASONING (ATB-VA3)
Refer to page 795.

COMMUNICATING EMPATHY
John Milnes and Harvey Bertcher

Adult

Purpose: Assesses verbal empathetic responses of adults and helps teach them to develop empathetic communication skills. Used for communication skills training. Appropriate for use by counselors, therapists, trainers, and those requiring management and leadership training.

Description: Assessment consists of an introduction, nine aurally administered paper-pencil exercises, and a conclusion, all of which comprise a full day's training program in empathetic communication skills. A cassette player and a quiet room are required. Examiner required. Suitable for small group use.

Untimed: 1 day

Scoring: Tape key

Cost: Complete (2 cassette tapes, 25 response forms, manual) $44.95

Publisher: University Associates, Inc.

Information and availability unconfirmed; no publisher response.

COMMUNICATION KNOWLEDGE INVENTORY
W.J. Reddin

Adult

Purpose: Assesses a manager's general knowledge of communication.

Description: 80-item paper-pencil test covering verbal and nonverbal communication fallacies. Self-administered. Suitable for group use.
CANADIAN PUBLISHER

Untimed: 20-30 minutes

Scoring: Hand key

Cost: Test kit (10 test copies, fact sheet, user's guide) $40.00; cash orders postpaid

Publisher: Organizational Tests (Canada) Ltd.

COMMUNICATION SENSITIVITY INVENTORY
W.J. Reddin

Adult

Purpose: Determines the characteristic response of a manager to whom others come with problems. Used as a pretest in courses in listening, coaching, and communication.

Description: 10-item paper-pencil multiple-choice test measuring a manager's reaction to problems expressed by subordinates. Responses are categorized as feeling, challenge, more information, or recommendation. Self-administered. Suitable for group use.
CANADIAN PUBLISHER

Untimed: 20-30 minutes

Scoring: Hand key

Cost: Test kit (10 test copies, fact sheet, user's guide) $40.00; cash orders postpaid

Publisher: Organizational Tests (Canada) Ltd.

CREE QUESTIONNAIRE
T.G. Thurstone and J.J. Mellinger

Adult

Purpose: Evaluates an individual's overall creative potential and the extent to which his behavior resembles that of identified creative individuals. Used for placement of managerial and professional personnel and career counseling.

Description: 145-item paper-pencil test measuring the 13 factorially determined dimensions of the creative personality: dominance vs. submission, indifference vs. involvement, independence vs. conformity, unstructured vs. structured work situation, selective vs. prescribed activity, work-involved vs. detached attitude, pressures vs. relaxed situation, high vs. low energy level, fast vs. slow reaction time, high vs. low ideational spontaneity, and strength of theoretical, artistic, and mechanical interests. Basic reading skills are required. Self-administered. Suitable for group use.

Untimed: 15-20 minutes

Scoring: Hand key; may be computer scored

Cost: Specimen set $10.00; 25 test booklets $15.00

Publisher: London House Press

CRITICAL REASONING TEST BATTERY: DIAGRAMMATIC SERIES (CRTB: DC3)
Saville & Holdsworth Ltd. Staff

Ages 16-adult

Purpose: Measures critical reasoning ability for thinking sequentially. Used in personnel screening and counseling.

Description: 40-item paper-pencil test assessing the logical or analytical ability to follow a sequence of diagrams and select the next one in a series from five alternatives. The test is used for technical research and computer programming positions. One of three tests in the Critical Reasoning Test Battery. Together, the three tests provide information on impor-

tant abilities related to junior management. Examiner required. Suitable for group use.
BRITISH PUBLISHER
Timed: 20 minutes
Scoring: Hand key; may be computer scored
Cost: 50 answer sheets $51.00; administration card $9.50; scoring key $9.50; 10 booklets $114.50
Publisher: Saville & Holdsworth Ltd.

CRITICAL REASONING TEST BATTERY: INTERPRETING DATA (CRTB: NC2)
Saville & Holdsworth Ltd. Staff

Ages 16-adult

Purpose: Measures ability to make correct decisions or inferences from numerical data. Used in personnel screening and counseling.

Description: 40-item paper-pencil test assessing the ability to interpret straightforward statistical and other numerical data, presented as tables or diagrams. Candidates select the correct answer to a question from five alternatives. The test is appropriate for jobs involving analysis or decision making based on numerical facts. One of three tests in the Critical Reasoning Test Battery. Together, the three tests provide information on important abilities related to junior management. Examiner required. Suitable for group use.
BRITISH PUBLISHER
Timed: 30 minutes
Scoring: Hand key; may be computer scored
Cost: 10 booklets $114.50; 50 answer sheets $51.00; administration card $9.50; scoring key $9.50; 10 data cards $27.50
Publisher: Saville & Holdsworth Ltd.

CRITICAL REASONING TEST BATTERY: VERBAL EVALUATION (CRTB: VC1)
Saville & Holdsworth Ltd. Staff

Ages 16-adult

Purpose: Measures ability to understand and evaluate the logic of arguments. Used in personnel screening and counseling.

Description: 60-item paper-pencil test of a supervisor's or general manager's ability to understand and evaluate the logic of various types of arguments. The examinee must decide if a statement is true or untrue or whether there is sufficient information to judge. One of three tests in the Critical Reasoning Test Battery. Together, the three tests provide information on important abilities related to junior management. Examiner required. Suitable for group use.
BRITISH PUBLISHER
Timed: 30 minutes
Scoring: Hand key; may be computer scored
Cost: 50 answer sheets $51.00; administration card $9.50; scoring key $9.50; 10 booklets $114.50
Publisher: Saville & Holdsworth Ltd.

EDUCATIONAL ADMINISTRATIVE STYLE DIAGNOSIS TEST
W. J. Reddin

Adult

Purpose: Measures the styles of educational administrators. Used as a training tool.

Description: Multiple-item paper-pencil test designed to provide scores on many styles based on the 3-D Theory of Leadership Effectiveness, including deserter, missionary, autocrat, compromiser, bureaucrat, developer, benevolent autocrat, task orientation, relationships orientation, and effectiveness. The administrator responds to such items as "He sees students as sources of competent help and welcomes suggestions from them." Self-administered. Suitable for group use.
CANADIAN PUBLISHER
Untimed: 20-30 minutes
Scoring: Hand key
Cost: Test kit (10 test copies, fact sheet, user's guide) $40.00; cash orders postpaid
Publisher: Organizational Tests (Canada) Ltd.

EMO QUESTIONNAIRE (EMOTIONAL ADJUSTMENT)
G.O. Baehr and Melany E. Baehr

Adult

Purpose: Determines an individual's personal-emotional adjustment. Used to evaluate the potential of managerial and professional personnel and to screen applicants for jobs requiring efficient performance under pressure.

Description: 140-item paper-pencil examination measuring 10 traditional psychodiagnostic categories (rationalization, inferiority feelings, hostility, depression, fear and anxiety, organic reaction, projection, unreality, sex, withdrawal) and 4 composite adjustment factors (internal, external, somatic, general). The results reflect both the individual's internal psychodynamics and his relationship with the external environment. In combination with other instruments, the test has been validated for selection of salespersons, police and security guards, and transit operators. In hospital settings, it is useful as a diagnosis of emotional health and as a course of psychotherapy. Basic reading skills are required. Examiner required. Suitable for group use. Available in French.

Untimed: 20-30 minutes

Scoring: Hand key; may be computer scored

Cost: Specimen set $16.00; 25 test booklets $15.00

Publisher: London House Press

EMPLOYEE APTITUDE SURVEY TEST #6—NUMERICAL REASONING (EAS #6)
Refer to page 802.

EMPLOYEE APTITUDE SURVEY TEST #7—VERBAL REASONING (EAS #7)
Refer to page 802.

EXECUTIVE PROFILE SURVEY (EPS)
Virgil R. Lang

Adult

Purpose: Measures executive potential and identifies individuals likely to succeed. Assesses an organizations' executive strengths and identifies future needs. Used for employee evaluation and placement, screening job applicants, and professional development.

Description: 94-item (61 on a 7-point Likert scale and 33 multiple-choice) paper-pencil test measuring self-attitudes, values, and beliefs of individuals in comparison with over 2,000 top-level executives. Based on a 10-year study of the "executive personality," EPS measures the 11 personality-profile dimensions most important in business, management, and executive settings. The profile dimensions include ambitious, assertive, enthusiastic, creative, spontaneous, self-considerate, open-minded, focused, and systematic traits of the individual. The survey also provides two validity scales. Norms, reliability, validity, and developmental background are explained in "Perspectives on the Executive Personality." Self-administered. Suitable for group use.

Untimed: 1 hour

Scoring: Computer scored

Cost: Profile (prepaid answer sheet) and interpretation via mail $20.00; contact publisher

Publisher: Institute for Personality and Ability Testing, Inc.

EXPERIENCE AND BACKGROUND INVENTORY (EBI)
Melany E. Baehr and E.C. Froemel

Adult

Purpose: Evaluates an individual's past performance and experience on 16 factorially determined dimensions of quantified personal background data. Used for selection, promotion, and career counseling of higher-level managerial and professional personnel.

Description: 107-item paper-pencil multiple-choice inventory assessing the following background areas: school achievement, choice of a college major, school activities, aspiration level, drive, leadership and group participation, vocational satisfaction, financial responsibility, husband-wife financial working partnership, general family responsibility, male-oriented family responsibility, female-oriented family responsibility, parental family adjustment, professional-successful parents, job and personal stability, and active relaxation pursuits. Different combinations of factors have been validated for selection and evaluation of potential for successful performance in higher-level managerial and professional positions. Basic reading skills are required. Self-administered. Suitable for group use.

Untimed: 15-20 minutes

Scoring: Hand key; may be computer scored

Cost: Specimen set $10.00; 25 test booklets $17.50

Publisher: London House Press

GRADUATE AND MANAGERIAL ASSESSMENT
Refer to page 399.

GROUP EXERCISES
Saville & Holdsworth Ltd. Staff

Adult

Purpose: Assesses leadership abilities of potential managers. Used for personnel screening, placement, and development.

Description: Three role-play exercises providing scores on leadership potential, interpersonal sensitivity, and the quality of an individual's contribution to a group situation. The Swedish Visit exercise has candidates plan a visit from members of an associated company. Individuals are to meet specified objectives within a budget. The Amalgamated Baths exercise gives candidates six assigned roles in a medium-small company in which costs must be reduced. The exercise provides a conflict situation and tests numerical abilities. The Jacquie Cosmetics exercise provides a competitive situation requiring understanding of people. Candidates are assigned roles in which each one has to speak for the selection of a management trainee. Examiner required. Suitable for group use.

BRITISH PUBLISHER

Untimed: Varies

Scoring: Examiner evaluated

Cost: Assessor's manual $89.50; initial training fee $945.00; 12 "Swedish Visit" booklets $75.60; 12 "Amalgamated Baths" booklets $75.60; 12 "Jacquie Cosmetics" booklets $75.60; 50 group exercise observation forms $38.00; 50 group exercise rating forms $38.00

Publisher: Saville & Holdsworth Ltd.

HEXAGON TAPS IN-TRAY EXERCISE
Saville & Holdsworth Ltd. Staff

Adult

Purpose: Assesses general managerial ability. Used for personnel screening, placement, and development.

Description: Multiple-item paper-pencil response test assessing organizing, forecasting, decision-making, and written communication skills. The test consists of separately timed exercises based on letters, memos, and other background information found in an in-box. The test simulates aspects of a general manager's job at a small subsidiary of a larger organization. Examiner required. Suitable for group use.

BRITISH PUBLISHER

Untimed: Not available

Scoring: Examiner evaluated

Cost: Administration set (includes initial training fee, assessor's manual, in-tray, exercise booklet, evaluation form) $88.50

Publisher: Saville & Holdsworth Ltd.

HOW SUPERVISE?
Q. W. File and H. H. Remmers

Adult

Purpose: Measures a supervisor's knowledge of human relations in work situations. Used for training, selecting, promoting, and counseling supervisors.

Description: Multiple-item paper-pencil test of beliefs about human relations in business and industry. The subjects indicate whether they believe certain supervisory practices, company policies, and supervisor opinions are desirable or undesirable. Materials include two alternate forms, A and B, dealing with the problems of supervisors. Form M consists of items from Forms A and B that are applicable to higher management levels. Examiner required. Suitable for group use.

Untimed: 40 minutes

Scoring: Hand key

Cost: 25 tests, manual, and key $21.00; key $6.00; manual $7.00 (specify form for each item ordered)

Publisher: The Psychological Corporation

I.P.I. APTITUDE—INTELLIGENCE TEST SERIES: JUDGMENT
Refer to page 813.

I.P.I. JOB TEST FIELD SERIES: FACTORY SUPERVISOR
Refer to page 817.

I.P.I. JOB TEST FIELD SERIES: OFFICE SUPERVISOR
Refer to page 819.

I.P.I. JOB TEST FIELD SERIES: SALES SUPERVISOR
Refer to page 820.

INCENTIVES MANAGEMENT INDEX (IMI)
Refer to page 1001.

INTERACTION INFLUENCE ANALYSIS
Paul Hersey and Joseph W. Keilty

Adult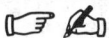

Purpose: Evaluates supervisor-subordinate relationships.

Description: 125-item paper-pencil test in which observers record behavior during several leader-follower interactions. Three types of interaction are evaluated: leader behavior (directing, open or closed questioning, supporting); effective follower behavior (attentive listening, accepting, rational responding); ineffective follower behavior (nonattentive listening, rejecting, irrational responding). Examiner required. Suitable for group use.

Untimed: Not available

Scoring: Hand key

Cost: 10-99 score sheets $2.95 each

Publisher: Center for Leadership Studies

THE JONES-MOHR LISTENING TEST
John E. Jones and Lawrence Mohr

Adult

Purpose: Provides feedback on listening accuracy. Used for manager and leadership assessment, interviewing, communication skills training, counseling, and family therapy training.

Description: Aurally administered paper-pencil test measuring how well a person understands intended meanings. The subject listens to a tape cassette and responds to test items. The subject then scores his own form according to taped instructions. A cassette player and a quiet room are required. Self-administered. Suitable for group use.

Timed: 30 minutes

Scoring: Tape key

Cost: Complete (cassette tape, 25 recording forms A and B, manual) $44.95

Publisher: University Associates, Inc.

Information and availability unconfirmed; no publisher response.

KIPNIS-SCHMIDT PROFILES OF ORGANIZATIONAL INFLUENCE STRATEGIES: INFLUENCING YOUR SUBORDINATES (POIS: FORM S)
Refer to page 920.

THE LAKE ST. CLAIR INCIDENT
Refer to page 920.

LEADER EFFECTIVENESS AND ADAPTABILITY DESCRIPTION (LEAD): SELF/OTHER
Paul Hersey and Kenneth H. Blanchard

Adult

Purpose: Evaluates an individual's leadership style and ascertains its appropriateness to certain situations and employees.

Description: 12-item situational paper-pencil test measuring an individual's leadership style range and style adaptability. The instrument is available in two forms. The Self form is filled out by the leader, and the Other form is completed by the leader's superiors, associates, or subordinates. Each form contains 12 situations to which the respondent chooses one of four alternative actions that the leader in question might select. The answers are transferred to a self-scoring sheet. Scores are transferred to a graph, which provides a three-dimensional display of the results. A data profile sheet is used for interpretation. A facilitator is recommended for interpretation, directions, and theory. Self-administered. Suitable for group use. Available in French.

Untimed: Not available

Scoring: Hand key

Cost: 10-99 forms (specify form) $2.95 each; 10-99 directions for self-scoring $1.95 each; 10-99 matrix profiles $1.95 each

Publisher: Center for Leadership Studies

LEADERSHIP ABILITY EVALUATION
Russell N. Cassel and Edward J. Stancik

Adolescent, adult
Grades 9 and above

Purpose: Measures leadership abilities, behavior, and style in adults and high-school students. Used for counseling and self-analysis.

Description: 50-item paper-pencil multiple-choice test consisting of eight pages of leadership-decision problems, each with four possible solutions. Responses reflect specific decision modes or social climate structures and classify decision-making patterns into one of four types: laissez faire, democratic-cooperative, autocratic-submissive, or autocratic-aggressive. The test was normed on 2,000 individuals; additional norms are provided for 400 outstanding leaders and 100 U.S. Air Force officers. Self-administered. Suitable for group use.

Untimed: 15 minutes

Scoring: Hand key

Cost: Kit (25 tests, manual) $22.50

Publisher: Western Psychological Services

LEADERSHIP OPINION QUESTIONNAIRE (LOQ)
Edwin A. Fleishman

Adult

Purpose: Measures supervisory leadership abilities. Provides a brief measure of leadership attitudes. Used in a variety of industrial and organizational settings for selection, appraisal, counseling, and training of employees.

Description: 40-item paper-pencil test measuring two aspects of leadership: consideration (how likely an individual's job relationship with subordinates is characterized by mutual trust, respect, and consideration) and structure (how likely an individual is to define and structure his and his subordinates' roles toward goal attainment. Self-administered. Suitable for group use.

Untimed: 10-15 minutes
Scoring: Hand key
Cost: 25 test booklets $29.00; examiner's manual $10.00
Publisher: Science Research Associates, Inc.

LEADERSHIP SCALE: MANAGER/STAFF MEMBER
Paul Hersey, Kenneth H. Blanchard, and Ronald K. Hambleton

Adult

Purpose: Assesses a leader's task and relationship behavior toward staff members. Aids in leadership and managerial training, HRD, team building, and problem solving.

Description: 125-item scale measuring task dimensions (goal setting, organizing, setting time lines, directing, controlling) and relationship behavior dimensions (providing support, communicating, facilitating interactions, active listening, providing feedback). The test is available in two forms. The manager uses the Manager Form to select 1-5 of a staff members most important objectives and rates his behavior in relation to those objectives. Using the Staff Member form, the staff member selects his most important objectives and rates the manager's behavior in relation to them. Self-administered. Suitable for group use.

Untimed: Not available
Scoring: Hand key
Cost: 10-99 scales (specify form) $2.95 each
Publisher: Center for Leadership Studies

THE MANAGEMENT AND GRADUATE ITEM BANK (MGIB)
Saville & Holdsworth Ltd. Staff

Adult

Purpose: Assesses verbal and numerical critical reasoning skills in managers and new graduate applicants.

Description: 92-item paper-pencil multiple-choice tests measuring verbal and numerical critical reasoning ability. Designed for use in the selection, develop-

ment, or guidance of personnel at the graduate level or in management positions. The tests are restricted to qualified users and are not available to educational institutions. Examiner required. Suitable for group use.
BRITISH PUBLISHER
Timed: Total 1 hour
Scoring: Hand key; may be computer scored
Cost: Manual and user's guide $42.00; administration set $105.00
Publisher: Saville & Holdsworth Ltd.

THE MANAGEMENT AND GRADUATE ITEM BANK (MGIB)— NMG1
Saville & Holdsworth Ltd. Staff

Adult

Purpose: Assesses numerical critical reasoning skills in managers and new graduate applicants.

Description: Paper-pencil multiple-choice test measuring understanding and reasoning rather than pure computation. Candidates are required to make decisions or inferences from numerical data presented in a variety of formats. In order to better simulate up-to-date working practices, the use of calculators is permitted. The format has a very clear relevance to management decision-making based on numerical or statistical data. Examiner required. Suitable for group use.
BRITISH PUBLISHER
Timed: 35 minutes
Scoring: Hand key; may be computer scored
Cost: 10 booklets $105.00; 50 answer sheets $63.00; scoring key $12.60; administration card $12.60
Publisher: Saville & Holdsworth Ltd.

THE MANAGEMENT AND GRADUATE ITEM BANK (MGIB)— VMG1
Saville & Holdsworth Ltd. Staff

Adult

Purpose: Assesses verbal critical reasoning skills in industry. Used with managers and new graduate applicants.

Description: Paper-pencil multiple-choice test measuring the ability to evaluate the logic of various kinds of argument within a realistic context. Candidates are given a passage of information followed by a series of statements. The candidates must decide whether a given statement is true or untrue or whether there is insufficient information to make the judgment. The test clearly relates to a key element in managerial or senior specialist jobs in which decisions or inferences have to be made or evaluated either on paper or in a meeting. Examiner required. Suitable for group use.

BRITISH PUBLISHER

Timed: 25 minutes

Scoring: Hand key; may be computer scored

Cost: 10 booklets $76.50; 50 answer sheets $63.00; scoring key $12.60; administration card $12.60

Publisher: Saville & Holdsworth Ltd.

MANAGEMENT APPRAISAL SURVEY (MAS)
Jay Hall, Jerry Harvey, and Martha S. Williams

Adult

Purpose: Assesses an individual's style of management from the subordinates' point of view. Used for management training and development and as a basis for discussion.

Description: Multiple-item paper-pencil inventory assessing subordinates' perceptions of their manager's practices. Analysis is based on the Blake-Mouton managerial grid—a model of management behavior that is an extension of Likert's production-morale theory relating production concerns with people concerns. The inventory provides a total score for each of the five management styles described by the model, as well as scores for each style on four components: philosophy, planning, implementation, and evaluation. The survey may be administered in conjunction with the Styles of Management Inventory to provide a comparison between subordinate ratings and

manager self-ratings on the SMI. Normative data are provided. Examiner required. Suitable for group use.

Untimed: Varies

Scoring: Examiner evaluated

Cost: Individual instrument $4.50

Publisher: Teleometrics International

Information and availability unconfirmed; no publisher response.

MANAGEMENT BURNOUT SCALE
Refer to page 921.

MANAGEMENT CHANGE INVENTORY
W.J. Reddin

Adult

Purpose: Measures a manager's knowledge of sound methods of introducing change at a worker and supervisory level. Used before or after training in change techniques.

Description: 80-item true-false paper-pencil test assessing a manager's likelihood to obtain cooperation in support of proposed changes. Topics covered include participation, speed degree of information, training, resistance, and planning. Self-administered. Suitable for group use.

CANADIAN PUBLISHER

Untimed: 20-30 minutes

Scoring: Hand key

Cost: Test kit (10 test copies, fact sheet, user's guide) $40.00; cash orders postpaid

Publisher: Organizational Tests (Canada) Ltd.

MANAGEMENT COACHING RELATIONS TEST (MCR)
W.J. Reddin

Adult

Purpose: Measures a manager's knowledge of sound methods of coaching subordinates who may be supervisors or managers. Used before or after a discussion of coaching.

Description: 80-item true-false paper-pencil test measuring knowledge of performance appraisal, effectiveness criteria, coaching interview, and training. Self-administered. Suitable for group use. CANADIAN PUBLISHER

Untimed: 20-30 minutes

Scoring: Hand key

Cost: Test kit (10 test copies, fact sheet, user's guide) $40.00; cash orders postpaid

Publisher: Organizational Tests (Canada) Ltd.

MANAGEMENT INTEREST INVENTORY (MII)
Saville & Holdsworth Ltd. Staff

Adult

Purpose: Identifies interests related to management functions and skills. Used with managers and other adults from a variety of educational backgrounds for personnel selection, placement, and counseling.

Description: 144-item paper-pencil inventory identifying preferences for a series of 12 management functions and 12 management skills. The management functions inventoried are production operations, technical services, research and development, distribution, sales, personnel and training, finance, administration, purchasing, marketing support, data processing, and legal and secretarial. The management skills inventoried are information collecting, information processing, problem solving, decision making, modeling, communicating orally, communicating in writing, organizing things, organizing people, persuading, developing people, and representing. The inventory also forms part of the Occupational Interest inventories. Self-administered. Suitable for group use.
BRITISH PUBLISHER

Untimed: 30 minutes

Scoring: Hand key; may be computer scored

Cost: Manual and user's guide $38.00; 10 nonreusable booklets $38.00; scoring key $51.00; computer disk (50 administrations) $472.50

Publisher: Saville & Holdsworth Ltd.

MANAGEMENT INVENTORY ON MANAGING CHANGE (MIMC)
Donald L. Kirkpatrick

Adult

Purpose: Measures a manager's attitudes and knowledge in regard to managing change within an organization. Used in conjunction with training programs aimed at teaching managers how to deal with change. Used with all levels of management from first-level supervisors and foremen to top executives.

Description: 65-item paper-pencil inventory measuring attitudes, knowledge, and opinions regarding principles and approaches for managing change. Items 1-50 are statements of beliefs or attitudes concerning organizational change and various ways of implementing such change. Individuals indicate whether they agree or disagree with each statement. Items 51-60 are free-response questions asking for a list of reasons why people might accept or resist change. Items 61-65 are multiple-choice items calling for an assessment of a situation involving change within an organization. An objective scoring key takes into account that more than one answer may be correct for some of the questions. The answer booklet provides the rationale for answers. Results of the test identify topics that should be emphasized in management training courses, serve as a tool for conference discussions, measure the effectiveness of training programs, provide information for on-the-job coaching, and assist in the selection and promotion of managers. Item content is intended to help managers understand their role in managing change, the reasons why people resist change, the reasons why people accept change, principles for effective management of change, and specific approaches for managing change in their department. Self-administered. Suitable for group use.

Untimed: 20 minutes

Scoring: Self-scored

Cost: 20 tests and answer booklets $20.00; instructor's manual $1.00

Publisher: Donald L. Kirkpatrick

MANAGEMENT INVENTORY ON MODERN MANAGEMENT (MIMM)
Donald L. Kirkpatrick

Adult

Purpose: Measures philosophy, principles, and approaches related to the effective performance of middle and upper-level managers. Used to determine need for training, as a tool for conference discussions, to evaluate effectiveness of a training program, provide information for on-the-job coaching, and assist in the selection of managers.

Description: 80-item paper-pencil agree/ disagree test of eight topics important to managers: leadership styles, selection and training, communicating, motivating, managing change, delegating, decision making, and managing time. Other available materials include an explanatory cassette, a book on communication, and a communication training kit. Examiner/ self-administered. Suitable for group use.

Untimed: 20 minutes

Scoring: Self-scored

Cost: 20 tests and answer booklets $20.00; instruction manual $1.00

Publisher: Donald L. Kirkpatrick

MANAGEMENT INVENTORY ON TIME MANAGEMENT (MITM)
Donald L. Kirkpatrick

Adult

Purpose: Measures a manager's knowledge and attitudes regarding effective management of time. Used in conjunction with training programs on time management.

Description: 60-item paper-pencil two-choice test assessing managers' knowledge of the principles and practices concerning the effective management of time. Test items are statements about time use within an organization. Individuals indicate for each item whether they agree or disagree with the statement. The answer booklet includes rationale for all correct answers. Test results identify topics that should be emphasized in training

programs, serve as a tool for conference discussions, measure the effectiveness of training programs, and provides information for on-the-job coaching. A list of books and films for use in time management training programs is included also. Self-administered. Suitable for group use.

Untimed: 15 minutes

Scoring: Self-scored

Cost: 20 tests and answer booklets $20.00; instructor's manual $1.00

Publisher: Donald L. Kirkpatrick

MANAGEMENT OF MOTIVES INDEX (MMI)
Jay Hall

Adult

Purpose: Assesses a manager's approach to employee motivation in terms of Maslow's need-hierarchy concept. Used for management training and development and as a basis for discussion.

Description: Multiple-item paper-pencil self-report inventory assessing a manager's theories of what stimulates subordinates, assumptions about why people work, and the approaches to motivation that result from those assumptions. The inventory yields five scores indicating the relative emphasis that managers place on each of Maslow's five need systems to manage others. Normative profiles provide a basis for comparing what managers emphasize with what subordinates say they need. The inventory may be administered in conjunction with the Work Motivation Inventory of subordinates for a more complete assessment of managerial motivational techniques. Self-administered. Suitable for group use.

Untimed: Varies

Scoring: Self-scored

Cost: Individual instrument $4.50

Publisher: Teleometrics International

Information and availability unconfirmed; no publisher response.

MANAGEMENT RELATIONS SURVEY (MRS)
Jay Hall

Adult

Purpose: Measures a manager's communications/employee relations skills from the subordinates' point of view. Used for employee training and development.

Description: Multiple-item paper-pencil inventory assessing management/employee relations from the subordinates' point of view. The inventory provides a manager with feedback from associates and subordinates and allows subordinates to examine their own practices with the manager. The inventory may be administered in conjunction with the Personnel Relations Survey for self-other comparisons of management communication skills and effectiveness. Normative data are provided. Examiner required. Suitable for group use.

Untimed: Varies

Scoring: Examiner evaluated

Cost: Individual instrument $4.50

Publisher: Teleometrics International

Information and availability unconfirmed; no publisher response.

MANAGEMENT STYLE DIAGNOSIS TEST
W.J. Reddin

Adult

Purpose: Measures managers and supervisors against the eight styles of the 3-D Theory of Leadership Effectiveness. Used in management and supervisory training seminars.

Description: Multiple-item paper-pencil test in which the manager responds "agree" or "disagree" to descriptive statements of a hypothetical manager's actions. Test scores relate to styles such as deserter, missionary, autocrat, compromiser, bureaucrat, developer, benevolent autocrat, task orientation, relationships orientation, and effectiveness. Self-administered. Suitable for group use.

CANADIAN PUBLISHER

Untimed: 20-30 minutes

Scoring: Hand key

Cost: Test kit (10 test copies, fact sheet, user's guide) $40.00; cash orders postpaid

Publisher: Organizational Tests (Canada) Ltd.

MANAGEMENT STYLE INVENTORY
J. Robert Hanson and Harvey F. Silver

Adult   Managers

Purpose: Identifies the management styles of administrators.

Description: 60-item paper-pencil instrument used for profiling an individual's management style, defining decision-making strengths, and identifying skills for development. Individuals relate their profiles to one of four management styles: sensing-thinking (implementor), sensing-feeling (communicator), intuitive-thinking (planner/analyst), and intuitive-feeling (designer, synthesizer, innovator). Detailed descriptions of the four styles are included. Self-administered. Suitable for group use.

Untimed: 30 minutes

Scoring: Self-scored

Cost: $5.00 per copy

Publisher: Hanson, Silver, Strong and Associates, Inc.

MANAGEMENT TRANSACTIONS AUDIT (MTA)
Jay Hall and C. Leo Griffith

Adult

Purpose: Assesses management communications skills in terms of Eric Berne's model of transactional analysis. Used for employee training and development and as a basis for discussion.

Description: Multiple-item paper-pencil self-report inventory measuring the size of the parent, adult, and child—the three positions from which individuals can communicate according to the model of transactional analysis—in a manager's transactions with subordinates, colleagues, and superiors. The inventory also provides scores for transaction contamination, crossed and complementary transactions, and constructive and disruptive tension. Normative data are provided. Examiner required. Suitable for group use.

Untimed: Varies

Scoring: Examiner evaluated

Cost: Individual instrument $4.50

Publisher: Teleometrics International

Information and availability unconfirmed; no publisher response.

THE MANAGER PROFILE RECORD
Richardson, Bellows, Henry and Company, Inc.

Adult

Purpose: Assesses the managerial qualities of employees or applicants. Used for predicting managerial success.

Description: Multiple-item computer-administered predictive inventory indicating the degree to which an individual resembles successful managerial employees in the areas of background, judgment, and perception. The test yields 17 separate scores for individuals with more than 10 full years of full-time work experience and 15 separate scores for those with 10 or less years of full-time work experience. Self-administered. Suitable for group use.

Untimed: Varies

Scoring: Not available

Cost: Contact publisher

Publisher: Richardson, Bellows, Henry and Company, Inc.

MANAGERIAL AND PROFESSIONAL JOB FUNCTIONS INVENTORY (MP-JFI)
Melany E. Baehr,
Wallace G. Lonergan,
and Bruce A. Hunt

Adult

Purpose: Assesses the relative importance of functions performed in higher-level managerial and professional positions and the incumbent's ability to perform them. Used to clarify job positions and organizational structure,

diagnose individual and group training needs, and classify higher-level positions.

Description: Multiple-item paper-pencil inventory assessing the relative importance of various job functions in the following 16 categories: setting organizational objectives, financial planning and review, improving work procedures and practices, interdepartmental coordination, developing technical ideas, judgment and decision-making, developing teamwork, coping with difficulties and emergencies, promoting safety attitudes and practices, communications, developing employee potential, supervisory practices, self-development and improvement, personnel practices, promoting community-organization relations, and handling outside contacts. Items are rated by incumbent employees for each position. The test also may be used to have incumbents rate their own relative abilities to perform the various job functions. Separate forms are available for rating the importance of the function and for self-rating of the incumbent's abilities. Examiner required. Suitable for group use.

Untimed: 45-60 minutes

Scoring: Hand key; may be machine scored

Cost: Specimen set $10.00; 25 test booklets $13.75

Publisher: London House Press

MANAGERIAL PHILOSOPHIES SCALE (MPS)
Jacob Jacoby and James Terborg

Adult

Purpose: Evaluates managers in terms of Douglas McGregor's Theory X and Theory Y types of managers. Differentiates between high-, average-, and low-achieving managers.

Description: Multiple-item paper-pencil self-report inventory measuring the degree to which managers adhere to either of two theories concerning the philosophical motivation behind management practice: Theory X and Theory Y. Theory X managers are authoritarian and intent on others' compliance with their commands. Theory Y managers see the potential of satisfaction and self-fulfillment for all who work. The inventory yields scores for both X and Y dimensions. Normative data and interpretive guidelines are provided for purposes of comparison, reflection, and evaluation. The inventory may be used for pre- and posttesting to measure the impact of training intervention programs. Examiner required. Suitable for group use.

Untimed: Varies

Scoring: Examiner evaluated

Cost: Individual instrument $4.50

Publisher: Teleometrics International

Information and availability unconfirmed; no publisher response.

MANAGERIAL STYLE QUESTIONNAIRE (MSQ-M) AND (MSQ-S)
Bruce A. Kirchhoff

Adult

Purpose: Evaluates the use of objectives and goals among managers. Identifies managers with goal-related problems. Used for management staff development.

Description: 47-item paper-pencil test measuring the extent to which managers use objectives in performing their managerial duties. Assesses seven dimensions: controlling, coordinating, motivating, appraisal, compensation, personnel selection, training, and developing. Two forms are available: a manager self-evaluation form (MSQ-M) and a form for subordinate-evaluation of the manager (MSQ-S). Application is limited to managerial and professional personnel. Self-administered. Suitable for group use. Available in Swedish, Dutch, French, and German.

Untimed: 10-15 minutes

Scoring: Hand key; may be computer scored

Cost: 25 evaluation forms or profiles $34.00; FORTRAN or BASIC computer programs and instructions $185.00; scoring service $22.50 per form

Publisher: BJK Associates

MATTOX PERFORMANCE APPRAISAL DATA SHEET
Robert J. Mattox

Adult   Managers

Purpose: Evaluates managers' performances on 15 critical managerial behaviors. Can be used before and after training to compare changes in performance.

Description: Multiple-item paper-pencil test covering 15 performance variables frequently encountered in management: upward communication and participation, clarification of goals and objectives, orderly work planning, management feedback, time management, controlling details, applying goal pressure, delegating, recognizing and reinforcing performance, manager approachability, team building, subordinate growth, and trust building. Test is completed by the supervisor about the manager being rated. Suitable for either blue or white collar managers. Examiner required. Suitable for group use.

Untimed: 10-20 minutes

Scoring: Examiner evaluated

Cost: 25 test booklets $50.00

Publisher: Bureau of Educational Measurements

MATURITY SCALE: SELF/ MANAGER
Ronald K. Hambleton, Kenneth H. Blanchard, and Paul Hersey

Adult

Purpose: Determines a person's willingness and ability to direct his own behavior. Used for leadership training, team building, and problem solving.

Description: 10-item paper-pencil test measuring job maturity in terms of job experience and knowledge and ability to solve problems, take responsibility, and meet deadlines. The instrument measures psychological maturity in terms of willingness to take responsibility, achievement motivation, persistence, work attitudes, and independence. The test is available in two forms: a Manager

Rating Form and a Self (employee) Rating Form. Each respondent selects up to five of the employee's most important objectives or responsibilities and rates the employee along the psychological and job maturity dimensions. Charting and interpretation materials are included with each test form, although a facilitator is recommended for theory, interpretation, and follow-up. Self-administered. Suitable for group use.

Untimed: Not available

Scoring: Hand key

Cost: 10-99 forms (specify form) $2.95 each

Publisher: Center for Leadership Studies

MATURITY STYLE MATCH: STAFF MEMBER/MANAGER
Paul Hersey, Kenneth H. Blanchard, and Joseph W. Keilty

Adult

Purpose: Evaluates the relationship between a manager's leadership style and an employee's maturity. Used for management and leadership training, HRD, team building, and conflict resolution.

Description: Multiple-item paper-pencil test measuring four leadership-style dimensions (telling, selling, participating, and delegating) in relation to the employee's ability and willingness to perform specific job tasks. The test is available in two forms: a Manager Rating Form and a Staff Member Rating Form. Although an interpretation text is included with the forms, a facilitator is recommended for theory and interpretation. Self-administered. Suitable for group use.

Untimed: Not available

Scoring: Hand key

Cost: 10-99 forms (specify form) $2.95

Publisher: Center For Leadership Studies

THE OLIVER ORGANIZATION DESCRIPTION QUESTIONNAIRE (OODQ)
John E. Oliver

Adult

Purpose: Evaluates the organizational form of a particular organization or its components.

Description: Multiple-item paper-pencil questionnaire measuring the extent to which four organizational forms exist within a particular organization. The forms are hierarchic (bureaucratic), professional (specialized), task (entrepreneurial), and group (socio-technical). The scoring guide discusses the form of the instrument, the four domains, scoring, potential uses of the scores, development of the instrument, interpretation of individual scores, and interpretation of organization scores. Examiner required. Suitable for group use.

Untimed: Varies

Scoring: Examiner evaluated

Cost: 50 questionnaires $15.00; scoring guide $2.50

Publisher: Organizational Measurement Systems Press

ORGANIZATION HEALTH SURVEY (OHS)
W.J. Reddin

Adult

Purpose: Reveals the attitudes of managers in an organization. Used as a training device or as feedback to top management.

Description: 80-item true-false paper-pencil test providing a separate score on productivity, leadership, organization structure, communication, conflict management, participation, human resource management, and creativity. Self-administered. Suitable for group use.
CANADIAN PUBLISHER

Untimed: 20-30 minutes

Scoring: Hand key

Cost: Test kit (10 test copies, fact sheet, user's guide) $40.00; cash orders postpaid

Publisher: Organizational Tests (Canada) Ltd.

PAPI SYSTEM: RATING OF JOB REQUIREMENTS—FORM A REVISED
Refer to page 930.

PAPI SYSTEM: RATING OF JOB REQUIREMENTS—FORM B REVISED

Refer to page 930.

PERSONAL RELATIONS SURVEY (PRS)
Jay Hall and Martha S. Williams

Adult

Purpose: Assesses the communications skills of managers. Used for employee training and development.

Description: Multiple-item paper-pencil self-report inventory assessing the communications tendencies of managers in three areas: with employees, with colleagues, and with superiors. Normative data provide a basis for comparison with the "average" manager on both the exposure and feedback dimensions. The inventory may be administered in conjunction with the Management Relations Survey for a more complete assessment of managers' communications skills. Self-administered. Suitable for group use.

Untimed: Varies

Scoring: Self-scored

Cost: Individual instruments $4.50

Publisher: Teleometrics International

Information and availability unconfirmed; no publisher response.

PERSONNEL PERFORMANCE PROBLEMS INVENTORY (PPPI)
Albert A. Canfield

Adult

Purpose: Assesses the use of delegation skills at all levels of management. Identifies specific elements in the delegation process which are creating problems. Used for manager/supervisor training and development.

Description: 30-item paper-pencil test assessing the effectiveness of a supervisor's delegation relationships in the following areas: mutual understanding of job responsibilities, authority, accountability, results expected, and employment conditions. Each test item describes a common performance problem of subordinates. The supervisor or manager must indicate the extent to which each is a problem with a present employee or group of employees. Test booklets contain complete descriptions of areas for improvement. Norms are provided for supervisors/managers to identify key areas for improvement. A bibliography for additional reading also is included. Self-administered. Suitable for group use.

Untimed: 30 minutes

Scoring: Self-scored

Cost: Demonstration kit (30 test booklets, manual) $45.95; specimen set (includes manual) $9.95

Publisher: Humanics Media

POWER MANAGEMENT INVENTORY (PMI)
Jay Hall and James Hawker

Adult

Purpose: Evaluates a manager's use of power. Used for management training and development and as a basis for discussion.

Description: Multiple-item paper-pencil self-report inventory assessing the motivations for power and power styles of managers. The first part of the inventory examines an individual's personal motivations for power, including needs for impact, strength, and influence that guide behavior. The second part of the inventory analyzes how the individual uses power and assesses two bipolar dimensions of power style: autocratic-democratic and permissive-authoritarian. The analysis of individual power dynamics includes assessments of both motive and style, focusing on the interaction between the two. Normative data are provided. The inventory may be administered in conjunction with the Power Management Profile to provide a comparison of the managers' self-ratings with the ratings of their subordinates. Self-administered. Suitable for group use.

Untimed: Varies

Scoring: Self-scored

Cost: Individual instrument $4.50

Publisher: Teleometrics International

Information and availability unconfirmed; no publisher response.

POWER MANAGEMENT PROFILE (PMP)
Jay Hall and James Hawker

Adult

Purpose: Evaluates a manager's use of power from the viewpoint of subordinates or associates. Used for management training and development and as a basis for discussion.

Description: Multiple-item paper-pencil inventory assessing a manager's power style and related behaviors as seen by the manager's subordinates or co-workers. Elicits feedback for managers concerning how their approaches to power are viewed by those on the receiving end of their behavior. Analysis of responses provides a structure for after-the-fact discussions with subordinates and develops a statement of the general morale that exists in the workplace as a function of the manager's use of power. Normative data are provided. The inventory may be administered in conjunction with the Power Management Inventory to provide a comparison of managers' self-ratings with those of his subordinates. Examiner required. Suitable for group use.

Untimed: Varies

Scoring: Examiner evaluated

Cost: Individual instrument $4.50

Publisher: Teleometrics International

Information and availability unconfirmed; no publisher response.

POWER PERCEPTION PROFILES: SELF/OTHER
Refer to page 935.

PRESS TEST
*Melany E. Baehr and
Raymond J. Corsini*

Adult

Purpose: Assesses adults' ability to work under pressure by providing objective

measures of reaction time. Used for career counseling and placement of high-level personnel, especially in occupations where efficiency must be maintained under pressure.

Description: 600-item paper-pencil test measuring speed of reaction to verbal stimuli, color stimuli, and color stimuli under distraction caused by interfering verbal stimuli. For valid results, stop-watch time limits and strict monitoring must be employed in the administration of the test, which is not designed to be completed in the allotted time. Reading skills are not required. The test has been used to select airline pilots. Examiner required. Suitable for group use. Can be administered in any language.

Timed: 90 seconds per part

Scoring: Hand key

Cost: Specimen set $10.00; 25 test booklets $23.75

Publisher: London House Press

PROBLEM-SOLVING DECISION-MAKING STYLE INVENTORY: SELF/OTHER
Paul Hersey and Walter E. Natemeyer

Adult

Purpose: Evaluates individual problem-solving and decision-making styles. Used in management training, team-building, HRD, and organizational development.

Description: 12-item paper-pencil multiple-choice examination measuring an individual's directive behavior (how he solves problems, makes decisions, and explains others' duties) and supportive behavior (how he engages in two-way communication and provides social and emotional support). The individual in question completes the Self Inventory, and an associate completes the Other Inventory. The two individuals compare and discuss scores. The test package includes score sheets, profile analysis, and interpretation materials. Self-administered. Suitable for group use.

Untimed: Not available

Scoring: Hand key

Cost: 10-99 forms (specify form) $2.95 each

Publisher: Center for Leadership Studies

PROFESSIONAL AND MANAGERIAL POSITION QUESTIONNAIRE (PMPQ)
J.L. Mitchell and Ernest J. McCormick

Adult

Purpose: Assesses characteristics of jobs. Used for analysis of professional, managerial, and related positions.

Description: Multiple-item paper-pencil measure of job characteristics. There are five scales: Part-of-the-job, Complexity, Impact, Responsibility, and Special. PMPQ items are divided into three sections: job functions, personal requirements, and other information. The analyst rates each item in terms of its relevance to the job. Special features include numerous computer processing options. Self-administered. Suitable for group use.

Untimed: 30 minutes

Scoring: Examiner evaluated; computer processing available

Cost: Questionnaire $1.40; computer processing from PAQ Services $1.60 to $100.00 based on processing option

Publisher: Purdue Research Foundation/ University Book Store

PROFESSIONAL EMPLOYMENT TEST
Refer to page 897.

PURDUE INDUSTRIAL SUPERVISORS WORD-MEANING TEST
Joseph Tiffin and Donald A. Long

Adult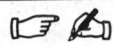

Purpose: Measures supervisors' understanding of words which appear frequently in material directed to them. Used for personnel evaluation.

Description: Multiple-item paper-pencil test of word comprehension used in conjunction with the Purdue Reading Test for Industrial Supervisors. Sale is restricted

to companies employing qualified personnel administrators and to psychologists using tests for instruction or vocational guidance. Examiner required. Suitable for group use.

Untimed: Not available

Scoring: Hand key

Cost: Specimen set $1.00; 25 tests, manual, key $6.00

Publisher: Purdue Research Foundation/ University Book Store

PURDUE RATING SCALE FOR ADMINISTRATORS AND EXECUTIVES
H.H. Remmers and R.L. Hobson

Adult

Purpose: Assesses effectiveness of executives/administrators based on ratings of subordinates and co-workers. Used to provide feedback on performance.

Description: 36-item paper-pencil test of three dimensions of executive and administrative effectiveness: fairness to subordinates, administrative achievement, and democratic orientation. The employee rates the administrator on each of 36 characteristics. Self-administered. Suitable for group use.

Untimed: 5 minutes

Scoring: Examiner evaluated

Cost: Contact publisher

Publisher: Purdue Research Foundation/ University Book Store

PURDUE READING TEST FOR INDUSTRIAL SUPERVISORS
Joseph Tiffin and Roy Dunlap

Adult

Purpose: Measures reading comprehension of paragraphs. Used for evaluation of supervisory personnel.

Description: Multiple-item paper-pencil test of ability to understand material frequently encountered by supervisors. The test is used in conjunction with the Purdue Industrial Supervisors Word-Meaning Test. Sale is restricted to companies employing qualified personnel administrators and to psychologists using tests for instruction or vocational guidance. Examiner required. Suitable for group use.

Untimed: Not available

Scoring: Hand key

Cost: Specimen set $1.00; 25 tests, manual, key $7.50

Publisher: Purdue Research Foundation/ University Book Store

STEIN SURVEY FOR ADMINISTRATORS
Morris I. Stein

Adult

Purpose: Determines a supervisor's or administrator's view of his role in research and development (R & D) organizations. Used to assess the organization from a supervisor's point of view.

Description: 95-item paper-pencil questionnaire measuring an individual's perception of his status and role requirements as a supervisor or administrator working with research and development organizations. The test is restricted to R & D organizations. Self-administered. Suitable for group use.

Untimed: 35 minutes

Scoring: Examiner evaluated

Cost: $2.50 per copy

Publisher: Morris I. Stein

Information and availability unconfirmed; no publisher response.

STYLES OF MANAGEMENT INVENTORY (SMI)
Jay Hall, Jerry B. Harvey, and Martha S. Williams

Adult

Purpose: Evaluates an individual's style of management in terms of the assumptions made about the relationship between production concerns and people concerns. Used for management training and development and as a basis for discussion.

Description: Multiple-item paper-pencil self-report inventory assessing styles of management based on the Blake-Mouton managerial grid, a model of management behavior based on Likert's morale-pro-

duction theory. The inventory yields a total score for each of the five styles described by the Blake-Mouton model, as well as subscores for each style on four components of management: philosophy, planning, implementation, and evaluation. The inventory provides managers with a way of relating their behavior with their on-the-job practices and discovering areas needing change. Normative data and conversion tables afford personal comparison with both the "average" manager and a theoretical ideal. The inventory may be administered in conjunction with the Management Appraisal Survey for a more complete assessment of management styles. Examiner required. Suitable for group use.

Untimed: Varies

Scoring: Examiner evaluated

Cost: Individual instrument $4.50

Publisher: Teleometrics International

Information and availability unconfirmed; no publisher response.

SUPERVISORY CHANGE RELATIONS TEST (SCHR)
W.J. Reddin

Adult

Purpose: Measures a supervisor's knowledge of sound methods of introducing change. Used before or after training in change techniques.

Description: 80-item true-false paper-pencil test measuring a supervisor's understanding of how change can be affected by participation, speed, degree of information, training, resistance, and planning. Suitable for blue- or white-collar supervision. The test is based on chapter 13 of Reddin, W.J., *Managerial Effectiveness*, McGraw-Hill, 1970. Self-administered. Suitable for group use.
CANADIAN PUBLISHER

Untimed: 20-30 minutes

Scoring: Hand key

Cost: Test kit (10 test copies, fact sheet, user's guide) $30.00; cash orders postpaid

Publisher: Organizational Tests (Canada) Ltd.

SUPERVISORY COACHING RELATIONS TEST (SCORE)
W.J. Reddin

Adult

Purpose: Measures a supervisor's knowledge of the methods of coaching subordinates. Used before or after coaching training.

Description: 80-item true-false paper-pencil test covering performance appraisal, effectiveness criteria, coaching interview, and training. Suitable for white- or blue-collar supervision. Self-administered. Suitable for group use. CANADIAN PUBLISHER

Untimed: 20-30 minutes

Scoring: Hand key

Cost: Test kit (10 test copies, fact sheet, user's guide) $30.00; cash orders postpaid

Publisher: Organizational Tests (Canada) Ltd.

SUPERVISORY COMMUNICATION RELATIONS TEST (SCOM)
W.J. Reddin

Adult

Purpose: Measures an individual's understanding of sound communication methods. Used before or after coaching training.

Description: 80-item true-false paper-pencil test covering communication with subordinates, co-workers, and superiors. The test also assesses the ability to give orders and introduce change. The test covers verbal and nonverbal communication. Suitable for either blue- or white-collar supervision. Self-administered. Suitable for group use. CANADIAN PUBLISHER

Untimed: 20-30 minutes

Scoring: Hand key

Cost: Test kit (10 test copies, fact sheet, user's guide) $30.00; cash orders postpaid

Publisher: Organizational Tests (Canada) Ltd.

SUPERVISORY HUMAN RELATIONS TEST (SHR)
W.J. Reddin

Adult

Purpose: Measures an individual's attitude toward others. Used before or after instruction in human relations.

Description: 80-item true-false paper-pencil test measuring an individual's attitude toward superiors, co-workers, and subordinates. The test is not recommended as a test-retest device to discover the effects of training. Suitable for white- or blue-collar supervision. Self-administered. Suitable for group use. CANADIAN PUBLISHER

Untimed: 20-30 minutes

Scoring: Hand key

Cost: Test kit (10 test copies, fact sheet, user's guide) $30.00

Publisher: Organizational Tests (Canada) Ltd.

SUPERVISORY INVENTORY ON COMMUNICATION (SIC)
Refer to page 943.

SUPERVISORY INVENTORY ON HUMAN RELATIONS (SIHR)
Refer to page 943.

SUPERVISORY INVENTORY ON SAFETY (SIS)
Donald L. Kirkpatrick

Adult

Purpose: Measures supervisors' knowledge of basic facts and principles concerning on-the-job safety and accident prevention. Used in training courses aimed at increasing job safety and reducing accidents.

Description: 80-item paper-pencil two-choice test assessing knowledge of the principles, facts, and techniques related to safety and accident prevention. Items are related to the job of foreman, supervisor, and manager in industry, business, and government. Test results identify topics that should be emphasized in training programs, serve as tools for conference discussions, measure the effectiveness of training programs, provide information for on-the-job coaching, and assist in the selection of supervisory personnel. The inventory was revised in 1980 to include new items based on the Occupational Safety & Health Act and recommendations from safety engineers. Norms are provided for first-level supervisors and foremen, middle- and top-level supervisors, and safety and personnel professionals. The answer booklet provides a rationale for all correct answers. Self-administered. Suitable for group use.

Untimed: 20 minutes

Scoring: Self-scored

Cost: 20 tests and answer booklets $20.00; instructor's manual $1.00

Publisher: Donald L. Kirkpatrick

SUPERVISORY JOB DISCIPLINE TEST (SJD)
W.J. Reddin

Adult

Purpose: Determines an individual's knowledge of accepted disciplinary techniques. Used before or after training in disciplinary training techniques.

Description: 80-item true-false paper-pencil test covering lateness, horseplay, appropriate punishments, corrective interview techniques, handling errors, long coffee breaks, visiting other departments, and eating lunch at desk. Suitable for either blue- or white-collar supervision. Self-administered. Suitable for group use.
CANADIAN PUBLISHER

Untimed: 20-30 minutes

Scoring: Hand key

Cost: Test kit (10 test copies, fact sheet, user's guide) $30.00; cash orders postpaid

Publisher: Organizational Tests (Canada) Ltd.

SUPERVISORY JOB INSTRUCTION TEST (SJI)
W.J. Reddin

Adult

Purpose: Measures an individual's knowledge of how to instruct others on the job. Used before or after job instruction training.

Description: 80-item true-false paper-pencil test measuring understanding of learning principles, teacher-learner relationships, learning aids, learning environment. Suitable for either blue- or white-collar supervision. Self-administered. Suitable for group use.
CANADIAN PUBLISHER

Untimed: 20-30 minutes

Scoring: Hand key

Cost: Test kit (10 test copies, fact sheet, user's guide) $30.00; cash orders postpaid

Publisher: Organizational Tests (Canada) Ltd.

SUPERVISORY JOB SAFETY TEST (SJS)
W.J. Reddin

Adult

Purpose: Measures an individual's attitudes toward an understanding of good safety practices. Used before or after safety training.

Description: 80-question true-false paper-pencil test covering safety instruction, safety devices, safety responsibilities, safety causes, corrective practices, work methods, types of accidents, hazard analysis, accident investigation, and role of supervisors. Suitable for either blue- or white-collar supervision. Self-administered. Suitable for group use.
CANADIAN PUBLISHER

Untimed: 20-30 minutes

Scoring: Hand key

Cost: Test kit (10 test copies, fact sheet, user's guide) $30.00; cash orders postpaid

Publisher: Organizational Tests (Canada) Ltd.

SUPERVISORY POTENTIAL TEST (SPT)
W.J. Reddin

Adult

Purpose: Measures an individual's understanding of supervisory methods, principles, and techniques. Used as a training tool.

Description: 80-item true-false paper-pencil test covering subordinate evaluation techniques, disciplinary principles, promotion criteria, change introduction, superior relations, new supervisor attachment, and subordinate motivation. Suitable for either blue- or white-collar supervision. Self-administered. Suitable for group use. CANADIAN PUBLISHER

Untimed: 20-30 minutes

Scoring: Hand key

Cost: Test kit (10 test copies, fact sheet, user's guide) $30.00; cash orders postpaid

Publisher: Organizational Tests (Canada) Ltd.

SUPERVISORY PRACTICE TEST (REVISED)
Martin M. Bruce

Adult

Purpose: Evaluates supervisory ability and potential in a business-world setting. Used for personnel selection, evaluation, and training.

Description: 50-item paper-pencil multiple-choice test indicating the extent to which the subject is able to choose a desirable course of action (as compared with the perceptions and attitudes of managers and subordinates) when presented with a business decision. Minority group data are available. Self-administered. Suitable for group use. Available in French and German.

Untimed: 20 minutes

Scoring: Hand key

Cost: Manual $6.15; key $1.10; package of tests $25.75

Publisher: Martin M. Bruce, Ph.D., Publishers

SUPERVISORY PRACTICES INVENTORY (SPI)
Judith S. Canfield and Albert A. Canfield

Adult

Purpose: Evaluates how an individual prefers to be supervised, how the individual's supervisor actually functions, and the difference between preferred and actual supervisory behaviors. Identifies areas in which to reduce "stress points" in supervisor/subordinate working relationships.

Description: 20-item paper-pencil inventory assessing a subordinate's view of 10 areas of supervisory behavior: setting objectives, planning, organization, delegation, problem identification, decision making, performance evaluation, subordinate development, team building, and conflict resolution. The test items consist of a list of supervisory behaviors, which the subordinate must rank first in order of personal preference and second to indicate how his supervisor actually functions. Questions measure supervisory behavior rather than trait or personality characteristics. Dissonance scores are developed from the difference between preferred and actual rankings. Test booklets include explanations of the scales and possible interpretations. Norms are available for supervisors/managers from diverse organizations. Self-administered. Suitable for group use.

Untimed: 20-40 minutes

Scoring: Self-scored

Cost: Demonstration kit (30 test booklets, manual) $45.95; specimen set (includes manual) $9.95

Publisher: Humanics Media

SUPERVISORY PROFILE RECORD
Richardson, Bellows, Henry and Company, Inc.

Adult

Purpose: Assesses qualities related to successful first-line supervision.

Description: Multiple-item paper-pencil computerized questionnaire system designed for predicting an individual's potential for success as a first-line supervisor. The Supervisory Profile Record Report yields information in the areas of background (present self-concept evaluation and present work-values orientation) and judgment (employee communication-motivation, employee training-evaluation, problem resolution, disciplinary practices, and general style-practices). Self-administered. Suitable for group use.

Untimed: Varies

Scoring: Computer scored

Cost: Contact publisher

Publisher: Richardson, Bellows, Henry and Company, Inc.

SUPERVISORY UNION RELATIONS TEST (SUR)
W. J. Reddin

Adult

Purpose: Measures a supervisor's attitudes toward unions. Used to evaluate supervisors' and managers' attitudes.

Description: 80-item true-false paper-pencil test covering motives of union leadership, the reasons men join unions, effective methods for working with unions, management rights, role of shop steward, foreman-union relationship, labor benefits, and company benefits. Respondents answer on the basis of what they believe is best for their position or company at the present time. Suitable for either blue- or white-collar supervision. Self-administered. Suitable for group use. CANADIAN PUBLISHER

Untimed: 20-30 minutes

Scoring: Hand key

Cost: Test kit (10 test copies, fact sheet, user's guide) $30.00; cash orders postpaid

Publisher: Organizational Tests (Canada) Ltd.

TEMPERAMENT COMPARATOR
Melany E. Baehr

Adult

Purpose: Determines the relatively permanent temperament traits characteristic of an individual's behavior. Used to evaluate the potential of higher-level managerial and professional personnel and for job screening and vocational counseling.

Description: 153-item paper-pencil test consisting of trait pairs derived from the application of a paired comparison technique to 18 individual traits. Emphasis is on individual variations in significant dimensions within the "normal" range of behavior. The factors measured are the 18 individual traits and five factorially-determined behavior factors: extroversive vs. reserved, emotionally responsive vs. emotionally controlled, self-reliant/individually oriented vs. dependent/group oriented, excitable vs. placid, and socially oriented vs. not socially oriented. The test provides a measure of internal consistency of response. Basic reading skills are required. Examiner required. Suitable for group use.

Untimed: 20-30 minutes

Scoring: Hand key; may be computer scored

Cost: Specimen set $12.00

Publisher: London House Press

TEST OF PRACTICAL JUDGMENT—FORM 62
Alfred J. Cardall

Adult

Purpose: Determines employee ability to use practical judgment in solving problems. Used to screen for management and sales positions.

Description: Multiple-item paper-pencil multiple-choice test of judgment factors that may be used in conjunction with intelligence testing. The test also may be used for screening and for selection and placement of individuals whose work involves thinking, planning, or getting along with people. The test examines such factors as empathy, drive, and social maturity. Materials include five tests, a key, and a manual. Examiner required. Suitable for group use. Available in French. CANADIAN PUBLISHER

Untimed: 30 minutes

Scoring: Hand key

Cost: Review set $5.00; 25 booklets $15.00

Publisher: Institute of Psychological Research, Inc.

Information and availability unconfirmed; no publisher response.

VALUES INVENTORY (VI)
W.J. Reddin

Adolescent, adult

Purpose: Reveals a manager's value system. Used in college and industry.

Description: Multiple-item paper-pencil test consisting of quotations among which the manager chooses preferred statements. The values tested are theoretical, power, effectiveness, achievement, human, industry, and profit. Self-administered. Suitable for group use.
CANADIAN PUBLISHER
Untimed: 20-30 minutes
Scoring: Hand key
Cost: Test kit (10 test copies, fact sheet, user's guide) $40.00; cash orders postpaid
Publisher: Organizational Tests (Canada) Ltd.

WOLFE MANAGER/SUPERVISOR STAFF SELECTOR

Adult

Purpose: Measures intellectual and personality characteristics of candidates for manager and supervisor positions.

Description: Multiple-item paper-pencil set of seven subtests in four formats for assessing logic, problem-solving, planning, and conceptualizing skills; numerical skills and reasoning; verbal fluency and communication skills; business judgment and ability to deal with peers; supervisory practices and practical leadership; emotional stability; and people contact skills. The test is used for selecting first- and second-line supervisors for all positions and as a screening test for middle and senior management candidates. Three subtests are timed. See the description of Wolfe Staff Selector Test Kits for further information. Examiner required. Suitable for group use. Available in French.

CANADIAN PUBLISHER
Timed/Untimed: 75 minutes
Scoring: Hand key or computer scored depending on format
Cost: $65.00 each
Publisher: Wolfe Personnel Testing and Training Systems, Inc.

WORK MOTIVATION INVENTORY (WMI)
Refer to page 950.

X-Y-Z INVENTORY
W.J. Reddin

Adult

Purpose: Reveals a manager's basic, underlying, philosophical assumptions about man. Used in business to help understand a manager's frame-of-reference in assessing employees' performances.

Description: Multiple-item inventory revealing some elements of a manager's assumptions that man is a beast (X), a self-actualizing being (Y), or a rational being (Z). The test is used prior to discussion of X, Y, and Z theories. Self-administered. Suitable for group use.
CANADIAN PUBLISHER
Untimed: 20-30 minutes
Scoring: Hand key
Cost: Test kit (10 test copies, fact sheet, user's guide) $40.00; cash orders postpaid
Publisher: Organizational Tests (Canada) Ltd.

Mechanical Abilities and Manual Dexterity

ACER MECHANICAL COMPREHENSION TEST

Adolescent, adult
Ages 13.6 and older

Purpose: Measures mechanical aptitude. Used for employee selection and placement for positions requiring some degree of mechanical aptitude.

Description: 45-item paper-pencil multiple-choice test consisting of problems in the form of diagrams which illustrate various mechanical principles and mechanisms. Australian norms are provided for various age groups, university and technical college groups, and national service trainees. Materials include a reusable booklet, separate answer sheet, scoring key, manual, and specimen set. Examiner required. Suitable for group use.
AUSTRALIAN PUBLISHER
Timed: 30 minutes
Scoring: Hand key
Cost: Contact publisher
Publisher: The Australian Council for Educational Research Limited

ACER MECHANICAL REASONING TEST (REVISED EDITION)

Adolescent, adult
Ages 15 and older

Purpose: Measures basic mechanical reasoning abilities. Used for employee selection and placement for positions requiring some degree of mechanical aptitude.

Description: Multiple-item paper-pencil multiple-choice test consisting of problems in the form of diagrams which illustrate various mechanical principles and mechanisms. This test is a shortened version of the ACER Mechanical Comprehension Test and contains some different items and less verbal content. Australian norms are provided for apprenticeship applicants for a variety of trades and for apprentices beginning training. Materials include a reusable booklet, answer sheet, score key, manual, and specimen set. Examiner required. Suitable for group use.
AUSTRALIAN PUBLISHER
Timed: 20 minutes
Scoring: Hand key
Cost: Contact publisher
Publisher: The Australian Council for Educational Research Limited

BENNETT MECHANICAL COMPREHENSION TEST (BMCT)
G.K. Bennett et. al.

Adult

Purpose: Measures ability to understand mechanical relationships and physical laws in practical situations. Used to screen job applicants for positions requiring practical application of mechanical principles, complex machine operation, and repair.

Description: Multiple-item multiple-choice paper-pencil test assessing understanding of mechanical relationships. Materials include two equivalent forms, S and T. Tapes of the test questions read aloud are available for applicants with limited reading skills. Examiner required. Suitable for group use.
Timed: 30 minutes
Scoring: Hand key; may be machine scored locally
Cost: Specimen set (includes tests, answer document, manual) $23.00; 25 tests $42.00; 50 answer documents $21.00; key (specify S or T) $8.00; manual $9.00; tape recording (specify reel-to-reel or cassette) $40.00
Publisher: The Psychological Corporation

CARD SORTING BOX

Adult

Purpose: Measures progress in motor learning where it is necessary to rapidly recognize materials and quickly coordinate visual discrimination with hand movements.

Description: Multiple-item task-performance test consisting of a 15-hole sorting box and 10 sets of 15 cards each. The individual is provided with the sorting box, a set of cards, and sorting instructions. The individual must place each card in the proper pigeon-hole. Problems of inhibition and facilitation can be studied by changing the pattern for appropriate pigeon-holes for given cards. Once the cards have been sorted, the backless sorting apparatus may be lifted and the cards readily picked up in packs for counting. An extra supply of numbers, which may be attached to the back of the three wood strips forming the first scoring key to form a second key, is provided. Examiner required. Not suitable for group use.

Timed: Varies

Scoring: Examiner evaluated

Cost: Test kit (sorting box, 150 cards, random scoring key) $98.00

Publisher: Lafayette Instrument Company, Inc.

CLOSURE FLEXIBILITY (CONCEALED FIGURES)
L.L. Thurstone and T.E. Jeffrey

Adult

Purpose: Measures visual and space perception skills. Used by vocational counselors to predict mechanical skills and possible success in the engineering and drafting professions.

Description: 49-item paper-pencil test measuring the ability to hold a configuration in mind despite distraction, as indicated by seeing a given figure embedded in a larger, more complex drawing. For example, after being presented with a figure, the test subject indicates in which of four drawings that figure appears. Examiner required. Suitable for group use.

Timed: 10 minutes

Scoring: Hand key; may be computer scored

Cost: Specimen set $8.00; 25 test booklets $11.25

Publisher: London House Press

CRAWFORD SMALL PARTS DEXTERITY TEST (CSPDT)
John Crawford

Adolescent, adult

Purpose: Measures fine eye-hand coordination. Used for selecting applicants for such jobs as engravers, watch repairers, and telephone installers.

Description: Two-part performance measure of dexterity. Part 1 measures dexterity in using tweezers to assemble pins and collars. Part 2 measures dexterity in screwing small screws with a screwdriver after placing them in threaded holes. The test may be administered in two ways. In the work-limit method, the subject completes the task and the total time is the score. Using the time-limit procedure, the score is the amount of work completed during a specified time. Materials include an assembly plate, pins, collars, and screws. Examiner required. Suitable for group use.

Timed: 10 to 15 minutes

Scoring: Examiner evaluated

Cost: Complete set (manual, spare parts) $298.00

Publisher: The Psychological Corporation

CURTIS SPATIAL TESTS: OBJECT COMPLETION TEST AND SPACE-FORM TEST
James W. Curtis

Adult

Purpose: Assesses perceptual efficiency. Used for screening applicants for jobs requiring manual skills.

Description: Two paper-pencil tests of perceptual efficiency. One test is two-dimensional and one is three-dimensional. The tests may be used in conjunction with Holmes' One Minute Per-Flu-Dex Tests for screening of factory aptitudes. Examiner required. Suitable for group use.

Timed: 1 minute per test

Scoring: Hand key
Cost: Specimen set $4.00; 25 tests (specify form) $3.50
Publisher: Psychometric Affiliates

EMPLOYEE APTITUDE SURVEY TEST #9—MANUAL SPEED AND ACCURACY (EAS #9)
Refer to page 802.

FINE FINGER DEXTERITY WORK TASK UNIT

Adult

Purpose: Assesses kinesthetic memory, bimanual coordination, finger dexterity, and frustration tolerance. Used for vocational evaluation and job placement of blind and visually impaired multiply handicapped persons.

Description: Multiple-task test evaluating a variety of work abilities. The individual is taught the task and then works for a 50-minute period. He receives feedback on the rate and accuracy of his work. The test provides an objective method of comparing a blind or visually impaired person's performance to that of an average sighted person. Materials include assembled testing equipment and a manual. Examiner required. Not suitable for group use.
Timed: 50 minutes
Scoring: Examiner evaluated
Cost: Manual $15.00; for the testing apparatus, contact George Aarons, Royal Maid Association for the Blind, P.O. Drawer 30, Hazlehurst, MS 39083; (601) 894-1771
Publisher: Mississippi State University Rehabilitation Research & Training Center/National Industries for the Blind

FOOT OPERATED HINGED BOX WORK TASK UNIT

Adult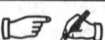

Purpose: Assesses hand-foot coordination, bimanual coordination and finger dexterity. Used for vocational evaluation and job placement of blind and visually impaired multiply handicapped persons.

Description: Multiple-task test evaluating a variety of work abilities. The individual is taught the task, works for a 50-minute period, and receives feedback on the rate and accuracy of his work. The test provides an objective method of comparing a blind or visually impaired person's performance to that of an average sighted person. Materials include assembled testing equipment and a manual. Examiner required. Not suitable for group use.
Timed: 50 minutes
Scoring: Examiner evaluated
Cost: Manual $15.00; for testing apparatus, contact George Aarons, Royal Maid Association for the Blind, P.O. Drawer 30, Hazlehurst, MS 39083; (601) 894-1771
Publisher: Mississippi State University Rehabilitation Research & Training Center/National Industries for the Blind

HAND-TOOL DEXTERITY TEST
G.K. Bennett

Adult

Purpose: Measures manipulative skill in using ordinary mechanic's tools, wrenches, and screwdrivers. Used in selecting applicants for mechanical and industrial jobs.

Description: Task test of mechanical skill in which the subject takes apart twelve assemblies of nuts, bolts, and washers from a wooden frame according to a prescribed sequence and then reassembles them. The score is time required. Materials include a wooden frame, nuts, bolts, washers, and tools. Examiner required. Not suitable for group use.
Timed: 7 minutes
Scoring: Score obtained by timing
Cost: Complete set (includes manual) $298.00; manual $15.00
Publisher: The Psychological Corporation

HINGED BOX WORK TASK UNIT

Adult

Purpose: Assesses tactual perception, material control, bimanual coordination, and frustration tolerance. Used for vocational evaluation and job placement of blind and visually impaired multiply handicapped individuals.

Description: Multiple-task test evaluating a variety of work abilities. The individual is taught the task, works for a 50-minute period, and receives feedback on the rate and accuracy of his work. The test provides an objective method of comparing a blind or visually impaired person's performance to that of an average sighted person. Materials include assembled testing equipment and a manual. Examiner required. Not suitable for group use.

Timed: 50 minutes

Scoring: Examiner evaluated

Cost: Manual $15.00; for testing apparatus, contact George Aarons, Royal Maid Association for the Blind, P.O. Drawer 30, Hazlehurst, MS 39083; (601) 894-1771

Publisher: Mississippi State University Rehabilitation Research & Training Center/National Industries for the Blind

---

I.P.I. APTITUDE—INTELLIGENCE TEST SERIES: DEXTERITY
Refer to page 812.

===

I.P.I. APTITUDE—INTELLIGENCE TEST SERIES: MOTOR
Refer to page 813.

===

I.P.I. JOB TEST FIELD SERIES: INSPECTOR
Refer to page 818.

===

INDEX CARD WORK TASK UNIT

Adult

Purpose: Assesses bimanual coordination, finger dexterity, frustration tolerance, and memory for sequence of operations. Used for vocational evaluation and job placement of blind and visually impaired multiply handicapped persons.

Description: Multiple-task test evaluating a variety of work abilities. The individual is taught the task, works for a 50-minute period, and receives feedback on the rate and accuracy of his work. The

---

test provides an objective method of comparing a blind or visually impaired person's performance to that of an average sighted person. Materials include assembled testing equipment and a manual. Examiner required. Not suitable for group use.

Timed: 50 minutes

Scoring: Examiner evaluated

Cost: Manual $15.00; for testing apparatus, contact George Aarons, Royal Maid Association for the Blind, P.O. Drawer 30, Hazlehurst, MS 39083; (601) 894-1771

Publisher: Mississippi State University Rehabilitation Research & Training Center/National Industries for the Blind

---

INTUITIVE MECHANICS (WEIGHTS AND PULLEYS)
L.L. Thurstone and T.E. Jeffrey

Adult

Purpose: Assesses mechanical aptitude of individuals, especially of engineering students. Used for vocational counseling.

Description: 32-item paper-pencil measure measuring the ability to understand mechanical relationships and visualize internal movement in a mechanical system. The test assesses, for example, students' ability to judge whether a diagrammed system is stable and/or stationary. Examiner required. Suitable for group use.

Timed: 3 minutes

Scoring: Hand key

Cost: Specimen set $8.00; 25 test booklets $8.75

Publisher: London House Press

MACQUARRIE TEST FOR MECHANICAL ABILITY
T.W. MacQuarrie

Adolescent, adult
Grades 7 and above

Purpose: Assesses an individual's motor skills abilities. Used for evaluating job candidates and by special educators with exceptional students.

Description: Multiple-item battery of seven reponse tests measuring finger dexterity, eye/hand coordination, and visualization abilities required in a wide variety of office and factory tasks. The seven subtests are tracing (50 seconds), tapping (30 seconds), dotting (30 seconds), copying (2½ minutes), location (2 minutes), blocks (2½ minutes), and pursuit (2½ minutes). The test is used in selecting inspectors, assemblers, draftsmen, blueprint readers, power sewing machine operators, machinists, tool and die designers, and employees for other skilled occupations. Examiner required. Suitable for group use.

Timed: 11 minutes, 20 seconds

Scoring: Hand key

Cost: Manual, 35 test booklets, scoring overlay per unit $25.20

Publisher: CTB/McGraw-Hill

MANUAL DEXTERITY TEST
E.I.T.S. Staff

Adult

Purpose: Measures manual dexterity as a skill needed in assembly and packaging tasks. Used for personnel placement and selection.

Description: Multiple-item paper-pencil test consisting of one subtest in manual speed and one in manual skill. Materials include booklets, the specimen set, and the manual. Examiner required. Suitable for group use.
BRITISH PUBLISHER

Timed: Part I 45 seconds; Part II 90 seconds

Scoring: Examiner evaluated

Cost: Contact publisher

Publisher: Educational and Industrial Test Services Ltd.

MECHANICAL ABILITY TEST
Refer to page 829.

MECHANICAL MOVEMENTS
L.L. Thurstone and T.E. Jeffrey

Adult

Purpose: Determines degree of mechanical interest and experience. Used for vocational counseling and to select per-

sons for mechanical occupations in industry.

Description: 38-item paper-pencil multiple-choice measure of mechanical comprehension indicating the ability to visualize a moving mechanical system in which there is internal movement or displacement of the parts. Basic reading skills are required. Examiner required. Suitable for group use.

Timed: 14 minutes

Scoring: Hand key

Cost: Specimen set $8.00; 25 test booklets $8.75

Publisher: London House Press

MINNESOTA MANUAL DEXTERITY TEST

Adolescent, adult
Ages 13 and older

Purpose: Measures an individual's capacity for the kind of rapid, simple hand-eye coordination needed for such semiskilled shop and clerical operations as wrapping, sorting, and packing.

Description: Two-phase nonverbal manual dexterity test measuring rate of hand movement and finger manipulation. Materials consist of a board with 58 holes 1⅜" in diameter spaced 2¼" apart, arranged in four rows containing 58 round pegs painted red on one side and black on the other. In the placing test, the taker is presented with the empty board and asked to transfer the pegs, presented same color up, back to the board using only one hand. In the turning test, the pegs are left in the board and the taker removes each peg one at a time with one hand, turns it over, transfers it to the other hand, and replaces it in the same position on the board until all pegs have been turned. Both tests are timed for four complete trials. Examiner required. Suitable for group use.

Untimed: 6-10 minutes

Scoring: Hand key

Cost: Complete test $108.00; replacement wooden cylinder $0.95 each; 50 record blanks $4.00

Publisher: Lafayette Instrument Company, Inc.

MINNESOTA RATE OF MANIPULATION TESTS
Employment Stabilization Research Institute, University of Minnesota

Adult

Purpose: Measures finger-hand-arm dexterity. Used for employee selection for jobs requiring manual dexterity and in vocational and rehabilitation training programs.

Description: Five-test battery measuring manual dexterity. The five tests are The Placing Test, The Turning Test, The Displacing Test, The One-Hand Turning and Placing Test, and The Two-Hand Turning and Placing Test. Materials consist of two test boards and 60 round blocks. Each test board contains 60 round holes in four rows, and each block is painted orange on the upper half and yellow on the lower half. In each of the tests, the blocks are manipulated in prescribed ways that require finger movement and hand-and-arm movement. Specific tests assess movements with the preferred hand and with both hands. The five tests may be administered separately. All tests are repeated for four complete trials. The Displacing and Turning tests are suitable for use with the blind. The board, blocks, 50 individual record forms, and a manual are included in a vinyl carrying case. Examiner required. Suitable for group use.

Timed: 10 minutes or less for each test

Scoring: Examiner evaluated

Cost: Complete kit $219.00

Publisher: American Guidance Service

MOBILE VOCATIONAL EVALUATION (MVE)
Refer to page 830.

MULTIFUNCTIONAL WORK TASK UNIT

Adult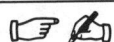

Purpose: Assesses bimanual coordination, material control, and kinesthetic memory. Used for vocational evaluation and job placement of blind and visually impaired multiply handicapped persons.

Description: Multiple-task test evaluating a variety of work abilities. The individual is taught the task, works for a 50-minute period, and receives feedback on the rate and accuracy of his work. The test provides an objective method of comparing a blind or visually impaired person's performance to that of an average sighted person. Materials include assembled testing equipment and a manual. Examiner required. Not suitable for group use.

Timed: 50 minutes

Scoring: Examiner evaluated

Cost: Manual $15.00; for testing apparatus, contact George Aarons, Royal Maid Association for the Blind, P.O. Drawer 30, Hazlehurst, MS 39083; (601) 894-1771

Publisher: Mississippi State University Rehabilitation Research & Training Center/National Industries for the Blind

O'CONNOR FINGER DEXTERITY TEST
Johnson O'Connor

Adult

Purpose: Measures finger dexterity. Used to determine individual aptitude for small assembly jobs requiring rapid hand work.

Description: Multiple-operation manual test using an 11″ x 5½″ board containing a shallow well, 100 -³⁄₁₆″ holes (arranged in 10 rows), and a set of 300 pins. The individual places three pins in each hole. The time required to fill the first 50 holes and the second 50 holes are recorded separately. The test helps predict success in the assembly of armatures, miniature parts, clocks, watches; the filling of vials; and small lathe and machine work. Examiner required. Suitable for group use.

Untimed: 8-16 minutes

Scoring: Hand key; examiner evaluated

Cost: Complete $65.75; 310 replacement pins $21.75

Publisher: Stoelting Company

O'CONNOR TWEEZER DEXTERITY TEST
Johnson O'Connor

Adolescent, adult
Ages 14 and older

Purpose: Measures fine eye-hand coordination and the ability to use small hand tools precisely and steadily. Used to identify vocational aptitude.

Description: Multiple-operation manual test using an 11" x 5½" board containing a shallow well, 100 small holes (arranged in 10 rows), and 100 one-inch pins. The individual places a pin in each of the holes using only small tweezers. The total elapsed time is recorded. A high score indicates an aptitude for tasks involving the use of small hand tools (e.g., forceps, needle-nose pliers, and tweezers) used by laboratory workers, medical personnel, watch repairers, and stamp collectors. Examiner required. Suitable for group use.

Untimed: 8-10 minutes

Scoring: Hand key; examiner evaluated

Cost: Complete $65.75; 105 replacement pins $13.50

Publisher: Stoelting Company

O'CONNOR WIGGLY BLOCK
Johnson O'Connor

Adult

Purpose: Measures ability to visualize structured design and three-dimensional space. Assesses aptitudes associated with machinists, tool and die makers, draftsmen, engineers, and architects.

Description: Task-assessment test measuring an individual's ability to visualize a completed project from the disassembled pieces. The test consists of assembling a 10" x 6" x 6" wooden block, which has been cut on two planes into nine irregular pieces. The subject assembles the block three times. The average time for the three trials is recorded. Examiner required. Suitable for group use.

Untimed: 15-30 minutes

Scoring: Hand key

Cost: Complete test $82.00; package of 50 record blanks $4.50

Publisher: Lafayette Instrument Company, Inc.

PENNSYLVANIA BI-MANUAL WORKSAMPLE
John R. Roberts

Adolescent, adult
Ages 16-39

Purpose: Measures manual dexterity and eye-hand coordination. Used for employee placement.

Description: Multiple-operation manual dexterity test utilizing an 8 x 24-inch board containing 100 holes arranged in 10 rows and a set of nuts and bolts to test finger dexterity of both hands, whole movement of both arms, eye-hand coordination, and bi-manual coordination. The employee grasps a nut between the thumb and index finger of one hand and a bolt between the thumb and index finger of the other hand, turns the bolt into the nut, and places both in a hole in the board. Twenty practice motions are allowed, and 80 motions are timed. Disassembly reverses the process and involves timing 100 motions. As many as four people can be tested simultaneously, provided each person has a separate board. Assembly and disassembly times can be converted to percentile ranks and standard scores. A special supplement contains directions for administering the test to blind employees. Materials include the board, nuts and bolts, 50 record forms, and a vinyl carrying case. Examiner required. Suitable for group use.

Timed: 12 minutes

Scoring: Examiner evaluated

Cost: Complete kit $130.00

Publisher: American Guidance Service

PHOENIX ABILITY SURVEY SYSTEM (PASS)
Refer to page 835.

PRIMARY MECHANICAL ABILITY TEST
Jack Harris Hazlehurst

Adult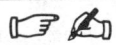

Purpose: Measures mechanical aptitude. Used to select and classify shop personnel from highly skilled engineers, draftsmen, and machinists to relatively unskilled workers and apprentices.

Description: 119-item paper-pencil multiple-choice test in four parts. Each part measures a separate aspect of mechanical aptitude: size discrimination, space perception, tool knowledge, and visualization. The manual provides technical data, instructions for administering and scoring, and norms. Examiner required. Suitable for group use.

Timed: 22 minutes

Scoring: Hand key

Cost: 25 batteries $25.00; manual $2.00

Publisher: Stevens, Thurow and Associates

PURDUE HAND PRECISION TEST

Adult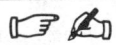

Purpose: Measures upper level perceptual-motor skills. Used to select hosiery mill operators and employees for other positions requiring precision perceptual-motor skills.

Description: Multiple-item task-performance test assessing an individual's ability to make contact between a hand-held stylus and a rapidly rotating shutter. The testing apparatus consists of a rotating shutter, variable speed control, and hand stylus. The speed control provides a continuously variable shutter speed from 30 to 60 rpm. Three measures may be recorded with this instrument: total number of correct responses, total number of attempts (recorded with an impulse counter), and actual shutter contacts (recorded with a stop clock). Examiner required. Not suitable for group use.

Timed: Varies

Scoring: Examiner evaluated

Cost: Testing apparatus (110 volt) $325.00; testing apparatus (220 volt) $395.00

Publisher: Lafayette Instrument Company, Inc.

PURDUE MECHANICAL ADAPTABILITY TEST
C.H. Lawshe and Joseph Tiffin

Adolescent, adult
Males 15 and older

Purpose: Assesses mechanical interests and abilities. Used to select job applicants.

Description: Multiple-item paper-pencil test identifying subjects who are "mechanically inclined." The test is restricted to companies employing qualified personnel administrators and to psychologists using tests for instruction or vocational guidance. Examiner required. Suitable for group use.

Untimed: Not available

Scoring: Hand key

Cost: Specimen set $1.00; 25 tests, manual, key $7.50

Publisher: Purdue Research Foundation/ University Book Store

PURDUE PEGBOARD TEST
Developed by Purdue Research Foundation under the direction of Joseph Tiffin

Adult

Purpose: Measures hand-finger-arm dexterity required for certain types of manual work. Used in the selection of business and industrial personnel.

Description: Multiple-operation manual test of gross- and fine-motor movements of hands, fingers, arms, and tip of fingers. The test measures the dexterity needed in assembly work, electronic production work, and similarly related jobs. Materials consist of a test board with two vertical rows of holes and four storage wells holding 50 pegs, 40 washers, and 20 collars. To test the right hand, the subject inserts as many pegs as possible in the holes, starting at the top of the right hand row. The test for the left hand uses the left row, moving top to bottom. Finally, both hands are used together to fill both rows top to bottom. In the Assembly Test, the subject picks up a peg with the right hand, inserts it in the top right hole, places a washer over the peg with the left hand, then places a collar with the right hand, and finally places a second washer with the left hand. This procedure constitutes one assembly. The subject must complete as many assemblies as possible in the allotted time. A revised test available through Lafayette Instrument Company, Inc. has useful applications for high-school vocational evaluations and development evaluations for children. Examiner required. Suitable for group use.

Timed: 5-10 minutes

Scoring: Hand key

Cost: Complete (board, manual) $188.00; 100 profiles $46.00; complete replacement set (pegs, washers, collars) $50.00; manual $10.00

Publisher: Science Research Associates, Inc.

PYRAMID PUZZLE

Adult

Purpose: Measures motor-learning and problem-solving abilities.

Description: Multiple-item task-performance test assessing problem solving, insight learning, and concept formation. The task involves placing a series of graduated blocks on one of three posts such that a larger block is never placed over a smaller block. Average solution time is about 20 minutes for the first trial. Repeated trials with the same individual will produce successively shorter solution times. Examiner required. Suitable for group use.

Timed: Varies

Scoring: Examiner evaluated

Cost: Test kit (test board with three posts, set of graduated blocks) $25.00

Publisher: Lafayette Instrument Company, Inc.

REVISED MINNESOTA PAPER FORM BOARD TEST
Rensis Likert and W.H. Quasha

Adolescent, adult

Purpose: Measures ability to visualize and manipulate objects in space. Used to select applicants for jobs requiring mechanical-spatial ability.

Description: Multiple-item paper-pencil test of spatial perception. The applicant is required to visualize the assembly of two-dimensional geometric shapes into a whole design. The test is related to both mechanical and artistic ability. Two equivalent forms, AA and BB (hand scoring) and MA and MB (machine scoring) are available. Examiner required. Suitable for group use. Available in a French-Canadian edition.

Timed: 20 minutes

Scoring: Hand key; may be machine scored locally

Cost: 25 tests, manual, key $21.00; 25 tests for use with separate answer documents $26.00; 50 IBM 805 answer documents for use with Form MA or MB $16.00; hand-scoring keys $8.00

Publisher: The Psychological Corporation

REVOLVING ASSEMBLY TABLE

Adult

Purpose: Assesses bimanual coordination, finger dexterity, kinesthetic memory, and ability to work with others. Used for vocational evaluation and job placement of blind and visually impaired multiply handicapped persons.

Description: Multiple-task test evaluating a variety of work abilities. The individual is taught the task, works for a 50-minute period, and receives feedback on the rate and accuracy of his work. The test provides an objective method of comparing a blind or visually impaired person's performance to that of an average sighted person. Materials include assembled testing equipment and a manual. Examiner required. Not suitable for group use.

Timed: 50 minutes

Scoring: Examiner evaluated

Cost: Manual $15.00; for testing appa-
ratus, contact George Aarons, Royal Maid
Association for the Blind, P.O. Drawer
30, Hazlehurst, MS 39083; (601) 894-1771

Publisher: Mississippi State University
Rehabilitation Research & Training
Center/National Industries for the Blind

ROEDER MANIPULATIVE
APTITUDE TEST
Refer to page 565.

SRA MECHANICAL APTITUDES
*Richardson, Bellows, Henry,
and Company, Inc.*

**Adolescent, adult
Grades 10 and above**

Purpose: Evaluates an individual's
mechanical aptitude. Used for employee
selection and placement.

Description: Three paper-pencil
aptitude tests measuring mechanical
knowledge, space relations, and shop
arithmetic. The Mechanical Knowledge
test consists of 46 pictures of common
tools and measures general mechanical
background. The Space Relations test (40
items) measures the ability to visualize
and mentally manipulate objects in space.
The Shop Arithmetic test (24 problems)
measures application of quantitative reasoning and fundamental math operations.
All three tests are presented in one booklet. Examiner required. Suitable for
group use.

Timed: 35 minutes

Scoring: Hand key

Cost: 25 reuseable test booklets $86.00;
25 answer sheets $18.00; 100 profile sheets
$20.00; examiner's manual $10.00

Publisher: Science Research Associates,
Inc.

SRA TEST OF MECHANICAL
CONCEPTS
*Steven J. Stanard and
Kathleen A. Bode*

Adult

Purpose: Measures an individual's ability
to visualize and understand basic
mechanical and spatial interrelationships.
Used for employee selection and screening for such jobs as assembler,
maintenance mechanic, machinist, and
factory production worker.

Description: Three paper-pencil subtests
measuring separate skills or abilities necessary for jobs requiring mechanical
ability. The Mechanical Interrelationships
test consists of 24 drawings depicting
mechanical movements and interrelationships. The Mechanical Tools and
Devices subtest consists of 30 items measuring knowledge of common mechanical
tools and devices. The Spatial Relations
subtest consists of 24 items measuring the
ability to visualize and manipulate objects
in space. The test is available in two
forms, A and B. Examiner required. Suitable for group use.

Untimed: 35-40 minutes

Scoring: Hand key

Cost: 25 test booklets (specify form)
$58.00; examiner's manual $10.00

Publisher: Science Research Associates,
Inc.

STEADINESS TESTER—GROOVE
TYPE

Adult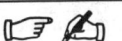

Purpose: Measures the steadiness aspect
of psychomotor control.

Description: Multiple-item task-performance test assessing the degree of
steadiness with which an individual can
move a stylus in a straight line on a fric-
tionless surface. The testing unit consists
of adjustable stainless steel plates, which
form the sides of a progressively narrowing slit. The sides are indexed in
centimeters to accurately measure an individual's performance. The bottom surface
of the unit is mirror-finished glass to

assure no friction artifact. The unit may be connected to a tone response unit for immediate feedback studies or to any number of data collection devices. A replacement stylus is available. Examiner required. Not suitable for group use.

Untimed: Varies

Scoring: Examiner evaluated

Cost: Testing apparatus $45.00

Publisher: Lafayette Instrument Company, Inc.

STEADINESS TESTER—HOLE TYPE

Ages 5-55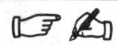

Purpose: Measures one aspect of the psychomotor phenomena of steadiness.

Description: Multiple-item task-performance test assessing the steadiness with which an individual can place a stylus in circular holes of varying sizes. The testing instrument provides nine holes of diminishing size. An analysis can be made of the subject's total score or for each hole separately. Considerable differences in performance may be determined for different individuals. The apparatus may be used with a counter or stop clock to record scores. The unit also may be connected to a tone reponse unit to provide immediate feedback. A replacement stylus is available. Examiner required. Not suitable for group use.

Timed: Varies

Scoring: Hand key

Cost: Testing apparatus $25.00; single impulse counter $72.00

Publisher: Lafayette Instrument Company, Inc.

STROMBERG DEXTERITY TEST (SDT)
E.L. Stromberg

Adult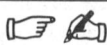

Purpose: Measures manipulative skill in sorting by color and sequence. Used to select applicants for jobs requiring manual speed and accuracy. Also used for assessing manual dexterity of handi-capped individuals in vocational training programs.

Description: Two-trial performance test of manual dexterity in which the applicant is asked to discriminate and sort biscuit-sized discs and to move and place them as fast as possible. The score is the number of seconds required to complete the two trials. Materials include assembly board and discs. Examiner required. Not suitable for group use.

Timed: 5-10 minutes

Scoring: Score obtained by timing

Cost: Complete set (includes manual) $350.00; manual $17.00

Publisher: The Psychological Corporation

TAPPING BOARD

Adult

Purpose: Measures elementary psychomotor skills.

Description: Multiple-item task-performance test assessing an individual's ability to tap with a stylus, as rapidly as possible, the two stainless steel plates located at each end of an 18-inch fiberesin board (stainless steel plates measure 3½" square). The test may be used to evaluate a number of basic psychomotor skills. A replacement stylus is available. Examiner required. Not suitable for group use.

Timed: Varies

Scoring: Examiner evaluated

Cost: Testing apparatus $25.00; single impulse counter $72.00

Publisher: Lafayette Instrument Company, Inc.

TWO ARM COORDINATION TEST

Adult

Purpose: Measures perceptual motor abilities involving the use of both arms together.

Description: 1-item task-performance test assessing an individual's ability to use both arms together in the performance of a fine-motor task. The testing unit consists of a stylus mounted on an apparatus with two handles. The individual grasps both handles simultaneously and moves the stylus around a 6-point star pattern. The testing unit may be connected to an impulse counter to record the number of errors and/or a stop clock to record the amount of time outside the path. A stop clock may be used to time the total test time. Examiner required. Not suitable for group use.

Timed: Varies

Scoring: Examiner evaluated

Cost: Testing apparatus $120.00; single impulse counter $72.00

Publisher: Lafayette Instrument Company, Inc.

VCWS 1—SMALL TOOLS (MECHANICAL)

Adult

Purpose: Measures an individual's understanding of small tools and ability to work with them. May be used with institutionally retarded, visually impaired, and hearing-impaired individuals.

Description: Manual test measuring understanding of small tools and the ability to work with them. The design of the test challenges the individual to demonstrate skill in working in small, confined spaces while using the fingers and hands to manipulate tools to perform the assigned task. The individual works through a small hole in the work sample in order to simulate working conditions in which an individual is unable to view the work he is doing. The individual completes five panels. In each panel, the individual uses a different set of tools to insert fasteners such as screws, bolts, and hitch pin clips. Performance indicates the ability to complete successfully jobs requiring various degrees of ability in using small tools and understanding their functions. A special administration procedure and kit (B-KIT) has been developed for use with the visually impaired. The test should not be used with individuals with severe impairment of the upper extremities. Examiner required. Not suitable for group use.

Timed: 1½ hours

Scoring: Examiner evaluated

Cost: $905.00

Publisher: Valpar International Corporation

VCWS 2—SIZE DISCRIMINATION

Adult

Purpose: Measures an individual's ability to perform tasks requiring visual size discrimination. Provides insight into problem-solving abilities, work organization, ability to follow directions, and psychomotor coordination. May be used with institutionally retarded, hearing-impaired, and visually impaired individuals.

Description: Manual test measuring an individual's ability to visually discriminate sizes. The individual must use his dominant hand to screw 49 hex nuts onto 32 bolt threads of various sizes. Both hands may be used to remove the nuts during disassembly. Performance indicates the ability to work successfully in occupations requiring visual size discrimination, eye-hand coordination, and bilateral dexterity. Work activities related to the test include examining and measuring for purposes of grading and sorting; performing work with close supervision using gauges, calipers, and other tools; and working within prescribed tolerances or standards. The test should not be used with individuals with severe impairment of the upper extremities. Examiner required. Not suitable for group use.

Timed: Not available

Scoring: Examiner evaluated

Cost: $795.00

Publisher: Valpar International Corporation

VCWS 4—UPPER EXTREMITY RANGE OF MOTION

Adult

Purpose: Measures an individual's upper extremity range of motion, including the shoulders, upper arms, forearms, elbows, wrists, and hands. Provides insight into factors such as neck and back fatigue, finger dexterity, and finger tactile sense.

May be used with institutionally retarded, hearing-impaired, and visually impaired individuals.

Description: Manual test measuring the range of motion and work tolerances of an individual in relation to his upper torso. The individual works through an opening in front of the work sample, the inside of which is half red and half blue. Using opposite hands for each color, the individual fastens two sizes of nuts to bolts on each of five panels. The design of the work sample allows the examiner to view muscle action in the individual's wrist and fingers. Performance indicates coordination, spatial, and perceptual skills, susceptibility to fatigue, and the ability to succeed in jobs requiring reaching, handling, fingering, feeling, and seeing. The test should not be used with individuals with severe impairment of the upper extremities. Examiner required. Not suitable for group use.

Timed: Not available

Scoring: Examiner evaluated

Cost: $845.00

Publisher: Valpar International Corporation

VCWS 7—MULTI-LEVEL SORTING

Adult

Purpose: Measures an individual's decision-making ability while performing tasks requiring physical manipulation and visual discrimination of colors, color-numbers, color-letters, and combinations of the three. May be used with institutionally retarded, hearing-impaired, and visually impaired individuals.

Description: Manual test measuring an individual's ability to make decisions while performing work tasks requiring physical manipulation and visual discrimination. The individual sorts 168 coded chips into 48 sorting slots showing on a board. Each chip is coded in one of the following ways: color; color and letter; color and number; or color, letter, and number. The test allows the examiner to observe the individual's orientation, approach, and organization in regard to the task, color, and letter; number discrimination skills; simple decision

making; and physical manipulation. A time/error score relating directly to the level of supervision the individual will need while performing a particular job is derived. The test should not be used with individuals with severe impairment of the upper extremities. Examiner required. Not suitable for group use.

Timed: Not available

Scoring: Examiner evaluated

Cost: $995.00

Publisher: Valpar International Corporation

VCWS 8—SIMULATED ASSEMBLY

Adult

Purpose: Measures an individual's ability to work at an assembly task requiring repetitive physical manipulation and evaluates bilateral use of the upper extremities. Determines standing and sitting tolerance.

Description: Manual test measuring an individual's ability to work at conveyor-assembly jobs. The individual stands or sits in front of two parts bins, one containing metal pins and the other containing a black washer and white cap. The individual must place the pin, then the washer, and then the cap on the assembly board, which rotates automatically at a constant speed. Correct assemblies are counted automatically, and all assemblies are recycled to the parts bins automatically. Work activities relating to the test include placing materials in or on automatic machines, following simple instructions, and starting, stopping, and observing the functioning of machines and equipment. The test should not be used with individuals with severe impairment of the upper extremities. Examiner required. Suitable for group use.

Timed: Not available

Scoring: Examiner evaluated

Cost: $1,185.00

Publisher: Valpar International Corporation

VCWS 9—WHOLE BODY RANGE OF MOTION

Adult

Purpose: Assesses the ability to perform successfully gross- and fine-finger dexterity tasks while in kneeling, crouching, stooping, bending, and stretching positions. May be used with hearing-impaired and visually impaired individuals.

Description: Nonmedical measurement of gross body movements of the trunk, hands, arms, legs, and fingers as they relate to an individual's functional ability to perform job tasks. The individual stands in front of the work sample, with the frame adjusted to approximately 6 inches above his head. The individual takes three colored shapes, one at a time, and transfers them from shoulder height to overhead. The individual then transfers the shapes to waist level, which requires bending forward at the waist; to knee level, which requires crouching or kneeling; and then back to shoulder height. In each transfer, the individual must remove a total of 22 nuts and then replace them, using only one hand, onto each of the three colored shapes, which are positioned in such a way that the individual is encouraged to twist the trunk to both the left and the right as he transfers the colored shapes. The individual makes a total of four transfers, requiring the removal and replacement of 176 nuts. The test relates to client functional ability in performing tasks such as stooping, kneeling, crouching, reaching, handling, fingering, feeling, and seeing. The test should not be used with individuals with severe impairment of the upper extremities. Examiner required. Not suitable for group use.

Timed: Not available
Scoring: Examiner evaluated
Cost: $1,135.00
Publisher: Valpar International Corporation

VCWS 11—EYE-HAND-FOOT COORDINATION

Adult

Purpose: Measures eye, hand, and foot coordination. Provides insight into individual concentration, learning, planning, spatial discrimination, and reaction to immediate positive and negative feedback. May be used with institutionally retarded and hearing-impaired individuals.

Description: Manual test measuring an individual's ability to use his eyes, hands, and feet simultaneously and in a coordinated manner. The examinee sits in front of the work sample and maneuvers nine steel balls, one at a time, through a maze containing 13 holes into which the steel balls may drop, thus ending the examinee's attempt to make it to the end of the maze with that particular ball. In order to move the ball, the examinee tilts the maze left and right with his hands, forward and backward with his feet, and traces the track of the ball with his eyes. Work activities related to the test include starting, stopping, and observing the function of machines; perceiving relationships between moving objects, fixtures, and surfaces; and planning the order of successive operations. The test should not be used with individuals with severe impairment of the upper or lower extremities. Examiner required. Not suitable for group use.

Timed: Not available
Scoring: Examiner evaluated
Cost: $985.00
Publisher: Valpar International Corporation

Municipal Services

APTITUDE TEST FOR POLICEMEN
McCann Associates, Inc.

Adult

Purpose: Assesses ability and learning aptitude of police officer candidates. Used for police department personnel selection.

Description: Multiple-item paper-pencil multiple-choice test in two forms: Form 62 (100 items) and Form 70 (130 items). Form 70 contains an additional 30 verbal learning-ability questions. The tests cover the ability to learn verbal and quantitative skills, total learning ability, interest in police work, common sense in police situations, and sense of public relations in the performance of police duties. Materials include test booklet, answer sheets, scoring stencil, and instruction manual with several norm tables for interpreting scores. Also available is a 50-item, multiple-choice observation test covering the candidate's ability to observe obvious and deduced facts about a picture of an accident scene. The tests are available only to qualified municipal officials and Civil Service Commissions. Examiner required. Suitable for group use.

Timed: 3 hours

Scoring: Hand key

Cost: 10 sets or less $50.00 each; 11-24 sets $4.40 each

Publisher: McCann Associates, Inc.

THE BIPOLAR PSYCHOLOGICAL INVENTORY (BPI)
Refer to page 121.

CHANGE AGENT QUESTIONNAIRE (CAQ)
Refer to page 911.

CORRECTIONAL OFFICERS' INTEREST BLANK (COIB)
Refer to page 902.

DELUXE FIRE PROMOTION TESTS
McCann Associates, Inc.

Adult

Purpose: Measures knowledge of firefighting and other job responsibilities. Used to evaluate candidates for promotion within fire departments.

Description: 100-item paper-pencil test of knowledge of fire attack, fire extinguishment, rescue, salvage, fire inspection, fire supervision, fire administration, first-aid practices, and other areas upon the request of individual departments. The tests are individually prepared according to job analysis. Separate tests are available for the positions of

driver, engineer, lieutenant, captain, battalion chief, deputy chief, assistant chief, and chief. The publisher scores each area and provides a total score, norms, means subtest and total scores, standard deviations, reliability coefficient, and an evaluation of each candidate. Materials include test booklets, answer sheets, identification sheets, envelopes, candidate study guides, and administration instructions. A list of references is provided also. The test is available on a rental basis only to Civil Service Commissions or qualified municipal officials. Examiner required. Suitable for group use.

Timed: 3½ hours

Scoring: Computer scored by publisher

Cost: First 5 candidates $485.00; next 5 candidates $29.00 each

Publisher: McCann Associates, Inc.

DELUXE POLICE PROMOTION TESTS
McCann Associates, Inc.

Adult

Purpose: Assesses abilities of candidates for police promotion. Used by municipal police departments for promotions to the level of sergeant, lieutenant, captain, assistant chief, chief, and detective.

Description: 100-item paper-pencil multiple-choice test. Each test is individually prepared according to an analysis of the job for which the subject is being tested. The test may include patrol techniques, investigative techniques, supervisory techniques, and administrative knowledge. The publisher scores each area and provides a total score, norms, means subtest and total scores, standard deviations, reliability coefficient, and an evaluation of each candidate. Materials include test booklets, answer sheets, identification sheets, envelopes, candidate study guides, and administration instructions. A list of reference sources is provided also. The test is available on a rental basis only to Civil Service Commissions or qualified municipal officials. Examiner required. Suitable for group use.

Timed: 3½ hours

Scoring: Computer scored by publisher

Cost: First 5 candidates $485.00; next 5 candidates $29.00 each

Publisher: McCann Associates, Inc.

ECONOMY FIRE PROMOTION SERIES
McCann Associates, Inc.

Adult

Purpose: Assesses candidate knowledge for promotion within a municipal fire department. Used for promotion to the positions of driver engineer, lieutenant, captain, battalion chief, deputy chief, assistant chief, and chief.

Description: 100-item paper-pencil multiple-choice test of fire attack knowledge, fire extinguishment knowledge, overhaul, salvage and rescue, fire prevention and investigation, supervision and administration. The number of questions in each subject matter area varies according to the rank being tested. Materials include test booklets, answer sheets, scoring key, norms, and manual. The test is available on a rental basis only to Civil Service Commissions or qualified municipal officials. Examiner required. Suitable for group use.

Timed: 3½ hours

Scoring: Hand key

Cost: First 5 candidates $200.00; next 5 candidates $8.00 each

Publisher: McCann Associates, Inc.

ECONOMY POLICE PROMOTION SERIES
McCann Associates, Inc.

Adult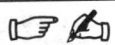

Purpose: Assesses candidate knowledge for police promotion. Used for positions of sergeant, lieutenant, captain, assistant chief, chief, and detective.

Description: 100-item paper-pencil multiple-choice test of patrol, other police knowledge, crime investigation, police supervision, police administration, and legal knowledge (i.e., laws generally applicable in most states). The number of questions in each section varies according to the rank being tested. Materials include test booklets, answer sheets, iden-

tification sheets, scoring stencil, norms charts for tabulating scores, and manual. Deluxe tests, in which law questions have been specifically checked with the state laws where the test is to be given, are available. The tests are available only on a rental basis to qualified municipal officials and Civil Service Commissions. Examiner required. Suitable for group use.

Timed: 3½ hours

Scoring: Hand key

Cost: First 5 candidates $200.00; next 5 candidates $8.00 each

Publisher: McCann Associates, Inc.

EMOTIONAL STABILITY SURVEY (ES SURVEY)
Refer to page 914.

ESV FIREFIGHTER
McCann Associates, Inc.

Adult

Purpose: Assesses candidates' ability to learn firefighting. Used by fire departments for job screening.

Description: 125-item criterion-validated paper-pencil multiple-choice test covering interest in firefighting, compatibility, map reading, spatial visualization, visual pursuit, understanding and interpreting table and test material about firefighting, basic building construction, and mechanical aptitude. The publisher scores each area and provides a total score, norms, mean subtest and total scores, standard deviations, reliability coefficient, and an evaluation of each candidate. Materials include test booklets, answer sheets, identification sheets, envelopes, candidate study guides, and administration instructions. The test is available on a rental basis only to Civil Service Commissions or qualified municipal officials. Examiner required. Suitable for group use.

Timed: 2 hours

Scoring: Computer scored by publisher

Cost: First 5 candidates $165.00; next 5 candidates $11.00 each

Publisher: McCann Associates, Inc.

FIRE COMPANY OFFICER FORMS 1, 2, AND A
McCann Associates, Inc.

Adult

Purpose: Assesses abilities of candidates for promotion in municipal fire departments.

Description: 100-item paper-pencil multiple-choice criterion-related validity test assessing fire attack knowledge, fire extinguishment knowledge, chemistry and physics of fire, and fireground supervision and management. The publisher scores each area and provides a total score, norms, means subtest and total scores, standard deviations, reliability coefficient, and an evaluation of each candidate. Materials include test booklets, answer sheets, identification sheets, candidate study guides, and administration instructions. A list of reference sources is provided also. The test is available only on a rental basis to Civil Service Commissions or qualified municipal officials. Examiner required. Suitable for group use.

Timed: 3½ hours

Scoring: Computer scored by publisher

Cost: First 5 candidates $450.00; next 5 candidates $27.00 each

Publisher: McCann Associates, Inc.

FIREFIGHTER SELECTION TEST

Adult

Purpose: Measures three abilities important for learning and performing the job of firefighter: mechanical comprehension, reading comprehension, and report interpretation. Used to select applicants for entry-level firefighter positions or training programs.

Description: 100-item paper-pencil multiple-choice test measuring the understanding of mechanical principles relevant to the firefighting job (39 items), the ability to read and interpret a passage (51 items), and the ability to read and interpret charts and reports (10 items). The items consist of drawings, passages based on firefighter training materials, and sample charts and reports presenting fire department data. For test security purposes, the test is available for lease only. Examiner required. Suitable for group use.

Timed: 2 hours, 30 minutes

Scoring: Hand key; may be computer scored

Cost: First packet of 20 tests $170.00; each additional packet $70.00; answer sheets $0.10 each; scoring key, administrator's manual, and technical report are included with each order

Publisher: Psychological Services, Inc.

FIREMAN ENTRANCE APTITUDE TESTS
McCann Associates, Inc.

Adult

Purpose: Assesses aptitude for ability to learn firefighting. Used by fire departments to select entrance-level personnel.

Description: Multiple-item paper-pencil multiple-choice test in two forms: Form 62A (100 items) and Form 70A (130 items). Booklet I of both tests includes 55 questions on verbal and quantitative learning ability. Booklet II of Form 62A contains 45 questions in three subtests: Common Sense, Interest in Firefighting Situations, and Mechanical Aptitude. Book II of Form 70A includes the same 45 questions as in Form 62A, as well as 30 easy-learning ability questions. Form 70A is easier and is intended for users who are legally required to use 70-75% as the minimum passing score. Materials include test booklets, answer sheets, scoring stencil, and instruction manual with norms. Because the format is identical to the McCann policeman test, the tests can be administered simultaneously. The test is available only to Civil Service Commissions or competent municipal officials. Examiner required. Suitable for group use.

Timed: 3 hours

Scoring: Hand key

Cost: 10 sets or less $50.00; 11-24 sets $4.40 each

Publisher: McCann Associates, Inc.

IPMA ENTRY-LEVEL FIRE SERVICE TESTS: B-3 FIREFIGHTER
Advanced Research Resources Organization

Adult

Purpose: Assesses the aptitude and abilities of candidates for entry-level firefighter positions.

Description: 97-item paper-pencil test assessing the following general abilities considered important for entry-level firefighters: reasoning, problem solving, and decision making (12 items); mathematical computations and comparisons (7 items); reading comprehension (63 items); and mechanical reasoning (15 items). Items were constructed from task data to assess the following performance dimensions: responding to alarms; firefighting and extinguishing operations; post-fire operations; emergency and rescue operations; first-aid and assistance; fire prevention; inspection and code-enforcing activities; apparatus and equipment maintenance; fire/arson investigation; training activities; general firehouse duties, including management, administration, and housewatch; and public relations and community activities. Examiner required. Suitable for group use.

Timed: 2 hours, 15 minutes

Scoring: Hand key; may be machine scored

Cost: 1-50 test booklets (rental): IPMA agency members $7.50 each; nonmembers $9.00 each

Publisher: International Personnel Management Association

IPMA ENTRY-LEVEL FIRE SERVICE TESTS: B-4 FIREFIGHTER
Advanced Research Resources Organization

Adult

Purpose: Assesses the aptitude and abilities of candidates for entry-level firefighter positions.

Description: 110-item paper-pencil test measuring the following general abilities considered important for entry-level firefighters: reasoning, problem solving, and decision making (9 items); mathematical computations and comparisons (7 items); reading comprehension (76 items); and mechanical reasoning (18 items). Items were constructed from task data to assess the following performance dimensions: responding to alarms; firefighting and extinguishing operations; post-fire operations; emergency and rescue operations; first-aid and assistance; fire prevention; inspection and code-enforcing activities; apparatus and equipment maintenance; fire/arson investigation; training activities; general firehouse duties; management, administration, and housewatch; and public relations and community activities. Examiner required. Suitable for group use.

Timed: 2½ hours

Scoring: Hand key; may be machine scored

Cost: 1-50 test booklets (rental): IPMA agency members $7.50 each; nonmembers $9.00 each

Publisher: International Personnel Management Association

IPMA ENTRY-LEVEL POLICE SERVICE TESTS: A-2 POLICE OFFICER
Advanced Research Resources Organization

Adult

Purpose: Assesses the general aptitude and abilities of candidates for entry-level police officer positions.

Description: 81-item paper-pencil test assessing the general aptitude and abilities of candidates for entry-level police officer positions. Subtests cover reasoning, problem solving, decision making (19 items), data/rule interpretation and understanding instructions (43 items), and reading comprehension (19 items). Items were constructed from task data to assess the following performance dimensions: preparing for duty, patrol activities, response to call for assistance, arrest and detention procedures, search and seizure, traffic control and investigation, public relations, investigation, court activities, and administrative duties. Examiner required. Suitable for group use.

Timed: 2 hours

Scoring: Hand key; may be machine scored

Cost: 1-50 test booklets (rental): IPMA agency members $7.50 each; nonmembers $9.00 each

Publisher: International Personnel Management Association

IPMA ENTRY-LEVEL POLICE SERVICE TESTS: MULTIJURISDICTIONAL POLICE OFFICER EXAMINATIONS (MPOE), FORMS 165.1 AND 165.2
Educational Testing Service

Adult

Purpose: Assesses the general aptitude and abilities of candidates for entry-level police officer positions.

Description: 150-item paper-pencil test assessing the general aptitude and abilities of candidates for entry-level police officer positions. Subscales measure verbal comprehension (15 items), spatial scanning (15 items), visualization (15 items), semantic ordering (15 items), memory for ideas (15 items), spatial orientation (15 items), problem sensitivity (15 items), induction (15 items), memory for relationship (15 items), and paired associates memory (15 items). Each applicant must be provided with a study guide (MPOE 1164.1) at least three weeks prior to test administration to enhance test fairness and reduce undesirable influences of reading ability. The study guide is comprised of 38 practice items with answers and a practice sheet. Available in two alternate forms, 165.1 and 165.2. Examiner required. Suitable for group use.

Timed: 2½ hours

Scoring: Hand key; may be machine scored

Cost: 1-50 test booklets (rental): IPMA agency members $7.00 each; nonmembers $7.50 each

Publisher: International Personnel Management Association

IPMA ENTRY-LEVEL POLICE SERVICE TESTS: POLICE OFFICER EXAMINATIONS (POE), FORMS 175.1 AND 175.2
Advanced Research Resources Organization

Adult

Purpose: Assesses the general aptitude and abilities of candidates for entry-level police officer positions.

Description: 140-item paper-pencil test assessing the general aptitude and abilities of candidates for entry-level police officer positions. The subtests cover verbal comprehension (32 items), memory for relationships (14 items), memory for ideas (11 items), paired-associate memory (33 items), spatial orientation (12 items), semantic ordering (6 items), problem sensitivity (11 items), spatial scanning (9 items), and induction (12 items). Items were constructed to assess performance dimensions derived from task data, including preparing for duty, patrol activities, response to call for assistance, arrest and detention procedures, search and seizure, traffic control and investigation, public relations, investigation, court activities, and administrative duties. Two forms of the test are available: 175.1 and 175.2. Each applicant must be provided with a study guide at least three weeks prior to administration to enhance test fairness and reduce undesirable influences of reading ability. Examiner required. Suitable for group use.

Timed: 2½ hours

Scoring: Hand key; may be machine scored

Cost: 1-50 test booklets (rental): IPMA agency members $7.50 each; nonmembers $8.50 each

Publisher: International Personnel Management Association

IPMA FIRE SERVICE TESTS: 307 RADIO OPERATOR

Adult

Purpose: Assesses the knowledge, skills, and abilities of candidates for the position of fire service radio operator.

Description: 100-item paper-pencil test assessing the following general abilities considered important for the position of fire service radio operator: reading comprehension (10 items), vocabulary (10 items), arithmetic (10 items), filing (10 items), English usage (10 items), pronunciation (10 items), radio operation (10 items), electricity (10 items), and Radio I knowledge—terminology, principles, equipment, and troubleshooting (20 items). Examiner required. Suitable for group use.

Timed: 2 hours

Scoring: Hand key; may be machine scored

Cost: 1-50 test booklets (rental): IPMA agency members $6.25 each; nonmembers $7.75 each

Publisher: International Personnel Management Association

IPMA FIRE SERVICE TESTS: 307 SENIOR RADIO OPERATOR

Adult

Purpose: Assesses the knowledge, skills, and abilities of candidates for the position of fire service senior radio operator.

Description: 130-item paper-pencil test covering the following general abilities considered important for the position of fire service senior radio operator: reading comprehension (10 items), vocabulary (10 items), arithmetic (10 items), filing (10 items), English usage (10 items), pronunciation (10 items), radio operation (10 items), electricity (10 items), Radio I knowledge—terminology, principles, equipment, troubleshooting (20 items), supervision (10 items), and Radio II knowledge—terminology, principles, equipment, troubleshooting (20 items). The first 100 items can be used for entry-level radio operator positions. Examiner required. Suitable for group use.

Timed: 2½ hours

Scoring: Hand key; may be machine scored

Cost: 1-50 test booklets (rental): IPMA agency members $6.25 each; nonmembers $7.75 each

Publisher: International Personnel Management Association

IPMA FIRE SERVICE TESTS: 575 FIRE SERVICE ADMINISTRATOR (BATTALION CHIEF)
Advanced Research Resources Organization

Adult

Purpose: Assesses the knowledge, skills, and abilities of candidates for the position of battalion fire chief.

Description: 175-item paper-pencil test covering the following general abilities considered important for the position of battalion fire chief: communication skills (19 items); fire protection and alarm systems (14 items); water supply, system analyses, and fire protection hydraulics (16 items); fire service administration (25 items); general physics (9 items); public speaking (11 items); personnel management (44 items); sociological aspects of fire protection (14 items); and major emergency planning (23 items). A reading list and documentation are available. Examiner required. Suitable for group use.

Timed: 2 hours, 55 minutes

Scoring: Hand key; may be machine scored

Cost: 1-50 test booklets (rental): IPMA agency members $7.75 each; nonmembers $9.25 each

Publisher: International Personnel Management Association

IPMA FIRE SERVICE TESTS: 576 FIRE SERVICE ADMINISTRATOR (DEPUTY CHIEF)

Adult

Purpose: Assesses the knowledge, skills, and abilities of candidates for the position of deputy fire chief.

Description: 175-item paper-pencil test covering fire safety (17 items), industrial fire protection (16 items), management/public administration (58 items), public finance/budgeting (30 items), fire suppression and detection systems (14 items), public relations (23 items), and fire protection and the law (17 items). A reading list and documentation are available. Examiner required. Suitable for group use.

Timed: 2 hours, 55 minutes

Scoring: Hand key; may be machine scored

Cost: 1-50 test booklets (rental): IPMA agency members $7.75 each; nonmembers $9.25 each

Publisher: International Personnel Management Association

IPMA FIRE SERVICE TESTS: R530 FIRE INSPECTOR

Adult

Purpose: Assesses the knowledge, skills, and abilities of candidates for the position of fire inspector.

Description: 125-item paper-pencil test assessing the following general abilities considered important for the position of fire inspector: reading comprehension (15 items), records and reports (10 items), public speaking (10 items), interviewing (10 items), combustible materials (15 items), fire inspection hazards (20 items), fire prevention (15 items), public relations (15 items), and fire safety (15 items). The test is composed of the first 125 items of the 160-item Senior Fire Inspector test. A reading list is available. Examiner required. Suitable for group use.

Timed: 2 hours, 15 minutes

Scoring: Hand key; may be machine scored

Cost: 1-50 test booklets (rental): IPMA agency members $6.25 each; nonmembers $7.75 each

Publisher: International Personnel Management Association

IPMA FIRE SERVICE TESTS: R530 SENIOR FIRE INSPECTOR

Adult

Purpose: Assesses the knowledge, skills, and abilities of candidates for the position of senior fire inspector.

Description: 160-item paper-pencil test covering the following general abilities considered important for the position of

senior fire inspector: reading comprehension (15 items), records and reports (10 items), public speaking (10 items), interviewing (10 items), combustible materials (15 items), fire inspection hazards (20 items), fire prevention (15 items), public relations (15 items), fire safety (15 items), supervision (5 items), evidence (15 items), and building inspection (15 items). The first 125 items can be used for testing candidates for entry-level fire inspector positions. A reading list is available. Examiner required. Suitable for group use.

Timed: 3 hours

Scoring: Hand key; may be machine scored

Cost: 1-50 test booklets (rental): IPMA agency members $6.25 each; nonmembers $7.75 each

Publisher: International Personnel Management Association

IPMA FIRE SERVICE TESTS: R577 FIRE ENGINEER

Adult

Purpose: Assesses the knowledge, skills, and abilities of candidates for the position of fire engineer.

Description: 110-item paper-pencil test covering the following general abilities considered important for the position of fire engineer: automotive terminology and operations (30 items); fire equipment, fire combat, and first aid (30 items); and pumps, gauges, and hydraulics (50 items). A reading list is available. Examiner required. Suitable for group use.

Timed: 2 hours

Scoring: Hand key; may be machine scored

Cost: 1-50 test booklets (rental): IPMA agency members $6.25 each; nonmembers $7.75 each

Publisher: International Personnel Management Association

IPMA PROMOTIONAL FIRE SERVICE TESTS: 539 FIRE SERVICE ADMINISTRATOR (CHIEF)

Adult

Purpose: Assesses the knowledge, skills, and abilities of candidates for the position of fire chief.

Description: 150-item paper-pencil test covering the following general abilities considered important for the position of fire chief: reading comprehension (10 items), special problems (5 items), combat techniques (5 items), fire command (10 items), pumpers (5 items), extinguishers (5 items), training (5 items), fire inspection (5 items), records and reports (5 items), combat equipment (5 items), hydraulics (5 items), fire chemistry (5 items), supervision (10 items), planning (5 items), standards (5 items), fire hazards (5 items), public relations (5 items), education (5 items), fire training (15 items), budget (5 items), personnel (5 items), and administration (20 items). A reading list is available. Examiner required. Suitable for group use.

Timed: 2 hours, 45 minutes

Scoring: Hand key; may be machine scored

Cost: 1-50 test booklets (rental): IPMA agency members $6.25 each; nonmembers $7.75 each

Publisher: International Personnel Management Association

IPMA PROMOTIONAL FIRE SERVICE TESTS: 573 FIRE SERVICE SUPERVISOR (SERGEANT, LIEUTENANT)
Advanced Research Resources Organization

Adult

Purpose: Assesses the knowledge, skills, and abilities of candidates for positions of fire service sergeant or lieutenant.

Description: 150-item paper-pencil test covering basic firefighting (22 items), leadership (16 items), fire prevention (19 items), fire suppression (9 items), fire pro-

tection (6 items), fire hazards and causes (12 items), building construction (12 items), codes and ordinances (3 items), strategy and tactics (24 items), chemistry (3 items), fire safety (9 items), fire investigation (6 items), and report writing (9 items). The ranks of sergeant and lieutenant are indicated as a general guide. The application of the test should be dictated by local policies. A reading list and documentation are available. Examiner required. Suitable for group use.

Timed: 2½ hours

Scoring: Hand key; may be machine scored

Cost: 1-50 test booklets (rental): IPMA agency members $7.75 each; nonmembers $9.25 each

Publisher: International Personnel Management Association

IPMA PROMOTIONAL FIRE SERVICE TESTS: 574 FIRE SERVICE ADMINISTRATOR (CAPTAIN)
Advanced Research Resources Organization

Adult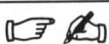

Purpose: Assesses the knowledge, skills, and abilities of candidates for the position of fire captain.

Description: 150-item paper-pencil test covering the following general abilities considered important for the position of fire captain: human relations and management (65 items), communication skills (22 items), technical mathematics (14 items), hazardous materials (25 items), and technical reports (24 items). A reading list and documentation are available. Examiner required. Suitable for group use.

Timed: 2½ hours

Scoring: Hand key; may be machine scored

Cost: 1-50 test booklets (rental): IPMA agency members $7.75 each; nonmembers $8.75 each

Publisher: International Personnel Management Association

IPMA PROMOTIONAL FIRE SERVICE TESTS: 578 FIRE SERVICE ADMINISTRATOR (CHIEF)

Adult

Purpose: Assesses the knowledge, skills, and abilities of candidates for the position of fire chief.

Description: 150-item paper-pencil test assessing the following general abilities considered important for the position of fire chief: master- and long-range planning (20 items), management information systems (28 items), labor relations (42 items), and public administration (60 items). The rank of chief indicated for the test is a general guide. Specific application depends on local policies. A reading list and documentation are available. Examiner required. Suitable for group use.

Timed: 3 hours

Scoring: Hand key; may be machine scored

Cost: 1-50 test booklets (rental): IPMA agency members $7.75 each; nonmembers $9.25 each

Publisher: International Personnel Management Association

IPMA PROMOTIONAL POLICE SERVICE TESTS: 47B POLICE RADIO DISPATCHER

Adult

Purpose: Assesses the knowledge, skills, and abilities of candidates for the position of police radio dispatcher.

Description: 120-item paper-pencil test assessing the knowledge, skills, and abilities of candidates for the position of police radio dispatcher. The subtests cover reading comprehension (10 items), abstract reasoning (10 items), arithmetic calculations (10 items), filing skills (10 items), tabular interpretation (10 items), pronunciation (10 items), terminology (10 items), radio equipment (10 items), radio dispatching (10 items), radio operations (5 items), radio logs (5 items), radio communications (5 items), radio repairs (10

items), and radio symbols (5 items). Examiner required. Suitable for group use.

Timed: 2 hours

Scoring: Hand key; may be machine scored

Cost: 1-50 test booklets (rental): IPMA agency members $6.25 each; nonmembers $7.25 each

Publisher: International Personnel Management Association

IPMA PROMOTIONAL POLICE SERVICE TESTS: 558 POLICE ADMINISTRATOR (CHIEF)

Adult

Purpose: Assesses the knowledge, skills, and abilities of candidates for the position of police chief.

Description: 180-item paper-pencil test covering the following general abilities considered important for the position of police chief: reading comprehension (10 items), tabular interpretation (5 items), crime classification (5 items), patrol (15 items), search and seizure (5 items), arrest (5 items), stolen property recovery (5 items), evidence (5 items), courts and trials (5 items), interrogation (5 items), investigation (5 items), accident investigation (5 items), traffic (10 items), criminology (5 items), identification (5 items), fingerprints (5 items), crime prevention (5 items), juvenile delinquency (5 items), vice (5 items), reports (5 items), special problems (5 items), supervision (20 items), training (5 items), personnel (10 items), public relations (5 items), administration (10 items), and crime statistics (5 items). The rank of chief is indicated as a general guide. The application of the test should be dictated by local policies. A reading list and documentation are available on request. Examiner required. Suitable for group use.

Timed: 2 hours, 25 minutes

Scoring: Hand key; may be machine scored

Cost: 1-50 test booklets (rental): IPMA agency members $6.25 each; nonmembers $7.75 each

Publisher: International Personnel Management Association

IPMA PROMOTIONAL POLICE SERVICE TESTS: 563 POLICE SUPERVISOR (CORPORAL, SERGEANT)

Adult

Purpose: Assesses the knowledge, skills, and abilities of candidates for supervisory-level police officer positions.

Description: 145-item paper-pencil test measuring the following general abilities considered important for supervisory-level police officer police positions: patrol (31 items), investigative (26 items), legal (20 items), administrative (15 items), supervision (46 items), and police role in the community (7 items). The rank of corporal or sergeant indicated for the test is a general guide. Specific application depends on local policies. A reading list and documentation are available. Examiner required. Suitable for group use.

Timed: 2½ hours

Scoring: Hand key; may be machine scored

Cost: 1-50 test booklets (rental): IPMA agency members $7.75 each; nonmembers $9.25 each

Publisher: International Personnel Management Association

IPMA PROMOTIONAL POLICE SERVICE TESTS: 564 POLICE ADMINISTRATOR
Advanced Research Resources Organization

Adult

Purpose: Assesses the knowledge, skills, and abilities of candidates for the position of police lieutenant.

Description: 145-item paper-pencil test covering the following general abilities considered important for the position of police lieutenant: patrol (15 items), investigation (14 items), legal (14 items), administration (44 items), supervision (44 items), and police role in the community (14 items). A reading list is available. The rank of lieutenant is indicated as a general

guide. The application of the test should be dictated by local policies. Examiner required. Suitable for group use.

Timed: 2½ hours

Scoring: Hand key; may be machine scored

Cost: 1-50 test booklets (rental): IPMA agency members $7.75 each; nonmembers $9.25 each

Publisher: International Personnel Management Association

IPMA PROMOTIONAL POLICE SERVICE TESTS: 565 POLICE ADMINISTRATOR (CAPTAIN)
Advanced Research Resources Organization

Adult

Purpose: Assesses the knowledge, skills, and abilities of candidates for the position of police captain.

Description: 170-item paper-pencil test covering the following general abilities considered important for the position of police captain: patrol (8 items), investigation (18 items), legal aspects (9 items), administration (65 items), supervision (49 items), and police role in the community (21 items). A reading list and documentation are available. The rank of captain is indicated as a general guide. The application of the test should be dictated by local policies. Examiner required. Suitable for group use.

Timed: 3 hours

Scoring: Hand key; may be machine scored

Cost: 1-50 test booklets (rental): IPMA agency members $7.75 each; nonmembers $9.25 each

Publisher: International Personnel Management Association

IPMA PROMOTIONAL POLICE SERVICE TESTS: 566 POLICE ADMINISTRATOR (ASSISTANT CHIEF)
Advanced Research Resources Organization

Adult

Purpose: Assesses the knowledge, skills, and abilities of candidates for the position of assistant police chief.

Description: 170-item paper-pencil test covering the following general abilities considered important for the position of assistant police chief: patrol (6 items), investigation (7 items), administration (95 items), supervision (34 items), and police role in the community (28 items). A reading list and documentation are available. The rank of assistant chief is indicated as a general guide. The application of the test should be dictated by local policies. Examiner required. Suitable for group use.

Timed: 3 hours

Scoring: Hand key; may be machine scored

Cost: 1-50 test booklets (rental): IPMA agency members $7.75 each; nonmembers $9.25 each

Publisher: International Personnel Management Association

IPMA PROMOTIONAL POLICE SERVICE TESTS: 568 POLICE ADMINISTRATOR (CHIEF)

Adult

Purpose: Assesses the knowledge, skills, and abilities of candidates for the position of police chief.

Description: 180-item paper-pencil test assessing the knowledge, skills, and abilities of police chief candidates. The subtests measure operational field activities (38 items), internal management (68 items), public relations (31 items), interaction with agencies in the criminal justice system (20 items), and interaction with local officials (23 items). The rank of chief indicated for the test is a general guide. Specific application depends on local policies. A reading list and documentation are available. Examiner required. Suitable for group use.

Timed: 3 hours

Scoring: Hand key; may be machine scored

Cost: 1-50 test booklets (rental): IPMA agency members $7.75 each; nonmembers $9.25 each

Publisher: International Personnel Management Association

IPMA PROMOTIONAL POLICE SERVICE TESTS: R552 POLICE DETECTIVE

Adult

Purpose: Assesses the knowledge, skills, and abilities of candidates for the position of police detective.

Description: 165-item paper-pencil test covering the following general abilities considered important for the position of police detective: reading comprehension (10 items), crime classification (15 items), patrol (5 items), search and seizure (10 items), arrest (10 items), interrogation (20 items), identification (10 items), criminology (10 items), crime prevention (10 items), vice (15 items), courts and trials (10 items), fingerprints (10 items), supervision (10 items), public relations (10 items), and juvenile delinquency (10 items). A reading list is available. Examiner required. Suitable for group use.

Timed: 3 hours

Scoring: Hand key; may be machine scored

Cost: 1-50 test booklets (rental): IPMA agency members $6.25 each; nonmembers $7.25 each

Publisher: International Personnel Management Association

POLICE OFFICER ESV-100
McCann Associates, Inc.

Adult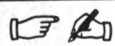

Purpose: Assesses abilities of candidates for police officer. Used by municipal police departments for job screening.

Description: 100-item criterion-validated paper-pencil multiple-choice test assessing observational ability, ability to exercise judgment and common sense, interest in police work, map reading, dealing with people, ability to read and comprehend policy text material, and reasoning ability. The publisher scores each area and provides a total score, norms, means subtest and total scores, standard deviations, reliability coefficient, and an evaluation of each candidate. Materials include test booklets, answer sheets, identification sheets, envelopes, candidate study guides, and administration instructions. The test is available on a rental basis only to Civil Service Commissions or qualified municipal officials. Examiner required. Suitable for group use.

Timed: 2 hours, 40 minutes

Scoring: Computer scored by publisher

Cost: First 5 candidates $165.00; next 5 candidates $11.00 each

Publisher: McCann Associates, Inc.

POLICE OFFICER ESV-125
McCann Associates, Inc.

Adult

Purpose: Assesses abilities of candidates for police officer. Used by municipal police departments for job screening.

Description: 125-item criterion-validated paper-pencil multiple-choice test assessing observational ability, police aptitude, police public relations, and police judgment. The publisher scores each area and provides a total score, norms, means subtest and total scores, standard deviations, reliability coefficient, and an evaluation of each candidate. Materials include test booklets, answer sheets, identification sheets, envelopes, candidate study guides, and administration instructions. The test is available on a rental basis only to Civil Service Commissions or qualified municipal officials. Examiner required. Suitable for group use.

Timed: 3 hours

Scoring: Computer scored by publisher

Cost: First 5 candidates $165.00; next 5 candidates $11.00 each

Publisher: McCann Associates, Inc.

POLICE SERGEANT (ESV)
McCann Associates, Inc.

Adult

Purpose: Assesses candidates for promotion to police sergeant. Used by municipal police departments.

Description: 100-item criterion-validated paper-pencil multiple-choice test of knowledge of police supervisory principles and practices; legal knowledge,

technical police knowledge, police judgment, and understanding and interpreting police table and text materials. The publisher scores each area and provides a total score, norms, means subtest and total scores, standard deviations, reliability coefficient, and an evaluation of each candidate. Materials include test booklets, candidate study guides, answer sheets, identification sheets, envelopes, and administration instructions. The test is available on a rental basis only to qualified municipal officials and Civil Service Commissions. Examiner required. Suitable for group use.

Timed: 3½ hours

Scoring: Computer scored by publisher

Cost: First 5 candidates $485.00; next 5 candidates $28.00 each

Publisher: McCann Associates, Inc.

PROBATION OFFICER TRAINEE
McCann Associates, Inc.

Adult college graduates

Purpose: Used by court systems and probation departments for job screening where a baccalaureate degree in probation and parole, one of the social sciences, or related curricula is required.

Description: 90-item paper-pencil multiple-choice test covering knowledge of basic psychology and the sociology of deviant behavior, interviewing and counseling knowledge and abilities, knowledge of criminal behavior and delinquency, knowledge of the principles and practices of probation, ability to deal effectively with others, reasoning ability, and verbal comprehension. Materials include test booklets, answer sheets, identification sheets, envelopes, candidate study guides, and complete monitoring instructions. The publisher scores answer sheets and provides a comprehensive report, including norms, means and standard deviations, reliability coefficient, and an evaluation of each candidate. The test is available on a rental basis only to personnel directors or other qualified examiners. Examiner required. Suitable for group use.

Timed: 3½ hours

Scoring: Computer scored by publisher

Cost: Contact publisher
Publisher: McCann Associates, Inc.

TRANSIT BUS OPERATOR SELECTION TEST BATTERY
G.O. Baehr and Melany E. Baehr

Adult

Purpose: Identifies applicants with good potential for long-term successful performance as municipal bus operators.

Description: Multiple-item paper-pencil test measuring aptitude for operating municipal buses. The test consists of three sections: Work Experience and Background (35 items), Skills and Abilities (96 items), and Self-Understanding and Experience (108 items). Together, the three sections predict performance on criteria such as accidents, sick days, and supervisor ratings. Examiner required. Suitable for group use.
Timed: 90 minutes for total battery
Scoring: Hand key; may be computer scored
Cost: $4.00-$12.00 per booklet depending on scoring method
Publisher: London House Press

Sales

APTITUDES ASSOCIATES TEST OF SALES APTITUDE
Martin M. Bruce

Adult

Purpose: Evaluates an individual's aptitude for selling. Used as an aid in vocational guidance and in the selection of sales personnel.

Description: 50-item paper-pencil test measuring the subject's knowledge and understanding of the principles of selling a wide variety of goods ranging from heavy industrial capital items to door-to-door housewares. Norms are available to compare the subject's score with salespeople, men, women, and selected "special sales groups." The subject reads the directions and completes the test. Self-administered. Suitable for group use.

Untimed: 20-30 minutes
Scoring: Hand key
Cost: Manual $6.15; key $1.10; package of tests $25.75
Publisher: Martin M. Bruce, Ph.D., Publishers

BIOGRAPHICAL INDEX
Refer to page 910.

CUSTOMER REACTION SURVEY (CRS)
Jay Hall and C. Leo Griffith

Adult

Purpose: Assesses customer reaction to a salesperson's interpersonal style and customer preferences regarding salesperson behavior. Used for employee training and development and as a basis for discussion.

Description: Multiple-item paper-pencil inventory assessing an individual's success as a salesperson from the customer's point of view. In the first part of the inventory, the customer rates the salesperson's use of exposure and feedback. In the second part, the customer states preferred salesperson behavior. The resulting profiles may be combined with self-ratings from the Sales Relations Survey to make sales training relevant to the realities of the field. Normative data are provided. Examiner required. Suitable for group use.
Untimed: Varies
Scoring: Examiner evaluated
Cost: Individual instrument $4.50
Publisher: Teleometrics International
Information and availability unconfirmed; no publisher response.

DIPLOMACY TEST OF EMPATHY
Willard A. Kerr

Adult

Purpose: Measures empathic ability. Used for selecting applicants for sales positions.

Description: Multiple-item paper-pencil test measuring the ability to sell, be persuasive, tactful, and diplomatic. Items correlate with the mean salary increases of executives but have little or no relationship with intelligence. Norms are available for general adults, management, sales, and sales management. Examiner required. Suitable for group use.

Untimed: 20 minutes

Scoring: Hand key

Cost: Specimen set $5.00; 25 tests $5.00; 25 answer sheets $5.00

Publisher: Psychometric Affiliates

ETSA TESTS 7-A—SALES APTITUDE
Refer to page 805.

GUILFORD-ZIMMERMAN APTITUDE SURVEY: NUMERICAL OPERATIONS (GZAS:NO)
Refer to page 810.

I.P.I. APTITUDE—INTELLIGENCE TEST SERIES: FLUENCY
Refer to page 812.

I.P.I. APTITUDE—INTELLIGENCE TEST SERIES: JUDGMENT
Refer to page 813.

I.P.I. APTITUDE—INTELLIGENCE TEST SERIES: MEMORY
Refer to page 813.

I.P.I. APTITUDE—INTELLIGENCE TEST SERIES: PERCEPTION
Refer to page 814.

I.P.I. APTITUDE—INTELLIGENCE TEST SERIES: SALES TERMS
Refer to page 814.

I.P.I. JOB TEST FIELD SERIES: SALES CLERK
Refer to page 820.

I.P.I. JOB TEST FIELD SERIES: SALES PERSON
Refer to page 820.

I.P.I. JOB TEST FIELD SERIES: SALES SUPERVISOR
Refer to page 820.

INCENTIVES MANAGEMENT INDEX (IMI)
Jay Hall and Norman J. Seim

Adult

Purpose: Assesses the incentives used by a sales manager to motivate the sales force. Used for training and development of sales managers and as a basis for discussion.

Description: Multiple-item paper-pencil self-report inventory identifying which incentives a sales manager emphasizes and assessing the sales manager's personal theories about what motivates the sales force. The inventory yields a managerial profile that may be used as feedback for the sales force. The inventory may be administered in conjunction with the Sales Motivation Survey (SMS) in two ways: to indicate areas in which the sales manager's own needs influence the incentives that are emphasized with the sales force and to assess the sales manager's own motivational theory in light of the needs of the sales force. Normative data are provided. Examiner required. Suitable for group use.

Untimed: Varies

Scoring: Examiner evaluated

Cost: Individual instrument $4.50

Publisher: Teleometrics International

Information and availability unconfirmed; no publisher response.

LIMRA CAREER PROFILE SYSTEM

Adult

Purpose: Evaluates the career experience and expectations of individuals considering an insurance sales career. Used for employee screening and selection.

Description: 183- or 158-item paper-pencil questionnaire assessing career information related to future success as an insurance salesperson. The 183-item Initial Career Profile is used with applicants who have no prior insurance sales experience. The 158-item Advanced Career Profile is used with experienced applicants. The questionnaire is available to insurance company home offices only. Examiner required. Suitable for group use. Both forms may be administered in Canada and are available in French.

Untimed: Varies

Scoring: Computer scored

Cost: Test booklet (specify profile) $5.00; Initial Career Profile answer sheet $10.00; Advanced Career Profile answer sheet $12.00; cost includes scoring

Publisher: Life Insurance Marketing and Research Association, Inc.

POPPLETON-ALLEN SALES APTITUDE TEST (PASAT)
S. Poppleton, E. Allen, and D. Garland

Adult

Purpose: Measures 15 different sales aptitudes, preferably of adults with previous work experience.

Description: 126-item paper-pencil test assessing social skills, organization and planning abilities, emotional expression, and motivation of potential sales people. Test items are based on job and factor analysis studies. Individuals select one of four or five alternative answers to questions. Norms are available for business and managment students and for sales people in various industries. Examiner/self-administered. Suitable for group use. BRITISH PUBLISHER

Untimed: 20-30 minutes

Scoring: Self-scored

Cost: Specimen set (test booklet, answer key, manual) £23.75

Publisher: The Test Agency Ltd.

RETAIL SALES BATTERY (RSB)

Adult

Purpose: Identifies job applicants who might engage in counterproductive behaviors in the workplace, assesses math skills required for financial transactions with customers, and includes a self-assessment of skills and abilities required of retail sales positions. Used for selecting candidates for retail sales positions.

Description: Test battery identifying job appplicants who might engage in counterproductive behavior in the workplace, assessing the mathematical skills required in financial transactions with customers and skills and abilities necessary for effective performance. The battery can result in a hire, not hire decision, or subscale scores that can be used in a selection process. The counterproductivity measure includes four subscale scores: theft, violence, drug abuse, and distortion. The applied mathematics and the skills and abilities test each result in one score. Basic literacy is required. Self-administered. Suitable for group use.

Untimed: 45 minutes

Scoring: Computer scored by phone

Cost: Complete $8.00-$12.00 depending on volume ordered

Publisher: London House Press

SALES ATTITUDE CHECKLIST
Erwin K. Taylor

Adult

Purpose: Measures attitudes and behaviors involved in sales and selling. Used for sales selection programs.

Description: 31-item paper-pencil test assessing basic attitudes toward selling and habits in the selling situation. Norms are provided for applicants for the following positions: sales and sales managerial positions, automobile salespersons, freight traffic salespersons, office equipment salespersons, and utility salespersons. Examiner required. Suitable for group use.

Untimed: 10-15 minutes

Scoring: Hand key

Cost: 25 test booklets $42.00; examiner's manual $10.00

Publisher: Science Research Associates, Inc.

SALES COMPREHENSION TEST
Martin M. Bruce

Adult

Purpose: Measures sales ability and potential based on the subject's understanding of the principles of selling. Used for evaluating prospective salespeople, vocational counseling, and training projects for salesmen.

Description: 30-item paper-pencil multiple-choice test measuring the subject's aptitude for selling. Standard test procedures are used. Available in French, Italian, Dutch, and German. Self-administered. Suitable for group use.

Untimed: 15-20 minutes

Scoring: Hand key

Cost: Manual $6.15; key $1.10; package of profile sheets $10.50; package of tests $25.75

Publisher: Martin M. Bruce, Ph.D., Publishers

SALES MOTIVATION INVENTORY
Martin M. Bruce

Adult

Purpose: Assesses interest in and motivation for sales work, both commission and wholesale/retail.

Description: 75-item paper-pencil test measuring sales motivation and drive. Consists of multiple-choice triads. Not intended for non-commissioned clerking or order-taking positions. Self-administered. Suitable for group use. Available in French.

Untimed: 20-30 minutes

Scoring: Hand key

Cost: Manual $6.15; key $1.10; package of profile sheets $10.50; package of tests $25.75

Publisher: Martin M. Bruce, Ph.D., Publishers

SALES MOTIVATION SURVEY (SMS)
Jay Hall and Norman J. Seim

Adult

Purpose: Assesses the needs and motivations of salespersons. Used for employee training and development and as a basis for discussion.

Description: Multiple-item paper-pencil self-report inventory measuring the personal needs and goals of salespersons. The inventory provides a profile of personal motivations. The results may serve as a basis for reordering personal priorities and better understanding of personal performance. Normative data are provided. The inventory may be administered in conjunction with the Incentive Management Index for assessment of sales managers. Self-administered. Suitable for group use.

Untimed: Varies

Scoring: Self-scored

Cost: Individual instrument $4.50

Publisher: Teleometrics International

Information and availability unconfirmed; no publisher response.

SALES PREFERENCE QUESTIONNAIRE
George W. Dudley

Adult

Purpose: Measures the fear of prospecting in direct sales personnel. Used for personnel selection/evaluation and for training/development purposes.

Description: 45-item paper-pencil or computerized inventory of an individual's feeling about making sales calls. The questionnaire measures nine areas of reluctance (threat-sensitivity, over-preparation, excuse-making, group presentations, calling on personal friends, pride in sales career, intrusion-sensitivity, up-market resistance, and calling on relatives) and provides scores on two additional scales (emotional energy spent resisting making calls and emotional freedom to initiate prospecting calls with prospective buyers). The report includes a graphic presentation of the basic scales, an analysis of various critical items, and a narrative discussion of those areas in which reluctance is significantly elevated. Self-administered. Suitable for group use.

Untimed: 15-20 minutes

Scoring: Computer scored

Cost: Contact publisher

Publisher: Behavioral Science Research Press, Inc.

SALES RELATIONS SURVEY (SRS)
Jay Hall

Adult

Purpose: Assesses an individual's interpersonal sales style. Used for employee training and development and as a basis for discussion.

Description: Multiple-item paper-pencil self-report inventory assessing the quality of a salesperson's relationships with customers along exposure and feedback dimensions. The inventory is used to introduce and assess concepts such as blindspots, facades, and hidden potentials. Scores may be used to plot Johari Window profiles for an entire sales force. Normative data are provided. The inventory may be administered in conjunction with the Customer Reaction Survey for a more complete assessment of an individual's interpersonal sales style. Examiner required. Suitable for group use.

Untimed: Varies

Scoring: Examiner evaluated

Cost: Individual instrument $4.50

Publisher: Teleometrics International

Information and availability unconfirmed; no publisher response.

THE SALES SENTENCE COMPLETION BLANK
Martin M. Bruce

Adult

Purpose: Aids in evaluating and selecting sales personnel by providing insight into how the applicant thinks and his social attitudes and general personality.

Description: 40-item paper-pencil test consisting of sentence fragments to be completed by the subject. The examiner assesses the results by scoring the responses on a 7-point scale, allowing a "projection" of the subject's attitudes about life, self, and others. Self-administered. Suitable for group use.

Untimed: 20-35 minutes

Scoring: Hand key

Cost: Manual $7.50; package of tests $27.25

Publisher: Martin M. Bruce, Ph.D., Publishers

SALES STYLE DIAGNOSIS TEST
W.J. Reddin and David Forman

Adult

Purpose: Measures a salesperson's selling style and effectiveness. Used to screen, coach, and train salespersons.

Description: Multiple-item paper-pencil test designed to provide scores on the following selling styles: deserter, missionary, autocrat, compromiser, bureaucrat, developer, benevolent autocrat, and executive. Task orientation, relationships orientation, and effectiveness are assessed as well. The individual responds to actions of a hypothetical salesperson and receives a score indicative of selling style. Self-administered. Suitable for group use.
CANADIAN PUBLISHER

Untimed: 20-30 minutes

Scoring: Hand key

Cost: Test kit (10 test copies, fact sheet, user's guide) $40.00; cash orders postpaid

Publisher: Organizational Tests (Canada) Ltd.

SALES TRANSACTION AUDIT (STA)
Jay Hall and C. Leo Griffith

Adult

Purpose: Assesses the interpersonal transactions of salespeople with their customers in terms of Eric Berne's model of transactional analysis. Used for employee training and development and as a basis for discussion.

Description: Multiple-item paper-pencil self-report inventory measuring the size of the parent, adult, and child—the three positions from which individuals can communicate according to the model of transactional analysis—in a salesperson's transactions with customers. The inventory also provides scores for transaction contamination, crossed and complementary transactions, and constructive and disruptive tension in the sales relationship. Normative data are provided. Examiner required. Suitable for group use.

Untimed: Varies

Scoring: Examiner evaluated

Cost: Individual instrument $4.50

Publisher: Teleometrics International

Information and availability unconfirmed; no publisher response.

SELLING JUDGMENT TEST
Martin M. Bruce

Adolescent, adult

Purpose: Measures the sales comprehension of high school students and adults. Used by sales trainers to develop discussion topics.

Description: 5-item paper-pencil multiple-choice test assessing sales competence in the retail and wholesale fields. The items in this test are taken from the Sales Comprehension Test and were chosen by the Associated Merchandising Corporation as particularly pertinent to the department retail store field. The test is used primarily for training and discussion purposes. The Sales Comprehension Test is more appropriate for assessment purposes. Self-administered. Suitable for group use.

Untimed: 3 minutes

Scoring: Hand key

Cost: 20 test booklets $9.95

Publisher: Martin M. Bruce, Ph.D., Publishers

TEST OF PRACTICAL JUDGMENT—FORM 62
Refer to page 972.

TEST OF RETAIL SALES INSIGHT (TRSI)
Russell N. Cassel

Adult

Purpose: Assesses degree of knowledge of retail selling. Used for in-service education of retail sales clerks and assessing progress in distributive education courses.

Description: 60-item multiple-choice paper-pencil test measuring five areas of retail sales: general sales knowledge, customer motivation and need, merchandise procurement and adaptation, sales promotion procedures, and sales closure. Five alternatives are provided for each item. A fifth-grade reading level is required. Examiner required. Suitable for group use.

Untimed: 30 minutes

Scoring: Hand key

Cost: Specimen set $8.00; 25 tests $25.00; 25 answer sheets $6.00; 25 profile sheets $7.50; keys $6.00; manual $6.00

Publisher: Psychologists and Educators, Inc.

WOLFE SALES STAFF SELECTOR

Adult

Purpose: Evaluates suitability of candidates for sales representative positions.

Description: Multiple-item paper-pencil set of seven subtests measuring numerical skills, problem-solving and logical-thinking abilities, verbal fluency and communication skills, comprehension of selling principles, sales motivation and career interests, emotional stability, and desire for people contact. The first three tests are timed speed tests. The tests are appropriate for sales/order desk applicants, sales applicants without prior experience, sales professionals, sales service applicants of all levels of experience, and marketing candidates. See description of Wolfe Staff Selector Test Kits for further information. Examiner required. Suitable for group use. Available in French.
CANADIAN PUBLISHER

Timed/Untimed: 75 minutes

Scoring: Hand key or computer scored depending on format

Cost: $50.00 each

Publisher: Wolfe Personnel Testing and Training Systems, Inc.

Teachers

TEACHER OCCUPATIONAL COMPETENCY TESTING: AIR CONDITIONING AND REFRIGERATION EXAMINATION

Adult

Purpose: Assesses competency in air conditioning and refrigeration. Used for providing evidence of competency to become a teacher or obtaining academic credit at participating educational institutions.

Description: Two-part test of skills and knowledge important in air conditioning and refrigeration work. The multiple-choice written test (200 items) covers domestic systems installation, domestic systems servicing, commercial systems installation, commercial systems servicing, residential air conditioning and heating installation, residential air conditioning and heating service, industrial refrigeration installation, and industrial refrigeration service. The performance test is evenly divided between three areas: domestic systems installation and service, commercial systems installation and servicing, and residential air conditioning and heating. Handbook and references will be provided for preparation. Personal tools may be used. Examiner required. The written test is suitable for group use.

Timed: Written test 3 hours; performance test 5 hours

Scoring: Examiner evaluated; may be computer scored

Cost: Contact publisher

Publisher: National Occupational Competency Testing Institute

TEACHER OCCUPATIONAL COMPETENCY TESTING: AIRFRAME AND POWER PLANT EXAMINATION

Adult

Purpose: Assesses competency in airframe and power plant trades. Used for providing evidence of competency to become a teacher or obtaining academic credit at participating educational institutions.

Description: Two-part test of skills and knowledge important in airframe and power plant work. The multiple-choice written test (200 items) covers general knowledge, airframe—systems and components, and power plant operation and maintenance—systems and components. The performance test measures skills in sheet metal work, generator service, use of airworthiness directives, hydraulic components and systems, engine ignition timing, engine valve service, and carburetor service. Shop manuals and specifications will be provided for preparation. Personal tools may be used. Examiner required. The written test is suitable for group use.

Timed: Written test 3 hours; performance test 5½ hours

Scoring: Examiner evaluated; may be computer scored

Cost: Contact publisher

Publisher: National Occupational Competency Testing Institute

TEACHER OCCUPATIONAL COMPETENCY TESTING: ARCHITECTURAL DRAFTING EXAMINATION

Adult

Purpose: Assesses competency in architectural drafting. Used for providing evidence of competency to become a teacher or obtaining academic credit at participating educational institutions.

Description: Two-part test of skills and knowledge important in architectural drafting positions. The multiple-choice written test (200 items) covers basic architectural data, planning and design, materials and methods of construction, structural systems, and administration. The performance test measures skills in sections, working drawings, structural items, electrical items, heating, and perspective and rendering. The applicant should bring a set of drawing instruments, drawing pencils (lead holder and leads), a slide rule, architect's erasers, and erasing shields. Applicants also may bring a lettering guide and Kidder's Handbook and Standards if desired. Examiner required. The written test is suitable for group use.

Timed: Written test 3 hours; performance test 5 hours

Scoring: Examiner evaluated; may be computer scored

Cost: Contact publisher

Publisher: National Occupational Competency Testing Institute

TEACHER OCCUPATIONAL COMPETENCY TESTING: AUDIO-VISUAL COMMUNICATIONS TECHNOLOGY

Adult

Purpose: Assesses competency in audiovisual communications technology. Used for providing evidence of competency to become a teacher or obtaining academic credit at participating educational institutions.

Description: Two-part test of skills and knowledge important in audio-visual communications technology. The multiple-choice written test (200 items) covers general information and theory; design and construction of visuals; catalog, storage, and distribution of audio-visual materials; and equipment identification and operation. The performance test measures skills in motion picture operation, photography, tape recorder operation, and transparency design. Over half the performance test focuses on photography. Examiner required. The written test is suitable for group use.

Timed: Written test 3 hours; performance test 3 hours, 40 minutes

Scoring: Examiner evaluated; may be computer scored

Cost: Contact publisher

Publisher: National Occupational Competency Testing Institute

TEACHER OCCUPATIONAL COMPETENCY TESTING: AUTO BODY REPAIR EXAMINATION

Adult

Purpose: Assesses competency in auto body repair. Used for providing evidence of competency to become a teacher or obtaining academic credit at participating educational institutions.

Description: Two-part test of skills and knowledge important in auto body repair. The multiple-choice written test (190 items) covers welding and brazing, sheet metal repair, refinishing, glass: trim and hardware, panel replacement, frame (unitized body repair), estimating: tools and equipment and safety, filling operations and plastics, and front end alignment. The performance test measures skills in sheet metal repair, refinishing, solder application, glass trim repair, and electrical work. Handbooks and reference material will be provided. Candidates should bring their own safety glasses and spray mask. Examiner required. The written test is suitable for group use.

Timed: Written test 3 hours; performance test 6 hours

Scoring: Examiner evaluated; may be computer scored

Cost: Contact publisher

Publisher: National Occupational Competency Testing Institute

TEACHER OCCUPATIONAL COMPETENCY TESTING: AUTO MECHANIC EXAMINATION

Adult

Purpose: Assesses competency in auto mechanics. Used for providing evidence of competency to become a teacher or obtaining academic credit at participating educational institutions.

Description: Two-part test of skills and knowledge important in auto mechanics. The multiple-choice written test (200 items) covers basic shop principles and practices, engines, emission systems, engine system analysis and repair, suspension, steering and braking, fuel systems, electrical, drive line and components, accessories, and shop management and control. The performance test measures skills in engines, basic automotive practices, fuel systems, electrical, batteries, air conditioning, charging systems, emission systems, engine analysis and repair, drive lines and components, suspension and steering, and brakes. Test equipment, shop manuals, and specifications are provided. Personal tools may be used. Examiner required. The written test is suitable for group use.

Timed: Written test 3 hours; performance test 5 hours

Scoring: Examiner required; may be computer scored

Cost: Contact publisher

Publisher: National Occupational Competency Testing Institute

TEACHER OCCUPATIONAL COMPETENCY TESTING: AUTOMOTIVE BODY AND FENDER

Adult

Purpose: Assesses competency in automotive body and repair. Used for providing evidence of competency to become a teacher or obtaining academic credit at participating educational institutions.

Description: Two-part test of skills and knowledge important in automotive body and fender work. The multiple-choice written test (200 items) covers metal forming, alignment, welding, refinishing, estimating, synthetics, accessory systems, and glass and trim. The performance test measures skills in metal forming, welding, and refinishing. Examiner required. The written test is suitable for group use.

Timed: Written test 3 hours; performance test 4 hours

Scoring: Examiner evaluated; may be computer scored

Cost: Contact publisher

Publisher: National Occupational Competency Testing Institute

TEACHER OCCUPATIONAL COMPETENCY TESTING: BAKER

Adult

Purpose: Assesses competency of individuals in bakery occupations. Used for providing evidence of competency to become a teacher or obtaining academic credit at participating institutions.

Description: Multiple-item paper-pencil and task-performance test in two parts assessing competencies of teachers of baking. The multiple-choice written test (183 items) covers definition of terms, classifications of ingredients, substitutions, sanitation and safety, weights and measurements, interaction of ingredients, handling and storage of ingredients, general baking knowledge, equipment preparation, and baking remedies. The performance test consists of dough preparation for and baking of bread, rolls, cakes, and pastries. Examiner required. Suitable for group use.

Timed: Written test 3 hours; performance test 4 hours

Scoring: Examiner evaluated; may be computer scored

Cost: Contact publisher

Publisher: National Occupational Competency Testing Institute

TEACHER OCCUPATIONAL COMPETENCY TESTING: BRICK MASONRY

Adult

Purpose: Assesses competency in brick masonry. Used for providing evidence of competency to become a teacher or obtaining academic credit at participating educational institutions.

Description: Two-part test of skills and knowledge important in brick masonry. The multiple-choice written test (200 items) covers brick, block, tile, and stone. The performance test measures skills in the same four areas. Both the written and performance tests emphasize brick. Examiner required. The written test is suitable for group use.

Timed: Written test 3 hours; performance test 4 hours
Scoring: Examiner evaluated; may be computer scored
Cost: Contact publisher
Publisher: National Occupational Competency Testing Institute

TEACHER OCCUPATIONAL COMPETENCY TESTING: BUILDING AND HOME MAINTENANCE SERVICES

Adult

Purpose: Assesses competency of individuals in building and home maintenance services. Used for providing evidence of competency to become a teacher or obtaining academic credit at participating institutions.

Description: Multiple-item paper-pencil and task-performance test measuring competencies of individuals teaching building and home maintenance services. The multiple-choice written test (162 items) determines knowledge of floor stripping, refinishing and buffing, carpet care, general electricity and repair, building security, fire prevention, records, general cleaning, plumbing, employee/staff relations, heating, and painting. The performance test consists of general cleaning of an office or a classroom and a restroom or a shower; floor stripping, refinishing, and buffing; welding or soldering; electrical repair; small hand/power tools; and interior/exterior painting. Examiner required. Suitable for group use.
Timed: Written test 3 hours; performance test 5 hours
Scoring: Examiner evaluated; may be computer scored
Cost: Contact publisher
Publisher: National Occupational Competency Testing Institute

TEACHER OCCUPATIONAL COMPETENCY TESTING: BUILDING CONSTRUCTION OCCUPATIONS EXAMINATION

Adult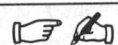

Purpose: Assesses competency in building construction occupations. Used for providing evidence of competency to become a teacher or obtaining academic credit at participating educational institutions.

Description: Two-part test of skills and knowledge important in building construction occupations. The multiple-choice written test (200 items) covers carpentry, electrical, plumbing, painting, masonry, building code and safety, and sheet metal. The performance test measures skills in masonry, carpentry, painting, sheet metal, plumbing, and electrical. Examiner required. The written test is suitable for group use.
Timed: Written test 3 hours; performance test 6 hours
Scoring: Examiner evaluated; may be computer scored
Cost: Contact publisher
Publisher: National Occupational Competency Testing Institute

TEACHER OCCUPATIONAL COMPETENCY TESTING: BUILDING TRADES MAINTENANCE EXAMINATION

Adult

Purpose: Assesses competency in building trade maintenance occupations. Used for providing evidence of competency to become a teacher or obtaining academic credit at participating educational institutions.

Description: Two-part test of skills and knowledge important in building trades maintenance occupations. The multiple-choice written test (200 items) covers heating, air conditioning and refrigeration, carpentry, masonry, custodial, electrical, painting and wallpapering, plumbing, management practices, sheet metal, and welding. The performance test measures skill in masonry, welding, carpentry, surface coating, electrical installation, plumbing, door hardware, glass installation, and custodial services. Examiner required. The written test is suitable for group use.
Timed: Written test 3 hours; performance test 5½ hours

Scoring: Examiner evaluated; may be computer scored

Cost: Contact publisher

Publisher: National Occupational Competency Testing Institute

TEACHER OCCUPATIONAL COMPETENCY TESTING: CABINET MAKING AND MILLWORK EXAMINATION

Adult

Purpose: Assesses competency in cabinet making and millwork occupations. Used for providing evidence of competency to become a teacher or obtaining academic credit at participating educational institutions.

Description: Two-part test of skills and knowledge important in carpentry. The multiple-choice written test consists of 200 items covering planning, safety, machines, hand tools, wood/stock selection, joinery, assembly, and finishing. The performance test measures skills in planning and layout, wood/stock selection, hand tools, safety, machine, joinery, assembly, and finish. References will be provided. Personal tools may be used. Examiner required. The written test is suitable for group use.

Timed: Written test 3 hours; performance test 5 hours

Scoring: Examiner required; may be computer scored

Cost: Contact publisher

Publisher: National Occupational Competency Testing Institute

TEACHER OCCUPATIONAL COMPETENCY TESTING: CARPENTRY EXAMINATION

Adult

Purpose: Assesses competency in carpentry. Used for providing evidence of competency to become a teacher or obtaining academic credit at participating educational institutions.

Description: Two-part test of skills and knowledge important in carpentry. The multiple-choice written test (200 items)

covers surveying, layout, and blueprint reading; foundation work; concrete walks; floors; step construction; floor framing; wall and ceiling framing; estimating scaffolding; roof framing and roofing; stair construction; interior finish; cabinetry; and exterior finish. The performance test measures skills in floor framing, wall framing, roof framing, roofing, and exterior finish. Personal tools may be used. Candidates are advised to bring their own portable power saw. Examiner required. The written test is suitable for group use.

Timed: Written test 3 hours; performance test 5 hours

Scoring: Examiner evaluated; may be computer scored

Cost: Contact publisher

Publisher: National Occupational Competency Testing Institute

TEACHER OCCUPATIONAL COMPETENCY TESTING: CIVIL TECHNOLOGY EXAMINATION

Adult

Purpose: Assesses competency in civil technology occupations. Used for providing evidence of competency to become a teacher or obtaining academic credit at participating educational institutions.

Description: Two-part test of skills and knowledge important in civil technology occupations. The multiple-choice written test (200 items) covers asphalt, concrete, surveying, instrumentation, steel structures, general engineering information, and drafting. The performance test measures skills in concrete, soils, asphalt, surveying, and drafting. All necessary tools, machinery, and handbooks are provided. Candidates should bring their own calculators and drafting instruments. Examiner required. The written test is suitable for group use.

Timed: Written test 3 hours; performance test 5 hours

Scoring: Examiner evaluated; may be computer scored

Cost: Contact publisher

Publisher: National Occupational Competency Testing Institute

TEACHER OCCUPATIONAL COMPETENCY TESTING: COMMERCIAL ART

Adult

Purpose: Assesses competency in commercial art. Used for providing evidence of competency to become a teacher or obtaining academic credit at participating educational institutions.

Description: Two-part test of skills and knowledge important in commercial art. The multiple-choice written test (125 items) covers production, drawing and rendering, design and typography, printing, and fundamentals of photography and basic knowledge of the field. The performance test measures skills in black and white rendering, magazine ad, and key-line/mechanical. Examiner required. The written test is suitable for group use.

Timed: Written test 3 hours; performance test 5 hours

Scoring: Examiner evaluated; may be computer scored

Cost: Contact publisher

Publisher: National Occupational Competency Testing Institute

TEACHER OCCUPATIONAL COMPETENCY TESTING: COMMERCIAL PHOTOGRAPHY

Adult

Purpose: Measures competency of individuals in commercial photography. Used for providing evidence of competency to become a teacher or obtaining academic credit at participating institutions.

Description: Multiple-item paper-pencil and task-performance test assessing knowledge and skills of commercial photography teachers. The multiple-choice written test (150 items) covers 35mm camera operation, photo printing, film processing, film characteristics, lighting, print finishing, composition, filters, light meters, light, and color. The performance test covers operating a 35mm camera, processing film, printing and enlarging, and lighting. Examiner required. Suitable for group use.

Timed: Written test 3 hours; performance test 5 hours-6 hours, 45 minutes

Scoring: Examiner evaluated; may be computer scored

Cost: Contact publisher

Publisher: National Occupational Competency Testing Institute

TEACHER OCCUPATIONAL COMPETENCY TESTING: COMPUTER TECHNOLOGY EXAMINATION

Adult

Purpose: Assesses competency in computer technology. Used for providing evidence of competency to become a teacher or obtaining academic credit at participating educational institutions.

Description: Two-part test of skills and knowledge important in computer technology. The multiple-choice written test (200 items) covers general information, data processing machine operations, computer programming, and system analysis and design. The performance test measures skills in file preparation, flowcharting, and source listing and output. The majority of the performance test covers source listing and output. The candidate must be able to operate a keypunch or a CRT with a keyboard. Examiner required. The written test is suitable for group use.

Timed: Written test 3 hours; performance test 5 hours

Scoring: Examiner evaluated; may be computer scored

Cost: Contact publisher

Publisher: National Occupational Competency Testing Institute

TEACHER OCCUPATIONAL COMPETENCY TESTING: COSMETOLOGY EXAMINATION

Adult

Purpose: Assesses competency in cosmetology. Used for providing evidence of competency to become a teacher or obtaining academic credit at participating educational institutions.

Description: Two-part test of skills and knowledge important in cosmetology. The multiple-choice written test (150 items) covers care of hands, chemical permanent waving, hair styling, hair coloring, hair pieces, hair and scalp, chemical hair straightening, hair shaping, care of face, and shop operation and management. The performance test measures skills in hair styling, haircutting, hair coloring, chemical permanent waving or chemical hair straightening, thermal waving, and manicuring or facial makeup. One live model and one manikin are required for the performance examination. The candidate supplies haircutting tools, hair clips, combs, brushes, protective gloves and apron, blow dryers, lotions, rollers, makeup, and curling irons. Towels, shampoo, cotton, and standard shop equipment will be furnished. The candidate must submit to the examiner at the time of testing a published plan and photograph of the hairstyle he intends to execute. A calculator may be used for both tests. Examiner required. The written test is suitable for group use.

Timed: Written test 3 hours; performance test 5 hours

Scoring: Examiner required; may be computer scored

Cost: Contact publisher

Publisher: National Occupational Competency Testing Institute

TEACHER OCCUPATIONAL COMPETENCY TESTING: DIESEL ENGINE REPAIR EXAMINATION

Adult

Purpose: Assesses competency in diesel engine repair. Used for providing evidence of competency to become a teacher or obtaining academic credit at participating educational institutions.

Description: Two-part test of skills and knowledge important in diesel engine repair. The multiple-choice written test (200 items) covers fuel injection pumps and nozzle repair and adjustment, hydraulic systems troubleshooting, electrical systems diagnosis and repair, power train operation and repair, and basic engine diagnosis and repair. The perform-

ance test includes fuel injection pump and nozzle repair, testing and callibrating pump systems, basic engine diagnosis and repair, electrical systems diagnosis and repair, and power train operation and repair. Examiner required. The written test is suitable for group use.

Timed: Written test 3 hours; performance test 4 hours

Scoring: Examiner evaluated; may be computer scored

Cost: Contact publisher

Publisher: National Occupational Competency Testing Institute

TEACHER OCCUPATIONAL COMPETENCY TESTING: DIESEL MECHANIC

Adult

Purpose: Measures competency in diesel mechanics. Used for providing evidence of competency to become a teacher or obtaining academic credit at participating institutions.

Description: Multiple-item paper-pencil and task-performance test assessing abilities of teachers of diesel mechanics. The multiple-choice written test assesses knowledge of engine service, diesel fuel systems service, lubrication systems service, electrical systems service, engine auxiliaries, cooling system service, internal and external systems service, dynamometer, and testing. The performance test covers engine service, fuel systems, electrical systems, cooling systems, and lubrication. Examiner required. Suitable for group use.

Timed: Written test 3 hours; performance test 4 hours

Scoring: Examiner evaluated; may be computer scored

Cost: Contact publisher

Publisher: National Occupational Competency Testing Institute

TEACHER OCCUPATIONAL COMPETENCY TESTING: DRAFTING OCCUPATIONS EXAMINATION

Adult

Purpose: Assesses competency in drafting occupations. Used for providing evidence of competency to become a teacher or obtaining academic credit at participating educational institutions.

Description: Two-part test of skills and knowledge important in drafting occupations. The multiple-choice written test (200 items) covers fundamentals, related trades, related mathematics, and related sciences. The performance test measures skills in orthographics, sectioning, any projection, revolutions, isometric and oblique, threads and fasteners, intersections, and development and drawing dimension. Examiner required. The written test is suitable for group use.

Timed: Written test 3 hours; performance test 5 hours

Scoring: Examiner evaluated; may be computer scored

Cost: Contact publisher

Publisher: National Occupational Competency Testing Institute

TEACHER OCCUPATIONAL COMPETENCY TESTING: ELECTRICAL INSTALLATION

Adult

Purpose: Assesses competency in electrical installation. Used for providing evidence of competency to become a teacher or obtaining academic credit at participating educational institutions.

Description: Two-part test of skills and knowledge important in electrical installation. The multiple-choice written test (200 items) covers basic principles of electricity and magnetism and their application in the trade, reading working instructions and trade calculations, lighting, motors and generators, wiring practices and procedures, transformers, and general trade information. The performance test measures skills in layout and print reading, installation, testing and operation of controls, code applications, installation of residential and commercial wiring, testing and trouble-shooting of installations, and safety. Applicants may bring their own reference materials and handbooks. Personal tools also may be used. Examiner required. The written test is suitable for group use.

Timed: Written test 3 hours; performance test 5 hours

Scoring: Examiner required; may be computer scored

Cost: Contact publisher

Publisher: National Occupational Competency Testing Institute

TEACHER OCCUPATIONAL COMPETENCY TESTING: ELECTRONICS COMMUNICATIONS EXAMINATION

Adult

Purpose: Assesses competency in electronics communications. Used for providing evidence of competency to become a teacher or obtaining academic credit at participating educational institutions.

Description: Two-part test of skills and knowledge important in electronics communications. The multiple-choice written test (200 items) covers basic electricity; measurements; standards and tolerances; conductors, insulators, and semiconductors; batteries; sources of voltage; vacuum tube and solid state devices; amplifiers in cascade for RF and AF; other concepts in electronics; inductive devices; alternating current; single phase circuits; electronic circuits; and methods and procedures. The performance test measures skills in radio equipment, recording equipment, and television service. Television service accounts for half the performance test. Personal tools may be used. The Electronics Data Handbook may be consulted. Examiner required. The written test is suitable for group use.

Timed: Written test 3 hours; performance test 4 hours

Scoring: Examiner required; may be computer scored

Cost: Contact publisher

Publisher: National Occupational Competency Testing Institute

TEACHER OCCUPATIONAL COMPETENCY TESTING: ELECTRONICS TECHNOLOGY

Adult

Purpose: Assesses competency in electronics technology. Used for providing evidence of competency to become a teacher or obtaining academic credit at participating educational institutions.

Description: Two-part test of skills and knowledge important in electronics technology. The multiple-choice written test (200 items) covers analysis, troubleshooting, instruments, electronic components, D.C. circuits/basic electricity, A.C. circuits/basic electronics, semiconductors/basic circuits, and basic digital electronics. The performance test measures skills in analysis, troubleshooting and repair, instrumentation, electronic components, basic theory, and fabrication and inspection. Examiner required. The written test is suitable for group use.

Untimed: Written test 3 hours; performance test 4 hours

Scoring: Examiner evaluated; may be computer scored

Cost: Contact publisher

Publisher: National Occupational Competency Testing Institute

TEACHER OCCUPATIONAL COMPETENCY TESTING: HEATING EXAMINATION

Adult

Purpose: Assesses competency in heating occupations. Used for providing evidence of competency to become a teacher or obtaining academic credit at participating educational institutions.

Description: Two-part test of skills and knowledge important in heating occupations. The multiple-choice written test (200 items) covers systems, heating plants, controls, and service and testing. The performance test measures skills in systems, heating plants, controls, and service and testing. Examiner required. The written test is suitable for group use.

Timed: Written test 3 hours; performance test 4 hours

Scoring: Examiner evaluated; may be computer scored

Cost: Contact publisher

Publisher: National Occupational Competency Testing Institute

TEACHER OCCUPATIONAL COMPETENCY TESTING: INDUSTRIAL ELECTRICIAN EXAMINATION #014

Adult

Purpose: Assesses competency of industrial electricians. Used for providing evidence of competency to become a teacher or obtaining academic credit at participating educational institutions.

Description: Two-part test of skills and knowledge important for industrial electricians. The multiple-choice written test (190 items) covers basic theory, D.C. circuits/calculations, A.C. circuits/calculations, D.C. machines, A.C. machines/polyphase circuits, N.E.C. code, motor control/symbols, and motor controls. The performance test measures skills in magnetic motor control circuits, bending rigid conduit, bending electrical metallic tubing, troubleshooting controls, and digital circuitry. Personal tools, a calculator, and the National Electrical Code Handbook may be used. Examiner required. The written test is suitable for group use.

Timed: Written test 3 hours; performance test 4 hours

Scoring: Examiner evaluated; may be computer scored

Cost: Contact publisher

Publisher: National Occupational Competency Testing Institute

TEACHER OCCUPATIONAL COMPETENCY TESTING: INDUSTRIAL ELECTRONICS EXAMINATION #016

Adult

Purpose: Assesses competency in industrial electronics occupations. Used for providing evidence of competency to become a teacher or obtaining academic credit at participating educational institutions.

Description: Two-part test of skills and knowledge important in industrial electronics. The multiple-choice written test (200 items) covers basic electronic fundamentals, digital circuits, network (passive), electronic control devices, amplifiers, detectors, active circuits, components, use of instruments, troubleshooting, electronic assembly precautions, computer technology, energy conversion, and transducers. The performance test measures skills in the use of measuring instruments; measuring, observing, and recording; the use of test equipment; and programming simple problems. Candidates must bring their own calculators. A handbook, manuals, and other reference materials are provided. Examiner required. The written test is suitable for group use.

Timed: Written test 3 hours; performance test 5 hours

Scoring: Examiner required; may be computer scored

Cost: Contact publisher

Publisher: National Occupational Competency Testing Institute

TEACHER OCCUPATIONAL COMPETENCY TESTING: MACHINE DRAFTING EXAMINATION

Adult

Purpose: Assesses competency in machine drafting occupations. Used for providing evidence of competency to become a teacher or obtaining academic credit at participating educational institutions.

Description: Two-part test of skills and knowledge important in machine drafting. The multiple-choice written test (180 items) covers drafting room practices; orthographic and sectional drawings; dimensioning, tolerance, and symbols; threads and fasteners; cams, gears, and pulleys; trade computations; shop practices; pictorial drawings; and applied science. The performance test measures orthographic projection, sectioning, auxil-

iary projection, revolutions, isometric, intersections, developments, and drawing and dimensioning. Examiner required. The written test is suitable for group use.

Timed: Written test 3 hours; performance test 4 hours

Scoring: Computer scoring provided

Cost: Contact publisher

Publisher: National Occupational Competency Testing Institute

TEACHER OCCUPATIONAL COMPETENCY TESTING: MACHINE TRADES EXAMINATION

Adult

Purpose: Assesses competency in machine trades. Used for providing evidence of competency to become a teacher or obtaining academic credit at participating educational institutions.

Description: Two-part test of skills and knowledge important in machine trades occupations. The multiple-choice written test (200 items) covers bench assembly work, layout, and inspection; machine sawing, filing, and multiple parts processing; milling processes and machines; drilling, tapping, lapping—machines and attachments; grinding and precision finishing— processes and machines; applied math and science; shaping and planning processes; turning; and electrical discharge machining. The performance test measures skills in bench and assembly, layout, and inspection; milling processes and machines; grinding and precision finishing; drilling, tapping, reaming— machines and attachments; and turning and processing. Personal tools (micrometors and scales) may be used. Safety glasses are required; candidates should bring their own. Examiner required. The written test is suitable for group use.

Timed: Written test 3 hours; performance test 5 hours

Scoring: Examiner required; may be computer scored

Cost: Contact publisher

Publisher: National Occupational Competency Testing Institute

TEACHER OCCUPATIONAL COMPETENCY TESTING: MAJOR APPLIANCE REPAIR EXAMINATION

Adult

Purpose: Assesses competency in major appliance repair. Used for providing evidence of competency to become a teacher or obtaining academic credit at participating educational institutions.

Description: Two-part test of skills and knowledge important in major appliance repair. The multiple-choice written test (200 items) covers fundamentals, power tools and small appliances, kitchen equipment, major heating devices, laundry equipment, and refrigeration. The performance test measures skills in major heating devices, laundry equipment, and refrigeration. Personal tools may be used. Handbooks and references are provided. Examiner required. The written test is suitable for group use.

Timed: Written test 3 hours; performance test 6 hours

Scoring: Examiner evaluated; may be computer scored

Cost: Contact publisher

Publisher: National Occupational Competency Testing Institute

TEACHER OCCUPATIONAL COMPETENCY TESTING: MASONRY EXAMINATION

Adult

Purpose: Assesses competency in masonry occupations. Used for providing evidence of competency to become a teacher or obtaining academic credit at participating educational institutions.

Description: Two-part test of skills and knowledge important in masonry. The multiple-choice written test (200 items) covers trade tools, terminology, estimating procedures, layout procedures, masonry practices, safety, and materials of the trade. The performance test measures skills in layout procedures, work practices, quality of completed work, and observation of safe practices. Personal

hand tools are required. Examiner required. The written test is suitable for group use.

Timed: Written test 2 hours; performance test 3 hours

Scoring: Examiner evaluated; may be computer scored

Cost: Contact publisher

Publisher: National Occupational Competency Testing Institute

TEACHER OCCUPATIONAL COMPETENCY TESTING: MASONRY OCCUPATIONS

Adult

Purpose: Assesses competency in masonry occupations. Used for providing evidence of competency to become a teacher or obtaining academic credit at participating educational institutions.

Description: Two-part test of skills and knowledge important in masonry occupations. The multiple-choice written test (200 items) covers concrete, stone, estimating, tile, plaster, and brick/block. The performance test measures skills in block, brick, stone, and tile. Examiner required. The written test is suitable for group use.

Timed: Written test 3 hours; performance test 4 hours

Scoring: Examiner evaluated; may be computer scored

Cost: Contact publisher

Publisher: National Occupational Competency Testing Institute

TEACHER OCCUPATIONAL COMPETENCY TESTING: MATERIALS HANDLING EXAMINATION

Adult

Purpose: Assesses competency in materials handling. Used for providing evidence of competency to become a teacher or obtaining academic credit at participating educational institutions.

Description: Two-part test of skills and knowledge important in materials handling. The multiple-choice written test

(200 items) covers warehousing, purchasing, shipping and distribution, transportation, receiving, materials handling equipment, material storage, and inventory control. The performance test measures skills in purchasing, shipping, equipment, receiving, storage, warehouse, and inventory. Examiner required. The written test is suitable for group use.

Timed: Written test 3 hours; performance test 4 hours, 25 minutes

Scoring: Examiner evaluated; may be computer scored

Cost: Contact publisher

Publisher: National Occupational Competency Testing Institute

TEACHER OCCUPATIONAL COMPETENCY TESTING: MECHANICAL TECHNOLOGY EXAMINATION

Adult

Purpose: Assesses competency in mechanical technology occupations. Used for providing evidence of competency to become a teacher or obtaining academic credit at participating educational institutions.

Description: Two-part test of skills and knowledge important in mechanical technology occupations. The multiple-choice written test (200 items) covers machine tool operations, metallurgy, statics, fluid mechanics, thermodynamics, electricity, strength of materials, physics, mathematics, and computer. The performance test measures skills in design, drawing, testing, and evaluation and reporting. The following personal tools are required: set of drawing instruments, drawing pencils, copy of Machinery Handbook, calculator, lettering guide, and pen. Examiner required. The written test is suitable for group use.

Timed: Written test 3 hours; performance test 6 hours

Scoring: Examiner evaluated; may be computer scored

Cost: Contact publisher

Publisher: National Occupational Competency Testing Institute

TEACHER OCCUPATIONAL COMPETENCY TESTING: PAINTING AND DECORATING EXAMINATION

Adult

Purpose: Assesses competency in painting and decorating. Used for providing evidence of competency to become a teacher or obtaining academic credit at participating educational institutions.

Description: Two-part test of skills and knowledge important in painting and decorating occupations. The multiple-choice written test (200 items) covers exterior and interior painting, wood finishing, wall covering, estimating, color and color harmony, and special wall finishes. The performance test measures abilities in exterior and interior painting, wood finishing, wall covering, color and color harmony, and clean up. Examiner required. The written test is suitable for group use.

Timed: Written test 3 hours; performance test 4 hours

Scoring: Examiner evaluated; may be computer scored

Cost: Contact publisher

Publisher: National Occupational Competency Testing Institute

TEACHER OCCUPATIONAL COMPETENCY TESTING: PLUMBING EXAMINATION

Adult

Purpose: Assesses competency in plumbing. Used for providing evidence of competency to become a teacher or obtaining academic credit at participating educational institutions.

Description: Two-part test of skills and knowledge important in plumbing. The multiple-choice written test (200 items) covers water supply and distribution—fixture units; physical properties and characteristics of commonly used materials and supplies; operating principles and installation of commonly used materials and supplies; installation and principles of operation of building drains and sewers; installation and operation of storm water drains; plumbing fixtures; industrial and special wastes; inspection and tests; and general trade information. The performance test measures abilities in working from builder's or architect's drawings, roughing in standard installation, installing fixtures and accessories on a variety of materials, and testing systems. Personal tools may be used. Handbooks and reference material also may be brought to the session. Installation will be tested on available facilities. Examiner required. The written test is suitable for group use.

Timed: Written test 3 hours; performance test 5 hours

Scoring: Examiner evaluated; may be computer scored

Cost: Contact publisher

Publisher: National Occupational Competency Testing Institute

TEACHER OCCUPATIONAL COMPETENCY TESTING: POWER SEWING EXAMINATION

Adult

Purpose: Assesses competency in power sewing. Used for providing evidence of competency to become a teacher or obtaining academic credit at participating educational institutions.

Description: Two-part test of skills and knowledge important in power sewing. The multiple-choice written test (200 items) covers power machine operation, apparel assembly, terminology, needle trade industry, and tools and attachments. The performance test measures abilities in assembling techniques, sewing machines, tools and attachments, finishing techniques, materials, and safety and clean up. Examiner required. The written test is suitable for group use.

Timed: Written test 3 hours; performance test 4 hours

Scoring: Examiner evaluated; may be computer scored

Cost: Contact publisher

Publisher: National Occupational Competency Testing Institute

TEACHER OCCUPATIONAL COMPETENCY TESTING: PRINTING EXAMINATION

Adult

Purpose: Assesses competency in printing. Used for providing evidence of competency to become a teacher or obtaining academic credit at participating educational institutions.

Description: Two-part test of skills and knowledge important in printing. The multiple-choice written test (200 items) covers typography, layout, and composition; camera photo mechanical; trade information; job safety; presswork; platemaking and stripping; binding and finishing. The performance test measures abilities in design and composition, photo preparatory—image carriers, image transfer, and bindery/finishing. Examiner required. The written test is suitable for group use.

Timed: Written test 3 hours; performance test 5 hours

Scoring: Examiner evaluated; may be computer scored

Cost: Contact publisher

Publisher: National Occupational Competency Testing Institute

TEACHER OCCUPATIONAL COMPETENCY TESTING: PRINTING (LETTERPRESS)

Adult

Purpose: Assesses competency in teachers of letterpress printing. Used for providing evidence of competency to become a teacher or obtaining academic credit at participating institutions.

Description: Multiple-item paper-pencil and task-performance test measuring knowledge and skills of letterpress printing teachers. The multiple-choice written test (183 items) covers typography, layout and composition, camera photo mechanicals, presswork, stripping and platemaking, binding and finishing, trade information, and job safety. The performance test covers design and composition, presswork, and binding and finishing. Examiner required. Suitable for group use.

Timed: Written test 3 hours; performance test 5 hours

Scoring: Examiner evaluated; may be computer scored

Cost: Contact publisher

Publisher: National Occupational Competency Testing Institute

TEACHER OCCUPATIONAL COMPETENCY TESTING: QUANTITY FOOD PREPARATIONS EXAMINATION

Adult

Purpose: Assesses competency in quantity food preparation. Used for providing evidence of competency to become a teacher or obtaining academic credit at participating educational institutions.

Description: Two-part test of skills and knowledge important in quantity food preparation. The multiple-choice written test (195 items) covers menu planning, guest service, food groups, equipment and tools, sanitation, purchasing, receiving and storage, cost control, and safety. The performance test measures abilities in recipes and menus; assembling and portioning ingredients; methods of food preparation; use of utensils and hand tools; use of equipment; use of preparation areas; and general knowledge. All required items are furnished. Examiner required. The written test is suitable for group use.

Timed: Written test 3 hours; performance test 3 hours

Scoring: Examiner evaluated; may be computer scored

Cost: Contact publisher

Publisher: National Occupational Competency Testing Institute

TEACHER OCCUPATIONAL COMPETENCY TESTING: QUANTITY FOODS EXAMINATION

Adult

Purpose: Assesses competency in quantity foods. Used for providing evidence of

competency to become a teacher or obtaining academic credit at participating educational institutions.

Description: Two-part test of skills and knowledge important in quantity foods. The multiple-choice written test (200 items) covers cost control and menu planning, safety and cleanliness, waitressing and customer service, food service occupations nutrition, food purchasing, food receiving and storage, and food preparation. The performance test measures abilities in work organization; selection of proper tools, utensils, and ingredients; cleanliness; safety practices; weights and measurements; and food preparation. Over half the performance test focuses on food preparation. Examiner required. The written test is suitable for group use.

Timed: Written test 3 hours; performance test 5½ hours

Scoring: Examiner evaluated; may be computer scored

Cost: Contact publisher

Publisher: National Occupational Competency Testing Institute

TEACHER OCCUPATIONAL COMPETENCY TESTING: RADIO/ TV REPAIR EXAMINATION

Adult

Purpose: Assesses competency in radio and TV repair. Used for providing evidence of competency to become a teacher or obtaining academic credit at participating educational institutions.

Description: Two-part test of skills and knowledge important in radio and TV repair. The multiple-choice written test (193 items) covers test equipment, fundamental electronic theory, solid state and tube circuitry, antenna and transmission lines, signal characteristics: TV and FM transmissions and reception, color and black and white receivers, and servicing. The performance test measures abilities in recording equipment, radio equipment, and TV service and repair. Examiner required. The written test is suitable for group use.

Timed: Written test 3 hours; performance test 4 hours, 10 minutes

Scoring: Examiner evaluated; may be computer scored

Cost: Contact publisher

Publisher: National Occupational Competency Testing Institute

TEACHER OCCUPATIONAL COMPETENCY TESTING: REFRIGERATION

Adult

Purpose: Assesses competency in refrigeration. Used for providing evidence of competency to become a teacher or obtaining academic credit at participating educational institutions.

Description: Two-part test of skills and knowledge important in refrigeration occupations. The multiple-choice written test (200 items) covers domestic service, commercial service, industrial service, commercial installation, and industrial installation. The performance test consists entirely of skills in assembly, installation, and service. Examiner required. The written test is suitable for group use.

Timed: Written test 3 hours; performance test 4 hours

Scoring: Examiner evaluated; may be computer scored

Cost: Contact publisher

Publisher: National Occupational Competency Testing Institute

TEACHER OCCUPATIONAL COMPETENCY TESTING: SHEET METAL EXAMINATION

Adult

Purpose: Assesses competency in sheet metal occupations. Used for providing evidence of competency to become a teacher or obtaining academic credit at participating educational institutions.

Description: Two-part test of skills and knowledge important in sheet metal work. The multiple-choice written test (169 items) covers layout and drafting, sheet metal machinery, bench and hand tools—processing, welding, computa-

tions, hazards, materials, fluxes, application of trade science, and sheet metal fabrication. The performance test measures abilities in pattern layout (stretchout), fabrication, and assembly. Candidates may bring their own tools. Examiner required. The written test is suitable for group use.

Timed: Written test 3 hours; performance test 5½ hours

Scoring: Examiner evaluated; may be computer scored

Cost: Contact publisher

Publisher: National Occupational Competency Testing Institute

TEACHER OCCUPATIONAL COMPETENCY TESTING: SMALL ENGINE REPAIR EXAMINATION #005

Adult

Purpose: Assesses competency in small engine repair. Used for providing evidence of competency to become a teacher or obtaining academic credit at participating educational institutions.

Description: Two-part test of skills and knowledge important for small engine repair. The multiple-choice written test (200 items) covers benchwork, testing, and inspection; engine operation; cylinder block servicing and overhaul; lubrication system and lubrication; cooling and exhaust systems; transmission of power and drive units; troubleshooting; fuel systems and carburetion; ignition and starting systems; trade-related information; preventive maintenance; trade application of science; and trade computations. The performance test measures abilities in benchwork, testing, and inspection; engine analysis; cooling and exhaust system; preventive maintenance; cylinder block servicing and overhaul; lubricating systems and lubrication; fuel systems and carburetion; ignition and starting systems; and troubleshooting. Personal tools may be used. Handbooks and references are provided; however, candidates may bring their own. Examiner required. The written test is suitable for group use.

Timed: Written test 3 hours; performance test 5 hours

Scoring: Examiner evaluated; may be computer scored

Cost: Contact publisher

Publisher: National Occupational Competency Testing Institute

TEACHER OCCUPATIONAL COMPETENCY TESTING: SMALL ENGINE REPAIR EXAMINATION #056

Adult

Purpose: Assesses competency in small engine repair. Used for providing evidence of competency to become a teacher or obtaining academic credit at participating educational institutions.

Description: Two-part test of skills and knowledge important in small engine repair. The multiple-choice written test (180 items) covers orientation, engine servicing, fuel system, electrical system, and parts and inventory. The performance test measures abilities in peripheral components, engine service and repair, fuel systems, and electrical systems. Examiner required. The written test is suitable for group use.

Timed: Written test 3 hours; performance test 4 hours

Scoring: Examiner evaluated; may be computer scored

Cost: Contact publisher

Publisher: National Occupational Competency Testing Institute

TEACHER OCCUPATIONAL COMPETENCY TESTING: TEXTILE PRODUCTION/ FABRICATION

Adult

Purpose: Assesses competency in textile production and fabrication. Used for providing evidence of competency to become a teacher or obtaining academic credit at participating educational institutions.

Description: Two-part test of skills and knowledge important in textile produc-

tion and fabrication. The multiple-choice written test (200 items) covers power machine operations, apparel assembly, pattern making, alterations, and textiles. The performance test measures abilities in the same five areas. Candidates should bring trousers with cuffs and a fly-type zipper, a skirt, a coat or jacket with vented sleeve, seam binding to match the skirt, a trouser zipper, hand sewing needles, fabric shears, nippers, a ripping instrument, and a thimble. Examiner required. The written test is suitable for group use.

Timed: Written test 3 hours; performance test 4 hours

Scoring: Examiner evaluated; may be computer scored

Cost: Contact publisher

Publisher: National Occupational Competency Testing Institute

TEACHER OCCUPATIONAL COMPETENCY TESTING: TOOL AND DIE MAKING EXAMINATION

Adult

Purpose: Assesses competency in tool and die making. Used for providing evidence of competency to become a teacher or obtaining academic credit at participating educational institutions.

Description: Two-part test of skills and knowledge important in tool and die making. The multiple-choice written test (200 items) covers inspection work, tool design and cost estimating, characteristics of metals, math, metallurgy/heat treat, physical mechanics, metal fabrication, profiling machines, surface finish pages, and extruding and molding. The performance test measures abilities in die making, tooling, and jig and fixture work. Examiner required. The written test is suitable for group use.

Timed: Written test 3 hours; performance test 5 hours

Scoring: Examiner evaluated; may be computer scored

Cost: Contact publisher

Publisher: National Occupational Competency Testing Institute

TEACHER OCCUPATIONAL COMPETENCY TESTING: WELDING EXAMINATION #021

Adult

Purpose: Assesses competency in welding. Used for providing evidence of competency to become a teacher or obtaining academic credit at participating educational institutions.

Description: Two-part test of skills and knowledge important in welding. The multiple-choice written test (200 items) covers general welder qualifications, welding symbols, joint design, welding defects and causes, testing, electricity, basic metallurgy, oxyfuel welding, brazing, hard surfacing, other processes, shielded arc welding, gas metal arc welding, and gas tungsten arc welding. The performance test measures abilities in shielded metal arc welding, oxyfuel welding, gas metal arc welding, and gas tungsten arc welding. Personal tools may be used. Candidates furnish appropriate work clothes and safety equipment. Examiner required. The written test is suitable for group use.

Timed: Written test 3 hours; performance test 4 hours

Scoring: Examiner evaluated; may be computer scored

Cost: Contact publisher

Publisher: National Occupational Competency Testing Institute

TEACHER OCCUPATIONAL COMPETENCY TESTING: WELDING EXAMINATION #057

Adult

Purpose: Assesses competency in welding occupations. Used for providing evidence of competency to become a teacher or obtaining academic credit at participating educational institutions.

Description: Two-part test of skills and knowledge important in welding occupations. The multiple-choice written test (200 items) covers general knowledge, shielded metal arc, oxyfuel welding, torch brazing, gas metal arc, and basic metal-

lurgy. The performance test measures abilities in shielded metal arc welding, oxyfuel welding, gas-metal arc welding, and gas-tungsten arc welding. Examiner required. The written test is suitable for group use.

Timed: Written test 3 hours; performance test 4 hours, 10 minutes

Scoring: Examiner evaluated; may be computer scored

Cost: Contact publisher

Publisher: National Occupational Competency Testing Institute

TEACHER OCCUPATIONAL COMPETENCY TESTS (TOCT)

Adult

Purpose: Assesses competency in skilled trades and occupations. Used for providing evidence of competency to become a teacher or obtaining academic credit at participating educational institutions.

Description: Multiple-item paper-pencil tests of skills and knowledge in 45 vocational fields: air conditioning and refrigeration, airframe and power plant, architectural drafting, audio visual communication, automotive body and fender, auto body repair, baking, brick masonry, building and home maintenance services, building construction occupations, building trades maintenance, cabinet making and millwork, carpentry, civil technology, commercial art, commercial photography, computer technology, cosmetology, diesel engine repair, drafting occupations, electrical installation, electronics communications, electronics technology, heating, industrial electrician, industrial electronics, machine drafting, machine trades, major appliance repair, masonry, materials handling, mechanical technology, painting and decorating, plumbing, power sewing, printing, quantity food preparation, radio/TV repair, refrigeration, sheet metal, small engine repair, textile production/fabrication, tool and die making, and welding. Each test consists of a written section and a performance section. The multiple-choice written tests cover factual knowledge, technical information, understanding of principles, and problem-solving abilities related to the occupation. The performance tests are administered in a laboratory, school shop, or clinical setting and enable the applicant to demonstrate knowledge and skills of competent craft persons. Examiner required. Suitable for group use.

Timed: Varies depending on test
Scoring: Examinator evaluated; may be computer scored
Cost: Contact publisher
Publisher: National Occupational Competency Testing Institute

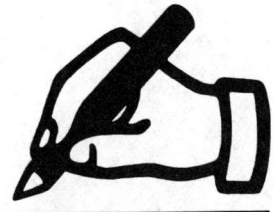

Indexes

Test Title Index

Note: Numbers in italics refer to pages on which cross-references appear.

Brigance® Diagnostic Assessment of Basic
Skills—Spanish Edition, The, 367, *578*
Brigance® Diagnostic Comprehensive
Inventory of Basic Skills (CIBS), The, 368
Brigance® Diagnostic Inventory of Basic
Skills, The, 368
Brigance® Diagnostic Inventory of Early
Development, The, 463, *5*
Brigance® Diagnostic Inventory of Essential
Skills, The, 369, *603*
Brigance® K & 1 Screen, The, 464
Brigance Preschool Screen, 464
Bristol Achievement Tests, Revised
Edition, 369
Bristol Social Adjustment Guides, American
Edition (BSAG), 667, *191, 590*
Bristol Social Adjustment Guides, British
Edition (BSAG), 668, *191, 603*
British Ability Scales, Revised
Edition The, 503, *20*
British Picture Vocabulary Scales, 503, *465*
Bruce Vocabulary Inventory, 890, *798*
Bruininks-Oseretsky Test of Motor
Proficiency, 559
Buffalo Reading Test, 798, *543*
Bulimia Test (BULIT), 122
Burks' Behavior Rating Scales, 191
Burks' Behavior Rating Scales, Preschool and
Kindergarten Edition, 102, *5*
Burt Word Reading Test, 518
Business Analyst Skills Evaluation
(BUSAN), 878
Business English Test (BET), 714
Business Judgment Test, 911
Buttons: A Projective Test for Pre-Adolescents
and Adolescents, 668, *192*
Bzoch-League Receptive-Expressive Emergent
Language Scale (REEL), The, 5, *619*
CAI Study Skills Test, 709
Cain-Levine Social Competency Scale, 590
California Achievement Tests: Forms C
and D (CAT/C&D), 370
California Achievement Tests: Forms E
and F, 370
California Adaptive Behavior Scale, 192
California Brief Life History Inventory
(CBLHI), 123
California Child Q-Set, 102, *218*
California Life Goals Evaluation
Schedules, 698
California Marriage Readiness Evaluation, 86
California Phonics Survey, 543
California Preschool Social Competency
Scale, 465
California Psychological Inventory (CPI), 123
California Q-Sort Deck, 123, *218*
California Verbal Learning Test, Research
Edition, 38
Callier-Azusa Scale: G-Edition, 5, *38, 465*
Cambridge Kindergarten Screening Test, 619
Camelot Behavioral Checklist, 591
Canadian Cognitive Abilities Test (CCAT),
Form 3, 1981, 370

Canadian Comprehensive Assessment
Program—Achievement Series, 371
Canadian Comprehensive Assessment
Program—Developing Cognitive Abilities
Test (DCAT), 709
Canadian Comprehensive Assessment
Program: School Attitude Measure
(SAM), 683
Canadian Occupational Interest Inventory
(COII), 902, *735*
Canadian Tests of Basic Skills: High School
Edition (CTBS), Form 5, 1981, 371
Canadian Tests of Basic Skills: Multilevel
Edition (CTBS), Forms 5 and 6, 1981, 371
Canadian Tests of Basic Skills: Primary Battery
(CTBS), 372
Candidate Profile Record, The, 856
Canfield Instructional Styles Inventory
(CIS), 775
Canfield Learning Styles Inventory
(CLS), 683, *698, 911*
Canter Background Interference Procedure
(BIP) for the Bender Gestalt Test, 38
Card Sorting Box, 974, *39*
Career Ability Placement Survey (CAPS), 762
Career Adaptive Behavior Inventory
(CAB), 735, *603*
Career and Vocational Form of the SOI-LA
Basic Test, 714
Career and Vocational Interest Inventory,
735, *902*
Career Assessment Inventories: For the
Learning Disabled (CAI), 578
Career Assessment Inventory (CAI), 736
Career Awareness Inventory (CAI), 762
Career Decision Scale (2nd Edition), 890, *736,
911*
Career Development Inventory (College and
University Form), 762
Career Development Inventory (School
Form), 763
Career Directions Inventory, 736, *902*
Career Exploration Profile (CEP), 736, *902*
Career Exploration Series (CES), 737, *902*
Career Guidance Inventory, 737
Career Interest Test (CIT), 902, *737*
Career Maturity Inventory (CMI), 737
Career Maturity Inventory: Attitude Scale, 738
Career Maturity Inventory: Competence
Test, 738
Career Orientation Placement and Evaluation
Survey (COPES), 738
Career Path Strategy, 763
Career Planning Program (CPP), 763
Career Problem Checklist, 738
Career Suitability Profile, The, 911
Career Survey, 739, *902*
Caring Relationship Inventory (CRI), 86
Carlson Psychological Survey (CPS), 123
Carolina Picture Vocabulary Test, 599
Carrow Auditory-Visual Abilities Test
(CAVAT), 656, *608, 619*

Executive Profile Survey (EPS), 953
Experience and Background Inventory
(EBI), 953
Experience and Background Questionnaire
(EBQ), 915
Experience Exploration, 743, *903*
Explore the World of Work (E-WOW),
743, *604*
Expression Grouping (SIEG), 196
Expressional Fluency (EF), 221
Expressive One-Word Picture Vocabulary Test
(EOWPVT), 504, *580, 626*
Expressive One-Word Picture Vocabulary Test:
Upper Extension (EOWPVT: UE), 627, *580*
Extended Merrill-Palmer Scale, 8, *22*
Eysenck Personality Inventory (EPI), 134
Eysenck Personality Questionnaire (EPQ), 135
Eysenck-Withers Personality Inventory, 196
Facial Recognition Test, 41
Familism Scale, A, 72
Familism Scale: Extended Family
Integration, A, 72
Familism Scale: Nuclear Family
Integration, A, 72
Family Adjustment Test (Elias Family Opinion
Survey), The, 72
Family Environment Scale, 73
Family History-Research Diagnostic Criteria
(FH-RDC), 135
Family Inventories, 73
Family Inventories: Adolescent Family
Inventory of Life Events and Changes (A-
FILE), 73
Family Inventories: Enriching and Nurturing
Relationship Issues, Communication and
Happiness (ENRICH), 88
Family Inventories: Family Adaptability and
Cohesion Evaluation Scales (FACES III), 74
Family Inventories: Family Coping Strategies
(F-COPE), 74
Family Inventories: Family Inventory of Life
Events and Changes (FILE), 74
Family Inventories: Family Satisfaction, 75
Family Inventories: Family Strengths, 75
Family Inventories: Parent-Adolescent
Communication, 75
Family Inventories: Quality of Life, 75
Family Pre-Counseling Inventory Program,
76, *700*
Family Relations Test—Adult Version, 76, *221*
Family Relations Test—Children's Version, 76
Family Relations Test—Married Couples
Version, 77, *221*
Family Relationship Inventory (FRI), 77
Family Violence Scale, 77
Famous Sayings (FS), 916, *221*
Farnsworth Dichotomous Test for Color
Blindness, 658, *806*
Farnsworth-Munsell 100 Hue Test, 806, *658*
Farnum Music Test, 255
Farnum String Scale, 255
Fast-Tyson Health Knowledge Test Form C,
1986 Revision, 316

Fear Survey Schedule (FSS), 135
Figure Classification Test, 892
Fine Finger Dexterity Work Task Unit, 976
Finger Localization Test, 42
Fire Company Officer Forms 1, 2, and A, 990
Firefighter Selection Test, 990
Fireman Entrance Aptitude Tests, 990
First Grade Readiness Checklist, The, 473
First Year French Test, 263
First Year Spanish Test, 263
Fisher Language Survey and Write-To-Learn
Program, Revised 1985, 580
Five P's: Parent Professional Preschool
Performance Profile, The, 473, *8*
Flanagan Aptitude Classification Tests
(FACT), 806, *764*
Flanagan Industrial Tests (FIT), 807
Fletcher Time-By-Count Test of
Diadochokinetic Syllable Rate, 627
Flint Infant Security Scale: For Infants Aged
3-24 Months, The, 8, *78*
Florida International Diagnostic-Prescriptive
Vocational Competency Profile, 764,
594, 604
Florida Kindergarten Screening
Battery, The, 524
Flowers Auditory Test of Selective Attention
(FATSA), 609
Flowers-Costello Tests of Central Auditory
Ability, 609
Fluency (FLU), 221
Fluharty Preschool Speech and Language
Screening Test, 627
Fogel Wp Operator Test, 879
Foot Operated Hinged Box Work Task
Unit, 976, *808*
Forer Structured Sentence Completion
Test, 136
Forer Vocational Survey: Men-Women,
743, *903*
Form Series Test A, 892
Formal Reading Inventory (FRI), 549
Forty-Eight Item Counseling Evaluation Test:
Revised, The, 136
Foster Mazes, 560
Four Picture Test, 197
Franck Drawing Completion Test, 197
Free Recall (FREEREC), 42
French Comprehension Tests, 263
Frenchay Dysarthria Assessment, 627, *42*
Frost Self-Description Questionnaire, 108, *700*
Frost Self-Description Questionnaire:
Extended Scale (FSDQ: Extended), 109
Frostig Developmental Test of Visual
Perception, 474
Frostig Movement Skills Test Battery
(Experimental Edition), 560
Fuld Object-Memory Evaluation, 42
Full-Range Picture Vocabulary Test
(FRPV), 22, *504, 600*
Fullerton Language Test for Adolescents
(Experimental Edition), 628, *43*
Functional Analysis of Behavior, 197

Personal Problems Checklist—Adult, 163
Personal Questionnaire/Occupational Values, 755, *933*
Personal Questionnaire Rapid Scaling Technique (PQRST), 164
Personal Reaction Index (PRI), 933
Personal Relations Survey (PRS), 965, *933*
Personal Resources Questionnaire: Form E-2, 933
Personal Skills Map (PSM), The, 934
Personal Strain Questionnaire: Form E-2, 934
Personality Descriptions, 207, *703*
Personality Inventory for Children (PIC), Revised Format, 110
Personality Rating Scale, 111, *703*
Personality Research Form (PRF), 207, *934*
Personnel Performance Problems Inventory (PPPI), 965
Personnel Reaction Blank, 906
Personnel Selection Inventory (PSI), 934
Personnel Test Battery (PTB), 831
Personnel Test Battery: Audio Checking (PTB:CP8), 832
Personnel Test Battery: Basic Checking (PTB:CP7), 832
Personnel Test Battery: Checking (PTB:CP3), 832
Personnel Test Battery: Classification (PTB:CP4), 833
Personnel Test Battery: Numerical Computation (PTB:NP2), 833
Personnel Test Battery: Numerical Reasoning (PTB:NP6), 833
Personnel Test Battery: Verbal Meaning (PTB:VP5), 833
Personnel Test Battery: Verbal Usage (PTB:VP1), 834
Personnel Tests for Industry (PTI), 834
Personnel Tests for Industry—Oral Directions Test (PTI-ODT), 834
Pertinent Questions, 224
Pet Attitude Scale, 164
Phoenix Ability Survey System (PASS), 835, *730*, *980*
Phoneme Discrimination Test, 54
Phonemic Synthesis: Blending Sounds Into Words, 637
Phonological Assessment of Child Speech, 638
Phonovisual Diagnostic Tests, 238
Photo Articulation Test (PAT), 638
Photoelectric Rotary Pursuit, 563
PHSF Relations Questionnaire—1970, 674, *164*
Physical Chemistry for the Life Sciences Test, 314
Physical Chemistry Tests, 314
Pictorial Study of Values, The, 164
Pictorial Test of Intelligence, 511, *29*, *602*
Picture Articulation and Screening Test (PALST), 638
Picture Identification Test, The, 164
Picture Personality Test for Indian South Africans (PPT-ISA), 165, *935*
Picture Situation Test, 935, *225*

Picture Spondee Threshold Test, 638
Picture Story Language Test (PSLT), The, 253, *54*
Picture Vocational Interest Questionnaire for Adults (PVI)—1981, 755
Piers-Harris Children's Self-Concept Scale (PHCSC), 111
Pikunas Adult Stress Inventory (PASI, 1984), 165
Pikunas Graphoscopic Scale (PGS), 207
Pill Scale, A, 96
Pimsleur Language Aptitude Battery, 267
PIP Developmental Charts, 15
Planning Career Goals (PCG), 755
Play and Tell Cards: A Therapeutic Game, 111
Plot Titles (PT), 225
Police Officer ESV-100, 998
Police Officer ESV-125, 999
Police Sergeant (ESV), 999
Politte Sentence Completion Test (PSCT), 703, *208*
Pollack-Branden Battery: For Identification of Learning Disabilities, Dyslexia, and Classroom Dysfunction, The, 584, *604*
Polyfactorial Study of Personality, 165
Polymer Chemistry Test, 314
Pope Inventory of Basic Reading Skills, 552
Poppleton-Allen Sales Aptitude Test (PASAT), 1002
Porch Index of Communicative Ability (PICA), 639
Porch Index of Communicative Ability in Children (PICAC), 639, *54*
Portable Tactual Performance Test (P-TPT), 54, *585*
Porteous Problem Checklist, 675, *166*
Porteus Mazes, 30
Portland Problem Behavior Checklist—Revised (PPBC-R), The, 675
Portland Prognostic Test for Mathematics, 294
Position Analysis Questionnaire (PAQ), 935
Possible Jobs (PJ), 225
Potential for Foster Parenthood Scale (PFPS), 83
Power Management Inventory (PMI), 965
Power Management Profile (PMP), 966
Power Perception Profiles: Self/Other, 935, *966*
Practical Articulation Kit: Game Cards and Screening Test, 639
Pragmatics Screening Test, 640
Pre-Academic Learning Inventory (PAL), 484
Pre-LAS, 640
Pre-Marital Counseling Inventory, 96
Premarital Communication Inventory, 96
Premarital Counseling Kit (PCK), The, 97
Pre-Mod, 675
Prereading Expectancy Screening Scale (PRESS), 534
Preschool and Early Primary Skills Survey (PEPSS), 484, *15*
Preschool and Kindergarten Interest Descriptor (PRIDE), 571, *485*

Senior South African Individual Scale (SSAIS)—1964, 31, *513*
Sentence Completion Test, 177, *706*
Sentence Comprehension Test-SCT-(Experimental Edition), 644
Sentence Imitation Screening Test (SIST), 645, *493*
Sequence Recall (SEQREC), 61, *594*
Sequenced Inventory of Communication Development, Revised Edition, 1984, 645, *594, 612*
Sequential Assessment of Mathematics Inventory-Individual Assessment Battery (SAMI), 295
Sequential Tests of Educational Progress (STEP II), 446
Sequential Tests of Educational Progress (STEP III), 446
Serial Digit Learning Test, 61
Sex Attitudes Survey (SAS), The, 97
Sex Knowledge and Attitude Test (SKAT), 98
Sex Knowledge Inventory—Form X (SKI-X), The, 98
Sex Knowledge Inventory—Form Y (SKI-Y), The, 98
Sexometer, 99
Sexual Communications Inventory (SCI), The, 99
Sexual Compatability Test, The, 99
Sexual Concerns Checklist (SCC), The, 99
Sexuality Experience Scales, 100
Shape Matching (MATCH), 61
Shapes Analysis Test, The, 838
Shapes Test, 838
Sherman Mental Impairment Test, 62
Ship Destination Test (SD), 898
Shipley Institute of Living Scale, 31
Shop Arithmetic Test, 838
Shorr Imagery Test (SIT), 177
Short Employment Tests, 873
Short Imaginal Process Inventory (SIPI), 178
Short Term Auditory Retrieval and Storage Test (STARS), 612
Short Tests of Clerical Ability (STCA), 873
Silver Drawing Test of Cognitive and Creative Skills, 513
Similes Test, The, 572, *239*
Simons Measurements of Music Listening Skills, 258
Singer-Loomis Inventory of Personality, Experimental Edition, 178
Single and Double Simultaneous Stimulation (SDSS), 62, *662*
Single and Double Simultaneous Stimulation Test (SDSST), 62
Sipay Word Analysis Test (SWAT), 538
Situational Preference Inventory, 178, *226*
Six-Factor Automated Vocational Assessment System (SAVAS), 758, *907*
Sixteen Personality Factor Questionnaire, 179, *940*
Sketches (SKET), 226

Skillcorp Computer Management System—Math, 296
Skillcorp Computer Management System—Reading, 538
Skills and Attributes Inventory, 839
Sklar Aphasia Scale: Revised 1983, 645, *62*
Slingerland Screening Tests for Identifying Children with Specific Language Disability, 587, *646*
Sloan Achromatopsia Test, 226, *662*
Slosson Articulation, Language Test with Phonology (SALT-P), 493, *646*
Slosson Drawing Coordination Test (SDCT), 62
Slosson Intelligence Test (SIT), 31, *513*
Slosson Oral Reading Test (SORT), 554
Slosson Post-Observational Testing Screen (SPOTS), 679
Slosson Pre-Observational Record Screen (SPORS), 679
Small College Goals Inventory (SCGI), 787
Smell Identification Test™, 839
Smith-Johnson Nonverbal Performance Scale, 17, *612, 646*
Smoking and Health, 318, *226*
Social and Prevocational Information Battery (SPIB), 594
Social and Prevocational Information Battery-T (SPIB-T), 595
Social Behavior Assessment (SBA), 706
Social Behavior Assessment Schedule, The, 179, *85*
Social-Emotional Dimension Scale (SEDS), 680
Social Intelligence Test, 706
Social Interaction and Creativity in Communication System (SICCS), 573
Social Translations (SIST), 680
Socio-Sexual Knowledge and Attitudes Test (SSKAT), 100, *595*
S.O.I. Learning Abilities Test, 490
SOI-Learning Abilities Test: Dental Receptionist Test, 839
SOI-Learning Abilities Test: Screening Form for Atypical Gifted, 573
SOI-Learning Abilities Test: Screening Form for Gifted, 574
SOI Primary Form (Form P), 513, *573, 605*
Somatic Inkblot Series (SIS), 180
Somatic Inkblot Series II, 180
Somatic Video Series II, 180
South African Individual Scale for the Blind (SAISB)—1979, The, 514, *32, 662*
South African Personality Questionnaire, 181
South African Wechsler Adult Individual Intelligence Scale, 32
South African Written Language Test (SAWLT)—1981, 239
Southern California Motor Accuracy Test, Revised 1980, 63, *566*
Southern California Ordinal Scales of Development, The, 566, *605*

Out-of-Print Tests

Note: This list was compiled via information provided by test publishers regarding tests recently declared out-of-print. Because in-print status is subject to change, the editors encourage test users to contact the test's author(s) or former publisher for information concerning the availability of a particular test.

ACER Lower Grades General Ability Scale

ACER Silent Reading Test-Form C

ACER Word Knowledge Test-Adult Form B

ACT Proficiency Examination Program—Criminal Justice: Criminal Investigation *The American College Testing Program*

ACT Proficiency Examination Program—Criminal Justice: Introduction to Criminal Justice *The American College Testing Program*

ACT Proficiency Examination Program—Nursing: Nursing Health Care *The American College Testing Program*

Activities for Assessing Classification Skills (Experimental Edition) *Rachel Gal-Choppin*

Advanced Reading Inventory *Jerry L. Johns*

AH Vocabulary Scale *A.W. Heim, K.P. Watts, and V. Simmonds*

AI3Q Measure of Obsessional or Anal Character *Paul Kline*

Applied Biological and Agribusiness Interest Inventory, The *Robert W. Walker and Glenn Z. Stevens*

Aptitude Index Battery (AIB) *LIMRA*

Aptitude Tests for Occupations *Wesley S. Roder*

Barsch Learning Style Inventory *Jeffery Barsch*

Basic Screening and Referral Form for Children with Suspected Learning and Behavioral Disabilities, A *Robert E. Valett*

Belwin-Mills Singing Achievement Test *Richard W. Bowles*

Brook Reaction Test of Interests and Temperament, The *A.W. Heim, K.P. Watts, and V. Simmonds*

California Neuropsych System: Computer Battery of Neuropsychological Tests and Procedures *Alan Fridlund and Dean Delis*

Chart of Initiative and Independence

Children's Scale of Social Attitudes *Glen D. Wilson, David K.B. Nias, and Paul M. Insel*

Classroom Learning Screening (CLS) *Carl H. Koenig and Harold P. Kunzelman*

Columbus: Picture Analysis of Growth Toward Maturity, Third Edition *M.J. Langeveld*

Comprehension Test: Early Primary, Primary and Intermediate *Marion L. McGuire and Marguerite J. Bumpus*

Cooper-McGuire Diagnostic Word Analysis Test *J. Louis Cooper and Marion L. McGuire*

Coping Inventory, The *Shirley Zeitlin*

Crowley Occupational Interests Blank *Tony Crowley*

CSMS Science Reasoning Tasks *M. Shayer, H. Wylam, P. Adey, and D. Kuchemann*

CSMS Science Reasoning Tasks: Chemical Combinations *M. Shayer, H. Wylam, P. Adey, and D. Kuchemann*

CSMS Science Reasoning Tasks: Equilibrium in the Balance *M. Shayer, H. Wylam, P. Adey, and D. Kuchemann*

CSMS Science Reasoning Tasks: Flexible Rods *M. Shayer, H. Wylam, P. Adey, and D. Kuchemann*

CSMS Science Reasoning Tasks: Inclined Plane *M. Shayer, H. Wylam, P. Adey, and D. Kuchemann*

CSMS Science Reasoning Tasks: Spatial Relationships *M. Shayer, H. Wylam, P. Adey, and D. Kuchemann*

CSMS Science Reasoning Tasks: The Pendulum *M. Shayer, H. Wylam, P. Adey, and D. Kuchemann*

CSMS Science Reasoning Tasks: Volume and Heaviness *M. Shayer, H. Wylam, P. Adey, and D. Kuchemann*

Cureton Multi-Aptitude Test (CMAT) *E.E. Cureton and L.W. Cureton et al.*

Deeside Picture Test *W.G. Emmett*

Developmental Task Analysis *Robert E. Valett*

Devereux Test of Extremity Coordination (DTEC) *The Devereux Foundation*

Dimock L. Inventory (DLI) *Hedly G. Dimock*

Driscoll Play Kit *G.P. Driscoll*

Driver Attitude Survey (DAS), The *Donald H. Schuster and J.P. Guilford*

Dynamic Personality Inventory (DPI) and Likes and Interests Test (LIT) *T.G. Grygier*

Effectiveness-Motivation Scale *J. Sharp and D.H. Stott*

Essentials of English Tests *Constance McCullough, Dora V. Smith, and Carolyn Greene*

Estes Attitude Scale: Measures of Attitude Toward School Subjects   *Thomas H. Estes, Julie Johnstone Estes, Herbert C. Richards, and Doris Roettger*

Everyday Skills Test (EDST)   *CTB/McGraw-Hill*

Everyday Skills Test: Mathematics

Everyday Skills Test: Reading

Factorial Interest Blank   *P.H. Sandall*

Fine Dexterity Test   *E.I.T.S. Staff*

First Grade Screening Test (FGST)   *John E. Pate and Warren W. Webb*

Fisher-Logemann Test of Articulation Competence   *Hilda B. Fisher and Jerilyn A. Logemann*

Five Task Test   *Charlotte Buhler and Kathryn Mandeville*

Freeman Anxiety Neurosis and Psychosomatic Test , The   *M.J. Freeman*

Garnett College Test in Engineering Science (Revised Edition)   *I. MacFarlane Smith*

General Tests of Language and Arithmetic for Students (GTLAS)—1972

Graded French Tests

Growth Process Inventory (GPI)   *Everett L. Shostrom*

Guilford-Holley L. Inventory (GHL)   *J.P. Guilford and J.W. Holley*

Harrower Psychodiagnostic Inkblot Test   *Molly Harrower*

Hilton Questionnaire—A Measure of Drinking Behavior , The   *Margaret Hilton*

Holborn Reading Scale (1980) , The   *A.F. Watts*

Hostility and Direction of Hostility Questionnaire (HDHQ)   *A.T.M. Caine, G.A. Foulds, and K. Hope*

Immediate Test (IT) , The   *Raymond J. Corsini*

Individual Problem Index (IPI)

Interactive Medical History (IMH)   *Based on the Harvard Medical History*

Inventory of Insurance Selling Potential

Inventory of Primary Skills , An   *Robert E. Valett*

Junior Inventory (J.I.)   *Hermann H. Remmers and Robert H. Bauernfeind*

Leadership Education and Development Scale (LEADS)   *Harley W. Mowry*

Learning Screen (LS)   *Carl H. Koenig and Harold P. Kunzelman*

MACC Behavioral Adjustment Scale: Revised Scale , The   *Robert B. Ellsworth*

Make a Picture Story (MAPS)   *E.S. Shneidman*

Management Inventory on Leadership and Motivation (MILM)   *Donald L. Kirkpatrick*

Manchester Scales of Social Adaptation   *E.A. Lunzer*

Manual Accuracy and Speed Test   *Peter F. Briggs and Auke Tellegen*

McGuire-Bumpus Diagnostic Comprehension Test   *Marion L. McGuire and Marguerite J. Bumpus*

Memory for Events (ME)   *J.P. Guilford*

Memory for Meanings (MM)   *Ralph Hoepfner and J.P. Guilford*

Mertens Visual Perception Test   *Marjorie K. Mertens*

Minnesota Preschool Scale   *Florence Goodenough, Katherine Maurer, and M.J. Van Wagenen*

Missouri Student Needs Survey, Form V

Monash Diagnostic Test of Lipreading Ability

Multiple Choice English and Progressive Multiple Choice English   *A.F. Bolt*

Multiple-Choice Biology and Advanced Multiple-Choice Biology   *R. Soper, D. Robinson, and S.T. Smith*

Multiple-Choice Chemistry and Advanced Multiple-Choice Chemistry   *J.A.S. Rees*

Multiple-Choice Physics   *R.W. Adams*

My Self Check List (MSCL)   *Robert E. Valett*

National Achievement Tests for Elementary Schools: Arithmetic and Mathematics— Arithmetic Reasoning   *Robert K. Speer and Samuel Smith*

National Achievement Tests: Health and Science Tests—General Biology   *Lester D. Crow and James G. Murray*

National Business Entrance Tests— Bookkeeping Test   *N.B.E.A. Test Committee*

National Business Entrance Tests—Business Fundamentals and General Information Test   *N.B.E.A. Test Committee*

National Business Entrance Tests—Machine Calculation Test   *N.B.E.A. Test Committee*

Naylor-Harwood Adult Intelligence Scale   *G.F.K. Naylor and E. Harwood*

Neale Analysis of Reading Ability—Braille Edition   *N.B. Neale*

Netherne Study Difficulties Battery for Student Nurses (SDB)   *James Patrick S. Robertson*

NIIP Clerical Tests

NLN Achievement Tests For Practical Nursing: Mental Health Concepts For Practical Nursing Students (Form 0481)

NLN Achievement Tests For Practical Nursing: Psychiatric Nursing Concepts For Practical Nursing Students (Form 4313)

NLN Achievement Tests For Registered Nursing: Comprehensive Nursing Achievement Test 1984 Edition (Form 3014)

NLN Achievement Tests For Registered Nursing: Nursing The Childbearing Family (Form 0581)

Occupational Check List   *Tony Crowley*

Oregon Academic Ranking Test   *Charles H. Derthick*

Organization Survey   *Human Resource Center, University of Chicago*

Orzeck Aphasia Evaluation   *Arthur Orzeck*

Otis Self Administering Test of Mental Ability   *Arthur S. Otis*
Otto Pre-Marital Counseling Schedules   *Herbert A. Otto*
Peer Attitudes Towards the Handicapped Scale (PATHS)   *Micheal T. Bayley and John F. Greene*
Peg Board   *E.I.T.S. Staff*
Personal Background Inventory   *Melany E. Baehr and Frances M. Burns*
Personal History Index   *M.E. Baehr, R.K. Burns, and R.N. McMurry*
Personality and Personal Illness Questionnaires   *T.M. Caine, G.A. Foulds, and K. Hope*
Personality Inventory , The   *Robert G. Bernreuter*
Piaget Task Kit   *Willard Stibal*
Picture World Test   *Charlotte Buhler and Morse P. Manson*
Preschool Attainment Record (Research Edition)   *Edgar A. Doll*
Psychoeducational Inventory of Basic Learning Abilities , A   *Robert E. Valett*
Rapid Exam for Early Referral (REFER)   *Carl H. Koenig and Harold P. Kunzelman*
Reading Level Tests (Using Cloze Procedure)
Reading Readiness Inventory   *J. Downing and Derek V. Thackray*
Reading Tests   *F.J. Schonell*
Rohde Sentence Completions   *Amanda R. Rohde*
Rorschach Concept Evaluation Technique   *Paul McReynolds*
School/Home Observation and Referral System (SHORS)   *Joyce Evans*
SCRE Profile Assessment System
Self-Rating Anxiety Scale (SAS)   *William W.K. Zung*
Senior English Test
Short Occupational Knowledge Tests (SOKT)   *Bruce A. Campbell and Suellen O. Johnson*
Shorthand Aptitude Test   *Queensland Department of Education*
South African Picture Analysis Test (PASAT), The   *B.F. Nel and A.J.K. Pelser*
Speed Scale for Determining Independent Reading Level   *Ward Cramer and Roger Trent*
Staffordshire Test of Computation , The   *M.E. Hebron and W. Pattinson*
Stanford-Ohwaki-Kohs Block Design Intelligence Test for the Blind: American Revision   *Richard M. Suinn and William L. Dauterman*
Stress Profile for Teachers   *Christopher F. Wilson*

Student Developmental Profile and Planning Record   *Roger B. Winston, Theodore K. Miller, and Judith S. Prince*
Survey of Object Visualization (SOV)   *Daniel R. Miller*
Survey of Space Relations Ability (SSRA)   *Harry W. Case and Floyd Ruch*
Symbol Identities   *Ralph Hoepfner*
System for the Administration and Interpretation of Neurological Tests (SAINT-II)   *Dennis Swiercinsky*
Test of Abstract Concept Learning (TACL)
Test of Behavioral Rigidity (TBR)   *K. Warner Schaie and Iris A. Parham*
Test of Children's Learning Ability— Individual Version   *J. Haynes, S. Hegarty, X. Perryer, and C. Gipps*
Test of Consumer Competencies (TCC)   *Thomas Stanley, E. Thomas Garman, and Richard Brown*
Test of Economic Achievement   *J.D. Thexton*
Test of Everyday Writing Skills (TEWS)   *CTB/McGraw-Hill*
Test Orientation Procedure   *G.K. Bennett and J.E. Doppelt*
Tests of Proficiency in English   *C. Gipps and E. Ewen*
Tests of Proficiency in English—Listening Tests   *C. Gipps and E. Ewen*
Tests of Proficiency in English—Reading Tests   *C. Gipps and E. Ewen*
Tests of Proficiency in English—Speaking Tests   *C. Gipps and E. Ewen*
Tests of Proficiency in English—Writing Tests   *C. Gipps and E. Ewen*
Tests on Newbery Medal Award Books
Time Appreciation Test   *John N. Buck*
Transitional Assessment Modules
Verbal Language Development Scale (VLDS)   *Merlin J. Mecham*
Verbal Power Test of Concept Equivalents   *E. Francesco*
Visual Pattern Recognition Test Diagnostic Schedule and Training Materials   *Diane Montgomery*
Washington Speech and Sound Discrimination Test   *E. Prather, A. Miner, M.A. Addicott, and L. Summerland*
Wessex Reading Analysis , The   *A. Hughes, P. Evans, and S. Moulton*
Wilson-Patterson Attitude Inventory   *Glenn D. Wilson*
Wing Standardised Tests of Musical Intelligence   *H.D. Wing*
Wittenborn Psychiatric Rating Scales (Revised)   *J.R. Wittenborn*
Word Orders Comprehension Test   *Gillian Fenn*
Work Environment Preference Schedule   *Leonard V. Gordon*
Youth Inventory (YI)   *Hermann H. Remmers and Benjamin Shimberg*

Hearing-Impaired Index

Note: This index was compiled via information provided by test publishers. It contains tests that assess the sense of hearing as well as tests that are suitable for use with individuals having hearing impairments. Both tests that have been designed for use specifically with hearing-impaired individuals and tests that may be adapted for use with such individuals are included. The editors encourage test users to contact the test publisher for specific information regarding the use of a particular test with hearing-impaired individuals.

Physically Impaired Index

Note: This index was compiled via information provided by test publishers. Both tests that have been designed for use specifically with physically impaired individuals and tests that may be adapted for use with such individuals are included. The editors encourage test users to contact the test publisher for specific information regarding the use of a particular test with physically impaired individuals.

Visually Impaired Index

Note: This index was compiled via information provided by test publishers. It contains tests that assess the sense of vision as well as tests that are suitable for use with individuals having visual impairments. Both tests that have been designed for use specifically with visually impaired individuals and tests that may be adapted for use with such individuals are included. The editors encourage test users to contact the test publisher for specific information regarding the use of a particular test with visually impaired individuals.

Foreign Language
Availability Index

Employee Aptitude Survey Test #7—Verbal
Reasoning (EAS #7), 802
Employee Aptitude Survey Test #10—Symbolic
Reasoning (EAS #10), 803
Reid Report, 937

PORTUGUESE

Children's Apperception Test (CAT-A),
The, 105
Children's Apperception Test—Human Figures
(CAT-H), The, 105
Defense Mechanisms Inventory, 130
McMaster Family Assessment Device
(FAD), 79
PAPI System, 928
PAPI System: How I See Myself, 929
PAPI System: How I See You, 929
PAPI System: PA Preference Inventory, 930
PAPI System: Rating of Job Requirements—
Form A Revised, 930
PAPI System: Rating of Job Requirements—
Form B Revised, 930
PAPI System: Rating of Job Requirements—
Form C Revised, 931
PAPI System: Rating of Job Requirements—
Form D Revised, 931
Reid Report, 937
Reid Survey, 938
Reid Survey (Retail), 938
Taylor-Johnson Temperament Analysis, 183

RUSSIAN

Rokeach Value Survey, 208

SERBO-CROATIAN

ACER Checklists for School Beginners, 459

SPANISH

ACER Checklists for School Beginners, 459
Adaptive Behavior Inventory of Children
(ABIC), 69
Adult Neuropsychological Questionnaire, 36
Affective Perception Inventory (API), The, 697
Analysis of Readiness Skills, 460
Annual High School Mathematics Examination
(AHSME), 300
Aptitude Assessment Battery: Programming
(AABP), 877
Assessment of Children's Language
Comprehension (ACLC), 617
Association Adjustment Inventory (AAI), 119
Autism Screening Instrument for Educational
Planning—The Autism Behavior
Checklist, 189
Ber-Sil Spanish Tests, The: Elementary
Test, 259
Boehm Test of Basic Concepts, 462
California Psychological Inventory (CPI), 123
Career Assessment Inventory (CAI), 736
Center for Epidemiologic Studies—Depression
Scale (CES-D), 124

Child Neuropsychological Questionnaire,
The, 39
Children's Apperception Test (CAT-A),
The, 105
Children's Apperception Test—Human Figure
(CAT-H), The, 105
Children's Apperception Test—Supplement
(CAT-S), The, 105
Children's Personality Questionnaire
(CPQ), 106
Columbia Mental Maturity Scale, 21
Comprehensive Assessment Program: School
Attitude Measure, 685
Comprehensive Identification Process
(CIP), 467
Comprehensive Tests of Basic Skills
(Forms S and T), 392
Comprehensive Tests of Basic Skills:
Forms U and V (CTBS/U and V), 392
Cooperative Preschool Inventory, 467
COPSystem Interest Inventory (COPS), 740
CPRI Questionnaires (Q-71, Q-74, Q-75,
Q-76), 686
Culture Fair Series: Scales 1, 2, 3, The, 21
Curtis Completion Form, 130
Dallas Pre-School Screening Test, The, 469
Denver Developmental Screening Test
(DDST), 7
Early Identification Screening Program, 471
Early School Personality Questionnaire
(ESPQ), 108
Educational Goal Attainment Tests, 781
Educational Goal Attainment Tests:
Careers, 782
Educational Goal Attainment Tests: Civics, 782
Educational Goal Attainment Tests: General
Knowledge, 783
Educational Goal Attainment Tests: Life
Skills, 784
Effective Study Test (EST), 710
Ego State Personality Profile (Egogram™), 133
Employee Aptitude Survey Test #2—Numerical
Ability (EAS #2), 800
Employee Aptitude Survey Test #3—Visual
Pursuit (EAS #3), 801
Employee Aptitude Survey Test #4—Visual
Speed and Accuracy (EAS #4), 801
Employee Aptitude Survey Test #6—Numerical
Reasoning (EAS #6), 802
Employee Aptitude Survey Test #7—Verbal
Reasoning (EAS #7), 802
Employee Aptitude Survey Test #10—Symbolic
Reasoning (EAS #10), 803
Expressive One-Word Picture Vocabulary Test
(EOWPVT), 504
Expressive One-Word Picture Vocabulary Test:
Upper Extension (EOWPVT: UE), 627
Eysenck Personality Inventory (EPI), 134
Frost Self-Description Questionnaire, 108
General Aptitude Test Battery (GATB), 808
Geriatric Depression Scale, 137
Hartman Value Profile (HVP), 199
Hay Aptitude Test Battery, 861

*The 16PF has been translated by users into over 40 different languages; the reader should contact Foreign Test Editor, Institute for Personality and Ability Testing, regarding availability and distribution of specific language versions.

Author Index

Wykoff, G.S., 245
Yamauchi, K.T., 224
Yanico, B., 890
Yoder, D., 634
Yonge, G.D., 161
Young, D., 238, 253, 288, 298, 510, 527
Young, E.C., 636
Youniss, R.P., 144

Yufit, R., 119
Yuker, H.E., 691
Zachman, L., 515, 635, 636, 655
Zaichkowsky, L.D., 702
Zalk, S.R., 687
Zehrbach, R.R., 467
Zeisloft, B., 9
Zeitlin, S., 699

Zimmerman, I.L., 640
Zimmerman, J.J., 325
Zimmerman, W.S., 139, 711, 744, 809, 810, 811
Zinkin, P., 489
Zoss, S.K., 202
Zucker, S.H., 409, 410
Zuckerman, M., 156
Zung, W.W.K., 177, 206
Zyzanski, S.J., 203

Publisher/Distributor Index

Behavior Science Systems, Inc., P.O. Box 1108, Minneapolis, Minnesota 55440; (612)929-6220—13, 482

Behavioral Science Research Press, 695 Villa Creek, Suite 180, Dallas, Texas 75234; (214)243-8543—1003

Belwin-Mills Publishing Company, 15800 N.W. 48th Avenue, Miami, Florida 33014; (305)620-1500—256

The Ber-Sil Company, 3412 Seaglen Drive, Rancho Palos Verdes, California 90274; (213)541-1074—259

Bilingual Media Productions, Inc., P.O. Box 9337, North Berkeley Station, Berkeley, California 94709; (415)548-3777—260

Bingham Button Test, 46211 North 125th Street East, Lancaster, California 93534; (805)943-3241—4

BJK Associates, 2104 South 135th Avenue, Omaha, Nebraska 68144; (402)330-3726—963

Bloom, Philip, 140 Cadman Plaza West, Apt. 3F, Brooklyn, New York 11201; no business phone—20

Blue Star Enterprises, c/o Claire R. Greenbaum, 792 Columbus Avenue, New York, New York 10025; (212)749-1916—239

Bond Publishing Company, 787 Willett Avenue, Riverside, Rhode Island 02915-9990; (401)437-0421—255

Book-Lab, 500 74th Street, North Bergen, New Jersey 07047; (201)861-6763 or (201)868-1305—442, 476, 550, 552, 584

Brador Publications, Inc., Education Division, 36 Main Street, Livonia, New York 14487; (716)346-3191—502, 536

Branden Press, Inc., 21 Station Street, P.O. Box 843, Brookline Village, Massachusetts 02147; (617)734-2045—260

Brink, T.L., 1044 Sylvan, San Carlos, California 94070; (415)593-7323—46, 64, 137, 142

Brook Educational Publishing Ltd., P.O. Box 1171, Guelph, Ontario N1H 6N3, Canada; (519)836-2920—579

William C. Brown Company Publishers, 2460 Kemper Boulevard, Dubuque, Iowa 52001; (319)588-1451—548

Brown/Butler Family Research Program, 345 Blackstone Boulevard, Providence, Rhode Island 02906; (401)456-3700—79

Bruce, Martin M., Ph.D., Publishers, 50 Larchwood Road, Larchmont, New York 10538; (914)834-1555—120, 165, 213, 256, 694, 790, 856, 890, 911, 917, 947, 971, 1000, 1003, 1004, 1005

Bureau of Business and Economic Research, College of Business Administration, University of Iowa, Iowa City, Iowa 52242; (319)353-2121—323

Bureau of Educational Measurements, Emporia State University, 1200 Commercial, Emporia, Kansas 66801; (316)343-1200—231, 233, 234, 235, 236, 237, 242, 244, 246, 262, 263, 267, 268, 270, 271, 286, 304, 307, 308, 309, 310, 315, 316, 320, 321, 322, 323, 324, 325, 523, 524, 556, 963

Callier Center for Communication Disorders, The University of Texas at Dallas, 1966 Inwood Road, Dallas, Texas 75235; (214)783-3000—5

Cambridge, The Adult Education Company, 888 Seventh Avenue, New York, New York 10106; west of the Mississippi or Louisiana, Alabama, Mississippi, and the Florida panhandle (800)221-4764, east of the Mississippi (except New York) (800)221-4600, in New York (212)957-2563—438, 544, 768

Camelot Behavioral Systems, P.O. Box 3447, Lawrence, Kansas 66044; (913)843-9159—591

Carlson, Bernadine P., c/o Western Michigan University, 720 Sprau Tower, Kalamazoo, Michigan 49008; (616)383-0788—247, 852

Carroll Publications, 704 South University, Mount Pleasant, Michigan 48858; (517)772-3956—540

C.C. Publications, Inc., P.O. Box 23699, Tigard, Oregon 97223-0108; (503)692-6800, (800)547-4800—619, 620, 627, 630, 635, 644, 654

Cedars Press, P.O. Box 29351, Columbus, Ohio 43229; (614)846-2849—706

Center for Advanced Study in Theoretical Psychology, University of Alberta, 6-102 Education North, Edmonton, Alberta, Canada T6G 2E9; (403)432-5271—704

Center for Child Development and Education, College of Education, University of Arkansas at Little Rock, 33rd and University, Little Rock, Arkansas 72204; (501)569-3422—9

Center for Cognitive Therapy, 133 South 36th Street, Room 602, Philadelphia, Pennsylvania 19104; (215)898-4100—120

Center for Leadership Studies (available from Learning Resources Corporation), 8517 Production Avenue, P.O. Box 26240, San Diego, California 92126; (714)578-5900—79, 82, 935, 955, 956, 957, 963, 966

The Center for Psychological Service, 1511 K Street N.W., Suite 430, Washington, D.C. 20005; (202)347-4069—438, 707

Center for the Study of Parental Acceptance and Rejection, The University of Connecticut, Storrs, Connecticut 06268; (203)486-4513—82

CFKR Career Materials, Inc., P.O. Box 437, Meadow Vista, California 95722; (800)553-3313, in California (916)878-0118—689, 737, 743, 747, 750, 758, 901

Chambers, Jay L., College of William and Mary, Williamsburg, Virginia 23185; (703)253-4000—164

Chandler, Louis A., Ph.D., 5D Forbes Quadrangle, Pittsburgh, Pennsylvania 15260; (412)624-1244—681

Chapman, Brook & Kent, 1215 De La Vina, Suite F, Santa Barbara, California 93101; (805)962-0055—465

CHECpoint Systems, Inc., 1520 North Waterman Avenue, San Bernadino, California 92404; (714)888-3296—618

The CHILD Center, Childhood Help in Learning and Development, P.O. Box 144, Kentfield, California 94914; (415)456-0440—372

Child Development Centers of the Bluegrass, Inc., 465 Springhill Drive, Lexington, Kentucky 40503; (606)278-0549—480

Childcraft Education Corporation, 20 Kilmer Road, Edison, New Jersey 08818; (800)631-5652, in New Jersey (201)572-6100—470, 471

Children's Hospital of San Francisco, Publication Department OPR-110, P.O. Box 3805, San Francisco, California; (415)387-8700—567, 614

Chronicle Guidance Publications, Inc., Moravia, New York 13118; (315)497-0330—743

Clinical Diagnostics, 300 East Mineral Avenue, Suite 6, Littleton, Colorado 80122; (800)521-4503, in Colorado (303)795-0438—581

Clinical Psychology Publishing Co., Inc., 4 Conant Square, Brandon, Vermont 05733; (802)247-6871—50, 154, 471, 496, 653

Clinical Psychometric Research, 1228 Wine Spring Lane, Towson, Maryland 21204; (301)321-6165—88, 118, 122, 131, 141, 169, 175

Coddington, R. Dean, M.D., P.O. Box 307, St. Clairsville, Ohio 43950; (614)695-4805—149

Coffin Associates, 21 Darling Street, Marblehead, Massachusetts 01945; (617)631-9491—320, 322

The College Board Publications, 45 Columbus Avenue, New York, New York 10023; (212)713-8000—327, 328, 329, 330, 331, 332, 353, 354, 355, 356, 357, 358, 359, 360, 361, 362, 363, 364, 374, 375, 376, 377, 378, 379, 380, 381, 382, 383, 384, 385, 386, 387, 388, 389

College-Hill Press, 4284 41st Street, San Diego, California 92105; (619)563-8899—627

Communication Research Associates, Inc., P.O. Box 11012, Salt Lake City, Utah 84147; (801)292-3880—589, 632, 643, 645, 653

Communication Skill Builders, Inc., 3130 North Dodge Boulevard, P.O. Box 42050, Tucson, Arizona 85733; (602)323-7500—101, 622, 623, 624, 625, 629, 636, 648, 652

Compuscore, P.O. Box 7035, Ann Arbor, Michigan 48107; (313)662-2040—96

Consulting Psychologists Press, Inc., 577 College Avenue, P.O. Box 60070, Palo Alto, California 94306; (415)857-1444—30, 73, 78, 94, 95, 102, 106, 107, 114, 117, 119, 123, 128, 129, 136, 138, 140, 142, 145, 147, 157, 166, 178, 181, 190, 194, 195, 197, 198, 199, 203, 204, 211, 216, 217, 218, 219, 220, 221, 465, 474, 485, 492, 496, 543, 560, 590, 596, 617, 628, 639, 681, 684, 695, 696, 698, 712, 751, 754, 762, 763, 770, 776, 901, 902, 906, 907, 908, 925, 937, 948

Counseling and Self-Improvement Programs, 710 Watson Drive, Natchitoches, Louisiana 71457; (318)352-5313—144, 917

C.P.S., Inc., P.O. Box 83, Larchmont, New York 10538; no business phone—105, 177

Crane Publishing Company, Division of MLP, 1301 Hamilton Avenue, P.O. Box 3713, Trenton, New Jersey 08629; (609)393-1111—261

Creative Learning Press, Inc., P.O. Box 320, Mansfield Center, Connecticut 06250; (203)423-8120—572, 687, 688, 690, 775

Creative Learning Systems, Inc., 9889 Hibert, San Diego, California 92131; (619)566-2880—588, 593, 605

Creative Therapeutics, P.O. Box R, Cresskill, New Jersey 07626; (201)567-8989—586

CTB/McGraw-Hill, Publishers Test Service, Del Monte Research Park, 2500 Garden Road, Monterey, California 93940; (800)538-9547, in California (800)682-9222 or (408)649-8400—10, 50, 241, 243, 247, 248, 262, 266, 268, 280, 283, 284, 285, 297, 304, 367, 370, 392, 444, 446, 452, 455, 467, 494, 519, 521, 534, 546, 553, 590, 594, 595, 606, 672, 676, 718, 737, 738, 752, 755, 977

Curriculum Associates, Inc., 5 Esquire Road, North Billerica, Massachusetts, 08162-2589; (800)225-0248, in Massachusetts (617)667-8000—287, 367, 368, 369, 464

Dallas Educational Services, P.O. Box 831254, Richardson, Texas 75083-1254; (214)234-6371—469, 570, 697, 706

Dansk Psykologisk Forlag, Hans Knudsens Plads 1A, DK-2100 København Ø, Denmark—101

Datascan, 1134 Bobbie Lane, Garland, Texas 75042; (214)276-3978—89, 95, 748

Dean, Raymond S., Ph.D., Ball State University, TC 521, Muncie, Indiana 47306; (317)285-8500—47

Delaware County Reading Council State Building, Sixth and Olive Streets, Media, Pennsylvania 19063; (215)565-4880—519, 520

Lawrence Erlbaum Associates, Inc., 365 Broadway, Hillsdale, New Jersey 07642; (201)666-4110 —516

Essay Press, P.O. Box 2323, La Jolla, California 92037; (619)565-6603—537

Evaluation Research Associates, P.O. Box 6503, Teall Station, Syracuse, New York 13217; (315)422-0064—211, 684, 685, 687, 928

Examinations Committee, American Chemical Society (ACS), University of South Florida, Chemistry, Room 112, Tampa, Florida 33620; (813)974-2730—308, 309, 310, 311, 312, 313, 314, 315

Exceptional Resources, Inc., 7701 Cameron Road, Suite 105, Austin, Texas 78766; (512)346-4964—603, 637

Eyberg, Sheila M., Ph.D., Department of Clinical Psychology, Box J-165, J.H.M.H.C., University of Florida, Gainesville, Florida 32610; (904)392-4558—85

Family Life Publications, Inc., Box 427, Saluda, North Carolina 28773; (704)749-4971—87, 90, 91, 92, 93, 94, 96, 97, 98, 99

Family Social Science, 290 McNeal Hall, University of Minnesota, St. Paul, Minnesota 55108; (612)373-1544—73, 74, 75, 88

Family Stress, Coping and Health Project, School of Family Resources and Consumer Sciences, University of Wisconsin, 1300 Linden Drive, Madison, Wisconsin 53706; (608)262-5712—69, 116

Charles G. Fast, Northeast Missouri State University, Kirksville, Missouri 63501; (816)785-4000—316

Federation of Societies for Coatings Technology, 1315 Walnut Street, Philadelphia, Pennsylvania 19107; (215)545-1506—798

Foreworks, P.O. Box 9747, North Hollywood, California 91609; (213)982-0467—566, 613

The Foundation for Knowledge in Development, KID Technology, 11715 East 51st Avenue, Denver, Colorado 80239; (303)373-1916—12

Freeman, Betty Jo, Ph.D., Neuropsychiatric Institute, 58-227A, 760 Westwood Plaza, Los Angeles, California 90024; (213)825-0458—102

Frost, Barry P., Ph.D., University of Calgary, 2500 University Drive N.W., Calgary, Alberta, Canada T2N 1N4; (403)284-5651—108, 109

Gallaudet College Press, Distribution Office, 800 Florida Avenue N.E., Washington, D.C. 20002; (202)651-5591 (voice) or (202)651-5355 (TDD)—254

Garrard Publishing Company, 1607 North Market Street, P.O. Box A, Champaign, Illinois 61820; (217)352-7685—517

Gesell Developmental Test Materials, Inc., P.O. Box 272391, Houston, Texas 77277-2391—16

G.I.A. Publications, 7404 South Mason Avenue, Chicago, Illinois 60638; (312)496-3800—255, 256, 257

Robert Gibson Publisher, 17, Fitzroy Place, Glasgow, Scotland G3 7BR; (041)248-5674—507

Girona, Ricardo, 428 Columbus Avenue, Sandusky, Ohio 44870; no business phone—118

Gough, Harrison G./Institute of Personality and Research, University of California, Berkeley, California 94720; (415)642-6000—672

Goyer, Robert S., Ph.D., Centre for Communication Studies, Ohio University, Athens, Ohio 45701; (602)965-5095—399

Grune & Stratton, Inc., Orlando, Florida 32887-0018; (305)345-4100—68, 109, 112, 209, 253, 540, 564, 577, 585, 640

Guidance Centre, Faculty of Education, University of Toronto, 10 Alcorn Avenue, Ontario, Canada M4V 2Z8—8, 291, 298, 371, 547, 683, 700, 701, 709, 757

Halgren Tests, 873 Persimmon Avenue, Sunnyvale, California 94807; (408)738-1342—208, 209

Hanson, Silver, Strong, & Associates, P.O. Box 402, Moorestown, New Jersey 08057; (609)234-2610—710, 711, 779, 961

Harding, Christopher, Harding Tests, P.O. Box 5271, Rockhampton Mail Centre, Q. 4702, Australia; no business phone—89, 251, 505, 506

Harvard University Press, 79 Garden Street, Cambridge, Massachusetts 02138; (617)495-2600—185

Haverly Systems, Inc., 78 Broadway, P.O. Box 919, Denville, New Jersey 07834; (201)627-1424—880

Hayes Educational Tests, 7040 North Portsmouth Avenue, Portland, Oregon 97203; (503)285-3745—292, 294

Heath, S. Roy, Ph.D., 1193 South East Street, Amherst, Massachusetts 01002; (413)253-7756—56, 205

Heinemann Educational Books, Inc., 70 Court Street, Portsmouth, New Hampshire 03801-4414—522

Heinemann Educational Books Limited, 26 Kilham Avenue, Auckland 9, P.O. Box 36064, New Zealand—522

Heinemann Publishers Australia Party Limited, 85 Abinger Street, P.O. Box 133, Richmond, Victoria 3121, Australia; (03)429 3622—524, 549

Hill, William Fawcett, California State Polytechnic University, Pomona, 3801 West Temple Avenue, Pomona, California 91768; (714)626-0128—194, 199, 200

The Hiskey-Nebraska Test, 5640 Baldwin, Lincoln, Nebraska 68507; (402)466-6145—600

Hodder & Stoughton Educational, A Division of Hodder & Stoughton Ltd., P.O. Box 702, Mill Road, Dunton Green, Sevenoaks, Kent TN13 2YD, England; (0732)450111—15, 125, 129, 196, 235, 238, 251, 253, 281, 287, 288, 289, 293, 298, 365, 408, 473, 477, 510, 518, 527, 537, 538, 539, 544, 560, 668, 749

Hodges, Kay, Ph.D., Duke University Medical Center, P.O. Box 2906, Durham, North Carolina 27710; (919)684-3044—103

Hoeflin, Ronald K., 439 West 50th Street, New York, New York 10019; (212)582-2326—27

Huber, Hans, Langgassstrasse 76, 3000 Bern 9, Switzerland—209

Human Sciences Center, P.O. Box 796, Yuma, Arizona 85364; (602)344-3397—206

Human Sciences Research Council, Private Bag X41, 0001 Pretoria, South Africa; (012)28-3944—23, 24, 31, 144, 165, 212, 213, 237, 239, 253, 257, 262, 265, 270, 283, 290, 310, 313, 318, 325, 326, 364, 365, 400, 401, 403, 440, 443, 444, 445, 492, 505, 507, 509, 514, 613, 648, 674, 701, 713, 714, 732, 733, 747, 748, 750, 752, 755, 760, 789, 843

Humanics Limited, 1389 Peachtree Street, N.E., Suite 201, P.O. Box 7447, Atlanta, Georgia 30309; (404)874-2176—105, 476, 477, 481, 698

Humanics Media, 5457 Pine Cone Road, La Crescenta, California 91214; (818)957-4332—683, 775, 900, 920, 946, 965, 971

Illinois Thinking Project, Education Building, University of Illinois, Urbana, Illinois 61801; (217)333-1000—393

Industrial Psychology Inc. (IPI), 515 Madison Avenue, New York, New York 10022; (212)355-5330—812, 813, 814, 815, 816, 817, 818, 819, 820, 821, 822, 823, 879

Institute for Character Development, 1209 West Main Street, Shelbyville, Kentucky 40065; (502)456-1990—124

Institute for Child Behavior Research, 4182 Adams Avenue, San Diego, California 92116; (619)281-7165—108

Institute for Educational Research and Development, Memorial University of Newfoundland, Canada A1B 3X8; (709)737-8685—453

Institute for Personality and Ability Testing, Inc. (IPAT), P.O. Box 188, 1602 Coronado Drive, Champaign, Illinois 61820; (217)352-4739—21, 103, 106, 108, 117, 125, 134, 140, 145, 158, 159, 173, 179, 201, 798, 925, 941, 953

Institute for Psycho-Imagination Therapy, c/o Joseph Shorr, Ph.D., 111 North La Cienega Boulevard #108, Beverly Hills, California 90211; (213)652-2922—139, 177

Institute for Psychosomatic & Psychiatric Research & Training/Daniel Offer, Michael Reese Hospital and Medical Center, Lake Shore Drive at 31st Street, Chicago, Illinois 60616; (312)791-3826—159, 160

Institute for the Advancement of Philosophy for Children, Montclair State College, Upper Montclair, New Jersey 07043; (201)893-4277—421

Institute for the Development of Human Resources, 1201 Second Street, Corpus Christi, Texas 78404; (512)883-6442—934

Institute of Psychological Research, Inc., 34, Fleury Street West, Montreal, Quebec, Canada H3L 1S9; (514)382-3000—29, 62, 182, 208, 222, 390, 483, 494, 511, 600, 610, 642, 644, 828, 945, 972

Instructional Materials & Equipment Distributors (IMED), 1520 Cotner Avenue, Los Angeles, California 90025; (213)879-0377—540, 541, 542, 579

Instructional Materials Laboratory, The Ohio State University, 1885 Neil Avenue, Columbus, Ohio 43210; (614)422-2345—717, 718, 719, 720, 721, 722, 723, 724, 725, 726, 727, 728, 729, 730

Integrated Professional Services, Inc. (IPS), 5211 Mahoning Avenue, Suite 135, Youngstown, Ohio 44515; (216)799-3282—145, 735

Interdatum, 600 Montgomery Street, 37th Floor, San Francisco, California 94111; (415)989-8226—181

International Personnel Management Association, 1617 Duke Street, Alexandria, Virginia; (703)549-7100—863, 864, 991, 992, 993, 994, 995, 996, 997, 998

The Interstate Printers and Publishers, Inc. (IPP), 19 North Jackson Street, P.O. Box 50, Danville, Illinois 61832; (217)466-0500—617, 628, 638, 639, 646, 655

IOX Assessment Associates, 11411 West Jefferson Boulevard, Culver City, California 90230; (213)391-6295—234, 242, 282, 301, 517, 543

Jamestown Publishers, P.O. Box 6743, 544 Douglas Avenue, Providence, Rhode Island 02940; (800)USA-READ or (401)351-1915—527, 528, 529, 534, 547

Jansky, Jeannette J., 120 East 89th Street, New York, New York 10028; (212)876-8894—529

Jastak Assessment Systems, 1526 Gilpin, Wilmington, Delaware 19806; (302)652-4990—216, 457, 544, 761, 769

Johnson, Suzanne Bennett, Ph.D., Shands Teaching Hospital, Psychiatry Service, Children's Mental Health Unit, Box J-234, J.H.M.H.C., University of Florida, Gainesville, Florida 32610—85, 107, 161

Joint Council on Economic Education, 1212 Avenue of the Americas, New York, New York 10036; (212)582-5150—319, 322, 323, 324

Kahn, Marvin W., Department of Psychology, The University of Arizona, Tucson, Arizona 85721; (602)626-2921—192

Katz, Martin M., Division of Psychology, Department of Psychiatry, Albert Einstein College of Medicine, Montefiore Hospital and Medical Center, Bronx Municipal Hospital Center, Pelham Parkway and Eastchester Boulevard, Bronx, New York 10461; (212)430-0551—147

Keeler Instruments, Inc., 456 Parkway, Lawrence Park Industrial District, Broomall, Pennsylvania; (800)523-5620, in Pennsylvania (215)353-4350—657

Kent Developmental Metrics, 126 West College Avenue, P.O. Box 3178, Kent, Ohio 44240-3178; (216)678-3589—11

Kew, Clifton E., 245 East 19th Street, New York, New York 10003; (212)473-3082—138

Keystone View, Division of Mast Development Company, 2212 East 12th Street, Davenport, Iowa 52803; (319)326-0141—660, 665

Khavari, Khalil A., Ph.D., Midwest Institute on Drug Use, Vogel Hall, University of Wisconsin-Milwaukee, Milwaukee, Wisconsin 53201; (414)963-4747—132

Kirkpatrick, Donald L., Ph.D., 1080 Lower Ridgeway, Elm Grove, Wisconsin 53122; (414)224-1891—943, 959, 960, 970

Kovacs, Maria, Ph.D., University of Pittsburgh, School of Medicine, Western Psychiatric Institute and Clinic, 3811 O'Hara Street, Pittsburgh, Pennsylvania 15213-2593; no business phone—193

Krantz, David S., Department of Medical Psychology, Uniformed Services, University of the Health Sciences, 4301 Jones Bridge Road, Bethesda, Maryland 20014; (301)295-3030—222

Robert E. Krieger Publishing Company, Inc., P.O. Box 9542, Melbourne, Florida 32901; (305)724-9542—188

Kundu, Ramanath, Department of Psychology, University of Calcutta, 92, Acharya Prafulla Chandra Road, Calcutta 700 009 India; (35)9666/7089—147, 148

Ladoca Publishing Foundation, Laradon Hall Training and Residential Center, East 51st Avenue and Lincoln Street, Denver, Colorado 80216; (303)629-6379—7, 78, 486, 608, 625

Lafayette Instrument Company, P.O. Box 5729, Lafayette, Indiana 47903; (317)423-1505—24, 43, 44, 48, 66, 563, 564, 565, 657, 661, 811, 830, 835, 974, 978, 980, 981, 982, 983, 984

LaForge, Rolfe, 83 Homestead Boulevard, Mill Valley, California 94941; (415)388-8121—143

David S. Lake Publishers, 19 Davis Drive, Belmont, California 94002; (415)592-7810—41

Larlin Corporation, P.O. Box 1523, Marietta, Georgia 30061; (404)424-6210—557

Lawrence, Trudys, 5916 Del Loma Avenue, San Gabriel, California 91775; (213)286-2027—700

Lea and Febiger, 600 Washington Square, Philadelphia, Pennsylvania 19106; (215)922-1330—38

Leach, Glenn C., Ed.D., Wagner College, 631 Howard Avenue, Staten Island, New York 10301; (212)390-3100—316, 317, 318

Learnco, Inc., 128 High Street, Greenland, New Hampshire 03840; (603)778-0813—556

Learning Publications, Inc., 5351 Gulf Drive, P.O. Box 1326, Holmes Beach, Florida 33509; (813)778-6818—574

Learning Time Products, 4436 Engle Road, Sacramento, California 95821; (916)483-6417—565, 584

Lentz Peace Research Laboratory, 6251 San Bonita, St. Louis, Missouri 63105; (314)721-8219—321, 686, 779

Lefkowitz, Monroe M., Ph.D., 106 Cliffwood Street, Lenox, Massachusetts 01240; (413)637-2113—110

Hal Leonard Publishing Corporation, 960 East Mark Street, Winona, Minnesota 55987; (507)454-2920—255, 258

Leonardo Press, P.O. Box 403, Yorktown Heights, New York 10598; no business phone—252

H.K. Lewis and Co. Ltd., 136 Gower Street, London, England WC1E 6BS; (01)387-4282—19, 21, 32, 407

Life Insurance Marketing and Research Association, Inc. (LIMRA), P.O. Box 208, Hartford, Connecticut 06141; (203)677-0033—1001

Life Office Management Association, Inc. (LOMA), 5770 Powers Ferry Road, Atlanta, Georgia 30327; (404)951-1770—823, 824, 825, 826, 827

Life Science Associates, 1 Fenimore Road, Bayport, New York 11705; (516)472-2111—41, 42, 47, 48, 49, 52, 56, 60, 61, 62, 63, 64, 66, 67, 69

Linguametrics Group, P.O. Box 3495, San Rafael, California 94912; (415)499-9350—568, 630, 640

LinguiSystems, Inc., 716 17th Street, Moline, Illinois 61265; (800)ALL-TIME, in Illinois (309)762-5112—515, 629, 635, 636, 655

Lippincott/Harper Publishers, Inc., Journals Division, 2350 Virginia Avenue, Hagerstown, Maryland 21740; (800)638-3030—14

Perceptual Learning Systems, P.O. Box 864, Dearborn, Michigan 48121; (313)277-6480—606, 609, 612

The Perfection Form Company, 8350 Hickman Road, Suite 15, Des Moines, Iowa 50322; (800)831-4190, in Iowa (800)432-5831—241, 243, 244, 245, 318, 319, 320, 324, 325

Person-O-Metrics, Inc., Evaluation and Development Services, 20504 Williamsburg Road, Dearborn Heights, Michigan 48127; no business phone—686, 691, 705

Phi Delta Kappa, Eighth and Union, P.O. Box 789, Bloomington, Indiana 47402; (812)339-1156—781, 782, 783, 784

The Phoenix Institute of California, 248 Blossom Hill Road, Los Gatos, California 95030; (408)354-6122—99

Phonic Ear Ltd., 7475 Kimbell Street, Mississauga, Ontario, Canada L5S 1E7; no business phone—627

Phonovisual Products, Inc., 12216 Parklawn Drive, P.O. Box 2007, Rockville, Maryland 20852; (301)881-4888—238

Pikunas, Justin, Ph.D., 335 Briggs Building, University of Detroit, Detroit, Michigan 48221; (313)927-1000—113, 165

Planet Press, 115 29th Street, Newport Beach, California 92663-3418; (714)675-7504/5994—185, 190, 192, 197

Polymath Systems, P.O. Box 795, Berkeley, California 94701; (415)492-0875—26, 254, 456

Precision People, 3452 North Ride Circle South, Jacksonville, Florida 32217; (904)262-1096—45, 736

Prep, Inc., 1007 Whitehead Road Extension, Trenton, New Jersey 08638; (800)257-5234, in New Jersey, Alaska, Hawaii, and Canada (609)882-2668—764, 828, 849, 854, 904, 915

Preventive Measures, Inc., 1115 West Campus Road, Lawrence, Kansas 66044; (913)842-5078—128

Price Systems, Inc., P.O. Box 3067, Lawrence, Kansas 66044; (913)843-7892—688, 936

Priority Innovations, Inc., P.O. Box 792, Skokie, Illinois 60076; (312)729-1434—483, 486, 493

PRO-ED, 5341 Industrial Oaks Boulevard, Austin, Texas 78735; (512)892-3142—5, 10, 33, 58, 240, 254, 284, 297, 395, 396, 461, 469, 539, 549, 550, 555, 567, 596, 604, 605, 618, 623, 634, 636, 642, 648, 650, 653, 666, 667, 680, 682, 715, 753

Programs for Education, Inc., Rosemont, New Jersey 08556; (609)397-2214—474, 475, 491

Psychodiagnostic Test Company, P.O. Box 859, East Lansing, Michigan 48823; no business phone—52

Psychodynamic Instruments, c/o Gerald Blum, P.O. Box 1172, Ann Arbor, Michigan 48106; no business phone—191

Psychological Assessment and Services, Inc., P.O. Box 1031, Iowa City, Iowa 52240; no business phone—78, 110

Psychological Assessment Resources, Inc., P.O. Box 98, Odessa, Florida 33556; (800)331-TEST or (813)977-3395—36, 37, 39, 51, 54, 68, 91, 107, 114, 126, 132, 137, 140, 158, 163, 169, 171, 172, 209, 524, 591, 785, 907, 908

The Psychological Corporation (PsyCor), A Subsidiary of Harcourt Brace Jovanovich, Inc., 555 Academic Court, San Antonio, Texas 78204; (512)299-1061—3, 6, 12, 19, 21, 22, 30, 32, 34, 35, 37, 38, 43, 68, 69, 125, 132, 138, 155, 161, 171, 200, 203, 257, 260, 266, 267, 295, 299, 326, 327, 350, 351, 352, 353, 355, 366, 367, 392, 397, 405, 406, 407, 409, 410, 439, 440, 448, 449, 450, 451, 462, 463, 472, 481, 482, 495, 502, 508, 509, 511, 514, 522, 525, 551, 552, 564, 567, 575, 592, 612, 621, 622, 626, 632, 633, 634, 640, 650, 651, 658, 666, 674, 694, 712, 715, 744, 754, 811, 828, 834, 852, 860, 865, 872, 875, 886, 890, 898, 954, 974, 975, 976, 982, 984

Psychological Documents, American Psychological Association, 1200 17th Street NW, Washington, D.C. 20036; (202)955-7600—71

Psychological Measurement Systems, 15 Princess Street, Sausalito, California 94965; (415)331-2133—84, 133

Psychological Publications, Inc., 5300 Hollywood Boulevard, Los Angeles, California 90027; (213)465-4163—77, 183

Psychological Service Center of Philadelphia, Suite 904, 1422 Chestnut Street, Philadelphia, Pennsylvania 19102; (215)568-2555—745

Psychological Services Bureau, P.O. Box 4, St. Thomas, Pennsylvania 17252; no business phone—441, 442, 545

Psychological Services, Inc., 370 Lake Forest Road, Bay Village, Ohio 44140; (216)871-7663—800, 801, 802, 803, 867, 868, 869, 870, 871, 872, 897, 990

Psychological Systems Corporation, 900 Jorie Boulevard, Suite 130, Oak Brook, Illinois 60521; (312)325-8000—910, 914, 947

Psychological Test Specialists, P.O. Box 9229, Missoula, Montana 59807; no business phone—22, 24, 30, 47, 50, 199, 201, 512, 759, 916

Search Institute, 122 West Franklin, Suite 525, Minneapolis, Minnesota 55404-9990; (612)870-3664—305, 306

Sensonics, Inc., 15 South Haddon Avenue, Haddonfield, New Jersey 08033; no business phone—839

Sewall Rehabilitation Center, 1360 Vine Street, Denver, Colorado 80206; (303)399-1800—17

Sheridan Psychological Services, Inc., P.O. Box 6101, Orange, California 92667; (714)639-2595—27, 139, 192, 196, 205, 217, 219, 221, 222, 223, 224, 225, 226, 227, 673, 680, 695, 741, 744, 809, 810, 811, 898

Skillcorp Software, Inc., 2300 West Fifth Avenue, Columbus, Ohio 43216; no business phone—296, 490, 538

Slosson Educational Publications, Inc., P.O. Box 280, East Aurora, New York 14052; (800)828-4800, in New York (716)652-0930—31, 62, 71, 188, 205, 248, 249, 284, 305, 493, 501, 504, 548, 554, 569, 572, 576, 586, 603, 643, 647, 651, 679, 706, 710

SOARES Associates, 111 Teeter Rock Road, Trumbull, Connecticut 06611; (203)375-5353—678-697

SOI Institute, 343 Richmond Street, El Segundo, California 90245; (213)322-5532—468

South, John C., Duquesne University, Pittsburgh, Pennsylvania 15282; (412)434-6000—887

Southern Illinois University Press, P.O. Box 3697, Carbondale, Illinois 62901; (618)453-2281—776

Special Child Publications (SCP), P.O. Box 33548, Seattle, Washington 98133; (206)771-5711—195, 513, 558, 663, 735

Speech and Hearing Clinic, 110 Moore Building, University Park, Pennsylvania 16802; (814)865-5414—614

Spivack, George and Swift, Marshall, Department of Mental Health Sciences, Hahnemann University, 1505 Race Street, Philadelphia, Pennsylvania 19102; no business phone—671

Springer Publishing Company, 200 Park Avenue South, New York, New York 10003; (212)475-2494—113, 167, 182

S.P. Medical and Scientific Books, 175-20 Wexford Terrace, Jamaica, New York 11432; (718)658-0888—48

The Stanton Corporation, 5701 Executive Center Drive, Suite 300, Charlotte, North Carolina 28229; (800)528-5745, in North Carolina (704)535-0060—941

Statistical Publishing Society, Indian Statistical Institute, 203 Barrackpore Trunk Road, Calcutta, India 700 035; no business phone—509

Steck-Vaughn Company, P.O. Box 2028, Austin, Texas 78768; (800)531-5015, in Texas (800)252-9317—398, 451

Stein, Morris, Graduate School of Arts and Sciences, Research Center for Human Relations, New York University, 6 Washington Place, 7th Floor, New York, New York 10003; (212)598-1212—888, 889, 932, 968

Stevens, Thurow and Associates, 100 West Monroe Street, Chicago, Illinois 60603; (312)332-6277—858, 859, 895, 981

Stoelting Company, 1350 South Costner Avenue, Chicago, Illinois 60623; (312)522-4500—4, 8, 9, 11, 20, 23, 25, 26, 27, 42, 60, 100, 121, 122, 133, 143, 148, 149, 190, 193, 212, 258, 475, 478, 480, 484, 485, 506, 508, 560, 561, 562, 569, 570, 571, 573, 580, 582, 600, 603, 633, 656, 658, 664, 680, 742, 764, 897, 898, 918, 979, 980

Stratton-Christian Press, Inc., P.O. Box 1055, University Place Station, Des Moines, Iowa 50311; no business phone—242, 244

Student Development Associates, 110 Crestwood Drive, Athens, Georgia 30605; (404)549-4122—693, 707, 770

SWETS and Zeitlinger B.V., Heereweg 347b, 2161 CA Lisse, The Netherlands; 02521-19113—44, 100, 197

Tabin, Johanna Krout, Ph.D., 162 Park Avenue, Glencoe, Illinois 60022; (312)835-0162—163, 213

TAV Selection System, 12807 Arminta Street, North Hollywood, California 91605; no business phone—945

Taylor & Francis Ltd., Rankine Road, Basingstoke, Hampshire, RG24 OPR, England; no business phone—627

Teachers College Press, Teachers College, Columbia University, 1234 Amsterdam Avenue, New York, New York 10027; (212)678-3929—183, 317, 466, 472, 524, 775

Teaching and Testing Resources, P.O. Box 984, Woden, A.C.T. 2606, Australia; (062)88 5777—292, 519, 539

T.E.D. Associates, 42 Lowell Road, Brookline, Massachusetts 02146; (617)734-5868—681

Teleometrics International, 1755 Woodstead Court, The Woodlands, Texas 77380; (713)367-0060—911, 912, 916, 921, 933, 936, 942, 945, 950, 958, 960, 961, 962, 965, 966, 968, 1000, 1001, 1003, 1004

Templer, Donald I., Ph.D., California School of Professional Psychology, 1350 M Street, Fresno, California 93721; (209)486-8420—164, 191, 195

The Test Agency Ltd., Cournswood House, North Dean, High Wycombe, Bucks, HP14 4NW, England; (024)3384—8, 22, 148, 198, 236, 664, 800, 838, 895, 905, 1002

Robert L. Williams & Associates, Inc., 6372-76 Delmar Boulevard, St. Louis, Missouri 63130; (314)862-0055—122, 187, 213

The Wilmington Press, 13315 Wilmington Drive, Dallas, Texas 75234; (214)620-8431—51, 97, 111, 170, 763

Windholz, George, Ph.D., Department of Psychology, University of North Carolina, Charlotte, North Carolina 28223; (704)497-4731—225

Wolfe Personnel Testing and Training Systems, Inc., P.O. Box 1104, St. Laurent Station, Montreal, Canada H4L 4W6; (201)265-5393—852, 861, 862, 876, 877, 878, 880, 881, 882, 883, 884, 886, 895, 932, 973, 1006

E.F. Wonderlic Personnel Test, Inc., 820 Frontage Road, Northfield, Illinois 60093; (312)446-8900—853, 861, 874, 875, 918, 919

Woolner, Rosetelle B., 3551 Aurora Circle, Memphis, Tennessee 38111; (901)454-2365—703

Word Making Productions, P.O. Box 15038, Salt Lake City, Utah 84115-0038; (801)484-3092—638

World of Work, Inc., 2923 North 67th Place, Scottsdale, Arizona 85251; (602)946-1884—909

Wyeth Laboratories, P.O. Box 8616, Philadelphia, Pennsylvania 19101; (215)688-4400—65

Yamauchi, Kent, Ph.D., The Advancement of Professional Psychology, 4210 Via Arbolado Road, Suite 102, Los Angeles, California 90042-5122; (818)578-7272—224

Yuker, H.E., Hofstra University, Hempstead, Long Island, New York 11550; (516)560-5635—691

Zalk, Susan Rosenberg, The Graduate School and University Center of The City University of New York; 33 West 42nd Street, New York, New York 10036; no business phone—687

Zung, William W.K., M.D., Veterans Administration Medical Center, 508 Fulton Street, Durham, North Carolina 27705; (919)286-0411—177, 206

About the Editors

RICHARD C. SWEETLAND, Ph.D. After completing his doctorate at Utah State University in 1968, Dr. Sweetland completed postdoctoral training in psychoanalytically oriented clinical psychology at the Topeka State Hospital in conjunction with the training program of the Menninger Foundation. Following appointments in child psychology at the University of Kansas Medical Center and in neuropsychology at the Kansas City Veterans Administration Hospital, he entered the practice of psychotherapy in Kansas City. In addition to his clinical work in neuropsychology and psychoanalytic psychotherapy, Dr. Sweetland has been involved extensively in the development of computerized psychological testing. Dr. Sweetland co-edited *Tests: First Edition* and *Tests: Supplement* and is co-editor of the *Test Critiques* series.

DANIEL J. KEYSER, Ph.D. Since completing postgraduate work at the University of Kansas in 1974, Dr. Keyser has worked in drug and alcohol rehabilitation and psychiatric settings. In addition, he has taught undergraduate psychology at Rockhurst College for 15 years. Dr. Keyser specializes in behavioral medicine—biofeedback, pain control, stress management, terminal care support, habit management, and wellness maintenance—and maintains a private clinical practice in the Kansas City area. Dr. Keyser co-edited *Tests: First Edition* and *Tests: Supplement*, is co-editor of the *Test Critiques* series, and has made significant contributions to computerized psychological testing.